# POLITICS IN AMERICA

## BRIEF CALIFORNIA EDITION

### Second Edition

## Thomas R. Dye

*Emeritus McKenzie*
*Professor of Government*
*Florida State University*

## with Milton Clarke

*Los Medanos College*

PEARSON

Prentice
Hall

Upper Saddle River, New Jersey 07458

*To my students over the years,*
*who taught me more than I taught them.*

**Editorial Director:** Charlyce Jones Owen
**Executive Editor:** Dickson Musslewhite
**Associate Editor:** Rob DeGeorge
**Editorial Assistant:** Jennifer Murphy
**Senior Marketing Manager:** Kate Mitchell
**Marketing Manager:** Emily Cleary
**Marketing Assistant:** Jennifer Lang
**Senior Managing Editor:** Lisa Iarkowski
**Production Liaison:** Fran Russello
**Permissions Coordinator:** Lisa Black
**Manufacturing Buyer:** Mary Ann Gloriande
**Design Manager:** Amy Rosen
**Interior Design:** Jonathan Boylan
**Cover Design:** Jonathan Boylan/Laura Gardner
**Cover Illustration/Photo:** Tomi/Photolink/Photodisc Green/Getty Images, Inc.
**Director, Image Resource Center:** Melinda Reo
**Manager, Rights and Permissions:** Zina Arabia
**Manager, Visual Research:** Beth Brenzel
**Manager, Cover Visual Research & Permissions:** Karen Sanatar
**Image Permission Coordinator:** Debbie Hewitson
**Photo Researcher:** Kathy Ringrose
**Composition/Full-Service Project Management:** Margaret Pinette/
Stratford Publishing Services, Inc.
**Printer/Binder:** Courier Companies, Inc.
**Cover Printer:** Phoenix Color Corp.

Credits and acknowledgments borrowed from other sources and reproduced, with permission, in this textbook appear on appropriate page within text (or on page PC-1).

Pearson Education LTD. London
Pearson Education Singapore, Pte. Ltd
Pearson Education, Canada, Ltd
Pearson Education–Japan

Pearson Education Australia PTY, Limited
Pearson Education North Asia Ltd
Pearson Educación de Mexico, S.A. de C.V.
Pearson Education Malaysia, Pte. Ltd

10 9 8 7 6 5 4 3 2 1

**ISBN 0-13-613195-6**
**ISBN 978-0-13-613195-3**

# BRIEF CONTENTS

*Preface*   *xiii*
*About the Author*   *xvii*

## Part One     POLITICS
CHAPTER 1     Politics: Who Gets What, When, and How     2
CHAPTER 2     Political Culture: Ideas in Conflict     24

## Part Two     CONSTITUTION
CHAPTER 3     The Constitution: Limiting Governmental Power     56
                **CONSTITUTION OF THE UNITED STATES**     87
CHAPTER 4     Federalism: Dividing Governmental Power     102

## Part Three     PARTICIPANTS
CHAPTER 5     Participation, Compaigns, and Elections:
                Deciding Who Governs     134
CHAPTER 6     Mass Media: Setting the Political Agenda     174
CHAPTER 7     Political Parties and Interest Groups: Organizing Politics     204

## Part Four     INSTITUTIONS
CHAPTER 8     Congress: Politics on Capitol Hill     244
CHAPTER 9     The President: White House Politics     302
CHAPTER 10    The Bureaucracy: Bureaucratic Politics     342
CHAPTER 11    Courts: Judicial Politics     384

## Part Five     OUTCOMES
CHAPTER 12    Politics, Personal Liberty, and Civil Rights     420
CHAPTER 13    Politics, Economics, and Social Welfare Policy     470
CHAPTER 14    Politics and National Security     496

## Part Six     CALIFORNIA POLITICS
CHAPTER 15    California: Historical Perspective     520
CHAPTER 16    Democracy, California Style: Political Participation     548
CHAPTER 17    The California State Legislature     584
CHAPTER 18    The California Executive and Bureaucracy     618
CHAPTER 19    The California Judiciary     648
CHAPTER 20    Local Government in California     676
CHAPTER 21    California Fiscal Policy     710
                **CALIFORNIA CONSTITUTION OF 1879**     738

## APPENDIX
The Declaration of Independence     A-1
*The Federalist*, No. 10, James Madison     A-2
*The Federalist*, No. 51, James Madison     A-5
Presidents and Vice Presidents     A-8
Supreme Court Justices     A-9
Presidential Elections and Voting     A-11
Party Control of Congress     A-15

# CONTENTS

PREFACE   xiii
ABOUT THE AUTHOR   xvii

## Part One   POLITICS

*The study of politics is the study of influence and the influential. . . .
The influential are those who get the most of what there is to get. Those
who get the most are elite; the rest are mass.*

Harold Lasswell

### 1  POLITICS: WHO GETS WHAT, WHEN, AND HOW   2

Politics and Political Science   3
Politics and Government   3

**WHAT DO YOU THINK?**
Can You Trust the Government?   6

The Purposes of Government   7

**A CONFLICTING VIEW**
Sometimes It's Right to Disobey the Law   8

The Meaning of Democracy   9

**WHAT DO YOU THINK?**
What Government Programs Do You Support?   10

**COMPARED TO WHAT?**
Freedom and Democracy around the World   11

The Paradox of Democracy   12
Direct versus Representative Democracy   14

**UP CLOSE**
Confidence in American Institutions   15

Who Really Governs?   16

**UP CLOSE**
Terrorism's Threat to Democracy   18

**A CONFLICTING VIEW**
Complaints about the American Political System   20

Democracy in America   21

**A CONSTITUTIONAL NOTE**
Representative Government,
  Not Direct Democracy   21

Summary Notes   22
Key Terms   22
Suggested Readings   23

### 2  POLITICAL CULTURE: IDEAS IN CONFLICT   24

Political Culture   25
Individual Liberty   26
Dilemmas of Equality   27

**WHAT DO YOU THINK?**
Beliefs about Fairness   30

Inequality of Income and Wealth   30

**COMPARED TO WHAT?**
Income and Inequality   31

Social Mobility   32

**A CONFLICTING VIEW**
Success Is Determined by the Bell Curve   33

Race, Ethnicity, and Immigration   34

**WHAT DO YOU THINK?**
Does Immigration Help or Hurt America?   38

**WHAT DO YOU THINK?**
Could You Pass the Citizenship Test?   39

Religion and Secularism in Politics   40
Ideologies: Liberalism and Conservatism   41

**ACROSS THE USA**
Liberalism and Conservatism   43

**PEOPLE IN POLITICS**
Bill O'Reilly, "The No Spin Zone"?   44

**PEOPLE IN POLITICS**
Barbara Boxer, Defending Liberalism in Congress   45

Dissent in the United States   46

**WHAT DO YOU THINK?**
Are You a Liberal or a Conservative?   49

**A CONSTITUTIONAL NOTE**
Natural Born versus Naturalized Citizenship   51

Summary Notes   52
Key Terms   53
Suggested Readings   53
Make It Real   53

## Part Two   CONSTITUTION

*The ascendancy of any elite depends upon the success of the practices
it adopts. . . . The Constitution, written and unwritten, embodies the
practices which are deemed most fundamental to the governmental
and social order.*

Harold Lasswell

### 3  THE CONSTITUTION: LIMITING GOVERNMENTAL POWER   56

Constitutional Government   57
The Constitutional Tradition   57

**PEOPLE IN POLITICS**
John Locke, Guiding the Founders   59

Troubles Confronting a New Nation    59
Consensus in Philadelphia    62
Conflict in Philadelphia    62

**PEOPLE IN POLITICS**
George Washington, Founder of a Nation    63

Resolving the Economic Issues    66

**A CONFLICTING VIEW**
An Economic Interpretation of the Constitution    67

Protecting National Security    68
The Structure of the Government    70

**UP CLOSE**
The Supremacy Clause at Work:
  Marijuana for Medical Use?    71

Separation of Powers and Checks and Balances    72

**A CONFLICTING VIEW**
Let the People Vote on National Issues    73

Conflict over Ratification    75

**PEOPLE IN POLITICS**
James Madison and the Control of "Faction"    77

A Bill of Rights    78
Constitutional Change    78

**A CONFLICTING VIEW**
Objections to the Constitution
  by an Anti-Federalist    82

**A CONSTITUTIONAL NOTE**
How Democratic Was the Constitution of 1787?    83

Summary Notes    84
Key Terms    85
Suggested Readings    85
Make It Real    85


**THE CONSTITUTION OF THE UNITED STATES**    87


4  FEDERALISM: DIVIDING
   GOVERNMENTAL POWER    102

Indestructible Union, Indestructible States    103
Why Federalism? The Argument for
  a "Compound Republic"    105

**COMPARED TO WHAT?**
The European Union    106

**UP CLOSE**
Federalism Is the Enemy of Uniformity    108

**UP CLOSE**
Katrina: Federalism Fails in a Crisis    110

The Original Design of Federalism    110

**A CONFLICTING VIEW**
The Dark Side of Federalism    112

The Evolution of American Federalism    114

**WHAT DO YOU THINK?**
Federalism and Same-Sex Marriage    115

**UP CLOSE**
Historical Markers in the Development
  of American Federalism    117

Federalism Revived?    121

**WHAT DO YOU THINK?**
Should Violence Against Women Be
  a Federal Crime?    123

Money and Power Flow to Washington    123

**UP CLOSE**
How Congress Set a National
  Drinking Age    124

**A CONFLICTING VIEW**
Liberals, Conservatives, and Federalism    127

Coercive Federalism: Preemptions
  and Mandates    127

**A CONSTITUTIONAL NOTE**
How Is National and State Power Divided?    129

Summary Notes    130
Key Terms    130
Suggested Readings    131
Make It Real    131

# Part Three  PARTICIPANTS

*People strive for power—to get the most of what there is to get.*
                                        Harold Lasswell

5  PARTICIPATION, CAMPAIGNS, AND
   ELECTIONS: DECIDING WHO
   GOVERNS    134

Individual Participation in Politics    135
Voters and Nonvoters    135
Elections in a Democracy    136

**COMPARED TO WHAT?**
Voter Turnout in Western Democracies    139

The Advantages of Incumbency    139

**UP CLOSE**
How to Run for Office    140

Campaign Strategies    143

**UP CLOSE**
Dirty Politics    145

How Much Does It Cost to Get Elected?   147
Raising Campaign Cash   149

**UP CLOSE**
How to Spend $7 Million on a
  Political Campaign   150

What Do Contributors "Buy"?   151
Regulating Campaign Finance   154

**UP CLOSE**
Midterm Congressional Elections, 2006:
  What Do They Mean?   156

The Presidential Campaign:
  The Primary Race   158
The Presidential Campaign: The General
  Election Battle   161

**UP CLOSE**
Bush v. Kerry, 2004   162

The Voter Decides   163

**UP CLOSE**
The Presidential Debates   164

**ACROSS THE USA**
How the States Voted   166

**A CONSTITUTIONAL NOTE**
Who Can Vote?   171

Summary Notes   172
Key Terms   173
Suggested Readings   173
Make It Real   173


6   MASS MEDIA: SETTING
    THE POLITICAL AGENDA   174

The Power of the Media   175

**UP CLOSE**
The Generation Gap in News   177

Sources of Media Power   178
The Business of the Media   181
The Politics of the News   183

**WHAT DO YOU THINK?**
Are the Media Biased?   186

**A CONFLICTING VIEW**
Fox News: "Fair and Balanced"?   187

Polarization of the Media   188
Mediated Elections   188

**UP CLOSE**
TV Network News Coverage of the Presidential
  Campaign, 2004   192

Freedom versus Fairness   193

**PEOPLE IN POLITICS**
Larry King Live   194

**COMPARED TO WHAT?**
America's TV Culture in Perspective   195

Libel and Slander   195
Politics and the Internet   196
Media Effects: Shaping Political Life   198

**UP CLOSE**
The Media Age   199

**A CONSTITUTIONAL NOTE**
Can the Federal Communications Commission Ban
  Profanity from Radio and Television?   202

Summary Notes   202
Key Terms   203
Suggested Readings   203


7   POLITICAL PARTIES AND
    INTEREST GROUPS:
    ORGANIZING POLITICS   204

The Power of Organization   205
Political Parties and Democratic Government   205

**WHAT DO YOU THINK?**
Which Party Does a Better Job?   208

Parties as Organizers of Elections   211

**UP CLOSE**
Off and Running, 2008   214

National Party Conventions   214

**UP CLOSE**
Democratic and Republican Platforms: Can You Tell
  the Difference?   216

Party Finances   217
Party Voters   217
Why the Two-Party System Persists   220

**ACROSS THE USA**
Red States, Blue States   222

Interest-Group Power   223
The Organized Interests in Washington   224

**UP CLOSE**
The Christian Coalition: Organizing the Faithful   228

The Washington Lobbyists   229
The Fine Art of Lobbying   231

**UP CLOSE**
AARP: The Nation's Most Powerful
  Interest Group   234

**UP CLOSE**
EMILY's List   236

Lobbying the Bureaucracy   236

**UP CLOSE**
Payback: Money and Medicare   237

Lobbying the Courts   238
Summary Notes   239
Key Terms   240
Suggested Readings   241
Make It Real   241

# Part Four  INSTITUTIONS

*Authority is the expected and legitimate possession of power.*
Harold Lasswell

## 8  CONGRESS: POLITICS ON CAPITOL HILL   244

The Powers of Congress   245
Congressional Apportionment
  and Redistricting   251

**ACROSS THE USA**
Reapportionment, 2000   252

Getting to Capitol Hill   256

**WHAT DO YOU THINK?**
Why Do Voters Reelect Members
  of an Unpopular Congress?   261

Party Fortunes in Congress   262

**ACROSS THE USA**
Urban, Surburban, and Rural Districts   265

**UP CLOSE**
The 110th Congress   266

Life in Congress   267

**PEOPLE IN POLITICS**
Hillary Rodham Clinton in the Senate   269

Home Style   272
Organizing Congress: Party and Leadership   273

**PEOPLE IN POLITICS**
Nancy Pelosi, Leading House Democrats   277

In Committee   278

**PEOPLE IN POLITICS**
Ted Kennedy: Keeping Liberalism Alive
  in the U.S. Senate   282

On the Floor   283

**WHAT DO YOU THINK?**
Should Presidential Appointments of Judges,
  Including Supreme Court Justices, Be Thwarted
  by Senate Filibusters?   285

Decision Making in Congress   286

**UP CLOSE**
Polarization on Capitol Hill   289

**UP CLOSE**
Tips on Lobbying Congress   291

Customs and Norms   292

**A CONFLICTING VIEW**
Congress Can Act Responsibly on Occasion   293

Congressional Ethics   296

**A CONSTITUTIONAL NOTE**
Congress as the First Branch   298

Summary Notes   299
Key Terms   300
Suggested Readings   300
Make It Real   301

## 9  THE PRESIDENT: WHITE HOUSE POLITICS   302

Presidential Power   303

**WHAT DO YOU THINK?**
How Would You Rate the Presidents?   304

Constitutional Powers of the President   306

**PEOPLE IN POLITICS**
George Bush and the War on Terrorism   308

**UP CLOSE**
Sex, Lies, and Impeachment   311

**UP CLOSE**
Watergate and the Limits of
  Presidential Power   313

Political Resources of the President   314
Personality versus Policy   317
Chief Executive   319

**UP CLOSE**
Contrasting Presidential Styles   321

Chief Legislator and Lobbyist   325
Global Leader   329
Commander-in-Chief   333
The Vice Presidential Waiting Game   336

**PEOPLE IN POLITICS**
Dick Cheney, Presidential Confidant   338

**A CONSTITUTIONAL NOTE**
How Broad Is the "Executive Power"?   339

Summary Notes   340
Key Terms   340
Suggested Readings   341
Make It Real   341

## 10 THE BUREAUCRACY: BUREAUCRATIC POLITICS   342

Bureaucratic Power   343

**WHAT DO YOU THINK?**
How Would You Rate These Federal
  Agencies?   346

The Federal Bureaucracy   349

**COMPARED TO WHAT?**
The Size of Government in
Other Nations   350

**UP CLOSE**
The Department of Homeland Security   352

**UP CLOSE**
Managing the Nation's Money   356

Bureaucracy and Democracy   357
Bureaucratic Politics   360
The Budgetary Process   362

**UP CLOSE**
Reorganizing Intelligence After 9/11   363

The Politics of Budgeting   369

**UP CLOSE**
Bureaucratic Budget Strategies   370

**WHAT DO YOU THINK?**
How Much Money Does
  the Government Waste?   371

Regulatory Battles   372

**A CONFLICTING VIEW**
Bureaucratic Regulations Are Suffocating
  America   373

Regulating America   375
Congressional Constraints on
  the Bureaucracy   376

**UP CLOSE**
How to Use the Freedom of
  Information Act   378

Interest Groups and Bureaucratic
  Decision Making   380
Judicial Constraints on the Bureaucracy   380

**A CONSTITUTIONAL NOTE**
Congress and the Budget   381

Summary Notes   382
Key Terms   383
Suggested Readings   383
Make It Real   383

## 11 COURTS: JUDICIAL POLITICS   384

Judicial Power   385

**PEOPLE IN POLITICS**
John Marshall and Early
  Supreme Court  Politics   387

**UP CLOSE**
William Jefferson Clinton v.
  Paula Corbin Jones   389

Activism versus Self-Restraint   390

Structure and Jurisdiction of
  Federal Courts   392

**ACROSS THE USA**
Geographic Boundaries of
  Federal Courts   395

**A CONFLICTING VIEW**
America Is Drowning Itself in a
  Sea of Lawsuits   396

The Special Rules of Judicial
  Decision Making   397
The Politics of Selecting Judges   399

**WHAT YOU THINK?**
Should Supreme Court Nominees Reveal
  Their Views on Key Cases before
  the Senate Votes to Confirm Them?   403

Who Is Selected?   403

**UP CLOSE**
Bush Scores, Then Fumbles,
  Then Scores Again   404

**UP CLOSE**
The Confirmation of Clarence Thomas   405

Supreme Court Decision Making   406
Politics and the Supreme Court   409
Checking Court Power   411

**UP CLOSE**
*Bush v. Gore* in the U.S.
  Supreme Court   413

**A CONSTITUTIONAL NOTE**
The Power of Judicial Review   415

Summary Notes   416
Key Terms   417
Suggested Readings   417
Make It Real   417

## Part Five    OUTCOMES

*That political science concentrates upon the influential does not imply the neglect of the total distribution of values throughout the community. . . . The emphasis upon the probability that the few (elite) will get the most does not imply that the many (mass) do not profit from some political changes.*

Harold Lasswell

## 12  POLITICS AND PERSONAL LIBERTY    420

Power and Individual Liberty    421
Freedom of Religion    422

**UP CLOSE**
Are We One Nation "Under God"?    428

Freedom of Speech    429
Privacy, Abortion, and the Constitution    431
Obscenity and the Law    433
The Right to Bear Arms    434

**WHAT DO YOU THINK?**
Gun Control?    435

Rights of Criminal Defendants    436

**WHAT DO YOU THINK?**
Are Persons Captured on the Battlefields of Afghanistan and Iraq Entitled to the Protections of the U.S. Constitution?    438

**A CONFLICTING VIEW**
Terrorism Requires Restrictions on Civil Liberties    439

The Death Penalty    441

**ACROSS THE USA**
The Death Penalty    443

The Politics of Equality    444
Slavery, Segregation, and the Constitution    444
The Civil Rights Acts    448

**PEOPLE IN POLITICS**
Martin Luther King Jr., "I Have a Dream"    450

Affirmative Action: Opportunity versus Results    451

**WHAT YOU THINK**
Do You Favor Affirmative Action?    454

**A CONFLICTING VIEW**
The Constitution Should Be Color-Blind    457

Hispanics in America    457

**ACROSS THE USA**
Hispanic Populations    459

Hispanic Politics    460

**UP CLOSE**
Republicans and the Latino Vote    462

Gender Equality and the Fourteenth Amendment    462
Gender Equality in the Economy    464

**WHAT DO YOU THINK?**
What Constitutes Sexual Harassment?    467

Summary Notes    468
Key Terms    469
Suggested Readings    469
Make It Real    469

## 13  POLITICS, ECONOMICS, AND SOCIAL WELFARE POLICY    470

Politics and Economics    471
The Performance of the American Economy    471
Economic Globalization    473
The Tax Burden    477

**WHAT DO YOU THINK?**
Does Globalization Help or Hurt America?    478

**COMPARED TO WHAT?**
Tax Burdens in Advanced Democracies    479

Tax Politics    480
Poverty in the United States    483

**UP CLOSE**
Who Are the Poor?    485

Social Welfare Policy    485
Politics and Welfare Reform    488

**UP CLOSE**
Is Welfare Reform Working?    489

Health Care in America    490

**A CONSTITUTIONAL NOTE**
Rights versus Entitlements    493

Summary Notes    494
Key Terms    494
Suggested Readings    495
Make It Real    495

## 14  POLITICS AND NATIONAL SECURITY    496

Power among Nations    497
The Legacy of the Cold War    499
Nuclear Threats    503
When to Use Military Force?    505

**A CONFLICTING VIEW**
We Should Defend Ourselves against a Ballistic
  Missile Attack  506

**UP CLOSE**
The Use of Force: Operation Desert Storm  508

The War on Terrorism  510

**PEOPLE IN POLITICS**
Condoleezza Rice  511

**COMPARED TO WHAT?**
World Opinion about America's War
  against Terrorism  513

Political Support for War in Iraq  514

**A CONSTITUTIONAL NOTE**
Congress versus the Commander-in-Chief  515

Summary Notes  516
Key Terms  517
Suggested Readings  517

**Part Six**    CALIFORNIA POLITICS

15  CALIFORNIA: HISTORICAL
    PERSPECTIVE  520

Introduction  521
A Lure and a Challenge: California's Land and
  Climate  522
Native American Settlement  525
Spanish Exploration and Settlement  525

**WHAT DO YOU THINK?**
Earthquakes: The Ultimate Doom or
  Reasonable Risk?  526

Mexican Control  528
U.S. Annexation  528

**COMPARED TO WHAT?**
The Spanish Heritage of California and Texas  530

Early Years of Statehood: The Big Four  533

**UP CLOSE**
Levi Strauss: Gold Rush Entrepreneur  534

Revolt against the Railroads: The Second California
  Constitution  537
The Progressive Era: Hiram Johnson and Clean
  Government  538
The Twentieth Century: Rapid Economic
  Growth  540

**PEOPLE IN POLITICS**
The Legacy of Upton Sinclair and EPIC  542

California in the New Millennium  544

Summary Notes  546

Key Terms  547
Suggested Readings  547

16  DEMOCRACY, CALIFORNIA STYLE:
    POLITICAL PARTICIPATION  548

Introduction  549
Voting: Who Can Vote?  550

**UP CLOSE**
Voter Rights  551

Elections  552

**UP CLOSE**
Circumventing Campaign Finance Law: California
Independent Expenditure Committees  554

Direct Democracy: California's Electoral
  Dilemma  555

**ACROSS THE USA**
Reforming Campaign Finance: California
  and Connecticut  556

Campaigning for Votes  570
Empowering California Voters  577
Vote-Counting Difficulties in California  578
Beyond Electoral Politics  579
California's Tradition of Unconventional
  Political Participation  580

Summary Notes  582
Key Terms  582
Suggested Readings  583

17  THE CALIFORNIA STATE
    LEGISLATURE  584

Introduction  585
The Role of the California Legislature  585
The Making of a California State Legislator  588

**UP CLOSE**
Latino Legislators: The Long and Difficult Road to
  the California Legislature  591

The Legislative Universe  593

**UP CLOSE**
An Ethical Legislature?  596

Leadership in the State Legislature  602

**PEOPLE IN POLITICS**
The Rapid Rise of Fabian Nuñez  607

The Legislative Committee System  609

**WHAT DO YOU THINK?**
Is California Ready for a Part-Time Legislature?  610

The Legislative Process  614
The Hidden View of Lawmaking  615

Summary Notes  616
Key Terms  617
Suggested Readings  617

## 18 THE CALIFORNIA EXECUTIVE AND BUREAUCRACY  618

Introduction  619
Governor: Supreme Executive Authority  620
Citizen-Governor Persona  623
Humble Background  623
Partner Wife  624
A Nonpublic Side  625
Becoming Governor  626

**PEOPLE IN POLITICS**
Susan Kennedy: Democrat Joins Schwarzenegger Republicans  627

The California Plural Executive  630
Attorney General  631

**UP CLOSE**
California's Problematic Health Care Safety Net  632

**WHAT DO YOU THINK?**
The California Performance Review—Quality Control or Just Hype?  642

**COMPARED TO WHAT?**
California and Nevada Governments Grapple with Gambling  644

Summary Notes  646
Key Terms  647
Suggested Readings  647

## 19 THE CALIFORNIA JUDICIARY  648

Introduction  649
The California Court System  650

**PEOPLE IN POLITICS**
Janice Rogers Brown: California's Controversial Justice Reaches U.S. Appellate Court  654

The Variations in California Law  656

**UP CLOSE**
The Wendland Case and the Right to Die  659

The California Jury System  661

**WHAT DO YOU THINK?**
The Evolving Dimensions of Capital Punishment  662

Police Powers and the Prosecution  666
The Prosecution  668
Trends in the California Judicial System  668
Punishment in California  671

Reforming the California Judicial System  672

**UP CLOSE**
Exonerations in California and Louisiana  673

Summary Notes  674
Key Terms  675
Suggested Readings  675

## 20 LOCAL GOVERNMENT IN CALIFORNIA  676

Introduction  677
California County Government  678

**WHAT DO YOU THINK?**
Public Power in California  682

**COMPARED TO WHAT?**
Smart-Growth in Oregon and California  684

Funding County Government  688
The Legal Framework and Formation of Cities  689
The City Council  690
The Municipal Bureaucracy  695

**WHAT DO YOU THINK?**
Differing Perspectives on Eminent Domain in California  698

Special Districts  690

**UP CLOSE**
LAFCO Rules  702

School Districts in California  703
Councils of Government  707
The Future of Local Government  707
Summary Notes  708
Key Terms  709
Suggested Readings  709

## 21 CALIFORNIA FISCAL POLICY  710

Introduction  711
The California Structural Budget Gap  713
The California Budget: Politics and Key Players  715
Major Sources of State Revenue  716

**COMPARED TO WHAT?**
California and Minnesota: Approaches to Fiscal Policy  718

Major State Expenditures  722

**UP CLOSE**
The Protection and Education of Children  723

Financing Local Government  726
The California Budget Process  727

**WHAT DO YOU THINK?**
Understanding Municipal Budgets    728

The Effect of Direct Democracy on the Budget
  Process    734
The State Economy: The Foundation of
  Fiscal Policy    735
The Future of the California
  Political Economy    736
Summary Notes    737
Key Terms    737
Suggested Readings    737

**CALIFORNIA CONSTITUTION OF 1879    738**

# APPENDIX

The Declaration of Independence    A-1
*The Federalist*, No. 10, James Madison    A-2
*The Federalist*, No. 51, James Madison    A-5
Presidents and Vice Presidents    A-8
Supreme Court Justices    A-9
Presidential Elections and Voting    A-11
Party Control of Congress    A-15
Glossary    G-1
Notes    N-1
Photo Credits    PC-1
Index    I-1

# PREFACE

Politics is an activity by which people try to get more of whatever there is to get. It is not about the pursuit of liberty as much as it is about the struggle over the allocation of values in society. Simply put, it is about "who gets what, when, and how."

By using Lasswell's classic definition of politics as the unifying framework, *Politics in America, Second Edition*, strives to present a clear, concise, and stimulating introduction to the American political system. Politics consists of all of the activities—reasonable discussion, impassioned oratory, campaigning, balloting, fund raising, advertising, lobbying, demonstrating, rioting, street fighting, and waging war—by which conflict is carried on. Managing conflict is the principal function of the political system and power is the ultimate goal.

By examining the struggle for power—the participants, the stakes, the processes, and the institutional arenas—*Politics in America, Second Edition*, introduces students to the political struggles that drive democracy.

## Why Politics in America?

Instructors teaching the Introductory American Government course find engaging their students to be the most difficult task facing them. *Politics in America, Second Edition*, is written to be lively and absorbing, reflecting the teaching philosophy that *stimulating students' interest in politics and public affairs is the most important goal of an introductory course.* Interesting examples and controversial debates spark students' interest and keep them connected to the material. The struggle for power in society is not a dull topic, and textbooks should not make it so.

*Politics in America, Second Edition*, strives for a balanced presentation, but "balanced" does not mean boring. It does not mean the avoidance of controversy. Liberal and conservative arguments are set forth clearly and forcefully. Race and gender are given particular attention, not because it is currently fashionable to do so, but because American politics has long been driven by these factors.

## Organization

Part I, "Politics," begins with Lasswell's classic definition of politics and proceeds to describe the nature and functions of government and the meaning of democracy. It poses the question, How democratic is the American political system? It describes the American political culture: its contradictions between law and liberty, political equality and economic inequality, equality of opportunity and inequality of results, and the role of ideology—liberalism and conservatism, thus laying the groundwork for understanding the struggle over who gets what.

Part II, "Constitution," describes the politics of constitution making—deciding how to decide. It describes how the struggle over the U.S. Constitution reflected the distribution of power in the new nation. It focuses on the classic arguments of the Founders for limiting and dividing governmental power and the structural arrangements designed to accomplish this end.

Part III, "Participants," begins by examining individual participation in politics—the way people acquire and hold political opinions and act on them through voting and protest activity. It examines the influences of family, school, gender, race, and the role of media in shaping political opinion. It describes how organization concentrates power—to win public office in the case of party organizations, and to influence policy in the case of interest groups. It assesses the role of personal ambition in politics and the role of money.

Part IV, "Institutions," describes the various governmental arenas in which the struggle for power takes place—the Congress, the presidency, the bureaucracy, the courts. More important, it evaluates the power that comes with control of each of these institutions.

Part V, "Outcomes," deals with public policies—the result of the struggle over the allocation of values. It is especially concerned with the two fundamental values of American society—liberty and equality. Each is examined in separate chapters, as are economic policies, welfare policies, and national security policies.

## New to the Second Edition

The struggle for political power in America has been particularly intense since the controversy over the election of George W. Bush in 2000. In that election Bush's opponent, Al Gore, won more popular votes than Bush, but following a bitter controversy over Electoral College votes from Florida—a controversy that was finally resolved by the Supreme Court—Bush occupied the White House. The bitterness of that election helped to polarize Americans—Democrats versus Republicans, liberals versus conservatives, religious versus secular, supporters versus opponents of the Iraq war, feminists versus nonfeminists, civil libertarians versus supporters of restrictive measures in the war on terror, supporters versus opponents of immigration, and a host of other conflicts. Americans seemed to become more polarized than at any other time since the Vietnam War. And all of these conflicts resounded in the halls of Congress, the White House, the Supreme Court, and the federal bureaucracy.

The second edition of *Politics in America* tries to capture these conflicts and how they affect our political system. Few of these conflicts were resolved with Bush's reelection in 2004. Indeed, it seemed as if the nation became even more polarized, especially as the war in Iraq continued unabated. A textbook focusing on conflict and the struggle for power seems more relevant today than in previous decades.

Among the topics given special attention in the second edition are the war in Iraq and its impact on domestic politics; the war on terror and its potential threats to civil liberty; religious and secular conflicts; immigration and its impact on politics and the economy; social issues, including abortion, marijuana for medical use, same-sex marriages, the conservative fight against the mainstream media, and the battle between liberal and conservative 527s; the continuing struggle over affirmative action, particularly in universities; the controversy over the extent of "executive power"; the reorganization of the intelligence community after 9/11; the heated controversies over the selection of Supreme Court justices; and the Democratic and Republican efforts to capture the growing Hispanic vote.

*Politics in America* is designed to invite controversy and spirited discussion in the classroom. It does not hesitate to raise all of the "politically incorrect" issues— affirmative action and "diversity" in education; when is it right to disobey the law; what is the appropriate justification for the use of military force; what, if any, restrictions should be placed on abortion; should the states or the federal government attempt to ban gay marriages; what constitutional rights, if any, should be given to enemy combatants captured on foreign battlefields or inside the United States; and even whether the Pledge of Allegiance should include the words "under God." Discussions of these conflicts and how and where they are carried on leads students to better understand our political system and how it works.

The congressional election of 2006 is described and analyzed in terms of popular perceptions of the role of Congress in resolving some of these conflicts. President Bush's policies and popularity are assessed as components of voters' decisions in the congressional election.

Educators and citizens have become distressed in recent years over the lack of knowledge of the U.S. Constitution by college graduates. To address this issue, the second edition of *Politics in America* not only includes an *annotated* Constitution, but also a new feature—*A Constitutional Note*—at the end of each chapter that discusses constitutional issues raised by the topic in that chapter.

# Supplementary Books and Readings for American Government

Each of the following books features specialized topical coverage allowing you to tailor your American Government course to suit the needs of your region or your particular teaching style. Featuring contemporary issues or timely readings, any of the following books are available for a discount when bundled with *Politics in America.* Please visit our Online Catalog at www.prenhall.com/dye for additional details.

*Government's Greatest Achievements:*
*From Civil Rights to Homeland Security,* 20th ed.
Paul C. Light, Brookings Institute
ISBN: 0-13-110192-7 © 2004

*Issues in American Political Life:*
*Money, Violence, and Biology,* 4th ed.
Robert Thobaben, Wright State University
Donna Schlagheck, Wright State University
Charles Funderburk, Wright State University
ISBN: 0-13-0336726 © 2002

*Choices: An American Government Reader—*
*Custom Publishing*
Gregory Scott, University of Central Oklahoma
Katherine Tate, University of California–Irvine
Ronald Weber, University of Wisconsin–Milwaukee
ISBN: 0-13-0219916 © 2002

*Civil Rights and Liberties:*
*Provocative Questions and Evolving Answers,* 2nd ed.
Harold Sullivan, The City University of New York
ISBN: 0-13-1174355 © 2001

*21 Debated: Issues in American Politics,* 2nd ed.
Gregory Scott, University of Central Oklahoma
Loren Gatch, University of Central Oklahoma
ISBN: 0-13-1841785 © 2005

*Government and Politics in the Lone Star State:*
*Theory and Practice,* 4th ed.
L. Tucker Gibson, Trinity University
Clay Robison, The Houston Chronicle
ISBN: 0-13-0340502 © 2002

*Rethinking California:*
*Politics and Policy in the Golden State*
Matthew Cahn, California State
University–Northridge
H. Eric Schockman, University of Southern California
David Shafie, Ohio University
ISBN: 0-13-0282677 © 2001

*Strategies for Active Citizenship*

Kateri M. Drexler

Gwen Garcelon

ISBN: 0-13-1172956 © 2005

*Political Science: Evaluating Online Resources with Research Navigator, 2005*

Melissa Payton

ISBN: 0-13-192288-2

*The Political Science Student Writer's Manual, 4th ed.*

Gregory M. Scott, University of Central Oklahoma

Stephen M. Garrison, University of Central Oklahoma

ISBN: 0-13-0404470 © 2002

*Smoking and Politics: Policy Making and the Federal Bureaucracy, 5th ed.*

A. Lee Fritschler, Dickinson College

James M. Hoefler, Dickinson College

ISBN: 0-13-4358015 © 1996

**Real Politics in America** series is another resource for contemporary instructional material. To bridge the gap between research and relevancy, we have launched a new series of supplemental books with the help of series editor Paul Herrnson of the University of Maryland. More descriptive than quantitative, more case study than data study, these books cut across all topics to bring students relevant details in current political science research. From exploring the growing phenomenon of direct democracy to who runs for the state legislature, these books show students that real political science is meaningful and exciting. Available for a discount when bundled with *Politics in America*. Please see your Prentice Hall representative or access www.prenhall.com for a complete listing of titles in the series.

# Acknowledgments

*Politics in America, Second Edition,* reflects the influence of many splendid teachers, students, and colleagues who have helped me over the years. I am grateful for the early guidance of Frank Sorauf, my undergraduate student adviser at Pennsylvania State University, and James G. Coke, my Ph.D. dissertation director at the University of Pennsylvania. Georgia Parthemos at the University of Georgia and Malcolm Parsons at Florida State University gave me my first teaching posts. But my students over the years contributed most to my education—notably Susan MacManus, Kent Portney, Ed Benton, James Ammons, Aubrey Jewitt, and especially John Robey. Several of my colleagues gave advice on various parts of this book. Glen Parker (on Congress), Suzanne Parker (on public opinion), James Gwartney (on economics), Robert Lichter (on the mass media), Charles Barrioux (on bureaucracy), and especially Harmon Zeigler, whose knowledge of politics is unbounded.

I would like to thank James Corey of High Point University for preparing the annotated Constitution and Chris Cardone for editorial management in the early stages of this second edition.

Finally, I would like to thank the many reviewers who evaluated the text and contributed invaluable advice:

Charles W. Chapman, University of Texas at Brownsville

John Pratt, Cedar Valley College

James Corey, High Point University

Christopher C. Lovett, Emporia State University

Kevin R. den Dulk, Grand Valley State University

Wayne Pryor, Brazosport College

James W. Lamare, Florida Atlantic University

Roger Marietta, Darton College

Paul Davis, Truckee Meadows Community College

Earl T. Sheridan, University of North Carolina

**Thomas R. Dye**

# ABOUT THE AUTHOR

**THOMAS R. DYE**, Emeritus McKenzie Professor of Government at Florida State University, regularly taught large introductory classes in American politics and was University Teacher of the Year in 1987. He received his B.A. and M.A. degrees from Pennsylvania State University and his Ph.D. degree from the University of Pennsylvania. He is the author of numerous books and articles on American government and public policy, including *The Irony of Democracy; Politics in States and Communities; Understanding Public Policy; Who's Running America; American Politics in the Media Age; Power in Society; Politics, Economics, and the Public;* and *American Federalism: Competition Among Governments.* His books have been translated into many languages, including Russian and Chinese, and published abroad. He has served as president of the Southern Political Science Association, president of the Policy Studies Organization, and secretary of the American Political Science Association. He has taught at the University of Pennsylvania, the University of Wisconsin, and the University of Georgia, and served as a visiting scholar at Bar-Ilan University, Israel, the Brookings Institution in Washington, D.C., and elsewhere. He is a member of Phi Beta Kappa, Omicron Delta Kappa, and Phi Kappa Phi and is listed in most major biographical directories. Additional information is available at www.thomasrdye.com.

**MILTON CLARKE** is currently a tenured political science instructor at Los Medanos College in Pittsburg, California. His research and publications have focused on a wide variety of topics that have included welfare reform, economic development, international trade, law enforcement and multiculturalism. Most recently, he coordinated a study of international commerce in East Contra Costa County, a project funded by the Chancellor's Office of the California Community Colleges. Clarke also directed a county funded economic impact study of the East Contra Costa County equestrian community and the publication of the Journal of Public Issues and Policy, another project funded by the Chancellor's Office of the California Community Colleges.

Clarke is the author of published articles such as "The African American Traveler in Europe," *Oakland Tribune;* "New Generation turns to heroin for the 'DL,'" *Pacific News Service;* "Young murder victims transform nature of urban morticians' work," *Pacific News Service* and featured in *San Francisco Chronicle;* and a series of articles for *From the Archives,* the journal of the African American Museum and Library in Oakland, California.

Clarke has been actively involved in mass media, producing a regular cable-access program on college activities which is supported by the California Community Colleges and is recognized as one of the "best practices" among "Fund For Student Success" projects. He has also produced other video projects addressing such issues as civic literacy and service learning. One of Clarke's most memorable media experiences was as a news reporter for KPFA Radio in Berkeley where he was awarded a grant from the Northern California Center for investigative journalism to write and produce the four part radio series, "Crack in the City."

As an instructor of American Government and International Relations courses, Clarke has been very active in campus affairs, developing and coordinating an intersegmental project that resulted in a "Guide to Studying the Social Sciences at Two and Four-Year Colleges." Based on a grant awarded by the Intersegmental Program at California State University at the East Bay, this project was designated as a "best practices" project. In 1997, Clarke was chosen as the Los Medanos College Most Valuable Player and recognized by the Los Medanos College Student Senate again in 2000.

# STUDENT TOOL KIT

## 1 POLITICS
### Who Gets What, When, and How

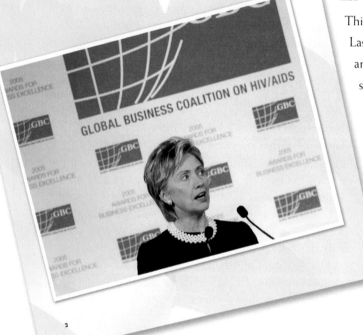

## A Provocative Theme and Lively Narrative

This balanced and exceedingly readable text uses Harold Laswell's classic definition of politics—"who gets what, when and how"—as a framework for presenting a clear, concise, and stimulating introduction to the American political system. The absorbing narrative examines this struggle for power— the participants, the stakes, the processes, and the institu- tions—in a way that provokes thinking and discussion.

## Contemporary and Relevant

The study of politics is the story of not just the past, but the present, of conflict and debate. It is also constantly changing. *Politics in America* captures the essence of politics today. Its many features help students see how our system works, and understand the timely and important issues that are currently challenging our political system. The text consistently helps students understand how what is happening in politics today affects their own lives.

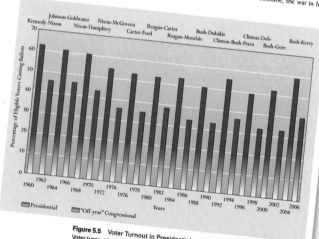

effects on actual turnout at the polls were very limited.[18] Apparently, easy regis- tration does not automatically increase voter turnout.

### Why Vote?

**turnout** Number of voters who actually cast ballots in an election, as a percentage of people eligible to register and vote.

Deciding whether to cast a vote in an election is just as important as deciding which candidate to vote for. *About half of the voting-age population in the United States typi- cally fails to vote, even in presidential elections.* Voter turnout—the number of actual voters in relation to the number of people eligible to register and vote—is even lower in off-year congressional and state elections, when presidential elections are not held. Turnout in local elections (for example, city, county, school board) is even lower when these elections are held separately from national elections. Voter turnout in presidential elections steadily declined for several decades (see Figure 5.5). The three-way presidential race in 1992 temporarily reversed the downward trend. But in 2004 voter turnout surged to levels not seen since the 1960s. Various explana- tions have been offered: the expected closeness of the election, the experience of 2000 when only a few votes in Florida decided the outcome, the war in Iraq,

**Figure 5.5**  Voter Turnout in Presidential and Congressional Elections
Voter turnout is always higher in years with a presidential election. However, voter turnout has generally declined since 1960, even in presidential election years. The exception came in 1992, when intense interest in the contest between George H.W. Bush and Bill Clinton— spiced by the entry of independent Ross Perot—led to a higher-than-normal turnout. In 1996 fewer than half of voting-age Americans bothered to cast ballots. However, in 2004 voter turnout rose to levels not seen since the 1960s.

# ENGAGING SPECIAL FEATURES

## What Do You Think?

This feature helps students to think critically about today's issues and political debates. Controversial questions and national opinion survey data on topics in the national news are included to stimulate classroom discussion.

## A Conflicting View

This feature challenges students to rethink conventional notions about American politics. They are designed to be controversial and to start students thinking about the push and pull that is politics.

## Compared to What?

Global context is essential to the study of American politics today. This feature provides comparisons of the United States with other nations. Discussions include "Freedom and Democracy around the World," as well as topics such as the size of government, tax burdens, voter turnout, television culture, and health care.

## People in Politics

This feature is designed to personalize politics, to illustrate that the participants in the struggle for power are real people. Students are introduced to some of the key participants who have helped shape American politics, their backgrounds, and careers.

## Up Close

This feature illustrates the struggles over who gets what and covers a wide variety of current political conflicts.

# The Constitution of the United States

### THE PREAMBLE

We the People of the United States, in Order to form a more perfect Union, establish Justice, insure domestic Tranquility, provide for the common defense, promote the general Welfare, and secure the Blessings of Liberty to ourselves and our Posterity, do ordain and establish this Constitution for the United States of America.

"We, the people." Three simple words, yet of profound importance and contentious origin. Every government in the world at the time of the Constitutional Convention was some type of monarchy wherein sovereign power flowed from the top. The Founders of our new country rejected monarchy as a form of government and proposed instead a republic, which would draw its sovereignty from the people.

The Articles of Confederation that governed the U.S. from 1776 until 1789 started with: "We the under signed Delegates of the States." Early drafts of the new constitution started with: "We, the states . . ." But again, the Founders were not interested in another union of states but rather the creation of a new national government. Therefore, "We, the states" was changed to "We, the people."

The remainder of the preamble describes the generic functions of government.

of Representatives) organization of the legislative branch.

### House of Representatives: Composition, Qualifications, Apportionment, Impeachment Power

*Section 2* Clause 1. The House of Representatives shall be composed of Members chosen every second Year by the People of the several States, and the Electors in each State shall have the Qualifications requisite for Electors of the most numerous Branch of the State Legislature.

This section sets the term of office for House members (2 years) and indicates that those voting for Congress will have the same qualifications as those voting for the state legislatures. Originally, states limited voters to white property owners. Some states even had religious disqualifications, such as Catholic or Jewish. Most property and religious qualifications for voting were removed by the 1840s, but race and gender restrictions remained, until the 15th and 19th amendments were passed.

Clause 2. No Person shall be a Representative who shall not have attained to the Age of twenty five Years, and been seven Years a Citizen of the United States, and who shall not, when elected, be an inhabitant of that State in which he shall be chosen.

## Annotated Constitution

*Politics in America* features the most integrated approach to the Constitution for the American Government class. An annotated constitution is included as part of the Constitution chapter. It provides extended commentary on key sections and clauses to give students a deeper insight into the intentions behind this important document.

## NEW! A Constitutional Note

A groundbreaking feature at the end of each chapter that expands and integrates coverage of the Constitution into the core concepts of the American Government course.

### A CONSTITUTIONAL NOTE

#### Campaign Finance and Free Speech

Both the Congress and the Supreme Court have confronted the issue of whether or not limiting campaign spending has the effect of limiting free speech. In 1976 in *Buckley v. Valeo*, the Supreme Court struck down Congress's limit on what an individual candidate or independent organization could spend to promote its own views it a campaign. "The First Amendment denies government the power to determine that spending to promote one's political views is... excessive. In the free society ordained by our Constitution, it is not the government but the people who must retain control over the quantity and range of debate in a political campaign."[a] This decision means that wealthy individuals can spend unlimited amounts on their own campaigns, and independent organizations can spend unlimited amounts as long as their spending is independent of a candidate's campaign. However, the Supreme

Court approved limits on *contributions* by individuals and organizations—distinguishing between contributions and expenditures. It approved the Federal Election Commission limits on individual and organizational contributions to political campaigns. Congress sought to remedy the many holes in the original Federal Election Campaign Act of 1974 in its Bipartisan Campaign Reform Act of 2002. It placed limits on "soft money" contributions to political parties, most of which found its way into candidate campaigns. However, Congress did not challenge the Court's *Buckley* decision by trying to prevent individuals or nonprofit organizations from spending money to broadcast their views. Limiting spending for political broadcasting would "place substantial and direct restrictions on the ability of candidates, citizens, and associations to engage in protected political speech."[b] The result was the emergence of independent organizations, known as "527s," in the 2004 election. These organizations spent heavily and played a major role in the presidential campaigns of both parties.

[a] *Buckley v. Valeo*, 424 U.S. 1 (1976).

[b] *McConnell v. Federal Election Commission*, 590 U.S. 93 (2003).

influential as in previous presidential races. The economy was cited as "most important" by about one-fifth of the voters in 2004 and Kerry won the vast majority of these voters.

**Issue Voting** Casting one's vote exclusively on the basis of the policy positions of the candidates is rare. Most voters are unaware of the specific positions taken by candidates on the issues. Indeed, voters often believe that their pre-

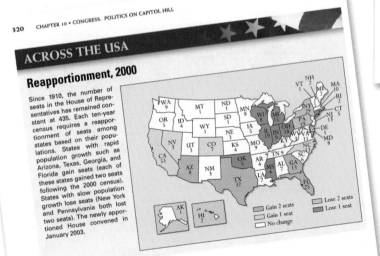

### ACROSS THE USA

#### Reapportionment, 2000

Since 1910, the number of seats in the House of Representatives has remained constant at 435. Each ten-year census requires a reapportionment of seats among states based on their populations. States with rapid population growth such as Arizona, Texas, Georgia, and Florida gain seats (each of these states gained two seats following the 2000 census). States with slow population growth lose seats (New York and Pennsylvania both lost two seats). The newly apportioned House convened in January 2003.

courts have ruled that only official U.S. Bureau of the Census figures may be used; estimated changes since the last census may *not* be used. In recent years, the courts have insisted on nearly exact mathematical equality in populations in congressional districts in a state.

## Across the USA

This collection of maps summarizes important statistical and demographic information relevant to American politics.

# STUDY AIDS FOR SUCCESS IN THE CLASSROOM

## Chapter Outline

Each chapter begins with an outline that gives students an overview of the topics that are covered.

## Thinking About Politics

A brief poll alerts students to crucial issues covered in the chapter. By taking the poll, students can understand their own beliefs on these issues before undertaking their study of the chapter content.

## Marginal Learning Aids

Each chapter contains a **running glossary** in the margin to help students master important concepts. **Website urls** provides sources from which students can obtain additional information. **Think Again** marginal questions are taken from the chapter opening poll to help students revisit their thinking on issues as they move through the content.

## End-of-Chapter Resources

**Summary Notes** and a list of **Key Terms** help students review and test their understanding of the chapter's main topics.

---

### Chapter Outline

- The Power of the Media
- Sources of Media Power
- The Business of the Media
- The Politics of the News
- Polarization of the Media
- Mediated Elections
- Freedom versus Fairness
- Libel and Slander
- Politics and the Internet
- Media Effects: Shaping Political Life

### Think About Politics

1 Are media professionals—news reporters, editors, anchors—the true voice of the people in public affairs?
Yes ☐ No ☐

2 Do the media mirror what is really news, rather than deciding themselves what's important and then making it news?
Yes ☐ No ☐

3 Is television your most important source of news?
Yes ☐ No ☐

4 Should the media report on all aspects of the private lives of public officials?
Yes ☐ No ☐

5 Do the media report equally fairly on Democratic and Republican candidates for office?
Yes ☐ No ☐

6 Should the media be legally required to be fair and accurate in reporting political news?
Yes ☐ No ☐

7 Are you more alienated than attracted by the media's coverage of politics?
Yes ☐ No ☐

8 Is your choice of candidates in elections affected by their advertising?
Yes ☐ No ☐

Ask yourself how much of your knowledge about politics in America comes from television and newspapers and the radio. What you know about politics and how you participate are, in fact, largely determined by the power of the media to decide what they want you to know.

★ ★ ★

### The Power of the Media

Politics—the struggle over who gets what, when, and how—is largely carried out in the **mass media**. The arenas of political conflict are the various media of mass communication—television, newspapers, magazines, radio, books, recordings, motion pictures, and the Internet. What we know about politics comes to us largely through these media. Unless we ourselves are admitted to the White House Oval Office or the committee rooms of Congress or dinner parties at foreign embassies, or unless we ourselves attend political rallies and demonstrations or travel to distant battlefields, we must rely on the mass media to tell us about politics. Furthermore, few of us ever have the opportunity to personally evaluate the character of presidential candidates or cabinet members or members of Congress, or to learn their views on public issues by talking with them face to face. Instead, we must learn about people as well as events from the mass media.

Great power derives from the control of information. Who knows what helps to determine who gets what. The media not only provide an arena for politics; they are also themselves players in that arena. The media not only report on the struggles for power in society; they are also themselves participants in those struggles. The media have long been referred to as America's "fourth branch" of government—and for good reason.[1]

**The Power of Television** Television is the most powerful medium of communication. It is the first true mass communication medium. Virtually every home in the United States has a television set, and the average home has the set turned on for about seven hours a day. Television is regularly chosen over other news media by Americans as the most common news source.

Americans turn to local TV news broadcasts as their most regular source of news. Daily newspapers are read by less than half of the adult public (see Figure 6.1). The national network evening news shows (NBC Nightly News, ABC World News Tonight, CBS Evening News) have lost viewership in recent years. But viewership of CNN, Fox News Cable, CNBC, and MSNBC is rising. Television weekly news magazines, notably CBS's 60 Minutes and ABC's 20/20 have also become major sources of news for many Americans.

169

---

**First Gov**
Official Web portal to all federal departments and agencies, information on government benefits, agency links, and so forth.
www.firstgov.gov

**bureaucracy** Departments, agencies, bureaus, and offices that perform the functions of government.

**chain of command** Hierarchical structure of authority in which command flows downward; typical of a bureaucracy.

**division of labor** Division of work among many specialized workers in a bureaucracy.

**impersonality** Treatment of all persons within a bureaucracy on the basis of "merit" and of all "clients" served by the bureaucracy equally according to rules.

Think Again
Do bureaucrats in Washington have too much power?

**implementation** Development by the federal bureaucracy of procedures and activities to carry out policies legislated by Congress; it includes regulation as well as adjudication.

1. *Needed Expertise and Technological Advances* Congress and the president do not have the time, energy, or expertise to handle the details of policy making. A related explanation is that the increasing complexity and sophistication of technology require technical experts ("technocrats") to actually carry out the intent of Congress and the president. Neither the president nor the 535 members of Congress can look after the myriad details involved in environmental protection, occupational safety, air traffic control, or thousands of other responsibilities of government. So the president and Congress create bureaucracies, appropriate money for them, and authorize them to draw up detailed rules, regulations, and "guidelines" that actually govern the nation. Bureaucratic agencies receive only vague and general directions from the president and Congress. Actual governance is in the hands of the Environmental Protection Agency, the Occupational Safety and Health Administration, the Federal Aviation Administration, and hundreds of similar agencies (see Figure 12.1).

2. *Symbolic Politics* But there are also political explanations for the growth of bureaucratic power. Congress and the president often deliberately pass vague and ambiguous laws. These laws allow elected officials to show symbolically their concerns for environmental protection, occupational safety, and so on, yet avoid the controversies surrounding actual application of those lofty principles. Bureaucracies must then give practical meaning to these symbolic measures by developing specific rules and regulations. If the rules and regulations prove unpopular, Congress and the president can blame the bureaucrats and pretend that these unpopular decisions are a product of an "ungovernable" Washington bureaucracy (see What Do You Think? "How Would You Rate These Federal Agencies?")

3. *Bureaucratic Explanation* There is also a bureaucratic explanation of the growth in the size and influence of government agencies. Bureaucracy has become its own source of power. Bureaucrats have a personal stake in expanding the size of their own agencies and budgets and adding to their own regulatory authority. They can mobilize their "client" groups (interest groups that directly benefit from the agency's programs, such as environmental groups on behalf of the Environmental Protection Agency, farm groups for the Department of Agriculture, the National Education Association for the Department of Education) in support of larger budgets and expanded authority.

4. *Popular Demands* Finally, it has been argued that "big government" is really an expression of democratic sentiments. People want to use the power of government to improve their lives—to regulate and develop the economy, to guarantee civil rights, to develop their communities, and so on. Conservative opponents of the government are really expressing their disdain for popular demands.[3]

**Bureaucratic Power: Implementation** Bureaucracies are not *constitutionally* empowered to decide policy questions. But they do so, nevertheless, as they perform their tasks of implementation, regulation, and adjudication.
**Implementation** is the development of procedures and activities to carry out policies legislated by Congress. It may involve creating new agencies or bureaus or assigning new responsibilities to old agencies. It often requires bureaucracies to translate laws into operational rules and regulations and usually to allocate resources—money, personnel, offices, supplies—to the new function. All of these tasks involve decisions by bureaucrats, decisions that drive how the law

# MEDIA RESOURCES
## AID LEARNING AND ASSESSMENT

### Make it Real 2.0

This comprehensive website contains dynamic simulations, activities on civic participation, interactive timelines and maps, quizzes, primary source documents, Census data, exercises in visual literacy, and self-study quizzes. Students will use information such as real election results, real demographics, maps and voting score cards. Self-study quizzes are available for the student to take to make sure they understand the concepts used in completing the simulations and other activities.
**www.prenhall.com/makeitreal2**

### New! MyPoliSciLab

An easy-to-use online resource that enables students to diagnose their progress by completing an online self-assessment test. Based on the results of this test, each student is provided with a customized study plan, including a variety of tools to help them fully master the material. MyPoliSciLab offers the major resources, including Make It Real online resources and ABC News video clip, in one convenient location. **www.mypoliscilab.com**

### Research Navigator

From finding the right articles and journals, to citing sources, drafting and writing effective papers, and completing research assignments, Research Navigator offers extensive help on the research process.

# Your instructor resources…

Politics in America is accompanied by an extensive supplements package that delivers classroom support in a variety of media.

A comprehensive Instructor's Resource Manual offers recent news and pop culture examples, discussion topics, activities, and assignments, and a list of related Internet activities for students all correlated to related content in each chapter.

The Faculty Resource CD-ROM contains PowerPoint presentations including a Lecture presentation that covers each chapter in detail, a Special Topic presentation for each chapter and a Graphics presentation that includes all of the chapter's graphs, charts, and illustrations. It also includes the Test Item File and Instructor's Manual.

### First Amendment Rights

**In what way can First Amendment rights be considered "preferred freedoms"?**

Copyright 2008 Prentice Hall

### First Amendment Rights: Freedom of Speech

**Free speech laws must balance individual liberties and societal interests**

Copyright 2006 Prentice Hall

# Custom solutions

It's your course. Why not teach from your book? The Pearson Custom Publishing program allows you to tailor the content and organization of Politics in America to the specific needs of your course, including the addition of your own course notes and original content. Pearson custom editions are available in groundbreaking full color. Contact your local Prentice Hall representative today to begin building your ideal text. Visit www.pearsoncustom.com for additional information.

# Part One
# POLITICS

## On the Edge

**ABCNEWS**
Originally Aired: **April 15, 2004**
Program: **Nightline**
Running Time: **16:16**

When we say "poor" or "poverty-stricken Americans," what image comes to mind? The homeless man sleeping on the grate? The unemployed person standing in line at the unemployment or welfare office? What about someone who has a full-time job making $9 an hour? That sounds like a decent wage, right? Well, that actually comes out to just above $18,000 a year, and for a family with one adult and three children, that means poverty. We've decided to launch a new, occasional series that looks at the working poor: the millions of Americans who live on the edge of poverty.

The genesis of tonight's show was a great new book by former *New York Times* reporter and Pulitzer Prize winner David Shipler. *The Working Poor* takes a comprehensive look at the lives of people set to plunge into the abyss of financial ruin if just one payment isn't met, if their car breaks down, or if they call in sick at work. Such seemingly minor events can have catastrophic effects on this segment of the population and Mr. Shipler has documented many of their lives, weaving economic analysis into the story of what these people face trying to survive from day to day. Ted Koppel sat down with Mr. Shipler for an extensive interview on his findings.

## Critical Thinking Questions

1. How does author David Shipler define "working poor"?

2. How does the video's title, "On the Edge," apply to the working poor?

3. The underlying problem of the working poor seems to be their vulnerability in every area of life. Explain how the working poor are vulnerable in ways not experienced by other economic groups.

4. Author David Shipler disagrees with the concept of a "culture of poverty." Instead, he speaks of an "ecological system of interactions." What does he mean?

5. What is the difference between an entitlement and a means-tested entitlement?

# 1 POLITICS
## Who Gets What, When, and How

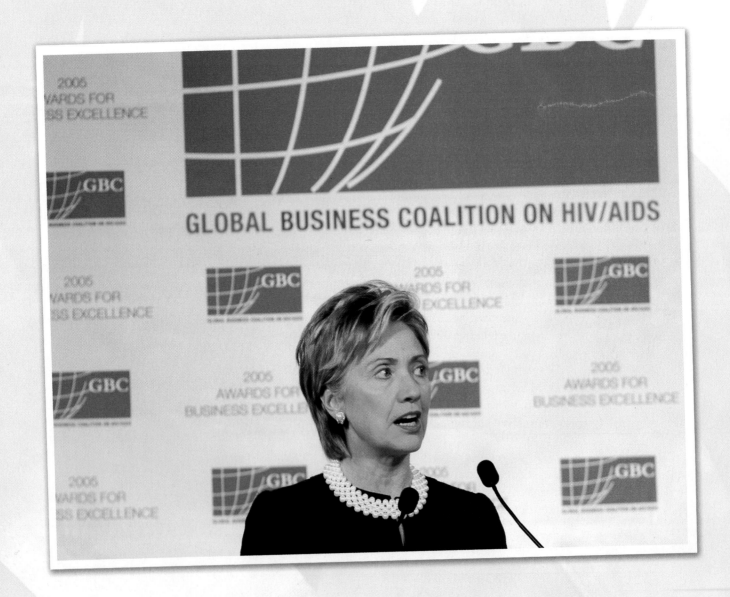

## Chapter Outline

- Politics and Political Science
- Politics and Government
- The Purposes of Government
- The Meaning of Democracy
- The Paradox of Democracy
- Direct Versus Representative Democracy
- Who Really Governs?
- Democracy in America

## Think About Politics

1 Can you trust the government to do what is right most of the time?
Yes ☐ No ☐

2 Should any group other than the government have the right to use force?
Yes ☐ No ☐

3 Is it ever right to disobey the law?
Yes ☐ No ☐

4 Should important decisions in a democracy be submitted to voters rather than decided by Congress?
Yes ☐ No ☐

5 Is the government run by a few big interests looking out for themselves?
Yes ☐ No ☐

6 In a democracy should "majority rule" be able to limit the rights of members of an unpopular or dangerous minority?
Yes ☐ No ☐

7 Is government trying to do too many things that should be left to individuals?
Yes ☐ No ☐

8 Does the threat of terrorism on American soil justify increased government surveillance of its citizens?
Yes ☐ No ☐

*Who has power and how they use it are the basis of all these questions. Issues of power underlie everything we call politics and the study of political science.*

★   ★   ★

## Politics and Political Science

**Politics** is deciding "who gets what, when, and how."[1] It is an activity by which people try to get more of whatever there is to get—money, prestige, jobs, respect, sex, even power itself. Politics occurs in many different settings. We talk about office politics, student politics, union politics, church politics, and so forth. But political science usually limits its attention to *politics in government.*

**Political science** is the study of politics, or the study of who gets what, when, and how. The *who* are the participants in politics—voters, special-interest groups, political parties, television and the press, corporations and labor unions, lawyers and lobbyists, foundations and think tanks, and both elected and appointed government officials, including members of Congress, the president and vice president, judges, prosecutors, and bureaucrats. The *what* of politics are public policies—the decisions that governments make concerning social welfare, health care, education, national defense, law enforcement, the environment, taxation, and thousands of other issues that come before governments. The *when* and *how* are the political process—campaigns and elections, political reporting in the news media, television debates, fund raising, lobbying, decision making in the White House and executive agencies, and decision making in the courts.

Political science is generally concerned with three questions. *Who governs? For what ends? By what means?* Throughout this book, we are concerned with who participates in politics, how government decisions are made, who benefits most from those decisions, and who bears their greatest costs (see Figure 1.1).

Politics would be simple if everyone agreed on who should govern, who should get what, who should pay for it, and how and when it should be done. But conflict arises from disagreements over these questions, and sometimes the question of confidence in the government itself underlies the conflict (see *What Do You Think?* "Can You Trust the Government?").

## Politics and Government

What distinguishes governmental politics from politics in other institutions in society? After all, parents, teachers, unions, banks, corporations,

**politics** Deciding who gets what, when, and how.

**political science** The study of politics: who governs, for what ends, and by what means.

**Figure 1.1**   Who Gets What, When, and How

Political science is the study of politics. The distinguished political scientist Harold Lasswell entitled his most popular book *Politics: Who Gets What, When and How.* The first topic of politics is "Who?" (that is, who are the participants in politics, both within and outside of government?), "When and how are political decisions made?" (that is, how do the institutions and processes of politics function?), and "What outcomes are produced?" (that is, what public policies are adopted?). Shown here are some of the topics of concern to political science.

## Who Governs: Participants

| *Governmental* | *Nongovernmental* |
|---|---|
| President and White House staff | Voters |
| Executive Office of the President, including Office of Management and Budget | Campaign contributors |
| | Interest-group leaders and members |
| Cabinet officers and executive agency heads | Party leaders and party identifiers in the electorate |
| Bureaucrats | Corporate and union leaders |
| Congress members | Media leaders, including press and television anchors and reporters |
| Congressional staff | |
| Supreme Court justices | Lawyers and lobbyists |
| Federal appellate and district judges | Think tanks and foundation personnel |

## When and How: Institutions and Processes

| *Institutions* | *Processes* |
|---|---|
| Constitution | Socialization and learning |
|   Separation of powers | Opinion formation |
|   Checks and balances | Party identification |
|   Federalism | Voting |
|   Judicial review | Contributing |
|   Amendment procedures | Joining organizations |
|   Electoral system | Talking politics |
| Presidency | Running for office |
| Congress | Campaigning |
|   Senate | Polling |
|   House of Representatives | Fund raising |
| | Parading and demonstrating |
| Courts | Nonviolent direct action |
|   Supreme Court | Violence |
|   Appellate courts | |
|   District courts | Agenda setting |
| | Lobbying |
| Parties | Logrolling |
|   National committees | Deciding |
|   Conventions | Budgeting |
|   State and local organizations | Implementing and evaluating |
| Press and television | Adjudicating |

## What Outcomes: Public Policies

| | |
|---|---|
| Civil liberties | Environmental protection |
| Civil rights | Economic development |
| Equality | Economic stability |
| Criminal justice | Taxation |
| Welfare | Government spending and deficits |
| Social Security | National defense |
| Health | Foreign affairs |
| Education | Homeland Security |
| Energy | |

— Think Again —

Should any group other than the government have the right to use force?

**government** Organization extending to the whole society that can legitimately use force to carry out its decisions.

and many other organizations make decisions about who gets what in society. The answer is that only **government** decisions can *extend to the whole society*, and only government can *legitimately use force*. Other institutions encompass only a part of society: for example, students and faculty in a college, members of a church or union, employees or customers of a corporation. And individuals have a legal right to voluntarily withdraw from *non*governmental organizations. But governments make decisions affecting everyone, and no one can voluntarily

Conflict exists in all political activities as participants struggle over who gets what, when, and how. From the streets to the Congress to the White House, participants in the political process compete to further their goals and ambitions.

withdraw from government's authority (without leaving the country, and thus becoming subject to some other government's authority). Some individuals and organizations—muggers, gangs, crime families—occasionally use physical force to get what they want. But only governments can use force legitimately—that is, people generally believe it is acceptable for the government to use force if necessary to uphold its laws, but they do not extend this right to other institutions or individuals.

Most people would say that they obey the law in order to avoid fines and stay out of prison. But if large numbers of people all decided to disobey the law at the same time, the government would not have enough police or jails to hold them all.

The government can rely on force only against relatively small numbers of offenders. Most of us, most of the time, obey laws out of habit—the habit of compliance. We have been taught to believe that law and order are necessary and that government is right to punish those who disobey its laws.

Government thus enjoys **legitimacy**, or rightfulness, in its use of force.[2] A democratic government has a special claim to legitimacy because it is based on the consent of its people, who participate in the selection of its leaders and the making of its laws. Those who disagree with a law have the option of working for its change by speaking out, petitioning, demonstrating, forming interest groups or parties, voting against unpopular leaders, or running for office themselves.

**American Political Science Association**
Association of college and university teachers advises students how to study political science.
*www.apsanet.org*

—— Think Again ——
Is violence ever justified as a means of bringing about political change?

**legitimacy** Widespread acceptance of something as necessary, rightful, and legally binding.

# WHAT DO YOU THINK?

## Can You Trust the Government?

Americans are suspicious of big government. Many do not trust the government in Washington to "do what is right." Trust in government has varied over the years, as measured by polls asking, "How much of the time do you think you can trust the government in Washington to do what is right? Just about always? Most of the time? Some of the time? None of the time?" Low levels of trust and confidence in government may represent profound disaffection with the political system, or more superficial dissatisfaction with current leaders or policies.[a] During the early years of the Johnson Administration (and even earlier, during the Kennedy and Eisenhower presidencies), public confidence in government was high. But in the late '60s and early '70s defeat and humiliation in Vietnam appeared to diminish public confidence. On the heels of the Vietnam experience came the Watergate scandal and President Richard Nixon's forced resignation in 1974—the first resignation of a president in U.S. history—causing public confidence in government to fall further.

Throughout the long years of decline in public confidence in government, television has broadcast many negative images of government and public policy. Television producers seldom consider good news

as "news" but instead focus on violence, scandal, corruption, and incompetence (see Chapter 6, "Mass Media: Setting the Political Agenda").

But public confidence in government can be at least partially restored, as it was in part during the Reagan presidency. Perhaps President Reagan's personal popularity was part of the reason that popular confidence in government rose.[b]

Economic recessions erode public confidence in government. People expect the president and Congress to lead them out of "hard times." George H. W. Bush's Gulf War success in 1991 raised public confidence only temporarily; the perceived failure of his administration to act decisively to restore the nation's economic health helped to send public confidence in government back down. Sustained growth in the economy during the 1990s under President Clinton improved public trust in government.

The terrorist attacks of September 11, 2001, rallied Americans behind their government as no other event since the Japanese attack on Pearl Harbor in 1941. American flags sprouted from homes, businesses, and automobiles. Trust in government "to do the right thing" leaped to levels not seen since the 1960s. This dramatic rise in trust after "9/11" leveled off in 2002, but still remained higher than at any time in recent years.

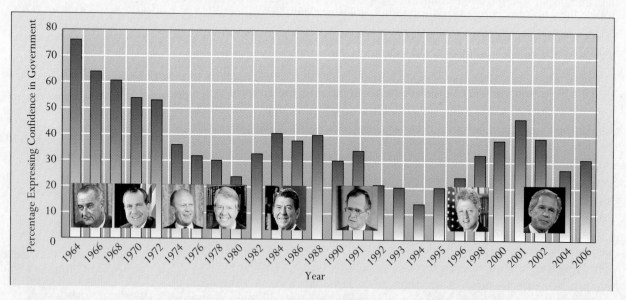

**Public Confidence, That the Federal Government Can Be Trusted to "Do What Is Right Most of the Time"**

[a]Timothy E. Cook and Paul Gronke, "The Skeptical American," *Journal of Politics* Vol. 67 (Aug., 2005) 784–803.

[b]Arthur H. Miller, "Confidence in Government during the 1980s," *American Politics Quarterly* 19 (April 1991): 147–73.

*Source:* 1992–2006 data from Gallup Opinion Polls (http://www.gallup.com/poll/topics/trust_gov.asd), Copyright © 1992–2004, The Gallup Organization.

Since people living in a democracy can effect change by "working within the system," they have a greater moral obligation to obey the law than people living under regimes in which they have no voice. However, there may be some occasions when "civil disobedience" even in a democracy may be morally justified (see *A Conflicting View:* "Sometimes It's Right to Disobey the Law").

## The Purposes of Government

All governments tax, penalize, punish, restrict, and regulate their people. Governments in the United States—the federal government in Washington, the 50 state governments, and the more than 87,000 local governments—take nearly 40 cents out of every dollar Americans earn. Each year, the Congress enacts about 500 laws; federal bureaucracies publish about 19,000 rules and regulations, the state legislatures enact about 25,000 laws; and cities, counties, school districts, and other local governments enact countless local ordinances. Each of these laws restricts our freedom in some way.

Why do people put up with governments? An answer to this question can be found in the words of the Preamble to the Constitution of the United States:

> We the people of the United States, in Order to form a more perfect Union, establish Justice, insure domestic Tranquility, provide for the common defense, promote the general Welfare, and secure the Blessings of Liberty to ourselves and our Posterity, do ordain and establish this Constitution for the United States of America.

**To Establish Justice and Insure Domestic Tranquility**   Government manages conflict and maintains order. We might think of government as a **social contract** among people who agree to allow themselves to be regulated and taxed in exchange for protection of their lives and property. No society can allow individuals or groups to settle their conflicts by street fighting, murder, kidnapping, rioting, bombing, or terrorism. Whenever government fails to control such violence, we describe it as "a breakdown in law and order." Without the protection of government, human lives and property are endangered, and only those skilled with fists and weapons have much of a chance of survival. The seventeenth-century English political philosopher Thomas Hobbes described life without government as "a war where every man is enemy to every man," where people live in "continual fear and danger of violent death."[3]

**To Provide for the Common Defense**   Many anthropologists link the origins of government to warfare—to the need of early communities to protect themselves from raids by outsiders and to organize raids against others. Since the Revolutionary War, the U.S. government has been responsible for the country's defense. During the long Cold War, when America confronted a nuclear-armed, expansionist-minded, communist-governed Soviet Union, the United States spent nearly half of the federal budget on national defense. With the end of the Cold War, defense spending fell to about 15 percent of the federal budget, but defense spending has begun to creep upward again as the nation confronts the new war on terrorism. National defense will always remain a primary responsibility of United States government.

**To Promote the General Welfare**   Government promotes the general welfare in a number of ways. It provides **public goods**—goods and services that private markets cannot readily furnish either because they are too expensive for individuals to buy for themselves (for example, a national park, a highway, or a

— Think Again —

Is it ever right to disobey the law?

**WWW  The King Center**   Atlanta-based center commemorates the life and teachings of Martin Luther King, Jr.
*www.theKingCenter.com*

**WWW  Internet Encyclopedia of Philosophy**   At this site, you can find a concise description of social contract theory along with a discussion of John Locke's writing.
*www.utm.edu/research/iep/*

**social contract**  Idea that government originates as an implied contract among individuals who agree to obey laws in exchange for protection of their rights.

**WWW  DefenseLink**   Official site of the U.S. Department of Defense, with current news as well as links to Army, Navy, Air Force, Marine, and other defense agencies.
*www.defenselink.gov*

**public goods**  Goods and services that cannot readily be provided by markets, either because they are too expensive for a single individual to buy or because if one person bought them, everyone else would use them without paying.

# A CONFLICTING VIEW

## Sometimes It's Right to Disobey the Law

Civil disobedience is the nonviolent violation of laws that people believe to be unjust. Civil disobedience denies the *legitimacy,* or rightfulness, of a law and implies that a higher moral authority takes precedence over unjust laws. It is frequently a political tactic of minorities. (Majorities can more easily change laws through conventional political activity.)

Why resort to civil disobedience in a democracy? Why not work within the democratic system to change unjust laws? In 1963 a group of Alabama clergy posed these questions to Martin Luther King, Jr., and asked him to call off mass demonstrations in Birmingham, Alabama. King, who had been arrested in the demonstrations, replied in his now famous "Letter from Birmingham City Jail":

> One may well ask, "How can you advocate breaking some laws and obeying others?" The answer is found in the fact that there are unjust laws. I would be the first to advocate obeying just laws. One has not only a legal but a moral responsibility to obey just laws. Conversely, one has a moral responsibility to disobey unjust laws.

King argued that *nonviolent direct action* was a vital aspect of democratic politics. The political purpose of civil disobedience is to call attention or "to bear witness" to the existence of injustices. Only laws regarded as unjust are broken, and they are broken openly, without hatred or violence. Punishment is actively sought rather than avoided, since punishment will further emphasize the injustice of the laws.

The objective of nonviolent civil disobedience is to stir the conscience of an apathetic majority and to win support for measures that will eliminate the injustices. By accepting punishment for the violation of an unjust law, persons practicing civil disobedience demonstrate their sincerity. They hope to shame the majority and to make it ask itself how far it is willing to go to protect the status quo. Thus, according to King's

*Dr. Martin Luther King, Jr., shown here marching in Mississippi with his wife, Coretta Scott King, and others, used civil disobedience to advance the rights of African Americans during the 1950s and 1960s. (Copyright © Flip Schulke)*

teachings, civil disobedience is clearly differentiated from hatred and violence:

> One who breaks an unjust law must do it openly, lovingly (not hatefully as the white mothers did in New Orleans when they were seen on television screaming "nigger, nigger, nigger") and with a willingness to accept the penalty. I submit that an individual who breaks a law that conscience tells him is unjust, and willingly accepts the penalty by staying in jail to arouse the conscience of the community over its injustice, is in reality expressing the very highest respect for law.

In 1964 Martin Luther King, Jr., received the Nobel Peace Prize in recognition of his extraordinary contributions to the development of nonviolent methods of social change.

*Source:* Martin Luther King, Jr., "Letter from Birmingham City Jail," April 16, 1963.

---

**free market** Free competition for voluntary exchange among individuals, firms, and corporations.

sewage disposal plant) or because if one person bought them, everyone else would "free-ride," or use them without paying (for example, clean air, police protection, or national defense).

Nevertheless, Americans acquire most of their goods and services on the **free market**, through voluntary exchange among individuals, firms, and corporations. The **gross domestic product (GDP)**—the dollar sum of all the goods and services produced in the United States in a year—amounts to more than $12 trillion.

Government spending in the United States—federal, state, and local governments combined—amounts to about $4 trillion, or an amount equivalent to 30 percent of the gross domestic product.

Governments also regulate society. Free markets cannot function effectively if individuals and firms engage in fraud, deception, or unfair competition, or if contracts cannot be enforced. Moreover, many economic activities impose costs on persons who are not direct participants in these activities. Economists refer to such costs as **externalities**. A factory that produces air pollution or wastewater imposes external costs on community residents who would otherwise enjoy cleaner air or water. A junkyard that creates an eyesore makes life less pleasant for neighbors and passersby. Many government regulations are designed to reduce these external costs.

To promote general welfare, governments also use **income transfers** from taxpayers to people who are regarded as deserving. Government agencies and programs provide support and care for individuals who cannot supply these things for themselves through the private job market, for example, ill, elderly, and disabled people, and dependent children who cannot usually be expected to find productive employment. The largest income transfer programs are Social Security and Medicare, which are paid to the elderly regardless of their personal wealth. Other large transfer payments go to farmers, veterans, and the unemployed, as well as to a wide variety of businesses. As we shall see, the struggle of individuals and groups to obtain direct government payments is a major motivator of political activity (see *What Do You Think?* "What Government Programs Do You Support?").

**To Secure the Blessings of Liberty**   All governments must maintain order, protect national security, provide public goods, regulate society, and care for those unable to fend for themselves. But *democratic* governments have a special added responsibility—to protect individual liberty by ensuring that all people are treated equally before the law. No one is above the law. The president must obey the Constitution and laws of the United States, and so must members of Congress, governors, judges, and the police. A democratic government must protect people's freedom to speak and write what they please, to practice their religion, to petition, to form groups and parties, to enjoy personal privacy, and to exercise their rights if accused of a crime.

# The Meaning of Democracy

Throughout the centuries, thinkers in many different cultures contributed to the development of democratic government. Early Greek philosophers contributed the word **democracy**, which means "rule by the many." But there is no single definition of *democracy*, nor is there a tightly organized system of democratic thought. It is better, perhaps, to speak of democratic traditions than of a single democratic ideology.

Unfortunately, the looseness of the term *democracy* allows it to be perverted by *anti*democratic governments. Hardly a nation in the world exists that does not *claim* to be "democratic." Governments that outlaw political opposition, suppress dissent, discourage religion, and deny fundamental freedoms of speech and press still claim to be "democracies," "democratic republics," or "people's republics" (for example, the Democratic People's Republic of Korea is the official name of Communist North Korea). These governments defend their use of the term *democracy* by claiming that their policies reflect the true interests of their people. But they are unwilling to allow political freedoms or to hold free elections in

**gross domestic product (GDP)** Measure of economic performance in terms of the nation's total production of goods and services for a single year, valued in terms of market prices.

**externalities** Costs imposed on people who are not direct participants in an activity.

**income transfers** Government transfers of income from taxpayers to persons regarded as deserving.

**Council for Excellence in Government**
A Washington-based think tank, relatively unbiased, that regularly publishes polls and studies on key issues facing the nation. *www.excelgov.org*

**democracy** Governing system in which the people govern themselves, from the Greek term meaning "rule by the many."

**U.S. Information Agency**
Official government site defining democracy, individual rights, and the culture of democracy. *www.usinfo.state.gov/products/ pubs/whatsdem*

## WHAT DO YOU THINK?

### What Government Programs Do You Support?

Although many Americans lack confidence in their government in general, they support many specific programs of the government. In somewhat of a paradox, Americans often express distrust in the federal government, yet at the same time approve of many of the programs and activities of that government.

The Council on Excellence in Government, which conducted this poll, believes that the most highly regarded programs are those that serve (or potentially serve) all Americans, rather than target groups.

**Support for Government Programs**

| Support a Great Deal | Percent |
| --- | --- |
| Social Security | 69 |
| The Armed Forces | 64 |
| Medicare | 64 |
| Enforcing workplace safety | 63 |
| Enforcing laws against discrimination | 61 |
| Programs for public schools | 61 |
| Enforcing food and drug safety | 60 |
| College student loans | 56 |
| Enforcing minimum wage laws | 56 |
| Enforcing environmental protection laws | 55 |
| Federal law enforcement, such as the FBI | 45 |
| Enforcing family and medical leave laws | 40 |
| NASA and the space program | 34 |
| Affirmative action programs | 29 |
| Welfare programs | 24 |

*Source:* Council Excellence in Government nationwide survey, February, 1997. www.excelgov.org. Reprinted by permission of Council on Excellence in Government.

order to find out whether their people really agree with their policies. In effect, they use the term as a political slogan rather than a true description of their government.

**democratic ideals**
Individual dignity, equality before the law, widespread participation in public decisions, and public decisions by majority rule, with one person having one vote.

The actual existence of **democratic ideals** varies considerably from country to country, regardless of their names (see *Compared to What?* "Freedom and Democracy around the World"). A meaningful definition of democracy must include the following ideals: 1) recognition of the dignity of every individual; 2) equal protection under the law for every individual; 3) opportunity for everyone to participate in public decisions; and 4) decision making by majority rule, with one person having one vote.

**Individual Dignity**   The underlying value of democracy is the dignity of the individual. Human beings are entitled to life and liberty, personal property, and equal protection under the law. These liberties are *not* granted by governments; they belong to every person born into the world. The English political philosopher John Locke (1632–1704) argued that a higher "natural law" guaranteed liberty to every person and that this natural law was morally superior to all human laws and governments. Each individual possesses "certain inalienable Rights, among these are Life, Liberty, and Property."[4] When Thomas Jefferson wrote his eloquent defense of the American Revolution in the Declaration of Independence for the Continental Congress in Philadelphia in 1776, he borrowed heavily from Locke (perhaps even to the point of plagiarism):

> We hold these truths to be self-evident, that all Men are created equal, that they are endowed by their Creator with certain unalienable Rights, that among these are Life, Liberty and the Pursuit of Happiness.

Individual dignity requires personal freedom. People who are directed by governments in every aspect of their lives, people who are "collectivized" and made into workers for the state, people who are enslaved—all are denied the personal

# COMPARED TO WHAT?

## Freedom and Democracy Around the World

Worldwide progress toward freedom over the past half-century has been impressive. In 1950 there were 22 democracies accounting for 31 percent of the world population that were said to be "free." Another 21 nations with restricted democratic practices were labeled "partly free"; they accounted for an additional 11.9 percent of the world population. By 2005, democracy had spread to 88 "free" countries that constituted 44 percent of the world population; an additional 21 percent lived in nations labeled "partly free." "Not-free" authoritarian and totalitarian regimes governed more than one-third of the world's population.[a]

Worldwide progress toward freedom and democracy has been evident since 1989 notably as a result of the collapse of communism in Eastern Europe and the demise of the Soviet Union.

One way to assess the degree of democracy in a governmental system is to consider its record in ensuring political freedoms—enabling citizens to participate meaningfully in government—and individual liberties. A checklist for political freedoms might include whether the chief executive and national legislature are elected; whether elections are generally fair, with open campaigning and honest tabulation of votes; and whether multiple candidates and parties participate. A checklist for individual liberties might include whether the press and broadcasting are free and independent of the government; whether people are free to assemble, protest, and form opposition parties; whether religious institutions, labor unions, business organizations, and other groups are free and independent of the government; and whether individuals are free to own property, travel, and move their residence.

The Freedom House is a New York-based think tank that regularly surveys political conditions around the world (see map). Russia's score was downgraded by Freedom House in 2004 and its classification remains only "partly free." Freedom House denounced President Vladimir Putin's government takeover of that nation's media.

[a]Freedom House, *Democracy's Century* (New York: Freedom House, 2001).

### Map of Freedom 2005

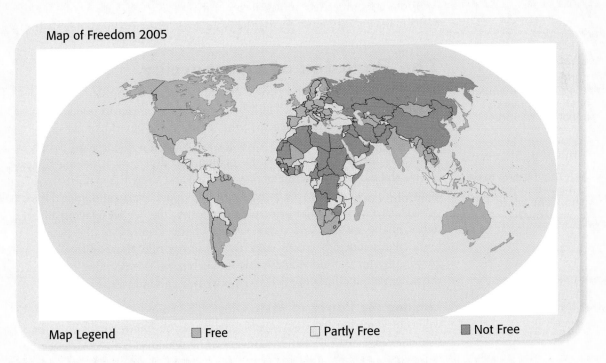

Map Legend    ▨ Free    ☐ Partly Free    ▓ Not Free

**Freedom House**
A think tank monitoring the ongoing evolution of global human rights and liberty; provides an annual world survey covering freedom's progress throughout the state system. *www.freedomhouse.org/*

— Think Again —

Should important decisions in a democracy be submitted to voters rather than decided by Congress?

**National Endowment for Democracy**
Private advocacy group for worldwide democracy and human rights. *www.ned.org*

— Think Again —

In a democracy should "majority rule" be able to limit the rights of members of an unpopular or dangerous minority?

— Think Again —

Is government trying to do too many things that should be left to individuals?

**paradox of democracy**
Potential for conflict between individual freedom and majority rule.

dignity to which all human beings are entitled. Democratic governments try to minimize the role of government in the lives of citizens.

**Equality**   True democracy requires equal protection of the law for every individual. Democratic governments cannot discriminate between blacks and whites, or men and women, or rich and poor, or any groups of people in applying the law. Not only must a democratic government refrain from discrimination itself, but it must also work to prevent discrimination in society generally. Today our notion of equality extends to equality of opportunity—the obligation of government to ensure that all Americans have an equal opportunity to develop their full potential.

**Participation in Decision Making**   Democracy means individual participation in the decisions that affect individuals' lives. People should be free to choose for themselves how they want to live. Individual participation in government is necessary for individual dignity. People in a democracy should not have decisions made *for* them but *by* them. Even if they make mistakes, it is better that they be permitted to do so than to take away their rights to make their own decisions. The true democrat would reject even a wise and benevolent dictatorship because it would threaten the individual's character, self-reliance, and dignity. The argument for democracy is not that the people will always choose wise policies for themselves, but that people who cannot choose for themselves are not really free.

**Majority Rule: One Person, One Vote**   Collective decision making in democracies must be by majority rule, with each person having one vote. That is, each person's vote must be equal to every other person's, regardless of status, money, or fame. Whenever any individual is denied political equality because of race, sex, or wealth, then the government is not truly democratic. Majorities are not always right. But majority *rule* means that all persons have an equal say in decisions affecting them. If people are truly equal, their votes must count equally, and a majority vote must decide the issue, even if the majority decides foolishly.

# The Paradox of Democracy

But what if a *majority* of the people decide to attack the rights of some unpopular individuals or minorities? What if hate, prejudice, or racism infects a majority of people and they vote for leaders who promise to "get rid of the Jews" or "put blacks in their place" or "bash a few gays"? What if a majority of people vote to take away the property of wealthy people and distribute it among themselves.[5] Do we abide by the principle of majority rule and allow the majority to do what it wants? Or do we defend the principle of individual liberty and limit the majority's power? If we enshrine the principle of majority rule, we are placing all our confidence in the wisdom and righteousness of the majority of the people. Yet we know that democracy means more than majority rule, that it also means freedom and dignity for the individual. How do we resolve this **paradox of democracy**— the potential for conflict between majority rule and individual freedom?

**Limiting the Power of Majorities**   The Founders of the American nation were not sure that freedom would be safe in the hands of the majority. In *The Federalist Papers* in 1787, James Madison warned against a direct democracy: "Pure democracy . . . can admit of no cure for the mischiefs of faction. . . . There is nothing to check the inducements to sacrifice the weaker party, or an obnoxious individual."[6] So the Founders wrote a Constitution and adopted a Bill of Rights that limited the power of government over the individual, that placed some personal liberties beyond the reach of majorities. They established the principle

The paradox of democracy balances the principles of majority rule against the principle of individual liberty. When the German people voted Adolf Hitler and the Nazi Party into power, did majority rule give the Nazis free rein to restrict the individual liberties of the people? Or did those who abhorred the trespasses of their government have the right to fight against its power?

of **limited government**—a government that is itself restrained by law. Under a limited government, even if a majority of voters wanted to, they could not prohibit communists or atheists or racists from speaking or writing. Nor could they ban certain religions, set aside the rights of criminal defendants to a fair trial, or prohibit people from moving or quitting their jobs. These rights belong to individuals, not to majorities or governments.

## Totalitarianism: Unlimited Government Power
No government can be truly democratic if it directs every aspect of its citizens' lives. Individuals must be free to shape their own lives, free from the dictates of governments or even majorities of their fellow citizens. Indeed, we call a government with *un*limited power over its citizens totalitarian. Under **totalitarianism**, the individual possesses no personal liberty. Totalitarian governments decide what people can say or write;

**limited government**
Principle that government power over the individual is limited, that there are some personal liberties that even a majority cannot regulate, and that government itself is restrained by law.

**totalitarianism** Rule by an elite that exercises unlimited power over individuals in all aspects of life.

Political sociologists have observed that the military in totalitarian societies has a distinct body language. Soldiers in Nazi Germany and, as seen here, communist North Korea used a "goose step" when on parade—a march in which the knee is unbent and the foot, encased in a heavy boot, is stamped on the ground, providing a powerful image of authority and force. In democratic societies, the goose step is not employed; indeed, it is regarded as somewhat ridiculous.

what unions, churches, or parties they can join, if any; where people must live; what work they must do; what goods they can find in stores and what they will be allowed to buy and sell; whether citizens will be allowed to travel outside of their country; and so on. Under a totalitarian government, the total life of the individual is subject to government control.

Totalitarian governments undertake to control all agencies of the government, including the military and the police, and virtually all other institutions of society including newspapers, television, schools, churches, businesses, banks, labor unions, and any other organization that might challenge their control. In contrast, democratic societies allow many other institutions to operate independently of the government (see *Up Close:* "Confidence in American Institutions").

**Authoritarianism**    In many countries throughout the world, a single individual or ruling group monopolizes all *political* power, but allows people to otherwise lead their lives as they wish. **Authoritarianism** is largely concerned with dominating government. People can conduct business and trade, join churches, live where they wish, and otherwise conduct their *private* lives without government interference. They have no role to play in politics, no control over their government, no competitive political parties, no elections, and are otherwise barred from political life. Authoritarianism appears somewhat less oppressive, at least in the everyday lives of the people, than totalitarianism.

> **authoritarianism** Monopoly of political power by an individual or small group that otherwise allows people to go about their private lives as they wish.

**Constitutional Government**    Constitutions, written or unwritten, are the principal means by which governmental powers are limited. Constitutions set forth the liberties of individuals and restrain governments from interfering with these liberties. Consider, for example, the opening words of the First Amendment to the U.S. Constitution: "Congress shall make no law respecting an establishment of religion, or prohibiting the free exercise thereof." This amendment places religious belief beyond the reach of the government. The government itself is restrained by law. It cannot, even by majority vote, interfere with the personal liberty to worship as one chooses. In addition, armed with the power of judicial review, the courts can declare unconstitutional laws passed by majority vote of Congress or state legislatures (see "Judicial Power" in Chapter 13).

Throughout this book we examine how well limited constitutional government succeeds in preserving individual liberty in the United States. We examine free speech and press, the mass media, religious freedom, the freedom to protest and demonstrate, and the freedom to support political candidates and interest groups of all kinds. We examine how well the U.S. Constitution protects individuals from discrimination and inequality. And we examine how far government should go in protecting society without destroying individual liberty (see *Up Close:* "Terrorism's Threat to Democracy" on page 18).

> **New Rules Project** An organization advocating local government solutions and "direct democracy," including the New England town meeting. *www.newrules.org*

# Direct Versus Representative Democracy

In the Gettysburg Address, Abraham Lincoln spoke about "a government of the people, by the people, for the people," and his ringing phrase remains an American ideal. But can we take this phrase literally? More than 300 million Americans are spread over 4 million square miles. If we brought everyone together, standing shoulder to shoulder, they would occupy 70 square miles. One round of five-minute speeches by everyone would take over 3,000 years. "People could be born, grow old, and die while they waited for the assembly to make one decision."[7]

> **direct democracy** Governing system in which every person participates actively in every public decision, rather than delegating decision making to representatives.

**Direct democracy** (also called pure or participatory democracy), where everyone actively participates in every decision, is rare. The closest approximation to direct democracy in American government may be the traditional New England

## UP CLOSE

### Confidence in American Institutions

American's confidence in their government varies over time, but overall it is much lower than a generation ago. Which institutions in society today enjoy the confidence of the American people? In somewhat of a paradox for a democratic society, the *military* enjoys the greatest confidence of Americans. The *police* also enjoyed a great deal of confidence, although "the criminal justice system" (defined by most respondents as the courts) does not. Among branches of the national government, the president and the Supreme Court rate fairly high in confidence. But Congress is rated very low.

*Q. I am going to read you a list of institutions in American society. Please tell me how much confidence you, yourself, have in each one: a great deal, quite a lot, some, or very little.*

|  | Percent Saying a Great Deal or Quite a Lot |
|---|---|
| The military | 74 |
| The police | 63 |
| Organized religion | 53 |
| Banks | 49 |
| The presidency | 44 |
| The medical system | 42 |
| The U.S. Supreme Court | 41 |
| Public schools | 37 |
| Television news | 28 |
| Newspapers | 28 |
| The criminal justice system | 26 |
| Organized labor | 24 |
| Congress | 22 |
| Big business | 22 |
| Health maintenance organizations (HMOs) | 17 |

*Source:* Copyright © 2005 The Gallup Organization.

*Americans' patriotism and love of the flag as a symbol of their freedom doesn't always translate into confidence in government institutions.*

town meeting, where all of the citizens come together face-to-face to decide about town affairs. But today most New England towns vest authority in a board of officials elected by the townspeople to make policy decisions between town meetings, and professional administrators are appointed to supervise the day-to-day town services. The town meeting is vanishing because citizens cannot spend so much of their time and energy in community decision making.

**Representative democracy** recognizes that it is impossible to expect millions of people to come together and decide every issue. Instead, representatives of the people are elected by the people to decide issues on behalf of the people. Elections must be open to competition so that the people can choose representatives who reflect their own views. And elections must take place in an environment of free speech and press, so that both candidates and voters can freely express their views. Finally, elections must be held periodically so that representatives can be thrown out of office if they no longer reflect the views of the majority of the people.

No government can claim to be a representative democracy, then, unless

1. Representatives are selected by vote of all the people.

2. Elections are open to competition.

**representative democracy**
Governing system in which public decision making is delegated to representatives of the people chosen by popular vote in free, open, and periodic elections.

Direct democracy still lives in many New England towns, where citizens come together periodically to pass laws, elect officials, and make decisions about such matters as taxation and land use.

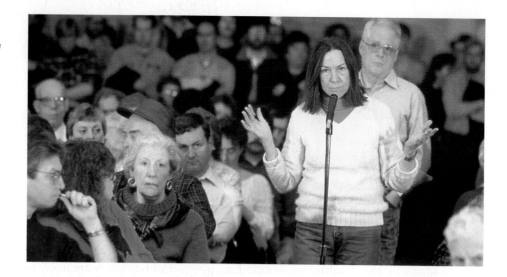

3. Candidates and voters can freely express themselves.

4. Representatives are selected periodically.

So when we hear of "elections" in which only one party is permitted to run candidates, candidates are not free to express their views, or leaders are elected "for life," then we know that these governments are not really democracies, regardless of what they may call themselves.

Throughout this book, as we examine how well representative democracy works in the United States, we consider such issues as participation in elections—why some people vote and others do not—whether parties and candidates offer the voters real alternatives, whether modern political campaigning informs voters or only confuses them, and whether elected representatives are responsive to the wishes of voters. These are the kinds of issues that concern political science.

## Who Really Governs?

Democracy is an inspiring ideal. But is democratic government really possible? Is it possible for millions of people to govern themselves, with every voice having equal influence? Or will a small number of people inevitably acquire more power than others? To what extent is democracy attainable in *any* society, and how democratic is the American political system? That is, who really governs?

**The Elitist Perspective**    "Government is always government by the few, whether in the name of the few, the one, or the many."[8] This quotation from political scientists Harold Lasswell and Daniel Lerner expresses the basic idea of **elitism**. All societies, including democracies, divide themselves into the few who have power and the many who do not. In every society, there is a division of labor. Only a few people are directly involved in governing a nation; most people are content to let others undertake the tasks of government. The *elite* are the few who have power; the *masses* are the many who do not.[9] This theory holds that an elite is inevitable in any social organization. We cannot form a club, a church, a business, or a government without selecting some people to provide leadership. And leaders will always have a perspective on the organization different from that of its members.[10]

In any large, complex society, then, whether or not it is a democracy, decisions are made by tiny minorities. Out of more than 300 million Americans, only

—Think Again—

Is the government run by a few big interests looking out for themselves?

**elitism**  Political system in which power is concentrated in the hands of a relatively small group of individuals or institutions.

a few thousand individuals at most participate directly in decisions about war and peace, wages and prices, employment and production, law and justice, taxes and benefits, health and welfare.

Elitism does *not* mean that leaders always exploit or oppress members. On the contrary, elites may be very concerned for the welfare of the masses. Elite status may be open to ambitious, talented, or educated individuals from the masses or may be closed to all except the wealthy. Elites may be very responsive to public opinion, or they may ignore the usually apathetic and ill-informed masses. But whether elites are self-seeking or public-spirited, open or closed, responsive or unresponsive, it is they and not the masses who actually make the decisions.

Most people do not regularly concern themselves with decision making in Washington. They are more concerned with their jobs, family, sports, and recreation than they are with politics. They are not well informed about tax laws, foreign policy, or even who represents them in Congress. Since the "masses" are largely apathetic and ill informed about policy questions, their views are likely to be influenced more by what they see and hear on television than by their own experience. Most communication flows downward from elites to masses. Elitism argues that the masses have at best only an indirect influence on the decisions of elites.

Opinion polls indicate that many Americans agree with the elitist contention that government is run by "a few big interests" (see Figure 1.2).

**The Pluralist Perspective**    No one seriously argues that all Americans participate in *all* of the decisions that shape their lives; that majority preferences *always* prevail; that the values of life, liberty, and property are *never* sacrificed; or that every American enjoys equality of opportunity. Nevertheless, most American political scientists argue that the American system of government, which they describe as "pluralist," is the best possible approximation of the democratic ideal in a large, complex society. Pluralism is designed to make the theory of democracy "more realistic."[11]

**Pluralism** is the belief that democracy can be achieved in a large, complex society by competition, bargaining, and compromise among organized groups and that individuals can participate in decision making through membership in these groups and by choosing among parties and candidates in elections.

Pluralists recognize that the individual acting alone is no match for giant government bureaucracies, big corporations and banks, the television networks,

**pluralism**  Theory that democracy can be achieved through competition among multiple organized groups and that individuals can participate in politics through group memberships and elections.

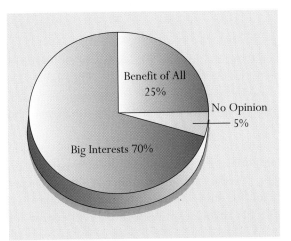

**Figure 1.2**  Public Opinion about Who Runs the Country

Would you say the government is pretty much run by a few big interests looking out for themselves or that it is run for the benefit of all the people?

*Source:* The Gallup Poll, July 6–9, 2000. Copyright © 1996–2004 by The Gallup Organization.

## UP CLOSE

# Terrorism's Threat to Democracy

The horrifying images of "9/11" will not be easily forgotten—America's tallest skyscrapers exploding in flames and crumbling to earth—images projected over and over again on the nation's television screens. Commercial airliners, loaded with fuel and passengers, flown at high speeds directly into the symbols of America's financial and military power—the World Trade Center in New York and the Pentagon in Washington. Within minutes, thousands of lives are lost on American soil—more than at any time since the Civil War. After September 11 America found itself in a new war, a war against worldwide networks of terrorists.

*The Goal of Terrorism* Terrorism is violence directed against innocent civilians to advance political goals. As barbaric as terrorism appears to civilized peoples, it is not without a rationale. Terrorists are not "crazies." Their first goal is to announce in the most dramatic fashion their own grievances, their commitment to violence, and their disregard for human life, often including their own. In its initial phase the success of a terrorist act is directly related to the publicity it receives. Terrorist groups jubilantly claim responsibility for their acts. The more horrendous, the more media coverage, the more damage, the more dead—all add to the success of the terrorists in attracting attention to themselves.

A prolonged campaign of terrorism is designed to inspire pervasive fear among people, to convince them that their government cannot protect them, and to undermine their confidence in their political system. If the government fails to suppress terrorism, people become ever more fearful, more willing to accept restrictions on liberties, and more open to

*The horrifying images of "9/11" will not be easily forgotten—America's tallest skyscrapers exploding and crumbling to earth—images projected over and over again on the nation's television screens.*

the appeals of demagogues who promise to restore order to protect people at any cost. Or a weakened government may resort to "negotiations" with the leaders of terrorist groups, implicitly granting them legitimacy and providing them the opportunity to advance their goals.

*America's Response* But America's response to the terrorist attacks of September 11, 2001, was precisely the *opposite* of the intention of the terrorists. National pride, confidence in national leadership, and faith in human nature, all soared among the American people in the aftermath of the attack. Patriotism flourished. Flags flew from businesses, homes, and automobiles. The attack united the country in a way that no other event since the 1941 Japanese attack on Pearl Harbor had done. Trust in government rose to highs not seen since the 1960s. Initial popular support for military action was overwhelming.

---

labor unions, or other powerful interest groups. Instead, pluralists rely on *competition* among these organizations to protect the interests of individuals. They hope that countervailing centers of power—big business, big labor, big government—will check one another and prevent any single group from abusing its power and oppressing individual Americans.

Individuals in a pluralist democracy may not participate directly in decision making, but they can join and support *interest groups* whose leaders bargain on their behalf in the political arena. People are more effective in organized groups—for example, the Sierra Club for environmentalists, the American Civil Liberties Union (ACLU) for civil rights advocates, the National Association for

**www Democracy Net**
Democracy site of the League of Women Voters linking ZIP codes to your federal, state, and local representatives. *www.dnet.org*

However, this "rally 'round the flag" effect could not be sustained. Mass support for the nation's elite over a long war on terrorism—with continuing terrorist attacks, daily casualties among American soldiers, and few reported victories in a largely hidden conflict—declined over time. Political partisanship again replaced national unity, and Washington began "the blame game." Support for the war on terrorism gradually eroded (see Chapter 18).

***Security vs. Liberty***   Threats to national security have historically resulted in challenges to individual liberty. Abraham Lincoln suspended the *writ of habeas corpus* (the requirement that authorities bring defendants before a judge and show cause for their detention) during the Civil War. (Only after the war did the U.S. Supreme Court hold that he had no authority to suspend the writ.[a])

In February 1942, shortly after the Japanese attack on Pearl Harbor, President Franklin D. Roosevelt authorized the removal and internment of Japanese Americans living on the West Coast. The U.S. Supreme Court upheld this flagrant violation of the Constitution;[b] not until 1988 did the U.S. Congress vote reparations and make public apologies to the surviving victims.

***New Restrictions on Liberty***   The "9/11" terrorist attack on America inspired Congress and the president to enact and enforce greater restrictions on individual liberty than the nation had experienced since World War II. Congress passed the Patriot Act with near-unanimous support of Democrats and Republicans. Among other things, the Act allows searches without notice to the suspect; grants "roving" wiretap warrants that allow government eavesdropping on any telephones used by suspects; allows the interception of e-mail; allows investiga-

tors to obtain information from credit card companies, banks, libraries, and other businesses; authorizes the seizure of properties used to commit or facilitate terrorism; and allows the detention of noncitizens charged with terrorism. President George W. Bush created a new Department of Homeland Security, reorganizing more than forty federal agencies that have a role in combating terrorism.

President Bush also announced that "enemy combatants" captured on the battlefields of Afghanistan and Iraq would be tried by military tribunals. Prisoners of war have never been entitled to constitutional protection. "Detainees" from the war on terrorism are not officially prisoners of war; most are being held at the U.S. base in Guantanamo Bay, Cuba. As military detainees, they were not given lawyers or access to courts, although a Supreme Court decision in 2004 ordered the U.S. to provide them with lawyers and hearings (see Chapter 14).[c]

***Terrorism and Democracy***   Terrorism has brought mixed blessings to American democracy. It has succeeded in uniting Americans, inspiring patriotism, and increasing their trust in government. But it has also inspired a greater willingness to accept new restrictions on individual liberty. In the past, restrictions on individual liberty have been relaxed when the perceived crisis has subsided. How long will the "war on terrorism" last? Will Americans be asked to sacrifice additional liberties in this war? How far are Americans willing to go in sacrificing individual liberty to achieve national security?

See Robert A. Pape, "The Strategic Logic of Suicide Terrorism," *American Political Science Review* 97 (August 2003): 343–361.

[a]Ex parte Milligan (1866).
[b]*Korematsu v. U.S.,* 323 U.S. 214 (1944).
[c]*Rasul v. Bush,* June 28, 2004.

the Advancement of Colored People (NAACP) and the Urban League for African Americans, the American Legion and Veterans of Foreign Wars for veterans, and the National Rifle Association (NRA) for opponents of gun control.

According to the pluralist view, the Democratic and Republican parties are really coalitions of groups: the national Democratic Party is a coalition of union members, big-city residents, blacks, Catholics, Jews, and, until recently, southerners; the national Republican Party is a coalition of business and professional people, suburbanites, farmers, and white Protestants. When voters choose candidates and parties, they are helping to determine which interest groups will enjoy a better reception in government.

**The Terrorism Research Center**
News and information on terrorist attacks around the world and list of terrorist organizations.
*www.terrorism.com*

# A CONFLICTING VIEW

## Complaints About the American Political System

Overall, Americans are very patriotic. Indeed, most polls conducted in United States and other democratic nations show Americans to be the most patriotic citizens in the free world.

Nonetheless, many Americans express serious reservations about their political system. They believe strongly in the ideals of democracy but they are realistic in their appraisal of its weaknesses as well. A majority of Americans describe as "a major problem": elected officials caring more about reelection than what's best for the country; good people being discouraged from running for office because of the high costs of campaigns; citizens who don't stay informed about politics; a decline in moral and ethical standards in government; and the role that money plays in elections and influencing decisions.

*Q. As I read each item, tell me how much of a problem you think it is for the political system today: a major problem, somewhat of a problem, or not much of a problem.*

*Women have achieved political prominence in their party and in the U.S. Senate. Hillary Clinton (D-NY), Elizabeth Dole (R-NC), and Kay Bailey Hutchinson (R-TX) are among women leaders in the Senate.*

| | Major Problem | Somewhat of a Problem | Not much of a Problem |
|---|---|---|---|
| Elected officials caring more about getting reelected than doing what is best for the country | 76% | 19% | 4% |
| The two major political parties not being responsive enough to people's concerns | 58% | 32% | 7% |
| Good people being discouraged from running for office by the high costs of campaigns | 71% | 22% | 6% |
| Political contributions having too much influence on elections and government policy | 66% | 25% | 7% |
| Citizens not making enough effort to vote or stay informed about politics and government | 68% | 26% | 5% |
| A decline in moral and ethical values in politics | 59% | 30% | 9% |
| Elected officials spending too much of their time raising money for election campaigns | 61% | 30% | 6% |
| Elected officials seeking or receiving political contributions while making decisions about issues of concern to those giving money | 65% | 27% | 6% |

*Source:* Adapted from *Beyond Red and Blue,* Pew Research Center for the People and the Press, May 10, 2005. Copyright © 2005 by The Pew Research Center. Reprinted by permission..

Pluralists contend that there are multiple leadership groups in society (hence the term *pluralism*). They contend that power is widely dispersed among these groups; that no one group, not even the wealthy upper class, dominates decision making; and that groups that are influential in one area of decision making are not necessarily the same groups that are influential in other areas of decision making. Different groups of leaders make decisions in different issue areas.

# A CONSTITUTIONAL NOTE

## Representative Government, Not Direct Democracy

Nowhere in the Constitution do we find a provision for national referenda voting on any topic, however important for the nation. Indeed, nowhere do we find the word "democracy" in the Constitution. Rather, the founders believed in "republican" government, that is, decision making by representatives of the people, *not* by the people themselves. James Madison wrote, "the public voice, pronounced by representatives of the people, will be more consonant to the public good than if pronounced by the people themselves."

It was not until over a century later that "populism"—a strong political movement mainly in the Midwestern and Western states that appealed especially to farmers—succeeded in getting the initiative and referendum adopted, allowing *state* voters to vote directly on some issues. (The initiative allows citizens to place issues on the ballot by obtaining a certain number of signatures on a petition. The referendum is a popular vote that decides whether the issue becomes part of the state constitution or state law.) Today about half of the states have the initiative and referendum. (The legislatures of all fifty states can place an issue on the ballot if they choose to do so, usually a change in the state constitution.) But Americans cannot vote directly on *national* issues.

---

Pluralism recognizes that public policy does not always coincide with majority preferences. Instead, public policy is the "equilibrium" reached in the conflict among group interests. It is the balance of competing interest groups, and therefore, say the pluralists, it is a reasonable approximation of society's preferences.

## Democracy in America

Is democracy alive and well in America today? Elitism raises serious questions about the possibility of achieving true democracy in any large, complex society. Pluralism is more comforting; it offers a way of reaffirming democratic values and providing some practical solutions to the problem of individual participation in a modern society.

There is no doubt about the strength of democratic *ideals* in American society. These ideals—individual dignity, equality, popular participation in government, and majority rule—are the standards by which we judge the performance of the American political system. But we are still faced with the task of describing the *reality* of American politics.

This book explores who gets what, when, and how in the American political system; who participates in politics; what policies are decided upon; and when and how these decisions are made. In so doing, it raises many controversial questions about the realities of democracy, elitism, and pluralism in American life. But this book does not supply the answers; as a responsible citizen, you have to provide your own answers. At the completion of your studies, you will have to decide for yourself whether the American political system is truly democratic. Your studies will help inform your judgment, but, in the end, you yourself must make that judgment. That is the burden of freedom.

# Summary Notes

- Politics is deciding who gets what, when, and how. It occurs in many different settings, but political science focuses on politics in government.

- Political science focuses on three central questions:
  Who governs?
  For what ends?
  By what means?

- Government is distinguished from other social organizations in that it
  Extends to the whole society
  Can legitimately use force

- The purposes of government are to
  Maintain order in society
  Provide for national defense
  Provide "public goods"
  Regulate society
  Transfer income
  Protect individual liberty

- The ideals of democracy include
  Recognition of individual dignity and personal freedom
  Equality before the law
  Widespread participation in decision making
  Majority rule, with one person equaling one vote

- The principles of democracy pose a paradox: How can we resolve conflicts between our belief in majority rule and our belief in individual freedom?

- Limited government places individual liberty beyond the reach of majorities. Constitutions are the principal means of limiting government power.

- Direct democracy, in which everyone participates in every public decision, is very rare. Representative democracy means that public decisions are made by representatives elected by the people, in elections held periodically and open to competition, in which candidates and voters freely express themselves.

- Threats to national security have historically reduced the scope of individual liberty in our nation. The terrorist attack on America of September 11, 2001, inspired greater unity, patriotism, and trust in government among the people. But it also brought greater restrictions on individual liberty.

- Who really governs? The elitist perspective on American democracy focuses on the small number of leaders who actually decide national issues, compared to the mass of citizens who are apathetic and ill informed about politics. A pluralist perspective focuses on competition among organized groups in society, with individuals participating through group membership and voting for parties and candidates in elections.

- How democratic is American government today? Democratic ideals are widely shared in our society. But you must make your own informed judgment about the realities of American politics.

# Key Terms

| | | | |
|---|---|---|---|
| politics  3 | public goods  7 | democracy  9 | authoritarianism  14 |
| political science  3 | free market  8 | democratic ideals  10 | direct democracy  14 |
| government  4 | gross domestic product (GDP)  9 | paradox of democracy  12 | representative democracy  15 |
| legitimacy  5 | externalities  9 | limited government  13 | elitism  16 |
| social contract  7 | income transfers  9 | totalitarianism  13 | pluralism  17 |

# Suggested Readings

Cronin, Thomas J. *Direct Democracy*. Cambridge, Mass.: Harvard University Press, 1989. A thoughtful discussion of direct versus representative democracy, as well as a review of initiative, referendum, and recall devices.

Dahl, Robert A. *Democracy and Its Critics*. New Haven, Conn.: Yale University Press, 1989. A defense of modern democracy from the pluralist perspective.

Dye, Thomas R., and Harmon Zeigler. *The Irony of Democracy*. 13th ed. New York: Wadsworth, 2005. An interpretation of American politics from the elitist perspective.

Fukuyama, Francis. *Trust*. New York: Free Press, 1995. Argues that the breakdown of trust in America—not only in the government but at a person-to-person level—is burdening the nation with formal rules and regulations, lengthy contracts, bureaucracy, lawyers, and lawsuits.

Katznelson, Ira, Mark Kesselman, and Alan Draper. *The Politics of Power: A Critical Introduction to American Government*, 5th ed. Belmont, Calif.: Wadsworth, 2006. An argument that the United States "is characterized by massive disparities in wealth, income, and political resources."

Lasswell, Harold. Politics: *Who Gets What, When, and How*. New York: McGraw-Hill, 1936. Classic description of the nature of politics and the study of political science by America's foremost political scientist of the twentieth century.

Mills, C. Wright. *The Power Elite*. New York: Oxford University Press, 1956. Classic Marxist critique of elitism in American society, setting forth the argument that "corporate chieftains," "military warlords," and a "political directorate" come together to form the nation's power elite.

Neiman, Max. *Defending Government: Why Big Government Works*. Upper Saddle River, N.J.: Prentice Hall, 2000. A spirited defense of how big government can improve the lives of people.

Putnam, Robert D. *Bowling Alone: The Collapse and Revival of the American Community*. New York: Simon & Schuster, 2001. An argument that Americans are increasingly disconnected from one another, harming the health of democracy.

Roskin, Michael G. *Political Science: An Introduction*, 9th ed. Upper Saddle River, N.J.: Prentice Hall, 2006. A text introduction to the basic theories and concepts of political science.

# 2 POLITICAL CULTURE
## Ideas in Conflict

## Chapter Outline

- Political Culture
- Individual Liberty
- Dilemmas of Equality
- Inequality of Income and Wealth
- Social Mobility
- Race, Ethnicity, and Immigration
- Ideologies: Liberalism and Conservatism
- Dissent in the United States

## Think About Politics

**1** Do you consider yourself politically conservative, moderate, or liberal?
Conservative ☐ Moderate ☐ Liberal ☐

**2** Are income differences in America widening?
Yes ☐ No ☐

**3** Is it the government's responsibility to reduce income differences between people?
Yes ☐ No ☐

**4** If incomes were made more equal, would people still be motivated to work hard?
Yes ☐ No ☐

**5** Do Americans today still have the opportunity to significantly improve their condition in life?
Yes ☐ No ☐

**6** Should the U.S. government curtail immigration to America?
Yes ☐ No ☐

**7** Should illegal immigrants be denied welfare benefits?
Yes ☐ No ☐

**8** Is American culture racist and sexist?
Yes ☐ No ☐

*Ask yourself if your answers to these questions are widely shared by most citizens of the United States. Your answers probably reflect not only your own beliefs and values but also those of the political culture to which you belong.*

## Political Culture

Ideas have power. We are all influenced by ideas—beliefs, values, symbols—more than we realize. Political institutions are shaped by ideas, and political leaders are influenced by them.

The term **political culture** refers to widely shared ideas about who should govern, for what ends, and by what means. **Values** are shared ideas about what is good and desirable. Values provide standards for judging what is right or wrong. **Beliefs** are shared ideas about what is true. Values and beliefs are often related. For example, if we believe that human beings are endowed by God with rights to life, liberty, and property, then we will value the protection of these rights. Thus beliefs can justify values.

Cultural descriptions are generalizations about the values and beliefs of many people in society, but these generalizations do not apply to everyone. Important variations in values and beliefs may exist within a society; these variations are frequently referred to as **subcultures** and may arise from such diverse bases as religion, racial or ethnic identity, or political group membership.

**Contradictions between Values and Conditions** Agreement over values in a political culture is no guarantee that there will not be contradictions between these values and actual conditions. People both in and out of politics frequently act contrary to their professed values. No doubt the most grievous contradiction between professed national beliefs and actual conditions in America is found in the long history of slavery, segregation, and racial discrimination. The contradiction between the words of the Declaration of Independence that "all men are created equal" and the practices of slavery and segregation became the "American dilemma."[1] But this contradiction does not mean that professed values are worthless; the very existence of the gap between values and behavior becomes *a motivation for change.* The history of the civil rights movement might be viewed as an effort to "bear witness" to the contradiction between the belief in equality and the existence of segregation and discrimination.[2] Whatever the obstacles to racial equality in America, these obstacles would be even greater if the nation's political culture did *not* include a professed belief in equality.

**Inconsistent Applications** And political culture does not mean that shared principles are always applied in every circumstance. For example,

25

**political culture** Widely shared views about who should govern, for what ends, and by what means.

**values** Shared ideas about what is good and desirable.

**beliefs** Shared ideas about what is true.

**subcultures** Variations on the prevailing values and beliefs in a society.

people may truly believe in the principle of "free speech for all, no matter what their views might be," and yet when asked whether racists should be allowed to speak on a college campus, many people will say no. Thus general agreement with abstract principles of freedom of speech, freedom of the press, and academic freedom does not always ensure their application to specific individuals or groups.[3] Americans are frequently willing to restrict the freedoms of particularly obnoxious groups. A generation ago it was alleged communists and atheists whose freedoms were questioned. Over time these groups have become less threatening, but today people are still willing to restrict the liberties of racists, pro-abortion or anti-abortion groups, "skinheads" and neo-Nazis, and people who resemble terrorists.

**Conflict**   The idea of political culture does not mean an absence of conflict over values and beliefs. Indeed, much of politics involves conflict over very fundamental values. The American nation has experienced a bloody civil war, political assassinations, rioting and burning of cities, the forced resignation of a president, and other direct challenges to its political foundations. Indeed, much of this book deals with serious political conflict. Yet Americans do share many common ways of thinking about politics.

## Individual Liberty

No political value has been more widely held in the United States than individual liberty. The very beginnings of our history as a nation were shaped by **classical liberalism**, which asserts the worth and dignity of the individual. This political philosophy emphasizes the rational ability of human beings to determine their own destinies, and it rejects ideas, practices, and institutions that submerge individuals into a larger whole and thus deprive them of their dignity. The only restriction on the individual is not to interfere with the liberties of others.

**classical liberalism** Political philosophy asserting the worth and dignity of the individual and emphasizing the rational ability of human beings to determine their own destinies.

**Political Liberty**   Classical liberalism grew out of the eighteenth-century Enlightenment, the Age of Reason in which great philosophers such as Voltaire, John Locke, Jean Jacques Rousseau, Adam Smith, and Thomas Jefferson affirmed their faith in reason, virtue, and common sense. Classical liberalism originated as an attack on the hereditary prerogatives and distinctions of a feudal society, the monarchy, the privileged aristocracy, and the state-established church.

Classical liberalism motivated America's Founders to declare their independence from England, to write the U.S. Constitution, and to establish the Republic. It rationalized their actions and provided ideological legitimacy for the new nation. The founders adopted the language of John Locke, who argued that a natural law, or moral principle, guaranteed every person "certain inalienable Rights," among them "Life, Liberty, and Property," and that human beings form a social contract with one another to establish a government to help protect their rights. Implicit in the social contract and the liberal notion of freedom is the belief that governmental activity and restrictions on the individual should be kept to a minimum.

**Philosophy Pages**
History of Western philosophy and discussion of major democratic philosophers, including John Locke, Jean Jacques Rousseau, and Thomas Hobbes, among others.
*www.philosophypages.com*

**capitalism** Economic system asserting the individual's right to own private property and to buy, sell, rent, and trade that property in a free market.

**Economic Freedom**   Classical liberalism as a political idea is closely related to capitalism as an *economic* idea. **Capitalism** asserts the individual's right to own private property and to buy, sell, rent, and trade that property in a free market. The economic version of freedom is the freedom to make contracts, to bargain for one's services, to move from job to job, to join labor unions, to start one's own business. In classical liberal *politics*, individuals are free to speak out, to form political parties, and to vote as they please—to pursue their political interests as they think best. In classical liberal *economics*, individuals are free to find work, to

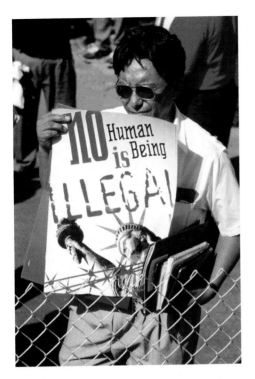

Illegal immigration became an issue in the 2006 congressional elections. Many Hispanic Americans have protested against bills targeting illegal immigrants.

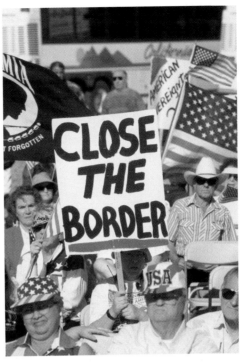

Opposition to illegal immigration is strong, especially among Anglos in the Southwest. Just prior to the 2006 congressional elections, Congress voted to strengthen border security

start businesses, and to spend their money as they please—to pursue their economic interests as they think best. The role of government is restricted to protecting private property, enforcing contracts, and performing only those functions and services that cannot be performed by the private market.

The value of liberty in these political and economic spheres has been paramount throughout our history. Only equality competes with liberty as the most honored value in the American political culture.

## Dilemmas of Equality

Since the bold assertion of the Declaration of Independence that "all men are created equal," Americans have generally believed that no person has greater worth than any other person. The principle of equal worth and dignity was a radical idea in 1776, when much of the world was dominated by hereditary monarchies, titled nobilities, and rigid caste and class systems.

As early as 1835 the French historian and visitor to America, Alexis de Tocqueville, wrote his classic analysis of American political culture, *Democracy in America*. He identified equality as a fundamental aspect of American society—the absence of a privileged nobility or notions of class that characterize European societies. Yet he also warned of the "tyranny of the majority"—the potential for the majority to trample the rights of minorities and individuals—and he believed that an independent judiciary formed a powerful barrier "against the tyranny of political assemblies."[4]

Belief in equality drove the expansion of voting rights in the early 1800s and ultimately destroyed the institution of slavery. Abraham Lincoln understood that equality was not so much a description of reality as an ideal to be aspired to: "a standard maxim for a free society which should be familiar to all, and revered by all; constantly looked to, constantly labored for, and even though never perfectly

**Heritage Foundation**
This think tank site includes a ranking of over 150 nations on an "Index of Economic Freedom." The U.S. ranks sixth; Hong Kong ranks first.
*www.heritage.org*

In the early 1800s, a visiting French historian, Alexis de Tocqueville, identified *equality* as a central American value that distinguished the new nation from European countries.

attained, constantly approximated and thereby augmenting the happiness and value of life to all people of all colors everywhere."[5] The millions who immigrated to the United States viewed this country as a land not only of opportunity but of *equal* opportunity, where everyone, regardless of birth, could rise in wealth and status based on hard work, natural talents, and perhaps good luck.

Today, most Americans agree that no one is intrinsically "better" than anyone else. This belief in equality, then, is fundamental to Americans, but a closer examination shows that throughout our history it has been tested, as beliefs and values so often are, by political realities.

**Political Equality**   The nation's Founders shared the belief that the law should apply equally to all—that birth, status, or wealth do not justify differential application of the laws. But *legal equality* did not necessarily mean **political equality**, at least not in 1787, when the U.S. Constitution was written. The Constitution left the issue of voter qualifications to the states to decide for themselves. At that time, all states imposed either property or taxpayer qualifications for voting. Neither women nor slaves could vote anywhere. The expansion of voting rights to universal suffrage required many bitter battles over the course of two centuries. The long history of the struggle over voting rights illustrates the contradictions between values and practices (see the section "Securing the Right to Vote" in Chapter 6). Yet in the absence of the *value* of equality, voting rights might have remained restricted.

**Equality of Opportunity**   The American ideal of equality extends to **equality of opportunity**—the elimination of artificial barriers to success in life. The term *equality of opportunity* refers to the ability to make of oneself what one can, to develop one's talents and abilities, and to be rewarded for one's work, initiative, and achievement. Equality of opportunity means that everyone comes to the same starting line in life, with the same chance of success, and that whatever differences develop over time do so as a result of abilities, talents, initiative, hard work, and perhaps good luck.

Americans do not generally resent the fact that physicians, engineers, airline pilots, and others who have spent time and energy acquiring particular skills

---

**political equality** Belief that the law should apply equally to all and that every person's vote counts equally.

**Center for Equal Opportunity**
Think tank advocating equality of opportunity over equality of results.
*www.ceousa.org*

**equality of opportunity** Elimination of artificial barriers to success in life and the opportunity for everyone to strive for success.

make more money than those whose jobs require fewer skills and less training. Neither do most Americans resent the fact that people who risk their own time and money to build a business, bring new or better products to market, and create jobs for others make more money than their employees. Nor do many Americans begrudge multimillion-dollar incomes to sports figures, rock stars, and movie stars whose talents entertain the public. And few Americans object when someone wins a million-dollar lottery, as long as everyone who entered the lottery had an equal chance at winning. Americans are generally willing to have government act to ensure equality of opportunity—to ensure that everyone has an equal chance at getting an education, landing a job, and buying a home, and that no barriers of race, sex, religion, or ethnicity bar individual advancement.

**Equality of Results**    **Equality of results** refers to the equal sharing of income and material rewards. Equality of results means that everyone starts *and finishes* the race together, regardless of ability, talent, initiative, or work. Those who argue on behalf of this notion of equality say that if individuals are truly equal, then everyone should enjoy generally equal conditions in life. According to this belief, we should appreciate an individual's contributions to society without creating inequalities of wealth and income. Government should act to *transfer* wealth and income from the rich to the poor to increase the total happiness of all members of society.

But equality of results, or absolute equality, is *not* a widely shared value in the United States. This notion of equality was referred to as "leveling" by Thomas Jefferson and generally has been denounced by the nation's political leadership— and by most Americans—then and now:

> To take from one, because it is thought his own industry and that of his fathers has acquired too much, in order to spare to others who have not exercised equal industry and skill, is to violate arbitrarily . . . the guarantee to everyone the free exercise of his industry and the fruits acquired by it.[6]

The taking of private property from those who acquired it legitimately, for no other reason than to equalize wealth or income, is widely viewed as morally wrong. Moreover, many people believe that society generally would suffer if incomes were equalized. Absolute equality, in this view, would remove incentives for people to work, save, or produce. Everyone would slack off, production would decline, goods would be in short supply, and everyone would end up poorer than ever. So some inequality may be essential for the well-being of society.

Thus Americans believe strongly in equality of opportunity but not necessarily equality of results (see *What Do You Think?* "Beliefs about Fairness"). Americans seek fairness rather than equality of wealth and income.

**Fairness**    Americans value "fairness" even though they do not always agree on what is fair. Most Americans support a "floor" on income and material well-being— a level that no one, regardless of his or her condition, should be permitted to fall below—even though they differ over how high that floor should be. Indeed, the belief in a floor is consistent with the belief in equality of opportunity; extreme poverty would deny people, especially children, the opportunity to compete in life.[7] But very few Americans want to place a "ceiling" on income or wealth. This unwillingness to limit top income extends to nearly all groups in the United States, the poor as well as the rich. Generally, Americans want people who cannot provide for themselves to be well cared for, especially children, the elderly, the ill, and the disabled. They are often willing to "soak the rich" when searching for new

**equality of results**  Equal sharing of income and material goods regardless of one's efforts in life.

**Monticello**  Biography, letters, and a "Day in the Life" of Thomas Jefferson.
*www.monticello.org*

Thomas Jefferson, the primary author of the Declaration of Independence, was a powerful advocate of equality of opportunity, but opposed government redistribution of wealth.

## WHAT DO YOU THINK?

### Beliefs about Fairness

Americans believe that there is "plenty of opportunity" to get ahead and that the economic system of the United States is "basically fair." They do NOT believe that everyone's income should be made more equal.

*Q. Some people say there's not much opportunity in America today—that the average person doesn't have much chance to really get ahead. Others say there's plenty of opportunity and anyone who works hard can go as far as they want. How do you feel about this?*

| | |
|---|---|
| Plenty of opportunity | 81% |
| Not much opportunity | 17 |
| Don't know | 2 |

*Q. Do you believe that incomes should be more equal because everybody's contribution to society is equally important?*

| | |
|---|---|
| Yes | 37% |
| No | 61 |
| No opinion | 2 |

*Q. People should be allowed to accumulate as much wealth as they can even if some make millions while others live in poverty.*

| | |
|---|---|
| Strongly agree or agree | 56% |
| Neither agree nor disagree | 11 |
| Strongly disagree or disagree | 30 |

*Sources:* James R. Kluegel and Eliot R. Smith, *Beliefs about Inequality* (New York: Aldine de Gruyter, 1986); Everett Ladd and Karlyn H. Bowman, *Attitudes toward Economic Inequality* (Washington, DC: AEI Press, 1998).

---

tax sources, believing that the rich can easily afford to bear the burdens of government. But, unlike citizens in other Western democracies, Americans generally do *not* believe that government should equalize incomes.

—— Think Again ——
Are income differences in America widening?

## Inequality of Income and Wealth

Conflict in society is generated more often by inequalities among people than by hardship or deprivation. Material well-being and standards of living are usually expressed in aggregate measures for a whole society—for example, gross domestic product per capita, income per capita, average life expectancy, infant mortality rate. These measures of societal well-being are vitally important to a nation and its people, but *political* conflict is more likely to occur over the *distribution* of well-being *within* a society. Unequal distributions can generate conflict even in a very affluent society with high levels of income and a high standard of living (see *Compared to What?* "Income and Inequality").

**Inequality of Income**   Let us examine inequality of income in the United States systematically. Figure 2.1 divides all American households into two groups—the lowest one-fifth in income and the highest one-fifth—and shows the shares (percentage) of total household income received by each of these groups over the years. (If perfect income equality existed, each fifth of American households would receive 20 percent of all personal income.) The poorest one-fifth received only 4.5 percent of all household income in 1929; today, this group does a little worse, at 3.5 percent of household income. The highest one-fifth received 54.0 percent of all household income in 1929; today, its percentage stands at 50.1.

However, while income differences in the United States have declined over the long run, inequality has actually *increased* in recent years. The income of the poorest households declined from 5.4 to 3.5 percent of total income between 1970 and 2004; the income of the highest quintile rose from 40.9 to 50.1 percent of total income. This reversal of historical trends has generated both political rhetoric and serious scholarly inquiry about both its causes and consequences.[8]

**Global Policy Forum**   Information on many global issues. Click to "social and economic policy" and then to "inequality of wealth and income" for cross-national data.
www.globalpolicy.org

# COMPARED TO WHAT?

## Income and Inequality

Capitalism has proven successful in creating wealth. The free market system has provided Americans with more purchasing power than any other people. ("Purchasing power parity" is a statistic used by international economists to adjust for the cost of living differences in measuring how much it costs to purchase a standard "basket" of goods and services.)

However, relatively high incomes of average Americans exist side by side with relatively high inequality among Americans. The United States ranks well below many European countries in measures of income inequality. (The "Gini index" is a statistic used by economists to measure income equality/inequality.) But poverty and inequality exists side by side in most of the world's less-developed countries (not ranked below).

### Rank by purchasing power

1. **United States**
2. Switzerland
3. Norway
4. Belgium
5. Denmark
6. Canada
7. Japan
8. Netherlands
9. Ireland
10. Australia
11. Germany
12. Finland
13. France
14. Sweden
15. United Kingdom
16. Italy
17. Taiwan
18. Israel
19. Spain
20. South Korea
21. Portugal
22. Greece
23. Czech Republic
24. Poland
25. Mexico

### Rank by equality (Gini index)

1. Denmark
2. Czech Republic
3. Japan
4. Sweden
5. Finland
6. Norway
7. Italy
8. Belgium
9. Germany
10. Canada
11. South Korea
12. Poland
13. Spain
14. Netherlands
15. Taiwan
16. France
17. Greece
18. Switzerland
19. Portugal
20. Israel
21. Ireland
22. United Kingdom
23. **United States**
24. Costa Rica
25. Mexico

*Sources:* Rank by purchasing power, *The Economist Pocket World in Figures,* 2003; rank by Gini index, Central Intelligence Agency, *The World Factbook,* 2003. Both sources rank many more nations.

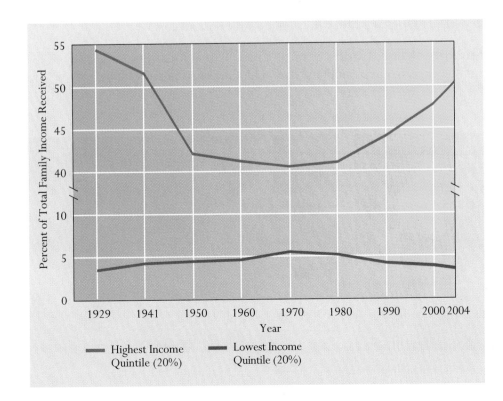

**Figure 2.1** Shares of Total Household Income Received by Highest and Lowest Income Groups

**Explaining Recent Increases in Income Inequality**   Recent increases in income inequality in the United States are a product of several social and economic trends: (1) the decline of the manufacturing sector of the economy (and the loss of many relatively high-paying blue-collar jobs) and the ascendancy of the communications, information, and service sectors of the economy (with a combination of high-paying and low-paying jobs); (2) the rise in the number of two-wage families, making single-wage, female-headed households relatively less affluent; (3) demographic trends, which include larger proportions of aged and larger proportions of female-headed families; and (4) global competition, which restrains wages in unskilled and semiskilled jobs while rewarding people in high-technology, high-productivity occupations.

## Social Mobility

**social mobility** Extent to which people move upward or downward in income and status over a lifetime or generations.

Political conflict over inequality might be greater in the United States if it were not for the prospect of **social mobility**. All societies are stratified, or layered, but societies differ greatly in the extent to which people move upward or downward in income and status over a lifetime or over generations. When there is social mobility, people have a good opportunity to get ahead if they study or work long and hard, save and invest wisely, or display initiative and enterprise in business affairs (however, see *A Conflicting View:* "Success Is Determined by the Bell Curve"). Fairly steep inequalities may be tolerated politically if people have a reasonable expectation of moving up over time, or at least of seeing their children do so.

**How Much Mobility?**   The United States describes itself as the land of opportunity. The really important political question may be how much real opportunity exists for individual Americans to improve their conditions in life relative to others. The impression given by Figure 2.1 is one of a static distribution system, with families permanently placed in upper or lower fifths of income earners. But there is considerable evidence of both upward and downward movement by people among income groupings.[9] Almost half of the families in the poorest one-fifth will move upward within a decade, and about half of families in the richest one-fifth will fall out of this top category.

**Mobility, Class Conflict, and Class Consciousness**   Social mobility and the expectation of mobility, over a lifetime or over generations, may be the

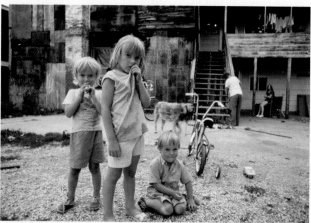

Income and wealth differences have increased in America in recent years.

# A CONFLICTING VIEW

## Success Is Determined by the Bell Curve

Most Americans believe in social mobility—the idea that anyone who studies or works hard, saves and invests wisely, and makes good use of his or her talents, initiative, and enterprise can get ahead. But a controversial book, *The Bell Curve* by Richard J. Herrnstein and Charles Murray, sets forth the argument that general intelligence largely determines success in life. General intelligence, the authors contend, is distributed among the population in a bell-shaped curve, with most people clustered around the median, smaller numbers with higher intelligence (a "cognitive elite") at one end, and an unfortunate few trailing behind at the other end (see graph). Over time, say Herrnstein and Murray, intelligence is becoming ever more necessary for the performance of key jobs in the "information society." The result will be the continuing enhancement of the power and wealth of the cognitive elite and the further erosion of the lifestyle of the less intelligent.

Even more controversial than the authors' claim that general intelligence determines success is their contention that general intelligence is mostly (60 percent) genetic. Because intelligence is mostly inherited, programs to assist the underprivileged are useless or even counterproductive.

**Population Distribution of IQ Scores**

*Source:* Adapted with the permission of The Free Press, a division of Simon & Schuster Adult Publishing Group, from *The Bell Curve: Intelligence and Class Structure in American Life* by Richard J. Herrnstein and Charles Murray. Copyright © 1994 by Richard J. Herrnstein and Charles Murray. All rights reserved.

The cognitive elite, the authors predict, will continue to distance themselves from the masses in knowledge, skills, technical competence, income, and power while social problems will be concentrated among the "dullest." Indeed, they amass statistics showing that educational deficiencies, emotional problems, welfare reliance, early childbirth, and even criminal behavior are disproportionately concentrated in low-intelligence groups (see table).

| Cognitive Class | High School Dropout | Women on Welfare Assistance | Mean Age at First Childbearing | Convictions (young white males) |
|---|---|---|---|---|
| I Very Bright | 0% | 0% | 27.2 years | 3% |
| II Bright | 0 | 2 | 25.6 | 7 |
| III Normal | 6 | 8 | 23.4 | 15 |
| IV Dull | 35 | 17 | 21.0 | 21 |
| V Very Dull | 55 | 31 | 19.8 | 14 |

*Source:* Adapted with the permission of The Free Press, a Division of Simon & Schuster Adult Publishing Group, from *The Bell Curve: Intelligence and Class Structure for American Life* by Richard J. Hernstein and Charles Murray. Copyright © 1994 by Richard J. Hernstein and Charles Murray. All rights reserved.

key to understanding why **class conflict**—conflict over wealth and power among social classes—is not as widespread or as intense in America as it is in many other nations. The *belief* in social mobility reduces the potential for class conflict because it diminishes **class consciousness**, the awareness of one's class position and the feeling of political solidarity with others in the same class in opposition to other classes. If class lines were impermeable and no one had any reasonable expectation of moving up or seeing his or her children move up, then class consciousness would rise and political conflict among classes would intensify.

**class conflict** Conflict between upper and lower social classes over wealth and power.

**class consciousness** Awareness of one's class position and a feeling of political solidarity with others within the same class in opposition to other classes.

Most Americans describe themselves as "middle class" rather than "rich" or "poor" or "lower class" or "upper class." There are no widely accepted income definitions of "middle class." The federal government officially defines a "poverty level" each year based on the annual cash income required to maintain a decent standard of living ($19,223 in 2004 for a family of four). Roughly 12 to 13 percent of the U.S. population lives with annual cash incomes below this poverty line. This is the only income group in which a majority of people describe themselves as poor. Large majorities in every other income group identify themselves as middle class. So it is no surprise that presidents, politicians, and political parties regularly claim to be defenders of America's "middle class"!

# Race, Ethnicity, and Immigration

America has always been an ethnically and racially pluralist society. All groups were expected to adopt the American political culture—including individual liberty, economic freedom, political equality, and equality of opportunity—and to learn American history and the English language. The nation's motto "E Pluribus Unum" (from many, one) is inscribed on its coins. Yet each of America's racial and ethnic groups brings its own traditions and values to the American political culture.

**African Americans**   Historically African Americans constituted the nation's largest minority. Blacks composed about 20 percent of the population at the time the U.S. Constitution was written in 1787 (although as we shall see in Chapter 3 an enslaved African American was to be counted as only 3/5ths of a person in the original Constitution). Heavy European immigration in the late nineteenth century diluted the black population to roughly 12 percent of the nation's total. As late as 1900, most African Americans (90 percent) were still concentrated in the Southern states. But World Wars I and II provided job opportunities in large cities of the Northeast and Midwest. Blacks could not cast ballots in most Southern counties, but they could "vote with their feet." The migration of African Americans from the rural South to the urban North was one of the largest internal migrations in our history. Today only about half of the nation's African Americans live in the South—still more than in any other region but less of a concentration than earlier in American history. Today the nation's 36 million African Americans comprise 12.3 percent of the total population of the United States (see Figure 2.2). This struggle has given African Americans a somewhat different perspective on American politics (see "Race and Opinion" in Chapter 6).

**Hispanic Americans**   Hispanics are now the nation's largest minority. The term *Hispanic* generally refers to persons of Spanish-speaking ancestry and culture; it includes Mexican Americans, Cuban Americans, and Puerto Ricans. Today there are an estimated 37 million Hispanics in the United States, or 12.5 percent of the total population. The largest subgroup is Mexican Americans, some of whom are descendants of citizens living in Mexican territory that was annexed to the United States in 1848, but most of whom have come to the United States in accelerating numbers in recent years. The largest Mexican American populations are found in Texas, Arizona, New Mexico, and California. The second-largest subgroup is Puerto Ricans, many of whom move back and forth from the island to the mainland, especially New York City. The third-largest subgroup is Cubans, most of whom have fled from Castro's Cuba. They

— Think Again —

Is American culture racist and sexist?

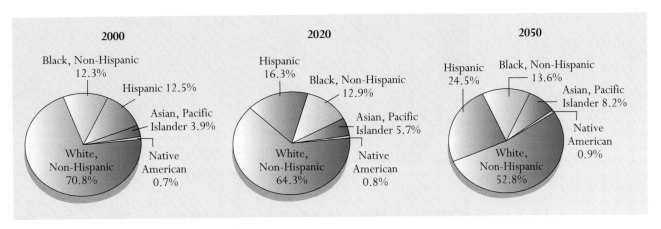

**Figure 2.2**   Racial and Ethnic Composition of the United States 2000, 2020, 2050

*Source:* U.S. Bureau of the Census (Middle Series).

live mainly in the Miami metropolitan area. The politics of each of these Hispanic groups differs somewhat (see "Hispanic Politics" in Chapter 12).

**A Nation of Immigrants**   The United States is a nation of immigrants, from the first "boat people" (Pilgrims) to the latest Haitian refugees and Cuban *balseros* ("rafters"). Historically, most of the people who came to settle in this country did so because they believed their lives would be better here, and American political culture today has been greatly affected by the beliefs and values they brought with them. Americans are proud of their immigrant heritage and the freedom and opportunity the nation has extended to generations of "huddled masses yearning to breathe free"—words emblazoned on the Statue of Liberty in New York's harbor. Today about 8 percent of the U.S. population is foreign-born.

Immigration policy is a responsibility of the national government. It was not until 1882 that Congress passed the first legislation restricting entry into the United States of persons alleged to be "undesirable" and virtually all Asians. After

Immigration places responsibility on public schools to provide for the needs of children from different cultures. Here, Latino pupils assemble in Santa Ana, California.

The U.S. Coast Guard may intercept boats at sea and return their occupants to their country of origin. But once immigrants reach the U.S. shore, they are entitled to a hearing in any deportation proceedings.

World War I, Congress passed the comprehensive Immigration Act of 1921, which established maximum numbers of new immigrants each year and set a quota for immigrants for each foreign country at 3 percent of the number of that nation's foreign-born who were living in the United States in 1910, later reduced to 2 percent of the number living here in 1890. These restrictions reflected antiimmigration feelings that were generally directed at the large wave of Southern and Eastern European Catholic and Jewish immigrants (from Poland, Russia, Hungary, Italy, and Greece) entering the United States prior to World War I (see Figure 2.3). It was not until the Immigration and Naturalization Act of 1965 that national origin

**Figure 2.3** Legal Immigration to the United States by Decades

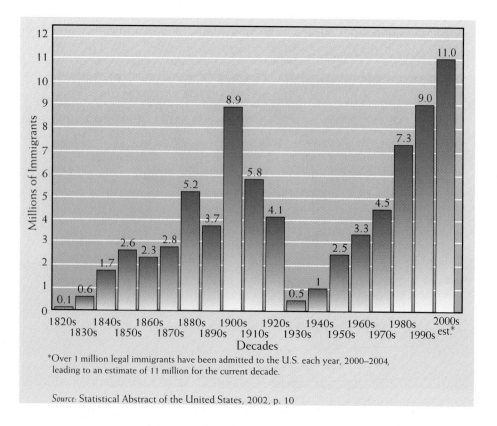

*Over 1 million legal immigrants have been admitted to the U.S. each year, 2000–2004, leading to an estimate of 11 million for the current decade.

*Source:* Statistical Abstract of the United States, 2002, p. 10

quotas were abolished, replaced by preference categories for close relatives of U.S. citizens, professionals, and skilled workers.

Immigration "reform" was the announced goal of Congress in the Immigration Reform and Control Act of 1986, also known as the Simpson-Mazzoli Act. It sought to control immigration by placing principal responsibility on employers; it set fines for knowingly hiring an illegal alien. However, it allowed employers to accept many different forms of easily forged documentation and at the same time subjected them to penalties for discriminating against legal foreign-born residents. To win political support, the act granted amnesty to illegal aliens who had lived in the United States since 1982. But the act failed to reduce the flow of either legal or illegal immigrants.

Today, more than a million people per year are admitted *legally* to the United States as "lawful permanent residents" (persons who have needed job skills or who have relatives who are U.S. citizens) or as "political refugees" (persons with "a well-founded fear of persecution" in their country of origin). In addition, each year more than 33 million people are awarded temporary visas to enter the United States for study, business, or pleasure (See *What Do You Think?* "Does Immigration Help or Hurt America?").

**Illegal Immigration**    The United States is a free and prosperous society with more than 5,000 miles of borders (2,000 with Mexico) and hundreds of international air- and seaports. In theory, a sovereign nation should be able to maintain secure borders, but in practice the United States has been unwilling and unable to do so. Estimates of illegal immigration vary widely, from the official U.S. Bureau of Immigration and Citizenship Services (formerly the Immigration and Naturalization Service, INS) estimate of 400,000 per year (about 45 percent of the legal immigration) to unofficial estimates ranging up to 3 million per year. The government estimates that about 4 million illegal immigrants currently reside in the United States; unofficial estimates range up to 12 million or more. Many illegal immigrants slip across U.S. borders or enter ports with false documentation; many more overstay tourist, worker, or student visas.[10] The total number of immigrants, legal and illegal, living in the United States is shown above.

As a free society, the United States is not prepared to undertake massive roundups and summary deportations of millions of illegal residents. The Fifth and Fourteenth Amendments to the U.S. Constitution require that every *person* (not just citizen) be afforded "due process of law." The government may turn back persons at the border or even hold them in detention camps. The Coast Guard may intercept boats at sea and return persons to their country of origin.[11] Aliens have no constitutional right to come to the United States. However, once in the United States, whether legally or illegally, every person is entitled to due process of law and equal protection of the laws. People are thus entitled to a fair hearing prior to any government attempt to deport them. Aliens are entitled to apply for asylum and present evidence at a hearing of their "well-founded fear of prosecution" if returned to their country. Experience has shown that the only way to reduce the flow of illegal immigration is to control it at the border, an expensive and difficult, but not impossible, task. Localized experiments in border enforcement have indicated that, with significant increases in personnel and technology, illegal immigration can be reduced by half or more.

**Citizenship**    Persons born in the United States are U.S. citizens. People who have been lawfully admitted into the United States and granted permanent

**Center for Immigration Studies**
Advocacy organization for strengthening enforcement of immigration law. *www.cis.org*

Source: Steve Kelley.

**Bureau of Citizenship and Immigration Services**
Official site with information on immigration laws, citizenship requirements, etc. (previously INS).
*www.immigration.gov*

# WHAT DO YOU THINK?

## Does Immigration Help or Hurt America?

Americans are divided over whether *legal* immigration is a "good thing" or a "bad thing." And they are divided over whether immigrants help the economy by taking low-paying hard labor jobs that most Americans shun, or whether they hurt the economy by driving down wages and burdening schools and social services.

*Q. On the whole, do you think immigration is a good thing or a bad thing for this country today?*

| | |
|---|---|
| Good thing | 52% |
| Bad thing | 42 |
| Mixed or no opinion | 6 |

*Q. Do you think immigrants mostly help the economy by providing low-cost labor, or mostly hurt the economy by driving wages down for many Americans?*

| | |
|---|---|
| Mostly hurt | 48% |
| Mostly help | 42 |
| Neither | 3 |
| Both | 1 |
| Don't know | 5 |

It is important to note, however, that most Americans oppose *illegal* immigration. They want illegal immigrants sent back to their home country "immediately" without court hearings, and they favor "stricter penalties" on illegal immigrants.

*Q. When people are caught trying to enter the United States illegally, which do you think should be government policy?*

| | |
|---|---|
| Immediately send them back to their home country | 61% |
| Allow them to appeal their case using legal representation and a court hearing | 35 |
| Neither, don't know | 4 |

*Q. Do you favor or oppose stricter penalties on illegal immigrants?*

| | |
|---|---|
| Favor | 77% |
| Oppose | 18 |
| Don't know | 5 |

*Q. Do you favor or oppose using the U.S. military to stop illegal immigration at the borders?*

| | |
|---|---|
| Favor | 67% |
| Oppose | 24 |
| Unsure | 9 |

*Source:* Various national polls reported in Public Agenda, www.publicagenda.com

**Number of Immigrants Living in the United States**

*Source:* Derived from figures published by the Center for Immigration Studies, 2004.

*Border Patrol officers apprehend illegal aliens in the U.S. border city of Nogales, Arizona*

residence, and who have resided in the United States for at least five years and in their home state for the last six months, are eligible for naturalization as U.S. citizens. Federal district courts as well as offices of the CIS may grant applications for citizenship. By law, the applicant must be over age eighteen, be able to read, write, and speak English, possess good moral character, and understand and

# WHAT DO YOU THINK?

## Could You Pass the Citizenship Test?

To ensure that new citizens "understand" the history, principles, and form of government of the United States, the CIS administers a citizenship test. Could you pass it today?

*Answer correctly at least 18 of 30 questions to pass:*

1. How many stars are there on our flag?
2. What do the stars on the flag mean?
3. What color are the stripes?
4. What do the stripes on the flag mean?
5. What is the date of Independence Day?
6. Independence from whom?
7. What do we call a change to the Constitution?
8. How many branches are there in our government?
9. How many full terms can a president serve?
10. Who nominates judges of the Supreme Court?
11. How many Supreme Court justices are there?
12. Who was the main writer of the Declaration of Independence?
13. What holiday was celebrated for the first time by American colonists?
14. Who wrote the Star-Spangled Banner?
15. What is the minimum voting age in the U.S.?
16. Who was president during the Civil War?
17. Which president is called the "Father of our Country"?
18. What is the 50th state of the Union?
19. What is the name of the ship that brought the Pilgrims to America?
20. Who has the power to declare war?
21. What were the 13 original states of the U.S. called?
22. In what year was the Constitution written?

*A large congregation at Calvary Chapel in Fort Lauderdale, Florida, hears a sermon in 2004 regarding faith and morals in politics and government.*

23. What is the introduction to the Constitution called?
24. Which president was the first Commander-in-Chief of the U.S. Army and Navy?
25. In what month do we vote for the president?
26. How many times may a senator be reelected?
27. Who signs bills into law?
28. Who elects the president of the U.S.?
29. How many states are there in the U.S.?
30. Who becomes president if both the president and V.P. die?

---

Answers to citizenship test: 1. 50; 2. One for each state in the Union; 3. Red and white; 4. They represent the 13 original states; 5. July 4; 6. England; 7. Amendments; 8. 3; 9. 2; 10. The president; 11. 9; 12. Thomas Jefferson; 13. Thanksgiving; 14. Francis Scott Key; 15. 18; 16. Abraham Lincoln; 17. George Washington; 18. Hawaii; 19. *The Mayflower;* 20. The Congress; 21. Colonies; 22. 1787; 23. The Preamble; 24. George Washington; 25. November; 26. There is no limit at the present time; 27. The president; 28. The Electoral College; 29. 50; 30. Speaker of the House of Representatives.

*Source:* Bureau of Citizenship and Immigration Services.

---

demonstrate an attachment to the history, principles, and form of government of the United States (see *What Do You Think?* "Could You Pass the Citizenship Test?").

Citizens of the United States are entitled to **passports**, issued by the U.S. State Department upon presentation of photos plus evidence of citizenship—a birth certificate or naturalization papers. A passport enables U.S. citizens to re-enter the country after travel abroad. When traveling abroad, your U.S. passport may be your most valuable possession. Fewer than one-quarter of the U.S.

**passport** Evidence of U.S. citizenship, allowing people to travel abroad and reenter the United States.

**visa** A document or stamp on a passport allowing a person to visit a foreign country.

population currently hold passports. **Visas** are documents or stamps on a passport, issued by a foreign country, that allow citizens of one nation to visit another. The U.S. allows citizens of some countries, mostly Western European, to visit the United States without visas.

# Religion and Secularism in Politics

The United States is one of the most religious societies in the world. Over 90 percent of Americans report in polls that they believe in God. Over 80 percent say that prayer is part of their daily lives, and 60 percent say that they attend church at least once a month. Over 80 percent claim some religious affiliation. Evangelical Protestants are the largest single group and the fastest-growing (see Figure 2.4).

At the same time, however, most Americans are concerned about religious leaders exercising influence in political life. Most respondents say it is "not appropriate for religious leaders to talk about their political beliefs as part of their religious activities" (61 percent), "religious leaders should not try to influence how people vote in elections" (64 percent), and "religious groups should not advance their beliefs by being involved in politics and working to affect policy" (54 percent).[12]

American's religious commitments and their belief in the separation of religion from politics sometimes clash.

**People for the American Way**
An influential interest group on the Left which, among other issues, strongly opposes religious symbols in public.
*www.pfaw.org*

**secular** In politics, a reference to opposition to religious practices and symbols in public life.

**Challenging Religion in Public Life**    There is a growing divide in America between religious faith and **secular** politics on a number of key public issues. The most religious among us, as determined by frequency of church attendance and

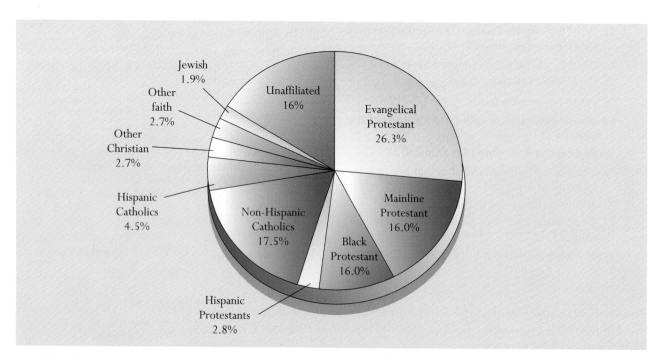

**Figure 2.4**    Religious Affiliations of Americans

*Source:* From Pew Forum on Religion & Public Life Survey of 4,000 U.S. adults in March–May 2004. Copyright © 2004 by The Pew Research Center. Reprinted by permission.

belief in the literal interpretation of the Bible, generally support limitations on abortion, including parental notification when minors seek abortions, and would prohibit partial-birth abortions. They also support abstinence in sex education; oppose same-sex marriage, support the phrase "under God" in the Pledge of Allegiance; support the display of religious symbols in public places; support the public funding of "faith-based" social service organizations; and generally believe that religion should play an important role in addressing "all or most of today's problems."

In contrast, challenges to religion in public life are increasingly being raised in American politics, especially in the courts. Organizations such as the American Civil Liberties Union and Americans United for the Separation of Church and State are challenging many traditional religious practices and symbols in public life. Most of these challenges are based upon the First Amendment's "no establishment of religion" clause. Among these challenges: removing "under God" from the Pledge of Allegiance and eliminating the national motto "In God We Trust" from our coins; removing religious symbols—Christmas displays, the Ten Commandments, etc.—from public places; supporting the teaching of evolution and opposing the teaching of "creationism" in the schools; opposing the use of public school vouchers to pay for students attending religious schools; supporting gay rights, including same-sex marriages; and threatening to remove tax exemptions from churches whose religious leaders endorse candidates or involve themselves in politics.

**Religious/Political Alignments**  Interestingly, the religious-versus-secular division on these issues does *not* depend upon *which* religion (for example, Protestants, Catholic, Jewish) that Americans identify themselves. Rather, this division appears to be more closely aligned with the intensity of people's religious commitments; in polls, for example, their self-identification as "born-again" or "evangelical"; their frequency of church attendance; and their agreement with statements such as "prayer is an important part of my daily life."

An overwhelming majority of Americans (80 percent) say they have "old-fashioned values about family and marriage." And in the 2004 presidential election "moral values" was cited as the single most important issue (see Chapter 5).

Increasingly, this division between religious and secular viewpoints is coming to correspond with the division between liberals and conservatives in American politics. Religious traditionalists are more likely to describe themselves as conservatives or moderates, while secularists are more likely to describe themselves as liberal in politics.[13]

# Ideologies: Liberalism and Conservatism

An **ideology** is a consistent and integrated system of ideas, values, and beliefs. A political ideology tells us who *should* get what, when, and how; that is, it tells us who *ought* to govern and what goals they *ought* to pursue. When we use ideological terms such as *liberalism* and *conservatism*, we imply reasonably integrated sets of values and beliefs. And when we pin ideological labels on people, we imply that those people are fairly consistent in the application of these values and beliefs in public affairs. In reality, neither political leaders nor citizens always display integrated or consistent opinions; many hold conservative views on some issues and liberal views on others.[14] Many Americans avoid ideological labeling, either by

**Americans United for Separation of Church and State**
An interest group formed to keep religion out of public places, especially schools. *www.au.org*

**Family Religious Council**
An interest group championing religion, family, and marriage, and government support of these values. *www.frc.org*

**ideology** Consistent and integrated system of ideas, values, and beliefs.

**Figure 2.5** Americans: Liberal, Moderate, Conservative

*Source:* General Social Surveys, National Opinion Research Center, University of Chicago; Updated from *The American Enterprise,* January/February 2000, and Gallup, 2005.

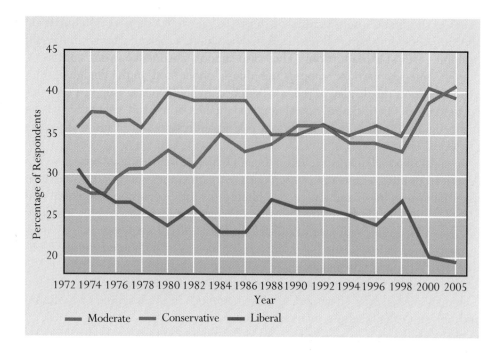

Think Again

Do you consider yourself politically conservative, moderate, or liberal?

**American Conservative Union**
Conservative news and views and rankings of Congress members on conservative index. *www.conservative.org*

**conservatism** Belief in the value of free markets, limited government, and individual self-reliance in economic affairs, combined with a belief in the value of tradition, law, and morality in social affairs.

**Bill O'Reilly**
Popular Web site for conservative views as well as promotion of O'Reilly programs, books, editorials, etc. *www.billoreilly.com*

describing themselves as "moderate" or "middle-of-the-road" or by simply declining to place themselves on an ideological scale. But as Figure 2.5 shows, among those who choose an ideological label to describe their politics, conservatives consistently outnumber liberals. (See also *Across the USA:* "Liberalism and Conservatism" on the facing page)

Despite inconsistencies in opinion and avoidance of labeling, ideology plays an important role in American politics. Political *elites*—elected and appointed officeholders; journalists, editors, and commentators; party officials and interest-group leaders; and others active in politics—are generally more consistent in their political views than nonelites and are more likely to use ideological terms in describing politics.[15]

**Modern Conservatism: Individualism plus Traditional Values** Modern **conservatism** combines a belief in free markets, limited government, and individual self-reliance in economic affairs with a belief in the value of tradition, law, and morality in social affairs. Conservatives wish to retain our historical commitments to individual freedom from governmental controls; reliance on individual initiative and effort for self-development; a free-enterprise economy with a minimum of governmental intervention; and rewards for initiative, skill, risk, and hard work. These views are consistent with the early classical liberalism of Locke, Jefferson, and the nation's Founders, discussed at the beginning of this chapter. The result is a confusion of ideological labels: modern conservatives claim to be the true inheritors of the (classical) liberal tradition.

Conservatism is less optimistic about human nature. Traditionally, conservatives have recognized that human nature includes elements of irrationality, ignorance, hatred, and violence. Thus they have been more likely to place their faith in *law* and *traditional values* than in popular fads, trends, or emotions. To conservatives, the absence of law does not mean freedom but, rather, exposure to the tyranny of terrorism and violence. They believe that without the guidance of traditional values, people would soon come to grief through the unruliness

## ACROSS THE USA

# Liberalism and Conservatism

States might be classified in terms of their voters' self-identification in opinion surveys as liberal, moderate, or conservative. The most conservative state is Utah (45 percent conservative, 37 percent moderate, 13 percent liberal), followed by Indiana (42 percent conservative, 39 percent moderate, 13 percent liberal). The most liberal states are Massachusetts (26 percent conservative, 42 percent moderate, 26 percent liberal), New York (29 percent conservative, 39 percent moderate, 26 percent liberal), and New Jersey (28 percent conservative, 40 percent moderate, 26 percent liberal).

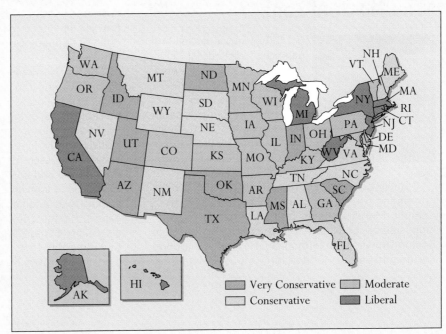

*Source:* Gerald C. Wright, Robert S. Erikson, and John P. McIver, "Public Opinion and Policy Liberalism in the American States," *American Journal of Political Science* 31 (November 1987): 980–1001. Reprinted by permission of the University of Wisconsin Press.

of their passions, destroying both themselves and others. Conservatives argue that strong institutions—family, church, and community—are needed to control individuals' selfish and immoral impulses and to foster civilized ways of life.

It is important to note that conservatism in America incorporates different views of the role of government in economic versus social affairs. Conservatives generally prefer *limited noninterventionist government in economic affairs*—a government that relies on free markets to provide and distribute goods and services; minimizes its regulatory activity; limits social welfare programs to the "truly needy"; keeps taxes low; and rejects schemes to equalize income or wealth. On the other hand, conservatives would *strengthen government's power to regulate social conduct.* They support restrictions on abortion; endorse school prayer; favor a war on drugs and pornography; oppose the legitimizing of homosexuality; support the death penalty; and advocate tougher criminal penalties.

### Modern Liberalism: Governmental Power to "Do Good"    Modern **liberalism** combines a belief in a strong government to provide economic security and protection for civil rights with a belief in freedom from government intervention in social conduct. Modern liberalism retains the classical liberalism commitment to individual dignity, but it emphasizes the importance of social and

**Young Americans for Freedom**
The "YAF" archives site contains background on the conservative organization and conservative views on key issues of the day.
*www.yaf.com*

**liberalism** Belief in the value of strong government to provide economic security and protection for civil rights, combined with a belief in personal freedom from government intervention in social conduct.

## PEOPLE IN POLITICS

### Bill O'Reilly, "The No Spin Zone"?

Bill O'Reilly assures "fair and balanced" broadcast journalism to Fox News viewers. He describes his popular TV show as a "no spin zone" and refers to himself as an "independent." Yet O'Reilly has emerged as the nation's most popular voice of conservatism on television.

O'Reilly boasts of an Irish Catholic working-class upbringing in Long Island. He graduated from Catholic Marist College, briefly taught in a Miami high school, and earned a master's degree from Boston University in journalism. He bounced around the country as a reporter for various TV stations,

and by 1986 he had become a top correspondent for ABC News. He eventually replaced David Frost as anchor of the TV tabloid *Inside Edition*, but left that job in 1995 to earn a master's degree from the John F. Kennedy School of Government at Harvard University.

The Fox News network recruited O'Reilly to create a new evening talk show, *The O'Reilly Factor*. The show quickly grew into the most watched program on cable news, outdistancing even *Larry King Live*.

O'Reilly mixes humor with bombast. He ferociously attacks liberals bold enough to come on his show as guests. He constantly interrupts guests, both liberal and conservative, to broadcast his own views. He is convinced that liberal "secularists" are waging war against religion and traditional moral values. His favorite targets include Hollywood liberals, Hillary Clinton, Jesse Jackson, and the American Civil Liberties Union. The occasional twinkle in his Irish eyes tempers his often venomous commentary.

---

**Americans for Democratic Action**
The ADA is the nation's oldest liberal political action organization.
*www.adaction.org*

**U.S. Senator Barbara Boxer**
The official Web site of U.S. Senator Barbara Boxer of California contains biographical material, information about Boxer's committee assignments, and her stands on various political issues. *www.senate.gov/~boxer/*

economic security for the whole population. In contrast to classical liberalism, which looked at governmental power as a potential threat to personal freedom, modern liberalism looks on the power of government as a positive force for eliminating social and economic conditions that adversely affect people's lives and impede their self-development. The modern liberal approves of the use of governmental power to correct the perceived ills of society (see *People in Politics:* "Barbara Boxer, Defending Liberalism in Congress").

The prevailing impulse is to "do good," to perform public services, and to assist the least fortunate in society, particularly the poor and minorities. Modern liberalism is impatient with what it sees as the slow progress of individual initiative and private enterprise toward solving socioeconomic problems, so it seeks to use the power of the national government to find solutions to society's troubles.

Modern liberalism contends that individual dignity and equality of opportunity depend in some measure on *reduction of absolute inequality* in society. Modern liberals believe that true equality of opportunity cannot be achieved where significant numbers of people are suffering from hopelessness, hunger, treatable illness, or poverty. Thus modern liberalism supports government efforts to reduce inequalities in society.

Liberals also have different views of the role of government in economic versus social affairs. Liberals generally prefer an *active, powerful government in economic affairs*—a government that provides a broad range of public services; regulates business; protects civil rights; protects consumers and the environment; provides generous unemployment, welfare, and Social Security benefits; and reduces economic inequality. But many of these same liberals would *limit the government's power to regulate social conduct.* They oppose restrictions on abortion; oppose school prayer; favor "decriminalizing" marijuana use and "victimless" offenses like public intoxication and vagrancy; support gay rights and tolerance toward alternative

## PEOPLE IN POLITICS

# Barbara Boxer, Defending Liberalism in Congress

Perhaps no one has been more successful in defending liberal causes in Congress than California's outspoken U.S. senator, Barbara Boxer. Her political résumé boasts awards and honors from such organizations as Planned Parenthood (family planning, reproductive health, and abortion rights), the Sierra Club (environmental causes), Mobilization against AIDS, Anti-Defamation League (civil rights), and Public Citizen (consumer affairs).

A graduate of Brooklyn College with a B.A. in economics, Boxer worked briefly as a stockbroker before moving to San Francisco, where she became a journalist and later a campaign aide to a local congressional representative. Her political career is based in Marin County, a trendy, upper-class, liberal community north of San Francisco, where she first won elected office as a member of the County Board of Supervisors. She was elected to the U.S. House of Representatives from her Marin County district in 1982 and quickly won a reputation as one of the most liberal members of the House. Appointed to the House Armed Services Committee, she became

a leading critic of defense spending and virtually every weapon requested by the military.

When her state's liberal Democratic senator, Alan Cranston, announced he would not seek reelection to the Senate in the wake of his censure in the Keating Five affair, Boxer sought the open seat. Her opponent, conservative Republican radio and TV commentator Bruce Herschensohn, hammered at Boxer's 143 overdrafts at the House bank, her frequent absenteeism, and her extensive use of congressional perks. But with the help of Clinton's 1992 landslide (47 to 32 percent) victory over George Bush in California, Boxer eked out a 48 to 46 percent victory over Herschensohn. Her victory, together with that of Dianne Feinstein, gave California a historical first—two women U.S. senators.

Boxer quickly emerged as a powerful force in the U.S. Senate on behalf of abortion rights. She led the Senate fight for a federal law protecting abortion clinics from obstruction by demonstrators. On the Environmental and Public Works Committee she helped block efforts to relax federal environmental regulations. She led the movement to oust Republican senator Bob Packwood from the Senate on charges of sexually harassing staff members. She helped lead the fight for the Family Medical Leave Act, passed in the early days of the Clinton administration, as well as the Freedom of Access to [Abortion] Clinics Act. She was reelected by a wide margin in 1998, 2004, and 2006.

lifestyles; oppose government restrictions on speech, press, and protest; oppose the death penalty; and strive to protect the rights of criminal defendants. Liberalism is the prevailing ideology among college professors (see Figure 2.6).

**The Ideological Battlefield**   If Americans aligned themselves along a single liberal-conservative dimension, politics in the United States would be easier to describe, but far less interesting. We have already defined liberals as supporting a strong government in economic affairs and civil rights, but opposing government intervention in social affairs. And we have described conservatives as supporting a limited government in economic affairs and civil rights, but favoring government regulation of social conduct. Thus neither liberals or conservatives are really consistent in their view of the role of government in society, each differentiating between economic and social affairs.

Yet some people consistently support strong government to regulate business and provide economic security, and also to closely regulate social conduct. While few people use the term *populist* to describe themselves, these people may actually make up a fairly large proportion of the electorate. Liberal politicians can appeal for their votes by stressing government intervention to provide economic security, while conservative politicians can appeal to them by stressing the maintenance of traditional social values.

**Figure 2.6**  Ideology Among Professors

*Source: American Enterprise*, vol. 2, July/August 1991, http://www. TAEmag.com. Published by the American Enterprise Institute for Public Policy Research, Washington, DC.

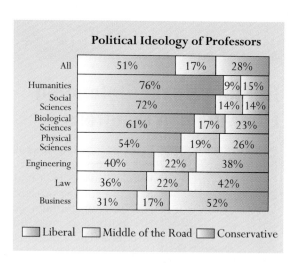

**libertarian**  Opposing government intervention in both economic and social affairs, and favoring minimal government in all sectors of society.

And some people, often referred to as **libertarians**, oppose government intervention in *both* economic affairs and in the private lives of citizens. They are against most environmental regulations, consumer protecton laws, antidrug laws, defense spending, foreign aid, and government restrictions on abortion. In other words, they favor minimal government intervention in all sectors of society.

The result may be a two-dimensional ideological battlefield—identifying more or less government intervention and separating economic from social affairs—resulting in four separate groups—liberals, conservatives, populists, and libertarians (see Figure 2.7).

**Youth and Ideology**  Young people are more likely to hold liberal views than their elders. Especially on social issues, young people, 18–24, are more likely to describe themselves as liberals (see Table 2.1). Older adults are more likely to describe themselves as conservatives on social as well as economic issues.

**left**  A reference to the liberal, progressive, and/or socialist side of the political spectrum.

**right**  A reference to the conservative, traditional, anticommunist side of the political spectrum.

**radicalism**  Advocacy of immediate and drastic changes in society, including the complete restructuring of institutions, values, and beliefs. Radicals may exist on either the extreme left or extreme right.

**extremism**  Rejection of democratic politics and the assertion of the supremacy of the "people" over laws, institutions, and individual rights.

## Dissent in the United States

Dissent from the principal elements of American political culture—individualism, free enterprise, democracy, and equality of opportunity—has arisen over the years from both the *left* and the *right*. The **left** generally refers to socialists and communists, but it is sometimes used to brand liberals. The **right** generally refers to fascists and extreme nationalists, although it is sometimes used to stamp conservatives. Despite their professed hostility toward each other, **radicals** on the left and right share many characteristics. Both are **extremist**. They reject democratic politics, compromise, and coalition building as immoral, and they assert the supremacy of the "people" over laws, institutions, and individual rights. Extremists view politics with hostility, although they may make cynical use of democratic politics as a short-term tactical means to their goals.

Conspiracy theories are popular among extremists. For example, the left sees a conspiracy among high government, corporate, and military chieftains to profit from war; the right sees a conspiracy among communists, intellectuals, the United Nations, and Wall Street bankers to subordinate the United States to a

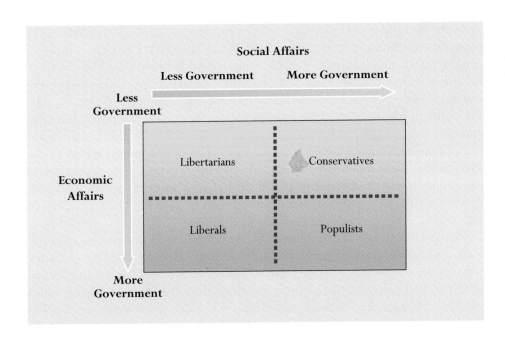

**Figure 2.7** Mapping the Ideological Battlefield
We can classify people's views on whether they prefer more or less government intervention, first, in economic affairs (the vertical axis), and, second, in social affairs (the horizontal axis). The result is a fourfold classification scheme distinguishing types (economic and social) of liberals and conservatives.

world government. The historian Richard Hofstadter has referred to this tendency as "the paranoid style of politics."[16] Both the left and right are intolerant of the opinions of others and are willing to disrupt and intimidate those with whom they disagree. Whether shouting down speakers or disrupting meetings or burning crosses and parading in hoods, the impulse to violence is often present in those who subscribe to radical politics.

**Antidemocratic Ideologies**   Dissent in the United States has historical roots in antidemocratic movements that originated primarily outside its borders. These movements have spanned the political spectrum from the far right to the far left.

**Table 2.1    Ideology and Age**

Thinking about social issues, would you say your views on social issues are conservative, moderate, or liberal?

| Age | Conservative | Moderate | Liberal |
|---|---|---|---|
| 18–24 | 27% | 36% | 36% |
| 25–38 | 33 | 34 | 31 |
| 39 plus | 40 | 38 | 19 |

Thinking about economic issues, would you say your views on economic issues are conservative, moderate, or liberal?

| Age | | | |
|---|---|---|---|
| 18–24 | 33% | 40% | 26% |
| 25–38 | 39 | 39 | 20 |
| 39 plus | 47 | 38 | 12 |

*Source:* Gallup Poll reported May 20, 2003. Copyright © 2003 by The Gallup Organization.

**fascism** Political ideology in which the state and/or race is assumed to be supreme over individuals.

At the far-right end of this spectrum lies **fascism**, an ideology that asserts the supremacy of the state or race over individuals. The goal of fascism is unity of people, nation, and leadership—in the words of Adolf Hitler: *"Ein Volk, Ein Reich, Ein Führer"* (One People, One Nation, One Leader). Every individual, every interest, and every class are to be submerged for the good of the nation. Against the rights of liberty or equality, fascism asserts the duties of service, devotion, and discipline. Its goal is to develop a superior type of human being, with qualities of bravery, courage, genius, and strength. The World War II defeat of the two leading fascist regimes in history—Adolf Hitler's Nazi Germany and Benito Mussolini's fascist Italy—did not extinguish fascist ideas. Elements of fascist thought are found today in extremist movements in both the United States and Europe.

**Marxism** The theories of Karl Marx, among them that capitalists oppress workers and that worldwide revolution and the emergence of a classless society are inevitable.

**Marxism** arose out of the turmoil of the Industrial Revolution as a protest against social evils and economic inequalities. Karl Marx (1818–83), its founder, was not an impoverished worker but rather an upper-middle-class intellectual unable to find an academic position. Benefiting from the financial support of his wealthy colleague Friedrich Engels (1820–95), Marx spent years writing *Das Kapital* (1867), a lengthy work describing the evils of capitalism, especially the oppression of factory workers (the proletariat) and the inevitability of revolution. The two men collaborated on a popular pamphlet entitled *The Communist Manifesto* (1848), which called for a workers' revolution: "Workers of the world, unite. You have nothing to lose but your chains."

**Leninism** The theories of Vladimir Lenin, among them that advanced capitalist countries turned toward war and colonialism to make their own workers relatively prosperous.

It fell to Vladimir Lenin (1870–1924) to implement Marx and Engels's revolutionary ideology in the Russian Revolution in 1917. According to **Leninism**, the key to a successful revolution is the organization of small, disciplined, hard-core groups of professional revolutionaries into a centralized totalitarian party. To explain why Marx's predictions about the ever-worsening conditions of the masses under capitalism proved untrue (workers' standards of living in Western democracies rose rapidly in the twentieth century), Lenin devised the theory of imperialism: advanced capitalist countries turned to war and colonialism, exploiting the Third World, in order to make their own workers relatively prosperous.

 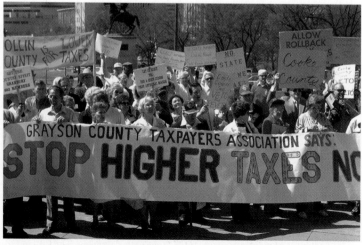

Liberals' concern about efforts to curtail social welfare programs reflects their support of strong government, whereas conservatives' demands for tax cuts reflect their preference for government that encourages self-reliance and individual initiative.

# WHAT DO YOU THINK?

## Are You a Liberal or a Conservative?

Not everyone consistently takes a liberal or a conservative position on every issue. But if you find that you agree with more positions under one of the following "liberal" or "conservative" lists, you are probably ready to label yourself ideologically.

| | You are *Liberal* If You Agree That | You Are *Conservative* If You Agree That |
|---|---|---|
| Economic policy | Government should regulate business to protect the public interest. | Free-market competition is better at protecting the public than government regulation. |
| | The rich should pay higher taxes to support public services for all. | Taxes should be kept as low as possible. |
| | Government spending for social welfare is a good investment in people. | Government welfare programs destroy incentives to work. |
| Crime | Government should place primary emphasis on alleviating the social conditions (such as poverty and joblessness) that cause crime. | Government should place primary emphasis on providing more police and prisons and stop courts from coddling criminals. |
| Social policy | Government should protect the right of women to choose abortion and fund abortions for poor women. | Government should restrict abortion and not use taxpayer money for abortions. |
| | Government should pursue affirmative action programs on behalf of minorities and women in employment, education, and so on. | Government should not grant preferences to anyone based on race or sex. |
| | Government should keep religious prayers and ceremonies out of schools and public places. | Government should allow prayers and religious observances in schools and public places. |
| National security policy | Government should support "human rights" throughout the world. | Government should pursue the "national interest" of the United States. |
| | Military spending should be reduced now that the Cold War is over. | Military spending must reflect a variety of new dangers in this post–Cold War period. |

**Communism** is the outgrowth of Marxist-Leninist ideas about the necessity of class warfare, the inevitability of a worldwide proletarian revolution, and the concentration of all power in the "vanguard of the proletariat"—the Communist Party. Communism justifies violence as a means to attain power by arguing that the bourgeoisie (the capitalistic middle class) will never voluntarily give up its control over "the means of production" (the economy). Democracy is only "window dressing" to disguise capitalist exploitation. The Communist Party justifies authoritarian single-party rule as the "dictatorship of the proletariat." In theory, after a period of rule by the Communist Party, all property will be owned by the government, and a "classless" society of true communism will emerge.

**communism** System of government in which a single totalitarian party controls all means of production and distribution of goods and services.

**Socialist Party USA** News and views from America's Socialist party. *http://sp-usa.org*

**Socialism** Socialism shares with communism a condemnation of capitalist profit making as exploitative of the working classes. Communists and socialists agree on the "evils" of industrial capitalism: the concentration of wealth, the insensitivity of the profit motive to human needs, the insecurities and suffering brought on by the business cycle, the conflict of class interests, and the tendency of capitalist nations to involve themselves in imperialist wars. However, socialists are committed to the democratic process as a means of replacing capitalism with collective ownership of economic enterprise. Socialists generally reject the notion of violent revolution as a way to replace capitalism and instead advocate

**socialism** System of government involving collective or government ownership of economic enterprise, with the goal being equality of results, not merely equality of opportunity.

Political extremists of the left and right often have more in common than they would like to admit. Although decidedly different in their political philosophies, both members of right-wing American neo-Nazi groups and members of left-wing communist groups reject democratic politics and assert the supremacy of the "people" over laws, institutions, and individual rights. Gregory Johnson (left) was the catalyst for the flag burning controversy that is still raging in Congress today. Buford O'Neal Furrow, Jr. (right), was arrested for opening fire on children in a Jewish day care center in California. Several children died in this attack.

peaceful, constitutional roads to bring about change. Moreover, many socialists are prepared to govern in a free society under democratic principles, including freedom of speech and press and the right to organize political parties and oppose government policy. Socialism is egalitarian, seeking to reduce or eliminate inequalities in the distribution of wealth. It attempts to achieve equality of results, rather than mere equality of opportunity.

**The End of History?** Much of the history of the twentieth century was the struggle between democratic capitalism and totalitarian communism. Thus the collapse of communism in Eastern Europe and the Soviet Union, symbolized by the tearing down of the Berlin Wall in 1989 as well as the worldwide movement toward free markets and democracy at the end of the twentieth century, has been labeled the **end of history**.[17] Democratic revolutions were largely inspired by the realization that free-market capitalism provided much higher standards of living than communism. The economies of Eastern Europe were falling further and further behind the economies of the capitalist nations of the West. Similar comparative observations of the successful economies of the Asian capitalist "Four Tigers"—South Korea, Taiwan, Singapore, and Hong Kong—even inspired China's communist leadership to undertake market reforms. Communism destroyed the individual's incentive to work, produce, innovate, save, and invest in the future. Under communism, production for government goals (principally a strong military) came first; production for individual needs came last. The result

**end of history** The collapse of communism and the worldwide movement toward free markets and political democracy.

# A CONSTITUTIONAL NOTE

## Natural Born Versus Naturalized Citizenship

The Fourteenth Amendment to the Constitution requires the states, and by implication the national government, to treat natural born and naturalized citizens the same: "all persons born or naturalized in United States, and subject to the jurisdiction thereof, are citizens of the United States. . . . No State shall make or enforce any law which shall abridge the privileges or immunities of citizens of the United States . . ." But there is one key difference between natural born and naturalized citizens written into the original Constitution of 1787: "No Person except a natural born Citizen, or a Citizen of the United States, at the time of the Adoption of this Constitution, shall be eligible to the Office of President . . ."

Requiring that the President be born in the United States is the only constitutional difference between born and naturalized citizens. Perhaps this difference made more sense in 1787 when many aspiring politicians had only recently moved into the country. But is it relevant today? Does it deny some very qualified people the opportunity to run for the nation's highest office?

was long lines at stores, shoddy products, and frequent bribery of bureaucrats to obtain necessary consumer items. More important, the concentration of both economic and political power in the hands of a central bureaucracy proved to be incompatible with democracy. Communism relies on central direction, force, and repression. Communist systems curtail individual freedom and prohibit the development of separate parties and interest groups outside of government.

Capitalism does not *ensure* democracy; some capitalist nations are authoritarian. But economic freedom inspires demands for political freedom. Thus market reforms, initiated by communist leaders to increase productivity, led to democracy movements, and those movements eventually dismantled the communist system in Eastern Europe and the old Soviet Union.

**Academic Radicalism**    Marxism survives on campuses today largely as an academic critique of the functioning of capitalism.[18] It provides some disaffected academics with ideas and language to attack everything that disturbs them about the United States—from poverty, racism, and environmental hazards to junk food, athletic scholarships, and obnoxious television advertising—conveniently blaming the "profit motive" for many of the ills of American society.

Contemporary radicals argue that the institutions of capitalism have conditioned people to be materialistic, competitive, and even violent. The individual has been transformed into a one-dimensional person in whom genuine humanistic values are repressed.[19] Profitability, rather than humanistic values, remains the primary criterion for decision making in the capitalist economy, and thus profitability is the reason for poverty and misery despite material abundance. Without capitalist institutions, life would be giving, cooperative, and compassionate. Only a *radical restructuring* of social and economic institutions will succeed in liberating people from these institutions to lead humanistic, cooperative lives.

To American radicals, the problem of social change is truly monumental, because capitalist values and institutions are deeply rooted in this country. Since most people are not aware that they are oppressed and victimized, the first step toward social change is consciousness raising—that is, making people aware of their misery.

The agenda of academic radicalism has been labeled **politically correct (PC)** thinking. Politically correct thinking views American society as racist, sexist, and homophobic. Overt bigotry is not the real issue, but rather Western institutions,

**National Association of Scholars**
Association of college and university professors opposed to PC restrictions on campus.
*www.nas.org*

**politically correct (PC)**
Repression of attitudes, speech, and writings that are deemed racist, sexist, homophobic (anti-homosexual), or otherwise "insensitive."

language, and culture, which systematically oppress and victimize women, people of color, gays, and others.

Academic radicalism "includes the assumption that Western values are inherently oppressive, that the chief purpose of education is political transformation, and that all standards are arbitrary.[20] In PC thinking, "everything is political." Therefore curriculum, courses, and lectures—even language and demeanor—are judged according to whether they are politically correct or not. Universities have always been centers for the critical examination of institutions, values, and culture, but PC thinking does not really tolerate open discussion or debate. Opposition is denounced as "insensitive," racist, sexist, or worse, and intimidation is not infrequent.

# Summary Notes

- Ideas are sources of power. They provide people with guides for determining right and wrong and with rationales for political action. Political institutions are shaped by the values and beliefs of the political culture, and political leaders are restrained in their exercise of power by these ideas.

- The American political culture is a set of widely shared values and beliefs about who should govern, for what ends, and by what means.

- Americans share many common ways of thinking about politics. Nevertheless, there are often contradictions between professed values and actual conditions, problems in applying abstract beliefs to concrete situations, and even occasional conflict over fundamental values.

- Individual liberty is a fundamental value in American life. The classical liberal tradition that inspired the nation's Founders included both political liberties and economic freedoms.

- Equality is another fundamental American value. The nation's Founders believed in equality before the law; yet political equality, in the form of universal voting rights, required nearly two centuries to bring about.

- Equality of opportunity is a widely shared value; most Americans are opposed to artificial barriers of race, sex, religion, or ethnicity barring individual advancement. But equality of results is not a widely shared value; most Americans support a "floor" on income and well-being for their fellow citizens but oppose placing a "ceiling" on income or wealth.

- Income inequality has increased in recent years primarily as a result of economic and demographic changes. Most Americans believe that opportunities for individual advancement are still available, and this belief diminishes the potential for class conflict.

- A great majority of Americans claim religious affiliation. But there is a growing divide between religious and secular viewpoints on the role of religion in public life. Secularists have challenged many traditional religious practices and symbols, such as the words "under God" in the Pledge of Allegiance.

- Liberal and conservative ideologies in American politics present somewhat different sets of values and beliefs, even though they share a common commitment to individual dignity and private property. Generally, liberals favor an active, powerful government to provide economic security and protection for civil rights but oppose government restrictions on social conduct. Generally, conservatives favor minimal government intervention in economic affairs and civil rights but support many government restrictions on social conduct.

- Many Americans who identify themselves as liberals or conservatives are not always consistent in applying their professed views. Populists are liberal on economic issues but conservative in their views on social issues. Libertarians are conservative on economic issues but liberal in their social views.

- The collapse of communism in Eastern Europe and the former Soviet Union and the worldwide movement toward free markets and democracy have undermined support for socialism throughout the world. Yet Marxism survives in academic circles as a critique of the functioning of capitalism.

# Key Terms

| | | | |
|---|---|---|---|
| political culture   26 | equality of results   29 | conservatism   42 | Marxism   48 |
| values   26 | social mobility   32 | liberalism   43 | Leninism   48 |
| beliefs   26 | class conflict   33 | libertarian   46 | communism   49 |
| subcultures   26 | class consciousness   33 | left   46 | socialism   49 |
| classical liberalism   26 | passport   39 | right   46 | end of history   50 |
| capitalism   26 | visa   40 | radicalism   46 | politically correct (PC)   51 |
| political equality   28 | secular   40 | extremism   46 | |
| equality of opportunity   28 | ideology   41 | fascism   48 | |

# Suggested Readings

Baradat, Leon P., *Political Ideologies: Their Origin and Impact*. 9th ed. Upper Saddle River, NJ: Prentice Hall, 2006. Text coverage of evolution of political ideologies over the past three centuries.

de Tocqueville, Alexis. *Democracy in America* (1835). Chicago: University of Chicago Press. 2000. Classic early assessment of American political culture by a French traveler.

Dolbeare, Kenneth M., and Michael S. Cummings, *American Political Thought*, 5th ed. Washington, DC: CQ Press, 2004. A compilation of key writings and speeches from Franklin, Madison, Adams, and Paine, to Bill Clinton, Ronald Reagan, Pat Buchanan, and the Green Party.

Ebenstein, Alan, William Ebenstein, and Edwin Fogelman. *Today's Isms: Communism, Fascism, Capitalism, Socialism*. 11th ed. Upper Saddle River, N.J.: Prentice Hall, 2000. A concise description and history of the major isms.

Herrnstein, Richard J., and Charles Murray. *The Bell Curve: Intelligence and Class Structure in American Life*. New York: Free Press, 1994. A controversial argument that success in life is mainly a result of inherited intelligence and that a very bright "cognitive elite" will continue to distance themselves from the duller masses.

Huntington, Samuel P. *American Politics: The Promise of Disharmony*. Cambridge, Mass.: Harvard University Press, 1981. An examination of the gaps between the promise of the American ideals of liberty and equality and the performance of the American political system.

Ingersoll, David E., Richard K. Matthews, and Andrew Davidson. *The Philosophical Roots of Modern Ideology: Liberalism, Communism, Fascism, Islamism*. 3rd ed. Upper Saddle River, N.J.: Prentice Hall, 2001. Overview of political ideologies, including extensive quotes from original sources, from Locke, Jefferson, Madison, Marx, and Lenin to Gorbachev, Hitler, and Khomeini.

Jacobs, Lawrence R., and Theda Skocpol, eds. *Inequality and American Democracy*. New York: Russell Sage Foundation, 2005. A series of essays on the political consequences of growing income inequality in America.

Ryscavage, Paul. *Income Inequality in America*. Armonk, N.Y.: M.E. Sharpe, 1999. A careful analysis of current trends toward income inequality in the United States.

Wolff, Edward N. *Top Heavy*. 2nd ed. New York: News Press, 2002. A fact-filled report on the increasing inequality of wealth in America, together with a proposal to tax wealth as well as income.

* * * *

# Make It Real

## POLITICAL CULTURE
Students take a look at the belief systems that make political movements possible.

# Part Two
# CONSTITUTION

## Moment of Crisis—System Failure

**ABCNEWS**

Originally Aired: **September 15, 2005**
Program: **Primetime**
Running Time: **29:12**

Katrina ranks as the country's most expensive natural disaster and one of the deadliest in U.S. history. It has killed more than 700 people, uprooted tens of thousands of families, destroyed countless homes, and forced the evacuation of a major American city. Two and a half weeks after the hurricane roared ashore, just east of New Orleans, the country is trying to make sense of the resulting failures of local, state, and federal government. On this program, ABC News will piece together what we know and where the breakdowns occurred.

Born as a garden-variety tropical depression, Katrina grew into a tropical storm and officially earned hurricane status on August 24, 2005. It initially made landfall north of Miami, causing serious flooding and eleven deaths. But only when it marched across the Florida peninsula and hit the warm waters of the Gulf of Mexico did Katrina rapidly intensify and unleash its full fury. And as it evolved into a monster storm, the National Hurricane Center issued pointed warnings to the target communities along the Gulf Coast. The director made phone calls to key officials, including the mayor of New Orleans, saying Katrina could be "the big one" officials had long feared. Simultaneously, weather service bulletins were issued with unusually apocalyptic language. One predicted a storm of "unprecedented strength," "the area will be uninhabitable for weeks," and went on to predict human suffering "incredible by modern standards."

Given the dire warnings, should the deaths and suffering throughout the Gulf region have been as great? Were the recommendations issued by the 9/11 Commission put into practice?

Ted Koppel hosts a Primetime special edition, "Moment of Crisis: System Failure," a moment-by-moment chronology of what went so terribly wrong in the horrific days following Katrina's strike on the Gulf Coast. This was America's first major test of emergency response since 9/11, a test that has received failing grades.

## Critical Thinking Questions

1. In "Moment of Crisis—System Failure," state and local officials blame federal officials for the grossly inadequate response to this natural disaster and federal officials blame state and local officials. What are the responsibilities of the federal government, particularly agencies such as the Federal Emergency Management Agency (FEMA) and the Department of Homeland Security, in regard to both natural and man-made disasters? What are the responsibilities of state and local governments?

2. How much of a role did poverty play in the tragic aftermath of Hurricane Katrina? Do you get the impression from viewing the program that race had any impact on the way the federal government responded to the crisis?

# 3 THE CONSTITUTION
## Limiting Governmental Power

## Chapter Outline

- Constitutional Government
- The Constitutional Tradition
- Troubles Confronting a New Nation
- Consensus in Philadelphia
- Conflict in Philadelphia
- Resolving the Economic Issues
- Protecting National Security
- The Structure of the Government
- Separation of Powers and Checks and Balances
- Conflict over Ratification
- A Bill of Rights
- Constitutional Change

## Think About Politics

**1** Was the original constitution of 1787 a truly democratic document?
Yes ☐ No ☐

**2** Should citizens be able to vote directly on national policies such as prayer in public schools or doctor-assisted suicides?
Yes ☐ No ☐

**3** Should a large state like California, with 32 million people, elect more U.S. senators than a small state like Wyoming, with only half a million people?
Yes ☐ No ☐

**4** Should federal laws always supersede state laws?
Yes ☐ No ☐

**5** In which do you have the most trust and confidence?
President ☐ Congress ☐ Supreme Court ☐

**6** Should the Constitution be amended to require Congress to pass only balanced budgets?
Yes ☐ No ☐

**7** Should the Constitution be amended to guarantee that equal rights shall not be denied based on sex?
Yes ☐ No ☐

*In a democracy "of the people, by the people, and for the people," who really has the power to govern? Are strong national government and personal liberty compatible? Can majorities limit individual rights? America's Founders struggled with such questions, and in resolving them established the oldest existing constitutional government.*

## Constitutional Government

Constitutions govern government. **Constitutionalism**—a government of laws, not of people—means that those who exercise governmental power are restricted in their use of it by a higher law. If individual freedoms are to be placed beyond the reach of government and beyond the reach of majorities, then a constitution must truly limit the exercise of authority by government. It does so by setting forth individual liberties that the government—even with majority support—cannot violate.

A **constitution** legally establishes government authority. It sets up governmental bodies (such as the House of Representatives, the Senate, the presidency, and the Supreme Court in the United States). It grants them powers. It determines how their members are to be chosen. And it prescribes the rules by which they make decisions.

Constitutional decision making is deciding how to decide; that is, it is deciding on the rules for policy making. It is not policy making itself. Policies will be decided later, according to the rules set forth in the constitution.

A constitution cannot be changed by the ordinary acts of governmental bodies; change can come only through a process of general popular consent.[1] The U.S. Constitution, then, is superior to ordinary laws of Congress, orders of the president, decisions of the courts, acts of the state legislatures, and regulations of the bureaucracies. Indeed, the Constitution is "the supreme law of the land."

## The Constitutional Tradition

Americans are strongly committed to the idea of a written constitution to establish government and limit its powers. In fact, the Constitutional Convention of 1787 had many important antecedents.

**The Magna Carta, 1215** English lords, traditionally required to finance the king's wars, forced King John to sign the Magna Carta, a document guaranteeing their feudal rights and setting the precedent of a limited government and monarchy.

**constitutionalism** A government of laws, not people, operating on the principle that governmental power must be limited and government officials should be restrained in their exercise of power over individuals.

**constitution** The legal structure of a political system, establishing governmental bodies, granting their powers, determining how their members are selected, and prescribing the rules by which they make their decisions. Considered basic or fundamental, a constitution cannot be changed by ordinary acts of governmental bodies.

**National Constitution Center**
Located in Philadelphia's Independence Mall, this museum is devoted to explaining the U.S. Constitution.
*www.constitutioncenter.org*

**The Mayflower Compact, 1620**   Puritan colonists, while still aboard the Mayflower, signed a compact establishing a "civil body politic . . . to enact just and equal laws . . . for the general good of the colony, unto which we promise all due submission and obedience." After the Puritans landed at Plymouth, in what is today Massachusetts, they formed a colony based on the Mayflower Compact, thus setting a precedent of a government established by contract with the governed.

**The Colonial Charters, 1624–1732**   The charters that authorized settlement of the colonies in America were granted by royal action. For some of the colonies, the British king granted official proprietary rights to an individual, as in Maryland (granted to Lord Baltimore), Pennsylvania (to William Penn), and Delaware (also to Penn). For other colonies, the king granted royal commissions to companies to establish governments, as in Virginia, Massachusetts, New Hampshire, New York, New Jersey, Georgia, and North and South Carolina. Royal charters were granted directly to the colonists themselves only in Connecticut and Rhode Island. These colonists drew up their charters and presented them to the king, setting a precedent in America for written contracts defining governmental power.

The "Charter Oak Affair" of 1685–88 began when King James II became displeased with his Connecticut subjects and issued an order for the repeal of the Connecticut Charter. In 1687 Sir Edmund Andros went to Hartford, dissolved the colonial government, and demanded that the charter be returned. But Captain John Wadsworth hid it in an oak tree. After the so-called Glorious Revolution in England in 1688, the charter was taken out and used again as the fundamental law of the colony. Subsequent British monarchs silently acquiesced in this restoration of rights, and the affair strengthened the notion of loyalty to the constitution rather than to the king.

**The Declaration of Independence, 1776**   The First Continental Congress, a convention of delegates from twelve of the thirteen original colonies, came together in 1774 to protest British interference in American affairs. But the Revolutionary War did not begin until April 19, 1775. The evening before, British regular troops marched out from Boston to seize arms stored by citizens in Lexington and Concord, Massachusetts. At dawn the next morning, the Minutemen—armed citizens organized for the protection of their towns—engaged the British regulars in brief battles, then harassed them all the way back to Boston. In June of that year, the Second Continental Congress appointed George Washington Commander-in-Chief of American forces and sent him to Boston to take command of the American militia surrounding the city. Still, popular support for the Revolution remained limited, and even many members of the Continental Congress hoped only to force changes—not to split off from Britain.

As this hope died, however, members of the Continental Congress came to view a formal Declaration of Independence as necessary to give legitimacy to their cause and establish the basis for a new nation. Accordingly, on July 2, 1776, the Continental Congress "Resolved, that these United Colonies are, and, of right, ought to be free and independent States." Thomas Jefferson had been commissioned to write a justification for the action, which he presented to the congress on July 4, 1776. In writing the Declaration of Independence, Jefferson lifted several phrases directly from the English political philosopher John Locke asserting the rights of individuals, the contract theory of government, and the

## PEOPLE IN POLITICS

# John Locke, Guiding the Founders

The English political philosopher John Locke had a profound influence on America's founders. Indeed, the Declaration of Independence may be thought of as a restatement of Locke's basic ideas. Writing in 1690, Locke rejected the notion of the divine right of kings to rule and asserted the rights of human beings who are "by nature free, equal, and independent" to establish their own government by "social contract" to gain security from an unstable "state of nature." In other words, people consent to be governed to protect themselves and their property. But if the government they create becomes arbitrary, enslaves its people, or takes away their property, then the people have the "right of revolution" against such a government. Locke had been read by most of the Founders, who accepted his ideas of a "social contract" as the origin of government, and even a "right of revolution" as a last resort to a despotic government.

right of revolution. The declaration was signed first by the president of the Continental Congress, John Hancock.

The Revolutionary War effectively ended when British General Charles Cornwallis surrendered at Yorktown, Virginia, in October 1781. But even as the war was being waged, the new nation was creating the framework of its government.

**The Articles of Confederation, 1781–1789**  Although Richard Henry Lee, a Virginia delegate to the Continental Congress, first proposed that the newly independent states form a confederation on July 6, 1776, the Continental Congress did not approve the Articles of Confederation until November 15, 1777, and the last state to sign them, Maryland, did not do so until March 1, 1781. Under the Articles, Congress was a single house in which each state had two to seven members but only one vote. Congress itself created and appointed executives, judges, and military officers. It also had the power to make war and peace, conduct foreign affairs, and borrow and print money. But Congress could *not* collect taxes or enforce laws directly; it had to rely on the states to provide money and enforce its laws. The United States under the Articles was really a confederation of nations. Within this "firm league of friendship" (Article III of the Articles of Confederation), the national government was thought of as an alliance of independent states, not as a government "of the people."

**U.S. History**
The Independence Hall Association Web site with "Documents of Freedom" including Mayflower Compact, Declaration of Independence, Articles of Confederation, etc.
*www.ushistory.org*

## Troubles Confronting a New Nation

Two centuries ago the United States was struggling to achieve nationhood. The new U.S. government achieved enormous successes under the Articles of Confederation: It won independence from Great Britain, the world's most powerful colonial nation at the time; it defeated vastly superior forces in a prolonged war for independence; it established a viable peace and won powerful allies (notably, France) in the international community; it created an effective army and navy, established a postal system, and laid the foundations for national unity. But despite these successes in war and diplomacy, the political arrangements under the Articles were unsatisfactory to many influential groups—notably, bankers and investors who held U.S. government bonds, plantation owners, real estate developers, and merchants and shippers.

**Constitution Society**

Web site includes comprehensive list of founding documents, essays, and commentaries on the Constitution.
*www.constitution.org*

**Financial Difficulties**    Under the Articles of Confederation, Congress had no power to tax the people directly. Instead, Congress had to ask the states for money to pay its expenses, particularly the expenses of fighting the long and costly War of Independence with Great Britain. There was no way to force the states to make their payments to the national government. In fact, about 90 percent of the funds requisitioned by Congress from the states was never paid, so Congress had to borrow money from wealthy patriot investors to fight the war. Without the power to tax, however, Congress could not pay off these debts. Indeed, the value of U.S. governmental bonds fell to about 10 cents for every dollar's worth because few people believed the bonds would ever be paid off. Congress even stopped making interest payments on these bonds.

**Commercial Obstacles**    Under the Articles of Confederation, states were free to tax the goods of other states. Without the power to regulate interstate commerce, the national government was unable to protect merchants from heavy tariffs imposed on shipments from state to state. Southern planters could not ship their agricultural products to northern cities without paying state-imposed tariffs, and northern merchants could not ship manufactured products from state to state without interference. Merchants, manufacturers, shippers, and planters all wanted to develop national markets and prevent the states from imposing tariffs or restrictions on interstate trade.

**Currency Problems**    Under the Articles, the states themselves had the power to issue their own currency, regulate its value, and require that it be accepted in payment of debts. States had their own "legal tender" laws, which required creditors to accept state money if "tendered" in payment of debt. As a result, many forms of money were circulating: Virginia dollars, Rhode Island dollars, Pennsylvania dollars, and so on. Some states (Rhode Island, for example) printed a great deal of money, creating inflation in their currency and alienating banks and investors whose loans were being paid off in this cheap currency. If creditors refused payment in a particular state's currency, the debt could be abolished in that state. So finances throughout the states were very unstable, and banks and creditors were threatened by cheap paper money.

In an attempt to prevent the foreclosure of farms by creditors, Revolutionary War veteran Daniel Shays led an armed mass of citizens in a march on a western Massachusetts courthouse. This uprising, which came to be known as Shays's Rebellion, exposed the Confederation's military weakness and increased support for a strong central government.

**Civil Disorder**    In several states, debtors openly revolted against tax collectors and sheriffs attempting to repossess farms on behalf of creditors who held unpaid mortgages. The most serious rebellion broke out in the summer of 1786 in western Massachusetts, where a band of 2,000 insurgent farmers captured the courthouses in several counties and briefly held the city of Springfield. Led by Daniel Shays, a veteran of the Revolutionary War battle at Bunker Hill, the insurgent army posed a direct threat to investors, bankers, creditors, and tax collectors by burning deeds, mortgages, and tax records to wipe out proof of the farmers' debts. Shays's Rebellion, as it was called, was finally put down by a small mercenary army, paid for by well-to-do citizens of Boston.

Reports of Shays's Rebellion filled the newspapers of the large Eastern cities. George Washington, Alexander Hamilton, James Madison, and many other prominent Americans wrote their friends about it. The event galvanized property owners to support the creation of a strong central government capable of dealing with "radicalism." Only a strong central government, they wrote one another, could "insure domestic tranquility," guarantee "a republican form of government," and protect property "against domestic violence." It is no accident that all of these phrases appear in the Constitution of 1787.

**The Road to the Constitutional Convention**    In the spring of 1785, some wealthy merchants from Virginia and Maryland met at Alexandria, Virginia, to try to resolve a conflict between the two states over commerce and navigation on the Potomac River and Chesapeake Bay. George Washington, the new nation's most prominent citizen, took a personal interest in the meeting. As a wealthy plantation owner and a land speculator who owned more than 30,000 acres of land upstream on the Potomac, Washington was keenly interested in commercial problems under the Articles of Confederation. He lent his great prestige to the Alexandria meeting by inviting the participants to his house at Mount Vernon. Out of this conference came the idea for a general economic conference for all of the states, to be held in Annapolis, Maryland, in September 1786.

The Annapolis Convention turned out to be a key stepping-stone to the Constitutional Convention of 1787. Instead of concentrating on commerce and navigation between the states, the delegates at Annapolis, including Alexander Hamilton and James Madison, called for a general constitutional convention to suggest remedies to what they saw as defects in the Articles of Confederation.

On February 21, 1787, the Congress called for a convention to meet in Philadelphia for the "sole and express purpose" of *revising* the Articles of Confederation and reporting to the Congress and the state legislatures "such alterations and provisions therein as shall, when agreed to in Congress and confirmed by the states, render the federal Constitution adequate to the exigencies of government and the preservation of the union." Notice that Congress did not authorize the convention to write a new constitution or to call constitutional conventions in the states to ratify a new constitution. State legislatures sent delegates to Philadelphia expecting that their task would be limited to revising the Articles and that revisions would be sent back to Congress and state legislatures for their approval. But that is not what happened.

**George Washington Papers**
The life of George Washington with images, maps, documents, and papers.
*http://gwpapers.virginia.edu*

**The Nation's Founders**    The fifty-five delegates to the Constitutional Convention, which met in Philadelphia in the summer of 1787, quickly discarded the congressional mandate to merely "revise" the Articles of Confederation. The Virginia delegation, led by James Madison, arrived before a quorum of seven states had assembled and used the time to draw up an entirely new constitutional document. After the first formal session opened on May 25 and George Washington was elected president of the convention, the Virginia Plan became the basis of discussion. Thus, at the very beginning of the convention, the decision was made to scrap the Articles of Confederation altogether, write a new constitution, and form a new national government.[2]

The Founders were very confident of their powers and abilities. They had been selected by their state legislatures (only Rhode Island, dominated by small farmers, refused to send a delegation). When Thomas Jefferson, then serving in the critical post of ambassador to France (the nation's military ally in the Revolutionary War), first saw the list of delegates, he exclaimed, "It is really an assembly of demigods." Indeed, among the nation's notables, only Jefferson and John Adams (then serving as ambassador to England) were absent. The eventual success of the convention, and the ratification of the new Constitution, resulted in part from the enormous prestige, experience, and achievements of the delegates themselves.

Above all, the delegates at Philadelphia were cosmopolitan. They approached political, economic, and military issues from a "continental" point of view. Unlike most Americans in 1787, their loyalties extended beyond their states. They were truly nationalists.[3]

**Our Documents**
National Archives
Web site with access to 100 "milestone documents" in American history.
*www.ourdocuments.gov*

┤Think Again├

Was the original Constitution of 1787 a truly democratic document?

# Consensus in Philadelphia

The Founders shared many ideas about government. We often focus our attention on *conflict* in the Convention of 1787 and the compromises reached by the participants, but the really important story of the Constitution is the *consensus* that was shared by these men of influence.

**Liberty and Property**   The Founders had read John Locke and absorbed his idea that the purpose of government is to protect individual liberty and property. They believed in a natural law, superior to any human-made laws, that endowed each person with certain inalienable rights—the rights to life, liberty, and property. They believed that all people were equally entitled to these rights. Most of them, including slave owners George Washington and Thomas Jefferson, understood that the belief in personal liberty conflicted with the practice of slavery and found the inconsistency troubling.

**Social Contract**   The Founders believed that government originated in an implied contract among people. People agreed to establish government, obey laws, and pay taxes in exchange for protection of their natural rights. This social contract gave government its legitimacy—a legitimacy that rested on the consent of the governed, not with gods or kings or force. If a government violated individual liberty, it broke the social contract and thus lost its legitimacy.

**Representative Government**   Although most of the world's governments in 1787 were hereditary monarchies, the Founders believed the people should have a voice in choosing their own representatives in government. They opposed hereditary aristocracy and titled nobility. Instead, they sought to forge a republic. **Republicanism** meant government by representatives of the people. The Founders expected the masses to consent to be governed by their leaders—men of principle and property with ability, education, and a stake in the preservation of liberty. The Founders believed the people should have only a limited role in directly selecting their representatives: they should vote for members of the House of Representatives, but senators, the president, and members of the Supreme Court should be selected by others more qualified to judge their ability.

**Limited Government**   The Founders believed unlimited power was corrupting and a concentration of power was dangerous. They believed in a written constitution that limited the scope of governmental power. They also believed in dividing power within government by creating separate bodies able to check and balance one another's powers.

**Nationalism**   Most important, the Founders shared a belief in **nationalism**—a strong and independent national (federal) government with power to govern directly, rather than through state governments. They sought to establish a government that would be recognized around the world as representing "We the people of the United States." Not everyone in America shared this enthusiasm for a strong federal government; indeed, opposition forces, calling themselves Anti-Federalists, almost succeeded in defeating the new Constitution. But the leaders meeting in Philadelphia in the summer of 1787 were convinced of the need for a strong central government that would share power with the states.

**republicanism** Government by representatives of the people rather than directly by the people themselves.

**nationalism** Belief that shared cultural, historical, linguistic, and social characteristics of a people justify the creation of a government encompassing all of them and that the resulting nation-state should be independent and legally equal to all other nation-states.

# Conflict in Philadelphia

Consensus on basic principles of government was essential to the success of the Philadelphia convention. But conflict over the implementation of these principles not only tied up the convention for an entire summer but also later

## PEOPLE IN POLITICS

# George Washington, Founder of a Nation

From the time he took command of the American Revolutionary forces in 1775 until he gave his Farewell Address to the nation in 1796 and returned to his Mount Vernon plantation, George Washington (1732–99) was, indeed, "First in war, first in peace, first in the hearts of his countrymen." His military success, combined with his diplomacy and practical political acumen, gave him overwhelming moral authority, which he used to inspire the Constitutional Convention, to secure the ratification of the Constitution, and then to guide the new nation through its first years.

Washington was raised on a Virginia plantation and inherited substantial landholdings, including his Mount Vernon plantation on the Potomac River. He began his career as a surveyor. His work took him deep into the wilderness of America's frontier. This experience later served him well when, at age twenty-one, he was appointed an officer in the Virginia militia. In 1754 he led a small force toward the French Fort Duquesne, but after a brief battle at makeshift "Fort Necessity" he was obliged to retreat. In 1755 British Major General Edward Braddock asked the young militia officer to accompany his heavy regiments on a campaign to dislodge the French from Fort Duquesne. Braddock disregarded Washington's warnings about concealed ways of fighting in the New World; Braddock's parading redcoat forces were ambushed by the French and Indians near Pittsburgh, and the general was killed. Washington rallied what remained of the British forces and led them in a successful retreat back to Virginia.

Washington was viewed by Virginians as a hero, and at age twenty-two he was appointed by the Virginia Assembly "Colonel of the Virginia Regiment and Commander in Chief of all Virginia Forces." But regular British officers ridiculed the militia forces and asserted their authority over Washington. British General John Forbes occupied Fort Duquesne, renamed it Fort Pitt, and gave Washington's men the task of garrisoning it.

In 1759, having completed his service in the French and Indian Wars, Washington left his military post and returned to plantation life. He married a wealthy widow, Martha Custis, expanded his plantation holdings, and prospered in western land speculation.

The Virginia legislature elected Washington to attend the First Continental Congress in September 1774. Washington was the most celebrated veteran of the French and Indian Wars who was still young enough (forty-two) to lead military forces in a new struggle. John Adams of Massachusetts was anxious to unite the continent in the coming contest, and he persuaded the Second Continental Congress to give the Virginian command of the American revolutionary forces surrounding the British army in Boston in 1775.

Throughout the Revolutionary War Washington persevered by employing many of the tactics later defined as the principles of guerrilla warfare. By retreating deep into Pennsylvania's Valley Forge, Washington avoided defeat and saved his army. His bold Christmas night attack against Hessian troops at Trenton, New Jersey, encouraged French intervention on America's behalf. Slowly Washington was able to wear down the British resolve to fight. In the end, he succeeded in trapping a British army at Yorktown, Virginia. Assisted by a French naval blockade, he accepted the surrender of Lord Cornwallis and 8,000 of his men on October 19, 1781.

Perhaps Washington's greatest contribution to democratic government occurred in 1783 in Newburgh, New York, near West Point, where the veterans of his Continental Army were encamped. Despite their hardships and ultimate victory in the Revolutionary War, these soldiers remained unpaid by Congress. Indeed, Congress ignored a series of letters, known as the Newburgh Addresses, that threatened military force if Congress continued to deny benefits to the veterans. Washington was invited to Newburgh by officers who hoped he would agree to lead a military coup against the Congress. But when Washington mounted the platform he denounced the use of force and the "infamous propositions" contained in their earlier addresses to Congress. There is little doubt that he could have chosen to march on the Congress with his veteran army and install himself as military dictator. World history is filled with revolutionary army leaders who did so. But Washington chose to preserve representative government.

One of the few noncontroversial decisions of the Constitutional Convention in 1787 was the selection of George Washington to preside over the meetings. He took little part in the debates; however, his enormous prestige helped to hold the convention together and later to win support for the new Constitution.

threatened to prevent the states from ratifying, or voting to approve, the document the convention produced.

**Representation** Representation was the most controversial issue in Philadelphia. Following the election of George Washington as president of the convention, Governor Edmund Randolph of Virginia rose to present a draft of a new constitution. This Virginia Plan called for a legislature with two houses: a lower house chosen by the people of the states, with representation according to population, and an upper house to be chosen by the lower house (see Table 3.1). Congress was to have the broad power to "legislate in all cases to which the separate States are incompetent, or in which the harmony of the United States may be interrupted." Congress was to have the power to nullify state laws that it believed violated the Constitution, thus ensuring the national government's supremacy over the states. The Virginia Plan also proposed a *parliamentary* form of government, in which the legislature (Congress) chose the principal executive officers of the government as well as federal judges. Finally, the Virginia Plan included a curious "council of revision," with the power to veto acts of Congress.

Delegates from New Jersey and Delaware objected strongly to the great power given to the national government in the Virginia Plan, the larger representation it proposed for the more populous states, and the plan's failure to recognize the role of the states in the composition of the new government. After several weeks of debate, William Paterson of New Jersey submitted a counterproposal.[4] The New Jersey Plan called for a single-chamber Congress in which each state, regardless of its population, had one vote, just as under the Articles of Confederation. But unlike the Articles, the New Jersey Plan proposed separate executive and judicial branches of government and the expansion of the powers of Congress to include levying taxes and regulating commerce. Moreover, the New Jersey Plan included a National Supremacy Clause, declaring that the Constitution and federal laws would supersede state constitutions and laws.

## Table 3.1 Constitutional Compromise

| The Virginia Plan | The New Jersey Plan | The Connecticut Compromise The Constitution of 1787 |
|---|---|---|
| Two-house legislature, with the lower house directly elected based on state population and the upper house elected by the lower. | One-house legislature, with equal state representation, regardless of population. | Two-house legislature, with the House directly elected based on state population and the Senate selected by the state legislatures; two senators per state, regardless of population. |
| Legislature with broad power, including veto power over laws passed by the state legislatures. | Legislature with the same power as under the Articles of Confederation, plus the power to levy some taxes and to regulate commerce. | Legislature with broad power, including the power to tax and to regulate commerce. |
| President and cabinet elected by the legislature. | Separate multiperson executive, elected by the legislature, removable by petition from a majority of the state governors. | President chosen by an Electoral College. |
| National judiciary elected by the legislature. | National judiciary appointed by the executive. | National judiciary appointed by the president and confirmed by the Senate. |
| "Council of Revision" with the power to veto laws of the legislature. | National Supremacy Clause similar to that found in Article VI of the 1787 Constitution. | National Supremacy Clause: the Constitution is "the supreme Law of the Land." |

Debate over representation in Congress raged into July 1787. At one point, the convention actually voted for the Virginia Plan, 7 votes to 3, but without New York, New Jersey, and Delaware, the new nation would not have been viable. Eventually, Roger Sherman of Connecticut came forward with a compromise. This Connecticut Compromise—sometimes called the Great Compromise— established two houses of Congress: in the upper house, the Senate, each state would have two members regardless of its size; in the lower body, the House of Representatives, each state would be represented according to population. Members of the House would be directly elected by the people; members of the Senate would be selected by their state legislatures. Legislation would have to pass both houses to be enacted. This compromise was approved by the convention on July 16.

**The Great Compromise**
James Madison University Web site on Madison with information on constitutional compromises, including the slavery compromise.
*www.jmu.edu/madison*

**Slavery**   Another conflict absorbing the attention of the delegates was slavery. In 1787 slavery was legal everywhere except in Massachusetts. Nevertheless, the delegates were too embarrassed to use the word *slave* or *slavery* in their debates or in the Constitution itself. Instead, they referred to "other persons" and "persons held to service or labour."

Delegates from the Southern states, where slaves were a large proportion of the population, believed slaves should be counted in representation afforded the states, but not counted if taxes were to be levied on a population basis. Delegates from the Northern states, with small slave populations, believed that "the people" counted for representation purposes should include only free persons. The Connecticut Plan included the now-infamous Three-Fifths Compromise: Three-fifths of the slaves of each state would be counted for purposes both of representation in the House of Representatives and for apportionment for direct taxes.

Slave owners also sought protection for their human "property" in the Constitution itself. They were particularly concerned about slaves running away to other states and claiming their freedom. So they succeeded in writing into the Constitution (Article IV, Section 2) a specific guarantee: "No person held to Service or Labour in one State . . . escaping into another, shall . . . be discharged from such Service or Labour, but shall be delivered up on Claim of the Party to whom such Service or Labour may be due."

Yet another compromise dealt with the slave trade. The capture, transportation, and "breaking in" of African slaves was considered a nasty business, even by Southern planters. Many wealthy Maryland and Virginia plantations were already well supplied with slaves and thus could afford the luxury of conscience to call for an end to slave importation. But other planters from the less-developed Southern states, particularly South Carolina and Georgia, wanted additional slave labor. The final compromise prohibited the slave trade—but not before the year 1808, thereby giving the planters twenty years to import all the slaves they needed before the slave trade ended.

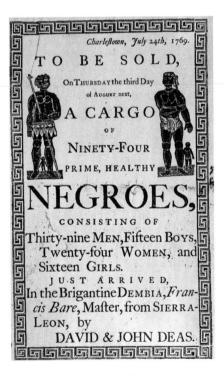

Slavery was protected in the Constitution as written in 1787. The buying and selling of slaves was common at the time in the Southern states. The slave trade from Africa to America was given protection for twenty years, until 1808.

**Voter Qualifications**   Another important conflict centered on qualifications for voting and holding office in the new government. Most of the delegates believed that voters as well as officeholders should be men of property. (Only Benjamin Franklin went so far as to propose universal *male* suffrage.) But delegates argued over the specific wording of property qualifications, their views on the subject reflecting the source of their own wealth. Merchants, bankers, and manufacturers objected to making the ownership of a certain amount of land a qualification for officeholding. James Madison, a plantation owner himself, was forced to admit that "landed possessions were no certain evidence of real wealth. Many enjoyed them who were more in debt than they were worth."

After much debate, the convention approved a constitution without any expressed property qualifications for voting or holding office, except those that the states might impose themselves: "The Electors in each State shall have the Qualifications requisite for Electors of the most numerous Branch of the State Legislature." At the time, every state had property qualifications for voting, and women were not permitted to vote or hold office. (The New Jersey Constitution of 1776 enfranchised women as well as men who owned property, but in 1787 a new state law limited the vote to "free white male citizens.")

## Resolving the Economic Issues

The Founders were just as concerned with "who gets what, when, and how" as today's politicians are. Important economic interests were at stake in the Constitution. Historian Charles A. Beard pointed out that the delegates to the Constitutional Convention were men of wealth: planters, slaveholders, merchants, manufacturers, shippers, bankers and investors, and land speculators. Moreover, most of the delegates owned Revolutionary War bonds that were now worthless and would remain so unless the national government could obtain the tax revenues to pay them off[5] (see *A Conflicting View:* "An Economic Interpretation of the Constitution"). But it is certainly not true that the Founders acted only out of personal interest. Wealthy delegates were found on both sides of constitutional debates, arguing principles as well as economic interests.[6]

**Levying Taxes**   A central purpose of the Constitution was to enable the national government to levy its own **taxes**, so that it could end its dependence on state contributions and achieve financial credibility. The very first power given to Congress in Article 1, Section 8, is the power to tax: "The Congress shall have Power to lay and collect Taxes, Duties, Imposts and Excises, to pay the Debts and provide for the common Defence and general Welfare."

The financial credit of the United States and the interests of Revolutionary War bondholders were guaranteed by Article VI in the Constitution, which specifically declared that the new government would be obligated to pay the debts of the old government. Indeed, the nation's first secretary of the treasury, Alexander Hamilton, made repayment of the national debt the first priority of the Washington Administration.

The original Constitution placed most of the tax burden on consumers in the form of **tariffs** on goods imported into the United States. For more than a century, these tariffs provided the national government with its principal source of revenue. Tariffs were generally favored by American manufacturers, who wished to raise the price paid for foreign goods to make their home-produced goods

**taxes**  Compulsory payments to the government.

**Constitutional Law**
Cornell University Law School overview of the Constitution.
*www.law.cornell.edu/topics/constitutional*

**tariff**  Tax imposed on imported products (also called a customs duty).

Under the Articles of Confederation, each state issued its own currency. Differences in currency regulation from state to state led to financial uncertainty and inflation. By creating a national currency and putting the national government in charge of the money supply, the Founders hoped to restore stability and control inflation.

# A CONFLICTING VIEW

## An Economic Interpretation of the Constitution

Charles Beard, historian and political scientist, provided the most controversial historical interpretation of the origin of American national government in his landmark book, *An Economic Interpretation of the Constitution of the United States* (1913). Not all historians agree with Beard's economic interpretation, but all concede that it is a milestone in understanding the U.S. Constitution. Beard closely studied unpublished financial records of the U.S. Treasury Department and the personal letters and financial accounts of the fifty-five delegates to the Philadelphia convention. He concluded that they represented the following five economic interest groups, each of which benefited from specific provisions of the Constitution:

- *Public security interests* (persons holding U.S. bonds from the Revolutionary War; thirty-seven of the fifty-five delegates). The taxing power was of great benefit to the holders of public securities, particularly when it was combined with the provision in Article VI that "all Debts contracted and Engagements entered into, before the Adoption of this Constitution, shall be as valid against the United States under this Constitution, as under the Confederation." That is, the national government would be obliged to pay off all those investors who held U.S. bonds, and the taxing power would give the national government the ability to do so on its own.
- *Merchants and manufacturers* (persons engaged in shipping and trade; eleven of the fifty-five delegates). The Interstate Commerce Clause, which eliminated state control over commerce, and the provision in Article I, Section 9, which prohibited the states from taxing exports, created a free-trade area, or "common market," among the thirteen states.
- *Bankers and investors* (twenty-four of fifty-five delegates). Congress was given the power to make bankruptcy laws, to coin money and regulate its value, to fix standards of weights and measures, to punish counterfeiting, to establish post offices and post roads, to pass copyright and patent laws to protect authors and inventors, and

to punish piracies and felonies committed on the high seas. Each of these powers is a specific asset to bankers and investors as well as merchants, authors, inventors, and shippers.

- *Western land speculators* (persons who purchased large tracts of land west of the Appalachian Mountains: fourteen of the fifty-five delegates). If western settlers were to be protected from the Indians, and if the British were to be persuaded to give up their forts in Ohio and open the way to American westward expansion, the national government could not rely on state militias but must have an army of its own. Western land speculators welcomed the creation of a national army that would be employed primarily as an Indian-fighting force over the next century.
- *Slave owners* (fifteen of the fifty-five delegates). Protection against domestic insurrection also appealed to the southern slaveholders' deep-seated fear of a slave revolt. The Constitution permitted Congress to outlaw the *import of slaves* after the year 1808. But most Southern planters were more interested in protecting their existing property and slaves than they were in extending the slave trade, and the Constitution provided an explicit advantage to slaveholders in Article IV, Section 2 (later revoked by the Thirteenth Amendment, which abolished slavery), by specifically requiring the forced return of slaves who might escape to free states.

Beard argued that the members of the Philadelphia convention who drafted the Constitution were, with a few exceptions, immediately, directly, and personally interested in, and derived economic advantages from, the establishment of the new system. But many historians disagree with Beard's emphasis on the economic motives of the Founders. The Constitution, they point out, was adopted in a society that was fundamentally democratic, and it was adopted by people who were primarily middle-class property owners, especially farmers, rather than owners of businesses. The Constitution was not just an economic document, although economic factors were certainly important. Since most of the people were middle class and owned private property, practically all Americans were interested in the protection of property.

more competitive. No taxes were permitted on *exports,* a protection for southern planters, who exported most of their tobacco and, later, cotton. Direct taxes on individuals were prohibited (Article 1, Section 2) except in proportion to *population.* This provision prevented the national government from levying direct taxes in proportion to income until the Sixteenth Amendment (income tax) was ratified in 1913.

The power to tax and spend was given to Congress, not to the president or executive agencies. Instead, the Constitution was very specific: "No Money shall be drawn from the Treasury, but in Consequence of Appropriations made by Law." This is the constitutional basis of Congress's "power of the purse."

**Regulating Commerce**    The new Constitution gave Congress the power to "regulate Commerce with foreign Nations, and among the several States" (Article 1, Section 8), and it prohibited the states from imposing tariffs on goods shipped across state lines (Article 1, Section 10). This power created what we call today a **common market**; it protected merchants against state-imposed tariffs and stimulated trade among the states. States were also prohibited from "impairing the Obligation of Contracts"—that is, passing any laws that would allow debtors to avoid their obligations to banks and other lenders.

**common market** Unified trade area in which all goods and services can be sold or exchanged free from customs or tariffs.

**Protecting Money**    The Constitution also ensured that the new national government would control the money supply. Congress was given the power to coin money and regulate its value. More important, the states were prohibited from issuing their own paper money, thus protecting bankers and creditors from the repayment of debts in cheap state currencies. (No one wanted to be paid for goods or labor in Rhode Island's inflated dollars.) If only the national government could issue money, the Founders hoped, inflation could be minimized.

# Protecting National Security

At the start of the Revolutionary War, the Continental Congress had given George Washington command of a small regular army—"Continentals"—paid for by Congress and also had authorized him to take command of state militia units. During the entire war, most of Washington's troops had been state militia. (The "militia" in those days was composed of every free adult male; each was expected to bring his own gun.) Washington himself had frequently decried the militia units as undisciplined, untrained, and unwilling to follow his orders. He wanted the new United States to have a *regular* army and navy, paid for by the Congress with its new taxing power, to back up the state militia units.

**War and the Military Forces**    Congress was authorized to "declare War," to raise and support a regular army and navy, and to make rules regulating these forces. It was also authorized to call up the militia, as it had done in the Revolution, in order to "execute the Laws of the Union, suppress Insurrections and repel Invasions." When the militia are called into national service, they come under the rule of Congress and the command of the president.

The United States relied primarily on militia—citizen-soldiers organized in state units—until World War I. The regular U.S. Army, stationed in coastal and frontier forts, directed most of its actions against Native Americans. The major actions in America's nineteenth-century wars—the War of 1812 against the British, the Mexican War of 1846–48, the Civil War in 1861–65, and the Spanish-American War in 1898—were fought largely by citizen-soldiers from these state units.

**Commander-in-Chief**    Following the precedent set in the Revolutionary War, the new president, whom everyone expected to be George Washington, was made "Commander-in-Chief of the Army and Navy of the United States, and

The president's role as Commander-in-Chief was designed at the Constitutional Convention with George Washington in mind, as a reflection of his exploits in the Revolutionary War. Here three wartime presidents—Franklin Delano Roosevelt, Lyndon Baines Johnson, and George W. Bush—are shown reviewing troops.

of the Militia of the several States, when called into the actual Service of the United States." Clearly, there is some overlap in responsibility for national defense: Congress has the power to declare war, but the president is Commander-in-Chief. During the next two centuries, the president would order U.S. forces into 200 or more military actions, but Congress would pass an official Declaration of War only five times. Conflict between the president and Congress over war-making powers continues to this day.

**Foreign Affairs**   The national government also assumed full power over foreign affairs and prohibited the states from entering into any "Treaty, Alliance, or Confederation." The Constitution gave the president, not Congress, the power to "make Treaties" and "appoint Ambassadors." However, the Constitution stipulated that the president could do these things only "by and with the Advice and Consent of the Senate," indicating an unwillingness to allow the president to act autonomously in these matters. The Senate's power to "advise and consent" to treaties and appointments, together with the congressional power over appropriations, gives the Congress important influence in foreign affairs. Nevertheless, the president remains the dominant figure in this arena.

# The Structure of the Government

The Constitution that emerged from the Philadelphia convention on September 17, 1787, founded a new government with a unique structure. That structure was designed to implement the Founders' beliefs in nationalism, limited government, republicanism, the social contract, and the protection of liberty and property. The Founders were realists; they did not have any romantic notions about the wisdom and virtue of "the people." James Madison wrote, "A dependence on the people is, no doubt, the primary control on the government, but experience has taught mankind the necessity of auxiliary precautions." The key structural arrangements in the Constitution—national supremacy, federalism, republicanism, separation of powers, checks and balances, and judicial review—all reflect the Founders' desire to create a strong national government while at the same time ensuring that it would not become a threat to liberty or property.

**National Supremacy**   The heart of the Constitution is the National Supremacy Clause of Article VI:

> This Constitution, and the Laws of the United States which shall be made in Pursuance thereof, and all Treaties made, or which shall be made, under the Authority of the United States, shall be the supreme Law of the Land, and the Judges in every State shall be bound thereby, any Thing in the Constitution or Laws of any State to the Contrary notwithstanding.

This sentence ensures that the Constitution itself is the supreme law of the land and that laws passed by Congress supersede state laws. This National Supremacy Clause establishes the authority of the Constitution and the U.S. government. (See *Up Close*: "The Supremacy Clause at Work: Marijuana for Medical Use?").

**Federalism**   The Constitution *divides power* between the nation and the states (see Chapter 4). It recognizes that both the national government and the state governments have independent legal authority over their own citizens: both can pass their own laws, levy their own taxes, and maintain their own courts. The states have an important role in the selection of national officeholders—in the apportionment of congressional seats and in the allocation of electoral votes for president. Most important, perhaps, both the Congress and three-quarters of the states must consent to changes in the Constitution itself.

**Republicanism**   To the Founders, a *republican* government meant the delegation of powers by the people to a small number of gifted individuals "whose wisdom may best discern the true interest of their country, and whose patriotism and love of justice, will be least likely to sacrifice it to temporary or partial considerations."[7] The Founders believed that enlightened leaders of principle and property with ability, education, and a stake in the preservation of liberty could govern the people better than the people could govern themselves. So they gave the voters only a limited voice in the selection of government leaders.

The Constitution of 1787 created *four* decision-making bodies, each with separate numbers of members, terms of office, and selection processes (see

---Think Again---

Should a large state like California, with 32 million people, elect more U.S. senators than a small state like Wyoming, with only half a million people?

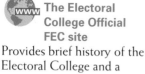

**The Electoral College Official FEC site**

Provides brief history of the Electoral College and a description of how it works. *www.fec.gov/pages/ecmenu*

## UP CLOSE

# The Supremacy Clause at Work: Marijuana for Medical Use?

Currently, marijuana prohibition applies to everyone across the nation, including the sick and dying. But many doctors, patients, and organizations contend that marijuana, medically known as cannabis, is valuable in the treatment of glaucoma, HIV-AIDS, nausea, and pain relief, especially in cancer patients. Since 1996 voters in nine states—Alaska, Arizona, California, Colorado, Maine, Maryland, Nevada, Oregon, and Washington—have adopted initiatives exempting patitents who use marijuana under a physician's supervision from state marijuana prohibitions. Wherever the issue has appeared on state referenda, it has passed by large margins. National polls regularly report that 75 percent of the American public support making marijuana legally available to seriously ill patients.

Congress, however, has never exempted the medical use of marijuana from its Controlled Substance Act, which makes it a federal crime "to manufacture, distribute, or dispense, or possess . . . a controlled substance." Various petitions to the federal Drug Enforcement Agency to declassify marijuana as a controlled substance and allow physicians to legally prescribe its use have been rejected.

Clearly, federal law is in direct conflict with the laws of many states in this issue. But the Supremacy Clause of the Constitution clearly requires that federal law prevail over state law in cases of conflict.

The issue reached the U.S. Supreme Court in 2001. The Court recognized that whether or not the activities of individuals or organizations regarding marijuana were legal under California law, they nonetheless violated federal law, notably the Controlled Substance Act. The Court further held that "medical necessity" does not allow anyone to violate the Controlled Substance Act; Congress made no exemption in this act for medical necessity. The Supreme Court recognized that the states have concurrent powers with the federal government in regulating drugs and medications. However, "Under the Supremacy Clause, any state law, however clearly within a state's acknowledged power, which interferes with or is contrary to federal laws must yield."[a]

Politically, the federal Drug Enforcement Agency realizes that prosecuting seriously ill patients or their doctors for using marijuana medically is very unpopular. Many individuals, especially in those states that have tried to legalize the medical use of marijuana, have continued to use the drug, knowing that they are violating federal law.

---

[a] *United States v. Oakland Cannabis Buyers Cooperatives* 523 U.S. 483 (2001).

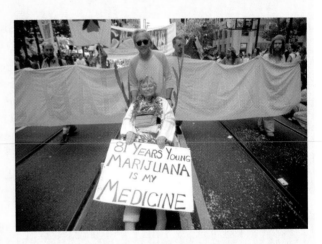

*The Supremacy Clause of the Constitution dictates that the laws of Congress prevail over those of the states. Some states have attempted to legalize the use of marijuana for medical purposes. But the laws of Congress have not (yet?) made an exception for such use.*

Table 1.2). Note that in the *original* Constitution only one of these four bodies— the House of Representatives—was to be directly elected by the people. The other three were removed from direct popular control: state legislatures selected U.S. senators; "electors" (chosen at the discretion of the state legislatures) selected the president; the president appointed Supreme Court and other federal judges.

**Democracy?**    The Founders believed that government rests ultimately on "the consent of the governed." But their notion of republicanism envisioned decision

**Table 3.2    Decision-Making Bodies in the Constitution of 1787**

| House of Representatives | Senate | President | Supreme Court |
|---|---|---|---|
| Members alloted to each state "according to their respective numbers," but each state guaranteed at least one member. | "Two senators from each state" (regardless of the size of the state). | Single executive. | No size specified in the Constitution, but by tradition nine. |
| Two-year term. No limits on number of terms that can be served. | Six-year term. No limits on number of terms that can be served. | Four-year term (later limited to two terms by the Twenty-second Amendment in 1951). | Life term. |
| Directly elected by "the People of the several States." | Selected by the state legislatures (later changed to direct election by the Seventeenth Amendment in 1913). | Selected by "Electors," appointed in each state "In such Manner as the Legislature thereof may direct" and equal to the total number of U.S. senators and House members to which the state is entitled in Congress. | Appointed by the president, "by and with the Advice and Consent of the Senate." |

making by *representatives* of the people, not the people themselves (see *A Conflicting View*: "Let the People Vote on National Issues"). The U.S. Constitution does not provide for *direct* voting by the people on national questions; that is, unlike many state constitutions today, it does *not* provide for national **referenda**. Moreover, as noted earlier, only the House of Representatives (sometimes referred to even today as "the people's house") was to be elected directly by voters in the states.

These republican arrangements may appear "undemocratic" from our perspective today, but in 1787 the U.S. Constitution was more democratic than any other governing system in the world. Although other nations were governed by monarchs, emperors, chieftains, and hereditary aristocracies, the Founders recognized that government depended on the *consent of the governed.* Later democratic impulses in America greatly altered the original Constitution (see "Constitutional Change" later in this chapter) and reshaped it into a much more democratic document.

**referenda** Proposed laws or constitutional amendments submitted to the voters for their direct approval or rejection, found in state constitutions, but not in the U.S. Constitution.

# Separation of Powers and Checks and Balances

The Founders believed that unlimited power was corrupting and that the concentration of power was dangerous. James Madison wrote, "Ambition must be made to counteract ambition." The **separation of powers** within the national government—the creation of separate legislative, executive, and judicial branches in Articles I, II, and III of the Constitution—was designed to place internal controls on governmental power. Power is not only apportioned among three branches of government, but, perhaps more important, each branch is given important **checks and balances** over the actions of the others (see Figure 3.1 on page 73). According to Madison, "The constant aim is to divide and arrange the several offices in such a manner as that each may be a check on the other." No bill can become a law without the approval of both the House and the Senate. The president shares legislative power through the power to sign or to veto laws of Congress, although

**separation of powers** Constitutional division of powers among the three branches of the national government—legislative, executive, and judicial.

**checks and balances** Constitutional provisions giving each branch of the national government certain checks over the actions of other branches.

## A CONFLICTING VIEW

# Let the People Vote on National Issues

"Direct democracy" means that the people themselves can initiate and decide policy questions by popular vote. The Founders were profoundly skeptical of this form of democracy. They had read about direct democracy in the ancient Greek city-state of Athens, and they believed the "follies" of direct democracy far outweighed any virtues it might possess. It was not until more than 100 years after the U.S. Constitution was written that widespread support developed in the American states for direct voter participation in policy making. Direct democracy developed in states and communities, and it is to be found today *only* in state and local government.

Why not extend our notion of democracy to include nationwide referenda voting on key public issues? Perhaps Congress should be authorized to place particularly controversial issues on a national ballot. Perhaps a petition signed by at least 1 million voters should also result in a question being placed on a national ballot.

*Proponents* of direct voting on national issues argue that national referenda would

- Enhance government responsiveness and accountability to the people.
- Stimulate national debate over policy questions.
- Increase voter interest and turnout on election day.
- Increase trust in government and diminish feelings of alienation from Washington.
- Give voters a direct role in policy making.

*Opponents* of direct democracy, from our nation's Founders to the present, argue that national referenda voting would

- Encourage majorities to sacrifice the rights of individuals and minorities.
- Lead to the adoption of unwise and unsound policies because voters are not sufficiently informed to cast intelligent ballots on many complex issues.
- Prevent consideration of alternative policies or modifications or amendments to the proposition set forth on the ballot. (In contrast, legislators devote a great deal of attention to writing, rewriting, and amending bills, as well as seeking out compromises among interests.)
- Enable special interests to mount expensive referendum campaigns; the outcomes of referenda would be heavily influenced by paid television advertising.

How would voters' decisions in national referenda differ from current government policies? National polls suggest that voters would approve of many policy initiatives that Congress has rejected, including a constitutional requirement to balance the budget (83% favor); making English the official language (82% favor); a constitutional amendment to limit the terms of Congress members (74% favor); and a constitutional amendment to allow prayer in public schools (73% favor).[a]

[a]*Gallup Poll Monthly*, May 1996.

Congress may override a presidential veto with a two-thirds vote in each house. The president may also suggest legislation, "give to the Congress Information of the State of the Union, and recommend to their Consideration such Measures as he shall judge necessary and expedient." The president may also convene special sessions of Congress.

However, the president's power of appointment is shared by the Senate, which confirms cabinet and ambassadorial appointments. The president must also secure the advice and consent of the Senate for any treaty. The president must execute the laws, but it is Congress that provides the money to do so. The president and the rest of the executive branch may not spend money that has not been appropriated by Congress. Congress must also authorize the creation of executive departments and agencies. Finally, Congress may impeach and remove the president from office for "Treason, Bribery, or other High Crimes and Misdemeanors."

| Think Again |
In which do you have the most trust and confidence? President, Congress, Supreme Court

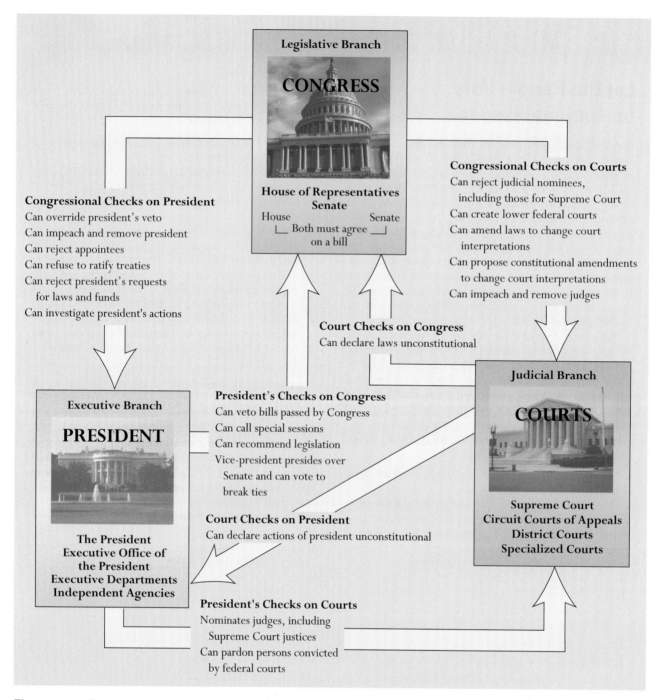

**Figure 3.1**   Checks and Balances

**judicial review** Power of the U.S. Supreme Court and federal judiciary to declare laws of Congress and the states and actions of the president unconstitutional and therefore legally invalid.

Members of the Supreme Court are appointed by the president and confirmed by the Senate. Traditionally, this court has nine members, but Congress may determine the number of justices. More important, Congress must create lower federal district courts as well as courts of appeal. Congress must also determine the number of these judgeships and determine the jurisdiction of federal courts. But the most important check of all is the Supreme Court's power of judicial review.

**Judicial review**, which is not specifically mentioned in the Constitution itself, is the power of the judiciary to overturn laws of Congress and the states and

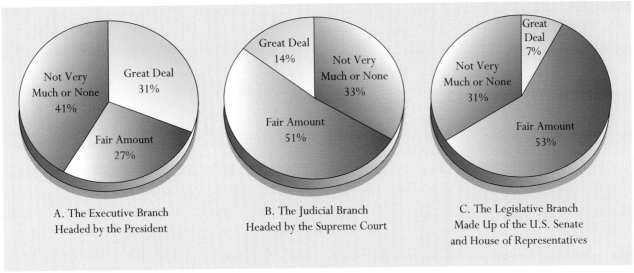

A. The Executive Branch
Headed by the President

B. The Judicial Branch
Headed by the Supreme Court

C. The Legislative Branch
Made Up of the U.S. Senate
and House of Representatives

**Figure 3.2** Trust and Confidence in the Three Branches of Government

As you know, the federal government is made up of three branches: an Executive branch, headed by the president, a Judicial branch, headed by the U.S. Supreme Court, and a Legislative branch, made up of the U.S. Senate and House of Representatives. How much trust and confidence do you have at this time: a great deal, a fair amount, not very much, or none at all?

*Source:* Gallup Poll, July, 2004. Copyright © 2004 by The Gallup Organization.

actions of the president that the courts believe violate the Constitution (see "Judicial Power" in Chapter 11). Judicial review, in short, ensures compliance with the Constitution.

Many Federalists, including Alexander Hamilton, believed the Constitution of 1787 clearly implied that the Supreme Court could invalidate any laws of Congress or presidential actions it believed to be unconstitutional. Hamilton wrote in 1787, "[Limited government] . . . can be preserved in no other way than through the medium of courts of justice, whose duty it is to declare all acts contrary to the manifest tenor of the Constitution void."[8] But it was not until *Marbury v. Madison* in 1803 that Chief Justice John Marshall asserted in a Supreme Court ruling that the Supreme Court possessed the power of judicial review over laws of Congress. (See *People in Politics:* "John Marshall and Early Supreme Court Politics" in Chapter 11.) Today the American people express more trust and confidence in the Supreme Court than in either the president or the Congress (see Figure 3.2).

# Conflict over Ratification

Today the U.S. Constitution is a revered document, but in the winter of 1787–88, the Founders had real doubts about whether they could get it accepted as "the supreme Law of the Land." Indeed, the Constitution was ratified by only the narrowest of margins in the key states of Massachusetts, Virginia, and New York.

The Founders adopted a **ratification** procedure that was designed to enhance chances for acceptance of the Constitution. The ratification procedure written into the new Constitution was a complete departure from what was then supposed to be the law of the land, the Articles of Confederation, in two major ways. First, the Articles of Confederation required that amendments be approved

**ratification** Power of a legislature to approve or reject decisions made by other bodies. State legislators or state conventions must have the power to ratify constitutional amendments submitted by Congress. The U.S. Senate has the power to ratify treaties made by the president.

**Figure 3.3** The Fight over Ratification.

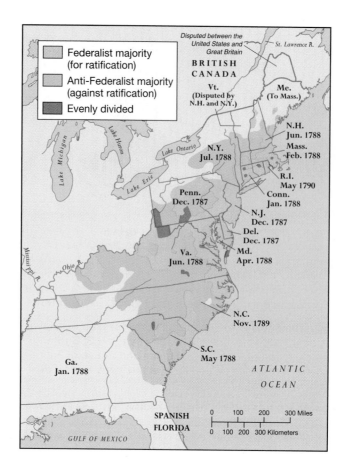

by *all* of the states. But since Rhode Island was firmly in the hands of small farmers, the Founders knew that unanimous approval was unlikely. So they simply wrote into their new Constitution that approval required only nine of the states. Second, the Founders called for special ratifying conventions in the states rather than risk submitting the Constitution to the state legislatures. Because the Constitution placed many prohibitions on the powers of states, the Founders believed that special constitutional ratifying conventions would be more likely to approve the document than would state legislatures.

The Founders enjoyed some important tactical advantages over the opposition. First, the Constitutional Convention was held in secret; potential opponents did not know what was coming out of it. Second, the Founders called for ratifying conventions to be held as quickly as possible so that the opposition could not get itself organized. Many state conventions met during the winter months, so it was difficult for some rural opponents of the Constitution to get to their county seats in order to vote (see Figure 3.3 above).

The Founders also waged a very professional (for 1787–88) media campaign in support of the Constitution. James Madison, Alexander Hamilton, and John Jay issued a series of eighty-five press releases, signed simply "Publius," on behalf of the Constitution. Major newspapers ran these essays, which were later collected and published as *The Federalist Papers*. The essays provide an excellent description and explanation of the Constitution by three of its writers and even today serve as a principal reference for political scientists and judges faced with constitutional ambiguities (see *People in Politics:* "James Madison and the Control

## PEOPLE IN POLITICS

# James Madison and the Control of "Faction"

The most important contributions to American democracy by James Madison (1751–1836) were his work in helping to write the Constitution and his insightful and scholarly defense of it during the ratification struggle. Indeed, Madison is more highly regarded by political scientists and historians as a *political theorist* than as the fourth president of the United States.

Madison's family owned a large plantation in Virginia. He graduated from the College of New Jersey (now Princeton University) at eighteen and assumed a number of elected and appointed positions in Virginia's colonial government. In 1776 Madison drafted a new Virginia Constitution. While serving in Virginia's Revolutionary assembly, he met Thomas Jefferson; the two became lifetime political allies and friends. In 1787 Madison represented Virginia at the Constitutional Convention and took a leading role in its debates over the form of a new federal government.

Madison's political insights are revealed in *The Federalist Papers*, a series of eighty-five essays published in major newspapers in 1787–88, all signed simply "Publius." Alexander Hamilton and John Jay contributed some of them, but Madison wrote the two most important essays: Number 10, which explains the nature of political conflict (faction) and how it can be "controlled", and Number 51, which explains the system of separation of powers and checks and balances (both reprinted in the Appendix of this textbook). According to Madison, "controlling faction" was the principal task of government.

What creates faction? Madison believed that conflict is part of human nature. In all societies, we find "a zeal for different opinions concerning religion, concerning government, and many other points," as well as "an attachment to different leaders ambitiously contending for preeminence and power." Even when there are no serious differences among people, these "frivolous and fanciful distinctions" will inspire "unfriendly passions" and "violent conflicts."

Clearly, Madison believed conflict could arise over just about any matter. Yet "the most common and durable source of factions, has been the various and unequal distribution of property." That is, economic conflicts between rich and poor and between people with different kinds of wealth and sources of income are the most serious conflicts confronting society.

Madison argued that factions could best be controlled in a republican government extending over a large society with a "variety of parties and interests." He. defended republicanism (representative democracy) over "pure democracy," which he believed "incompatible with personal security, or the rights of property." And he argued that protection against "factious combinations" can be achieved by including a great variety of competing interests in the political system so that no one interest will be able to "outnumber and oppress the rest." Modern pluralist political theory (see Chapter 1) claims Madison as a forerunner.

of 'Faction'"). Two of the most important *Federalist Papers* are reprinted in the Appendix to this textbook.

Nevertheless, opponents of the Constitution—the Anti-Federalists—almost succeeded in defeating the document in New York and Virginia. They charged that the new Constitution would create an "aristocratic tyranny" and pose a threat to the "spirit of republicanism." They argued that the new Senate would be an aristocratic upper house and the new president a ruling monarch. They complained that neither the Senate nor the president was directly elected by the people. They also argued that the new national government would trample state governments and deny the people of the states the opportunity to handle their own political and economic affairs. Virginia patriot Patrick Henry urged the defeat of the Constitution "to preserve the poor Commonwealth of Virginia." Finally, their most effective argument was that the new Constitution lacked a bill of rights to protect individual liberty from government abuse (see A *Conflicting View*: "Objections to the Constitution by an Anti-Federalist" on page 82).

# A Bill of Rights

It may be hard to imagine today, but the original Constitution had no **Bill of Rights**. This was a particularly glaring deficiency because many of the new state constitutions proudly displayed these written guarantees of individual liberty.

**Bill of Rights** Written guarantees of basic individual liberties; the first ten amendments to the U.S. Constitution.

The Founders certainly believed in limited government and individual liberty, and they did write a few liberties into the body of the Constitution, including protection against ex post facto laws, a limited definition of treason, a guarantee of the writ of habeas corpus, and a guarantee of trial by jury (see Chapter 14).

The Federalists argued that there was really no need for a bill of rights because (1) the national government was one of **enumerated powers** only, meaning it could not exercise any power not expressly enumerated, or granted, in the Constitution; (2) the power to limit free speech or press, establish a religion, or otherwise restrain individual liberty was not among the enumerated powers; (3) therefore it was not necessary to specifically deny these powers to the new government. But the Anti-Federalists were unwilling to rest fundamental freedoms on a thin thread of logical inference from the notion of enumerated powers. They wanted specific written guarantees that the new national government would not interfere with the rights of individuals or the powers of the states. So Federalists at the New York, Massachusetts, and Virginia ratifying conventions promised to support the addition of a bill of rights to the Constitution in the very first Congress.

**enumerated powers** Powers specifically mentioned in the Constitution as belonging to the national government.

A young member of the new House of Representatives, James Madison, rose in 1789 and presented a bill of rights that he had drawn up after reviewing more than 200 recommendations sent from the states. Interestingly, the new Congress was so busy debating new tax laws that Madison had a difficult time attracting attention to his bill. Eventually, in September 1789, Congress approved a Bill of Rights as ten **amendments**, or formal changes, to the Constitution and sent them to the states. (Congress actually passed twelve amendments. One was never ratified; another, dealing with pay raises for Congress, was not ratified by the necessary three-quarters of the states until 1992.) The states promptly ratified the first ten amendments to the Constitution (see Table 3.3), and these changes took effect in 1791.

**amendment** Formal change in a bill, law, or constitution.

The Bill of Rights was originally designed to limit the powers of the new *national* government. The Bill of Rights begins with the command "Congress shall make no law. . . ." It was not until after the Civil War that the Constitution was amended to also prohibit states from violating individual liberties. The Fourteenth Amendment, ratified in 1868, includes the command "No State shall. . . ." It prohibits the states from depriving any person of "life, liberty or property, without due process of law," or abridging "the privileges or immunities of citizens of the United States," or denying any person "equal protection of the laws." Today virtually all of the liberties guaranteed in the Constitution protect individuals not only from the national government but also from state governments.

**James Madison**
The legacy of Madison organized by topic.
*www.jmu.edu/madison*

## Constitutional Change

The purpose of a constitution is to govern government—to place limits on governmental power. Thus government itself must not be able to alter or amend a constitution easily. Yet the U.S. Constitution has changed over time, sometimes by formal amendment and other times by judicial interpretation, presidential and congressional action, and general custom and practice.

┤Think Again├

Should the Constitution be amended to guarantee that equal rights shall not be denied based on sex?

## Table 3.3    The Bill of Rights

**_Guaranteeing Freedom of Expression_**
First Amendment prohibits the government from abridging freedoms of speech, press, assembly, and petition.

**_Guaranteeing Religious Freedom_**
First Amendment prohibits the government from establishing a religion or interfering with the free exercise of religion.

**_Affirming the Right to Bear Arms and Protecting Citizens from Quartering Troops_**
Second Amendment guarantees the right to bear arms.

Third Amendment prohibits troops from occupying citizens' homes in peacetime.

**_Protecting the Rights of Accused Persons_**
Fourth Amendment protects against unreasonable searches and seizures.

Fifth Amendment requires an indictment by a grand jury for serious crimes; prohibits the government from trying a person twice for the same crime; prohibits the government from taking life, liberty, or property without due process of law; and prohibits the government from taking private property for public use without fair compensation to the owner.

Sixth Amendment guarantees a speedy and public jury trial, the right to confront witnesses in court, and the right to legal counsel for defense.

Seventh Amendment guarantees the right to a jury trial in civil cases.

Eighth Amendment prohibits the government from setting excessive bail or fines or inflicting cruel and unusual punishment.

**_Protecting the Rights of People and States_**
Ninth Amendment protects all other unspecified rights of the people.

Tenth Amendment reserves to the states or to the people those powers neither granted to the federal government nor prohibited to the states in the Constitution.

**Amendments**    A constitutional amendment must first be proposed, and then it must be ratified. The Constitution allows two methods of *proposing* a constitutional amendment: (1) by passage in the House and the Senate with a two-thirds vote, or (2) by passage in a national convention called by Congress in response to petitions by two-thirds of the state legislatures. Congress then chooses the method of *ratification,* which can be either (1) by vote in the legislatures of three-fourths of the states, or (2) by vote in conventions called for that purpose in three-fourths of the states (see Figure 3.4).

Of the four possible combinations of proposal and ratification, the method involving proposal by a two-thirds vote of Congress and ratification by three-quarters of the legislatures has been used for all the amendments except one. Only for the Twenty-first Amendment's repeal of Prohibition did Congress call for state ratifying conventions (principally because Congress feared that southern Bible Belt state legislatures would vote against repeal). The method of proposal by national convention has never been used.

In addition to the Bill of Rights, most of the constitutional amendments ratified over the nation's 200 years have expanded our notion of democracy. Today

**The Anti-Federalist Papers**
Essays by Anti-Federalists opposed to the ratification of the Constitution.
*www.thisnation.com/library/ antifederalist*

**Figure 3.4**
Constitutional
Amendment Process

The Constitution set up two alternative routes for proposing amendments and two for ratifying them. One of the four possible combinations has actually been used for all except one (the Twenty-first) amendment. However, in our time there have been persistent calls for a constitutional convention to propose new amendments permitting school prayer, making abortion illegal, and requiring a balanced national budget.

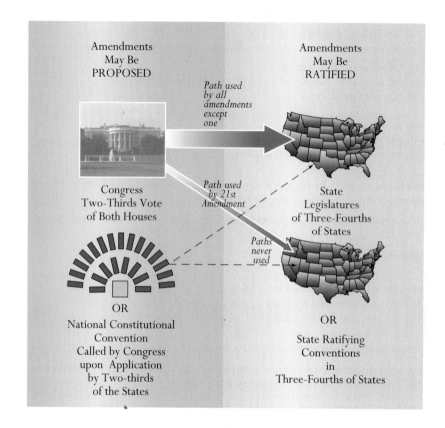

**Equal Rights Amendment (ERA)**  Proposed amendment to the Constitution guaranteeing that equal rights under the law shall not be denied or abridged on account of sex. Passed by Congress in 1972, the amendment failed to win ratification by three of the necessary three-fourths of the states.

the Constitution includes 27 amendments, which means that only 17 (out of more than 10,000) proposed amendments have been ratified since the passage of the Bill of Rights. It is possible to classify the amendments that have been ratified into the broad categories of constitutional processes, Prohibition, income tax, individual liberty, and voting rights (see Table 3.4).

Amending the U.S. Constitution requires not only a two-thirds vote in both houses of Congress, reflecting *national* support, but also ratification by three-fourths of the states, reflecting widespread support within the states. The fate of the **Equal Rights Amendment**, popularly known as the ERA, illustrates the need for nationwide consensus in order to amend the Constitution. The Equal Rights Amendment is a simple statement to which the vast majority of Americans agree, according to public opinion polls: "Equality of rights under the law shall not be denied or abridged by the United States or any state on account of sex." Congress passed the ERA in 1972 with far more than the necessary two-thirds vote; both Republicans and Democrats supported the ERA, and it was endorsed by Presidents Nixon, Ford, and Carter as well as most other national political leaders and organizations. By 1978, thirty-five state legislatures had ratified the amendment— three states short of the necessary thirty-eight (three-quarters). (Five states subsequently voted to rescind, or cancel, their earlier ratification. However, because there is no language in the Constitution regarding rescission, there is some disagreement about the constitutionality of this action.) Promising that the "ERA won't go away," proponents of the amendment have continued to press their case. But to date Congress has not acted to resubmit the ERA to the states.

**Judicial Interpretations**   Some of the greatest changes in the Constitution have come about not by formal amendment but by interpretations of the document by federal courts, notably the U.S. Supreme Court.

## Table 3.4    Amendments to the Constitution Since the Bill of Rights

**Perfecting Constitutional Processes**

Eleventh Amendment (1798) forbids federal lawsuits against a state by citizens of another state or nation.

Twelfth Amendment (1804) provides separate ballots for president and vice president in the Electoral College to prevent confusion.

Twentieth Amendment (1933) determines the dates for the beginning of the terms of Congress (January 3) and the president (January 20).

Twenty-second Amendment (1951) limits the president to two terms.

Twenty-fifth Amendment (1967) provides for presidential disability.

Twenty-seventh Amendment (1992) prevents Congress from raising its own pay in a single session.

**The Experiment with Prohibition**

Eighteenth Amendment (1919) prohibits the manufacture, sale, or transportation of intoxicating liquors.

Twenty-first Amendment (1933) repeals the Eighteenth Amendment.

**The Income Tax**

Sixteenth Amendment (1913) allows Congress to tax incomes.

**Expanding Liberty**

Thirteenth Amendment (1865) abolishes slavery.

Fourteenth Amendment (1868) protects life, liberty, and property and the privileges and immunities of citizenship and provides equal protection of the law.

**Expanding Voting Rights**

Fifteenth Amendment (1870) guarantees that the right to vote shall not be denied because of race.

Seventeenth Amendment (1913) provides for the election of senators by the people of each state.

Nineteenth Amendment (1920) guarantees that the right to vote shall not be denied because of sex.

Twenty-third Amendment (1961) gives the District of Columbia electoral votes for presidential elections.

Twenty-fourth Amendment (1964) guarantees that the right to vote shall not be denied because of failure to pay a poll tax or other tax.

Twenty-sixth Amendment (1971) guarantees that the right to vote shall not be denied to persons eighteen years of age or older.

---

Indeed, through **judicial review**, the U.S. Supreme Court has come to play the central role in giving meaning to the Constitution. Judicial review is the power of federal courts, and ultimately the Supreme Court, to declare laws of Congress and actions of the president unconstitutional and therefore invalid. This power was first asserted by Chief Justice John Marshall in the case of *Marbury v. Madison* in 1803 (see *People in Politics:* "John Marshall and Early Supreme Court Politics" in Chapter 11). It is now an important part of the system of checks and balances (see Figure 3.1). This power is itself an interpretation of the Constitution, because it is not specifically mentioned in the document.

Supreme Court interpretations of the Constitution have given specific meaning to many of our most important constitutional phrases. Among the most important examples of constitutional change through judicial interpretation are

**judicial review** The power of federal courts to declare laws of Congress and actions of the president unconstitutional.

# A CONFLICTING VIEW

## Objections to the Constitution by an Anti-Federalist

Virginia's George Mason was a delegate to the Constitutional Convention of 1787, but he refused to sign the final document and became a leading opponent of the new Constitution. Mason was a wealthy plantation owner and a heavy speculator in western (Ohio) lands. He was a friend of George Washington, but he considered most other political figures of his day to be "babblers" and he generally avoided public office. However, in 1776 he authored Virginia's Declaration of Rights, which was widely copied in other state constitutions and later became the basis for the Bill of Rights. Although an ardent supporter of states' rights, he attended the Constitutional Convention of 1787 and, according to James Madison's notes on the proceedings, was an influential force in shaping the new national government. His refusal to sign the Constitution and his subsequent leadership of the opposition to its ratification made him the recognized early leader of the Anti-Federalists.

Mason's first objection to the Constitution was that it included no Bill of Rights. But he also objected to the powers given to the Senate, which was not directly elected by the people in the original document; to the federal courts; and to the president. He was wary of the Necessary and Proper Clause, which granted Congress the power to "make all laws which shall be necessary and proper" for carrying out the enumerated powers—those specifically mentioned in the Constitution. Mason correctly predicted that this clause would be used to preempt the powers of the states.

In his "objections to the Constitution" Mason wrote,

There is no declaration of rights; and the laws of the general government being paramount to the laws and constitutions of the several States, the declaration of rights in the separate States are no security.

Senators are not the representatives of the people, or amenable to them.

The judiciary of the United States is so constructed and extended as to absorb and destroy the judiciaries of the several States; thereby rendering law as tedious, intricate and expensive . . .

Under their own construction of the general clause at the end of the enumerated powers, the Congress may . . . extend their power as far as they shall think proper; so that the State Legislatures have no security for the powers now presumed to remain to them; or the people for their rights.

Note that virtually all of Mason's objections to the original Constitution had to be remedied at a later date. The Bill of Rights was added as the first ten amendments. Eventually (1913) the Seventeenth Amendment, for the direct election of U.S. senators, was passed. And Mason correctly predicted that the federal judiciary would eventually render the law "tedious, intricate, and expensive" and that the Necessary and Proper Clause, which he refers to as "the general clause at the end of the enumerated powers," would be used to expand congressional powers at the expense of the states.

---

the meanings given to the Fourteenth Amendment, particularly its provisions that "No State shall . . . deprive any person of life, liberty, or property, without due process of law; nor deny to any person within its jurisdiction the equal protection of the laws":

- Deciding that "equal protection of the laws" requires an end to segregation of the races (*Brown v. Board of Education of Topeka*, 1954, and subsequent decisions).

- Deciding that "liberty" includes a woman's right to choose an abortion, and that the term *person* does not include the unborn fetus (*Roe v. Wade*, 1973, and subsequent decisions).

- Deciding that "equal protection of the laws" requires that every person's vote should be weighed equally in apportionment and districting plans for the House of Representatives, state legislatures, city councils, and so on (*Baker v. Carr*, 1964, and subsequent decisions).

**Presidential and Congressional Action**   Congress and the president have also undertaken to interpret the Constitution. Nearly every president, for example, has argued that the phrase "executive Power" in Article II includes more than the specific powers mentioned afterward. Thomas Jefferson purchased the Louisiana Territory from France in 1803 even though there is no constitutional authorization for the president, or even the national government, to acquire new territory. Presidents from George Washington to Richard Nixon have argued that Congress cannot force the executive branch to turn over documents it does not wish to disclose (see Chapter 9).

Congress by law has tried to restrict the president's power as Commander-in-Chief of the Armed Forces by requiring the president to notify Congress when U.S. troops are sent to "situations where imminent involvement in hostilities is clearly indicated" and limiting their stay to sixty days unless Congress authorizes an extension. This War Powers Resolution (1973), passed by Congress over President Richard Nixon's veto in the immediate aftermath of the Vietnam War, has been ignored by every president to date (see Chapter 9). Yet it indicates that Congress has its own ideas about interpreting the Constitution.

**Custom and Practice**   Finally, the Constitution changes over time as a result of generally accepted customs and practice. It is interesting to note, for example, that the Constitution never mentions political parties. (Many of the Founders disapproved of parties because they caused "faction" among the people.) But soon after Thomas Jefferson resigned as President Washington's first secretary of state (in part because he resented the influence of Secretary of the Treasury Alexander Hamilton), the Virginian attracted the support of Anti-Federalists, who believed the national government was too strong. When Washington retired from office, most Federalists supported John Adams as his successor. But many Anti-Federalists ran for posts as presidential electors, promising to be "Jefferson's men." Adams won the presidential election of 1796, but the Anti-Federalists organized themselves into a political party, the Democratic-Republicans, to oppose Adams in the

# A CONSTITUTIONAL NOTE

## How Democratic Was the Constitution of 1787?

The Constitution established *four* decision-making bodies—the House and the Senate in the legislative branch (Article I); the president in the executive branch (Article II); and the Supreme Court and "such inferior Courts as the Congress may from time to time ordain and establish" in the judicial branch (Article III). But in 1787 only one of these bodies was to be elected by the people—the House of Representatives. The other three bodies were removed from direct popular control: State legislatures selected U.S. Senators; "electors," chosen in a fashion decided by state legislatures, chose the president;

and the president appointed the Supreme Court and other federal judges "with the Advice and Consent of the [then unelected] Senate." Of course, over time state legislatures provided for the direct election of presidential electors and the Seventeenth Amendment provided for the direct election of U.S. Senators.

The Constitution of 1787 also recognized slavery—"persons held to Service or Labor" (Article IV, Section 2)—and even protected it, by requiring states that capture runaway slaves to "deliver up," that is, to return them to their owners. And in terms of representation, the Constitution of 1787 distinguishes between "free persons" and three-fifths of "all other Persons" (Article I, Section 2), that is, slaves.

election of 1800. The party secured pledges from candidates for presidential elector to cast their electoral vote for Jefferson if they won their post, and then the party helped win support for its slate of electors. In this way the Electoral College was transformed from a deliberative body where leading citizens from each state came together to decide for themselves who should be president into a ceremonial body where pledged electors simply cast their presidential vote for the candidate who had carried their state in the presidential election.

# Summary Notes

■ The true meaning of constitutionalism is the limitation of governmental power. Constitutions govern governments; they are designed to restrict those who exercise governmental power. Constitutions not only establish governmental bodies and prescribe the rules by which they make their decisions, but, more important, they also limit the powers of government.

■ The American tradition of written constitutions extends back through the Articles of Confederation, the colonial charters, and the Mayflower Compact to the thirteenth-century English Magna Carta. The Second Continental Congress in 1776 adopted a written Declaration of Independence to justify the colonies' separation from Great Britain. All of these documents strengthened the idea of a written contract defining governmental power.

■ The movement for a Constitutional Convention in 1787 was inspired by the new government's inability to levy taxes under the Articles of Confederation, its inability to fund the Revolutionary War debt, obstacles to interstate commerce, monetary problems, and civil disorders, including Shays's Rebellion.

■ The nation's Founders—fifty-five delegates to the Constitutional Convention in Philadelphia in 1787—shared a broad consensus on liberty and property, the social contract, republicanism, limited government, and the need for a national government.

■ The Founders compromised their differences over representation by creating two co-equal houses in the Congress: the House of Representatives, with members apportioned to the states on the basis of population and directly elected by the people for two-year terms, and the Senate, with two members allotted to each state regardless of its population and originally selected by state legislatures for six-year terms.

■ The infamous slavery provisions in the Constitution—counting each slave as three-fifths of a person for purposes of taxation and representation, guaranteeing the return of escaped slaves, and postponing the end of the slave trade for twenty years—were also compromises. Voter qualifications in national elections were left to the states to determine.

■ The structure of the national government reflects the Founders' beliefs in national supremacy, federalism, republicanism, separation of powers, checks and balances, and judicial review.

■ The original Constitution gave the people very little influence on their government: only members of the House of Representatives were directly elected; senators were elected by state legislatures; the president was elected indirectly by "electors" chosen in each state; and members of the Supreme Court and federal judiciary were appointed for life by the president and confirmed by the Senate. Over time, the national government became more democratic through the expansion of voting rights, the direct election of senators, the emergence of political parties, and the practice of voting for presidential electors pledged to cast their vote for the candidates of one party.

■ The separation of powers and checks and balances written into the Constitution were designed, in Madison's words, "to divide and arrange the several offices in such a manner as that each may be a check on the other." Judicial review was not specifically described in the original Constitution, but the Supreme Court soon asserted its power to overturn laws of Congress and the states, as well as presidential actions, that the Court determined to be in conflict with the Constitution.

■ Opposition to the new Constitution was strong. Anti-Federalists argued that it created a national government that was aristocratic, undemocratic, and a threat to the rights of the states and the people. Their concerns resulted in the Bill of Rights: ten amendments added to the original Constitution, all designed to limit the power of the national government and protect the rights of individuals and states.

■ Over time, constitutional changes have come about as a result of formal amendments, judicial interpretations, presidential and congressional actions, and changes in custom and practice. The most common method of constitutional amendment has been proposal by two-thirds vote of both houses of Congress followed by ratification by three-fourths of the state legislatures.

# Key Terms

constitutionalism  58
constitution  58
republicanism  62
nationalism  62
taxes  66

tariff  66
common market  68
referenda  72
separation of powers  72

checks and balances  72
judicial review  74
ratification  75
Bill of Rights  78

enumerated powers  78
amendment  78
Equal Rights Amendment (ERA)  80
judicial review  81

# Suggested Readings

Beard, Charles. *An Economic Interpretation of the Constitution*. New York: Macmillan, 1913. A classic work setting forth the argument that economic self-interest inspired the Founders in writing the Constitution.

Finkelman, Paul. *Slavery and the Founders*. 2nd ed. Armonk, NY: M.E. Sharpe, 2000. A critical account of the Founders' attitudes toward slavery and the resulting three-fifth's compromise.

Frohren, Bruce, ed. *The American Republic: Primary Sources*. Indianapolis: Liberty Fund Inc., 2002. Excellent collection of earliest American documents, from the Mayflower Compact to the Declaration of Independence.

Madison, James, Alexander Hamilton, and John Jay. *The Federalist Papers*. New York: Modern Library, 1937. These eighty-five collected essays, written in 1787–88 in support of ratification of the Constitution, remain the most important commentary on that document. Numbers 10 and 51 (reprinted in the Appendix) ought to be required reading for all students of American government.

Mason, Alpheus Thomas, and Donald Grier Stephenson Jr. *American Constitutional Law*. 14th ed. Upper Saddle River, NJ: Prentice Hall, 2004. The now classic introduction to the Constitution and the Supreme Court through essays and case excerpts.

McDonald, Forrest B. *Novus Ordo Seculorum*. Lawrence: University Press of Kansas, 1986. A description of the intellectual origins of the Constitution and the "new secular order" that it represented.

Peltason, J. W., and Sue Davis. *Understanding the Constitution*. 16th ed. New York: Harcourt Brace, 2004. Of the many books that explain the Constitution, this is one of the best. It contains explanations of the Declaration of Independence, the Articles of Confederation, and the Constitution. The book is written clearly and well suited for undergraduates.

Rossiter, Clinton L. *1787, The Grand Convention*. New York: Macmillan, 1960. A very readable account of the people and events surrounding the Constitutional Convention in 1787, with many insights into the conflicts and compromises that took place there.

Storing, Herbert J. *What the Anti-Federalists Were For*. Chicago: University of Chicago Press, 1981. An examination of the arguments of the Anti-Federalists in opposition to the ratification of the Constitution.

# Make It Real

## CONSTITUTIONAL DEMOCRACY
This module includes a look at the *Federalist Papers* and the Articles of Confederation.

# ★ ★ On Reading the Constitution ★ ★

More than 218 years after its ratification, our Constitution remains the operating charter of our republic. It is neither self-explanatory nor a comprehensive description of our constitutional rules. Still, it remains the starting point. Many Americans who swear by the Constitution have never read it seriously, although copies can be found in most American government and American history textbooks.

Justice Hugo Black, who served on the Supreme Court for 34 years, kept a copy of the Constitution with him at all times. He read it often. Reading the Constitution would be a good way for you to begin (and then reread again to end) your study of the government of the United States. We have therefore included a copy of it at this point in the book. Please read it carefully.

# The Constitution of the United States

We the People of the United States, in Order to form a more perfect Union, establish Justice, insure domestic Tranquility, provide for the common defense, promote the general Welfare, and secure the Blessings of Liberty to ourselves and our Posterity, do ordain and establish this Constitution for the United States of America.

**"We, the people." Three simple words, yet of profound importance and contentious origin. Every government in the world at the time of the Constitutional Convention was some type of monarchy wherein sovereign power flowed from the top. The Founders of our new country rejected monarchy as a form of government and proposed instead a republic, which would draw its sovereignty from the people.**

**The Articles of Confederation that governed the U.S. from 1776 until 1789 started with: "We the under signed Delegates of the States." Early drafts of the new constitution started with: "We, the states . . ." But again, the Founders were not interested in another union of states but rather the creation of a new national government. Therefore, "We, the states" was changed to "We, the people."**

**The remainder of the preamble describes the generic functions of government.**

## ARTICLE I—THE LEGISLATIVE ARTICLE

### Legislative Power

**The very first article in the Constitution established the legislative branch of the new national government. Why did the framers start with the legislative power instead of the executive branch? Under the Articles of Confederation, the legislature was the only functional instrument of government. Therefore, the framers truly believed it was the most important component of the new government.**

*Section 1* All legislative Powers herein granted shall be vested in a Congress of the United States, which shall consist of a Senate and House of Representatives.

**Section 1 established a bicameral (two-chamber) legislature of an upper (Senate) and lower (House of Representatives) organization of the legislative branch.**

### House of Representatives: Composition; Qualifications; Apportionment; Impeachment Power

*Section 2* Clause 1. The House of Representatives shall be composed of Members chosen every second Year by the People of the several States, and the Electors in each State shall have the Qualifications requisite for Electors of the most numerous Branch of the State Legislature.

**This section sets the term of office for House members (2 years) and indicates that those voting for Congress will have the same qualifications as those voting for the state legislatures. Originally, states limited voters to white property owners. Some states even had religious disqualifications, such as Catholic or Jewish. Most property and religious qualifications for voting were removed by the 1840s, but race and gender restrictions remained, until the 15th and 19th amendments were passed.**

Clause 2. No Person shall be a Representative who shall not have attained to the Age of twenty five Years, and been seven Years a Citizen of the United States, and who shall not, when elected, be an inhabitant of that State in which he shall be chosen.

**This section sets forth the basic qualifications of a representative: at least 25 years of age, a U.S. citizen for at least 7 years, and a resident of a state. Note that the Constitution does not require a person to be a resident of the district he or she represents. At the time the Constitution was written, life expectancy was about 43 years of age. So a person 25 years old was middle aged. Considering today's life expectancy of about 78 years, the equivalent age of 25 would be about 45. The average age of a current representative is 53.**

**Clause 2 does not specify how many terms a Representative can serve in Congress. Calls for Congress members to be term limited have never been enacted. Some states passed legislation to limit the terms of their U.S. Representatives. Because of the specificity of the qualifications for office, the USSC ruled in *U.S. Term Limits, Inc. v. Thomton*, 514 U.S. 779 (1995) that term limits for U.S. legislators could not be imposed by any state but would require a constitutional amendment.**

Clause 3. Representatives and direct Taxes[1] shall be apportioned among the several States which may be included within this Union, according to their respective Numbers, which shall be determined by adding to the whole Number of free Persons, including those bound to Service for a Term of Years, and excluding Indians not taxed, three fifths of all other Persons.[2] The actual Enumeration shall be made within three Years after the first Meeting of the Congress of the United States, and within every subsequent Term of ten Years in such Manner as they shall by Law direct. The Number of Representatives shall not exceed one for every thirty Thousand, but each State shall have at Least one Representative, and until such enumeration shall be made, the State of New Hampshire shall be entitled to chuse three, Massachusetts eight, Rhode Island and Providence Plantations one, Connecticut five, New York six, New Jersey four, Pennsylvania eight, Delaware one, Maryland six, Virginia ten, North Carolina five, South Carolina five, and Georgia three.

**This clause contains the Three-Fifths Compromise wherein American Indians and Blacks were only counted as 3/5 of a person for congressional representation purposes. This clause also addresses the question of congressional reapportionment every 10 years, which requires a census. Since the 1911 Reapportionment Act, the size of the House of Representatives has been set at 435. This is the designated size that is reapportioned every 10 years. Based on changes of population, some states gain and some states lose representatives. This clause also provides that every state, regardless of population, will have at least one (1) representative. Currently, seven states have only one representative.**

Clause 4. When vacancies happen in the Representation from any State, the Executive Authority thereof shall issue Writs of Election to fill such Vacancies.

**This clause provides a procedure for replacing a U.S. representative in the case of death, resignation, or expulsion from the House. Generally, if less than half a term is left, the governor will appoint a successor. If more than half a term is remaining, most states require a special election to fill the vacancy.**

Clause 5. The House of Representatives shall chuse their Speaker and other Officers, and shall have the sole Power of Impeachment.

**Only one officer of the House is specified—the Speaker. All other officers are decided by the House. This clause also gives the House authority for impeachments (accusations) against officials of the executive and judicial branches.**

### Senate Composition: Qualifications, Impeachment Trials

*Section 3*  Clause 1. The Senate of the United States shall be composed of two Senators from each State, chosen by the Legislature thereof,[3] for six Years and each Senator shall have one Vote.

**This clause treats each state equally—all have two senators each. Originally, senators were chosen by state legislators, but since passage and ratification of the 17th Amendment, they are now elected by popular vote. This clause also establishes the term of a senator—6 years—three times that of a House member.**

Clause 2. Immediately after they shall be assembled in Consequence of the first Election, they shall be divided as equally as may be into three Classes. The Seats of the Senators of the first Class shall be vacated at the Expiration of the second Year, of the second Class at the Expiration of the fourth Year, and of the third Class at the Expiration of the sixth Year, so that one third may be chosen every second Year and if Vacancies happen by Resignation, or otherwise, during the Recess of the Legislature of any State, the Executive thereof may make temporary Appointments until the next Meeting of the Legislature which shall then fill such Vacancies.[4]

**To prevent a wholesale election of senators every six years, this clause provides that one-third of the Senate will be elected every two years. Senate vacancies are filled similar to the House—either appointment by the governor or a special election.**

Clause 3. No person shall be a Senator who shall not have attained to the Age of thirty Years, and been nine Years a Citizen of the United States, and who shall not, when elected, be an Inhabitant of that State for which he shall be chosen.

**This clause sets forth the qualifications for U.S. senator: at least 30 years old, a U.S. citizen for at least nine years, and a citizen of a state. The equivalent age of 30 today would be 54 years old. The average age of a U.S. senator at present is 58.3 years.**

Clause 4. The Vice President of the United States shall be President of the Senate but shall have no Vote, unless they be equally divided.

**The only constitutional duty of the vice president is specified in this clause—president of the Senate. This official only has a vote if there is a tie vote in the Senate; then the vice president's vote breaks the tie.**

Clause 5. The Senate shall chuse their other Officers, and also a President pro tempore, in the Absence of the Vice President, or when he shall exercise the Office of President of the United States.

**One official office in the U.S. Senate is specified—temporary president, who fills in during the vice president's absence (which is normally the case). All other Senate officers are designated and selected by the Senate.**

Clause 6. The Senate shall have the sole Power to try all Impeachments. When sitting for that Purpose, they shall be on Oath or Affirmation. When the President of the United States is tried, the Chief Justice shall preside. And no Person shall be convicted without the Concurrence of two thirds of the Members present.

Judgment in Cases of impeachment shall not extend further than to removal from Office, and disqualification to hold and enjoy any Office of honor, Trust or Profit under the United States, but the Party convicted shall nevertheless be liable and subject to Indictment, Trial, Judgment and Punishment according to Law.

---

[1]Modified by the 16th Amendment
[2]Replaced by Section 2, 14th Amendment
[3]Repealed by the 17th Amendment

[4]Modified by the 17th Amendment

The Senate acts as a trial court for impeached federal officials. If the accused is the president, the Chief Justice of the U.S. Supreme Court presides. Otherwise, the vice president normally presides. Conviction of the charges requires a 2/3 majority vote of those senators present at the time of the vote. Conviction results in the federal official's removal from office and disqualification to hold any other federal appointed office. Removal from office does not bar further prosecution under applicable criminal or civil laws, nor does it apparently bar one from elected office. A current representative, Alcee L. Hastings, was impeached and removed as a federal district judge. He subsequently ran for Congress and now represents Florida's 23rd Congressional District.

### Congressional Elections: Times, Places, Manner

*Section 4*   The Times, Places and Manner of holding Elections for Senators and Representatives, shall be prescribed in each State by the Legislature thereof, but the Congress may at any time by Law make or alter such Regulations, except as to the Places of chusting Senators.

The Congress shall assemble at least once in every Year, and such Meeting shall be on the first Monday in December, unless they shall by Law appoint a different Day.[5]

The states determine the place and manner of electing representatives and senators, but Congress has the right to make or change these laws or regulations, except for the election sites. Congress is required to meet annually, and now, by law, annual meetings begin in January.

### Powers and Duties of the Houses

*Section 5*   Clause 1. Each House shall be the Judge of the Elections, Returns and Qualifications of its own Members, and a Majority of each shall constitute a Quorum to do Business, but a smaller Number may adjourn from day to day, and may be authorized to compel the Attendance of absent Members, in such Manner, and under the Penalties as each House may provide.

This clause enables each legislative branch to essentially make its own rules. Normally, to take a vote, a quorum is necessary. But if no votes are scheduled, fewer than a quorum can convene a session.

Clause 2. Each House may determine the Rules of its Proceedings, punish its Members for disorderly Behaviour, and with the Concurrence of two thirds, expel a Member.

Essentially, each branch promulgates its own rules and punishes its own members. The ultimate punishment is expulsion of the member, which requires a 2/3 vote. Expulsion does not prevent the member from running again.

Clause 3. Each House shall keep a Journal of its Proceedings, and from time to time publish the same, excepting such Parts as may in their Judgment require Secrecy, and the Yeas and Nays of the Members of either House on any question shall, at the Desire of one fifth of those Present, be entered on the Journal.

An official record called the Congressional Record, House Journal, etc., is kept for all sessions. It is a daily account of House and Senate floor debates,

[5]Changed by the 20th Amendment

votes, and members' remarks. However, a record is not printed if a proceeding is closed to the public for security reasons. Many votes are by voice vote, and if at least 1/5 of the members request, a recorded vote of Yeas and Nays will be conducted and recorded. This procedure permits analysis of congressional roll-call votes.

Clause 4.  Neither House, during the Session of Congress shall, without the Consent of the other, adjourn for more than three days, nor to any other Place than that in which the two Houses shall be sitting.

This clause prevents one branch from adjourning for a long period or to some other location without the consent of the other branch.

### Rights of Members

*Section 6*   Clause 1. The Senators and Representatives shall receive a Compensation for their Services, to be ascertained by Law, and paid out of the Treasury of the United States. They shall in all Cases, except Treason, Felony and Breach of the Peace, be privileged from Arrest during their Attendance at the Session of their respective Houses, and in going to and returning from the same, and for any Speech or Debate in either House, they shall not be questioned in any other Place.

This section ensures that senators and congressional representatives will be paid a salary from the U.S. Treasury. This salary is determined by no other than the legislature. According to the Library of Congress legislative Web site THOMAS "The current salary for members of Congress is $165,200. A small number of leadership positions, like Speaker of the House, receive a somewhat higher salary." In addition, members of Congress receive many other benefits: free health care, fully funded retirement system, free gyms, 26 free round trips to their home state or district, etc. This section also provides immunity from arrest or prosecution for congressional actions on the floor or in travel to and from the Congress. For example, few members of Congress have ever been charged with drunk driving.

Clause 2.  No Senator or Representative, shall, during the Time for which he was elected, be appointed to any civil Office under the Authority of the United States, which shall have been created, or the Emoluments whereof shall have been encreased during such time; and no Person holding any Office under the United States, shall be a Member of either House during his Continuance in Office.

This section prevents the U.S. from adopting a parliamentary democracy, since congressional members cannot hold executive offices and members of the executive branch cannot be members of Congress.

### Legislative Powers: Bills and Resolutions

*Section 7*   Clause 1. All Bills for raising Revenue shall originate in the House of Representatives; but the Senate may propose or concur with Amendments as on other Bills.

This clause specifies one of the few powers specific to the U.S. House—revenue bills.

Clause 2. Every Bill which shall have passed the House of Representatives and the Senate, shall, before it becomes a Law, be presented to the President of the United States; If he approve he shall sign it, but if not he shall return it, with his Objections to that House in which it shall have originated, who shall enter the Objections at large on their Journal, and proceed to reconsider it. If after such Reconsideration two thirds of that House shall agree to pass the Bill, it shall be sent, together with the Objections, to the other House, by which it shall likewise be reconsidered, and if approved by two thirds of that House, it shall become a Law. But in all such Cases the Votes of both Houses shall be determined by yeas and Nays, and the Names of the Persons voting for and against the Bill shall be entered on the Journal of each House respectively. If any Bill shall not be returned by the President within ten Days (Sundays excepted) after it shall have been presented to him, the Same shall be a Law, in like Manner as if he had signed it, unless the Congress by their Adjournment prevent its Return, in which Case it shall not be a Law.

**The heart of the checks and balances system is contained in this clause. Both the House and Senate must pass a bill and present it to the president. If the president fails to act on the bill within 10 days (not including Sundays), the bill will automatically become law. If the president signs the bill, it becomes law. If the president vetoes the bill and sends it back to Congress, this body may override the veto by a 2/3 vote in each house. This vote must be a recorded vote.**

Clause 3. Every Order, Resolution, or Vote to which the Concurrence of the Senate and House of Representatives may be necessary (except on a question of Adjournment) shall be presented to the President of the United States; and before the Same shall take Effect, shall be approved by him, or being disapproved by him, shall be repassed by two thirds of the Senate and House of Representatives, according to the Rules and Limitations prescribed in the Case of a Bill.

**This clause covers every other type of legislative action other than a bill. Essentially, the same procedures apply in most cases. There are a few exceptions. For example, a joint resolution proposing a new congressional amendment is not subject to presidential veto.**

### Powers of Congress

*Section 8*   Clause 1. The Congress shall have Power to lay and collect Taxes, Duties, Imposts and Excises, to pay the Debts and provide for the common Defence and general Welfare of the United States, but all Duties, Imposts and Excises shall be uniform throughout the United States.

To borrow Money on the credit of the United States;

To regulate Commerce with foreign Nations, and among the several States, and with the Indian Tribes;

To establish an uniform Rule of Naturalization, and uniform Laws on the subject of Bankruptcies throughout the United States;

To coin Money, regulate the Value thereof, and of foreign Coin, and fix the Standard of Weights and Measures;

To provide for the Punishment of counterfeiting the Securities and current Coin of the United States;

To establish Post Offices and post Roads;

To promote the Progress of Science and useful Arts, by securing for limited Times to Authors and Inventors the exclusive Right to their respective Writings and Discoveries;

To constitute Tribunals inferior to the supreme Court;

To define and punish Piracies and Felonies committed on the high Seas, and Offences against the Law of Nations;

To declare War, grant Letters of Marque and Reprisal, and make Rules concerning Captures on Land and Water;

To raise and support Armies, but no Appropriation of Money to that Use shall be for a longer Term than two Years;

To provide and maintain a Navy;

To make Rules for the Government and Regulation of the land and naval Forces;

To provide for calling for the Militia to execute the Laws of the Union, suppress Insurrections and repel Invasions;

To provide for organizing, arming, and disciplining, the Militia, and for governing such Part of them as may be employed in the Service of the United States, reserving to the States respectively, the Appointment of the Officers, and the Authority of training the Militia according to the discipline prescribed by Congress.

**This *extensive* clause establishes what are known as the "expressed" or "specified" powers of Congress. In theory, this serves as a limit or brake on congressional power.**

Clause 2. To exercise exclusive Legislation in all Cases whatsoever, over such District (not exceeding ten Miles square) as may, by Cession of particular States, and the Acceptance of Congress, become the Seat of the Government of the United States, and to exercise like Authority over all Places purchased by the Consent of the Legislature of the State in which the Same shall be, for the Erection of Forts, Magazines, Arsenals, dock Yards, and other needful Buildings—And

**This clause establishes the seat of the federal government, which was first started in New York but eventually was moved to Washington, D.C., when both Maryland and Virginia ceded land to the new national government, which then established the District of Columbia.**

Clause 3. To make all Laws which shall be necessary and proper for carrying into Execution the foregoing Powers, and all other Powers vested by this Constitution in the Government of the United States, or in any Department or Officer thereof.

**This clause, known as the "Elastic Clause," provides the basis for the doctrine of "implied" congressional powers, which was first introduced in the U.S. Supreme Court case of *McCulloch v. Maryland,* 1819. This doctrine tremendously expanded the power of Congress to pass legislation and make regulations.**

### Powers Denied to Congress

*Section 9*   Clause 1. The Migration or Importation of such Persons as any of the States now existing shall think proper to admit, shall not be prohibited by the Congress prior to the Year one thousand eight hundred and eight, but a Tax or duty may be imposed on such Importation, not exceeding ten dollars for each Person.

**This clause was part of the Three-Fifths Compromise. Essentially, the new Congress was prohibited from stopping the importation of slaves until 1808, but it could impose a head tax, not to exceed ten dollars for each slave.**

Clause 2. The Privilege of the Writ of Habeas Corpus shall not be suspended, unless when in Cases of Rebellion or Invasion the public Safety may require it.

Congress cannot suspend the writ of habeas corpus except in cases of rebellion or invasion. The writ of habeas corpus permits a judge to inquire about the legality of detention or deprivation of liberty of any citizen.

Clause 3. No Bill of Attainder or ex post facto Law shall be passed.

This provision prohibits Congress from passing either a bill of attainder (forfeiture of property in capital cases) or ex post facto laws (retroactive crimes after passage of legislation). Similar restrictions were enshrined in many state constitutions.

Clause 4. No Capitation, or other direct Tax shall be laid, unless in Proportion to the Census or Enumeration herein before directed to be taken.[6]

This clause prevented Congress from passing an Income tax. Only with passage of the 16th Amendment in 1913 did Congress gain this power.

Clause 5. No Tax or Duty shall be laid on Articles exported from any State.

This section establishes free trade within the U.S. The federal government cannot tax state exports.

Clause 6. No Preference shall be given by any Regulation of Commerce or Revenue to the Ports of one State over those of another; nor shall Vessels bound to, or from one State, be obliged to enter, clear, or pay Duties in another.

This clause also applies to free trade within the U.S. The national government cannot show any preference to any state or maritime movements among the states.

Clause 7. No Money shall be drawn from the Treasury, but in Consequence of Appropriations made by Law, and a regular Statement and Account of the Receipts and Expenditures of all public Money shall be published from time to time.

This provision of the Constitution prevents any expenditure unless it has been specifically provided for in an appropriations bill. At the beginning of most fiscal years, Congress has not completed its work on the budget. Technically, the government cannot spend any money according to this provision and would have to shut down. So Congress normally passes a Continuing Resolution providing temporary authority to continue to spend money until the final budget is approved and signed into law.

Clause 8. No Title of Nobility shall be granted by the United States. And no Person holding any Office of Profit or Trust under them, shall, without the Consent of Congress, accept of any present, Emolument, Office, or Title, of any kind whatever, from any King, Prince, or foreign State.

Feudalism would not be established in the new country. We would have no nobles. No federal official can even accept a title of nobility (even honorary) without permission of Congress.

[6]Modified by the 16th Amendment.

### Powers Denied to the States

This section sets out the prohibitions on state actions.

Section 10 Clause 1. No State shall enter into any Treaty, Alliance, or Confederation, grant Letters of Marque and Reprisal, coin Money, emit Bills of Credit, make any Thing but gold and silver Coin a Tender in Payment of Debts, pass any Bill of Attainder, ex post facto Law, or Law impairing the Obligation of Contracts of grant any Title of Nobility.

This particular clause is a laundry list of denied powers. Note that these restrictions cannot even be waived by Congress. States are not to engage in foreign relations, nor acts of war. A letter of Marque and Reprisal was used during these times to provide legal cover for privateers. The federal government's currency monopoly is established. The sanctity of contracts is specified. And similar state prohibitions are specified for bills of attainder, ex post facto, etc.

Clause 2. No State shall, without the Consent of the Congress, lay any Imposts or Duties on Imports or Exports, except what may be absolutely necessary for executing its inspection Laws: and the net Produce of all Duties and Imposts, laid by any State on Imports or Exports, shall be for the Use of the Treasury of the United States, and all such Laws shall be subject to the Revision and Controul of the Congress.

This section establishes the monopoly control of the national government in matters of both national and international trade. The only concession to states is health and safety inspections.

Clause 3. No State shall, without the Consent of Congress, lay any Duty of Tonnage, keep Troops, or Ships of War in time of Peace, enter into any Agreement or Compact with another State, or with a foreign Power, or engage in War, unless actually invaded, or in such imminent Danger as will not admit of delay.

This final section of the Legislative article establishes the war monopoly power of the national government. The only exception to state action is actual invasion or threat of imminent danger.

### ARTICLE II—THE EXECUTIVE ARTICLE

This article establishes an entirely new concept in government—an elected executive power.

### Nature and Scope of Presidential Power

Section 1 Clause 1. The executive Power shall be vested in a President of the United States of America. He shall hold his Office during the Term of four Years and, together with the Vice President, chosen for the same Term, be elected, as follows.

This clause establishes the executive power in the office of the president of the United States of America. It also establishes a second office—vice president. A four-year term was established, but no limit on the number of terms. A limit was later established by the 22nd Amendment.

Clause 2. Each State shall appoint, in such Manner as the Legislature thereof may direct, a Number of Electors, equal to the whole Number of Senators and Representatives to which the State may be entitled in the Congress: but no Senator or Representative, or Person holding an Office of Trust or Profit under the United States, shall be appointed an Elector.

**This paragraph essentially establishes the Electoral College to choose the president and vice president.**

Clause 3. The Electors shall meet in their respective States, and vote by Ballot for two Persons, of whom one at least shall not be an Inhabitant of the same State with themselves. And they shall make a List of all the Persons voted for, and of the Number of Votes for each; which List they shall sign and certify, and transmit sealed to the Seat of the Government of the United States, directed to the President of the Senate. The President of the Senate shall, in the Presence of the Senate and House of Representatives, open all the Certificates, and the Votes shall then be counted. The Person having the greatest Number of Votes shall be the President, if such Number be a Majority of the whole Number of Electors appointed; and if there be more than one who have such Majority and have an equal Number of Votes, then the House of Representatives shall immediately chuse by Ballot one of them for President; and if no Person have a Majority, then from the five highest on the List the said House shall in like Manner chuse the President. But in chusing the President, the Votes shall be taken by States, the Representation from each State having one Vote; a quorum for this Purpose shall consist of a Member or Members from two thirds of the States, and a Majority of all the States shall be necessary to a Choice. In every Case, after the Choice of the President, the Person having the greatest Number of Votes of the Electors shall be the Vice President. But if there should remain two or more who have equal Votes, the Senate shall chuse from them by Ballot the Vice President.[7]

**This paragraph has been superseded by the 12th Amendment. The original language did not require a separate vote for president and vice president. This resulted in a tied vote in the Electoral College in 1800 when both Thomas Jefferson and Aaron Burr received 73 electoral votes. The 12th Amendment requires a separate vote for each. Only one of the two can be from the state of the elector. This means that it is highly unlikely that the presidential and vice presidential candidates would be from the same state. This question arose in the 2000 election when Dick Cheney, who lived and worked in Texas, had to reestablish his residence in Wyoming.**

**The original language provided for a House election in the case of no majority vote or a tie vote among the top five candidates. The amendment lowered the number of candidates to the top three. The Senate is to select the vice president if a candidate does not have an electoral majority or in the case of a tie vote. The Senate considers only the top two candidates. The amendment also clarifies that the qualifications of the vice president are the same as those for president.**

Clause 4. The Congress may determine the Time of chusing the Electors, and the Day on which they shall give their Votes; which Day shall be the same throughout the United States.

**Congress is given the power to establish a uniform day and time for the state selection of electors.**

Clause 5. No Person except a natural born Citizen, or a Citizen of the United States, at the time of the Adoption of this Constitution, shall be eligible to the Office of President; neither shall any Person be eligible to that Office who shall not have attained to the Age of thirty five Years, and been fourteen Years a Resident within the United States.

**The qualifications for the offices of president and vice president are specified here—at least 35 years old, 14 years' resident in the U.S., and a natural-born citizen or citizen of the U.S. The 14th Amendment clarified who is a citizen of the U.S.: a person born or naturalized in the U.S. and subject to its jurisdiction. But the term "natural-born citizen" is unclear and has never been further defined by the judicial branch. Does it mean born in the U.S. or born of U.S. citizens in the U.S. or somewhere else in the world? Unfortunately, there is no definitive answer.**

Clause 6. In Case of the Removal of the President from Office, or of his Death, Resignation, or Inability to discharge the Powers and Duties of the said Office, the Same shall devolve on the Vice President, and the Congress may by Law provide for the Case of Removal, Death, Resignation, or Inability, both of the President and Vice President, declaring what Officer shall then act as president, and such Officer shall act accordingly, until the Disability be removed, or a President shall be elected.[8]

**This clause has been modified by the 25th Amendment. Upon the death, resignation, or impeachment and conviction of the president, the vice president becomes president. The new president nominates a new vice president, who assumes the office, if approved by a majority vote in both congressional branches. The president is also now able to notify the Congress of his inability to perform his office.**

Clause 7. The President shall, at stated Times, receive for his Services, a Compensation which shall neither be increased nor diminished during the Period of which he shall have been elected, and he shall not receive within that Period any other Emolument from the United States, or any of them.

**This section covers the compensation of the president, which cannot be increased or decreased during his office. The current salary is $400,000/year.**

Clause 8. Before he enter on the Execution of his Office, he shall take the following Oath or Affirmation—"I do solemnly swear (or affirm) that I will faithfully execute the Office of President of the United States, and will to the best of my Ability, preserve, protect and defend the Constitution of the United States."

**This final clause in Section 1 is the oath of office administered to the new president.**

### Powers and Duties of the President

*Section 2*   Clause 1. The President shall be the Commander in Chief of the Army and Navy of the United States, and of the

---

[7]Changed by the 12th and 20th Amendments

[8]Modified by the 25th Amendment

Militia of the several States; when called into the actual Service of the United States, he may require the Opinion, in writing, of the principal Officer in each of the executive Departments, upon any Subject relating to the Duties of their respective Offices, and he shall have the Power to grant Reprieves and Pardons for Offences against the United States, except in Cases of Impeachment.

**This clause establishes the president as Commander-in-Chief of the U.S. armed forces. George Washington actually led U.S. armed forces during the Whiskey Rebellion. The second provision provides the basis for cabinet meetings that are used to acquire the opinions of executive department heads. The last provision provides an absolute pardon or reprieve power from the president. The provision was controversial, but legal, when President Gerald Ford pardoned Richard Nixon following the Watergate scandal.**

Clause 2. He shall have Power, by and with the Advice and Consent of the Senate to make Treaties, provided two thirds of the Senators present concur, and he shall nominate, and by and with the Advice and Consent of the Senate, shall appoint Ambassadors, other public Ministers and Consuls, Judges of the supreme Court, and all other Officers of the United States, whose Appointments are not herein otherwise provided for, and which shall be established by Law but the Congress may by Law vest the Appointment of such inferior Officers, as they think proper in the President alone, in the Courts of Law, or in the Heads of Departments.

**This clause covers two important presidential powers, treaty making and appointments. The president (via the State Department) can negotiate treaties with other nations, but these do not become official until ratified by a 2/3 vote of the U.S. Senate. The president is empowered to appoint judges, ambassadors, and other U.S. officials (cabinet officers, military officers, agency heads, etc.) subject to Senate approval. The Congress can and does delegate this approval to the president in the case of inferior officers. For example, junior military officer promotions are not submitted to the Senate, but senior officer promotions are.**

Clause 3. The President shall have Power to fill up all Vacancies that may happen during the Recess of the Senate, by granting Commissions which shall expire at the End of their next Session.

**This provision allows recess appointments of the officials listed in Clause 2 above. These commissions automatically expire unless approved by the Senate by the end of the next session. Presidents have used this provision to fill jobs when the nomination process is stalled. Some of these appointments have been very controversial. The regular nomination was stalled because the Senate did not want to confirm the nominee.**

*Section 3*　He shall from time to time give to the Congress Information of the State of the Union, and recommend to their Consideration such Measures as he shall judge necessary and expedient, he may, on extraordinary Occasions convene both Houses, or either of them and in Case of Disagreement between them, with Respect to the Time of Adjournment, he may adjourn them to such Time as he shall think proper, he shall receive

Ambassadors and other public Ministers, he shall take Care that the Laws be faithfully executed, and shall Commission all the Officers of the United States.

**This section provides for the annual State of the Union address to a joint session of Congress and the American people. The president is also authorized to call special meetings of either the House or Senate. If there is disagreement between the House and Senate regarding adjournment, the president is empowered to adjourn them. This would be extremely rare. The president formally receives other nations' ambassadors. The next to last provision to faithfully execute laws provides the basis for the whole administrative apparatus of the presidency. All officers of the U.S. receive a formal commission from the president (most of these are signed with a signature machine).**

*Section 4*　The President, Vice President and all civil Officers of the United States, shall be removed from Office on Impeachment for, and Conviction of, Treason, Bribery, or other high Crimes and Misdemeanors.

**This section provides the constitutional authority for the impeachment and trial of the president, vice president, and all civil officers of the U.S. for treason, bribery, or other high crimes and misdemeanors (the exact meaning of this phrase is unclear and is often more political than judicial).**

### Article III—The Judicial Article

#### Judicial Power, Courts, Judges

*Section 1*　The judicial Power of the United States, shall be vested in one supreme Court, and in such inferior Courts as the Congress may from time to time ordain and establish. The Judges, both of the supreme and inferior Courts, shall hold their Offices during good Behaviour, and shall, at stated Times, receive for their Services, a Compensation, which shall not be diminished during their Continuance in Office.

**This section establishes the judicial branch in very general terms. It specifically provides only for the Supreme Court. Congress is given the responsibility to flesh out the court system. It initially did so in the Judiciary Act of 1789, when it established 13 district courts (one for each state), and 3 appellate courts. All federal judges hold their offices for life and can only be removed for breaches of good behavior—a very nebulous term. Federal judges have been removed for drunkenness, accepting bribes, and other misdemeanors. To date, no justice of the U.S. Supreme Court has ever been removed.**

**The salary of federal judges is set by congressional act, but can never be reduced. Although the American Bar Association and the Federal Bar Association consider federal judges' salaries inadequate, most Americans would probably disagree. Federal district judges earn $165,200/year, appellate judges $174,600, and Supreme Court justices $203,000. The Chief Justice is paid $212,100. These are lifetime salaries, even upon retirement.**

### Jurisdiction

*Section 2* The judicial Power shall extend to all Cases, in Law and Equity, arising under this Constitution, the Laws of the United States, and Treaties made, or which shall be made, under their Authority,—to all Cases affecting Ambassadors, other public Ministers and Consuls;—to all Cases of admiralty and maritime Jurisdiction;—to Controversies to which the United States shall be a Party;—to Controversies between two or more States; between a State and Citizens of another State;[9]—between Citizens of different States;—between Citizens of the same State claiming Lands under Grants of different States, and between a State, or the Citizens thereof, and foreign States, Citizens, or Subjects.

In all Cases affecting Ambassadors, other public Ministers and Consuls, and those in which a State shall be Party, the supreme Court shall have original Jurisdiction. In all the other Cases before mentioned, the supreme Court shall have appellate Jurisdiction, both as to Law and Fact, with such Exceptions, and under such Regulations as Congress shall make.

The Trial of all Crimes, except in Cases of Impeachment, shall be by Jury; and such Trial shall be held in the State where the said Crimes shall have been committed; but when not committed within any State, the Trial shall be at such Place or Places as the Congress may by Law have directed.

**This section establishes the original and appellate jurisdiction of the U.S. Supreme Court. With the Congress of Vienna's 1815 establishment of "diplomatic immunity," the U.S. Supreme Court no longer hears cases involving ambassadors. Since 1925, the Supreme Court no longer hears every case on appeal but can select which cases it will accept, which is now only about 150 cases per year. This section also establishes the right of trial by jury for federal crimes.**

### Treason

*Section 3* Treason against the United States, shall consist only in levying War against them, or in adhering to their Enemies, giving them Aid and Comfort. No Person shall be convicted of Treason unless on the Testimony of two Witnesses to the same overt Act, or on Confession in open Court.

The Congress shall have Power to declare the Punishment of Treason, but no Attainder of Treason shall work Corruption of Blood, or Forfeiture except during the Life of the Person attainted.

**Treason is the only crime defined in the U.S. Constitution. Congress established the penalty of death for treason convictions. Note that two witnesses are required to convict anyone of treason. Even in cases of treasonable conduct, seizure of estates is prohibited.**

### ARTICLE IV—INTERSTATE RELATIONS

### Full Faith and Credit Clause

*Section 1* Full Faith and Credit shall be given in each State to the public Acts, Records, and judicial Proceedings of every other State. And the Congress may by general Laws prescribe the Manner in which such Acts, Records and Proceedings shall be proved, and the Effect thereof.

**This section provides that the official acts and records of one state will be recognized and given credence by other states, e.g., marriages and divorces.**

### Privileges and Immunities, Interstate Extradition

*Section 2* Clause 1. The Citizens of each State shall be entitled to all Privileges and Immunities of Citizens in the several States.

**This clause requires states to treat citizens of other states equally. For example, when driving in another state, one's driver's license is recognized. One area not so clear is that of charging higher tuitions at state educational institutions for out-of-state students.**

Clause 2. A person charged in any State with Treason, Felony or other Crime, who shall flee from Justice, and be found in another State, shall on Demand of the executive Authority of the State from which he fled, be delivered up, to be removed to the State having Jurisdiction of the Crime.

**Extradition is the name of this clause. A criminal fleeing to another state, if captured, can be returned to the state where the crime was committed. But this is not an absolute. A state's governor can refuse, for good reason, to extradite someone to another state.**

Clause 3. No person held to Service or Labour in one State, under the Laws thereof, escaping into another, shall, in Consequence of any Law or Regulation therein, be discharged from such Service or Labour, but shall be delivered up on Claim of the Party to whom such Service or Labour may be due.[10]

**This clause was included to cover runaway slaves. It has been made inoperable by the 13th Amendment, which abolished slavery.**

### Admission of States

*Section 3* New States may be admitted by the Congress into this Union but no new State shall be formed or erected within the Jurisdiction of any other State, nor any State to be formed by the Junction of two or more States, or Parts of States, without the Consent of the Legislatures of the States concerned as well as of the Congress.

The Congress shall have Power to dispose of and make all needful Rules and Regulations respecting the Territory or other Property belonging to the United States, and nothing in this Constitution shall be so construed as to Prejudice any Claims of the United States, or of any particular State.

**This section concerns the admission of new states to the Union. In theory, no state can be created from part of another state without permission of the state legislature. But West Virginia was formed from Virginia during the Civil War without the permission of Virginia, which was part of the Confederacy. With fifty states now part of the Union, this section has not been used for many decades. The only future use may be in the case of Puerto Rico or perhaps Washington, D.C.**

### Republican Form of Government

*Section 4* The United States shall guarantee to every State in this Union a Republican Form of Government, and shall protect each of them against Invasion, and on Application of the Legislature, or of the Executive (when the Legislature cannot be convened) against domestic Violence.

---

[9]Modified by the 11th Amendment

[10]Repealed by the 13th Amendment

This section commits the federal government to guarantee a republican form of government to each state and protect the state against foreign invasion or domestic insurrection.

### ARTICLE V—THE AMENDING POWER

The Congress, whenever two thirds of both Houses shall deem it necessary, shall propose Amendments to this Constitution, or, on the Application of the Legislatures of two thirds of the several States, shall call a Convention for proposing Amendments, which, in either Case, shall be valid to all Intents and Purposes, as Part of this Constitution, when ratified by the Legislatures of three fourths of the several States, or by Conventions in three fourths thereof, as the one or the other Mode of Ratification may be proposed by the Congress; Provided that no Amendment which may be made prior to the Year One thousand eight hundred and eight shall in any Manner affect the first and fourth Clauses in the Ninth Section of the first Article; and that no State, without its Consent, shall be deprived of its equal Suffrage in the Senate.

Amendment to the U.S. Constitution can be originated by a 2/3 vote in both the U.S. House and Senate or by 2/3 of the state legislatures asking for a convention to propose amendments. Proposed amendments, by either route, must be approved by 3/4 of state legislatures or by 3/4 of conventions convened in the states for purposes of ratification. Only one amendment has been ratified by the convention method—Amendment 21 to repeal the 18th Amendment establishing Prohibition.

Thousands of amendments have been proposed; few have been passed by 2/3 vote in each branch of Congress. The Equal Rights Amendment was one such case, but it was not ratified by 3/4 of state legislatures. There have only been 27 successful amendments to the U.S. Constitution.

### ARTICLE VI—THE SUPREMACY CLAUSE

Clause 1. All Debts contracted and Engagements entered into, before the Adoption of this Constitution, shall be as valid against the United States under the Constitution, as under the Confederation.

This clause made the new national government responsible for all debts incurred during the Revolutionary War. This was very important to banking and commercial Interests.

Clause 2. This Constitution, and the Laws of the United States which shall be made in Pursuance thereof, and all Treaties made, or which shall be made, under the Authority of the United States, shall be the supreme Law of the Land; and the Judges in every State shall be bound thereby any Thing in the Constitution or Laws of any State to the Contrary notwithstanding.

This is the National Supremacy Clause, which provides the basis for the supremacy of the national government.

Clause 3. The Senators and Representatives before mentioned, and the Members of the several State Legislatures, and all executive and judicial Officers, both of the United States and of the several States, shall be bound by Oath or Affirmation, to support this Constitution, but no religious Test shall ever be required as a

Qualification to any Office or public Trust under the United States.

This clause requires essentially all federal and state officials to swear or affirm their allegiance to and support of the U.S. Constitution. Note that a religious test was prohibited for federal office. However, some states used religious tests for voting and office qualification until the 1830s.

### ARTICLE VII—RATIFICATION

The Ratification of the Conventions of nine States, shall be sufficient for the Establishment of this Constitution between the States so ratifying the Same.

Done in Convention by the Unanimous Consent of the States present the Seventeenth Day of September in the Year of our Lord one thousand seven hundred and Eighty seven and of the Independence of the United States of America the Twelfth. *In Witness whereof We have hereunto subscribed our Names.*

Realizing the unanimous ratification of the 13 states of the new Constitution might never have occurred, the framers wisely specified that only 9 states would be needed for ratification. Even this proved to be a test of wills between Federalists and Anti-Federalists, leading to publication of the great political work *The Federalist Papers*.

### AMENDMENTS
### THE BILL OF RIGHTS

[The first ten amendments were ratified on December 15, 1791, and form what is known as the "Bill of Rights."]

The Bill of Rights applied initially only to the federal government and not to state or local governments. Beginning in 1925 in the case of *Gitlow v. New York,* the U.S. Supreme Court began to selectively incorporate the Bill of Rights, making its provisions applicable to state and local governments. There are only three exceptions, which will be discussed at the appropriate amendment.

### AMENDMENT 1—RELIGION, SPEECH, ASSEMBLY, AND POLITICS

Congress shall make no law respecting an establishment of religion, or prohibiting the free exercise thereof; or abridging the freedom of speech, or of the press; or the right of the people peaceably to assemble, and to petition the Government for a redress of grievances.

This is the godfather of all amendments in that it protects five fundamental freedoms: religion, speech, press, assembly, and petition. Note that the press is the only business that is specifically protected by the U.S. Constitution. Freedom of religion and speech are two of the most contentious issues and generate a multitude of Supreme Court cases.

### AMENDMENT 2—MILITIA AND THE RIGHT TO BEAR ARMS

A well-regulated Militia, being necessary to the security of a free State, the right of the people to keep and bear Arms, shall not be infringed.

**There is also controversy as to the meaning of this amendment. Some believe that it specifically refers to citizen militias, which were common at the time of the Constitution but now have been replaced by National Guard units. Therefore, is the amendment still applicable? Do private citizens need weapons for the security of a free state?**

### AMENDMENT 3—QUARTERING OF SOLDIERS

No Soldier shall, in time of peace be quartered in any house, without the consent of the Owner, nor in time of war, but in manner to be prescribed by law.

**It was the practice of the British government to insist that colonists provide room and board to British troops. This amendment was designed to prohibit this practice. Today, military and naval bases provide the necessary quarters.**

### AMENDMENT 4—SEARCHES AND SEIZURES

The right of the people to be secure in their persons, houses, papers, and effects, against unreasonable searches and seizures, shall not be violated, and no Warrants shall issue, but upon probable cause, supported by Oath or affirmation, and particularly describing the place to be searched, and the persons or things to be seized.

**This is an extremely important amendment to prevent the abuse of state police powers. Essentially, unreasonable searches or seizures of homes, persons, or property cannot be undertaken without probable cause or a warrant that specifically describes the place to be searched, the person involved, and suspicious things to be seized.**

### AMENDMENT 5—GRAND JURIES, SELF-INCRIMINATION, DOUBLE JEOPARDY, DUE PROCESS, AND EMINENT DOMAIN

No person shall be held to answer for a capital, or otherwise infamous crime, unless on a presentment or indictment of a Grand jury, except in cases arising in the land or naval forces, or in the Militia, when in actual service in time of War or public danger; nor shall any person be subject for the same offence to be twice put in jeopardy of life or limb, nor shall be compelled in any criminal case to be a witness against himself, nor be deprived of life, liberty, or property, without due process of law, nor shall private property be taken for public use, without just compensation.

**Only a grand jury can indict a person for a federal crime. This provision does not apply to state/local governments. This amendment also covers double jeopardy, or being tried twice for the same crime in the same jurisdiction. Note that since the federal government and state governments are different jurisdictions, one could be tried in each jurisdiction for essentially the same crime. For example, it is a federal crime to kill a congressperson. It is also a state crime to murder anyone. Further, this amendment also covers the prohibition of self-incrimination. Pleading the 5th Amendment is common among defendants. The deprivation of life, liberty, or property by any level of government is prohibited unless due process of law is applied. Finally, private property may not be taken under**

**the doctrine of "eminent domain" unless the government provides just compensation and the taking is for public purposes.**

### AMENDMENT 6—CRIMINAL COURT PROCEDURES

In all criminal prosecutions, the accused shall enjoy the right to a speedy and public trial, by an impartial jury of the State and district wherein the crime shall have been committed, which district shall have been previously ascertained by law, and to be informed of the nature and cause of the accusation, to be confronted with the witnesses against him, to have compulsory process for obtaining witnesses in his favor, and to have the Assistance of Counsel for his defence.

**This amendment requires public trials by jury for criminal prosecutions. Anyone accused of a crime is guaranteed the right to be informed of the charges; confront witnesses; to subpoena witnesses for his or her defense; and to have a lawyer for his or her defense. The government must provide a lawyer for a defendant unable to afford one.**

### AMENDMENT 7—TRIAL BY JURY IN COMMON LAW CASES

In Suits at common law, where the value in controversy shall exceed twenty dollars, the right of trial by jury shall be preserved, and no fact tried by a jury shall be otherwise re-examined in any Court of the United States, than according to the rules of the common law.

**This amendment is practically without meaning in modern times. Statutory law has largely superseded common law. Federal civil law suits with a guaranteed jury are now restricted to cases that exceed $50,000. The Bill of Rights, which includes the right to trial by jury, applied orginally only to the national government. Beginning in 1925, the USSC began a selective process of incorporating provisions of the Bill of Rights, applicable to state/local governments as well. There are just a few provisions that have not been thus incorporated. Trial by jury is one. Some state/local governments have trials by judges, not by juries.**

### AMENDMENT 8—BAIL, CRUEL AND UNUSUAL PUNISHMENT

Excessive bail shall not be required, nor excessive fines imposed, nor cruel and unusual punishments inflicted.

**Capital punishment is covered by this amendment, which also prohibits excessive bail. But this is relative. Million-dollar bails are not uncommon in some cases. One federal judge offered voluntary castration for sex offenders in lieu of jail time. Higher courts held this to be a cruel or unusual punishment. But it is the death penalty that generates the most heated controversy. Court cases challenging the constitutionality of capital punishment cite this amendment's language prohibiting cruel and unusual punishment. For a period of 4 years, the USSC banned capital punishment. When states modified their statutes to provide a two-part judicial process of guilt determination and punishment, the USSC allowed the reinstitution of capital punishment by the states.**

## AMENDMENT 9—RIGHTS RETAINED BY THE PEOPLE

The enumeration in the Constitution of certain rights, shall not be construed to deny or disparage others retained by the people.

**This amendment implies that there may be other rights of the people not specified by the previous amendments. Indeed, the Warren Court established the right to privacy even though it is not specifically mentioned in any previous amendment.**

## AMENDMENT 10—RESERVED POWERS OF THE STATES

The powers not delegated to the United States by the Constitution, nor prohibited by it to the States, are reserved to the States respectively, or to the people.

**The 10th Amendment was seen as the reservoir of reserved powers for state governments. If the national government had been limited only to expressed powers in Article 1, Section 8, of the Constitution, this would have been the case. But the doctrine of implied national government powers, which was established by the U.S. Supreme Court in *McCulloch v. Maryland* in 1819, made the intent of this amendment almost meaningless. What reserved powers that were retained by the states were virtually removed by the U.S. Supreme Court's decision in the *Garcia v. San Antonio Metropolitan Transit Authority* case in 1985, which basically told state/local governments not to look to the courts to protect their residual rights but rather to their political representatives. In subsequent cases, the USSC has retreated somewhat from this position when the court found the federal government encroaching in state jurisdictional areas.**

## AMENDMENT 11—SUITS AGAINST THE STATES

### [Ratified February 7, 1795]

The Judicial power of the United States shall not be construed to extend to any suit in law or equity, commenced or prosecuted against one of the United States by Citizens of another State, or by Citizens or Subjects of any Foreign State.

**Article 3 of the U.S. Constitution originally allowed federal jurisdiction in cases of one state citizen against another state citizen or state. This amendment removes federal jurisdiction in this area. In essence, states may not be sued in federal court by citizens of another state or country.**

## AMENDMENT 12—ELECTION OF THE PRESIDENT

### [Ratified June 15, 1804]

The Electors shall meet in their respective states, and vote by ballot for President and Vice-President, one of whom, at least, shall not be an inhabitant of the same state with themselves; they shall name in their ballots the person voted for as President, and in distinct ballots the person voted for as Vice-President, and they shall make distinct lists of all persons voted for as President, and of all persons voted for as Vice-President, and of the number of votes for each, which lists they shall sign and certify, and transmit sealed to the seat of the government of the United States, directed to the President of the Senate;—The President of the Senate shall, in presence of the Senate and House of Representatives, open all the certificates and the votes shall then be counted;—The person having the greatest number of votes for President, shall be the President, if such number be a majority of the whole number of Electors appointed; and if no person have such majority, then from the persons having the highest numbers not exceeding three on the list of those voted for as President, the House of Representatives shall choose immediately, by ballot, the President. But in choosing the President, the votes shall be taken by states, the representation from each state having one vote; a quorum for this purpose shall consist of a member or members from two-thirds of the states, and a majority of all states shall be necessary to a choice. And if the House of Representatives shall not choose a President whenever the right of choice shall devolve upon them, before the fourth day of March next following, then the Vice-President shall act as President, as in the case of the death or other constitutional disability of the President.[11] The person having the greatest number of votes as Vice-President, shall be the Vice-President, if such a number be a majority of the whole numbers of Electors appointed, and if no person have a majority, then from the two highest numbers on the list, the Senate shall choose the Vice-President, a quorum for the purpose shall consist of two-thirds of the whole number of Senators, and a majority of the whole number shall be necessary to a choice. But no person constitutionally ineligible to the office of President shall be eligible to that of Vice-President of the United States.

**This was a necessary amendment to correct a flaw in the Constitution covering operations of the Electoral College. In the election of 1800, both Thomas Jefferson and Aaron Burr, of the same Democratic-Republican Party, received the same number of electoral votes, 73, for president. Article II of the original Constitution specified that each elector would cast two ballots. It did not specify for whom. This amendment clarifies that the electoral vote must be specific for president and vice president. The original Constitution provided that if no candidate received a majority of electoral votes, the House would decide from the candidates with the top five vote totals. This amendment reduces the candidate field to the top three vote totals. If the House delays in this selection past the fourth day of March, the elected vice president will act as president until the House selects the president. The original Constitution provided that the candidate with the second highest number of electoral votes would become vice president.**

**This amendment, which requires a separate vote tally for vice president, provides for selection by the U.S. Senate if no vice presidential candidate receives an electoral vote majority.**

## AMENDMENT 13—PROHIBITION OF SLAVERY

### [Ratified December 6, 1865]

*Section 1* Neither slavery nor involuntary servitude, except as a punishment for crime whereof the party shall have been duly convicted, shall exist within the United States, or any place subject to their jurisdiction.

*Section 2* Congress shall have power to enforce this article by appropriate legislation.

---

[11]Changed by the 20th Amendment

**This is the first of the three Civil War amendments. Slavery is prohibited under all circumstances. In-voluntary servitude is also prohibited unless it is a punishment for a convicted crime.**

### Amendment 14—Citizenship, Due Process, and Equal Protection of the Laws

#### [Ratified July 9, 1868]

*Section 1*   All persons born or naturalized in the United States, and subject to the jurisdiction thereof, are citizens of the United States and of the State wherein they reside. No State shall make or enforce any law which shall abridge the privileges or immunities of citizens of the United States; nor shall any State deprive any person of life, liberty, or property, without due process of law; nor deny to any person within its jurisdiction the equal protection of the laws.

**This section defines the meaning of U.S. citizenship and protection of these citizenship rights. It also establishes the Equal Protection Clause that each state must guarantee to its citizens. It extended the provisions of the 5th Amendment of due process and protection of life, liberty, and property and made these applicable to the states.**

*Section 2*   Representatives shall be apportioned among the several States according to their respective numbers, counting the whole number of persons in each State, excluding Indians not taxed. But when the right to vote at any election for the choice of electors for President and Vice President of the United States, Representatives in Congress, the Executive and Judicial officers of a State, or the members of the Legislature thereof, is denied to any of the male inhabitants of such State, being twenty-one[12] years of age, and citizens of the United States, or in any way abridged, except for participation in rebellion, or other crime, the basis of representation therein shall be reduced in the proportion which the number of such male citizens shall bear to the whole number of male citizens twenty-one years of age in such State.

**This section changes the Three-Fifths Clause of the original Constitution. Now all male citizens, 21 or older, will be used to calculate representation in the House of Representatives. If a state denies the right to vote to any male 21 or older, the number of denied citizens will be deducted from the over-all state total to determine representation.**

*Section 3*   No person shall be a Senator or Representative in Congress, or elector of President and Vice President, or hold any office, civil or military under the United States, or under any State, who, having previously taken an oath, as a member of Congress, or as an officer of the United States, or as a member of any State legislature, or as an executive or judicial officer of any State, to support the Constitution of the United States, shall have engaged in insurrection or rebellion against the same, or given aid or comfort to the enemies thereof. But Congress may by a vote of two-thirds of each House, remove such disability.

**This section disqualifies from federal office or elector for president or vice president anyone who rebelled or participated in an insurrection against the Constitution. This was specifically directed against citizens of Southern states. Congress by a 2/3 vote could override this provision.**

*Section 4*   The validity of the public debt of the United States, authorized by law, including debts incurred for payment of pensions and bounties for services in suppressing insurrection or rebellion, shall not be questioned. But neither the United States nor any State shall assume or pay any debt or obligation incurred in aid of insurrection or rebellion against the United States or any claim for the loss or emancipation of any slave, but all such debts, obligations and claims shall be held illegal and void.

*Section 5*   The Congress shall have power to enforce, by appropriate legislation, the provisions of this article.

**These sections guarantee payment of Civil War debts incurred by the U.S. government but declare void any debts incurred by the Confederacy.**

### Amendment 15—The Right to Vote

#### [Ratified February 3, 1870]

*Section 1*   The right of citizens of the United States to vote shall not be denied or abridged by the United States or by any State on account of race, color, or previous condition of servitude.

*Section 2*   The Congress shall have power to enforce this article by appropriate legislation.

**This final Civil War amendment guarantees that voting rights cannot be denied by any states on account of race, color, or previous servitude. Unfortunately, it did not mention gender. Accordingly, all male citizens 21 or over were guaranteed the right to vote by this amendment.**

### Amendment 16—Income Taxes

#### [Ratified February 3, 1913]

The Congress shall have power to lay and collect taxes on incomes, from whatever source derived, without apportionment among the several States, and without regard to any census or enumeration.

**Article 1, Section 9, of the original Constitution prohibited Congress from enacting a direct tax (head tax) unless in proportion to a census. Congress in 1894 passed an income tax law, levying a 2 percent tax on incomes over $4,000. In 1895, the U.S. Supreme Court in a split decision (5–4) found that the income tax was a direct tax not apportioned among the states and was thus unconstitutional. Thus, Congress proposed an amendment allowing it to enact an income tax. Once this amendment was ratified, the flow of tax money to Washington increased tremendously.**

### Amendment 17—Direct Election of Senators

#### [Ratified April 8, 1913]

The Senate of the United States shall be composed of two Senators from each State, elected by the people thereof, for six years and each Senator shall have one vote. The electors in each State shall have the qualifications requisite for electors of the most numerous branch of the State legislatures.

When vacancies happen in the representation of any State in the Senate, the executive authority of such State shall issue writs of election to fill such vacancies: Provided, That the legislature of any State may empower the executive thereof to make temporary

---

[12]Changed by the 26th Amendment

appointment until the people fill the vacancies by election as the legislature may direct.

This amendment shall not be so construed as to affect the election or term of any Senator chosen before it becomes valid as part of the Constitution.

**Prior to this amendment, U.S. senators were selected by state legislatures. Now U.S. senators would be selected by popular vote in each state. Further, the governor of each state may fill vacancies, subject to state laws.**

### AMENDMENT 18—PROHIBITION

### [Ratified January 16, 1919, Repealed December 5, 1933 by Amendment 21]

*Section 1* After one year from the ratification of this article the manufacture, sale, or transportation of intoxicating liquors within, the importation thereof into, or the exportation thereof from the United States and all territory subject to the jurisdiction thereof for beverage purposes is hereby prohibited.

*Section 2* The Congress and the several States shall have concurrent power to enforce this article by appropriate legislation.

*Section 3* This article shall be inoperative unless it shall have been ratified as an amendment to the Constitution by the legislatures of the several States, as provided in the Constitution, within seven years from the date of the submission hereof to the States by the Congress.[13]

**This amendment was largely the work of the Women's Christian Temperance Union and essentially banned the manufacture, sale, or transportation of alcoholic beverages. Unintended consequences of this attempt to legislate morality were the brewing of "bathtub gin" and moonshine liquor, and the involvement of the mob in importing liquor from Canada. This ill-fated social experiment was corrected by the 21st Amendment. This is also the first amendment for which Congress fixed a period for ratification—7 years.**

### AMENDMENT 19—WOMEN'S SUFFRAGE

### [Ratified August 18, 1920]

The right of the citizens of the United States to vote shall not be denied or abridged by the United States or by any State on account of sex.

Congress shall have power to enforce this article by appropriate legislation .

**At long last, women achieved voting parity with men.**

### AMENDMENT 20—THE LAME DUCK AMENDMENT

### [Ratified January 23, 1933]

*Section 1* The terms of the President and Vice President shall end at noon on the 20th day of January, and the terms of the Senators and Representatives at noon on the 3d day of January, of the years in which such terms would have ended if this article had not been ratified, and the terms of their successors shall then begin.

*Section 2* The Congress shall assemble at least once in every year, and such meeting shall begin at noon on the 3d day of January, unless they shall by law appoint a different day.

*Section 3* If, at the time fixed for the beginning of the term of the President, the President elect shall have died, the Vice President elect shall become President. If a President shall not have been chosen before the time fixed for the beginning of his term, or if the President elect shall have failed to qualify, then the Vice President elect shall act as President until a President shall have qualified, and the Congress may by law provide for the case wherein neither a President elect nor a Vice President elect shall have qualified, declaring who shall then act as President, or the manner in which one who is to act shall be selected, and such person shall act accordingly until a President or Vice President shall have qualified.

*Section 4* The Congress may by law provide for the case of the death of any of the persons from whom the House of Representatives may choose a President whenever the right of choice shall have devolved upon them, and for the case of the death of any of the persons from whom the Senate may choose a Vice President whenever the right of choice shall have devolved upon them.

*Section 5* Sections 1 and 2 shall take effect on the 15th day of October following the ratification of this article.

*Section 6* This article shall be inoperative unless it shall have been ratified as an amendment to the Constitution by the legislatures of three-fourths of the several States within seven years from the date of its submission.

**Called the Lame Duck amendment, this amendment fixes the dates for the end of presidential and legislative terms. A new president is elected in November, but the current president remains in office until January 20 of the following year. Thus, the term "lame duck." Legislative terms begin earlier, on January 3.**

### AMENDMENT 21—REPEAL OF PROHIBITION

### [Ratified December 5, 1933]

*Section 1* The eighteenth article of amendment to the Constitution of the United States is hereby repealed.

*Section 2* The transportation or importation into any State, Territory, or possession of the United States for delivery or use therein of intoxicating liquors, in violation of the laws thereof, is hereby prohibited.

*Section 3* This article shall be inoperative unless it shall have been ratified as an amendment to the Constitution by conventions in the several States, as provided in the Constitution, within seven years from the date of the submission hereof to the States by the Congress.

**This unusual amendment nullified the 18th Amendment. It ended federal Prohibition; now only state laws regulate liquors.**

### AMENDMENT 22—NUMBER OF PRESIDENTIAL TERMS

### [Ratified February 27, 1951]

*Section 1* No person shall be elected to the office of the President more than twice, and no person who has held the office of President, or acted as President, for more than two years of a term to which some other person was elected President shall be elected to the office of the President more than once. But this article shall not apply to any person holding the office of President when this article was proposed by the Congress, and shall

---

[13]Repealed by the 21st Amendment

not prevent any person who may be holding the office of President, or acting as President, during the term within which this article becomes operative from holding the office of President or acting as President during the remainder of such term.

*Section 2*　This article shall be inoperative unless it shall have been ratified as an amendment to the Constitution by the legislatures of three-fourths of the several states within seven years from the date of its submission to the states by the Congress.

**This amendment could be called the Franklin D. Roosevelt amendment. It was FDR who broke the previous unwritten custom of no more than two-term presidents. Democrat Roosevelt won an unprecedented four terms as president. When the Republicans took control of the Congress in 1948, they pushed through the 22nd Amendment, limiting the U.S. president to a lifetime of two full four-year terms of office.**

### AMENDMENT 23—PRESIDENTIAL ELECTORS FOR THE DISTRICT OF COLUMBIA

#### [Ratified March 29, 1961]

*Section 1*　The District constituting the seat of government of the United States shall appoint in such manner as the Congress may direct:

A number of electors of President and Vice President equal to the whole number of Senators and Representatives in Congress to which the District would be entitled if it were a state, but in no event more than the least populous state, they shall be in addition to those appointed by the states, but they shall be considered for the purposes of the election of President and Vice President, to be electors appointed by a state, and they shall meet in the District and perform such duties as provided by the twelfth article of amendment.

*Section 2*　The Congress shall have power to enforce this article by appropriate legislation.

**This amendment gave electoral votes to the citizens of Washington, D.C., which is not a state and thus not included in the original scheme of state electoral votes. Currently, Washington, D.C., has 3 electoral votes, bringing the total of presidential electoral votes to 538. Puerto Ricans are citizens of the U.S. but have no electoral votes.**

### AMENDMENT 24—THE ANTI-POLL TAX AMENDMENT

#### [Ratified January 23, 1964]

*Section 1*　The right of citizens of the United States to vote in any primary or other election for President or Vice President, for electors for President or Vice President or for Senator or Representative in Congress, shall not be denied or abridged by the United States or any state by reason of failure to pay any poll tax or other tax.

*Section 2*　The Congress shall have power to enforce this article by appropriate legislation.

**The poll tax was a procedure used mostly in southern states to discourage poor white and black voters from registering to vote. Essentially, one would have to pay a tax to register to vote. The tax was usually not much. But for a poor white or black voter, this might not be disposable income. As part of the assault against disenfran-**

**chisement of voters, the poll tax was abolished. Literacy tests, another device to disqualify voters, were abolished by the Voting Rights Act of 1965.**

### AMENDMENT 25—PRESIDENTIAL DISABILITY, VICE PRESIDENTIAL VACANCIES

#### [Ratified February 10, 1967]

*Section 1*　In case of the removal of the President from office or his death or resignation, the Vice President shall become President.

*Section 2*　Whenever there is a vacancy in the office of the Vice President, the President shall nominate a Vice President who shall take the office upon confirmation by a majority vote of both Houses of Congress.

*Section 3*　Whenever the President transmits to the President pro tempore of the Senate and the Speaker of the House of Representatives his written declaration that he is unable to discharge the powers and duties of his office, and until he transmits to them a written declaration to the contrary, such powers and duties shall be discharged by the Vice President as Acting President.

*Section 4*　Whenever the Vice President and a majority of either the principal officers of the executive departments or of such other body as Congress may by law provide, transmit to the President pro tempore of the Senate and the Speaker of the House of Representatives their written declaration that the President is unable to discharge the powers and duties of his office, the Vice President shall immediately assume the powers and duties of the office as Acting President.

Thereafter, when the President transmits to the President pro tempore of the Senate and the Speaker of the House of Representatives his written declaration that no inability exists, he shall resume the powers and duties of his office unless the Vice President and a majority of either the principal officers of the executive departments, or of such other body as Congress may by law provide, transmit within four days to the President pro tempore of the Senate and the Speaker of the House of Representatives their written declaration that the President is unable to discharge the powers and duties of his office. Thereupon Congress shall decide the issue, assembling within forty-eight hours for that purpose if not in session. If the Congress, within twenty-one days after receipt of the latter written declaration, or, if Congress is not in session, within twenty-one days after Congress is required to assemble, determines by two-thirds vote of both Houses that the President is unable to discharge the powers and duties of his office, the Vice President shall continue to discharge the same as Acting President; otherwise the President shall resume the powers and duties of his office.

**During the administration of President Woodrow Wilson, his final year in office, in 1919, was marked by serious illness. It is rumored that his wife acted as president. There was no constitutional provision to cover an incapacitating illness of a president. So this amendment provides a procedure for this eventuality. The president can inform congressional leaders of his incapacitation and the vice president takes over. When he recovers, the president can so inform congressional leaders and he resumes office.**

**But the amendment also recognizes that the president may not be able or wish to indicate this debilitation; so the vice president and a majority of cabinet members can inform congressional leaders and the vice president takes over. When the president informs congressional leadership that**

he is back in form, he resumes the presidency unless the vice president and a majority of the cabinet disagree. Then Congress must decide. The likelihood that this procedure will ever be used is very small.

The most immediate importance of this amendment concerns the office of vice president. The original Constitution did not address the issue of a vacancy in this office. So the 25th Amendment established the procedure, just in time! This amendment was ratified in 1967. In 1973, the sitting vice president, Spiro Agnew, resigned his office. Under the provisions of this amendment, President Nixon nominated Gerald Ford as vice president. A former member of the House, the Congress quickly approved him. But a year later, President Nixon also resigned. Now Vice President Ford became President Ford, and he in turn appointed Nelson Rockefeller as the new vice president. For the first time in our history, we had both a president and vice president, neither of whom was elected by the Electoral College.

### AMENDMENT 26—EIGHTEEN-YEAR-OLD VOTE

#### [Ratified July 1, 1971]

*Section 1*   The right of citizens of the United States, who are 18 years of age or older, to vote, shall not be denied or abridged by the United States or by any state on account of age.

*Section 2*   The Congress shall have power to enforce this article by appropriate legislation.

During the Vietnam War, 18-year-olds were being drafted and sent out to possibly die in the service of their country. Yet they did not even have the right to vote. This incongruity led to the 26th Amendment, which lowered the legal voting age from 21 to 18.

### AMENDMENT 27—CONGRESSIONAL SALARIES

#### [Ratified May 7, 1992]

No law varying the compensation for the services of the Senators and Representatives shall take effect until an election of Representatives shall be intervened.

This is a "sleeper" amendment that was part of 12 amendments originally submitted by the first Congress to the states for ratification. The states only ratified 10 of the 12, which collectively became known as the Bill of Rights. But since Congress did not set a time limit for ratification, the other two amendments remained on the table. Much to the shock of the body politic, in 1992, 3/4 of the states ratified original amendment 12 of 12. This reflected the disgust of seeing Congress continuing to increase its salary and benefits. The amendment delays any increase of compensation for at least one election cycle.*

---

*Annotations by James Corey, High Point University.

# 4 FEDERALISM
## Dividing Governmental Power

## Chapter Outline

- Indestructible Union, Indestructible States
- Why Federalism? The Argument for a "Compound Republic"
- The Original Design of Federalism
- The Evolution of American Federalism
- Federalism Revived?
- Money and Power Flow to Washington
- Coercive Federalism: Preemptions and Mandates
- Summary Notes

## Think About Politics

**1** Which level of government deals best with the problems it faces?
Federal ☐ State ☐ Local ☐

**2** In which level of government do you have the most confidence?
Federal ☐ State ☐ Local ☐

**3** Should the national government be able to prosecute a high school student for bringing a gun to school?
Yes ☐ No ☐

**4** Should welfare benefits be the same in all states?
Yes ☐ No ☐

**5** Should each state determine its own minimum age for drinking alcohol?
Yes ☐ No ☐

**6** Should each state determine its own maximum highway speed limit?
Yes ☐ No ☐

**7** When the federal government requires states to provide safe drinking water, clean air, or access for the handicapped, should it provide funds to carry out these mandates?
Yes ☐ No ☐

*What should be the relationship between the national government and the states? Questions like these lie at the heart of the issue of who gets what, when, and how. They affect employment, transportation, health, education, the very air we breathe. And when there has been disagreement, the nation has been plunged into conflict at best and the bloodiest war in its history at worst.*

## Indestructible Union, Indestructible States

In December 1860 South Carolina seceded from the Union and in April 1861 authorized its state militia to expel U.S. troops from Fort Sumter in Charleston harbor. Although there is no provision in the Constitution for states leaving the Union, eleven southern states—South Carolina, Mississippi, Florida, Alabama, Georgia, Louisiana, Texas, Virginia, Arkansas, Tennessee, and North Carolina, in that order—argued that the Union was a voluntary association and they were entitled to withdraw.[1] President Abraham Lincoln declared these states to be in armed rebellion and sent federal troops to crush the "rebels." The result was the nation's bloodiest war: more than 250,000 battle deaths and another 250,000 deaths from disease and privation, out of a total population of less than 30 million.

Following the Civil War, Chief Justice Salmon P. Chase confirmed what had been decided on the battlefield. "The Constitution in all its provisions looks to an indestructible union, composed of indestructible states."[2]

**Federalism** divides power between two separate authorities—the nation and the states—each of which enforces its own laws directly on its citizens. Both the nation and the states pass laws, impose taxes, spend money, and maintain their own courts. Neither the nation nor the states can dissolve the Union or amend the Constitution without the consent of the other. The Constitution itself is the only legal source of authority for both the states and the nation, the states do not get their power from the national government, and the national government does not get its power from the states. Both national and state governments derive their power directly from the people.

American federalism differs from a **unitary system** of government, in which formal authority rests with the national government, and whatever powers are exercised by states, provinces, or subdivisions are given to those governments by the national government. Most of the world's governments—including France and Britain—are unitary. Federalism also differs from a **confederation** of states, in which the national government relies on the states for its authority, not the people (see Figure 4.1). Under

**Figure 4.1**   The Federal, Confederation, and Unitary Systems of Government

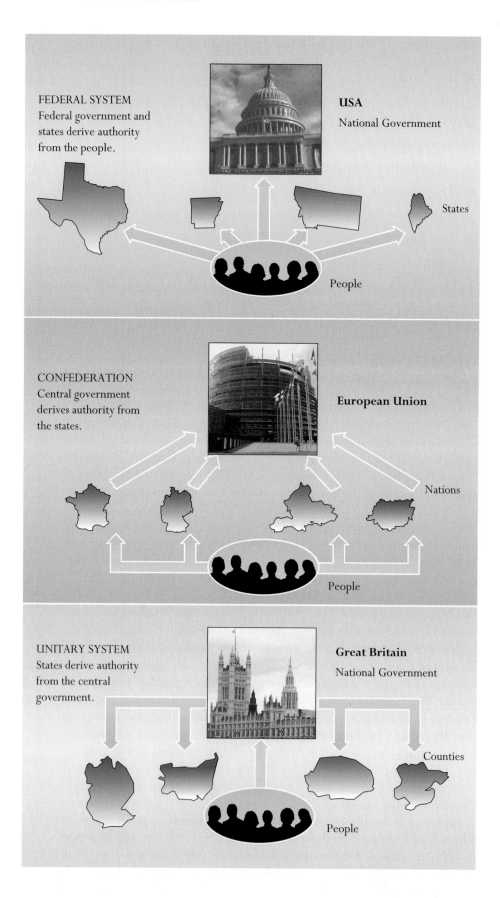

**Table 4.1   How Many American Governments?**

| | |
|---|---|
| U.S. government | 1 |
| States | 50 |
| Counties | 3,034 |
| Municipalities | 19,429 |
| Townships | 16,504 |
| Special districts | 35,052 |
| School districts | 13,506 |
| **All governments** | **87,525** |

Source: *Statistical Abstract of the United States*, 2006, p. 272.

the Articles of Confederation of 1781, the United States was a confederation. The national government could not even levy taxes; it had to ask the states for revenue. Like the United States, a number of other countries were confederations before establishing federal systems, and today new types of confederations with limited functions are being formed (see *Compared to What?* "The European Union").

People in the United States often think of the *federal government* when the word *government* comes up. In fact, today there are more than 87,000 American governments. These state and local governments are important in American life, for they provide such essential day-to-day services as schools, water, and police and fire departments (see Table 4.1). However, the U.S. Constitution, the supreme law of the land, recognizes the existence of only the national government and the states. Local governments have no guarantees of power—or even existence—under the U.S. Constitution. Whatever powers they have are given to them by their state governments. States can create or abolish local governments, grant or withhold their powers, or change their boundaries without their consent. Some local governments have powers guaranteed in *state* constitutions, and some are even given **home rule**—the power to pass laws affecting local affairs, so long as those laws do not conflict with state or federal laws. About 60,000 of these 87,000 governments have the power to levy taxes to support activities authorized by state law.

In short, the American federal system is large and complex, with three levels of government—national, state, and local—sharing power. Indeed, the numbers and complexity of governments in the United States make **intergovernmental relations**—all of the interactions among these governments and their officials—a major concern of political scientists and policy makers.

# Why Federalism? The Argument for a "Compound Republic"

The nation's Founders believed that "republican principles" would help make government responsible to the people, but they also argued that "auxiliary precautions" were necessary to protect the liberties of minorities and individuals. They believed that majority rule in a democratic government made it particularly important to devise ways to protect minorities and individuals from "unjust" and "interested" *majorities*. They believed that federalism would better protect liberty, disperse power, and manage "faction" (conflict).

**federalism** A constitutional arrangement whereby power is divided between national and subnational governments, each of which enforces its own laws directly on its citizens and neither of which can alter the arrangement without the consent of the other.

**unitary system** Constitutional arrangement whereby authority rests with the national government; subnational governments have only those powers given to them by the national government.

**confederation** Constitutional arrangement whereby the national government is created by and relies on subnational governments for its authority.

**home rule** Power of local government to pass laws affecting local affairs, so long as those laws do not conflict with state or federal laws.

— Think Again —
Which level of government deals best with the problems it faces?

**intergovernmental relations** Network of political, financial, and administrative relationships between units of the federal government and those of state and local governments.

# COMPARED TO WHAT?

## The European Union

The European Union (EU) incorporates features of both federalism and confederation. The EU now includes twenty-five member nations and embraces more than 455 million people. It grew slowly from a European Economic Community established in 1957 (designed to reduce and eventually abolish all tariffs among member nations), through a European Community established in 1965 (designed to create a single market free of all barriers to the movement of goods, services, capital, and labor), to its much more unified European Union established in 1991.

### European Parliament

Deputies of the European Parliament are directly elected every five years by the EU's 455 million citizens. The major political parties operating in each of the member nations nominate candidates. The Parliament oversees the EU budget and passes on proposals to the Council of Ministers and the Commission. The Parliament also passes on new applicants to the EU.

### Distribution of Seats in the European Parliament

| | | | |
|---|---|---|---|
| Austria | 18 | Latvia | 9 |
| Belgium | 24 | Lithuania | 13 |
| Cyprus | 6 | Luxembourg | 6 |
| Czech Republic | 24 | Malta | 5 |
| Denmark | 14 | Netherlands | 27 |
| Estonia | 6 | Poland | 54 |
| Finland | 14 | Portugal | 24 |
| France | 78 | Slovakia | 14 |
| Germany | 99 | Slovenia | 7 |
| Greece | 24 | Spain | 54 |
| Hungary | 24 | Sweden | 19 |
| Ireland | 13 | United Kingdom | 78 |
| Italy | 78 | | |

### Council of the EU

The Council is the EU's principal decision-making body. It is composed of the foreign ministers of the member nations. Each country takes the presidency for six months; the Council votes by majority, although each country's vote is weighted differently.

### The Commission

The Commission of the EU supervises the implementation of EU treaties, implements EU policies, and manages EU funds. It is composed of 20 commissioners appointed by member governments. The five largest countries—France, Germany, Italy, Spain, and the United Kingdom—appoint two commissioners each; the remaining countries appoint one commissioner each.

### The Court of Justice

A Court of Justice hears complaints about member governments' treaty violations and interprets EU treaties and legislation. Its fifteen justices are appointed by the member governments and serve six-year terms.

### The "Euro"

Perhaps the most far-reaching accomplishment of the EU was the introduction of the "euro"—a single European currency for use in all member states. The euro was first introduced January 1, 1999, and officially replaced old national currencies—such as francs, marks, pesetas, and lira—on January 1, 2002. However, the United Kingdom, Sweden, and Denmark have refused to substitute the euro for their own currency.

### The Future of the Union

The future of the EU remains under discussion. A lengthy EU Constitution was to be submitted to

---

**Protecting Liberty**   Constitutional guarantees of individual liberty do not enforce themselves. The Founders argued that to guarantee liberty, government should be structured to encourage "opposite and rival" centers of power *within* and *among* governments. So they settled on both *federalism*—dividing powers between the national and state governments—and *separation of powers*—the dispersal of power among branches within the national government.

**European Union Online Official EU site**
Describes the structure of the organization, its membership, current issues, and so forth.
*www.europa.eu.int*

In the compound republic of America, the power surrendered by the people is first divided between two distinct governments, and then the portion allotted to each is subdivided among distinct and separate departments. Hence a double security arises to the rights of the people. The different governments will control each other, at the same time that each will be controlled by itself.[3]

the voters in each nation. Ten nations approved it, but in 2005 voters in France and the Netherlands rejected it. Inasmuch as all twenty-five nations must approve it in order for it to go into effect, its future is in serious doubt.

At present the EU is more of an economic alliance than a sovereign political state. Voters in member nations may not be as yet willing to enact a common Bill of Rights or depend upon a central government (in Brussels) for the protection of their individual liberties. How much power will be allocated to the central EU government relative to the powers of member nations? Note that these and similar questions were the same as many of those discussed in the American Constitutional Convention of 1787 (see Chapter 3).

This map, produced by the EU, uses the languages of the nations portrayed. Test yourself by translating these names into English, for example Osterreich = Austria.

*Source:* Reprinted from http://www.europa.eu.int/abc/maps/index_en.htm. Copyright © European Communities, 1995–2006.

Thus the Founders deliberately tried to create competition within and among governmental units as a means of protecting liberty. Rather than rely on the "better motives" of leaders, the Founders sought to construct a system in which governments and government officials would be constrained by competition with other governments and other government officials: "Ambition must be made to counteract ambition."[4]

**Dispersing Power** Federalism distributes power widely among different sets of leaders, national as well as state and local officeholders. The Founders believed that multiple leadership groups offered more protection against tyranny than a single set of all-powerful leaders. State and local government offices also provide a political base for the opposition party when it has lost a national election. In this way, state and local governments contribute to party competition in the

**Council of State Governments**
Official Organization of U.S. states, providing information on their governmental structures, officials, and current issues. *www.csg.org*

## UP CLOSE

# Federalism Is the Enemy of Uniformity

Should taxes and services be uniform throughout the United States? Or should federalism allow variations among the states in tax burdens as well as provided?

Federalism allows citizens in each state to decide levels of public services (schools, transportation, police and fire protection, and so forth, and other state and local functions), as well as how much they pay in state and local taxes. If some voters want more public services and are willing to pay higher taxes for them, and other voters want fewer public services and enjoy lower taxes, then federalism allows for a better match between citizen preferences and public policy. Of course, the result is a lack of uniformity across the states.

Consider, for example, differences in per capita state and local taxes paid by residents of different states.

**Ten high-tax states**

| | |
|---|---|
| New York | $4,640 |
| Connecticut | 4,373 |
| New Jersey | 4,038 |
| Massachusetts | 3,721 |
| Minnesota | 3,673 |
| Maryland | 3,646 |
| Wyoming | 3,644 |
| Maine | 3,567 |
| California | 3,440 |
| Wisconsin | 3,421 |

**Ten low-tax states**

| | |
|---|---|
| Oregon | $2,558 |
| Oklahoma | 2,516 |
| Idaho | 2,451 |
| South Dakota | 2,423 |
| Arkansas | 2,387 |
| South Carolina | 2,376 |
| Montana | 2,346 |
| Mississippi | 2,275 |
| Tennessee | 2,241 |
| Alabama | 2,170 |

### States Without Income Taxes

| | | |
|---|---|---|
| Alaska | New Hampshire[a] | Texas |
| Florida | South Dakota | Washington |
| Nevada | Tennessee[a] | Wyoming |

### States Taxing Individual Income (rate ranges in parentheses)

| | | |
|---|---|---|
| Alabama (2.0–5.0) | Kentucky (2.0–6.0) | North Carolina (6.0–8.25) |
| Arizona (2.8–5.0) | Louisiana (2.0–6.0) | North Dakota (2.1–15.6) |
| Arkansas (1.0–7.0) | Maine (2.0–8.5) | Ohio (0.7–7.5) |
| California (1.0–9.3) | Maryland (2.0–4.8) | Oklahoma (0.5–6.75) |
| Colorado (4.6) | Massachusetts (5) | Oregon (5.0–9.0) |
| Connecticut (3.0–5) | Michigan (4) | Pennsylvania (2.8) |
| Delaware (2.2–6.0) | Minnesota (5.3–7.8) | Rhode Island (26% federal)[b] |
| Georgia (1.0–6.0) | Mississippi (3.0–5.0) | South Carolina (2.5–7.0) |
| Hawaii (1.4–8.25) | Missouri (1.5–6.0) | Utah (2.3–7.0) |
| Idaho (1.6–7.8) | Montana (2.0–11.0) | Vermont (3.6–9.5) |
| Illinois (3.0) | Nebraska (2.5–6.8) | Virginia (2.0–5.75) |
| Indiana (3.4) | New Jersey (1.4–6.4) | West Virginia (3.0–6.5) |
| Iowa (0.4–9.0) | New Mexico (1.7–6.8) | Wisconsin (4.6–6.8) |
| Kansas (3.5–6.5) | New York (4.0–7.7) | |

[a]State income tax is limited to dividends and interest only.

[b]State income taxes determined as a percentage of federal income tax liability.

*Source:* Data from Council of State Governments, *Book of the States, 2004–05* (Lexington, KY: Council of State Governments, 2005).

United States by helping to tide over the losing party after electoral defeat at the national level so that it can remain strong enough to challenge incumbents at the next election. And finally, state and local governments often provide a training ground for national political leaders. National leaders can be drawn from a pool of leaders experienced in state and local government.

**Increasing Participation**    Federalism allows more people to participate in the political system. With more than 87,000 governments in the United States—state, county, municipality, township, special district, and school district—nearly a million people hold some kind of public office.

**Improving Efficiency**    Federalism also makes government more manageable and efficient. Imagine the bureaucracy, red tape, and confusion if every governmental activity—police, schools, roads, fire fighting, garbage collection, sewage disposal, and so forth—in every local community in the nation were controlled by a centralized administration in Washington. Government can become arbitrary when a bureaucracy far from the scene directs local officials. Thus decentralization often softens the rigidity of law.

**Ensuring Policy Responsiveness**    Federalism encourages policy responsiveness. The existence of multiple governments offering different packages of benefits and costs allows a better match between citizen preferences and public policy. Americans are very mobile. People and businesses can "vote with their feet" by relocating to those states and communities that most closely conform to their own policy preferences. This mobility not only facilitates a better match between citizen preferences and public policy but also encourages competition between states and communities to offer improved services at lower costs.[5]

**Encouraging Policy Innovation**    The Founders hoped that federalism would encourage policy experimentation and innovation. Today federalism may seem like a "conservative" idea, but it was once the instrument of liberal reformers. Federal programs as diverse as the income tax, unemployment compensation, Social Security, wage and hour legislation, bank deposit insurance, and food stamps were all state programs before becoming national undertakings. Today much of the current "liberal" policy agenda—mandatory health insurance for workers, child-care programs, notification of plant closings, government support of industrial research and development—has been embraced by various states. The phrase **laboratories of democracies** is generally attributed to the great progressive jurist Supreme Court Justice Louis D. Brandeis, who used it in defense of state experimentation with new solutions to social and economic problems.[6]

**laboratories of democracy**
A reference to the ability of states to experiment and innovate in public policy.

**Some Important Reservations**    Despite the strengths of federalism, it has its problems. First of all, federalism can obstruct action on national issues. Although decentralization may reduce conflict at the national level, it may do so at the price of "sweeping under the rug" very serious national injustices (see *A Conflicting View:* "The Dark Side of Federalism" on page 112). Federalism also permits local leaders and citizens to frustrate national policy, to sacrifice national interest to local interests. Decentralized government provides an opportunity for local NIMBYs (people who subscribe to the motto *"Not In My Back Yard"*) to obstruct airports, highways, waste disposal plants, public housing, drug rehabilitation centers, and many other projects that would be in the national interest.

—Think Again—
In which level of government do you have the most confidence?

## UP CLOSE

# Katrina: Federalism Fails in a Crisis

Hurricane Katrina was the nation's largest natural disaster. Perhaps it was inevitable that government—federal, state, and local—would be unable to respond to such a crisis. But the lack of competence among city, state, and federal officials, the bureaucratic inertia and stupidity, the disorganized relief that led directly to the deaths of many, all combined to make Katrina "the worst man-made relief disaster ever."[a]

Katrina was a powerful Category Four hurricane when it hit east of New Orleans, practically leveling the city of Biloxi, Mississippi. The first day New Orleans seemed to be spared, but the next day the levees began to crumble—levees that had protected the below-sea-level "Big Easy" for over a century. Soon water submerged 80 percent of the city and 100,000 people were stranded with little or no food and water and no electricity. For three days emergency efforts floundered badly. Survivors gathered on rooftops and highway flyovers. The country watched on television as babies, old people, the sick, and diabetic died on live television. Reporters got themselves to the scenes of tragedies, but government agents failed to do so. Soon armed looters appeared on the streets. Hospitals functioned in the dark and in the heat; doctors and nurses cried out for rescue of their patients.

The first rescuers, including private citizens with small boats, dropped people off on highway overpasses, with 100-degree heat and no water or food. Other makeshift rescue efforts took over 25,000

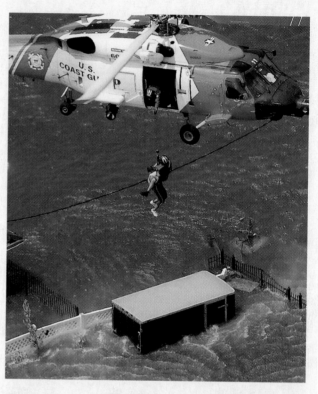

*Federal, state, and local government agencies performed poorly in response to Hurricane Katrina's devastation of New Orleans and the Mississippi Gulf Coast. Only the U.S. Coast Guard, shown here rescuing survivors, was given high marks for its work during the disaster.*

# The Original Design of Federalism

The U.S. Constitution *originally* defined American federalism in terms of (1) the powers expressly delegated to the national government plus the powers implied by those that are specifically granted, (2) the concurrent powers exercised by both states and the national government, (3) the powers reserved to the states, (4) the powers denied by the Constitution to both the national government and the states, and (5) the constitutional provisions giving the states a role in the composition of the national government (see Figure 4.2).

**Delegated Powers**  The U.S. Constitution lists seventeen specific grants of power to Congress, in Article I, Section 8. These are usually referred to as the **delegated, or enumerated, powers**. They include authority over war and foreign affairs, authority over the economy ("interstate commerce"), control over the money supply, and the power to tax and spend "to pay the debts and provide for the common defence and general welfare." After these specific grants of power comes the power "to make all laws which shall be necessary and proper for carrying

**delegated, or enumerated, powers** Powers specifically mentioned in the Constitution as belonging to the national government.

survivors to the leaking Superdome, where there were no light, no air, and no working toilets. Stories of individual bravery as well as bureaucratic bungling were carried on national television.

No one was in charge. Local, state, and federal leaders failed to lead, bureaucrats battled over turf, and government was paralyzed. The mayor urged residents to evacuate, but tens of thousands, especially the poor, had no cars or other means of transportation. The mayor hesitated to order a mandatory evacuation; when he finally did, hundreds of city buses were underwater. Some city police abandoned their posts to help their own families. Some nursing homes were overlooked in evacuation efforts and some elderly died unnecessarily.

Meanwhile, the mayor, FEMA officials, the governor, and even the president were giving press conferences boasting of all the aid that was on its way. But the governor refused to request federal troops or to place the Louisiana National Guard under federal authority. President Bush could have done so on his own, but he hesitated, waiting for the governor's request. The governor, a Democrat, feared that Republican federal officials would claim political credit for rescuing the city. She instructed National Guardsmen to keep people out of the city; in many instances they interpreted that order to keep out rescue workers from other states. Only the U.S. Coast Guard and military helicopters seemed to perform well—indeed heroically, in many cases rescuing survivors from rooftops.

But FEMA's performance was even worse. FEMA's authority is only to "coordinate" relief efforts in a crisis. FEMA had recently been transformed from an independent agency to a bureau in the Department of Homeland Security. Many newer appointees, including its director, had little or no disaster experience.

For three days FEMA sat and waited to be called by the governor. When asked by a TV reporter what he intended to do about the horrid conditions in the Superdome, conditions that had been shown on TV for days, the FEMA director responded that he did not know that anyone was in the Superdome. Hundreds of FEMA house trailers sat outside the city unused, as did truckloads of food and water. As flames consumed buildings in New Orleans, FEMA held back 600 firefighters in order to lecture them on equal opportunity, sexual harassment, and customer service.[b] At the airport, frustrated medics waited in empty helicopters to evacuate patients while FEMA delayed over paperwork. When outside doctors and nurses tried to help, FEMA rejected their assistance because they "weren't certified members of a National Disaster Medical Team." "FEMA kept stonewalling us with paperwork. Meanwhile, every 30 or 40 minutes someone was dying."[c] About 150 trucks full of ice purchased for hurricane victims sat uselessly in a parking lot in Maine.[d] The FEMA emergency number was out of service.

The president was on vacation in Crawford, Texas. Initially he and his advisers failed to understand the seriousness of the situation. When the full extent of the tragedy became known in Crawford, the president flew over New Orleans and later, in a series of speeches, pledged billions to rebuild the city. He finally relieved the FEMA director of his job. But the president's approval ratings fell to their lowest point since he first entered office.

[a]*U.S. News and World Report*, September 19, 2005, p. 30.
[b]*Time*, September 19, 2005, p. 18.
[c]*New York Times*, September 18, 2005.
[d]*Ft. Lauderdale Sun-Sentinel*, October 7, 2005, p. 1.

---

into execution the foregoing powers, and all other powers vested by this Constitution in the government of the United States or in any department or officer thereof." This statement is generally known as the **Necessary and Proper Clause**, and it is the principal source of the national government's **implied powers**— powers not specifically listed in the Constitution but inferred from those that are.

**National Supremacy**   The delegated and implied powers, when coupled with the assertion of "national supremacy" (in Article VI), ensure a powerful national government. The **National Supremacy Clause** is very specific in asserting the supremacy of federal laws over state and local laws.

> This Constitution, and the laws of the United States which shall be made in pursuance thereof, and all treaties made, or which shall be made, under the authority of the United States, shall be the supreme law of the land, and the Judges in every state shall be bound thereby, any thing in the constitution or laws of any state to the contrary notwithstanding.

**Concurrent and Reserved Powers**   Despite broad grants of power to the national government, the states retain considerable governing power. **Concurrent powers** are those recognized in the Constitution as belonging to *both* the national

**Necessary and Proper Clause** Clause in Article I, Section 8, of the U.S. Constitution granting Congress the power to enact all laws that are "necessary and proper" for carrying out those responsibilities specifically delegated to it. Also referred to as the Implied Powers Clause.

**implied powers** Powers not mentioned specifically in the Constitution as belonging to Congress but inferred as necessary and proper for carrying out the enumerated powers.

# A CONFLICTING VIEW

## The Dark Side of Federalism

Segregationists once regularly used the argument of "states' rights" to deny equal protection of the law to African Americans. Indeed, *states' rights* became a code word for opposition to federal civil rights laws. In 1963 Governor George Wallace invoked the states' rights argument when he stood in a doorway at the University of Alabama to prevent the execution of a federal court order that the university admit two African American students and thus integrate. Federal marshals were on hand to enforce the order, and Wallace only temporarily delayed them. Shortly after his dramatic stand in front of the television cameras, he retreated to his office. Later in his career, Wallace sought African American votes, declaring, "I was wrong. Those days are over."

Federalism in America remains tainted by its historical association with slavery, segregation, and discrimination. In the Virginia and Kentucky Resolutions of 1798, Thomas Jefferson and James Madison asserted the doctrine of "nullification," claiming that states could nullify unconstitutional laws of Congress. Although the original intent of this doctrine was to counter congressional attacks on a free press under the Alien and Sedition Acts of 1798, it was later revived to defend slavery. John C. Calhoun of South Carolina argued forcefully in the years before the Civil War that slavery was an issue for the states to decide and the Constitution gave Congress no power to interfere with slavery in the southern states or in the new western territories.

In the years immediately following the Civil War, the issues of slavery, racial inequality, and African American voting rights were *nationalized.* Nationalizing these issues meant removing them from the jurisdiction of the states and placing them in the hands of the national government. The Thirteenth, Fourteenth, and Fifteenth Amendments to the Constitution were enforced by federal troops in the southern states during the post–Civil War Reconstruction era. But after the Compromise of 1876 led to the withdrawal of federal troops from the southern states, legal and social segregation of African Americans became a "way of life" in the region. Segregation was *denationalized,*

which reduced national conflict over race but exacted a high price from the nation's African American population. Segregationists asserted the states' rights argument so often in defense of racial discrimination that it became a code phrase for racism. Not until the 1950s and 1960s were questions of segregation and equality again made into national issues. The civil rights movement asserted the supremacy of national law and in 1954 won a landmark decision in the case of *Brown v. Board of Education of Topeka,* when the U.S. Supreme Court ruled that segregation enforced by state (or local) officials violated the Fourteenth Amendment's guarantee that no state could deny any person the equal protection of the law. Later the *national* Civil Rights Act of 1964 outlawed discrimination in private employment and businesses serving the public.

Only now that national constitutional and legal guarantees of equal protection of the law are in place is it possible to reassess the true worth of federalism. Having established that federalism will not mean racial inequality, Americans are now free to explore the values of decentralized government.

*In an attempt to block the admission of two African American students to the University of Alabama in 1963, Governor George Wallace barred the door with his body in the face of U.S. federal marshals. The tactic did not succeed, and the two students were admitted.*

**National Supremacy Clause** Clause in Article VI of the U.S. Constitution declaring the constitution and laws of the national government "the supreme law of the land" superior to the constitutions and laws of the states.

and state governments, including the power to tax and spend, make and enforce laws, and establish courts of justice. The Tenth Amendment reassured the states that "the powers not delegated to the United States . . . are reserved to the States respectively, or to the people." Through these **reserved powers**, the states generally retain control over property and contract law, criminal law, marriage and divorce, and the provision of education, highways, and social welfare activities. The states control the organization and powers of their own local governments. Finally, the states, like the federal government, retain the power to tax and spend for the general welfare.

## POWERS GRANTED BY THE CONSTITUTION

**NATIONAL GOVERNMENT**
Delegated Powers

**Military Affairs and Defense**
- Provide for the common defense (I-8).
- Declare war (I-8).
- Raise and support armies (I-8).
- Provide and maintain a navy (I-8).
- Define and punish piracies (I-8).
- Define and punish offenses against the law of nations (I-8).
- Provide for calling forth the militia to execute laws, suppress insurrections, and repel invasions (I-8).
- Provide for organizing, arming, and disciplining the militia (I-8).
- Declare the punishment of treason (III-3).

**Economic Affairs**
- Regulate commerce with foreign nations, among the several states, and with Indian tribes (I-8).
- Establish uniform laws on bankruptcy (I-8).
- Coin money and regulate its value (I-8).
- Fix standards of weights and measures (I-8).
- Provide for patents and copyrights (I-8).
- Establish post offices and post roads (I-8).

**Governmental Organization**
- Constitute tribunals inferior to the Supreme Court (I-8, III-1).
- Exercise exclusive legislative power over the seat of government and over certain military installations (I-8).
- Admit new states (IV-3).
- Dispose of and regulate territory or property of the United States (IV-3).

**"Implied" Powers**
- Make laws necessary and proper for carrying the expressed powers into execution (I-8).

**NATIONAL AND STATE GOVERNMENTS**
Concurrent Powers

- Levy taxes (I-8).
- Borrow money (I-8).
- Contract and pay debts (I-8).
- Charter banks and corporations (I-8).
- Make and enforce laws (I-8).
- Establish courts (I-8).
- Provide for the general welfare (I-8).

**STATE GOVERNMENTS**
Reserved to the States

- Regulate intrastate commerce.
- Conduct elections.
- Provide for public health, safety, and morals.
- Establish local government.
- Maintain the militia (National Guard).
- Ratify amendments to the federal Constitution (V).
- Determine voter qualifications (I-2).

**"Reserved" Powers**

- Powers not delegated to national government nor denied to the States by the Constitution (X).

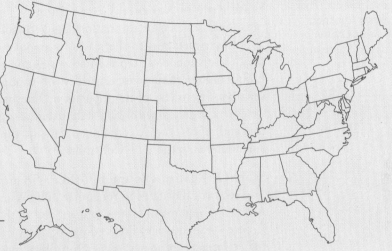

## POWERS DENIED BY THE CONSTITUTION

**NATIONAL GOVERNMENT**

- Give preference to the ports of any state (I-9).
- Impose a tax or duty on articles exported from any state (I-9).
- Directly tax except by apportionment among the states on a population basis (I-9), now superseded as to income tax (Amendment XVI).
- Draw money from the Treasury except by appropriation (I-9).

**NATIONAL AND STATE GOVERNMENTS**

- Grant titles of nobility (I-9).
- Limit the suspension of habeas corpus (I-9).
- Issue bills of attainder (I-10).
- Make ex post facto laws (I-10).
- Establish a religion or prohibit the free exercise of religion (Amendment I).
- Abridge freedom of speech, press, assembly, or right of petition (Amendment I).
- Deny the right to bear arms (Amendment II).
- Quarter soldiers in private homes (Amendment III).
- Conduct unreasonable searches or seizures. (Amendment IV).
- Deny guarantees of fair trials (Amendment V, Amendment VI, and Amendment VII).
- Impose excessive bail or unusual punishments (Amendment VII).
- Take life, liberty, or property without due process (Amendment V).
- Permit slavery (Amendment XIII).
- Deny life, liberty, or property without due process of law (Amendment XIV).
- Deny voting because of race, color, previous servitude (Amendment XV), sex (Amendment XIX), or age if 18 or over (Amendment XXVI).
- Deny voting because of nonpayment of any tax (Amendment XXIV).

**STATE GOVERNMENTS**

**Economic Affairs**
- Use legal tender other than gold or silver coin (I-10).
- Issue separate state coinage (I-10).
- Impair the obligation of contracts (I-10).
- Emit bills of credit (I-10).
- Levy import or export duties, except reasonable inspection fees, without the consent of Congress (I-10).
- Abridge the privileges and immunities of national citizenship (Amendment XIV)
- Make any law that violates federal law (Amendment VI).
- Pay for rebellion against the United States or for emancipated slaves (Amendment XIV).

**Foreign Affairs**
- Enter into treaties, alliances, or confederations (I-10).
- Make compact with a foreign state, except by congressional consent (I-10).

**Military Affairs**
- Issue letters of marque and reprisal (I-10).
- Maintain standing military forces in peace without congressional consent (I-10).
- Engage in war, without congressional consent, except in imminent danger or when invaded (I-10).

**Figure 4.2**   Original Constitutional Distribution of Powers

Under the Constitution of 1787, certain powers were delegated to the national government, other powers were shared by the national and state governments, and still other powers were reserved for state governments alone. Similarly, certain powers were denied by the Constitution to the national government, other powers were denied to both the national and state governments, and still other powers were denied only to state governments. Later amendments especially protected individual liberties.

**concurrent powers**  Powers exercised by both the national government and state governments in the American federal system.

**reserved powers**  Powers not granted to the national government or specifically denied to the states in the Constitution that are recognized by the Tenth Amendment as belonging to the state governments. This guarantee, known as the Reserved Powers Clause, embodies the principle of American federalism.

"Look, the American people don't want to be bossed around by federal bureaucrats. They want to be bossed around by state bureaucrats."

**Powers Denied to the States**    The Constitution denies the states some powers in order to safeguard national unity. States are specifically denied the power to coin money, enter into treaties with foreign nations, interfere with the "obligation of contracts," levy taxes on imports or exports, or engage in war.

**Powers Denied to the Nation and the States**    The Constitution denies some powers to both national and state government—namely, the powers to abridge individual rights. The Bill of Rights originally applied only to the national government, but the Fourteenth Amendment, passed by Congress in 1866 and ratified by 1868, provided that the states must also adhere to fundamental guarantees of individual liberty.

**State Role in National Government**    The states are basic units in the organizational scheme of the national government. The House of Representatives apportions members to the states by population, and state legislatures draw up the districts that elect representatives. Every state has at least one member in the House of Representatives, regardless of its population. Each state elects two U.S. senators, regardless of its population. The president is chosen by the electoral votes of the states, with each state having as many electoral votes as it has senators and representatives combined. Finally, three-fourths of the states must ratify amendments to the U.S. Constitution.

**State Obligations to Each Other**    To promote national unity, the Constitution requires the states to recognize actions and decisions taken by other states. Article IV requires the states to give "Full Faith and Credit . . . to the public Acts, Records, and judiciary Proceedings of every other State." This provision ensures that contracts, property ownership, insurance, civil judgments, marriages and divorces, among other things, made in one state are recognized in all states (see *What Do You Think?:* "Federalism and Same-Sex Marriages").

Recently, controversy has arisen over recognition of gay and lesbian marriages or "civil unions." A strict reading of Article IV would suggest that if any state legalized same-sex marriages, all states would be obliged to recognize them. (In 1999 the Vermont Supreme Court prohibited discrimination against gay marriages.) Anticipating this issue, the Congress passed a Defense of Marriage Act in 1996 stating that "No State . . . shall be required to give effect to any public act, record, or judicial proceeding of any other State respecting a relationship between persons of the same sex that is treated as a marriage . . ." The Congress relied on language in the next sentence of Article IV: "the Congress may by general law prescribe the Manner in which such Acts, Records and Proceedings shall be proved, *and the Effect thereof*" (italics added). It is not altogether clear whether this constitutional language in the second sentence allows Congress to nullify the "Full Faith and Credit" clause in the first sentence. If Vermont or any other state persists in recognizing gay marriages, the issue may end up in the Supreme Court (see also "Privacy and the Constitution" in Chapter 12).

# The Evolution of American Federalism

American federalism has evolved over 200 years from a state-centered division of power to a national-centered system of government. Although the original constitutional wordings have remained in place, *power has flowed toward the national government since the earliest days of the Republic.* American federalism has been forged in the fires of political conflicts between states and nation, conflicts that have usually been resolved in favor of the national government. (See *Up Close:* "Historical Markers in the Development of American Federalism.") Generalizing about the

# WHAT DO YOU THINK?

## Federalism and Same-Sex Marriage

Traditionally, states outlawed sodomy (anal penetration, whether practiced by homo- or heterosexuals). The U.S. Supreme Court upheld these laws in 1986: "There is no constitutional right to sodomy."[a] But in 2003 the Supreme Court reversed itself and held that homosexuals' "right to liberty under the Due Process Clause gives them the full right to engage in private conduct without government interference."[b] This decision was a important victory for the gay rights movement in America and generated additional cases involving the legal status of homosexual relations.

Among the issues confronting homosexuals is that of same-sex marriage. The Supreme Court's decision that homosexual activity among consenting adults was a constitutionally protected liberty inspired several state courts to consider whether the denial of marriage to homosexual couples was discriminatory. Anticipating that some state courts might rule that same-sex marriages were constitutionally protected in their states, Congress passed a Defense of Marriage Act in 1996. This act was designed to circumvent the Full Faith and Credit clause of Article IV of the Constitution requiring every state to recognize the public acts and judiciary proceedings of every other state. The act stated that "No state. . . . shall be required to give effect to any public act, record, or judicial proceeding of any other state respecting a relationship between persons of the same-sex that is treated as a marriage. . . ." The Congress relied on the language of the next sentence of Article IV: "The Congress may by general law prescribe the Manner in which such Acts, Records and Proceedings shall be proved, and the Effect thereof." Congress was trying to prevent the recognition of same-sex marriages by all states if one or more states decided to legalize such marriages.

Public opinion is strongly opposed to same-sex *marriage*, but many Americans have no objection to the alternative of *civil unions* for same-sex couples.[c]

*Q. Do you think marriages between homosexuals should or should not be recognized by the law as valid, with the same rights as traditional marriages?"*

| Should be valid | Should not be | Unsure |
|---|---|---|
| 28% | 68% | 4% |

[a]*Bowers v. Hardwick*, 478 U.S. 186 (1986).
[b]*Lawrence v. Texas*, June 26, 2003.
[c]*ABC News Poll*, April 24, 2005; *CNN/USA Today* Poll, March 20, 2005.

*Q. "Do you think same-sex couples should be allowed to legally marry, should be allowed legally to form civil unions but not to marry, should not be allowed to obtain legal recognition of their relationships?"*

| Marriage | Civil unions | No legal recognition | Unsure |
|---|---|---|---|
| 27% | 29% | 40% | 4% |

Vermont decided in 2000 to sanction "civil unions" between same-sex couples. While avoiding the term "marriage," the Vermont law allows ceremonies to be performed by a judge or clergy member and the couple to be entitled to all the benefits, protections, and responsibilities that are granted to married couples. And in 2003 the Massachusetts Supreme Court ruled that same-sex couples had a right to marriage under the Massachusetts state constitution.[d]

In 2005, forty states had laws against same-sex marriages, many adapted by a statewide voter referendum. It is not altogether clear whether the Congress has a power under the language of Article IV to nullify in effect the Full Faith and Credit clause. It is quite possible that the U.S. Supreme Court will hold that it does not, and that states are obliged to recognize same-sex marriages performed lawfully in any state.

Finally, *if* the federal courts, with the approval of the U.S. Supreme Court, were to decide that denying licenses for same-sex marriages violated the Equal Protection Clause of the Fourteenth Amendment to the Constitution, that such denial was discriminatory, *then all* states would be obliged to grant such licenses and recognize such marriages.

[d]*Goodridge v. Department of Health*, 798 N.E. 2d 941 (2003).

*Does the Constitution's "full faith and credit clause" oblige all states to recognize same-sex marriages performed in any state? Congress's "Protection of Marriage Act" says no, but the U.S. Supreme Court has yet to speak on the issue. Here television celebrity Rosie O'Donnell leaves the courthouse following her marriage ceremony.*

Battles over same-sex marriages are currently being fought in state capitals across the country. The Constitution requires every state to give "Full Faith and Credit" to the official acts of other states. But Congress' Defense of Marriage Act relieves states from recognizing same-sex marriages consummated in other states. The Supreme Court may end up deciding the issue.

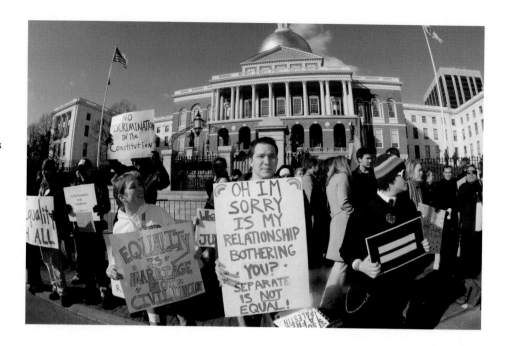

evolution of American federalism is no easy task. But let us try to describe broadly some major periods in the evolution of federalism and then look at five specific historical developments that had far-reaching impact on that evolution.

**State-Centered Federalism, 1787–1868**   From the adoption of the Constitution of 1787 to the end of the Civil War, the states were the most important units in the American federal system. It is true that during this period the legal foundation for the expansion of national power was being laid, but people looked to the states for resolving most policy questions and providing most public services. Even the issue of slavery was decided by state governments. The supremacy of the national government was frequently questioned, first by the Anti-Federalists (including Thomas Jefferson) and later by John C. Calhoun and other defenders of slavery.

**Dual Federalism, 1868–1913**   The supremacy of the national government was decided on the battlefields of the Civil War. Yet for nearly a half-century after that conflict, the national government narrowly interpreted its delegated powers, and the states continued to decide most domestic policy issues. The resulting pattern has been described as **dual federalism**. Under this pattern, the states and the nation divided most governmental functions. The national government concentrated its attention on the "delegated" powers—national defense, foreign affairs, tariffs, interstate commerce, the coinage of money, standard weights and measures, post office and post roads, and the admission of new states. State governments decided the important domestic policy issues—education, welfare, health, and criminal justice. The separation of policy responsibilities was once compared to a layer cake, with local governments at the base, state governments in the middle, and the national government at the top.[7]

**Cooperative Federalism, 1913–64**   The distinction between national and state responsibilities gradually eroded in the first half of the twentieth century. American federalism was transformed by the Industrial Revolution and the development of a national economy, by the federal income tax in 1913, which shifted financial resources to the national government, and by the challenges of two world wars and the Great Depression. In response to the Great Depression of the

**dual federalism** Early concept of federalism in which national and state powers were clearly distinguished and functionally separate.

## UP CLOSE

# Historical Markers in the Development of American Federalism

Among the most important events in the development of American federalism: (1) the Supreme Court's decision in *McCulloch v. Maryland* in 1819 giving a broad interpretation of the Necessary and Proper Clause; (2) the victory of the national government in the Civil War 1861–65; (3) the establishment of a national system of civil rights based on the Fourteenth Amendment culminating in the Supreme Court's desegregation decision in *Brown v. Board of Education;* (4) the expansion of the national government's power under the Interstate Commerce Clause during the Great Depression of the 1930s; and (5) the growth of federal revenues after the passage of the Sixteenth (income tax) Amendment in 1913.

### *McCulloch v. Maryland* and the Necessary and Proper Clause

Political conflict over the scope of national power is as old as the nation itself. In 1790 Secretary of the Treasury Alexander Hamilton proposed the establishment of a national bank. Congress acted on Hamilton's suggestion in 1791, establishing a national bank to serve as a depository for federal money and to aid the federal government in borrowing funds. Jeffersonians believed the national bank was a dangerous centralization of government. They objected that the power to establish the bank was nowhere to be found in the enumerated powers of Congress.

Hamilton replied that Congress could derive the power to establish a bank from grants of authority in the Constitution relating to money, in combination with the clause authorizing Congress "to make all laws which shall be necessary and proper for carrying into execution the foregoing powers."

The question finally reached the Supreme Court in 1819, when the State of Maryland levied a tax on the national bank and the bank refused to pay it. In the case of *McCulloch v. Maryland*, Chief Justice Marshall accepted the broader Hamiltonian version of the Necessary and Proper Clause: "Let the end be legitimate, let it be within the scope of the Constitution, and all means which are appropriate, which are plainly adopted to that end, which are not prohibited but consistent with the letter and the spirit of the Constitution, are constitutional."[a]

The *McCulloch* case firmly established the principle that the Necessary and Proper Clause gives Congress the right to choose its means in carrying out the enumerated powers of the national government. Because of this broad interpretation of the Necessary and Proper Clause, today Congress can devise programs, create agencies, and establish national laws on the basis of long chains of reasoning from the most meager phrases of the constitutional text.

### Secession and Civil War

The Civil War was the greatest crisis of the American federal system. Did a state have the right to oppose national law to the point of secession, that is, withdrawing from the federal Union? The question of secession was decided on Civil War battlefields between 1861 and 1865. Yet the states' rights doctrine and political disputes over the character of American federalism did not disappear with General Robert E. Lee's surrender at Appomattox. In addition to establishing that states cannot secede from the federal union, the Civil War led to three constitutional amendments clearly aimed at limiting state power in the interests of individual freedom. The Thirteenth Amendment eliminated slavery in the states; the Fifteenth Amendment prevented states from denying the vote on the basis of race, color, or previous enslavement; and the Fourteenth Amendment declared,

> No State shall make or enforce any law which shall abridge the privileges or immunities of citizens of the United States; nor shall any state deprive any person of life, liberty, or property, without due process of law; nor deny to any person within its jurisdiction the equal protection of the laws.

### National Guarantees of Civil Rights

In the twentieth century, the Supreme Court began to build a national system of civil rights based on the Fourteenth Amendment. First, the Court held that the Fourteenth Amendment prevented states from interfering with free speech, free press, or religious practices. But it was not until 1954, in the desegregation decision in *Brown v. Board of Education of Topeka,* that the Court began to call for the full assertion of national authority on behalf of civil rights.[b] When it decided that the Fourteenth Amendment prohibited the states from segregating the races in public schools, the Court was asserting national authority over longstanding practices in many of the states.

But in the years following *Brown,* some state officials tried to prevent the enforcement of a national law. Governor Orval Faubus called out the Arkansas National Guard to prevent a federal court from desegregating Little Rock Central High School in 1957. President Dwight D. Eisenhower responded by

[a]*McCulloch v. Maryland,* 4 Wheaten 316 (1819).

[b]*Brown v. Board of Education of Topeka, Kansas,* 347 U.S. 483 (1954).

ordering the Arkansas National Guard removed and sent units of the U.S. Army to enforce national authority. This presidential action reinforced the principle of national supremacy in the American political system.

### The Expansion of Interstate Commerce

The growth of national power under the Interstate Commerce Clause of the Constitution is another important development in the evolution of American federalism. For many years, the U.S. Supreme Court narrowly defined *interstate commerce* to mean only the movement of goods and services across state lines. Until the late 1930s, it insisted that agriculture, mining, manufacturing, and labor relations were outside the reach of the delegated powers of the national government. However, when confronted with the Great Depression of the 1930s and Franklin Roosevelt's threat to add enough members to the Supreme Court to win favorable rulings, the Court yielded. It redefined

*interstate commerce* to include any activity that "substantially affects" the national economy.[c] Indeed, the Court frequently approved of congressional restrictions on economic activities that had only very indirect effects on interstate commerce.[d]

### The Income Tax and Federal Grants

In the famous Northwest Ordinance of 1787, which provided for the governing of the territories west of the Appalachian Mountains, Congress made grants of land for the establishment of public schools. Then in the Morrill Land Grant Act of 1862, Congress provided grants of land to the states to promote higher education, especially agricultural and mechanical studies. Federal support for "A and M" or "land grant" universities continues today.

With the money provided to Washington by the passage of the Sixteenth (income tax) Amendment in 1913, Congress embarked on cash grants to the states. Among the earliest cash grant programs were the Federal Highway Act of 1916 and the Smith-Hughes Act of 1917 (vocational education). With federal money came federal direction. For example, states that wanted federal money for highways after 1916 had to accept uniform standards of construction and even a uniform road-numbering system (U.S. 1, U.S. 30, and so on). Shortly after these programs began, the U.S. Supreme Court considered the claim that these federal grants were unconstitutional intrusions into areas "reserved" for the states. But the Court upheld grants as a legitimate exercise of Congress's power to tax and spend for the general welfare.[e]

[c]*National Labor Relations Board v. Jones & Laughlin Steel Corporation*, 301 U.S. 1 (1937).
[d]*Wickard v. Filburn*, 317 U.S. 128 (1938).
[e]*Massachusetts v. Mellon, Framingham v. Mellon*, 262 U.S. 447 (1923).

1930s, state governors welcomed massive federal public works projects under President Franklin D. Roosevelt's New Deal program. In addition, the federal government intervened directly in economic affairs, labor relations, business practices, and agriculture. Through its grants of money, the national government cooperated with the states in public assistance, employment services, child welfare, public housing, urban renewal, highway building, and vocational education.

**cooperative federalism**
Model of federalism in which national, state, and local governments work together exercising common policy responsibilities.

This new pattern of federal-state relations was labeled **cooperative federalism**. Both the nation and the states exercised responsibilities for welfare, health, highways, education, and criminal justice. This merging of policy responsibilities was compared to a marble cake: "As the colors are mixed in a marble cake, so functions are mixed in the American federal system."[8] Yet even in this period of shared national-state responsibility, the national government emphasized cooperation in achieving common national and state goals. Congress generally acknowledged that it had no direct constitutional authority to regulate public health, safety, or welfare. Instead, it relied primarily on its powers to tax and spend for the general welfare, providing financial assistance to state and local governments to achieve shared goals. Congress did not usually legislate directly on local matters.

**Centralized Federalism, 1964–80**    Over the years, it became increasingly difficult to maintain the fiction that the national government was merely assisting the states to perform their domestic responsibilities. By the time President Lyndon B. Johnson launched the Great Society program in 1964, the federal government clearly had its own *national* goals. Virtually all problems confronting American society—from solid-waste disposal and water and air pollution to consumer safety, home insulation, noise abatement, and even "highway beautification"—were declared to be national problems. Congress legislated directly on any matter it chose, without regard to its *enumerated powers* and without pretending to render only financial assistance. The Supreme Court no longer concerned itself with the reserved powers of the states, and the Tenth Amendment lost most of its meaning. The pattern of national-state relations became **centralized federalism**. As for the cake analogies, one commentator observed, "The frosting had moved to the top, something like a pineapple upside-down cake."[9]

**New Federalism, 1980–85**    New federalism was a phrase frequently applied to efforts to reverse the flow of power to Washington and to return responsibilities to states and communities. (The phrase originated in the administration of Richard M. Nixon, 1969–74, who used it to describe general revenue sharing—making federal grants to state and local governments with few strings attached.) New Federalism was popular early in the administration of President Ronald Reagan, who tried to reduce federal involvement in domestic programs and encourage states and cities to undertake greater policy responsibilities themselves. The result was that state and local governments were forced to rely more on their own sources of revenue and less on federal money. Still, centralizing tendencies in the American federal system continued. While the general public usually gave better marks to state and local governments than to the federal government, paradoxically that same public also favored greater federal involvement in policy areas traditionally thought to be state or local responsibilities (see Figure 4.3).

**The Close Up Foundation**

A nonprofit, nonpartisan citizenship education organization with excellent historical materials about federalism's evolution and information about federalism issues. A related link on the Close Up site contains the complete text of the pro-states' rights 1798 Kentucky and Virginia Resolutions (authored by Jefferson and Madison). *www.closeup.org*

**centralized federalism**
Model of federalism in which the national government assumes primary responsibility for determining national goals in all major policy areas and directs state and local government activity through conditions attached to money grants.

**new federalism**    Attempts to return power and responsibility to the states and reduce the role of the national government in domestic affairs.

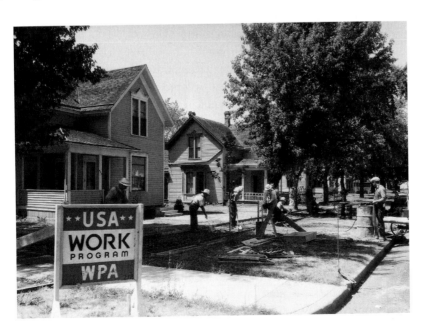

During the Great Depression of the 1930s, the massive public works projects sponsored by the federal government under President Franklin Roosevelt's New Deal reflected the emergence of cooperative federalism. Programs of the Works Progress Administration, like the one shown here, were responsible for the construction of buildings, bridges, highways, and airports throughout the country.

**Figure 4.3** Public Views about Which Level of Government Should Run Various Programs

*Source:* Gallup/CNN/*USA Today* Poll, reported in *The Polling Report*, February 10, 1997. Copyright © 1996–2004 by The Gallup Organization.

**Which level of government should run the following programs?**

**Service to immigrants**
Federal 60%
State 15%
Local 6%

**Welfare**
Federal 40%
State 38%
Local 17%

**Health care for the disabled, poor, and elderly**
Federal 36%
State 28%
Local 18%

**Opportunity for minorities**
Federal 35%
State 30%
Local 28%

**Air/water quality**
Federal 35%
State 40%
Local 22%

**Public education**
Federal 21%
State 47%
Local 30%

**Child care**
Federal 16%
State 34%
Local 29%

**Employment and job training**
Federal 15%
State 59%
Local 24%

**Law enforcement**
Federal 15%
State 36%
Local 45%

**Representational Federalism, 1985–95**   Despite centralizing tendencies, it was still widely assumed prior to 1985 that the Congress could not directly legislate how state and local governments should go about performing their traditional functions. However, in its 1985 *Garcia v. San Antonio Metropolitan Transit Authority* decision, the U.S. Supreme Court appeared to remove all barriers to direct congressional legislation in matters traditionally reserved to the states. The case arose after Congress directly ordered state and local governments to pay minimum wages to their employees. The Court dismissed arguments that the nature of American federalism and the Reserved Powers Clause of the Tenth Amendment prevented Congress from directly legislating in state affairs. It said that the only protection for state powers was to be found in the states' role in electing U.S. senators, members of the U.S. House of Representatives, and the president. The Court's ruling asserts a concept known as **representational federalism**: Federalism is defined by the role of the states in electing members of Congress and the president, not by any constitutional division of powers. The United States is said to retain a federal system because its national officials are selected from subunits of government—the president through the allocation of Electoral College votes to the states and the Congress through the allocation of two Senate seats per state and the apportionment of representatives based on state population. Whatever protection exists for state power and independence

**representational federalism**
Assertion that no constitutional division of powers exists between the nation and the states but the states retain their constitutional role merely by selecting the president and members of Congress.

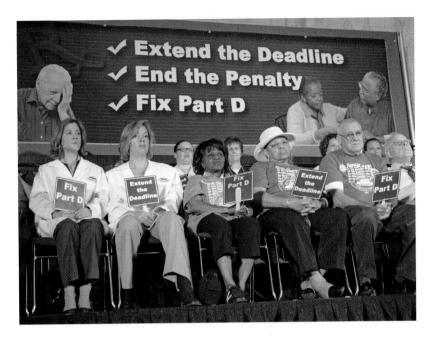

Medicare was begun in 1965 as part of President Lyndon B. Johnson's Great Society agenda. A Republican Congress added prescription drug coverage (Part D) beginning in 2004, but protestors like these shown here criticize gaps in coverage.

must be found in the national political process, in the influence of state and district voters on their senators and representatives. In a strongly worded dissenting opinion in *Garcia,* Justice Lewis Powell argued that if federalism is to be retained, the Constitution—not Congress—should divide powers. "The states' role in our system of government is a matter of constitutional law, not legislative grace. . . . [This decision] today rejects almost 200 years of the understanding of the constitutional status of federalism."[10]

## Federalism Revived?

In recent years federalism has experienced a modest revival. The U.S. Supreme Court today appears to be somewhat more respectful of the powers of states and somewhat less willing to see these powers trampled upon by the national government.[11]

In 1995 the U.S. Supreme Court issued its first opinion in more than sixty years that recognized a limit on Congress's power over interstate commerce and reaffirmed the Founders' notion of a national government with only the powers enumerated in the Constitution.[12] The Court found that the federal Gun-Free School Zones Act was unconstitutional because it exceeded Congress's powers under the Interstate Commerce Clause. When a student, Alfonso Lopez, was apprehended at his Texas high school carrying a .38 caliber handgun, federal agents charged him with violating the *federal* Gun-Free School Zones Act of 1990.

The U.S. government argued that the act was a constitutional exercise of its interstate commerce power, because "violent crime reduces the willingness of individuals to travel to areas within the country that are perceived to be unsafe." But after reviewing virtually all of the key commerce clause cases in its history, the Court determined that an activity must *substantially affect* interstate commerce in order to be regulated by Congress. Chief Justice William H. Rehnquist, writing for the majority in a 5 to 4 decision in *U.S. v. Lopez,* even cited James Madison with approval: "The powers delegated by the proposed Constitution to the federal government are few and defined. Those which are to remain in the state governments are numerous and indefinite" (*Federalist,* No. 45).

**─── Think Again ───**
**Should the national government be able to prosecute a high school student for bringing a gun to school?**

 **National Conference of State Legislatures**
This conference site provides information on 50 state legislatures and the issues they confront. *www.ncsl.org*

In another victory for federalism, the U.S. Supreme Court ruled in 1996 in *Seminole Tribe v. Florida* that the Eleventh Amendment shields states from lawsuits by private parties that seek to force states to comply with federal laws enacted under the commerce power.[13] And in 1999 in *Alden v. Maine,* the Supreme Court held that states were also shielded in their own courts from lawsuits in which private parties seek to enforce federal mandates. In an opinion that surveyed the history of American federalism, Justice Kennedy wrote: "Congress has vast power but not all power. . . . When Congress legislates in matters affecting the states it may not treat these sovereign entities as mere prefectures or corporations."[14]

In defense of federalism, the Supreme Court invalidated a provision of a very popular law of Congress—the Brady Handgun Violence Protection Act. The Court decided in 1997 that the law's command to local law enforcement officers to conduct background checks on gun purchasers violated "the very principle of separate state sovereignty." The Court affirmed that the federal government "may neither issue directives requiring the states to address particular problems, nor command the states' officers, or those of their political subdivisions, to administer or enforce the federal regulatory program" (*Printz v. U.S.,* 521 U.S. 890 (1997).[15] And the Court held that in the Violence against Women Act, Congress also invaded the reserved police power of the states[16] (see *What Do You Think?* "Should Violence Against Women Be a Federal Crime?").

The Supreme Court's apparent revival of federalism has been greeted with cautious optimism. However, all of the recent Supreme Court rulings reaffirming federalism have come in narrow 5 to 4 decisions. The closeness of these votes, together with these decisions' contrast to more than a half-century of case law in support of national power, provide no guarantee that in the future the Supreme Court will continue to move in the direction of strengthening federalism.

Former presidential press secretary James Brady was permanently disabled in the assassination attempt on President Reagan in 1981. Brady and his wife led the effort to pass the Brady Act, which, among other things, ordered state and local officials to conduct background checks on gun purchasers. The Supreme Court held that portion of the act to be an unconstitutional violation of the principle of federalism.

## WHAT DO YOU THINK?

# Should Violence Against Women Be a Federal Crime?

When a student at VPI (Virginia Polytechnic Institute) was raped, she argued that the attack violated the federal Violence against Women Act of 1994, a popular bill that passed overwhelmingly in Congress and was signed by President Bill Clinton. The act allowed victims of "gender-motivated violence," including rape, to sue their attackers for monetary damages in *federal* court. The U.S. government defended its constitutional authority to involve itself in crimes against women by citing the Interstate Commerce Clause, arguing that crimes against women interfered with interstate commerce, the power over which is given to the national government in Article I of the Constitution.

But in 2000 the U.S. Supreme Court said, "If accepted, this reasoning would allow Congress to regulate any crime whose nationwide, aggregated impact has substantial effects on employment, production, transit, or consumption. Moreover, such reasoning will not limit Congress to regulating violence, but may be applied equally as well to family law and other areas of state regulation since the aggregate effect of marriage, divorce, and childrearing on the national economy is undoubtedly significant." The Court reasoned that "the Constitution requires a distinction between what is truly national and what is truly local, and there is no better example of the police power, which the Founders undeniably left reposed in the States and denied the central government." In Justice Scalia's opinion, allowing Congress to claim that violence against women interfered with interstate commerce would open the door to federalizing all crime because all crime affects interstate commerce.

*Source: U.S. v. Morrison, May 15, 2000.*

# Money and Power Flow to Washington

Over the years, power in the federal system has flowed to Washington because tax money has flowed to Washington. With its financial resources, the federal government has been able to offer assistance to state and local governments and thereby involve itself in just about every governmental function performed by these governments. Today the federal government is no longer one of *enumerated* or *delegated* powers. No activities are really *reserved* to the states. Through its power to tax and spend for the *general welfare*, the national government is now deeply involved in welfare, education, transportation, police protection, housing, hospitals, urban development, and other activities that were once the exclusive domain of state and local government (see *Up Close:* "How Congress Set a National Drinking Age").

*Think Again*

When the federal government requires states to provide safe drinking water, clean air, or access for the handicapped, should it provide funds to carry out these mandates?

**Grants-in-aid**   Today grant-in-aid programs are the single most important source of federal influence over state and local activity. A **grant-in-aid** is defined as "payment of funds by one level of government (national or state) to be expended by another level (state or local) for a specified purpose, usually on a matching-funds basis (the federal government puts up only as much as the state or locality) and in accordance with prescribed standards of requirements."[17] No state or local government is *required* to accept grants-in-aid. Participation in grant-in-aid programs is voluntary. So in theory, if conditions attached to the grant money are too oppressive, state and local governments can simply decline to participate and pass up these funds.

About one-quarter of all state and local government revenues currently come from federal grants. Federal grants are available in nearly every major category of state and local government activity. Over 500 separate grant programs are administered by various federal agencies. So numerous and diverse are these

**grants-in-aid** Payments of funds from the national government to state or local governments or from a state government to local governments for specific purposes.

## UP CLOSE

## How Congress Set a National Drinking Age

Traditionally the *reserved* powers of the states included protection of the health, safety, and well-being of their citizens. The *enumerated* powers of Congress in the Constitution did not include regulating the sale and consumption of alcoholic beverages. Every state determined its own minimum age for drinking.

But the minimum drinking age became a national issue as a result of emotional appeals by groups such as Mothers Against Drunk Driving (MADD). Tragic stories told at televised committee hearings by grieving relatives of dead teenagers swept away federalism arguments. A few Congress members tried to argue that a national drinking age infringed on the powers of the state in a matter traditionally under state control. However, the new law, enacted in 1984, did not directly mandate a national drinking age. Instead, it ordered the withholding of 10 percent of all federal highway funds from any state that failed to raise its minimum drinking age to twenty-one. States retained the rights to ignore the national minimum and give up a portion of their highway funds. (Congress used this same approach in 1974 in establishing a national 55-mile-per-hour speed limit.) Opponents of this device labeled it federal blackmail and a federal intrusion into state responsibilities. For some state officials, then, the issue was not teen drinking but rather the preemption of state authority.

From a purely constitutional perspective, Congress simply exercised its power to spend money for the general welfare; it did not *directly* legislate in an area *reserved* to the states. Technically, states remain free to set their own minimum drinking age. Despite heated arguments in many state legislatures, all of the states adopted the twenty-one-year-old minimum national drinking age by 1990.

*Appeals by groups such as Mothers Against Drunk Driving (MADD) helped overcome concerns that legislation effectively setting a national drinking age would infringe on state authority.*

grants that state and local officials often lack information about their availability, purpose, and requirements. "Grantsmanship"—knowing where and how to obtain federal grants—is highly valued in state and local governments. Federal grants can be obtained to preserve historic buildings, develop minority-owned businesses, aid foreign refugees, drain abandoned mines, control riots, subsidize school milk programs, and so on. However, welfare (including cash benefits and food stamps) and health (including Medicaid for the poor) account for two-thirds of federal aid money (see Figure 4.4).

Thus many of the special projects and ongoing programs carried out today by state and local governments are funded by grants from the federal government. These funds have generally been dispersed as either categorical grants or block grants.

- *Categorical Grant:* A grant for a specific, narrow project. The project must be approved by a federal administrative agency. About 90 percent of federal aid money is distributed in the form of categorical grants. Categorical grants can be distributed on a project basis or a formula basis. Grants made on a project basis

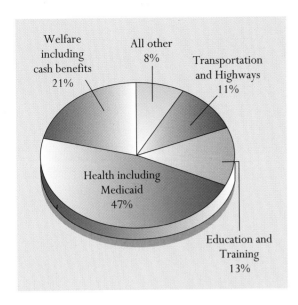

**Figure 4.4** Purposes of Federal Grants to State and Local Governments
Over one-fifth of all state and local government revenues are derived from federal grants. Federal grants-in-aid to state and local governments are especially vital in the areas of health and welfare.

*Source:* Budget of United States Government, 2007.

are distributed by federal administrative agencies to state or local governments that compete for project funds in their applications. Federal agencies have a great deal of discretion in selecting specific projects for support, and they can exercise direct control over the projects. Most categorical grants are distributed to state or local governments according to a fixed formula set by Congress. Medicaid and Food Stamps (see Chapter 13) are the largest categorical grant programs.

■  *Block Grant:*   A grant for a general governmental function, such as health, social services, law enforcement, education, or community development. State and local governments have fairly wide discretion in deciding how to spend federal block grant money within a functional area. For example, cities receiving "community development" block grants can decide for themselves about specific neighborhood development projects, housing projects, community facilities, and so on. All block grants are distributed on a formula basis set by Congress. Federal administrative agencies may require reports and adherence to rules and guidelines, but they do not choose which specific projects to fund.

**State–Local Dependency on Federal Grants**   Prior to 1980 and the presidential administration of Ronald Reagan, state and local governments throughout the United States were becoming increasingly dependent upon federal grant money. From 1960 to 1980 federal grants as a percent of state–local spending rose from 14.8 percent to 27.4 percent. President Reagan made significant cutbacks in the flow of federal funds to state and local governments, and by 1990 federal grants constituted only 18.9 percent of state–local spending (see Figure 4.5). Reagan achieved most of this reduction by transforming categorical grants into block grants and then reducing the size of the block grants below the sum of the categorical grants. But following Reagan's efforts, federal grants again began to creep up under Presidents Bill Clinton and George W. Bush, and today federal grants again account for about one-quarter of all state and local government spending.

**"Devolution"**   Controversy over federalism—what level of government should do what and who should pay for it—is as old as the nation itself (see *A Conflicting View:* "Liberals, Conservatives, and Federalism"). Beginning in 1995,

**Figure 4.5** State and Local Government Dependency on Federal Grants

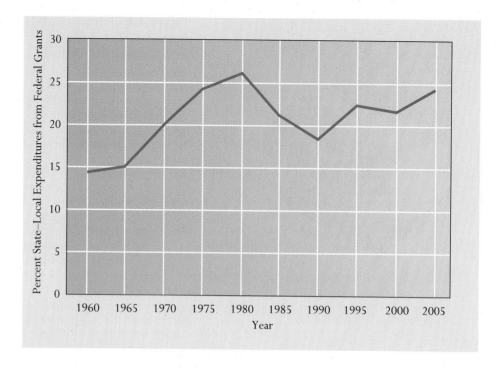

**devolution** Passing down of responsibilities from the national government to the states.

with a new Republican majority in both houses of Congress and Republicans holding a majority of state governorships, debates over federalism were renewed. The new phrase was **devolution**—the passing down of responsibilities from the national government to the states.

Welfare reform turned out to be the key to devolution. Bill Clinton once promised "to end welfare as we know it," but it was a Republican Congress in 1996 that did so. After President Clinton had twice vetoed welfare reform bills, he and Congress finally agreed to merge welfare reform with devolution. A new Temporary Assistance to Needy Families program (see Chapter 13) replaced direct federal cash aid welfare "entitlements." The new program:

- Establishes block grants with lump-sum allocations to the states for cash welfare payments.

- Grants the states broad flexibility in determining eligibility and benefit levels for persons receiving such aid.

- Limits the use of federally aided cash grants for most recipients to two continuing years and five years over their lifetime.

- Allows states to deny additional cash payments for children born to women already receiving welfare assistance and allowing states to deny cash payments to parents under eighteen who do not live with an adult and attend school.

Since Franklin D. Roosevelt's New Deal, with its federal guarantee of cash Aid to Families with Dependent Children (AFDC), low-income mothers and children had enjoyed a federal "entitlement" to welfare payments. But welfare reform, with its devolution of responsibility to the states, ended this sixty-year-old federal entitlement. Note, however, that Congress continues to place "strings" on the use of federal welfare funds, including a two-year limit on continuing payments to beneficiaries and a five-year lifetime limit.

## A CONFLICTING VIEW

# Liberals, Conservatives, and Federalism

From the earliest days of the Republic, American leaders and scholars have argued over federalism. Political interests that constitute a majority at the national level and control the national government generally praise the virtue of national supremacy. Political interests that do not control the national government but exercise controlling influence in one or more states generally see great merit in preserving the powers of the states.

In recent years, political conflict over federalism—over the division between national versus state and local responsibilities and finances—has tended to follow traditional "liberal" and "conservative" political cleavages. Generally, liberals seek to enhance the power of the *national* government because they believe people's lives can be changed— and bettered—by the exercise of national governmental power. The government in Washington has more power and resources than do state and local governments, which many liberals regard as too slow, cumbersome, weak, and unresponsive. Thus liberalism and centralization are closely related in American politics.

In contrast, conservatives generally seek to return power to *state and local* governments. Conservatives are skeptical about the "good" that government can do and believe that adding to the power of the national government is not an effective way of resolving society's problems. On the contrary, they argue that "government is the problem, not the solution." Excessive government regulation, burdensome taxation, and inflationary government spending combine to restrict individual freedom, penalize work and savings, and destroy incentives for economic growth. Government should be kept small, controllable, and close to the people.

There is no way to settle the argument over federalism once and for all. Debates about federalism are part of the fabric of American politics.

**Political Obstacles to Devolution and Federalism** Politicians in Washington are fond of the rhetoric of federalism. They know that Americans generally prefer governments closer to home. Yet at the same time they confront strong political pressures to "DO SOMETHING!" about virtually every problem that confronts individuals, families, or communities, whether or not doing so may overstep the enumerated powers of the national government. Politicians gain very little by telling their constituents that a particular problem—violence in the schools, domestic abuse, physician-assisted suicide, and so on—is not a federal responsibility and should be dealt with at the state or local level of government. So both federal and state politicians compete to address well-publicized problems.[18]

Moreover, neither presidents nor members of Congress are inclined to restrain their own power. Both liberals and conservatives in Washington are motivated to tie their own strings to federal grant-in-aid money, issue their own federal mandates, and otherwise "correct" what they perceive to be errors or inadequacies of state policies.

**Urban Institute** Washington think tank offers viewpoints on federalism and issues confronting state/local government. *www.urban.org*

# Coercive Federalism: Preemptions and Mandates

Traditionally, Congress avoided issuing direct orders to state and local governments. Instead, it sought to influence them by offering grants of money with federal rules, regulations, or "guidelines" attached. In theory at least, states and communities were free to forgo the money and ignore the strings attached to it. But increasingly Congress has undertaken direct regulation of areas traditionally reserved to the states and restricted state authority to regulate these areas. And it has issued direct orders to state and local governments to perform various services and comply with federal law in the performance of these services.

**preemption** Total or partial federal assumption of power in a particular field, restricting the authority of the states.

**total preemption** Federal government's assumption of all regulatory powers in a particular field.

**partial preemption** Federal government's assumption of some regulatory powers in a particular field, with the stipulation that a state law on the same subject as a federal law is valid if it does not conflict with the federal law in the same area.

**standard partial preemption** Form of partial preemption in which the states are permitted to regulate activities already regulated by the federal government if the state regulatory standards are at least as stringent as the federal government's.

**mandate** Perception of popular support for a program or policy based on the margin of electoral victory won by a candidate who proposed it during a campaign; direct federal orders to state and local governments requiring them to perform a service or to obey federal laws in the performance of their functions.

**Federal Preemptions**  The supremacy of federal laws over those of the states, spelled out in the National Supremacy Clause of the Constitution, permits Congress to decide whether or not there is **preemption** of state laws in a particular field by federal law. In **total preemption**, the federal government assumes all regulatory powers in a particular field—for example, copyrights, bankruptcy, railroads, and airlines. No state regulations in a totally preempted field are permitted. **Partial preemption** stipulates that a state law on the same subject is valid as long as it does not conflict with the federal law in the same area. For example, the Occupational Safety and Health Act of 1970 specifically permits state regulation of any occupational safety or health issue on which the federal Occupational Safety and Health Administration (OSHA) has *not* developed a standard; but once OSHA enacts a standard, all state standards are nullified. A specific form of partial preemption called **standard partial preemption** permits states to regulate activities in a field already regulated by the federal government, as long as state regulatory standards are at least as stringent as those of the federal government. Usually states must submit their regulations to the responsible federal agency for approval; the federal agency may revoke a state's regulating power if that state fails to enforce the approved standards. For example, the federal Environmental Protection Agency (EPA) permits state environmental regulations that meet or exceed EPA standards.

**Federal Mandates**  Federal **mandates** are direct orders to state and local governments to perform a particular activity or service or to comply with federal laws in the performance of their functions. Federal mandates occur in a wide variety of areas, from civil rights to minimum-wage regulations. Their range is reflected in some recent examples of federal mandates to state and local governments:

- *Age Discrimination Act, 1986:*  Outlaws mandatory retirement ages for public as well as private employees, including police, firefighters, and state college and university faculty.

- *Asbestos Hazard Emergency Act, 1986:*  Orders school districts to inspect for asbestos hazards and remove asbestos from school buildings when necessary.

- *Safe Drinking Water Act, 1986:*  Establishes national requirements for municipal water supplies; regulates municipal waste treatment plants.

- *Clean Air Act, 1990:*  Bans municipal incinerators and requires auto emission inspections in certain urban areas.

- *Americans with Disabilities Act, 1990:*  Requires all state and local government buildings to promote handicapped access.

- *National Voter Registration Act, 1993:*  Requires states to register voters at driver's license, welfare, and unemployment compensation offices.

- *No Child Left Behind Act, 2001:*  Requires states and their school districts to test public school pupils.

State and local governments frequently complain that the costs imposed on them by complying with such federal mandates are seldom reimbursed by Washington.

**"Unfunded" Mandates**  Federal mandates often impose heavy costs on states and communities. When no federal monies are provided to cover these

## A CONSTITUTIONAL NOTE

### How Is National and State Power Divided?

The Constitution gives to Congress—that is, to the national government—seventeen specific grants of power, the so-called "enumerated powers." These are followed by an eighteenth "necessary and proper" power—"to make all laws which shall be necessary and proper for carrying into Execution the foregoing powers, and all other Powers vested by this Constitution in the Government of the United States . . ." (Article I, Section 8). It is this last "implied powers" or "elastic" clause that has been used extensively by the national government to greatly expand its power.

But what of the states? The Founders believed that the Constitution left all other governmental powers to the states. The Tenth Amendment solidified that idea: "The powers not delegated to the United States by the Constitution, nor prohibited by it to the States, are reserved to the States respectively, or to the people." The "reserved powers" of the states are limited only by a few paragraphs in the text of the Constitution, notably Article I, Section 10, which, among other things, prohibits the states from entering into treaties with other nations, or coining money, or passing laws impairing the obligation of contracts, or granting any title of nobility, or placing taxes or duties on imports or exports, or engaging in war with a foreign power "unless actually invaded."

In brief, the original Constitution envisioned the states as having the principal responsibility for the health, safety, education, welfare, law enforcement, and protection of their people. This constitutional "division of power" remains in the Constitution, despite great shifts in power to the national government. Subsequent amendments prohibited slavery in the states (Amendment 13); prohibited states from abridging the privileges or immunities of citizens of the United States, or depriving any person of life, liberty, or property without due process of law, or denying any person within this jurisdiction equal protection of the laws (Amendment 14); or prohibiting citizens the right to vote because of race, color, or previous condition of servitude (Amendment 15); or denying the right to vote for failure to pay any poll tax or other tax (Amendment 24); or denying anyone eighteen years of age or older the right to vote on account of age (Amendment 26).

So anyone reading the Constitution, without knowledge of the history of constitutional change in United States, would not really understand the nature of our government.

---

costs, the mandates are said to be **unfunded mandates**. Governors, mayors, and other state and local officials have often urged Congress to stop imposing unfunded mandates on states and communities. Private industries have long voiced the same complaint. Regulations and mandates allow Congress to address problems while pushing the costs of doing so onto others.

**Homeland Security**  The Constitution gives the federal government the responsibility for national defense. The terrorist attacks on the World Trade Center in New York and the Pentagon in Washington, on September 11, 2001, began what President George W. Bush described as a long and difficult "war on terrorism." Washington reorganized itself, creating a new Department of Homeland Security (see Chapter 10), and allocated billions of dollars for homeland defenses. But the "first responders" to any terrorist attack are state and local police, fire, medical, and other emergency agencies. States, counties, and cities now face unprecedented and permanent responsibilities in homeland security, even including dealing with the results of nuclear, biological, and chemical attacks. Governors, mayors, city and county officials, and especially police, fire, and emergency officers, have urged the Congress to provide more federal funding and resources to state and local agencies for homeland security. Congress has responded with billions of dollars in additional aid, but states and communities claim that assistance for their "first responders" is inadequate.

**unfunded mandates**
Mandates that impose costs on state and local governments (and private industry) without reimbursement from the federal government.

# Summary Notes

- The struggle for power between the national government and the states over two centuries has shaped American federalism today.

- Federalism is the division of power between two separate authorities, the nation and the state, each of which enforces its own laws directly on its citizens and neither of which can change the division of power without the consent of the other.

- American federalism was designed by the Founders as an additional protection for individual liberty by providing for the division and dispersal of power among multiple units of government.

- Federalism has also been defended as a means of increasing opportunities to hold public office, improving governmental efficiency, ensuring policy responsiveness, encouraging policy innovation, and managing conflict.

- However, federalism can also obstruct and frustrate national action. Narrow state interests can sometimes prevail over national interests or the interests of minorities within states. Segregation was long protected by theories of states' rights. Federalism also results in uneven levels of public services through the nation.

- Power has flowed to the national government over time, as the original state-centered division of power has evolved into a national-centered system of government. Among the most important historical influences on this shift in power toward Washington have been the Supreme Court's broad interpretation of national power, the national government's victory over the secessionist states in the Civil War, the establishment of a national system of civil rights based on the Fourteenth Amendment, the growth of a national economy governed by Congress under its interstate commerce power, and the national government's accumulation of power through its greater financial resources.

- Federal grants to state and local governments have greatly expanded the national government's powers in areas previously regarded as *reserved* to the states.

- Federal grants are available for most state and local government activities, but health and welfare account for about two-thirds of these grants. Grant money flows unevenly to the states, causing complaints from states that send more tax dollars then they get back.

- Although Congress has generally refrained from directly legislating in areas traditionally *reserved* to the states, federal power in local affairs has grown as a result of federal rules, regulations, and guidelines established as conditions for the receipt of federal funds.

- The Supreme Court in its *Garcia* decision in 1985 removed all constitutional barriers to direct congressional legislation in matters traditionally reserved to the states. Establishing the principle of representational federalism, the Court said that states could defend their own interests through their representation in the national government.

- Representational federalism focuses on the role of the states in electing national officials—the president through the allocation of Electoral College votes to the states, the Senate through the allocation of two seats for each state, and the House through the apportionment of representatives based on the state's population.

- Recent efforts at the "devolution" of federal responsibilities for welfare resulted in an end to federal individual "entitlements" to cash welfare payments and their replacement with block grants for cash aid to the states. But Congress continues to place "strings" on the use of federal welfare grants to the states.

# Key Terms

| | | | |
|---|---|---|---|
| federalism 105 | delegated, or enumerated, powers 110 | reserved powers 114 | devolution 126 |
| unitary system 105 | | dual federalism 116 | preemption 128 |
| confederation 105 | Necessary and Proper Clause 111 | cooperative federalism 118 | total preemption 128 |
| home rule 105 | implied powers 111 | centralized federalism 119 | partial preemption 128 |
| intergovernmental relations 105 | National Supremacy Clause 112 | new federalism 119 | standard partial preemption 128 |
| laboratories of democracy 109 | concurrent powers 114 | representational federalism 120 | mandate 128 |
| | | grants-in-aid 123 | unfunded mandates 129 |

# Suggested Readings

Beer, Samuel H. *To Make a Nation: The Rediscovery of American Federalism*. Cambridge, Mass.: Harvard University Press, 1993. A historical account of the development of both federalism and nationalism in American political philosophy.

Dye, Thomas R. *American Federalism: Competition among Governments*. Lexington, Mass.: Lexington Books, 1990. A theory of "competitive federalism" arguing that rivalries among governments improve public services while lowering taxes, restrain the growth of government, promote innovation and experimentation in public policies, inspire greater responsiveness to the preferences of citizen-taxpayers, and encourage economic growth.

Ehrenhalt, Alan, ed. *Governing: Issues and Applications from the Front Lines of Government*, 2nd ed. Washington D.C.: CQ Press, 2005. A collection of essays and case studies on state and local government management, with federal relations given prominence.

Elazar, Daniel J. *The American Partnership*. Chicago: University of Chicago Press, 1962. Classic study of the historical evolution of federalism, stressing the nation-state sharing of policy concerns and financing, from the early days of the Republic, and the politics behind the gradual growth of national power.

Nagel, Robert F. *The Implosion of Federalism*. New York: Oxford University Press, 2001. America's political institutions are collapsing into the center, reducing the opportunity for competition and participation.

Ostrum, Vincent. *The Meaning of American Federalism*. San Francisco: ICS Press, 1991. A theoretical examination of federalism, setting forth the conditions for a self-governing society and arguing that multiple, overlapping units of government, with various checks on one another's power, provide a viable democratic system of conflict resolution.

O'Toole, Laurence J., ed. *American Intergovernmental Relations*. 3rd ed. Washington, D.C.: CQ Press, 1999. A collection of readings, both classic and contemporary, describing the theory, history, and current problems of intergovernmental relations in America.

Peterson, Paul E. *The Price of Federalism*. Washington, D.C.: Brookings Institution, 1995. Historical, theoretical, and empirical perspectives merged into a new, timely model of federalism that would allocate social welfare functions to the national government and education and economic development to states and communities.

Van Horn, Carl E. *The State of the States*. 4th ed. Washington, D.C.: CQ Press, 2005. An assessment of the challenges facing state governments as a result of the devolution revolution.

# Make It Real

## FEDERALISM
This unit delves into *McCulloch v. Maryland* and Katrina.

# Part Three
# PARTICIPANTS

## God and Country

**ABCNEWS**

Originally Aired: **November 26, 2002**
Program: **Nightline**
Running Time: **12:41**

Over the last couple of years, what has come to be called the Christian Right has become more and more active in supporting the Sharon government in its war with the Palestinians. And their political clout with the Bush administration is considerable. They are opposed to giving the Palestinians any land, taking a much harder line than many Americans. The reason? Prophecy. Many believe that what is playing out now in the Middle East is all part of the process leading toward the Second Coming. The existence of the state of Israel is crucial to that process and many believe that Israel must cover all of the land, including the occupied territories, in order for this process to move forward. So they send money, take trips to Israel, meet regularly with Israeli officials, including Sharon, and at the same time, seem to be breaking what was a strong alliance between American Jews and the Democratic Party. That would certainly change the political landscape in this country as well. Israel needs friends now, facing serious criticism from much of the world over its tactics in the current conflict.

And so both sides are sort of glossing over a theological issue. According to the prophecies that many Christians believe, as part of the Second Coming, Jews will have the opportunity to either convert to Christianity or perish. In other words, they will disappear as a people, or religion, one way or the other. You might think this would be a point of contention between the two religions but it doesn't appear to be. Ted Koppel interviews Pat Robertson, founder and chairman of the Christian Broadcasting Network. He is a former presidential candidate and arguably one of the most recognized leaders of the evangelical Christian community.

## Critical Thinking Questions

1. In "God and Country," conservative Christians explain their strong support for Israel, especially their support of Jewish occupation of the West Bank. Briefly discuss the reasons they give for this support.

2. Not all Jews welcome the support of conservative American Christians. What implications of that support concern them?

3. As a general rule, interest groups rarely have a decisive role in the formulation of foreign policy. How might conservative Christian support for Israel be an exception to that rule?

# 5 PARTICIPATION, CAMPAIGNS, AND ELECTIONS:
## Deciding Who Governs

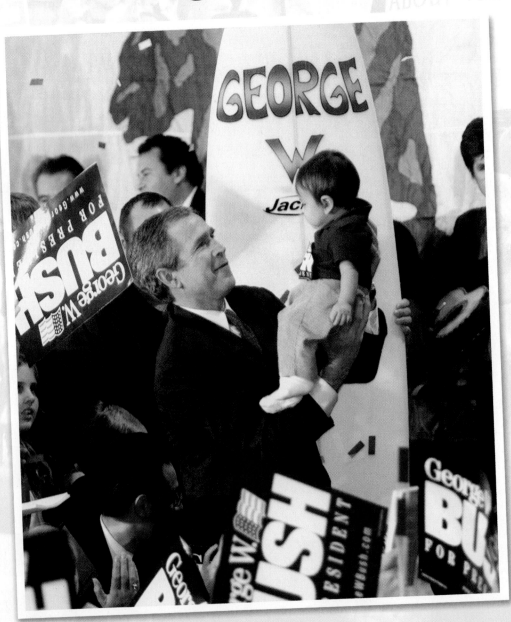

## Chapter Outline

- Individual Participation in Politics
- Voters and Nonvoters
- Elections in a Democracy
- The Advantages of Incumbency
- Campaign Strategies
- How Much Does It Cost to Get Elected?
- Raising Campaign Cash
- What Do Contributors "Buy"?
- Regulating Campaign Finance
- The Presidential Campaign: The Primary Race
- The Presidential Campaign: The General Election Battle
- The Voter Decides

## Think About Politics

**1** Is our government really legitimate when only about half the people vote in presidential elections?
Yes ☐ No ☐

**2** Should people vote on the basis of a candidate's personal character rather than his or her policy positions?
Yes ☐ No ☐

**3** Would you vote for a candidate who used negative ads to discredit an opponent?
Yes ☐ No ☐

**4** Do political campaign contributions have too much influence on elections and government policy?
Yes ☐ No ☐

**5** Are high campaign costs discouraging good people from becoming candidates?
Yes ☐ No ☐

*What real power do you have in a democracy? By casting ballots, citizens in a democracy have the power to determine who will represent them, who will make up the government under which they live. You, then, are an integral part of the democratic process every time you vote in an election.*

## Individual Participation in Politics

Democracies provide a variety of ways for individuals to participate in politics. People may run for, and win, public office; take part in marches, demonstrations, and protests; make financial contributions to political candidates or causes; attend political meetings, speeches, and rallies; write letters to public officials or to newspapers; wear a political button or place a bumper sticker on their car; belong to organizations that support or oppose particular candidates or take stands on public issues; attempt to influence friends while discussing candidates or issues; and vote in elections. Individuals may also participate in politics passively, by simply following political issues and campaigns in the media, acquiring knowledge, forming opinions about public affairs, and expressing their views to others. These forms of political participation can be ranked according to their order of frequency (see Figure 5.1). Only a little more than half of the voting-age population vote in presidential elections, and far fewer vote in congressional and state and local elections (see Figure 5.2).

## Voters and Nonvoters

Who votes and who doesn't? The perceived benefits and costs of voting apparently do not fall evenly across all social groups. Nonvoting would generate less concern if voters were a representative cross section of nonvoters. But voters differ from nonvoters in politically important ways.

Voters are better educated than nonvoters. Education appears to be the most important determinant of voter turnout (see Figure 5.3). It may be that schooling promotes an interest in politics, instills the ethic of citizen participation, or gives people a better awareness of public affairs and an understanding of the role of elections in a democracy. Education is associated with a sense of confidence and political *efficacy*, the feeling that one can indeed have a personal impact on public affairs.

Age is another factor affecting voter participation. Perhaps because young people have more distractions, more demands on their time in

**Figure 5.1** Political Participation

Only a small percentage of the American people are actively engaged in the political process, yet they receive most of the media attention. Less than 1 percent of the population runs for office at any level of government, and only about half of all voting-age Americans bother to go to the polls even in a presidential election.

*Source: National Election Studies Cumulative File.* See also M. Margaret Conway, *Political Participation in the United States,* 3rd ed. (Washington, D.C.: CQ Press, 2000).

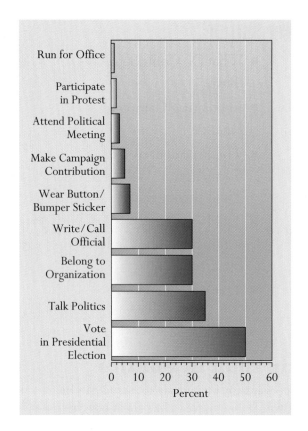

school, work, or new family responsibilities, nonvoting is greatest among eighteen- to twenty-four-year-olds. In contrast, older Americans are politically influential in part because candidates know they turn out at the polls.

High-income people are more likely to vote than are low-income people. Most of this difference stems from the fact that high-income people are more likely to be well educated and older. But poor people may also feel alienated from the political system—they may lack a sense of political efficacy; they may feel they have little control over their own lives, let alone over public affairs. Or poor people may simply be so absorbed in the problems of life that they have little time or energy to spend on registering and voting.[1]

Income and education differences between participants and nonparticipants are even greater when other forms of political participation are considered. Higher-income, better-educated people are much more likely to be among those who make campaign contributions, who write or call their elected representatives, and who join and work in active political organizations.[2]

Historically, race was a major determinant of nonvoting. Black voter turnout, especially in the South, was markedly lower than white voter turnout. African Americans continue today to have a slightly lower overall voter turnout than whites, but most of the remaining difference is attributable to differences between blacks and whites in educational and income levels. Blacks and whites at the same educational and income levels register and vote with the same frequency. Indeed, in cities where African Americans are well organized politically, black voter turnout may exceed white voter turnout.[3]

## Elections in a Democracy

Democratic government is government by "the consent of the governed." Elections give practical meaning to this notion of "consent." Elections allow people

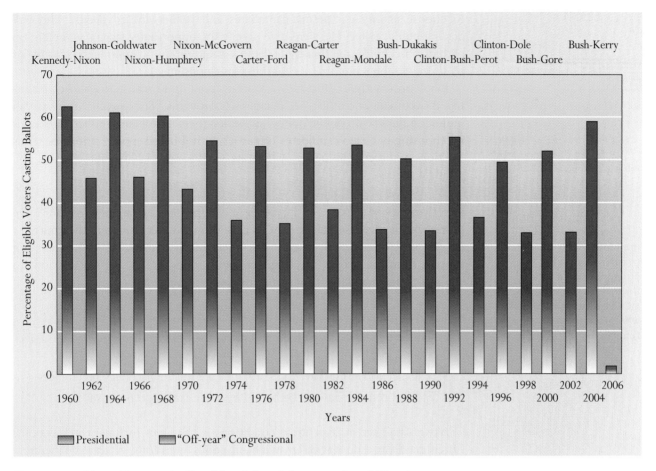

**Figure 5.2**    Voter Turnout in Presidential and Congressional Elections

Voter turnout is always higher in years with a presidential election. However, voter turnout has generally declined since 1960, even in presidential election years. The exception came in 1992, when intense interest in the contest between George H.W. Bush and Bill Clinton—spiced by the entry of independent Ross Perot—led to a higher-than-normal turnout. In 1996 fewer than half of voting-age Americans bothered to cast ballots. However, in 2004 voter turnout rose to levels not seen since the 1960s.

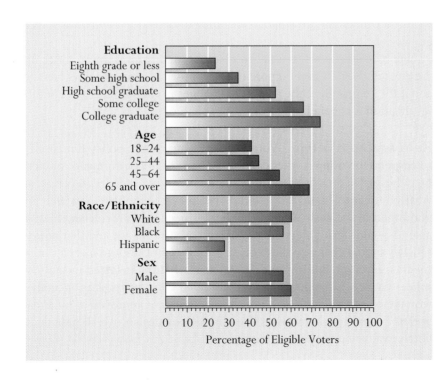

**Figure 5.3**    Voter Turnout by Social Groups

Although there is virtually no gender gap in who goes to the polls, voter turnout increases with education, age, and income. Major efforts to "get out the vote" in the African American community have raised voter turnout to nearly that of whites, but turnout among Hispanics continues to lag.

*Source:* U.S. Bureau of the Census, *Statistical Abstract of the United States,* 2006. Data for 2004 presidential election.

to choose among competing candidates and parties and to decide who will occupy public office. Elections give people the opportunity to pass judgment on current officeholders, either by reelecting them (granting continued consent) or by throwing them out of office (withdrawing consent).

In a representative democracy, elections function primarily to choose personnel to occupy public office—to decide "who governs." But elections also have an indirect influence on public policy, allowing voters to influence policy directions by choosing between candidates or parties with different policy priorities. Thus elections indirectly influence "who gets what"—that is, the outcomes of the political process.

**Elections as Mandates?**   However, it is difficult to argue that elections serve as "policy mandates"—that is, that elections allow voters to direct the course of public policy. Frequently, election winners claim a **mandate**—overwhelming support from the people—for their policies and programs. But for elections to serve as policy mandates, four conditions have to be met:

**mandate** Perception of popular support for a program or policy based on the margin of electoral victory won by a candidate who proposed it during a campaign.

1. Competing candidates have to offer clear policy alternatives.
2. The voters have to cast their ballots on the basis of these policy alternatives alone.
3. The election results have to clearly indicate the voters' policy preferences.
4. Elected officials have to be bound by their campaign promises.[4]

As we shall see, *none* of these conditions is fully met in American elections. Often candidates do not differ much on policy questions, or they deliberately obscure their policy positions to avoid offending groups of voters. Voters themselves frequently pay little attention to policy issues in elections but rather vote along traditional party lines or group affiliations, or on the basis of the candidate's character, personality, or media image.

Moreover, even in elections in which issues seem to dominate the campaign, the outcome may not clearly reflect policy preferences. Candidates take stands on a variety of issues. It is never certain on which issues the voters agreed with the winner and on which issues they disagreed yet voted for the candidate anyway.

Finally, candidates often fail to abide by their campaign promises once they are elected. Some simply ignore their promises, assuming voters have forgotten about the campaign. Others point to changes in circumstances or conditions as a justification for abandoning a campaign pledge.

**Retrospective Voting**   Voters can influence future policy directions through **retrospective voting**—votes cast on the basis of the performance of incumbents, by either reelecting them or throwing them out of office.[5] Voters may not know what politicians will do in the future, but they can evaluate how well politicians performed in the past. When incumbent officeholders are defeated, it is reasonable to assume that voters did not like their performance and that newly elected officials should change policy course if they do not want to meet a similar fate in the next election. But it is not always clear what the defeated incumbents did in office that led to their ouster by the voters. Nor, indeed, can incumbents who won reelection assume that all of their policies are approved of by a majority of voters. Nevertheless, retrospective voting provides an overall judgment of how voters evaluate performance in office.

**retrospective voting** Voting for or against a candidate or party on the basis of past performance in office.

─── Think Again ───
Should elected officials be bound by their campaign promises?

# COMPARED TO WHAT?

## Voter Turnout in Western Democracies

Other Western democracies regularly report higher voter turnout rates than the United States (see figure). Yet in an apparent paradox, Americans seem to be more supportive of their political institutions, less alienated from their political system, and even more patriotic than citizens of Western European nations. Why, then, are voter turnouts in the United States so much lower than in these other democracies?

The answer to this question lies primarily in the legal and institutional differences between the United States and the other democracies. First of all, in Austria, Australia, Belgium, and Italy, voting is *mandatory.* Penalties and the level of enforcement vary within and across these countries. Moreover, registration laws in the United States make voting more difficult than in other countries. In Western Europe, all citizens are required to register with the government and obtain identification cards. These cards are then used for admission to the polls. In contrast, voter registration is entirely voluntary in the United States, and voters must reregister if they change residences. Nearly 50 percent of the U.S. population changes residence at least once in a five-year period, thus necessitating reregistration.

Parties in the United States are more loosely organized, less disciplined, and less able to mobilize voters than are European parties. Moreover, many elections in the United States, notably elections for Congress, are not very competitive. The United States organizes congressional elections by district with winner-take-all rules, whereas many European parliaments are selected by proportional representation, with seats allocated to parties based on national vote totals. Proportional representation means every vote counts toward seats in the legislative body. Thus greater competition and proportional representation may encourage higher voter turnout in European democracies.

But cultural differences may also contribute to differences in turnout. The American political culture, with its tradition of individualism and self-reliance and its reluctance to empower government (see Chapter 2), encourages Americans to resolve their problems through their own efforts rather than looking to government for solutions. Government is not as central to Americans as it is to Europeans, and therefore getting to the polls on election day is not seen as so important.

### Average Turnout, 1991–2000

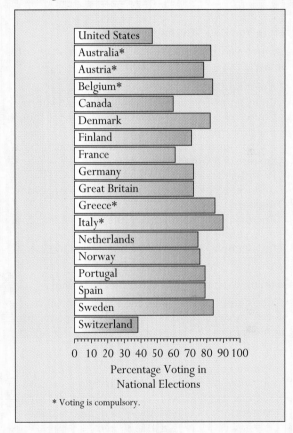

*Source:* Center for Voting and Democracy, 2002, *www.fairvote.org.* Reprinted by permission.

## The Advantages of Incumbency

In theory, elections offer voters the opportunity to "throw the rascals out." But in practice, voters seldom do so. **Incumbents**, people already holding public office, have a strong advantage when they seek reelection. The reelection rates of incumbents for *all* elective offices—city council, mayor, state legislature, governor, and especially Congress—are very high. Since 1950, more than 90 percent of all members of the House of Representatives who have sought reelection have been successful. The success rate of U.S. Senate incumbents is not as great, but it is still impressive; since 1950, more than 70 percent of senators seeking reelection have been successful.[6]

**incumbent** Candidate currently in office seeking reelection.

## UP CLOSE

# How to Run for Office

Many rewards come with elected office—the opportunity to help shape public policy, public attention and name recognition, and many business, professional, and social contacts. But there are many drawbacks as well—the absence of privacy; a microscopic review of one's past; constant calls, meetings, interviews, and handshaking; and, perhaps most onerous of all, the continual need to solicit campaign funds.

### Before You Run—Getting Involved

Get involved in various organizations in your community:

- Neighborhood associations.
- Chambers of commerce, business associations.
- Churches and synagogues (become an usher, if possible, for visibility).
- Political groups (Democratic or Republican clubs, League of Women Voters, and so on).
- Parent-Teacher Associations (PTAs).
- Service clubs (Rotary, Kiwanis, Civitan, Toastmasters).
- Recreation organizations (Little League, flag football, soccer leagues, running and walking clubs, for example, as participant, coach, or umpire).

### Deciding to Run—Know What You're Doing

In deciding to run, and choosing the office for which you wish to run, you should become thoroughly familiar with the issues, duties, and responsibilities.

- Attend council or commission meetings, state legislative sessions, and/or committee hearings.
- Become familiar with current issues and officeholders, and obtain a copy of and read the budget.
- Learn the demographics of your district (racial, ethnic, and age composition; occupational mix; average income; neighborhood differences). If you do not fit the prevailing racial, ethnic, or age composition, think about moving to another district.
- Memorize a brief (preferably less than seven seconds) answer to the question, "Why are you running?"

### Getting in the Race

Contact your county elections department to obtain the following:

- Qualifying forms and information.
- Campaign financing forms and regulations.

- District and street maps for your district.
- Recent election results in your district.
- Election-law book or pamphlet.
- Voter registration lists (usually sold as lists, or labels, or tapes).
- Contact your party's county chairperson for advice; convince the party's leaders that you can win. Ask for a list of their regular campaign contributors.

### Raising Money

The easiest way to finance a campaign is to be rich enough to provide your own funds. Failing that, you must:

- Establish a campaign fund, according to the laws of your state.
- Find a treasurer/campaign-finance chairperson who knows many wealthy, politically involved people.
- Invite wealthy, politically involved people to small coffees, cocktail parties, dinners; give a brief campaign speech and then have your finance chairperson solicit contributions.
- Follow up fund-raising events and meetings with personal phone calls.
- Be prepared to continue fund-raising activities throughout your campaign; file accurate financial disclosure statements as required by state law.

### Getting Organized

Professional campaign managers and management firms almost always outperform volunteers. If you cannot afford professional management, you must rely on yourself or trusted friends to perform the following:

- Draw up a budget based on reasonable expectations of campaign funding.
- Interview and select a professional campaign-management firm, or appoint a trusted campaign manager.
- Ask trusted friends from various clubs, activities, neighborhoods, churches, and so on, to meet and serve as a campaign committee. If your district is racially or ethnically diverse, make sure all groups are represented on your committee.
- Decide on a campaign theme; research issues important to your community; develop brief, well-articulated positions on these issues.
- Open a campaign headquarters with desks and telephones. Buy a cell phone; use call forwarding; stay in contact. Use your garage if you can't afford an office.

- Arrange to meet with newspaper editors, editorial boards, TV station executives, and political reporters. Be prepared for tough questions.
- Hire a media consultant or advertising agency, or appoint a volunteer media director who knows television, radio, and newspaper advertising.
- Arrange a press conference to announce your candidacy. Notify all media well in advance. Arrange for overflow crowd of supporters to cheer and applaud.
- Produce eyecatching, inspirational 15- or 30-second television and radio ads that present a favorable image of you and stress your campaign theme.
- Prepare and print attractive campaign brochures, signs, and bumper stickers.
- Hire a local survey-research firm to conduct telephone surveys of voters in your district, asking what they think are the most important issues, how they stand on them, whether they recognize your name and your theme, and how they plan to vote. Be prepared to change your theme and your position on issues if surveys show strong opposition to your views.

### On the Campaign Trail

Campaigns themselves may be primarily media centered or primarily *door-to-door* ("retail") or some combination of both.

- Buy media time as early as possible from television and radio stations; insist on prime-time slots before, during, and after popular shows.
- Buy newspaper ads; insist on their placement in popular, well-read sections of the paper.
- Attend every community gathering possible, just to be seen, even if you do not give a speech. Keep all speeches short. Focus on one or two issues that your polls show are important to voters.
- Recruit paid or unpaid volunteers to hand out literature door-to-door. Record names and addresses of voters who say they support you.
- Canvass door-to-door with a brief (seven-second) self-introduction and statement of your reasons for running. Use registration lists to identify members of your own party, and try to address them by name. Also canvass offices, factories, coffee shops, shopping malls—anywhere you find a crowd.
- Organize a phone bank, either professional or volunteer. Prepare *brief* introduction and phone statements. Record names of people who say they support you.

- Know your opponent: Research his or her past affiliations, indiscretions if any, previous voting record, and public positions on issues.
- Be prepared to "define" your opponent in negative terms. Negative advertising works. But be fair: Base your comments on your opponent's public record. Emphasize his or her positions that clearly deviate from your district voters' known preferences.

### Primary versus General Elections

Remember that you will usually have to campaign in two elections—your party's primary and the general election.

- Before the primary, identify potential opposition in your own party, try to dissuade them from running.
- Allocate your budget first to win the primary election. If you lose the primary, you won't need any funds for the general election.
- In general elections, you must broaden your appeal without distancing your own party supporters. Deemphasize your party affiliation unless your district regularly elects members of your party; in a close district or a district that regularly votes for the opposition party, stress your independence and your commitment to the *district's* interests.

### On Election Day

Turning out your voters is the key to success. Election day is the busiest day of the campaign for you and your staff.

- Use your phone bank to place as many calls as possible to party members in your district (especially those who have indicated in previous calls and visits that they support you). Remind them to vote; make sure your phone workers can tell each voter where to go to cast his or her vote.
- Solicit volunteers to drive people to the polls.
- Assign workers to as many polling places as possible. Most state laws require that they stay a specified distance from the voting booths. But they should be in evidence with your signs and literature to buttonhole voters before they go into the booths.
- Show up at city or county election office on election night with prepared victory statement thanking supporters and pledging your service to the district. (Also draft a courteous concession statement pledging your support to the winner, in case you lose.)
- Attend victory party with your supporters; meet many "new" friends.

Why do incumbents win so often? This is a particularly vexing question, inasmuch as so many people are distrustful of government and hold politicians in low esteem. Congress itself is the focal point of public disapproval and even ridicule. Yet people seem to distinguish between Congress as an institution—which they distrust—and their own members of Congress—whom they reelect. The result is something of a contradiction: popular members of Congress serving in an unpopular Congress (see *What Do You Think?* "Why Do Voters Reelect Members of an Unpopular Congress?" in Chapter 8). Three major advantages tend to enhance incumbents' chances of winning: name recognition, campaign contributions, and the resources of office.

**name recognition** Public awareness of a political candidate—whether they know his or her name.

**Name Recognition**   One reason for incumbents' success is that they begin the campaign with greater **name recognition** than their challengers, simply because they are the incumbent and their name has become familiar to their constituents over the previous years. Much of the daily work of all elected officials, especially members of Congress, is really public relations. Name recognition is a strategic advantage at the ballot box, especially if voters have little knowledge of policy positions or voting records. Voters tend to cast ballots for recognizable names over unknowns. Cynics have concluded that there is no such thing as bad publicity, only publicity. Even in cases of well-publicized scandals, incumbent members of Congress have won reelection; presumably, voters preferred "the devil they knew" to the one they did not.

**challengers** In politics, a reference to people running against incumbent officeholders.

**Campaign Contributions**   Incumbents have a strong advantage in raising campaign funds, simply because individuals and groups seeking access to those already in office are inspired to make contributions (see Table 5.1). **Challengers** have no immediate favors to offer; they must convince a potential contributor that they will win office and also that they are devoted to the interests of their financial backers.[7]

Contributing individuals and interest groups show a strong preference for incumbents over challengers. They do not wish to offend incumbent officeholders by contributing to their challengers; doing so risks both immediate retribution and future "freezing out" in the likely event of the challengers' defeat. Thus only when an incumbent has been especially hostile to an organization's interest, or in rare cases in which an incumbent seems especially vulnerable, will an interest group support a challenger. Yet challengers need even larger campaign war chests than incumbents to be successful. Challengers must overcome the greater name recognition of incumbents, their many office resources, and their records of constituency service. Thus even if incumbents and challengers had equal campaign treasuries, incumbents would enjoy the advantage.

**Table 5.1   Incumbent Advantage in Fund Raising**

|  | 2002 | 2004 | 2006 |
|---|---|---|---|
| **Senate** | | | |
| Average Incumbent Raised | $5,803,639 | $7,212,068 | $10,634,268 |
| Average Challenger Raised | 1,013,314 | 869,688 | 1,615,177 |
| **House** | | | |
| Average Incumbent Raised | 898,382 | 982,941 | 1,155,276 |
| Average Challenger Raised | 197,608 | 171,551 | 244,340 |

*Source:* Center for Responsive Politics; figures for 2002, 2004, and 2006 Congressional elections.

**Resources of Office**   Successful politicians use their offices to keep their names and faces before the public in various ways—public appearances, interviews, speeches, and press releases. Congressional incumbents make full use of the **franking privilege** (free use of the U.S. mails) to send self-promotional newsletters to tens of thousands of households in their district at taxpayers' expense. They travel on weekends to their district virtually year-round, using tax-funded travel allowances, to make local appearances, speeches, and contacts.

Members of Congress have large staffs working every day over many years with the principal objective of ensuring the reelection of their members. Indeed, Congress is structured as an "incumbent-protection society" organized and staffed to help guarantee the reelection of its members (see "Home Style" in Chapter 8). Service to constituents occupies the energies of congressional office staffs both in Washington and in local district offices established for this purpose. Casework wins voters one at a time: tracing lost Social Security checks, ferreting out which federal loans voters qualify for and helping them with their applications, and performing countless other personal favors. These individual "retail-level" favors are supplemented by larger-scale projects that experienced members of Congress can bring to their district or state (roads, dams, post offices, buildings, schools, grants, contracts), as well as undesirable projects (landfills, waste disposal sites, halfway houses) that they can keep out of their district. The longer incumbents have occupied the office, the more favors they have performed and the larger their networks of grateful voters.

## Campaign Strategies

Campaigning is largely a media activity, especially in presidential and congressional campaigns. Media campaigns are highly professionalized, relying on public relations and advertising specialists, professional fund-raisers, media consultants, and pollsters. Campaign management involves techniques that strongly resemble those employed in marketing commercial products. Professional media campaign management includes developing a **campaign strategy**: compiling computerized mailing lists and invitations for fund-raising events; selecting a campaign theme and coming up with a desirable candidate image; monitoring the progress of the campaign with continual polling of the voters; producing television tapes for commercials, newspaper advertisements, signs, bumper stickers, and radio spots; selecting clothing and hairstyles for the candidate; writing speeches and scheduling appearances; and even planning the victory party.

**Selecting a Theme**   Finding the right theme or "message" for a campaign is essential; this effort is not greatly different from that of launching an advertising campaign for a new detergent. A successful theme or "message" is one that characterizes the candidate or the electoral choice confronting the voters. A campaign theme need not be controversial; indeed, it need not even focus on a specific issue. It might be as simple as "a leader you can trust"—an attempt to "package" the candidate as competent and trustworthy.

Most media campaigns focus on candidates' personal qualities rather than on their stands on policy issues. Professional campaigns are based on the assumption that a candidate's "image" is the most important factor affecting voter choice. This image is largely devoid of issues, except in very general terms: for example, "tough on crime," "stands up to the special interests," "fights for the taxpayer," or "cares about you."

**Negative Campaigning: "Defining" the Opponent**   A media campaign also seeks to "define" the opponent in negative terms. The original negative TV

**franking privilege** Free use of the U.S. mails granted to members of Congress to promote communication with constituents.

**campaign strategy** Plan for a political campaign, usually including a theme, an attempt to define the opponent or the issues, and an effort to coordinate images and messages in news broadcasts and paid advertising.

**Campaigns and Elections**
The Web site for *Campaigns and Elections*, a magazine directed toward candidates, campaign managers, political TV advertisers, political consultants, and lobbyists.
*www.campaignline.com*

**negative campaigning**
Speeches, commercials, or advertising attacking a political opponent during a campaign.

ad is generally identified as the 1964 "Daisy Girl" commercial, aired by the Lyndon B. Johnson presidential campaign (see *Up Close:* "Dirty Politics"). Negative ads can serve a purpose in exposing the record of an opponent. But **negative campaigning** risks an opponent's counterattack charges of "mudslinging," "dirty tricks," and "sleaze."

Research into the opponent's public and personal background ("oppo research") provides the data for negative campaigning. Previous speeches and writings can be mined for embarrassing or mean-spirited statements. The voting record of the opponent can be scrutinized for unpopular policy positions. Any evils that occurred during an opponent's term of office can be attributed to him or her, either directly ("She knew and conspired in it") or indirectly ("He should have known and done something about it"). Personal scandals or embarrassments can be developed as evidence of "character." If campaign managers fear that highly personal attacks on an opponent will backfire, they may choose to leak the information to reporters and try to avoid attribution of the story to themselves or their candidate.

Negative advertising is often blamed on television's dominant role in political campaigns. "The high cost of television means now that you have to go for the jugular."[8] A political consultant summarized the current rules of political engagement as follows:

1. Advertise early if you have the money. . . .
2. Go negative early, often, and right through Election Day, if necessary.
3. Appeal to the heart and gut, rather than to the head.
4. Define your opponent to the voters before he or she can define him/herself or you.
5. If attacked, hit back even harder.
6. It's easier to give voters a negative impression of your opponent than it is to improve their image of you.[9]

**Using Focus Groups and Polling** Focus group techniques can help in selecting campaign themes and identifying negative characteristics in opponents. A **focus group** is a small group of people brought together to view videotapes, listen to specific campaign appeals, and respond to particular topics and issues. Media professionals then develop a campaign strategy around "hot-button" issues—issues that generate strong responses by focus groups—and avoid themes or issues that fail to elicit much interest.

**focus group** In a political context, a small number of people brought together in a comfortable setting to discuss and respond to themes and issues, allowing campaign managers to develop and analyze strategies.

The results of focus group work can then be tested in wider polling. Polling is a central feature of professional campaigning. Serious candidates for national and statewide offices almost always employ their own private polling firms, distinct from the national survey organizations that supply the media with survey data. Initial polling is generally designed to determine candidates' name recognition—the extent to which the voters recognize the candidates—and whatever positive and negative images are already associated with their names.

Campaign polling is highly professionalized, with telephone banks, trained interviewers, and computer-assisted-telephone-interviewing (CATI) software that records and tabulates responses instantly and sends the results to campaign managers. In well-financed campaigns, polling is continual throughout the campaign, so that managers can assess progress on a daily basis. Polls chart the candidate's progress and, perhaps more important, help assess the effectiveness of specific campaign themes. If the candidate appears to be gaining support, the campaign stays on course. But if the candidate appears to be falling in the polls,

**Think Again**

Would you vote for a candidate who used negative ads to discredit an opponent?

# UP CLOSE

## Dirty Politics

Political campaigning frequently turns ugly with negative advertising that is vicious and personal. It is widely believed that television's focus on personal character and private lives—rather than on policy positions and governmental experience—encourages negative campaigning. But vicious personal attacks in political campaigns began long before television. They are nearly as old as the nation itself.

"If Jefferson is elected," proclaimed Yale's president in 1800, "the Bible will be burned and we will see our wives and daughters the victims of legal prostitution." In 1864 *Harper's Weekly* decried the "mudslinging" of the day, lamenting that President Abraham Lincoln was regularly referred to by his opponent as a "filthy storyteller, despot, liar, thief, braggart, buffoon, monster, Ignoramus Abe, robber, swindler, tyrant, fiend, butcher, and pirate."

Television's first memorable attack advertisement was the "Daisy Girl" commercial broadcast by Lyndon Johnson's presidential campaign in 1964 against his Republican opponent, Barry Goldwater. Although never mentioning Goldwater by name, the purpose of the ad was to "define" him as a warmonger who would plunge the world into a nuclear holocaust. The ad opens with a small, innocent girl standing in an open field plucking petals from a daisy and counting, "1, 2, 3 . . ." When she reaches 9, an ominous adult male voice begins a countdown: "10, 9, 8 . . ." as the camera closes in on the child's face. At "zero," a mushroom cloud appears, reflected in her eyes, and envelops the screen. Lyndon Johnson's voice is heard: "These are the stakes."

The infamous Willie Horton ad, broadcast by an independent organization supporting Republican George H. W. Bush in 1988, portrayed Democrat Michael Dukakis as weak on crime prevention. It featured a close-up mug shot of a very threatening convicted murderer, Willie Horton, with a voice proclaiming, "Dukakis not only opposes the death penalty, he allowed first-degree murderers to have weekend passes from prison. One was Willie Horton, who murdered a boy in a robbery, stabbing him nineteen times. Despite a life sentence, Horton received ten weekend passes from prison." A final photo shows Dukakis, with a voice-over announcing, "Weekend prison passes, Dukakis weak on crime."

"Attack ads" have multiplied in recent elections at all levels of government. John Kerry had volunteered for Vietnam following his graduation from Yale. In four months as commander of a small "swift boat" he won a Silver Star, a Bronze Star, and three Purple Hearts. But an independent group, Swift Boat Veterans for the Truth, challenged the legitimacy of Kerry's medals in a series of TV ads. Later, the Swift Boat group redirected their attacks toward Kerry's post-Vietnam behavior as a leader in the Vietnam Veterans against the War. These ads showed a young Kerry at a congressional hearing accusing his fellow veterans of terrible atrocities, "murdering civilians, cutting off heads, and burning villages." These ads corresponded to a slight drop in Kerry's poll numbers.

But Bush's service in the Texas National Guard during the Vietnam War was also a target of attack. Bush joined the Guard with the possible help of family friends, but he won his wings as a fighter pilot and was honorably discharged after five years. The Texas Guard was never called to active duty and Bush never saw combat. But a CBS News report by Dan Rather, based on forged documents, asserted that Bush failed to meet all of his Guard responsibilities. Later CBS News recanted the charge. The affair may have helped Bush somewhat, by convincing viewers that Dan Rather and others at CBS were biased against him.

What are the effects of negative advertising? First of all, it works more often than not. Controlled experiments indicate that targets of attack ads are rated less positively by people who have watched these ads. But another effect of negative advertising is to make voters more cynical about politics and government in general. There is conflicting evidence about whether negative campaigning by opposing candidates reduces voter turnout.

What, if anything, can be done? Government regulation of political speech directly contravenes the First Amendment. American democracy has survived negative campaigning for a long time.

*Source:* Kathleen Hall Jamieson, *Dirty Politics, Deception, Distraction, and Democracy* (New York: Oxford University Press, 1992); also Stephen Ansolabehere et al., "Does Attack Advertising Demobilize the Electorate?" *American Political Science Review* 88 (December, 1994): 829–38; Kim Fridkin Kahn and Patrick J. Kenney, "Do Negative Campaigns Mobilize or Suppress Turnout?" *American Political Science Review* 93 (December, 1999): 877–89.

Frames from Lyndon Johnson's 1964 "Daisy Girl" commercial.

the campaign manager comes under intense pressure to change themes and strategies. As election day nears, the pressure increases on the trailing candidate to "go negative"—to launch even more scathing attacks on the opponent.

**Incumbent versus Challenger Strategies**   Campaign strategies vary by the offices being sought, the nature of the times, and the imagination and inventiveness of the candidates' managers. But incumbency is perhaps the most important factor affecting the choice of a strategy. The challenger must attack the record of the incumbent, deplore current conditions in the city, state, or nation; and stress the need for change. Challengers are usually freer to take the offensive; incumbents must defend their record in office and either boast of accomplishments during their term or blame the opposition for blocking them. Challengers frequently opt for the "outsider" strategy, capitalizing on distrust and cynicism toward government.

**News Management**   News management is the key to the media campaign. News coverage of the candidates is more credible in the eyes of viewers than paid advertisements. The campaign is planned to get the maximum favorable "free" exposure on the evening news. Each day a candidate must do something interesting and "newsworthy," that is, likely to be reported as news. Pictures are as important as words. Candidates must provide good **photo ops** for the media—opportunities where they can be photographed in settings or backgrounds that emphasize their themes. For example, if the theme is patriotism, then the candidate appears with war veterans, at a military base, or at a flag factory. If the theme is education, the candidate appears at a school; if crime control, then with police officers; if environmentalism, then in a wilderness area; if the economy, then at a closed factory or unemployment line or soup kitchen for the homeless.

Themes must be stated in concise and catchy **sound bites** that will register in the viewers' minds. Candidates now understand that the news media will select only a few seconds of an entire day of speech making for broadcast. The average length of a network news sound bite has shrunk from forty-five to seven seconds over the last thirty years. Thus, extended or serious discussion of issues during a campaign is sacrificed to the need for one-liners on the nightly news. Indeed, if a campaign theme cannot fit on a bumper sticker, it is too complex.

**Paid Advertising**   Television "spot" ads must be prepared prior to and during the campaign. They involve employing expensive television advertising and production firms well in advance of the campaign and keeping them busy revising and producing new ads throughout the campaign to respond to changing issues or opponents' attacks. Commercial advertising is the most expensive aspect of the campaign. Heavy costs are incurred in the production of the ads and in the purchase of broadcast time. The Federal Communications Commission (FCC) does not permit television networks or stations to charge more than standard commercial rates for political ads, but these rates are already high. Networks and stations are required to offer the same rates and times to all candidates, but if one candidate's campaign treasury is weak or exhausted, an opponent can saturate broadcast airtime.

Paid spot ads on television are usually only fifteen or thirty seconds long, owing to the expense of television time. The result is that these ads pay relatively little attention to issues but rather try to appeal to the viewers' emotions. There is some evidence that simply showing enthusiasm for the candidate motivates participation and activates existing supporters to get out and vote, whereas appealing to fear is somewhat more effective in changing behavior, including swinging the votes of undecideds. However, advertising campaigns, whether they are directed at inspiring enthusiasm for the candidate or fear of a candidate's

**photo ops** Staged opportunities for the media to photograph the candidate in a favorable setting.

**sound bites** Concise and catchy phrases that attract media coverage.

opponent, must be kept going over time. Bursts of emotion are likely to fade if the ad campaign does not keep the drumbeat going.[10] An accumulation of short spot ads, all aimed at the same theme, can have a meaningful impact on the course of an election.

Television ads are much maligned by scholars and commentators. And it is easy to identify particular ads that are silly, offensive, uninformative, and even misleading. Nevertheless, there is increasing evidence that paid political advertising does create a somewhat more attentive, more informed, and more-likely-to-vote citizenry. Moreover, paid ads appear to affect people with less political information and less interest in politics more than the better-informed and more active citizens. Thus, campaign ads are often petty, sometimes offensive, and seldom uplifting. But they do serve an important political function.[11]

**Free Airtime**    All candidates seek free airtime on news and talk shows, but the need to gain free exposure is much greater for underfunded candidates. They must go to extremes in devising media events, and they must encourage and participate in free televised debates. The debate format is particularly well suited for candidates who cannot match their opponents in paid commercial advertising. Thus, well-funded and poorly funded candidates may jockey over the number and times of public debates.

**The Effects of Campaigning**    Campaigns serve primarily to activate a candidate's supporters—to ensure that they go to the polls on Election Day. They serve secondarily to try to persuade undecideds to become supporters. Campaigns are designed to **mobilize** core supporters more than to persuade undecideds or opponents to vote for candidates.[12] Undecideds must be both persuaded *and* mobilized to vote—a more difficult task than simply activating core supporters. Observers may wonder why candidates appear before partisan crowds, visit with supporters, and advertise in areas that appear to support them anyway. "Core party voters are more likely to receive and respond to campaign information, implying that successful campaigns are those that mobilize their supporters enough to translate their natural predispositions into actual votes."

**mobilize** In politics, to activate supporters to work for candidates and turn out on Election Day.

# How Much Does It Cost to Get Elected?

Getting elected to public office has never been more expensive. The professionalization of campaigning and the heavy costs of television advertising drive up the costs of running for office. Campaign costs are rising with each election cycle (see Figure 5.4). In the presidential election year 2004, campaign spending by *all* presidential and congressional candidates, the Democratic and Republican parties, and independent political organizations is estimated to have topped *$4 billion.*

— Think Again —
Are high campaign costs discouraging good people from becoming candidates?

**Congressional Costs**    The typical winning campaign for a seat in the House of Representatives costs nearly $1 million. House members seeking to retain their seats must raise this amount *every two years.* The typical winning campaign for a U.S. Senate seat costs $5 to $7 million. But Senate campaign costs vary a great deal from state to state; Senate seats in the larger states may cost $20 million to $40 million or more.

The upward spiral in congressional campaign spending continued through 2006 with over $1.2 *billion* spent by all House and Senate candidates (see Table 5.2). New York's high-profile Senate race in 2002 between Democrat Hillary Clinton and Republican Rick Lazio attracted a combined $85 million in contributions from across the nation. A new individual spending record was set

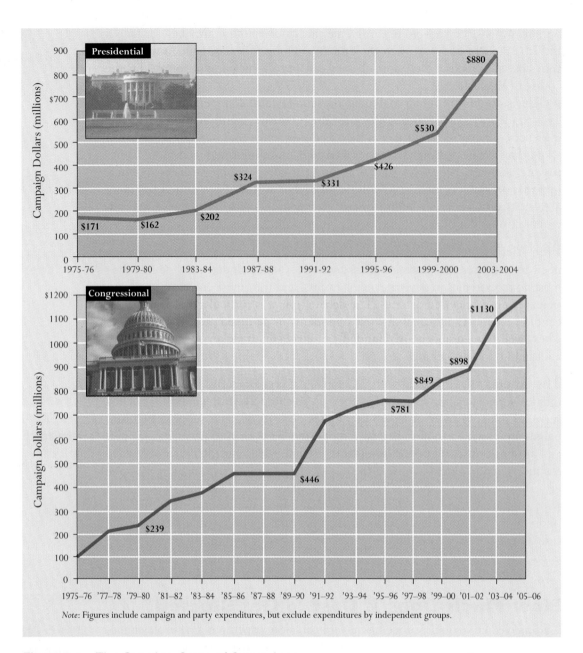

**Figure 5.4** The Growing Costs of Campaigns

*Source:* Reprinted by permission of the Center for Responsive Politics.

by multimillionaire Democrat Jon Corzine in his successful bid for a U.S. Senate seat from New Jersey in 2002; Corzine spent about $60 million of his *own* money.

Spending for House seats also varies a great deal from one race to another. (The spending record for a House seat is held by former Speaker Republican Newt Gingrich of Georgia, who spent more than $7.5 million seeking reelection in 1998.) In nearly two-thirds of all House districts, one candidate (almost always the incumbent) outspends his or her opponent by a factor of ten to one or more. Only about 16 percent of House campaigns are financially competitive, that is, neither candidate spends more than twice as much as his or her opponent. In the remaining 84 percent of House campaigns, one candidate spends more than twice as much as his or her opponent.[13]

| Table 5.2 | The Cost of Getting Elected to Congress |
|---|---|

**Senate**

| | |
|---|---|
| Average Democratic Incumbent | $8,582,559 |
| Average Democratic Challenger | $772,381 |
| Average Republican Incumbent | $5,750,211 |
| Average Republican Challenger | $1,126,857 |
| Most Expensive Campaign | Tom Daschle (D-S.D.) $17.4 million (lost) |

**House of Representatives**

| | |
|---|---|
| Average Democratic Incumbent | $918,481 |
| Average Democratic Challenger | $174,694 |
| Average Republican Incumbent | $1,041,327 |
| Average Republican Challenger | $192,960 |
| Most Expensive Campaign | Martin Frost (D-Tex.), $3.9 million (lost) |

*Source:* Center for Responsive Politics. Figures for 2004.

# Raising Campaign Cash

Fund raising to meet the high costs of campaigning is the most important hurdle for any candidate for public office. Campaign funds come from a wide range of sources—small donors, big donors, interest group PACs of every stripe, labor unions, even taxpayers. In some cases, candidates pay their own way (or most of it). More typically, however, candidates for high public office—particularly incumbents—have become adept at running their campaigns using other people's money, not their own.

**Public Money**    Presidential campaigns can be partly funded with taxpayer money through an income tax checkoff system. Each year taxpayers are urged to check the box on their tax forms that authorizes $3 of their tax payment to go to the Federal Elections Commission for distribution to presidential candidates' campaigns as well as to political party conventions. However, taxpayers are becoming less and less willing to allow their tax monies to go into political campaigning (even though the $3 checkoff does not add to the taxpayers' total taxes). Only about 11 percent of taxpayers currently check the box. The Presidential Election Campaign Fund has been in jeopardy of not having enough money to make its promised payments to the candidates and parties.

Presidential candidates may opt out of taxpayer-financed funding if they choose to do so. This allows them to spend as much money as they wish, but they receive no public money. Nonetheless, all presidential candidates, and all candidates for Congress, must abide by federal campaign finance laws (see below).

**Small Donations**    Millions of Americans participate in campaign financing, either by giving directly to candidates or the parties or by giving to political action committees, which then distribute their funds to candidates. For members of Congress, small donors typically make up less than 20 percent of their campaign funds. The proportion is higher for presidential candidates. For donations under $200, contributors' names and addresses are recorded only by the candidates and parties, not passed along to the Federal Election Commission as part of the public record.

**Large Individual Donors**    "Fat cats" are the preferred donors. These are the donors whose names are on the candidates' Rolodexes. They are the ones in

**Center for Responsive Politics**
The site of an organization devoted to the study of campaign finance laws, the role of money in elections, PACs, "soft money," and special-interest groups.
*www.opensecrets.org*

## UP CLOSE

# How to Spend $7 Million on a Political Campaign

How do you spend $7 million dollars on a Senate campaign? It may sound like a lot of money, but it can disappear quickly in a heated Senate campaign. Indeed, $7 million is the *average* expenditure of winning senators. (U.S. Senator Jon Corzine [D-N.J.] spent $60 million of his own personal wealth to win his New Jersey seat.)

Television advertising is the biggest cost. It may consume 40 to 65 percent of the campaign budget, depending on how many "media markets" (separate cities with groups of TV stations) are in the state and

how expensive television time is in each market. Staff salaries may consume a good portion of the budget. Experienced professionals and/or professional campaign management firms do not come cheap; volunteers are helpful, but no match for professionals in knowing how to run a campaign. Polling firms are needed throughout the campaign to keep track of progress or decline and to continue to evaluate the effectiveness of campaign themes, policy positions, negative hits on the opponent, and so on. Travel is another large item, whether the candidate and staff fly by private jet or rent a bus. Lawyers and accountants must supervise spending, submit FEC reports, and see that everyone adheres to campaign laws. A typical Senate campaign budget follows.

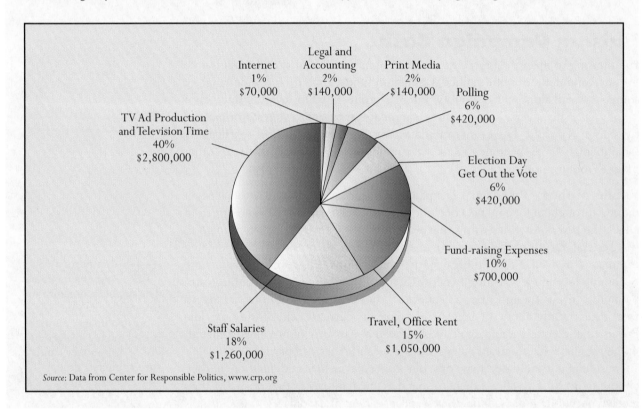

Internet
1%
$70,000

Legal and
Accounting
2%
$140,000

Print Media
2%
$140,000

Polling
6%
$420,000

TV Ad Production
and Television Time
40%
$2,800,000

Election Day
Get Out the Vote
6%
$420,000

Fund-raising Expenses
10%
$700,000

Staff Salaries
18%
$1,260,000

Travel, Office Rent
15%
$1,050,000

*Source*: Data from Center for Responsible Politics, www.crp.org

attendance when the president, the Speaker of the House, or other top political dignitaries travel around the country doing fund-raisers. They are also the ones who are wined, dined, prodded, and cajoled in a seemingly ceaseless effort by the parties and the candidates to raise funds for the next election.

In its 2002 campaign finance reform legislation, Congress raised the maximum individual contribution to federal candidates to $2,000 (up from $1,000 in the 2000 election). Fat cats are expected to give the maximum, and indeed even more. They can do so by giving their maximum $2,000 once in the primary election and a second time in the general election. And their spouses can do the same. And, of course, they can also give to the parties and to independent political organizations committed to helping their preferred candidates.

New Jersey Governor Jon Corzine at his inauguration in 2006. The multimillionaire Corzine still holds the record for a self-financed U.S. senate campaign. There are no limits on the amounts of their personal money that candidates can spend on their own campaigns.

**Candidate Self-Financing** Candidates for federal office also pump millions into their own campaigns. There are no federal restrictions on the amount of money individuals can spend on their own campaign.[14] Senate and House candidates frequently put $50,000 to $100,000 or more of their own money into their campaigns, through outright gifts or personal loans. (Candidates who loan themselves the money to run are able to pay themselves back later from outside contributions.)

**Issue Ads** Issue ads advocate policy positions rather than explicitly advising voters to cast their ballots for or against particular candidates. But most of these ads leave little doubt about which candidate is being supported or targeted. There are no dollar limits on the size of contributions to sponsoring groups (often referred to as 527s from the section of the Internal Revenue code under which they operate).

**issue ads** Ads that advocate policy positions rather than explicitly supporting or opposing particular candidates.

## What Do Contributors "Buy"?

What does money buy in politics? A cynic might say that money can buy anything—for example, special appropriations for public works directly benefiting the contributor, special tax breaks, special federal regulations. Public opinion views big-money contributions as a major problem in the American political system. Scandals involving the direct (quid pro quo) purchase of special favors, privileges, exemptions, and treatments have been common enough in the past, and they are likely to continue in the future. But campaign contributions are rarely made in the form of a direct trade-off for a favorable vote. Such an arrangement risks exposure as bribery and may be prosecuted under the law. Campaign contributions are more likely to be made without any *explicit* quid pro quo but rather with a general understanding that the contributor has confidence in the candidate's good judgment on issues directly affecting the contributor. The contributor expects the candidate to be smart enough to figure out how to vote in order to keep the contributions coming in the future.

**Think Again**

Do political campaign contributions have too much influence on elections and government policy?

**The Big-Money Contributors** Big-money contributors—businesses, unions, professional associations—pump millions into presidential and congressional

| Rank | Contributor | Total Contributions | % Dem. | % Rep. | Rank | Contributor | Total Contributions | % Dem. | % Rep. |
|---|---|---|---|---|---|---|---|---|---|
| 1. | American Federation of State/County/Municipal Employees | $34,944,356 | 98% | 1% | 25. | National Rifle Assn | $14,345,042 | 13% | 86% |
| | | | | | 26. | AFL-CIO | $14,143,542 | 88% | 11% |
| 2. | National Assn of Realtors | $24,159,780 | 50% | 49% | 27. | American Bankers Assn | $13,753,323 | 39% | 60% |
| 3. | National Education Assn | $23,382,034 | 86% | 13% | 28. | Time Warner | $13,408,561 | 70% | 28% |
| 4. | Assn of Trial Lawyers of America | $23,310,366 | 89% | 10% | 29. | SBC Communications | $13,032,502 | 34% | 65% |
| | | | | | 30. | Verizon Communications | $12,617,393 | 38% | 61% |
| 5. | Communications Workers of America | $21,968,716 | 98% | 1% | 31. | BellSouth Corp | $12,427,578 | 43% | 56% |
| | | | | | 32. | Microsoft Corp | $12,327,062 | 58% | 41% |
| 6. | Service Employees International Union | $21,865,215 | 88% | 11% | 33. | National Beer Wholesalers Assn | $12,207,798 | 30% | 69% |
| 7. | Intl Brotherhood of Electrical Workers | $21,522,812 | 96% | 3% | 34. | EMILY's List | $11,777,389 | 100% | 0% |
| | | | | | 35. | Sheet Metal Workers Union | $11,687,901 | 97% | 2% |
| 8. | Carpenters & Joiners Union | $20,995,637 | 68% | 31% | 36. | Ernst & Young | $11,672,581 | 31% | 67% |
| 9. | Teamsters Union | $20,838,115 | 85% | 13% | 37. | Lockheed Martin | $11,486,880 | 39% | 60% |
| 10. | American Medical Assn | $20,632,636 | 28% | 71% | 38. | JP Morgan Chase & Co | $11,455,069 | 49% | 50% |
| 11. | Altria Group (Philip Morris) | $20,567,067 | 41% | 57% | 39. | RJR Nabisco/ RJ Reynolds Tobacco | $10,959,872 | 11% | 88% |
| 12. | FedEx Corp | $20,500,993 | 33% | 66% | 40. | American Dental Assn | $10,898,735 | 43% | 56% |
| 13. | Laborers Union | $20,497,632 | 86% | 13% | 41. | Morgan Stanley | $10,850,938 | 34% | 65% |
| 14. | United Auto Workers | $19,832,550 | 98% | 0% | 42. | Blue Cross/Blue Shield | $10,757,914 | 42% | 57% |
| 15. | AT&T | $19,484,567 | 47% | 52% | 43. | American Hospital Assn | $10,748,440 | 44% | 55% |
| 16. | American Federation of Teachers | $19,291,514 | 99% | 0% | 44. | National Assn of Insurance & Financial Advisors | $10,629,255 | 37% | 62% |
| 17. | Goldman Sachs | $18,607,643 | 50% | 49% | | | | | |
| 18. | Machinists & Aerospace Workers Union | $18,429,464 | 98% | 0% | 45. | General Electric | $10,596,818 | 46% | 53% |
| | | | | | 46. | American Institute of CPAs | $10,381,169 | 37% | 62% |
| 19. | United Food & Commercial Workers Union | $18,318,526 | 98% | 1% | 47. | Union Pacific Corp | $10,131,658 | 22% | 77% |
| | | | | | 48. | Credit Union National Assn | $10,110,853 | 43% | 56% |
| 20. | Citigroup Inc | $17,080,206 | 48% | 50% | | | | | |
| 21. | United Parcel Service | $16,859,844 | 29% | 70% | 49. | Deloitte Touche Tohmatsu | $10,108,211 | 28% | 71% |
| 22. | National Auto Dealers Assn | $16,474,442 | 29% | 70% | | | | | |
| 23. | National Assn of Home Builders | $14,930,228 | 38% | 61% | 50. | United Steelworkers of America | $10,089,196 | 97% | 2% |
| 24. | National Assn of Letter Carriers | $14,608,734 | 71% | 27% | | | | | |

**Figure 5.5**  The Big-Money Contributors

*Source:* Center for Responsive Politics, *The Big Picture* (Washington, D.C., 2001). Reprinted by permission of the Center for Responsive Politics.

elections. Figure 5.5 lists the top fifty contributors to candidates and parties since 1989. Note that union contributions are heavily weighted toward Democrats, as are the contributions of the Association of Trial Lawyers. Businesses and business associations tend to split their contributions between the parties, but Republicans usually get the largest share.

**Buying Access to Policymakers**  Large contributors expect to be able to call or visit and present their views directly to "their" officeholders. At the presidential level, major contributors who cannot get a meeting with the president expect to meet at least with high-level White House staff or cabinet officials. At the congressional level, major contributors usually expect to meet or speak directly with their representative or senator. Members of Congress boast of responding to letters, calls, or visits by any constituent, but contributors can expect a more immediate and direct response than noncontributors can. Lobbyists for contributing organizations routinely expect and receive a hearing from members of Congress.

**Political Action Committees**   Political action committees (PACs) are the most reliable source of money for reelection campaigns in Congress. Corporations and unions are not allowed to contribute directly to campaigns from corporate or union funds, but they may form PACs to seek contributions from managers and stockholders and their families, or union workers and their families. PACs are organized not only by corporations and unions but also by trade and professional associations, environmental groups, and liberal and conservative ideological groups. The wealthiest PACs are based in Washington, D.C. PACs are very cautious; their job is to get a maximum return on their contributions, winning influence and goodwill with as many lawmakers as possible in Washington. There's no return on their investment if their recipients lose at the polls; therefore, most PACs—particularly business PACs—give most of their dollars to incumbents seeking reelection.

**Individual Contributors**   Most individual contributors are ideologically motivated. They make their contributions based on their perception of the ideological position of the candidate (or perhaps their perception of the candidate's opponent). They may make contributions to congressional candidates across the country who share their policy views. Liberal and conservative networks of contributors can be contacted through specialized mailing lists—for example, liberals through television producer Norman Lear's People for the American Way. Feminists have been effective in soliciting individual contributions across the country and funneling them very early in a campaign to women candidates through EMILY's List. Ideological contributors may only get the satisfaction of knowing that they are financially backing their cause in the political process. Some contributors simply enjoy the opportunity to be near and to be seen with high-ranking politicians. Politicians pose for photos with contributors, who later frame the photos and hang them in their office to impress their friends, associates, and customers. Contributors are disproportionately high-income, older people with strong partisan views (see Figure 5.6).

**Buying Government Assistance**   Many large contributors do business with government agencies. They expect any representative or senator they have supported to intervene on their behalf with these agencies, sometimes acting to cut red tape, ensure fairness, and expedite their cases, and other times pressuring the agencies for a favorable decision. Officials in the White House or the cabinet may also be expected to intervene on behalf of major contributors. There is little question raised when the intervention merely expedites consideration of a contributor's case, but pressure to bend rules or regulations to get favorable decisions raises ethical problems for officeholders (see "Congressional Ethics" in Chapter 8).

**Fund-Raising Chores**   Fund-raising occupies more of a candidate's time than any other campaign activity. Candidates must personally contact as many individual contributors as possible. They work late into the evening on the telephone with potential contributors. Fund-raising dinners, cocktail parties, barbecues, fish frys, and so on, are scheduled nearly every day of a campaign. The candidate is expected to appear personally to "press the flesh" of big contributors. Movie and rock stars and other assorted celebrities may also be asked to appear at fund-raising affairs to generate attendance. Dinners may run to $2,000 a plate in presidential affairs, although often less in Senate or House campaigns. Tickets may be "bundled" to well-heeled individual contributors or sold in blocks to organizations. Fund-raising techniques are limited only by the imagination of the campaign manager.

**political action committees (PACs)** Organizations that solicit and receive campaign contributions from corporations, unions, trade associations, and ideological and issue-oriented groups, and their members, then distribute these funds to political candidates.

**Figure 5.6**
Characteristics of Individual Political Contributors

Contributors to political campaigns generally are older and have higher incomes than most Americans. Whites and males contribute more than blacks and females, and conservatives contribute more than liberals.

*Source:* John Green, Paul Herrnson, Lynda Powell, and Clyde Wilcox, "Individual Congressional Campaign Contributions," press release, June 9, 1998, Center for Responsive Politics.

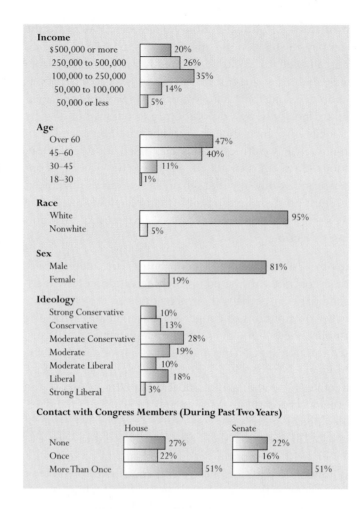

## Regulating Campaign Finance

**Federal Election Commission (FEC)** Agency charged with enforcing federal election laws and disbursing public presidential campaign funds.

The **Federal Election Commission (FEC)** is responsible for enforcing limits on individual and organizational contributions to all federal elections, administering the public funding of presidential campaigns, and requiring full disclosure of all campaign financial activity in presidential and congressional elections. Enforcement of these federal election and campaign finance laws lies in the hands of the six-member FEC. Appointed by the president to serve staggered six-year terms, commission members are traditionally split 3 to 3 between Republicans and Democrats.

**Limits on Contributions** The FEC now limits direct individual contributions to a candidate's campaign to $2,000 per election and organizational contributions to $5,000 per election. But there are many ways in which individuals and organizations can legally surmount these limits. Contributors may give a candidate $2,000 for each member of their family in a primary election and then another $2,000 per member in the general election. Organizations may generate much more than the $5,000 limit by bundling (combining) $2,000 additional contributions from individual members. (Soft-money contributions—unregulated amounts given to the national parties officially for "party building" but actually used in support of candidates—were banned in 2002.) Independent organizations can spend whatever they wish in order to promote their political views, so long as these organizations do so "without cooperation or consultation with the candidate of his or her campaign." Finally, as noted, individuals may spend as much of their own money on their own campaigns as they wish.[15]

**Federal Election Commission**
The FEC Web site contains ample information on the important regulations and statutes relating to campaign finance. *http://www.fec.gov*

Candidates often seek the help of celebrities in raising campaign money. Here Senator Ted Kennedy (D-MA) appears at a 2006 concert with singer Bono and cellist Yo Yo Ma.

**Federal Funding of Presidential Elections**   Federal funding, financed by the $3 checkoff box on individual income tax returns, is available to presidential candidates in primary and general elections, as well as to major-party nominating conventions. Candidates seeking the nomination in presidential primary elections can qualify for federal funds by raising $5,000 from private contributions no greater than $250 each in each of twenty states. In the general election, Democratic and Republican nominees are funded equally at levels determined by the FEC. In order to receive federal funding, presidential candidates must agree to FEC limits on their campaign spending in both primary and general elections.

Federal funding pays about one-third of the primary campaign costs of presidential candidates and all the *official* presidential campaign organization costs in the general election. The parties also receive federal funds for their nominating conventions.

**Campaign Finance Reform**   Unregulated soft-money contributions to the parties grew rapidly during the 1990s. These contributions represented a giant black hole in the original Federal Election Campaign Act of 1974. Contributions made directly to a candidate's campaign—hard-money contributions—were limited (originally to $1,000). But individuals, organizations, corporations, and unions could contribute as much as they wanted to the Democratic and Republican national parties. These contributions were supposed to be for party building, voter registration, getting out the vote, and so on, but in fact went into candidate campaigning.

In the 2000 Republican presidential primaries, U.S. Senator John McCain made campaign finance reform his principal issue. He surprised the Republican Party leaders by defeating George W. Bush in the New Hampshire primary that year. Bush and both Democratic and Republican leaders decided to jump on the campaign finance reform bandwagon, although with little real enthusiasm. In 2002 a somewhat reluctant Congress finally passed the Bipartisan Campaign Finance Reform Act (see Table 5.3).

Among other things, this act eliminates soft-money contributions to the parties; increases the individual contribution limit to candidates' campaigns from

## UP CLOSE

# Midterm Congressional Elections, 2006: What Do They Mean?

Tip O'Neill, the former Democratic Speaker of the House and wily Boston Irish politician, once said, "All politics is local." Usually midterm congressional elections are decided by personalities, issues, and events with 435 separate House districts and one-third of the states electing U.S. Senators. But in 2006 the war in Iraq was the top concern of voters everywhere. Nearly two of every three Americans cited Iraq as "the top priority for the president and Congress to deal with."[a]

Traditionally the party of a two-term president loses congressional seats in the sixth year of his tenure. The party out of power usually calls for "change," even if it does not make the direction of the change very clear. But the 2006 congressional elections appeared to be in large measure a referendum on George Bush's presidency. Throughout the election year Bush's approval ratings stayed below 40 percent. As U.S. troop casualties in Iraq grew, a large majority of voters turned against the war and especially against Bush's conduct of the war and the decisions of Secretary of Defense Donald Rumsfeld. An early indication of voter dissatisfaction was the defeat of incumbent U.S. Senator Joseph Lieberman in his own Democratic primary in Connecticut. (The defeat of an incumbent senator in his own party's primary is practically unheard-of in American politics.) Lieberman had voted for the war, and although he defeated his primary opponent in the general election, the antiwar handwriting was on the wall.

Throughout the campaign Bush defended the war in Iraq as a necessary part of the broader war on terrorism. He portrayed Democrats as wanting to "cut and run" and argued that a U.S. defeat in Iraq would encourage terrorists around the world. Democratic congressional campaigns attacked Bush's initial decision to go into Iraq, as well as his subsequent conduct of the war. Yet few Democrats proposed any real strategy for U.S. withdrawal from Iraq. Even New York Democratic senatorial candidate Hillary Clinton opposed an immediate and complete withdrawal of U.S. troops.

*Senator Hillary Clinton (D-NY) campaigning for reelection in Buffalo, New York, with her husband, former president Bill Clinton, in 2006. He is a popular campaign speaker for Democratic candidates throughout the country.*

Democrats captured control of both the House of Representatives and the Senate in the 2006 midterm elections. (The GOP had held the House for the previous 12 years, since 1994.) The new House opened its 2007 session with 232 Democrats and 203 Republicans, and the Democrats held a razor-thin majority—51 to 49 in the U.S. Senate. On the morning after the election, the president announced that he had accepted the resignation of Secretary of Defense Donald Rumsfeld. The immediate replacement of Rumsfeld (with former CIA Director Robert Gates) suggested that Bush understood the unpopularity of the war in Iraq and was prepared to change direction (although exactly what the new direction would be remained unclear).

Only a handful of seats changed from Republican to Democratic. But it was enough to change party control of the House and Senate, to shake up the balance of power in Washington, to cause the president to rethink national security policy, and to bring back divided party government to the nation.

[a] Gallup poll, November 3, 2006. *www.gallup.com*

## Table 5.3   Campaign Finance Rules, 2006

**General**

All federal election contributions and expenditures must be reported to the Federal Election Commission, which may investigate and prosecute violators.

All contributions over $200 must be reported, with name, address, and occupation of contributor.

No foreign contributions can be made.

There are no restrictions on how much individuals may spend on their own campaigns *(Buckley v. Valeo).*

No large contributions (soft money) may be made to the national parties; party contributions by individuals and committees are limited.

**Presidential Primaries**

Federal matching funds are available for money raised by candidates from individual donors giving $250 dollars or less. To be eligible, the primary candidate must raise $5,000 in each of twenty states in contributions of $250 or less.

**Presidential Elections**

The federal government pays all campaign costs of major party candidates and contributes to the costs of party conventions. The federal government will also pay part of the costs of minor party candidates who win between 5 and 25 percent of the vote.

**Limits on Contributions**

| Donor | Candidate | PAC | National Party | State/Local | Special |
|---|---|---|---|---|---|
| Individual | $2,100[a] | $5,000 | $25,000 | $10,000 | Biennial total: $101,400[a] |
| National party | 5,000 | 5,000 | — | — | — |
| State/local party | 5,000 | 5,000 | — | — | — |
| PAC (multi-candidate) | 5,000 | 5,000 | 1,500 | 5,000 | — |
| PAC (single-candidate) | 2,100[a] | 5,000 | 26,700[a] | 10,000 | — |

**Millionaire Amendment**

If a candidate spends more of his own money beyond specified thresholds (e.g., $350,000 for House candidates), contribution limits for his or her opponent are tripled.

**Independent Group Expenditures**

Independent individuals or groups airing TV or radio ads must not coordinate with candidates or parties in order to avoid contribution limits.

**Election Communications**

Independent individuals or groups may not broadcast TV or radio ads referring to a candidate 60 days prior to a general election or 30 days prior to the primary election.

[a]Contribution limit for 2006. Limits rise with inflation.

Note: This table summarizes the Bipartisan Campaign Finance Reform Act of 2002.

*Source:* FEC, 2006.

$1,000 to $2,000; prohibits independent groups from coordinating their campaign spending with candidates or parties; does not allow independent groups to mention the name of a candidate in their issue ads; and bans independent groups from broadcasting their views in the final days of a campaign.

But contributions to nonprofit independent groups remain unregulated. Big-money contributors who can no longer provide large amounts of cash to candidates or to parties *can* establish nonprofit independent groups (known as "527s," referring to their Internal Revenue Service code) to accept big contributions to enable them to produce and broadcast campaign advertisements.

The act was challenged as a violation of First Amendment free speech rights but upheld by the U.S. Supreme Court.[16]

# The Presidential Campaign: The Primary Race

The phrase *presidential fever* refers to the burning political ambition required to seek the presidency. The grueling presidential campaign is a test of strength, character, endurance, and determination. It is physically exhausting and mentally and emotionally draining. Every aspect of the candidates' lives—and the lives of their families—is subject to microscopic inspection by the news media. Most of this coverage is critical, and much of it is unfair. Yet candidates are expected to handle it all with grace and humor, from the earliest testing of the waters through a full-fledged campaign.

**Media Mentions**   Politicians with presidential ambitions may begin by promoting presidential *mentions* by media columnists and commentators. The media help to identify "presidential timber" years in advance of a presidential race simply by drawing up lists of potential candidates, commenting on their qualifications, and speculating about their intentions. Mentions are likely to come to prominent governors or senators who start making speeches outside their states, who grab the media spotlight on a national issue, or who simply let it be known to the media "off the record" that they are considering a presidential race. Visiting New Hampshire and Iowa and giving speeches there is viewed as "testing the waters" and a signal of presidential ambitions.

**The Decision to Run**   The decision to run for president involves complex personal and political calculations. Ambition to occupy the world's most powerful office must be weighed against the staggering costs—emotional as well as financial—of a presidential campaign.

Serious planning, organizing, and fund-raising must begin at least two years before the general election. A staff must be assembled—campaign managers and strategists, fund-raisers, media experts, pollsters, issues advisers and speechwriters, lawyers and accountants—and supporters must be identified in key states throughout the nation. Paid and volunteer workers must be assembled (see Figure 5.7). Leaders among important interest groups must be contacted. A general campaign strategy must be developed, an organization put in place, and several millions of dollars in campaign contributions pledged in advance of the race. Often the decision to run hinges on whether initial pledges of campaign contributions appear adequate. The serious candidate must be able to anticipate contributions of $25 million or more for primary elections. Most of this work must be accomplished in the preprimary season—the months after Labor Day of the year preceding the election, and before the first primary election.

**A Strategy for the Primaries**   The road to the White House consists of two separate races: the primary elections and caucuses leading to the Democratic and Republican party nominations, and the general election. Each of these races requires a separate strategy. The primary race requires an appeal to party activists and the more ideologically motivated primary voters in key states. The general election requires an appeal to the less partisan, less attentive, more ideologically moderate general election voters. Thus the campaign strategy developed to win the nomination must give way after the national conventions to a strategy to win the November general election.

**Primary Campaigns**   Primary campaigns come in different varieties. An incumbent president with no serious competition from within his own party can safely glide through his party's primaries, saving campaign money for the general election. In contrast, the party out of the White House typically goes through a

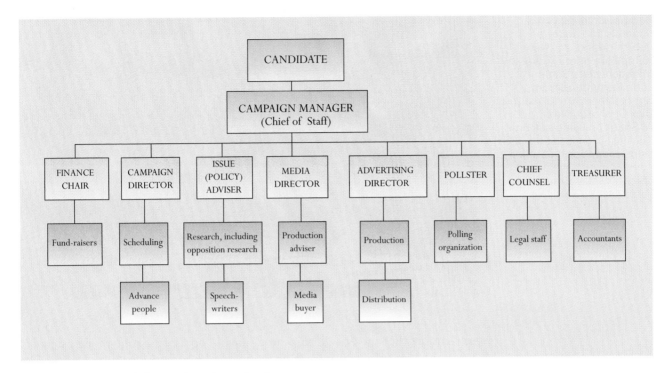

**Figure 5.7** Typical Campaign Organization
Campaign organizations vary, but most assign someone to perform these tasks: funding, scheduling appearances, speech writing, media production and buying, polling, advertising, legal compliance, and check writing, even if, in local campaigns, all these tasks must be performed by the candidate or his or her family members.

rough-and-tumble primary (and preprimary) season, with multiple presidential aspirants. And when no incumbent president is running for reelection, both parties experience heavy party infighting among multiple presidential hopefuls.

Candidates strive during the preprimary season to win media attention, to climb the poll ratings, and raise campaign funds. Early front-runners must beware of stumbles and gaffes; they must be prepared for close scrutiny by the media; and they must expect to be the targets of their competitors. Not infrequently, early front-runners lose their momentum even before the first primary elections.[17]

Primary voters are heavily weighted toward party activists, who are more ideologically motivated than the more moderate voters in general elections. Democratic primary voters are more liberal, and Republican primary voters are more conservative, than the voters in the November general election. Democratic primary voters include large numbers of the party's core constituents—union members, public employees, minorities, environmentalists, and feminists.

Presidential candidates must try to appeal not only to the ideological predispositions of their party's primary voters but also convince them of their "electability"—the likelihood that they can win the party's nomination and, more important, go on to win the presidential election. Often primary voters are torn between voting for their favorite candidate based on his or her ideological and issue positions, or voting for the most electable candidate.

**The New Hampshire Primary** The primary season begins in the winter snows of New Hampshire, traditionally the first state to hold a presidential primary election. New Hampshire is far more important *strategically* to a presidential campaign than it is in delegate strength. As a small state, New Hampshire supplies fewer than 1 percent of the delegates at the Democratic and Republican

Democratic presidential hopefuls line up for a debate prior to the New Hampshire primary, won by Massachusetts Senator John Kerry (third from right). Others are Missouri's Dick Gephardt, New York's Al Sharpton, Ohio's Dennis Kucinich, Connecticut's Joe Lieberman, North Carolina's John Edwards, Illinois' Carol Moseley-Braun, and Vermont's Howard Dean.

**retail politics** Direct candidate contact with individual voters.

conventions. But the New Hampshire primary looms very large in media coverage and hence in overall campaign strategy. Although the popular Democratic Iowa party caucuses are held even earlier, New Hampshire is the nation's first primary, and the media begin speculating about its outcome and reporting early state-poll results months in advance.

The New Hampshire primary inspires **retail politics**—direct candidate contact with the voters. Presidential aspirants begin visiting New Hampshire in the year preceding the primary elections, speaking at town hall meetings, visiting with small groups, standing outside of supermarkets, walking through restaurants, greeting workers at factories and offices, and so on. These personal contacts bypass the media's filtering and interpreting of the candidate's personality and message. Retail politics is largely confined to New Hampshire, a small state and a year of preprimary time to reach voters personally. And there is some evidence that voters who actually meet candidates come away with a more favorable view of them.[18]

New Hampshire provides the initial *momentum* for the presidential candidates. "Momentum" is more than just a media catchword. The Democratic and Republican winners in New Hampshire have demonstrated their voter appeal, their "electability." Favorable New Hampshire results inspire more financial contributions and thus the resources needed to carry the fight into the next group of primary elections. Unfavorable New Hampshire results tend to dry up contributions; weaker candidates may be forced into an early withdrawal.

**front-end strategy** Presidential political campaign strategy in which a candidate focuses on winning early primaries to build momentum.

**The Front-End Strategy** A **front-end strategy** places heavy emphasis on the results from New Hampshire and other early primary states. This strategy involves spending all or most of the candidate's available resources—time, energy, and money—on the early primary states, in the hopes that early victories will provide the momentum, in media attention and financial contributions, to continue the race.

The "expectations" game is played with a vengeance in the early primaries. Media polls and commentators set the candidates' expected vote percentages, and the candidates and their spokespersons try to deflate these expectations. On election night, the candidates' **spin doctors** sally forth among the crowds of television and newspaper reporters to give a favorable interpretation of the outcome. The candidates themselves appear at campaign headquarters (and, they hope, on

**spin doctor** Practitioner of the art of spin control, or manipulation of media reporting to favor one's own candidate.

national television) to give the same favorable spin to the election results. But the media itself—particularly the television network anchors and reporters and commentators—interpret the results for the American people, determining the early favorites in the presidential horse race.

**Front-Loading**    Presidential nominees are now selected by early March. State legislators in a number of states expressed their frustration over the media attention given to tiny New Hampshire by moving up the dates of their presidential primary elections. (The New Hampshire legislature responded by officially setting its primary date one week earlier than any other state's primary.) Today many big states, including California, Connecticut, Georgia, Massachusetts, Minnesota, New York, Ohio, Florida, and Texas hold their primary in March.

This **front-loading** of presidential primaries appears to favor the candidate who peaks in the polls in the first six weeks of the primary season.[19]

**front-loading** The scheduling of presidential primary elections early in the year.

**Convention Showplace**    Once a presidential candidate has enough votes to assure nomination, this uncrowned winner must prepare for the party's convention. Organizing and orchestrating convention forces, dominating the platform and rules writing, enjoying the nominating speeches and the traditional roll call of the state delegations, mugging for the television camera when the nominating vote goes over the top, submitting the vice presidential nominee's name for convention approval, and preparing and delivering a rousing acceptance speech to begin the fall campaign are just a few of the many tasks awaiting the winner—and the winner's campaign team.

# The Presidential Campaign: The General Election Battle

Buoyed by the conventions—and often by postconvention bounces in the polls—the new nominees must now face the general electorate.

**General Election Strategies**    Strategies in the general election are as varied as the imaginations of campaign advisers, media consultants, pollsters, and the candidates themselves. As noted earlier, campaign strategies are affected by the nature of the times and the state of the economy; by the incumbent or challenger status of the candidate; by the issues, conditions, scandals, or events currently being spotlighted by the media; and by the dynamics of the campaign itself as the candidates attack and defend themselves (see *Up Close:* "Bush v. Kerry, 2004").

Presidential election campaigns must focus on the **Electoral College**. The president is not elected by the national popular vote total but rather by a majority of the *electoral* votes of the states. Electoral votes are won by plurality, winner-take-all popular voting in most of the states. (Exceptions are Nebraska and Maine.) Thus a narrow plurality win in a state delivers *all* of that state's electoral votes. Big-state victories, even by very narrow margins, can deliver big electoral prizes. The biggest prizes are California with 55 electoral votes, New York with 31, and Texas with 34. With a total of 538 electoral votes at stake, *the winner must garner victories in states that total a minimum of 270 electoral votes.*

**Electoral College** The 538 presidential electors apportioned among the states according to their congressional representation (plus three for the District of Columbia) whose votes officially elect the president and vice president of the United States.

**Targeting the Swing States**    In focusing on the most populous states, with their large electoral votes, candidates must decide which of these states are "winnable," then direct their time, energy, and money to these **swing states.** Candidates cannot afford to spend too much effort in states that already seem to be solidly in their column, although they must avoid the perception that they are

**swing states** States that are not considered to be firmly in the Democratic or Republican column.

## UP CLOSE

## Bush v. Kerry, 2004

John F. Kerry wrapped up the Democratic nomination in the early spring, and his poll numbers quickly matched those of President Bush. Despite one of the most liberal voting records in Congress, Kerry appeared to be a "moderate" in contrast to his boisterous primary opponent, Vermont Governor Howard Dean. At the Democratic National Convention Kerry took the stage with a snappy military salute, "I'm John Kerry and I'm reporting for duty!" The early intent was to use his war hero's status to demonstrate his ability to be Commander-in-Chief in time of war. It was a risky strategic decision because President Bush was perceived in all of the polls as a "strong leader" in the war on terrorism. But events thirty-five years ago seemed irrelevant in 2004. Kerry got very little "bounce" from the Democratic Convention.

George Bush had little choice but to make the war on terrorism his major theme. Bush's advisors believed it was to their candidate's advantage to make terrorism the "chief concern" of Americans, rather than the economy. They believed that in wartime most voters wanted a "strong leader," "decisive," and a "man of his word"—qualities in which the polls indicated Bush was strongest. Kerry was to be cast as a "waffler"—first voting to authorize military force against Iraq and then later voting against a bill to finance operations there. Kerry supported continuing U.S. military efforts in Iraq, but he attacked Bush's decision to invade Iraq without the support of other United Nations members. He referred to Iraq as "the wrong war, the wrong place, the wrong time," and accused Bush of a "colossal error of judgment" in shifting anti-terrorist efforts to catch Osama bin Laden in Afghanistan to the attack on Iraq.

Bush maintained a slim lead in the polls throughout the spring and summer, a lead that he was to lose briefly after the first presidential debate in October. Kerry's carefully crafted image in the debate seemed to reassure many Americans that he too would make a strong Commander-in-Chief. He claimed that Bush had "misled" the American people about the existence of weapons of mass destruction in Iraq, that he failed to "exhaust the

remedies of the United Nations," and that he, Kerry, would not commit American troops to battle without satisfying "the global test." Bush jumped on the phrase "the global test" to claim that Kerry would place America's security in the hands of the United Nations: "I'll never turn over America's national security needs to leaders of other countries." Kerry was judged by the polls as the winner of the debates. But Bush had found a theme—that Kerry was indecisive, that he flip-flopped, and that he would hesitate to act when confronted with threats to national security. Within a week, Bush regained his slim lead in the polls.

As Election Day neared, the rhetoric became more bitter. Bush had "lied" about the reasons for the war in Iraq, rather than simply being misinformed by the intelligence community about the existence of weapons of mass destruction in Saddam's hands. It was charged that Bush secretly intended to bring back the draft and that he would cut Social Security benefits for the elderly. Kerry was "unfit for command": early in his career he had accused his fellow veterans of committing atrocities in Vietnam. The terrorists were hoping for a Kerry victory. The nation would not be "safe" if Kerry won.

Bush succeeded in making Iraq part of the war on terrorism: "We will fight the terrorists abroad, rather than fight them at home." Kerry could never fully take advantage of the controversial war: He had voted for it in the first place. He said he would call upon our allies in the United Nations to help in Iraq, but it seemed unlikely to many Americans that UN members who opposed the war would want to assist the United States.

Contrary to expectations, Americans went to the polls in record numbers. And while Iraq and terrorism ranked high among their concerns, they cited "moral values"as the most important issue in the election. Bush's folksy image and his moral values seemed to match their own. He was "honest and trustworthy," he "took a clear stand," he was "decisive" and "better at handling the war on terrorism." He not only won a majority of the popular vote (51 to 48%), but also helped to increase the Republican majorities in the House and Senate.

ignoring these strong bases of support. Neither can candidates waste much effort on states that already appear to be solidly in their opponent's column. So the swing states receive most of the candidates' time, attention, and television advertising money.

**The Presidential Debates**   The nationally televised presidential debates are the central feature of the general election campaign. These debates attract more viewers than any other campaign event. Moreover, they enable a candidate to reach undecided voters and the opponent's supporters, as well as the candidate's own partisans. Even people who usually pay little attention to politics may be drawn in by the drama of the confrontation (see *Up Close: "The Presidential Debates"* on page 164).

The debates allow viewers an opportunity to see and hear candidates together and to compare their responses to questions as they stand side by side. The debates give audiences a better view of the candidates than they can get from thirty-second commercial ads or seven-second news sound bites. Viewers can at least judge how the candidates react under pressure.

However, the debates emphasize candidate image over substantive policy issues. Candidates must appear presidential. They must appear confident, compassionate, concerned, and good-humored. They must not appear uncertain or unsure of themselves, or aloof or out of touch with viewers, or easily upset by hostile questions. They must avoid verbal slips or gaffes or even unpolished or awkward gestures. They must remember that the debates are not really debates so much as joint press conferences in which the candidates respond to questions with rehearsed mini-speeches and practiced sound bites.

**Hitting the Talk Shows**    Candidates know that more people watch entertainment talk shows than news shows. Oprah Winfrey, Regis Philbin, Larry King, David Letterman, Jay Leno, and Conan O'Brien all have larger audiences than *Meet the Press, Hardball, Hannity and Colmes, The O'Reilly Factor,* and others. Moreover, entertainment hosts rarely ask policy questions but rather toss "softball" queries about family, feelings, and personal qualities. Responding to these questions "humanizes" the candidate. And these entertainment shows reach audiences that have relatively little political knowledge or awareness. This provides an opportunity for a candidate to actually win over undecideds and persuadable opposition voters with a likable personality, good humor, and a good rapport with the host.[20] Beginning in 2000, presidential candidates expended considerable effort to get themselves on as many entertainment talk shows as possible.

**The Electoral College Vote**    In recent presidential elections, the Democratic candidates (Clinton in 1992 and 1996 and Gore in 2000) have won the Northeastern states, including New York; the upper Midwestern states, including Michigan and Illinois; and, perhaps most important, the West Coast, including California (see *Across the USA: "How the States Voted"* on page 166). Republican presidential candidates (Bush in 1992, Dole in 1996, and Bush in 2000 and 2004) have shown greater strength in the Great Plains and Rocky Mountain states and in the southeastern states (forming a Republican "L" on the Electoral College map). If these patterns continue in presidential elections, Democrats can depend on two of the four largest Electoral College vote states, California (55) and New York (31), whereas Republicans can feel comfortable in the other two, Texas (34) and Florida (27). The Electoral College battleground may be states such as Ohio, Pennsylvania, and Missouri—"swing states" that have cast their votes alternatively for Democratic and Republican candidates in recent presidential elections.

**The Center for Voting and Democracy**
A site with material on possible changes in the Electoral College.
*www.fairvote.org*

# The Voter Decides

Understanding the reasons behind the voters' choice at the ballot box is a central concern of candidates, campaign strategists, commentators, and political scientists. Perhaps no other area of politics has been investigated as thoroughly as voting behavior. Survey data on voter choice have been collected for presidential elections for the past half century.[21] We know that voters cast ballots for and

## UP CLOSE

# The Presidential Debates

Presidential debates attract more viewers than any other campaign activity. Most campaign activities—speeches, rallies, motorcades—reach only supporters. Such activities may inspire supporters to go to the polls, contribute money, and even work to get others to vote their way. But televised debates reach undecided voters as well as supporters, and they allow candidates to be seen by supporters of their opponent. Even if issues are not really discussed in depth, people see how presidential candidates react as human beings under pressure.

### Kennedy-Nixon

Televised presidential debates began in 1960 when John F. Kennedy and Richard M. Nixon confronted each other on a bare stage before an America watching on black-and-white TV sets. Nixon was the vice president in the popular presidential administration of Dwight Eisenhower; he was also an accomplished college debate-team member. He prepared for the debates as if they were college debates, memorizing facts and arguments. But he failed to realize that image triumphs over substance on television. By contrast, Kennedy was handsome, cool, confident; whatever doubts the American people may have had regarding his youth and inexperience were dispelled by his polished manner. Radio listeners tended to think that Nixon won, and debate coaches scored him the winner. But television viewers preferred the glamorous young Kennedy. The polls shifted in Kennedy's direction after the debate, and he won in a very close general election.

### Carter-Ford

President Lyndon Johnson avoided debating in 1964, and Nixon, having learned his lesson, declined to debate in 1968 and 1972. Thus televised presidential debates did not resume until 1976, when incumbent president Gerald Ford, perceiving he was behind in the polls, agreed to debate challenger Jimmy Carter. Ford made a series of verbal slips. Carter was widely perceived as having won the debate, and he went on to victory in the general election.

### Reagan-Carter and Reagan-Mondale

It was Ronald Reagan who demonstrated the true power of television. Reagan had lived his life in front of a camera. It was the principal tool of both of his trades—actor and politician. In 1980 incumbent president Jimmy Carter talked rapidly and seriously about programs, figures, and budgets. But Reagan was master of the stage; he was relaxed, confident, joking. He appeared to treat the president of the United States as an overly aggressive, impulsive younger man, regrettably given to exaggeration. When it was all over, it was clear to most viewers that Carter had been bested by a true professional in media skills.

However, in the first of two televised debates with Walter Mondale in 1984, Reagan's skills of a lifetime seemed to desert him. He stumbled over statistics and groped for words. Reagan's poor performance raised the only issue that might conceivably defeat him—his age. The president had looked and sounded *old.* But in the second debate, Reagan laid the perfect trap for his questioners. When asked about his age and capacity to lead the nation, he responded with a serious dead-pan expression to a hushed audience and waiting America: "I want you to know that I will not make age an issue in this campaign. I am not going to exploit for political purposes [pause] my opponent's youth and inexperience." The studio audience broke into uncontrolled laughter. Even Mondale had to laugh. With a classic one-liner, Reagan buried the age issue and won not only the debate but also the election.

### Bush-Dukakis

In 1988 Michael Dukakis ensured his defeat with a cold, detached performance in the presidential debates, beginning with the very first question. When CNN anchor Bernard Shaw asked, "Governor, if Kitty Dukakis were raped and murdered, would you favor an irrevocable death penalty for the killer?" The question demanded an emotional reply. Instead, Dukakis responded with an impersonal recitation of his stock position on law enforcement. Bush seized the opportunity to establish a more personal relationship with the viewers: Voters responded to Bush, electing him.

### Clinton-Bush-Perot

The three-way presidential debates of 1992 drew the largest television audiences in the history of presidential debates. In the first debate, Ross Perot's Texas twang and down-home folksy style stole the show. Chided by his opponents for having no governmental experience, he shot back, "Well, they have a point. I don't have any experience in running up a $4 trillion dollar debt." But it was Bill Clinton's smooth performance in the second debate, with its talk-show format, that seemed to wrap up the election. Ahead in the polls, Clinton appeared at ease walking about the stage and responding to audience questions with sympathy and sincerity. By contrast, George Bush appeared stiff and formal, and somewhat ill-at-ease with the "unpresidential" format.

### Clinton-Dole

A desperate Bob Dole, running 20 points behind, faced a newly "presidential" Bill Clinton in their two 1996 debates. (Perot's poor standing in the polls led to his exclusion.) Dole tried to counter his image as a grumpy old man in the first encounter; his humor actually won more laughs from the audience than Clinton's. Dole injected more barbs in the second debate, complaining of "ethical problems in the White House." But Clinton remained cool and comfortable, ignoring the challenger and focusing on the nation's economic health. Viewers, most of whom were already in Clinton's court, judged him the winner of both debates.

### Bush-Gore

Separate formats were agreed upon for three debates—the traditional podium, a conference, table, and a town hall setting. Gore was assertive, almost to the point of rudeness, but both candidates focused on policy differences rather than on personal attacks. Viewers gave Gore the edge in these debates but they found Bush more likable. Bush appeared to benefit more in the postdebate polls.

### Bush-Kerry

Kerry prepared well for the three debates. He appeared tall, earnest, confident, well-informed, and "presidential." He spoke forcefully, avoiding the qualifying clauses and lengthy sentences that had plagued his speeches in the past. Bush appeared uncomfortable, scowling at Kerry's answers, often repeating himself, and failing to "connect" with his audiences. Polls showed Kerry winning each debate.

# ACROSS THE USA

## How the States Voted

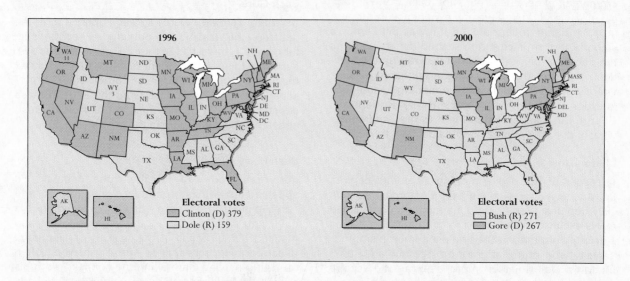

**1996**

Electoral votes
- Clinton (D) 379
- Dole (R) 159

**2000**

Electoral votes
- Bush (R) 271
- Gore (D) 267

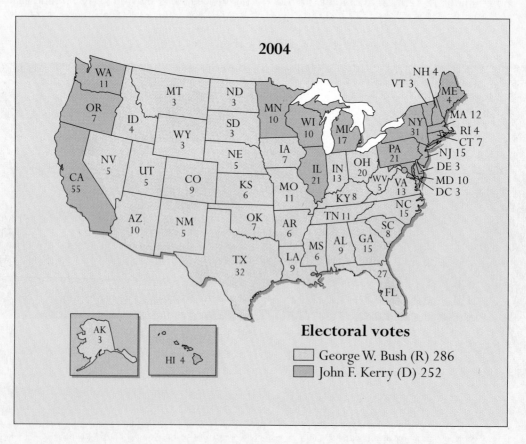

**2004**

### Electoral votes
- George W. Bush (R) 286
- John F. Kerry (D) 252

against candidates for a variety of reasons—party affiliation, group interests, characteristics and images of the candidates themselves, the economy, and policy issues. But forecasting election outcomes remains a risky business.

**Party Affiliation**    Although many people claim to vote for "the person, not the party," party identification remains a powerful influence in voter choice. Party ties among voters have weakened over time, with increasing proportions of voters labeling themselves as independents or only weak Democrats or Republicans, and more voters opting to split their tickets or cross party lines than did so a generation ago (see Chapter 7). Nevertheless, party identification remains one of the most important influences on voter choice. Party affiliation is more important in congressional than in presidential elections, but even in presidential elections the tendency to see the candidate of one's own party as "the best person" is very strong.

Consider the three presidential elections in Figure 5.8. Self-identified Republicans voted overwhelmingly for Bush in 1992, for Dole in 1996, and for George W. Bush in 2000 and 2004. Self-identified Democrats voted overwhelmingly for Clinton in 1992 and 1996, for Gore in 2000, and for Kerry in 2004.

Because Republican identifiers are outnumbered in the electorate by Democratic identifiers, Republican presidential candidates, and many Republican congressional candidates as well, *must* appeal to independent and Democratic crossover voters.

**Group Voting**    We already know that various social and economic groups give disproportionate support to the Democratic and Republican parties (see Chapter 7). So it comes as no surprise that recent Democratic presidential candidates have received disproportionate support from African Americans, Catholics, Jews, the less-educated, and union workers; Republican presidential candidates have fared better among whites, Protestants, and better-educated voters (see Figure 5.9). That is, these groups have given a larger percentage of their vote to the Democratic or Republican candidates than the candidate received from the total electorate.

**Race and Gender Gaps**    Among the more interesting group voting patterns is the serious *gender gap* affecting recent Republican candidates. Although Reagan won the women's vote in both 1980 and 1984, his vote percentages among men were considerably higher than among women. George H. W. Bush lost the women's vote in both 1988 and 1992. In 1996 the gender gap widened, with 54 percent of women voting for Clinton as opposed to only 38 percent for Dole, and continued in 2000 with women giving Gore 54 percent of the vote as opposed to Bush's 43 percent. Again in 2004 women gave Democrat John F. Kerry 54 percent of their vote. African Americans have long constituted the most loyal group of Democratic voters, regularly giving the Democratic presidential nominee up to 90 percent or more of their vote. The overall Hispanic vote is Democratic, although a significant portion of Hispanics, notably Cuban Americans in Florida, vote Republican.

**Candidate Image**    In an age of direct communication between candidates and voters via television, the image of candidates and their ability to relate to audiences have emerged as important determinants of voter choice. Candidate image is most important in presidential contests, inasmuch as presidential candidates are personally more visible to the voter than candidates for lesser offices.[22]

It is difficult to identify exactly what personal qualities appeal most to voters. Warmth, compassion, strength, confidence, honesty, sincerity, good humor, appearance, and "character" all seem important. "Character" has become a central

> **Think Again**
>
> Should people vote on the basis of a candidate's personal character rather than his or her policy positions?

| 2004 | Kerry(Democrat) | Bush (Republican) |
|---|---|---|
| **Party** | | |
| Democrat | 90% | 9% |
| Republican | 7% | 92% |
| Independent | 45% | 48% |
| **Ideology** | | |
| Liberal | 84% | 12% |
| Moderate | 45% | 53% |
| Conservative | 18% | 80% |
| **Economy** | | |
| Excellent | 10% | 88% |
| Good | 14% | 82% |
| Not Good | 80% | 16% |

| 2000 | Gore (Democrat) | Bush (Republican) |
|---|---|---|
| **Party** | | |
| Democrat | 86% | 11% |
| Republican | 8% | 91% |
| Independent | 45% | 47% |
| **Ideology** | | |
| Liberal | 80% | 13% |
| Moderate | 52% | 44% |
| Conservative | 17% | 81% |
| **Economy** | | |
| Excellent | 53% | 46% |
| Good | 37% | 53% |
| Not Good | 47% | 49% |

| 1996 | Clinton (Democrat) | Dole (Republican) |
|---|---|---|
| **Party** | | |
| Democrat | 84% | 10% |
| Republican | 13% | 80% |
| Independent | 43% | 35% |
| **Ideology** | | |
| Liberal | 78% | 11% |
| Moderate | 57% | 33% |
| Conservative | 20% | 71% |
| **Economy** | | |
| Better | 66% | 26% |
| Same | 46% | 45% |
| Worse | 27% | 57% |

**Figure 5.8**  Party, Ideology, and Nature of the Times in Presidential Voting
Those who identify themselves as members of a major political party are highly likely to vote for the presidential candidates of their party. Likewise, those who identify themselves as liberals are more likely than average to vote for Democrats, and those who identify themselves as conservatives are more likely to vote for Republicans in presidential elections. In addition, voters who see the economic picture as better are more likely to vote for the incumbent, and those who are concerned about the nation's economy are more likely to vote against the incumbent.

*Source:* Election exit polls, Voter News Service, National Election Pool.

feature of media coverage of candidates (see Chapter 6). Reports of extramarital affairs, experimentation with drugs, draft dodging, cheating in college, shady financial dealings, conflicts of interest, or lying or misrepresenting facts receive heavy media coverage because they attract large audiences. But it is difficult to estimate how many voters are swayed by so-called character issues.

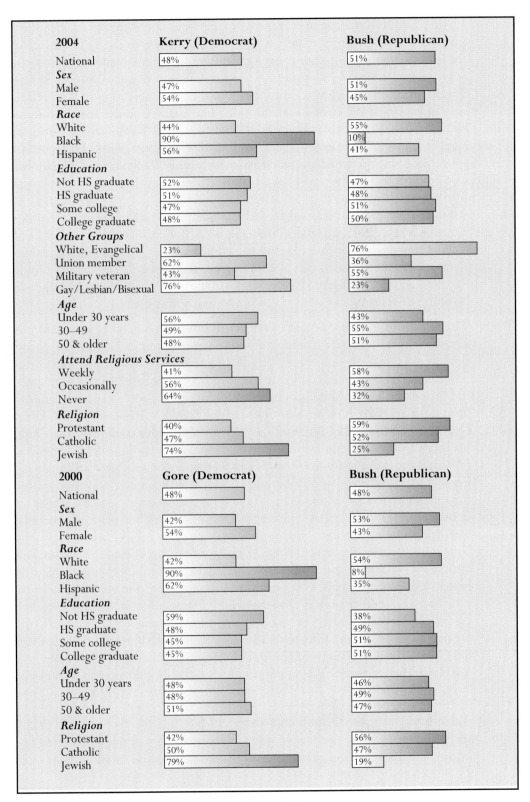

**Figure 5.9**    Group Voting in Presidential Elections

Democratic presidential candidates regularly do better among African American, Hispanic, lower income, less-educated voters. The gender gap—men tending to vote Republican and women Democratic—first emerged in the Reagan years. Increasingly, white religious voters are casting their ballots for Republican candidates.

*Source:* Election exit polls, Voter News Service, National Election Pool.

Attractive personal qualities can win support from opposition-party identifiers and people who disagree on the issues. John F. Kennedy's handsome and youthful appearance, charm, self-confidence, and disarming good humor defeated the heavy-jowled, shifty-eyed, defensive, and ill-humored Richard Nixon. Ronald Reagan's folksy mannerisms, warm humor, and comfortable rapport with television audiences justly earned him the title "The Great Communicator." Reagan disarmed his critics by laughing at his own personal flubs—falling asleep at meetings, forgetting names—and by telling his own age jokes. His personal appeal won more Democratic voters than any other Republican candidate has won in modern history, and he won the votes of many people who disagreed with him on the issues.

Bush's resolute position on Iraq and the war on terrorism created a popular image of him as "a strong leader," someone who "has clear stands on issues," and is "honest and trustworthy." He is also seen as having a "strong religious faith." Kerry was seen as someone who "will bring needed change," "cares about people like me," and is "intelligent" (see Table 5.4). Bush was also seen as friendly and likeable, while Kerry was seen as somewhat aloof and austere.

**The Economy**   Fairly accurate predictions of voting outcomes in presidential elections can be made from models of the American economy. Economic conditions at election time—recent growth or decline in personal income, the unemployment rate, consumer confidence, and so on—are related to the vote given the incumbent versus the challenger. Ever since the once-popular Republican incumbent Herbert Hoover was trounced by Franklin Roosevelt as the Great Depression of the 1930s deepened, politicians have understood that voters hold the incumbent party responsible for hard economic times.

Perhaps no other lesson has been as well learned by politicians: Hard economic times hurt incumbents and favor challengers. The economy may not be the only important factor in presidential voting, but it is certainly a factor of great importance.[23] Some evidence indicates that it is not voters' *own* personal economic well-being that affects their vote but rather voter perception of *general* economic conditions. People who perceive the economy as getting worse are likely to vote against the incumbent party, whereas people who think the economy is getting better support the incumbent.[24] Thus voters who thought the economy was getting *worse* in 1992 supported challenger Bill Clinton over incumbent president George H.W. Bush. But the reverse was true in 1996; more people thought the economy was better, and the people who thought so voted heavily for incumbent Bill Clinton. In 2000, Gore won the votes of those who thought the economy was "excellent," but economic voting did not seem to be as influential as in previous

**Table 5.4   Images of Bush and Kerry 2004**

Considering the following qualities and characteristics, please state whether you think each one better describes John F. Kerry or George W. Bush.

| Percentage who said: | Voted for: | Kerry | Bush |
|---|---|---|---|
| 25% | Will bring needed change | 95% | 4% |
| 17 | Has clear stand on issues | 23 | 75 |
| 16 | Strong leader | 14 | 85 |
| 11 | Honest, trustworthy | 28 | 70 |
| 10 | Cares about people like me | 76 | 23 |
| 8 | Intelligent | 91 | 7 |
| 7 | Strong religious faith | 9 | 90 |

# A CONSTITUTIONAL NOTE

## Who Can Vote?

The Founders generally believed that only property-owning free white males, twenty-one or older, should be entitled to vote. But they failed to include these qualifications in the original Constitution of 1787. Instead, they left to the states to decide who should vote: ". . . the Electors in each State shall have the Qualifications requisite for Electors of the most numerous Branch of the State Legislature" (Article I, Section 2). Why leave it up to the states to decide the voter qualifications for national elections? In committee and in floor discussions the delegates could not agree on what kind of property should qualify a person to vote. Plantation owners argued for qualifications to be expressed in land acreage; bankers wanted them expressed in the size of one's bank account; shippers and businessmen, in the value of their inventories or ships; and so on.

In frustration, the delegates dropped the issue into the laps of the states secure in the knowledge that in 1787 all of the states had some form of property qualifications and no state permitted women, slaves, or persons under twenty-one to vote. But this opening in the Constitution began a long journey toward full voting rights in the United States. Jacksonian democracy swept the nation in the 1840s and property qualifications were dropped by the states themselves. Not until after the Civil War was the Constitution amended to prevent the states from denying the right to vote on account of race (Fifteenth Amendment, 1870). The long fight for women's suffrage finally resulted in a constitutional guarantee of women's right to vote (Nineteenth Amendment, 1920); poll taxes were constitutionally banned (Twenty-fourth Amendment, 1964); and eighteen-year-olds secured the constitutional right to vote (Twenty-sixth Amendment, 1971).

presidential races. The economy was cited as "most important" by about one-fifth of the voters in 2004 and Kerry won the vast majority of these voters.

**Issue Voting**   Casting one's vote exclusively on the basis of the policy positions of the candidates is rare. Most voters are unaware of the specific positions taken by candidates on the issues. Indeed, voters often believe that their preferred candidate agrees with them on the issues, even when this is not the case. In other words, voters project their own policy views onto their favorite candidate more often than they decide to vote for a candidate because of his or her position on the issues.

However, when asked specifically about issues, voters are willing to name those they care most about (see Table 5.5). Voters do not always make their choices based on a candidate's stated policy positions, but voters *do* strongly favor candidates whose policy views they assume match their own. Only when a key issue takes center stage do voters really become aware of what the candidates actually propose to do. In the 1992, 1996, and 2000 elections, the economy was

**Table 5.5   Issues the Voters Cared about in 2004**

**Presidential Vote of Those Who Listed Issue as "Most Important"**

| | | | Who they voted for: | |
| --- | --- | --- | --- | --- |
| Rank | Percentage who said: | | Kerry | Bush |
| 1 | 21% | Moral values | 19% | 78% |
| 2 | 20 | Economy/jobs | 82 | 16 |
| 3 | 18 | Terrorism | 15 | 85 |
| 4 | 15 | Iraq | 76 | 23 |
| 5 | 8 | Health care | 79 | 20 |
| 6 | 5 | Taxes | 47 | 53 |
| 7 | 4 | Education | 75 | 24 |

the issue that voters cared about most. In all three elections, Clinton and Gore won the votes of the people most concerned about the economy (see Table 5.5).

To the surprise of many commentators, "moral values" was cited as the most important issue by voters leaving the polls in 2004.[25] Bush won over three-quarters of these voters. Faith and family appeared to underlie concern with moral values. Bush had never disguised his religious faith. Bans on same-sex marriage were on referenda ballots in eleven states and may have helped inspire a heavy turnout for Bush.

Bush had tried to portray the war in Iraq as part of a broader war on terrorism. Although Bush won the votes of people concerned with terrorism, Kerry won the votes of those concerned with the war in Iraq. Voters opposed to the war in Iraq went heavily for Kerry, whereas supporters of the war voted heavily for Bush.

# Summary Notes

- Public opinion commands the attention of elected public officials in a democracy, yet many Americans are poorly informed and unconcerned about politics; their opinions on public issues are often changeable and inconsistent. Only a few highly salient issues generate strong and stable opinions.

- Ideology also shapes opinion, especially among politically interested and active people who employ fairly consistent liberal or conservative ideas in forming their opinions on specific issues.

- Race and gender also influence public opinion. Blacks and whites differ over the extent of discrimination in the United States, as well as over its causes and remedies. Men and women tend to differ over issues involving the use of force. In recent years, women have tended to give greater support to the Democratic Party than men have.

- Individuals can exercise power in a democratic political system in a variety of ways. They can run for public office, take part in demonstrations and protests, make financial contributions to candidates, attend political events, write letters to newspapers or public officials, belong to political organizations, vote in elections, or simply hold and express opinions on public issues.

- About half of the voting-age population fails to vote even in presidential elections. Voter turnout has steadily declined in recent decades. Voter registration is a major obstacle to voting. Turnout is affected by competition as well as by feelings of political alienation and distrust of government. Young people have the poorest record of voter turnout of any age group.

- Although winning candidates often claim a mandate for their policy proposals, in reality few campaigns present clear policy alternatives to the voters, few voters cast their ballots on the basis of policy considerations, and the policy preferences of the electorate can seldom be determined from election outcomes.

- Nevertheless, voters can influence future policy directions through retrospective judgments about the performance of incumbents, returning them to office or turning them out. Most retrospective voting appears to center on the economy.

- Incumbents begin campaigns with many advantages: name recognition, financial support, goodwill from services they perform for constituents, large-scale public projects they bring to their districts, and the other resources of office.

- Campaigning for office is largely a media activity, dominated by professional advertising specialists, fund-raisers, media consultants, and pollsters.

- The professionalization of campaigning and the heavy costs of a media campaign drive up the costs of running for office. These huge costs make candidates heavily dependent on financial support from individuals and organizations. Fund-raising occupies more of a candidate's time than any other campaign activity.

- Campaign contributions are made by politically active individuals and organizations, including political action committees. Many contributions are made in order to gain access to policymakers and assistance with government business. Some contributors are ideologically motivated; others merely seek to rub shoulders with powerful people.

- Presidential primary election strategies emphasize appeals to party activists and core supporters, including the more ideologically motivated primary voters.

- In the general election campaign, presidential candidates usually seek to broaden their appeal to moderate, centrist voters while holding on to their core supporters. Campaigns must focus on states where the candidate has the best chance of gaining the 270 electoral votes needed to win.

- Voter choice is influenced by party identification, group membership, perceived image of the candidates, economic conditions, and, to a lesser extent, ideology and issue preferences.

# Key Terms

mandate   138
retrospective voting   138
incumbent   139
name recognition   142
challengers   142
franking privilege   143

campaign strategy   143
negative campaigning   144
focus group   144
photo ops   146
sound bites   146
mobilize   147

issue ads   151
political action committees
   (PACs)   153
Federal Election
   Commission (FEC)   154
retail politics   160

front-end strategy   160
spin doctor   160
front-loading   161
Electoral College   161
swing states   161

# Suggested Readings

Conway, M. Margaret, *Political Participation in the United States.* 3rd ed. Washington, D.C.: CQ Press, 2000. A comprehensive summary of who participates in politics and why.

Conway, M. Margaret, Gertrude A. Stevernagel, and David Ahern. *Women and Political Participation.* 2nd ed. Washington, D.C.: CQ Press, 2004. An examination of cultural change and women's participation in politics, including treatment of the gender gap in political attitudes and the impact of women's membership in the political elite.

Drexler, Kateri M., and Gwen Garcelon. *Strategies for Active Citizenship.* Upper Saddle River, N.J.: Prentice Hall, 2005. A handbook for becoming active in politics.

Erikson, Robert S., and Kent L. Tedin. *American Public Opinion,* 6th ed. Longman, 2002. A comprehensive review of the forces influencing public opinion and an assessment of the influence of public opinion in American politics.

Flanigan, William H., and Nancy H. Zingale. *Political Behavior of the American Electorate.* 11th ed. Washington, D.C.: CQ Press, 2002. A brief but comprehensive summary of the extensive research literature on the effects of party identification, opinion, ideology, the media, and candidate image on voter choice and election outcomes.

Iyengar, Shanto, and Stephen Ansolabehere. *Going Negative: How Political Advertisements Shrink and Polarize the Electorate.* New York: Free Press, 1996. The real problem with negative political ads is not that they sway voters to support one candidate over another, but that they reinforce the belief that all are dishonest and cynical.

Page, Benjamin I., and Robert Y. Shapiro. *The Rational Public.* Chicago: University of Chicago Press, 1992. An examination of fifty years of public opinion polls convinces these authors that American government is generally responsive to the views of the majority.

Wald, Kenneth D. *Religion and Politics in the United States.* 4th ed. Rowman & Littlefield, 2003. An explanation of the impact of religion on American political culture, the policy process, and voting behavior.

Walton, Hanes, and Robert C. Smith. *African American Politics and the African American Quest for Universal Freedom.* New York: Pearson Longman, 2002. A comprehensive American government textbook emphasizing the diversity of African American opinions and behavior.

Zaller, John R. *The Nature and Origins of Mass Opinion.* New York: Cambridge University Press, 1992. An effort to develop and test a conceptual model of how people form political preferences, how political views and arguments diffuse through the population, and how people evaluate this information and convert their reactions into public opinion.

# ★ Make It Real

## PUBLIC OPINION, PARTICIPATION AND VOTING

Students look at the 2000 presidential election and how the outcome was affected by using congressional districts to allocate presidential electors.

# 6 MASS MEDIA
## Setting the Political Agenda

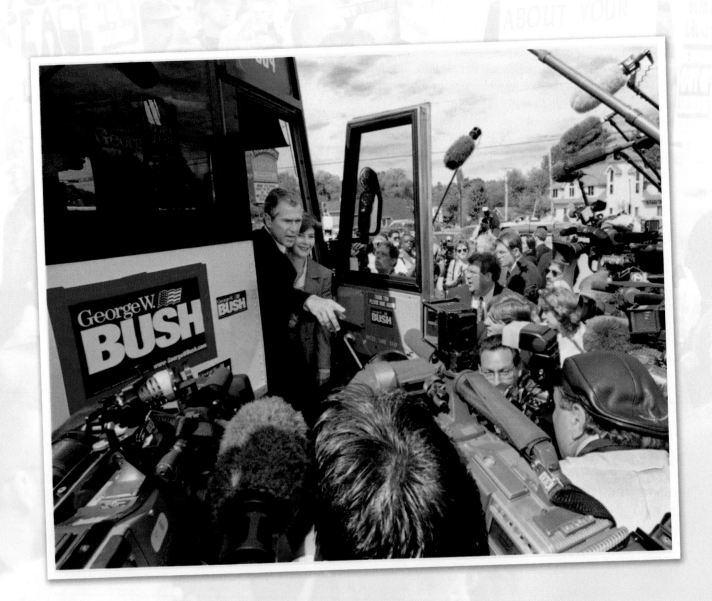

## Chapter Outline

- The Power of the Media
- Sources of Media Power
- The Business of the Media
- The Politics of the News
- Polarization of the Media
- Mediated Elections
- Freedom versus Fairness
- Libel and Slander
- Politics and the Internet
- Media Effects: Shaping Political Life

## Think About Politics

**1** Are media professionals—news reporters, editors, anchors—the true voice of the people in public affairs?
Yes ☐ No ☐

**2** Do the media mirror what is really news, rather than deciding themselves what's important and then making it news?
Yes ☐ No ☐

**3** Is television your most important source of news?
Yes ☐ No ☐

**4** Should the media report on all aspects of the private lives of public officials?
Yes ☐ No ☐

**5** Do the media report equally fairly on Democratic and Republican candidates for office?
Yes ☐ No ☐

**6** Should the media be legally required to be fair and accurate in reporting political news?
Yes ☐ No ☐

**7** Are you more alienated than attracted by the media's coverage of politics?
Yes ☐ No ☐

**8** Is your choice of candidates in elections affected by their advertising?
Yes ☐ No ☐

*Ask yourself how much of your knowledge about politics in America comes from television and newspapers and the radio. What you know about politics and how you participate are, in fact, largely determined by the power of the media to decide what they want you to know.*

★   ★   ★

# The Power of the Media

Politics—the struggle over who gets what, when, and how—is largely carried out in the **mass media**. The arenas of political conflict are the various media of mass communication—television, newspapers, magazines, radio, books, recordings, motion pictures, and the Internet. What we know about politics comes to us largely through these media. Unless we ourselves are admitted to the White House Oval Office or the committee rooms of Congress or dinner parties at foreign embassies, or unless we ourselves attend political rallies and demonstrations or travel to distant battlefields, we must rely on the mass media to tell us about politics. Furthermore, few of us ever have the opportunity to personally evaluate the character of presidential candidates or cabinet members or members of Congress, or to learn their views on public issues by talking with them face to face. Instead, we must learn about people as well as events from the mass media.

Great power derives from the control of information. *Who knows what* helps to determine *who gets what.* The media not only provide an arena for politics; they are also themselves players in that arena. The media not only report on the struggles for power in society; they are also themselves participants in those struggles. The media have long been referred to as America's "fourth branch" of government—and for good reason.[1]

**The Power of Television**   Television is the most powerful medium of communication. It is the first true *mass* communication medium. Virtually every home in the United States has a television set, and the average home has the set turned on for about seven hours a day. Television is regularly chosen over other news media by Americans as the most common news source.

Americans turn to *local* TV news broadcasts as their most regular source of news. Daily newspapers are read by less than half of the adult public (see Figure 6.1). The national network evening news shows (*NBC Nightly News, ABC World News Tonight, CBS Evening News*) have lost viewership in recent years. But viewership of CNN, Fox News Cable, CNBC, and MSNBC is rising. Television weekly news magazines, notably CBS's *60 Minutes* and ABC's *20/20* have also become major sources of news for many Americans.

**Figure 6.1** Where Americans Get Their News

Note: More than one answer accepted in survey, so the sum adds up to well over 100%.

*Source:* Data from Pew Research Center for the People and the Press, *http://people-press.org*, June 2, 2005.

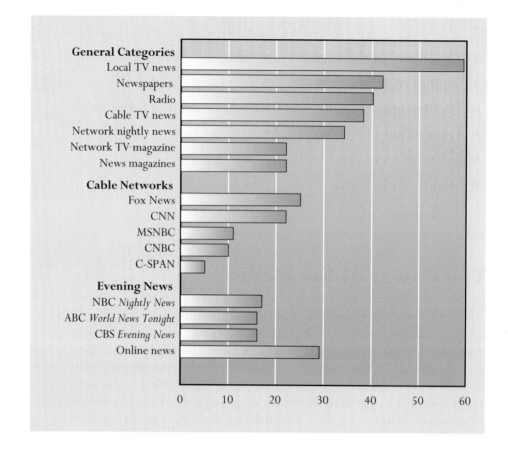

**mass media** All means of communication with the general public, including television, newspapers, magazines, radio, books, recordings, motion pictures, and the Internet.

A growing number of Americans, especially young people, are turning to online news sources (see *Up Close:* "The Generation Gap in News").

During a national crisis—for example, the terrorist attack of 9/11—Americans become even more dependent on television for their news. When asked "Where would you go first," for information during a crisis, 66 percent of Americans said they would turn on their TV sets. CNN was mentioned most often.[2]

**Believability** Television is also rated by Americans as the most *believable* medium of communication. Compared to television news, print sources are generally seen as less believable, with one exception, the *Wall Street Journal*. CNN is rated highest among all news sources (see Figure 6.2). Not many people rate the tabloids as very believable.

**Newspapers and Magazines** Less than one-half of the adult population reads one or another of the nation's 1,500 daily newspapers. But the nation's prestige newspapers—the *New York Times, Washington Post*, and *Wall Street Journal*—are regularly read by government officials, corporate chiefs, interest-group leaders, and other media people. Stories appearing in these newspapers are generally picked up by daily papers around the country, and these stories almost always appear on national network television.

The leading weekly newsmagazines—*Time, Newsweek*, and *U.S. News & World Report*—reach a smaller but more politically attentive audience than do newspapers. Magazines of political commentary—for example, the *Nation* (liberal), *New Republic* (liberal), *National Review* (conservative), *American Spectator* (conservative), *Weekly Standard* (conservative), *Public Interest* (neo-conservative), and *Washington Monthly* (neo-liberal)—reach very small but politically active audiences.

## UP CLOSE

# The Generation Gap in News

Young people are far less likely to spend time watching the news than older people. Indeed, people 65 and older are nearly twice as likely as those under 30 to watch television news. And older people are more than twice as likely to read a newspaper.

However, young people are more likely than older people to hear radio news, perhaps because radio news periodically interrupts music programming. And young people are the principal consumers of online news. Yet overall, young people are exposed to far less news than seniors.

### The News Generation Gap

|  | 18–29 | 30–49 | 50–64 | 65+ |
| --- | --- | --- | --- | --- |
| Watch TV news | 40% | 52% | 62% | 73% |
| Local TV | 28 | 41 | 49 | 52 |
| Network evening news | 17 | 25 | 38 | 46 |
| Cable TV news | 16 | 23 | 30 | 35 |
| Morning TV news | 11 | 16 | 21 | 27 |
| Read newspaper | 26 | 37 | 52 | 59 |
| Listen to radio news | 34 | 49 | 42 | 29 |
| News magazines | 12 | 13 | 15 | 13 |
| Online news | 31 | 30 | 24 | 7 |
| No news (yesterday) | 33 | 19 | 15 | 12 |

*Source:* Pew Research Center for the People and the Press. *http://people-press.org.* Reprinted by permission of Pew Research Center for the People and the Press.

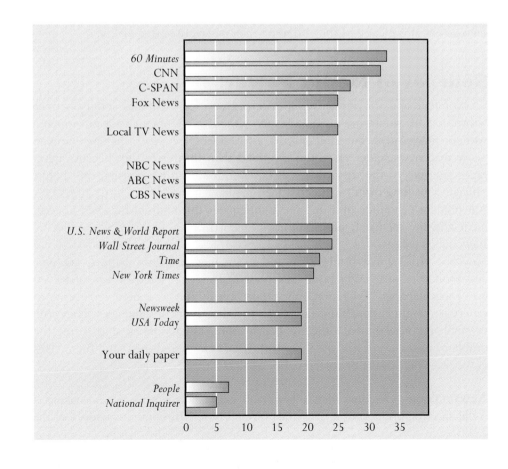

**Figure 6.2** Believability of the Media

*Source:* Data from Pew Research Center for the People and the Press, *http://people-press.org* June 2, 2005.

**Think Again**

Do the media mirror what is really news, rather than deciding themselves what's important and then making it news?

**newsmaking** Deciding what events, topics, presentations, and issues will be given coverage in the news.

**Television's Emotional Communication**   The power of television derives not only from its large audiences, but also from its ability to communicate emotions as well as information. Television's power is found in its visuals—angry faces in a rioting mob, police beating an African American motorist, wounded soldiers being unloaded from a helicopter—scenes that convey an emotional message. Gripping pictures can inflame public opinion, inspire a clamor for action, and even pressure the government into hasty action. (This "CNN effect"—pictures of starving children and brutal fighting—has been cited as a cause of the disastrous American intervention in Somalia in 1992.)

Moreover, television focuses on the faces of individuals as well as on their words, portraying honesty or deception, humility or arrogance, compassion or indifference, humor or meanness, and a host of other personal characteristics. Skillful politicians understand that *what* one says may not be as importants as *how* one says it. Image triumphs over substance on television.[3]

**Influence on Decision Makers**   The media's impact on political decision makers is vastly more significant than their impact on ordinary viewers. Media stories often relate more directly to the immediate concerns of politicians and government officials. They are more attentive to these stories; they are often asked to respond or comment upon news stories. They correctly perceive that media coverage of particular events and issues sets the agenda for public discussion. Even media stories that have relatively little widespread public interest can create a buzz "inside the Beltway," that is, within Washington circles.

**The Myth of the Mirror**   Media people themselves often deny that they exercise great power. They sometimes claim that they only "mirror" reality. They like to think of themselves as unbiased reporters who simply narrate happenings and transmit videotaped portrayals of people and events as they really are. But whether or not the editors, reporters, producers, or anchors acknowledge their own power, it is clear that they do more than passively mirror reality.

## Sources of Media Power

Government and the media are natural adversaries. (Thomas Jefferson once wrote that he would prefer newspapers without government to a government without newspapers. But after serving as president, he wrote that people who never read newspapers are better informed than those who do, because ignorance is closer to the truth than the falsehoods spread by newspapers.) Public officials have long been frustrated by the media. But the U.S. Constitution's First Amendment guarantee of a free press anticipates this conflict between government and the media. It prohibits government from resolving this conflict by silencing its critics.

Media professionals—television and newspaper reporters, editors, anchors, and producers—are not neutral observers of American politics but rather are active participants. They not only report events but also discover events to report, assign them political meaning, and predict their consequences. They seek to challenge government officials, debate political candidates, and define the problems of society. They see their profession as a "sacred trust" and themselves as the true voice of the people in public affairs.

**Newsmaking**   Deciding what is "news" and who is "newsworthy"—**newsmaking**—is the most important source of media power. It is only through the media that the

Politicians have a "love-hate" relationship with the media. Democratic presidential candidate John Kerry complains here to reporters that thousands of voters were wrongly prevented from voting in the 2004 presidential election.

general public comes to know about events, personalities, and issues. Media attention makes topics public, creates issues, and elevates personalities from obscurity to celebrity. Each day, editors, producers, and reporters must select from millions of events, topics, and people those that will be videotaped, written about, and talked about. The media can never be a "picture of the world" because the whole world cannot be squeezed into the picture. The media must decide what is and is not "news."

Politicians have a love-hate relationship with the media. They need media attention to promote themselves, their message, and their programs. They crave the exposure, the name recognition, and the celebrity status that the media can confer. At the same time, they fear attack by the media. They know the media are active players in the political game, not just passive spectators. The media seek sensational stories of sin, sexuality, corruption, and scandal in government to attract viewers and readers, and thus the media pose a constant danger to politicians. Politicians understand the power of the media to make or break their careers.

**Agenda Setting**  Agenda setting is the power to decide what will be decided. It is the power to define society's "problems," to create political issues, and to set forth alternative solutions. Deciding which issues will be addressed by government may be even more important than deciding how the issues will be resolved. The distinguished political scientist E. E. Schattschneider once wrote, "He who determines what politics is about runs the country."[4]

The real power of the media lies in their ability to set the political agenda for the nation. This power grows out of their ability to decide what is news. Media coverage determines what both citizens and public officials regard as "crises" or "problems" or "issues" to be resolved. Conditions ignored by the media seldom get on the agenda of political leaders. Media attention forces public officials to speak on the topic, take positions, and respond to questions. Media inattention allows problems to be ignored by government. "TV is the Great Legitimator. TV confers reality. Nothing happens in America, practically everyone seems to agree, until it happens on television."[5]

**Newspaper Web Sites**
Virtually all major daily newspapers have Web sites that summarize each day's stories. For national news the most frequently consulted sites are *USA Today, Wall Street Journal, New York Times, Washington Post*.
www.usatoday.com
www.nytimes.com
www.washingtonpost.com
www.wallstreetjournal.com

**agenda setting** Deciding what will be decided, defining the problems and issues to be addressed by decision makers.

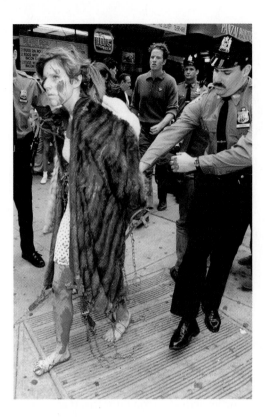

Groups hoping for free media coverage of their cause can improve their chances by framing their protests in dramatic form. Here, members of an animal-rights group attract the press by getting arrested during a protest against the fur industry, in which they painted themselves with red paint and wore leghold traps.

Political issues do not just "happen." The media are crucial to their development. Organized interest groups, professional public relations firms, government bureaucracies, political candidates, and elected officials all try to solicit the assistance of the media in shaping the political agenda. Creating an issue, publicizing it, dramatizing it, turning it into a "crisis," getting people to talk about it, and ultimately forcing government to do something about it are the tactics of agenda setting. The participation of the mass media is vital to their success.[6]

**Interpreting**    The media not only decide what will be news; they also interpret the news for us. Editors, reporters, and anchors provide each story with an *angle*, an interpretation that places the story in a context and speculates about its meaning and consequences. The interpretation tells us what to think about the news.

News is presented in "stories." Reporters do not report facts; they tell stories. The story structure gives meaning to various pieces of information. Some common angles or themes of news stories are these:

- *Good guys versus bad guys:* for example, corrupt officials, foreign dictators, corporate polluters, and other assorted villains versus honest citizens, exploited workers, endangered children, or other innocents.

- *Little guys versus big guys:* for example, big corporations, the military, or insensitive bureaucracies versus consumers, taxpayers, poor people, or the elderly.

- *Appearance versus reality:* for example, the public statements of government officials or corporate executives versus whatever contradicting facts hardworking investigative reporters can find.

News is also "pictures." A story without visuals is not likely to be selected as television news in the first place. The use of visuals reinforces the angle. A close-up shot can reveal hostility, insincerity, or anxiety on the face of villains or can show fear, concern, sincerity, or compassion on the face of innocents. To emphasize elements of a story, an editor can stop the action, use slow motion, zoom the lens, add graphics, cut back and forth between antagonists, cut away for audience reaction, and so on. Videotaped interviews can be spliced to make the interviewees appear knowledgeable, informed, and sincere or, alternatively, ignorant, insensitive, and mean-spirited. The media jealously guard the right to edit interviews themselves, rejecting virtually all attempts by interviewees to review and edit their own interviews.

**Socializing**    The media have power to socialize audiences to the political culture. News, entertainment, and advertising all contribute to **socialization**—to the learning of political values. Socialization through television and motion pictures begins in early childhood and continues throughout life. Most of the political information people learn comes to them through television—specific facts as well as general values. Election coverage, for example, shows "how democracy works," encourages political participation, and legitimizes the winner's control of government. Advertising shows Americans desirable middle-class standards of living even while it encourages people to buy automobiles, detergent, and beer, and entertainment programming socializes them to "acceptable" ways of life. Political values such as racial tolerance, sexual equality, and support for law enforcement are reinforced in movies, situation comedies, and police shows.

**socialization** The learning of a culture and its values.

**Persuading**    The media, in both paid advertising and news and entertainment programming, engage in direct efforts to change our attitudes, opinions, and behavior. Newspaper editorials have traditionally been employed for direct persuasion. A great deal of the political commentary on television news and interview programs is aimed at persuading people to adopt the views of the commentators. Even many entertainment programs and movies are intended to promote specific political viewpoints. But most direct persuasion efforts come to us through paid advertising.

**Center for Media and Public Affairs**
Studies of news and entertainment media, including election coverage. *www.cmpa.com*

Political campaigning is now largely a media battle, with paid political advertisements as the weapons. Candidates rely on professional campaign-management firms, with their pollsters, public relations specialists, advertising-production people, and media consultants, to carry on the fight (see Chapter 5).

Governments and political leaders must rely on persuasion through the mass media to carry out their programs. Presidents can take their message directly to people in televised speeches, news conferences, and the yearly State of the Union message. Presidents by custom are accorded television time whenever they request it. In this way, they can go over the heads of Congress and even the media executives and reporters themselves to communicate directly with the people.

In short, persuasion is central to politics, and the media are the key to persuasion.

## The Business of the Media

The business of the media is to gather mass audiences to sell to advertisers. Economic interest drives all media to try to attract and hold the largest numbers of readers and viewers in order to sell time and space to advertisers. Over one-quarter of all prime-time television (8–11 P.M.) is devoted to commercial advertising. Americans get more than one minute of commercials for every three minutes of news and entertainment. Television networks and commercial stations charge advertisers on the basis of audience estimates made by rating services. One rating service, A. C. Nielsen, places electronic boxes in a national sample of television homes and calculates the proportion of these homes that watch a program (the rating), as well as the proportion of homes with their television sets turned on that watch a particular program (the share). Newspapers' and magazines' advertising revenue is based primarily on circulation figures (see Table 6.1).

**National Association of Broadcasters**
News and views of the media industry from their trade association. *www.nab.org*

**Table 6.1**  The Largest Circulation U.S. Newspapers and Magazines

| Daily Newspapers | | | Magazines | | |
| --- | --- | --- | --- | --- | --- |
| **Rank** | **Newspaper** | **Circulation** | **Rank** | **Magazine** | **Circulation** |
| 1. *USA Today* (Arlington, Va.) | | 2,199,052 | 1. *AARP Modern Maturity* | | 22,668,583 |
| 2. *Wall Street Journal* (New York, N.Y.) | | 1,888,621 | 2. *Reader's Digest* | | 10,155,054 |
| 3. *The New York Times* (New York, N.Y.) | | 1,121,623 | 3. *TV Guide* | | 9,015,866 |
| 4. *The Los Angeles Times* (Los Angeles) | | 907,997 | 4. *Better Homes and Gardens* | | 7,627,256 |
| 5. *The Washington Post* (Washington, D.C.) | | 740,947 | 5. *National Geographic* | | 6,471,803 |
| 6. *Daily News* (New York, N.Y.) | | 708,713 | 6. *Good Housekeeping* | | 4,631,527 |
| 7. *New York Post* (New York, N.Y.) | | 652,149 | 7. *Family Circle* | | 4,252,730 |
| 8. *Chicago Tribune* (Chicago) | | 663,996 | 8. *Woman's Day* | | 4,130,507 |
| 9. *Houston Chronicle* (Houston) | | 477,493 | 9. *Ladies' Home Journal* | | 4,114,353 |
| 10. *Dallas Morning News* (Dallas) | | 527,744 | 10. *TIME* | | 4,034,272 |

*Source: Editor and Publisher International Yearbook 2005.* Copyright © 2005 VNU Business Media, Inc. Used with permission.

**Soft Fluff versus Hard Programming**  Lightweight entertainment—"soft fluff"—prevails over serious programming in virtually all media, but particularly on television. Critics of the "boob tube" abound in intellectual circles, but the mass public clearly prefers fluffy entertainment programming. Political scientist Doris Graber writes:

> Although "lightweight" programming draws the wrath of many people, particularly intellectual elites, one can argue that their disdain constitutes intellectual snobbery. Who is to say that the mass public's tastes are inferior to those of elites? . . . Proof is plentiful that the mass public does indeed prefer light entertainment to more serious programs.[7]

And it is the mass public that advertisers want to reach. Channels devoted to highbrow culture, including public television stations, languish with low ratings.

**News as TV Entertainment**  Increasingly news is being presented as television entertainment. In recent years there has been a dramatic increase in the number of entertainment-oriented, quasi-news programming, sometimes referred to as the "soft news media."[8] Soft news comes mainly in two formats: talk shows, both daytime and nighttime; and tabloid news programs (see Table 6.2). Even late-night entertainment

**Table 6.2**  TV Soft News Programming

| Network news magazines | Network TV soft news |
| --- | --- |
| *Dateline NBC* | *Extra* |
| *20/20* | *Entertainment Tonight* |
| *Primetime Live* | *Inside Edition* |
| *48 Hours* | *A Current Affair* |
| *60 Minutes* | *Access Hollywood* |
| **Late-night TV talk shows** | **Cable TV soft news** |
| Jay Leno | E! Network |
| David Letterman | Black Entertainment Television |
| Conan O'Brien | Comedy Central's *Daily Show* |
| *Politically Incorrect* | MTV News |
| **Daytime TV talk shows** | |
| Oprah Winfrey | |
| *Regis and Kelly* | |

The media are biased in favor of bad news over good. Wars, disasters, scandals, crimes are all well reported. Good news about improved health, a cleaner environment, or rising standards of living is generally overlooked.

programs—Jay Leno, David Letterman, Conan O'Brien, *Politically Incorrect*—include comedy monologues that occasionally refer to political events or issues.

Soft news is a major source of information for people who are not interested in politics or public affairs. It is true, of course, that most soft news programming favors celebrity gossip, murder trials, sex scandals, disasters, and other human interest stories. But on some high-profile news issues these programs provide an otherwise inattentive public with what little information it absorbs.

*Sixty Minutes* attracts more viewers than any other soft news program. *Dateline* and *20/20* are not far behind. (Arguably these programs are oriented toward a somewhat more sophisticated audience than talk shows or tabloid news programs.) These programs, as well as *Entertainment Tonight* and Oprah Winfrey, attract more viewers than any of the nightly network newscasts.

Politicians themselves have come to understand the importance of soft news programming in reaching segments of the public that seldom watch news programs, speeches or debates, or campaign advertising. Presidential candidates welcome invitations to appear with Oprah, or Leno, or Letterman, and try to reformulate their messages in a light, comedic style that fits the program.

**The Media Conglomerates**   Mega-mergers in recent years have created corporate empires that spread across multiple media—television, film, newspapers, music, and the Internet. Conglomerate media corporations combine television broadcasting and cable programming, movie production and distribution, magazine and book publication, music recording, Internet access, and even sports and recreation. The six multinational corporations listed in Table 6.3 currently dominate world media and cultural interests.

## The Politics of the News

The politics of the news media are shaped by (1) their *economic interest*, (2) their *professional environment*, and (3) their *ideological leanings*.

**Sensationalism**   The economic interest of the media—the need to capture and hold audience attention—creates a bias toward "hype" in the selection of news, its presentation, and its interpretation. To attract viewers and readers, the media bias the news toward violence, conflict, scandal, corruption, sex, scares of various sorts, and the personal lives of politicians and celebrities. News is selected primarily for its emotional impact on audiences; its social, economic, or political significance is secondary to the need to capture attention.

News must "touch" audiences personally, arouse emotions, and hold the interest of people with short attention spans. Scare stories—street crime, drug use, AIDS, nuclear power plant accidents, global warming, and a host of health alarms—make "good" news, for they cause viewers to fear for their personal

## Table 6.3   The Media Empires

**Time Warner Inc. (formerly known as AOL Time Warner)**

*Television:* HBO, TNT, TBS, CNN, CNNSI, CNNFN, Cinemax, Time Warner Cable
*Motion Pictures:* Warner Brothers, New Line Cinema, Castle Rock, Looney Tunes
*Magazines: Time, People, Sports Illustrated, Fortune,* plus twenty-eight other specialty magazines
*Books:* Warner Books; Little, Brown Publishing; Book-of-the-Month Club
*Music:* Warner Brothers Records, Atlantic Records, Elektra
*Sports and Entertainment:* Atlanta Braves, Atlanta Hawks, World Championship Wrestling
*Internet:* AOL, Netscape, CompuServe

**Walt Disney**

*Television:* ABC-TV, plus ten stations; ESPN, ESPN-2, Disney Channel, A&E, E!, Lifetime
*Motion Pictures:* Walt Disney Pictures, Miramax, Touchstone
*Music:* Walt Disney Records, Mammoth, Buena Vista Records
*Sports and Recreation:* Disney theme parks in Florida, California, France, Japan; Disney Cruise Line; Anaheim Mighty Ducks
*Consumer Products:* Disney stores, Disney toys.

**Viacom**

*Television:* CBS, plus forty TV stations: MTV, TNN, Nickelodeon, Showtime, VH1, Nick-At-Nite, Spike TV, BET, Comedy Central
*Motion Pictures:* Paramount Pictures, Spelling, Viacom
*Books:* Simon & Schuster, Scribner, Free Press
*Radio:* Infinity Broadcasting
*Music:* Famous Music Publishing
*Sports and Recreation:* SportsLine, plus five Paramount parks

**NewsCorp (Fox)**

*Television:* Fox Network plus thirty-five TV stations; Fox News, Fox Entertainment, Fox Sports, Fox Family Channel, National Geographic Channel, DirecTV
*Motion Pictures:* 20th Century Fox, Searchlight
*Books:* HarperCollins
*Newspaper: New York Post*
*Magazines: TV Guide*
*Music:* Mushroom Records
*Sports and Recreation:* Los Angeles Lakers, Los Angeles Kings

**Sony**

*Television:* Game Show Network, *Jeopardy, Wheel of Fortune*
*Motion Pictures:* Columbia Pictures, Sony Pictures, Tri Star
*Music:* Columbia Records, Epic Records, Sony, Nashville
*Sports and Recreation:* Sony Theaters

**NBC-Universal**

*Television:* NBC Network plus thirteen TV stations; CNBC, MSNBC, Telemundo, Bravo, USA, SciFi
*Motion Pictures:* Universal Pictures
*Sports and Recreation:* Universal Studios theme parks in California and Florida
*Music:* Motown, Geffen, MCA

*Source:* Thomas R. Dye, *Who's Running America? The Bush Restoration,* 6th ed. (Upper Saddle River, N.J.: Prentice Hall, 2002). Updated by the author.

safety. The sex lives of politicians, once by custom off-limits to the press, are now public "affairs." Scandal and corruption among politicians, as well as selfishness and greed among business executives, are regular media themes.[9]

**Negativism**   The media are biased toward bad news. Bad news attracts larger audiences than good news. Television news displays a pervasive bias toward the negative in American life—in government, business, the military, politics, education, and everywhere else. Bad-news stories on television vastly outnumber good-news stories.

Good news gets little attention. For example, television news watchers are not likely to know that illegal drug use is declining in the United States, that both the air and water are measurably cleaner today than in past decades, that the nuclear power industry has the best safety record of any major industry in the United States, and that the aged in America are wealthier and enjoy higher incomes than the nonaged. The violent crime rate is down 50 percent since 1990. Teenage pregnancies and abortion rates are both down significantly. Television has generally failed to report these stories or, even worse, has implied that the opposite is true. Good news—stories about improved health statistics, longer life spans, better safety records, higher educational levels, for example—seldom provides the dramatic element needed to capture audience attention. The result is an overwhelming bad-news bias, especially on television.[10]

**Muckraking**  The professional environment of reporters and editors predisposes them toward an activist style of journalism once dubbed **muckraking**. Reporters today view themselves as "watchdogs" of the public trust. They see themselves in noble terms—enemies of corruption, crusaders for justice, defenders of the disadvantaged. "The watchdog function, once considered remedial and subsidiary. . .[is now] paramount: the primary duty of the journalists is to focus attention on problems and deficits, failures and threats."[11] Their professional models are the crusading "investigative reporters" who expose wrongdoing in government, business, the military, and every other institution in society—except the media.

**muckraking** Journalistic exposés of corruption, wrongdoing, or mismanagement in government, business, and other institutions of society.

**The "Feeding Frenzy"**  Occasionally, muckraking episodes grow into "**feeding frenzies**"—intense coverage of a scandal or event that blocks out most other news. Political scientist Larry Sabato describes the feeding frenzy: "In such situations a development is almost inevitably magnified and overscrutinized, the crush of cameras, microphones, and people, combined with the pressure of instant deadlines and live broadcasts, hype events and make it difficult to keep them in perspective. When a frenzy begins to gather, the intensity grows exponentially. . . . Television news time is virtually turned over to the subject of the frenzy."[12] Increasingly stiff competition among the media for attention and the need for round-the-clock cable news to fill long hours contribute to feeding frenzies.

**"feeding frenzy"** Intense media coverage of a scandal or event that blocks out most other news.

**Liberalism in the Newsroom**  The activist role that the media have taken upon themselves means that the personal values of reporters, editors, producers, and anchors are a very important element of American politics. The political values of the media are decidedly liberal and reformist. Political scientist Doris A. Graber writes about the politics of the media: "Economic and social liberalism prevails, especially in the most prominent media organizations. So does a preference for an internationalist foreign policy, caution about military intervention, and some suspicion about the ethics of established large institutions, particularly big business and big government."[13] Most Americans agree that media news coverage is biased and the bias is in a liberal direction (see *What Do You Think?* "Are the Media Biased?").

**Liberalism in Hollywood**  With a few exceptions, Hollywood producers, directors, writers, studio executives, and actors are decidedly liberal in their political views, especially when compared with the general public. Of the Hollywood elite, more than 60 percent describe themselves as liberal and only 14 percent as conservative,[14] whereas in the general public, self-described conservatives outnumber liberals by a significant margin. Hollywood leaders are five times more likely to be Democrats than Republicans, and Hollywood is a major source of Democratic Party campaign funds. On both economic and social issues, the Hollywood elite is significantly more liberal than the nation's general public or college-educated public.[15] (However, see *A Conflicting View,* "Fox News: Fair and Balanced'?").

**People for the American Way** Web site founded by Hollywood "liberals" to combat "right-wing" influence. *www.pfaw.org*

# WHAT DO YOU THINK?

## Are the Media Biased?

Are the media biased, and if so in what direction—liberal or conservative? Arguments over media bias have grown in intensity as the media have come to play a central role in American politics.

Nearly three out of four Americans (74 percent) see "a fair amount" or "a great deal" of media bias in news coverage (see the following table). And of those who see a bias, over twice as many see a liberal bias rather than a conservative bias. Indeed, even liberals see a liberal bias in the news; it is not a perception limited to conservatives, although they are more likely to see it. The liberal bias is much more likely to be seen by college graduates than by people who did not finish high school. It is also more likely to be seen by political activists than by those who engage in little or no political activity. However, African Americans are likely to see a conservative bias in the news, in contrast to the liberal bias perceived more often by whites.

At the same time, Americans have high expectations of the role of the media in society: they expect the media to protect them from "abuse of power" by government, to hold public officials accountable, and to point out and help solve the problems of society.

### Perceptions of Media Bias

| | How Much Bias? "A Great Deal" or "Fair Amount" (%) | Direction of Bias | |
| --- | --- | --- | --- |
| | | Liberal (%) | Conservative (%) |
| **All** | 74 | 43 | 19 |
| **Race** | | | |
| White | 75 | 46 | 15 |
| Black | 64 | 24 | 40 |
| **Education** | | | |
| Less than high school | 56 | 29 | 33 |
| High school graduate | 75 | 42 | 19 |
| College graduate | 81 | 57 | 19 |
| **Ideology** | | | |
| Liberal | 70 | 41 | 22 |
| Moderate | 70 | 30 | 16 |
| Conservative | 81 | 57 | 19 |
| **Political Activism** | | | |
| High | 82 | 54 | 14 |
| Low | 76 | 42 | 22 |
| None | 65 | 34 | 22 |

**www Accuracy in Media** A self-described watchdog organization critical of liberal bias in the media. *www.aim.org*

**Conservatism on Talk Radio**   Talk radio is the one medium where conservatism prevails. The single most listened-to talk radio show is the *Rush Limbaugh Show,* whose host regularly bashes "limousine liberals," "femi-Nazis," "environmental wackos," and "croissant people."[16] Talk radio might be portrayed as "call-in democracy." Callers respond almost immediately to reported news events. Call-in shows are the first to sense the public mood. Callers are not necessarily representative of the general public. Rather they are usually the most intense and outraged of citizens. But their complaints are early warning signs for wary politicians.

**Televised Incivility and Political Trust**   Does watching political shows on television, in which hosts, guests, pundits, and others hurl insults at each other, interrupt and shout over each other, and use especially contentious and uncivil

## A CONFLICTING VIEW

# Fox News: "Fair and Balanced"?

For many years conservatives complained about the liberal tilt of television news. But despite their ample financial resources, conservative investors failed to create their own network or purchase an existing one. It was an Australian billionaire, Rupert Murdoch, who eventually came to the rescue of American conservatives.

Murdoch's global media empire, News Corp, includes Fox Network, Fox News Cable, 20th Century Fox, the *New York Post, The Times* and *The Sun* of London, HarperCollins Publishing, thirty-five local TV stations, and the Los Angeles Dodgers. He began his career by injecting glitz and vulgarity into previously dull Australian newspapers he inherited. The formula worked worldwide: The *New York Post* became a noisy tabloid after Murdoch took over (most memorable headline: "HEADLESS BODY FOUND IN TOPLESS BAR"), and Fox TV entertainment airs even more vulgar shows than the mainstream networks.

Murdoch himself is not particularly conservative in his politics, but he recognized an unfilled market for conservative views on American television. In 1996 he founded Fox News and hired Roger Ailes (former TV ad producer for Richard Nixon, Ronald Reagan, and George H. W. Bush) to head up the new network. Ailes quickly signed Bill O'Reilly (see *People in Politics* in Chapter 2) for an hourlong nightly conservative talk show. Brit Hume, one of the few prominent TV reporters considered to be a conservative, was made managing editor.

Fox proclaims "fair and balanced" news—"We report, you decide." The implication is that mainstream media has a liberal bias and that Fox is rectifying it with its own fair and balanced reporting. According to Fox, if its reporting appears conservative, it is only because the country has become so accustomed to left-leaning media that a truly balanced network just seems conservative.

Regular news reporting on Fox is not much different than other networks, except that Fox may cover some stories ignored by the mainstream media, e.g. political correctness running amok on college campuses, ridiculous environmental regulations, hypocrisy among Hollywood liberals, etc. But it is the talk and commentary shows that outrage liberals and warm the hearts of conservatives. Liberals bold enough to appear on Fox are badgered mercilessly, while conservative guests are tossed softball questions.

The bottom line, financially as well as politically, is that Fox News is now the most watched cable news network, even surpassing CNN. Whatever its flaws, Fox News had added diversity of views to American television.

language, reduce levels of trust in politicians and government? Programs such as *The O'Reilly Factor, Meet the Press, Crossfire, Capital Gang,* and *Hardball* regularly resort to confrontational talk, replete with hyperbole and venomous invective. One experiment, with some viewers watching friendly, polite, and simple political discussions, and other viewers watching rude, emotional, quarrelsome political confrontations, concluded that incivility has a detrimental effect on trust in government and attitudes toward political leaders.[17] Yet it is not likely that televised politics will ever become more civil. Politics for most people cannot compete with entertainment shows for TV audiences, so increasingly political shows are creating dramatic tension and uncivil conflict to gain viewers.

**News versus Entertainment**  Cable television and the Internet have produced dramatic increases in available political information. Yet overall political knowledge and turnout have not changed noticeably. The key to understanding this apparent paradox is the vast expansion in choices now available to viewers.[18] People can now choose from numerous cable channels and Web sites. Increasingly there is a division between people who prefer entertainment programming and those who prefer news shows. There is some evidence that people who prefer news shows acquire greater political knowledge and go to the polls more often than those who mainly watch entertainment shows. Greater media choice, then, appears to widen the "knowledge gap." Because people who like news and take advantage of additional information in the media gain political knowledge, while people who prefer entertainment programming learn less about politics, the mean levels of political knowledge in the population have essentially remained constant.

## Polarization of the Media

Increasingly, media audiences are becoming politically polarized, with Republicans and conservatives, and Democrats and liberals, choosing to listen to and view separate media outlets. Listeners and viewers are choosing sides in their sources of news (see Table 6.4).

News audiences in the aggregate are somewhat more conservative than the general public. The Pew Research Center reports that of those who regularly watch, read, or listen to the news, conservatives comprise 36 percent, moderates 38 percent, and liberals 18 percent. The favorites of conservatives are the *Rush Limbaugh Show* on radio and the *O'Reilly Factor* on Fox television, followed by religious radio, Fox News, business magazines, and call-in radio shows. Moderates and liberals turn to *Larry King Live*, the nightly ABC, CBS, and NBC news, National Public Radio, and literary magazines.

## Mediated Elections

Political campaigning is largely a media activity, and the media, especially television, shape the nation's electoral politics.

**The Media and Candidate-Voter Linkage**   The media are the principal link between candidates and the voters. At one time, political party organizations performed this function, with city, ward, and precinct workers knocking on

---

**Table 6.4   Ideology and News Sources**

| Of those who regularly watch, read or listen to . . . | Conservative | Moderate | Liberal | Don't Know |
|---|---|---|---|---|
| *Rush Limbaugh Show* | 77% | 16% | 7% | 0% |
| *O'Reilly Factor* | 72 | 23 | 4 | 1 |
| Religious radio | 53 | 26 | 12 | 9 |
| Fox News | 52 | 30 | 13 | 5 |
| Business magazines | 49 | 35 | 14 | 2 |
| Call-in radio shows | 45 | 33 | 18 | 4 |
| Local news | 38 | 41 | 15 | 6 |
| Morning news | 38 | 39 | 17 | 6 |
| Newspaper | 37 | 41 | 17 | 5 |
| Network News Magazines | 37 | 40 | 17 | 6 |
| Political magazines | 37 | 29 | 29 | 5 |
| CNN | 36 | 39 | 20 | 5 |
| *Larry King Live* | 35 | 41 | 16 | 8 |
| CNBC | 35 | 40 | 18 | 7 |
| Letterman/Leno | 34 | 41 | 21 | 4 |
| MSNBC | 33 | 41 | 22 | 4 |
| Nightly Network news | 33 | 41 | 18 | 8 |
| NPR | 31 | 33 | 30 | 6 |
| Literary magazines | 19 | 38 | 36 | 7 |

*Source:* Pew Research Center for the People and the Press, June 8, 2004, *http://people-press.org.*

Conservative talk-show host
Rush Limbaugh has
become a symbol of the
talk-radio phenomenon.

doors, distributing campaign literature, organizing rallies and candidate appearances, and getting out the vote on election day. But television has largely
replaced party organizations and personal contact as the means by which candidates communicate with voters. Candidates come directly into the living room
via television—on the nightly news, in broadcast debates and interviews, and in
paid advertising (see Table 6.5).

Media campaigning requires candidates to possess great skill in communications. Candidates must be able to project a favorable media *image*. The image is a
composite of the candidate's words, mannerisms, appearance, personality,
warmth, friendliness, humor, and ease in front of a camera. Policy positions have
less to do with image than the candidate's ability to project personal qualities—
leadership, compassion, strength, and character.

**The Media and Candidate Selection**  The media strongly influence the
early selection of candidates. Media coverage creates **name recognition**, an
essential quality for any candidate. Early media "mentions" of senators, governors, and other political figures as possible presidential contenders help to sort
out the field even before the election year begins. Conversely, media inattention
can condemn aspiring politicians to obscurity.

Serious presidential campaigns now begin at least six months to a year before
the New Hampshire primary (or almost two years before the November presidential election). This early time period, "the invisible primary," is increasingly critical
for campaigns.[19] Candidates must position themselves relative to competitors in
their own party—build their name recognition, raise poll numbers, and build a
campaign war chest. Inasmuch as campaign contributions are just beginning to
come in, candidates have relatively little money to spend on paid advertising.
They are forced to focus their efforts on attracting media attention by staging
media events and issuing press releases. But from the media's perspective, campaign news is neither timely nor immediately relevant. Candidates must try to win
media coverage by catering to the conflict and horse race stories preferred by the
media. Press releases and speeches focused on issues are most likely to be ignored.

The media sort out the serious candidates early in a race. They even assign
front-runner status, which may be either a blessing or a curse, depending on subsequent media coverage. In presidential primaries, the media play the *expectations*

**name recognition** Public
awareness of a candidate—
whether they even know his
or her name.

**Table 6.5    Sources of Political Campaign News in Presidential Election Years**

Overtime, network news (ABC, CBS, NBC) has been declining as a major source of campaign news, while cable news (CNN, MSNBC, Fox) has been gaining. The Internet has also gained ground as a source of campaign news.

| News Sources | 1992 | 1996 | 2000 | 2004 |
|---|---|---|---|---|
| Television | 82% | 72% | 70% | 76% |
| Cable | 29 | 21 | 36 | 40 |
| Network | 55 | 36 | 22 | 29 |
| Local | 29 | 23 | 21 | 12 |
| Newspapers | 57 | 60 | 39 | 46 |
| Radio | 12 | 19 | 15 | 22 |
| Internet | — | 3 | 11 | 21 |
| Magazines | 9 | 11 | 4 | 6 |

*Note:* Respondents were asked, "How did you get most of your news about the presidential election campaign? From television, from newspapers, from radio, from magazines or from the Internet?" Television users were then asked, "Did you get most of your news about the presidential campaign from network TV news, from local TV news, or from cable news networks such as CNN or MSNBC?" Respondents could name two sources.

*Source:* Pew Research Center for the People and the Press, November 10–12, 2000, and November 11, 2004, *www.people-press.org*.

*game,* setting vote margins that the front-runner must meet in order to maintain *momentum.* If the front-runner does not win by a large enough margin, the media may declare the runner-up the "real" winner. This sorting out of candidates by the media influences not only voters, but—more important—financial contributors. The media-designated favorite is more likely to receive campaign contributions; financial backers do not like to waste money on losers. And as contributions roll in, the favorite can buy more television advertising, adding momentum to the campaign.

In presidential elections, the media sorting process places great emphasis on the early primary states, particularly New Hampshire, whose primary in early February is customarily the first contest in a presidential election year. Less than 1 percent of convention delegates are chosen by this small state, but media coverage is intense, and the winner quickly becomes the media-designated front-runner.[20]

**The Media as Kingmakers**   In the early months of a campaign, media coverage of candidates and their standing in public opinion polls tend to move together. Candidates who receive heavy media coverage usually do well in the polls. Good poll ratings create more media coverage. Good poll ratings and increased media coverage inspire campaign contributions, which then allow candidates to buy television advertising to further increase their poll numbers. Media-sponsored public opinion polls play an important role in kingmaking. The CBS/*New York Times* poll, the NBC/*Associated Press* poll, the ABC/*Washington Post* poll, and the CNN/*USA Today* poll are widely reported; they become the benchmarks for voters, telling them who the winners and losers are.

The name of the game for candidates early in the race is *exposure.* Even appearances on entertainment shows, once considered "unpresidential," are now highly valued by political candidates. They vie to appear on *Larry King Live* and on late-night talk shows hosted by Jay Leno, David Letterman, and Conan O'Brien.

**Drudge Report**
Controversial site that links to stories not always carried by mainstream media. Links to all major media outlets.
*www.drudgereport.com*

Democratic supporters of Colorado Attorney General Ken Salazar Watch early results in the presidential election at a hotel ballroom in Denver, Colorado, on Tuesday night, Nov. 2, 2004. Salazar is in a close race against beer magnate Pete Coors for the open U. S. Senate seat.

**Media Effects on the Campaign**    Political candidates are aware of the importance of the media to their success. Their campaign managers must be "media-savvy" and they must hire media consultants early in the campaign. Candidates are advised to arrange daily newsworthy events to keep their name and image in the news. Television producers, reporters, and editors do not like to receive position papers on substantive issues or to present "talking heads"—shots only of the faces of speakers. Rather they prefer attention-getting, action-oriented, emotion-laden videotape. Candidates and their managers know this and so they attract media attention and resort to *media events*—staged activities designed to polish the image of the candidate. Candidates arrange to appear at police conventions, at schools, at hazardous waste sites, on aircraft carriers, at flag factories, and so on in order to project an image on television of their concern for crime, education, the environment, national defense, patriotism, and the like. (See also "Campaign Strategies" in Chapter 5.)

**The Media and the Horse Race**    The media give election campaigns **horse-race coverage**: reporting on who is ahead or behind, what the candidates' strategies are, how much money they are spending, and, above all, what their current standing in the polls is. Such stories account for more than half of all television news coverage of an election. Additional stories are centered on *campaign* issues—controversies that arise on the campaign trail itself, including verbal blunders by the candidate—and *character* issues, such as the sex life of the candidate. In contrast, *policy* issues typically account for only about one-third of the television news stories in a presidential election campaign.[21]

**horse-race coverage**    Media coverage of electoral campaigns that concentrates on who is ahead and who is behind, and neglects the issues at stake.

**The Bad News Bias**    The media's bad-news bias is evident in election campaigns as well as in general news reporting. Negative stories about all presidential candidates usually outnumber positive stories. The media generally see their function in political campaigns as reporting on the weaknesses, blunders, and vulnerabilities of the candidates. It might be argued that exposing the flaws of the candidates is an important function in a democracy. But the media's negative reporting about candidates and generally skeptical attitude toward their campaign speeches, promises, and advertisements may contribute to political alienation and cynicism among voters.

The media focus intense scrutiny on the personal lives of candidates—their marriages, sex lives, drug or alcohol use, personal finances, past friendships, military service, club memberships, and other potential sources of embarrassment.

## UP CLOSE

### TV Network News Coverage of the Presidential Campaign, 2004

How did the major TV networks cover the 2004 presidential campaign between Republican George W. Bush and Democrat John Kerry? More time and more stories were devoted to the 2004 campaign than any other campaign since the Clinton–Bush contest in 1996. And in a reversal of past trends, almost as much time was devoted to policy issues as to the horse race.

More people (21 percent) reported that they relied "most" on Fox News, followed by CNN (15 percent), NBC (13 percent), ABC (11 percent), and CBS (9 percent).

But as in previous elections, stories broadcast by the traditional networks—ABC, CBS, and NBC—favored the Democratic candidate by a large margin. Only Fox News reported more favorably on Bush (53 percent of stories with positive evaluations) than Kerry (21 percent of stories with positive evaluations).

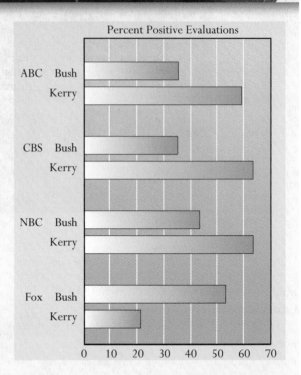

*Source:* Data derived from various issues of *Media Monitor*, the publication of the Center for Media and Public Affairs.

Virtually any past error in judgment or behavior by a candidate is given heavy coverage. But the media defend their attention to personal scandal on the ground that they are reporting on the "character issue." They argue that voters must have information on candidates' character as well as on their policy positions.

**The Shrinking Sound Bite**   Reporters and newsroom anchors dominate television broadcasting. They report roughly three-quarters of all campaign news themselves. The candidates are allocated less than 15 percent of the time devoted to campaign news stories. (Other sources—pundits, commentators, voters, and so forth—account for the remaining airtime.) The candidates themselves have very little direct contact with audiences in network news. The average **sound bite**—time allowed the candidates to speak on their own behalf—has shrunk to less than eight seconds!

**sound bites** Concise and catchy phrases that attract media coverage.

**The Media and Political Bias**   The media are very sensitive to charges of bias toward candidates or parties. Media people are overwhelmingly liberal and Democratic but generally try to deflect charges of political bias during an election campaign by giving almost equal coverage to both Democratic and Republican candidates. Moreover, the media report negatively on both Republicans and Democrats, although some scholars count more negative stories about Republican candidates.

The media are generally more critical of front-runners than of underdogs during a campaign. A horse race loses audience interest if one horse gets too far ahead, so the media tend to favor the underdog. During the presidential primary season, media attacks on an early favorite may result in gains for the underdog, who then becomes the new object of attack.

# Freedom versus Fairness

Complaints about the fairness of media are as old as the printing press. Most early newspapers in the United States were allied with political parties; they were not expected to be fair in their coverage. It was only in the early 1900s that many large newspapers broke their ties with parties and proclaimed themselves independent. And it was not until the 1920s and 1930s that the norms of journalistic professionalism and accuracy gained widespread acceptance.

The Constitution protects the *freedom* of the press; it was not intended to guarantee *fairness*. The First Amendment's guarantee of freedom of the press was originally designed to protect the press from government attempts to silence criticism. Over the years, the U.S. Supreme Court has greatly expanded the meaning of the free-press guarantee.

**No Prior Restraint**   The Supreme Court has interpreted freedom of the press to mean that government may place no **prior restraint** on speech or publication (that is, before it is said or published). Originally, this doctrine was designed to prevent the government from closing down or seizing newspapers. Today, the doctrine prevents the government from censoring any news items. In the famous case of the Pentagon Papers, the *New York Times* and *Washington Post* undertook to publish secret information stolen from the files of the State Department and Defense Department regarding U.S. policy in Vietnam while the war was still going on. No one disputed the fact that stealing the secret material was illegal. What was at issue was the ability of the government to prevent the publication of stolen documents in order to protect national security. The Supreme Court rejected the national security argument and reaffirmed that the government may place no prior restraint on publication.[22] If the government wishes to keep military secrets, it must not let them fall into the hands of the American press.

**Press versus Electronic Media**   In the early days of radio, broadcast channels were limited, and anyone with a radio transmitter could broadcast on any frequency. As a result, interference was a common frustration of early broadcasters. The industry petitioned the federal government to regulate and license the assignment and use of broadcast frequencies.

The Federal Communications Commission (FCC) was established in 1934 to allocate broadcast frequencies and to license stations for "the public interest, convenience and necessity." The act clearly instructed the FCC: "Nothing in this Act shall be understood or construed to give the Commission the power of censorship." However, the FCC views a broadcast license and exclusive right to use a particular frequency as a *public trust*. Thus broadcasters, unlike newspapers and magazines, are licensed by a government agency and supposed to operate in the *public interest*.

**Decency**   Recently the FCC decided to crack down on "indecency" on radio and television, presumably doing so in the "public interest." CBS was fined for the Super Bowl halftime "wardrobe malfunction" by singer Janet Jackson. "Shock-jock" Howard Stern incurred millions of dollars in fines for himself and his stations before giving up regular programming and moving to unregulated satellite radio. Government suppression of "indecency" is constitutionally permitted over broadcast waves on the theory that these channels are limited, they belong to the public, and government licenses broadcasters. Otherwise, mere "indecency" that does not constitute "obscenity" is constitutionally protected by the First Amendment (see Chapter 12).

**The Equal-Time Requirement**   The FCC requires radio and television stations that provide airtime to a political candidate to offer competing candidates

---

**Think Again**

Should the media be legally required to be fair and accurate in reporting political news?

---

**prior restraint**   Government actions to restrict publication of a magazine, newspaper, or books on grounds of libel, obscenity, or other legal violations prior to actual publication of the work.

---

**Federal Communication Commission**
The FCC's official Web site with announcements and consumer information.
*www.fcc.gov*

## PEOPLE IN POLITICS

# Larry King Live

Who turned presidential politics into talk-show entertainment? A strong argument can be made that Larry King was personally responsible for changing the nature of presidential campaigning. It was Larry King who nudged frequent talk-show guest Ross Perot into the presidential arena. And it was Larry King who demonstrated to the candidates that the talk-show format was a good way to reach out to the American people.

Larry King's supremacy in talk-show politics came late in life, after a half-century of hustling and hard knocks, no college education, bouts of gambling followed by bankruptcy, and multiple marriages. King has written five books about himself, describing his rise from Brooklyn neighborhoods; his friendships with Jackie Gleason, Frank Sinatra, and other celebrities; and his hardscrabble life. As he tells it, he hung around a New York radio station for five years before taking a bus to Miami to try his luck first as a disk jockey and later as a sports announcer. After a decade in Miami, he had his own TV interview show, a talk show on radio, and a newspaper column, and he was color commentator for the Miami Dolphins. He lived the fast life, running up huge debts and dealing in shady financial transactions. He was arrested in 1971 on grand larceny charges; they were dropped only because the statute of limitations had expired. He lost his TV and radio shows and his newspaper column. He ended up in Shreveport, Louisiana, doing play-by-play for the World Football League. In 1975 he was bankrupt but back in Miami doing radio. In 1978 he moved to Washington to launch his Mutual Network radio talk show. As radio talk shows gained popularity, so did King. When CNN started twenty-four-hour broadcasting in 1982, the network turned to King to

do an evening interview show, *Larry King Live*. At first, the show merely filled the space between the evening and the late news. A decade later, the show was making news itself.

King's success is directly attributable to his accommodating style. He actually listens to his guests; he lets them speak for themselves; he unashamedly plugs their books, records, and movies. He does *not* attack his guests; he does not assume the adversarial, abrasive style preferred by reporters like Mike Wallace, or interviewers like Bill O'Reilly. An old-fashioned liberal himself, King appears comfortable interviewing politicians of every stripe. He lets guests talk about themselves. He tosses "softball" questions: "If I were to interview the president about an alleged sexual affair, I wouldn't ask if he'd had one, I'd ask him, 'How does it feel to read these things about yourself?'"

With his emphasis on feelings, emotions, and motives rather than on facts, it is little wonder that King's style attracts politicians . . . or that *Larry King Live* is the highest rated show on CNN.

---

**equal-time rule** Federal Communications Commission (FCC) requirement that broadcasters who sell time to any political candidate must make equal time available to opposing candidates at the same price.

the same amount of airtime at the same price. Stations are not required to give free time to candidates, but if stations choose to give free time to one candidate, they must do so for the candidate's opponents. But this **equal-time rule** does *not* apply to newscasts, news specials, or even long documentaries, nor does it apply to talk shows like *Larry King Live* (see *People in Politics:* "Larry King Live"). Nor does it apply to presidential press conferences or presidential addresses to the nation, although the networks now generally offer free time for a "Democratic response" to a Republican president, and vice versa. A biased news presentation does not require the network or station to grant equal time to opponents of its views. And it is important to note that newspapers, unlike radio and television, have never been required to provide equal time to opposing views (see *Compared to What?* "America's TV Culture in Perspective").

## COMPARED TO WHAT?

# America's TV Culture in Perspective

America is a TV culture. Americans rely more on television for news and entertainment than people in other advanced industrial nations do. Perhaps more important, Americans have greater confidence in the media than other peoples do. Consider, for example, the question "Would you say you have a great deal of confidence, only some confidence, hardly any confidence, or no confidence at all in the media—press, radio, and television?" When this question was asked of a national sample of Americans, 69 percent responded that they had a great deal or at least some confidence in the media. But majorities in four other countries—France, Great Britain, Germany, and Spain—said they had little or no confidence in the media (see "confidence in the media" figure).

How much do the media influence key decisions in society? A majority of people in both the United States and these same European nations believe the media exert a large influence on public opinion. Americans appear to be closer to unanimity on this point (88 percent) than are Europeans. When people are asked how much influence the media exerts on particular governing institutions—the executive, the legislature, and the judiciary—Americans are much more likely to perceive strong media influence than are Europeans (see "media influence" figure).

*Source:* Adapted from Laurence Parisot, "Attitudes about the Media: A Five Country Study," *Public Opinion* 43 (January/February 1988): 18, 60.

**Have confidence in the media**

| | |
|---|---|
| France | 48% |
| Germany | 42% |
| Great Britain | 38% |
| Spain | 46% |
| USA | 69% |

**Agree that media influence is large or somewhat large on the judiciary**

| | |
|---|---|
| France | 46% |
| Germany | 29% |
| Great Britain | 40% |
| Spain | 32% |
| USA | 69% |

**Agree that media influence is large or somewhat large on the legislature**

| | |
|---|---|
| France | 37% |
| Germany | 44% |
| Great Britain | 48% |
| Spain | 38% |
| USA | 78% |

**Agree that media influence is large or somewhat large on the executive**

| | |
|---|---|
| France | 48% |
| Germany | 40% |
| Great Britain | 44% |
| Spain | 41% |
| USA | 81% |

**Agree that media influence is large or somewhat large on public opinion**

| | |
|---|---|
| France | 77% |
| Germany | 71% |
| Great Britain | 80% |
| Spain | 70% |
| USA | 88% |

## Libel and Slander

Communications that wrongly damage an individual are known in law as **libel** (when written) and **slander** (when spoken). The injured party must prove in court that the communication caused actual damage and was either false or defamatory. A damaging falsehood or words or phrases that are defamatory (such as "Joe Jones is a rotten son of a bitch") are libelous and are not protected by the First Amendment from lawsuits seeking compensation.

**Public Officials**    Over the years, the media have sought to narrow the protection afforded public officials against libel and slander. In 1964 the U.S. Supreme Court ruled in the case of *New York Times v. Sullivan* that public officials did not have a right to recover damages for false statements unless they are made with "malicious intent."[23] The **Sullivan rule** requires public officials not only to show that the media

**libel** Writings that are false and malicious and are intended to damage an individual.

**slander** Oral statements that are false and malicious and are intended to damage an individual.

" INTERESTING.....IT'S LIKE A PORTABLE 500K FILE and YOU DON'T HAVE TO WAIT FOR IT TO DOWNLOAD.... AND YOU SAY IT'S CALLED A NEWSPAPER ? "

(©1997 Jim Borgman, Cincinnati Enquirer. Reprinted with permission of King Features Syndicate.)

──── Think Again ────

Should the media report on all aspects of the private lives of public officials?

**Sullivan rule** Court guideline that false and malicious statements regarding public officials are protected by the First Amendment unless it can be proven they were known to be false at the time they were made or were made with "reckless disregard" for their truth or falsehood.

published or broadcast false and damaging statements but also to prove they did so knowing that their statements were false and damaging or that they did so with "reckless disregard" for the truth or falsehood of their statements. The effect of the Sullivan rule is to free the media to say virtually anything about public officials. Indeed, the media have sought to expand the definition of "public officials" to "public figures"—that is, to include anyone they choose as the subject of a story.

**"Absence of Malice"**   The First Amendment protects the right of the media to be biased, unfair, negative, sensational, and even offensive. Indeed, even *damaging falsehoods* may be printed or broadcast as long as the media can show that the story was not deliberately fabricated by them with malicious intent, that is, if the media can show an "absence of malice."

**Shielding Sources**   The media argue that the First Amendment allows them to refuse to reveal the names of their sources, even when this information is required in criminal investigations and trials. Thus far, the U.S. Supreme Court has not given blanket protection to reporters to withhold information from court proceedings. However, a number of states have passed *shield laws* protecting reporters from being forced to reveal their sources.

## Politics and the Internet

The development of any new medium of communications invariably affects political life. Just as, first, radio and, later, television reshaped politics in America, today the Internet is having its own unique impact on public affairs. The Internet provides a channel for *interactive mass participation* in politics. It is unruly and chaotic by design. It offers the promise of abundant and diverse information and the opportunity for increased political participation. It empowers everyone who can design a Web site to spread their views, whether their views are profound and public-spirited or hateful and obscene.

**Chaotic by Design**   During the Cold War, the RAND Corporation, a technological research think tank, proposed the Internet as a communications network that might survive a nuclear attack. It was deliberately designed to operate

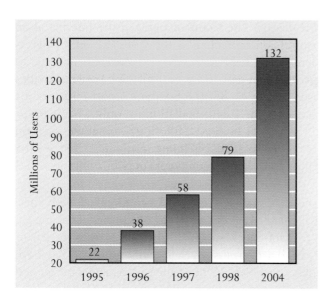

**Figure 6.3**  Growth of Internet Users

*Source: Statistical Abstract of the United States, 2004–05, p. 731.*

without any central authority or organization. Should any part of the system be destroyed, messages would still find their way to their destinations. The later development of the World Wide Web language allowed any connected computer in the world to communicate with any other connected computer. And introduction of the World Wide Web in 1992 also meant that users no longer needed computer expertise to communicate. By 1995 Americans were buying more computers than television sets and sending more e-mail than "snail mail." Since then, Internet usage has continued to mushroom (see Figure 6.3).

**Political Web Sites Abound**   The Internet is awash in political Web sites. The simple query "politics" on a standard search program can return well over a million matches. Almost all federal agencies, including the White House, Congress, the federal judiciary, and executive departments and agencies, maintain Web sites. Individual elected officeholders, including all members of Congress, maintain sites that include personal biographies, committee assignments, legislative accomplishments, issue statements, and press releases. The home pages of the Democratic and Republican parties offer political news, issue positions, opportunities to become active in party affairs, and invitations to send them money. No serious candidate for major public office lacks a Web site; these campaign sites usually include flattering biographies, press releases, and, of course, invitations to contribute financially to the candidates' campaigns. All major interest groups maintain Web sites—business, trade, and professional groups; labor unions; ideological and issue groups; women's, religious, environmental, and civil rights groups. Indeed, this virtual tidal wave of politics on the Internet may turn out to offer too much information in too fragmented a fashion, thereby simply adding to apathy and indifference.[24]

**Internet Uncensored**   The Internet allows unrestricted freedom of expression, from scientific discourses on particle physics and information on the latest developments in medical science, to invitations to join in paramilitary "militia" and offers to exchange pornographic photos and messages. Commercial sex sites outnumber any other category on the Web.

Congress unsuccessfully attempted to outlaw "indecent" and "patently offensive" material on the Internet with its Communications Decency Act of 1996. But the U.S. Supreme Court gave the Internet First Amendment protection in 1997

**Annenberg Public Policy Center**
The Annenberg Center of the University of Pennsylvania conducts research on political use of the media, including the Internet.
*www.appcpenn.org*

in *Reno v. American Civil Liberties Union.*[25] The Court recognized the Internet as an important form of popular expression protected by the Constitution. Congress had sought to make it a federal crime to send or display "indecent" material to persons under 18 years of age (material describing or displaying sexual activities or organs in "patently offensive" fashion). But the Supreme Court reiterated its view that government may not limit the adult population to "only what is fit for children." The Court decision places the burden of filtering Internet messages on parents. Filtering software can be installed on home computers, but a First Amendment issue arises when it is installed on computers in public libraries.

**The Bloggers**   The Internet has spawned a myriad of individual Web sites, commonly known as "blogs," that frequently criticize the professional media. The more reputable blog sites fact-check stories in the mainstream media, or publish stories ignored by them, as well as toss in their own opinions. They have been labeled the media's "back-seat" drivers. (One of the earliest and most quoted bloggers is the "Drudge Report," posted by maverick journalist Matt Drudge.) While many bloggers offer little more than their own often-heated opinions, bloggers have forced the mainstream media to cover stories they may not otherwise have covered, as well as forcing some professional journalists to check the accuracy of their stories before publication.

## Media Effects: Shaping Political Life

What effects do the media have on public opinion and political behavior? Let us consider media effects on (1) information and agenda setting, (2) values and opinions, and (3) behavior. These categories of effects are ranked by the degree of influence the media are likely to have over us. The strongest effects of the media are on our information levels and societal concerns. The media also influence values and opinions, but the strength of media effects in these areas is diluted by many other influences. Finally, it is most difficult to establish the independent effect of the media on behavior.

**Information and Agenda-Setting Effects**   The media strongly influence what we know about our world and how we think and talk about it. Years ago, foreign-policy expert Bernard Cohen, in the first book to assess the effects of the media on foreign policy, put it this way: "The mass media may not be successful in telling people what to think, but the media are stunningly successful in telling their audience what to think about"[26] (see *Up Close:* "The Media Age").

However, **information overload** diminishes the influence of the media in determining what we think about. So many communications are directed at us that we cannot possibly process them all. A person's ability to recall a media report depends on repeated exposure to it and reinforcement through personal experience. For example, an individual who has a brother in a trouble spot in the Middle East is more likely to be aware of reports from that area of the world. But too many voices with too many messages cause most viewers to block out a great deal of information.

Information overload may be especially heavy in political news. Television tells most viewers more about politics than they really want to know. Political scientist Austin Ranney writes, "The fact is that for most Americans politics is still far from being the most interesting and important thing in life. To them, politics is usually confusing, boring, repetitive, and above all irrelevant to the things that really matter in their lives."[27]

---

— Think Again —

Is your choice of candidates in elections affected by their advertising?

**information overload**
Situation in which individuals are subjected to so many communications that they cannot make sense of them.

**American Journalism Review**
Features articles on current topics in print and television reporting, together with links to newspapers, television networks and stations, radio stations, media companies, and so forth. *www.ajr.org*

# UP CLOSE

## The Media Age

The print media—newspapers, magazines, and books—have played a major role in American politics since colonial times. But today the electronic media—radio, television, and cable television—dominate in political communication.

Radio was widely introduced into American homes in the 1920s and 1930s, allowing President Franklin D. Roosevelt to become the first "media president," directly communicating with the American people through radio "fireside chats." After World War II, the popularity of television spread quickly; between 1950 and 1960, the percentage of homes with TV sets grew from 9 to 87.

Some notable political media innovations over the years:

- **1952:** The first paid commercial TV ad in a presidential campaign appeared, on behalf of Dwight D. Eisenhower. The black-and-white ad began with a voice-over—"Eisenhower answers the nation!"—followed by citizens asking favorable questions and Eisenhower responding, and ending with a musical jingle: "I like Ike." Although crude by current standards, it nevertheless set a precedent in media campaigning.

- **1952:** The "Checkers speech" by Eisenhower's running mate, Richard M. Nixon, represented the first direct television appeal to the people over the heads of party leaders. Nixon was about to be dumped from the Republican ticket for hiding secret slush-fund money received from campaign contributors. He went on national television with an emotional appeal, claiming that the only personal item he ever took from a campaign contributor was his daughters' little dog, Checkers. Thousands of viewers called and wired in sympathy. Ike kept Nixon on the ticket.

- **1960:** The first televised debate between presidential candidates featured a youthful, handsome John F. Kennedy against a shifty-eyed Richard M. Nixon with a pronounced "five o'clock shadow." Nixon doggedly scored debater points, but JFK presented a cool and confident image and spoke directly to the viewers. The debate swung the popular tide toward Kennedy, who won in a very tight contest. Nixon attributed his defeat to his failure to shave before the broadcast.

- **1964:** The first "negative" TV ad was the "Daisy Girl" commercial sponsored by the Lyndon Johnson campaign against Republican conservative Barry Goldwater. It implied that Goldwater would start a nuclear war. It showed a little girl picking petals off a daisy while an ominous voice counted down "10-9-8-7 . . ." to a nuclear explosion, followed by a statement that

Lyndon Johnson could be trusted to keep the peace.

- **1976:** President Gerald Ford was the first incumbent president to agree to a televised debate. (No televised presidential debates were held in the Nixon-Humphrey race in 1968 or in the Nixon-McGovern race in 1972. Apparently Nixon had learned his lesson.) Ford stumbled badly, and Jimmy Carter went on to victory.

- **1982:** CNN (Cable News Network), introduced by the maverick media mogul Ted Turner, began twenty-four-hour broadcasting.

- **1991:** The Persian Gulf War was the first war to be fought live on television. (Although film and videotape reports of the Vietnam War had been important molders of public opinion in America, the technology of that era did not allow live reporting.) In the Gulf War, the Iraqi government permitted CNN to continue live broadcasts from Baghdad, including spectacular coverage of the first night's air raids on the city.

- **1992:** In the presidential election, television talk shows became a major focus of the campaign. Wealthy independent candidate Ross Perot actually conducted an all-media campaign, rejecting in-person appearances in favor of such media techniques as half-hour "infomercials."

- **1994–95:** The arrest and trial of celebrity O.J. Simpson on murder charges so dominated the national news that more television time was devoted to the O.J. story than to the actions of the president and Congress.

- **1996:** The presidential election was given less television time and newspaper space than previous elections. Clinton's large lead throughout the campaign, public boredom with Whitewater and other scandals, and Dole's lackluster performance frustrated reporters in search of drama. Network TV news gave Clinton twice as much positive coverage as Dole.

- **1997–98:** Sex scandals involving Bill Clinton dominated the news and talk shows, but public opinion polls gave the president the highest approval ratings of his two terms in office.

- **2000:** On election night, the networks prematurely called the presidential election, first for Gore and then for Bush, causing confusion among the public and embarrassment for the networks. A "Florida feeding frenzy" ensued over the next month as television blanketed every phase of that state's recount, from local election officials staring at punch-card ballots to state and U.S. Supreme Court arguments.

- **2001:** Dramatic television coverage of commercial aircraft crashing into the World Trade Center and videotape of the collapse of the twin giant

The first televised presidential election debates were in 1960 between Senator John F. Kennedy and Vice President Richard Nixon. Nixon came armed with statistics, but his dour demeanor, "five o'clock shadow," and stiff presentation fared poorly in contrast to Kennedy's open, relaxed, confident air.

buildings shocked Americans and inspired the "War on Terrorism."

■ **2003:**  Reporters were "embedded" with American troops in the Iraqi War, providing ground-level narratives and video of combat.

■ **2004:**  Photos from Ahu Ghraib prison in Iraq showing abuse of detainees were broadcast worldwide, inspiring intense opposition in the Muslim world.

**selective perception**
Mentally screening out information or opinions with which one disagrees.

**Effects on Values and Opinions**    The media often tell us how we *should* feel about news events or issues, especially those about which we have no prior feelings or experiences. The media can reinforce values and attitudes we already hold. However, the media seldom *change* our preexisting values or opinions. Media influence over values and opinions is reduced by **selective perception**, mentally screening out information or opinions we disagree with. People tend to see and hear only what they want to see and hear. For example, television news concentration on scandal, abuse, and corruption in government has not always produced the liberal, reformist values among viewers that media people expected. On the contrary, the focus of network executives on governmental scandals—Watergate, the Iran-Contra scandal, the sexual antics of politicians, congressional check kiting, and so on—has produced feelings of general political distrust and cynicism toward government and the political system. These feelings have been labeled **television malaise**, a combination of social distrust, political cynicism, feelings of powerlessness, and disaffection from parties and politics that seems to stem from television's emphasis on the negative aspects of American life.

**television malaise**
Generalized feelings of distrust, cynicism, and powerlessness stemming from television's emphasis on the negative aspects of American life.

The media do not *intend* to create television malaise; they are performing their self-declared watchdog role. They expect their stories to encourage liberal reform of our political institutions. But the result is often alienation rather than reform.

**Direct Effects on Public Opinion**    Can the media change public opinion, and if so, how? For many years, political scientists claimed that the media had only minimal effects on public opinions and behavior. This early view was based largely on the fact that newspaper editorial endorsements seldom affected people's votes. But serious research on the effects of television tells a different story.

In an extensive study of eighty policy issues over fifteen years, political scientists examined public opinion polls on various policy issues at a first point in time,

— Think Again —

Are media professionals—news reporters, editors, anchors—the true voice of the people in public affairs?

Late-night television is now a popular campaign forum. Young people rely heavily on the Jay Leno, David Letterman, and Conan O'Brien shows for their political news.

then media content over a following interval of time, and finally public opinion on these same issues at the end of the interval. The purpose was to learn if media content—messages scored by their relevance to the issue, their salience in the broadcast, their pro/con direction, the credibility of the news source, and quality of the reporting—changed public opinion. Most people's opinions remained constant over time (opinion at the first point in time is the best predictor of opinion at the second point in time). However, when opinion did change, it changed in the direction supported by the media. "News variables alone account for nearly half the variance in opinion change." Other findings include the following:

■ Anchors, reporters, and commentators have the greatest impact on opinion change. Television newscasters have high credibility and trust with the general public. Their opinions are crucial in shaping mass opinion.

■ Independent experts interviewed by the media have a substantial impact on opinion, but not as great as newscasters themselves.

■ A popular president can also shift public opinion somewhat. Unpopular presidents do not have much success as opinion movers, however.

■ Interest groups on the whole have a slightly negative effect on public opinion. "In many instances they seem actually to have antagonized the public and created a genuine adverse effect"; such cases include Vietnam War protesters, nuclear freeze advocates, and other demonstrators and protesters, even peaceful ones.[28]

**Effects on Behavior**    Many studies have focused on the effects of the media on behavior: studies of the effects of TV violence, studies of the effects of television on children, and studies of the effects of obscenity and pornography.[29] Although it is difficult to generalize from these studies, television appears more likely to reinforce behavioral tendencies than to change them. For example, televised violence may trigger violent behavior in children who are already predisposed to such behavior, but televised violence has little behavioral effect on average children.[30] Nevertheless, we know that television advertising sells products. And we know that political candidates spend millions to persuade audiences to go out and vote for them on election day. Both manufacturers and politicians create name recognition, employ product differentiation, try to associate with

# A CONSTITUTIONAL NOTE

## Can the Federal Communications Commission Ban Profanity from Radio and Television?

When the Bill of Rights was passed by the nation's first Congress, the First Amendment's reference to freedom of the press could hardly have envisioned radio, television, or the Internet. When radio broadcasting began in the 1920s, there was a scarcity of broadcast frequencies. Stations fought over frequencies and even jammed each other's programming. The industry welcomed the Federal Communications Act of 1934 which created the Federal Communications Commission (FCC) to license stations for the exclusive use of radio frequencies. The law stated that the use of a frequency was a "public trust" and that the FCC should ensure that it was used in "the public interest." Although technology has vastly multiplied radio and television channels, the FCC has continued

to fine broadcasters for indecency or profanity. The Supreme Court has continued to uphold the powers of the FCC. "Shock-jock" radio personality Howard Stern has been fined almost $2 million. Janet Jackson's "wardrobe malfunction" during the 2004 Super Bowl half-time performance also cost her network a large fine. In short, the FCC has retained its power over radio and television despite the fact that its original rationale, the scarcity of broadcast frequencies, has disappeared. We can contrast the control that the Supreme Court allows the government to exercise over radio and television with the freedom the same Court grants to users of the Internet. The Supreme Court held that the Communications Decency Act of 1996, making it a federal crime to send or display "indecent" material to persons under eighteen years of age over the Internet, was unconstitutional. The Supreme Court held that the government may not limit the adult population to "only what is fit for children."[a] Commercial sex sites deluge the Internet.

[a]*Reno v. American Civil Liberties Union*, 521 U.S. 471 (1997).

---

audiences, and use repetition to communicate their messages. These tactics are designed to affect our behavior both in the marketplace and in the election booth.

Political ads are more successful in motivating a candidate's supporters to go to the polls than they are in changing opponents into supporters. It is unlikely that voters who dislike a candidate will be persuaded by political advertising to change their votes. But many potential voters are undecided, and the support of many others is dubbed "soft." Going to the polls on Election Day requires effort—people have errands to do, it may be raining, they may be tired. Television advertising is more effective with the marginal voters.

## Summary Notes

- The mass media in America not only report on the struggle for power, they are also participants themselves in that struggle.

- It is only through the media that the general public comes to know about political events, personalities, and issues. Newsmaking—deciding what is or is not "news"—is a major source of media power. Media coverage not only influences popular discussion but also forces public officials to respond.

- Media power also derives from the media's ability to set the agenda for public decision making—to determine what citizens and public officials will regard as "crises," "problems," or "issues" to be resolved by government.

- The media also exercise power in their interpretation of the news. News is presented in story form; pictures, words, sources, and story selection all contribute to interpretation.

- The media play a major role in socializing people to the political culture. Socialization occurs in news, entertainment, and advertising.

- The politics of the media are shaped by their economic interest in attracting readers and viewers. This interest largely accounts for the sensational and negative aspects of news reporting.

- The professional environment of newspeople encourages an activist, watchdog role in politics. The politics of most newspeople are liberal and Democratic.

- Political campaigning is largely a media activity. The media have replaced the parties as the principal linkage between candidates and voters. But the media tend to report the campaign as a horse race, at the expense of issue coverage, and to focus more on candidates' character than on their voting records or issue positions.

- The First Amendment guarantee of freedom of the press protects the media from government efforts to silence or censor them and allows the media to be "unfair" when they choose to be. The Federal Communications Commission exercises some modest controls over the electronic media, since the rights to exclusive use of broadcast frequencies is a *public trust.*

- Public officials are afforded very little protection by libel and slander laws. The Supreme Court's Sullivan rule allows even damaging falsehoods to be written and broadcast as long as newspeople themselves do not deliberately fabricate lies with "malicious intent" or "reckless disregard."

- Media effects on political life can be observed in (1) information and agenda setting, (2) values and opinions, and (3) behavior—in that order of influence. The media strongly influence what we know about politics and what we talk about. The media are less effective in changing existing opinions, values, and beliefs than they are in creating new ones. Nevertheless, the media can change many people's opinions, based on the credibility of news anchors and reporters. Direct media effects on behavior are limited. Political ads are more important in motivating supporters to go to the polls, and in swinging undecided or "soft" voters, than in changing the minds of committed voters.

# Key Terms

| | | | |
|---|---|---|---|
| mass media   176 | "feeding frenzy"   185 | equal-time rule   194 | selective perception   200 |
| newsmaking   178 | name recognition   189 | libel   195 | television malaise   200 |
| agenda setting   179 | horse-race coverage   191 | slander   195 | |
| socialization   181 | sound bites   192 | Sullivan rule   196 | |
| muckraking   185 | prior restraint   193 | information overload   198 | |

# Suggested Readings

Alterman, Eric. *What Liberal Media?* New York: Simon & Schuster, 2003. A contrarian argument that the media does *not* have a liberal bias but rather bends over backward to include conservative views.

Ansolabehere, Stephen, Roy Behr, and Shanto Iyengar. *The Media Game: American Politics in the Television Age.* New York: Longman, 1993. A comprehensive text assessing the changes in the political system brought about by the rise of television since the 1950s.

Fallows, James. *Breaking the News: How the Media Undermine American Democracy.* New York: Pantheon, 1996. An argument that today's arrogant, cynical, and scandal-minded news reporting is turning readers and viewers away and undermining support for democracy.

Goldberg, Bernard. *Bias: A CBS Insider Exposes How the Media Distort the News.* New York: Perennial, 2003. The title says it all.

Graber, Doris A. *Mass Media and American Politics.* 7th ed. Washington, D.C.: CQ Press, 2005. A wide-ranging description of media effects on campaigns, parties, and elections, as well as on social values and public policies.

Lichter, Robert S., Stanley Rothman, and Linda S. Lichter. *The Media Elite.* Bethesda, Md.: Adler and Adler, 1986. A thorough study of the social and political values of top leaders in the mass media, based on extensive interviews of key people in the most influential media outlets.

Patterson, Thomas E. *Out of Order.* New York: Random House, 1994. The antipolitical bias of the media poisons national election campaigns; policy questions are ignored in favor of the personal characteristics of candidates, their campaign strategies, and their standing in the horse race.

Prindle, David F. *Risky Business.* Boulder, Colo.: Westview Press, 1993. An examination of the politics of Hollywood, its liberalism, activism, self-indulgence, and celebrity egotism.

Sabato, Larry J. *Feeding Frenzy: How Attack Journalism Has Transformed American Politics.* New York: Free Press, 1992. A strong argument that the media prefer "to employ titillation rather than scrutiny" and as a result produce " trivialization rather than enlightenment."

West, Darrell M. *Air Wars: Television Advertising in Election Campaigns.* 4th ed. Washington, D.C.: CQ Press, 2005. The evolution of campaign advertising from 1952 to 2004 and how voters are influenced by television ads.

# 7 POLITICAL PARTIES AND INTEREST GROUPS
## Organizing Politics

## Chapter Outline

- The Power of Organization
- Political Parties and Democratic Government
- Parties as Organizers of Elections
- National Party Conventions
- Party Finances
- Party Voters
- Why the Two-Party System Persists
- Interest-Group Power
- The Organized Interests in Washington
- The Washington Lobbyists
- The Fine Art of Lobbying
- Lobbying the Bureaucracy
- Lobbying the Courts

## Think About Politics

1 Generally speaking, how would you identify yourself: as a Republican, Democrat, independent, or something else?
Republican ☐ Democrat ☐ Independent ☐ Other ☐

2 Which major party does a better job of protecting the Social Security system?
Republican ☐ Democrat ☐

3 Which major party does a better job of handling foreign affairs?
Republican ☐ Democrat ☐

4 Should elected officials be bound by their party's platform?
Yes ☐ No ☐

5 Do special-interest groups in America obstruct the majority of citizens' wishes on public policy?
Yes ☐ No ☐

6 Should interest groups be prohibited from making large campaign contributions in their effort to influence public policy?
Yes ☐ No ☐

7 If a lobbyist makes a campaign contribution to a Congress member, hoping to gain support for a bill, is this a form of bribery?
Yes ☐ No ☐

*How much power do political parties really have to determine who gets what in America? What role do interest groups play in politics? Their organization, their money, and their influence in Washington raise the possibility that interest groups, rather than individuals, may in fact hold the real power in politics.*

## The Power of Organization

In the struggle for power, organization grants advantage. Italian political scientist Gaetano Mosca once put it succinctly: "A hundred men acting uniformly in concert, with a common understanding, will triumph over a thousand men who are not in accord and can therefore be dealt with one by one."[1] Thus politics centers on organization—on organizing people to win office and to influence public policy.

Political organizations—parties and interest groups—function as intermediaries between individuals and government. They organize individuals to give them power in selecting government officials—who governs—and in determining public policy—for what ends. Generally, **political parties** are more concerned with winning public office in elections than with influencing policy, whereas interest groups are more directly concerned with public policy and involve themselves with elections only to advance their policy interests (see Figure 7.1). In other words, parties and interest groups have an informal division of functions, with parties focusing on personnel and interest groups focusing on policy. Yet both organize individuals for more effective political action.

## Political Parties and Democratic Government

"Political parties created democracy, and modern democracy is unthinkable save in terms of the parties."[2] Traditionally, political scientists have praised parties as indispensable to democratic government. They have argued that parties are essential for organizing popular majorities to exercise control over government. The development of political parties in all the democracies of the world testifies to the underlying importance of parties to democratic government. But political parties in the United States have lost their preeminent position as instruments of democracy. Other structures and organizations in society—interest groups, the mass media, independent campaign organizations, primary elections, social welfare agencies—now

205

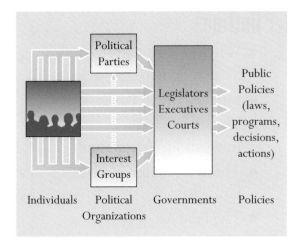

**Figure 7.1**  Political Organizations as Intermediaries

All political organizations function as intermediaries between individuals and government. Parties are concerned primarily with winning elected office; interest groups are concerned with influencing policy.

**political parties**
Organizations that seek to achieve power by winning public office.

**Democratic Party**
Web site of the Democratic National Committee (DNC), with news, press releases, policy positions, and so forth.
*www.democrat.org*

**Republican Party**
Web site of the Republican National Committee (RNC), with GOP news, press releases, policy positions, and so forth.
*www.rnc.org*

— Think Again —
Should elected officials be bound by their party's platform?

**responsible party model**
System in which competitive parties adopt a platform of principles, recruiting candidates and directing campaigns based on the platform, and holding their elected officials responsible for enacting it.

perform many of the functions traditionally regarded as prerogatives of political parties. Nevertheless, the Democratic and Republican parties remain important organizing structures for politics in the United States (see Figure 7.2).

**"Responsible" Parties in Theory**   In theory, political parties function in a democracy to organize majorities around broad principles of government in order to win public office and enact these principles into law. A "responsible" party should:

- Adopt a platform setting forth its principles and policy positions.

- Recruit candidates for public office who agree with the party's platform.

- Inform and educate the public about the platform.

- Organize and direct campaigns based on platform principles.

- Organize the legislature to ensure party control in policy making.

- Hold its elected officials responsible for enacting the party's platform.

*If* responsible, disciplined, policy-oriented parties competed for majority support, *if* they offered clear policy alternatives to the voters, and *if* the voters cast their ballots on the basis of these policy options, *then* the winning party would have a "policy mandate" from the people to guide the course of government. In that way, the democratic ideal of government by majority rule would be implemented.

**But Winning Wins over Principle**   However, the **responsible party model** never accurately described the American party system. The major American parties have been loose coalitions of individuals and groups seeking to attract sufficient votes to gain control of government. *Winning has generally been more important than any principles or policies.* America's major parties must appeal to tens of millions of voters in every section of the nation and from all walks of life. If a major party is to acquire a majority capable of controlling the U.S. government, it cannot limit its appeal by relying on a single unifying principle. Instead, it must form coalitions of voters from as many sectors of the population as it can. Major American parties therefore usually do not emphasize particular principles or ideologies so much as try to find a common ground of agreement among many different people. This emphasis does not mean no policy differences exist between the American parties. On the contrary, each party tends to appeal to a distinctive coalition of interests, and therefore each party expresses somewhat distinctive policy views (see *What Do You Think?* "Which Party Does a Better Job?").

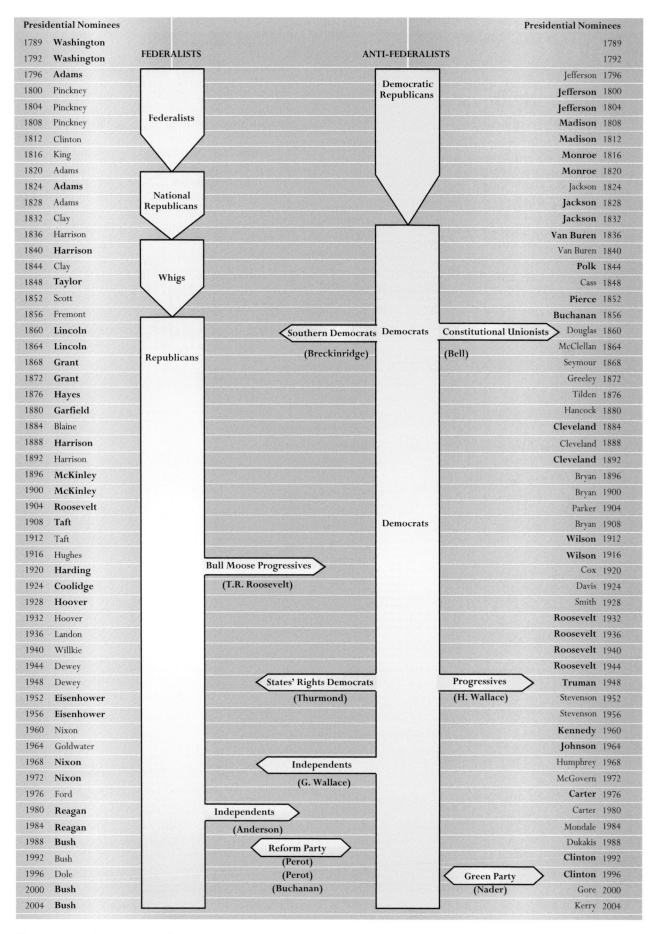

**Figure 7.2**   Change and Continuity in the American Party System

# WHAT DO YOU THINK?

## Which Party Does a Better Job?

What do Americans think of the Democratic and Republican parties? Generally speaking, the Democratic Party has been able to maintain an image of "the party of the common people," and the Republican Party has long been saddled with an image of "favoring the rich."

But when it comes to popular perceptions of each party's ability to deal with problems confronting the nation, the Democratic and Republican parties appear evenly matched. The Republican Party is trusted to "do a better job" in handling foreign affairs and maintaining a strong national defense. It also enjoys a reputation of being better at "holding down taxes."

The Democratic Party enjoys its greatest advantage on "compassion issues" such as helping poor, elderly, and homeless people. And the Democrats have long enjoyed the support of the high-voter-turnout over-sixty-five age group because it is trusted to do a better job "protecting the Social Security system."

*Source:* Various polls reported in *The Polling Report,* November 22, 1999, September 10, 2001, January 28, 2002, August 11, 2003.

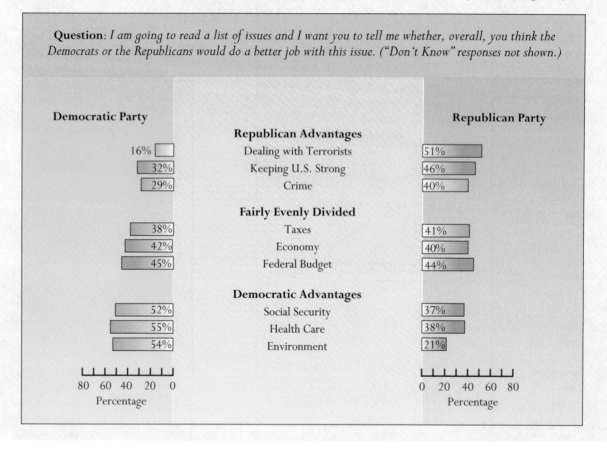

**Question:** *I am going to read a list of issues and I want you to tell me whether, overall, you think the Democrats or the Republicans would do a better job with this issue. ("Don't Know" responses not shown.)*

| Democratic Party | | Republican Party |
|---|---|---|
| | **Republican Advantages** | |
| 16% | Dealing with Terrorists | 51% |
| 32% | Keeping U.S. Strong | 46% |
| 29% | Crime | 40% |
| | **Fairly Evenly Divided** | |
| 38% | Taxes | 41% |
| 42% | Economy | 40% |
| 45% | Federal Budget | 44% |
| | **Democratic Advantages** | |
| 52% | Social Security | 37% |
| 55% | Health Care | 38% |
| 54% | Environment | 21% |

80 60 40 20 0
Percentage

0 20 40 60 80
Percentage

In their efforts to win, major American political parties strive to attract the support of the large numbers of people near the center of public opinion. Generally more votes are at the center of the ideological spectrum—the middle-of-the-road—than on the extreme liberal or conservative ends. Thus *no real incentive exists for vote-maximizing parties to take strong policy positions in opposition to each other* (see Figure 7.3).

**Party and Ideology** Despite incentives for the parties to move to the center of the political spectrum, the Republican and Democratic parties are perceived by the public as ideologically separate. The electorate tends to perceive the Republican Party as conservative and the Democratic Party as liberal.

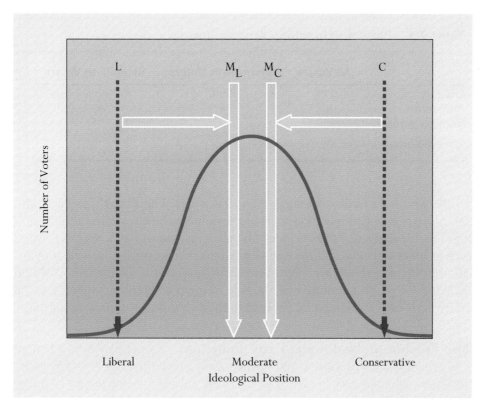

**Figure 7.3** Winning versus Principle

Why don't we have a party system based on principles, with a liberal party and a conservative party, each offering the voters a real ideological choice? Let's assume that voters generally choose the party closest to their own ideological position. If the liberal party (L) took a strong ideological position to the left of most voters, the conservative party (C) would move toward the center, winning more moderate votes, even while retaining its conservative supporters, who would still prefer it to the more liberal opposition party. Likewise, if the conservative party took a strong ideological position to the right of most voters, the liberal party would move to the center and win. So both parties must abandon strong ideological positions and move to the center, becoming moderate in the fight for support of moderate voters.

Indeed, polls suggest that Republican voters described themselves as conservatives far more often than as liberals. And Democratic voters are more likely to identify themselves as liberals than as conservatives, although many like to think of themselves as moderates (see Table 7.1).

This relationship between ideological self-identification and party self-identification is relatively stable over time. It suggests that the parties are not altogether empty jars. Later we will observe that Democratic and Republican party activists (notably, delegates to the party conventions) are even more ideologically separate than Democratic and Republican Party voters.

Democratic and Republican party activists have become more ideologically separate in recent years. And voters have become increasingly aware of this **party polarization**. Indeed many voters are now prepared to say that the Democratic Party is more liberal and the Republican Party is more conservative on a variety of high-profile issues, including government services and spending, government provision of health insurance, and government help to African Americans.[3]

The Republican Party tends to include defenders of the free enterprise system and opponents of government regulation, together with strongly religious

**party polarization** The tendency of the Democratic Party to take more liberal positions and the Republican Party to take more conservative positions on key issues.

**Table 7.1    Party and Ideology Among Voters**

|  | All Voters | Democratic Voters | Republican Voters |
| --- | --- | --- | --- |
| Liberals | 21% | 85% | 13% |
| Moderates | 45 | 54 | 45 |
| Conservatives | 34 | 15 | 84 |

*Source:* As reported at www.CNN.com, November 17, 2004.

people who hold traditional views on moral issues. The Republican Party also appeals to people strongly supportive of the military and an assertive foreign policy. The Democratic Party includes liberals with strong views on social issues such as homosexuality, abortion, and environmental protection, as well as opposition to the use of military force. Yet another part of the Democratic coalition includes the people supportive of the role of government in providing a social safety net—efforts to provide jobs, help to the needy, and economic opportunity for all.

**The Erosion of Traditional Party Functions**    Parties play only a limited role in campaign organization and finance. *Campaigns are generally directed by professional campaign management firms or by the candidates' personal organizations, not by parties.* Party organizations have largely been displaced in campaign activity by advertising firms, media consultants, pollsters, and others hired by the candidates themselves (see Chapter 5).

*Most political candidates today are self-recruited.* American political parties also play only a limited role in recruiting candidates for elected office. People initiate their own candidacies, first contacting friends and financial supporters. Often in state and local races, candidates contact party officials only as a courtesy, if at all.

*The major American political parties cannot really control who their **nominee**—the party's entry in a general election race—will be.* Rather, party **nominations** for most elected offices are won in *primary elections.* In a **primary election**, registered voters select who will be their party's nominee in the general election. Party leaders may endorse a candidate in a primary election and may even work to try to ensure the victory of their favorite, but the voters in that party's primary select the nominee.

*Candidates usually communicate directly with voters through the mass media.* Television has replaced the party organization as the principal medium of communication between candidates and voters. Candidates no longer rely much on party workers to carry their message from door to door. Instead, candidates can come directly into the voters' living rooms via television.

Even if the American parties wanted to take stronger policy positions and to enact them into law, they would not have the means to do so. *American political parties have no way to bind their elected officials to the party platform or even to their campaign promises.* Parties have no strong disciplinary sanctions to use against members of Congress who vote against the party's policy position. The parties cannot deny them renomination. At most, the party's leadership in Congress can threaten the status, privileges, and pet bills of disloyal members (see Chapter 8). Party cohesion, where it exists, is more a product of like-mindedness than of party discipline.

*American political parties no longer perform social welfare functions*—trading off social services, patronage jobs, or petty favors in exchange for votes. Traditional party organizations, or **machines**, especially in large cities, once helped immigrants get settled in, found **patronage** jobs in government for party workers, and occasionally

**nominee**  Political party's entry in a general election race.

**nomination**  Political party's selection of its candidate for a public office.

**primary elections**  Elections to choose party nominees for public office; may be open or closed.

**machine**  Tightly disciplined party organization, headed by a boss, that relies on material rewards—including patronage jobs—to control politics.

**patronage**  Appointment to public office based on party loyalty.

provided aid to impoverished but loyal party voters. But government bureaucracies have replaced the political parties as providers of social services. Government employment agencies, welfare agencies, civil service systems, and other bureaucracies now provide the social services once undertaken by political machines in search of votes.

**Divided Party Government**    Finally, to further confound the responsible party model, Americans seem to prefer **divided party government**—in which one party controls the executive branch while the other party controls one or both houses of the legislative branch. Over the last forty years, American presidents have been more likely to face a Congress in which the opposition party controls one or both houses than to enjoy their own party's full control of Congress.[4] (Divided party government in the states—in which one party controls the governorship and the opposition party controls one or both houses of the state legislature—is also increasing over time.)[5] Divided party control of government makes it difficult for either party to fully enact its platform.

It is noteworthy that American public opinion seems to prefer divided party government over unified party control: *"Do you think it is better when one party controls both the presidency and the Congress, better when control is split between the Democrats and Republicans, or doesn't it matter?"*: Better one party—23.8%; Better control split—52.4%; Doesn't matter—23.8%.[6]

**divided party government**
One party controls the presidency while the other party controls one or both houses of Congress.

# Parties as Organizers of Elections

Despite the erosion of many of their functions, America's political parties survive as the principal institutions for organizing elections. Party nominations organize electoral choice by narrowing the field of aspiring office seekers to the Democratic and Republican candidates in most cases. Very few independents or third-party candidates are elected to high political office in the United States. **Nonpartisan elections**—elections in which there are no party nominations and all candidates run without an official party label—are common only in local elections, for city council, country commission, school board, judgeships, and so on. Only Nebraska has nonpartisan elections for its unicameral (one-house) state legislature. Party conventions are still held in many states in every presidential year, but these conventions seldom have the power to determine the parties' nominees for public office.

**nonpartisan elections**
Elections in which candidates do not officially indicate their party affiliation; often used for city, country, school board, and judicial elections.

**Party Conventions**    Historically, party nominations were made by caucus or convention. The **caucus** was the earliest nominating process; party leaders (party chairs, elected officials, and "bosses") would simply meet several months before the election and decide on the party's nominee themselves. The early presidents—Thomas Jefferson, James Madison, James Monroe, and John Quincy Adams—were nominated by caucuses of Congress members. Complaints about the exclusion of the people from this process led to nominations by convention—large meetings of delegates sent by local party organizations—starting in 1832. Andrew Jackson was the first president to be nominated by convention. The convention was considered more democratic than the caucus.

**caucus** Nominating process in which party leaders select the party's nominee.

For nearly a century, party conventions were held at all levels of government—local, state, and national. City or county conventions included delegates from local **wards** and **precincts**, who nominated candidates for city or county office, for the state legislature, or even for the House of Representatives when a congressional district fell within the city or county. State conventions included delegates from counties, and they nominated governors, U.S. senators, and other

**ward** Division of a city for electoral or administrative purposes or as a unit for organizing political parties.

**precinct** Subdivision of a city, county, or ward for election purposes.

(a)

(b)

(c)

(d)

Political parties as organizers of elections. (a) The Executive Committee of the Republican National Convention in Chicago in 1880. Conventions emerged as the main way for parties to select candidates in the nineteenth century. (b) Senator Ted Kennedy (D-MA) and Senate Minority Leader Harry Reid (D-NV) lead the Democratic opposition to the policies of Republican President George W. Bush, at a news conference in 2006. (c) Parties also seek to attract voters through registration drives. (d) George W. Bush campaigning on his way to the Republican National Convention in Philadelphia. Parties provide the organizational structure for political campaigns.

statewide officers. State parties chose delegates to the Republican and Democratic national conventions every four years to nominate a president.

**Party Primaries**  Today, primary elections have largely replaced conventions as the means of selecting the Democratic and Republican nominees for public office.[7] Primary elections, introduced as part of the progressive reform movement of the early twentieth century, allow the party's *voters* to choose the party's nominee directly. The primary election was designed to bypass the power of party organizations and party leaders and to further democratize the nomination process. It generally succeeded in doing so, but it also had the effect of seriously weakening political parties, since candidates seeking a party nomination need only appeal to party *voters*—not *leaders*—for support in the primary election.[8]

**Types of Primaries**  There are some differences among the American states in how they conduct their primary elections. **Closed primaries** allow only voters who have previously registered as Democrats or Republicans (or in some states voters who choose to register as Democrats or Republicans on primary election

**closed primaries**  Primary elections in which voters must declare (or have previously declared) their party affiliation and can cast a ballot only in their own party's primary election.

day) can cast a ballot in their chosen party's primary. Closed primaries tend to discourage people from officially registering as independents, even if they think of themselves as independent, because persons registered as independents cannot cast a ballot in either party's primary.

**Open primaries** allow voters to choose on election day which party primary they wish to participate in. Anyone, regardless of prior party affiliation, may choose to vote in either party's primary election. Voters simply request the ballot of one party or the other.[9] Open primaries provide opportunities for voters to cross over party lines and vote in the primary of the party they usually do not support. Opponents of open primaries have argued that these types of primary elections allow for **raiding**—organized efforts by one party to get its members to cross over to the opposition party's primary and defeat an attractive candidate and thereby improve the raiding party's chances of winning the general election. But there is little evidence to show that large numbers of voters connive in such a fashion.

Louisiana is unique in its nonpartisan primary elections. All candidates, regardless of their party affiliation, run in the same primary election. If a candidate gets over 50 percent of the vote, he or she wins the office, without appearing on the general election ballot. If no one receives over 50 percent of the primary election votes, then the top two vote-getters, regardless of party, face each other in the general election.

Some states hold a **runoff primary** when no candidate receives a majority or a designated percentage of the vote in the party's first primary election. A runoff primary is limited to the two highest vote-getters in the first primary. Runoff elections are more common in the southern United States. In most states, only a plurality of votes is needed to win a primary election.

**General Elections**   Several months after the primaries and conventions, the **general election** (usually held in November, on the first Tuesday after the first Monday for presidential and most state elections) determines who will occupy elective office. Winners of the Democratic and Republican primary elections must face each other—and any independent or third-party candidates—in the general election. Voters in the general election may choose any candidate, regardless of how they voted earlier in their party's primary or whether they voted in the primary at all.

**open primaries**  Primary elections in which a voter may cast a ballot in either party's primary election.

**raiding**  Organized efforts by one party to get its members to cross over in a primary and defeat an attractive candidate in the opposition party's primary.

**runoff primary**  Additional primary held between the top two vote-getters in a primary in which no candidate has received a majority of the vote.

**general election**  Election to choose among candidates nominated by parties and/or independent candidates who gained access to the ballot by petition.

Voter turnout among 18- to 21-year-olds is lower than any other age group. Here, University of New Hampshire students register to vote in the 2000 election.

## UP CLOSE

# Off and Running, 2008

Campaigning for the next election begins the day after the polls close from the last election. In presidential politics, candidates have about three years of "precampaigning" before officially announcing their candidacies. During this time, they must seek "media mentions" as possible presidential contenders, get their names in presidential polls, begin recruiting a campaign staff, give speeches to organizations influential in their party, meet with party officials across the country, travel to Iowa and New Hampshire, and, most of all, make contacts with wealthy potential campaign contributors. Knowing that they must first win their party's nomination, most of these activities take place *within* party circles.

Early frontrunners in the polls do not always win their party's nomination. Three or four years is a long time in politics. Relative unknowns have won their party's nomination in the final year, for example, Jimmy Carter in 1976, and Bill Clinton in 1992. But prominence in the polls helps to raise campaign funds and often deters potential competitors.

### 2008

| Democratic Candidates | | Republican Candidates | |
|---|---|---|---|
| **Respondents: Registered Democrats** | | **Respondents: Registered Republicans** | |
| Hillary Clinton | 36% | Rudy Giuliani | 28% |
| Al Gore | 16% | John McCain | 24% |
| John Edwards | 12% | Newt Gingrich | 8% |
| John Kerry | 11% | Mitt Romney | 6% |
| Wesley Clark | 4% | Bill Frist | 6% |
| Joe Biden | 4% | George Allen | 5% |
| Other/None | 21% | Other/None | 23% |

*Source:* Gallup Poll, November 2006.

---

**convention** Nominating process in which delegates from local party organizations select the party's nominees.

**presidential primaries** Primary elections in the states in which voters in each party can choose a presidential candidate for its party's nomination. Outcomes help determine the distribution of pledged delegates to each party's national nominating convention.

Independent and minor-party candidates can get on the general election ballot, although the process is usually very difficult. Most states require independent candidates to file a petition with the signatures of several thousand registered voters. The number of signatures varies from state to state and office to office, but it may range up to 5 or 10 percent of *all* registered voters, a very large number that, in a big state especially, presents a difficult obstacle. The same petition requirements usually apply to minor parties, although some states automatically carry a minor party's nominee on the general election ballot if that party's candidate or candidates received a certain percentage (for example, 10 percent) of the vote in the previous general election.

## National Party Conventions

The Democratic and Republican parties are showcased every four years at the national party **convention**. The official purpose of these four-day fun-filled events is the nomination of the presidential candidates and their vice presidential running mates. Yet the presidential choices have usually already been made in the parties' **presidential primaries** and caucuses earlier in the year. By midsummer convention time, delegates pledged to cast their convention vote for one or another of the presidential candidates have already been selected. Not since 1952, when the Democrats took three convention ballots to select Adlai Stevenson as their presidential candidate, has convention voting gone beyond the first ballot.[10] The possibility exists that in some future presidential race no candidate will win a majority of delegates in the primaries and caucuses, and the result will be a *brokered* convention in which delegates will exercise independent power to select the party nominee. But this event is unlikely.

The Democratic and Republican national conventions are really televised party rallies, designed to showcase the presidential nominee, confirm the nominee's choice for a running mate, and inspire television viewers to support the party and its candidates in the forthcoming general election. Indeed, the national party conventions are largely media events, carefully staged to present an attractive image of the party and its nominees. Party luminaries jockey for key time slots at the podium, and the party prepares slick videotaped commercials touting its nominee for prime-time presentation.

**Convention Delegates**   Over time, the spread of presidential primary elections has taken the suspense out of the national party conventions. As late as 1968, fewer than half of the delegates were selected in primary elections. But today, the selection of more than 80 percent of pledged delegates by the party's primary voters has greatly diminished the role of party officials in presidential selection.

Both parties award **delegates** to each state in rough proportion to the number of party voters in the state. Convention delegates are generally party activists, ideologically motivated and strongly committed to their presidential candidates. Democratic delegates are much more *liberal* than Democratic voters, and Republican delegates are more *conservative* than Republican voters (see Figure 7.4). There is a slight tendency for Democratic and Republican delegates to differ in social backgrounds; usually more African Americans, women, public employees, and union members are found among Democratic delegates than among Republican delegates.

**Party Platforms**   National conventions also write party **platforms**, setting out the party's goals and policy positions. Because a party's platform is not binding on its nominees, platform *planks* are largely symbolic, although they often provide heated arguments and provide distinct differences between the parties to present to voters (see *Up Close:* "Democratic and Republican Platforms: Can You Tell the Difference?").

**delegates** Accredited voting members of a party's national presidential nominating convention.

**platform** Statement of principles adopted by a political party at its national convention (specific portions of the platform are known as planks); a platform is not binding on the party's candidates.

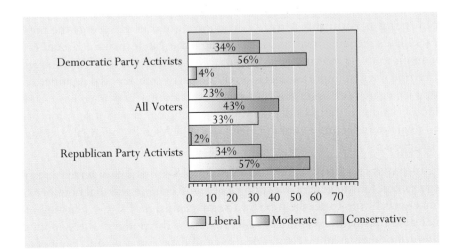

**Figure 7.4**   Ideologies of Voters versus Party Activists
Democratic and Republican party activists (convention delegates in 2000) are far more likely to hold divergent liberal and conservative views than voters generally.

*Source:* As reported in the *New York Times,* August 14, 2000.

## UP CLOSE

# Democratic and Republican Platforms: Can You Tell the Difference?

### Iraq

A "We cannot allow a failed state in Iraq that inevitably would become a haven for terrorists and a destabilizing force in the Middle East."

B "... today there are more than 50 million newly freed people in the nation of Afghanistan and Iraq— America is safer."

### Taxes

A "We will roll back the tax cuts for those making more than $200,000."

B "Tax reform is necessary to achieve tax simplicity, efficiency, fairness, and predictability. . . . In particular we must: Make the tax relief of 2001 and 2003 permanent."

### Foreign Policy

A "They rush to force before exhausting diplomacy. They bully rather than persuade. They act alone when they could assemble a team."

B "We are defending the peace by taking the fight to the enemy. We are confronting terrorists overseas so that we do not have to confront them here at home."

### Health Care

A "We will offer individuals and businesses tax credits to make quality, reliable health coverage more affordable."

B "Enact Health Savings Accounts that allow individuals to save and pay for their healthcare tax-free."

### Social Security

A "We are absolutely committed to preserving Social Security."

B "Social Security needs to be strengthened and enhanced for our children and grandchildren . . . Each of today's workers should be free to direct a portion of their payroll taxes to personal investments for their retirement."

### Other

A "Their energy policy is simple: government by big oil, of big oil, and for big oil."

B "We will curb the burden of frivolous lawsuits . . . One of their nominees made his fortune as a trial lawyer . . . They offer no hope for reform of this badly broken system."

A "We will raise the minimum wage to $7.00."

B "We strongly support the policy that prevents taxpayers' dollars from being used to encourage the future destruction of human embryos."

A "We will create new jobs and protect existing ones by ending tax breaks for companies that ship jobs overseas."

B "We support legislation requiring a supermajority vote in both houses of Congress to raise taxes."

*Source:* Excerpts from Democratic [A] and Republican [B] party platforms, 2004.

**Selecting a Running Mate**   The convention *always* accepts the presidential candidate's recommendation for a running mate. No formal rules require the convention to do so, but it would be politically unacceptable for the convention to override the first important decision of the party's presidential nominee. Convention delegates set aside any personal reservations they may have and unanimously endorse the presidential nominee's choice. (For a discussion of various strategies in selecting a running mate, see "The Vice Presidential Waiting Game" in Chapter 9.)

**The Polling Report**
Up-to-date polling information from a variety of polls on Democratic and Republican party preferences.
*www.pollingreport.com*

**Campaign Kickoff**   The final evening of the national conventions is really the kickoff for the general election campaign. The presidential nominee's acceptance speech tries to set the tone for the fall campaign. Party celebrities, including defeated presidential candidates, join hands at the podium as a symbol of party unity. Presidential and vice presidential candidates, spouses, and families assemble

**Table 7.2    Party Finances (million $)**

|  | 2000 | 2002 | 2004 |
|---|---|---|---|
| **Totals** | | | |
| Democratic Party | $520 | $463 | $618 |
| Republican Party | 715 | 691 | 744 |
| **National Committees** | | | |
| Dem. National Com. | 260 | 162 | 299 |
| Rep. National Com. | 379 | 284 | 330 |
| **House Party Committees** | | | |
| Dem. Cong. Camp. Com. | 105 | 103 | 76 |
| Nat'l Rep. Cong. Com. | 145 | 211 | 156 |
| **Senate Party Committees** | | | |
| Dem. Senatorial Camp. Com. | 104 | 143 | 76 |
| Nat'l Rep. Senatorial Camp. Com. | 96 | 125 | 69 |

*Source:* Federal Elections Commission.

under balloons and streamers, amid the happy noise and hoopla, to signal the start of the general election campaign. TV coverage helps provide the parties with small postconvention "bumps" in the polls.[11]

# Party Finances

Parties as well as candidates raise hundreds of millions of dollars in every election year. (Later, in Chapter 8, we will examine campaign financing by candidates themselves.) At the national level, contributions to the parties go to the Democratic and Republican National Committees, and to the Democratic and Republican House and Senatorial Committees (see Table 7.2).

**The Partisan Tilt of Campaign Contributions**    The Republican Party has generally been able to raise and spend more money in each election cycle than the Democratic Party. But the dollar differences have narrowed over the years. Perhaps more interesting are the differences in sources of support for each party. Broken down by sector (as in Table 7.3), the Democratic Party relies more heavily on lawyers and law firms; on the TV, movie and music industry (Hollywood); teachers and public sector employee unions; and industrial and building trade unions. Business interests divide their contributions, but they tilt toward the Republican Party, notably the health care industry, insurance, manufacturing, oil and gas, automotive, and general and special contractors.

# Party Voters

Traditionally, the Democratic Party has been able to claim to be the majority party in the United States (see Figure 7.5). In opinion polls, those who "identify" with the Democratic Party generally outnumber those who "identify" with the Republican Party. (**Party identification** is determined by response to the question, "Generally speaking, how would you identify yourself: as a Republican, Democrat, independent, or something else?") But the Democratic Party advantage among the voters eroded over time, partly as a result of a gradual increase in the number of people who call themselves independents.

**party identification** Self-described identification with a political party, usually in response to the question, "Generally speaking, how would you identify yourself: as a Republican, Democrat, independent, or something else?"

**Table 7.3** Contributors to the Republican and Democratic Parties by Sector

| Democratic Party | Republican Party |
| --- | --- |
| 1. Lawyers/law firms | 1. Real estate |
| 2. Securities/investment | 2. Health professionals |
| 3. Real estate | 3. Securities/investment |
| 4. TV/movies/music | 4. Lawyers/law firms |
| 5. Business services | 5. Insurance |
| 6. Health professionals | 6. Manufacturing/distributing |
| 7. Education | 7. Oil and gas |
| 8. Lobbyists | 8. Business services |
| 9. Computers/Internet | 9. General contractors |
| 10. Insurance | 10. Automotive |
| 11. Public sector unions | 11. Computers/Internet |
| 12. Commercial banks | 12. Commercial banks |
| 13. Industrial unions | 13. Special trade contractors |
| 14. Building trade unions | 14. Retail sales |
| 15. Liberal/ideological | 15. Food and beverage |

*Source:* Center for Responsive Politics. Candidate committees, miscellaneous, and "retired" excluded from this table. Data from 2004 presidential election.

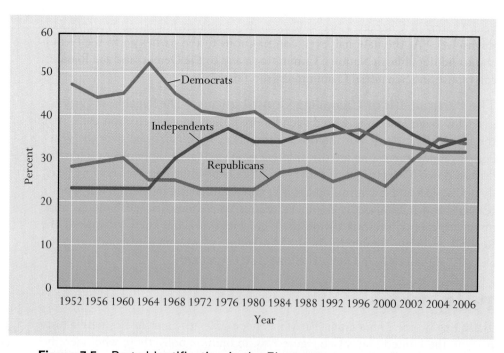

**Figure 7.5** Party Identification in the Electorate

For many years, the Democratic Party enjoyed a substantial lead in party identification among voters. This Democratic lead eroded in the late 1960s as more people began to identify themselves as independents. Independent identification suggests that many voters have become disillusioned with both parties.

*Source:* Data from *National Election Studies,* University of Michigan; 2000–2006, data from Gallup Polls.

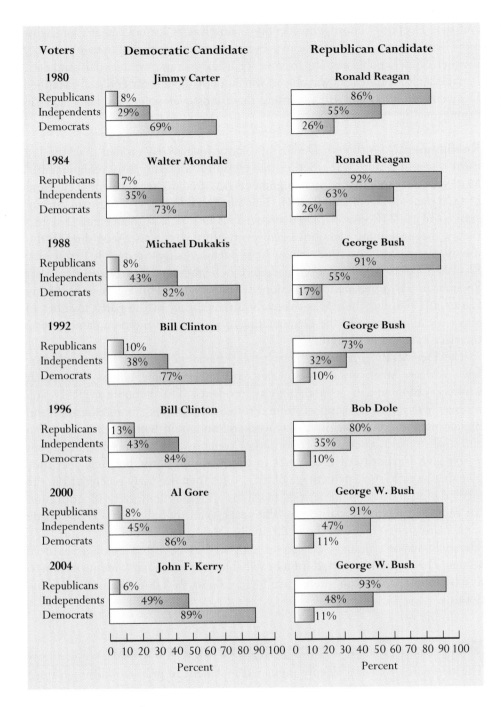

**Figure 7.6** Republican, Democratic, and Independent Voters in Presidential Elections

As the percentages here indicate, in recent years registered Democrats have been more likely to "cross over" and vote for a Republican candidate for president than registered Republicans have been to vote for the Democratic presidential candidate.

*Source: New York Times.*

**Dealignment** Dealignment describes the decline in attractiveness of the political parties to the voters, the growing reluctance of people to identify themselves with either party, and a decrease in reliance on a candidate's party affiliation in voter choice. Dealignment is evident not only in the growing numbers of self-described independents, but also in the declining numbers of those who identify themselves as "strong" Democrats or Republicans. In short, the electorate is less partisan than it once was.

**dealignment** Declining attractiveness of the parties to the voters, a reluctance to identify strongly with a party, and a decrease in reliance on party affiliation in voter choice.

**Party Loyalty in Voting** Despite the decline in partisan identification in the electorate, it is important to note that *party identification is a strong influence in voter choice in elections.* Most voters cast their ballot for the candidate of their party. This is true in presidential elections (see Figure 7.6) and even more true in congressional and state elections. Those who identify themselves as Democrats are somewhat more likely to vote for a Republican presidential candidate than those who identify themselves as Republicans are to vote for a Democratic presidential candidate. Republican Ronald Reagan was able to win more than one-quarter of self-identified Democrats in 1980 and 1984, earning these crossover voters the label "Reagan Democrats."[12]

**realignment** Long-term shift in social-group support for various political parties that creates new coalitions in each party.

**Realignment?** Although Democratic Party loyalty has eroded over the last thirty years, it is not clear whether this erosion is a classic party **realignment**.[13] Most scholars agree that party realignments occurred in the presidential elections of 1824 (Jackson, Democrats), 1860 (Lincoln, Republicans), 1896 (Bryan, Democrats), and 1932 (Roosevelt, Democrats). This historical sequence gave rise to a theory that realigning elections occur every thirty-six years. According to this theory, the election of 1968 should have been a realigning one. It is true that Richard Nixon's 1968 victory marked the beginning of a twenty-four-year Republican era in presidential election victories that was broken only by Jimmy Carter in 1976. But there was relatively little shifting of the party loyalties of major social groups, and the Democratic Party remained the dominant party in the electorate and in Congress.

The Democratic Party still receives *disproportionate* support from Catholics, Jews, African Americans, less-educated and lower-income groups, blue-collar workers, union members, and big-city residents. The Republican Party still receives *disproportionate* support from Protestants, whites, more-educated and higher-income groups, white-collar workers, nonunion workers, and suburban and small-town dwellers. Disproportionate support does not mean these groups *always* give a majority of their votes to the indicated party, but only that they give that party a larger percentage of their votes than the party receives from the general electorate. This pattern of social-group voting and party identification has remained relatively stable over the years, even though the GOP has made some gains among many of the traditionally Democratic groups (see Figure 7.7). The only major *shift* in social-group support has occurred among Southern whites. This group has shifted from heavily Democratic in party identification to a substantial Republican preference[14] (see *Across the USA:* "Red States, Blue States").

## Why the Two-Party System Persists

The two-party system is deeply ingrained in American politics. Although third parties have often made appearances in presidential elections, no third-party candidate has ever won the Oval Office. (Lincoln's new Republican Party in 1860 might be counted as an exception, but it quickly became a major party.) Very few third-party candidates have won seats in Congress. Many other democracies have multiple-party systems, so the question arises as to why the United States has had a two-party system throughout its history.[15]

**Third-Party Prospects** In recent years, polls have reported that a majority of Americans favor the idea of a third party. But support for the *general* idea of a third party has never been matched by voter support for *specific* third-party or independent presidential candidates (see Table 7.4). Moreover, it is very difficult for a third party or independent candidate to win electoral votes. Only Theodore Roosevelt, Robert M. La Follette, and George C. Wallace managed to win any electoral votes

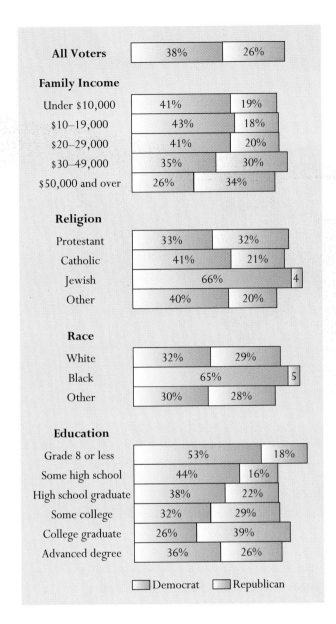

**Figure 7.7** Social-Group Support for the Democratic and Republican Parties
The Democratic Party draws disproportionate support from low-income, less-educated, Catholic, Jewish, and African American voters. The Republican Party relies more heavily on support from high-income, college-educated, white Protestant voters.

*Source:* Data from *National Election Studies,* University of Michigan.

in the past century. The Reform Party, founded by billionaire Ross Perot in 1992, was the latest serious yet unsuccessful attempt to create a nationwide third party.

**Cultural Consensus**   One explanation of the nation's continuing two-party system focuses on the broad consensus supporting the American political culture (see Chapter 2). The values of democracy, capitalism, free enterprise, individual liberty, religious freedom, and equality of opportunity are so widely shared that no party challenging these values has ever won much of a following. There is little support in the American political culture for avowedly fascist, communist, authoritarian, or other antidemocratic parties. Moreover, the American political culture includes a strong belief in the separation of church and state. Political parties with religious affiliations, common in European democracies, are absent from American politics. Socialist parties have frequently appeared on the scene under various labels—the Socialist Party, the Socialist Labor Party, and the Socialist Workers Party. But the largest popular vote ever garnered by a socialist candidate in a

# ACROSS THE USA

## Red States, Blue States

The Democratic and Republican Parties compete in every state. But sectionalism was and is evident in the strength of the Republican Party in the Mountain, Plains, and Southern states. The Democratic Party is becoming bicoastal—strong in the Northeast and the Pacific Coasts. Of the four largest states, California and New York lean Democratic, whereas Texas and Florida lean Republican. At least this has been the pattern in the last few presidential elections; congressional and gubernatorial elections are not quite so sectionalized.

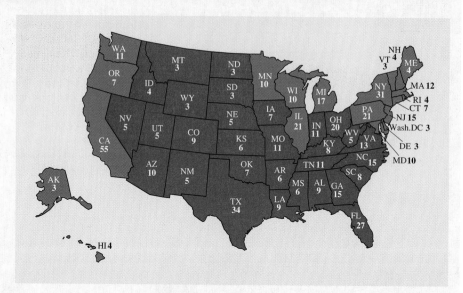

presidential election was the 6 percent won by Eugene V. Debs in 1912. In contrast, socialist parties have frequently won control of European governments.

On broad policy issues, most Americans cluster near the center. This general consensus tends to discourage multiple parties. There does not appear to be sufficient room for them to stake out a position on the ideological spectrum that would detach voters from the two major parties.

## Table 7.4    Twentieth-Century Third-Party Presidential Votes

| Third-Party Presidential Candidates | Popular Vote (percentage) | Electoral Votes (number) |
|---|---|---|
| Theodore Roosevelt (1912), Progressive (Bull Moose) Party | 27.4% | 88 |
| Robert M. La Follette (1924), Progressive Party | 16.6 | 13 |
| George C. Wallace (1968), American Independent Party | 13.5 | 46 |
| John Anderson (1980), Independent | 6.6 | 0 |
| Ross Perot (1992), Independent | 18.9 | 0 |
| Ross Perot (1996), Reform Party | 8.5 | 0 |
| Ralph Nader (2000), Green Party | 2.7 | 0 |
| Ralph Nader (2004) Independent | 0.4 | 0 |

This cultural explanation blends with the influence of historical precedents. The American two-party system has gained acceptance through custom. The nation's first party system developed from two coalitions, Federalists and Anti-Federalists, and this dual pattern has been reinforced over two centuries.

**Winner-Takes-All Electoral System**    Yet another explanation of the American two-party system focuses on the electoral system itself. Winners in presidential and congressional elections, as well as in state gubernatorial and legislative elections, are usually determined by a plurality, winner-takes-all vote. Even in elections that require a majority of more than 50 percent to win—which may involve a runoff election—only one party's candidate wins in the end. Because of the winner-takes-all nature of U.S. elections, parties and candidates have an overriding incentive to broaden their appeal to a plurality or majority of voters. Losers come away empty-handed. There is not much incentive in such a system for a party to form to represent the views of 5 or 10 percent of the electorate.

Americans are so accustomed to winner-takes-all elections that they seldom consider alternatives. In some countries, legislative bodies are elected by **proportional representation**, whereby all voters cast a single ballot for the party of their choice and legislative seats are then apportioned to the parties in proportion to their total vote in the electorate. Minority parties are assured of legislative seats, perhaps with as little as 10 or 15 percent of the vote. If no party wins 50 percent of the votes and seats, the parties try to form a coalition of parties to establish control of the government. In these nations, party coalition building to form a governing majority occurs *after* the election rather than *before* the election, as it does in winner-takes-all election systems.

**proportional representation**
Electoral system that allocates seats in a legislature based on the proportion of votes each party receives in a national election.

**Legal Access to the Ballot**    Another factor in the American two-party system may be electoral system barriers to third parties. The Democratic and Republican nominees are automatically included on all general election ballots, but third-party and independent candidates face difficult obstacles in getting their names listed. In presidential elections, a third-party candidate must meet the varied requirements of fifty separate states to appear on their ballots along with the Democratic and Republican nominees. These requirements often include filing petitions signed by up to 5 or 10 percent of registered voters. In addition, states require third parties to win 5 or 10 percent of the vote in the last election in order to retain their position on the ballot in subsequent elections. In 1980 independent John Anderson gained access to the ballot in all fifty states, as did independent Ross Perot in 1992. But just doing so required a considerable expenditure of effort and money that the major parties were able to avoid.

# Interest-Group Power

Organization is a means to power—to determining who gets what in society. The First Amendment to the Constitution recognizes "the right of the people peaceably to assemble and to petition the government for a redress of grievances." Americans thus enjoy a fundamental right to organize themselves to influence government.

**Electoral versus Interest-Group Systems**    The *electoral system* is organized to represent geographically defined constituencies—states and congressional districts in Congress. The *interest-group system* is organized to represent economic,

**interest group** Organization seeking to directly influence government policy.

professional, ideological, religious, racial, gender, and issue constituencies. In other words, the interest-group system supplements the electoral system by providing people with another avenue of participation. Individuals may participate in politics by supporting candidates and parties in elections, and also by joining **interest groups**, organizations that pressure government to advance their interests.[16]

Interest group activity provides more *direct* representation of policy preferences than electoral politics. At best, individual voters can influence government policy only indirectly through elections (see Chapter 8). Elected politicians try to represent many different—and even occasionally conflicting—interests. But interest groups provide concentrated and direct representation of policy views in government.

**Checking Majoritarianism**    The interest-group system gives voice to special interests, whereas parties and the electoral system cater to the majority interest. Indeed, interest groups are often defended as a check on **majoritarianism**, the tendency of democratic governments to allow the faint preferences of a majority to prevail over the intense feelings of minorities. However, the interest-group system is frequently attacked because it obstructs the majority from implementing its preferences in public policy.

**majoritarianism** Tendency of democratic governments to allow the faint preferences of the majority to prevail over the intense feelings of minorities.

**Concentrating Benefits While Dispersing Costs**    Interest groups seek special benefits, subsidies, privileges, and protections from the government. The costs of these *concentrated* benefits are usually *dispersed* to all taxpayers, none of whom individually bears enough added cost to merit spending time, energy, or money to organize a group to oppose the benefit. Thus the interest-group system concentrates benefits to the few and disperses costs to the many. The system favors small, well-organized, homogeneous interests that seek the expansion of government activity at the expense of larger but less well-organized citizen-taxpayers. Over long periods of time, the cumulative activities of many special-interest groups, each seeking concentrated benefits to themselves and dispersed costs to others, result in what has been termed **organizational sclerosis**, a society so encrusted with subsidies, benefits, regulations, protections, and special treatments for organized groups that work, productivity, and investment are discouraged and everyone's standard of living is lowered.

**organizational sclerosis** Society encrusted with so many special benefits to interest groups that everyone's standard of living is lowered.

# The Organized Interests in Washington

There are more than 1 million nonprofit organizations in the United States, several thousand of which are officially registered in Washington as lobbyists.[17] Trade and professional associations and corporations are the most common lobbies in Washington, but unions, public-interest groups, farm groups, environmental groups, ideological groups, religious and civil rights organizations, women's groups, veterans and defense-related groups, groups organized around a single issue (e.g., Mothers Against Drunk Driving), and even organizations representing state and local governments also recognize that they need to be "where the action is." Among this huge assortment of organizations, many of which are very influential in their highly specialized field, there are a number of well-known organized interests. Even a partial list of organized interest groups (see Table 7.5) demonstrates the breadth and complexities of interest-group life in American politics.

**Business and Trade Organizations**    Traditionally, economic organizations have dominated interest-group politics in Washington. There is ample evidence

— Think Again—

Do special-interest groups in America obstruct the majority of citizens' wishes on public policy?

## Table 7.5    Major Organized Interest Groups, by Type

**Business**
Business Roundtable
National Association of
  Manufacturers
National Federation of Independent
  Businesses
National Small Business Association
U.S. Chamber of Commerce

**Trade**
American Bankers Association
American Gas Association
American Iron and Steel Institute
American Petroleum Institute
American Truckers Association
Automobile Dealers Association
Home Builders Association
Motion Picture Association of
  America
National Association of Broadcasters
National Association of Real Estate
  Boards

**Professional**
American Bar Association
American Medical Association
Association of Trial Lawyers
National Education Association

**Union**
AFL-CIO
American Federation of State,
  County, and Municipal Employees
American Federation of Teachers
International Brotherhood of
  Teamsters
International Ladies' Garment
  Workers Union
National Association of Letter
  Carriers
United Auto Workers
United Postal Workers
United Steelworkers

**Agricultural**
American Farm Bureau Federation
National Cattlemen's Association
National Farmers Union
National Grange
National Milk Producers Federation
Tobacco Institute

**Women**
League of Women Voters
National Organization for Women

**Public Interest**
Common Cause
Consumer Federation of America
Public Citizen
Public Interest Research Groups

**Ideological**
American Conservative Union
Americans for Constitutional Action
  (conservative)
Americans for Democratic Action
  (liberal)
People for the American Way (liberal)
MoveOn (liberal)

**Single Issue**
Mothers Against Drunk Driving
NARAL Pro-Choice America
National Rifle Association
National Right to Life Committee
Planned Parenthood Federation of
  America
National Taxpayers Union

**Environmental**
Environmental Defense Fund
Greenpeace
National Wildlife Federation
National Resources Defense Council
Nature Conservancy
Sierra Club
Wilderness Society

**Religious**
American Israel Public Affairs
  Committee
Anti-Defamation League of B'nai
  B'rith
Christian Coalition
National Council of Churches
U.S. Catholic Conference

**Civil Rights**
American Civil Liberties Union
American Indian Movement
Mexican-American Legal Defense and
  Education Fund
National Association for the
  Advancement of Colored People
National Urban League
Rainbow Coalition
Southern Christian Leadership
  Conference

**Age Related**
American Association of Retired
  Persons
Children's Defense Fund

**Veterans**
American Legion
Veterans of Foreign Wars
Vietnam Veterans of America

**Defense**
Air Force Association
American Security Council
Army Association
Navy Association

**Government**
National Association of Counties
National Conference of State
  Legislators
National Governors Association
National League of Cities
U.S. Conference of Mayors

---

that economic interests continue to play a major role in national policy making, despite the rapid growth over the last several decades of consumer and environmental organizations. Certainly in terms of the sheer number of organizations with offices and representatives in Washington, business and professional groups and occupational and trade associations predominate. More than half of the organizations with offices in Washington are business or **trade associations**, and all together these organizations account for about 75 percent of all of the reported lobbying expenditures.[18]

**trade associations** Interest groups composed of businesses in specific industries.

**Professional Associations**    Professional associations rival business and trade organizations in lobbying influence. The American Bar Association (ABA), the American Medical Association (AMA), and the National Education Association

(NEA) are three of the most influential groups in Washington. For example, the ABA, which includes virtually all of the nation's practicing attorneys, and its more specialized offspring, the American Association of Trial Lawyers, have successfully resisted efforts to reform the nation's tort laws (see *A Conflicting View:* "America Is Drowning in a Sea of Lawsuits," Chapter 11).

**Organized Labor** Labor organizations have declined in membership over the last several decades. The percentage of the total workforce belonging to unions has declined from about 37 percent in the 1950s to about 13 percent today. Workers in the private sector have largely deserted unions (see Figure 7.8). The major industrial unions—for example, the United Steelworkers of America, United Automobile Workers, United Mine Workers—have shrunk in membership. Only the unions of government employees—for example, the American Federation of State, Country, and Municipal Employees, the National Education Association—and some transportation and service workers unions—for example, Teamsters Union, Service Employees International, International Brotherhood of Electrical Workers—have gained members in recent years.

Nevertheless, labor unions remain a major political influence in Congress and the Democratic Party. The AFL-CIO is a federation of sixty-eight separate unions with more than 13 million members. The AFL-CIO has long maintained a large and capable lobbying staff in Washington, and it provides both financial contributions and campaign services (registration, get-out-the-vote, information, endorsements) for members of Congress it favors. Many of the larger individual unions also maintain offices in Washington and offer campaign contributions and services.

Today union influence is greatest among government employees, including teachers. About 38 percent of all public sector employees are unionized. The American Federation of State, County, and Municipal Employees (AFSCME), the National Education Association (NEA), the American Federation of Teachers (AFT), and the Teamsters Union (which recruits public employees in sanitation and transportation) are among the few unions growing in membership.

**AFL-CIO**
Homepage of labor confederation; includes information on wages, unemployment, strikes, as well as news and press releases on union affairs.
*www.alfcio.org*

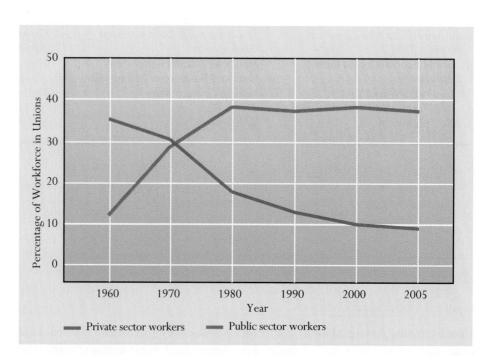

**Figure 7.8** Unions and the American Workforce

Labor union political campaign contributions remain a major source of union influence in Washington. The AFSCME, NEA, Teamsters, United Auto Workers, United Steelworkers, Electrical Workers, Machinists, and Letter Carriers, as well as the AFL-CIO itself, are regularly ranked among the top contributors in congressional elections. Almost all union campaign contributions go to Democratic candidates.

**Women's Organizations**    Women's organizations date back to the antislavery societies in pre-Civil War America. The first generation of feminists—Lucretia Mott, Elizabeth Cady Stanton, Lucy Stone, and Susan B. Anthony—learned to organize, hold public meetings, and conduct petition campaigns as abolitionists. After the Civil War, women were successful in changing many state laws that abridged the rights of married women and otherwise treated them as "chattel" (property) of their husbands. Women were also prominent in the Anti-Saloon League, which succeeded in outlawing prostitution and gambling in every state except Nevada and provided a major source of support for the Eighteenth Amendment (Prohibition). In the early twentieth century, the feminist movement concentrated on obtaining the vote (suffrage) for women. Today the League of Women Voters—a broad-based organization that provides information to voters—backs registration and get-out-the-vote drives and generally supports measures seeking to ensure honesty and integrity in government.

Interest in feminist politics revived in the wake of the civil rights movement of the 1960s. New organizations sprang up to compete with the conventional activities of the League of Women Voters by taking a more activist stance toward women's issues. The largest of these organizations is the National Organization for Women (NOW), founded in 1966.

**Religious Groups**    Churches and religious groups have a long history of involvement in American politics—from the pre-Civil War antislavery crusades, to the prohibition effort in the early twentieth century, to the civil rights movement of the 1960s. The leadership for the historic Civil Rights Act of 1964 came from the Reverend Martin Luther King Jr. and his Southern Christian Leadership Conference. Today religious groups span the political spectrum, from liberal organizations such as the National Council of Churches and Anti-Defamation League of B'nai B'rith, to conservative and fundamentalist organizations, such as the Christian Coalition, often referred to as the "religious right" (see *Up Close:* "The Christian Coalition: Organizing the Faithful").

**Christian Coalition**
Organization "defending our godly heritage" by giving "people of faith a voice in government."
*www.cc.org*

**Public-Interest Groups**    **Public-interest groups** claim to represent broad classes of people—consumers, voters, reformers, or the public as a whole. Groups with lofty-sounding names, such as Common Cause, Public Citizen, and the Consumer Federation of America, perceive themselves as balancing the narrow, "selfish" interests of business organizations, trade associations, unions, and other "special" interests. Public-interest groups generally lobby for greater government regulation of consumer products, public safety, campaign finance, and so on. Their reform agenda, as well as their call for a larger regulatory role for government, makes them frequent allies of liberal ideological groups, civil rights organizations, and environmental groups.[19]

Many public-interest groups were initially formed in the 1970s by "entrepreneurs" who saw an untapped "market" for the representation of these interests. Among the most influential public-interest groups are Common Cause, a self-styled "citizens' lobby," and the sprawling network of organizations created by consumer advocate Ralph Nader. Common Cause tends to focus on election-law

**public-interest groups**
Interest groups that claim to represent broad classes of people or the public as a whole.

**Public Citizen**
Organization founded by Ralph Nader; devotes its site to "protecting health, safety and democracy" as well as lobbying for "strong citizen and consumer protection laws."
*www.publiccitizen.com*

## UP CLOSE

# The Christian Coalition: Organizing the Faithful

Christian fundamentalists, whose religious beliefs are based on a literal reading of the Bible, have become a significant political force in the United States through effective organization. Perhaps the most influential Christian fundamentalist organization today is the Christian Coalition, with nearly 2 million active members throughout the country.

Fundamentalist Christians are opposed to abortion, pornography, and homosexuality; they favor the recognition of religion in public life, including prayer in schools; and they despair at the decline of traditional family values in American culture, including motion pictures and television broadcasting. Historically, fundamentalist Protestant churches avoided politics as profane and concentrated evangelical efforts on saving individual souls. Their few ventures into worldly politics—notably the prohibition movement in the early twentieth century—ended in defeat. Their strength tended to be in the southern, rural, and poorer regions of the country. They were widely ridiculed in the national media.

In the 1960s, television evangelism emerged as a religious force in the United States. The Reverend Pat Robertson founded the Christian Broadcasting Network (CBN) and later purchased the Family Channel. But efforts by social conservatives to build a "moral majority" for political action largely failed, as did Robertson's presidential candidacy in 1988. Televangelists, including Jerry Falwell and Tammy Faye Bakker, suffered popular disdain following some well-publicized scandals.

Although officially nonpartisan, the Coalition became an important force in Republican politics; religious fundamentalists may constitute as much as one-third of the party's voter support. The Christian Coalition does not officially endorse candidates, but its voter guides at right clearly indicate which candidates reflect the coalition's position on major issues. The political influence of the Christian Coalition in Republican politics, and the "religious right" generally, ensures that most GOP candidates for public office publicly express support for a "profamily" agenda. This agenda includes a constitutional amendment allowing prayer in public schools; vouchers for parents to send their children to private, religious schools; banning late-term abortions as well as banning the use of taxpayer funds to pay for abortions; restrictions on pornography on cable television and the Internet; and opposition to human embryo research and human cloning.

*Religious groups can play a key role in elections by informing their members about candidates and getting out the vote. The Christian Coalition is one of the most active religious groups.*

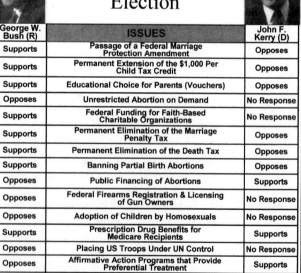

# 2004 Christian Coalition
## VOTER GUIDE

### PRESIDENTIAL Election

| George W. Bush (R) | ISSUES | John F. Kerry (D) |
|---|---|---|
| Supports | Passage of a Federal Marriage Protection Amendment | Opposes |
| Supports | Permanent Extension of the $1,000 Per Child Tax Credit | Opposes |
| Supports | Educational Choice for Parents (Vouchers) | Opposes |
| Opposes | Unrestricted Abortion on Demand | No Response |
| Supports | Federal Funding for Faith-Based Charitable Organizations | No Response |
| Supports | Permanent Elimination of the Marriage Penalty Tax | Opposes |
| Supports | Permanent Elimination of the Death Tax | Opposes |
| Supports | Banning Partial Birth Abortions | Opposes |
| Opposes | Public Financing of Abortions | Supports |
| Opposes | Federal Firearms Registration & Licensing of Gun Owners | No Response |
| Opposes | Adoption of Children by Homosexuals | No Response |
| Supports | Prescription Drug Benefits for Medicare Recipients | Supports |
| Opposes | Placing US Troops Under UN Control | No Response |
| Opposes | Affirmative Action Programs that Provide Preferential Treatment | Supports |
| Supports | Allowing Younger Workers to Invest a Portion of their Social Security Tax in a Private Account | Opposes |

www.georgewbush.com                www.johnkerry.com

Each candidate was sent a 2004 Federal Issue Survey by certified mail and/or facsimile machine. When possible, positions of candidates on issues were verified or determined using voting records and/or public statements.

Authorized by the Christian Coalition of America; PO Box 37030 - Washington, DC 20013

The Christian Coalition of America is a pro-family, citizen action organization. This voter guide is provided for educational purposes only and is not to be construed as an endorsement of any candidate or party.

Please visit our website at www.cc.org, and the Texas website at www.texascc.org

### Vote on November 2          F

*Photo courtesy: Christian Coalition of America*

reform, public financing of elections, and limitations on political contributions. The Nader organization began as a consumer protection group focusing on auto safety but soon spread to encompass a wide variety of causes.

**Single-Issue Groups**    Like public-interest groups, **single-issue groups** appeal to principle and belief. But as their name implies, single-issue groups concentrate their attention on a single cause. They attract the support of individuals with a strong commitment to that cause. Single-issue groups have little incentive to compromise their position. Among the most vocal single-issue groups in recent years have been the organizations on both sides of the abortion issue. NARAL Pro-Choice America describes itself as "pro-choice" and opposes any restrictions on a woman's right to obtain an abortion. The National Right-to-Life Committee describes itself as "pro-life" and opposes abortion for any reason other than to preserve the life of the mother. Other prominent single-issue groups include the National Rifle Association (opposed to gun control) and Mothers Against Drunk Driving (MADD).

**single-issue groups** Organizations formed to support or oppose government action on a specific issue.

**Ideological Groups**    **Ideological organizations** pursue liberal or conservative agendas, often with great passion and considerable financial resources derived from true-believing contributors. The ideological groups rely heavily on computerized mailings to solicit funds from persons identified as holding liberal or conservative views. The oldest of the established ideological groups is the liberal Americans for Democratic Action (ADA), well known for its annual liberalism ratings of members of the Congress according to their support for or rejection of programs of concern. The American Conservative Union (ACU) also rates members of Congress each year.

**ideological organizations** Interest groups that pursue ideologically based (liberal or conservative) agendas.

**Government Lobbies**    The federal government's grant-in-aid programs to state and local governments (see Chapter 4) have spawned a host of lobbying efforts by these governments in Washington, D.C. Thus state- and local-government taxpayers foot the bill to lobby Washington to transfer federal taxpayers' revenues to states and communities. The National Governors Association occupies a beautiful marble building, the Hall of the States, in Washington, along with representatives of the separate states and many major cities. The National League of Cities and the National Association of Counties also maintain large Washington offices, as does the U.S. Conference of Mayors. The National Conference of State Legislators sends its lobbyists to Washington from its Denver headquarters. These groups pursue a wide policy agenda and often confront internal disputes. But they are united in their support for increased federal transfers of tax revenues to states and cities.

**National Rifle Association**
The National Rifle Association site is devoted to opposing gun control legislation as well as employing the Second Amendment in its anti–gun control argument.
*www.nra.org*

# The Washington Lobbyists

Washington is a labyrinth of interest representatives—lawyers and law firms; independent consultants; public and governmental relations firms; business, professional, and trade associations; and advocates of special causes. It is estimated that more than 15,000 people in Washington fit the definition of **lobbyist**, a person working to influence government policies and actions. This figure suggests at least twenty-eight lobbyists for every member of Congress. Roughly $2.2 *billion* are spent on direct lobbying activities *each year*.[20] This figure does *not* include political campaign contributions. The top spenders for direct lobbying are listed in Table 7.6.

**lobbyist** Person working to influence government policies and actions.

**Table 7.6   Top Lobbying Spenders, 1998–2005**

| Rank | Organization | Total |
|------|--------------|-------|
| 1 | U.S. Chamber of Commerce | $243,564,680 |
| 2 | American Medical Assn. | 138,415,500 |
| 3 | Pharmaceutical Rsrch & Mfrs of America | 133,156,515 |
| 4 | General Electric | 118,430,000 |
| 5 | American Hospital Assn. | 111,436,891 |
| 6 | Edison Electric Institute | 94,752,628 |
| 7 | Business Roundtable | 88,280,000 |
| 8 | National Assn. of Realtors | 80,750,000 |
| 9 | Northrop Grumman | 79,182,509 |
| 10 | Philip Morris | 75,500,000 |
| 11 | Blue Cross/Blue Shield | 75,242,355 |
| 12 | AARP | 73,700,000 |
| 13 | Freddie Mac | 73,470,000 |
| 14 | Lockheed Martin | 70,469,965 |
| 15 | Boeing Co. | 69,048,310 |
| 16 | SBC Communications | 64,593,327 |
| 17 | Verizon Communications | 63,126,522 |
| 18 | General Motors | 62,373,483 |
| 19 | Fannie Mae | 60,957,000 |
| 20 | Ford Motor Co. | 57,950,808 |

*Source:* Reprinted by permission of the Center for Responsive Politics, *Influence, Inc.* There is considerable change from year to year in the list, depending on the nature of the legislation before Congress.

**Who Are the Lobbyists?**   Lobbyists in Washington share a common goal—to influence the making and enforcing of laws—and common tactics to achieve this goal. Many lobbyists are the employees of interest-group organizations who devote all of their efforts to their sponsors.

Other lobbyists are located in independent law, consulting, or public relations firms that take on clients for fees. Independent lobbyists, especially law firms, are often secretive about whom they represent, especially when they represent foreign governments. Lobbyists frequently prefer to label their activities as "government relations," "public affairs," "regulatory liaison," "legislative counseling," or merely "representation."

In reality, many independent lawyers and lobbyists in Washington are "fixers" who offer to influence government policies for a price. Many are former government officials—former Congress members, cabinet secretaries, White House aides, and the like—who "know their way around." Their personal connections help to "open doors" to allow their paying clients to "just get a chance to talk" with top officials.

Some lobbying organizations rely heavily on their campaign contributions to achieve lobbying power; others rely on large memberships, and still others on politically active members who concentrate their attention on a narrow range of issues.

Washington's army of lobbyists includes many former members of Congress. Lobbying is a favorite occupation of former members; they can command much higher salaries as lobbyists than they did as Congress members. Lobbying firms are pleased to have people who know the lawmaking process from the inside and who can easily "schmooze" with their former colleagues.

# The Fine Art of Lobbying

Any activity directed at a government decision maker with the hope of influencing decisions is a form of **lobbying**. (The term arose from the practice of waiting in the lobbies of legislative chambers to meet and persuade legislators.) For organized interests, lobbying is continuous—in congressional committees, in congressional staff offices, at the White House, at executive agencies, at Washington cocktail parties. If a group loses a round in Congress, it continues the fight in the agency in charge of executing the policy, or it challenges the policy in the courts. The following year it resumes the struggle in Congress: It fights to repeal the offending legislation, to weaken amendments, or to reduce the agency's budget enough to cripple enforcement efforts.

Lobbying techniques are as varied as the imagination of interest-group leaders, but such activities generally fall into seven categories: (1) public relations; (2) access; (3) information; (4) grassroots mobilization; (5) protests and demonstrations; (6) coalition building; and (7) campaign support. In the real world of Washington power struggles, all these techniques may be applied simultaneously or innovative techniques may be discovered and applied at any time (see Figure 7.9).

**Public Relations**   Many interest groups actually spend more of their time, energy, and resources on **public relations**—developing and maintaining a favorable climate of opinion in the nation—than on direct lobbying of Congress. The mass media—television, magazines, newspapers—are saturated with expensive ads by oil companies, auto companies, chemical manufacturers, trade associations, teachers' unions, and many other groups, all seeking to create a favorable image for themselves with the general public. These ads are designed to go well beyond promoting the sale of particular products; they portray these organizations as

 **American League of Lobbyists**
Lobbyists have their own Web site, one devoted to "ethical conduct" in the lobbying process and the "advancement of the lobbying profession."
*www.alldc.org*

**lobbying** Activities directed at government officials with the hope of influencing their decisions.

**public relations** Building and maintaining goodwill with the general public.

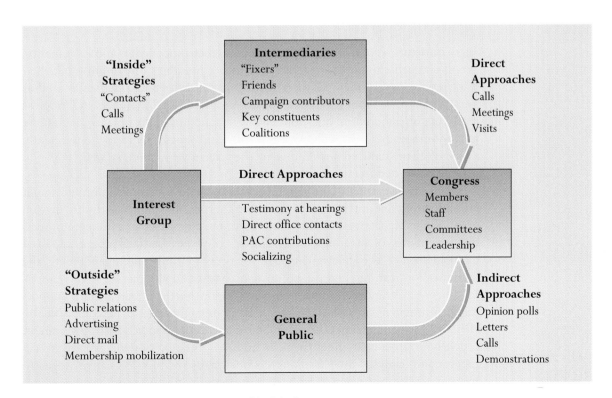

**Figure 7.9**   A Guide to the Fine Art of Lobbying
Interest groups seek to influence public policy both directly through lobbying and campaign contributions (inside strategy) and indirectly through public relations efforts to mold public opinion (outside strategy).

patriotic citizens, protectors of the environment, providers of jobs, defenders of family values, and supporters of the American way of life. Generally, business interests have an advantage in the area of public relations because public relations and sales and marketing activities are synonymous. But paid advertising is less credible than news stories and media commentary. Hence interest groups generate a daily flood of press releases, media events, interviews, reports, and studies for the media. Media news stories appear to favor liberal public interest groups.[21]

**access** Meeting and talking with decision makers, a prerequisite to direct persuasion.

**Access**   "Opening doors" is a major business in Washington. To influence decision makers, organized interests must first acquire **access** to them. Individuals who have personal contacts in Congress, the White House, or the bureaucracy (or who say they do) sell their services at high prices. Washington law firms, public relations agencies, and consultants—often former insiders—all offer their connections, along with their advice, to their clients. The personal prestige of the lobbyist, together with the group's perceived political influence, helps open doors in Washington.

Washington socializing is often an exercise in access—rubbing elbows with powerful people. Well-heeled lobbyists regularly pay hundreds, even thousands, of dollars per plate at fund-raising dinners for members of Congress. Lobbyists regularly provide dinners, drinks, travel, vacations, and other amenities to members of Congress, their families, and congressional staff, as well as to White House and other executive officials. These favors are rarely provided on a direct quid pro quo basis in exchange for votes. Rather, they are designed to gain access—"just a chance to talk."

"Schmoozing," building personal relationships, consumes much of a lobbyist's time and the client's money. It is difficult to know how much this contributes to actual success in passing, defeating, or amending legislation. But, to quote one client: "I figured that half of the money I spend on lobbying is wasted. Trouble is, I don't know which half."[22]

**Information**   Once lobbyists gain access, their knowledge and information become valuable resources to those they lobby. Members of Congress and their staff look to lobbyists for *technical expertise* on the issue under debate as well as *political information* about the group's position on the issue. Members of Congress must vote on hundreds of questions each year, and it is impossible for them to be fully informed about the wide variety of bills and issues they face. Consequently many of them (and administrators in the executive branch as well) come to depend on trusted lobbyists.

Lobbyists also spend considerable time and effort keeping informed about bills affecting their interests. They must be thoroughly familiar with the "ins and outs" of the legislative process—the relevant committees and subcommittees, their schedules of meetings and hearings, their key staff members, the best moments to act, the precise language for proposed bills and amendments, the witnesses for hearings, and the political strengths and weaknesses of the legislators themselves. In their campaign to win congressional and bureaucratic support for their programs, lobbyists engage in many different types of activities. Nearly all testify at congressional hearings and make direct contact with government officials on issues that affect them. In addition, lobbyists provide the technical reports and analyses used by congressional staffs in their legislative research. Engaging in protest demonstrations is a less common activity, in part because it involves a high risk of alienating some members of Congress.

Experienced lobbyists develop a reputation for accurate information. Most successful lobbyists do not supply faulty information; their success depends on

**AARP**
The AARP site covers issues and provides information relevant to the concerns of citizens who are 50 years of age or older.
*www.aarp.org*

maintaining the trust and confidence of decision makers. A reputation for honesty is as important as a reputation for influence.

**Grassroots Mobilization**    Many organized interests lobby Congress from both the *outside* and the *inside*. From the outside, organizations seek to mobilize **grassroots lobbying** of members of Congress by their constituents. Lobbyists frequently encourage letters and calls from "the folks back home." Larger organized interests often have local chapters throughout the nation and can mobilize these local affiliates to apply pressure when necessary. Lobbyists encourage influential local people to visit the office of a member of Congress personally or to make a personal phone call on behalf of the group's position. And, naturally, members are urged to vote for or against certain candidates, based on their policy stances (see *Up Close:* "AARP: The Nation's Most Powerful Interest Group").

Experienced lawmakers recognize attempts by lobby groups to orchestrate "spontaneous" grassroots outpourings of cards and letters. Pressure mail is often identical in wording and content. Nevertheless, members of Congress dare not ignore a flood of letters and telegrams from home, for the mail shows that constituents are aware of the issue and care enough to sign their names.

**Protests and Demonstrations**    Interest groups occasionally employ protests and demonstrations to attract media attention to their concerns and thereby apply pressure on officials to take action. For these actions to succeed in getting issues on the agenda of decision makers in Congress, in the White House, and in executive agencies, participation by the media, especially television, is essential. The media carry the message of the protest or demonstration both to the general public and directly to government officials.

**Coalition Building**    Interest groups frequently seek to build **coalitions** with other groups in order to increase their power. Coalitions tend to form among groups with parallel interests: for example, the National Organization for Women, the League of Women Voters, and NARAL Pro-Choice America on women's issues. Coalitions usually form temporarily around a single piece of legislation in a major effort to secure or prevent its passage.

**Campaign Support**    Perhaps the real key to success in lobbying is the campaign contribution. Interest-group contributions not only help lobbyists gain access and a favorable hearing but also help elect people friendly to the group's goals. As the costs of campaigning increase, legislators must depend more heavily on the contributions of organized interests.

**Lobbying Ethics**    Experienced lobbyists also avoid offering a campaign contribution in exchange for a specific vote.[23] Crude "vote buying" (bribery) is illegal and risks repulsing politicians who refuse bribes. **Bribery**, when it occurs, is probably limited to very narrow and specific actions—payments to intervene in a particular case before an administrative agency; payments to insert a very specific break in a tax bill or a specific exemption in a trade bill; payments to obtain a specific contract with the government. Bribery on major issues is very unlikely; there is too much publicity and too many participants for bribery to be effective.

To the skeptical, "lobbying ethics" may seem to be an oxymoron. Lobbyists regularly send Congress members and even their staffs on expensive junkets around the world and entertain them back in Washington with golf outings, free meals at expensive restaurants, luxury skybox seats at sporting events, and a host of other perks. And, of course, they direct their clients' campaign contributions to Congress members who support their cause. Prudent lobbyists report these

**grassroots lobbying**
Attempts to influence government decision making by inspiring constituents to contact their representatives.

**coalition** A joining together of interest groups (or individuals) to achieve a common goal.

**bribery** Giving or offering anything of value in an effort to influence government officials in the performance of their duties.

## UP CLOSE

# AARP: The Nation's Most Powerful Interest Group

The American Association of Retired Persons (AARP) is the nation's largest and most powerful interest group, with more than 36 million members. The AARP's principal interests are the Social Security and Medicare system programs, the nation's largest and most expensive entitlements.

Like many other interest groups, the AARP has grown in membership not only by appealing to the political interests of retired people but also by offering a wide array of material benefits. For a $12.50 annual fee, members are offered a variety of services, including discounted rates on home, auto, life and health insurance; discounted mail-order drugs, tax advisory services; discounted rates on hotels, rental cars, and so on; a newsletter, *The AARP Bulletin*; a semi-monthly magazine, *Modern Maturity*, and for babyboomers now reaching their 50s, a new magazine, *My Generation*.

The political power of senior citizens is so great that prospects for limiting current or even future increases in government benefits for the elderly are slim. President Bush's proposal to allow workers to invest part of their Social Security taxes in private accounts was defeated largely by the work of the AARP. Social Security is said to be the "third rail of American politics—touch it and you're dead."

Critics of the AARP argue that its lobbyists in Washington do not fairly represent the views of the nation's senior citizens, that few of its members know what its lobbying arm does at the nation's capital. Indeed, in the struggle over prescription drug coverage under Medicare in 2003, the AARP leadership was accused of favoring its own interest in selling private insurance over the interests of its members in receiving government-paid insurance. AARP keeps its dues low, and consequently its membership high, through its business ties with insurance companies, its magazine advertising revenue, and commercial royalties revenues for endorsing products and services.

*Source:* Reprinted, with permission, from the April 1997 issue of *Reason Magazine,* Copyright 2000 by the Reason Foundation, 3415 S. Sepulveda Blvd. Suite 400, Los Angeles, CA, 90034, *www.reason.com.*

contributions and avoid any direct communications that would suggest that the contributions were made in exchange for a particular official action. But ethical problems remain. In 2005 lobbyist Jack Abramoff was indicted for defrauding Indian tribes of millions in fees and campaign contributions that had been given by the tribes to gain favorable treatment of their gambling enterprises. Abramoff kept millions for himself, but he also distributed millions to hundreds of Congress members both directly and indirectly through organizations he created. Following his indictment, many Congress members rushed to rid themselves of his contributions by giving them to charity.

**Distributing PAC Money**    Because political action committee (PAC) contributions are in larger lumps than individual contributions, PAC contributions often attract more attention from members of Congress. The PACs listed in Table 7.7 gave millions of dollars to finance the campaigns of their potential allies in 2004.

Most PACs use their campaign contributions to acquire access and influence with decision makers. Corporate, trade, and professional PAC contributions go overwhelmingly to incumbents, regardless of party. Leaders of these PACs know that incumbents are rarely defeated, and they do not wish to antagonize even unsympathetic members of Congress by backing challengers. However, ideological and issue-oriented PACs are more likely to allocate funds according to the candidates' policy positions and voting records. Labor PACs give almost all of their contributions to Democrats. Ideological and issue-oriented PACs give money to challengers as well as incumbents; in recent years, these groups collectively favored Democrats as women's, environmental, abortion rights, and elderly groups proliferated. (See *Up Close:* "EMILY's List.") Business, trade and professional PACs usually split their contributions in order to ensure access to both Democrats and Republicans. But Republicans generally garner a larger share of the money from these PACs.

PAC money is less important in the Senate than in the House. PAC contributions account for about 35 percent of House campaign contributions; they account for only about 20 percent of Senate campaign contributions. Actually, PACs contribute more *dollars* to the average senator than to the average House member. But because Senate campaigns cost so much more than House campaigns, PAC contributions are *proportionally* less. Senators must rely more on individual contributions than House members do.

**EMILY's List**
Political network for pro-choice Democratic women that raises early money for women candidates.
*www.emilyslist.org*

**Table 7.7    The Big Money PACs in 2004**

| Rank | Organization | Total Amount | Dem Pct | Repub Pct |
|------|--------------|--------------|---------|-----------|
| 1 | National Assn. of Realtors | $3,787,083 | 47% | 52% |
| 2 | Laborers Union | $2,684,250 | 86 | 14 |
| 3 | National Auto Dealers Assn. | $2,603,300 | 27 | 73 |
| 4 | Intl. Brotherhood of Electrical Workers | $2,369,500 | 96 | 4 |
| 5 | National Beer Wholesalers Assn. | $2,314,000 | 24 | 76 |
| 6 | National Assn. of Home Builders | $2,201,500 | 33 | 67 |
| 7 | Assn. of Trial Lawyers of America | $2,181,499 | 93 | 6 |
| 8 | United Parcel Service | $2,142,679 | 28 | 72 |
| 9 | American Medical Assn. | $2,092,425 | 21 | 79 |
| 10 | United Auto Workers | $2,075,700 | 98 | 1 |
| 11 | Carpenters & Joiners Union | $2,074,560 | 74 | 26 |
| 12 | Credit Union National Assn. | $2,065,678 | 42 | 58 |
| 13 | Service Employees International Union | $1,985,000 | 85 | 15 |
| 14 | American Bankers Assn. | $1,978,013 | 36 | 64 |
| 15 | SBC Communications | $1,955,116 | 35 | 65 |
| 16 | Machinists/Aerospace Workers Union | $1,942,250 | 99 | 1 |
| 17 | Teamsters Union | $1,917,413 | 88 | 11 |
| 18 | American Hospital Assn. | $1,769,326 | 44 | 56 |
| 19 | American Federation of Teachers | $1,717,372 | 97 | 3 |
| 20 | Wal-Mart Stores | $1,677,000 | 22 | 78 |

*Source:* Center for Responsive Politics.

## UP CLOSE

## EMILY's List

Fund-raising is the greatest obstacle to mounting a successful campaign against an incumbent. And the most difficult problem facing challengers is raising money *early* in the campaign, when they have little name recognition and little or no standing in the polls.

EMILY's List is a politically adroit and effective effort to support liberal Democratic women candidates by infusing *early money* into their campaigns. EMILY stands for Early Money Is Like Yeast, because "it makes the dough rise." Early contributions provide the initial credibility that a candidate, especially a challenger, needs in order to solicit additional funds from individuals and organizations. EMILY is a fund-raising network of thousands of contributors, each of whom pays $100 to join and pledges to give at least $100 to two women from a list of candidates prepared by EMILY's leaders. Most of the contributors are professional women who appreciate EMILY's screening of pro-choice, liberal women candidates around the country.

EMILY's List was begun in 1985 by a wealthy heir to a founder of IBM, Ellen Malcolm. Women challengers for congressional races traditionally faced frustration in fund-raising. Incumbent male office-holders enjoyed a huge fund-raising advantage because contributors expected them to win and therefore opened their wallets to gain access and goodwill. EMILY's List has helped to overcome defeatism among both women candidates and contributors.

EMILY's List supports *only* Democratic women candidates who are strong supporters of abortion rights. When the list was founded, there were no women in the Senate and only a very few in the House. In 2006 there were thirteen women in the Senate (eleven supported by Emily's List) and forty-nine in the House (forty-three supported by Emily's List). EMILY's List currently boasts of more than 100,000 members; they have contributed more than $43 million dollars to pro-choice Democratic women.

Senator Barbara Milkulski, Democrat of Maryland and an early beneficiary of EMILY's List, at a news conference.

**Payback**    Representatives of organized interest groups say that their PAC contributions are designed to buy access—"a chance to talk"—with members of Congress, their staffs, and executives in the administration (see "What Do Contributors Buy?" in Chapter 5). Both interest groups and government officials usually deny that campaign contributions can "buy" support.

Nevertheless, the pattern of campaign contributions by major industries corresponds closely with the pattern of congressional voting on many key issues. Congress members who receive the largest PAC contributions from an industry group tend to vote in favor of that group's position. Congress members who oppose the industry's position generally receive far less (see *Up Close:* "Payback: Money and Medicare").

## Lobbying the Bureaucracy

Lobbying does not cease after a law is passed. Rather, interest groups try to influence the implementation of the law. Interest groups know that bureaucrats exercise considerable discretion in policy implementation (see "Bureaucratic

## UP CLOSE

# Payback: Money and Medicare

After years of struggle, Congress finally passed a prescription drug benefit for Medicare recipients in 2003. The bill was one of the most heavily lobbied pieces of legislation in the Congress in many years. The House and Senate passed very different measures, and the conference committee required months of behind-the-scenes negotiations before sending the bill to both chambers for final passage.

The principal beneficiaries of the bill were supposed to be the nation's senior citizens. And indeed the AARP was heavily involved in every stage of the bill's progress. But the biggest campaign contributors, and arguably the biggest beneficiaries of the final bill, were the drug manufacturers, the health maintenance organizations (HMOs), and the insurance industry.

The House passed the final bill by a close vote of 220–215. An analysis of congressional voting on the bill shows that lawmakers who voted to approve the legislation received an average of roughly twice as much in campaign contributions from the drug companies, HMOs, and insurance companies, as those who voted against the bill.

Republicans controlled the House as well as the Senate, and Republicans were generally more favorable toward the positions taken by these industries. So it is no surprise that Republican Congress members on average received much larger contributions from these industries than Democrats, even Democrats who supported the industries' positions.

### PAC Contributions and the Prescription Drug Vote in the House

|  | Average Contributions 1990–2003 | |
| --- | --- | --- |
|  | Supporters | Opponents |
| Drug manufacturers | $27,618 | $11,308 |
| HMOs | $11,582 | $ 6,630 |
| Health insurers | $19,510 | $10,128 |

Power" in Chapter 10). Thus many interests spend as much as or more time and energy trying to influence executive agencies as they do Congress.

Lobbying the bureaucracy involves various types of activities, including monitoring regulatory agencies for notices of new rules and regulatory changes; providing reports, testimony, and evidence in administrative hearings; submitting contract and grant applications and lobbying for their acceptance; and monitoring the performance of executive agencies on behalf of group members.

Groups may try to influence the creation of a new agency to carry out the law or influence the assignment of implementation to an existing "friendly" agency. They may try to influence the selection of personnel to head the implementing agency. They may lobby the agency to devote more money and personnel to enforcement of the law (or less, depending on a group's preference). They may argue for strict rules and regulations—or loose interpretations of the law—by the implementing agencies. Lobbyists frequently appear at administrative hearings to offer information. They often undertake to sponsor test cases of administrative regulations on behalf of affected members. In short, lobbying extends throughout the government.[24]

**Iron Triangles**   In general, interest groups strive to maintain close working relationships with the departments and agencies that serve their members or regulate their industries. Conversely, bureaucracies seek to nourish relationships with powerful "client" groups that are capable of pressuring Congress to expand their authority and increase their budgets. Both bureaucracies and interest groups seek close working relationships with the congressional committees that exercise jurisdiction over their policy function. Finally, members of Congress seek the political and financial support of powerful interest groups, and members also seek to influence bureaucrats to favor supportive interest groups.

The mutual interests of congressional committee members, organized groups, and bureaucratic agencies come together to form what has been labeled the "iron triangles" of American government. **Iron triangles** refer to stable relationships among interest groups, congressional committees, and administrative agencies functioning in the same policy area. Each of the three sides of these triangles depends on the support of the other two; their cooperation serves their own interests (see Figure 7.10).

In an iron triangle, bureaucracies, interest groups, and congressional committees "scratch each other's backs." Bureaucrats get political support from interest groups in their requests for expanded power and authority and increased budgetary allocations. Interest groups get favorable treatment of their members by the bureaucracy. Congressional committee members get political and financial support from interest groups, as well as favorable treatment for their constituents and contributors who are served or regulated by the bureaucracy.

**Revolving Doors**   It is not uncommon in Washington for people in a particular policy field to switch jobs, moving from a post in the government to a job in the private sector, or vice versa, or moving to different posts within the government. In one example, an individual might move from a job in a corporation (Pillsbury or General Mills) to the staff of an interest group (American Farm Bureau Federation), and then to the executive agency charged with implementing policy in the field (U.S. Department of Agriculture) or to the staff of a House or Senate committee with jurisdiction over the field (House Agricultural Committee or Senate Agriculture, Nutrition, and Forestry Committee). The common currency of moves within a network is both policy expertise and contacts within the field.

The term **revolving doors** is often used to criticize people who move from a government post (where they acquired experience, knowledge, and personal contacts) to a job in the private sector as a consultant, lobbyist, or salesperson. Defense contractors may recruit high-ranking military officers or Defense Department officials to help sell weapons to their former employers. Trade associations may recruit congressional staffers, White House staffers, or high-ranking agency heads as lobbyists, or these people may leave government service to start their own lobbying firms. Attorneys from the Justice Department, the Internal Revenue Service, and federal regulatory agencies may be recruited by Washington law firms to represent clients in dealings with their former employers.

Former members of Congress are considered the most viable commodity a lobby firm can offer their clients. The Center for Responsive Politics reports that 125 to 150 former Congress members are lobbyists, many of them among the highest paid in the profession. When asked, lobbyists themselves, especially former members of Congress, acknowledge that their success depends mostly on "schmoozing" with their former colleagues.[25]

## Lobbying the Courts

Interest groups play an important role in influencing federal courts. Many of the key cases brought to the federal courts are initiated by interest groups. Indeed, **litigation** is becoming a favored instrument of interest-group politics. Groups that

---

**iron triangles** Mutually supportive relationships among interest groups, government agencies, and legislative committees with jurisdiction over a specific policy area.

**revolving doors** The movement of individuals from government positions to jobs in the private sector, using the experience, knowledge, and contacts they acquired in government employment.

**litigation** Legal dispute brought before a court.

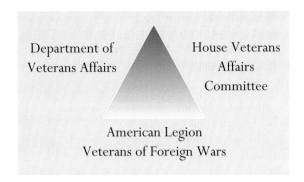

**Figure 7.10** Iron Triangles
The iron triangle approach provides a convenient way to look at the interrelationship among interest groups, executive agencies, and congressional committees. As this example shows, veterans' interest groups work closely with both the Department of Veterans Affairs (executive agency) and the House Veterans Affairs Committee.

oppose a new law or an agency's action often challenge it in court as unconstitutional or as violating the law. Interest groups bring issues to the courts by (1) supplying the attorneys for individuals who are parties to a case; (2) bringing suits to the courts on behalf of classes of citizens; or (3) filing companion *amicus curiae* (literally "friend of the court") arguments in cases in which they are interested.

The nation's most powerful interest groups all have legal divisions specializing in these techniques. The American Civil Liberties Union is one of the most active federal court litigants on behalf of criminal defendants. The early civil rights strategy of the National Association for the Advancement of Colored People (NAACP) was directed by its Legal Defense and Education Fund under the leadership of Thurgood Marshall (see *People in Politics:* "Thurgood Marshall" in Chapter 12). The NAACP chose to sponsor a suit by Linda Brown against the Board of Education in her hometown—Topeka, Kansas—in order to win the historic 1954 desegregation decision.[26] NARAL Pro-Choice America is active in sponsoring legal challenges to abortion restrictions. The Environmental Defense Fund and the Natural Resources Defense Council specialize in environmental litigation.

The special rules of judicial decision making preclude direct lobbying of judges by interest groups (see "The Special Rules of Judicial Decision Making" in Chapter 11). Directly contacting federal judges about a case, letter writing, telephoning, and demonstrating outside of federal courtrooms are all considered inappropriate conduct. They inspire more resentment than support among federal judges. However, interest groups have been very active in direct lobbying of Congress over judicial appointments. Key interest groups supporting abortion rights—NARAL Pro-Choice America, People for the American Way, the National Organization for Women, and so on—have played a central role in confirmation battles (see *Up Close:* "The Confirmation of Clarence Thomas" in Chapter 12).

**amicus curiae** Person or group other than the defendant or the plaintiff or the prosecution that submits an argument in a case for the court's consideration.

# Summary Notes

- Organization grants advantage in the struggle for power. Political parties organize individuals and groups to exercise power in democracies by winning elected office.

- In theory, political parties are "responsible" organizations that adopt a principled platform, recruit candidates who support the platform, educate the public about it, direct

an issue-oriented campaign, and then organize the legislature and ensure that their candidates enact the party's platform.

- But in the American two-party system, winning office by appealing to the large numbers of people at the center of the political spectrum becomes more important than promoting strong policy positions. American parties cannot bind elected officials to campaign promises anyway.

■ American parties have lost many of their traditional functions over time. Party nominations are won by individual candidates in primary elections rather than through selection by party leaders. Most political candidates are self-selected; they organize their own campaigns. Television has replaced the party as the principal means of educating the public. And government bureaucracies, not party machines, provide social services.

■ Party nominations are won in primary elections as earlier caucus and convention methods of nomination have largely disappeared. Party primary elections in the various states may be open or closed and may or may not require runoff primaries. The nominees selected in each party's primary election then battle each other in the general election.

■ The parties battle in three major arenas. The *party-in-the-electorate* refers to party identification among voters. The *party-in-the-government* refers to party identification and organization among elected officials. The *party organization* refers to party offices at the local, state, and national levels.

■ Since presidential nominations are now generally decided in primary elections—with pledged delegates selected before the opening of the national conventions and with party platforms largely symbolic and wholly unenforceable on the candidates—the conventions have become largely media events designed to kick off the general election campaign.

■ *Dealignment* refers to a decline in the attractiveness of the parties to the voters, a growing reluctance of people to identify strongly with either party, and greater voter willingness to cross party lines. Despite dealignment, party identification remains a strong influence in voter choice.

■ The interest-group system supplements the electoral system as a form of representation. The electoral system is designed to respond to broad, majority preferences in geographically defined constituencies. The interest-group system represents narrower, minority interests in economic, professional, ideological, religious, racial, gender, and issue constituencies.

■ Washington lobbying groups represent a wide array of organized interests. But business, trade, and professional associations outnumber labor union, women's, public-interest, single-issue, and ideological groups.

■ Lobbying activities include advertising and public relations, obtaining access to government officials, providing them with technical and political information, mobilizing constituents, building coalitions, organizing demonstrations, and providing campaign support. Bribery is illegal, and most lobbyists avoid exacting specific vote promises in exchange for campaign contributions.

■ The mutual interests of organized groups, congressional committees, and bureaucratic agencies sometimes come together to form "iron triangles" of mutual support and cooperation in specific policy areas. In many policy areas, loose "policy networks" emerge among people who share an interest and expertise—although not necessarily opinions—about a policy and are in regular contact with each other.

■ The "revolving door" problem emerges when individuals use the knowledge, experience, and contacts obtained through government employment to secure high-paying jobs with corporations, law firms, lobbying and consulting firms, and interest groups doing business with their old agencies.

■ Interest groups influence the nation's courts not only by providing financial and legal support for issues of concern to them but also by lobbying Congress over judicial appointments.

# Key Terms

political parties   206
responsible party
   model   206
party polarization   209
nominee   210
nomination   210
primary election   210
machine   210
patronage   210
divided party
   government   211
nonpartisan elections   211

caucus   211
ward   211
precinct   211
closed primaries   212
open primaries   213
raiding   213
runoff primary   213
general election   213
convention   214
presidential primaries   214
delegates   215
platform   215

party identification   217
dealignment   219
realignment   220
proportional
   representation   223
interest group   224
majoritarianism   224
organizational sclerosis   224
trade associations   225
public-interest groups   227
single-issue groups   229
ideological

organizations   229
lobbyist   229
lobbying   231
public relations   231
access   232
grassroots lobbying   233
coalition   233
bribery   233
iron triangles   238
revolving doors   238
litigation   238
*amicus curiae*   239

# Suggested Readings

Beck, Paul, and Marjorie Hershey. *Party Politics in America*. 11th ed. New York: Longman, 2005. An authoritative text on the American party system—party organizations, the parties-in-government, and the parties-in-the-electorate.

Berry, Jeffrey M. *The New Liberalism: The Rising Power of Citizen Groups*. Washington, D.C.: Brookings Institution Press, 1999. A description of the increasing number and activities of liberal interest groups in Washington and their success in defeating both business and conservative groups.

Cigler, Allan J., and Burdett, A. Loomis, eds. *Interest Group Politics*. 6th ed. Washington, D.C.: CQ Press, 2002. A collection of essays examining interest-group politics.

Downs, Anthony. *An Economic Theory of Democracy*. New York: Harper & Row, 1957. The classic work describing rational choice-winning strategies for political parties and explaining why there is no incentive for vote-maximizing parties in a two-party system to adopt widely separate policy positions.

Goldstein, Kenneth M. *Interest Groups, Lobbying and Participation in America*. New York: Cambridge University Press, 2003. When and why people join interest groups, how they are recruited, and how groups try to influence legislation.

Hernson, Paul S., Ronald G. Shaiko, and Clyde Wilcox. The *Interest Group Connection: Electioneering, Lobbying and Policy-making*. 2nd ed. Washington D.C.: CQ Press 2004. Interest group activities in the electoral, legislative, judicial, and policy-making processes.

Keefe, William J., and Marc E. Hetherington. *Parties, Politics, and Public Policy in America*. 9th ed. Washington, D.C.: CQ Press, 2003. A comprehensive survey of American political parties, from the nominating process to campaign finance and the changing affiliations of voters.

Lowi, Theodore J. *The End of Liberalism*. New York: Norton, 1969. The classic critique of "interest-group liberalism," describing how special interests contribute to the growth of government and the development of "clientism."

Rozell, Mark J., Clyde Wilcox, and David Madland. *Interest Groups in American Campaigns*. Washington, D.C.: CQ Press, 2005. The role of interest groups in campaigns, including their adjustments to the Bipartisan Campaigns Reform Act of 2002 and the creation of "527s" to circumvent the act.

# ★ Make It Real

## POLITICAL PARTIES

In this module, students have the opportunity to write their own party platforms.

## INTEREST GROUPS

This unit lets students represent an interest group and try to get their legislation passed.

# Part Four

# INSTITUTIONS

## Price of Victory

**ABCNEWS**

Originally Aired: **March 15, 2005**
Program: **Nightline**
Running Time: **14:34**

It was meant to be a victory that could be savored all the way through the 2004 election. When the president signed the Medicare bill into law last December, it was a landmark event. This bill had managed to achieve what seniors had been demanding for years—prescription drug coverage. That's definitely something to celebrate. Well, a funny thing happened on the way to the bill's becoming law: accusations of bribery, lying, intimidation, political shenanigans—it has become quite a Washington drama. A bureaucrat who you probably wouldn't normally hear about testified on Capitol Hill. Richard Foster is the chief actuary of the Medicare program and he says that his boss threatened to fire him if he publicized his estimates of how much the Medicare bill would actually cost. His boss happens to be a political appointee. The bill that passed had a cost estimate of around $400 billion. Foster's estimate—$534 billion—became public a month after the signing of the bill. Needless to say, people are furious, including Republicans who now say if they knew then what they know now, they would not have voted for the bill.

Then there is the story of the endless vote in the House—a fifteen-minute roll call that stayed open for three hours. A lot of arm-twisting occurred that night, including allegations that retiring Congressman Nick Smith (R-Michigan) was told that if he voted for the bill his son would get $100,000 worth of help for his upcoming congressional race. Smith voted against the bill, but there is another investigation of this allegation.

There are some people who roll their eyes at the very thought of the congressional process. But this is a dramatic one. People are really emotional about it, as you will see in this program.

## Critical Thinking Questions

1. In "Price of Victory," of what does Medicare actuary Richard Foster accuse the administration?

2. In the process of passing the 2003 Medicare bill, what was unusual in regard to the timing of the vote?

3. In "Price of Victory," of what does Representative Nick Smith accuse the House leadership?

4. Your text describes the process by which bills become laws. How does the process in the text differ from the process in the video?

# 8 CONGRESS
## Politics on Capitol Hill

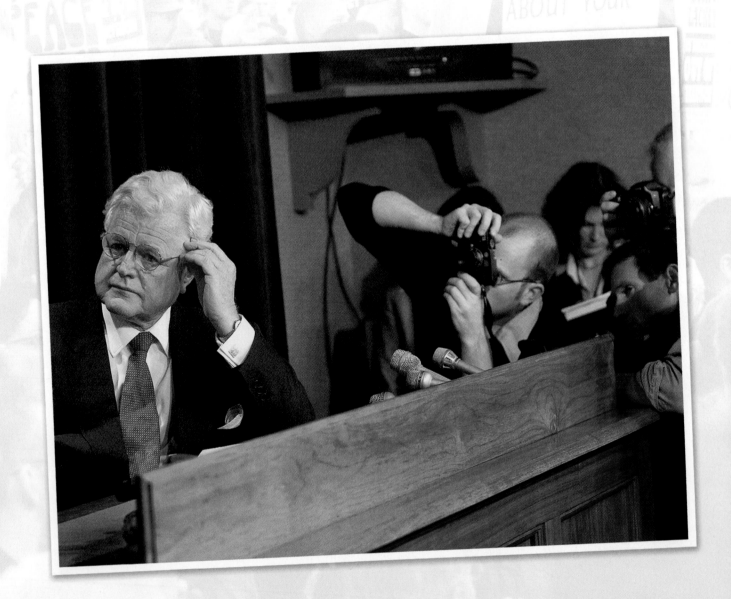

## Chapter Outline

- The Powers of Congress
- Congressional Apportionment and Redistricting
- Getting to Capitol Hill
- Party Fortunes in Congress
- Life in Congress
- Home Style
- Organizing Congress: Party and Leadership
- In Committee
- On the Floor
- Decision Making in Congress
- Customs and Norms
- Congressional Ethics

# The Powers of Congress

The Constitution gives very broad powers to Congress. "All legislative Powers herein granted shall be vested in a Congress of the United States, which shall consist of a Senate and House of Representatives." *The nation's Founders envisioned Congress as the first and most powerful branch of government.* They equated national powers with the powers of Congress and gave Congress the most clearly specified role in national government.

Article I empowers Congress to levy taxes, borrow and spend money, regulate interstate commerce, establish a national money supply, establish a post office, declare war, raise and support an army and navy, establish a court system, and pass all laws "necessary and proper" to implement these powers. Congress may also propose amendments to the Constitution or (with a two-thirds vote of both the House and the Senate) admit new states. In the event that no presidential candidate receives a majority of votes in the Electoral College, the House of Representatives selects the president. The Senate has two additional powers: It is called on for advice and consent to treaties, and it confirms presidential nominations to executive and judicial posts. The House has the power to impeach, and the Senate to try any officer of the U.S. government, including the president. Each **congressional session** convenes on January 3 following congressional elections in November of even-numbered years.

**Institutional Conflict** Over two centuries, the three separate branches of the national government—the Congress, the presidency and the executive branch, and the Supreme Court and federal judiciary—have struggled for power and preeminence in governing. This struggle for power among the separate institutions is precisely what the Founders envisioned. In writing the Constitution, they sought to create "opposite and rival interests" among the separate branches of the national government. "The constant aim," explained Madison, "is to divide and arrange the several offices in such a manner as that each may be a check on the other."[1] (see Appendix, *Federalist Papers*, No. 51). From time to time, first the Congress, then the presidency, and occasionally the Supreme Court have appeared to become the most powerful branch of government.

**congressional session** Each Congress elected in November of even-numbered years meets the following January 3 and remains in session for two years. Since the first Congress to meet under the Constitution in 1789, Congresses have been numbered by session (for example, 107th Congress 2001–2003, 108th Congress 2003–2005, 109th Congress 2005–2007).

**U.S. House of Representatives**
Official Web site of the House, with schedule of floor and committee actions, legislative information, and links to every Representative's Web site and every committee Web site.
*www.house.gov*

**bicameral** Any legislative body that consists of two separate chambers or houses; in the United States, the Senate represents 50 statewide voter constituencies, and the House of Representatives represents voters in 435 separate districts.

**"The President Initiates, Congress Deliberates"** Throughout much of the twentieth century, Congress ceded leadership in national policy making to the president and the executive branch. Congress largely responded to the policy initiatives and spending requests originating from the president, executive agencies, and interest groups. Congress did not merely ratify or "rubber-stamp" these initiatives and requests; it played an independent role in the policymaking process. But this role was essentially a deliberative one, in which Congress accepted, modified, amended, or rejected the policies and budget requests initiated by others.

It is easier for the Congress to obstruct the policy initiatives of the president than it is to assume policy leadership itself. Congress can defeat presidential policy proposals, deny presidential budget requests, delay or reject presidential appointments, investigate executive agencies, hold committee hearings to spotlight improprieties, and generally immobilize the executive branch. It can investigate and question nominees for the Supreme Court and the federal judiciary; it can legislate changes in the jurisdiction of the federal courts; and it can try to reverse court decisions by amending laws or the Constitution itself. The Congress can even threaten to impeach the president or federal judges. But these are largely reactive, obstructionist actions, usually accompanied by a great deal of oratory.

**Dividing Congressional Power: House and Senate** Congress must not only share national power with the executive and judicial branches of government; it must also share power within itself. The framers of the Constitution took the advice of the nation's eldest diplomat, Benjamin Franklin: "It is not enough that your legislature should be numerous; it should also be divided. . . . One division should watch over and control the other, supply its wants, correct its blunders, and cross its designs, should they be criminal or erroneous."[2] Accordingly, the U.S. Congress is **bicameral**—composed of two houses (see Figure 8.1).

No law can be passed and no money can be spent unless both the House of Representatives and the Senate pass identical laws. Yet the House and the Senate have very different constituencies and terms. The House consists of 435 voting members, elected from districts within each state apportioned on the basis of equal population. (The average congressional district since the 2000 census has a population of about 650,000; the House also includes nonvoting delegates from Puerto Rico, the District of Columbia, Guam, the Virgin Islands, and American Samoa.) All House members face election every two years. The Senate consists of 100 members serving six-year terms, elected by statewide constituencies. Senate terms are staggered so that one-third of senators are elected every two years (see Table 8.1).

The House of Representatives, with its two-year terms, was designed to be more responsive to the popular mood. Representatives are fond of referring to their chamber as "the people's House," and the Constitution requires that all revenue-raising bills originate in the House. The Senate was designed to be a smaller, more deliberative body, with its members serving six-year terms. Indeed, the Senate is the more prestigious body. House members frequently give up their seats to run for the Senate; the reverse has seldom occurred. Moreover, the Senate exercises certain powers not given to the House: the power to ratify treaties and the power to confirm federal judges, ambassadors, cabinet members, and other high executive officials.

**Domestic versus Foreign and Defense Policy** Congress is more powerful in domestic than in foreign and military affairs. It is freer to reject presidential initiatives in domestic policy areas such as welfare, health, education, the environment,

HOUSE OF REPRESENTATIVES                                              SENATE

**Figure 8.1**   Corridors of Power in Congress

The architecture and floor plan of the Capitol Building in Washington reflect the bicameral division of Congress, with one wing for the House of Representatives and one for the Senate.

and taxation. But Congress usually follows presidential leadership in foreign and defense policy even though constitutionally the president and Congress share power in these arenas. The president is "Commander-in-Chief" of the armed forces, but only Congress can "declare war." The president appoints and receives ambassadors and "makes treaties," but the Senate must confirm appointments and provide "advice and consent" to treaties. Historically presidents have led the nation in matters of war and peace.

**www U.S. Senate**
Official Senate Web site, with floor and committee schedules, Senate news, and links to each Senator's Web site.
*www.senate.gov*

---

**Table 8.1   Comparing the House and Senate**

|  | House of Representatives | Senate |
|---|---|---|
| *Terms* | Two years | Six years |
| *Members* | 435 | 100 |
| *Elections* | All every two years | One-third every two years |
| *Constituencies* | Congressional districts | States |
| *Unique powers* | Originate tax bills | Advise and consent to (ratify) treaties by |
|  | Bring impeachment charges | two-thirds vote |
|  |  | Confirm appointments |
|  |  | Try impeachment charges |
| *Debate on bills* | Limited by Rules Committee | Unlimited, except by unanimous consent or vote of cloture (three-fifths) |
| *Member prestige* | Modest; smaller personal staffs, fewer committee assignments | High: larger personal staffs, more committee assignments, always addressed as "Senator" |
| *Leadership* | Hierarchical, with speaker, majority and minority leaders and whips and committees, especially Rules, concentrating power | Less hierarchical, with each senator exercising more influence on leadership, committees, and floor votes |
| *Committees* | Twenty standing and select committees | Twenty standing and select committees |
|  | Each member on about five committees | Each member on about seven committees |
|  | Difficult to bypass | Easier to bypass |

The Vietnam experience inspired Congress to try to reassert its powers over war and peace. Military embarrassment, prolonged and indecisive fighting, and accumulating casualties—all vividly displayed on national television—encouraged Congress to challenge presidential war-making power. The War Powers Resolution of 1973, passed over the veto of President Richard Nixon, who was weakened by the Watergate scandal, sought to curtail the president's power to commit U.S. military forces to combat (see "Commander-in-Chief" in Chapter 9). But this legislation has not proven effective, and both Republican and Democratic presidents have continued to exercise war-making powers.

**power of the purse**
Congress's exclusive constitutional power to authorize expenditures by all agencies of the federal government.

**The Power of the Purse**   Congress's real power in both domestic and foreign (defense) policy centers on its **power of the purse**—its power over federal taxing and spending. Only Congress can "lay and collect Taxes, Duties, Imposts and Excises" (Article I, Section 8), and only Congress can authorize spending: "No Money shall be drawn from the Treasury, but in Consequence of Appropriations made by Law" (Article I, Section 9).

Congress jealously guards these powers. Presidents initiate taxing and spending policies by sending their budgets to the Congress each year (see "The Budgetary Process" in Chapter 10 for details). But Congress has the last word on taxing and spending. The most important bills that Congress considers each year are usually the budget resolutions setting ceilings on various categories of expenditures and the later appropriations bills authorizing specific expenditures. It is often in these appropriations bills that Congress exercises its greatest influence over national policy. Thus, for example, the Congress's involvement in foreign affairs centers on its annual consideration of appropriations for foreign aid, its involvement in military affairs centers on its annual deliberations over the defense appropriations bill, and so on.

**oversight** Congressional monitoring of the activities of executive branch agencies to determine if the laws are being faithfully executed.

**Oversight of the Bureaucracy**   Congressional **oversight** of the federal bureaucracy is a continuing process by which Congress reviews the activities of the executive branch. The *formal* rationale of oversight is to determine whether the purposes of laws passed by Congress are being achieved by executive agencies and whether appropriations established by Congress are being spent as intended. Often the *real* purpose is to influence executive branch decisions, secure favorable treatment for friends and constituents, embarrass presidential appointees, undercut political support for particular programs or agencies, lay the political groundwork for budgetary increases or decreases for an agency, or simply enhance the power of congressional committees and subcommittees and those who chair them.

Oversight is carried out primarily through congressional committees and subcommittees. Individual senators and representatives can engage in a form of oversight simply by writing or calling executive agencies, but committees and their staffs carry on the bulk of oversight activity. Because committees and subcommittees specialize in particular areas of policy making, each tends to focus its oversight activities on particular executive departments and agencies. Oversight is particularly intense during budget hearings. Subcommittees of both the House and the Senate Appropriations Committees are especially interested in how money is being spent by the agencies they oversee.

**advice and consent** The constitutional power of the U.S. Senate to reject or ratify (by a two-thirds vote) treaties made by the president.

**Senate Advice and Consent and Confirmation of Presidential Appointments**   The Constitution provides that the president must obtain the **advice and consent** of the Senate for treaties "provided that two-thirds of the Senators present concur." In fact, the Senate has seldom provided "advice" to the

Senate committee confirmation hearings provide an opportunity for senators to lecture presidential nominees about how they should perform their jobs. The Senate must vote to confirm high executive branch nominees, including the Federal Reserve Board Chairman, Ben Bernanke, shown here testifying in 2005.

president regarding treaties prior to their submission to the Senate for "consent." The president enjoys a high degree of autonomy over U.S. foreign policy (see "Global Leader" in Chapter 9). The process of treaty ratification begins when a president submits an already negotiated treaty to the Senate. Once submitted, treaties are automatically referred to the Senate Foreign Relations Committee. That Committee cannot make changes in the treaty itself; it can either reject the treaty or forward it to the full Senate. The Senate itself cannot make changes in the formal treaty but must accept or reject it. Ratification requires a two-thirds vote. The Senate can, however, express its reservations to a treaty and/or instruct the president how the treaty is to be interpreted.[3]

The Senate also exercises a special power over the president and the executive branch of government through its constitutional responsibility for approving presidential appointments of key executive officers, including Cabinet members, ambassadors, and other high officials (see "Congressional Constraints on the Bureaucracy" in Chapter 10). And the Senate exercises a special power over the judicial branch through its constitutional responsibility for the **confirmation** of presidential appointments to the federal judiciary including the Supreme Court (see "The Politics of Selecting Judges" in Chapter 11).

**Agenda Setting and Media Attention**   **Congressional hearings** and investigations often involve agenda setting—bringing issues to the public's attention and placing them on the national agenda. For agenda-setting purposes, congressional committees or subcommittees need the assistance of the media. Televised hearings and investigations are perhaps the most effective means by which Congress can attract attention to issues as well as to itself and its members.

Hearings and investigations are similar in some ways, but hearings are usually held on a specific bill in order to build a record of both technical information (what is the problem and how legislation might be crafted to resolve it) and political information (who favors and who opposes various legislative options).

**confirmation** The constitutionally required consent of the Senate to appointments of high-level executive officials by the president and appointments of federal judges.

**congressional hearings** Congressional committee sessions in which members listen to witnesses who provide information and opinions on matters of interest to the committee, including pending legislation.

**congressional investigation**
Congressional committee hearings on alleged misdeeds or scandals.

In contrast, investigations are held on alleged misdeeds or scandals. Although the U.S. Supreme Court has held that there must be some "legislative purpose" behind a **congressional investigation**, that phrase has been interpreted very broadly indeed.[4]

The *formal* rationale for congressional investigations is that Congress is seeking information to assist in its lawmaking function. But from the earliest Congress to the present, the investigating powers of Congress have often been used for political purposes: to rally popular support for policies or programs favored by Congress; to attack the president, other high officials in the administration, or presidential policies or programs; to focus media attention and public debate on particular issues; or simply to win media coverage and popular recognition for members of Congress.

Congressional investigators have the legal power to subpoena witnesses (force them to appear), administer oaths, compel testimony, and initiate criminal charges for contempt (refusing to cooperate) and perjury (lying). These powers can be exercised by Congress's regular committees and subcommittees and by committees appointed especially to conduct a particular investigation.

Congress cannot impose criminal punishments as a result of its investigations. But the information uncovered in a congressional investigation can be turned over to the U.S. Department of Justice, which may proceed with its own criminal investigation and perhaps indictment and trial of alleged wrongdoers in federal courts.

Congressional investigations have long been used as an opportunity for Congress to expose wrongdoing on the part of executive branch officials. The first congressional investigation (1792) examined why General Arthur St. Clair had been defeated by the Indians in Ohio; the Crédit Mobilier investigations (1872–73) revealed scandals in the Grant administration; the Select Committee on Campaign Practices, known universally as the "Watergate Committee," exposed the activities of President Richard Nixon's inner circle that led to impeachment charges and Nixon's forced resignation; a House and Senate Joint Select Committee conducted the Iran-Contra investigation in the Reagan Administration; the Senate Special Whitewater Committee investigated matters related to Bill and Hillary Clinton's real estate investments in Arkansas.

**Impeachment and Removal**   Potentially Congress's most formidable power is that of impeaching and removing from office the president, other officers of the United States, and federal judges, including Supreme Court justices. Congress can do so only for "Treason, Bribery or other High Crimes and Misdemeanors." The House of Representatives has the sole authority to bring charges of impeachment, by a simple majority vote. Impeachment is analogous to a criminal indictment; it does not remove an officer but merely subjects him or her to trial by the Senate. Only the Senate, following a trial, can remove the federal official from office, and then only by a two-thirds vote.

Bill Clinton is the second president in the nation's history to be impeached by the U.S. House of Representatives. (Andrew Johnson was the first in 1867; after a one-month trial in the Senate, the "guilty" vote fell one short of two-thirds needed for removal. President Richard Nixon resigned just prior to an impending impeachment vote in 1974.) The 1998 House impeachment vote split along partisan lines, with Republicans voting "yes" and Democrats voting "no." Two Articles of Impeachment were passed, one for perjury before a grand jury and one for obstruction of justice. In the subsequent Senate trial, only 45 senators (less than a majority and far less than the needed two-thirds) voted to convict

President Clinton on the first charge, and only 50 voted to convict on the second (see *Up Close:* "Sex, Lies, and Impeachment" in Chapter 9).

# Congressional Apportionment and Redistricting

The Constitution states that "Representatives . . . shall be apportioned among the several states . . . according to their respective Numbers." It orders an "actual enumeration" (census) every ten years. And it provides that every state shall have at least one representative, in addition to two senators, regardless of population. But the Constitution is silent on the size of the House of Representatives. Congress itself determines its own size; for more than a century, it allowed itself to grow to accommodate new states and population growth. In 1910 it fixed the membership of the House at 435.

The effect of doing so has been to expand the population of House districts over the years. Following the 2000 census, House districts have populations of about 650,000. It is sometimes argued that such large House constituencies prevent meaningful communication between citizens and their representatives. (The Framers originally envisioned House districts of no more than 30,000 people.) But expanding the size of the House would complicate its work, reduce the influence of individual members, require more procedural controls, and probably strengthen the power of party leaders.

**Apportionment**    Apportionment refers to the allocation of House seats to the states after each ten-year census. The Constitution does not specify a mathematical method of apportionment; Congress adopted a complex "method of equal proportion" in 1929, which so far has withstood court challenges (see *Across the USA:* "Reapportionment, 2000," which shows the current apportionment, together with the states that gained and lost seats after the 2000 census).

**Malapportionment**    Historically, state legislatures were notorious for their **malapportionment**—congressional (and state legislative) districts with grossly unequal numbers of people. Some congressional districts had twice the average number of people per district, and others had only half as many. In a district twice the size of the average district, the value of an individual's vote was heavily diluted. In a district half the size of the average, the value of an individual's vote was greatly magnified.

**Enter the Supreme Court**    Prior to 1962, the Supreme Court refused to intervene in apportionment, holding that this question belonged to the state legislatures and that the federal courts should avoid this "political thicket." So the Supreme Court's decision in the landmark case *Baker v. Carr* (1962) came as a surprise. The Court ruled that inequalities in voters' influence resulting from different-size districts violated the Equal Protection Clause of the Fourteenth Amendment. The case dealt with a complaint about Tennessee's state legislative districts, but the Court soon extended its holding to congressional districts as well.[5] "The conception of political equality from the Declaration of Independence to Lincoln's Gettysburg Address, to the Fourteenth, Fifteenth, Seventeenth, and Nineteenth Amendments, can mean only one thing—one person, one vote."[6]

The shift in the Supreme Court's policy raised a new question: How equal must districts be in order to guarantee voters "equal protection of the law"? The

---

**Think Again**

Should congressional districts be drawn to ensure that minorities win seats in Congress in rough proportion to their populations in the states?

---

**apportionment** The allocation of legislative seats to jurisdictions based on population. Seats in the U.S. House of Representatives are apportioned to the states on the basis of their population after every ten-year census.

**malapportionment** Unequal numbers of people in legislative districts resulting in inequality of voter representation.

# ACROSS THE USA

## Reapportionment, 2000

Since 1910, the number of seats in the House of Representatives has remained constant at 435. Each ten-year census requires a reapportionment of seats among states based on their populations. States with rapid population growth such as Arizona, Texas, Georgia, and Florida gain seats (each of these states gained two seats following the 2000 census). States with slow population growth lose seats (New York and Pennsylvania both lost two seats). The newly apportioned House convened in January 2003.

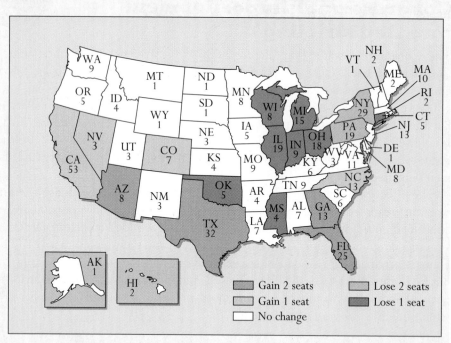

courts have ruled that only official U.S. Bureau of the Census figures may be used: estimated changes since the last census may *not* be used. In recent years, the courts have insisted on nearly exact mathematical equality in populations in congressional districts in a state.

**"Enumeration"**   The U.S. Constitution is very specific in its wording: It calls for an "actual Enumeration" (Article I, Section 2) of the population in each ten-year census. However, the U.S. Bureau of the Census has considered the use of samples and estimates to correct what it perceives to be "undercounts." Undercounting is said to occur when certain populations are difficult to identify and count on an individual basis, populations such as recent non-English-speaking immigrants or residents of neighborhoods likely to mistake government census takers for law enforcement officers or other unwelcome government officials. Political leaders (usually Democrats) of states and cities with large immigrant and minority populations have favored the substitution of samples and estimates for actual head counts. However, the U.S. Supreme Court held in 1999 that the Census Act of 1976 prohibits sampling for purposes of apportioning House members among the states.[7] Congress may use sampling for determining the allocation of grant-in-aid funds if it wishes.

**Redistricting**   Redistricting refers to the drawing of boundary lines of congressional districts following the census. After each census, some states gain and others lose seats, depending on whether their populations have grown faster or slower than the nation's population. In addition, population shifts within a state

**redistricting** Drawing of legislative district boundary lines following each ten-year census.

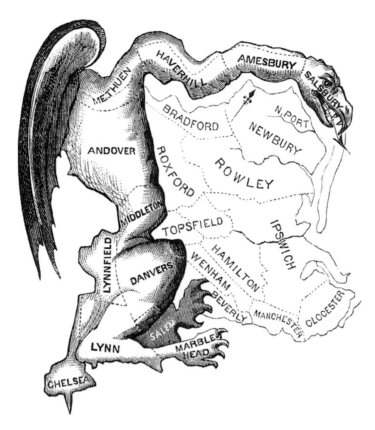

**Figure 8.2** The Original Gerrymander

The term *gerrymander* immortalizes Governor Elbridge Gerry (1744–1814) of Massachusetts, who in 1811 redistricted the state legislature to favor Democrats over Federalists. A district north of Boston was designed to concentrate, and thus "waste," Federalist votes. This political cartoon from the *Boston Gazette,* March 26, 1812, depicted the new district lines as a salamander, dubbing the process the "gerrymander."

may force districting changes. Congressional district boundaries are drawn by state legislatures in each state; a state's redistricting act must pass both houses of the state legislature and win the governor's signature (or be passed over a gubernatorial veto). The U.S. Justice Department and the federal judiciary are also deeply involved in redistricting issues, particularly questions of whether or not redistricting disadvantages African Americans or other minorities.

**Gerrymandering**   Gerrymandering is the drawing of district lines for political advantage (see Figure 8.2). The population of districts may be equal, yet the district boundaries are drawn in such a fashion as to grant advantage or disadvantage to specific groups of voters. Gerrymandering has long been used by parties in control of the state legislatures to maximize their seats in Congress and state legislatures.

Gerrymandering, with the aid of sophisticated computer-mapping programs and data on past voting records of precincts, is a highly technical task. But consider a simple example where a city is entitled to three representatives and the eastern third of the city is Republican but the western two-thirds is Democratic (see Figure 8.3). If the Republicans could draw the district lines, they might draw them along a north-south direction to allow their party to win in one of the three districts. In contrast, if Democrats could draw the district lines, they might draw them along an east-west direction to allow their party to win all three districts by diluting the Republican vote. Such dividing up and diluting of a strong minority to deny it the power to elect a representative is called **splintering**. Often gerrymandering is not as neat as our example; district lines may twist and turn, creating grotesque patterns in order to achieve the desired effects. Another

**gerrymandering** Drawing district boundary lines for political advantage.

**splintering** Redistricting in which a strong minority is divided up and diluted to prevent it from electing a representative.

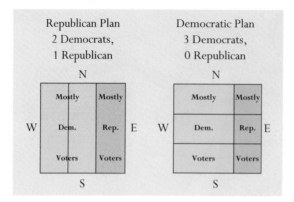

**Figure 8.3**
**Gerrymandering in Action**
Depending on how an area is divided into districts, the result may benefit one party or the other. In this example, dividing the area so one district has virtually all the Republicans gives that party a victory in that district while ceding the other two districts to the Democrats. In contrast, Democrats benefit when Republican voters are divided among the three districts so that their votes are splintered.

**packing** Redistricting in which partisan voters are concentrated in a single district, "wasting" their majority vote and allowing the opposition to win by modest majorities in other districts.

gerrymandering strategy—**packing**—is the heavy concentration of one party's voters in a single district in order to "waste" their votes and allow modest majorities of the party doing the redistricting to win in other districts.

**Partisan Gerrymandering**    Partisan gerrymandering does not violate federal court standards for "equal protection" under the Fourteenth Amendment. There is no constitutional obligation to allocate seats "to the contending parties in proportion to what their anticipated statewide vote will be."[8] For several years the Supreme Court threatened to intervene to correct partisan gerrymandering,[9] but in 2004 it finally decided that the issue was "nonjusticiable"—there were no "judicially manageable standards for adjudicating [party] claims." The Court decided that "'Fairness' is not a judicially manageable standard."[10] Parties are free to try to advantage themselves in redistricting.

**Re-redistricting**    The redrawing of congressional districts usually occurs after each ten-year census. However, several states have been embroiled in a second round of redistricting, notably Texas. (If one party dominated a state legislature during the first redistricting after the census and drew district lines in a partisan fashion, there is then a strong temptation for the opposition party to undertake a second round of partisan redistricting if it subsequently wins control of the state legislature.) It is theoretically possible that redistricting could be undertaken every time a state legislature changes party control.

In a controversial case, the Supreme Court upheld the practice of reredistricting. After a protracted partisan struggle in 2003, a new Republican majority in the Texas Legislature redrew congressional boundaries that had been drawn by a Democratic-controlled legislature after the 2000 Census. The result was a significant increase in Republican congressional seats and a corresponding decrease in Democratic seats in that state. But the Supreme Court declined to intervene: "Neither the Constitution nor Congress has stated any explicit prohibition on middecade redistricting to change districts drawn earlier in conformance with a decennial census."[11] And the Court approved of middecade redistricting when racial or ethnic groups appeared to have been disadvantaged by earlier redistricting.

**Incumbent Gerrymandering**   Yet another problem confronting state legislatures in redistricting is the preservation of incumbent Congress members, that is, **incumbent gerrymandering**. Incumbents generally have sufficient political clout with their state parties to inspire efforts in the legislature to protect their districts.

Incumbent gerrymandering means drawing district lines in such a way as to ensure that districts of incumbents include enough supporters of their party to provide a high probability of their reelection. But often ensuring incumbents' security and maximizing the party's total number of seats are conflicting goals. It is not always possible to redraw district lines in such a way as to protect incumbents and at the same time ensure the largest number of party seats in a state. Incumbents themselves want the largest number of their party's voters packed in their district. But this tactic may result in losses for their party in other districts that have been robbed of party voters. Redistricting almost always confronts incumbents with new voters—voters who were previously in a different incumbent's district. As a result, incumbents usually have a somewhat more difficult reelection campaign following redistricting than in other elections.[12]

**Racial Gerrymandering**   Racial gerrymandering to disadvantage African Americans and other minorities violates both the Equal Protection Clause of the Fourteenth Amendment and the Voting Rights Act of 1965. The Voting Rights Act specifies that redistricting in states with a history of voter discrimination or low voter participation must be "cleared" in advance with the U.S. Justice Department. The act extends special protection not only to African American voters but also to Hispanic, Native American, Alaska Native, and Asian voters.

In 1982 Congress strengthened the Voting Rights Act by outlawing any electoral arrangement that has the effect of weakening minority voting power. This *effects test* replaced the earlier *intent test*, under which redistricting was outlawed only if boundaries were intentionally drawn to dilute minority political influence. In *Thornburg v. Gingles* (1986), the Supreme Court interpreted the effects test to require state legislatures to redistrict their states in a way that maximizes minority representation in Congress and the state legislatures.[13] The effect of this ruling was to require **affirmative racial gerrymandering**—the creation of predominantly African American and minority districts (labeled "majority-minority" districts) whenever possible. Following the 1990 census, redistricting in legislatures in states with large minority populations was closely scrutinized by the U.S. Justice Department and the federal courts. The result was a dramatic increase in African American and Hispanic representation in Congress (see Figure 8.7 later in this chapter).

However, the Supreme Court later expressed constitutional doubts about bizarre-shaped districts based *solely* on racial composition. In a controversial 5 to 4 decision in *Shaw v. Reno* (1993), Justice Sandra Day O'Connor wrote, "Racial gerrymandering, even for remedial purposes, may balkanize us into competing racial factions. . . . A reapportionment plan that includes in one district individuals who have little in common with one another but the color of their skin bears an uncomfortable resemblance to political apartheid"[14] (see Figure 8.4). Later the Court held that the use of race as the "predominant factor" in drawing district lines is unconstitutional: "When the state assigns voters on the basis of race, it engages in the offensive and demeaning assumption that voters of a particular race, because of their race, think alike, share the same political interests and will prefer the same candidates at the polls."[15] But the Court has stopped short of saying that *all* race-conscious districting is unconstitutional.

**incumbent gerrymandering** Drawing legislative district boundaries to advantage incumbent legislators.

**affirmative racial gerrymandering** Drawing district boundary lines to maximize minority representation.

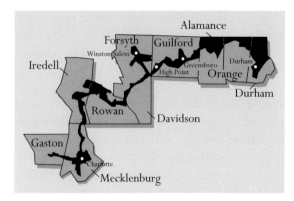

**Figure 8.4** Affirmative Racial Gerrymandering

North Carolina's Twelfth Congressional District was drawn up to be a "majority-minority" district by combining African American communities over a wide region of the state. The U.S. Supreme Court in *Shaw v. Reno* (1993) ordered a court review of this district to determine whether it incorporated any common interest other than race. The North Carolina legislature redrew the district in 1997, lowering its black population from 57 to 46 percent, yet keeping its lengthy connection of black voters from Charlotte to Greensboro.

**Partisanship Interacts with Race** Racial gerrymandering appears to help Republican congressional candidates. If African American voters are concentrated in heavily black districts, the effect is to "bleach" surrounding districts of Democratic-leaning black voters and thus improve the chances for Republican victories. Republican Party congressional gains in the South during the 1990s may be partly attributed to racial gerrymandering.[16] In what has been described as a "paradox of representation," the creation of majority-minority districts brought more minority members to Congress, but it also led to a more conservative House of Representatives, as Republicans gained seats previously held by white liberal Democrats.[17]

Republican-led efforts to "pack" black (Democratic) voters into relatively few districts suffered a setback in 2003 when the U.S. Supreme Court recognized that doing so might diminish the power of African American voters overall. The Court approved of a plan that "unpacked" some heavily concentrated majority-minority districts in Georgia. The Court reasoned that the result would be to create additional black "influence" districts where African American voters would not be in a majority but would be a large influential voting bloc.[18]

## Getting to Capitol Hill

Members of Congress are independent political entrepreneurs—selling themselves, their services, and their personal policy views to the voters in 435 House districts and 50 states across the country. They initiate their own candidacies, raise most of their campaign funds from individual contributors, put together personal campaign organizations, and get themselves elected with relatively little help from their party. Their reelection campaigns depend on their ability to raise funds from individuals and interest groups and on the services and other benefits they provide to their constituents.

Every two years all House members and one-third of the Senate face reelection. Here Democratic House Minority Leader Nancy Pelosi (D-CA) and Representative Meehan (D-MA) share a joke during a meeting at Pelosi's Capitol Hill office.

**Who Runs for Congress?**   Members of Congress come from a wide variety of backgrounds, ranging from acting and professional sports to medicine and the ministry. However, exceptionally high percentages of senators and representatives have prior experience in at least one of three fields—law, business, or public service (see Table 8.2). Members of Congress are increasingly career politicians, people who decided early in life to devote themselves to running for and occupying public office.[19] The many lawyers, by and large, are *not* practicing attorneys. Rather, the typical lawyer-legislator is a political activist with a law degree. These are people who graduated from law school and immediately sought public jobs— as federal or state prosecuting attorneys, as attorneys for federal or state agencies, or as staff assistants in congressional, state, or city offices. They used their early job experiences to make political contacts and learn how to organize a political campaign, find financial contributors, and deal with the media. Another group of Congress members are former businesspeople—not employees of large corporations, but people whose personal or family businesses brought them into close contact with government and their local community, in real estate, insurance, franchise dealerships, community banks, and so forth.

**Competition for Seats**   Careerism in Congress is aided by the electoral advantages enjoyed by incumbents over challengers. Greater name recognition, advantages in raising campaign funds, and the resources of congressional offices all combine to limit competition for seats in Congress and to reelect the vast majority of incumbents (see "The Advantages of Incumbency" in Chapter 5). The result is an incumbent reelection percentage for House members that usually exceeds 90 percent. The average reelection rate for U.S. senators is more than 80 percent (see Figure 8.5).

Aspirants for congressional careers are well advised to wait for open seats. **Open seats** in the House of Representatives are created when incumbents retire or vacate the seat to run for higher office. These opportunities occur on average in about 10 percent of House seats in each election. But every ten years reapportionment

**Think Again**

Are there too many lawyers in Congress?

**Roll Call**
   This online magazine covers a variety of current topics about Congress but is especially strong on stories dealing with running for Congress and/or campaign financing. *www.rollcall.com*

**open seat** Seat in a legislature for which no incumbent is running for reelection.

---

### Table 8.2    Backgrounds of Congress Members

#### Occupations

Many members cite more than one occupation. Members are especially likely to cite previous public service jobs as their principal occupation. (This is especially true for Democrats.) Traditionally, lawyers predominated, and they may still do so because many lawyers prefer to claim public service as their occupation. But as far as self-identification is concerned, public service prevails. Businessmen have a slight advantage over lawyers. An increasing number of congress members are coming from education.

|                      | Total |
|----------------------|------:|
| Public service       | 254   |
| Business             | 245   |
| Law                  | 242   |
| Education            | 104   |
| Real estate          | 42    |
| Agriculture          | 34    |
| Medicine             | 20    |
| Journalism           | 18    |
| Labor/blue collar    | 12    |
| Law enforcement      | 9     |

#### Religion

Catholics have long been the single largest religious group in Congress. But all Protestants combined—Baptists, Methodists, Presbyterians, Episcopalians, Lutherans, and others—make up a solid majority. Jews comprise about 10 percent of the Congress.

| Roman Catholics   | 153 |
|-------------------|----:|
| Baptists          | 72  |
| Methodists        | 62  |
| Presbyterians     | 50  |
| Episcopalians     | 42  |
| Lutherans         | 21  |
| Jews              | 37  |
| Mormons           | 16  |
| Other religions   | 81  |

#### Top 10 Universities in Congress

It might not always seem so, especially when Congress is in gridlock or unable to address itself to important national problems, but in fact Congress members on the whole are very well educated. Indeed, the largest number of university graduates obtained their degree at prestigious Harvard University, followed by Georgetown University and Yale University. The overall Top 10 are

| Harvard University           | 39 |
|------------------------------|---:|
| Georgetown University        | 20 |
| Yale University              | 16 |
| University of Virginia       | 14 |
| Stanford University          | 13 |
| University of Michigan       | 12 |
| George Washington University | 11 |
| University of Florida        | 10 |
| University of Pittsburgh     | 10 |
| University of Texas          | 9  |

*Source: Congressional Quarterly Weekly Report, January 31, 2005.*

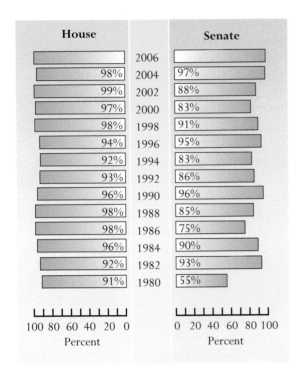

| House | | Senate |
|---|---|---|
| | 2006 | |
| 98% | 2004 | 97% |
| 99% | 2002 | 88% |
| 97% | 2000 | 83% |
| 98% | 1998 | 91% |
| 94% | 1996 | 95% |
| 92% | 1994 | 83% |
| 93% | 1992 | 86% |
| 96% | 1990 | 96% |
| 98% | 1988 | 85% |
| 98% | 1986 | 75% |
| 96% | 1984 | 90% |
| 92% | 1982 | 93% |
| 91% | 1980 | 55% |

100 80 60 40 20 0
Percent

0 20 40 60 80 100
Percent

**Figure 8.5** Incumbent Advantage

Despite periodic movements to "throw the bums out," voters in most districts and states routinely reelect their members of Congress. In recent years, more than 90 percent of representatives and 80 percent of senators who have sought reelection have been returned to Congress by votes in their districts or states.

creates many new opportunities to win election to Congress. Reapportionment creates new seats in states gaining population, just as it forces out some incumbents in states losing population. Redistricting also threatens incumbents with new constituencies, where they have less name recognition, no history of casework, and perhaps no common racial or ethnic identification. Thus forced retirements and electoral defeats are more common in the first election following each ten-year reapportionment and redistricting of Congress.

**Winning Big**   Not only do incumbent Congress members usually win, they usually also win big. Over 70 percent of House members win by margins of 60 percent or more or run unopposed. (In recent years, 10 to 18 percent of House members have had no opposition in the general election.) Senate races are somewhat more competitive. Senate challengers are usually people who have political experience and name recognition as members of the House, governors, or other high state officials. Even so, most Senate incumbents seeking reelection are victorious over their challengers. Most members of Congress, then, sit comfortably in **safe seats**—that is, they regularly win reelection by a large margin of the vote.

**safe seat** Legislative district in which the incumbent regularly wins by a large margin of the vote.

**Turnover**   Despite a high rate of reelection of incumbents in Congress, about 15 percent of members arrive new to their jobs each session. **Turnover** occurs more frequently as a result of retirement, resignation (sometimes to run for higher office), or reapportionment (and the loss of an incumbent's seat) than it does as a result of an incumbent's defeat in a bid for reelection. Roughly 10 percent of Congress members voluntarily leave office when their term expires.[20]

**turnover** Replacement of members of Congress by retirement or resignation, by reapportionment, or (more rarely) by electoral defeat, usually expressed as a percentage of members newly elected.

**Congressional Term Limits?**   Public distrust of government helped to fuel a movement in the states to limit congressional terms. Several states attempted to limit their state's House members to four two-year terms and their senators to

—Think Again—

Should members of Congress be limited in the number of terms they can serve?

two six-year terms. Proponents of congressional term limits argued that career politicians become isolated from the lives and concerns of average citizens, that they acquire an "inside the Beltway" (the circle of highways that surround Washington) mentality. They also argued that term limits would increase competition, creating "open-seat" races on a regular basis and encouraging more people to seek public office.

Opponents of congressional term limits argued that they infringe on the voters' freedom of choice. If voters are upset with the performance of their Congress members, they can limit their terms by not reelecting them. But if voters wish to keep popular and experienced legislators in office, they should be permitted to do so. Opponents also argued that inexperienced Congress members would be forced to rely more on the policy information supplied them by bureaucrats, lobbyists, and staff people—thus weakening the institution of Congress.

But the U.S. Supreme Court ruled in 1995 that the states themselves cannot limit the terms of their members of Congress. "If the qualifications set forth in the text of the Constitution are to be changed, that text must be amended."[21] In a controversial 5 to 4 decision, the Court held that the Founders intended age, citizenship, and residency to be the *only* qualifications for members of Congress.

It is not likely that the necessary two-thirds of both houses of Congress will ever vote for a constitutional amendment to limit their own stay in office. Thus, the Supreme Court's decision effectively killed the movement for congressional term limits.

**The Congressional Electorate**  Congressional elections generally fail to arouse much interest among voters. Indeed, only about 60 percent of the general public can name one U.S. senator from their state, and only about 40 percent can name both of their U.S. senators. Members of the House of Representatives fare no better: less than half of the general public can name their representative. But even constituents who know the names of their congressional delegation seldom know anything about the policy positions of these elected officials or about their votes on specific issues. Turnout in congressional *general elections* averages only about 35 percent in off-year (nonpresidential) elections. Turnout in congressional *primary elections* seldom exceeds 15 to 20 percent of persons eligible to vote. This lack of public attentiveness to congressional elections gives a great advantage to candidates with high name recognition, generally the incumbents (see *What Do You Think?* "Why Do Voters Reelect Members of an Unpopular Congress?").

**Independence of Congressional Voting**  Congressional voting is largely independent of presidential voting. The same voters who elected Republican presidents in 1968, 1972, 1980, 1984, and 1988 simultaneously elected Democratic majorities to the House of Representatives. And while reelecting Democratic President Bill Clinton in 1996, voters simultaneously reelected Republican majorities in the House and Senate. In 2000, Republicans maintained a razor-thin margin in the House, despite Gore's popular vote victory. Only in 2004 did voters elect a Republican president and *add* to Republican majorities in the House and Senate. It is unlikely that voters deliberately seek to impose *divided party government* on the nation. Rather, they cast their presidential and congressional votes on the basis of differing expectations of presidents versus members of Congress. Divided party government reappeared in Washington in 2006, when Democrats captured control of both houses of Congress, confronting Republican George Bush with a legislature from the opposing party in his final two years in the White House.[22]

# WHAT DO YOU THINK?

## Why Do Voters Reelect Members of an Unpopular Congress?

Congress is the least popular branch of government. Public approval of Congress is well below that of the presidency and the Supreme Court. What accounts for this lack of popularity? The belief that members of Congress "spend more time thinking about their own political futures than they do in passing legislation" may contribute to this sentiment.

But public disapproval of Congress may also arise from a misunderstanding of democratic government. "People do not wish to see uncertainty, conflicting options, long debate, competing interests, confusion and compromised imperfect solutions. . . . They often see a patently unrealistic form of democracy."[a]

But in an apparent paradox, most voters *approve of their own* representative (see figure below), even while Congress itself is the object of popular distrust and ridicule. A majority of voters believe that their own representatives "deserve reelection."

This apparent contradiction is explained in part by differing expectations: Americans expect Congress to deal with national issues, but they expect their own representatives to deal with local concerns and even personal problems. Members of Congress understand this concern and consequently devote a great deal of their time to constituent service. Indeed, many members of Congress try to dissociate themselves from Congress, attacking Congress in their own campaigns and contributing to negative images of the institution. Finally, the national news media are highly critical of Congress, but local news media frequently portray local members of Congress in a more favorable light.

Q. *Do you approve of the way the U.S. Congress is handling its job?"*

Q. *"Do you approve or disapprove of the way the representative from your own congressional district is handling his or her job?"*

[a]John R. Hibbing and Elizabeth Theiss-Morse, *Congress as Public Enemy* (Cambridge: Cambridge University Press, 1995), p. 147. Also cited by Roger H. Davidson and Walter J. Oleszak, *Congress and Its Members* 9th ed. (Washington, D.C.: CQ Press, 2004), p. 487.

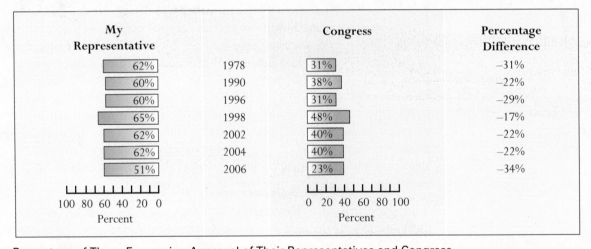

| My Representative | Year | Congress | Percentage Difference |
|---|---|---|---|
| 62% | 1978 | 31% | −31% |
| 60% | 1990 | 38% | −22% |
| 60% | 1996 | 31% | −29% |
| 65% | 1998 | 48% | −17% |
| 62% | 2002 | 40% | −22% |
| 62% | 2004 | 40% | −22% |
| 51% | 2006 | 23% | −34% |

Percentage of Those Expressing Approval of Their Representatives and Congress.

*Source:* Data from various surveys, as reported in *www.thepollingreport.com*

**Congressional Campaign Financing**    Raising the $900,000 it can take to win a House seat or the $5 to $10 million for a successful Senate campaign is a major job in and of itself (see "How Much Does It Cost to Get Elected?" in Chapter 5). Even incumbents who face little or no competition still work hard at fund-raising, "banking" contributions against some future challenger. Large campaign chests, assembled well in advance of an election, can also be used to frighten off would-be challengers. Campaign funds can be used to build a strong personal organization back home, finance picnics and other festivities for constituents, expand the margin of victory, and develop a reputation for invincibility that may someday protect against an unknown challenger.[23]

Does money buy elections? In about 90 percent of all congressional races, the candidate who spends the most money wins. However, because most winning candidates are incumbents, the money probably reflects the expected political outcome rather than shaping it. But even in open-seat races, the candidate who spends the most money usually wins.

## Party Fortunes in Congress

For forty years (1954–94) Democrats enjoyed an advantage in congressional races; in fact, the Democratic Party was said to have a "permanent majority" in the House of Representatives (see Figure 8.6). The Republican victory in the congressional election of 1994 was widely described as a political "earthquake." It gave the GOP control of the House for the first time in four decades, as well as control of the Senate. Republicans have remained in control of the House and the Senate (except for a brief period in 2001–02) through the 2004 elections.

**The Historic Democratic Party Dominance of Congress**   The historic Democratic dominance of Congress was attributed to several factors. First, over those four decades more voters identified themselves with the Democratic Party than with the Republican Party (see Chapter 7). Party identification plays a significant role in congressional voting; it is estimated that 75 percent of those who identify themselves with a party cast their vote for the congressional candidate of their party.[24] Second, the Democratic advantage was buttressed by the fact that many voters considered local rather than national conditions when casting congressional votes. Voters may have wanted to curtail *overall* federal spending in Washington (a traditional Republican promise), but they wanted a member of Congress who would "bring home the bacon." Although both Republican and Democratic congressional candidates usually promised to bring money and jobs to their districts, Democratic candidates appeared more creditable on such promises because their party generally supported large domestic-spending programs. Finally, Democratic congressional candidates over those years enjoyed the many advantages of incumbency. It was thought that only death or retirement would dislodge many of them from their seats.

**The Republican "Revolution"?**   The sweeping Republican victory in 1994—especially the party's capturing control of the House of Representatives—surprised many analysts.[25] Just two years after a Democratic president won election and Democrats won substantial majorities in both houses of Congress, the GOP gained its most complete victory in many years. How did it happen?

First of all, the Republican congressional candidates, under the leadership of Newt Gingrich, largely succeeded in *nationalizing* the midterm congressional election. That is, Republican candidates sought to exploit the voters' general skepticism about government and disenchantment with its performance. Voters were often unfamiliar with specific Republican promises, but they correctly sensed that the Republicans favored "less government."

The GOP's capture of control of both houses of Congress in 1994 for the first time in forty years raised conservatives' hopes of a "revolution" in public policy.

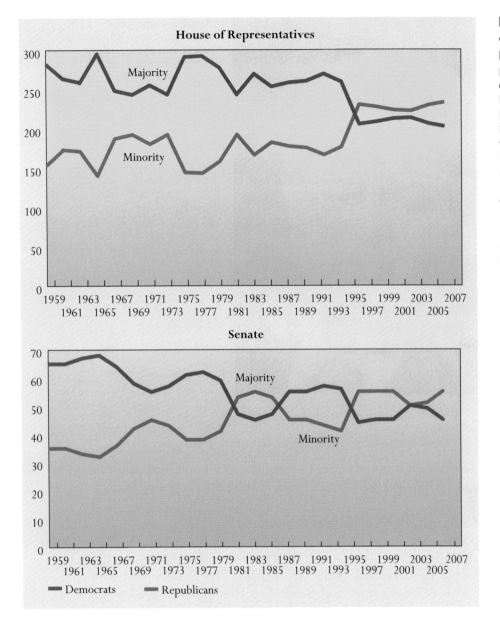

**House of Representatives**

**Senate**

■ Democrats   ■ Republicans

**Figure 8.6** Party Control of the House and Senate
Except for two very brief periods, Democrats continuously controlled both the House of Representatives and the Senate for more than forty years. The Democratic Party's "permanent" control of Congress was ended in 1994, when Republicans won majorities in both houses. Republicans retained control of Congress despite President Clinton's victory in 1996, and retained control by a slim margin in the House in 1998, 2000, and 2002. President George W. Bush's reelection victory in 2004 increased Republican margins in both the House and Senate.

The new Republican House Speaker, Newt Gingrich, was the acknowledged leader of the revolution, with Republican Senate Majority Leader Bob Dole in tow. But soon the revolution began to fizzle out. Two key Republican campaign promises failed to pass the Congress: the House failed to muster the necessary two-thirds majority for a constitutional amendment to impose congressional term limits, and the Senate failed to do so on behalf of a balanced budget amendment.

**The Democratic Revival**  Republicans succeeded in maintaining their control of Congress despite Clinton's reelection in 1996. But Democrats gained House seats in both the 1996 and 1998 congressional elections. Although the GOP retained a slim majority in the House of Representatives, the 1998 midterm election stunned Republicans. They had expected to benefit from Clinton's acknowledged sexual misconduct and the House impeachment investigation. But voters

Newt Gingrich (R-Ga.) led the Republican Party to victory in the House of Representatives in 1994 after forty years of Democratic control of that body.

generally sided with Clinton. Democrats were encouraged because historically the party controlling the White House had *lost* seats in midterm elections.

**Congress Divided**   The congressional elections of 2000 reflected the close partisan division of the nation. Republicans barely held on to their majority in the House of Representatives. The election produced a historic 50–50 tie in the Senate. Formal control of the Senate should have rested with Republicans, owing to the tie-breaking vote of Republican Vice President Dick Cheney. But in a precedent-shattering midsession shift of power, Democrats took control of the Senate in 2001, when Republican Senator Jim Jeffords from Vermont abandoned his party, declared himself an Independent, but gave his vote to the Democrats in the Senate. Other senators had defected from their party in the past, but no previous switch ever produced a change in party control. The new 51–49 Democratic majority took control of all Senate committees as well as the floor of that body.

**Bush Leads GOP to Victories in 2002 and 2004**   Traditionally, the party that had won the White House in the previous presidential election *lost* seats in the following midterm congressional election. (Indeed, since Abraham Lincoln was president, the party holding the presidency *lost* House seats in every midterm election except three—1902, 1934, and 1998.) It was theorized that presidential popularity tended to wane after two years in office, and that voters usually sought to check presidential power in the following midterm election. It was also believed that even popular presidents had little impact on midterm congressional elections; these elections were thought to be decided by the popularity of individual candidates and local district issues.

# ACROSS THE USA

## Urban, Suburban, and Rural Districts

Congressional House districts can be divided into urban, suburban, rural, and mixed, each with a distinctly Republican or Democratic tilt. Most residents of *urban districts* live in the central cities of metropolitan areas; most residents of *suburban districts* live in the metropolitan area but outside of the central city; most residents of *rural districts* live outside of metropolitan areas outside cities of more than 25,000; *mixed districts* are those in which there is no majority in any of the other categories.

**Urban Districts**

Number 90
Party (2004)
| | |
|---|---|
| Democrats | 76% |
| Republicans | 24% |

Ethnicity
| | |
|---|---|
| White | 46% |
| Black | 20% |
| Hispanic | 24% |
| Other | 10% |

**Suburban Districts**

Number 220
Party (2004)
| | |
|---|---|
| Democrats | 39% |
| Republicans | 61% |

Ethnicity
| | |
|---|---|
| White | 73% |
| Black | 10% |
| Hispanic | 11% |
| Other | 4% |

**Rural Districts**

Number 61
Party (2004)
| | |
|---|---|
| Democrats | 44% |
| Republicans | 56% |

Ethnicity
| | |
|---|---|
| White | 83% |
| Black | 9% |
| Hispanic | 4% |
| Other | 4% |

**Mixed Districts**

Number 64
Party (2004)
| | |
|---|---|
| Democrats | 44% |
| Republicans | 66% |

Ethnicity
| | |
|---|---|
| White | 76% |
| Black | 9% |
| Hispanic | 9% |
| Other | 6% |

*Source:* Derived from information in *Congressional Quarterly Weekly Report,* July 27, 2005, pp. 1714–24.

But in 2002 President George W. Bush designated himself as "Campaigner-in-Chief," traveling about the country raising campaign money and lending his popularity to Republican House and Senate candidates. His continuing high approval rating throughout the year following the "9/11" terrorist attack on America made him a highly welcomed campaigner in districts and states across the nation. In his campaign stops, Bush talked about the war on terrorism and his need for "allies" in the Congress. President Bush appeared to influence just enough voters in key districts and states to reverse the historic pattern of presidential midterm congressional losses. The GOP won back control of the U.S. Senate and strengthened its majority in the House of Representatives.

Again in 2004 President Bush appeared to help GOP congressional candidates across the country. Republicans increased their control of the Senate from 51 to 55. They picked up several seats of retiring older-generation Southern Democrats. And they even succeeded in defeating the Democratic Senate Minority Leader, Tom Daschle of South Dakota. The 2004 election also made the Senate slightly more "diverse": African American Barack Obama was elected from Illinois, and Hispanic Mel Martinez was elected from Florida. In the House, Republicans also increased their margin of control. President Bush was quick to claim that winning the White House, the Senate, and the House of Representatives meant that the American People supported his "agenda."

After twelve years of Republican majorities in the House of Representatives, Democrats captured control of that body in 2006. Some 30 seats switched from Republican to Democratic. Although this was only about seven percent of the

## UP CLOSE

# Divided Government: The 110th Congress

Divided government does not *necessarily* mean policy gridlock, yet that is often the result. The bitter partisanship that has infected Washington in recent years may prevent the Republican president and the Democratic Congress from working together to pass much significant legislation.

The substantial Democratic majority in the House of Representatives is likely to be a major stumbling block to any policy initiatives by President Bush. And the president is likely to threaten vetoes to any major new social spending program initiated by the congressional leadership.

Democratic Speaker of the House Nancy Pelosi has a reputation for strong partisan attacks on Republicans. Leadership itself may tend to moderate her rhetoric, and many of the newly elected Democratic House members won office by projecting a "moderate" image. Yet the senior Democratic leadership in both the House and the Senate are committed to a liberal agenda, and the strong liberal base of the Democratic Party will push for that agenda to be enacted.

The president is the Commander-in-Chief, and there is little that Congress can do by itself to com-

pel changes in strategy in Iraq. In theory, Congress can cut off funds for the war, but it is politically unthinkable that Congress would vote to deny funds for American troops in the field.

The policy agenda for the congressional leadership includes strengthening congressional ethics rules, increasing the minimum wage, authorizing the government to negotiate with drug companies for lower prices, and reducing interest rates on student loans. And Bush's "comprehensive"immigration reform proposal—a guest worker program with earnable citizenship for immigrants who are here now, as well as increased border enforcement—may succeed with Democratic cooperation. (It was primarily congressional opposition from the president's own party that doomed efforts at comprehensive reform in the last Congress.)

Perhaps the most contentious issue between the Democratic-controlled Congress and the Republican president is taxation. Bush's first-term tax cuts are set to expire in 2010 unless Congress makes them permanent. Republicans characterize a failure to do so as a "tax increase." Democrats call Bush's cuts "tax cuts for the rich" and oppose making them permanent.

*Bipartisanship* is a popular term in political rhetoric, but it seldom describes what actually occurs in Washington, especially with divided party government.

Democratic senator Harry Reid of Nevada, center and House Minority Leader Nancy Pelosi, center, left, are surrounded by House and Senate Democrats during an event highlighting the Democrats' approach to homeland security.

Democrat Barack Obama (D–IL) clasps hands with his grandmother, who lives in Kenya. Obama is a rapidly rising star in the Democratic party.

435-member House, it was enough to change the balance of power in Washington. In the Senate only six seats switched from Republican to Democratic, but that too was enough to change party control of that chamber.

# Life in Congress

"All politics is local," declared former House Speaker Thomas P. "Tip" O'Neill, himself once the master of both Boston ward politics and the U.S. House of Representatives. Attention to the local constituency is the key to survival and success in congressional politics. If Congress often fails to deal responsibly with national problems, the explanation lies in part with the design of the institution. House members must devote primary attention to their districts and Senate members to their states. Only *after* their constituencies are served can they turn their attention to national policy making.

**The "Representativeness" of Congress**   The Constitution requires only that members of the House of Representatives be (1) residents of the state they represent (they need not live in their congressional district, although virtually all do so); (2) U.S. citizens for at least seven years; and (3) at least twenty-five years old. Senators must also be residents of the state they represent, but they must be at least thirty years old and U.S. citizens for at least nine years.

■ *African Americans*   African Americans were first elected to Congress following the Civil War—seven black representatives and one black senator served in 1875. But with the end of Reconstruction, black membership in Congress fell to a single seat in the House from 1891 to 1955. Following the Civil Rights Act of 1964 and the Voting Rights Act of 1965, black membership in Congress rose steadily. Redistricting following the 1990 census resulted in many new "majority-minority" congressional districts. After the 1992 elections, black membership in the House rose dramatically (see Figure 8.7), with most elected from predominantly African American districts.[26] As a result, although African Americans today make up a little more than 12 percent of the U.S. population, they make up less than 9 percent of the House membership. African American, Carol Moseley Braun of Illinois served in

**Figure 8.7** Women, African Americans, and Hispanics in the House of Representatives

Although the House of Representatives is still far short of "looking like America," in recent years the number of African Americans, Hispanics, and female members has risen noticeably. Particularly impressive advances were made in the 1992 elections, following court-ordered creation of "majority–minority" districts.

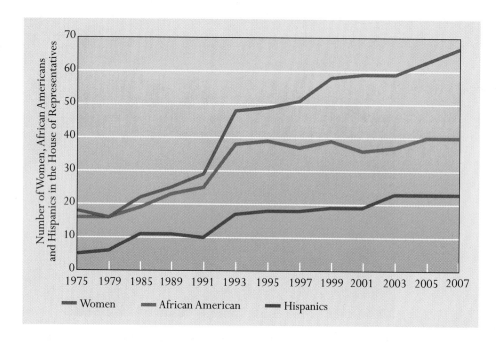

the Senate from 1993 to 1999, and Barack Obama won a Senate seat in the same state in 2004. He is currently the only African American in the U.S. Senate.

- *Hispanics* Hispanics now comprise the nation's largest minority, with slightly more than 12 percent of the U.S. population. But Hispanic representation in the Congress lags considerably behind their population growth. Currently only about 5 percent of House members are Hispanic, and just one Hispanic serves in the U.S. Senate. The Voting Rights Act of 1965 protects "language minorities" as well as racial and ethnic minorities. Prior to the 1990 census and the creation of many court-ordered "majority-minority" congressional districts, very few Hispanics served in the Congress. But with the creation of new Hispanic majority districts, Hispanic representation began to increase in the House of Representatives. Most Hispanic House members come from California, Florida, and Texas. In the 110th Congress (2007–09), 00 Hispanics served in the House; 00 were Democrats, and 00 (all from Florida) were Republicans.

- *Women* Women have made impressive gains in both the House and the Senate in the last decade. The "year of the woman" election in 1992 brought a significant increase in the number of women in the House of Representatives. Since then, women's representation in the House continued upward; fifty-nine women serve in the House in 108th Congress (2003–05), divided between thirty-eight Democrats and twenty-one Republicans. In the Senate, fourteen women serve. California is represented by two Democratic women, Dianne Feinstein and Barbara Boxer. They are joined by seven other Democratic women Senators, including former First Lady Hillary Rodham Clinton. (See *People in Politics:* "Hillary Rodham Clinton in the Senate.") Five Republican women serve in the Senate: Elizabeth Dole from North Carolina, Kay Hutchinson from Texas, Olympia Snowe and Susan Collins from Maine, and Lisa Murkowski from Alaska. Although this is the largest delegation of women ever to serve together in the U.S. Senate, it is still only 14 percent of that body. The number of women in Congress has grown as result of many factors, including strides that women have made in the workplace and other societal institutions. Yet stereotypes

## PEOPLE IN POLITICS

# Hillary Rodham Clinton in the Senate

Hillary Rodham Clinton is the first First Lady ever elected to the Congress and the first woman senator from New York. Her celebrity attracts the media wherever she goes, sometimes causing resentment among her ninety-nine other Senate colleagues, all of whom think of themselves as stars in their own right. Her initial efforts in the Senate have been directed toward establishing herself as a serious, knowledgeable, and effective legislator. And she tries particularly hard to identify herself with the interests of her adopted state, New York.

Hillary Rodham grew up in suburban Chicago, the daughter of wealthy parents who sent her to the private, prestigious Wellesley College. A 1969 honors graduate with a counterculture image—horn-rimmed glasses, long, straggling hair, no makeup—she was chosen by her classmates to give a commencement speech—a rambling statement about "more immediate, ecstatic, and penetrating modes of living."

At Yale Law School Hillary met a long-haired, bearded Rhodes scholar from Arkansas, Bill Clinton, who was just as politically ambitious as she was. Both Hillary and Bill received their law degrees in 1973. Bill returned to Arkansas to build a career in state politics, and Hillary went to Washington as an attorney—first for a liberal lobbying group, the Children's Defense Fund, and later on the staff of the House Judiciary Committee seeking to impeach President Richard Nixon. But Rodham and other Yale grads traveled to Arkansas to help Clinton run, unsuccessfully, for Congress in 1974. Hillary decided to stay with Bill in Little Rock: they married before his next campaign, a successful run for state attorney general in 1976. Hillary remained Hillary Rodham, even as her husband went on to the governorship in 1978.

Her husband's 1980 defeat for reelection as governor was blamed on his liberal leanings; therefore, in his 1982 comeback Bill repackaged himself as a moderate and centrist. Hillary cooperated by becoming Mrs. Bill Clinton, shedding her horn-rims for contacts, blonding her hair, and echoing her husband's more moderate line. These tactics helped propel them back into the governor's mansion. Hillary soon became a full partner in Little Rock's Rose law firm, regularly earning more than $200,000 a year (while Bill earned only $35,000 as Arkansas governor). She won national recognition as one of the "100 most influential lawyers in the United States," according to the *American National Law Journal.* She chaired the American Bar Association's Commission on Women and the Profession.

Hillary's steadfast support of Bill during the White House sex scandals and subsequent impeachment by the House of Representatives in all likelihood saved his presidency. Her approval ratings in public opinion polls skyrocketed during the affair. Whatever she thought in private, she never chastised her husband in public and blamed much of the scandal on "a vast right-wing conspiracy."

Her Senate race attracted national media attention as well as campaign contributions from supporters throughout the nation. When New York City's Mayor Rudolph Giuliani announced that he would *not* run for the Senate, Hillary was relieved to confront a little-known opponent, Congressman Rick Lazio. New York voters were unimpressed with charges that Hillary was not a true New Yorker. She studied New York problems diligently, and overwhelmed Lazio in the campaign. Over $85 million were spent by the candidates, making the campaign the most expensive congressional campaign in history.

Senator Clinton has developed a reputation as an advocate for children and families. Her early work with the Children's Defense Fund and Marian Wright Edelman (see *People in Politics:* "Marian Wright Edelman, Lobbying for the Poor" in Chapter 7) was carried forward in her book *It Takes a Village* in 1997. She was prominently mentioned in all of the early 2004 presidential polls, but she declined to run. She crushed her Republican opponent in her 2006 reelection to the Senate, setting the stage for a possible presidential campaign in 2008.

---

about women as politicians remain. Generally, voters view women as better able to handle "feminine" issues, such as health care, child care and education, but less able to handle "masculine" issues, including the economy and war. In the past, some women candidates tried to counter these stereotypes by emphasizing their toughness, especially on crime. But new evidence suggests that women candidates can use female stereotypes to their advantage by focusing the campaign on gender-owned issues—health, welfare, education, and other compassion issues.[27]

**Congressional Staff**   Congress is composed of a great deal more than 535 elected senators and representatives. Congressional staff and other support personnel now total some 25,000 people. Each representative has a staff of twenty or more people, usually headed by a chief of staff or administrative assistant and including legislative assistants, communications specialists, constituent-service personnel, office managers, secretaries, and aides of various sorts. Senators frequently have staffs of thirty to fifty or more people. All representatives and senators are provided with offices both in Washington and in their home districts and states. In addition, representatives receive more than $500,000 apiece for office expenses, travel, and staff; and senators receive $2 million or more, depending on the size of their state's population. Overall, Congress spends more than $2 *billion* on itself each year.

Congressional staff people exercise great influence over legislation. Many experienced "Hill rats" have worked for the same member of Congress for many years. They become very familiar with "their" member's political strengths and vulnerabilities and handle much of the member's contacts with interest groups and constituents. Staff people, more than members themselves, move the legislative process—scheduling committee hearings, writing bills and amendments, and tracking the progress of such proposals through committees and floor proceedings. By working with the staff of other members of Congress or the staff of committees and negotiating with interest-group representatives, congressional staff are often able to work out policy compromises, determine the wording of legislation, or even outline "deals" for their member's vote (all subject to later approval by their member). With multiple demands on their time, members of Congress come to depend on their staff not only for information about the content of legislation but also for political recommendations about what position to take regarding it.

**Support Agencies**   In addition to the thousands of personal and committee staff who are supposed to assist members of Congress in research and analysis, four congressional support agencies provide Congress with information:

- The Library of Congress and its Congressional Research Service (CRS) are the oldest congressional support agencies. Members of Congress can turn to the Library of Congress for references and information. The CRS responds to direct requests of members for factual information on virtually any topic. It tracks major bills in Congress and produces summaries of each bill introduced. This information is available on computer terminals in members' offices.

**Government Accountability Office**   The GAO Web site provides latest reports evaluating government programs and spending. *www.gao.gov*

- The **Government Accountability Office** (GAO) has broad authority to oversee the operations and finances of executive agencies, to evaluate their programs, and to report its findings to Congress. Established as an arm of Congress in 1921, the GAO largely confined itself to financial auditing and management studies in its early years but expanded to more than five thousand employees in the 1970s and undertook a broad agenda of policy research and evaluation. Most GAO studies and reports are requested by members of Congress and congressional committees, but the GAO also undertakes some studies on its own initiative.

- The Congressional Budget Office (CBO) was created by the Congressional Budget and Impoundment Act of 1974 to strengthen Congress's role in the budgeting process. It was designed as a congressional counterweight to the president's Office of Management and Budget (see Chapter 12). The CBO supplies the House and Senate budget committees with its own budgetary analyses and economic forecasts, sometimes challenging those found in the president's annual budget.

■ The Government Printing Office (GPO), created in 1860 as the publisher of the *Congressional Record*, now distributes over 20,000 different government publications in U.S. government bookstores throughout the nation.

**Workload** Members of Congress claim to work twelve- to fifteen-hour days: two to three hours in committee and subcommittee meetings; two to three hours on the floor of the chamber; three to four hours meeting with constituents, interest groups, other members, and staff in their offices; and two to three hours attending conferences, events, and meetings in Washington.[28] Members of Congress may introduce anywhere from ten to fifty bills in a single session of Congress. Most bills are introduced merely to exhibit the member's commitment to a particular group or issue. Cosigning a popular bill is a common practice; particularly popular bills may have 100 or 200 cosigners in the House of Representatives. Although thousands of bills are introduced, only 400 to 800 are passed in a session.[29]

**Pay and Perks** Taxpayers can relate directly to what members of Congress spend on themselves, even while millions—and even billions—of dollars spent on government programs remain relatively incomprehensible. Taxpayers thus were enraged when Congress, in a late-night session in 1991, raised its own pay from $89,500 to $129,000. Congress claimed the pay raise was a "reform," since it was coupled with a stipulation that members of Congress would no longer be allowed to accept honoraria from interest groups for their speeches and appearances, thus supposedly reducing members' dependence on outside income. Many angry taxpayers saw only a 44 percent pay raise, in the midst of a national recession, for a Congress that was doing little to remedy the nation's problems. By

**Congressional Budget Office**
The Web site of the CBO is an excellent source of data on federal finances, economic projections, and the budgetary process.
*www.cbo.gov*

Democratic House Member John Lewis is congratulated for success in passing a Voting Rights Act reauthorization bill. Lewis regularly wins his Atlanta congressional seat by large margins.

2006, automatic cost-of-living increases, also enacted by Congress, had raised members' pay to $165,200. House and Senate members receive the same pay; leaders in both houses receive $183,500 and the speaker of the House $212,000. Benefits, including retirement pay, are very generous.

As the pay-raise debate raged in Washington, several states resurrected a constitutional amendment originally proposed by James Madison. Although passed by the Congress in 1789, it had never been ratified by the necessary three-quarters of the states. The 203-year-old amendment, requiring a House election to intervene before a congressional pay raise can take effect, was added as the Twenty-seventh Amendment when ratified by four states (for a total of thirty-nine) in 1992.

## Home Style

**home style** Activities of Congress members specifically directed at their home constituencies.

**casework** Services performed by legislators or their staff on behalf of individual constituents.

**pork barreling** Legislation designed to make government benefits, including jobs and projects used as political patronage, flow to a particular district or state.

Members of Congress spend as much time politically cultivating their districts and states as they do legislating. **Home style** refers to the activities of senators and representatives in promoting their images among constituents and personally attending to constituents' problems and interests.[30] These activities include members' allocations of their personnel and staff resources to constituent services; members' personal appearances in the home district or state to demonstrate personal attention; and members' efforts to explain their Washington activities to the voters back home.

**Casework** Casework is really a form of "retail" politics. Members of Congress can win votes one at a time by helping constituents on a personal level. Casework can involve everything from tracing lost Social Security checks and Medicare claims to providing information about federal programs, solving problems with the Internal Revenue Service, and assisting with federal job applications. Over time, grateful voters accumulate, giving incumbents an advantage at election time. Congressional staff do much of the actual casework, but letters go out over the signature of the member of Congress. Senators and representatives blame the growth of government for increasing casework, but it is also clear that members solicit casework, frequently reminding constituents to bring their problems to their member of Congress.[31]

**Pork Barrel** Pork barreling describes the efforts of senators and representatives to "bring home the bacon"—to bring federally funded projects, grants, and contracts that primarily benefit a single district or state to their home constituencies. Opportunities for pork barreling have never been greater: roads, dams, parks, and post offices are now overshadowed by redevelopment grants to city governments, research grants to universities, weapons contracts to local plants, "demonstration" projects of all kinds, and myriad other "goodies" tucked inside each year's annual appropriations bills. Members of Congress understand the importance of supporting each other's pork barrel projects, cooperating in the "incumbent-protection society." Even though pork barreling adds to the public's negative image of Congress as an institution, individual members gain local popularity for the benefits they bring to home districts and states.

**Pressing the Flesh** Senators and representatives spend a great deal of time in their home states and districts. Although congressional sessions last virtually all year, members of Congress find ways to spend more than a hundred days per year at home.[32] It is important to be seen at home—giving speeches and attending dinners, fund-raising events, civic occasions, and so on. To accommodate this aspect of home style, Congress usually follows a Tuesday-to-Thursday schedule of legislative business, allowing members to spend longer weekends in their home districts. Congress also enjoys long recesses during the late summer and over holidays.

**Puffing Images**   To promote their images back home, members make generous use of their **franking privilege** (free mailing) to send their constituents newsletters, questionnaires, biographical material, and information about federal programs. Newsletters "puff" the accomplishments of the members; questionnaires are designed more to flatter voters than to assess opinions; and informational brochures tout federal services members claim credit for providing and defending. Congress's penchant for self-promotion has also kept pace with the media and electronic ages. Congress now provides its members with television studios and support for making videotapes to send to local stations in home districts, and all members maintain Web sites on the Internet designed to puff their images.

**franking privilege**   Free mail service afforded members of Congress.

**Hill Styles and Home Styles**   Members of Congress spend their lives "moving between two contexts, Washington and home, and between two activities, governing and campaigning."[33] They must regularly ask themselves how much time they should spend at home with their constituents versus how much time they should spend on lawmaking assignments in Washington. It is no surprise that freshman legislators spend more time in their districts; indeed, very few first-termers move their families to Washington. Long-term incumbents spend more time in Washington, but all Congress members spend more time at home in an election year.

Much of the time spent at home—with small groups of constituents, among contributors, in public speeches, and appearances on radio and television—is devoted to explaining issues and justifying the member's vote on them. "Often members defend their own voting record by belittling Congress—portraying themselves as knights errant battling sinister forces and feckless colleagues."[34]

**www Congressional Quarterly (CQ)**
The *Congressional Quarterly Weekly Report* provides the most comprehensive coverage of events in Congress, including key issues, House and Senate roll call votes, backgrounds of members, and political and election information. The CQ Press is a major publisher of books on politics and government. *www.cq.com*

# Organizing Congress: Party and Leadership

Congress is composed of people who think of themselves as leaders, not followers. They got elected without much help from their party. Yet they realize that their chances of attaining their personal goals—getting reelected and influencing policy—are enhanced if they cooperate with each other.

**Party Organizations in Congress**   The Democratic and Republican party organizations within the House of Representatives and the Senate are the principal bases for organizing Congress (see Figure 8.8). The leadership of each house of Congress, although nominally elected by the entire chamber, is actually chosen by secret ballot of the members of each party at a "conference" or caucus (see Table 8.3).

The parties and their leaders do not choose congressional candidates, nor can they deny them renomination; all members of Congress are responsible for their own primary and general election success. But party leadership in each chamber can help incumbents achieve their reelection goals. Each party in the House and Senate sponsors a campaign committee that channels some campaign funding to party members seeking reelection, although these Republican and Democratic congressional and senatorial campaign committees contribute less money than either PACs or individuals to the candidates.[35] Rather, good relations between

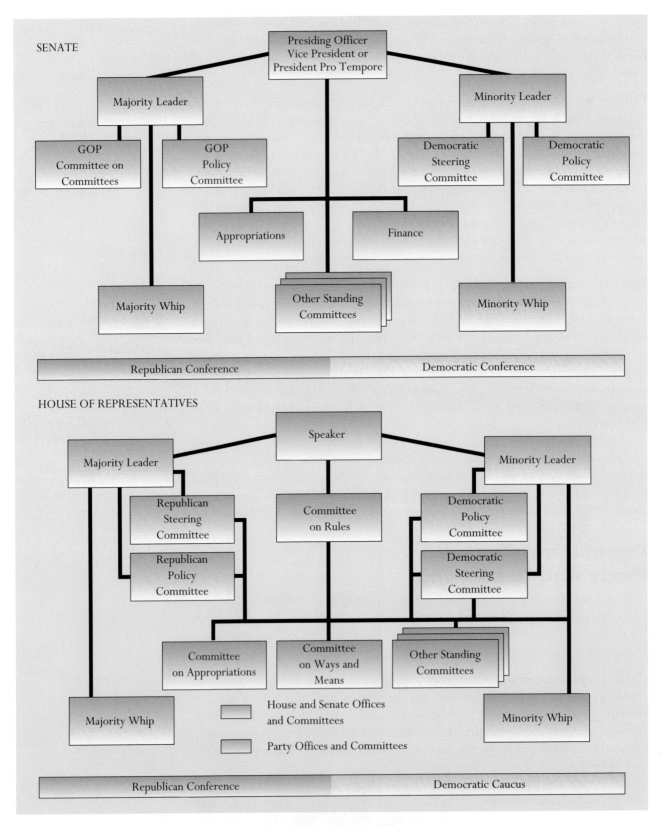

**Figure 8.8** The Organization of Congress

Aside from naming the Speaker of the House as head of that body's operations and the vice president as overseer of Senate deliberations, the Constitution is silent on the organization of Congress. Political parties have filled this gap: both majority and minority parties have their own leadership, which governs the appointment of members to the various committees, where much of the work of Congress actually takes place.

**Table 8.3  Leadership in Congress**

| | **Senate** |
|---|---|
| President Pro Tempore | An honorary post, usually the senior member of the majority party |
| Majority Leader | Top Senate post, elected by majority party members |
| Majority Whip | Second-ranking post in the majority party |
| Minority Leader | Leader of the minority opposition party |
| Minority Whip | Second-ranking post in the minority party |
| | **House** |
| Speaker | Powerful presiding officer, elected with the votes of the majority party |
| Majority Leader | Officially the leader of the majority party but second in power to the Speaker |
| Majority Whip | Third-ranking leader of the majority party |
| Minority Leader | Top post in the minority party |
| Minority Whip | Second-ranking post in the minority party |

members and their party's leadership are more important in the quest for power and influence in Washington.

Majority status confers great power on the party that controls the House and the Senate. The majority party chooses the leadership in each body, selects the chairs of every committee, and ensures that every committee has a majority of members from the majority party. In other words, if Republicans are in the majority in either the House or the Senate or both, Republicans will occupy all leadership positions, chair every committee, and constitute a majority of the members of every committee, and, of course, the Democrats enjoy the same advantages when they capture a majority of either body. Majority-party members in each house even take in more campaign contributions than minority members.[36]

**In the House: "Mr. Speaker"**   In the House of Representatives, the key leadership figure is the **Speaker of the House**, who serves as both presiding officer of the chamber and leader of the majority party. In the House, the Speaker has many powers. The Speaker decides who shall be recognized to speak on the floor and rules on points of order (with advice from the parliamentarian), including whether a motion or amendment is germane (relevant) to the business at hand. The Speaker decides to which committees new bills will be assigned and can schedule or delay votes on a bill. The Speaker appoints members of select, special, and conference committees and names majority-party members to the Rules Committee. And the Speaker controls both patronage jobs and office space in the Capitol. Although the norm of fairness requires the Speaker to apply the rules of the House consistently, the Speaker is elected by the majority party and is expected to favor that party.

Over the years, different Speakers have displayed different leadership styles. Republican Speaker Newt Gingrich was an ideological leader with a dramatic and aggressive agenda—a "Contract with America"—who contributed to partisan rancor in the House. In contrast, Republican Speaker Dennis Hastert has been a pragmatic leader who deals with his colleagues in an accommodating fashion.[37]

**Speaker of the House**
Presiding officer of the House of Representatives.

Republican Speaker of the House Dennis Hastert leads the Republican majority.

**majority leader** In the House, the majority-party leader and second in command to the Speaker; in the Senate, the leader of the majority party.

**minority leader** In both the House and Senate, the leader of the opposition party.

**whips** In both the House and Senate, the principal assistants to the party leaders and next in command to those leaders.

**House Leaders and Whips** The Speaker's principal assistant is the **majority leader**. The majority leader formulates the party's legislative program in consultation with other party leaders and steers the program through the House. The majority leader also must persuade committee leaders to support the aims of party leaders in acting on legislation before their committees. Finally, the majority leader arranges the legislative schedule with the cooperation of key party members.

The minority party in the House selects a **minority leader** whose duties correspond to those of the majority leader, except that the minority leader has no authority over the scheduling of legislation. The minority leader's principal duty has been to organize the forces of the minority party to counter the legislative program of the majority and to pass the minority party's bills. It is also the minority leader's duty to consult ranking minority members of House committees and to encourage them to adopt party positions and to follow the lead of the president if the minority party controls the White House (see *People in Politics:* "Nancy Pelosi, Leading House Democrats)".

In both parties, **whips** assist leaders in keeping track of the whereabouts of party members and in pressuring them to vote the party line. Whips are also responsible for ensuring the attendance of party members at important roll calls and for canvassing their colleagues on their likely support for or opposition to party-formulated legislation. Finally, whips are involved regularly in the formation of party policy and the scheduling of legislation.

**In the Senate: "Mr. President"** The Constitution declares the vice president of the United States to be the presiding officer of the Senate. But vice presidents seldom exercise this senatorial responsibility, largely because the presiding officer of the Senate has very little power. Having only 100 members, the Senate usually does not restrict debate and has fewer scheduling constraints than the House. The only significant power of the vice president is the right to cast a deciding vote in the event of a tie on a Senate roll call. In the usual absence of the vice president, the Senate is presided over by a *president pro tempore.* This honorific position is traditionally granted by the majority party to one of its senior stalwarts. The job of presiding over the Senate is so boring that neither the vice president nor the president pro tempore is found very often in the chamber. Junior senators are often asked to assume the chore. Nevertheless, speeches on

## PEOPLE IN POLITICS

### Nancy Pelosi, Leading House Democrats

Nancy Pelosi is the first woman in the history of the U.S. Congress to lead a major party. In 2001 her Democratic colleagues elected her Minority Leader, the highest-ranking leadership position among Democratic members. Pelosi has represented her San Francisco district since her first election to the Congress in 1986.

Congresswoman Pelosi comes from a highly political family. Her father, Thomas D'Alesandro, served five terms in Congress and later 12 years as mayor of Baltimore. Pelosi's brother also served as mayor of Baltimore. Young Nancy grew up in Washington and graduated from that city's Trinity College in 1962. She served as a congressional intern to her Maryland senator. She married Paul Pelosi, moved to his hometown of San Francisco, and raised five children. Prior to her election to Congress, she served on the National Democratic Committee.

In her years in Congress, Pelosi built a solid liberal reputation, serving on the powerful Appropriations Committee. She won the post as Democratic whip in 2001 in a close election against a more moderate Democrat. But Pelosi's real strength within the Democratic Party has long been her fund-raising ability. Her San Francisco district is the home of some of the party's wealthiest individual donors, and Democrats across the nation rely heavily upon money from California. Pelosi created her own leadership PAC and handed out over $1 million to her Democratic colleagues in 2000. She spends relatively little (about $400,000) on her own reelection races in her heavily Democratic district.

In 2002, Pelosi was reelected with an astonishing 80 percent of the vote in her California district. She has continued to win by 80 percent or more of the vote through 2006.

the Senate floor begin with the salutation "Mr. President," referring to the president of the Senate, *not* the president of the United States.

**Senate Majority and Minority Leaders**    Senate leadership is actually in the hands of the Senate majority leader, but the Senate majority leader is not as powerful in that body as the Speaker is in the House. With fewer members, all of whom perceive themselves as powerful leaders, the Senate is less hierarchically organized than the House. The Senate majority leader's principal power is scheduling the business of the Senate and recognizing the first speaker in floor debate. To be effective in policy making, the majority leader must be skilled in interpersonal persuasion and communication. Moreover, in the media age, the Senate majority leader must also be a national spokesperson for the party, along with the Speaker of the House. Republican Senate Leader Bill Frist and Republican Speaker of the House Dennis Hastert are their party's leading congressional spokesmen. The minority-party leader in the Senate represents the opposition in negotiations with the majority leader over Senate business. With the majority leader, the minority-party leader tends to dominate floor debate in the Senate.

**Career Paths within Congress**    Movement up the party hierarchy in each house is the most common way of achieving a leadership position. The traditional succession pattern in the House is from whip to majority leader to Speaker. In the Senate, Republicans and Democrats frequently resort to election contests in choosing their party leaders, yet both parties have increasingly adopted a two-step succession route from whip to leader.[38]

**Leadership PACs**    House and Senate leaders, and members who aspire to become leaders, often ingratiate themselves to their colleagues by distributing campaign funds to them. In recent years, *leadership PACs* have proliferated on Capitol Hill.

# In Committee

**Library of Congress**
The Thomas system allows the tracing of bills from their introduction, through the committee system, floor schedule vote, and so on. *http://thomas.loc.gov*

Much of the real work of Congress is done in committee. The floor of Congress is often deserted; C-SPAN focuses on the podium, not the empty chamber. Members dash to the floor when the bell rings throughout the Capitol signaling a roll-call vote. Otherwise they are found in their offices or in the committee rooms, where the real work of Congress is done.

**Standing Committees** The committee system provides for a division of labor in the Congress, assigning responsibility for work and allowing members to develop some expertise (see Table 8.4). The committee system is as old as the Congress itself: the very first Congress regularly assigned the task of wording bills to selected members who were believed to have a particular expertise. Soon a system of **standing committees**—permanent committees that specialize in a particular area of legislation—emerged. House committees have forty to sixty or more members and Senate committees fifteen to twenty-five members each. The proportions of Democrats and Republicans on each committee reflect the proportions of Democrats and Republicans in the House and Senate as a whole. Thus the majority party has a majority of members on every committee; and every committee is chaired by a member of the majority party. The minority membership on each committee is led by the **ranking minority member**, the minority-party committee member with the most seniority.

**standing committee**
Permanent committee of the House or Senate that deals with matters within a specified subject area.

**ranking minority member**
The minority-party committee member with the most seniority.

The principal function of standing committees is the screening and drafting of legislation. With 8,000 to 10,000 or more bills introduced each session, the screening function is essential. The standing committees are the gatekeepers of Congress; less than 10 percent of the legislation introduced will pass the Congress. With rare exceptions, bills are not submitted to a vote by the full membership of the House or Senate without prior approval by the majority of a standing committee. Moreover, committees do not merely sort through bills assigned to them to find

Congressional committee hearings provide an opportunity for members of Congress to gather information and at the same time promote their own images. Celebrity witnesses increase media coverage. Shown here testifying at a House committee hearing on steroid use in sports are baseball stars Curt Schilling, Rafael Palmeiro, Mark McGwire, and Sammy Sosa.

what they like. Rather, committees—or more often their subcommittees—draft (write) legislation themselves. Committees may amend, rewrite, or write their own bills. Committees are "little legislatures" within their own policy jurisdictions. Each committee guards its own policy jurisdiction jealously; jurisdictional squabbles between committees are common.

**The Pecking Order of Committees**    The most powerful standing committees, and, therefore, the most sought-after committee assignments, are the Appropriations Committees in the House and the Senate. These committees hold the federal purse strings, arguably Congress's most important power. These committees are closely followed in influence and desirability by the Ways and Means Committee in the House and the Senate Finance Committee; these committees must pass on all tax matters, as well as Social Security and Medicare financing. In the House, the Rules Committee is especially powerful, owing to its control over floor consideration of every bill submitted to the full House. The Senate Judiciary Committee is especially influential because of its influence over all presidential nominees to the federal judiciary, including Supreme Court justices. The Senate Foreign Relations Committee is also a highly valued assignment. Perhaps the *least* desirable committee assignments are those on the Senate Ethics Committee and the House Standards of Official Conduct Committee; these ethics panels are obliged to sit in judgment of their own colleagues.

**Decentralization and Subcommittees**    Congressional **subcommittees** within each standing committee further decentralize the legislative process. At present, the House has about 90 subcommittees and the Senate about 70 subcommittees, each of which functions independently of its full committee (see Table 8.4). Subcommittees have fixed jurisdictions (for example, the House International Relations Committee has subcommittees on Africa, Asia and the Pacific, International Economic Policy, International Operations and Human Rights, and the Western Hemisphere); they meet and schedule their own hearings; and they have their own staffs and budgets. However, bills recommended by a subcommittee still require full standing-committee endorsement before being reported to the floor of the House or Senate. Full committees usually, but not always, ratify the decisions of their subcommittees.

Chairing a committee or subcommittee gives members of Congress the opportunity to exercise power, attract media attention, and thus improve their chances of reelection. Often committees have become "fiefdoms" over which their chairs exercise complete control and jealously guard their power. This situation allows a very small number of House and Senate members to block legislation. Many decisions are not really made by the whole Congress. Rather, they are made by subcommittee members with a special interest in the policy under consideration. Although the committee system may satisfy the desire of members to gain power, prestige, and reelection opportunities, it weakens responsible government in the Congress as a whole.

**Committee Membership**    Given the power of the committee system, it is not surprising that members of Congress have a very keen interest in their committee assignments. Members strive for assignments that will give them influence in Congress, allow them to exercise power in Washington, and ultimately improve their chances for reelection. For example, a member from a big city may seek a seat on Banking, Housing, and Urban Affairs, a member from a farm district may seek a seat on Agriculture, and a member from a district with a large military base may seek a seat on National Security or Veterans Affairs. Everyone seeks a seat

**subcommittees** Specialized committees within standing committees; subcommittee recommendations must be approved by the full standing committee before submission to the floor.

**Table 8.4    Committees in Congress**

**Senate**

| | |
|---|---|
| Agriculture, Nutrition, and Forestry | Health, Education, Labor and Pensions |
| Appropriations | Homeland Security and |
| Armed Services | Environmental Affairs |
| Banking, Housing, and Urban Affairs | Judiciary |
| Budget | Rules and Administration |
| Commerce, Science, and | Small Business and |
| Transportation | Entrepreneurship |
| Energy and Natural Resources | Select Aging |
| Environment and Public Works | Select Ethics |
| Finance | Select Indian |
| Foreign Relations | Select Intelligence |
| | Veterans Affairs |

**House**

| | |
|---|---|
| Agriculture | Judiciary |
| Appropriations | Resources |
| Armed Forces | Rules |
| Budget | Science |
| Energy and Commerce | Small Business |
| Education and the Workforce | Standards of Official Conduct |
| Financial Services | Transportation and Infrastructure |
| Government Reform | Veterans Affairs |
| Homeland Security | Ways and Means |
| House Administration | Select Intelligence |
| International Relations | |

**Joint Committees**

Joint Economic Committee
Joint Taxation
Joint Committee on Printing
Joint Committee on the Library

on Appropriations, because both the House and the Senate Appropriations committees have subcommittees in each area of federal spending.[39]

Party leadership in both the House and the Senate largely determines committee assignments. These assignments are given to new Democratic House members by the Democratic Steering and Policy Committee; new Democratic senators receive their assignments from the Senate Democratic Steering Committee. New Republican members receive their committee assignments from the Republican Committee on Committees in both houses. The leadership generally tries to honor new members' requests and improve their chances for reelection, but because incumbent members of committees are seldom removed, openings on powerful committees are infrequent.

**Seniority**    Committee chairs are elected in the majority-party caucus. But the **seniority system** governs most movement into committee leadership positions. The seniority system ranks all committee members in each party according to the length of time they have served on the committee. If the majority-party chair exits the Congress or leaves the committee, that position is filled by the next *ranking majority-party member.* New members of a committee are initially added to the bottom of the ranking of their party; they climb the seniority ranking by remaining on the committee and accruing years of seniority. Members who stay

**seniority system** Custom whereby the member of Congress who has served the longest on the majority side of a committee becomes its chair and the member who has served the longest on the minority side becomes its ranking member.

in Congress but "hop" committees are usually placed at the bottom of their new committee's list.

The seniority system has a long tradition in the Congress. The advantage is that it tends to reduce conflict among members, who otherwise would be constantly engaged in running for committee posts. It also increases the stability of policy direction in committees over time. Critics of the system note, though, that the seniority system grants greater power to members from "safe" districts— districts that offer little electoral challenge to the incumbent. (Historically in the Democratic Party, these districts were in the conservative South, and opposition to the seniority system developed among liberal northern Democrats. But in recent years, many liberal Democrats gained seniority and the seniority system again became entrenched (see People in Politics: "'Ted' Kennedy, Keeping Liberalism Alive in the U.S. Senate"). The seniority rule for selecting committee chairs has been violated on only a few notable occasions.

**Committee Hearings**    The decision of a congressional committee to hold public hearings on a bill or topic is an important one. It signals congressional interest in a particular policy matter and sets the agenda for congressional policy making. Ignoring an issue by refusing to hold hearings on it usually condemns it to oblivion. Public hearings allow interest groups and government bureaucrats to present formal arguments to Congress. Testimony comes mostly from government officials, lobbyists, and occasional experts recommended by interest groups or committee staff members. Hearings are usually organized by the staff under the direction of the chair. Staff members contact favored lobbyists and bureaucrats and schedule their appearances. Committee hearings are regularly listed in the *Washington Post* and are open to the public. Indeed, the purpose of many hearings is not really to inform members of Congress but instead to rally public support behind an issue or a bill. The media are the real target audience of many public hearings, with committee members jockeying in front of the cameras for a "sound bite" on the evening news.

**Markup**    Once hearings are completed the committee's staff is usually assigned the task of writing a report and **drafting a bill**. The staff's bill generally reflects

**drafting a bill** Actual writing of a bill in legal language.

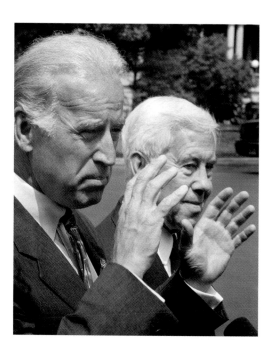

Senator Joe Biden (left), of the Senate Foreign Relations Committee, speaks to reporters after meeting with President Bush about the arms treaty with Russia.

## PEOPLE IN POLITICS

### Ted Kennedy: Keeping Liberalism Alive in the U.S. Senate

To the American public, Massachusetts Senator, Edward M. "Ted" Kennedy is largely a symbol of his family's legendary triumphs and tragedies. But in the U.S. Senate, Kennedy has established himself over the years as the recognized leader of liberal Democrats and a highly effective legislator.

Ted Kennedy's father, Joseph P. Kennedy, was a wealthy banker and stock market manipulator who provided key financial backing for the 1932 presidential campaign of Franklin D. Roosevelt. FDR later appointed "Old Joe" as ambassador to England. The senior Kennedy fathered nine children, including Joseph P. Jr., who was killed in World War II; President John F. Kennedy, who was assassinated in 1963; Senator Robert F. Kennedy, who was assassinated in 1968; and the youngest, Edward M. "Ted" Kennedy.

Although born to great wealth (he received his first communion from the Pope), Ted Kennedy acquired the sense of competition fostered in the large Kennedy household. In 1951, suspended from Harvard for cheating on an examination, he joined the Army and served two years in Germany. He was later readmitted to Harvard from which he graduated in 1956. Rejected by Harvard Law School, he enrolled instead in the University of Virginia Law School and completed his law degree in 1959. When he was just 30 years old, the minimum age for a U.S. senator, he announced his candidacy for the Massa-

chusetts Senate seat formerly held by his brother, who was then president. His 1962 election to the U.S. Senate reflected the esteem that Massachusetts voters have always held for his family.

But Ted's personal life was marred by accident, tragedy, and scandal. He nearly died in a 1964 plane crash in which he suffered a broken back. He was frequently the object of romantic gossip in Washington. In 1969, a young woman died when the car Kennedy was driving plunged off a narrow bridge on Chappaquiddick Island after a late-night party. Missing for ten hours after the accident, Kennedy later made a dramatic national television appearance claiming that the tragedy had been an accident that he had been too confused to report until the next day. He pled guilty to the minor charge of leaving the scene of the accident. Senate Democrats removed Kennedy from his position as majority party whip.

Kennedy deliberately avoided Democratic presidential battles in both 1972 and 1976, believing that the public's memory of Chappaquiddick was still too fresh. However, in late 1979, with President Jimmy Carter standing at a near all-time low for presidents in opinion polls, Kennedy announced his presidential candidacy. But shortly thereafter, Soviet troops invaded neighboring Afghanistan. Support for the president was equated with support for America, and Carter benefited from this "rally round the flag" effect. Carter defeated Kennedy in the Democratic primaries.

As the ranking Democrat on the Senate Health, Education, and Labor Committee, Kennedy has undertaken the lead in a variety of important legislative issues. He helped pass the Family Leave Act of 1993, the Kennedy-Kassebaum Act of 1996 that mandated health insurance "portability" (see Chapter 13), and increases in the minimum wage. In 2000 he was elected to his seventh full term as U.S. senator from Massachusetts with fully 70 percent of the vote.

**markup** Line-by-line revision of a bill in committee by editing each phrase and word.

the chair's policy views. But the staff draft is subject to committee **markup**, a line-by-line consideration of the wording of the bill. Markup sessions are frequently closed to the public in order to expedite work. Lobbyists are forced to stand in the hallways, buttonholing members as they go into and out of committee rooms.

It is in markup that the detailed work of lawmaking takes place. Markup sessions require patience and skill in negotiation. Committee or subcommittee chairs may try to develop consensus on various parts of the bill, either within the whole committee or within the committee's majority. In marking up a bill, members of a subcommittee must always remember that the bill must pass both in the full committee and on the floor of the chamber. Although they have considerable freedom

Seniority is a valuable resource in the U.S. Senate. Senators Ted Kennedy (D-MA) and Robert Byrd (D-WV) together have served over eighty years in the Senate.

in writing their own policy preferences into law, especially on the details of the legislation, they must give some consideration to the views of these larger bodies. Consultations with party leadership are not infrequent.

Most bills die in committee. Some are voted down, but most are simply ignored. Bills introduced simply to reassure constituents or interest groups that a representative is committed to "doing something" for them generally die quietly. But House members who really want action on a bill can be frustrated by committee inaction. The only way to force a floor vote on a bill opposed by a committee is to get a majority (218) of House members to sign a **discharge petition**. Out of hundreds of discharge petition efforts, only a few dozen have succeeded. The Senate also can forcibly "discharge" a bill from committee by simple majority vote; but because senators can attach any amendment to any bill they wish, there is generally no need to go this route.

**discharge petition** Petition signed by at least 218 House members to force a vote on a bill within a committee that opposes it.

## On the Floor

A favorable "report" by a standing committee of the House or Senate places a bill on the "calendar." The word *calendar* is misleading, because bills on the calendar are not considered in chronological order and many die on the calendar without ever reaching the floor.

**House Rules Committee**  Even after a bill has been approved by a standing committee, getting it to the floor of the House of Representatives for a vote by the full membership requires favorable action by the Rules Committee. The Rules Committee acts as a powerful "traffic cop" for the House. In order to reach the floor, a bill must receive a rule from the Rules Committee. The Rules Committee can kill a bill simply by refusing to give it a rule. A **rule** determines when the bill will be considered by the House and how long the debate on the bill will last. More important, a rule determines whether amendments from the floor will be

**rule** Stipulation attached to a bill in the House of Representatives that governs its consideration on the floor, including when and for how long it can be debated and how many (if any) amendments may be appended to it.

**closed rule** Rule that forbids adding any amendments to a bill under consideration by the House.

**restricted rule** Rule that allows specified amendments to be added to a bill under consideration by the House.

**open rule** Rule that permits unlimited amendments to a bill under consideration by the House.

**unanimous consent agreement** Negotiated by the majority and minority leaders of the Senate, it specifies when a bill will be taken up on the floor, what amendments will be considered, and when a vote will be taken.

**filibuster** Delaying tactic by a senator or group of senators, using the Senate's unlimited debate rule to prevent a vote on a bill.

**cloture** Vote to end debate—that is, to end a filibuster—which requires a three-fifths vote of the entire membership of the Senate.

**rider** Amendment to a bill that is not germane to the bill's purposes.

permitted and, if so, how many. A **closed rule** forbids House members from offering any amendments and speeds up consideration of the bill in the form submitted by the standing committee. A **restricted rule** allows certain specified amendments to be considered. An **open rule** permits unlimited amendments. Most key bills are brought to the floor of the House with fairly restrictive rules. In recent sessions, about three-quarters of all bills reaching the floor were restricted, and an additional 10 to 15 percent were fully closed. Only a few bills were open.

**Senate Floor Traditions** The Senate has no rules committee but relies instead on a **unanimous consent agreement** negotiated between the majority and minority leader to govern consideration of a bill. The unanimous consent agreement generally specifies when the bill will be debated, what amendments will be considered, and when the final vote will be taken. But as the name implies, a single senator can object to a unanimous consent agreement and thus hold up Senate consideration of a bill. Senators do not usually do so, because they know that a reputation for obstructionism will imperil their own favorite bills at a later date. Once accepted, a unanimous consent agreement is binding on the Senate and cannot be changed without another unanimous consent agreement. To get unanimous consent, Senate leaders must consult with all interested senators. Unanimous consent agreements have become more common in recent years as they have become more specific in their provisions.

The Senate cherishes its tradition of unrestricted floor debate. Senators may speak as long as they wish or even try to **filibuster** a bill to death by talking nonstop and tying up the Senate for so long that the leadership is forced to drop the bill in order to go on to other work. Senate rules also allow senators to place a "hold" on a bill, indicating their unwillingness to grant unanimous consent to its consideration. Debate may be ended only if *sixty* or more senators vote for **cloture**, a process of petition and voting that limits the debate. A cloture vote requires a petition signed by sixteen senators; two days must elapse between the petition's introduction and the cloture vote. If cloture passes, then each senator is limited to one hour of debate on the bill. But getting the necessary sixty votes for cloture is difficult. Recently Democrats, although a minority in the Senate, have defeated cloture motions in order to derail President Bush's nominees for federal judgeships (see *What Do You Think?* "Should Presidential Appointments of Judges, Including Supreme Court Justices, Be Thwarted by Senate Filibusters?").

Senate floor procedures also permit unlimited amendments to be offered, even those that are not germane to the bill. A **rider** is an amendment to a bill that is not germane to the bill's purposes.

These Senate traditions of unlimited debate and unrestricted floor amendments give individual senators considerably more power over legislation than individual representatives enjoy.

**Floor Voting** The key floor votes are usually on *amendments* to bills rather than on their final passage. Indeed, "killer amendments" are deliberately designed to defeat the original purpose of the bill. Other amendments may water down the bill so much that it will have little policy impact. Thus the true policy preferences of senators or representatives may be reflected more in their votes on amendments than their vote on final passage. Members may later claim to have supported legislation on the basis of their vote on final passage, even though they earlier voted for amendments designed to defeat the bill's purposes.

# WHAT DO YOU THINK?

## Should Presidential Appointments of Judges, Including Supreme Court Justices, Be Thwarted by Senate Filibusters?

The Constitution gives a president the power to make judicial appointments, including appointments to the Supreme Court, "by and with the Advice and Consent of the Senate." The Constitution requires only a majority vote of the Senate to consent to the president's appointment.

But from the earliest days of the Senate the idea of "unlimited debate" was enshrined in Senate rules and customs. For over a century, the "filibuster" was honored as "insurance against the will of a majority of states being imposed over the wishes of a minority of states." Over the years, liberals and progressives in the Senate came to loathe the filibuster rule. President Woodrow Wilson (formerly a political science professor at Princeton University and author of a book on Congress) persuaded the Senate to adopt a "cloture rule" (see p. 352 in this chapter) which called for cutting off debate with a two-thirds vote of Senators president and voting. For decades afterward, liberals sought to completely eliminate the filibuster, as it became an important tool of opponents of civil rights legislation. (The Civil Right Act of 1964 was passed only after a successful cloture vote ended a Southern filibuster.) In 1975 the Senate lowered the vote requirement for cloture to sixty, that is, three-fifths rather than two-thirds.

By the 1990s filibusters became more common as partisanship in the Senate began to rise. Democrats and Republicans both regularly threatened filibusters to stop legislation they opposed. This meant that controversial bills could not get through the Senate without sixty votes, rather than a simple majority of fifty-one.

Senate Democrats began to use the filibuster to thwart judicial nominees submitted by Republican President George W. Bush. Republican Senate Majority Leader Bill Frist argued that such a use violated the Constitution, which requires only a majority vote for judicial confirmations. Several key appeals court nominations were held up by Democrats threatening filibusters. Republicans had only fifty-five members in the Senate, not the sixty needed to end debate. So in 2005 Frist threatened "the nuclear option"—having the presiding officer of the Senate, Republican Vice President Richard Cheney, declare the filibuster rule for judicial nominations to be unconstitutional. This

*Senate filibusters can be ended only by persuasion or by a three-fifths vote (60 members). Inasmuch as at least one filibustering member must remain continuously on the floor of the Senate, beds are often prepared in Senate offices for periodic alternating-member breaks.*

ruling would then be upheld by a simple majority vote of the Senate.

But a temporary truce was fashioned in which several Bush judicial appointments were confirmed and the filibuster rule was undisturbed. Senators promised to use it only under "extraordinary circumstances," a phrase left undefined. Republicans promised not to use the nuclear option unless the Democrats fail to abide by the agreement.

Generally, Americans appear to support the filibuster, even against judicial nominees:

*Q.* "*As you know there are 100 senators. How many senators' votes should it take to move ahead to confirm a Supreme Court nominee? Should a majority of 51 votes be required, or is this something that should require a larger majority of 60 votes?*

| 51 votes | 60 votes | Unsure |
|----------|----------|--------|
| 31% | 64% | 5% |

*Q.* "*How do you feel about this issue? Do you favor or oppose changing the rules of the Senate to stop the use of filibusters against judicial nominees?*"

| Favor | Oppose | Unsure |
|-------|--------|--------|
| 28% | 37% | 35% |

*Source:* Pew Research Center for the People and the Press, May 15, 2005.

**roll-call vote** Vote of the full House or Senate at which all members' individual votes are recorded and made public.

Members may also obscure their voting records by calling for a voice vote—simply shouting "aye" or "nay"—and avoiding recording of their individual votes. In contrast, a **roll-call vote** involves the casting of individual votes, which are reported in the *Congressional Record* and are available to the media and the general public. Electronic voting machines in the House allow members to insert their cards and record their votes automatically. The Senate, truer to tradition, uses no electronic counters.

**Conference Committees** The Constitution requires that both houses of Congress pass a bill with identical wording. However, many major bills pass each house in different forms, not only with different wording but sometimes with wholly different provisions. Occasionally the House or the Senate will resolve these differences by reconsidering the matter and passing the other chamber's version of the bill. But about 15 percent of the time, serious differences arise and bills are assigned to **conference committees** to reach agreement on a single version for resubmission to both houses. Conference committees are temporary, with members appointed by the leadership in each house, usually from among the senior members of the committees that approved the bills.

**conference committee** Meeting between representatives of the House and Senate to reconcile differences over provisions of a bill passed by both houses.

Conference committees can be very powerful. Their final bill is usually (although not always) passed in both houses and sent to the president for approval. In resolving differences between the House and the Senate versions, the conference committee makes many final policy decisions. Although conference committees have considerable leeway in striking compromises, they focus on points of disagreement and usually do not change provisions already approved by both houses. Figure 8.9 summarizes the lawmaking process.

# Decision Making in Congress

How do senators and representatives decide about how they will vote on legislation? From an almost limitless number of considerations that go into congressional decision making, a few factors recur across a range of voting decisions: party loyalty, presidential support or opposition, constituency concerns, interest-group pressures, and the personal values and ideologies of members themselves.

**party vote** Majority of Democrats voting in opposition to a majority of Republicans.

**Party Voting** Party appears to be the most significant influence on congressional voting. **Party votes** are roll-call votes on which a majority of voting Democrats oppose a majority of voting Republicans. Traditionally, party votes occurred on roughly *half* of all roll-call votes in Congress. Partisanship in Congress, as reflected in the percentage of party votes, rose during the 1990s but may be moderating somewhat today (see Figure 8.10 on page 288).

**party unity** Percentage of Democrats and Republicans who stick with their party on party votes.

**Party unity** is measured by the percentage of Democrats and Republicans who stick by their party on party votes. Both Democratic and Republican Party unity has remained at fairly constant levels (85–95 percent) in both the House and the Senate over the past ten years. This is higher than in previous decades when party unity was regularly 50–60 percent in both the House and Senate. Greater party unity suggests increased partisan polarization in congress.

**Sources of Partisanship** Why do Democrats and Republicans in Congress vote along party lines? First of all, the Democratic Party has become more liberal and the Republican Party has become more conservative over the years (see *Up Close:* "Polarization on Capitol Hill"). Conservative Democrats, once very common in southern politics, are rapidly disappearing. At the same time, the ranks of liberal Republicans, mostly from the Northeast, have thinned. Second,

| **HOUSE** | **SENATE** |
|---|---|
| Bill is introduced and assigned to a committee, which refers it to the appropriate subcommittee. | Bill is introduced and assigned to a committee, which refers it to the appropriate subcommittee. |
| **Subcommittee**<br>Subcommittee holds hearings and "marks up" the bill. If the bill is approved in some form, it goes to the full committee.<br>**Committee**<br>Full committee considers the bill. If the bill is approved in some form, it is "reported" to the full House and placed on the House calendar. | **Subcommittee**<br>Subcommittee holds hearings, debates provisions and "marks up" the bill. If a bill is approved, it goes to the full committee.<br>**Committee**<br>Full committee considers the bill. If the bill is approved in some form, it is "reported" to the full Senate and placed on the Senate calendar. |
| **Rules Committee**<br>Rules Committee issues a rule to govern debate on the floor. Sends it to the full House.<br>**Full House**<br>Full House debates the bill and may amend it. If the bill passes and it is in a form different from the Senate version, it must go to a conference committee. | **Leadership**<br>Majority and minority leaders negotiate "unanimous consent" agreements scheduling full Senate debate and vote on the bill.<br>**Full Senate**<br>Full Senate debates the bill. Senate may amend it. If the bill passes and is in a form different from the House version, it must go to a conference committee. |

**Conference Committee**
Conference committee of senators and representatives meets to reconcile differences between bills. When agreement is reached, a compromise bill is sent back to both the House and the Senate.

**President**
President signs or vetoes the bill. Congress can override a veto by a two-thirds majority vote in both the House and Senate.

LAW

**Figure 8.9**  How a Bill Becomes a Law
This diagram depicts the major hurdles a successful bill must overcome in order to be enacted into law. Few bills introduced travel this full path; less than 10 percent of bills introduced are passed by Congress and sent to the president for approval or veto. Bills fail at every step along the path, but most die in committees and subcommittees, usually from inaction rather than from being voted down.

**Figure 8.10** Party Voting in Congress
Partisanship varies over time in Congress. For many years, between 30 and 40 percent of votes in the House and Senate were party votes—votes on which a majority of Democrats were in opposition to a majority of Republicans—but during the 1990s the percentage rose, indicating an increasingly partisan environment in Congress.

*Note:* Data indicate the percentage of all recorded votes on which a majority of voting Democrats opposed a majority of voting Republicans.

*Source:* Based on data from *Congressional Quarterly Weekly Report,* January 12, 2002, p. 136; December 11, 2005, pp. 29–53.

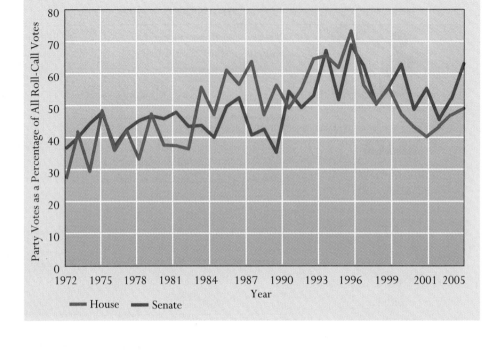

**bipartisanship** Agreement by members of both the Democratic and the Republican parties.

**divided party government** One party controls the presidency while the other party controls one or both houses of Congress.

the decline in voter turnout, especially in primary elections, has added to the importance of well-organized and ideologically motivated groups. In primary elections Republicans must be more concerned with pleasing conservative activists (e.g., the Christian Coalition, National Right-to-Life Committee, National Rifle Association, etc.), and Democrats must be more concerned with pleasing liberal groups (National Education Association, American Federation of State, County, and Municipal Employees, Sierra Club, etc.). And third, the rising costs of campaigning make members ever more dependent upon the financial support of these interests.

Conflict between the parties occurs frequently on domestic social and economic issues—welfare, housing and urban affairs, health, business regulation, taxing, and spending. Traditionally, **bipartisanship** was the goal of both presidents and congressional leaders on foreign and defense policy issues. Since the Vietnam War, however, Democrats in the Congress have been more critical of U.S. military involvements (and defense spending in general) than have Republicans.

**Presidential Support or Opposition** Presidential influence in congressional voting is closely tied to party. Presidents almost always receive their greatest support from members of their own party (see Figure 8.11). Indeed, policy gridlock is often associated with **divided party government**—in past decades, a Republican president and a Democratic-controlled Congress, but beginning in 1995 a Democratic president and a Republican-controlled Congress.

The decentralization of power in the congressional committee system also limits the president's ability to influence voting. The president cannot simply negotiate with the leadership of the House and Senate but instead must deal with scores of committee and subcommittee chairs and ranking members. To win the support of so many members of Congress, presidents often must agree to insert pork into presidential bills, promise patronage jobs, or offer presidential assistance in campaign fund raising.

## UP CLOSE

# Polarization on Capitol Hill

The Democratic and Republican parties in Congress are further apart ideologically than ever before. The Republicans are more uniformly conservative, and the Democrats more liberal, than in previous decades. "The proportion of political moderates—conservative Democrats or liberal Republicans—hovered at about 30 percent in the 1960s and 1970s. . . . Fewer than one in ten of today's lawmakers fall into this centrist category."[a] Conservative Southern Democrats once represented a third of their party's members, and a "conservative coalition" of Republicans and Southern Democrats was once a strong force in the Senate. Indeed, in the early 1980s President Ronald Reagan won the support of many moderate-to-conservative Democrats for his tax cutting measures. But today conservative Democrats account for less than 10 percent of their party's membership in Congress; with the retirement of several Southern Democratic senators in 2004, conservative Democrats have practically disappeared from the Senate. An even rarer breed—the liberal Republican—is also nearing extinction.

Partisanship and ideology are closely connected in this polarization on Capitol Hill. The result is more conflict, less bipartisan cooperation, and more acrimony in the halls of Congress.

The most common explanation for this polarization is the realignment of Southern voters from the Democratic to the Republican party. Southern conservatives moved almost en bloc into the Republican Party in the 1980s. As conservatives in the Republican Party gained strength, liberal Republicans, mostly from the Northeast, lost ground. Geographically, the Republican Party became centered in the Mountain states and the South, while the Democratic Party held the Northeast and West Coast. Finally, more polarizing issues—abortion, term limits, budget balancing—and a more aggressive leadership style, beginning with Republican Speaker Newt Gingrich in the 1990s and carried on by Democratic leader Nancy Pelosi since 2004, also contributes to party polarization.[b]

[a]Roger H. Davidson and Walter Oleszek. *Congress and Its Members.* 9th ed. Washington, D.C.: CQ Press, 2004, p. 276.

[b]Jason M. Roberts and Steven S. Smith, "Procedure Contexts, Party Strategy, and Conditional Party Voting in the U.S. House of Representatives, 1971–2000." *American Journal of Political Science* 47 (April 2003): pp. 305–317.

If negotiations break down, presidents can "go over the heads" of Congress, using the media to appeal directly to the people to support presidential programs and force Congress to act. The president has better access to the media than Congress has. But such threats and appeals can only be effective when (1) the president himself is popular with the public; and (2) the issue is one about which constituents can be made to feel intensely.

Finally, presidents can threaten to veto legislation. This threat, expressed or implied, confronts congressional leaders, committee chairs, and sponsors of a bill with several options. They must decide whether to (1) modify the bill to overcome the president's objections; (2) try to get two-thirds of both houses to commit to overriding the threatened veto; or (3) pass the bill and dare the president to veto it, then make a political issue out of the president's opposition. Historically, less than 5 percent of vetoes have been overridden by the Congress. Unless the president is politically very weak (as Richard Nixon was during the Watergate scandal), Congress cannot count on overriding a veto. If members of Congress truly want to address an important problem and not just define a political issue, they must negotiate with the White House to write a bill the president will sign.

**Constituency Influence**   **Constituency** influence in congressional voting is most apparent on issues that attract media attention and discussion and generate intense feelings among the general public. If many voters in the home state or district know about an issue and have intense feelings about it, members of Congress

**constituency** The votes in a legislator's home district.

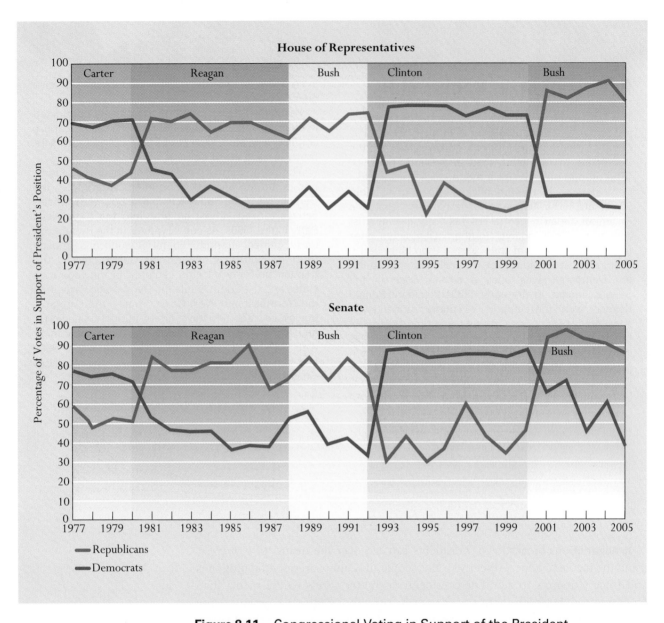

**Figure 8.11** Congressional Voting in Support of the President

Presidents always receive more support in Congress from members of their own party. Democratic Presidents Jimmy Carter and Bill Clinton could count on winning large majorities of Democratic members' votes, Republican Presidents Ronald Reagan and George Bush won large majorities of GOP members' votes. Percentages indicate congressional votes supporting the president on votes on which the president took a position.

*Source:* Norman J. Ornstein, Thomas E. Mann, and Michael J. Malbin, Vital Statistics on Congress 1999–2000 (Washington, D.C.: CQ Press, 2000), pp. 254–55; and *Congressional Quarterly Weekly Report,* December 11, 1999, p. 2987, January 12, 2002, p. 136; December 14, 2003, p. 3275; January 3, 2004, p. 53; December 11, p. 2946.

─Think Again─

Are members of Congress obliged to vote the way their constituents wish, even if they personally disagree?

are likely to defer to their constituents' feeling, regardless of the position of their party's leadership or even their own personal feelings. Members of Congress from *safe seats* seem to be just as attuned to the interests of their constituents as members from competitive seats (see *Up Close:* "Tips on Lobbying Congress").

Constituencies may also exercise a subtle influence by conditioning the personal views of members. Many members were born, were raised, and continue to live in

## UP CLOSE

## Tips on Lobbying Congress

YourCongress.com has some good suggestions about how to lobby Congress.

1. Keep it short and to the point. (Good lobbyists tell exactly what they want and why, in the fewest amount of words.)
2. Say thank you. (So few people say anything positive to members of Congress or their staff. If you know that they've done something good, say thank you. They'll remember it.)
3. Get to know the staff. (Good lobbyists don't complain when they don't get to meet the member of Congress. The staff does most of the work anyway, and has a knack for making requests disappear if given a reason to do so.)
4. Tell the whole story. (Good lobbyists don't patronize. They acknowledge when something is difficult and are up front about the opposition.)
5. Timing is everything. (Good lobbyists know the process of Congress, mention the proper deadlines, and don't ask for requests at the last minute.)
6. Always one page, and always written up in advance. (Good lobbyists have already written a draft of what they want before they ask for it, and are always happy to leave it or send it over.)
7. Capitol Hill is the last place to burn bridges. (Good lobbyists don't go ballistic when they are told no. They regroup and wait for another chance. D.C. is a very small place, and being a jerk will only mean you quickly get a reputation for being a jerk.)

the towns they represent; over a lifetime they have absorbed and internalized the views of their communities. Moreover, some members of Congress feel an obligation to represent their constituents' opinions even when they personally disagree.

However, members of Congress have considerable latitude in voting against their constituents' opinions if they choose to do so. Constituents, as noted earlier, lack information about most policy issues and the voting records of their senators and representatives. Even when constituents know about an issue and feel strongly about it, members can afford to cast a "wrong" vote from time to time. A long record of homestyle politics—casework, pork barreling, visits, public appearances, and so on—can isolate members of Congress from the wrath generated by their voting records. Only a long string of "wrong" votes on issues important to constituents is likely to jeopardize an incumbent.

**Interest-Group Influence**    Inside the Washington Beltway, the influence of interest groups, lobbyists, and fund-raisers on members of Congress is well understood. This influence is seldom talked about back home or on the campaign trail, except perhaps by challengers. Lobbyists have their greatest effects on the *details* of public policy. Congressional decisions made in committee rooms, at markup sessions, and around conference tables can mean billions of dollars to industries and tens of millions to individual companies. Pressures from competing interest groups can be intense as lobbyists buttonhole lawmakers and try to win legislative amendments that can make or break business fortunes. One of the most potent tools in the lobbyist's arsenal is money. The prohibitive cost of modern campaigning has dictated that dollars are crucial to electoral victory, and virtually all members of Congress spend more time than they would like courting it, raising it, and stockpiling it for the next election. (See also Lobbying Ethics in Chapter 7.)

Voters may be wrong when they think that all members of Congress are crooks, but they are not far off the mark when they worry that their own representatives may be listening to two competing sets of constituents—the real constituents back home in the district and the "cash constituents" who come calling in Washington.[40]

— Think Again —
Is it ethical for Congress members to pay special attention to requests for assistance by people who make large campaign contributions?

**trustees** Legislators who feel obligated to use their own best judgment in decision making.

**delegates** Legislators who feel obligated to present the views of their home constituents.

**Personal Values**    It was the eighteenth-century English political philosopher Edmund Burke, himself a member of Parliament, who told his constituents; "You choose a member indeed; but when you have chosen him, he is not a member of Bristol, but he is a member of *Parliament.*" Burke defended the classic notion of representatives as **trustees** who feel obligated to use their own best judgment about what is good for the nation as a whole. In this theory, representatives are not obligated to vote the views of their constituents. This notion contrasts with the idea of representatives as **delegates** who feel obligated to vote according to the views of "the folks back home" regardless of their own personal viewpoint. Most legislators *claim* to be trustees, perhaps because of the halo effect generated by the independence implied in the term.

Democratic political philosophers have pondered the merits of trustee versus delegate representation over the centuries, but the question only rarely arises in actual congressional deliberations. In many cases, members' own personal views and those of their constituents are virtually identical. Even when legislators perceive conflicts between their own views and those of their constituents, most attempt to find a compromise between these competing demands rather than choose one role or another exclusively. The political independence of members of Congress—their independence from party, combined with the ignorance of their constituents about most policy issues—allows members to give great weight to their own personal ideologies in voting.

## Customs and Norms

Over time, institutions develop customs and norms of behavior to assist in their functioning. These are not merely quaint and curious folkways; they promote the purposes of the institution. Congressional customs and norms are designed to help members work together, to reduce interpersonal conflict, to facilitate bargaining and promote compromise.

**Civility**    Traditionally, members of Congress understood that uncivil behavior—expressions of anger, personal attacks on character, ugly confrontations, flaming rhetoric—undermined the lawmaking function. Indeed, civility was encouraged by the longstanding custom of members of Congress referring to each other in elaborately courteous terms: "my distinguished colleague from Ohio," "the honorable representative from Pennsylvania," and the like. By custom, even bitter partisan enemies in Congress were expected to avoid harsh personal attacks on each other. The purpose of this custom was to try to maintain an atmosphere in which people who hold very different opinions can nevertheless function with some degree of decorum. Unfortunately, many of these customs and norms of behavior are breaking down. Individual ambition and the drive for power and celebrity have led to a decline in courtesy, cooperation, and respect for traditional norms. One result is that it has become increasingly difficult for Congress to reach agreement on policy issues. Another result is that life in Congress is increasingly tedious, conflict-filled, and unpleasant (see *A Conflicting View:* "Congress Can Act Responsibly on Occasion").

**The Demise of the Apprenticeship Norm**    Years ago, "the first rule"[41] of congressional behavior was that new members were expected to be seen but not heard on the floor, to be studious in their committee work, and to be cooperative with party leaders. But the institutional norm of apprenticeship has been swept aside as increasingly ambitious and independent senators and representatives arrive on Capitol Hill. Today new members of Congress feel free to grab the spotlight on

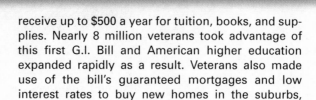

# A CONFLICTING VIEW

## Congress Can Act Responsibly on Occasion

Congress is not always mired in partisanship, squabbling, and gridlock. On occasion it acts responsibly in the national interest. Indeed, consider the following congressional landmarks in U.S. history:

### Louisiana Purchase (1803)

President Thomas Jefferson offered to purchase from France nearly 830,000 square miles between the Mississippi and the Rockies for $15 million—about three cents an acre. There is no constitutional provision authorizing the federal government to buy foreign territory, but the Senate, accepting Jefferson's broad interpretation of the Constitution, approved the purchase. The House appropriated the money to consummate the deal. On December 29, 1803, the United States took possession of North America's heartland, doubling the nation's size with territory that would comprise thirteen states.

### Homestead Act (1862)

This Civil War–era legislation allowed any family head or adult male to claim 160 acres of prairie land for a $10 registration fee and a promise to live there continuously for five years. It opened up the midwestern United States for immediate settlement. The act drew thousands of English, Irish, Germans, Swedes, Danes, Norwegians, and Czechs to the United States, pushing settlement farther west.

### Social Security Act (1935)

The act was designed to secure "the men, women, and children of the nation against certain hazards and vicissitudes of life," explained President Franklin Roosevelt. The act's best-known measure is the social insurance system that provides monthly checks to the elderly.

### National Labor Relations Act (1935)

By declaring workers had a right to join unions and bargain collectively with employers for pay raises and improved working conditions, the act spurred the growth of the nation's major industrial unions. Labor's Magna Carta also provided workers with the legal weapons to improve plant conditions and protect themselves from employer harassment.

### G.I. Bill of Rights (1944)

The G.I. Bill of Rights, known officially as the Serviceman's Readjustment Act of 1944, offered to pay tuition for college or trade education to ex–World War II servicemen. It also mandated that they receive up to $500 a year for tuition, books, and supplies. Nearly 8 million veterans took advantage of this first G.I. Bill and American higher education expanded rapidly as a result. Veterans also made use of the bill's guaranteed mortgages and low interest rates to buy new homes in the suburbs, inspiring a development boom.

### Truman Doctrine (1947) and NATO (1949)

The Truman Doctrine initiated U.S. resistance to expansion of the Soviet Union into Western Europe following World War II, and the NATO treaty has provided the framework for European security for half a century. Truman declared to a joint session of Congress, "I believe that it must be the policy of the United States to support free people who are resisting attempted subjugation by armed minorities or by outside pressures."

### Federal Highway Act (1956)

President Dwight D. Eisenhower was right when he said, "More than any single action by the government since the end of the war, this one would change the face of America." The most expensive public-works project in U.S. history, the highway act built the 41,000-mile nationwide interstate highway system.

### Civil Rights Act of 1964

Only Congress could end racial segregation in privately owned businesses and facilities. It did so by an overwhelming vote of both houses in the Civil Rights Act of 1964. Injustices endure, but the end of segregated restaurants, theaters, and drinking fountains provided new opportunities for African Americans and helped change white attitudes. In addition, Title VII of the act prohibits gender discrimination and serves as the legal bulwark for women's rights.

### Voting Rights Act of 1965

President Lyndon B. Johnson signed this act in the same room in the Capitol where Abraham Lincoln had penned the Emancipation Proclamation. This legislation guaranteed all Americans the most fundamental of all rights—the right to vote. Between the 1964 and 1968 presidential elections, black voter registration increased 50 percent across the nation, even in the reluctant Southern states, giving African Americans newfound political clout.

### Medicare and Medicaid (1965)

Congress amended the Social Security Act of 1935 to provide for national health insurance for the aged (Medicare) and for the poor (Medicaid). In 2003 (28 years later) Congress added prescription drug coverage to Medicare.

the floor, in committee, and in front of television cameras. "The evidence is clear, unequivocal, and overwhelming: the [apprenticeship] norm is simply gone."[42] Nevertheless, experienced members are more active and influential in shaping legislation than are new members.[43]

**Specialization and Deference**   The committee system encourages members of Congress to specialize in particular policy areas. Even the most independent and ambitious members can perceive the advantage of developing power and expertise in an area especially relevant to their constituents. Traditionally, members who developed a special expertise and accumulated years of service on a standing committee were deferred to in floor proceedings. These specialists were "cue givers" for party members when bills or amendments were being voted on. Members are still likely to defer to specialized committee members when the issues are technical or complicated, or when the issue is outside of their own area of policy specialization, but deference is increasingly rare on major public issues.

**Bargaining**   Bargaining is central to the legislative process. Little could be achieved if individual members were unwilling to bargain with each other for votes both in committees and on the floor. A willingness to bargain is a long-standing functional norm of Congress.

Members of Congress are not expected to violate their consciences in the bargaining process. On the contrary, members respect one another's issues of conscience and receive respect in return. On most issues, however, members can and do bargain their support. "Horse trading" is very common in committee work. Members may bargain in their own personal interest, in the interests of constituents or groups, or even in the interests of their committee with members of other committees. Because most bargaining occurs in a committee setting, it is seldom a matter of public record. The success and reputation of committee chairs largely depend on their ability to work out bargains and compromises.

Bargaining can assume different forms. Explicit trade-offs such as "If you vote for my bill, I'll vote for yours" are the simplest form of bargaining, but implicit understandings may be more common. Members may help other members in anticipation of receiving reciprocal help at some future unspecified time. Moreover, representatives who refuse to cooperate on a regular basis may find little support for their own bills. Mutual "back scratching" allows members to develop a reservoir of IOUs for the future. Building credit is good business for most members; one can never tell when one will need help in the future.

Bargaining requires a certain kind of integrity. Members of Congress must stick to their agreements. They must not consistently ask too high a price for their cooperation. They must recognize and return favors. They must not renege on promises. They must be trustworthy.

Conference-committee bargaining is essential if legislation acceptable to both houses is to be written. Indeed, it is expected that conferees from each house will bargain and compromise their differences. "Every House-Senate conference is expected to proceed via the methods of 'give and take,' 'trading back and forth,' 'pulling and hauling,' 'horse-trading and compromise,' 'splitting the difference,' etc."[44]

**Reciprocity**   The norm of *reciprocity*—favors rendered should be repaid in kind—supports the bargaining process. Members willing to accept "half a loaf" traditionally accomplished more than those who insisted on a "whole loaf." But the norm of reciprocity may have weakened in recent years.

**Logrolling**  Perhaps the most celebrated and reviled form of reciprocity, **logrolling** is mutual agreement to support projects that primarily benefit individual members of Congress and their constituencies. Logrolling is closely associated with pork-barrel legislation. Yet it can occur in virtually any kind of legislation. Even interest-group lobbyists may logroll with each other, promising to support each other's legislative agendas.

**Leader-Follower Relations**  Because leaders have few means of disciplining members, they must rely heavily on their bargaining skills to solicit cooperation and get the work of Congress accomplished. Party leaders can appeal to members' concerns for their party image among the voters. Individual majority members want to keep their party in the majority—if for no other reason than to retain their committee and subcommittee chairs. Individual minority members would like their party to win control of their house in order to assume the power and privileges of committee and subcommittee chairs. Party leaders must appeal to more than partisanship to win cooperation, however.

To secure cooperation, leaders can grant—or withhold—some tangible benefits. A member of the House needs the Speaker's support to get recognition, to have a bill called up, to get a bill scheduled, to see to it that a bill gets assigned to a preferred committee, to get a good committee assignment, and to help a bill get out of the Rules Committee, for example.

Party leaders may also seek to gain support from their followers by doing favors that ease their lives in Washington, advance their legislative careers, and help them with their reelection. Favors from party leaders oblige members to respond to leaders' requests at a later time. Members themselves like to build up a reservoir of good feeling and friendship with the leadership, knowing that eventually they will need some favors from the leadership (see *People in Politics:* "Bill Frist, M.D., Leading the Senate").

**Gridlock**  Congress is often criticized for legislative **gridlock**—the failure to enact laws, including appropriations acts, that are widely perceived to have merit. Indeed, much of the popular frustration with Congress relates to gridlock arising from policy and budgetary stalemates. Research has suggested that the following factors contribute to congressional gridlock:[45]

- Divided party control of the presidency and Congress

- Divided party control of the House and Senate

- Greater ideological polarization (liberal versus conservative) of the parties

- In the Senate, the willingness of members to filibuster against a bill, requiring 60 votes to overcome the opposition

In contrast, the factors that appear to lessen gridlock and encourage significant legislative accomplishment include

- Unified party control of the presidency, House, and Senate

- Larger numbers of moderates among Democrats and Republicans in Congress (as opposed to larger numbers of strong liberals and strong conservatives)

- Overwhelming public support for new legislation

Note that the constitutional structure of American government—separation of powers and checks and balances, as well as bicameralism—plays a major role in gridlock, as does the American two-party system. Overcoming gridlock

Fourteen women served in the U.S. Senate in 2005–2006, nine Democrats and seven Republicans. But this number is only 14 percent of that 100-member body.

requires a willingness of members of both parties in both houses of Congress, as well as the White House, to bargain and compromise over legislation. And it requires strong public opinion in support of congressional action.

## Congressional Ethics

Although critics might consider the phrase *congressional ethics* to be an oxymoron, the moral climate of Congress today is probably better than in earlier eras of American history. Nevertheless, Congress as an institution has suffered from well-publicized scandals that continue to prompt calls for reform.

**Ethics Rules**   Congress has an interest in maintaining the integrity of the institution itself and the trust of the people. Thus Congress has established its own rules of ethics. These rules include the following:

- *Financial disclosure:* All members must file personal financial statements each year.

- *Honoraria:* Members cannot accept fees for speeches or personal appearances.

- *Campaign funds:* Surplus campaign funds cannot be put to personal use. (A loophole allowed members elected before 1980 to keep such funds if they left office before January 1, 1993. A record number of House members resigned in 1992; many of them kept substantial amounts of campaign money.)

- *Gifts:* Members may not accept gifts worth more than $50 (with annual increases in these amounts for inflation).

- *Free travel:* Members may not accept free travel from private corporations or individuals for more than four days of domestic travel and seven days of international travel per year. (Taxpayer-paid "junkets" to investigate problems at home or abroad or attend international meetings are not prohibited.)

- *Lobbying:* Former members may not lobby Congress for at least one year after retirement.

But these limited rules have not gone very far in restoring popular trust in Congress.

**Gray Areas: Services and Contributions** Congress members are expected to perform services for their political contributors. However, a direct *quid pro quo*—receiving a financial contribution specifically for the performance of official duty—is illegal. Few Congress members would be so foolish as to openly state a price to a potential contributor for a specific service, and most contributors know not to state a dollar amount that would be forthcoming if the member performed a particular service for them. But what if the contribution and the service occur close together? A Senate Ethics Committee once found that a close relationship between a service and a contribution to be an "impermissible pattern of conduct [that] violated established norms of behavior in the Senate . . . [and] was improper and repugnant."[46] But the Ethics Committee offered little in the way of a future guidance in handling services for campaign contributors.

**Expulsion** The Constitution gives Congress the power to discipline its own members. "Each House may . . . punish its Members for disorderly Behaviour, and, with the Concurrence of two thirds, expel a Member." But the Constitution fails to define *disorderly behavior.*

It seems reasonable to believe that criminal conduct falls within the constitutional definition of disorderly behavior. Bribery is a criminal act: it is illegal to solicit or receive anything of value in return for the performance of a government duty. During its notorious Abscam investigation in 1980, the Federal Bureau of Investigation set up a sting operation in which agents posing as wealthy Arabs offered bribe money to members of Congress while secretly videotaping the transactions. Six representatives and one senator were convicted. But criminal conviction does not automatically result in expulsion from Congress. In the Abscam case, only one defendant, Representative Michael "Ozzie" Myers (D-Pa.),

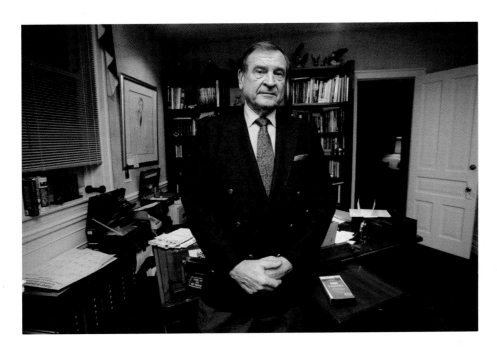

Democrat Dan Rostenkowski was the powerful Chairman of the House Ways and Means (taxation) Committee before he was indicted and convicted of misuse of public funds in 1994. He refused to resign, but his Chicago constituents voted him out of office.

# A CONSTITUTIONAL NOTE

## Congress as the First Branch

The Founders believed that the Congress would be the first and most powerful branch of government. Thus, Article I establishes the Congress, describes its structure, and sets forth its powers. Note that its powers *are* the enumerated powers of the national government. Following the English precedent of two houses of the legislature, a House of Commons and a House of Lords, the Founders created two separate houses, a House of Representatives and a Senate. They did so in part as a result of the Connecticut Compromise, which balanced large population states in the House with the small population states' demands for equality in the Senate. But the Founders also wanted a Senate elected by state legislatures, not the people, "as a defense to the people against their own temporary errors and delusions."

The Founders believed that the Senate would balance the interests and numerical superiority of common citizens with the property interests of the less numerous landowners, bankers, and merchants, who they expected to be sent to the Senate by the state legislatures. This defense against "temporary errors and delusions" of the people was strengthened by different lengths of tenure for the House and Senate. All House members were elected every two years, but Senate members were elected for six-year terms, one-third of the Senate elected every two years. The longer terms of the Senate were designed to protect senators from temporary popular movements. Not until the Seventeenth Amendment was ratified in 1913, over a century later, were senators directly elected by the people. In short, the original Constitution of 1787 was careful to limit the role of the people in lawmaking.

was expelled, becoming the first member to be expelled since the Civil War. (Two other House members and the senator resigned rather than face expulsion, and the other three representatives were defeated for reelection.) Perhaps the most interesting result of the Abscam investigation: Only one member of Congress approached by the FBI, Democratic Senator Larry Presler of South Dakota, turned down the bribe. The powerful chair of the House Ways and Means Committee, Democrat Dan Rostenkowski (Ill.), was indicted by a federal grand jury in 1994 for misuse of congressional office funds; he refused to resign from Congress, but his Chicago constituents voted him out of office. Democratic Representative Mel Reynolds (Ill.) resigned in 1995, following his criminal conviction on charges of sexual misconduct. (A special election to fill his vacated seat was won by Jesse Jackson Jr., son of the popular preacher, commentator, and former Democratic presidential contender.) Republican Senator Robert Packwood (Oreg.) resigned in 1995 in order to avoid official expulsion following a Senate Ethics Committee report charging him with numerous counts of sexual harassment of female staff. Representative James A. Traficant (D-Ohio) was expelled in 2002 following his conviction on ten federal corruption charges. And Representative Randy Cunningham (D-Calif.) resigned in 2005 after pleading guilty to charges of accepting $2.4 million in bribes from lobbyists.

**censure** Public reprimand for wrongdoing, given to a member standing in the chamber before Congress.

**Censure**   A lesser punishment in the Congress than expulsion is official **censure**. Censured members are obliged to "stand in the well" and listen to the charges read against them. It is supposed to be a humiliating experience and fatal to one's political career. In 1983 two members of Congress, Barney Frank (D-Mass.) and Gerry Studds (D-Mass.), were censured for sexual misconduct with teenage congressional pages. Both were obliged to "stand in the well." In 2002 New Jersey Democratic Senator Robert Torricelli was "severely admonished" by the Senate Ethics Committee for "at least the appearance of impropriety" for improperly accepting gifts and campaign contributions. Torricelli abruptly dropped out of his reelection race.

Lesser forms of censure include a public reprimand or admonition by the Ethics Committee expressing disapproval of the Congress member's behavior. And the Ethics Committee may also order a member to repay funds improperly received.

# Summary Notes

- The Constitution places all of the delegated powers of the national government in the Congress. The Founders expected Congress to be the principal institution for resolving national conflicts, balancing interests, and deciding who gets what. Today, Congress is a central battleground in the struggle over national policy. Congress generally does not initiate but responds to policy initiatives and budget requests originating from the president, the bureaucracy, and interest groups. Over time, the president and the executive branch, together with the Supreme Court and federal judiciary, have come to dominate national policy making.

- The Congress represents local and state interests in policy making. The Senate's constituencies are the 50 states, and the House's constituencies are 435 separate districts. Both houses of Congress, but especially the House of Representatives, wield power in domestic and foreign affairs primarily through the "power of the purse."

- Congressional powers include oversight and investigation. These powers are exercised primarily through committees. Although Congress claims these powers are a necessary part of lawmaking, their real purpose is usually to influence agency decision making, to build political support for increases or decreases in agency funding, to lay the political foundation for new programs and policies, and to capture media attention and enhance the power of members of Congress.

- Congress is gradually becoming more "representative" of the general population in terms of race and gender. Redistricting, under federal court interpretations of the Voting Rights Act, has increased African American and Hispanic representation in Congress. And women have significantly increased their presence in Congress in recent years. Nevertheless, women and minorities do not occupy seats in Congress proportional to their share of the general population.

- Members of Congress are independent political entrepreneurs. They initiate their own candidacies, raise their own campaign funds, and get themselves elected with very little help from their party. Members of Congress are largely career politicians who skillfully use the advantages of incumbency to stay in office. Incumbents outspend challengers by large margins. Interest-group political action committees and individual contributors strongly favor incumbents. Congressional elections are seldom focused on great national issues but rather on local issues and personalities and the ability of candidates to "bring home the bacon" from Washington and serve their constituents.

- Congress as an institution is not very popular with the American people. Scandals, pay raises, perks, and privileges reported in the media have hurt the image of the institution. Nevertheless, individual members of Congress remain popular with their districts' voters.

- Members of Congress spend as much time on "home style" activities—promoting their images back home and attending to constituents' problems—as they do legislating. Casework wins votes one at a time, gradually accumulating political support back home, and members often support each other's "pork-barrel" projects.

- Despite the independence of members, the Democratic and Republican party structures in the House and Senate remain the principal bases for organizing Congress. Party leaders in the House and Senate generally control the flow of business in each house, assigning bills to committees, scheduling or delaying votes, and appointing members to committees. But leaders must bargain for votes; they have few formal disciplinary powers. They cannot deny renomination to recalcitrant members.

- The real legislative work of Congress is done in committees. Standing committees screen and draft legislation; with rare exceptions, bills do not reach the floor without approval by a majority of a standing committee. The committee and subcommittee system decentralizes power in Congress. The system satisfies the desires of members to gain power, prestige, and electoral advantage, but it weakens responsible government in the Congress as a whole. All congressional committees are chaired by members of the majority party. Seniority is still the major determinant of power in Congress.

- In order to become law, a bill must win committee approval and withstand debate in both houses of Congress. The rules attached to a bill's passage in the House can significantly help or hurt its chances. Bills passed with differences in the two houses must be reworked in a conference committee composed of members of both houses and then passed in identical form in both.

- In deciding how to vote on legislation, Congress members are influenced by party loyalty, presidential support or opposition, constituency concerns, interest-group pressures, and their own personal values and ideology. Party majorities oppose each other on roughly half of all roll-call votes in Congress. Presidents receive the greatest support in Congress from members of their own party.

- The customs and norms of Congress help reduce interpersonal conflict, facilitate bargaining and compromise, and make life more pleasant on Capitol Hill. They include the recognition of special competencies of members, a willingness to bargain and compromise, mutual "back scratching"

and logrolling, reciprocity, and deference toward the leadership. But traditional customs and norms have weakened over time as more members have pursued independent political agendas. And partisanship and incivility in Congress have risen in recent years.

- Congress establishes its own rules of ethics. The Constitution empowers each house to expel its own members for "disorderly conduct" by a two-thirds vote, but expulsion has seldom occurred. Some members have resigned to avoid expulsion; others have been officially censured yet remained in Congress.

# Key Terms

| | | | |
|---|---|---|---|
| congressional session 246 | incumbent | whips 276 | cloture 284 |
| bicameral 246 | gerrymandering 255 | standing committee 278 | rider 284 |
| power of the purse 248 | affirmative racial | ranking minority | roll-call vote 286 |
| oversight 248 | gerrymandering 255 | member 278 | conference committee 286 |
| advice and consent 248 | open seat 257 | subcommittees 279 | party vote 286 |
| confirmation 249 | safe seat 259 | seniority system 281 | party unity 286 |
| congressional | turnover 259 | drafting a bill 281 | bipartisanship 288 |
| hearings 249 | Government Accoutability | markup 282 | divided party |
| congressional | Office 270 | discharge petition 283 | government 288 |
| investigation 250 | home style 272 | rule 283 | constituency 289 |
| apportionment 251 | casework 272 | closed rule 284 | trustees 292 |
| malapportionment 251 | pork barreling 272 | restricted rule 284 | delegates 292 |
| redistricting 252 | franking privilege 273 | open rule 284 | logrolling 295 |
| gerrymandering 253 | Speaker of the House 275 | unanimous consent | gridlock 295 |
| splintering 253 | majority leader 276 | agreement 284 | censure 298 |
| packing 254 | minority leader 276 | filibuster 284 | |

# Suggested Readings

Bond, Jon R., and Richard Fleisher, eds. *Polarized Politics: Congress and the President in a Partisan Era.* Washington, D.C.: CQ Press, 2000. Essay on the rise of partisanship in Washington and its effect on congressional-presidential relations.

Davidson, Robert H., and Walter J. Oleszek. *Congress and Its Members.* 10th ed. Washington, D.C.: CQ Press, 2005. Authoritative text on Congress covering the recruitment of members, elections, House styles and Hill styles, leadership, decision making, and relations with interest groups, presidency, and courts. Emphasizes tension between lawmaking responsibilities and desire to be reelected.

Fenno, Richard F. *Home Style.* Boston: Little, Brown, 1978. The classic description of how attention to constituency by members of Congress enhances their reelection prospects. Home style activities, including casework, pork barreling,

travel and appearances back home, newsletters, and surveys, are described in detail.

Herrnson, Paul S. *Playing Hardball: Campaigning for the U.S. Congress.* Upper Saddle River, N.J.: Prentice Hall, 2001. Congressional candidates' strategies, targeting, fund raising, and getting out the vote.

Herrnson, Paul S. *Congressional Elections: Campaigning at Home and in Washington.* 4th ed. Washington, D.C.: CQ Press, 2003. Interviews with candidates, campaign aides, and political consultants to paint a comprehensive portrait of congressional campaigns.

Jones, Charles O. *Separate but Equal Branches: Congress and the Presidency.* 2nd ed. Washington, D.C.: CQ Press, 1999. Presidential–congressional relations under Johnson, Nixon, Ford, Carter, Reagan, Bush, and Clinton.

Oleszek, Walter J. *Congressional Procedures and Policy Processes.* 6th ed. Washington, D.C.: CQ Press, 2003. The definitive work on congressional rules, procedures and traditions and their effect on the course and content of legislation.

Ornstein, Norman J., Thomas E. Mann, and Michael J. Malbin. *Vital Statistics on Congress.* Washington, D.C.: CQ Press, 2006. Published biennially. Excellent source of data on members of Congress, congressional elections, campaign finance, committees and staff, workload, and voting alignments.

Sinclair, Barbara. *Unorthodox Lawmaking.* 2nd ed. Washington, D.C.: CQ Press, 2000. A description of the various detours and shortcuts a major bill is likely to take in Congress, including five case studies.

Stathis, Stephen W. *Landmark Legislation 1774–2002.* Washington, D.C.: CQ Press, 2003. A summary of major congressional legislation over 225 years, in a single volume.

# ★ Make It Real

## CONGRESS
The simulation makes the student a member of Congress.

# 9 THE PRESIDENT
## White House Politics

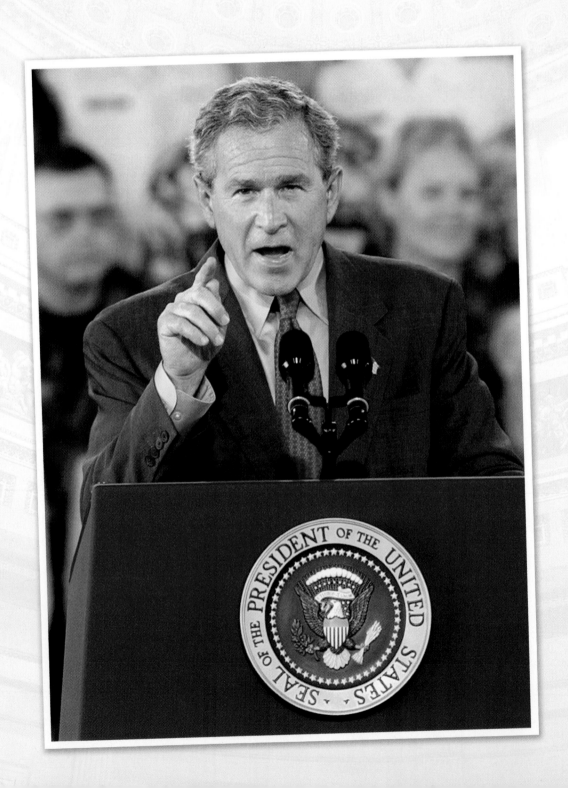

## Chapter Outline

- Presidential Power
- Constitutional Powers of the President
- Political Resources of the President
- Personality versus Policy
- Chief Executive
- Chief Legislator and Lobbyist
- Global Leader
- Commander-in-Chief
- The Vice Presidential Waiting Game

## Think About Politics

1 Do you approve of the way the president is handling his job?
Yes ☐ No ☐

2 Should presidents have the power to take actions not specifically authorized by law or the Constitution that they believe necessary for the nation's well-being?
Yes ☐ No ☐

3 Should the American people consider private moral conduct in evaluating presidential performance?
Yes ☐ No ☐

4 Should Congress rally to support a president's decision to send U.S. troops into action even if it disagrees with the decision?
Yes ☐ No ☐

5 Should Congress have the authority to call home U.S. troops sent by the president to engage in military actions overseas?
Yes ☐ No ☐

6 Should Congress impeach and remove a president whose policy decisions damage the nation?
Yes ☐ No ☐

7 Is presidential performance more related to character and personality than to policy positions?
Yes ☐ No ☐

8 Do you think the situation in Iraq was worth going to war?
Yes ☐ No ☐

*How much power does the president of the United States really have— over policies, over legislation, over the budget, over how this country is viewed by other nations, even over how it views itself?*

★　　★　　★

# Presidential Power

Americans look to their president for "Greatness." The presidency embodies the popular "great man" view of history and public affairs—attributing progress in the world to the actions of particular individuals. Great presidents are those associated with great events: George Washington with the founding of the nation, Abraham Lincoln with the preservation of the Union, Franklin D. Roosevelt with the nation's emergence from economic depression and victory in World War II (see *What Do You Think?* "How Would You Rate the Presidents?"). People tend to believe that the president is responsible for "peace and prosperity" as well as for "change." They expect their president to present a "vision" of America's future and to symbolize the nation.

**The Symbolic President**  The president personifies American government for most people. People expect the president to act decisively and effectively to deal with national problems. They expect the president to be "compassionate"—to show concern for problems confronting individual citizens.[1] The president, while playing these roles, is the focus of public attention and the nation's leading celebrity. Presidents receive more media coverage than any other person in the nation, for everything from their policy statements to their favorite foods to their dogs and cats.

**Managing Crises**  In times of crisis, the American people look to their president to take action, to provide reassurance, and to protect the nation and its people. It is the president, not the Congress or the courts, who is expected to speak on behalf of the American people in times of national triumph and tragedy.[2] The president gives expression to the nation's pride in victory. The nation's heroes are welcomed and its championship sports teams are feted in the White House Rose Garden.

The president also gives expression to the nation's sadness in tragedy and strives to help the nation go forward. How presidents respond to crises often defines their place in history. Franklin D. Roosevelt raised public morale during the Great Depression of the 1930s by reassuring Americans that "the only thing we have to fear is fear itself." Later he led the nation into war following the Japanese attack on Pearl Harbor, December 7, 1941, "a day which will live in infamy." When the *Challenger* spaceship disintegrated before the eyes of millions of television viewers in 1986, Ronald

# How Would You Rate the Presidents?

From time to time, historians have been polled to rate U.S. presidents (see table). The survey ratings given the presidents have been remarkably consistent. Abraham Lincoln, George Washington, and Franklin Roosevelt are universally recognized as the greatest American presidents. It is more difficult for historians to rate recent presidents; the views of historians are influenced by their own (generally liberal and reformist) political views. Richard Nixon once commented, "History will treat me fairly. Historians probably won't."

Historians may tend to rank activist presidents who led the nation through war or economic crisis higher than passive presidents who guided the nation in peace and prosperity. Initially Dwight Eisenhower, who presided in the relatively calm 1950s, was ranked low by historians. But later, after comparing his performance with those who came after him, his steadiness and avoidance of war raised his ranking dramatically.

| Arthur M. Schlesinger (1948) | Arthur M. Schlesinger, Jr. (1962) | Robert Murray (1982) | Arthur M. Schlesinger, Jr. (1996) | W. J. Ridings, S. B. McIver (1997) |
|---|---|---|---|---|
| **Great** | **Great** | **Presidential Rank** | **Great** | **Overall Ranking** |
| 1. Lincoln | 1. Lincoln | 1. Lincoln | 1. Lincoln | 1. Lincoln |
| 2. Washington | 2. Washington | 2. F. Roosevelt | 2. Washington | 2. F. Roosevelt |
| 3. F. Roosevelt | 3. F. Roosevelt | 3. Washington | 3. F. Roosevelt | 3. Washington |
| 4. Wilson | 4. Wilson | 4. Jefferson | **Near Great** | 4. Jefferson |
| 5. Jefferson | 5. Jefferson | 5. T. Roosevelt | 4. Jefferson | 5. T. Roosevelt |
| 6. Jackson | **Near Great** | 6. Wilson | 5. Jackson | 6. Wilson |
| **Near Great** | 6. Jackson | 7. Jackson | 6. T. Roosevelt | 7. Truman |
| 7. T. Roosevelt | 7. T. Roosevelt | 8. Truman | 7. Wilson | 8. Jackson |
| 8. Cleveland | 8. Polk | 9. J. Adams | 8. Truman | 9. Eisenhower |
| 9. J. Adams | 8. Truman (tie) | 10. L. Johnson | 9. Polk | 10. Madison |
| 10. Polk | 10. J. Adams | 11. Eisenhower | **High Average** | 11. Polk |
| **Average** | 11. Cleveland | 12. Polk | 10. Eisenhower | 12. L. Johnson |
| 11. J. Q. Adams | **Average** | 13. Kennedy | 11. J. Adams | 13. Monroe |
| 12. Monroe | 12. Madison | 14. Madison | 12. Kennedy | 14. J. Adams |
| 13. Hayes | 13. J. Q. Adams | 15. Monroe | 13. Cleveland | 15. Kennedy |
| 14. Madison | 14. Hayes | 16. J. Q. Adams | 14. L. Johnson | 16. Cleveland |
| 15. Van Buren | 15. McKinley | 17. Cleveland | 15. Monroe | 17. McKinley |
| 16. Taft | 16. Taft | 18. McKinley | 16. McKinley | 18. J. Q. Adams |
| 17. Arthur | 17. Van Buren | 19. Taft | **Average** | 19. Carter |
| 18. McKinley | 18. Monroe | 20. Van Buren | 17. Madison | 20. Taft |
| 19. A. Johnson | 19. Hoover | 21. Hoover | 18. J. Q. Adams | 21. Van Buren |
| 20. Hoover | 20. B. Harrison | 22. Hayes | 19. B. Harrison | 22. Bush |
| 21. B. Harrison | 21. Arthur | 23. Arthur | 20. Clinton | 23. Clinton |
| **Below Average** | 21. Eisenhower (tie) | 24. Ford | 21. Van Buren | 24. Hoover |
| 22. Tyler | 23. A. Johnson | 25. Carter | 22. Taft | 25. Hayes |
| 23. Coolidge | **Below Average** | 26. B. Harrison | 23. Hayes | 26. Reagan |
| 24. Fillmore | 24. Taylor | 27. Taylor | 24. Bush | 27. Ford |
| 25. Taylor | 25. Tyler | 28. Tyler | 25. Reagan | 28. Arthur |
| 26. Buchanan | 26. Fillmore | 29. Fillmore | 26. Arthur | 29. Taylor |
| 27. Pierce | 27. Coolidge | 30. Coolidge | 27. Carter | 30. Garfield |
| **Failure** | 28. Pierce | 31. Pierce | 28. Ford | 31. B. Harrison |
| 28. Grant | 29. Buchanan | 32. A. Johnson | **Below Average** | 32. Nixon |
| 29. Harding | **Failure** | 33. Buchanan | 29. Taylor | 33. Coolidge |
| | 30. Grant | 34. Nixon | 30. Coolidge | 34. Tyler |
| | 31. Harding | 35. Grant | 31. Fillmore | 35. W. Harrison |
| | | 36. Harding | 32. Tyler | 36. Fillmore |
| | | | **Failure** | 37. Pierce |
| | | | 33. Pierce | 38. Grant |
| | | | 34. Grant | 39. A. Johnson |
| | | | 35. Hoover | 40. Buchanan |
| | | | 36. Nixon | 41. Harding |
| | | | 37. A. Johnson | |
| | | | 38. Buchanan | |
| | | | 39. Harding | |

*Note:* These ratings result from surveys of scholars ranging in number from 55 to 950.

*Sources:* Arthur Murphy, "Evaluating the Presidents of the United States," *Presidential Studies Quarterly* 14 (1984): 117–26; Arthur M. Schlesinger, Jr., "Rating the Presidents: Washington to Clinton," *Political Science Quarterly* 112 (1997): 179–90; William J. Ridings and Stuart B. McIver, *Rating the Presidents* (Secaucus, N.J.: Citadel Press, 1997).

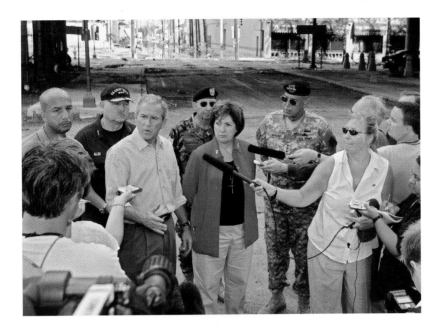

Crisis management is a key presidential responsibility. People look to the president for reassurance in times of national tragedy. President Bush is shown here during one of his many visits to the New Orleans area following Hurricane Katrina in 1995.

Reagan gave voice to the nation's feelings about the disaster: "I want to say something to the schoolchildren of America who were watching the live coverage of the shuttle's takeoff. I know it is hard to understand, but sometimes painful things like this happen. The future doesn't belong to the faint-hearted. It belongs to the brave." And the terrorist attack on America, September 11, 2001, transformed President George W. Bush in the eyes of the nation:

> Tonight we are a country awakened to danger and called to defend freedom. Our grief has turned to anger, and anger to resolution. Whether we bring our enemies to justice, or bring justice to our enemies, justice will be done.[3]

**The White House** This official White House site provides up-to-date information or news about the current president's policies, speeches, appointments, proclamations, and cabinet members.
*www.whitehouse.gov*

**Providing Policy Leadership**   The president is expected to set policy priorities for the nation. Most policy initiatives originate in the White House and various departments and agencies of the executive branch and then are forwarded to Congress with the president's approval. Presidential programs are submitted to Congress in the form of messages, including the president's annual State of the Union Address, and in the Budget of the United States Government, which the president presents each year to Congress.

As a political leader, the president is expected to mobilize political support for policy proposals. It is not enough for the president to send policy proposals to Congress. The president must rally public opinion, lobby members of Congress, and win legislative battles. To avoid being perceived as weak or ineffective, presidents must get as much of their legislative programs through Congress as possible. The president is responsible for "getting things done" in the policy arena.

**Managing the Economy**   The American people hold the president responsible for maintaining a healthy economy. Presidents are blamed for economic downturns, whether or not governmental policies had anything to do with market conditions. The president is expected to "Do Something!" in the face of high unemployment, declining personal income, high mortgage rates, rising inflation, high gasoline prices, or a stock market crash. Herbert Hoover in 1932, Gerald Ford in 1976, Jimmy Carter in 1980, and George Bush in 1992—all incumbent presidents defeated for reelection during recessions—learned the hard way that the general public holds the president responsible for hard economic times.

Presidents must have an economic "game plan" to stimulate the economy—tax incentives to spur investments, spending proposals to create jobs, plans to lower interest rates (see Chapter 13).

**Managing the Government**   As the chief executive of a mammoth federal bureaucracy with 2.8 million civilian employees, the president is responsible for implementing policy, that is, for achieving policy goals. Policy making does not end when a law is passed. Policy implementation involves issuing orders, creating organizations, recruiting and assigning personnel, disbursing funds, overseeing work, and evaluating results. It is true that the president cannot perform all of these tasks personally. But the ultimate responsibility for implementation—in the words of the Constitution, "to take Care that the Laws be faithfully executed"—rests with the president.

**The Global President**   Nations strive to speak with a single voice in international affairs; for the United States, the global voice is that of the president. As Commander-in-Chief of the armed forces of the United States, the president is a powerful voice in foreign affairs. Efforts by Congress to speak on behalf of the nation in foreign affairs and to limit the war-making power of the president have been generally unsuccessful. It is the president who orders American troops into combat (see *People in Politics:* "George Bush and the War on Terrorism").

## Constitutional Powers of the President

Popular expectations of presidential leadership far exceed the formal constitutional powers granted to the president. Compared with the Congress, the president has only modest constitutional powers (see Table 9.1). Nevertheless, presidents have pointed to a variety of clauses in Article II to support their rights to do everything from doubling the land area of the nation (Thomas Jefferson) to routing out terrorists from Afghanistan and invading Iraq (George W. Bush).

**Who May Be President?**   To become president, the Constitution specifies that a person must be a natural-born citizen at least thirty-five years of age and a resident of the United States for fourteen years.

Initially, the Constitution put no limit on how many terms a president could serve. George Washington set a precedent for a two-term maximum that endured until Franklin Roosevelt's decision to run for a third term in 1940 (and a fourth term in 1944). In reaction to Roosevelt's lengthy tenure, in 1947 Congress proposed the Twenty-second Amendment (ratified in 1951), which officially restricts the president to two terms (or one full term if a vice president must complete more than two years of the previous president's term).

**Presidential Succession**   Until the adoption of the Twenty-fifth Amendment in 1967, the Constitution had said little about presidential succession, other than designating the vice president as successor to the president "in Case of the Removal, . . . Death, Resignation, or Inability" and giving Congress the power to decide "what Officer shall then act as President" if both the president and vice president are removed. The Constitution was silent on how to cope with serious presidential illnesses. It contained no provision for replacing a vice president. The incapacitation issue was more than theoretical: James A. Garfield lingered months after being shot in 1881; Woodrow Wilson was an invalid during his last years in office (1919–20); Dwight Eisenhower suffered major heart attacks in office; and Ronald Reagan was in serious condition following an assassination attempt in 1981.

**American Presidents**
Biographical facts and key events in the lives of all U.S. presidents.
*www.americanpresidents.org*

**Table 9.1   The Constitutional Powers of the President**

**Chief Executive**

Implement policy: "take Care that the Laws be faithfully executed" (Article II, Section 3)
Supervise executive branch of government
Appoint and remove executive officials (Article II, Section 2)
Prepare executive budget for submission to Congress (by law of Congress)

**Chief Legislator**

Initiate policy: "give to the Congress Information of the State of the Union, and recommend to their Consider-
    ation such Measures as he shall judge necessary and expedient" (Article II, Section 3)
Veto legislation passed by Congress, subject to override by a two-thirds vote in both houses
Convene special session of Congress "on extraordinary Occasions" (Article II, Section 3)

**Chief Diplomat**

Make treaties "with the Advice and Consent of the Senate" (Article II, Section 2)
Exercise the power of diplomatic recognition: "receive Ambassadors" (Article II, Section 3)
Make executive agreements (by custom and international law)

**Commander-in-Chief**

Command U.S. armed forces: "The president shall be Commander-in-Chief of the Army and Navy" (Article II,
    Section 2)
Appoint military officers

**Chief of State**

"The executive Power shall be vested in a President" (Article II, Section 1)
Grant reprieves and pardons (Article II, Section 2)
Represent the nation as chief of state
Appoint federal court and Supreme Court judges (Article II, Section 2)

The Twenty-fifth Amendment stipulates that when the vice president and a majority of the cabinet notify the Speaker of the House and the president pro tempore of the Senate in writing that the president "is unable to discharge the powers and duties of his office," then the vice president becomes *acting* president. To resume the powers of office, the president must then notify Congress in writing that "no inability exists." If the vice president and a majority of cabinet officers do not agree that the president is capable of resuming office, then the Congress "shall decide the issue" within twenty-one days. A two-thirds vote of both houses is required to replace the president with the vice president.

The disability provisions of the amendment have never been used, but the succession provisions have been. The Twenty-fifth Amendment provides for the selection of a new vice president by presidential nomination and confirmation by a majority vote of both houses of Congress. When Vice President Spiro Agnew resigned in the face of bribery charges in 1973, President Richard Nixon nominated the Republican leader of the House, Gerald Ford, as vice president; and when Nixon resigned in 1974, Ford assumed the presidency and made Nelson Rockefeller, governor of New York, his vice president. Thus Gerald Ford's two-year tenure in the White House marked the only time in history when the man serving as president had not been elected to either the presidency or the vice presidency. (If the offices of president and vice president are both vacated, then Congress by law has specified the next in line for the presidency as the Speaker of the House of Representatives, followed by the president pro tempore of the Senate, then the cabinet officers, beginning with the secretary of state.)

## PEOPLE IN POLITICS

# George Bush and the War on Terrorism

In times of crisis for the nation, presidents matter. What they say, and what they do, create indelible images that determine how their presidencies are viewed by history. George W. Bush's place in history will likely be measured by his ability to inspire and mobilize the American public for the war on terrorism.

### An Unpromising Start

George W. Bush was born into his family's tradition of wealth, privilege, and public service. (Bush's grandfather, investment banker Prescott Bush, was a U.S. senator from Connecticut and chairman of the Yale Corporation, the university's governing board.)

He grew up in Midland, Texas, where his father had established himself in the oil business before going into politics—first as a Houston congressman, then Republican National Chairman, director of the CIA, ambassador to China, and finally vice president and president of the United States. George W. followed in his father's footsteps to Yale University, but he was not the scholar-athlete that his father had been. Rather, he was a friendly, likable, heavy-drinking president of his fraternity. Upon graduation in 1968, he joined the Texas Air National Guard, completed flight school, but never faced combat in Vietnam. He earned an [MBA] degree from Harvard Business School and returned to Midland to enter the oil business himself. Later in his career he would acknowledge his "youthful indiscretions," including a drunk driving arrest in 1976.

### Texas Governor

George W. Bush had never held public office before running for governor of Texas in 1994. But he had gained valuable political experience serving as an unofficial adviser to his father during his presidential campaigns. He went up against the sharp-tongued incumbent Democratic Governor Ann Richards, who ridiculed him as the "shrub" (little Bush). Bush heavily outspent Richards and won 54 percent of the vote, to become Texas's second Republican governor in modern times.

George W.'s political style fit comfortably with the Texas "good old boys" in both parties. Although the Texas legislature was controlled by Democrats, Bush won most of his early legislative battles. Bush's style was to meet frequently and privately with his Democratic opponents and to remain on friendly personal terms with them. He easily won reelection as governor in 1998.

### Running for President

Bush denies that his father ever tried to influence his decision to run for president, but many of his father's friends and political associates did, believing that only he could reclaim the White House for the GOP. They compared "Dubya" to Ronald Reagan—amiable, charming, and good-humored, even if a little vague on the details of public policy. His mother's 10,000-name Christmas card list of closest family friends helped in building a bankroll of more than $100 million before the campaign even began. And the GOP establishment stuck with him when he was challenged in the early primary elections by maverick Arizona Republican Senator and Vietnam war hero John McCain.

### His Father's Friends

While "Dubya's" father remained in the background, the president's White House and cabinet appointments indicated his reliance on experienced people to run the government. People who served in the Reagan and earlier Bush administrations surround George W. Bush. Bush chose Richard Cheney as his vice president, even though Cheney, as a former small state (Wyoming) congressman, brought no significant electoral votes to the ticket. But Cheney had won the confidence of the Bushes as secretary of defense during the Gulf War. Bush also brought the former chairman of the Joint Chiefs of Staff, Colin Powell, into his administration as secretary of state. President Gerald Ford's secretary of defense, Donald Rumsfeld, was reappointed to his old job. National

---

**impeachment** Equivalent of a criminal charge against an elected official; removal of the impeached official from office depends on the outcome of a trial.

**Impeachment** The Constitution grants Congress the power of **impeachment** over the president, vice president, and "all civil Officers of the United States" (Article II, Section 4). Technically, impeachment is a charge similar to a criminal indictment brought against an official. The power to bring charges of impeachment is given to the House of Representatives. The power to try all impeachments is given to the Senate, and "no Person shall be convicted without the Concurrence

Security Adviser Condoleezza Rice brought a reputation for brilliance and independence to her position. It was clear that "Dubya" was not afraid of being overshadowed by "heavyweights" in his administration.

### "9/11"

The terrorist attack on America, September 11, 2001, dramatically changed the political landscape in Washington and the nation. The attack became the defining moment in the presidency of George W. Bush. He grew in presidential stature, respect, and decisiveness. His public appearances and statements reassured the American people. He promptly declared a "War on Terrorism" against both the terrorist organizations themselves and the nations that harbor and support them.

Military action in Afghanistan followed quickly. Bush showed no hesitation, no indecision, no willingness to negotiate with terrorists. His public approval ratings skyrocketed: 90 percent of Americans approved of the way he was handling his job, a figure that even exceeded his father's approval ratings during the Gulf War. The rapid collapse of the hated Taliban government in Afghanistan seemed to confirm the wisdom of Bush's actions.

### Good Versus Evil

George Bush convinced the American people that the war on terrorism is "a monumental struggle of good versus evil." In his 2002 State of the Union message he specifically identified an "axis of evil"— Iraq, Iran, and North Korea. While many in the media scoffed at Bush's portrayal of the war on terrorism as a struggle between good and evil, most Americans heralded what they saw as Bush's "moral clarity" and the firmness of his convictions. Bush failed to win the support of the United Nations to oust Saddam Hussein from power in Iraq. (Only Britain, under the leadership of Tony Blair, gave Bush significant support.) But Bush succeeded in getting Congress to pass the joint resolution granting him authority to launch a preemptive military strike against Iraq. The early military phase of the war in Iraq went well; U.S. forces captured Baghdad in a mere 21 days, with precious few casualties. But remnants of Saddam's forces together with terrorists and other hard-line organizations began a guerrilla war against American and other coalition forces. Confronted with a prolonged struggle, costing lives and money, critics at home and abroad questioned American purposes in Iraq. Bush's high approval ratings began a slow decline. Throughout most of 2004, polls showed Bush running neck and neck with John Kerry in the presidential race. Kerry won the debates, but Bush remained "better at handling the war on terrorism." Election day brought the highest turnout in almost thirty years, and exit polls reported that "moral values" were the single most important concern of voters. These voters seemed to appreciate Bush's commitment to faith and family. He won 51 percent of the popular vote.

### Second Term Troubles

But Bush's second term turned out to be troublesome. His approval ratings plummeted into the 30s, and a majority of people turned against his "stay the course" policy in Iraq. He failed to get any significant legislation passed by a Republican Congress, despite impassioned pleas for Social Security and immigration reform. The election of a Democratic-controlled Congress in 2006 promised even more difficulties in his final two years in office. Bush was obliged to signal changes in Iraq policy by accepting the resignation of Defense Secretary Donald Rumsfeld the day after the midterm election.

After the September 11 terrorist attacks, U.S. troops moved quickly into Afghanistan to eliminate the Taliban.

of two thirds of the Members present" (Article I, Section 3). Impeachment by the House and conviction by the Senate only remove an official from office; a subsequent criminal trial is required to inflict any other punishment.

The Constitution specifies that impeachment and conviction can only be for "Treason, Bribery, or other High Crimes and Misdemeanors." These words indicate that Congress is not to impeach presidents, federal judges, or any other officials simply because Congress disagrees with their decisions or policies. Indeed, the phrase implies that only serious criminal offenses, not political conflicts, can result in impeachment. Nevertheless, politics was at the root of the impeachment of President Andrew Johnson in 1867. Johnson was a southern Democrat who had remained loyal to the Union. Lincoln had chosen him as vice president in 1864 as a gesture of national unity. A Republican House impeached him on a party-line vote, but after a month-long trial in the Senate, the "guilty" vote fell one short of the two-thirds needed for removal.[4] And partisan politics played a key role in the House impeachment and later Senate trial of Bill Clinton (see *Up Close:* "Sex, Lies, and Impeachment").

**Presidential Pardons**   The Constitution grants the president the power to "grant Reprieves and Pardons." This power derives from the ancient right to appeal to the king to reverse errors of law or justice committed by the court system. It is absolute: The president may grant pardons to anyone for any reason. The most celebrated use of the presidential pardon was President Ford's blanket pardon of former President Nixon "for all offenses against the United States which he, Richard Nixon, has committed or may have committed or taken part in." Ford defended the pardon as necessary to end "the bitter controversy and divisive national debate," but his actions may have helped cause his defeat in the 1976 election.

**Executive Power**   The Constitution declares that the "executive Power" shall be vested in the president, but it is unclear whether this statement grants the president any powers that are not specified later in the Constitution or given to the president by acts of Congress. In other words, does the grant of "executive Power" give presidents constitutional authority to act as they deem necessary *beyond* the actions specified elsewhere in the Constitution or specified in laws passed by Congress?

Contrasting views on this question have been offered over two centuries. President William Howard Taft provided the classic narrow interpretation of executive power: "The president can exercise no power which cannot be fairly and reasonably traced to some specific grant of power or justly implied and included within such express grant as proper and necessary to its exercise.[5] Theodore Roosevelt, Taft's bitter opponent in a three-way race for the presidency in 1912, expressed the opposite view: "My belief was that it was not only his right but his duty to do anything that the needs of the nation demanded, unless such action was forbidden by the Constitution or by the laws."[6] Although the constitutional question has never been fully resolved, history has generally sided with those presidents who have taken an expansive view of their powers.

**Some Historical Examples**   U.S. history is filled with examples of presidents acting independently, beyond specific constitutional powers or laws of Congress. Among the most notable:

- George Washington issued a Proclamation of Neutrality during the war between France and Britain following the French Revolution, thereby establishing the president's power to make foreign policy.

- Thomas Jefferson, who prior to becoming president argued for a narrow interpretation of presidential powers, purchased the Louisiana Territory despite the fact that the Constitution contains no provision for the acquisition of territory, let alone authorizing presidential action to do so.

---

— Think Again —

Should presidents have the power to take actions not specifically authorized by law or the Constitution that they believe necessary for the nation's well-being?

---

Center for the Study of the Presidency

Studies of the presidency and publication of the scholarly journal *Presidential Studies Quarterly*.

*www.thepresidency.org*

## UP CLOSE

# Sex, Lies, and Impeachment

Bill Clinton is the second president in the nation's history (following Andrew Johnson in 1867) to be impeached by the U.S. House of Representatives. (President Richard Nixon resigned just prior to an impeachment vote in 1974.)

Clinton's impeachment followed a report to the House by Independent Counsel Kenneth Starr in 1998 that accused the president of perjury, obstruction of justice, witness tampering, and "abuse of power." The Starr Report describes in graphic and lurid detail Clinton's sexual relationship with young White House intern Monica Lewinsky.

Does engaging in extramartial sex and lying about it meet the Constitution's standard for impeachment? "Treason, Bribery, or other High Crimes and Misdemeanors"? Perjury—knowingly giving false testimony in a sworn legal proceeding—is a criminal offense. But does the Constitution envision more serious misconduct? According to Alexander Hamilton in the *Federalist*, No. 65, impeachment should deal with "the abuse or violation of some public trust." Is Clinton's acknowledged "inappropriate behavior" a private affair or a violation of the public trust?

How are such questions decided? Despite pious rhetoric in Congress about the "search for truth," "impartial investigation," and "unbiased constitutional judgment," the impeachment process, whatever the merits of the charges against a president, is *political,* not judicial.

The House vote to impeach Clinton on December 19, 1998 (228 to 205) was largely along partisan lines, with all but five Republicans voting "yes" and all but five Democrats voting "no." And the vote in Clinton's Senate "trial" on February 12, 1999, was equally partisan. Even on the strongest charge—that Clinton had tried to obstruct justice—the Senate failed to find the president guilty. Removing Clinton failed to win even a majority of Senate votes, far less than the required two-thirds. All forty-five Democrats were joined by five Republicans to create a 50–50 tie vote that left Clinton tarnished but still in office.

Most Americans believed the president had a sexual affair in the White House and subsequently lied about it; however, they also *approved* of the way Clinton was performing his job as president. Indeed, the public appeared to rally around the president following the allegations of sexual misconduct.

Various explanations have been offered for this apparent paradox—a public that believed the president had an affair in the White House and lied about it, yet gave the president the highest approval ratings of his career. Many Americans believe that private sexual conduct is irrelevant to the performance

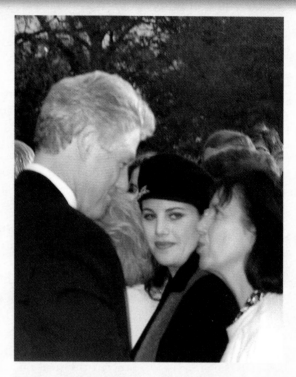

President Clinton greets well-wishers, including Monica Lewinsky, at a Democratic Party event in January 1996. Clinton's acknowledged "inappropriate behavior" and his efforts to conceal his relationship with Lewinsky were the subjects of the impeachment investigation opened against him by the House in 1998.

of public duties. Private morality is viewed as a personal affair about which Americans should be nonjudgmental. Some people said, "If it's okay with Hillary, why should we worry?" Haven't we had adulterous presidents before, from Thomas Jefferson to John F. Kennedy, presidents who were ranked highly in history? And many Americans believe that "they all do it."

Others argue, nonetheless, that private character counts in presidential performance, indeed, that it is a prerequisite for public trust. The president, in this view, performs a symbolic role that requires dignity, honesty, and respect. A president publicly embarrassed by sexual scandal, diminished by jokes, and laughed at by late-night television audiences cannot perform this role. The acceptance of a president's adulterous behavior, according to one commentator, lowers society's standards of behavior. "The president's legacy . . . will be a further vulgarization and demoralization of society."[a]

[a]Gertrude Himmelfarb, "Private Lives, Public Morality," *New York Times,* February 9, 1998.

- Andrew Jackson ordered the removal of federal funds from the national bank and removed his secretary of the treasury from office, establishing the president's power to *remove* executive officials, a power not specifically mentioned in the Constitution.

- Abraham Lincoln, asking, "Was it possible to lose the nation yet preserve the Constitution?" established the precedent of vigorous presidential action in national emergencies: He blockaded southern ports, declared martial law in parts of the country, and issued the Emancipation Proclamation—all without constitutional or congressional authority.

- Franklin D. Roosevelt, battling the Great Depression during the 1930s, ordered the nation's banks to close temporarily. Following the Japanese attack on Pearl Harbor in 1941, he ordered the incarceration without trial of many thousands of Americans of Japanese ancestry living on the West Coast.

**Checking Presidential Power**    President Harry Truman believed that "the president has the right to keep the country from going to hell," and he was willing to use means beyond those specified in the Constitution or authorized by Congress. In 1952, while U.S. troops were fighting in Korea, steelworkers at home were threatening to strike. Rather than cross organized labor by forbidding the strike under the terms of the Taft-Hartley Act of 1947 (which he had opposed), Truman chose to seize the steel mills by executive order and continue their operations under U.S. government control. The U.S. Supreme Court ordered the steel mills returned to their owners, however, acknowledging that the president may have inherent powers to act in a national emergency but arguing that Congress had provided a legal remedy, however distasteful to the president. Thus the president can indeed act to keep the country from "going to hell," but if Congress has already acted to do so, the president must abide by the law.[7]

The most dramatic illustration of the checking of presidential power was the forced resignation of Richard M. Nixon in 1974 (for details, see *Up Close:* "Watergate and the Limits of Presidential Power"). Nixon's conduct inspired the intense hostility of the nation's media, particularly the prestigious *Washington Post.* His high public approval ratings following the Vietnam peace agreement plummeted. A Democratic-controlled Senate created a special committee to investigate **Watergate** that produced damaging revelations almost daily. Congressional Republicans began to desert the embattled president. The Supreme Court ordered him to turn over White House audiotapes to a special investigator, tapes that implicated Nixon in cash payments to the men who had burglarized the Democratic National Committee offices during his 1972 reelection campaign. Facing the enmity of the media, the loss of public approval, opposition from his own party in the Congress, and the failure of his constitutional claim of "executive privilege" in the Supreme Court, Nixon became the only president of the United States ever to resign that office.

**Executive Privilege**    Over the years, presidents and scholars have argued that the Constitution's establishment of a separate executive branch of government entitles the president to **executive privilege**—the right to keep confidential communications from other branches of government. Public exposure of internal executive communications would inhibit the president's ability to obtain candid advice from subordinates and would obstruct the president's ability to conduct negotiations with foreign governments or to command military operations.

---

— Think Again —

Should Congress have the authority to call home U.S. troops sent by the president to engage in military actions overseas?

**Watergate**  The scandal that led to the forced resignation of President Richard M. Nixon. Adding "gate" as a suffix to any alleged corruption in government suggests an analogy to the Watergate scandal.

**executive privilege**  Right of a president to withhold from other branches of government confidential communications within the executive branch; although posited by presidents, it has been upheld by the Supreme Court only in limited situations.

## UP CLOSE

# Watergate and the Limits of Presidential Power

Richard Nixon was the only president ever to resign the office. He did so to escape certain impeachment by the House of Representatives and a certain guilty verdict in trial by the Senate. Yet Nixon's first term as president included a number of historic successes. He negotiated the first ever strategic nuclear arms limitation treaty, SALT I, with the Soviet Union. He changed the global balance of power in favor of the Western democracies by opening relations with the People's Republic of China and dividing the communist world. In his second term, he withdrew U.S. troops from Vietnam, negotiated a peace agreement, and ended one of America's longest and bloodiest wars. But his remarkable record is forever tarnished by his failure to understand the limits of presidential power.

On the night of June 17, 1972, five men with burglary tools and wiretapping devices were arrested in the offices of the Democratic National Committee in the Watergate Building in Washington. Also arrested were E. Howard Hunt, Jr., G. Gordon Liddy, and James W. McCord Jr., all employed by the Committee to Reelect the President (CREEP). All pleaded guilty and were convicted, but U.S. District Court Judge John J. Sirica believed that the defendants were shielding whoever had ordered and paid for the operation.

Although there is no evidence that Nixon himself ordered or had prior knowledge of the break-in, he discussed with his chief of staff, H. R. Haldeman, and White House advisers John Ehrlichman and John Dean the advisability of payoffs to buy the defendants' silence. Nixon hoped his landslide electoral victory in November 1972 would put the matter to rest.

But a series of sensational revelations in the *Washington Post* kept the story alive. Using an inside source known only as Deep Throat, Bob Woodward and Carl Bernstein, investigative reporters for the *Post,* alleged that key members of Nixon's reelection committee, including its chairman, former Attorney General John Mitchell, and White House staff were actively involved in the break-in and, more important, in the subsequent attempts at a cover-up.

In February 1973 the U.S. Senate formed a Special Select Committee on Campaign Activities—the "Watergate Committee"—to delve into Watergate and related activities. The committee's nationally televised hearings enthralled millions of viewers with lurid stories of "the White House horrors."

*Richard Nixon was the only president ever to resign the office. He did so in 1974 to avoid impeachment following the Watergate scandal. He is shown here leaving the White House for the last time.*

John Dean broke with the White House and testified before the committee that he had earlier warned Nixon the cover-up was "a cancer growing on the presidency." Then, in a dramatic revelation, the committee—and the nation—learned that President Nixon maintained a secret tape-recording system in the Oval Office. Hoping that the tapes would prove or disprove charges of Nixon's involvement in the cover-up, the committee issued a subpoena to the White House. Nixon refused to comply, arguing that the constitutional separation of powers gave the president an "executive privilege" to withhold his private conversations from Congress. However, the U.S. Supreme Court, voting 8 to 0 in *United States v. Richard M. Nixon,* ordered Nixon to turn over the tapes.

Despite the rambling nature of the tapes, committee members interpreted them as confirming Nixon's involvement in the payoffs and cover-up. Informed by congressional leaders of his own party that impeachment by a majority of the House and removal from office by two-thirds of the Senate were assured, on August 9, 1974, Richard Nixon resigned his office.

On September 8, 1974, new President Gerald R. Ford pardoned former President Nixon "for all offenses against the United States which he, Richard Nixon, has committed or may have committed or taken part in" during his presidency. Upon his death in 1994, Nixon was eulogized for his foreign policy successes.

But Congress has never recognized executive privilege. It has frequently tried to compel the testimony of executive officials at congressional hearings. Presidents have regularly refused to appear themselves at congressional hearings and have frequently refused to allow other executive officials to appear or divulge specific information, citing executive privilege. The federal courts have generally refrained from intervening in this dispute between the executive and legislative branches. However, the Supreme Court has ruled that the president is not immune from court orders when illegal acts are under investigation. In *United States v. Nixon* (1974), the U.S. Supreme Court acknowledged that although the president might legitimately claim executive privilege where military or diplomatic matters are involved, such a privilege cannot be invoked in a criminal investigation. The Court ordered President Nixon to surrender tape recordings of White House conversations between the president and his advisors during the Watergate scandal.[8] (See *Up Close:* "Watergate and the Limits of Presidential Power.")

**Presidential Impoundment**   The Constitution states that "no Money shall be drawn from the Treasury, but in Consequence of appropriations made by Law" (Article I, Section 9). Clearly the president cannot spend money *not* appropriated by Congress. But the Constitution is silent on whether the president *must* spend all of the money appropriated by Congress for various purposes. Presidents from Thomas Jefferson onward frequently refused to spend money appropriated by Congress, an action referred to as **impoundment**. But taking advantage of a presidency weakened by the Watergate scandal, the Congress in 1974 passed the Budget and Impoundment Control Act, which requires the president to spend all appropriated funds. The act does provide, however, that presidents may send Congress a list of specific **deferrals**—items on which they wish to postpone spending—and **rescissions**—items they wish to cancel altogether. Congress by *resolution* (which cannot be vetoed by the president) may restore the deferrals and force the president to spend the money. Both houses of Congress must approve a rescission; otherwise the government must spend the money.

**Responsibility to the Courts**   The president is not "above the law"; that is, his conduct is not immune from judicial scrutiny. The president's official conduct must be lawful; federal courts may reverse presidential actions found to be unconstitutional or violative of laws of Congress. And presidents are not immune from criminal prosecution; they cannot ignore demands to provide information in criminal cases. However, the Supreme Court has held that the president has "absolute immunity" from civil suits "arising out of the execution of official duties."[9] In other words, the president cannot be sued for damages caused by actions or decisions that are within his constitutional or legal authority.

But can the president be sued for *private* conduct beyond the scope of his official duties? In 1997 the U.S. Supreme Court rejected the notion of presidential immunity from civil claims arising from actions outside of the president's official duties.[10] (See *Up Close:* "William Jefferson Clinton v. Paula Corbin Jones," in Chapter 11.)

# Political Resources of the President

The real sources of presidential power are not found in the Constitution. The president's power is the *power to persuade*. As Harry Truman put it, "I sit here all day trying to persuade people to do things they ought to have sense enough to do without my persuading them. . . . That's all the powers of the president amount to."[11]

The president's political resources are potentially very great. The nation looks to the president for leadership, for direction, for reassurance. The president is

**impoundment** Refusal by a president to spend monies appropriated by Congress; outlawed except with congressional consent by the Budget and Impoundment Control Act of 1974.

**deferrals** Items on which a president wishes to postpone spending.

**rescissions** Items on which a president wishes to cancel spending.

the focus of public and media attention. The president has the capacity to mobilize public opinion, to communicate directly with the American people, and to employ the symbols of office to advance policy initiatives in both foreign and domestic affairs.

**The Reputation for Power**    A reputation for power is itself a source of power. Presidents must strive to maintain the image of power in order to be effective. A president perceived as powerful can exercise great influence abroad with foreign governments and at home with the Congress, interest groups, and the executive bureaucracy. A president perceived as weak, unsteady, bumbling, or error prone will soon become unpopular and ineffective.

**Presidential Popularity**    Presidential popularity with the American people is a political resource. Popular presidents cannot always transfer their popularity into foreign policy successes or legislative victories, but popular presidents usually have more success than unpopular presidents.

Presidential popularity is regularly tracked in national opinion polls. For more than forty years, national surveys have asked the American public: "Do you approve or disapprove of the way _____ is handling his job as president?" (see Figures 9.1 and 9.2). Analyses of variations over time in these poll results suggest some generalizations about presidential popularity (see Figure 9.1).

> **Think Again**
>
> Is presidential performance more related to character and personality than to policy positions?

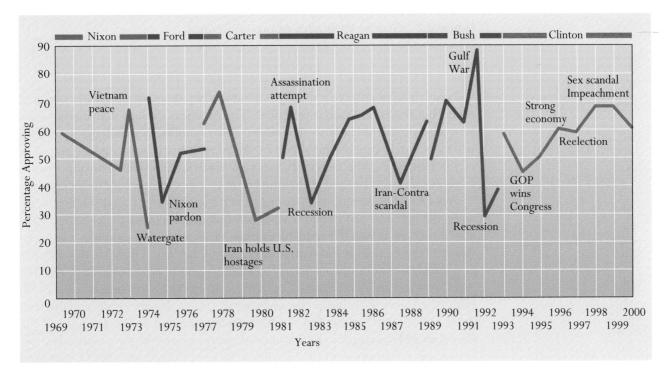

**Figure 9.1**    Presidential Popularity over Time

Americans expect a great deal from their presidents and are quick to give these leaders the credit—and the blame—for major events in the nation's life. In general, public approval (as measured by response to the question "Do you approve or disapprove of the way _____ is handling the job of president?") is highest at the beginning of a new president's term in office and declines from that point. Major military confrontations generally raise presidential ratings initially but can (as in the case of Lyndon Johnson) cause dramatic decline if the conflict drags on. In addition, public approval of the president is closely linked to the nation's economic health. When the economy is in recession, Americans tend to take a negative view of the president.

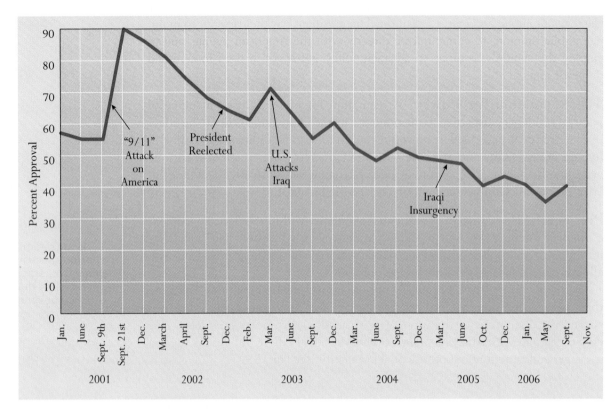

**Figure 9.2** George W. Bush's Approval Ratings

Presidential popularity is usually high at the beginning of a president's term of office, but this period can be very brief. The American public's high expectations for a new president can turn sour within a few months. A president's popularity will vary a great deal during a term in office, with sharp peaks and steep valleys in the ratings. But the general trend is downward.[12] Presidents usually recover some popularity at the end of their first term as they campaign for reelection.

Presidential popularity rises during crises. People "rally 'round the president" when the nation is confronted with an international threat or the president initiates a military action.[13] President George H.W. Bush, for example, registered nearly 90 percent approval during the Persian Gulf War. Likewise, the invasion of Grenada in 1983 and Panama in 1989 rallied support to the president. And the "9/11" terrorist attack on America rallied the American people behind George W. Bush (see Figure 9.2). But prolonged warfare and stalemate erode popular support. In both the Korean and the Vietnam wars, initial public approval of the president and support for the war eroded over time as military operations stalemated and casualties mounted.[14]

Major scandals *may* also hurt presidential popularity and effectiveness. The Watergate scandal produced a low of 22 percent approval for Nixon just prior to his resignation. Reagan's generally high approval ratings were blemished by the Iran-Contra scandal hearings in 1987, although he ultimately left office with a high approval rate. But highly publicized allegations of sexual improprieties against President Clinton in early 1998 appeared to have the opposite effect; Clinton's approval ratings went *up*. Perhaps the public differentiates between private sexual conduct and performance in office.

Finally, economic recessions erode presidential popularity. Every president in office during a recession has suffered loss of popular approval, including President

Reagan during the 1982 recession. But no president suffered a more precipitous decline in approval ratings than George H.W. Bush, whose popularity plummeted from its Gulf War high of 89 percent in 1991 to a low of 37 percent in only a year, largely as a result of recession.

**Access to the Media**    The president dominates the news more than any other single person. All major television networks, newspapers, and newsmagazines have reporters (usually their most experienced and skilled people) covering the "White House beat." The presidential press secretary briefs these reporters daily, but the president also may appear in person in the White House press room at any time. Presidents regularly use this media access to advance their programs and priorities.[15]

The **White House press corps** is an elite group of reporters assigned to cover the president. It includes the prestige press—the *New York Times, Washington Post, Wall Street Journal, Time, Newsweek, U.S. News and World Report*, as well as the television networks—ABC, CBS, NBC, CNN, FOX, and even the foreign press. Indeed, more than 1,800 journalists have White House press credentials. Fortunately, however, not all show up at once (there are only 48 seats in the White House briefing room, and attendance at press conferences is usually about 300). The great majority of daily newspapers have no Washington correspondents, but instead rely on national news services such as the Associated Press.

Formal press conferences are a double-edged sword for the president. They *can* help mobilize popular support for presidential programs. Presidents often try to focus attention on particular issues, and they generally open press conferences with a policy statement on these issues. But reporters' questions and subsequent reporting often refocus the press conference in other directions. Often the lead media story emerging from a press conference has nothing to do with the president's purpose in holding the conference. The president cannot control questions or limit the subject matter of press conferences.

Presidents may also use direct television addresses from the White House. (President Reagan made heavy use of national prime time television appeals to mobilize support for his programs; he was exceptionally successful in generating telephone calls, wires, and letters to Congress in support of his programs.) President George W. Bush has also used direct addresses to try to mobilize support for the war on terrorism, including military actions in Afghanistan and Iraq.

However, there is some evidence that with the multiplication of channels available to the public, presidential addresses may have less impact today on public opinion than in previous years. Television ratings for presidential addresses have been declining, and in reaction some broadcast networks have declined to cover presidential addresses.[16] Even the State of the Union Address attracts fewer viewers than in the past. Nonetheless, presidents continue to receive more television and press coverage than any other political figure. And a combination of national speeches, press conferences, speeches to various groups around the country, and media interviews, together with public appearances by members of their administrations, can move public opinion in the president's direction.[17]

**White House press corps**
Reporters from both print and broadcast media assigned to regularly cover the president.

# Personality versus Policy

A president with an engaging personality—warmth, charm, and good humor—can add to his political power. And, of course, a president who seems distant, uncaring, or humorless can erode his political resources. (Richard Nixon's seeming mean-spiritedness contributed to the collapse of his approval ratings during the Watergate scandal; Jimmy Carter's often cold and distant appearance failed

President George W. Bush answers questions during a press conference. These meetings with the press can be a double-edged sword. They give the president an opportunity to present his point of view to the public, but they also allow the press to raise issues a president might rather avoid.

to inspire much popular support for his programs; and George H. W. Bush appeared to be uncaring about the economic circumstances of ordinary Americans.) The public evaluates presidents as much on style as on policy substance.[18] (Perhaps no other president in recent times enjoyed such personal popularity while pursuing relatively unpopular policies as Ronald Reagan.) If the public thinks the president understands and cares about their problems, they may be willing to continue to approve of the job he is doing despite policy setbacks. In other words, the public evaluates the president by how much they like him as a person. (President Bill Clinton's likability kept his public approval ratings high during the sex scandal and impeachment effort.) Yet, as we have seen, public approval ratings of presidents can rise or fall based on wars and crises, scandals, and economic prosperity or recession, even while their personal style remains unaltered.

Bush's presidential campaigns, both against Al Gore in 2000 and John Kerry in 2004, rested largely on his personal appeal to voters—his perceived trustworthiness, warmth, good humor, and general "likability." With a strong economy, budget surpluses, relative peace, and a popular president to follow, Al Gore should have won the 2000 presidential election. But compared to Bush, Gore seemed stiff, wooden, artificial, and out of touch with common people. Bush mangled his sentences (and even joked about it) and offered fewer details about public policy issues.

Bush never hid his religious faith. He admitted to giving up drinking and carousing and finding religion earlier in his life. In 2004 Democratic Presidential candidate John Kerry appeared presidential, strong-voiced, articulate, and well-informed on the issues. He won the presidential debates but failed to shed his image as aloof, austere, and lacking in strong commitment to issues that mattered. Bush was able to characterize him as a "waffler" and a "flip-flopper." Bush, despite all his flaws, was seen as strong, uncomplicated, and "willing to take a stand."

**Party Leadership** Presidents are leaders of their party, but this role is hardly a source of great strength. It is true that presidents select the national party chair, control the national committee and its Washington staff, and largely direct the national party convention. Incumbent presidents can use this power to help defeat challengers *within* their own parties. President Ford used this power to help defeat challenger Ronald Reagan in 1976; President Carter used it to help defeat challenger Ted Kennedy in 1980; and President Bush used it against challenger Pat Buchanan in 1992. But the role of party leader is of limited value to a president because the parties have few direct controls over their members (see Chapter 7).

Nevertheless, presidents enjoy much stronger support in Congress from members of their own party than from members of the opposition party (see "Decision Making in Congress" in Chapter 8). Some of the president's party support in Congress is a product of shared ideological values and policy positions. But Republican Congress members do have some stake in the success of a Republican president, as do Democratic members in the success of a Democratic president. Popular presidents may produce those few extra votes that make the difference for party candidates in close congressional districts.

**Policy Leadership**   Presidents feel an obligation to exercise policy leadership—develop a policy agenda, to present it to the Congress, sell it to the American people, and lobby it through to success. Presidents are less likely than most politicians to pander to public opinion. Rather, they expect to be able to manipulate public opinion themselves.[19]

Nevertheless, there are times when presidents prudently decide to follow public opinion, rather than try to change it. First of all, presidents who are approaching a reelection contest become more responsive to public opinion. They are less likely to go off into new policy directions or to support unpopular policies. Generally, presidents present their policy initiatives at the beginning of their terms. This period usually corresponds to a president's high public approval rating. Indeed, throughout a presidential term, the higher their approval rating, the more likely they are to present new policy directions and even to take unpopular policy positions. In contrast, presidents experiencing low approval ratings are much less likely to present new policy initiatives or to pursue unpopular policies.[20]

# Chief Executive

The president is the chief executive of the nation's largest bureaucracy: 2.8 million civilian employees, 60 independent agencies, 15 departments, and the large Executive Office of the President. The formal organizational chart of the federal government places the president at the head of this giant structure (see Figure 10.1, "The Federal Bureaucracy," in Chapter 10). But the president cannot command this bureaucracy in the fashion of a military officer or a corporation president. When Harry Truman was preparing to turn over the White House to Dwight Eisenhower, he predicted that the general of the army would not understand the presidency: "He'll sit here and say 'Do this! Do that!' and nothing will happen. Poor Ike—it won't be a bit like the army. He'll find it very frustrating." Truman vastly underestimated the political skills of the former general, but the crusty Missourian clearly understood the frustrations confronting the nation's chief executive. The president does not command the executive branch of government but rather stands at its center—persuading, bargaining, negotiating, and compromising to achieve goals (see *Up Close:* "Contrasting Presidential Styles").

**The Constitutional Executive**   The Constitution is vague about the president's authority over the executive branch. It vests executive power in the presidency and grants the president authority to appoint principal officers of the government "by and with the Advice and Consent of the Senate." Under the Constitution, the president may also "require the Opinion, in writing, of the principal Officer in each of the executive Departments, upon any Subject relating to the Duties of their respective Offices." This awkward phrase presumably gives the president the power to oversee operations of the executive departments. Finally, and perhaps most important, the president is instructed to "take Care that the Laws be faithfully executed."

At the same time, Congress has substantial authority over the executive branch. Through its lawmaking abilities, Congress can establish or abolish executive departments and regulate their operations. Congress's "power of the purse" allows it to determine the budget of each department each year and thus to limit or broaden or even "micromanage" the activities of these departments. Moreover, Congress can pressure executive agencies by conducting investigations, calling administrators to task in public hearings, and directly contacting agencies with members' own complaints or those of their constituents.

**executive order** Formal regulation governing executive branch operations issued by the president.

**Executive Orders**  Presidents frequently use **executive orders** to implement their policies. Executive orders may direct specific federal agencies to carry out the president's wishes, or they may direct all federal agencies to pursue the president's preferred course of action. In any case, they must be based on either a president's constitutional powers or on powers delegated to the president by laws of Congress. Presidents regularly issue 50 to 100 executive orders each year, but some stand out. In 1942 President Franklin D. Roosevelt issued Executive Order 9066 for the internment of Japanese Americans during World War II. In 1948 President Harry Truman issued Executive Order 9981 to desegregate the U.S. armed forces. In 1965 President Lyndon Johnson issued Executive Order 11246 to require that private firms with federal contracts institute affirmative action programs. A president can even declare a national emergency by executive order, a step that authorizes a broad range of unilateral actions.

Executive orders have legal force when they are based on the president's constitutional or statutory authority. And presidents typically take an expansive view of their own authority. (President George Washington issued an executive order declaring American neutrality in the war between France and England in 1793. While the Constitution gave the power to "declare war" to Congress, Washington assumed the authority to declare neutrality.) Federal courts have generally upheld presidential executive orders. However, the Supreme Court overturned an order by President Harry Truman in 1951 during the Korean War seizing the nation's steel mills.[21] Research on the frequency of executive orders suggests that: Democratic presidents issue more orders than Republican presidents; presidents may issue executive orders to circumvent Congress but only when they believe that Congress will not overturn their orders; and presidents issue more executive orders when they are running for reelection.[22]

**Appointments**  Presidential power over the executive branch derives in part from the president's authority to appoint and remove top officials. Presidents can shape policy by careful attention to top appointments—cabinet secretaries, assistant secretaries, agency heads, and White House staff. The key is to select people who share the president's policy views and who have the personal qualifications to do an effective job. However, in cabinet appointments political considerations weigh heavily: unifying various elements of the party; appealing for interest-group support; rewarding political loyalty; providing a temporary haven for unsuccessful party candidates; achieving a balance of racial, ethnic, and gender representation.[23] The appointment power gives the president only limited control over the executive branch of government. Of the executive branch's 2.8 million civilian employees, the president actually appoints only about 3,000. The vast

## UP CLOSE

# Contrasting Presidential Styles

Every president brings to the White House his own personal administrative style. Some presidents work almost constantly, putting in twelve to fourteen hour days (Carter, Clinton). Others pursue a more leisurely schedule, leaving the Oval Office at 5 or 6 P.M. and spending weekends at the presidential retreat at Camp David or their home (Eisenhower, Reagan, Bush). Some presidents delegate a great deal of responsibility to Cabinet members and White House aides (Eisenhower, Reagan, Bush). Others closely monitor what is happening in executive departments and agencies (Johnson, Carter, Clinton). Some pursue a great many policy initiatives (Clinton), while others focus on a few key priorities (Reagan, Bush). Some are well informed about the specifics of public policy (Carter, Clinton), while others care more about overall goals and directions of their administration (Reagan, Bush). Some operate informally, communicating frequently with staff, Cabinet members, and others (Clinton). Other presidents function in a more business-like fashion, communicating mostly through their chief-of-staff (Eisenhower, Reagan). Below are the differences between the Bush and Clinton administrative styles as seen by two prominent political scientists.

### Differences Between the Bush and Clinton Presidencies

| George W. Bush | Bill Clinton |
| --- | --- |
| Disciplined White House | Less disciplined White House |
| Scripted presidency | Unscripted presidency |
| Strict focus on few key priorities | Wide-ranging policy focus |
| More reliance on vice president | Less reliance on vice president |
| Punctuality required for meetings with clear starting and ending times | Meetings start late and seldom end on time |
| Little use of the bully pulpit | More use of the bully pulpit |
| Direct public communicator | Skillful public communicator |
| Frequent reliance on experts to provide policy overviews | Well informed on policy issues |
| Somewhat more attentive to Congress and its members | Less attentive to Congress and its members |
| Large responsibilities delegated to aides | Close supervisory role maintained over all top aides |
| Preference for executive summaries | Enamored of thick briefing books |
| Regular working days observed insofar as practicable | A "24/7" president |

Source: Roger H. Davidson and Walter J. Oleszak, *Congress and Its Members*. 9th ed. (Washington, D.C.: CQ Press, 2004), p. 302.

majority of federal executive branch employees are civil servants—recruited, paid, and protected under civil service laws—and are not easily removed or punished by the president. Cabinet secretaries and heads of independent regulatory agencies require congressional confirmation, but presidents can choose their own White House staff without the approval of Congress.

Presidents have only limited power to remove the heads of independent regulatory agencies. By law, Congress sets the terms of these officials. Federal Communications Commission members are appointed for five years; Securities and Exchange Commission members for five years; and Federal Reserve Board members, responsible for the nation's money supply, enjoy the longest term of any executive officials—fourteen years. Congress's responsibility for term length for regulatory agencies is supposed to insulate those agencies, in particular their quasi-judicial responsibilities, from "political" influence.

**Budget** Presidential authority also derives from the president's role in the budgetary process. The Constitution makes no mention of the president with regard to expenditures; rather, it grants the power of the purse to Congress. Indeed, for nearly 150 years, executive departments submitted their budget requests directly to the Congress without first submitting them to the president. But with the passage of the Budget and Accounting Act in 1921, Congress established the Office of Management and Budget (OMB) (originally named the Bureau of the Budget) to assist the president in preparing an annual Budget of the United States Government for presentation to the Congress. The president's budget is simply a set of recommendations to the Congress. Congress must pass appropriations acts before the president or any executive department or agency may spend money. Congress can and frequently does alter the president's budget recommendations (see "The Politics of Budgeting" in Chapter 10).

**The Cabinet** The **cabinet** is not mentioned in the U.S. Constitution; it has no formal powers. It consists of the secretaries of the fifteen executive departments and others the president may designate, including the vice president, the Administrator of the Environmental Protection Agency, the Director of the Office of Management and Budget, the Director of National Drug Control Policy, and the Special Trade Representative. According to custom, cabinet officials are ranked by the date their departments were created (see Table 9.2). Thus the secretary of state is the senior cabinet officer, followed by the secretary of the treasury. They sit next to the president at cabinet meetings; heads of the newest departments sit at the far ends of the table.

The cabinet rarely functions as a decision-making body. Cabinet officers in the United States are powerful because they head giant administrative organizations. The secretary of state, the secretary of defense, the secretary of the treasury, the attorney general, and, to a lesser extent, the other departmental secretaries are all people of power and prestige. But seldom does a strong president hold a cabinet meeting to decide important policy questions. More

**cabinet** The heads (secretaries) of the executive departments together with other top officials accorded cabinet rank by the president; only occasionally does it meet as a body to advise and support the president.

**Cabinet**
The White House site provides the names of the current president's cabinet as well as those individuals with "cabinet-rank" status.
*www.whitehouse.gov/governme nt/cabinet.html*

---

**Table 9.2  The Cabinet Departments**

| Department | Created |
|---|---|
| State | 1789 |
| Treasury | 1789 |
| Defense* | 1947 |
| Justice | 1789 |
| Interior | 1849 |
| Agriculture† | 1889 |
| Commerce | 1913 |
| Labor | 1913 |
| Health and Human Services‡ | 1953 |
| Housing and Urban Development | 1965 |
| Transportation | 1966 |
| Energy | 1977 |
| Education | 1979 |
| Veterans' Affairs | 1989 |
| Homeland Security | 2002 |

*Formerly the War and Navy Departments, created in 1789 and 1798, respectively.

†Agriculture Department created in 1862, made part of cabinet in 1889.

‡Originally Health, Education, and Welfare; reorganized in 1979, with the creation of a separate Department of Education.

The Constitution designates the president as the nation's chief executive officer. The president names his cabinet secretaries (with the confirmation of the Senate). But the cabinet rarely meets as a body, and when it does, it is usually to allow the president to promote his views. President Bush is shown here with his cabinet in 2005.

frequently, presidents know what they want and hold cabinet meetings only to help promote their views.

The Constitution requires that "Officers of the United States" be confirmed by the Senate. In the past, the Senate rarely rejected a presidential cabinet nomination; the traditional view was that presidents were entitled to pick their own people and even make their own mistakes. In recent years, however, the confirmation process has become more partisan and divisive, with the Senate conducting lengthy investigations and holding public hearings on presidential cabinet nominees. The intense public scrutiny and potential for partisan attacks, together with financial disclosure and conflict-of-interest laws, may be discouraging some well-qualified people from accepting cabinet posts.

**The National Security Council**   The **National Security Council (NSC)** is really an "inner cabinet" created by law in 1947 to advise the president and coordinate foreign, defense, and intelligence activities. The president is chair, and the vice president, Secretary of State, Secretary of Defense and Secretary of the Treasury are participating members. The chair of the Joint Chiefs of Staff and the Director of Central Intelligence serve as advisers to the NSC. The President's National Security Advisor also sits on the NSC and heads its staff. The purposes of the council are to advise and coordinate policy; but in the Iran-Contra scandal in 1987, a staff member of the NSC, Lt. Col. Oliver North, undertook to *implement* security policy by directly channeling funds and arms to Nicaraguan "contras" fighting a communist-dominated government. Various investigative committees strongly recommended that the NSC staff confine itself to an advisory role.

**National Security Council (NSC)** "Inner cabinet" that advises the president and coordinates foreign, defense, and intelligence activities.

 **National Security Council**
Site provides brief history of NSC plus new releases dealing with national security.
*www.whitehouse.gov/nsc*

**White House Staff**   Today, presidents exercise their powers chiefly through the White House staff. This staff includes the president's closest aides and advisers. Over the years, the White House staff has grown from Roosevelt's small "brain trust" of a dozen advisers to several hundred people.

Senior White House staff members are trusted political advisers, often personal friends and long-time associates of the president. Some enjoy office space in the White House itself and daily contact with the president (see Figure 9.3). Appointed without Senate confirmation, they are loyal to the president alone, not to departments, agencies, or interest groups. Their many tasks include the following:

- Providing the president with sound advice on everything from national security to congressional affairs, policy development, and electoral politics.

**Figure 9.3**  The White House Corridors of Power
Presidents allocate office space in the White House according to their own desires.
An office located close to the president's is considered an indication of the power
of the occupant. This diagram shows the office assignments during the Clinton
Administration.

- Monitoring the operations of executive departments and agencies and evaluating the performance of key executive officials.

- Setting the president's schedule, determining whom the president will see and call, where and when the president will travel, and where and to whom the president will make personal appearances and speeches.

- Above all, the staff must protect their boss, steering the president away from scandal, political blunders, and errors of judgment.

The senior White House staff normally includes a chief of staff, the national security adviser, a press secretary, the counsel to the president (an attorney), a director of personnel (patronage appointments), and assistants for political affairs, legislative liaison, management, and domestic policy. Staff organization depends on each president's personal taste. Some presidents have organized their staffs hierarchically, concentrating power in the chief of staff. Others have maintained direct contact with several staff members.

**Presidential Perks**  Presidential perks are many, from the use of Air Force One to the living quarters of the White House. The president receives a salary of $400,000 per year, including a $50,000 expense allowance. Many presidential expenses are shifted to the budgets of other departments, especially the Department of Defense. Even after leaving the White House, benefits are generous; former President Bill Clinton receives an annual pension of $151,800 plus $150,000 for expenses. Presidents, First Ladies, and their children under 16, receive round-the-clock protection from the Secret Service.

# Chief Legislator and Lobbyist

The president has the principal responsibility for the initiation of national policy. Indeed, about 80 percent of the bills considered by Congress originate in the executive branch. Presidents have a strong incentive to fulfill this responsibility: the American people hold them responsible for anything that happens in the nation during their term of office, whether or not they have the authority or capacity to do anything about it.

**Policy Initiation**  The Founders understood that the president would be involved in policy initiation. The Constitution requires the president to "give to the Congress Information of the State of the Union," to "recommend to their Consideration such Measures as he shall judge necessary and expedient" (Article II, Section 3). "On extraordinary Occasions" the president may call a recessed Congress into special session. Each year the principal policy statement of the president comes in the State of the Union message to Congress. It is followed by the president's Budget of the United States Government, which sets forth the president's programs with price tags attached. Many other policy proposals are developed by executive departments and agencies, transmitted to the White House for the president's approval or "clearance," and then sent to Congress.

Congress may not accept all or even most of the president's proposals. Indeed, from time to time it may even try to develop its own legislative agenda in competition with the president's. But the president's legislative initiatives usually set the agenda of congressional decision making. As one experienced Washington lobbyist put it, "Obviously when the president sends up a bill, it takes first place in the queue. All other bills take second place."[24]

Presidents are expected to provide policy leadership and to work for congressional passage of their policy proposals. President Bush is shown here with the leadership of both the Democratic and Republican parties in the House and Senate.

**White House Lobbying**   Presidents do not simply send their bills to Congress and then await the outcome. The president is also expected to be the chief lobbyist on behalf of the administration's bills as they make their way through the legislative labyrinth. The White House staff includes "legislative liaison" people—lobbyists for the president's programs. They organize the president's legislative proposals, track them through committee and floor proceedings, arrange committee appearances by executive department and agency representatives, count votes, and advise the president on when and how to "cut deals" and "twist arms."

Presidents are not without resources in lobbying Congress. They may exchange many favors, large and small, for the support of individual members. They can help direct "pork" to a member's district, promise White House support for a member's pet project, and assist in resolving a member's problems with the bureaucracy. Presidents also may issue or withhold invitations to the White House for prestigious ceremonies, dinners with visiting heads of state, and other glittering social occasions—an effective resource because most members of Congress value the prestige associated with close White House "connections."

The president may choose to "twist arms" individually—by telephoning and meeting with wavering members of Congress. Arm twisting is generally reserved for the president's most important legislative battles. There is seldom time for a president to contact individual members of Congress personally about many bills in various stages of the legislative process—in subcommittee, full committee, floor consideration, conference committee, and final passage—in both the House and the Senate. Instead, the president must rely on White House staff for most legislative contacts and use personal appeals sparingly.

**honeymoon period** Early months of a president's term in which his popularity with the public and influence with the Congress are generally high.

**The Honeymoon**   The **honeymoon period** at the very start of a president's term offers the best opportunity to get the new administration's legislative proposals enacted into law. Presidential influence in Congress is generally highest at this time both because the president's personal popularity is typically at its height and because the president can claim the recent election results as a popular mandate for key programs. Sophisticated members of Congress know that votes cast for a presidential candidate are not necessarily votes cast for that candidate's policy position (see "The Voter Decides" in Chapter 5). But election results signal members of Congress, in a language they understand well, that the president is politically popular and that they must give the administration's programs careful consideration. President Lyndon Johnson succeeded in getting the bulk of his Great Society program enacted in the year following his landslide victory in 1964. Ronald Reagan pushed through the largest tax cut in American history in

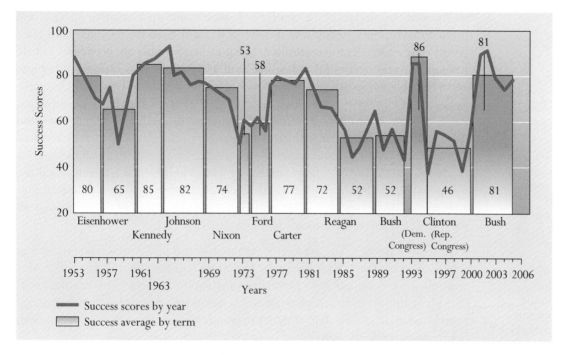

**Figure 9.4** Presidential Success Scores in Congress

Presidential "box scores"—the percentage of times that a bill endorsed by the president is enacted by Congress—are closely linked to the strength of the president's party in Congress. For example, both Dwight D. Eisenhower and Ronald Reagan benefited from having a Republican majority in the Senate in their first terms and suffered when Democrats gained control of the Senate in their second terms. Democratic control of both houses of Congress resulted in significantly higher box scores for Democratic presidents John Kennedy, Lyndon Johnson, and Jimmy Carter than for Republicans Richard Nixon, Gerald Ford, and George Bush. Clinton was very successful in his first two years, when the Democrats controlled Congress, but when the Republicans won control following the 1994 midterm election, Clinton's box score plummeted. Bush enjoyed a Republican Congress and therefore succeeded in passing over 80 percent of his bills.

the year following his convincing electoral victory over incumbent president Jimmy Carter in 1980. Bill Clinton was most successful with the Congress during his first year in office, in 1993, even winning approval for a major tax increase as part of a deficit-reduction package. And George W. Bush succeeded in getting a tax cut through Congress in his first six months in office. Both Democrat Clinton and Republican Bush benefited from having their party control the Congress during their first months in office.

**Presidential "Box Scores"**    How successful are presidents in getting their legislation through Congress? *Congressional Quarterly* regularly compiles "box scores" of presidential success in Congress—percentages of presidential victories on congressional votes on which the president took a clear-cut position. The measure does not distinguish between bills that were important to the president and bills that may have been less significant. But viewed over time (see Figure 9.4), the presidential box scores provide interesting insights into the factors affecting the president's legislative success.

The most important determinant of presidential success in Congress is party control. Presidents are far more successful when they face a Congress controlled by their own party. Democratic presidents John F. Kennedy and Lyndon Johnson enjoyed the support of Democratic-controlled Congresses and posted average success scores over 80 percent. Jimmy Carter was hardly a popular president, but he enjoyed the support of a Democratic Congress and an average of 76.8 percent presidential support. Republican presidents Richard Nixon and Gerald Ford fared poorly with Democratic-controlled Congresses. Republican president Ronald Reagan was very successful in his first term when he faced a Democratic House and a Republican Senate, but after Democrats took over both houses of Congress, Reagan's success rate plummeted. During the Reagan and Bush presidencies, divided party control of government (Republicans in the White House and Democrats controlling one or both houses of Congress) was said to produce **gridlock**, the political inability of the government to act decisively on the nation's problems. President Bill Clinton's achievements when Democrats controlled the Congress (1993–94), contrasted with his dismal record in dealing with Republican-controlled Congresses (1995–99), provide a vivid illustration of the importance of party in determining a president's legislative success.

**The Veto Power**    The **veto** is the president's most powerful weapon in dealing with Congress. The veto is especially important to a president facing a Congress controlled by the opposition party. Even the *threat* of a veto enhances the president's bargaining power with Congress.[25] Confronted with such a threat, congressional leaders must calculate whether they can muster a two-thirds vote of both houses to override the veto.

To veto a bill passed by the Congress, the president sends to Congress a veto message specifying reasons for not signing it. If the president takes no action for ten days (excluding Sundays) after a bill has been passed by Congress, the bill becomes law without the president's signature. However, if Congress has adjourned within ten days of passing a bill and the president has not signed it, then the bill does not become law; this outcome is called a **pocket veto**.

A bill returned to Congress with a presidential veto message can be passed into law over the president's opposition by a two-thirds vote of both houses. (A bill that has received a pocket veto cannot be overridden because the Congress is no longer in session.) In other words, the president needs only to hold the loyalty of more than one-third of *either* the House or the Senate to sustain a veto. If congressional leaders cannot count on the votes to **override**, they are forced to bargain with the president. "What will the president accept?" becomes a key legislative question.

The president's bargaining power with Congress has been enhanced over the years by a history of success in sustaining presidential vetoes.[26] From George Washington to Bill Clinton, more than 96 percent of all presidential vetoes have been sustained (see Table 9.3). For example, although George H.W. Bush was unable to achieve much success in getting his own legislative proposals enacted by a Democratic Congress, he was extraordinarily successful in saying no. Of Bush's many vetoes, only one (regulation of cable TV) was overridden by Congress. Clinton did not veto any bills when Democrats controlled Congress, but he began a series of vetoes in his struggle with the Republican Congress elected in 1994. He was able to sustain almost all of his vetoes because Republicans did not have two-thirds of the seats in both houses and most Democratic Congress members stuck with their president.

**Line-Item Veto Power Denied**    For many years, presidents, both Democratic and Republican, petitioned Congress to give them the **line-item veto**, the ability to veto some provisions of a bill while accepting other provisions. The lack of presidential line-item veto power was especially frustrating when dealing with appropriations bills because the president could not veto specific pork-barrel provisions from major spending bills for defense, education, housing, welfare, and so on. Finally, in 1996 Congress granted the president authority to

**gridlock**  Political stalemate between the executive and legislative branches arising when one branch is controlled by one major political party and the other branch by the other party.

**veto**  Rejection of a legislative act by the executive branch; in the U.S. federal government, overriding of a veto requires a two-thirds majority in both houses of Congress.

**pocket veto**  Effective veto of a bill when Congress adjourns within ten days of passing it and the president fails to sign it.

**override**  Voting in Congress to enact legislation vetoed by the president; requires a two-thirds vote in both the House and Senate.

**line-item veto**  Power of the chief executive to reject some portions of a bill without rejecting all of it.

**Table 9.3**  **Presidential Vetoes**

| President | Total Vetoes* | Vetoes Overridden | Percentage of Vetoes Sustained |
|---|---|---|---|
| F. Roosevelt | 633 | 9 | 99% |
| Truman | 250 | 12 | 95 |
| Eisenhower | 181 | 2 | 99 |
| Kennedy | 21 | 0 | 100 |
| L. Johnson | 30 | 0 | 100 |
| Nixon | 43 | 5 | 90 |
| Ford | 66 | 12 | 85 |
| Carter | 31 | 2 | 94 |
| Reagan | 78 | 8 | 91 |
| Bush | 46 | 1 | 98 |
| Clinton | 37 | 2 | 95 |
| Bush | 1 | 0 | — |

*Regular vetoes plus pocket vetoes.

*Source:* Harold W. Stanley and Richard G. Niemi, *Vital Statistics on American Politics, 1999–2000* (Washington, D.C.: CQ Press, 2000), p. 256. Updated by author.

"cancel" spending items in any appropriation act and any limited tax benefit. Such cancellation would take effect immediately unless blocked by a special "disapproval bill" passed by Congress.

However, opponents of the line-item veto successfully challenged its constitutionality, arguing that it transfers legislative power—granted by the Constitution only to Congress—to the president. The U.S. Supreme Court agreed: "There is no provision in the Constitution that authorizes the president to enact or amend or repeal statutes." The line-item veto, the Court said, "authorizes the president himself to elect to repeal laws, for his own policy reasons" and therefore violates the law-making procedures set forth in Article I of the Constitution.[27]

# Global Leader

The president of the United States is the leader of the world's largest and most powerful democracy. During the cold war, the president of the United States was seen as the leader of the "free world." The threat of Soviet expansionism, the huge military forces of the Warsaw Pact, and Soviet-backed guerrilla wars around the world all added to the global role of the American president as the defender of democratic values. In today's post–cold war world, Western Europe and Japan are formidable economic competitors and no longer routinely defer to American political leadership. But if a new stable world order based on democracy and self-determination is to emerge, the president of the United States must provide the necessary leadership.

Global leadership is based on a president's powers of persuasion. Presidents are more persuasive when the American economy is strong, when American military forces are perceived as ready and capable, and when the president is seen as having the support of the American people and Congress. America's allies as well as its enemies perceive the president as the controlling force over U.S. foreign and military policy. Only occasionally do they seek to bypass the president and appeal to the Congress or to American public opinion.

The president is recognized throughout the world as the American "head of state"; this power aids him in dominating American foreign and defense policy making. British Prime Minister Tony Blair was one of the very few foreign leaders to support Bush's policies in Iraq, support that eventually led to Blair's replacement.

Presidents sometimes prefer their global role to the much more contentious infighting of domestic politics. Abroad, presidents are treated with great dignity as head of the world's most powerful state. In contrast, at home presidents must confront hostile and insulting reporters, backbiting bureaucrats, demanding interest groups, and contentious members of Congress.

**State Department**
Official site includes news, travel warnings, international issues, and background notes on countries of the world.
*www.state.gov*

**Foreign Policy**   As the nation's chief diplomat, the president has the principal responsibility for formulating U.S. foreign policy. The president's constitutional powers in foreign affairs are relatively modest. Presidents have the power to make treaties with foreign nations "with the Advice and Consent of the Senate." Presidents may negotiate with nations separately or through international organizations such as the North Atlantic Treaty Organization (NATO) or the United Nations, where the president determines the U.S. position in that body's deliberations. The Constitution also empowers the president to "appoint Ambassadors, other public Ministers, and Consuls" and to "receive Ambassadors." This power of **diplomatic recognition** permits a president to grant legitimacy to or withhold it from ruling groups around the world (to declare or refuse to declare them "rightful"). Despite controversy, President Franklin Roosevelt officially recognized the communist regime in Russia in 1933, Richard Nixon recognized the communist government of the People's Republic of China in 1972, and Carter recognized the communist Sandinistas' regime in Nicaragua in 1979. To date, all presidents have withheld diplomatic recognition of Fidel Castro's government in Cuba.

**diplomatic recognition**
Power of the president to grant "legitimacy" to or withhold it from a government of another nation (to declare or refuse to declare it "rightful").

Presidents have expanded on these modest constitutional powers to dominate American foreign policy making. In part, they have done so as a product of their role as Commander-in-Chief. Military force is the ultimate diplomatic language. During wartime, or when war is threatened, military and foreign policy become inseparable. The president must decide on the use of force and, equally important, when and under what conditions to order a cease-fire or an end to hostilities.

Presidents have also come to dominate foreign policy as a product of the customary international recognition of the head of state as the legitimate voice of a government. Although nations may also watch the words and actions of the American Congress, the president's statements are generally taken to represent the official position of the U.S. government.

**Treaties**    Treaties the president makes "by and with the Advice and Consent of the Senate" are legally binding upon the United States. The Constitution specifies that "all Treaties made . . . under the Authority of the United States, shall be the supreme Law of the Land, and the Judges in every State shall be bound thereby" (Article VI). Thus treaty provisions are directly enforceable in federal courts.

Although presidents may or may not listen to "advice" from the Senate on foreign policy, no formal treaty is valid unless "two-thirds of the Senators present concur" to its ratification. Although the Senate has ratified the vast majority of treaties, presidents must be sensitive to Senate concerns. The Senate defeat of the Versailles Treaty in 1920, which formally ended World War I and established the League of Nations, prompted Presidents Roosevelt and Truman to include prominent Democratic and Republican members of the Senate Foreign Relations Committee in the delegation that drafted the United Nations Charter in 1945 and the NATO Treaty in 1949.

President Clinton was sharply reminded of the need to develop bipartisan support for treaties in the Senate in 1999 when that body rejected the Comprehensive Test Ban Treaty. This treaty would have prohibited all signatory nations from conducting any tests of nuclear weapons. Most Western European nations had already signed and ratified the nuclear test ban, but North Korea, Iraq, Iran, India, and Pakistan, among other nations, had rejected it. China and Russia appeared to be waiting for the United States to act first. The president argued that the United States should take moral leadership in worldwide nonproliferation of nuclear weapons. His opponents in the Senate argued that too many rogue nations would ignore the treaty and continue their own nuclear testing. Despite the Senate's rejection of the treaty, Clinton continued by executive order his own moratorium on nuclear testing by the United States (see Chapter 14).

**Executive Agreements**    Over the years, presidents have come to rely heavily on **executive agreements** with other governments rather than formal treaties. An executive agreement signed by the president of the United States has much the same effect in international relations as a treaty. However, an executive agreement does not require Senate ratification. Presidents have asserted that their constitutional power to execute the laws, command the armed services, and determine foreign policy gives them the authority to make agreements with other nations and heads of state without obtaining approval of the U.S. Senate. However, unlike treaties, executive agreements do not supersede laws of the United States or of the states with which they conflict, but they are otherwise binding on the United States.

The use of executive agreements in important foreign policy matters was developed by President Franklin Roosevelt. Prior to his administration, executive agreements had been limited to minor matters. But in 1940, Roosevelt agreed to trade fifty American destroyers to England in exchange for naval bases in Newfoundland and the Caribbean. Roosevelt was intent on helping the British in their struggle against Nazi Germany, but before the Japanese attack on Pearl Harbor in 1941, isolationist sentiment in the Senate was too strong to win a two-thirds ratifying vote for such an agreement. Toward the end of World War II, Roosevelt at the Yalta Conference and Truman at the Potsdam Conference negotiated secret executive agreements dividing the occupation of Germany between the Western Allies and the Soviet Union.

Congress has sometimes objected to executive agreements as usurping its own powers. In the Case Act of 1972, Congress required the president to inform Congress of all executive agreements within sixty days, but the act does not limit the president's power to make agreements. It is easier for Congress to renege on executive agreements than on treaties that the Senate has ratified. In 1973 President

**Treaties in Force**
Complete list of all treaties of the U.S. in force as of January 1, 2000.
*www.state.gov/www/global/legalaffairs*

**executive agreement**
Agreement with another nation signed by the president of the United States but less formal (and hence potentially less binding) than a treaty because it does not require Senate confirmation.

President Bush, acting as the United States' "Chief Diplomat," with British Prime Minister Tony Blair as they begin two days of talks dominated by the rise of violence in the Middle East.

Nixon signed an executive agreement with South Vietnamese President Nguyen Van Thieu pledging that the United States would "respond with full force" if North Vietnam violated the Paris Peace Agreement that ended American participation in the Vietnam War. But when North Vietnam reinvaded the south in 1975, Congress rejected President Gerald Ford's pleas for renewed military aid to the South Vietnamese government, and Ford knew that it had become politically impossible for the United States to respond with force.

**Intelligence**   The president is responsible for the intelligence activities of the United States. Presidents have undertaken intelligence activities since the founding of the nation. During the Revolutionary War, General George Washington nurtured small groups of patriots living behind British lines who supplied him with information on Redcoat troop movements.[28] Today, the National Intelligence Director (NID) is appointed by the president (subject to Senate confirmation) and reports directly to the president.

The NID coordinates the activities of the "intelligence community" (see *Up Close:* "Reorganizing Intelligence After 9/11" in Chapter 10). Some elements of the intelligence community—the Central Intelligence Agency, the Defense Intelligence Agency, the National Security Agency, the National Reconnaissance Office, and the National Geo-Spacial Agency—deal exclusively with intelligence collection, analysis and distribution. Other elements of the intelligence community are located in the Department of Defense, Department of Homeland Security, Federal Bureau of Investigation, Department of State, Department of Energy, and Department of the Treasury. Indeed, the fragmentation of the intelligence community may be its principal weakness.[29]

**covert action** Secret intelligence activity outside U.S. borders undertaken with specific authorization by the president; acknowledgment of U.S. sponsorship would defeat or compromise its purpose.

**The Central Intelligence Agency**   The CIA provides intelligence on national security to the president, the NID, the National Security Council, and other top Washington decision makers. The CIA is responsible for (1) assembly, analysis, and dissemination of intelligence information from all agencies in the intelligence community; (2) collection of human intelligence from abroad; (3) with specific "presidential findings," the conduct of **covert actions**, including paramilitary special operations.

Covert actions refer to activities in support of the national interest of United States that would be ineffective if their sponsorship were made public. For example, one of the largest covert actions ever undertaken by the United States was the support, for nearly ten years, of the Afghan rebels fighting Soviet occupation of their country during the Afghanistan war (1978–88). Public acknowledgment of such aid would have assisted the Soviet-backed regime in Afghanistan to claim that the rebels were not true patriots but rather "puppets" of the United States. The rebels themselves did not wish to acknowledge U.S. aid publicly, even though they knew it was essential to the success of their cause. Hence Presidents Carter and Reagan aided the Afghan rebels through covert action.

Covert action is, by definition, secret. And secrecy spawns elaborate conspiracy theories and flamboyant tales of intrigue and deception. In fact, most covert actions consist of routine transfers of economic aid and military equipment to pro-U.S. forces that do not wish to acknowledge such aid publicly. Although most covert actions would have widespread support among the American public if they were done openly, secrecy opens the possibility that a president will undertake to do by covert action what would be opposed by Congress and the American people if they knew about it.

In the atmosphere of suspicion and distrust engendered by the Watergate scandal, Congress passed intelligence oversight legislation in 1974 requiring a written "presidential finding" for any covert action and requiring that members of the House and Senate Intelligence Committees be informed of all covert actions. The president does not have to obtain congressional approval for covert actions; but Congress can halt such actions if it chooses to do so.

**Central Intelligence Agency**
The CIA site provides information about the agency's mission, organization, values, press releases, and congressional testimony along with employment possibilities.
*www.CIA.gov*

## Commander-in-Chief

Global power derives primarily from the president's role as Commander-in-Chief of the armed forces of the United States. Presidential command over the armed forces is not merely symbolic; presidents may issue direct military orders to

Although still part of the "Big Three," along with Prime Minister Winston Churchill of Great Britain (right) and Marshal Josef Stalin of the Soviet Union (left), it was a gravely ill President Franklin Roosevelt (middle) who traveled to Yalta, a port on Russia's Crimean peninsula, and negotiated secret executive agreements dividing Germany among the Allies in 1945. Germany remained divided until 1989, when protesters tore down the Berlin Wall and the Soviet Union under Mikhail Gorbachev acquiesced in the unification of Germany under a democratic government.

troops in the field. As president, Washington personally led troops to end the Whiskey Rebellion in 1794; Abraham Lincoln issued direct orders to his generals in the Civil War; Lyndon Johnson personally chose bombing targets in Vietnam; and George H. W. Bush personally ordered the Gulf War cease-fire after 100 hours of ground fighting. All presidents, whether they are experienced in world affairs or not, soon learn after taking office that their influence throughout the world is heavily dependent upon the command of capable military forces.

**War-making Power**   Constitutionally, war-making power is divided between the Congress and the president. Congress has the power "to declare war," but the president is the "Commander-in-Chief of the Army and Navy of the United States."

In reality, however, presidents have exercised their powers as Commander-in-Chief to order U.S. forces into military action overseas on many occasions—from John Adams's ordering of U.S. naval forces to attack French ships (1798–99) to Harry Truman's decision to intervene in the Korean War (1951–53) to Lyndon Johnson's and Richard Nixon's conduct of the Vietnam War (1965–73), to George H. W. Bush's Operation Desert Storm (1991), to Bill Clinton's interventions in Bosnia and Kosovo (1998–99), to George W.'s military actions in Afghanistan (2001) and Iraq (2003). The Supreme Court has consistently refused to hear cases involving the war powers of the president and Congress.[30]

Thus, although Congress retains the formal power to "declare war," in modern times wars are seldom "declared." Instead, they begin with direct military actions, and the president, as Commander-in-Chief of the armed forces, determines what those actions will be. Historically, Congress accepted the fact that only the president has the information-gathering facilities and the ability to act with the speed and secrecy required for military decisions during periods of crisis. Not until the Vietnam War was there serious congressional debate over whether the president has the power to commit the nation to war.

**War Powers Resolution**   In the early days of the Vietnam War, the liberal leadership of the nation strongly supported Democratic President Lyndon Johnson's power to commit the nation to war. By 1969, however, many congressional leaders had withdrawn their support of the war. With a new Republican president, Richard Nixon, and a Democratic Congress, congressional attacks on presidential policy became much more partisan.

Antiwar members of Congress made several attempts to end the war by cutting off money for U.S. military activity in Southeast Asia. Such legislation only passed after President Nixon announced a peace agreement in 1973, however. It is important to note that Congress has *never* voted to cut off funds to support American armies while they were in the field.

Congress also passed the **War Powers Resolution**, designed to restrict presidential war-making powers, in 1973. (President Nixon vetoed the bill, but the Watergate affair undermined his support in Congress, which overrode his veto.) The act has four major provisions:

1. In the absence of a congressional declaration of war, the president can commit armed forces to hostilities or to "situations where imminent involvement in hostilities is clearly indicated by the circumstances" only:

   ■ To repel an armed attack on the United States or to forestall the "direct and imminent threat of such an attack."

   ■ To repel an armed attack against U.S. armed forces outside the United States or to forestall the threat of such attack.

**DefenseLink**
Official site of U.S. Department of Defense, with news and links to Army, Navy, Air Force, and Marine Corps Web sites and other defense agencies and commands.
*www.defenselink.gov*

**War Powers Resolution** Bill passed in 1973 to limit presidential war-making powers; it restricts when, why, and for how long a president can commit U.S. forces and requires notification of and, in many cases, approval by Congress.

- To protect and evacuate U.S. citizens and nationals in another country if their lives are threatened.

2. The president must report promptly to Congress the commitment of forces for such purposes.

3. Involvement of U.S. forces must be no longer than sixty days unless Congress authorizes their continued use by specific legislation.

4. Congress can end a presidential commitment by resolution, an action that does not require the president's signature.

**Presidential Noncompliance** The War Powers Resolution raises constitutional questions. A Commander-in-Chief clearly can order U.S. forces to go anywhere. Presumably, Congress cannot constitutionally command troops, yet that is what the act attempts to do by specifying that troops must come home if Congress orders them to do so or if Congress simply fails to endorse the president's decision to commit them. No president—Democrat or Republican—can allow Congress to usurp this presidential authority. Thus, since the passage of the War Powers Resolution, presidents have continued to undertake military actions on their own initiative (see Table 14.1 in Chapter 14).

Politically, it is often important for the president to show the world, and especially enemies of the United States, that he has congressional support for going to war. For this reason, presidents have asked Congress for resolutions in support of using military means to achieve specific goals. President George H. W. Bush asked for and received (by a close vote) a resolution of support to use military force to oust Iraqi forces from Kuwait in 1991. President George W. Bush won strong support for a congressional resolution in 2002 to allow him to use military force to make Saddam Hussein comply with U.N. resolutions. Both presidents claimed that they had the constitutional authority as Commander-in-Chief to use military force even *without* such resolutions. But politically such resolutions strengthen the president when he chooses to use military force. (See "Political Support for War in Iraq" in Chapter 14.)

**Presidential Use of Military Force in Domestic Affairs** Democracies are generally reluctant to use military force in domestic affairs. Yet the president has the constitutional authority to "take Care that the Laws be faithfully executed" and, as Commander-in-Chief of the armed forces, can send them across the nation as well as across the globe. The Constitution appears to limit presidential use of military forces in domestic affairs to protecting states "against domestic Violence" and only "on Application of the [state] Legislature or the [state] Executive (when the Legislature cannot be convened)" (Article IV, Section 4). Although this provision would seem to require states themselves to request federal troops before they can be sent to quell domestic violence, historically presidents have not waited for state requests to send troops when federal laws, federal court orders, or federal constitutional guarantees are being violated.

Relying on their constitutional duty to "faithfully execute" federal laws and their command over the nation's armed forces, presidents have used military force in domestic disputes since the earliest days of the Republic. Perhaps the most significant example of a president's use of military force in domestic affairs was Dwight Eisenhower's 1957 dispatch of U.S. troops to Little Rock, Arkansas, to enforce a federal court's desegregation order. In this case, the president acted directly *against* the expressed wishes of the state's governor, Orval Faubus, who had posted state units of the National Guard at the entrance of Central High School to prevent the admission of black students, which had been ordered by the federal court. Eisenhower officially called Arkansas's National Guard units into federal service, took

—Think Again—

Should Congress have the authority to call home U.S. troops sent by the president to engage in military actions overseas?

Despite a Supreme Court ruling that segregation in education was illegal, many southern states continued to try to keep their schoolhouse doors closed to black students. Here Elizabeth Eckford, a fifteen-year-old resident of Little Rock, Arkansas, is denied entry to Central High School by a member of the National Guard under the orders of Governor Orval Faubus. Not until President Dwight Eisenhower sent the 101st Airborne Division to Little Rock were the high court's desegregation orders enforced.

AP Wide World Photos

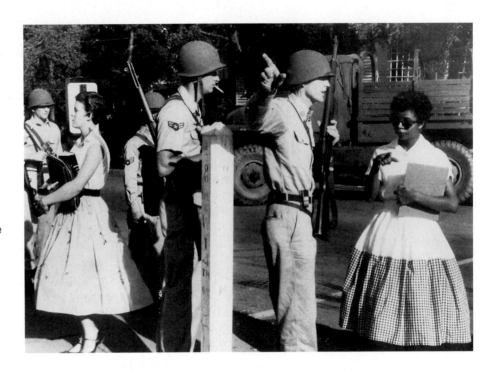

personal command of them, and then ordered them to leave the high school. Ike then replaced the Guard units with U.S. federal troops under orders to enforce desegregation. Eisenhower's action marked a turning point in the struggle over school desegregation. The Supreme Court's historic desegregation decision in *Brown v. Board of Education of Topeka* might have been rendered meaningless had not the president chosen to use military force to secure compliance.

## The Vice Presidential Waiting Game

Historically, the principal responsibility of the vice president is to be prepared to assume the responsibilities of the president. Eight vice presidents have become president following the death of their predecessor. But vice presidents have not always been well prepared: Harry Truman, who succeeded Franklin Roosevelt while World War II still raged, had never even been informed about the secret atomic bomb project.

**Political Selection Process**   The political process surrounding the initial choice of vice presidential candidates does not necessarily produce the persons best qualified to occupy the White House. It is, indeed, a "crap shoot"[31]; if it produces a person well qualified to be president, it is only by luck. Candidates may *claim* that they select running mates who are highly qualified to take over as president, but this claim is seldom true.

Traditionally, vice presidential candidates have been chosen to give political "balance" to the ticket, to attract voters who might otherwise desert the party or stay home. Democratic presidential candidates sought to give ideological and geographical balance to the ticket. Northern liberal presidential candidates (Adlai Stevenson, John Kennedy) selected southern conservatives (John Sparkman, Estes Kefauver, Lyndon Johnson) as their running mates. Walter Mondale selected New

York Congresswoman Geraldine Ferraro in a bold move to exploit the gender gap. Liberal Massachusetts Governor Michael Dukakis returned to the earlier Democratic tradition, choosing to run with conservative Texas Senator Lloyd Bentsen. Bill Clinton sought a different kind of balance: Al Gore's military service in Vietnam and his unimpeachable family life helped offset reservations about Clinton's avoidance of the draft and his past marital troubles. Massachusetts Senator John Kerry was viewed as serious, sober, and reserved, so the choice of the cheerful, enthusiastic, and outgoing North Carolinian John Edwards seemed to balance the ticket in both image and geography.

Republican presidential candidates sought to accommodate either the conservative or moderate wing of their party in their vice presidential selections. Moderate Eisenhower chose conservative Nixon. Conservative Barry Goldwater's selection of William Miller, an unknown conservative member of the House, ensured his loss of moderate support in 1964. In 1980 conservative Reagan first asked his moderate predecessor Gerald Ford to join him on the ticket before turning to his moderate primary opponent George Bush, who in 1988 tapped conservative Senator Dan Quayle. In 1996 Bob Dole gambled big in choosing the popular and charismatic—but opinionated and unpredictable— Jack Kemp as his running mate. Far behind in the polls, Dole could not afford a "safe" choice. He needed the former star quarterback of the Buffalo Bills to add excitement to the ticket, even at the risk of seeing Kemp call plays not approved by the coach.

Running behind in the polls prior to the 2000 Democratic convention, Al Gore believed he needed a dramatic choice of a running mate to stir interest in his campaign. Connecticut Senator Joe Lieberman would make history as the first Jew to run on a major party national ticket. Moreover, his moderate voting record balanced Gore's appeal to liberals.

Bush's dream running mate, General Colin Powell, turned down the offer. So Bush turned to Dick Cheney, secretary of defense in his father's administration during the Gulf War. It was hoped that Cheney would add *gravitas* (experience and wisdom) to the ticket. And Cheney's conservative voting record, as a former Congressman from Wyoming, helped reassure conservatives in the Republican Party that Bush was not overlooking them. Cheney's public approval ratings dropped as the Iraq war lengthened. Bush was urged to replace him with the popular former New York City Mayor Rudolph Giuliani. But Bush remained loyal to his family's old adviser.

**Vice Presidential Roles**    Presidents determine what role their vice presidents will play in their administration. Constitutionally, the only role given the vice president is to preside over the Senate and to vote in case of a tie in that body. Presiding over the Senate is so tiresome that vice presidents perform it only on rare ceremonial occasions, but they have occasionally cast important tie-breaking votes. If the president chooses not to give the vice president much responsibility, the vice presidency becomes what its first occupant, John Adams, described as "the most insignificant office that ever the invention of man contrived or his imagination conceived." One of Franklin Roosevelt's three vice presidents, the salty Texan John Nance Garner, put it more pithily, saying that the job "ain't worth a bucket of warm spit" (reporters of that era may have substituted "spit" for Garner's actual wording).

The political functions of vice presidents are more significant than their governmental functions. Vice presidents are obliged to support their president and the administration's policies. But sometimes a president will use the vice president

# PEOPLE IN POLITICS

## Dick Cheney, Presidential Confidant

For many weeks after the "9/11" attack on America, Vice President Dick Cheney remained out of sight "in a secure undisclosed location." A direct attack on the White House was viewed as a distinct possibility, and Cheney's absence from Washington was designed to ensure "continuity of government."

Yet during the crisis—indeed, throughout George W. Bush's presidency—Dick Cheney has been his chief's closest adviser—a prime minister, a *consigliere,* pal, tutor, and big brother to the president. Reportedly, Cheney and Bush confer several times a day, and Cheney's recommendations are seldom ignored. Cheney exercises more influence in the White House than perhaps any previous vice president.

Why does Bush place so much trust in his vice president? Cheney served as secretary of defense for Bush's father and served in the Nixon and Ford administrations. He also served as a Republican Congress member from Wyoming and a leader of the conservatives in the House of Representatives. But perhaps his most valued characteristic as vice president is his absence of political ambition. Unlike any other recent vice president, Cheney has no plans to run for president, no personal agenda other than to give his best advice to his president. This elevates the level of trust between the two men.

Dick Cheney has experienced four heart attacks and quadruple bypass heart surgery and wears a surgically implanted heart pacemaker. Yet he follows a very demanding schedule, including lengthy trips to the Middle East and elsewhere in the world.

Cheney was reported to be a strong supporter of the Iraq invasion, and his public approval ratings tumbled as the war lengthened. When he accidentally wounded a friend on a hunting trip, the media ridiculed him and his approval ratings fell even further. But he remained Bush's closest adviser.

to launch strongly partisan political attacks on opponents while the president remains "above" the political squabbles and hence more "presidential." Richard Nixon served as a partisan "attack dog" for Eisenhower, and then gave Spiro Agnew this task in his own administration. George Bush was a much more reserved vice president, but Dan Quayle renewed the tradition of the vice president as political "hit man." The attack role allows the vice president also to help cement political support for the president among highly partisan ideologues. Vice presidents are also useful in campaign fund-raising. Large contributors expect a personal touch; the president cannot be everywhere at once, so the vice president is frequently a guest at political fund-raising events. Presidents also have traditionally sent their vice presidents to attend funerals of world leaders and placed them at the head of governmental commissions.

Vice presidents themselves strive to play a more significant policy-making role, often as senior presidential adviser and confidant. Recent presidents have encouraged the development of the vice presidency along these lines. Walter Mondale, the first modern vice president to perform this function, had an office in the White House next to the president's, had access to all important meetings and policy decisions, and was invited to lunch privately each week with President Carter. Vice President Al Gore was routinely stationed behind President Clinton during major policy pronouncements. Clinton reportedly gave great weight to Gore's views on the environment, on cost savings in government, and on information technology. Gore also spoke out aggressively in defense of Clinton's policies. Thus the senior advisory role is becoming institutionalized over time (see *People in Politics:* "Dick Cheney, Presidential Confidant").

## A CONSTITUTIONAL NOTE

# How Broad is the "Executive Power"?

The Constitution states that "The executive Power shall be vested in a President of the United States of America" (Article II). The Constitution also gives the president specific powers; for example "to take care that the laws be faithfully executed"; to appoint and remove executive officials; "to give to the Congress information on the State of the Union and recommend to their Consideration such Measures as he shall judge necessary and expedient"; to veto legislation passed by Congress, subject to override by a two-thirds vote of both houses; to convene special sessions of Congress; to make treaties "with the Advice and Consent of the Senate"; to receive ambassadors; to grant pardons; to appoint federal court and Supreme Court judges, subject to Senate confirmation; and to serve as Commander-in-Chief of the Armed Forces. And the Congress may by law add to the president's powers. But does the Constitution's general grant of "executive power" give the president any powers that are not specified later in the Constitution or given to the president by acts of Congress? Most presidents have asserted a general "executive power," or, as Theodore Roosevelt said, "My belief was that it was not only his right but his duty to do anything that the needs of the nation demanded, unless such action was forbidden by the Constitution or by the laws." But when the Congress has addressed a problem by law, the president is obliged to follow the law, whether he likes it or not.[a] Closely related to the question of executive power is the question of "executive privilege." Can a president withhold information from the Congress or the courts to preserve confidentiality within the executive branch? The Supreme Court has acknowledged a constitutional protection for the "president's need for complete candor and objectivity from advisers" and for "military, diplomatic, or sensitive national security secrets,"[b] But the president cannot withhold information from the courts in a criminal investigation not related to defense or diplomacy, as Richard Nixon found to his dismay in the Watergate affair.

[a]*Youngstown Sheet & Tube Co. v. Sawyer*, 343 U.S. 579 (1952).

[b]*United States v. Nixon*, 418 U.S. 683 (1974).

**The Waiting Game**   Politically ambitious vice presidents are obliged to play a torturous waiting game. They can use their time in office to build a network of contacts that can later be tapped for campaign contributions, workers, and support in their own race for the presidency, should they decide to run. But winning the presidency following retirement of their former boss requires a delicate balance. They must show loyalty to the president in order to win the president's endorsement and also to help ensure that the administration in which they participated is judged a success by voters. At the same time, vice presidents must demonstrate that they have independent leadership qualities and a policy agenda of their own to offer voters. This dilemma becomes more acute as their boss's term nears its end.

Historically, only a few sitting vice presidents have won election to the White House: John Adams (1797), Thomas Jefferson (1801), Martin Van Buren (1837), and George H. W. Bush (1988). In addition, four vice presidents won election in their own right after entering the Oval Office as a result of their predecessors' death: Theodore Roosevelt (1901), Calvin Coolidge (1923), Harry Truman (1945), and Lyndon Johnson (1963). Only one nonsitting former vice president has been elected president: Richard Nixon (1968, after losing to Kennedy in 1960). Thus, out of the forty-seven men who served the nation as vice president through 2000, only nine were ever elected to higher office.

# Summary Notes

- The American presidency is potentially the most powerful office in the world. As head of state, the president symbolizes national unity and speaks on behalf of the American people to the world. And as Commander-in-Chief of the armed forces, the president has a powerful voice in national and international affairs. The president also symbolizes government for the American people, reassuring them in times of hardship and crises.

- As head of the government, the president is expected to set forth policy priorities for the nation, to manage the economy, to mobilize political support for the administration's programs in Congress, to manage the giant federal bureaucracy, and to recruit people for policy-making positions in both the executive and judicial branches of government.

- Popular expectations of presidential leadership far exceed the formal constitutional powers of the president: chief administrator, chief legislator, chief diplomat, Commander-in-Chief, and chief of state. The vague reference in the Constitution to "executive Power" has been used by presidents to justify actions beyond those specified elsewhere in the Constitution or in laws of Congress.

- It is the president's vast political resources that provide the true power base of the presidency. These include the president's reputation for power, personal popularity with the public, access to the media, and party leadership position.

- Presidential popularity and power are usually highest at the beginning of the term of office. Presidents are more likely to be successful in Congress during this honeymoon period. Presidents' popularity also rises during crises, especially during international threats and military actions. But prolonged indecision and stalemate erode popular support, as do scandals and economic recessions.

- As chief executive, the president oversees the huge federal bureaucracy. Presidential control of the executive branch is exercised through executive orders, appointments and removals, and budgetary recommendations to Congress. But the president's control of the executive branch is heavily circumscribed by Congress, which establishes executive departments and agencies, regulates their activities by law, and determines their budgets each year.

- Presidents are expected not only to initiate programs and policies but also to shepherd them through Congress. Presidential success scores in Congress indicate that presidents are more successful early in their term of office. Presidents who face a Congress controlled by the opposition party are far less successful in winning approval for their programs than presidents whose party holds a majority.

- The veto is the president's most powerful weapon in dealing with Congress. The president needs to hold the loyalty of only one more than one-third of either the House or the Senate to sustain a veto. Few vetoes are overridden. The threat of a veto enables the president to bargain in Congress for more acceptable legislation.

- During the long years of the Cold War, the president of the United States was the leader of the "free world." In the post–Cold War world, the president is still the leader of the world's most powerful democracy and is expected to exercise global leadership on behalf of a stable world order.

- Presidents have come to dominate foreign policy through treaty making, executive agreements, control of intelligence activities, and international recognition of their role as head of state. Above all, presidents have used their power as Commander-in-Chief of the armed forces to decide when to make war and when to seek peace.

- The global power of presidents derives primarily from this presidential role as Commander-in-Chief. Constitutionally, war-making power is divided between Congress and the president, but historically it has been the president who has ordered U.S. military forces into action. In the War Powers Resolution, Congress tried to reassert its war-making power after the Vietnam War, but the act has failed to restrain presidents. Presidents have also used the armed forces in domestic affairs to "take Care that the Laws be faithfully executed."

- The principal responsibility of the vice president is to be prepared to assume the responsibilities of the president. However, the selection of the vice president is dominated more by political concerns than by consideration of presidential qualifications. Aside from officially presiding over the U.S. Senate, vice presidents perform whatever roles are assigned them by the president.

# Key Terms

impeachment   308
Watergate   312
executive privilege   312
impoundment   314
deferrals   314
rescissions   314

White House press
   corps   317
executive order   320
cabinet   322
National Security
   Council (NSC)   323

honeymoon period   326
gridlock   328
veto   328
pocket veto   328
override   328
line-item veto   328

diplomatic recognition   330
executive agreement   331
covert action   332
War Powers Resolution   334

# Suggested Readings

Barber, James David. *The Presidential Character: Predicting Performance in the White House.* 4th ed. Upper Saddle River, N.J.: Prentice Hall, 1992. Barber's original thesis that a president's performance in office is largely a function of active/passive and positive/negative character; includes classifications of twentieth-century presidents through Reagan.

Brody, Richard A. *Assessing Presidents: The Media, Elite Opinion, and Public Support.* Stanford, Calif.: Stanford University Press, 1991. Develops the thesis that media and elite interpretations of presidential actions shape public evaluations of the president; includes analysis of the president's "honeymoon," "rally round the president" events, and the rise and fall of public approval ratings.

DiClerico, Robert E. *The American President.* 5th ed. Upper Saddle River, N.J.: Prentice Hall, 2000. Comprehensive text on the presidency, focusing on selection, power, accountability, decision making, personality, and leadership.

Edwards, George C. and Stephen J. Wayne. *Presidential Leadership.* 6th ed. Belmont, Calif.: Wadsworth, 2003. Comprehensive text covering nomination and election of the president, relations with the public, the media, the bureaucracy, Congress and the courts.

Lowi, Theodore. *The Personal President.* Ithaca, N.Y.: Cornell University Press, 1987. An examination of the presidency from the perspective of the public and its reliance on the president for reassurance in crises.

Milkus, Stanley, and Michael Nelson. *The American Presidency: Origins and Development, 1776–2002.* 4th ed. Washington, D.C.: CQ Press, 2003. A comprehensive history of the presidency that argues that the institution is best understood by examining its development over time, describes the significant presidential actions in the early days of the Republic that shaped the office, as well as the modern era in which the president has replaced Congress and the political parties as the leading instrument of popular rule.

Nelson, Michael, ed. *The Presidency and the Political System.* 8th ed. Washington D.C.: CQ Press, 2005. A series of influential essays on the presidency.

Neustadt, Richard E. *Presidential Power.* New York: Wiley, 1960. The classic argument that the president's power is the power to persuade, that the formal constitutional powers of the presidency provide only a framework for the president's use of persuasion, public prestige, reputation for power, and other personal attributes to exercise real power.

Pika, Joseph A., John Maltese, and Norman C. Thomas. *The Politics of the Presidency.* Rev. 6th ed. Washington, D.C.: CQ Press, 2005. An overview of the institution of the presidency, including George W. Bush as a wartime president.

Schultz, Jeffrey D. *Presidential Scandals.* Washington, D.C.: CQ Press, 1999. An historical survey of scandals in presidential administrations, from George Washington to Bill Clinton.

Van Tassel, Emily Field, and Paul Finkelman. *Impeachable Offenses.* Washington, D.C.: CQ Press, 1999. A documentary history of impeachment from 1787 to the present.

# ✴ Make It Real

### THE PRESIDENT
This module allows students to pick the next Supreme Court Justice.

# 10 THE BUREAUCRACY
## Bureaucratic Politics

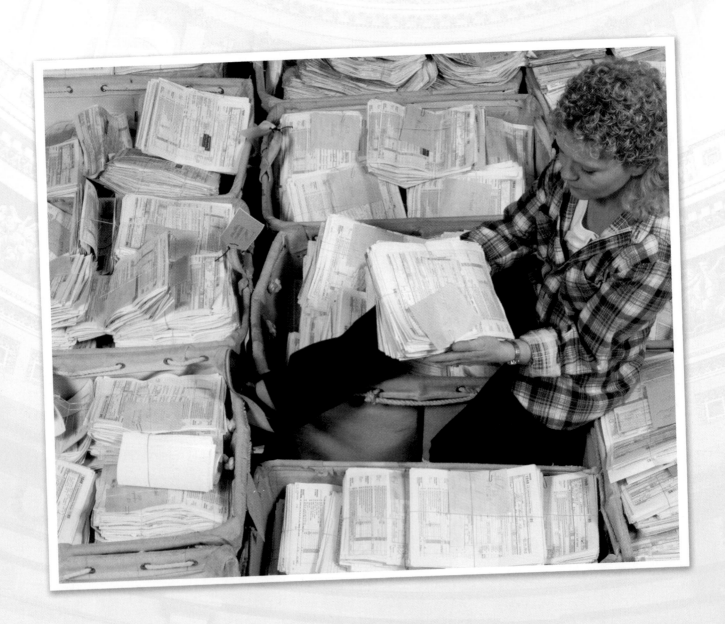

## Chapter Outline

- Bureaucratic Power
- The Federal Bureaucracy
- Bureaucracy and Democracy
- Bureaucratic Politics
- The Budgetary Process
- The Politics of Budgeting
- Regulatory Battles
- Regulating America
- Congressional Constraints on the Bureaucracy
- Interest Groups and Bureaucratic Decision Making
- Judicial Constraints on the Bureaucracy

## Think About Politics

1 Do bureaucrats in Washington have too much power?
Yes ☐ No ☐

2 Should the federal bureaucracy be managed by nonpartisan professionals rather than people politically loyal to the president?
Yes ☐ No ☐

3 Should the federal bureaucracy at all levels reflect the gender and minority ratios of the total civilian work force?
Yes ☐ No ☐

4 Do you believe the bureaucrats in Washington waste a lot of the money we pay in taxes?
Yes ☐ No ☐

5 Do you believe the federal government is spending more money but delivering less service?
Yes ☐ No ☐

6 Do you believe that the overall costs of federal regulatory activity are justified by the benefits?
Yes ☐ No ☐

7 Do you believe bureaucratic regulations of all kinds are hurting America's competitiveness in the global economy?
Yes ☐ No ☐

*Power in Washington is not only exercised by the president, Congress, and courts, but also by 2.8 million federal bureaucrats—neither elected nor accountable to ordinary citizens—who determine in large measure who gets what in America.*

## Bureaucratic Power

Political conflict does not end after a law has been passed by Congress and signed by the president. The arena for conflict merely shifts from Capitol Hill and the White House to the **bureaucracy**—to the myriad departments, agencies, and bureaus of the federal executive branch that implement the law. Despite the popular impression that policy is decided by the president and Congress and merely implemented by the federal bureaucracy, in fact policy is also made by the bureaucracy. Indeed, it is often remarked that "implementation is the continuation of policy making by other means." The Washington bureaucracy is a major base of power in the American system of government—independent of Congress, the president, the courts, and the people. Indeed, controlling the bureaucracy has become a major challenge of democratic government.

**The Nature of Bureaucracy**   "Bureaucracy" has become a negative term equated with red tape,[1] paper shuffling, duplication of effort, waste and inefficiency, impersonality, senseless regulations, and unresponsiveness to the needs of "real" people. But bureaucracy is really a form of social organization found not only in governments but also in corporations, armies, schools, and many other societal institutions. The German sociologist Max Weber described bureaucracy as a "rational" way for society to organize itself that has the following characteristics: a **chain of command** (hierarchical structure of authority in which command flows downward); a **division of labor** (work divided among many specialized workers in an effort to improve productivity); and **impersonality** (all persons within the bureaucracy treated on "merit" principles, and all "clients" served by the bureaucracy treated equally according to rules; all activities undertaken according to rules; records maintained to assure rules are followed).[2] Thus, according to Weber's definition, General Motors and IBM, the U.S. Marine Corps, the U.S. Department of Education, and all other institutions organized according to these principles are "bureaucracies."

**The Growth of Bureaucratic Power**   Bureaucratic power has grown with advances in technology and increases in the size and complexity of society. There are a variety of explanations for this growth of power.

**bureaucracy** Departments, agencies, bureaus, and offices that perform the functions of government.

**chain of command** Hierarchical structure of authority in which command flows downward; typical of a bureaucracy.

**division of labor** Division of work among many specialized workers in a bureaucracy.

**impersonality** Treatment of all persons within a bureaucracy on the basis of "merit" and of all "clients" served by the bureaucracy equally according to rules.

— Think Again —

Do bureaucrats in Washington have too much power?

1. *Needed Expertise and Technological Advances*   Congress and the president do not have the time, energy, or expertise to handle the details of policy making. A related explanation is that the increasing complexity and sophistication of technology require technical experts ("technocrats") to actually carry out the intent of Congress and the president. Neither the president nor the 535 members of Congress can look after the myriad details involved in environmental protection, occupational safety, air traffic control, or thousands of other responsibilities of government. So the president and Congress create bureaucracies, appropriate money for them, and authorize them to draw up detailed rules, regulations, and "guidelines" that actually govern the nation. Bureaucratic agencies receive only vague and general directions from the president and Congress. Actual governance is in the hands of the Environmental Protection Agency, the Occupational Safety and Health Administration, the Federal Aviation Administration, and hundreds of similar agencies (see Figure 10.1).

2. *Symbolic Politics*   But there are also political explanations for the growth of bureaucratic power. Congress and the president often deliberately pass vague and ambiguous laws. These laws allow elected officials to show symbolically their concerns for environmental protection, occupational safety, and so on, yet avoid the controversies surrounding actual application of those lofty principles. Bureaucracies must then give practical meaning to these symbolic measures by developing specific rules and regulations. If the rules and regulations prove unpopular, Congress and the president can blame the bureaucrats and pretend that these unpopular decisions are a product of an "ungovernable" Washington bureaucracy (see *What Do You Think?* "How Would You Rate These Federal Agencies?")

3. *Bureaucratic Explanation*   There is also a bureaucratic explanation of the growth in the size and influence of government agencies. Bureaucracy has become its own source of power. Bureaucrats have a personal stake in expanding the size of their own agencies and budgets and adding to their own regulatory authority. They can mobilize their "client" groups (interest groups that directly benefit from the agency's programs, such as environmental groups on behalf of the Environmental Protection Agency, farm groups for the Department of Agriculture, the National Education Association for the Department of Education) in support of larger budgets and expanded authority.

4. *Popular Demands*   Finally, it has been argued that "big government" is really an expression of democratic sentiments. People want to use the power of government to improve their lives—to regulate and develop the economy, to guarantee civil rights, to develop their communities, and so on. Conservative opponents of the government are really expressing their disdain for popular demands.[3]

**Bureaucratic Power: Implementation**   Bureaucracies are not *constitutionally* empowered to decide policy questions. But they do so, nevertheless, as they perform their tasks of implementation, regulation, and adjudication.

**Implementation** is the development of procedures and activities to carry out policies legislated by Congress. It may involve creating new agencies or bureaus or assigning new responsibilities to old agencies. It often requires bureaucracies to translate laws into operational rules and regulations and usually to allocate resources—money, personnel, offices, supplies—to the new function. All of these tasks involve decisions by bureaucrats, decisions that drive how the law

**implementation** Development by the federal bureaucracy of procedures and activities to carry out policies legislated by Congress; it includes regulation as well as adjudication.

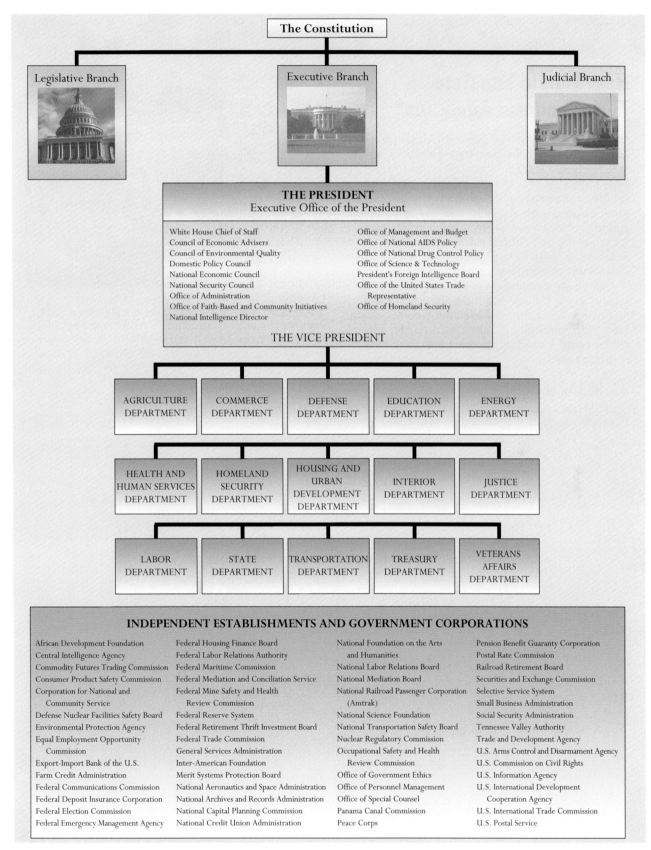

**Figure 10.1**   The Federal Bureaucracy

Although the president has constitutional authority over the operation of the executive branch, Congress creates departments and agencies and appropriates their funds, and Senate approval is needed for presidential appointees to head departments.

# WHAT DO YOU THINK?

## How Would You Rate These Federal Agencies?

Many federal agencies have come under close scrutiny following the devastating terrorist attacks of 9/11, deadly anthrax letters, and economic recession, the threat of a bird flu epidemic, and a space shuttle explosion. A poll near the end of 2003 asked Americans to rate some of the key government agencies charged with protecting the American public. While the poll did not ask about all government agencies, it does give a sense of how the public views some of the more prominent of them.

Overall, Americans rate individual agencies fairly highly. Even though the opinion polls regularly report that Americans believe "the federal government in Washington" has "too much power" (60 percent), individual agencies are given reasonably good marks.

*The Federal Emergency Management Agency, FEMA, was charged with bureaucratic mismanagement during Hurricane Katrina and its aftermath. Survivors endured long lines and inadequate service.*

Q. How would you rate the job being done by _____? Would you say it is doing an excellent, good, only fair, or poor job?

**Percentage saying "excellent" or "good"**

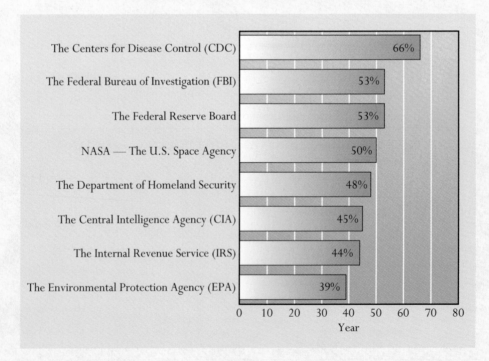

| Agency | Percentage |
|---|---|
| The Centers for Disease Control (CDC) | 66% |
| The Federal Bureau of Investigation (FBI) | 53% |
| The Federal Reserve Board | 53% |
| NASA — The U.S. Space Agency | 50% |
| The Department of Homeland Security | 48% |
| The Central Intelligence Agency (CIA) | 45% |
| The Internal Revenue Service (IRS) | 44% |
| The Environmental Protection Agency (EPA) | 39% |

*Source:* Gallup poll, September 30, 2003. Copyright © 1996–2004 by The Gallup Organization.

will actually affect society. In some cases, bureaucrats delay the development of regulations based on a new law, assign enforcement responsibility to existing offices with other higher priority tasks, and allocate few people with limited resources to the task. In other cases, bureaucrats act forcefully in making new regulations, insist on strict enforcement, assign responsibilities to newly created aggressive offices with no other assignments, and allocate a great deal of staff time and agency resources to the task. Interested groups have a strong stake in these decisions, and they actively seek to influence the bureaucracy.

**Bureaucratic Power: Regulation**   Regulation involves the development of formal rules for implementing legislation. The federal bureaucracy publishes about 80,000 pages of rules in the *Federal Register* each year. The Environmental Protection Agency (EPA) is especially active in developing regulations governing the handling of virtually every substance in the air, water, or ground. The rule-making process for federal agencies is prescribed by an Administrative Procedures Act, first passed in 1946 and amended many times. Generally, agencies must:

1. Announce in the *Federal Register* that a new regulation is being considered.
2. Hold hearings to allow interested groups to present evidence and arguments regarding the proposed regulation.
3. Conduct research on the proposed regulation's economic and environmental impacts.
4. Solicit "public comments" (usually the arguments of interest groups).
5. Consult with higher officials, including the Office of Management and Budget.
6. Publish the new regulation in the *Federal Register.*

Regulatory battles are important because formal regulations that appear in the *Federal Register* have the effect of law. Congress can amend or repeal a regulation only by passing new legislation and obtaining the president's signature. Controversial bureaucratic regulations often remain in place because Congress is slow to act, because key committee members block corrective legislation, or because the president refuses to sign bills overturning the regulation.

**Bureaucratic Power: Adjudication**   Adjudication involves bureaucratic decisions about individual cases. Rule making resembles the legislative process, and adjudication resembles the judicial process. In adjudication, bureaucrats decide whether a person or firm is failing to comply with laws or regulations and, if so, what penalties or corrective actions are to be applied. Regulatory agencies and commissions—for example, the National Labor Relations Board, the Federal Communications Commission, the Equal Employment Opportunity Commission, the Federal Trade Commission, the Securities and Exchange Commission—are heavily engaged in adjudication. Their elaborate procedures and body of previous decisions closely resemble the court system. Losers may appeal to the federal courts, but the record of agency success in the federal courts discourages many appeals.

**Bureaucratic Power: Administrative Discretion**   Much of the work of bureaucrats is administrative routine—issuing Social Security checks, printing forms, delivering the mail. Routines are repetitive tasks performed according to established rules and procedures. Yet bureaucrats almost always have some discretion in performing even the most routine tasks. Discretion is greatest when cases do not exactly fit established rules, or when more than one rule might be applied to the same case, resulting in different outcomes. The Internal Revenue

**regulation** Development by the federal bureaucracy of formal rules for implementing legislation.

**American Society for Public Administration**
Organization of scholars and practitioners in public administration. Site includes information on careers, job listings, etc. *www.apsanet.org*

**adjudication** Decision making by the federal bureaucracy as to whether or not an individual or organization has complied with or violated government laws and/or regulations.

An Internal Revenue Service processing center. The IRS administers the nation's complex tax code, leaving wide discretion to its agents to determine how to apply the rules to individual taxpayers.

Service administers the hundreds of thousands of rules developed to implement the U.S. Tax Code, but each IRS auditing agent has wide discretion in deciding which rules to apply to a taxpayer's income, deductions, business expenses, and so on. Indeed, identical tax information submitted to different IRS offices almost always results in different estimates of tax liability. But even in more routine tasks, from processing Medicare applications to forwarding mail, individual bureaucrats can be friendly and helpful or hostile and obstructive.[4]

**Bureaucratic Power and Budget Maximization** Bureaucrats generally believe strongly in the value of their programs and the importance of their tasks. Senior military officers and civilian officials of the Department of Defense believe in the importance of a strong national defense, and top officials in the Social Security Administration are committed to maintaining the integrity of the retirement system and serving the nation's senior citizens. Beyond these public-spirited motives, bureaucrats, like everyone else, seek higher pay, greater job security, and added power and prestige for themselves.

These public and private motives converge to inspire bureaucrats to seek to expand the powers, functions, and budgets of their departments and agencies. Rarely do bureaucrats request a reduction in authority, the elimination of a program, or a decrease in their agency's budget. Rather, over time, **budget maximization**—expanding the agency's budget, staff, and authority as much as possible—becomes a driving force in government bureaucracies. This is especially true of discretionary funds. **Discretionary funds** are those that bureaucrats have flexibility in deciding how to spend, rather than money committed by law to specific purposes.[5] Thus, bureaucracies continually strive to add new functions, acquire more authority and responsibility, and increase their budgets and personnel. Bureaucratic expansion is just one of the reasons that government grows over time.

**budget maximization**
Bureaucrats' tendencies to expand their agencies' budgets, staff, and authority.

**discretionary funds**
Budgeted funds not earmarked for specific purposes but available to be spent in accordance with the best judgment of a bureaucrat.

**Figure 10.2** Corridors of Power in the Bureaucracy

This map shows the Capitol, the White House, and the major departments of the federal bureaucracy in Washington, D.C.

# The Federal Bureaucracy

The federal bureaucracy—officially part of the executive branch of the U.S. government—consists of about 2.8 million civilian employees (plus 1.4 million persons in the armed forces) organized into 15 cabinet departments, more than 60 independent agencies, and a large Executive Office of the President (see Figure 10.2). The expenditures of *all* governments in the United States—the

## COMPARED TO WHAT?

# The Size of Government in Other Nations

How does the size of the public sector in the United States compare with the size of the public sector in other economically advanced, democratic countries? There is a great deal of variation in the size of government across countries. Government spending accounts for nearly two-thirds of the total output in Sweden. Government spending exceeds one-half of the total output of Denmark, Netherlands, Finland, Germany, Italy, Austria, Belgium, and France. The high level of government spending in these countries primarily reflects greater public-sector involvement in the provision of housing, health care, retirement insurance, and aid to the unemployed. The sizes of the public sectors in Australia, Japan, and Switzerland are only slightly higher than that of United States.

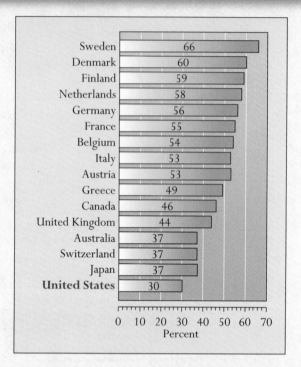

**Governmental Percentage of Gross Domestic Product**

*Source:* Joint Economic Committee of Congress, "The Size and Function of Government" (Washington, D.C.: 1998). United States updated to 2002.

federal government, the 50 state governments, and some 86,000 local governments—now amount to about $4.0 *trillion* (roughly 30 percent of the U.S. gross domestic product, or GDP, of $13.4 *trillion*). About two-thirds of this—about $2.8 *trillion* a year (about 20 percent of GDP)—is spent by the *federal* government. Government spending in the United States remains relatively modest compared to that of many nations (see *Compared to What?* "The Size of Government in Other Nations").

**Cabinet Departments**    Cabinet departments employ about 60 percent of all federal workers (see Table 10.1). Each department is headed by a secretary (with the exception of the Justice Department, which is headed by the attorney general) who is appointed by the president and must be confirmed by the Senate. Each department is hierarchically organized; each has its own organization chart.

Cabinet status confers great legitimacy on a governmental function and prestige on the secretary, thus strengthening that individual's voice in the government. Therefore the elevation of an executive agency to cabinet level often reflects political considerations as much as or more than national needs. Strong pressures from "client" interest groups (groups principally served by the department), as well as presidential and congressional desires to pose as defenders and promoters of particular interests, account for the establishment of all of the

**Fed World**    Run by the U.S. Commerce Department, this site contains information about federal/state–local agency links, government jobs, IRS forms, Supreme Court decisions, and the vast array of governmental services. *www.fedworld.gov*

## Table 10.1    Cabinet Departments and Functions

| Department and Date Created | Function |
| --- | --- |
| *State* (1789) | Advises the president on the formation and execution of foreign policy; negotiates treaties and agreements with foreign nations; represents the United States in the United Nations and in more than fifty major international organizations and maintains U.S. embassies abroad; issues U.S. passports and, in foreign countries, visas to the United States. |
| *Treasury* (1789) | Serves as financial agent for the U.S. government; issues all payments of the U.S. government according to law; manages the debt of the U.S. government by issuing and recovering bonds and paying their interest; collects taxes owed to the U.S. government; collects taxes and enforces laws on alcohol, tobacco, and firearms and on customs duties; manufactures coins and currency. |
| *Defense* (1947: formerly the War Department, created in 1789, and the Navy Department, created in 1798) | Provides the military forces needed to deter war and protect the national security interest; includes the Departments of the Army, Navy, and Air Force. |
| *Justice* (1789) | Enforces all federal laws, including consumer protection, antitrust, civil rights, drug, and immigration and naturalization; maintains federal prisons. |
| *Interior* (1849) | Has responsibility for public lands and natural resources, for American Indian reservations, and for people who live in island territories under U.S. administration; preserves national parks and historical sites. |
| *Agriculture* (1889) | Works to improve and maintain farm income and to develop and expand markets abroad for agricultural products; safeguards standards of quality in the food supply through inspection and grading services; administers rural development, credit, and conservation programs; administers food stamp program. |
| *Commerce* (1913) | Encourages the nation's international trade, economic growth, and technological advancement; conducts the census; provides social and economic statistics and analyses for business and government; maintains the merchant marine; grants patents and registers trademarks. |
| *Labor* (1913) | Oversees working conditions; administers federal labor laws; protects workers' pension rights; sponsors job training programs; keeps track of changes in employment, price, and other national economic indicators. |
| *Health and Human Services* (1953 as Health, Education, and Welfare; reorganized with Education as a separate department in 1979) | Administers social welfare programs for the elderly, children, and youths; protects the health of the nation against impure and unsafe foods, drugs, and cosmetics; operates the Centers for Disease Control; funds the Medicare and Medicaid programs. |
| *Housing and Urban Development* (1965) | Is responsible for programs concerned with housing needs, fair housing opportunities, and the improvement and development of the nation's communities; administers mortgage insurance programs, rental subsidy programs, and neighborhood rehabilitation and preservation programs. |
| *Transportation* (1966) | Is responsible for the nation's highway planning, development, and construction; also urban mass transit, railroads, aviation, and the safety of waterways, ports, highways, and oil and gas pipelines. |
| *Energy* (1977) | Is responsible for the research, development, and demonstration of energy technology; marketing of federal electric power; energy conservation; the nuclear weapons program; regulation of energy production and use; and collection and analysis of energy data. |
| *Education* (1979) | Administers and coordinates most federal assistance to education. |
| *Veterans Affairs* (1989) | Operates programs to benefit veterans and members of their families. |
| *Homeland Security* (2002) | Prevents terrorist attacks within the United States, reduces the vulnerability of the nation to terrorism, and minimizes the damage and assists in recovery from terrorist attacks. |

*Source: The United States Government Manual* (Washington, D.C.: Government Printing Office, annual).

## UP CLOSE

# The Department of Homeland Security

Presidents often create new bureaucratic organizations to symbolize their commitment to a policy direction. On October 8, 2001, less than one month after the "9/11" terrorist attack on America, President George W. Bush issued an executive order establishing the Office of Homeland Security and naming Pennsylvania's popular governor Tom Ridge as its director with "cabinet-level" status. Ridge was expected to coordinate the counterterrorism activities of 46 separate bureaucracies, but he was not given direct control over any government department or agency.

In 2002, in response to growing concerns that he had not done enough to reassure the American public of the federal government's commitment to protect them from terrorism, President Bush proposed a new Department of Homeland Security. Its mission is to prevent terrorist attacks within the United States, to reduce vulnerability of the United States to terrorism, and to minimize damage and assist recovery when and if terrorist attacks occur within the country.

The new department does more than just "coordinate" other federal agencies. In a major reorganization, the Department of Homeland Security has been given responsibility over agencies concerned with border protection, transportation security, and emergency preparedness, including the U.S. Border Patrol, the U.S. Customs Service, the Immigration and Naturalization Service, the U.S. Coast Guard, the Secret Service, the Federal Emergency Management Agency, and the newly created Transportation Security Administration.

But the Department of Homeland Security does *not* have authority over the Federal Bureau of Investigation in the Justice Department or the independent Central Intelligence Agency. So questions

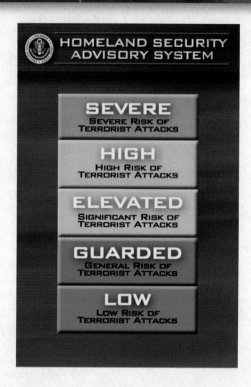

remain as to whether these two law enforcement and intelligence organizations can coordinate information among themselves and with the new Department of Homeland Security.

A new secretary was named in early 2005—former U.S. Court of Appeals Judge Michael Chertoff. But Chertoff had little time to prepare the department, especially the Federal Emergency Management Agency (FEMA), for the devastating Hurricane Katrina that laid waste to vast areas of New Orleans and the Mississippi Coast. The failures of FEMA in that disaster tarnished the image of the new Department (see *Up Close*: "Katrina: Federalism Fails in a Crisis" in Chapter 4).

newer departments. President Woodrow Wilson appealed to the labor movement in 1913 when he separated out a Department of Labor from the earlier business-dominated Department of Commerce and Labor. In 1965 President Lyndon Johnson created the Department of Housing and Urban Development to demonstrate his concern for urban problems. Seeking support from teachers and educational administrators, President Jimmy Carter created a separate Department of Education in 1979 and changed the name of the former Department of Health, Education, and Welfare to the Department of Health and Human Services (perhaps finding the phrase "human services" more politically acceptable than "welfare"). President Ronald Reagan tried, and failed, to "streamline" government by abolishing the Department of Education. But Reagan himself added a cabinet post, elevating the Veterans Administration to the Department of Veterans Affairs in an attempt to ingratiate himself with veterans. President George W. Bush created a new Department of Homeland Security in 2002 in response to the "9/11" terrorist attack on America and the threat of future attacks directly on the soil of the United States (see *Up Close:* "The Department of Homeland Security").

**Cabinet Department Functions**   The relative power and prestige of each cabinet-level department is a product not only of its size and budget but also of the importance of its function. By custom, the "pecking order" of departments—and therefore the prestige ranking of their secretaries—is determined by their years of origin. Thus the Departments of State, Treasury, Defense (War), and Justice, created by the First Congress in 1789, head the protocol list of departments. Overall, the duties of the fifteen cabinet-level departments of the executive branch cover an enormous range—everything from providing mortgage insurance, to overseeing the armed forces of the United States (see Table 10.1).

**Cabinet Appointments**   The Constitution requires that "Officers of the United States" be confirmed by the Senate. In the past, the Senate rarely rejected a presidential cabinet nomination; the traditional view was that presidents were entitled to pick their own people and even make their own mistakes. In recent years, however, the confirmation process has become more partisan and divisive, with the Senate conducting lengthy investigations and holding public hearings on presidential cabinet nominees. In 1989 the Senate rejected President Bush's nomination of John Tower as secretary of defense in a partisan battle featuring charges that the former Texas senator was a heavy drinker. The intense public scrutiny and potential for partisan attacks, together with financial disclosure and conflict-of-interest laws, may be discouraging some well-qualified people from accepting cabinet posts.

**Independent Regulatory Commissions**   Independent regulatory commissions differ from cabinet departments in their function, organization, and accountability to the president. Their function is to *regulate* a sector of society—transportation, communications, banking, labor relations, and so on (see Table 10.2). These commissions are empowered by Congress both to make and to enforce rules, and they thus function in a legislative and judicial fashion. To symbolize their impartiality, many of these organizations are headed by *commissions,* usually with five to ten members, rather than by a single secretary. Major policy decisions are made by majority vote of the commission. Finally, these agencies are more independent of the president than are cabinet departments. Their governing commissions are appointed by the president and confirmed by the Senate in the same fashion as cabinet secretaries, but their terms are fixed; they cannot be removed by the president.[6] These provisions are designed to insulate regulators from direct partisan or presidential pressures in their decision making.

A few powerful regulatory agencies remain inside cabinet departments. The most notable are the Food and Drug Administration (FDA), which remains in the Department of Health and Human Services and has broad authority to prevent the sale of drugs not deemed by the agency to be both "safe" and "effective"; the Occupational Health and Safety Administration (OSHA) in the Department of Labor, with authority to make rules governing any workplace in America; and

**Internal Revenue Service**
The tax-collecting IRS is potentially the most powerful of all government agencies, with financial records on every tax-paying American. *www.irs.gov*

**Food and Drug Administration**
The Food and Drug Administration site is a reflection of the agency's mission "to promote and protect the public health by helping safe and effective products reach the market in a timely way." *www.fda.gov*

**Table 10.2  Major Regulatory Bureaucracies**

| Commission | Date Created | Primary Functions |
|---|---|---|
| *Federal Communications Commission* (FCC) | 1934 | Regulates interstate and foreign communications by radio, television, wire, and cable. |
| *Food and Drug Administration* (FDA) | 1930 | Sets standards of safety and efficacy for foods, drugs, and medical devices. |
| *Federal Home Loan Bank* | 1932 | Regulates savings and loan associations that specialize in making home mortgage loans. |
| *Federal Maritime Commission* | 1961 | Regulates the waterborne foreign and domestic offshore commerce of the United States. |
| *Federal Reserve Board* (FRB) | 1913 | Regulates the nation's money supply by making monetary policy, which influences the lending and investing activities of commercial banks and the cost and availability of money and credit. |
| *Federal Trade Commission* (FTC) | 1914 | Regulates business to prohibit unfair methods of competition and unfair or deceptive acts or practices. |
| *National Labor Relations Board* (NLRB) | 1935 | Protects employees' rights to organize; prevents unfair labor practices. |
| *Securities and Exchange Commission* (SEC) | 1934 | Regulates the securities and financial markets (such as the stock market). |
| *Occupational Safety and Health Administration* (OSHA) | 1970 | Issues workplace regulations; investigates, cites, and penalizes for noncompliance. |
| *Consumer Product Safety Commission* (CPSC) | 1972 | Protects the public against product-related deaths, illnesses, and injuries. |
| *Commodity Futures Trading Commission* | 1974 | Regulates trading on the futures exchanges as well as the activities of commodity exchange members, public brokerage houses, commodity salespersons, trading advisers, and pool operators. |
| *Nuclear Regulatory Commission* (NRC) | 1974 | Regulates and licenses the users of nuclear energy. |
| *Federal Energy Regulatory Commission* (formerly Federal Power Commission) | 1977 | Regulates the transportation and sale of natural gas, the transmission and sale of electricity, the licensing of hydroelectric power projects, and the transportation of oil by pipeline. |
| *Equal Employment Opportunity Commission* (EEOC) | 1964 | Investigates and rules on charges of racial, gender, and age discrimination by employers and unions, in all aspects of employment. |
| *Environmental Protection Agency* (EPA) | 1970 | Issues and enforces pollution control standards regarding air, water, solid waste, pesticides, radiation, and toxic substances. |
| *Federal Elections Commission* (FEC) | 1975 | Administers and enforces federal campaign finance laws. |

*Source:* FirstGov, www.firstgov.gov/agencies

the most powerful government agency of all, the Internal Revenue Service in the Treasury Department, with its broad authority to interpret the tax code, maintain records on every American, and investigate and punish alleged violations of the tax code.

**Independent Agencies**  Congress has created a number of independent agencies outside of any cabinet department. Like cabinet departments, these agencies are hierarchically organized with a single head—usually called an "administrator"—who is appointed by the president and confirmed by the Senate. Administrators have no fixed terms of office and can be dismissed by the president; thus they are independent only insofar as they report directly to the

Cleaning up an oil spill on a California beach. The Environmental Protection Agency is perhaps the most powerful independent agency in the bureaucracy.

president rather than through a cabinet secretary. Politically, this independence ensures that their interests and budgets will not be compromised by other concerns, as may occur in agencies located within departments. (For more on their operations, see "Regulatory Battles" later in this chapter.)

One of the most powerful independent agencies is the Environmental Protection Agency (EPA), which is responsible for implementing federal legislation dealing with clean air, safe drinking water, solid waste disposal, pesticides, radiation, and toxic substances. EPA establishes and enforces comprehensive and complex standards for thousands of substances in the environment. It enjoys the political support of influential environmental interest groups, including the Environmental Defense Fund, Friends of the Earth, National Audubon Society, National Wildlife Federation, Natural Resources Defense Council, Sierra Club, and the Wilderness Society.

The Federal Reserve System is the most independent of all federal government agencies. The function of the "Fed" is to regulate the supply of money and thereby avoid both inflation and recession (see Chapter 13). The Federal Reserve System is independent of either the president or Congress. Its seven-member Board of Governors is appointed for *14-year terms*. Members are appointed by the president, with the consent of the Senate, but they may not be removed from the board except for "cause." No member has ever been removed since the creation of the board in 1913. The chairman of the board serves only a four-year term, but the chairman's term overlaps that of the president, so that new presidents

## UP CLOSE

## Managing the Nation's Money

Economist Alan Greenspan served as Chairman of the Board of Governors of the Federal Reserve System for eighteen years. He was initially appointed by President Ronald Reagan and served under four presidents—Reagan, Bush, Clinton, and Bush. His management of the Fed was widely praised by both Democrats and Republicans. He successfully fought inflationary trends during the nation's economic expansion in the 1990s by raising interest rates. When recession threatened in 2001, he led the Fed in bringing down interest rates to an all-time low, preventing a deep recession. During Greenspan's years inflation averaged only a modest 3 percent per year and unemployment averaged only 5.5 percent. (This compares with an inflation rate of 6.5 percent and an unemployment rate of 6.8 percent in the eighteen

years prior to his assuming the job.) Greenspan received his Ph.D. in economics from New York University; prior to serving as Fed Chairman, he had served as a member of the Council of Economic Advisors.

Ben Bernanke received his Ph.D. from MIT and also served on the Council of Economic Advisors before being appointed Fed chairman to replace the retiring Greenspan in 2005. Bernanke promptly announced his intention to "maintain continuity" with Greenspan's policies. But trying to keep a balance between inflation and recession requires "reading the tea leaves"—carefully evaluating economic reports to estimate the direction of the economy and initiate stabilizing policies as early as possible. Economists agree that Greenspan was a master at the art. It remains to be seen whether Bernanke will be as successful as his predecessor.

www **Occupational Safety and Health Administration**
This site covers news and information directly related to OSHA's mission "to ensure safe and healthful workplaces in America." *www.osha.gov*

www **Federal Reserve System**
This Federal Reserve System site covers general information about "Fed" operations, including monetary policy, reserve bank services, international banking, and supervisory and regulatory functions. *www.federalreserve.gov*

www **Amtrak**
The Amtrak Web site provides valuable information about trip planning, reservations, train schedules, and train fares. *www.amtrak.com*

cannot immediately name their own chair (see *Up Close:* "Managing the Nation's Money").

**Government Corporations**   Government corporations are created by Congress to undertake independent commercial enterprises. They resemble private corporations in that they typically charge for their services. Like private corporations, too, they are usually governed by a chief executive officer and a board of directors, and they can buy and sell property and incur debts.

Presumably, government corporations perform a service that the private enterprise system has been unable to carry out adequately. The first government corporation was the Tennessee Valley Authority, created by President Franklin Roosevelt during the Depression to build dams and sell electricity at inexpensive rates to impoverished citizens in the mid-South. In 1970 Congress created Amtrak to restore railroad passenger service to the United States. The U.S. Post Office had originally been created as a cabinet-level department, but in 1971 it became the U.S. Postal Service, a government corporation with a mandate from Congress to break even.

**Contractors and Consultants**   How has the federal government grown enormously in power and size, yet kept its number of employees at roughly the same level in recent years? The answer is found in the spectacular growth of private firms that live off federal contracting and consulting fees. Nearly one-fifth of all federal government spending flows through private contractors: for supplies, equipment, services, leases, and research and development. An army of scientists, economists, education specialists, management consultants, transportation experts, social scientists, and others are scattered across the country in universities, think tanks, consulting firms, and laboratories. Many are concentrated in the "beltway bandit" firms surrounding Washington, D.C.

The federal grant and contracting system is enormously complex; an estimated 150,000 federal contracting offices in nearly 500 agencies oversee thousands of outside contractors and consultants.[7] Although advertised bidding is sometimes required by law, most contracts and grants are awarded without competition through negotiation with favored firms or "sole source contracts" with organizations believed by bureaucrats to be uniquely qualified. Even when federal agencies issue public requests for proposals (RFPs), often a favored contractor has been alerted and advised by bureaucrats within the agency about how to win the award.

# Bureaucracy and Democracy

Traditionally, conflict over government employment centered on the question of partisanship versus competence. Should the federal bureaucracy be staffed by people politically loyal to the president, the president's party, or key members of Congress? Or should it be staffed by nonpartisan people selected on the basis of merit and protected from "political" influence?

**The Spoils System**    Historically, government employment was allocated by the **spoils system**—selecting employees on the basis of party loyalty, electoral support, and political influence. Or, as Senator William Marcy said in 1832, "They see nothing wrong in the rule that to the victors belong the spoils of the enemy."[8] The spoils system is most closely associated with President Andrew Jackson, who viewed it as a popular reform of the earlier tendency to appoint officials on the basis of kinship and class standing. Jackson sought to bring into government many of the common people who had supported him. Later in the nineteenth century, the bartering and sale of government jobs became so scandalous and time-consuming that presidents complained bitterly about the task. When President James Garfield was shot and killed in 1881 by a disgruntled job seeker, the stage was set for reform.

**The Merit System**    The **merit system**—government employment based on competence, neutrality, and protection from partisanship—was introduced in the Pendleton Act of 1883. The act created the Civil Service Commission to establish a system for selecting government personnel based on merit, as determined by competitive examinations. In the beginning, "civil service" coverage included only about 10 percent of total federal employees. Over the years, however, more and more positions were placed under civil service, primarily at the behest of presidents who sought to "freeze in" their political appointees. By 1978 more than 90 percent of federal employees were covered by civil service or other merit systems.

The civil service system established a uniform General Schedule (GS) of job grades from GS 1 (lowest) to GS 15 (highest), with an Executive Schedule added later for top managers and pay ranges based on an individual's time in the grade. Each grade has specific educational requirements and examinations. College graduates generally begin at GS 5 or above; GS 9 through GS 12 are technical and supervisory positions; and GS 13, 14, and 15 are midlevel management and highly specialized positions. The Executive Schedule (the "supergrades") are reserved for positions of greatest responsibility. (In 2006 annual pay ranged from roughly $32,000 to $44,000 for Grades 5–8, up to $85,000 to $120,000 for Grades 13–15, and $183,500 for some Executive Schedule positions.)

About two-thirds of all federal civilian jobs come under the General Schedule system, with its written examinations and/or training, experience, and educational requirements. Most of the other one-third of federal civilian employees are

---

**spoils system** Selection of employees for government agencies on the basis of party loyalty, electoral support, and political influence.

---

— Think Again —

Should the federal bureaucracy be managed by nonpartisan professionals rather than people politically loyal to the president?

---

**merit system** Selection of employees for government agencies on the basis of competence, with no consideration of an individual's political stance and/or power.

---

USA Jobs

This site is the official source for federal employment information.
*www.usajobs.opm.gov*

During the administration of Andrew Jackson, the spoils system was perhaps more overt than at any other time in the history of the U.S. federal government. Jackson claimed he was trying to involve more of the "common folk" in the government, but his selection of advisers on the basis of personal friendship rather than qualifications sometimes caused him difficulties.

part of the "excepted services"; they are employed by various agencies that have their own separate merit systems, such as the Federal Bureau of Investigation, the Central Intelligence Agency, the U.S. Postal Service, and the State Department Foreign Service. The military also has its own system of recruitment, promotion, and pay.

**Political Involvement**   Congress passed the Hatch Act in 1939, a law that prohibited federal employees from engaging in partisan political activity, including running for public office, soliciting campaign funds, or campaigning for or against a party or candidate. It also protected federal merit system employees from dismissal for partisan reasons. But over the years many federal employees came to believe that the Hatch Act infringed on their rights as citizens. In 1993, a Democratic-controlled Congress repealed major portions of the Hatch Act, allowing civil servants to hold party positions and involve themselves in political fund-raising and campaigning. They still may not be candidates for public office in partisan elections, or solicit contributions from subordinate employees or people who do business with—or have cases before—their agencies.

**The Problem of Responsiveness**   The civil service system, like most other "reforms," eventually created problems at least as troubling as those in the system it replaced. First of all, there is the problem of a *lack of responsiveness* to presidential direction. Civil servants, secure in their protected jobs, can be less than cooperative toward their presidentially appointed department or agency heads. They can slow or obstruct policy changes with which they personally disagree. Each bureau and agency develops its own "culture," usually in strong support of the governmental function or client group served by the organization. Changing the culture of an agency is extremely difficult, especially when a presidential administration is committed to reducing its resources, functions, or services. Bureaucrats' powers of policy obstruction are formidable: They can help mobilize interest-group support against the president's policy; they can "leak" damaging information to sympathizers in Congress or the media to undermine the president's policy; they can delay and/or "sabotage" policies with which they disagree.

**The Problem of Productivity**    Perhaps the most troublesome problem in the federal bureaucracy has involved *productivity*—notably the inability to improve job performance because of the difficulties in rewarding or punishing civil servants. "Merit" salary rewards have generally proven ineffective in rewarding the performance of federal employees. More than 99 percent of federal workers regularly receive annual "merit" pay increases. Moreover, over time, federal employees have secured higher grade classifications and hence higher pay for most of the job positions in the General Schedule. This "inflation" in GS grades, combined with regular increases in salary and benefits, has resulted in many federal employees enjoying higher pay and benefits than employees in the private sector performing similar jobs.

At the same time, very poor performance often goes largely unpunished. Once hired and retained through a brief probationary period, a federal civil servant cannot be dismissed except for "cause." Severe obstacles to firing a civil servant result in a rate of dismissal of about one-tenth of 1 percent of all federal employees (see Table 10.3). It is doubtful that only such a tiny fraction are performing unsatisfactorily. A federal executive confronting a poorly performing or nonperforming employee must be prepared to spend more than a year in extended proceedings to secure a dismissal. Often costly substitute strategies are devised to work around or inspire the resignation of unsatisfactory federal employees—assigning them meaningless or boring tasks, denying them promotions, transferring them to distant or undesirable locations, removing secretaries or other supporting resources, and the like.

**Civil Service Reform**    Presidents routinely try to remedy some of the problems in the system. The Civil Service Reform Act of 1978, initiated by President Jimmy Carter, replaced the Civil Service Commission with the Office of Personnel Management (OPM) and made OPM responsible for recruiting, examining, training, and promoting federal employees. Unlike the Civil Service Commission, OPM is headed by a single director responsible to the president. The act

---

**Table 10.3    Firing a Bureaucrat: What Is Required to Dismiss a Federal Employee**

- Written notice at least thirty days in advance of a hearing to determine incompetence or misconduct.
- A statement of cause, indicating specific dates, places, and actions cited as incompetent or improper.
- The right to a hearing and decision by an impartial official, with the burden of proof falling on the agency that wishes to fire the employee.
- The right to have an attorney and to present witnesses in the employee's favor at the hearing.
- The right to appeal any adverse action to the Merit Systems Protection Board.
- The right to appeal any adverse action by the board to the U.S. Court of Appeals.
- The right to remain on the job and be paid until all appeals are exhausted.

**Table 10.4    Women and Minorities in the Federal Bureaucracy**

|  | Percentage Female | Percentage White, Non-Hispanic | Percentage African American | Percentage Hispanic |
|---|---|---|---|---|
| Overall | 45.0% | 69.3% | 16.9% | 6.9% |
| By pay grade |  |  |  |  |
| GS 1–4 | 64.8 | 56.7 | 24.6 | 8.9 |
| GS 5–8 | 65.9 | 59.0 | 24.7 | 8.4 |
| GS 9–12 | 46.2 | 71.6 | 15.3 | 6.9 |
| GS 13–15 | 32.3 | 79.6 | 10.3 | 4.2 |
| Executive | 9.1 | 86.4 | 6.8 | 3.3 |
| U.S. population (2000) | 50.9 | 75.2 | 12.3 | 12.5 |

Table excludes Native Americans, Alaska Natives, and Asian and Pacific Islanders.

*Source:* Office of Personnel Management. Democratic Profile of the Federal Workforce. *www.opm.gov*

also sought to (1) streamline procedures through which individuals could be disciplined for poor performance; (2) establish merit pay for middle-level managers; and (3) create a Senior Executive Service (SES) composed of about 8,000 top people designated for higher Executive Schedule grades and salaries who also might be given salary bonuses, transferred among agencies, or demoted, based on performance.

But like many other reforms, this act failed to resolve the major problems—the responsiveness and productivity of the bureaucracy. No senior executives were fired, demoted, or involuntarily transferred. The bonus program proved difficult to implement: There are few recognized standards for judging meritorious work in public service, and bonuses often reflect favoritism as much as merit. Because the act created a separate Merit Systems Protection Board to hear appeals by federal employees from dismissals, suspensions, and demotions, rates of dismissal for all grades have not changed substantially from earlier days.

**Bureaucracy and Representation**    In addition to the questions of responsiveness and productivity, there is also the question of the representativeness of the federal bureaucracy. About 45 percent of the total civilian workforce is female, 16.9 percent is black, and 6.9 is Hispanic. However, a close look at *top* bureaucratic positions reveals far less diversity. As Table 10.4 shows, only 9.1 percent of federal "executive" positions (levels GS 16–18) are filled by women, only 6.8 percent by blacks, and only 3.3 percent by Hispanics. Thus the federal bureaucracy, like other institutions in American society, is *un*representative of the general population in its top executive positions.

## Bureaucratic Politics

To whom is the federal bureaucracy really accountable? The president, Congress, or itself? Article II, Section 2, of the Constitution places the president at the head of the executive branch of government, with the power to "appoint Ambassadors, other public Ministers and Consuls, Judges of the Supreme Court, and all other Officers of the United States . . . which shall be established by Law." Appointment of these officials requires "the Advice and Consent of the Senate"—that is,

—Think Again—

Should the federal bureaucracy at all levels reflect the gender and minority ratios of the total civilian work force?

a majority vote in the Senate. The Constitution also states that "the Congress may by Law vest the Appointment of such inferior Officers, as they think proper, in the President alone." If the bureaucracy is to be made accountable to the president, we would expect the president to directly appoint *policy-making* executive officers. But it is difficult to determine exactly how many positions are truly "policy making."

**Presidential "Plums"**    The president retains direct control over about 3,000 federal jobs. Some 700 of these jobs are considered policy-making positions. They include presidential appointments authorized by law—cabinet and subcabinet officers, judges, U.S. marshals, U.S. attorneys, ambassadors, and members of various boards and commissions. The president also appoints a large number of "Schedule C" jobs throughout the bureaucracy, described as "confidential or policy-determining" in character. Each new administration goes through many months of high-powered lobbying and scrambling to fill these posts. Applicants with congressional sponsors, friends in the White House, or a record of loyal campaign work for the president compete for these "plums." Political loyalty must be weighed against administrative competence.[9]

**Rooms at the Top**    The federal bureaucracy has "thickened" at the top, even as total federal employment has declined. Over time, departments and agencies have added layers of administrators, variously titled "deputy secretary," "undersecretary," "assistant secretary," "deputy assistant secretary," and so on. Cabinet departments have become top-heavy with administrators, and the same multiplication of layers of executive management has occurred in independent agencies as well.[10]

**Whistle-Blowers**    The question of bureaucratic responsiveness is complicated by the struggle between the president and Congress to control the bureaucracy. Congress expects federal agencies and employees to respond fully and promptly to its inquiries and to report candidly on policies, procedures, and expenditures. Whistle-blowers are federal employees (or employees of a firm supplying the government) who report government waste, mismanagement, or fraud to the media or to congressional committees or who "go public" with their policy disputes with their superiors. Congress generally encourages whistle-blowing as a means of getting information and controlling the bureaucracy, but the president and agency heads whose policies are under attack are often less kindly disposed toward whistle-blowers. In 1989 Congress passed the Whistleblower Protection Act, which established an independent agency to guarantee whistle-blowers protection against unjust dismissal, transfer, or demotion.

**Agency Cultures**    Over time, every bureaucracy tends to develop its own "culture"—beliefs about the values of the organization's programs and goals and close associations with the agency's client groups and political supporters. Many government agencies are dominated by people who have been in government service most of their lives, and most of these people have worked in the same functional field most of their lives. They believe their work is important, and they resist efforts by either the president or Congress to reduce the activities, size, or budget of their agency. Career bureaucrats tend to support enlargement of the public sector—to enhance education, welfare, housing, environmental and consumer protection, and so on. Bureaucrats not only share a belief in the need for government expansion but also stand to benefit directly from increased authority, staffing, and funding as government takes on new and enlarged responsibilities.

 **Center for Public Integrity**
Reform organization committed to "exposing" corruption, mismanagement, and waste in government.
*www.publicintegrity.org*

**whistle-blower** Employee of the federal government or of a firm supplying the government who reports waste, mismanagement, and/or fraud by a government agency or contractor.

**Friends and Neighbors** Bureaucracies maintain their own cultures in part by staffing themselves. Informal practices in recruitment often circumvent civil service procedures. Very few people ever get hired by taking a federal civil service examination administered by OPM and then sitting and waiting to be called for an interview by an agency. Most bureaucratic hiring actually comes about through "networks" of personal friends and professional associates. People inside an agency contact their friends and associates when a position first becomes vacant; they then send their friends to OPM to formally qualify for the job. Thus inside candidates learn about an opening well before it appears on any list of vacant positions and can tailor their applications to the job description. Agencies may even send a "name request" to OPM, ensuring that the preselected person will appear on the list of qualified people. In this way, individuals sometimes move through many jobs within a specific policy network—for example, within environmental protection, within transportation, or within social welfare— shifting between the federal bureaucracy, state or local government, and private firms or interest groups in the same field. Network recruiting generally ensures that the people entering a bureaucracy will share the same values and attitudes of the people already there.

**"Reinventing" Government** Reformers lament "the bankruptcy of bureaucracy"—the waste, inefficiency, impersonality, and unresponsiveness of large government organizations. They decry "the routine tendency to protect turf, to resist change, to build empires, to enlarge one's sphere of control, to protect projects and programs regardless of whether or not they are any longer needed."[11] Many bureaucratic reform efforts have foundered, from Hoover Commission studies in the Truman and Eisenhower years to the Grace Commission work in the Reagan Administration. Clinton assigned a "reinventing government" task to Vice President Al Gore. Gore produced a report designed to put the "customer" (U.S. citizen) first, to "empower" government employees to get results, to cut red tape, to introduce competition and a market orientation wherever possible, and to decentralize government decision making.[12] The most impressive result was the overall decline in federal employment during the Clinton Administration, from 3.1 million to 2.8 million civilian employees.

**Presidential Initiative** Presidents can create some new agencies by executive order. Often Congress gives presidents the authority to reorganize agencies by legislation (see *Up Close:* "Reorganizing Intelligence After 9/11"). But presidents have also acted on their own to create new agencies. Indeed, one study concludes that presidents have created about 40 percent of all new agencies[13]— perhaps the most famous was President Kennedy's Peace Corps. Of course, Congress has the last word, inasmuch as the continuation of a presidentially created agency requires funding and Congress controls the purse strings. It can end an agency's existence by cutting off its funds.

---

> **Think Again**
>
> Do you believe the bureaucrats in Washington waste a lot of the money we pay in taxes?

## The Budgetary Process

The federal government's annual budget battles are the heart of the political process. Budget battles decide who gets what and who pays the cost of government. The budget is the single most important policy statement of any government.

The president is responsible for submitting the annual *Budget of the United States Government*—with estimates of revenues and recommendations for expenditures— for consideration, amendment, and approval by the Congress. But the president's budget reflects the outcome of earlier bureaucratic battles over who gets what. Despite highly publicized wrangling between the president and Congress each year—and occasional declarations that the president's budget is "DOA" (dead on arrival)—final congressional appropriations rarely deviate by more than 2 or 3 percent from the original presidential budget. Thus the president and the Office of Management and Budget in the Executive Office of the President have real budgetary power.

## UP CLOSE

# Reorganizing Intelligence After 9/11

"Imagination is not a gift usually associated with bureaucracies." There were reports at lower levels of the intelligence community prior to 9/11 that Al Qaeda was planning a major attack on the United States, that the World Trade Center might be a target because it had been a target of a car bomb in 1992, that Muslim fanatics were in the country and some had been taking flying lessons, and that various intelligence agencies had considered the possibilities of terrorists using aircraft as weapons. But no specifics were reported—time, location, or individuals involved—and the *9/11 Commission: The National Commission on Terrorist Attacks upon the United States* concluded that no agency or individual was to blame for the failure to anticipate the tragedy. Simply, "No one connected the dots."

### 9/11 Commission

President Bush authorized the 9/11 Commission in 2002, after pressure mounted in Washington for a thorough investigation of the 9/11 attack. The Commission's Final Report makes for exciting reading; it carefully reconstructs what happened in the days and months prior to the tragedy, as well as the events on that day itself; and it describes what each relevant federal agency knew and did not know about the possibility of such an attack. Finally, the commission issued a series of recommendations regarding reorganization of the intelligence community: to unify the intelligence community and operational planning against terrorists; to unify the many agencies participating in counterterrorism; and to strengthen homeland defense.

### The Intelligence Community

The intelligence community consists of a series of agencies, each with a specialized responsibility, together with elements of the Department of Defense, the Department of Homeland Security, the

Federal Bureau of Investigation, the Department of State, the Department of Energy, and the Department of the Treasury. The Central Intelligence Agency (CIA) was the lead agency in assembly, analysis, and dissemination of intelligence from all other agencies in intelligence community. It prepared the President's Daily Briefing (PDB), which summarizes all intelligence reports from all agencies for the president each day. The CIA also prepared National Intelligence Estimates (NIE's)—more thorough studies of specific topics, for example, North Korea's nuclear capabilities. In addition the CIA is charged with responsibility for human intelligence collection (recruiting agents around the world and supervising their work), and it also has responsibility for covert operations under the direction of the President (see "The Central Intelligence Agency" in Chapter 11). The National Security Agency (NSA) collects and processes foreign signals intelligence—all electronic emissions from radio to satellite communication. The National Reconnaissance Office (NRO) collects information from satellite reconnaissance. The National Imagery and Mapping Agency (NIMA) is responsible for geographic and geospatial intelligence. The Defense Intelligence Agency (DIA) is responsible for delivering tactical military intelligence directly to war fighters as well as policy makers.

### National Intelligence Director

The key recommendation of the 9/11 Commission was the creation of a new office—the National Intelligence Director (NID)—to oversee the entire intelligence community. The new NID would replace the CIA director's role as the principal intelligence advisor to the president. The CIA director would concentrate on the responsibilities of the CIA itself. The NID would unify the budget for national intelligence as well as approve and submit nominations for individuals to head various agencies of the intelligence community. The NID would also manage the nation's counterterrorism effort, with the assistance of a new National Counterterrorism Center, which would assemble and analyze information on terrorists gathered both at home and abroad.

### Military Intelligence

The Defense Department objected to giving the NID budget and personnel responsibility for intelligence agencies located within the department. Army, Navy, Air Force, and Marine intelligence are closely integrated with their respective military commands. The issue was compromised in Congress, with the military retaining direct control over intelligence activities within the Defense Department and the NID only consulting on these issues. The same compromise was reached regarding intelligence activities in the Department of Homeland Security, Department of State, Department of Energy, and Department of the Treasury.

### Integrating Foreign and Domestic Intelligence

Perhaps the most troublesome problem in intelligence and counterterrorism in the past had been the lack of coordination between the CIA and the FBI. Fighting global terrorism requires close surveillance of individuals and terrorist organizations both within and outside of the United States. But in the original National Security Act of 1947, establishing the CIA, this agency was specifically prohibited from engaging in any activities, including surveillance of individual organizations, *inside the borders of the United States*. Only the FBI has the authority to act against terrorists inside the United States. Intelligence reorganization encouraged greater cooperation between these agencies. And the USA PATRIOT Act now permits both agencies to undertake surveillance of communications relevant to terrorism both within the United States and abroad. In a separate reorganization within the FBI, a new National Security Center was established with responsibility for counterterrorism. The NID was given budgetary and personnel authority over the new center. However, the FBI and the intelligence community each continue to operate largely separately from the other, and it is not clear whether the problems of communication and coordination between these agencies has been resolved.

### FISA and Domestic Surveillance

In the Foreign Intelligence Surveillance Act of 1978 (FISA) Congress created a special FISA court to oversee the collection of electronic intelligence within the United States. It required all intelligence agencies, including the National Security Agency, which is responsible for the collection of electronic intelligence, to obtain warrants upon a showing that the surveillance is required for investigation of possible attacks upon the nation. The FISA court is secret and the persons under surveillance are not notified.

Nevertheless, President Bush authorized the National Security Agency to intercept international calls to and from Americans—calls involving known or suspected terrorists—without a FISA warrant. The president claimed that he has inherent constitutional powers as Commander-in-Chief to gather intelligence during war or armed conflict, and that the United States is currently at war with international terrorists. The president also claims that a joint resolution of Congress passed following the 9/11 terrorist attack on American included "authorization for the use of military force" and that such authorization includes warrantless surveillance of suspected terrorists both inside and outside of the United States.

Opponents of warrantless surveillance argue that the president is bound by the FISA Act, which specifically requires court warrants for surveillance within United States, including international calls. Congress did not authorize warrantless surveillance in its 9/11 joint resolution. Moreover, Congress did authorize surveillance of American citizens in terrorist investigations *but only* with a warrant issued by the FISA court. Congress was direct and specific on the subject of domestic surveillance in the FISA Act even during wartime. And as far back as 1952, the Supreme Court held that when Congress has addressed a specific issue by law, the president is obliged to follow that law in dealing with the issue.[a] The president, opponents claim, is acting unconstitutionally and unlawfully in authorizing warrantless surveillance of American citizens.

[a]*Youngstown Sheet & Tube Co. v. Sawyer*, 343 U.S. 579 (1952).

**Office of Management and Budget (OMB)**
The OMB site includes all budget documents and information on regulatory oversight. *www.omb.gov*

**The Office of Management and Budget**   The Office of Management and Budget (OMB) has the key responsibility for budget preparation. In addition to this major task, OMB has related responsibilities for improving the organization and management of the executive agencies, for coordinating the extensive statistical services of the federal government, and for analyzing and reviewing proposed legislation.

Preparation of the budget begins when OMB, after preliminary consultations with the executive agencies and in accord with presidential policy, develops targets or ceilings within which the agencies are encouraged to build their requests

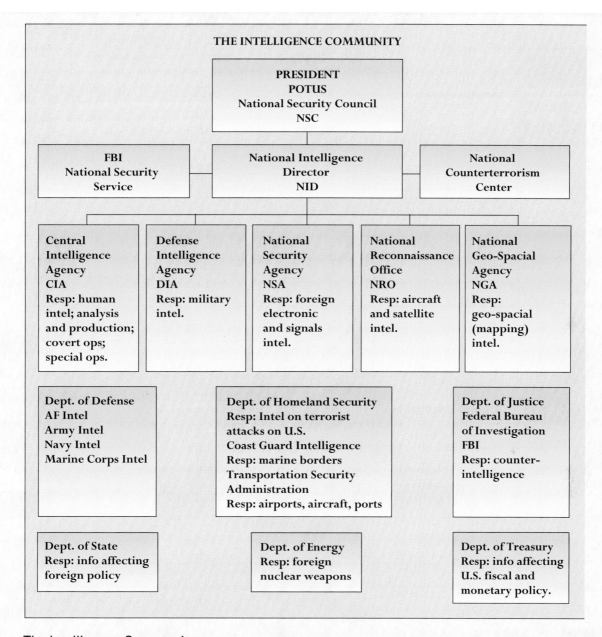

## THE INTELLIGENCE COMMUNITY

**PRESIDENT**
**POTUS**
National Security Council
**NSC**

**FBI**
National Security
Service

**National Intelligence**
**Director**
**NID**

**National**
**Counterterrorism**
**Center**

**Central**
**Intelligence**
**Agency**
**CIA**
Resp: human
intel; analysis
and production;
covert ops;
special ops.

**Defense**
**Intelligence**
**Agency**
**DIA**
Resp: military
intel.

**National**
**Security**
**Agency**
**NSA**
Resp: foreign
electronic
and signals
intel.

**National**
**Reconnaissance**
**Office**
**NRO**
Resp: aircraft
and satellite
intel.

**National**
**Geo-Spacial**
**Agency**
**NGA**
Resp:
geo-spacial
(mapping)
intel.

**Dept. of Defense**
**AF Intel**
**Army Intel**
**Navy Intel**
**Marine Corps Intel**

**Dept. of Homeland Security**
**Resp: Intel on terrorist**
**attacks on U.S.**
**Coast Guard Intelligence**
**Resp: marine borders**
**Transportation Security**
**Administration**
**Resp: airports, aircraft, ports**

**Dept. of Justice**
**Federal Bureau**
**of Investigation**
**FBI**
Resp: counter-
intelligence

**Dept. of State**
Resp: info affecting
foreign policy

**Dept. of Energy**
Resp: foreign
nuclear weapons

**Dept. of Treasury**
Resp: info affecting
U.S. fiscal and
monetary policy.

The Intelligence Community

*Note:* The CIA, DIA, NSA, NRO, and NGA are concerned exclusively with intelligence. The Departments of Defense, Homeland Security, Justice, State, Energy, and Treasury are concerned primarily with other missions but do have some intelligence responsibilities.

(see Figure 10.3). Budget materials and instructions then go to the agencies, with the request that the forms be completed and returned to OMB. This request is followed by about three months of arduous work by agency budget officers, department heads, and the "grass-roots" bureaucracy in Washington, D.C., and out in the field. Budget officials at the bureau and departmental levels check requests from the smaller units, compare them with previous years' estimates, hold conferences, and make adjustments. The heads of agencies are expected to submit their completed requests to OMB by July or August. Although these requests usually remain within target levels, occasionally they include some

| | WHO | WHAT | WHEN |
|---|---|---|---|
| **Presidential budget making** | President and OMB | OMB presents long-range forecasts for revenues and expenditures to the president. President and OMB develop general guidelines for all federal agencies. Agencies are sent guidelines and forms for their budget requests. | January February March |
| | Executive agencies | Agencies prepare and submit budget requests to OMB. | April May June July |
| | OMB and agencies | OMB reviews agency requests and holds hearings with agency officials. | August September October |
| | OMB and president | OMB presents revised budget to president. President and OMB write budget message for Congress. | November December January |
| | President | President presents budget for the next fiscal year to Congress. | February |
| **Congressional budget process** | CBO and congressional committees | CBO reviews taxing and spending proposals and reports to House and Senate budget committees. | February–April |
| | Congress; House and Senate budget committees | Committees present first concurrent resolution, which sets overall total for budget outlays in major categories. Full House and Senate vote on resolution. Committees are instructed to stay within Budget Committee's resolution. | May June |
| | Congress; House and Senate appropriations committees and budget committees | Appropriations committees and subcommittees draw up detailed appropriations bills and submit them to budget committees for second concurrent resolution. The full House and Senate vote on "reconciliations" and second (firm) concurrent resolution. | July August September |
| | Congress and president | House and Senate pass various appropriations bills (nine to sixteen bills, by major functional category, such as "defense"). Each is sent to president for signature. (If successfully vetoed, a bill is revised and resubmitted to the president.) | September October |
| **Executive budget implementation** | Congress and president | Fiscal year for all federal agencies begins October 1. If no appropriations bill for an agency has been passed by Congress and signed by the president, Congress must pass and the president sign a continuing resolution to allow the agency to spend at last year's level until a new appropriations bill is passed. If no continuing resolution is passed, the agency must officially cease spending government funds and must officially shut down. | After October 1 |

**Figure 10.3** The Budget Process

Development, presentation, and approval of the federal budget for any fiscal year takes almost two full years. The executive branch spends more than a year on the process before Congress even begins its review and revision of the president's proposals. The problems of implementing the budgeted programs then fall to the federal bureaucracy.

"overceiling" items (requests above the suggested ceilings). With the requests of the spending agencies at hand, OMB begins its own budget review, including hearings at which top agency officials support their requests as convincingly as possible. Frequently OMB must say "no," that is, reduce agency requests. On rare occasions, dissatisfied agencies may ask the budget director to take their cases to the president.

**The President's Budget**   In December, the president and the OMB director devote much time to the key document, *The Budget of the United States Government,* which by now is approaching its final stages of assembly. Each budget is named for the **fiscal year** in which it *ends.* The federal fiscal year begins on October 1 and ends the following September 30. (Thus *The Budget of the United States Government Fiscal Year* 2009 begins October 1, 2008, and ends September 30, 2009.) Although the completed document includes a revenue plan with general estimates for taxes and other income, it is primarily an expenditure budget. (Revenue and tax policy staff work centers in the Treasury Department, not in the Office of Management and Budget.) In late January, the president presents Congress with

**fiscal year** Yearly government accounting period, not necessarily the same as the calendar year. The federal government's fiscal year begins October 1 and ends September 30.

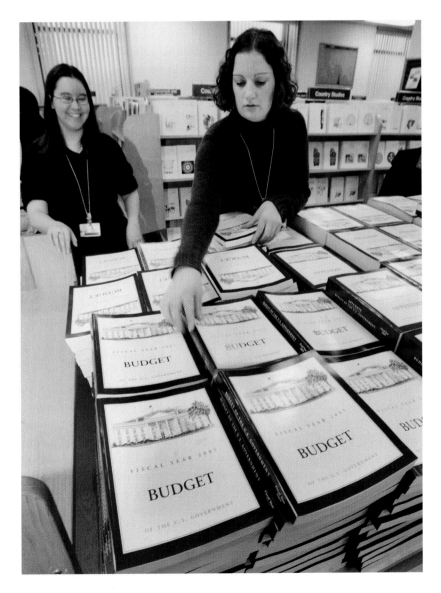

The 2005 Budget of the United States government shows total outlays of $2.4 trillion, with a deficit of nearly $365 billion. The deficit is in part a product of increased spending for defense and homeland security.

*The Budget of the United States Government* for the fiscal year beginning October 1. After the budget is in legislative hands, the president may recommend further alterations as needs dictate.

**House and Senate Budget Committees**   The Constitution gives Congress the authority to decide how the government should spend its money: "No money shall be drawn from the Treasury, but in Consequence of Appropriations made by Law" (Article 1, Section 9). The president's budget is sent initially to the House and Senate Budget Committees, which rely on their own bureaucracy, the Congressional Budget Office (CBO), to review the president's budget. Based on the CBO's assessment, these committees draft a first **budget resolution** (due May 15) setting forth target goals to guide congressional committees regarding specific appropriations and revenue measures. If proposed spending exceeds the targets in the budget resolution, the resolution comes back to the floor in a reconciliation measure. A second budget resolution (due September 15) sets binding budget figures for committees and subcommittees considering appropriations. In practice, however, these two budget resolutions are often folded into a single measure because Congress does not want to argue the same issues twice.

**Congressional Appropriations Committees**   Congressional approval of each year's spending is usually divided into thirteen separate appropriations bills (acts), each covering separate broad categories of spending (for example, defense, labor, human services and education, commerce, justice). These appropriations bills are drawn up by the House and Senate Appropriations Committees and their specialized subcommittees, which function as overseers of agencies included in their appropriations bills. Committee work in the House of Representatives is usually more thorough than it is in the Senate; the committee in the Senate tends to be a "court of appeal" for agencies opposed to House action. Each committee, moreover, has about ten largely independent subcommittees, each reviewing the requests of a particular agency or a group of related functions. Specific appropriations bills are taken up by the subcommittees in hearings. Departmental officers answer questions on the conduct of their programs and defend their requests for the next fiscal year; lobbyists and other witnesses testify. Although committees and subcommittees have broad discretion in allocating funds to the agencies they monitor, they must stay within overall totals set forth in the second budget resolution adopted by Congress.

**Appropriations Acts**   In examining the interactions between Congress and the federal bureaucracy over spending, it is important to distinguish between appropriations and authorization. An **authorization** is an act of Congress that establishes a government program and defines the amount of money it may spend. Authorizations may be for one or several years. However, an authorization does not actually provide the money that has been authorized; only an **appropriations act** can do that. In fact, appropriations acts, which are usually for a single fiscal year, are almost always *less* than authorizations; deciding how much less is the real function of the Appropriations Committees and subcommittees. (By its own rules, Congress cannot appropriate money for programs it has not already authorized.) Appropriations acts include both obligational authority and outlays.

  **Obligational authority** permits a government agency to enter into contracts that will require the government to make payments beyond the fiscal years in question. **Outlays** must be spent in the fiscal year for which they are appropriated.

**Continuing Resolutions and "Shutdowns"**   All appropriations acts *should* be passed by both houses and signed by the president into law before October 1,

---

**budget resolution**
Congressional bill setting forth target budget figures for appropriations to various government departments and agencies.

**authorization**   Act of Congress that establishes a government program and defines the amount of money it may spend.

**appropriations act**
Congressional bill that provides money for programs authorized by Congress.

**obligational authority**
Feature of some appropriations acts by which an agency is empowered to enter into contracts that will require the government to make payments beyond the fiscal year in question.

**outlays**   Actual dollar amounts to be spent by the federal government in a fiscal year.

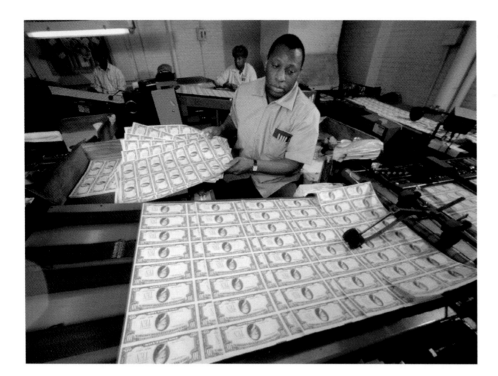

Much of the work of the federal bureaucracy is routine, including the printing of money.

the date of the start of the fiscal year. However, it is rare for Congress to meet this deadline, so the government usually finds itself beginning a new fiscal year without a budget. Constitutionally, any U.S. government agency for which Congress does not pass an appropriations act may not draw money from the Treasury and thus is obliged to shut down. To get around this problem, Congress usually adopts a **continuing resolution** that authorizes government agencies to keep spending money for a specified period at the same level as in the previous fiscal year.

A continuing resolution is supposed to grant additional time for Congress to pass, and the president to sign, appropriations acts. But occasionally this process has broken down in the heat of political combat over the budget: the time period specified in a continuing resolution has expired without agreement on appropriations acts or even on a new continuing resolution. Shutdowns occurred during the bitter battle between President Bill Clinton and the Republican-controlled Congress over the Fiscal Year 1996 budget. In theory, the absence of either appropriations acts or a continuing resolution should cause the entire federal government to "shut down," that is, to cease all operations and expenditures for lack of funds. But in practice, such shutdowns have been only partial, affecting only "nonessential" government employees and causing relatively little disruption.

**continuing resolution**
Congressional bill that authorizes government agencies to keep spending money for a specified period at the same level as in the previous fiscal year; passed when Congress is unable to enact final appropriations measures by October 1.

## The Politics of Budgeting

Budgeting is very political. Being a good "bureaucratic politician" involves (1) cultivating a good base of support for requests among the public at large and among people served by the agency; (2) developing interest, enthusiasm, and support for one's program among top political figures and congressional leaders; (3) winning favorable coverage of agency activities in the media; and (4) following strategies that exploit opportunities (see *Up Close:* "Bureaucratic Budget Strategies").

## UP CLOSE

# Bureaucratic Budget Strategies

How do bureaucrats go about "maximizing" their resources? Some of the most common budgetary strategies of bureaucrats are listed here. Remember that most bureaucrats believe strongly in the importance of their tasks; they pursue these strategies not only to increase their own power and prestige but also to better serve their client groups and the entire nation.

- **Spend it all:** Spend all of your current appropriation. Failure to use up an appropriation indicates the full amount was unnecessary in the first place, which in turn implies that your budget should be cut next year.

- **Ask for more:** Never request a sum less than your current appropriation. It is easier to find ways to spend up to current appropriation levels than it is to explain why you want a reduction. Besides, a reduction indicates your program is not growing, an embarrassing admission to most government administrators. Requesting an increase, at least enough to cover "inflation," demonstrates the continued importance of your program.

- **Put vital programs in the "base":** Put top priority programs into the basic budget—that is, that part of the budget within current appropriation levels. The Office of Management and Budget (OMB) and legislative committees seldom challenge programs that appear to be part of existing operations.

- **Make new programs appear "incremental":** Requested increases should appear to be small and should appear to grow out of existing operations. Any appearance of a fundamental change in a budget should be avoided.

- **Give them something to cut:** Give the OMB and legislative committees something to cut. Normally it is desirable to submit requests for substantial increases in existing programs and many requests for new programs, in order to give higher political authorities something to cut. This approach enables authorities to "save" the public untold millions of dollars and justify their claim of promoting "economy" in government. Giving them something to cut also diverts attention from the basic budget with its vital programs.

- **Make cuts hurt:** If your agency is faced with a real budget cut—that is, a reduction from last year's appropriation—announce pending cuts in vital and popular programs in order to stir up opposition to the cut. For example, the National Park Service might announce the impending closing of the Washington Monument. Never acknowledge that cuts might be accommodated by your agency without reducing basic services.

**incremental budgeting**
Method of budgeting that focuses on requested increases in funding for existing programs, accepting as legitimate their previous year's expenditures.

**Budgeting Is "Incremental"** The most important factor determining the size and content of the budget each year is last year's budget. Decision makers generally use last year's expenditures as a *base;* active consideration of budget proposals generally focuses on new items and requested increases over last year's base. The budget of an agency is almost never reviewed as a whole. Agencies are seldom required to defend or explain budget requests that do *not* exceed current appropriations; but requested increases *do* require explanation and are most subject to reduction by OMB or Congress.

The result of **incremental budgeting** is that many programs, services, and expenditures continue long after there is any real justification for them. When new needs, services, and functions arise, they do not displace older ones but rather are *added* to the budget. Budget decisions are made incrementally because policy makers do not have the time, energy, or information to review every dollar of every budget request every year. Nor do policy makers wish to refight every political battle over existing programs every year. So they generally accept last year's base spending level as legitimate and focus attention on proposed increases for each program.

## WHAT DO YOU THINK?

### How Much Money Does the Government Waste?

Bureaucracy is often associated in the public's mind with waste and inefficiency. But it is very difficult to determine objectively how much money government really wastes. People disagree on the value of various government programs. What is "waste" to one person may be a vital governmental function to another. But even those who believe a government program is necessary may still believe some of the money going to that program is wasted by the bureaucracy.

Indeed, over the last twenty years, nearly two-thirds of Americans have described the government as wasting "a lot" of money rather than "some" or "not very much" (see graph). Americans believe that there is more waste in domestic spending than in military spending.

Is public opinion correct in estimating that "a lot" of money is wasted? The Government Accountability Office (GAO) is an arm of Congress with broad authority to audit the operations and finances of federal agencies. GAO audits have frequently found fraud and mismanagement amounting to 10 percent or more of the spending of many agencies it has reviewed, which suggests that *$200 billion* of the overall federal budget of $2.1 trillion may be wasted.[a] Citizens' commissions studying the federal bureaucracy place an even higher figure on waste. The

Grace Commission estimated waste at more than 20 percent of federal spending.[b]

[a]General Accounting Office, *Federal Evaluation Issues* (Washington, D.C., 1989).

[b]*President's Private Sector Survey on Cost Control* (Grace Commission Report) (Washington, D.C.: Government Printing Office, 1984).

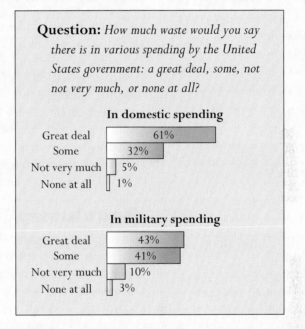

**Question:** *How much waste would you say there is in various spending by the United States government: a great deal, some, not not very much, or none at all?*

**In domestic spending**

| | |
|---|---|
| Great deal | 61% |
| Some | 32% |
| Not very much | 5% |
| None at all | 1% |

**In military spending**

| | |
|---|---|
| Great deal | 43% |
| Some | 41% |
| Not very much | 10% |
| None at all | 3% |

*Source:* Copyright © 2001, *The Washington Post*, Reprinted with permission.

---

Reformers have proposed "sunset" laws requiring bureaucrats to justify their programs every five to seven years or else the programs go out of existence, as well as **zero-based budgeting** that would force agencies to justify every penny requested—not just requested increases. In theory, sunset laws and zero-based budgeting would regularly prune unnecessary government programs, agencies, and expenditures and thus limit the growth of government and waste in government (see *What Do You Think?* "How Much Money Does the Government Waste?"). But in reality, sunset laws and zero-based budgeting require so much effort in justifying already accepted programs that executive agencies and legislative committees grow tired of the effort and return to incrementalism.

The "incremental" nature of budgetary politics helps reduce political conflicts and maintain stability in governmental programs. As bruising as budgetary battles are today, they would be much worse if the president or Congress undertook to review the value of *all* existing expenditures and programs each year. Comprehensive budgetary review would "overload the system" with political conflict by refighting every policy battle every year.

### Budgeting Is Nonprogrammatic
Budgeting is *nonprogrammatic* in that an agency budget typically lists expenditures under ambiguous phrases: "personnel

**zero-based budgeting**
Method of budgeting that demands justification for the entire budget request of an agency, not just its requested increase in funding.

services," "contractual services," "travel," "supplies," "equipment." It is difficult to tell from such a listing exactly what programs the agency is spending its money on. Such a budget obscures policy decisions by hiding programs behind meaningless phrases. Even if these categories are broken down into line items (for example, under "personnel services," the line-item budget might say, "John Doaks, Assistant Administrator, $85,000"), it is still next to impossible to identify the costs of various programs.

For many years, reformers have called for budgeting by programs. **Program budgeting** would require agencies to present budgetary requests in terms of the end products they will produce or at least to allocate each expense to a specific program. However, bureaucrats are often unenthusiastic about program budgeting; it certainly adds to the time and energy devoted to budgeting, and many agencies are reluctant to describe precisely what it is they do and how much it really costs to do it. Moreover, some political functions are best served by *non*program budgeting. Agreement comes more easily when the items in dispute can be treated in dollars instead of programmatic differences. Congressional Appropriations Committees can focus on increases or decreases in overall dollar amounts for agencies rather than battle over even more contentious questions of which individual programs are worthy of support.

**program budgeting**
Identifying items in a budget according to the functions and programs they are to be spent on.

## Regulatory Battles

Bureaucracies regulate virtually every aspect of American life. Interest rates on loans are heavily influenced by the Federal Reserve Board. The National Labor Relations Board protects unions and prohibits "unfair labor practices." Safety in automobiles and buses is the responsibility of the National Transportation Safety Board. The Federal Deposit Insurance Corporation insures bank accounts. The Federal Trade Commission orders cigarette manufacturers to place a health warning on each pack. The Equal Employment Opportunity Commission investigates complaints about racial and sexual discrimination in jobs. The Consumer Product Safety Commission requires that toys be large enough that they cannot be swallowed by children. The Federal Communications Commission bans tobacco advertisements on television. The Environmental Protection Agency requires automobile companies to limit exhaust emissions. The Occupational Safety and Health Administration requires construction firms to place portable toilets at work sites. The Food and Drug Administration decides what drugs your doctor can prescribe. The list goes on and on. Indeed, it is difficult to find an activity in public or private life that is not regulated by the federal government (see *A Conflicting View:* "Bureaucratic Regulations Are Suffocating America").

Federal regulatory bureaucracies are legislators, investigators, prosecutors, judges, and juries—all wrapped into one. They issue thousands of pages of rules and regulations each year; they investigate thousands of complaints and conduct thousands of inspections; they require businesses to submit hundreds of thousands of forms each year; they hold hearings, determine "compliance" and "noncompliance," issue corrective orders, and levy fines and penalties. Most economists agree that regulation adds to the cost of living, is an obstacle to innovation and productivity, and hinders economic competition. Most regulatory commissions are independent; they are not under an executive department, and their members are appointed for long terms by a president who has little control over their activities.

**Traditional Agencies: Capture Theory** The **capture theory of regulation** describes how some regulated industries come to benefit from government

— Think Again —
Do you believe bureaucratic regulations of all kinds are hurting America's competitiveness in the global economy?

— Think Again —
Do you believe that the overall costs of federal regulatory activity are justified by the benefits?

**capture theory of regulation** Theory describing how some regulated industries come to benefit from government regulation and how some regulatory commissions come to represent the industries they are supposed to regulate rather than representing "the people."

## A CONFLICTING VIEW

# Bureaucratic Regulations Are Suffocating America

Today, bureaucratic regulations of all kinds—environmental controls, workplace safety rules, municipal building codes, government contracting guidelines—have become so numerous, detailed, and complex that they are stifling initiative, curtailing economic growth, wasting billions of dollars, and breeding popular contempt for law and government.

Consider, for example, the Environmental Protection Agency's rules and regulations, now *seventeen volumes* of fine print. Under one set of rules, before any land on which "toxic" waste was once used can be reused by anyone for any purpose, it must be cleaned to near perfect purity. The dirt must be made cleaner than soil that has never been used for anything. The result is that most new businesses choose to locate on virgin land rather than incur the enormous expense of cleaning dirt, and a great deal of land previously used by industry sits vacant while new land is developed.

These and similar examples of "the death of common sense" in bureaucratic regulations are set forth by critic Philip K. Howard, who argues, "We have constructed a system of regulatory law that basically outlaws common sense."[a]

The explosive growth in federal regulations in the last two decades has added heavy costs to the American economy. The costs of regulations do not appear in the federal budget: rather, they are paid for by businesses, employees, and consumers.

[a]Philip K. Howard. *The Death of Common Sense: How Law Is Suffocating America* (New York: Random House, 1995), pp. 10–11.

Indeed, politicians prefer a regulatory approach to the environment, health, and safety precisely because it forces costs on the private sector—costs that are largely invisible to voters and taxpayers. Yet as the costs of regulation multiply for American businesses, the prices of their products rise in world markets.

How large is the regulatory bill? Proponents of a regulatory activity usually object to estimating its cost. Politicians who wish to develop an image as protectors of the environment, of consumers, of the disabled, and so on, do not want to call attention to the costs of their legislation. Only recently has the Office of Management and Budget (OMB) even attempted to estimate the costs of federal regulatory activity. Overall, regulatory activity costs Americans between $300 billion (OMB estimate) and $700 billion a year (estimate by Center for the Study of American Business), an amount equal to over one-third of the total federal budget.

Regulation also places a heavy burden on innovations and productivity. The costs and delays in winning permission for a new product tend to discourage invention and to drive up prices. For example, new drugs are difficult to introduce in the United States because the Food and Drug Administration (FDA) typically requires up to ten years of testing. Western European nations are many years ahead in their number of life-saving drugs available; they speak of the "drug lag" in the United States. Critics charge that if aspirin were proposed for marketing today, it would not be approved by the FDA. Recently activists have succeeded in speeding up FDA approval of drugs to treat AIDS, but the agency has continued to delay the introduction of drugs to treat other diseases.

regulation and how some regulatory commissions come to represent the industries they are supposed to regulate rather than representing "the people." Historically, regulatory commissions have acted against only the most wayward members of an industry. By attacking those businesses that gave the industry bad publicity, the commissions actually helped improve the public's opinion of the industry as a whole. Regulatory commissions provided symbolic reassurance to the public that the behavior of the industry was proper. Among the traditional regulatory agencies that have been accused of becoming too close to their regulated industry are the Federal Communications Commission (FCC, regulator of the communications industry, including the television networks), the Securities and Exchange Commission (SEC, the securities industry and stock exchanges), the Federal Reserve Board (FRB, the banking industry), and National Labor Relations Board (NLRB, unions).

Agencies need not be actually "captured" by the industries they regulate but rather simply provide "protection" to these industries, especially to the largest corporations within them. Larger corporations are better able to meet agency requirements and to respond to changes in these requirements than smaller corporations or individual firms. In product approval, licensing, permitting, and grant making, for example, larger corporations are better able to jump through bureaucratic hoops.[14]

Commission members often come from the industry they are supposed to regulate, and after a few years in government, the "regulators" return to high-paying jobs in the industry, creating the *revolving door problem* described in Chapter 9. Over the years, then, some industries have come to support their regulatory bureaucracies. Industries have often strongly opposed proposals to reduce government controls. Proposals to deregulate railroads, interstate trucking, and airlines have met with substantial opposition from both the regulatory bureaucracies and the regulated industries, working together.

**The Newer Regulators: The Activists**   In recent decades, Congress created several new "activist" regulatory agencies in response to the civil rights movement, the environmental movement, and the consumer protection movement. Unlike traditional regulatory agencies, the activist agencies do not regulate only a single industry; rather, they extend their jurisdiction to all industries. The Equal Employment Opportunity Commission (EEOC), the Environmental Protection Agency (EPA), and the Occupational Safety and Health Administration (OSHA) pose serious challenges to the business community. Many businesspeople argue that EEOC rules designed to prevent racial and sexual discrimination in employment and promotion (affirmative action guidelines) ignore the problems of their industry or their labor market and overlook the costs of training or the availability of qualified minorities. Likewise, many of OSHA's thousands of safety regulations appear costly and ridiculous to people in industry. The complaint about EPA is that it seldom considers the cost of its rulings to business or the consumer. Industry representatives contend that EPA should weigh the costs of its regulations against the benefits to the environment.

**deregulation** Lifting of government rules and bureaucratic supervision from business and professional activity.

**Deregulation**   The demand to deregulate American life was politically very popular during President Ronald Reagan's administration in the 1980s. But **deregulation** made only limited progress in curtailing the power of the regulatory bureaucracies. Arguments for deregulation centered on the heavy costs of compliance with regulations, the burdens these costs imposed on innovation and productivity, and the adverse impact of regulatory activity on the global competitiveness of American industry. In 1978 Jimmy Carter succeeded in getting Congress to deregulate the airline industry. Against objections by the industry itself, which *wanted* continued regulation, the Civil Aeronautics Board was stripped of its powers to allocate airline routes to various carriers and to set rates. At the end of 1984, the board went out of existence, the first major regulatory agency ever to be abolished. With the airlines free to choose where to fly and what to charge, competition on heavily traveled routes (such as from New York to Los Angeles) reduced fares dramatically while prices rose on less traveled routes served by a single airline. Overall the cost of airline travel declined by 25 to 30 percent.[15] Competition caused airline profits to decline and financially weak airlines to declare bankruptcy. Also, during the 1980s the Interstate Commerce Commission (ICC), the first regulatory commission ever established by the federal government, dating from 1887, was stripped of most of its power to set railroad and trucking rates. The ICC itself was finally abolished in 1995. Prices to consumers of railroad and trucking services declined dramatically.

The deregulation of the airline industry contributed to the development of the hub-and-spoke system currently used by most airlines to reduce their costs. Here American Airlines aircraft congregate at the airline's hub in Dallas/Fort Worth. Although deregulation has caused fares to decrease on heavily competitive routes, critics charge that it has contributed to higher rates on noncompetitive routes.

**Reregulation**   Deregulation threatens to diminish politicians' power and to eliminate bureaucrats' jobs. It forces industries to become competitive and diminishes the role of interest group lobbyists. So in the absence of strong popular support for deregulation, pressures to continue and expand regulatory activity will always be strong in Washington.

Airline deregulation brought about a huge increase in airline travel. The airlines doubled their seating capacity and made more efficient use of their aircraft through the development of "hub-and-spoke" networks. Air safety continued to improve; fatalities per millions of miles flown declined; and by taking travelers away from far more dangerous highway travel, overall transportation safety was enhanced. But these favorable outcomes were overshadowed by complaints about congestion at major airports and increased flight delays, especially at peak hours. The major airports are publicly owned, and governments have been very slow in responding to increased air traffic. Congestion and delays are widely publicized, and politicians respond to complaints by calling for reregulation of airline travel.

The political incentives to create new regulatory agencies, grant additional powers to existing agencies, and add to the accumulation of federal regulations are great. Politicians want to be seen "doing something" about any well-publicized problem in America. When the media reports accidents, health scares, environmental dangers, etc., politicians are interviewed for their response, and most feel obliged to call for new laws and regulations, with little regard to their likely costs or effectiveness.

# Regulating America

Federal regulatory agencies continually add more rules to American life. Roughly 4,000 new rules, all with the force of law, are issued by regulatory agencies each year. The Environmental Protection Agency (EPA) leads in making new

**Code of Federal Regulations**
All fifty titles of federal regulations can be found at the Cornell Law School site.
*www.cfr.law.cornell.edu*

rules, closely followed by the Internal Revenue Service (IRS) and the Federal Communications Commission (FCC).

Over 50 federal agencies have rule-making power. These agencies must publish proposed rules in the *Federal Register* and allow time for interested groups to "comment" on them. "Major rules," those estimated to cost Americans at least $100 or more per year in compliance, are sent to the Office of Management and Budget before being finalized.

**Multiplying Regulations**   Inasmuch as proposed new regulations must be published in the *Federal Register,* the size of this publication is often used as an indicator of overall federal regulatory activity. In 1970, the *Federal Register* included roughly 20,000 pages; by 1980 it had expanded to over 73,000 pages. Only during the presidency of Ronald Reagan, who promised to reduce federal regulatory activity, did the size of the *Federal Register* decline somewhat. But by 2000 it was again over 80,000 pages.

The accumulated regulations of federal government are published in the Code of Federal Regulations. The Code includes all regulations currently in effect. The Code has now expanded to over 150,000 pages, 50 titles, and 205 volumes.

**The Costs of Regulation**   Regulatory activity incurs costs for American businesses, employers, and consumers—costs which do not appear in the federal budget. (The official budgets of all federal regulatory agencies combined add up to "only" about $15 billion.) Indeed, it is precisely because these costs do not appear in the federal budget that politicians prefer a regulatory approach to many of the nation's problems. Regulation shifts costs from the government itself onto the private sector, costs that are largely invisible to voters and taxpayers. Even when agencies themselves are supposed to calculate the costs of their regulations, their calculations vary in quality and almost always underestimate the true costs.[16] One independent estimate of the total costs of federal regulation sets the figure at $700 *billion*, or about 7 percent of the nation's Gross Domestic Product.[17]

Regulations impose costs on Americans in a variety of ways. First of all, there are the direct costs of compliance. Direct costs include everything from adding pollution control devices and making businesses accessible to the disabled, to the overhead costs of paperwork, attorney and accounting fees, and staff time needed to negotiate the federal regulatory maze. Secondly, there are indirect economic costs—costs incurred by devoting resources to compliance that otherwise would be used to increase productivity. This lost economic output may amount to *$1 trillion* per year.[18] All of these costs, which typically are imposed on businesses, are ultimately passed on to American consumers in the form of higher prices.

# Congressional Constraints on the Bureaucracy

Bureaucracies are unelected hierarchical organizations, yet they must function within democratic government. To wed bureaucracy to democracy, ways must be found to ensure that bureaucracy is responsible to the people. Controlling the bureaucracy is a central concern of democratic government. The federal bureaucracy is responsible to all three branches of government—the president, the Congress, and the courts. Although the president is the nominal head of the executive agencies, Congress—through its power to create or eliminate and fund or fail to fund these agencies—exerts its full share of control. Most of the structure of the executive branch of government (see Figure 10.1) is determined by

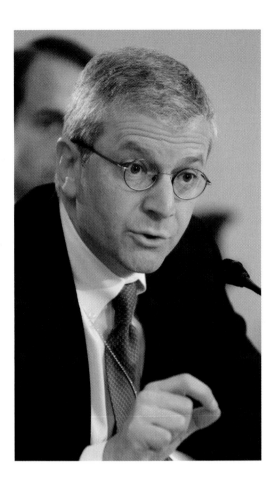

The Director of the Office of Management and Budget is one of the most influential bureaucrats in Washington. Yet he is seldom seen on national television. Here, President Bush's OMB Director Joshua B. Bolten (now White House Chief of Staff) testifies before a congressional committee.

laws of Congress. Congress has the constitutional power to create or abolish executive departments and independent agencies, or to transfer their functions, as it wishes. Congress can by law expand or contract the discretionary authority of bureaucrats. It can grant broad authority to agencies in vaguely written language, thereby adding to the power of bureaucracies, which can then determine themselves how to define and implement their own authority. In contrast, narrow and detailed laws place constraints on the bureaucracy.

In addition to specific constraints on particular agencies, Congress has placed a number of general constraints on the entire federal bureaucracy. Among the more important laws governing bureaucratic behavior are the following:

- *Administrative Procedures Act (1946):* Requires that agencies considering a new rule or policy give public notice in the *Federal Register,* solicit comments, and hold public hearings before adopting the new measures.

- *Freedom of Information Act (1966):* Requires agencies to allow citizens (and the media) to inspect all public records, with some exceptions for intelligence, current criminal investigations, and personnel actions (see *Up Close:* "How to Use the Freedom of Information Act").

- *Privacy Act (1974):* Requires agencies to keep confidential the personal records of individuals, notably their Social Security files and income tax records.

**Senate Confirmation of Appointments**   The U.S. Senate's power to confirm presidential appointments gives it some added influence over the bureaucracy.[19] It is true that once nominated and confirmed, cabinet secretaries and

## UP CLOSE

## How to Use the Freedom of Information Act

The Freedom of Information Act (FOIA) of 1966 requires agencies of the federal government to provide any member of the public records of the agencies. As amended by the Privacy Act of 1974, individuals can obtain their personal records held by government agencies and are given the right to correct information that is inaccurate. The FOIA does not apply to Congress, the federal courts, state and local government agencies (unless a state has a similar law), military plans and weapons, law enforcement investigations, records of financial institutions, or records which would invade the privacy of others. An agency must respond within ten days to an FOIA request, but it may charge fees for the costs of searching for the documents and duplicating them.

A good request must "reasonably describe" the records that are being sought; it must be specific enough that an agency employee will be able to locate the records within a reasonable amount of time. A good FOIA request letter includes:

Attention: Freedom of Information/Privacy Request Name and Address of Agency

This is a request under the Freedom of Information Act, 5 U.S.C. Sec.552

I request a copy of the following documents be provided for me.

_____

_____

I am aware that if my request is denied I am entitled to know the grounds for this denial and make an administrative appeal.

I am willing to pay fees for this request up to a maximum of $___. If you estimate that fees will succeed this limit, please inform me first.

Thank you for your prompt attention.

Signature

Address

---

regulatory commission members can defy the Congress; only the president can remove them from office. Senators usually try to impress their own views on presidential appointees seeking confirmation, however. Senate committees holding confirmation hearings often subject appointees to lengthy lectures on how the members believe their departments or agencies should be run. In extreme cases, when presidential appointees do not sufficiently reflect the views of Senate leaders, their confirmation can be held up indefinitely or, in very rare cases, defeated in a floor vote on confirmation.

**Congressional Oversight**    Congressional oversight of the federal bureaucracy is a continuing activity.[20] Congress justifies its oversight activities on the ground that its lawmaking powers require it to determine whether the purposes of the laws it passed are being carried out. Congress has a legitimate interest in communicating legislative *intent* to bureaucrats charged with the responsibility for implementing laws of Congress. But often oversight activities are undertaken to influence bureaucratic decision making. Members of Congress may seek to secure favorable treatment for friends and constituents, try to lay the political groundwork for increases or decreases in agency appropriations, or simply strive to enhance their own power or the power of their committees or subcommittees over the bureaucracy.

Oversight is lodged primarily in congressional committees and subcommittees (see "In Committee" in Chapter 8) whose jurisdictions generally parallel those of executive departments and agencies. However, all too frequently, agencies are

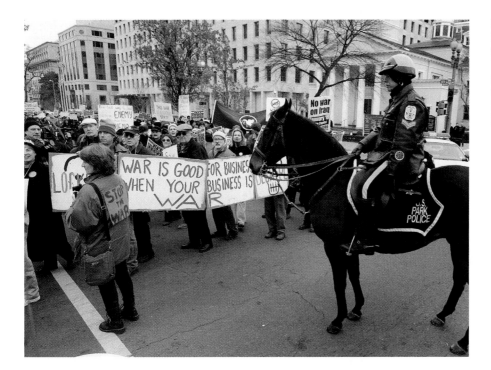

Protests are frequent in Washington, especially near the White House in Lafayette Park. Topics of protests vary widely. The war in Iraq has spawned more protests in recent years than any other issue.

required to respond to multiple committee inquiries in both the House and the Senate.

**Congressional Appropriations**   The congressional power to grant or to withhold the budget requests of bureaucracies and the president is perhaps Congress's most potent weapon in controlling the bureaucracy. Spending authorizations for executive agencies are determined by standing committees with jurisdiction in various policy areas, such as armed services, judiciary, education, and labor (see Table 8.4 in Chapter 8), and appropriations are determined by the House and Senate Appropriations Committees and, more specifically, their subcommittees with particular jurisdictions. These committees and subcommittees exercise great power over executive agencies. The Defense Department, for example, must seek *authorizations* for new weapons systems from the House and Senate Armed Services Committees and *appropriations* to actually purchase these weapons from the House and Senate Appropriations Committees, especially their Defense Appropriations subcommittees.

**Congressional Investigation**   Congressional investigations offer yet another tool for congressional oversight of the bureaucracy. Historically, congressional investigations have focused on scandal and wrongdoing in the executive branch (see "Oversight of the Bureaucracy" in Chapter 8). Occasionally, investigations even produce corrective legislation, although they more frequently produce changes in agency personnel, procedures, or policies. Investigations are more likely to follow media reports of waste, fraud, or scandal than to uncover previously unknown problems. In other words, investigations perform a political function for Congress—assuring voters that the Congress is taking action against bureaucratic abuses. Studies of routine bureaucratic performance are likely to be undertaken by the Government Accountability Office (GAO), an arm of Congress and frequent critic of executive agencies. GAO may undertake studies of the operations of executive agencies on its own initiative but more often responds to requests for studies by specific members of Congress.

**casework** Services performed by legislators and their staffs on behalf of individual constituents.

**Casework**  Perhaps the most frequent congressional oversight activities are calls, letters, and visits to the agencies by individual members of Congress seeking to influence particular actions on behalf of themselves or their constituents. A great deal of congressional **casework** involves intervening with executive agencies on behalf of constituents[21] (see Chapter 8). Executive departments and agencies generally try to deal with congressional requests and inquiries as favorably and rapidly as the law allows. Pressure from a congressional office will lead bureaucrats to speed up an application, correct an error, send information, review a case, or reinterpret a regulation to favor a client with congressional contacts. But bureaucrats become very uncomfortable when asked to violate established regulations on behalf of a favored person or firm. The line between serving constituents and unethical or illegal attempts to influence government agencies is sometimes very difficult to discern.

## Interest Groups and Bureaucratic Decision Making

Interest groups understand that great power is lodged in the bureaucracy. Indeed, interest groups exercise an even closer oversight of bureaucracy than do the president, Congress, and courts, largely because their interests are directly affected by day-to-day bureaucratic decisions. Interest groups focus their attention on the particular departments and agencies that serve or regulate their own members or that function in their chosen policy field. For example, the American Farm Bureau Federation monitors the actions of the Department of Agriculture; environmental lobbies—such as the National Wildlife Federation, the Sierra Club, and the Environmental Defense Fund—watch over the Environmental Protection Agency as well as the National Park Service; the American Legion, Veterans of Foreign Wars, and Vietnam Veterans "oversee" the Department of Veterans Affairs. Thus, specific groups come to have a proprietary interest in "their" specific departments and agencies. Departments and agencies understand that their "client" groups have a continuing interest in their activities.

Many bureaucracies owe their very existence to strong interest groups that successfully lobbied Congress to create them. The Environmental Protection Agency owes its existence to the environmental groups, just as the Equal Employment Opportunity Commission owes its existence to civil rights groups. Thus, many bureaucracies nourish interest groups' support to aid in expanding their authority and increasing their budgets (see "Iron Triangles and Policy Networks" in Chapter 7).

Interest groups can lobby bureaucracies directly by responding to notices of proposed regulations, testifying at public hearings, and providing information and commentary. Or interest groups can lobby Congress either in support of bureaucratic activity or to reverse a bureaucratic decision. Interest groups may also seek to "build fires" under bureaucrats by holding press conferences, undertaking advertising campaigns, and soliciting media support for agency actions. Or interest groups may even seek to influence bureaucracies through appeals to the federal courts.

## Judicial Constraints on the Bureaucracy

Judicial oversight is another source of restraint on the bureaucracy. Bureaucratic decisions are subject to review by the federal courts. Federal courts can even issue *injunctions* (orders) to an executive agency *before* it issues or enforces a regulation or undertakes a particular action. Thus, the judiciary poses a check on bureaucratic power.

# A CONSTITUTIONAL NOTE

## Congress and the Budget

The Constitution places "the power of the purse" firmly in the hands of Congress: "No money shall be drawn from the Treasury, but in Consequence of Appropriations made by Law" (Article I, Section 9). The Congress has multiple means of controlling the bureaucracy. It can create, eliminate, or reorganize agencies, and it can alter their functions and rules of operation as it sees fit. And the Senate can confirm or withhold confirmation of presidential appointments. In the exercise of these powers Congress can hold hearings, conduct investigations, and interrogate executive officials. But the power over appropriations for departments and agencies remains the most important instrument of congressional control over the bureaucracy. The president, of course, is head of the executive branch and the Constitution charges him to "take care that the laws be faithfully executed" (Article II, Section 3). Prior to 1921, executive departments and agencies submitted their budgets directly to the Congress with very little presidential input or control. But the Budget and Accounting Act of that year established a Bureau of the Budget which later was placed in the White House directly under the president. The act required all executive agencies to submit their budgets to the Bureau of the Budget, now called the Office of Management and Budget (OMB), and to the president. The president and OMB draw up the *Budget of the United States Government* each year for submission to Congress. The Budget Committees of the House and Senate by resolution set overall totals for budget outlays in major categories. These committees are under no obligation to follow the president's budget recommendations. Later, the Appropriations Committees and subcommittees of each house write up specific appropriations bills. If it wishes, Congress can ignore items in the president's budget and appropriate whatever funds to whatever agencies it chooses. The Appropriations Committees of the House and Senate jealously guard Congress's "power of the purse."

**Judicial Standards for Bureaucratic Behavior** Historically, the courts have stepped in when agency actions have violated laws passed by Congress, when agencies have exceeded the authority granted them under the laws, when the agency actions have been adjudged "arbitrary and unreasonable," and when agencies have failed in their legal duties under the law. The courts have also restrained the bureaucracy on procedural grounds—ensuring proper notice, fair hearings, rights of appeal, and so on. In short, appeals to the courts must cite failures of agencies to abide by substantive or procedural laws.

Judicial oversight tends to focus on (1) whether or not agencies are acting beyond the authority granted them by Congress; and (2) whether or not they are abiding by rules of procedural fairness. It is important to realize that the courts do not usually involve themselves in the *policy* decisions of bureaucracies. If policy decisions are made in accordance with the legal authority granted agencies by Congress, and if they are made with procedural fairness, the courts generally do not intervene.

**Bureaucrats' Success in Court** Bureaucracies have been very successful in defending their actions in federal courts.[22] Individual citizens and interest groups seeking to restrain or reverse the actions or decisions of executive agencies have been largely *unsuccessful.* What accounts for this success? Bureaucracies have established elaborate administrative processes to protect their decisions from challenge on procedural grounds. Regulatory agencies have armies of attorneys, paid for out of tax monies, who specialize in these narrow fields of law. It is very expensive for individual citizens to challenge agency actions. Corporations and interest groups must weigh the costs of litigation against the costs of compliance before undertaking a legal challenge of the bureaucracy. Excessive delays in court proceedings, sometimes extending to several years, add to the time and expense of challenging bureaucratic decisions.

# Summary Notes

- The Washington bureaucracy—the departments, agencies, and bureaus of the executive branch of the federal government—is a major base of power in American government. Political conflict does not end when a law is passed by Congress and signed by the president. The arena merely shifts to the bureaucracy.

- Bureaucratic power has grown with increases in the size of government, advances in technology, and the greater complexity of modern society. Congress and the president do not have the time, resources, or expertise to decide the details of policy across the wide range of social and economic activity in the nation. Bureaucracies must draw up the detailed rules and regulations that actually govern the nation. Often laws are passed for their symbolic value; bureaucrats must give practical meaning to these laws. And the bureaucracy itself is now sufficiently powerful to get laws passed adding to its authority, size, and budget.

- Policy implementation is the development of procedures and activities and the allocation of money, personnel, and other resources to carry out the tasks mandated by law. Implementation includes regulation—the making of detailed rules based on the law—as well as adjudication—the application of laws and regulations to specific cases. Bureaucratic power increases with increases in administrative discretion.

- Bureaucracies usually seek to expand their own powers, functions, and budgets. Most bureaucrats believe strongly in the value of their own programs and the importance of their tasks. And bureaucrats, like everyone else, seek added power, pay, and prestige. Bureaucratic expansion contributes to the growth of government.

- The federal bureaucracy consists of 2.8 million civilian employees in fourteen cabinet departments and more than sixty independent agencies, as well as a large Executive Office of the President. Federal employment is not growing, but federal spending, especially for Social Security, Medicare, and Medicaid, is growing rapidly.

- Today federal spending amounts to about 20 percent of GDP, and federal, state, and local government spending combined amounts to about 30 percent of GDP.

- Historically, political conflict over government employment centered on the question of partisanship versus competence. Over time, the "merit system" replaced the "spoils system" in federal employment, but the civil service system raised problems of responsiveness and productivity in the bureaucracy. Civil service reform efforts have not really resolved these problems.

- The president's control of the bureaucracy rests principally on the powers to appoint and remove policy-making officials, to recommend increases and decreases in agency budgets, and to recommend changes in agency structure and function.

- But the bureaucracy has developed various means to insulate itself from presidential influence. Bureaucrats have many ways to delay and obstruct policy decisions with which they disagree. Whistle-blowers may inform Congress or the media of waste, mismanagement, or fraud. A network of friends and professional associates among bureaucrats, congressional staffs, and client groups helps create a "culture" within each agency and department. The bureaucratic culture is highly resistant to change.

- Women and minorities are represented in overall federal employment in proportion to their percentages of the U.S. population. However, women and minorities are not proportionately represented in the higher levels of the bureaucracy.

- Budget battles over who gets what begin in the bureaucracy as departments and agencies send their budget requests forward to the president's Office of Management and Budget. OMB usually reduces agency requests in line with the president's priorities. The president submits spending recommendations to Congress early each year in *The Budget of the United States Government*. Congress is supposed to pass its appropriations acts prior to the beginning of the fiscal year, October 1, but frequently falls behind schedule.

- Budgeting is incremental, in that last year's agency expenditures are usually accepted as a base and attention is focused on proposed increases. Incrementalism saves time and effort and reduces political conflict by not requiring agencies to justify every dollar spent, only proposed increases each year. Nonprogrammatic budgeting also helps reduce conflict over the value of particular programs. The result, however, is that many established programs continue long after the need for them has disappeared.

- Bureaucracies regulate virtually every aspect of our lives. The costs of regulation are borne primarily by business and consumers; they do not appear in the federal budget. In part for this reason, a regulatory approach to national problems appeals to elected officials who seek to obscure the costs of government activity. It is difficult to calculate the true costs and benefits of much regulatory activity. After a brief period of deregulation in the 1980s, regulation has regained popular favor.

- Congress can exercise control over the bureaucracy in a variety of ways: by creating, abolishing, or reorganizing departments and agencies; by altering their authority and functions; by requiring bureaucrats to testify before congressional committees; by undertaking investigations and studies through the Government Accountability Office; by intervening directly on behalf of constituents; by instructing presidential nominees in Senate confirmation hearings and occasionally delaying or defeating nominations; and especially by withholding or threatening to withhold agency appropriations or by writing very specific provisions into appropriations acts.

■ Interest groups also influence bureaucratic decision making directly by testifying at public hearings and providing information and commentary, and indirectly by contacting the media, lobbying Congress, and initiating lawsuits.

■ Judicial control of the bureaucracy is usually limited to determining whether agencies have exceeded the authority granted them by law or have abided by the rules of procedural fairness. Federal bureaucracies have a strong record of success in defending themselves in court.

## Key Terms

| | | | |
|---|---|---|---|
| bureaucracy 344 | budget maximization 348 | authorization 368 | zero-based |
| chain of command 344 | discretionary funds 348 | appropriations act 368 | budgeting 371 |
| division of labor 344 | spoils system 357 | obligational | program budgeting 372 |
| impersonality 344 | merit system 357 | authority 368 | capture theory of |
| implementation 344 | whistle-blower 361 | outlays 368 | regulation 372 |
| regulation 347 | fiscal year 367 | continuing resolution 369 | deregulation 374 |
| adjudication 347 | budget resolution 368 | incremental budgeting 370 | casework 380 |

## Suggested Readings

Henry, Nicholas. *Public Administration and Public Affairs.* 9th ed. Upper Saddle River, N.J.: Prentice Hall, 2004. Authoritative introductory textbook on public organizations (bureaucracies), public management, and policy implementation.

Howard, Philip K. *The Death of Common Sense: How Law Is Suffocating America.* New York: Random House, 1995. Outrageous stories of bureaucratic senselessness coupled with a plea to allow bureaucrats flexibility in achieving the purposes of laws and holding them accountable for outcomes.

Kettl, Donald F., and James W. Fesler. *The Politics of the Administrative Process.* 3rd ed. Washington D.C.: CQ Press, 2005. Introduction to bureaucracy and public administration, including a case appendix with illustrations complementing each chapter.

Kerwin, Cornelius M. *Rulemaking: How Government Agencies Write Law and Make Policy.* 3rd ed. Washington D.C.: CQ Press, 2003. Argues that rulemaking actually defines the laws of Congress and describes the political activity surrounding rulemaking.

Maxwell, Bruce. *CQ's Insider's Guide to Finding a Job in Washington.* Washington, D.C.: CQ Press, 2000. How to locate job vacancies, make contacts, "market" oneself, and build a career in the Washington bureaucracy.

Neiman, Max. *Defending Government: Why Big Government Works.* Upper Saddle River, N. J.: Prentice Hall, 2000. A spirited defense of big government as a product of people's desire to improve their lives.

Osborne, David, and Ted Gaebler. *Reinventing Government.* New York: Addison-Wesley, 1992. The respected manual of the "reinventing government" movement, with recommendations to overcome the routine tendencies of bureaucracies and inject "the entrepreneurial spirit" into them.

Schick, Allen. *The Federal Budget: Politics, Policy, Process.* Rev. ed. Washington, D.C.: Brookings Institution, 2000. A comprehensive explanation of the federal budgetary process.

Smith, Robert W., and Thomas D. Lynch. *Public Budgeting in America.* 5th ed. Upper Saddle River N.J.: Prentice Hall, 2004. Standard text describing public budget processes, behaviors, and administration.

Wilson, James Q. *Bureaucracy: What Government Agencies Do and Why They Do It.* New York: Basic Books, 1989. In the author's words, "an effort to depict the essential features of bureaucratic life in the government agencies of the United States." Examining what really motivates middle-level public servants, Wilson argues that congressional attempts to "micromanage" government activities hamper the ability of bureaucrats to do their jobs.

## Make It Real

### BUREAUCRACY

In this unit, the student plays the role of a bureaucrat.

# 11 COURTS
## Judicial Politics

## Chapter Outline

- Judicial Power
- Activism versus Self-Restraint
- Structure and Jurisdiction of Federal Courts
- The Special Rules of Judicial Decision Making
- The Politics of Selecting Judges
- Who Is Selected?
- Supreme Court Decision Making
- Politics and the Supreme Court
- Checking Court Power

## Think About Politics

**1** Have the federal courts grown too powerful?
Yes ☐ No ☐

**2** Is it really democratic to allow federal court judges, who are appointed, not elected, and who serve for life, to overturn laws of an elected Congress and president?
Yes ☐ No ☐

**3** Should the Constitution be interpreted in terms of the original intentions of the Founders rather than the morality of society today?
Yes ☐ No ☐

**4** Are the costs of lawsuits in America becoming too burdensome on the economy?
Yes ☐ No ☐

**5** Should presidents appoint only judges who agree with their judicial philosophy?
Yes ☐ No ☐

**6** Should the Senate confirm Supreme Court appointees who oppose abortion?
Yes ☐ No ☐

**7** Should the Supreme Court overturn the law of Congress that prohibits federal funding of abortions for poor women?
Yes ☐ No ☐

**8** Is there a need to appoint special prosecutors to investigate presidents and other high officials?
Yes ☐ No ☐

*Do the Supreme Court and the federal judiciary in fact have the real power to shape public policies in the United States?*

## Judicial Power

"There is hardly a political question in the United States which does not sooner or later turn into a judicial one."[1] This observation by French diplomat and traveler Alexis de Tocqueville, although made in 1835, is even more accurate today. It is the Supreme Court and the federal judiciary, rather than the president or Congress, that has taken the lead in deciding many of the most heated issues of American politics. It has undertaken to:

- Eliminate racial segregation and decide about affirmative action.

- Ensure separation of church and state and decide about prayer in public schools.

- Determine the personal liberties of women and decide about abortion.

- Define the limits of free speech and free press and decide about obscenity, censorship, and pornography.

- Ensure equality of representation and require legislative districts to be equal in population.

- Define the rights of criminal defendants, prevent unlawful searches, limit the questioning of suspects, and prevent physical or mental intimidation of suspects.

- Protect private homosexual acts between consenting adults from criminal prosecution.

- Decide the life-or-death issue of capital punishment.

Courts are "political" institutions. Like Congress, the president, and the bureaucracy, courts decide who gets what in American society. Judges do not merely "apply" the law to specific cases. Years ago, former Supreme Court Justice Felix Frankfurter explained why this mechanistic theory of judicial objectivity fails to describe court decision making.

The meaning of "due process" and the content of terms like "liberty" are not revealed by the Constitution. It is the Justices who make the meaning. They read into the neutral language of the Constitution their own economic and social views. . . . Let us face the fact that five Justices of the Supreme Court are the molders of policy rather than the impersonal vehicles of revealed truth.[2]

—Think Again—

Have the federal courts grown too powerful?

**Constitutional Power of the Courts**    The Constitution grants "the judicial Power of the United States" to the Supreme Court and other "inferior Courts" that Congress may establish. The Constitution guarantees that the Supreme Court and federal judiciary will be politically independent: judges are appointed, not elected, and hold their appointments for life (barring commission of any impeachable offenses). It also guarantees that their salaries will not be reduced during their time in office. The Constitution goes on to list the kinds of cases and controversies that the federal courts may decide. Federal judicial power extends to any case arising under the Constitution and federal laws and treaties, to cases in which officials of the federal government or of foreign governments are a party, and to cases between states or between citizens of different states.

**Interpreting the Constitution: Judicial Review**    The Constitution is the "supreme Law of the Land" (Article VI). Judicial power is the power to decide cases and controversies and, in doing so, to decide what the Constitution and laws of Congress really mean. This authority—together with the guaranteed independence of judges—places great power in the Supreme Court and the federal judiciary. Indeed, because the Constitution takes precedence over laws of Congress as well as state constitutions and laws, it is the Supreme Court that ultimately decides whether Congress, the president, the states, and their local governments have acted constitutionally.

**judicial review** Power of the courts, especially the Supreme Court, to declare laws of Congress, laws of the states, and actions of the president unconstitutional and invalid.

The power of **judicial review** is the power to invalidate laws of Congress or of the states that conflict with the U.S. Constitution. Judicial review is not specifically mentioned in the Constitution but has long been inferred from it. Even before the states had approved the Constitution, Alexander Hamilton wrote in 1787 that "limited government . . . can be preserved in practice no other way than through the medium of courts of justice, whose duty it is to declare all acts contrary to the manifest tenor of the Constitution void."[3] But it was the historic decision of *Marbury v. Madison* (1803)[4] that officially established judicial review as the most important judicial check on congressional power (see *People in Politics:* "John Marshall and Early Supreme Court Politics"). Writing for the majority, Chief Justice Marshall constructed a classic statement in judicial reasoning as he proceeded step by step to infer judicial review from the Constitution's Supremacy (Article VI) and Judicial Power (Article III, Section 1) clauses:

- The Constitution is the supreme law of the land, binding on all branches of government: legislative, executive, and judicial.

- The Constitution deliberately establishes a government with limited powers.

- Consequently, "an act of the legislature repugnant to the Constitution is void." If this were not true, the government would be unchecked and the Constitution would be an absurdity.

- Under the judicial power, "It is emphatically the province and duty of each of the judicial departments to say what the law is."

- "So if a law be in opposition to the Constitution . . . the court must determine which of these conflicting rules governs the case. This is the very essence of judicial duty."

## PEOPLE IN POLITICS

# John Marshall and Early Supreme Court Politics

John Marshall was a dedicated Federalist. A prominent Virginia lawyer, he was elected a delegate to Virginia's Constitution-ratifying convention, where he was instrumental in winning his state's approval of the document in 1788. Later Marshall served as secretary of state in the administration of John Adams, where he came into conflict with Adams's vice president, Thomas Jefferson.

In the election of 1800, Jefferson's Democratic-Republicans crushed Adams's Federalist Party. But Adams, taking advantage of the fact that his term of office would not expire until the following March,[a] sought to pack the federal judiciary with Federalists. The lame duck Federalist majority in the Senate confirmed the appointments, and John Marshall was sworn in as Chief Justice of the Supreme Court on February 4, 1801. Many of these "midnight appointments" came at the very last hours of Adams's term of office.

At that time, a specified task of the secretary of state was to deliver judicial commissions to new judges. When Marshall left his position as secretary of state to become Chief Justice, several of these commissions were still undelivered. Jefferson and the Democratic-Republicans were enraged over this last-minute Federalist chicanery, so when Jefferson assumed office in March, he ordered his new secretary of state, James Madison, not to deliver the remaining commissions. William Marbury, one of the disappointed Federalist appointees, brought a lawsuit to the Supreme Court, asking it to issue a writ of mandamus ("we command") to James Madison, ordering him to do his duty and deliver the valid commission.

The Judiciary Act of 1789, which established the federal court system, had included a provision granting original jurisdiction to the Supreme Court to issue writs of mandamus. The case, therefore, came directly to new Chief Justice John Marshall, who had failed to deliver the commission in the first place. (Today, we expect justices who are personally involved in a case to "recuse" themselves—that is, not to participate in that case, allowing the other justices to make the decision—but Marshall's actions were typical of his time.)

John Marshall realized that if he issued a direct order to Madison to deliver the commission, Madison would probably ignore it. The Court had no way to enforce such an order, and Madison had the support of President Jefferson. Issuing the writ would create a constitutional crisis in which the Supreme Court would most likely lose power. But if the Court failed to pronounce Madison's actions unlawful, it would lose legitimacy.

Marshall resolved his political dilemma with a brilliant judicial ploy. Writing for the majority in *Marbury v. Madison,* he announced that Madison was wrong to withhold the commission but that the Supreme Court could not issue a writ of mandamus because Section 13 of the Judiciary Act of 1789, which gave the Court *original* jurisdiction in the case, was unconstitutional. Giving the Supreme Court *original* jurisdiction conflicted with Article III, Section 2, of the Constitution, which gives the Supreme Court original jurisdiction only in cases affecting "Ambassadors, other public Ministers and Consuls, and those in which a State shall be a Party." "In all other Cases," the Constitution states that the Court shall have appellate jurisdiction. Thus Section 13 of the Judiciary Act was unconstitutional.

By declaring part of an act of Congress unconstitutional, Marshall accomplished multiple political objectives. He avoided a showdown with the executive branch that would undoubtedly have weakened the Court. He left Jefferson and Madison with no Court order to disobey. At the same time, Marshall forced Jefferson and the Democratic-Republicans to acknowledge the Supreme Court's power of judicial review—the power to declare an act of Congress unconstitutional. (To do otherwise would have meant acknowledging Marbury's claim.) Thus Marshall sacrificed Marbury's commission to a greater political goal, enhancing the Supreme Court's power.

[a]Not until the adoption of the Twentieth Amendment in 1933 was the president's inauguration moved up to January.

- "If, then, the courts are to regard the Constitution, and the Constitution is superior to any ordinary act of the legislature, the Constitution, and not such ordinary act, must govern the case to which they both apply."

- Hence, if a law is repugnant to the Constitution, the judges are duty bound to declare that law void in order to uphold the supremacy of the Constitution.

**Judicial Review of State Laws**   The power of the federal courts to invalidate *state* laws and constitutions that conflict with federal laws or the federal Constitution is easily defended. Article VI states that the Constitution and federal laws and treaties are the supreme law of the land, "any Thing in the Constitution or Laws of any State to the Contrary notwithstanding." Indeed, the Constitution specifically obligates state judges to be "bound" by the Constitution and federal laws and to give these documents precedence over state constitutions and laws in rendering decisions. Federal court power over state decisions is probably essential to maintaining national unity: fifty different state interpretations of the meaning of the Constitution or of the laws and treaties of Congress would create unimaginable confusion. Thus the power of federal judicial review over state constitutions, laws, and court decisions is seldom questioned.

The Supreme Court has used its power of judicial review more frequently to invalidate state laws than laws of Congress. Some of these decisions had impact far beyond the individual states on trial. For example, the historic 1954 decision in *Brown v. Board of Education of Topeka*, declaring segregation of the races in public schools to be unconstitutional, struck down the laws of twenty-one states[5] (see Chapter 10). The 1973 *Roe v. Wade* decision, establishing the constitutional right to abortion, struck down antiabortion laws in more than forty states.[6] In 2003 the Court again struck down the laws of more than forty states by holding that private homosexual acts by consenting adults were protected by the constitution.[7]

**Judicial Review of Laws of Congress**   Judicial review is potentially the most powerful weapon in the hands of the Supreme Court. It enables the Court to assert its power over the Congress, the president, and the states and to substitute its own judgment for that of other branches of the federal government and the states. However, the Supreme Court has been fairly restrained in its use of judicial review to void acts of Congress. Prior to the Civil War, the Supreme Court invalidated very few laws of any kind. Since that time, however, the general trend has been for the U.S. Supreme Court to strike down more *state* laws as unconstitutional. In contrast, the Court has been relatively restrained in its rejection of *federal* laws; over two centuries the Court has struck down fewer than 150 of the more than 60,000 laws passed by Congress.

Nevertheless, some of the laws overturned by the Supreme Court have been very important. In *Buckley v. Valeo* (1976)[8] the Court struck down provisions of the Federal Election Campaign Act that had limited the amount individuals could spend to finance their own campaigns or express their own independent political views. In *United States v. Morrison* (2000), the Supreme Court struck down Congress's Violence Against Women Act[9] as an unconstitutional expansion of the interstate commerce power and an invasion of powers reserved to the states (see *What Do You Think?* "Should Violence Against Women Be a Federal Crime?" in Chapter 4). Overall, however, the Supreme Court's use of judicial review against the Congress has been restrained.

**Judicial Review of Presidential Actions**   The Supreme Court has only rarely challenged presidential power. The Court has overturned presidential

## UP CLOSE

# William Jefferson Clinton v. Paula Corbin Jones

The president is not "above the law"; that is, his conduct is not immune from judicial scrutiny. The president's official conduct must be lawful; federal courts may reverse presidential actions found to be unconstitutional or violative of laws of Congress. And presidents are not immune from criminal prosecution; they cannot ignore demands to provide information in criminal cases.[a] However, the Supreme Court has held that the president has "absolute immunity" from civil suits "arising out of the execution of official duties."[b] In other words, the president cannot be sued for damages caused by actions or decisions that are within his constitutional or legal authority.

But can the president be sued for *private* conduct beyond the scope of his official duties? In 1994 Paula Corbin Jones sued William Jefferson Clinton in federal district court in Arkansas, alleging that he made "abhorrent" sexual advances toward her in Little Rock in 1991 while he was governor and she was a state employee.

The president's lead attorney, Robert Bennett (brother of conservative commentator and former Reagan cabinet official William Bennett), stated that Clinton "has no recollection of ever meeting this woman" and "did not engage in any inappropriate or sexual conduct with this woman." But the president's defense team also argued that the president should be immune from civil actions, especially those arising from events alleged to occur *before* he assumed office. They argued that the president's constitutional responsibilities are so important and demanding that he must devote his undivided time and attention to them. He cannot be distracted by civil suits; otherwise a large volume of politically motivated frivolous litigation might undermine his ability to function effectively in office. At the very least, the president's attorney argued, the president should be given "temporary immunity" by postponing the case until after he leaves office.

However, in 1997 the U.S. Supreme Court rejected the notion of presidential immunity (as well as temporary immunity) from civil claims arising from actions outside of the president's official duties. Although advising lower courts to give "utmost deference to Presidential responsibilities" in handling the case, the Court held that "the doctrine of separation of powers does not require federal courts to stay all private actions against the president until he leaves office."[c]

Subsequently, after reviewing the case, federal district judge Susan Wright dismissed Jones's charges as insufficient to prove sexual assault or harassment.[d] Clinton later settled the case with a financial payment to Jones, but with no admission or apology. The settlement ended Jones's appeals and avoided possible reopening of the case.

[a]*United States v. Nixon* (1974).
[b]*Nixon v. Fitzgerald* (1982).

[c]*Clinton v. Jones*, May 27, 1997.
[d]*Jones v. Clinton*, April 1, 1998.

policies both on the grounds that they conflicted with laws of Congress and on the grounds that they conflicted with the Constitution. In *Ex parte Milligan* (1866)[10] for example, the Court held (somewhat belatedly) that President Abraham Lincoln could not suspend the writ of habeas corpus in rebellious states during the Civil War. In *Youngstown Sheet & Tube Co. v. Sawyer*, in 1952,[11] it declared President Harry Truman's seizure of the nation's steel mills during the Korean War to be illegal. In 1974 it ordered President Richard Nixon to turn over taped White House conversations to the special Watergate prosecutor, leading to Nixon's forced resignation.[12] And in 1997 the Court held that President Bill Clinton was obliged to respond to a civil suit even while serving in the White House.[13] (See *Up Close:* "William Jefferson Clinton versus Paula Corbin Jones.")

**Interpreting Federal Laws**    The power of the Supreme Court and the federal judiciary does not rest on judicial review alone. The courts also make policy in their interpretation of **statutory laws**—the laws of Congress. Frequently, Congress decides that an issue is too contentious to resolve. Members of Congress cannot themselves agree on specific language, so they write, sometimes deliberately,

**statutory laws** Laws made by act of Congress or the state legislatures, as opposed to constitutional law.

vague, symbolic language into the law—words and phrases like "fairness," "equitableness," "good faith," "good cause," and "reasonableness"—effectively shifting policy making to the courts by giving courts the power to read meaning into these terms.

## Activism versus Self-Restraint

**judicial self-restraint** Self-imposed limitation on judicial power by judges deferring to the policy judgments of elected branches of government.

Supreme Court Justice Felix Frankfurter once wrote: "The only check upon our own exercise of power is our own sense of self-restraint. For the removal of unwise laws from the statute books, appeal lies not to the courts but to the ballot and to the processes of democratic government."[14]

**Judicial Self-Restraint**    The idea behind **judicial self-restraint** is that judges should not read their own philosophies into the Constitution and should avoid direct confrontations with Congress, the president, and the states whenever possible. The argument for judicial self-restraint is that federal judges are not elected by the people and therefore should not substitute their own views for the views of elected representatives. The courts should defer to the judgments of the other branches of government unless there is a clear violation of constitutional principle. The benefit of the doubt should be given to actions taken by elected officials. Courts should only impose remedies that are narrowly tailored to correct specific legal wrongs. As Justice Sandra Day O'Connor argued in her Senate confirmation hearings, "The courts should interpret the laws, not make them. . . . I do not believe it is a function of the Court to step in because times have changed or social mores have changed."[15]

**Wisdom versus Constitutionality**    A law may be unwise, unjust, or even stupid and yet still be constitutional. One should not equate the wisdom of a law with its constitutionality, and the Court should decide only the constitutionality and not the wisdom of a law. Justice Oliver Wendell Holmes once lectured a younger colleague, sixty-one-year-old Justice Harlan Stone, on this point:

> Young man, about 75 years ago I learned that I was not God. And so, when the people . . . want to do something I can't find anything in the Constitution expressly forbidding them to do, I say, whether I like it or not, "Goddamn it, let 'em do it."[16]

However, the actual role of the Supreme Court in the nation's power struggles suggests that the Court indeed often equates wisdom with constitutionality. People frequently cite broad phrases in the Fifth and Fourteenth Amendments establishing constitutional standards of "due process of law" and "equal protection of the laws" when attacking laws they believe are unfair or unjust. Most Americans have come to believe that unwise laws must be unconstitutional. If so, then the courts must be the final arbiters of fairness and justice.

**original intent** Judicial philosophy under which judges attempt to apply the values of the Founders to current issues.

**Original Intent**    Should the Constitution be interpreted in terms of the intentions of the Founders or according to the morality of society today? Most jurists agree the Constitution is a living document, that it must be interpreted by each generation in the light of current conditions, and to do otherwise would soon render the document obsolete. But in interpreting the document, whose values should prevail—the values of the judges or the values of the Founders? The doctrine of **original intent** takes the values of the Founders as expressed in the text of the Constitution and attempts to apply these values to current conditions. Defenders of original intent argue that the words in the document must be given their historical meaning and that meaning must restrain the courts as well as the legislative and executive branches of government. That is, the Supreme Court should not set aside laws made by elected representatives unless they conflict with the original intent of the Founders. Judges who set aside laws that do not accord with their personal views of today's moral standards are simply substituting their own morality for that of elected bodies. Such decisions lack democratic legitimacy because there is no reason why judges' moral views should prevail over those of elected representatives.

**Judicial Activism**   However, the doctrine of original intent carries little weight with proponents of judicial activism. The idea behind **judicial activism** is that the Constitution is a living document whose strength lies in its flexibility, and judges should shape constitutional meaning to fit the needs of contemporary society. The argument for judicial activism is that viewing the Constitution as a broad and flexible document saves the nation from having to pass dozens of new constitutional amendments to accommodate changes in society. Instead, the courts need to give contemporary interpretations to constitutional phrases, particularly general phrases such as "due process of law" (Fifth Amendment), "equal protection of the laws" (Fourteenth Amendment), "establishment of religion" (First Amendment), and "cruel and unusual punishment" (Eighth Amendment). Courts have the responsibility to review the actions of other branches of government vigorously, to strike down unconstitutional acts, and to impose far-reaching remedies for legal wrongs whenever necessary.[17]

**judicial activism** Making of new law through judicial interpretations of the Constitution.

**Stare Decisis**   Conflicts between judicial activism and judicial self-restraint are underscored by questions of whether to let past decisions stand or to find constitutional support for overturning them. The principle of **stare decisis**, which means the issue has already been decided in earlier cases, is a fundamental notion in law. Reliance on **precedent** gives stability to the law; if every decision were new law, then no one would know what the law is from day to day. Yet the Supreme Court has discarded precedent in many of its most important decisions: *Brown v. Board of Education* (1954), which struck down laws segregating the races; *Baker v. Carr* (1962), which guaranteed equal representation in legislatures; *Roe v. Wade* (1973), which made abortion a constitutional right; and many other classic cases. Former Justice William O. Douglas, a defender of judicial activism, justified disregard of precedent as follows:

**stare decisis** Judicial precept that the issue has already been decided in earlier cases and the earlier decision need only be applied in the specific case before the bench; the rule in most cases, it comes from the Latin for "the decision stands."

**precedent** Legal principle that previous decisions should determine the outcome of current cases; the basis for stability in law.

> The decisions of yesterday or of the last century are only the starting points. . . . A judge looking at a constitutional decision may have compulsions to revere the past history and accept what was once written. But he remembers above all else that it is the Constitution which he swore to support and defend, not the gloss which his predecessors may have put on it. So he comes to formulate his own laws, rejecting some earlier ones as false and embracing others. He cannot do otherwise unless he lets men long dead and unaware of the problems of the age in which he lives do his thinking for him.[18]

**Rules of Restraint**   Even an activist Supreme Court adheres to some general rules of judicial self-restraint, however, including the following:

- The Court will pass on the constitutionality of legislation only in an actual case; it will not advise the president or Congress on constitutional questions.

- The Court will not anticipate a question on constitutional law; it does not decide hypothetical cases.

- The Court will not formulate a rule of constitutional law broader than that required by the precise facts to which it must be applied.

- The Court will not decide on a constitutional question if some other ground exists on which it may dispose of the case.

- The Court will not decide on the validity of a law if the complainants fail to show that they have been injured by the law.

- When doubt exists about the constitutionality of a law, the Court will try to interpret the law so as to give it a constitutional meaning and avoid the necessity of declaring it unconstitutional.

- Complainants must have exhausted all remedies available in lower federal courts or state courts before the Supreme Court will accept review.

- The Court will invalidate a law only when a constitutional issue is crucial to the case and is substantial, not trivial.

- Occasionally the Court defers to Congress and the president, classifies an issue as a political question, and refuses to decide it. The Court has generally stayed out of foreign and military policy areas.

- If the Court holds a law unconstitutional, it will confine its decision to the particular section of the law that is unconstitutional; the rest of the statute stays intact.

## Structure and Jurisdiction of Federal Courts

The federal court system consists of three levels of courts—the Supreme Court, the Courts of Appeals, and the district courts—together with various special courts (see Figure 11.1). Only the Supreme Court is established by the Constitution, although the number of justices is determined by Congress. Article III authorizes Congress to establish such "inferior Courts" as it deems appropriate. Congress has designed a hierarchical system with a U.S. Court of Appeals divided into twelve regional circuit courts, a federal circuit, and ninety-four district courts in the fifty states and one each in Puerto Rico and the District of Columbia. Table 11.1 describes their **jurisdiction** and distinguishes between **original jurisdiction**—where cases are begun, argued, and initially decided—and **appellate jurisdiction**—where cases begun in lower courts are argued and decided on **appeal**.

The Supreme Court is the "court of last resort" in the United States, but it hears only a very small number of cases each year. In a handful of cases, the Supreme Court has original jurisdiction; these concern primarily disputes between states (or states and residents of other states), disputes between a state and the federal government, and disputes involving foreign dignitaries. However, most Supreme Court cases are appellate decisions involving cases from state supreme courts or cases tried first in a U.S. district court.

**District Courts**   **District courts** are the original jurisdiction trial courts of the federal system. Each state has at least one district court, and larger states have more (New York, for example, has four). There are about eight hundred federal district judges, each appointed for life by the president and confirmed by the Senate. The president also appoints a U.S. marshal for each district to carry out orders of the court and maintain order in the courtroom. District courts hear criminal cases prosecuted by the Department of Justice as well as civil cases. As

**jurisdiction**  Power of a court to hear a case in question.

**original jurisdiction**  Refers to a particular court's power to serve as the place where a given case is initially argued and decided.

**appellate jurisdiction** Particular court's power to review a decision or action of a lower court.

**appeal**  In general, requests that a higher court review cases decided at a lower level. In the Supreme Court, certain cases are designated as appeals under federal law; formally, these must be heard by the Court.

**U.S. Courts**
The goal of this site is "to function as a clearinghouse for information from and about the Judicial Branch of the U.S. government." The site covers the U.S. Supreme Court, U.S. Courts of Appeals, U.S. District Courts, and U.S. Bankruptcy Courts.
*www.uscourts.gov*

**district courts**  Original jurisdiction trial courts of the federal system.

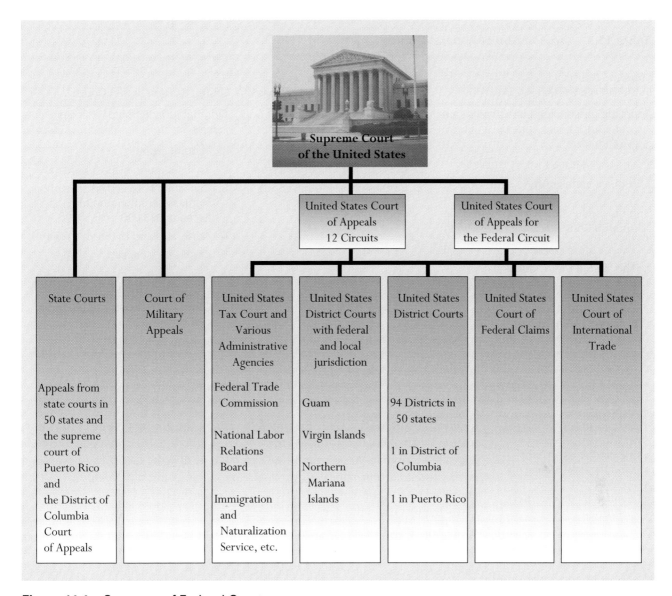

**Figure 11.1**   Structure of Federal Courts

The federal court system of the United States is divided into three levels: the courts of original jurisdiction (state courts, military courts, tax courts, district courts, claims courts, and international trade courts), U.S. Courts of Appeals (which hear appeals from all lower courts except state and military panels), and the U.S. Supreme Court, which can hear appeals from all sources.

trial courts, the district courts make use of both **grand juries** (called to hear evidence and, if warranted, to indict a defendant by bringing formal criminal charges) and **petit (regular) juries** (which determine guilt or innocence). District courts may hear 270,000 civil cases in a year and 70,000 criminal cases.

**Courts of Appeals**   Federal **circuit courts** (see *Across the USA:* "Geographic Boundaries of Federal Courts") are appellate courts. They do not hold trials or accept new evidence but consider only the records of the trial courts and oral or written arguments (**briefs**) submitted by attorneys. Federal law guarantees everyone the right to appeal, so the Court of Appeals has little discretion in this regard. Appellate judges themselves estimate that more than 80 percent of all appeals are frivolous—that is, without any real basis. There are more than a

**grand juries** Juries called to hear evidence and decide whether defendants should be indicted and tried.

**petit (regular) juries** Juries called to determine guilt or innocence.

**circuit courts** The twelve appellate courts that make up the middle level of the federal court system.

**Table 11.1   Jurisdiction of Federal Courts**

| Supreme Court of the United States | United States Courts of Appeals | United States District Courts |
| --- | --- | --- |
| Appellate jurisdiction (cases begin in a lower court); hears appeals, at its own discretion, from:<br><br>1. Lower federal courts<br>2. Highest state courts<br><br>Original jurisdiction (cases begin in the Supreme Court) over cases involving:<br><br>1. Two or more states<br>2. The United States and a state<br>3. Foreign ambassadors and other diplomats<br>4. A state and a citizen of a different state (if begun by the state) | No original jurisdiction; hear only appeals from:<br><br>1. Federal district courts<br>2. U.S. regulatory commissions<br>3. Certain other federal courts | Original jurisdiction over cases involving:<br><br>1. Federal crimes<br>2. Civil suits under the federal law<br>3. Civil suits between citizens of states where the amount exceeds $75,000<br>4. Admiralty and maritime cases<br>5. Bankruptcy cases<br>6. Review of actions of certain federal administrative agencies<br>7. Other matters assigned to them by Congress |

**briefs** Documents submitted by an attorney to a court, setting out the facts of the case and the legal arguments in support of the party represented by the attorney.

**Supreme Court Cases**

This Cornell Law School's Legal Information Institute site contains up-to-date information about important legal decisions rendered by federal and state courts along with an exhaustive online law library available to researchers.
*www.law.cornell.edu*

hundred circuit judges, each appointed for life by the president subject to confirmation by the Senate. Normally, these judges serve together on a panel to hear appeals. More than 90 percent of the cases decided by the Court of Appeals end at this level. Further appeal to the Supreme Court is not automatic; it must be approved by the Supreme Court itself. Because the Supreme Court hears very few cases, in most cases the decision of the circuit court becomes law.

**Supreme Court**   The Supreme Court of the United States is the final interpreter of all matters involving the Constitution and federal laws and treaties, whether the case began in a federal district court or in a state court. Appeals to the U.S. Supreme Court may come from a state court of last resort (usually a state's supreme court) or from lower federal courts. The Supreme Court determines whether to accept an appeal and consider a case. It may do so when there is a "substantial federal question" presented in a case or when there are "special and important reasons," or it may reject a case—with or without explaining why.

In the early days of the Republic, the size of the Supreme Court fluctuated, but since 1869 the membership has remained at nine: the Chief Justice and eight associate justices. The Supreme Court is in session each year from October through June, hearing oral arguments, accepting written briefs, conferring, and rendering opinions.

**Appeals from State Courts**   Each of the fifty states maintains its own courts. The federal courts are not necessarily superior to those courts; state and federal courts operate independently. State courts have original jurisdiction in most criminal and civil cases. Because the U.S. Supreme Court has appellate jurisdiction over state supreme courts as well as over lower federal courts, the Supreme Court oversees the nation's entire judicial system, but the great bulk of cases begin and end in the state court systems. The federal courts do not interfere once a case has been started in a state court except in very rare circumstances. And Congress has

## ACROSS THE USA

# Geographic Boundaries of Federal Courts

For administrative convenience, the U.S. District Courts are organized into twelve circuits (regions), plus the Federal Circuit (Washington, D.C.). Within each region, circuit court judges form panels to hear appeals from district courts. U.S. Circuit Courts of Appeals are numbered. U.S. District Courts are named for geographic regions of the states (East, West, North, South, Middle), for example, U.S. District Court for Northern California.

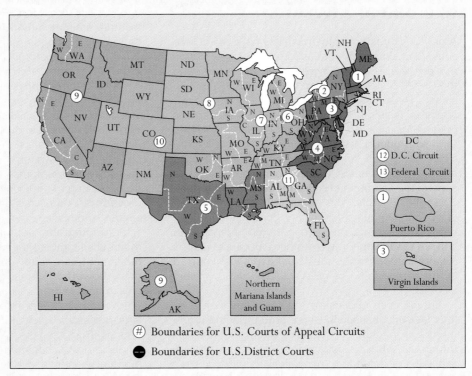

ⓐ Boundaries for U.S. Courts of Appeal Circuits

➖ Boundaries for U.S. District Courts

stipulated that legal disputes between citizens of different states must involve $75,000 or more to be heard in federal courts. Moreover, parties to cases in state courts must "exhaust their remedies"—that is, appeal their case all the way through the state court system—before the federal courts will hear an appeal. Appeals from state supreme courts go directly to the U.S. Supreme Court and not to a federal district or circuit court. Such appeals are usually made on the grounds that a federal question is involved in the case—that is, a question has arisen regarding the application of the Constitution or a federal law.

**Federal Cases**   Some 10 million civil and criminal cases are begun in the nation's courts each year (see *A Conflicting View:* "America Is Drowning Itself in a Sea of Lawsuits" on page 396). About 270,000 (3 percent) of the cases are begun in the federal courts. About 8,000 are appealed to the Supreme Court each year, but only about 125 of them are openly argued and decided by signed opinions. The Constitution "reserves" general police powers to the states. That is, civil disputes and most crimes—murder, robbery, assault, and rape—are normally state offenses rather than federal crimes and thus are tried in state and local courts.

Federal court caseloads have risen in recent years (see Figure 11.2), in part because more civil disputes are being brought to federal courts. In addition, the U.S. Justice Department is prosecuting more criminal cases as federal law enforcement agencies—such as the Federal Bureau of Investigation (FBI), Drug Enforcement Administration (DEA), Internal Revenue Service (IRS), and Bureau of Alcohol,

**The U.S. Supreme Court**

Official site provides recent decisions, case dockets, oral arguments, public information, etc.
*www.supremecourtus.gov*

**Law Info**

Web site offering legal documents, legal help guides, attorney references, and so forth. *www.lawinfo.com*

# A CONFLICTING VIEW

## America Is Drowning Itself in a Sea of Lawsuits

America is threatening to drown itself in a sea of law-suits. Civil suits in the nation's courts exceed *10 million* per year. There are more than 805,000 lawyers in the United States (compared to about 650,000 physicians). These lawyers are in business, and their business is litigation. Generating business means generating lawsuits. And just as businesses search for new products, lawyers search for new legal principles on which to bring lawsuits. They seek to expand legal liability for civil actions—that is, to expand the definition of civil wrongdoings, or torts.

Unquestionably, the threat of lawsuits is an important safeguard for society, compelling individuals, corporations, and government agencies to behave responsibly toward others. Because victims require compensation for *actual* damages incurred by the wrongdoing of others, liability laws protect all of us.

But we need to consider the social costs of frivolous lawsuits, especially those brought without any merit but initiated in the hope that individuals or firms will offer a settlement just to avoid the expenses of defending themselves. Legal expenses and excessive jury awards leveled against corporations increase insurance premiums for businesses and service providers. The Insurance Information Institute estimates that the overall costs of civil litigation in America is many times more than that of other industrial nations, perhaps amounting to over 2 percent of our nation's GDP. For example, the risk of lawsuits forces physicians to practice "defensive medicine," ordering expensive tests, multiple consultations with specialists, and expensive procedures, not because they are adjudged medically necessary, but rather to protect themselves from the possibility of a lawsuit.

Insurance premiums have risen sharply for physicians seeking malpractice insurance, as have premiums for recreation facilities, nurseries and day-care centers, motels, and restaurants.

Reforming the nation's liability laws presents major challenges to the political system. The reform movement can count on support from some normally powerful interest groups—insurance companies, manufacturers, drug companies, hospitals, and physicians. But legal reform is an anathema to the legal profession itself, notably the powerful Association of Trial Lawyers. And lawyers compose the single largest occupational background of Congress members—indeed, of politicians generally.

**Figure 11.2** Caseloads in Federal Courts

Increasing caseloads in the federal courts have placed a heavy burden on prosecutors and judges. Although the increase in civil suits in the federal courts is the result of more plaintiffs insisting on taking their cases to the federal level both originally and on appeal, the increase in criminal cases is the result of Congress's decision to make more crimes— especially drug-related crimes—federal offenses and to pursue such criminals more vigorously.

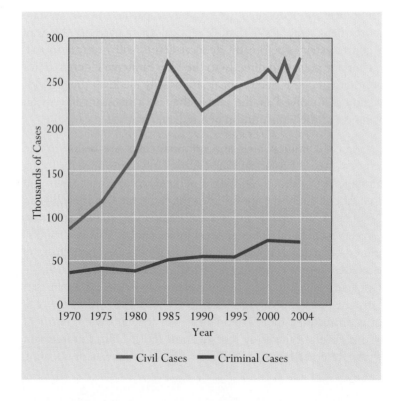

Tobacco, Firearms, and Explosives (ATF)—have stepped up their investigations. Most of this recent increase is attributable to enforcement of federal drug laws.

Traditionally, federal crimes were offenses directed against the U.S. government, its property, or its employees or were offenses involving the crossing of state lines. Over the years, however, Congress has greatly expanded the list of federal crimes so that federal and state criminal court jurisdictions often overlap, as they do, for example, in most drug violations.

# The Special Rules of Judicial Decision Making

Courts are political institutions that resolve conflict and decide about public policy. But unlike Congress, the presidency, and the bureaucracy, the courts employ highly specialized rules in going about their work.

**Cases and Controversies**   Courts do not initiate policy but rather wait until a case or controversy is brought to them for resolution. A case must involve two disputing parties, one of which must have incurred some real damage as a result of the action or inaction of the other. They do *not* issue policy declarations or decide hypothetical cases. Rather, the courts wait until disputing parties bring a case to them that requires them to interpret the meaning of a law or determine its constitutionality in order to resolve the case. Only then do courts render opinions.

The vast majority of cases do *not* involve important policy issues. Courts determine the guilt or innocence of criminal defendants. Courts enforce contracts and award damages to victims of negligence in **civil cases**. And courts render these decisions on the basis of established law. Only occasionally do courts make significant policy decisions.

**civil cases** Noncriminal court proceedings in which a plaintiff sues a defendant for damages in payment for harm inflicted.

**Adversarial Proceedings**   Underlying judicial decision making is the assumption that the best way to decide an issue is to allow two disputing parties to present arguments on each side. Judges in the United States do not investigate cases, question witnesses, or develop arguments themselves (as they do in some European countries). This **adversarial system** depends on quality of argument on each side, which means it often depends on the capabilities of attorneys. There is no guarantee that the adversarial process will produce the best policy outcomes.

**adversarial system** Method of decision making in which an impartial judge or jury or decision maker hears arguments and reviews evidence presented by opposite sides.

**Standing**   To bring an issue into court as a case, individuals or firms or interest groups must have **standing**; that is, they must be directly harmed by a law or action. People cannot "go to court" simply because they do not like what the government is doing. Merely being taxpayers does not entitle people to claim that they are damaged by government actions.[19] Individuals or firms automatically have standing when they are prosecuted by the government for violation of laws or regulations. Thus, one way to gain standing in order to challenge the legality of a regulation or the constitutionality of a law is to violate the regulation or law and invite the government to prosecute.

**standing** Requirement that the party who files a lawsuit have a legal stake in the outcome.

To sue the government, plaintiffs must show they have suffered financial damages, loss of property, or physical or emotional harm as a direct result of the government's action. (The party initiating a suit and claiming damages is the **plaintiff**; the party against whom a suit is brought is the **defendant**.) The ancient legal doctrine of **sovereign immunity** means that one cannot sue the government without the government's consent. But by law, the U.S. government allows itself to be sued in a wide variety of contract and negligence cases. A citizen can also personally sue to force government officials to carry out acts that they are

**plaintiff** Individual or party who initiates a lawsuit.

**defendants** Parties against whom a criminal or civil suit is brought.

**sovereign immunity** Legal doctrine that individuals can sue the government only with the government's consent.

required by law to perform or for acting contrary to law. The government does not allow suits for damages as a result of military actions.

**class action suits** Cases initiated by parties acting on behalf of themselves and all others similarly situated.

**Class Action Suits** Class action suits are cases brought into court by individuals on behalf not only of themselves but also of all other persons "similarly situated." That is, the party bringing the case is acting on behalf of a "class" of people who have suffered the same damages from the same actions of the defendant. One of the most famous and far-reaching class action suits was *Brown v. Board of Education of Topeka* (1954). The plaintiff, Linda Brown of Topeka, Kansas, sued her local board of education on behalf of herself and all other black pupils who were forced to attend segregated schools, charging that such schools violated the Equal Protection Clause of the Fourteenth Amendment. When she won the case, the Court's ruling affected not only Linda Brown and the segregated public schools in Topeka but also all other black pupils similarly situated across the nation (see Chapter 10).

——Think Again——

Are the costs of lawsuits in America becoming too burdensome on the economy?

Class action suits have grown in popularity. These suits have enabled attorneys and interest groups to bring multimillion-dollar suits against corporations and governments for damages to large numbers of people, even when none of them has individually suffered sufficient harm to merit bringing a case to court. For example, an individual overcharged by an electric utility would not want to incur the expense of suing for the return of a few dollars. But if attorneys sue the utility on behalf of a large number of customers similarly overcharged, the result may be a multimillion-dollar settlement from which the attorneys can deduct their hefty fees.

**Legal Fees** Going to court requires financial resources. Criminal defendants are guaranteed an attorney, without charge if they are poor, by the Sixth Amendment's guarantee of "Assistance of Counsel" (see Chapter 10).[20] However, persons who wish to bring a *civil* suit against governments or corporations must still arrange for the payment of legal fees. The most common arrangement is the

The Supreme Court of the United States is the final interpreter of the Constitution and federal laws and treaties. Two new members were added to the Court in 2005 and 2006: Chief Justice John Roberts (center, bottom) and Associate Justice Samuel Alito Jr. (top, right).

**contingency fee**, in which plaintiffs agree to pay expenses and share one-third or more of the money damages with their lawyers if the case is won. If the case is lost, neither plaintiffs nor their lawyers receive anything for their labors. Lawyers do not usually participate in such arrangements unless the prospects for winning the case are good and the promised monetary reward is substantial. Civil suits against the government have increased since Congress enacted a law requiring governments to pay the attorneys' fees of citizens who successfully bring suit against public officials for violation of their constitutional rights.

**contingency fees** Fees paid to attorneys to represent the plaintiff in a civil suit and receive in compensation an agreed-upon percentage of damages awarded (if any).

**Remedies and Relief**    Judicial power has vastly expanded through court determination of **remedies and relief**. These are the orders of a court following a decision that are designed to correct a wrong. In most cases, judges simply fine or sentence criminal defendants to jail or order losing defendants in civil suits to pay monetary damages to the winning plaintiffs. In recent years, however, federal district court judges have issued sweeping orders to governments to correct constitutional violations. For example, a federal district judge took over operation of the Boston public schools for more than ten years to remedy *de facto* (an existing, although not necessarily deliberate, pattern of) racial segregation. A federal district judge ordered the city of Yonkers, New York, to build public housing in white neighborhoods. A federal district judge took over the operation of the Alabama prison system to ensure proper prisoner treatment. A federal district judge ordered the Kansas City, Missouri, school board to increase taxes to pay for his desegregation plan.[21]

**remedies and relief** Orders of a court to correct a wrong, including a violation of the Constitution.

**Independent Counsels?**    The Ethics in Government Act of 1978 (passed in the wake of the Watergate scandal) granted federal courts the power, upon request of the attorney general, to appoint an **independent counsel**, or "special prosecutor," to investigate and prosecute violations of federal law by the president and other high officials. This act was challenged in the U.S. Supreme Court as a transferral of executive power ("to take care that the laws be faithfully executed"— Article II) to the judicial branch of government in violation of the separation of powers in the U.S. Constitution. But the Court upheld the law, noting that the attorney general, an executive branch official appointed by the president, had to request the judiciary to appoint the independent counsel.[22]

**independent counsel ("special prosecutor")** A prosecutor appointed by a federal court to pursue charges against a president or other high official. This position was allowed to lapse by Congress in 1999 after many controversial investigations by these prosecutors.

Whatever the original intent of the act, special prosecutors were often accused of *bringing politics into* the criminal justice system. Indeed, special prosecutor Kenneth Starr's dogged pursuit of Bill and Hillary Clinton (in "Whitewater" real estate deals and later the Monica Lewinsky sex scandal) was deemed a "witch hunt" by friends of the president. The First Lady linked Starr to "a vast right-wing conspiracy" trying to reverse the outcome of two presidential elections.

Congress allowed the independent counsel law to lapse in 1999. Democrats, infuriated by Starr's investigations, joined Republicans, who had earlier complained when Reagan and Bush administration officials were the targets of prosecution, in killing the act. Getting rid of the law, said its opponents, will help to "decriminalize" politics in Washington.

# The Politics of Selecting Judges

The Constitution specifies that all federal judges, including justices of the Supreme Court, shall be appointed by the president and confirmed by a majority vote of the Senate. Judicial recruitment is a political process: presidents almost always appoint members of their own party to the federal courts. More than 80 percent of federal judges have held some political office prior to their appointment to the court. More important, political philosophy now plays a major role in

Class action suits initiated by attorneys or interest groups on behalf of large numbers of people are increasingly popular. Here an attorney announces a suit against the nation's tobacco companies on behalf of flight attendants previously subjected to smoke.

the selection of judges. Thus the appointment of federal judges has increasingly become an arena for conflict between presidents and their political opponents in the Senate.

**The Politics of Presidential Selection**   Presidents have a strong motivation to select judges who share their political philosophy. Judicial appointments are made for life. The Constitution stipulates that federal judges "shall hold their Offices during good Behaviour." A president cannot remove a judge for any reason, and Congress cannot impeach judges just because it dislikes their decisions.

This independence of the judiciary has often frustrated presidents and Congresses. Presidents who have appointed people they thought were liberals or conservatives to the Supreme Court have sometimes been surprised by the decisions of their appointees. An estimated one-quarter of the justices of the Supreme Court have deviated from the political expectations of the presidents who appointed them.[23]

It is important to recognize that presidents' use of political criteria in selecting judges has a democratic influence on the courts. Presidents can campaign on the pledge to make the courts more liberal or conservative through their appointive powers, and voters are free to cast their ballots on the basis of this pledge.

**Political Litmus Test**   Traditionally, presidents and senators have tried to discern where a Supreme Court candidate fits on the continuum of liberal activism versus conservative self-restraint. Democratic presidents and senators usually prefer liberal judges who express an activist philosophy. Republican presidents usually prefer conservative judges who express a philosophy of judicial self-restraint. Until very recently, both the president and the Senate denied using any political "litmus test" in judicial recruitment. A **litmus test** generally refers to recruitment based on a nominee's stand on a single issue. Since the Supreme Court ruling on *Roe v. Wade* (1973), however, the single issue of abortion has come to dominate the politics of judicial recruitment. President Clinton was forthright in his pledge to nominate only justices who specifically support the *Roe v. Wade* decision. Republican presidents have denied using a litmus test, but they have insisted that nominees generally support a philosophy of judicial self-restraint.

───Think Again───
Should presidents appoint only judges who agree with their judicial philosophy?

**litmus test**  In political terms, a person's stand on a key issue that determines whether he or she will be appointed to public office or supported in electoral campaigns.

**The Politics of Senate Confirmation**   All presidential nominations for the federal judiciary, including the Supreme Court, are sent to the Senate for confirmation. The Senate refers them to its powerful Judiciary Committee, which holds hearings, votes on the nomination, and then reports to the full Senate, where floor debate may precede the final confirmation vote.

The Senate's involvement in federal district judgeships traditionally centered on the practice of **senatorial courtesy**. If senators from the president's party from the same state for which an appointment was being considered disapproved of a nominee, their Senate colleagues would defeat the nomination. But if the president and senators from that party agreed on the nomination, the full Senate, even if controlled by the opposition, customarily confirmed the nomination. During the Reagan-Bush years, however, partisan divisions between these Republican presidents and Senate Democrats eroded the tradition of senatorial courtesy.

Supreme Court nominations have always received close political scrutiny in the Senate. Over the last two centuries, the Senate has rejected or refused to confirm about 20 percent of presidential nominees to the high court, but only five nominees in this century (see Table 11.2). In the past, most senators believed that presidents deserved to appoint their own judges; the opposition party would get its own opportunity to appoint judges when it won the presidency. Only if the Senate found some personal disqualification in a nominee's background (for example, financial scandal, evidence of racial or religious bias, judicial incompetence) would a nominee likely be rejected. But publicity and partisanship over confirmation of Supreme Court nominees have increased markedly in recent years.[24]

> **senatorial courtesy** Custom of the U.S. Senate with regard to presidential nominations to the judiciary to defer to the judgment of senators from the president's party from the same state as the nominee.

**The Bork Battle**   The U.S. Senate's rejection of President Ronald Reagan's nomination of Judge Robert H. Bork in 1987 set a new precedent in Senate confirmation of Supreme Court nominees. The Senate rejected Bork because of his views, not because he lacked judicial qualifications. Bork had a reputation for "conservative activism"—a desire better to reflect the "original intent" of the Constitution's Framers by rolling back some of the Supreme Court's broad interpretations of privacy rights, including *Roe v. Wade*, free speech, and equal protection of the law. Unlike previous nominees, Bork was subjected by the Senate Judiciary Committee to extensive case-by-case questioning in nationally televised confirmation hearings. The Democrat-controlled U.S. Senate rejected his nomination. Victory in the Bork battle encouraged liberal interest groups to closely scrutinize the personal lives and political views of subsequent nominees. Indeed, the Bork battle set the stage for an even more controversial political struggle—the confirmation of Justice Clarence Thomas (see *Up Close*: "The Confirmation of Clarence Thomas").

**Filibustering Court Nominees**   The Constitution requires only a majority vote of the Senate to "advise and consent" to a presidential nominee for a federal court judgeship, including a seat on the Supreme Court. However, recent partisan battles over nominees have centered on the Senate's filibuster rule and the sixty votes required for cloture to end a filibuster. The Democrats in the Senate control more than forty votes, so they can deny the majority the ability to end debate: This means they can deny the vote on a federal court nominee indefinitely and thereby effectively kill the nomination. The president cannot force an up-or-down vote on a court nominee.[25]

President George W. Bush suffered several key defeats of judicial nominees for seats on the U.S. Court of Appeals by failing to get sixty votes to end filibusters

**Table 11.2  Senate Confirmation Votes on Supreme Court Nominations since 1950**

| Nominee | President | Year | Vote |
|---|---|---|---|
| Earl Warren | Eisenhower | 1954 | NRV[a] |
| John Marshall Harlan | Eisenhower | 1955 | 71–11 |
| William J. Brennan | Eisenhower | 1957 | NRV |
| Charles Whittaker | Eisenhower | 1957 | NRV |
| Potter Stewart | Eisenhower | 1959 | 70–17 |
| Byron White | Kennedy | 1962 | NRV |
| Arthur Goldberg | Kennedy | 1962 | NRV |
| Abe Fortas | Johnson | 1965 | NRV |
| Thurgood Marshall | Johnson | 1967 | 69–11 |
| Abe Fortas[b] | Johnson | 1968 | Withdrawn[c] |
| Homer Thornberry | Johnson | 1968 | No action |
| Warren Burger | Nixon | 1969 | 74–3 |
| Clement Haynsworth | Nixon | 1969 | Defeated 45–55 |
| G. Harrold Carswell | Nixon | 1970 | Defeated 45–51 |
| Harry Blackmun | Nixon | 1970 | 94–0 |
| Lewis Powell | Nixon | 1971 | 89–1 |
| William Rehnquist | Nixon | 1971 | 68–26 |
| John Paul Stevens | Nixon | 1975 | 98–0 |
| Sandra Day O'Connor | Reagan | 1981 | 99–0 |
| William Rehnquist[b] | Reagan | 1986 | 65–33 |
| Antonin Scalia | Reagan | 1986 | 98–0 |
| Robert Bork | Reagan | 1987 | Defeated 42–58 |
| Douglas Ginsburg | Reagan | 1987 | Withdrawn |
| Anthony Kennedy | Reagan | 1988 | 97–0 |
| David Souter | Bush | 1990 | 90–9 |
| Clarence Thomas | Bush | 1991 | 52–48 |
| Ruth Bader Ginsburg | Clinton | 1993 | 96–3 |
| Stephen G. Breyer | Clinton | 1994 | 87–9 |
| John G. Roberts Jr. | Bush | 2005 | 78–22 |
| Harriet Miers | Bush | 2005 | Withdrawn |
| Samuel Alito Jr. | Bush | 2005 | 58–42 |

[a]No recorded vote.

[b]Elevation to Chief Justice.

[c]Nomination withdrawn after Senate vote failed to end filibuster against nomination; vote was 45 to 43 to end filibuster, and two-thirds majority was required.

*Source:* Congressional Quarterly, *The Supreme Court: Justice and the Law* (Washington, D.C.: Congressional Quarterly, 1983), p. 179; updated by the author.

over these nominations. All of his nominations were qualified from a judicial point of view, but all were considered conservatives by leading Democrats in the Senate. Republican Majority Leader Bill Frist threatened to try to end the filibuster rule for judicial nominations. He argued that the constitution itself specifies a "majority vote of the Senate," not a three-fifths vote for confirmation. But ending the filibuster rule, even for only judicial nominations, would challenge a sacred tradition of the Senate. (Some senators referred to it as the "nuclear option.") A shaky compromise was reached in 2005 when some previously rejected appellate court nominees were confirmed, and Democrats in the Senate promised to use the filibuster only in extraordinary cases. The Democrats chose *not* to filibuster the Supreme Court nomination of John Roberts or Samuel Alito.

# WHAT DO YOU THINK?

## Should Supreme Court Nominees Reveal Their Views on Key Cases before the Senate Votes to Confirm Them?

U.S. Senators on the Judiciary Committee, questioning presidents' Supreme Court nominees, have traditionally been frustrated by the refusal of nominees to comment on issues that are likely to come before the court in future cases. The nominees have argued that giving specific opinions may impinge upon their judicial impartiality when faced with specific cases. A true judicial approach requires that they examine specific facts in a case, listen to the arguments on both sides, and confer with their colleagues on the Court before rendering an opinion. They should not approach cases with preconceived opinions. Thus, when asked if he supported *Roe v. Wade*, John Roberts simply stated that the case was now precedent in constitutional law and entitled to "due respect." "I should stay away from issues that may come before the court again."

But Democratic Sen. Joseph R. Biden Jr. insisted that Roberts could at least discuss his views about abortion and the right of privacy, as well as other general legal views. "Without any knowledge of your understanding of the law, because you will not share it with us, we are rolling the dice with you, judge."

Polls reveal that the general public wants to know the Supreme Court nominee's views on important issues.

Q. *"When the Senate votes on a nominee for the U.S. Supreme Court should it consider only that person's legal qualifications and background, or, along with legal background, should the Senate also consider how that nominee might vote on major issues the Supreme Court decides?"*

| Legal background only | Issues too | Unsure |
|---|---|---|
| 36% | 51% | 10% |

Q. *"Before senators vote on whether John Roberts should be confirmed as the Chief Justice of the Supreme Court, how important do you think it is for the Senate to know his position on issues such as abortion and affirmative action?"*

| Very Important | Somewhat Important | Not Very Important | Not At All Important | Unsure |
|---|---|---|---|---|
| 46% | 31% | 9% | 13% | 1% |

*Sources: Congressional Quarterly Weekly Report,* September 19, 2005, p. 2497; *New York Times,* September 14, 2005.

## Who Is Selected?

What background and experiences are brought to the Supreme Court? Despite often holding very different views on the laws, the Constitution, and their interpretation, the justices of the U.S. Supreme Court tend to share a common background of education at the nation's most prestigious law schools and prior judicial experience.

**Law Degrees**   There is no constitutional requirement that Supreme Court justices be attorneys, but every person who has ever served on the High Court has been trained in law. Moreover, a majority of the justices have attended one or another of the nation's most prestigious law schools (see Table 11.3).

**Judicial Experience**   Historically, about half of all Supreme Court justices have been federal or state court judges. Many justices have served some time as U.S. attorneys in the Department of Justice early in their legal careers. Relatively few have held elected political office, but one chief justice—William Howard Taft—previously held the nation's highest elected post, the presidency.

**Age**   Most justices have been in their fifties when appointed to the Court. Presumably this is the age at which people acquire the necessary prominence and experience to bring themselves to the attention of the White House and Justice

**Find Law for Students**
Law school information for schools A–Z, state bar information, job listings, law school rankings, and so forth.
*http://stu.findlaw.com*

## UP CLOSE

# Bush Scores, Then Fumbles, Then Scores Again

President George W. Bush was successful in his first Supreme Court nomination, John G. Roberts Jr. as Chief Justice. Roberts was eminently qualified: B.A., Harvard; J.D., Harvard Law School; editor of the *Harvard Law Review*; clerk for Supreme Court Justice William Rehnquist; assistant to the Attorney General; partner in the prestigious Washington law firm of Hogan and Harrison; Deputy Solicitor General; and since 2003 Judge on the D.C. Circuit Court of Appeals. As a lawyer he argued thirty-one cases before the Supreme Court. At the Senate Judiciary Committee hearings he was pleasant, courteous, and extraordinarily knowledgeable about the law. He testified for days without any notes. He promised judicial restraint—to interpret the law, not make it—but appeared more moderate than conservative in judicial philosophy. He declined, with grace and deference to the committee, to answer questions that might come before the Court in the future. His nomination was confirmed by 78–22, with all Republicans and half of the Democrats supporting him.

But President Bush followed Roberts's nomination with the nomination of Harriet Miers, a long-time personal friend serving as counselor to the president. Miers received her B.A. and law degrees from Southern Methodist University, worked at a Dallas law firm, served two years on the Dallas City Commission, and was appointed Texas Lottery Commissioner. She had never served in a judicial capacity; she had no record of past decisions. Lacking any public record, the Senate Judiciary Committee summoned all her communications with the president while she had served in the White House. Many conservative Republicans expressed their disappointment; they wanted a strong voice for conservatism on the Court. Democrats complained that "her lack of judicial experience, coupled with close personal ties to President Bush, cast a shadow over her nomination." Finally after weeks of personal visits with Senators, Miers withdrew her nomination, citing the Senate's demand for White House internal documents, a demand "that would undermine the president's ability to receive candid counsel."

President Bush promptly nominated Samuel A. Alito Jr., a judge with fifteen years of experience on the Third Circuit Court of Appeals. Alito received his B.A. from Princeton and his law degree from Yale. Yale was a hothouse of liberal activism while Alito was a student (Bill and Hillary Clinton were two years ahead of him). But Alito remained above the fray, concentrating on the complexities of the law, precedent, and reason. Following graduation, he became a Reagan Justice Department official and wrote many

*Presidential appointments to the Supreme Court require Senate confirmation. Here Senator Robert Byrd (D-WV) meets with Supreme Court nominee John Roberts prior to Roberts's confirmation in 2005.*

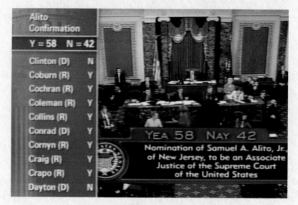

*This television image shows the final confirmation vote on the nomination of Samuel Alito Jr. to the Supreme Court in 2006. Alito replaced retiring Justice Sandra Day O'Connor.*

memos in support of Reagan policies. Liberals would later accuse him of personally endorsing these policies, but Alito responded that he was only serving his client as any lawyer would do. Later, on the Third Circuit Court of Appeals, his decisions were consistently narrow and respectful of precedent. He did not inject his personal views into his decisions. Liberal opponents of his nomination were unable to focus on any controversial decisions or statements. At the Senate Judiciary Committee hearings he was respectful of questioning Senators but stopped short of providing any views on pending cases that might later come before the Court (as had all preceding nominees). Regarding *Roe v. Wade* (the 1973 case declaring abortion a constitutional right), he declined to say whether he "supported" it, but he acknowledged that it was established precedent, that it had been relied upon by the Court many times, and that it was entitled to due respect. Overall he gave the impression that he would be a moderate on the Court, rather than a regular member of the conservative block. His nomination was confirmed by the Senate by a 58 to 42 vote.

## UP CLOSE

# The Confirmation of Clarence Thomas

Television coverage of Senate confirmation hearings on Clarence Thomas's appointment to the Supreme Court in 1991 captivated a national audience. The conflict raised just about every "hot-button" issue in American politics, from abortion rights and affirmative action to sexual harassment.

Born to a teenage mother who earned $10 a week as a maid, Clarence Thomas and his brother lived in a dirt-floor shack in Pin Point, Georgia, where they were raised by strict, hardworking grandparents who taught young Clarence the value of education and sacrificed to send him to a Catholic school. He excelled academically and went on to mostly white Immaculate Conception Seminary College in Missouri to study for the Catholic priesthood. But when he overheard a fellow seminarian express satisfaction at the assassination of Dr. Martin Luther King Jr., Thomas left the seminary in anger and enrolled at College of the Holy Cross, where he helped found the college's Black Student Union, and went on to graduate with honors and to win admission to Yale Law School.

Upon graduating from Yale, Thomas took a job as assistant attorney general in Missouri and later became a congressional aide to Republican Missouri Senator John Danforth. In 1981 he accepted the post as head of the Office of Civil Rights in the Department of Education. In 1982 he was named chair of the Equal Employment Opportunity Commission (EEOC), where he successfully eliminated much of that agency's financial mismanagement and aggressively pursued individual cases of discrimination. But at the same time, he spoke out against racial "quotas." In 1989 President Bush nominated him to the U.S. Court of Appeals, and he was easily confirmed by the Senate.

In tapping Thomas for the Supreme Court, the White House reasoned that the liberal groups who had blocked the earlier nomination of conservative Robert Bork would be reluctant to launch personal attacks on an African American. With the opposition fractured, the White House saw an opportunity to push a strong conservative nominee through the Democrat-dominated Senate Judiciary Committee and win confirmation by the full Senate.

But behind the scenes, liberal interest groups, including the National Abortion Rights Action League, People for the American Way, and the National Organization for Women, were searching for evidence to discredit Thomas. A University of Oklahoma law professor, Anita Hill, a former legal assistant to Thomas both at the Department of Education and later at the Equal Employment Opportunity Commission, charged, in a nationally televised press conference, that Thomas had sexually harassed her in both jobs. Thomas himself flatly denied the charges.

Democrats on the committee treated Hill with great deference, asking her to talk about her feelings and provide even more explicit details of Thomas's alleged misconduct. Given an opportunity to rebut Hill's charges, Thomas did so very emphatically: "This is a circus. It's a national disgrace. And from my standpoint as a black American, as far as I'm concerned, it is a high-tech lynching for uppity blacks who in any way deign to think for themselves."

In the end, there was no way to determine who was telling the truth, and "truth" in Washington is, at any rate, often determined by opinion polls. A majority of blacks as well as whites, and a majority of women as well as men, sided with the nominee.[a] In a fitting finale to the bitter and sleazy conflict, the final Senate confirmation vote was 52 to 48, the closest vote in the history of such confirmations. The best that can be said about the affair was that it placed the issue of sexual harassment on the national agenda.

[a]*Gallup Opinion Reports,* October 15, 1991, p. 209.

**Table 11.3   The Supreme Court**

| Justice | Age at Appointment | President Who Appointed | Law School | Position at Time of Appointment | Years as a Judge before Appointment |
|---|---|---|---|---|---|
| John Paul Stevens | 50 | Ford (1976) | Northwestern | U.S. Court of Appeals | 5 |
| Antonin Scalia | 50 | Reagan (1988) | Harvard | U.S. Court of Appeals | 4 |
| Anthony M. Kennedy | 51 | Reagan (1988) | Harvard | U.S. Court of Appeals | 12 |
| David H. Souter | 50 | Bush (1990) | Harvard | State Supreme Court | 13 |
| Clarence Thomas | 43 | Bush (1991) | Yale | U.S. Court of Appeals | 2 |
| Ruth Bader Ginsburg | 60 | Clinton (1993) | Columbia | U.S. Court of Appeals | 13 |
| Stephen G. Breyer | 56 | Clinton (1994) | Harvard | U.S. Court of Appeals | 14 |
| John G. Roberts Jr. Chief Justice | 50 | Bush (2005) | Harvard | U.S. Court of Appeals | 2 |
| Samuel A. Alito Jr. | 55 | Bush (2005) | Yale | U.S. Court of Appeals | 15 |

Department as potential candidates. At the same time, presidents seek to make a lasting imprint on the Court, and candidates in their fifties can be expected to serve on the Court for many more years than older candidates with the same credentials.

**Race and Gender**   No African American had ever served on the Supreme Court until President Lyndon Johnson's appointment of Thurgood Marshall in 1967. A Howard University Law School graduate, Marshall had served as counsel for the National Association for the Advancement of Colored People Legal Defense Fund and had personally argued the historic *Brown v. Board of Education* case before the Supreme Court in 1954. He served as solicitor general of the United States under President Lyndon Johnson before his elevation to the high court. Upon Marshall's retirement in 1991, President George Bush sought to retain minority representation on the Supreme Court, yet at the same time to reinforce conservative judicial views, with his selection of Clarence Thomas.

No woman had served on the Supreme Court prior to the appointment of Sandra Day O'Connor by President Ronald Reagan in 1981. O'Connor was Reagan's first Supreme Court appointment. Although a relatively unknown Arizona state court judge, she had the powerful support of Arizona Republican Senator Barry Goldwater and Stanford classmate Justice William Rehnquist. The second woman to serve on the High Court, Ruth Bader Ginsburg, had served as an attorney for the American Civil Liberties Union while teaching at Columbia Law School and had argued and won several important gender discrimination cases. President Jimmy Carter appointed her in 1980 to the U.S. Court of Appeals; President Bill Clinton elevated her to the Supreme Court in 1993.

# Supreme Court Decision Making

The Supreme Court sets its own agenda: it decides what it wants to decide. Of the more than 8,000 requests for hearing that come to its docket each year, the

Court issues opinions on only about 150 cases. Another 150 or so cases are decided *summarily* (without opinion) by a Court order either affirming or reversing the lower court decision. The Supreme Court refuses to rule at all on the vast majority of cases that are submitted to it. Thus the rhetorical threat to "take this all the way to the Supreme Court" is usually an empty one. It is important, however, to realize that a refusal to rule also creates law by allowing the decision of the lower court to stand. That is why the U.S. Circuit Courts of Appeals are powerful bodies.

**Setting the Agenda: Granting Certiorari**   Most cases reach the Supreme Court when a party in a case appeals to the Court to issue a **writ of certiorari** (literally to "make more certain"), a decision by the Court to require a lower federal or state court to turn over its records on a case.[26] To "grant certiorari"—that is, to decide to hear arguments in a case and render a decision—the Supreme Court relies on its **rule of four**: four justices must agree to do so. Deciding which cases to hear takes up a great deal of the Court's time.

What criteria does the Supreme Court use in choosing its policy agenda—that is, in choosing the cases it wishes to decide? The Court rarely explains why it accepts or rejects cases, but there are some general patterns. First, the Court accepts cases involving issues that the justices are interested in. The justices are clearly interested in the area of First Amendment freedoms—speech, press, and religion. Members of the Court are also interested in civil rights issues under the Equal Protection Clause of the Fourteenth Amendment and the civil rights laws and in overseeing the criminal justice system and defining the Due Process Clauses of the Fifth and Fourteenth Amendments.

In addition, the Court seems to feel an obligation to accept cases involving questions that have been decided differently by different circuit courts of appeals. The Supreme Court generally tries to see to it that "the law" does not differ from one circuit to another. Likewise, the Supreme Court usually acts when lower courts have made decisions clearly at odds with Supreme Court interpretations in order to maintain control of the federal judiciary. Finally, the Supreme Court is more likely to accept a case in which the U.S. government is a party and requests a review, especially when an issue appears to be one of overriding importance to the government. In fact, the U.S. government is a party in almost half of the cases decided by the Supreme Court.

**Hearing Arguments**   Once the Supreme Court places a case on its decision calendar, attorneys for both sides submit written briefs on the issues. The Supreme Court may also allow interest groups to submit **amicus curiae** (literally, "friend of the court") briefs. This process allows interest groups direct access to the Supreme Court. In the affirmative action case of *University of California Regents v. Bakke* (1978)[27] the Court accepted 59 *amicus curiae* briefs representing more than 100 interest groups. The U.S. government frequently submits *amicus curiae* arguments in cases in which it is not a party. The **solicitor general** of the United States is responsible for presenting the government's arguments both in cases in which the government is a party and in cases in which the government is merely an *amicus curiae*.

Oral arguments before the Supreme Court are a time-honored ritual of American government. They take place in the marble "temple"—the Supreme Court building across the street from the U.S. Capitol in Washington, D.C. (see Figure 11.3). The justices, clad in their black robes, sit behind a high "bench" and peer down at the attorneys presenting their arguments. Arguing a case before the

**writ of certiorari**  Writ issued by the Supreme Court, at its discretion, to order a lower court to prepare the record of a case and send it to the Supreme Court for review. Most cases come to the Court as petitions for writs of certiorari.

**rule of four**  At least four justices must agree to hear an appeal (writ of certiorari) from a lower court in order to get a case before the Supreme Court.

**amicus curiae**  Literally, "friend of the court"; a person, private group or institution, or government agency that is not a party to a case but participates in the case (usually through submission of a brief) at the invitation of the court or on its own initiative.

**solicitor general**  Attorney in the Department of Justice who represents the U.S. government before the Supreme Court and any other courts.

**Figure 11.3** Corridors of Power in the Supreme Court

This cutaway shows the location of the principal offices and chambers of the Supreme Court building.

THE SUPREME COURT

1. Courtyards
2. Solicitor General's Office
3. Lawyers' Lounge
4. Marshal's Office
5. Main Hall
6. Courtroom
7. Conference and Reception Rooms

**majority opinion** Opinion in a case that is subscribed to by a majority of the judges who participated in the decision.

Supreme Court is said to be an intimidating experience. Each side is usually limited to either a half-hour or an hour of argument, but justices frequently interrupt with their own pointed questioning. Court watchers sometimes try to predict the Court's decision from the tenor of the questioning. Oral argument is the most public phase of Supreme Court decision making, but no one really knows whether these arguments ever change the justices' minds.

**In Conference**   The actual decisions are made in private conferences among the justices. These conferences usually take place on Wednesdays and Fridays and cover the cases argued orally during the same week. The Chief Justice presides, and only justices (no law clerks) are present. It is customary for the Chief Justice to speak first on the issues, followed by each associate justice in order of seniority. A majority must decide which party wins or loses and whether a lower court's decision is to be affirmed or reversed.

**Writing Opinions**   The *written* opinion determines the actual outcome of the case (votes in conference are not binding). When the decision is unanimous, the Chief Justice traditionally writes the opinion. In the case of a split decision, the Chief Justice may take on the task of writing the **majority opinion** or assign it to another justice in the majority. If the Chief Justice is in the minority, the senior justice in the majority makes the assignment. Writing the opinion of the Court is the central task in Supreme Court policy making. Broadly written opinions may effect sweeping policy changes; narrowly written opinions may decide a particular case but have very little policy impact. The reasons cited for the decision become binding law, to be applied by lower courts in future cases. Yet despite the crucial role of opinion writing in Court policy making, most opinions are actually written by law clerks who are only recent graduates of the nation's prestigious law schools. The justices themselves read, edit, correct, and sometimes rewrite drafts prepared by clerks, but clerks may have a strong influence over the position taken by justices on the issues.

A draft of the opinion is circulated among members of the majority. Any majority member who disagrees with the reasoning in the opinion, and thus disagrees with the policy that is proposed, may either negotiate changes in the opinion with others in the majority or write a concurring opinion. A **concurring opinion** agrees with the decision about which party wins the case but sets forth a different reason for the decision, proposing, in effect, a different policy position.

Justices in the minority often agree to present a **dissenting opinion**. The dissenting opinion sets forth the views of justices who disagree with both the decision and the majority reasoning. Dissenting opinions do not have the force of law. They are written both to express opposition to the majority view and to appeal to a future Court to someday modify or reverse the position of the majority. Occasionally, the Court is unable to agree on a clear policy position on particularly vexing questions. If the majority is strongly divided over the reasoning behind their decision and as many as four justices dissent altogether from the decision, lower courts will lack clear guidance and future cases will be decided on a case-by-case basis, depending on multiple factors occurring in each case (see, for example, "Affirmative Action in the Courts" in Chapter 10). The absence of a clear opinion of the Court, supported by a unified majority of the justices, invites additional cases, keeping the issue on the Court's agenda until such time (if any) as the Court establishes a clear policy on the issue.

**concurring opinion**
Opinion by a member of a court that agrees with the result reached by the court in the case but disagrees with or departs from the court's rationale for the decision.

**dissenting opinion** Opinion by a member of a court that disagrees with the result reached by the court in the case.

**American Bar Association (ABA)**
ABA news and views; information for law students.
*www.abanet.org*

## Politics and the Supreme Court

The political views of Supreme Court justices have an important influence on Court decisions. Justices are swayed primarily by their own ideological views; but public opinion, the president's position, and the arguments of interest groups all contribute to the outcome of cases.

**Liberal and Conservative Voting Blocs**    Although liberal and conservative voting blocs on the Court are visible over time, on any given case particular justices may deviate from their perceived ideological position. Many cases do not present a liberal-conservative dimension. Each case presents a separate set of facts, and even justices who share a general philosophy may perceive the central facts of a case differently. Moreover, the liberal-versus-conservative dimension sometimes clashes with the activist-versus-self-restraint dimension. Although we generally think of liberals as favoring activism and conservatives self-restraint, occasionally those who favor self-restraint are obliged to approve of legislation that violates their personal conservative beliefs because opposing it would substitute their judgment for that of elected officials. So ideological blocs are not always good predictors of voting outcomes on the Court.

Over time, the composition of the Supreme Court has changed, as has the power of its various liberal and conservative voting blocs (see Table 11.4). The liberal bloc, headed by Chief Justice Earl Warren, dominated Court decision making from the mid-1950s through the end of the 1960s. The liberal bloc gradually weakened following President Richard Nixon's appointment of Warren Burger as Chief Justice in 1969, but not all of Nixon's appointees joined the conservative bloc; Justice Harry Blackmun and Justice Lewis Powell frequently joined in voting with the liberal bloc. Among Nixon's appointees, only William Rehnquist consistently adopted conservative positions. President Gerald Ford's only appointee to the Court, John Paul Stevens, began as a moderate and drifted to the liberal bloc. As a result, the Burger Court, although generally not as activist as the Warren Court, still did not reverse any earlier liberal holdings.

**Table 11.4    Liberal and Conservative Voting Blocs on the Supreme Court**

|              | The Warren Court | The Burger Court | The Rehnquist Court | The Roberts Court* |
|--------------|------------------|------------------|---------------------|--------------------|
| Liberal      | 1968<br>Earl Warren<br>Hugo Black<br>William O. Douglas<br>Thurgood Marshall<br>William J. Brennan<br>Abe Fortas | 1975<br>William O. Douglas<br>Thurgood Marshall<br>William J. Brennan | 2004<br>John Paul Stevens<br>Ruth Bader Ginsburg<br>Stephen G. Breyer | 2006<br>John Paul Stevens<br>Ruth Bader Ginsburg<br>Stephen G. Breyer<br>David Souter |
| Moderate     | Potter Stewart<br>Byron White | Potter Stewart<br>Byron White<br>Lewis Powell<br>Harry Blackmun | Anthony Kennedy<br>Sandra Day O'Connor<br>David Souter | Anthony Kennedy<br>John Roberts |
| Conservative | John Marshall Harlan | Warren Burger<br>William Rehnquist | William Rehnquist<br>Antonin Scalia<br>Clarence Thomas | Samuel Alito<br>Antonin Scalia<br>Clarence Thomas |

*All blocs have been designated by the author; blocs on the Roberts Court are more speculative, inasmuch as this court has yet to decide many cases.

President Ronald Reagan, who had campaigned on a pledge to restrain the liberal activism of the Court, tried to appoint conservatives. His first appointee, Sandra Day O'Connor, turned out to be less conservative than expected, especially on women's issues and abortion rights. When Chief Justice Burger retired in 1986, Reagan seized on the opportunity to strengthen the conservative bloc by elevating Rehnquist to Chief Justice. Reagan also appointed Antonin Scalia, another strong conservative, to the Court. Reagan added Anthony Kennedy to the Court in 1988, hoping to give Rehnquist and the conservative bloc the opportunity to form a majority. Had President Reagan succeeded in getting the powerful conservative voice of Robert Bork on the Court, it is possible that many earlier liberal decisions, including *Roe v. Wade*, would have been reversed. But the Senate rejected Bork; David Souter, the man ultimately confirmed, eventually drifted toward the liberal bloc.

Liberals worried that the appointment of conservative Clarence Thomas as a replacement for the liberal Thurgood Marshall would give the conservative bloc a commanding voice in Supreme Court policy making. But no solid conservative majority emerged. Justices Rehnquist, Scalia, and Thomas were considered the core of the conservative bloc, but they had to win over at least two of the more moderate justices in order to form a majority in a case. President Bill Clinton's appointees, Ruth Bader Ginsburg and Stephen G. Breyer, have consistently supported liberal views on the Supreme Court. On key questions, the moderate bloc has the deciding vote.

While the moderate bloc currently holds the balance of power on the Court, the Court as a whole has moved in a conservative direction since the high-watermark of judicial liberalism during the era of Chief Justice Earl Warren (1953–68). Liberalism on the Court—as measured by pro-individual rights decisions against the government in civil liberties cases, pro-defendant decisions in criminal cases, and pro-women and minorities decisions in civil rights cases—has declined significantly since the 1960s.[28] It has yet to be determined whether the Roberts Court will continue in a conservative direction.

**Public Opinion**   "By all arguable evidence of the modern Supreme Court, the Court appears to reflect public opinion about as accurately as other policy makers."[29] And indeed, on the liberal-conservative dimension, it can be argued that Supreme Court decisions have generally followed shifts in American public opinion. However, the Court appears to lag behind public opinion. It is doubtful that the justices read opinion polls; their jobs do not depend on public approval ratings. Rather, it is more likely that the justices, whose nomination and confirmation depended on an elected president and Senate, generally share the views of those who put them on the bench. Thus, public opinion affects the Court only indirectly, through the nomination and confirmation process.

**Presidential Influence**   Even after a president's initial appointment of a Justice to the High Court, a president may exercise some influence over judicial decision making. The Office of the **U.S. Solicitor General** is charged with the responsibility of presenting the government's (the president's) views in cases not only to which the U.S. government is a party, but also in cases in which the president and the Attorney General have a strong interest and present their arguments in amicus curiae briefs. The Solicitor General's Office, in both Democratic and Republican presidential administrations, has compiled an enviable record in Supreme Court cases. When representing federal agencies that are parties to cases, the Solicitors General have won two-thirds of their cases before the Supreme Court over the years. And in cases where the Solicitor General has offered an amicus curiae brief, he has won about three-quarters of the cases. In contrast, the states have won fewer than half of the cases before the Supreme Court in which a state has been a party.

**U.S. Solicitor General** The U.S. governement's chief legal counsel, presenting the government's arguments in cases in which it is a party or in which it has an interest.

**Interest-Group Influence**   Interest groups have become a major presence in Supreme Court cases. First of all, interest groups (for example, Planned Parenthood, National Association for the Advancement of Colored People, American Civil Liberties Union) sponsor many cases themselves. They find persons they believe to be directly damaged by a public policy, initiate litigation on their behalf, and provide the attorneys and money to pursue these cases all the way to the Supreme Court. Second, it is now a rare case that comes to the Court without multiple amicus curiae briefs filed by interest groups.

How influential are interest groups in Supreme Court decisions? Certainly interest groups have a significant influence in bringing issues before the Supreme Court through their sponsorship of cases. It is unlikely that the Court would have acted when it did on many key issues from racial segregation in 1954 (*Brown v. Board of Education* sponsored by the NAACP) to abortion in 1992 (*Planned Parenthood v. Casey* sponsored by Planned Parenthood) in the absence of interest-group activity. And interest-group *amicus curiae* briefs are now mentioned (cited) in about two-thirds of the written decisions of the Court. However, these briefs may not have much *independent* effect on decisions, that is, they may not have convinced the justices to decide a case one way or another. Several studies have found that interest-group briefs have had very little effect on Supreme Court decisions.[30]

# Checking Court Power

Many people are concerned about the extent to which we now rely on a nonelected judiciary to decide key policy issues rather than depending on a democratically elected president or Congress.

**Legitimacy as a Restraint on the Judiciary**   Court authority derives from legitimacy rather than force. By that we mean that the courts depend on their authority being seen as rightful, on people perceiving an obligation to abide by court decisions whether they agree with them or not. The courts have no significant force at their direct command. Federal marshals, who carry out the orders of federal courts, number only a few thousand. Courts must rely primarily on the executive branch for enforcement of their decisions.

Today most Americans believe that Supreme Court decisions are authoritative statements about the Constitution and that people have an obligation to obey these decisions whether they agree with them or not.[31] Thus public opinion constrains other public officials—from the president, to governors, to school superintendents, to law enforcement officials—to obey Supreme Court decisions. Their constituents do not hold them personally responsible for unpopular actions ordered by the Supreme Court or federal judges. On the contrary, their constituents generally expect them to comply with court decisions.

**Compliance with Court Policy**   Federal and state court judges must apply Supreme Court policies when ruling on cases in their own courts. Occasionally lower courts express their disagreement with the Supreme Court in an opinion, even when they feel obliged to carry out the High Court's policy. At times, lower federal and state courts try to give a narrow interpretation to a Supreme Court decision with which they disagree. But judges who seek to defy the Supreme Court face the ultimate sanction of reversal on appeal by the losing party. Professional pride usually inspires judges to avoid reversals of their judgments by higher courts even though a long record of reversals is not grounds for impeachment or removal of a federal judge.

Public officials who defy Supreme Court rulings risk lawsuits and court orders mandating compliance. Persons injured by noncompliance are likely to file suit against noncomplying officials, as are interest groups that monitor official compliance with the policies they support. These suits are expensive, time consuming, and potentially embarrassing to government officials and agencies. Once a court order is issued, continued defiance can result in fines and penalties for contempt of court.

The president of the United States is subject to federal court orders. Historically, this notion has been challenged: early presidents believed they were separate and at least co-equal to the courts and that their own determination about the legality or constitutionality of their own acts could not be overturned by the courts. President Andrew Jackson could—and did—say: "John Marshall has made his decision. Now let him enforce it," expressing the view that the president was not obliged to enforce court decisions he disagreed with.[32] But in the course of 200 years, the courts—not the president—have gained in legitimacy as the final authority on the law and the Constitution. Today a president who openly defied the Supreme Court would lose any claims to legitimacy and would risk impeachment by Congress.

The case of Richard Nixon illustrates the weakness of a modern president who would even consider defying the Supreme Court. When Nixon sought to invoke executive privilege to withhold damaging tapes of White House conversations in the Watergate investigation (see *Up Close:* "Watergate and the Limits of Presidential Power" in Chapter 9), federal district judge John Sirica rejected his claim and ordered that the tapes be turned over to the special prosecutor in the case. In arguments before the Supreme Court, Nixon's lawyers contended that the president would not have to comply with a Supreme Court decision to turn over the tapes.

## UP CLOSE

# *Bush v. Gore* in the U.S. Supreme Court

The presidential election of 2000 was unique in American history in that the outcome was decided by the Supreme Court of the United States. The Supreme Court's decision on December 12, 2000, in *Bush v. Gore,* rested on constitutional issues, but the 5–4 decision of the justices raised the question of the High Court's political partisanship.[a]

### "Too Close to Call"

On the morning after Election Day, it became clear that the outcome of the presidential election depended on Florida's twenty-five electoral votes. Florida's Secretary of State (separately elected Republican Katherine Harris) initially reported a margin of 1,784 for Bush out of over 6 million votes cast in the state. But because Florida law provides for a recount when the margin of victory is less than one-half of 1 percent, the recount of machine votes was conducted as well as a count of absentee ballots. Bush's lead was reduced to a slim 930 votes. The Florida Secretary of State declined to accept any recount returns from the counties after November 14, the date set by Florida law as the final date for submission of returns to the Secretary.

### Judicial Maneuvering

But immediately after Election Day armies of lawyers descended on Florida's capital city, Tallahassee. The stakes were high—the presidency of the United States. Gore's legal team was headed by former Secretary of State Warren Christopher, and the Bush team by former Secretary of State James Baker (although neither argued directly before the courts). The Gore team demanded *manual* recounts of the ballots in the state's three largest (and most Democratic) counties—Miami-Dade, Broward (Fort Lauderdale), and Palm Beach. The case was first argued before a Leon County (Tallahassee) trial judge, who dismissed Gore's petition. But the case was quickly appealed to the Florida Supreme Court (with its seven justices, all appointed by Democratic governors). That Court set aside the state's legal deadline for recounts, and county canvassing boards began a tedious hand count of punch card ballots.

The Bush legal team appealed directly to the U.S. Supreme Court, arguing first of all that the U.S. Constitution gives the power to appoint presidential electors "in such Manner as the *Legislature* thereof may direct" (Article II, Section 1), and that the Florida Supreme Court overreached its authority when it set aside legislative-enacted provisions of the election laws of the state, including the deadline for recounts. They also argued that hand counts in counties were late, unreliable, subjective, and open to partisan bias. The U.S. Supreme Court responded initially by ordering a halt to the recounts and remanding (sending back) the case to the Florida Supreme Court for clarification as to the grounds on which it had been decided.

The Florida Supreme Court was apparently not intimidated by the U.S. Supreme Court's implied judgment that it had erred in its decision. It ordered a manual recount of all legal votes in the state, especially undercounts (where ballots failed to register a vote for president). It specified that "the intent of the voter" should be the criterion for deciding how to count a ballot. The Florida Supreme Court decision, Gore v. Harris,[b] was immediately appealed to the U.S. Supreme Court.

By now more than a month had passed with the nation not knowing who would be its next president. It became clear that Al Gore had won the nationwide popular vote. But most Americans acknowledged that the popular vote was of secondary importance to the Constitution of the United States in its provisions for choosing the president by state electoral votes. Only the U.S. Supreme Court seemed to possess sufficient legitimacy to resolve the first contested presidential election in over a century.

### A Divided Supreme Court

The Supreme Court held that "the use of standardless manual recounts violates the Equal Protection and Due Process Clauses [of the U.S. Constitution] . . . . Moreover, the [Florida] court's interpretation of "legal vote," and hence its decision to order a contest-period recount, plainly departed from the legislative scheme. Florida statutory law cannot reasonably be thought to require the counting of improperly marked ballots. The judgment of the Supreme Court of Florida is reversed."

The narrow 5–4 decision appeared to follow partisan lines, with Justices O'Connor, Kennedy, Rehnquist, Scalia, and Thomas voting in the majority to allow Florida's Secretary of State to certify that state's electoral votes for Bush. Justices Souter, Stevens, Ginsburg, and Breyer dissented, arguing that the U.S. Supreme Court should not interfere with the Florida Supreme Court's order for a manual recount. Indeed, Justice Stevens implied that the Supreme Court's decision would undermine "the nation's confidence in the judge as an impartial guardian of the rule of law."

[a]*Bush v. Gore*, 531 U.S. 98, 2000.

[b]*Gore v. Harris*, Florida Supreme Court, December 8, 2000.

Yet when the Court ruled unanimously against him, Nixon felt bound to comply and released tapes that were very damaging to his cause. But Nixon understood that refusal to abide by a Supreme Court decision would most assuredly have resulted in impeachment. Under the circumstances, compliance was the better of two unattractive choices.

**Presidential Influence on Court Policy**   The president and Congress can exercise some restraint over court power through the checks and balances built into the Constitution. Using the office's powers of appointment, presidents have effectively modified the direction of Supreme Court policy and influenced lower federal courts as well. Certainly presidents must await the death or retirement of Supreme Court justices and federal judges, and presidents are constrained by the need to secure Senate confirmation of their appointees. However, over time presidential influence on the courts can be significant. During their combined twelve years in the White House, Ronald Reagan and his successor George H. W. Bush were able to fill 70 percent of federal district and appellate court judgeships and six of nine Supreme Court positions with their own appointees. As noted earlier, however, their appointees did not always reflect these presidents' philosophy of judicial self-restraint in rendering decisions. Nevertheless, the federal courts tilted in a somewhat more conservative direction. President Bill Clinton's appointments generally strengthened liberal, activist impulses throughout the federal judiciary, and George W. Bush's appointees generally supported a conservative, restrained judiciary.

**Congressional Checks on the Judiciary**   The Constitution gives Congress control over the structure and jurisdiction of federal district and appellate courts, but congressional use of this control has been restrained. Only the Supreme Court is established by the Constitution; Article III gives Congress the power to "ordain and establish" "inferior" courts. In theory, Congress could try to limit court jurisdiction to hear cases that Congress did not wish it to decide. Congress has used this power to lighten the federal courts' workload; for example, Congress has limited the jurisdiction of federal courts in cases between citizens of different states by requiring that the dispute involve more than $50,000. But Congress has never used this power to change court policy—for example, by removing federal court jurisdiction over school prayer cases or desegregation cases. Indeed federal courts would probably declare unconstitutional any congressional attempt to limit their power to interpret the Constitution by limiting jurisdiction.

Likewise, although Congress could, in theory, expand membership on the Supreme Court, the custom of a nine-member Supreme Court is now so deeply ingrained in American government that "court packing" is politically unthinkable. Franklin Roosevelt's unsuccessful 1937 attempt to expand the Supreme Court was the last serious assault on its membership.

A more common congressional constraint on the Supreme Court is amending statutory laws to reverse federal court interpretations of these laws that Congress believes are in error. Thus when the Supreme Court decided that civil rights laws did not mandate a cutoff of *all* federal funds to a college upon evidence of discrimination in a single program but only the funds for that program,[33] Congress amended its own laws to require the more sweeping remedy. Although members of Congress frequently berate the Court for what they see as misreading of the laws, all Congress needs to do to reverse a Court interpretation of those laws is to pass amendments to them.

Constitutional amendment is the only means by which the Congress and the states can reverse a Supreme Court interpretation of the Constitution itself. After

## A CONSTITUTIONAL NOTE

### The Power of Judicial Review

Nowhere in the Constitution do we find any mention of the power of "judicial review." It is true that the Constitution's Supremacy Clause (Article VI, Section 2) makes the Constitution and national laws and treaties "the supreme law of the land, anything in the Constitution or laws of any *state* to the contrary notwithstanding." The Founders clearly believed that federal court power over state decisions was essential to maintaining national unity. But at the *national* level, why should an appointed court's interpretation of the Constitution prevail over the views of an elected Congress and an elected president? All are pledged to uphold the Constitution. The answer is that the Founders distrusted popular majorities and elected officials subject to their influence. So the Founders deliberately insulated the courts from popular majorities; by appointing judges for life terms, they sought to ensure their independence. Alexander Hamilton viewed the federal courts as a final bulwark against threats to

principle and property. Writing in *The Federalist* in late 1787 he said: "Limited government . . . can be preserved in practice no other way than through the medium of courts of justice, whose duty it is to declare all acts contrary to the manifest tenor of the Constitution void." But it was not until the case of *Marbury v. Madison* in 1803 that John Marshall first assumed the power of Judicial review. He argued persuasively that (1) the Constitution is declared "the supreme law of the land," and national as well as state laws must be congruent with it; (2) Article III gives the Supreme Court the "judicial power," which includes the power to interpret the meaning of laws and, in case of conflict between laws, to decide which law shall prevail; and (3) the courts are sworn to uphold the Constitution, so they must declare void any law that conflicts with the Constitution. Despite the logic of the argument, judicial review—the ability of an *un*elected judiciary, serving for life, to invalidate laws of Congress and actions of the president—would appear to be an undemocratic feature of the Constitution.

the Civil War, the Thirteenth Amendment abolishing slavery reversed the Supreme Court's *Dred Scott* decision (1857) that slavery was constitutionally protected. The Sixteenth Amendment (1913) gave Congress the power to impose an income tax, thus reversing the Supreme Court's earlier decision in *Pollock v. Farmer's Loan*[34] holding income taxes unconstitutional (1895). But recent attempts to reverse Supreme Court interpretations of the Constitution by passing constitutional amendments on the issues of prayer in public schools, busing, and abortion have all failed to win congressional approval. The barriers to a constitutional amendment are formidable: a two-thirds vote of both houses of Congress and ratification by three-quarters of the states. Thus, for all practical purposes, the Constitution is what the Supreme Court says it is.

Congress can impeach federal court judges, but only for "cause" (committing crimes), not for their decisions. Although impeachment is frequently cited as a constitutional check on the judiciary, it has no real influence over judicial policy making. Only five federal court judges have ever been impeached by the House, convicted by the Senate, and removed from office, although two others were impeached and another nine resigned to avoid impeachment. In 1989 Federal District Court Judge Alcee Hastings became the first sitting judge in more than fifty years to be impeached, tried, and found guilty by the Congress. He was convicted by the Senate of perjury and conspiracy to obtain a $150,000 bribe; but a federal district court judge later ruled that he should have been tried by the full Senate, not a special committee of the Senate. Hastings declared the ruling a vindication; in 1992 he won a congressional seat in Florida, becoming the first person ever to become a member of the House after being impeached by that same body. Even criminal convictions do not ensure removal from office, although judges have resigned under fire.

# Summary Notes

- Great power is lodged in the Supreme Court of the United States and the federal judiciary. These courts have undertaken to resolve many of the most divisive conflicts in American society. The judicial power is the power to decide cases and controversies, and in so doing to decide the meaning of the Constitution and laws of Congress.

- The power of judicial review is the power to invalidate laws of Congress or of the states that the federal courts believe conflict with the U.S. Constitution. This power is not specifically mentioned in the Constitution but was derived by Chief Justice John Marshall from the Supremacy Clause and the meaning of judicial power in Article III.

- The Supreme Court has been fairly restrained in its use of judicial review with regard to laws of Congress and actions of presidents; it has more frequently overturned state laws. The federal courts also exercise great power in the interpretation of the laws of Congress, especially when statutory language is vague.

- Arguments over judicial power are reflected in the conflicting philosophies of judicial activism and judicial self-restraint. Advocates of judicial restraint argue that judges must not substitute their own views for those of elected representatives and the remedy for unwise laws lies in the legislature, not the courts. Advocates of judicial activism argue that the courts must view the Constitution as a living document and its meaning must fit the needs of a changing society.

- The federal judiciary consists of three levels of courts—the Supreme Court, the U.S. Courts of Appeals, and the U.S. District Courts. The district courts are trial courts that hear both civil and criminal cases. The courts of appeals are appellate courts and do not hold trials but consider only the record of trial courts and the arguments (briefs) of attorneys. More than 90 percent of federal cases end in appeals courts. The Supreme Court can hear appeals from state high courts as well as lower federal courts. The Supreme Court hears only about 200 cases a year.

- Courts function under general rules of restraint that do not bind the president or Congress. The Supreme Court does not decide hypothetical cases or render advisory opinions. The principle of stare decisis, or reliance on precedent, is not set aside lightly.

- The selection of Supreme Court justices and federal judges is based more on political considerations than legal qualifications. Presidents almost always appoint judges from their own party, and presidents increasingly have sought judges who share their ideological views. However, because of the independence of judges once they are appointed, presidents have sometimes been disappointed in the decisions of their appointees. In addition, Senate approval of

nominees has become increasingly politicized, with problems most evident when different parties control the White House and the Senate.

- The Supreme Court sets its own agenda for policy making, usually by granting or withholding certiorari. Generally four justices must agree to grant certiorari for a case to be decided by the Supreme Court. The Supreme Court has been especially active in policy making in interpreting the meaning of the Fourteenth Amendment's guarantee of "equal protection of the laws," as well as of the civil rights and voting rights acts of Congress. It has also been active in defining the meaning of freedom of press, speech, and religion in the First Amendment and "due process of law" in the Fifth Amendment. The federal courts are active in overseeing government regulatory activity. But federal courts have generally left the areas of national security and international relations to the president and Congress. In addition, the Court tends to accept cases involving questions decided differently by different courts of appeal, cases in which lower courts have challenged Supreme Court interpretations, and cases in which the U.S. government is a party and it requests review.

- Liberal and conservative blocs on the Supreme Court can be discerned over time. Generally, liberals have been judicial activists and conservatives have been restraintists. Today a moderate bloc appears to hold the balance of power.

- The Supreme Court risked its reputation for political impartiality when it intervened in the 2000 presidential election and issued a decision that in effect gave Florida's 25 electoral votes to George W. Bush and by so doing won him a majority in the Electoral College.

- Court power derives primarily from legitimacy rather than force. Most Americans believe that Supreme Court decisions are authoritative statements about the Constitution and people have an obligation to obey these decisions whether they agree with them or not. Although early presidents thought of themselves as constitutional co-equals with the Supreme Court and not necessarily bound by Court decisions, today it would be politically unthinkable for a president to ignore a court order.

- There are very few checks on Supreme Court power. Presidents may try to influence Court policy through judicial nominations, but once judges are confirmed by the Senate they can pursue their own impulses. Congress has never used its power to limit the jurisdiction of federal courts in order to influence judicial decisions.

- Only by amending the Constitution can Congress and the states reverse a Supreme Court interpretation of its meaning. Congress can impeach federal judges only for committing crimes, not for their decisions.

# Key Terms

judicial review   386

statutory laws   389

judicial self-restraint   390

original intent   390

judicial activism   391

stare decisis   391

precedent   391

jurisdiction   392

original jurisdiction   392

appellate jurisdiction   392

appeal   392

district courts   392

grand juries   393

petit (regular) juries   393

circuit courts   393

briefs   394

civil cases   397

adversarial system   397

standing   397

plaintiff   397

defendants   397

sovereign immunity   397

class action suits   398

contingency fee   399

remedies and relief   399

independent counsel ("special prosecutor")   399

litmus test   400

senatorial courtesy   401

writ of certiorari   407

rule of four   407

amicus curiae   407

solicitor general   407

majority opinion   408

concurring opinion   409

dissenting opinion   409

U.S. Solicitor General   411

# Suggested Readings

Baum, Lawrence. *The Supreme Court.* 8th ed. Washington, D.C.: CQ Press, 2003. Readable introduction to the Supreme Court as a political institution, covering the selection and confirmation of judges, the nature of the issues decided by courts, the process of judicial decision making, and the impact of Supreme Court decisions.

Bork, Robert H. *Coercing Virtue.* Washington DC: AEI Press, 2003. An argument that judges, rather than legislators, are making and repealing law and deciding cases with partisan and ideological subjectivity.

Carp, Robert A., and Ronald Stidham. *The Federal Courts.* 4th ed. Washington, D.C.: CQ Press, 2001. Overview of the federal judicial system, arguing that federal judges and Supreme Court justices function as part of the political system and engage in policy making that influences all our lives.

Epstein, Lee, and Thomas G. Walker. *Constitutional Law for a Changing America: Institutional Power and Constraints.* 5th ed. Washington, D.C.: CQ Press, 2004. Commentary and selected excerpts from cases dealing with the structure and powers of government.

Johnson, Charles, and Danette Buickman. *Independent Counsel: The Law and the Investigations.* Washington, D.C.: CQ Press, 2001. A comprehensive history of the independent counsel law and the investigations conducted under it since 1978, from Watergate to Whitewater.

Neubauer, David W. and Stephen S. Weinhold. *Judicial Politics: Law, Courts, and Politics in the United States.* Belmont, Calif.: Wadsworth, 2004. Introduction to the judicial process with controversial cases in each chapter.

U.S. Supreme Court decisions are available at most public and university libraries as well as at law libraries in volumes of *United States Reports.* Court opinions are cited by the names of the parties, for example, *Brown v. Board of Education of Topeka,* followed by a reference number such as 347 U.S. 483 (1954). The first number in the citation (347) is the volume number; "U.S." refers to *United States Reports;* the subsequent number is the page on which the decision begins; the year the case was decided is in parentheses.

# Make It Real

## THE JUDICIARY

This module allows students to become Supreme Court Justices.

# Part Five

# Outcomes

## Illegal Immigrant Workers

**ABCNEWS**

Originally Aired: **December 14, 2004**
Program: **Nightline**
Running Time: **15:22**

When Bernard Kerik, President Bush's first choice to run the Department of Homeland Security, withdrew his nomination because of a nanny who was an undocumented worker that he hired and failed to pay taxes on, it was a story that probably sounded familiar. Cabinet nominees have been tripped on this issue before in both the Clinton and Bush administrations. So the question is, why does this keep happening?

One of the reasons it keeps happening is that it is pretty easy to get by hiring undocumented workers. It seems that the only way to get tripped up is if you undergo a background check for an important government post. You would be hard pressed to find any aspect of the nation's economy where undocumented workers are not making a contribution. It could be in the service industry or the construction business. You will eat something today that has been brought to you as a result of the labor of illegal immigrants working here. A conservative estimate is that at least 50 percent of agricultural laborers are undocumented workers. So is this a result of American employers being cheap, or is it a result of the efficiency of market forces? Many employers say it is not easy to find Americans willing to do a lot of the low-paying, menial, and tedious tasks that immigrants are willing to do. Labor advocates say that illegal immigrants depress the wage market so Americans are shut out of these jobs. Everyone can find statistics to back their argument.

So what is the solution? When the president announced a proposal in 2006 to grant legal status to millions of undocumented workers in the United States, it wasn't greeted with unanimous enthusiasm. "Out of common sense and fairness, our laws should allow willing workers to enter our country and fill jobs that Americans are not filling," the president said. He wasn't calling for amnesty but a temporary guest worker program. But will that satisfy both sides? Michel Martin examines the arguments advanced on something that has always been a hot-button issue. We also speak with Senator John McCain of Arizona. His state has addressed the illegal immigration issue by voting for a sweeping proposition that bans all government services to illegal immigrants. He says that this is an issue that the nation has to wake up to and start dealing with as a high priority.

## Critical Thinking Questions

1. Why aren't immigration laws more strictly enforced?

2. Explain the "geographic" component to immigration law enforcement.

3. The inability to bar illegal aliens from entering the country is not a question of power. Rather, the problems are political and practical. Briefly explain what this means.

# 12 POLITICS, PERSONAL LIBERTY, AND CIVIL RIGHTS

## Chapter Outline

- Power and Individual Liberty
- Freedom of Religion
- Freedom of Speech
- Privacy, Abortion, and the Constitution
- Obscenity and the Law
- The Right to Bear Arms
- Rights of Criminal Defendants
- The Death Penalty
- The Politics of Equality
- Slavery, Segregation, and the Constitution
- The Civil Rights Acts
- Affirmative Action: Opportunity versus Results
- Hispanics in America
- Hispanic Politics
- Gender Equality and the Fourteenth Amendment
- Gender Equality in the Economy

## Think About Politics

**1** Do you think the government has become so large and powerful that it poses a threat to the rights and freedoms of ordinary citizens?
Yes ☐ No ☐

**2** Do you believe that using tax funds to pay tuition at church-affiliated schools violates the separation of church and state?
Yes ☐ No ☐

**3** Is the death penalty a "cruel and unusual" punishment?
Yes ☐ No ☐

**4** Does the U.S. Constitution require the government to be color-blind with respect to different races in all its laws and actions?
Yes ☐ No ☐

**5** Do you generally favor affirmative action programs for women and minorities?
Yes ☐ No ☐

**6** Do dirty jokes and foul language at work constitute sexual harassment?
Yes ☐ No ☐

*Government power defends your most basic rights to life, liberty, and the pursuit of happiness while at the same time ensuring that all other Americans have the same rights. The Founders guaranteed individual liberty in the earliest days of our nation through the first ten amendments to the Constitution—our Bill of Rights.*

# Power and Individual Liberty

To the authors of the Declaration of Independence, individual liberty was inherent in the human condition. It was not derived from governments or even from constitutions. Rather, governments and constitutions existed to make individual liberty more secure.

> We hold these truths to be self-evident, that all men are created equal, that they are endowed by their Creator with certain unalienable Rights, that among these are Life, Liberty and the pursuit of Happiness. That to secure these rights, Governments are instituted among Men, deriving their just powers from the consent of the governed.

The authors of the Bill of Rights (the first ten amendments to the Constitution) did *not* believe that they were creating individual rights, but rather that they were recognizing and guaranteeing rights that belonged to individuals by virtue of their humanity.

**Authority and Liberty** To avoid the brutal life of a lawless society, where the weak are at the mercy of the strong, people form governments and endow them with powers to secure peace and self-preservation. People voluntarily relinquish some of their individual freedom to establish a government that is capable of protecting them from their neighbors as well as from foreign aggressors. This government must be strong enough to maintain its own existence or it cannot defend the rights of its citizens.

But what happens when a government becomes too strong and infringes on the liberties of its citizens? How much liberty must individuals surrender to secure an orderly society? This is the classic dilemma of free government: People must create laws and governments to protect their freedom, but the laws and governments themselves restrict freedom.

421

**Democracy and Personal Liberty**    When democracy is defined only as a *decision-making process*—widespread popular participation and rule by majority—it offers little protection for individual liberty. Democracy must also be defined to include *substantive values*—a recognition of the dignity of all individuals and their equality under law. Otherwise, some people, particularly "the weaker party, or an obnoxious individual," would be vulnerable to deprivations of life, liberty, or property simply by decisions of majorities (see "The Paradox of Democracy" in Chapter 1). Indeed, the "great object" of the Constitution, according to James Madison, was to preserve popular government yet at the same time to protect individuals from "unjust" majorities.[1]

The purpose of the Constitution—and especially its Bill of Rights, passed by the First Congress in September 1789—is to limit governmental power over the individual, that is, to place personal liberty beyond the reach of government (see Table 12.1). Each individual's rights to life, liberty, and property, due process of law, and equal protection of the law are not subject to majority vote. Or, as Supreme Court Justice Robert Jackson once declared, "One's right to life, liberty, and property, to free speech, a free press, freedom of worship and assembly, and other fundamental rights may not be submitted to vote: they depend on the outcome of no elections."[2]

# Freedom of Religion

Americans are a very religious people. Belief in God and church attendance are more widespread in the United States than in any other advanced industrialized nation. Although many early American colonists came to the new land to escape religious persecution, they frequently established their own government-supported churches and imposed their own religious beliefs on others. Puritanism was the official faith of colonial Massachusetts, and Virginia officially established the Church of England. Only two colonies (Maryland and Rhode Island) provided for full religious freedom. In part to lessen the potential for conflict among the states, the Framers of the Bill of Rights sought to prevent the new national government from establishing an official religion or interfering with religious exercises. The very first words of the First Amendment set forth *two* separate prohibitions on government: "Congress shall make no law respecting an *establishment of religion*, or prohibiting the *free exercise* thereof." These two restrictions on government power—the Free Exercise Clause and the No Establishment Clause—guarantee separate religious freedoms.

**Free Exercise Clause** Clause in the First Amendment to the Constitution that prohibits government from restricting religious beliefs and practices that do not harm society.

**Free Exercise of Religion**    The **Free Exercise Clause** prohibits government from restricting religious beliefs or practices. Although the wording of the First Amendment appears absolute ("Congress shall make *no* law . . ."), the U.S. Supreme Court has never interpreted the phrase to protect any conduct carried on in the name of religion. In the first major decision involving this clause, the Court ruled in 1879 that polygamy could be outlawed by Congress in Utah Territory even though some Mormons argued that it was part of their religious faith. The Court distinguished between belief and behavior, saying that "Congress was deprived of all legislative power over mere opinion [by the First Amendment], but was left free to reach actions which were in violation of social duties."[3] The Court also employed the Free Exercise Clause to strike down as unconstitutional an attempt by a state to prohibit private religious schools and force all children to attend public schools.[4] This decision protects the entire structure of private religious schools in the nation.

## Table 12.1   Constitutionally Protected Rights

### The Bill of Rights

The first ten amendments to the Constitution of the United States, passed by the First Congress of the United States in September 1789 and ratified by the states in December 1791.

| Amendments | Protections |
| --- | --- |
| **First Amendment: Religion, Speech, Press, Assembly, Petition** | |
| Congress shall make no law respecting an establishment of religion, or prohibiting the free exercise thereof, or abridging the freedom of speech, or of the press; or the right of the people peaceably to assemble, and to petition the Government for a redress of grievances. | Prohibits government establishment of religion. Protects the free exercise of religion. Protects freedom of speech. Protects freedom of the press. Protects freedom of assembly. Protects the right to petition government "for a redress of grievances." |
| **Second Amendment: Right to Bear Arms** | |
| A well regulated Militia, being necessary to the security of a free State, the right of the people to keep and bear Arms, shall not be infringed. | Protects the right of people to bear arms and states to maintain militia (National Guard) units. |
| **Third Amendment: Quartering of Soldiers** | |
| No Soldier shall, in time of peace, be quartered in any house, without the consent of the Owner, nor in time of war, but in a manner to be prescribed by law. | Prohibits forcible quartering of soldiers in private homes in peacetime, or in war without congressional authorization. |
| **Fourth Amendment: Searches and Seizures** | |
| The right of the people to be secure in their persons, houses, papers, and effects, against unreasonable searches and seizures, shall not be violated, and no Warrants shall issue, but upon probable cause, supported by Oath or affirmation, and particularly describing the place to be searched, and the persons or things to be seized. | Protects against "unreasonable searches and seizures." Requires warrants for searches of homes and other places where there is a reasonable expectation of privacy. Judges may issue search warrants only with "probable cause," and such warrants must be specific regarding the place to be searched and the things to be seized. |
| **Fifth Amendment: Grand Juries, Double Jeopardy, Self-Incrimination, Due Process, Protection against Government Takings of Property** | |
| No person shall be held to answer for a capital, or otherwise infamous crime, unless on a presentment or indictment of a grand jury, except in cases arising in the land or naval forces, or in the Militia, when in actual service in time of war or public danger; nor shall any person be subject for the same offence to be twice put in jeopardy of life or limb, nor shall he be compelled in any criminal case to be a witness against himself, nor be deprived of life, liberty, or property, without due process of law; nor shall private property be taken for public use, without just compensation. | Requires that, before trial for a serious crime, a person (except military personnel) must be indicted by a grand jury. Prohibits double jeopardy (trial for the same offense a second time after being found innocent). Prohibits the government from forcing any person in a criminal case to be a witness against himself or herself. Prohibits the government from taking life, liberty, or property "without due process of law." Prohibits government from taking private property without paying "just compensation." |

*(continued)*

**Table 12.1    Constitutionally Protected Rights (continued)**

| Amendments | Protections |
|---|---|
| **Sixth Amendment: Fair Trial** | |
| In all criminal prosecutions, the accused shall enjoy the right to a speedy and public trial, by an impartial jury of the State and district wherein the crime shall have been committed, which district shall have been previously ascertained by law, and to be informed of the nature and cause of the accusation; to be confronted with the witnesses against him; to have compulsory process for obtaining witnesses in his favor, and to have the Assistance of Counsel for his defense. | Requires that the accused in a criminal case be given a speedy and public trial, and thus prohibits prolonged incarceration without trial or secret trials. Requires that trials be by jury and take place in the district where the crime was committed. Requires that the accused be informed of the charges, have the right to confront witnesses, have the right to force supporting witnesses to testify, and have the assistance of counsel. |
| **Seventh Amendment: Trial by Jury in Civil Cases** | |
| In Suits at common law, where the value in controversy shall exceed twenty dollars, the right of trial by jury shall be preserved, and no fact tried by a jury, shall be otherwise reexamined in any Court of the United States, than according to the rules of the common law. | Requires a jury trial in civil cases involving more than $20. Limits the degree to which factual questions decided by a jury may be reviewed by another court. |
| **Eighth Amendment: Bail, Fines and Punishment** | |
| Excessive bail shall not be required, nor excessive fines imposed, nor cruel and unusual punishments inflicted. | Prohibits excessive bail. Prohibits excessive fines. Prohibits cruel and unusual punishment. |
| **Ninth Amendment: Unspecified Rights Retained by People** | |
| The enumeration in the Constitution, of certain rights, shall not be construed to deny or disparage others retained by the people. | Protection of unspecified rights (including privacy) that are not listed in the Constitution. The Constitution shall not be interpreted to be a complete list of rights retained by the people. |
| **Tenth Amendment: Rights Reserved to the States** | |
| The powers not delegated to the United States by the Constitution, nor prohibited by it to the States, are reserved to the States respectively, or to the people. | States retain powers that are not granted by the Constitution to the national government or prohibited by it to the states. |

### Rights in the Text of the Constitution

Several rights were written into the text of the Constitution in 1787 and thus precede in time the adoption of the Bill of Rights.

| | |
|---|---|
| **Article 1 Section 9: Habeas Corpus, Bills of Attainder, and Ex Post Facto Laws** | |
| The privilege of the Writ of Habeas Corpus shall not be suspended, unless when in Cases of Rebellion or Invasion the public Safety may require it. No Bill of Attainder or ex post facto Law shall be passed. | Habeas corpus prevents imprisonment without a judge's determination that a person is being lawfully detained. Prohibition of bills of attainder prevents Congress (and states) from deciding people guilty of a crime and imposing punishment without trial. Prohibition of ex post facto laws prevents Congress (and states) from declaring acts to be criminal that were committed before the passage of a law making them so. |

**Table 12.1    Constitutionally Protected Rights (continued)**

### Thirteenth and Fourteenth Amendments

The Bill of Rights begins with the words "Congress shall make no law . . ." indicating that it initially applied only to the *federal* government. Although states had their own constitutions that guarantee many of the same rights, for more than a century the Bill of Rights did not apply to state and local governments. Following the Civil War, the Thirteenth, Fourteenth, and Fifteenth (voting rights) Amendments were passed, restricting *state* governments and their local subdivisions. But not until many years later did the U.S. Supreme Court, in a long series of decisions, apply the Bill of Rights against the states.

**Thirteenth Amendment**

Neither slavery nor involuntary servitude, except as a punishment for crime whereof the party shall have been duly convicted, shall exist within the United States, or any place subject to their jurisdiction.

Prohibits slavery or involuntary servitude except for punishment by law; applies to both governments and private citizens.

**Fourteenth Amendment**

All persons born or naturalized in the United States, and subject to the jurisdiction thereof, are citizens of the United States and of the State wherein they reside. No State shall make or enforce any law which shall abridge the privileges or immunities of citizens of the United States; nor shall any State deprive any person of life, liberty, or property, without due process of law; nor deny to any person within its jurisdiction the equal protection of the laws.

Protects "privileges and immunities of citizenship." Prevents deprivation of life, liberty, or property "without due process of law"; this phrase incorporates virtually all of the rights specified in the Bill of Rights. Prevents denial of "equal protection of the laws" for all persons.

---

**What Constitutes "Establishment"?** It has proven difficult for the Supreme Court to reconcile this wall-of-separation interpretation of the First Amendment with the fact that religion plays an important role in the life of most Americans. Public meetings, including sessions of the Congress, often begin with prayers;[5] coins are inscribed with the words "In God We Trust"; and the armed forces provide chaplains for U.S. soldiers.

The Supreme Court has set forth a three-part **Lemon test** for determining whether a particular state law constitutes "establishment" of religion and thus violates the First Amendment. To be constitutional, a law affecting religious activity:

1. Must have a secular purpose.
2. As its primary effect, must neither advance nor inhibit religion.
3. Must not foster "an excessive government entanglement with religion."[6]

Using this three-part test, the Supreme Court held that it was unconstitutional for a state to pay the costs of teachers' salaries or instructional materials in parochial schools. The justices argued that this practice would require excessive government controls and surveillance to ensure that funds were used only for secular instruction and thus involved "excessive entanglement between government and religion."

However, the Court has upheld the use of tax funds to provide students attending church-related schools with nonreligious textbooks, lunches, transportation, sign-language interpreting, and special education teachers. And the

**Americans United for Separation of Church and State** Organization advocating elimination of religious activity from public life. *www.au.org*

---

**Lemon test** To be constitutional, a law must have a secular purpose; its primary effect must neither advance nor inhibit religion; and it must not foster excessive government entanglement with religion.

A Menorah lighting ceremony celebrating Chanukah on public property near the White House. The Supreme Court is divided over whether such public displays violate the No Establishment Clause of the First Amendment.

 **Anti-Defamation League of B'nai B'rith**
Organization opposing anti-Semitism and securing justice for the Jewish people.
*www.adl.org*

Court has upheld a state's granting of tax credits to parents whose children attend private schools, including religious schools.[7] The Court has also upheld government grants of money to church-related colleges and universities for secular purposes.[8] The Court has ruled that if public buildings are open to use for secular organizations, they must also be opened to use by religious organizations.[9] And the Court has held that a state institution (the University of Virginia) not only can but must grant student activity fees to religious organizations on the same basis as it grants these fees to secular organizations.[10]

The Supreme Court has upheld tax exemptions for churches on the grounds that "the role of religious organizations as charitable associations, in furthering the secular objectives of the state, has become a fundamental concept in our society."[11] It held that schools must allow after-school meetings on school property by religious groups if such a privilege is extended to nonreligious groups.[12] Deductions on federal income tax returns for church contributions are also constitutional. The Supreme Court allows states to close stores on Sundays and otherwise set aside that day, as long as there is a secular purpose—such as "rest, repose, recreation and tranquility"—in doing so.[13]

But the Court has not always acted to "accommodate" religion. In a controversial case, the Court held that a Christmas nativity scene sitting alone on public property was an official "endorsement" of Christian belief and therefore violated the No Establishment Clause. However, if the Christian display was accompanied by a Menorah, a traditional Christmas tree, Santa Claus and reindeer, it would simply be "taking note of the season" and not an unconstitutional endorsement of religion.[14] And in another case, the Supreme Court held that a Louisiana law requiring the teaching of "creationism" along with evolution in the public schools was an unconstitutional establishment of a religious belief.[15]

**Prayer in the School**   The Supreme Court's most controversial interpretation of the No Establishment Clause involved the question of prayer and Bible-reading ceremonies conducted by public schools. The practice of opening the school day with prayer and Bible-reading ceremonies was once widespread in American public schools. To avoid the denominational aspects of these ceremonies, New York State's Board of Regents substituted the following nondenominational prayer,

Although the Supreme Court ruled in 1962 (*Engel v. Vitale*) that even voluntary prayer in public schools was an unconstitutional violation of the separation of church and state under the First Amendment, the question of prayer in the schools remains a heated one. Indeed, recent court rulings regarding nondenominational prayers at graduation ceremonies and sporting events have, if anything, further confused the issue.

which it required to be said aloud in each class in the presence of a teacher at the beginning of each school day: "Almighty God, we acknowledge our dependence upon Thee, and we beg Thy blessings upon us, our parents, our teachers, and our country." New York argued that this brief prayer did not violate the No Establishment Clause, because the prayer was denominationally neutral and because student participation in the prayer was voluntary. However, in *Engel v. Vitale* (1962), the Supreme Court stated that "the constitutional prohibition against laws respecting an establishment of a religion must at least mean in this country it is no part of the business of government to compose official prayers for any group of the American people to recite as part of a religious program carried on by government." The Court pointed out that making prayer voluntary did not free it from the prohibitions of the No Establishment Clause, and that clause prevented the *establishment* of a religious ceremony by a government agency regardless of whether the ceremony was voluntary.[16]

One year later, in the case of *Abington Township v. Schempp*, the Court considered the constitutionality of Bible-reading ceremonies in the public schools. Here again, even though the children were not required to participate, the Court found that Bible reading as an opening exercise in the schools was a religious ceremony. The justices went to some trouble in the majority opinion to point out that they were not "throwing the Bible out of the schools." They specifically stated that the *study* of the Bible or of religion, when presented objectively and as part of a secular program of education, did not violate the First Amendment; but religious *ceremonies* involving Bible reading or prayer established by a state or school did.[17]

**"Voluntary" Prayer**    State efforts to encourage "voluntary prayer" in public schools have also been struck down by the Supreme Court as unconstitutional. When the state of Alabama authorized a period of silence for "meditation or voluntary prayer" in public schools, the Court ruled that this action was an "establishment of religion." The Court said the law had no secular purpose, that it conveyed "a message of state endorsement and promotion of prayer," and that its real intent was to encourage prayer in public schools.[18] In a stinging dissenting opinion, Justice William Rehnquist noted that the Supreme Court itself opened its session with a prayer and that both houses of Congress opened every session with prayers led by official chaplains paid by the government. In 1992 the Court held that invocations and benedictions at public high school graduation ceremonies were an unconstitutional establishment of religion.[19] And in 2000 the Court ruled that

**Christian Coalition**    Organization dedicated to "take America back" from the "judicial tyranny" that would remove religion from public life. *www.cc.org*

# UP CLOSE

## Are We One Nation "Under God"?

For over one hundred years the years the Pledge of Allegiance has been recited in public school rooms at the beginning of each day. In 1954, at the height of the cold war, Congress added the words "under God" after "one nation," to emphasize that the United States acknowledged spiritual values in contrast to "godless communism." President Dwight D. Eisenhower, upon signing the bill, said it would strengthen "those spiritual weapons which forever will be our country's most powerful resource in peace and war."

As early as 1943, the Supreme Court declared that public school pupils could not be *required* to recite the pledge. The opinion was widely praised as an expression of our constitutional freedoms: "If there is any fixed star in our constitutional constellation, it is that no official, high or petty, can prescribe what shall be orthodox in politics, nationalism, religion, or other matters of opinion, or force citizens to confess by word or act their faith therein."[a] Pupils who did not wish to take the pledge were free to stand silent in the classroom while the pledge was being recited.

The Supreme Court was called upon to review the phrase "under God" in 2002 when the father of a public school pupil argued that these words constituted an establishment of religion by an instrument of the government, namely the schools, whether or not his daughter was required to participate in the ceremony. He argued that the pledge with "under God" constituted "a ritual proclaiming that there is a God" and therefore violated the No Establishment Clause of the First Amendment. The words "under God" asserted monotheism and possibly offended atheists, the nonreligious, and others who did not wish to swear an oath of allegiance to a monotheistic deity.

The U.S. Court of Appeals for the Ninth Circuit (with jurisdiction for California and other West Coast states and arguably the most liberal Circuit Court in the nation) agreed that the words "under God" were not neutral and represented a swearing of allegiance to monotheism. The effect of this appeals court's opinion was to remove the words "under God" from the Pledge. However, subsequently it was revealed that the father (who was divorced) did not have custody over his daughter, and that the custodial mother did not wish her daughter to bring suit over this issue. The Supreme Court, therefore, dismissed the case on this technicality and avoided the substantive issue of whether the words "under God" in the Pledge of Allegiance violated the No Establishment Clause.[b] The effect of the Supreme Court's decision was to retain the words.

It can be argued that these words do not refer to any specific religion or deity but simply acknowledge the nation's religious heritage. References to God have long been part of our national identity. Our coins invoke the blessing "In God We Trust," chaplains are provided for the Armed Forces, prayers open the sessions of both chambers of Congress as well as the Supreme Court itself. A strong majority (84 percent) of Americans support the inclusion of the words "under God" in the Pledge of Allegiance.

[a]*West Virginia Board of Education v. Barnette*, 319 U.S. 624 (1943).

[b]*El Grove United School District v. Newdow*, 542 U.S. 277 (2004).

student-led "invocations" at football games were unconstitutional. A Texas school district that allowed students to use its public address system at football games "to solemnize the event" was violating the No Establishment Clause. "The Constitution demands that schools not force on students the difficult choice between whether to attend these games or to risk facing a personally offensive religious ritual."[20] (See *Up Close*: "Are We One Nation Under God"?)

# Freedom of Speech

Although the First Amendment is absolute in its wording ("Congress shall pass no law . . . abridging the freedom of speech"), the Supreme Court has never been willing to interpret this statement as a protection of *all* speech. What kinds of speech does the First Amendment protect from government control, and what kinds of speech may be constitutionally prohibited?

**Clear and Present Danger Doctrine**    The classic example of speech that can be prohibited was given by Justice Oliver Wendell Holmes in 1919: "The most stringent protection of free speech would not protect a man in falsely shouting 'fire' in a theater and causing a panic."[21] Although Holmes recognized that the government may prevent speech that creates a serious and immediate danger to society, he objected to government attempts to stifle critics of its policies, such as the Espionage Act of 1917 and the Sedition Act of 1918. The Sedition Act prohibited, among other things, speech that was meant to discourage the sale of war bonds and "disloyal" speech about the government, the Constitution, the military forces, or the flag of the United States. In the case of *Gitlow v. New York*, the majority supported the right of the government to curtail any speech that "tended to subvert or imperil the government," but Holmes dissented, arguing that "every idea is an incitement. It offers itself for belief and if believed it is acted on unless some other belief outweighs it."[22] Unless the expression of an idea created a *serious and immediate danger*, Holmes argued that it should be tolerated and combated or defeated only by the expression of better ideas. This standard for determining the limits of free expression became known as the **clear and present danger doctrine**. Government should not curtail speech merely because it *might tend* to cause a future danger: "The question in every case is whether the words used are used in such circumstances and are of such a nature as to create a clear and present danger that they will bring about the substantive evils that Congress has a right to prevent."[23] Holmes's dissent inspired a long struggle in the courts to strengthen constitutional protections for speech and press.

Although Holmes was the first to use the phrase "clear and present danger," it was Justice Louis D. Brandeis who later developed the doctrine into a valuable constitutional principle that the Supreme Court gradually came to adopt. Brandeis explained that the doctrine involved two elements: (1) the clearness or seriousness of the expression; and (2) the immediacy of the danger flowing from the speech. With regard to immediacy he wrote,

> No danger flowing from speech can be deemed clear and present, unless the incidence of the evil apprehended is so imminent that it may befall before there is opportunity for full discussion. If there be time to expose through discussion the falsehood and fallacies, to avert the evil by the processes of education, the remedy to be applied is more speech, not enforced silence.

And with regard to seriousness he wrote,

> Moreover, even imminent danger cannot justify resort to prohibition [of speech] . . . unless the evil apprehended is relatively serious. Prohibition of free speech and assembly is a measure so stringent that it would be inappropriate as the means for averting a relatively trivial harm to society. . . . There must be the probability of serious injury to the State.[24]

**Preferred Position Doctrine**    Over the years, the Supreme Court has given the First Amendment freedoms of speech, press, and assembly a special **preferred**

**clear and present danger doctrine** Standard used by the courts to determine whether speech may be restricted; only speech that creates a serious and immediate danger to society may be restricted.

**preferred position** Refers to the tendency of the courts to give preference to the First Amendment rights to speech, press, and assembly when faced with conflicts.

position in constitutional law. These freedoms are especially important to the preservation of democracy. If speech, press, or assembly are prohibited by government, the people have no way to correct the government through democratic processes. Thus the burden of proof rests on the *government* to justify any restrictions on speech, writing, or assembly.[25] In other words, any speech or writing is presumed constitutional unless the government proves that a serious and immediate danger would ensue if the speech were allowed.

**Symbolic Speech**   The First Amendment's guarantees of speech, press, and assembly are broadly interpreted to mean **freedom of expression**. Political expression encompasses more than just words. For example, when Mary Beth Tinker and her brothers were suspended for wearing black armbands to high school to protest the Vietnam War, they argued that the wearing of armbands constituted **symbolic speech** protected by the First Amendment. The Supreme Court agreed, noting that the school did not prohibit all wearing of symbols but instead singled out this particular expression for disciplinary action.[26]

The Supreme Court continues to wrestle with the question of what kinds of conduct are symbolic speech protected by the First Amendment and what kinds of conduct are outside of this protection. Symbolic speech, like speech itself, cannot be banned just because it offends people. "If there is only one bedrock principle underlying the First Amendment, it is that the Government may not prohibit the expression of an idea simply because society finds the idea itself offensive or disagreeable."[27]

For example, flag desecration is a physical act, but it also has symbolic meaning—for example, hatred of the United States or opposition to government policies. In the case of Texas v. Johnson (1989), a majority of Supreme Court justices argued that "Johnson's burning of the flag was conduct sufficiently imbued with elements of communication to implicate the First Amendment." They declared that when speech and conduct are combined in the same expressive act, the government must show that it has "a sufficiently important interest in regulating the non-speech element to justify incident limitations on First Amendment freedoms." In this case, "preserving the flag as a symbol of nationhood and national unity" was not deemed sufficiently important to justify limiting Johnson's freedom of expression.[28]

However, in 2003 the Court upheld a Virginia statute that prohibited the burning of a cross "with the intent of intimidating any person or group" and asserting that "any such burning . . . shall be prima facie evidence of an intent to intimidate." The Supreme Court cited the long history of cross burnings as a form of intimidation and a threat of impending violence. "As the history of cross burning in this country shows, that act is often intimidating, intended to create a pervasive fear in victims that they are a target of violence." Therefore, "The First Amendment permits Virginia to outlaw cross burnings done with the intent to intimidate because burning a cross is a particularly virulent form of intimidation."[29]

**Campus Speech**   Many colleges and universities have undertaken to ban speech that is considered racist, sexist, homophobic, or otherwise "insensitive" to the feelings of women and minorities. Varieties of "speech codes," "hate codes," and sexual harassment regulations that prohibit verbal expressions raise serious constitutional questions, especially at state-supported colleges and universities. The First Amendment includes insulting or offensive racist or sexist words or comments in its protection. Many of these college and university regulations would not withstand a judicial challenge if students or faculty undertook to oppose them in federal court.

---

**freedom of expression**
Collectively, the First Amendment rights to free speech, press, and assembly.

**symbolic speech** Actions other than speech itself but protected by the First Amendment because they constitute political expression.

**Libel and Slander**   Libel and slander have never been protected by the First Amendment against subsequent punishment (see "Libel and Slander" in Chapter 6). Once a communication is determined to be libelous or slanderous, it is outside of the protection of the First Amendment. The courts have traditionally defined "libel" as a "damaging falsehood." However, if plaintiffs are public officials they must prove that the statements made about them are not only false and damaging but also "made with actual malice"—that is, with knowledge that they are false or with "reckless disregard" of the truth—in order to prove libel.[30]

# Privacy, Abortion, and the Constitution

A right of "privacy" is not expressly provided for anywhere in the Constitution. But does the word *liberty* in the First and Fourteenth Amendments include a constitutional right to privacy?

**Finding a Right to Privacy**   The U.S. Supreme Court found a right of privacy in the Constitution when it struck down a Connecticut law prohibiting the use of contraceptives in 1965. Estelle Griswold had opened a birth control clinic on behalf of the Planned Parenthood League of that state and was distributing contraceptives in violation of the state statute prohibiting their use. She challenged the constitutionality of the statute, even though there is no direct reference to birth control in the Bill of Rights. The Supreme Court upheld Griswold's challenge, finding a right of privacy, according to Justice William O. Douglas, in the "penumbras formed by the emanations from" the First, Third, Fourth, Fifth, Ninth, and Fourteenth Amendments. "Various guarantees create a zone of privacy. . . . Would we allow the police to search the sacred precincts of marital bedrooms for telltale signs of the use of contraceptives? The very idea is repulsive to the notion of privacy surrounding the marriage relationship." In concurrent opinions, other justices found the right of privacy in the Ninth Amendment: "The enumeration in the Constitution of certain rights, shall not be construed to deny or disparage others retained by the people."[31]

***Roe v. Wade***   The fact that the *Griswold* case dealt with reproduction gave encouragement to groups advocating abortion rights. In 1969 Norma McCorvey sought an abortion in Texas but was refused by doctors who cited a state law prohibiting abortion except to save a woman's life. McCorvey challenged the Texas law in federal courts on a variety of constitutional grounds, including the right to privacy. McCorvey became "Jane Roe," and the case became one of the most controversial in the Supreme Court's history.[32]

The Supreme Court ruled that the constitutional right of privacy as well as the Fourteenth Amendment's guarantee of "liberty" included a woman's decision to bear or not to bear a child. The Court held that the word "person" in the Constitution did *not* include the unborn child; therefore, the Fifth and Fourteenth Amendments' guarantee of "life, liberty, or property" did not protect the "life" of the fetus. The Court also ruled that a state's power to protect the health and safety of the mother could not justify any restriction on abortion in the first three months of pregnancy. Between the third and sixth months of pregnancy, a state could set standards for abortion procedures in order to protect the health of women, but a state could not prohibit abortions. Only in the final three months could a state prohibit or regulate abortion to protect the unborn.

Rather than end the political controversy over abortion, *Roe v. Wade* set off a conflagration. Congress defeated efforts to pass a constitutional amendment restricting abortion or declaring that life begins at conception. However, when

**Pro-Choice America** Formerly the National Abortion Rights Action League (NARAL), with information on current legislation and court cases.
*www.prochoiceamerica.org*

**National Right to Life Committee**
Leading anti-abortion organization with information on current legislation and court cases.
*www.nrlc.org*

Congress banned the use of federal funds under Medicaid (medical care for the poor) for abortions except to protect the life of a woman, the Supreme Court upheld the ban, holding that there was no constitutional obligation for governments to *pay* for abortions.[33]

**Reaffirming *Roe v. Wade*** Abortion has become such a polarizing issue that "pro-choice" and "pro-life" groups are generally unwilling to search out a middle ground. Yet the current Supreme Court appears to have chosen a policy of affirming a woman's right to abortion while upholding modest restrictions, as evidenced by the Court's ruling in *Planned Parenthood of Pennsylvania v. Casey* (1992).[34]

In this case, the Supreme Court considered a series of restrictions on abortion enacted by Pennsylvania: Physicians must inform women of risks and alternatives; women must wait twenty-four hours after requesting an abortion before having one; and the parents of minors must be notified. It struck down a requirement that spouses be notified. Later, the court struck drawn a parental notification law that did not provide an exception for a judge to withhold notification when it would not be in the best interest of the minor.

Justice Sandra Day O'Connor took the lead in forming a moderate, swing bloc on the Court. Her majority opinion strongly reaffirmed the fundamental right of abortion, both on the basis of the Fourteenth Amendment and on the principle of stare decisis. But the majority also upheld states' rights to protect any fetus that reached the point of "viability." The Court went on to establish a new standard for constitutionally evaluating restrictions: they must not impose an "undue burden" on women seeking abortion or place "substantial obstacles" in her path. All of Pennsylvania's restrictions met this standard and were upheld except spousal notification.

**"Partial Birth Abortion"** A number of states have attempted to outlaw an abortion procedure known as "intact dilation and evacuation" or "partial birth" abortion. This procedure, which is used in very few abortions, involves partial delivery of the fetus feet-first, then vacuuming out the brain and crushing the skull to ease complete removal. In a surprise 5 to 4 decision, with Justice O'Connor supporting the majority, the Supreme Court declared a Nebraska law prohibiting the procedure to be an unconstitutional "undue burden" on a woman's right to an abortion. The Nebraska law failed to make an exception in its prohibition of the procedure "for the preservation of the health of the mother."[35]

**Sexual Conduct** "Liberty gives substantial protection to adult persons in deciding how to conduct their lives in matters pertaining to sex." This Supreme Court ruling in *Lawrence v. Texas* (2003) struck down a state law against homosexual sodomy. The ruling overturned an earlier case in which the Court held that the Constitution granted no "fundamental right to homosexuals to engage in acts of consensual sodomy."[36] Rather, the Supreme Court decided that "The liberty protected by the Constitution allows homosexual persons the right to choose to enter upon relationships in the confines of their homes and their own private lives and still retain their dignity as free persons."[37]

**Gay Marriage** The Supreme Court has not yet spoken out on gay marriages—marriages between persons of the same sex. Several state courts, including the Supreme Court of Massachusetts, have held that the Equal Protection Clause of the Fourteenth Amendment entitles gay couples to marry, that to deny them marriage rights while recognizing heterosexual marriages amounts to discrimination. The issue is complicated by the constitutional provision that requires all states to give "Full Faith and Credit" to judicial proceedings of other states (see *What Do You Think:* "Federalism and Same-Sex Marriages" in Chapter 4). This provision implies that gay marriages in any state must be recognized in all states. Congress passed a Defense of Marriage Act in 1996 declaring that no state need recognize a gay marriage. But Congress failed to pass a constitutional amendment banning same-sex marriage.

# Obscenity and the Law

Obscene materials of all kinds—words, publications, photos, videotapes, films— are *not* protected by the First Amendment. Most states ban the publication, sale, or possession of obscene material, and Congress bans its shipment in the mails. Because obscene material is not protected by the First Amendment, it can be banned without even an attempt to prove that it results in antisocial conduct. In other words, it is not necessary to show that obscene material would result in a clear and present danger to society, the test used to decide the legitimacy of *speech.* In order to ban obscene materials, the government need only prove that they are *obscene.*

Defining "obscenity" has confounded legislatures and the courts for years, however. State and federal laws often define pornography and obscenity in such terms as "lewd," "lascivious," "filthy," "indecent," "disgusting"—all equally as vague as "obscene." "Pornography" is simply a synonym for "obscenity." *Soft-core pornography* usually denotes nakedness and sexually suggestive poses; it is less likely to confront legal barriers. *Hard-core pornography* usually denotes explicit sexual activity. After many fruitless efforts by the Supreme Court to come up with a workable definition of "pornography" or "obscenity," a frustrated Justice Potter Stewart wrote in 1974, "I shall not today attempt further to define [hard-core pornography]. . . . But *I know it when I see it.*"[38]

**Porn on the Internet**   New technologies continue to challenge courts in the application of First Amendment principles. Currently the Internet, the global computer communication network, allows users to gain access to information worldwide. Thousands of electronic bulletin boards give computer users access to everything from bomb-making instructions and sex conversations to obscene photos and even child pornography. Many commercial access services ban obscene messages and exclude bulletin boards with sexually offensive commentary. Software programs that screen out pornography Web sites are readily available to consumers. But can *government* try to ban such material from the Internet without violating First Amendment freedoms?

Congress tried unsuccessfully to ban "indecent" and "patently offensive" communications from the Internet in its Communications Decency Act of 1996. Proponents of the law cited the need to protect children from pornography. But in 1997 the Supreme Court held the act unconstitutional: "Notwithstanding the legitimacy and importance of the Congressional goal of protecting children from harmful materials, we agree that the statute abridges freedom of speech protected by the First Amendment." Government cannot limit Internet messages "to only what is fit for children." The Supreme Court agreed with the assertion that "as the most participatory form of mass speech yet developed [the Internet] deserves the highest protection from government intrusion."[39]

**Internet Freedom** Organization opposed to all forms of censorship and content regulation on the Internet. *www.netfreedom.org*

— Think Again —

Do law-abiding citizens have a constitutional right to carry a handgun for self-protection?

**Right to Keep and Bear Arms**

Organizations advocating self-defense rights with information on legislation, court cases, and so forth.
*www.rkba.org*

**Brady Campaign**
The nation's leading gun control organization, with facts, legislation, and a "report card" on each state.
*www.bradycampaign.org*

**Bureau of Alcohol, Tobacco, Firearms, and Explosives**
Federal agency responsible for regulation of alcohol, tobacco, firearms, and explosives; site includes publications on gun crimes.
*www.atf.gov*

# The Right to Bear Arms

The Second Amendment to the U.S. Constitution states: "A well regulated Militia, being necessary to the security of a free State, the right of the people to keep and bear Arms, shall not be infringed."

**Bearing Arms**   What is meant by the right of the people "to keep and bear arms"? One view is that the Second Amendment confers on Americans an *individual* constitutional right, like the First Amendment freedom of speech or press. The history surrounding the adoption of the Second Amendment reveals the concern of colonists with attempts by despotic governments to confiscate the arms of citizens and render them helpless to resist tyranny. James Madison wrote in the *Federalist Papers*, No. 46 that "the advantage of being armed which the Americans possess over the people of almost every other nation, forms a barrier against the enterprise of [tyrannical] ambition.[40] The Second Amendment was adopted with little controversy; most state constitutions at the time, like Pennsylvania's, declared that "the people have a right to bear arms for the defense of themselves and the state." Early American political rhetoric was filled with praise for an armed citizenry able to protect its freedoms by force if necessary.

**State Militias**   But many constitutional scholars argue that the Second Amendment protects only the *collective* right of the states to form militias—that is, their right to maintain National Guard units. They focus on the qualifying phrase "a well-regulated Militia, being necessary to the security of a free State." The Second Amendment merely prevents Congress from denying the states the right to organize their own military units. If the Founders had wished to create an individual right to bear arms, they would not have inserted the phrase about a "well-regulated militia." (Opponents of this view argue that the original definition of a militia included all free males over eighteen.) Interpreted in this fashion, the Second Amendment does *not* protect private groups who form themselves into militias, nor does it guarantee citizens the right to own guns.

The Second Amendment's "right to bear arms" can be interpreted to guarantee an individual's right to own guns (as asserted by these protestors), or only as a grant of power to the states to maintain National Guard units.

# WHAT DO YOU THINK?

## Gun Control?

New controls on guns are a common policy demand following highly publicized murders or assassination attempts. The Federal Gun Control Act of 1968 was a response to the assassinations of Sen. Robert F. Kennedy and Martin Luther King Jr. in that year, and efforts to legislate additional restrictions occurred after attempts to assassinate presidents Gerald Ford and Ronald Reagan. Today various federal gun control laws include the following:

- A ban on interstate and mail-order sales of handguns
- Prohibition of the sale of firearms to convicted felons
- A requirement that all firearms *dealers* be licensed by the federal Bureau of Alcohol, Tobacco, Firearms, and Explosives
- Requirements that manufacturers record the serial number of all firearms and that dealers record all sales
- Restrictions of private ownership of automatic weapons and military weapons.

Finally there is the *Brady Law* requirement for a five-day waiting period for the purchase of a handgun. (The law was named for James S. Brady, former press secretary to President Ronald Reagan, who was severely wounded in the 1981 attempted assassination of the president.) Handgun dealers must send police agencies a form completed by the buyer; police agencies have five days to make certain the purchaser is not a convicted felon.

### Gun Laws and Crime

There is no systematic evidence that gun control laws reduce violent crime. If we compare violent crime rates in jurisdictions with very restrictive gun laws (for example, New York, Massachusetts, New Jersey, Illinois, and the District of Columbia, all of which prohibit the possession of handguns by citizens) to crime rates in jurisdictions with very loose controls, we find no difference in rates of violent crime that cannot be attributed to social conditions.[a]

### The Second Amendment

Proponents of gun control cite the 1939 Supreme Court decision in *United States v. Miller*, a case in which a defendant challenged a federal law prohibiting the transportation of sawed-off shotguns in interstate commerce.[b] The defendant claimed that the law infringed upon his right to keep and bear arms. But the Supreme Court held that a sawed-off shotgun had no "relationship to the preservation or efficiency of a well regulated militia" and rejected the defendant's challenge to the law. The clear implication of this decision is that the right to bear arms refers only to a state's right to maintain a militia. However, a U.S. Court of Appeals in 2001 ruled that: "All of the evidence indicates that the Second Amendment like other parts of the Bill of Rights, applies to and protects individual Americans ... in their right to keep and bear arms whether or not they are a member of a select militia or performing active military service."[c]

### Public Opinion

Public opinion clearly opposes a nationwide prohibition on the sale of handguns to citizens. Various polls report that 65 to 75 percent of the public does *not* wish to deprive citizens of the right to own guns. However, there is considerable support for various laws respecting gun owners.[d]

[a]Douglas R. Murray, "Handguns, Gun Control Laws and Firearms Violence," *Social Problems*, 23 (June 1975, 26–35); James D. Wright and Peter H. Rossi, *Weapons, Crime and Violence in America* (Washington, D.C.: National Institute of Justice, 1981); Gary Kleck, *Targeting Guns* (New York: Aldine de Gruyter, 1997).

[b]*United States v. Miller*, 307 U.S. 174 (1939).

[c]*United States v. Emerson*, 5th Cir., Oct. 2001.

[d]Various polls from Public Agenda, *www.publicagenda.org*.

| | Favor | Oppose |
|---|---|---|
| Background checks on people buying guns | 92% | 6% |
| Trigger locks on stored guns | 81 | 15 |
| A ban on the sale of assault weapons | 71 | 27 |
| Requiring gun owners to attend a course on gun safety | 84 | 12 |
| A ban on people carrying concealed weapons | 49 | 48 |

Perhaps most controversial is the proposal to require all gun owners to register with the government. The National Rifle Association (NRA) believes that this is the first step in the government effort to seize all citizen-owned guns. However, the general public seems to favor gun registration.

| | | |
|---|---|---|
| Requiring gun owners to register with the government | 75 | 24 |

Think Again

Do you believe that the seizure of property believed by police to be used in drug trafficking, without a judicial hearing or trial, violates civil liberty?

**writ of habeas corpus**
Court order directing public officials who are holding a person in custody to bring the prisoner into court and explain the reasons for confinement; the right to habeas corpus is protected by Article I of the Constitution.

# Rights of Criminal Defendants

While society needs the protection of the police, it is equally important to protect society from the police. Arbitrary searches and arrests, imprisonment without trial, forced confessions, beatings and torture, secret trials, tainted witnesses, excessive punishments, and other human rights violations are all too common throughout the world. The U.S. Constitution limits the powers of the police and protects the rights of the accused (see Table 12.2).

### The Guarantee of the Writ of Habeas Corpus
One of the oldest and most revered rights in English common law is the right to obtain a **writ of habeas corpus**, which is a court order directing public officials who are holding a person in custody to bring the prisoner into court and explain the reasons for confinement. If a judge finds that the prisoner is being unlawfully detained, or finds insufficient evidence that a crime has been committed or that the prisoner could have committed it, the judge must order the prisoner's release. Thus the writ of habeas corpus is a means to test the legality of any imprisonment (see *What Do You Think?*: "Are Persons Captured on the Battlefields of Afghanistan and Iraq Entitled to Protections of the U.S. Constitution?").

The writ of habeas corpus was considered so fundamental to the Framers of the Constitution that they included it in the original text of Article I: "The privilege of the Writ of Habeas Corpus shall not be suspended, unless when in Cases of Rebellion or Invasion the public Safety may require it." Despite the qualifying phrase, the Supreme Court has never sanctioned suspension of the writ of habeas corpus even during wartime. President Abraham Lincoln suspended the writ of habeas corpus in several areas during the Civil War, but in the case of *Ex parte Milligan* (1866), the Supreme Court ruled that the president had acted unconstitutionally.[41] (With the war over, however, the Court's decision had no practical effect.).

### The Prohibition of Bills of Attainder and Ex Post Facto Laws
Like the guarantee of habeas corpus, protection against bills of attainder and ex post facto laws was considered so fundamental to individual liberty that it was included in the original text of the Constitution. A **bill of attainder** is a legislative act inflicting punishment without judicial trial. An **ex post facto law** is a retroactive criminal law that works against the accused—for example, a law that makes an act criminal after the act is committed or a law that increases the punishment for a crime and applies it retroactively. Both the federal government and the states are prevented from passing such laws.

The fact that relatively few cases of bills of attainder or ex post facto laws have come to the federal courts does not diminish the importance of these protections. Rather, it testifies to the widespread appreciation of their importance in a free society.

**bill of attainder** Legislative act inflicting punishment without judicial trial; forbidden under Article I of the Constitution.

**ex post facto law**
Retroactive criminal law that works against the accused; forbidden under Article I of the Constitution.

### Unreasonable Searches and Seizures
Individuals are protected by the Fourth Amendment from "unreasonable searches and seizures" of their private "persons, houses, papers, and effects." The Fourth Amendment lays out specific rules for searches and seizures of evidence: "No warrants shall issue, but upon probable cause, supported by Oath or affirmation, and particularly describing the place to be searched, and the persons or things to be seized." Judges cannot issue a **search warrant** just to let police see *if* an individual has committed a crime; there must be "probable cause" for such issuance. The indiscriminate searching of whole neighborhoods or groups of people is unconstitutional and is prevented by the Fourth Amendment's requirement that the place to be searched must be specifically described in the warrant. The requirement that the things to be

**search warrant** Court order permitting law-enforcement officials to search a location in order to seize evidence of a crime; issued only for a specified location, in connection with a specific investigation, and on submission of proof that "probable cause" exists to warrant such a search.

## Table 12.2 Individual Rights in the Criminal Justice Process

| Rights | Process |
| --- | --- |
| **Fourth Amendment: Protection against unreasonable searches and seizures**<br><br>Warranted searches for sworn "probable cause." Exceptions: consent searches, safety searches, car searches, and searches incident to a valid arrest. | **Investigation by law-enforcement officers**<br>Expectation that police act lawfully. |
| **Fifth Amendment: Protection against self-incrimination**<br>Miranda rules (see Figure 12.1, p. 527).<br><br>**Habeas corpus**<br>Police holding a person in custody must bring that person before a judge with cause to believe that a crime was committed and the prisoner committed it. | **Arrest**<br>Arrests based on warrants issued by judges and magistrates.<br>Arrests based on crimes committed in the presence of law enforcement officials.<br>Arrests for "probable cause." |
| **Eighth Amendment: No excessive bail**<br>Defendant considered innocent until proven guilty; release on bail and amount of bail depends on seriousness of crime, trustworthiness of defendant, and safety of community. | **Hearing and bail**<br>Preliminary hearing in which prosecutor presents testimony that a crime was committed and probable cause for charging the accused. |
| **Fifth Amendment: Grand jury (federal)**<br>Federal prosecutors (but not necessarily state prosecutors) must convince a grand jury that a reasonable basis exists to believe the defendant committed a crime and he or she should be brought to trial. | **Indictment**<br>Prosecutor, or a grand jury in federal cases, issues formal document naming the accused and specifying the charges. |
| **Sixth Amendment: Right to counsel**<br>Begins in investigation stage, when officials become "accusatory"; extends throughout criminal justice process. Free counsel for indigent defendants. | **Arraignment**<br>Judge reads indictment to the accused and ensures that the accused understands charges and rights and has counsel.<br>Judge asks defendant to choose a plea: Guilty, *nolo contendere* (no contest), or not guilty. If defendant pleads guilty or no contest, a trial is not necessary and defendant proceeds to sentencing. |
| **Sixth Amendment: Right to a speedy and public trial**<br>Impartial jury. Right to confront witnesses. Right to compel favorable witnesses to testify.<br><br>**Fourth Amendment: Exclusionary rule**<br>Illegally obtained evidence cannot be used against defendant. | **Trial**<br>Impartial judge presides as prosecuting and defense attorneys present witnesses and evidence relevant to guilt or innocence of defendant and make arguments to the jury. Jury deliberates in secret and issues a verdict. |
| **Eighth Amendment: Protection against cruel and unusual punishments** | **Sentencing**<br>If the defendant is found not guilty, the process ends. Defendants who plead guilty or no contest and defendants found guilty by jury are sentenced by fine, imprisonment, or both by the judge. Sentences imposed must be commensurate to the crimes committed. |
| **Fifth Amendment: Protection against double jeopardy**<br>Government cannot try a defendant again for the same offense. | **Appeal**<br>Defendants found guilty may appeal to higher courts for reversal of verdict or a new trial based on errors made anywhere in the process. |

# WHAT DO YOU THINK?

## Are Persons Captured on the Battlefields of Afghanistan and Iraq Entitled to the Protections of the U.S. Constitution?

The United States has held 6,000 or more "enemy combatants" captured on the battlefields of Afghanistan and Iraq for several years. Some are held at the U.S. base in Guantanamo Bay, Cuba.

Prisoners of war have never been entitled to constitutional protection. Prisoners of war are uniformed members of the military forces of a nation. (The U.S. held tens of thousands of German and Japanese prisoners of war during World War II.) They are entitled only to "humane treatment" under the Geneva Accords. They are not released until the war is ended.

"Detainees" from the war on terrorism are not officially prisoners of war, inasmuch as they are not uniformed soldiers of any nation. The United States has pledged humane treatment even though the government argues that these detainees are not protected by the Geneva Accords. They are not held on U.S. soil. As military detainees, they were not given lawyers or access to courts or, in most cases, even identified by name. The U.S. military decides whether or not, or if, they will face a military tribunal or be released to their home countries. They fall in a "legal black hole."

But in a controversial decision in 2004 the Supreme Court held that enemy combatants captured on the battlefield and "imprisoned in territory over which the United States exercises an exclusive jurisdiction and control" are entitled to constitutional rights including habeas corpus—the right to bring their case to U.S. courts.[a] President Bush proceeded to set up special military commissions to try detainees. But the Supreme Court struck down these commissions because Congress had not established them by law, and they did not operate under the rules of the Uniform Code of Military justice which Congress had enacted years ago.[b] The Court said that the president's powers as Commander-in-Chief did *not* grant him the power to hold and try detainees without congressional legislation. Bush promptly asked Congress for the power to establish special military tribunals with special rules to try detainees, and Congress quickly did so.

[a]*Rasul v. Bush*, 542 U.S. 466 (2004).
[b]*Hamdan v. Rumsfeld*, June 29, 2006.

seized must be described in the warrant is meant to prevent "fishing expeditions" into an individual's home and personal effects on the possibility that some evidence of unknown illegal activity might crop up. The only exception is if police, in the course of a valid search for a specified item, find other items whose very possession is a crime—for example, illicit drugs.

But the courts also permit police to undertake various other "reasonable" searches *without* a warrant: searches in connection with a valid arrest; searches to protect the safety of police officers; searches to obtain evidence in the immediate vicinity and in the suspect's control; searches to preserve evidence in danger of being immediately destroyed; and searches with the consent of a suspect. Indeed, most police searches today take place without warrant under one or another of these conditions. (See also *A Conflicting View:* "Terrorism Requires Restrictions on Civil Liberties.")

**Arrests**   The Supreme Court permits *arrests without warrants* (1) when a crime is committed in the presence of an officer; and (2) when an arrest is supported by "probable cause" to believe that a crime has been committed by the person apprehended.[42] However, the Court has held that police may not enter a home to arrest its occupant without either a warrant for the arrest or the consent of the owner.[43]

**Self-Incrimination and the Right to Counsel**   Freedom from self-incrimination had its origin in English common law; it was originally designed to prevent persons from being tortured into confessions of guilt. It is also a logical extension of the notion that individuals should not be forced to contribute to their own prosecution, that the burden of proof rests on the state. The Fifth

# A CONFLICTING VIEW

## Terrorism Requires Restrictions on Civil Liberties

The terrorist attack on America of September 11, 2001, was the most horrific violence committed against innocent American citizens in recent times. It created a new examination of Americans' commitment to personal freedoms and their willingness to trade these freedoms for the safety and security of society. All of the polls taken shortly after the attack indicated that Americans were prepared to accept many new restrictions on their freedom—more surveillance of their papers and communications, more searches of their belongings, roundups of suspected immigrants, and even prolonged detention without recourse to the courts. As time passed, however, fewer Americans expressed a willingness to sacrifice basic civil liberties to prevent additional acts of terrorism.[a]

Following the attack, Congress moved swiftly to enact the "PATRIOT" Act, officially the Uniting and Strengthening America Act by Providing Appropriate Tools Required to Intercept and Obstruct Terrorism of 2001. President Bush and Attorney General John Ashcroft successfully lobbied Congress to increase the federal government's powers of search, seizure, surveillance, and detention of suspects. The concerns of civil libertarians were largely swept aside. The act was passed nearly unanimously in the Senate (98–1) and overwhelmingly in the House (357–66), with the support of both Democrats and Republicans. The act was extended in 2005, with only minor changes.

Among the key provisions of the USA PATRIOT Act:

- *Roving wiretaps:* Allows wiretaps of any telephones that suspects might use, instead of requiring separate warrants for each line.
- *Internet tracking:* Allows law enforcement authorities to track Internet communications, that is, to "surf the Web" without obtaining warrants.
- *Business records:* Allows investigators to obtain information from credit cards, bank records, con-

sumer purchases, hospitals, libraries, schools and colleges, and so forth with secret warrants.
- *Foreign Intelligence Surveillance Court:* A special Foreign Intelligence Surveillance Court, originally established in 1978 to separate intelligence investigations from criminal investigation, may issue search warrants on an investigator's assertion that the information sought is relevant to a terrorist investigation. No showing of "probable cause" is required. The warrant is not made public, in order to avoid "tipping off" the subject.
- *Property seizure:* Authorizes the seizure of the property of suspected terrorists. Persons whose property is seized bear the burden of proof that the property was not used for terrorist purposes in order to secure the return of their property.
- *Detention:* Allows the detention of suspected terrorists for lengthy periods without judicial recourse.
- *Aliens reporting and detention:* Authorizes the Immigration and Customs Enforcement, or ICE (formerly the Immigration and Naturalization Service, or INS), to indefinitely detain illegal aliens suspected of terrorist connections.
- *Prohibits harboring of terrorists:* Creates a new federal crime—knowingly harboring persons who have committed, or are about to commit, a terrorist act.

What factors affect Americans' willingness to trade off restrictions on civil liberties in order to provide for safety and security from terrorism? Political science research suggests that the greater people's sense of threat, the greater their support for restrictions on civil liberties. The lower people's trust in government, the less willing they are to trade off civil liberties for security. Liberals are less willing to trade off civil liberties than moderates or conservatives. Overall it seems clear that Americans' commitment to civil liberties is highly contingent on their concerns about threats to national or personal security.

[a]Darren W. Davis and Brian D. Silver, "Civil Liberties vs. Security: Public Opinion in the Context of the Terrorist Attacks on America," *American Journal of Political Science* 48 (January 2004): 28–46.

---

Amendment protects people from both physical and psychological coercion.[44] It protects not only accused persons at their own trial but also witnesses testifying in trials of other persons, civil suits, congressional hearings, and so on. Thus "taking the Fifth" has become a standard phrase in our culture: "I refuse to answer that question on the grounds that it might tend to incriminate me." The protection also means that judges, prosecutors, and juries cannot use the refusal of people to take the stand at their own trial as evidence of guilt. Indeed, a judge or attorney is not even permitted to imply this to a jury, and a judge is obligated to instruct a jury not to infer guilt from a defendant's refusal to testify.

The Supreme Court under Chief Justice Earl Warren greatly strengthened the Fifth Amendment protection against self-incrimination and the right to counsel in a series of rulings in the 1960s:

- *Mapp v. Ohio (1961)*: Illegally obtained evidence of and confessions may not be used against the defendant in criminal trials. This exclusionary rule is one of the more controversial procedural rights that the Supreme Court has extended to criminal defendants. The rule provides enforcement for the Fourth Amendment guarantee against unreasonable searches and seizures, as well as the Fifth Amendment guarantee against self-incrimination and the guarantee of counsel.[45,46]

- *Gideon v. Wainwright (1963)*: Equal protection under the Fourteenth Amendment requires that free legal counsel be appointed for all indigent defendants in all criminal cases.[47]

- *Escobedo v. Illinois (1964)*: Suspects are entitled to confer with counsel as soon as police investigation focuses on them or once "the process shifts from investigatory to accusatory."[48]

- *Miranda v. Arizona (1966)*: Before questioning suspects, a police officer must inform them of all their constitutional rights, including the right to counsel (appointed at no cost to the suspect if necessary) and the right to remain silent. Although suspects may knowingly waive these rights, the police cannot question anyone who at any point asks for a lawyer or declines "in any manner" to be questioned. If the police commit an error in these procedures, the accused goes free, regardless of the evidence of guilt.[49]

**The Exclusionary Rule**  Illegally obtained evidence and confessions may not be used in criminal trials. If police find evidence of a crime in an illegal search or if they elicit statements from suspects without informing them of their rights to remain silent or to have counsel, the evidence or statements produced are not admissible in a trial. This **exclusionary rule** is one of the more controversial procedural rights that the Supreme Court has extended to criminal defendants. The rule is also unique to the United States: in Great Britain evidence obtained illegally may be used against the accused, although the accused may bring charges against the police for damages.

The rule provides *enforcement* for the Fourth Amendment guarantee against unreasonable searches and seizures, as well as the Fifth Amendment guarantee against compulsory self-incrimination and the guarantee of counsel. Initially applied only in federal cases, in *Mapp v. Ohio* (1961) the Supreme Court extended the exclusionary rule to all criminal cases in the United States.[50] A *good faith exception* is made "when law enforcement officers have acted in objective good faith or their transgressions have been minor."[51] And police are *not* prohibited from tricking a suspect into giving them incriminating evidence.[52] But the exclusionary rule is frequently attacked for the high price it extracts from society—the release of guilty criminals. Why punish society because of the misconduct of police? Why not punish police directly, perhaps with disciplinary measures imposed by courts that discover errors, instead of letting guilty persons go free?

**Fair Trial**  The original text of the Constitution guaranteed jury trials in criminal cases, and the Sixth Amendment went on to correct weaknesses the Framers saw in the English justice system at that time—closed proceedings, trials in

**exclusionary rule** Rule of law that evidence found in an illegal search or resulting from an illegally obtained confession may not be admitted at trial.

absentia (where the defendant is not present), secret witnesses, long delays between arrest and trial, biased juries, and the absence of defense counsel. Specifically, the Sixth Amendment guarantees the following:

- The right to a speedy and public trial. ("Speedy" refers to the time between arrest and trial, not the time between the crime itself and trial,[53] but the Supreme Court has declined to set a specific time limit that defines "speedy."[54])

- An impartial jury chosen from the state or district where the crime was committed.

- The right to confront (cross-examine) witnesses against the accused.

- The right of the accused to compel (subpoena) favorable witnesses to appear.

- The right of the accused to be represented by counsel.

**Plea Bargaining**   Few criminal cases actually go to trial. More than 90 percent of criminal cases are plea bargained.[55] In **plea bargaining**, the defendant agrees to plead guilty and waives the right to a jury trial in exchange for concessions made by the prosecutor, perhaps the dropping of more serious charges against the defendant or a pledge to seek a reduced sentence or fine. Some critics of plea bargaining view it as another form of leniency in the criminal justice system that reduces its deterrent effects. Other critics view plea bargaining as a violation of the Constitution's protection against self-incrimination and guarantee of a fair jury trial. Prosecutors, they say, threaten defendants with serious charges and stiff penalties in order to force a guilty plea. Still other critics see plea bargaining as an "under-the-table" process that undermines respect for the criminal justice system.

Yet it is vital to the nation's court system that most defendants plead guilty. The court system would quickly break down from overload if any substantial proportion of defendants insisted on jury trials.

**plea bargaining** Practice of allowing defendants to plead guilty to lesser crimes than those with which they were originally charged in return for reduced sentences.

**Double Jeopardy**   The Constitution appears to bar multiple prosecutions for the same offense: "Nor shall any person be subject for the same offense to be twice put in jeopardy of life or limb" (Fifth Amendment). But very early the Supreme Court held that this clause does not protect an individual from being tried a second time if jurors are deadlocked and cannot reach a verdict in the first trial (a "hung" jury).[56] Moreover, the Supreme Court has held that federal and state governments may separately try a person for the same offense if it violates both federal and state laws.[57].

# The Death Penalty

Perhaps the most heated debate in criminal justice policy today concerns capital punishment. Opponents of the death penalty argue that it violates the prohibition against "cruel and unusual punishments" in the Eighth Amendment to the Constitution. They also argue that the death penalty is applied unequally. A large proportion of those executed have been poor, uneducated, and nonwhite. In contrast, many Americans feel that justice demands strong retribution for heinous crimes—a life for a life. A mere jail sentence for a multiple murderer or rapist-murderer seems unjust compared with the damage inflicted on society and the victims. In many cases, a life sentence means less than ten years in prison under the current early-release and parole policies in many states. Convicted murderers have been set free, and some have killed again.

*Think Again*

Is the death penalty a "cruel and unusual" punishment?

**Prohibition against Unfair Application**   Prior to 1971, the death penalty was officially sanctioned by about half of the states. Federal law also retained the death penalty. However, no one had actually suffered the death penalty since 1967 because of numerous legal tangles and direct challenges to the constitutionality of capital punishment.

In *Furman v. Georgia* (1972), the Supreme Court ruled that capital punishment, as then imposed, violated the Eighth and Fourteenth Amendment prohibitions against cruel and unusual punishment and due process of law. The justices' reasoning in the case was very complex. Only Justices William J. Brennan and Thurgood Marshall declared that capital punishment itself is cruel and unusual. The other justices in the majority felt that death sentences had been applied unfairly; some individuals received the death penalty for crimes for which many others received much lighter sentences. These justices left open the possibility that capital punishment would be constitutional if it was specified for certain kinds of crime and applied uniformly.[58]

After this decision, a majority of states rewrote their death penalty laws to try to ensure fairness and uniformity of application. Generally, these laws mandate the death penalty for murders committed during rape, robbery, hijacking, or kidnapping; murder of prison guards; murder with torture; and multiple murders. They call for two trials to be held—one to determine guilt or innocence and another to determine the penalty. At the second trial, evidence of "aggravating" and "mitigating" factors must be presented; if there are aggravating factors but no mitigating factors, the death penalty is mandatory.

**Death Penalty Reinstated**   The revised death penalty laws were upheld in a series of cases that came before the Supreme Court in 1976. The Court concluded that "the punishment of death does *not* invariably violate the Constitution." The majority decision noted that the Framers of the Bill of Rights had accepted death as a common penalty for crime. Although acknowledging that the Constitution and its amendments must be interpreted in a dynamic fashion, reflecting changing moral values, the Court's majority noted that most state legislatures have been willing to reenact the death penalty and hundreds of juries have been willing to impose that penalty. Thus "a large proportion of American society continues to regard it as an appropriate and necessary criminal sanction."

Do retribution and deterrence justify the use of the death penalty? Perhaps the most heated debate in criminal justice policy today concerns capital punishment.

## ACROSS THE USA

# The Death Penalty

Today the death penalty is rarely imposed. Twelve states have no death penalty in their laws. An additional seven states have the death penalty in their laws but have not carried out any executions since 1977 (following the Supreme Court's 1976 decision in *Gregs v. Georgia*). The federal government itself has a death penalty, but the executions of Timothy

McVeigh and Juan Garza in 2001 marked the first death sentences carried out by the federal government in several decades. There are more than 3,500 prisoners across the country convicted and sentenced to death. Over half of these "death row" inmates have been held for more than five years. Executions have slowed as judges and governors have reviewed cases with new DNA evidence.

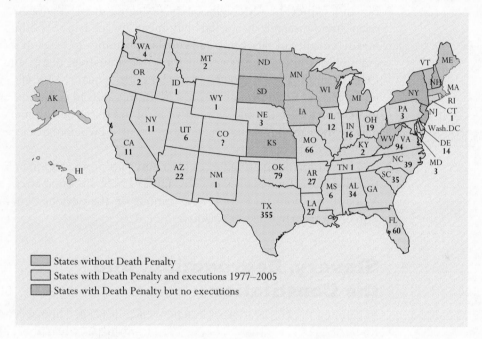

Note: In 2005 the New York Supreme Court ruled that the death penalty violated that state's constitution. Connecticut held its first execution in 2005. The year 2005 saw the one hundredth execution since the death penalty was resumed in 1976.

Moreover, the Court held that the social purposes of retribution and deterrence justify the use of the death penalty; this ultimate sanction is "an expression of society's moral outrage at particularly offensive conduct."[59]

The Court reaffirmed that *Furman v. Georgia* struck down the death penalty only where it was invoked in "an arbitrary and capricious manner." A majority of the justices upheld the death penalty in states where the trial is a two-part proceeding, provided that during the second part the jury is given relevant information and standards for deciding whether to impose the death penalty. The Court approved the consideration of "aggravating and mitigating circumstances." Later the Court held that the jury, not a judge acting alone, must find aggravating circumstances in order to impose the death sentence.[60] The Court also called for automatic review of all death sentences by state supreme courts to ensure that none is imposed under the influence of passion or prejudice, that aggravating factors are supported by the evidence, and that the sentence is not disproportionate to the crime. However, the court disapproved of state laws making the death penalty mandatory in all first-degree murder cases, holding that such laws were "unduly harsh and unworkably

**Bureau of Justice Statistics**
Federal statistics on jails, prisons, probation, and capital punishment. Click to capital punishment for numbers of executions and persons under sentence of death. *www.ojp.usdoj.gov/bjs*

rigid." The Court has held that executions of the mentally retarded are "cruel and unusual punishments" prohibited by the Eighth Amendment.[61] And in 2005 the Court held that the Eighth Amendment prohibited executions of offenders who were under age 18 when their crimes were committed.[62]

## The Politics of Equality

*Equality* has been the central issue of American politics throughout the history of the nation. It is the issue that sparked the nation's only civil war, and it continues today to be the nation's most vexing political concern.

Conflict begins over the very definition of "equality" (see "Dilemmas of Equality" in Chapter 2). Although Americans agree in the abstract that everyone is equal, they disagree over what they mean by "equality." Traditionally, equality meant "equality of *opportunity*": an equal opportunity to develop individual talents and abilities and to be rewarded for work, initiative, merit, and achievement. Over time, the issue of equality has shifted to "equality of *results*": an equal sharing of income and material rewards. With this shift in definition has come political conflict over the question of what, if anything, government should do to narrow the gaps between rich and poor, men and women, blacks and whites, and all other groups in society.

The nation's long struggle over equality has produced a number of constitutional and legal milestones in civil rights. These are summarized in Table 12.3. Much of the politics of civil rights centers on the development and interpretation of these guarantees of equality.

## Slavery, Segregation, and the Constitution

In penning the Declaration of Independence in 1776, Thomas Jefferson affirmed that "All men are created equal." Yet from 1619, when the first slaves were brought to Jamestown, Virginia, until 1865, when the Thirteenth Amendment to the Constitution outlawed the practice, slavery was a way of life in the United States. Africans were captured, enslaved, transported to America, bought and sold, and used as personal property.

**Think Again**

Does the U.S. Constitution require the government to be color-blind with respect to different races in all its laws and actions?

**Slavery and the Constitution** The Constitution of 1787 recognized and protected slavery in the United States. Article I stipulated that slaves were to be counted as three-fifths of a person for purposes of representation and taxation; it also prohibited any federal restriction on the importation of slaves until 1808. Article IV even guaranteed the return of escaped slaves to their owners. The Founders were aware that the practice of slavery contradicted their professed belief in "equality," and this contradiction caused them some embarrassment. Thus they avoided the word "slave" in favor of the euphemism "person held to Service or Labour" in writing the Constitution.

Supreme Court Chief Justice Roger Taney, ruling in the notorious case of *Dred Scott v. Sandford* in 1857, reflected the racism that prevailed in early America:

> They had for more than a century before been regarded as beings of an inferior order, and altogether unfit to associate with the white race, either in social or political relations; and so far inferior, that they had no rights which the white man was bound to respect; and that the negro might justly and lawfully be reduced to slavery for his benefit.[63]

## Table 12.3   Guarantees of Civil Rights

**Thirteenth Amendment (1865)**

Neither slavery nor involuntary servitude, except as a punishment for crime whereof the party shall have been duly convicted, shall exist within the United States, or any place subject to their jurisdiction.

**Fourteenth Amendment (1868)**

No State shall make or enforce any law which shall abridge the privileges or immunities of citizens of the United States; nor shall any State deprive any person of life, liberty, or property, without due process of law; nor deny to any person within its jurisdiction the equal protection of the laws.

**Fifteenth Amendment (1870)**

The rights of the citizens of the United States to vote shall not be denied or abridged by the United States or by any State on account of race, color, or previous condition of servitude.

**Nineteenth Amendment (1920)**

The right of the citizens of the United States to vote shall not be denied or abridged by the United States or by any State on account of sex.

**Civil Rights Acts of 1866, 1871, and 1875**

Acts passed by the Reconstruction Congress following the Civil War. The Civil Rights Act of 1866 guaranteed newly freed persons the right to purchase, lease, and use real property. The Civil Rights Act of 1875 outlawed segregation in privately owned businesses and facilities, but in the Civil Rights Cases (1883), the Supreme Court declared the act an unconstitutional expansion of federal power, ruling that the Fourteenth Amendment limits only "State" actions. Other provisions of these acts were generally ignored for many decades. But the Civil Rights Act of 1871 has been revived in recent decades; the act makes it a federal crime for any person acting under the authority of state law to deprive another of rights protected by the Constitution.

**Civil Rights Act of 1957**

The first civil rights law passed by Congress since Reconstruction. It empowers the U.S. Justice Department to enforce voting rights, established the Civil Rights Division in the Justice Department, and created the Civil Rights Commission to study and report on civil rights in the United States.

**Civil Rights Act of 1964**

A comprehensive enactment designed to erase racial discrimination in both public and private sectors of American life. Major titles of the act: I. outlaws arbitrary discrimination in voter registration and expedites voting rights suits; II. bars discrimination in public accommodations, such as hotels and restaurants, that have a substantial relation to interstate commerce; III. and IV. authorizes the national government to bring suits to desegregate public facilities and schools; V. extends the life and expands the power of the Civil Rights Commission; VI. provides for withholding federal funds from programs administered in a discriminatory manner; VII. establishes the right to equality in employment opportunities.

**Civil Rights Act of 1968**

Prohibits discrimination in the advertising, financing sale, or rental of housing, based on race, religion, or national origin and, as of 1974, sex. A major amendment to the act in 1988 extended coverage to the handicapped and to families with children.

**Voting Rights Act**

Enacted by Congress in 1965 and renewed and expanded in 1970, 1975, and 1982, this law has sought to eliminate restrictions on voting that have been used to discriminate against blacks and other minority groups. Amendments in 1975 (1) required bilingual ballots in all states; (2) required approval by the Justice Department or a federal court of any election law changes in states covered by the act; (3) extended legal protection of voting rights to Hispanic Americans, Asian Americans, and Native Americans. The 1982 act provides that *intent* to discriminate need not be proven if the *results* demonstrate otherwise. Although the 1982 extension does not require racial quotas for city councils, school boards, or state legislatures, a judge may under the law redraw voting districts to give minorities maximum representation.

---

Taney's decision in this case interpreted the Constitution in terms of the *original intent* of the Founders. The ruling upheld slavery and the constitutional guarantee given slave owners for the return of slaves escaping to nonslave states.

**Emancipation and the Fourteenth Amendment**   The Civil War was the nation's bloodiest war. (Combined deaths of Union and Confederate forces

**Emancipation Proclamation**
Lincoln's 1862 Civil War declaration that all slaves residing in rebel states were free. It did not abolish all slavery; that would be done by the Thirteenth Amendment in 1865.

matched the nation's losses in World War II, even though the nation's population in 1860 was only 31 million compared to 140 million during World War II.) Very few families during the Civil War did not experience a direct loss from that conflict. As casualties mounted, northern Republicans joined abolitionists in calling for emancipating, or freeing, the slaves simply to punish the Rebels. They knew that much of the South's power depended on slave labor. Lincoln also knew that if he proclaimed the war was being fought to free the slaves, military intervention by the British on behalf of the South was less likely. Accordingly, on September 22, 1862, Lincoln issued his **Emancipation Proclamation**. Claiming his right as Commander-in-Chief of the army and navy, he declared that, as of January 1, 1863, "all persons held as slaves within any State, or designated part of a State, the people whereof shall then be in rebellion against the United States, shall be then, thenceforward, and forever free." The Emancipation Proclamation did not come about as a result of demands by the people. It was a political and military action by the president intended to help preserve the Union.

The Emancipation Proclamation freed slaves in the seceding states, and the Thirteenth Amendment in 1865 abolished slavery everywhere in the nation. But freedom did not mean civil rights. The post–Civil War Republican Congress attempted to "reconstruct" southern society. The Fourteenth Amendment, ratified in 1868, made "equal protection of the laws" a command for every state to obey. The Fifteenth Amendment, passed in 1869 and ratified in 1870, prohibited federal and state governments from abridging the right to vote "on account of race, color, or previous condition of servitude." In addition, Congress passed a series of civil rights laws in the 1860s and 1870s guaranteeing the newly freed slaves protection in the exercise of their constitutional rights.

**The Imposition of Segregation**  But political support for Reconstruction policies soon began to erode. In the Compromise of 1877, the national government agreed to end military occupation of the South, give up its efforts to rearrange Southern society, and lend tacit approval to white supremacy in that region. In return, the Southern states pledged their support to the Union, accepted national supremacy, and agreed to permit the Republican presidential candidate, Rutherford B. Hayes, to assume the presidency, although the Democratic candidate, Samuel Tilden, had received more popular votes in the disputed election of 1876.

**Jim Crow**  Second-class-citizen status conferred on blacks by southern segregation laws; derived from a nineteenth-century song-and-dance act (usually performed by a white man in blackface) that stereotyped blacks.

Segregation became the social instrument by which African Americans were "kept in their place"—that is, denied social, economic, educational, and political equality. In many states, **Jim Crow** followed them throughout life: birth in segregated hospital wards, education in segregated schools, residence in segregated housing, employment in segregated jobs, eating in segregated restaurants, and burial in segregated graveyards. Segregation was enforced by a variety of public and private sanctions, from lynch mobs to country club admission committees. But government was the principal instrument of segregation in both the Southern and the border states of the nation.

**separate but equal**  Ruling of the Supreme Court in the case of *Plessy v. Ferguson* (1896) to the effect that segregated facilities were legal as long as the facilities were equal.

**Early Court Approval of Segregation**  Segregation was imposed despite the Fourteenth Amendment's guarantee of "equal protection of the laws." In the 1896 case of *Plessy v. Ferguson*, the Supreme Court upheld state laws requiring segregation. Although segregation laws involved state action, the Court held that segregation of the races did not violate the Equal Protection Clause of the Fourteenth Amendment as long as people in each race received equal treatment. Schools and other public facilities that were **separate but equal** were constitutional, the Court ruled. The effect of this decision was to give constitutional approval to segregation; the decision was not reversed until 1954.

**The NAACP and the Legal Battle** The National Association for the Advancement of Colored People (NAACP) and its Legal Defense and Education Fund led the fight to abolish lawful segregation. As chief legal counsel to the fund, Thurgood Marshall, later to become the first African American to sit on the U.S. Supreme Court, began a long legal campaign to ensure equal protection of the law for African Americans. Initially, the NAACP's strategy focused on achieving the "equal" portion of the separate-but-equal doctrine. Segregated facilities, including public schools, were seldom "equal," even with respect to physical conditions, teachers' salaries and qualifications, curricula, and other tangible factors. In other words, southern states failed to live up even to the segregationist doctrine of separate but equal. In a series of cases, Marshall and other NAACP lawyers convinced the Supreme Court to act when segregated facilities were clearly unequal.[64]

But Marshall's goal was to prove that segregation *itself* was inherently unequal whether or not facilities were equal in all tangible respects. In other words, Marshall sought a reversal of *Plessy v. Ferguson* and a ruling that separation of the races was unconstitutional. In 1952 Marshall led a team of NAACP lawyers in a suit to admit Linda Brown to the white public schools of Topeka, Kansas, one of the few segregated school systems where white and black schools were equal with respect to buildings, curricula, teachers' salaries, and other tangible factors. In choosing the *Brown* suit, the NAACP sought to prevent the Court from simply ordering the admission of black pupils because tangible facilities were not equal and to force the Court to review the doctrine of segregation itself.

**Brown v. Board of Education of Topeka** On May 17, 1954, the Court rendered its historic decision in the case of *Brown v. Board of Education of Topeka*:

> Segregation of white and colored children in public schools has a detrimental effect upon the colored children. The impact is greater when it has the sanction of law, for the policy of separating the races is usually interpreted as denoting the inferiority of the Negro group. A sense of inferiority affects the motivation of a child to learn. Segregation with the sanction of law, therefore, has a tendency to retard the educational and mental development of Negro children and to deprive them of some of the benefits they would receive in a racially integrated school system. Whatever may have been the extent of psychological knowledge of the time of *Plessy v. Ferguson*, this finding is amply supported by modern authority. Any language in *Plessy v. Ferguson* contrary to this source is rejected. . . . We conclude that in the field of public education the doctrine of "separate but equal" has no place. Separate educational facilities are inherently unequal.[65]

**Enforcing Desegregation** The *Brown* ruling struck down the laws of twenty-one states as well as congressional laws segregating the schools of the District of Columbia (see Figure 12.1).[66] Such a far-reaching exercise of judicial power was bound to meet with difficulties in enforcement, and the Supreme Court was careful not to risk its own authority. It did not order immediate national desegregation but rather required state and local authorities, under the supervision of federal district courts, to proceed with "all deliberate speed" in desegregation.[67] For more than fifteen years, state and school districts in the South waged a campaign of resistance to desegregation. Delays in implementing school desegregation continued until 1969, when the Supreme Court rejected a request by Mississippi officials for further delay, declaring that all school districts were obligated to end their dual school systems "at once" and "now and hereafter" to operate only integrated schools.[68] The Court was careful to note, however, that racial imbalance in schools is not itself grounds for ordering these remedies unless it is also shown that some present or past governmental action contributed to the imbalance.

**NAACP Legal Defense Fund**
Founded in 1940 by Thurgood Marshall to provide legal assistance to poor African Americans. Originally affiliated with the NAACP; now a separate organization.
*www.naacpldf.org*

**Figure 12.1**
Segregation Laws in the
United States in 1954

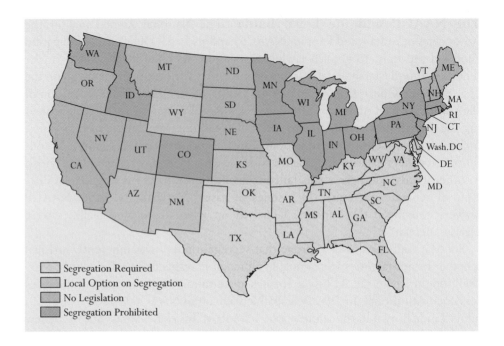

De Facto Segregation    However, in the absence of any past or present governmental actions contributing to racial imbalance, states and school districts are not required by the Fourteenth Amendment to integrate their schools. For example, where central-city schools are predominantly black and suburban schools are predominantly white owing to residential patterns, cross-district busing is not required unless some official action brought about these racial imbalances. Thus in 1974 the Supreme Court threw out a lower federal court order for massive busing of students between Detroit and fifty-two suburban school districts.[69] Although Detroit city schools were 70 percent black and the suburban schools almost all white, none of the area school districts segregated students within their own boundaries. This important decision means that largely black central cities surrounded by largely white suburbs will remain segregated in practice because there are not enough white students living within the city boundaries to achieve integration.

**de facto segregation** Racial imbalances not directly caused by official actions but rather by residential patterns.

De facto segregation is more common in the northern metropolitan areas than in the South. The states with the largest percentages of African American students attending schools that have 90 to 100 percent minority enrollments are Illinois, Michigan, New York, and New Jersey. The persistence of de facto segregation, together with a renewed interest in the quality of education, has caused many civil rights organizations to focus their attention on improving the quality of schools in urban areas rather than trying to desegregate these schools.

## The Civil Rights Acts

The early goal of the civil rights movement was to eliminate discrimination and segregation practiced by *governments*, particularly states and school districts. When the civil rights movement turned to *private* discrimination—discrimination practiced by private owners of restaurants, hotels, motels, and stores; private employers, landlords, and real estate agents; and others who were not government officials—it had to take its fight to the Congress. The Constitution does not govern the activities of private individuals. Only Congress at the national level could outlaw discrimination in the private sector. Yet prior to 1964, Congress had been

**The King Center**
Biography of M. L. K. Jr., together with news and information from Atlanta King Center.
*http://thekingcenter.com*

content to let the courts struggle with the question of civil rights. New political tactics and organizations were required to put the issue of equality on the agenda of Congress.

**Martin Luther King Jr. and Nonviolent Direct Action**   Leadership in the struggle to eliminate discrimination and segregation from private life was provided by a young African American minister, Martin Luther King Jr. (see *People in Politics:* "Martin Luther King Jr., 'I Have a Dream' "). Under King, the civil rights movement developed and refined political techniques for use by American minorities, including **nonviolent direct action**. Nonviolent direct action is a form of protest that involves breaking "unjust" laws in an open, "loving," nonviolent fashion. The purpose of nonviolent direct action is to call attention—to "bear witness"—to the existence of injustice. In the words of Martin Luther King Jr., such civil disobedience "seeks to dramatize the issue so that it can no longer be ignored"[70] (see also *A Conflicting View:* "Sometimes It's Right to Disobey the Law" in Chapter 1).

King formed the Southern Christian Leadership Conference (SCLC) in 1957 to develop and direct the growing nonviolent direct action movement. During the next few years, the SCLC overshadowed the older NAACP in leading the fight against segregation. Where the NAACP had developed its strategy of court litigation to combat discrimination by *governments*, now the SCLC developed nonviolent direct action tactics to build widespread popular support and to pressure Congress to outlaw discrimination by *private businesses*.

The year 1963 was perhaps the most important for nonviolent direct action. The SCLC focused its efforts in Birmingham, Alabama, where King led thousands of marchers in a series of orderly and peaceful demonstrations. When police attacked the marchers with fire hoses, dogs, and cattle prods—in full view of national television cameras—millions of viewers around the country came to understand the injustices of segregation. The Birmingham action set off demonstrations in many parts of the country. The theme remained one of nonviolence, and it was usually whites rather than blacks who resorted to violence in these demonstrations. Responsible black leaders remained in control of the movement and won widespread support from the white community.

The culmination of King's nonviolent philosophy was a huge yet orderly march on Washington, D.C., held on August 28, 1963. More than 200,000 blacks and whites participated in the march, which was endorsed by many civic leaders, religious groups, and political figures. The march ended at the Lincoln Memorial, where Martin Luther King Jr. delivered his most eloquent appeal, entitled "I Have a Dream." Congress passed the Civil Rights Act of 1964 by better than a two-thirds favorable vote in both houses; it won the overwhelming support of both Republican and Democratic members of Congress.

**The Civil Rights Act of 1964**   Signed into law on July 4, 1964, the Civil Rights Act of 1964 ranks with the Emancipation Proclamation, the Fourteenth Amendment, and the *Brown* case as one of the most important steps toward full equality for all minorities, including African Americans. Among its most important provisions are the following:

*Title II:* It is unlawful to discriminate against or segregate persons on the grounds of race, color, religion, or national origin in any public accommodation, including hotels, motels, restaurants, movies, theaters, sports arenas, entertainment houses, and other places that offer to serve the public. This prohibition extends to all business establishments whose operations affect interstate commerce or whose discriminatory practices are supported by state action.

**nonviolent direct action**
Strategy used by civil rights leaders such as Martin Luther King Jr., in which protesters break "unjust" laws openly but in a "loving" fashion in order to bring the injustices of such laws to public attention.

**U.S. Department of Justice, Civil Rights Division**
Responsible for enforcement of U.S. civil rights laws. Site includes information on cases. *www.usdoj.gov/crt*

# PEOPLE IN POLITICS

## Martin Luther King Jr., "I Have a Dream"

If a man hasn't discovered something he will die for, he isn't fit to live.[a]

For Martin Luther King Jr. (1929–68), civil rights was something to die for, and before he died for the cause, he would shatter a century of Southern segregation and set a new domestic agenda for the nation's leaders. King's contributions to the development of nonviolent direct action won him international acclaim and the Nobel Peace Prize.

King's father was the pastor of one of the South's largest and most influential African American congregations, the Ebenezer Baptist Church in Atlanta, Georgia. Young Martin was educated at Morehouse College in Atlanta and received a Ph.D. in religious studies at Boston University. Shortly after beginning his career as a Baptist minister in Montgomery, Alabama, in 1955, a black woman, Rosa Parks, refused to give up her seat to whites on a Montgomery bus, setting in motion a year-long bus boycott in that city. Only twenty-six years old, King was thrust into national prominence as the leader of that boycott, which ended in the elimination of segregation on the city's buses. In 1957 King founded the Southern Christian Leadership Conference (SCLC) to provide encouragement and leadership to the growing nonviolent protest movement against segregation.

Perhaps the most dramatic application of nonviolent direct action occurred in Birmingham, Alabama, in the spring of 1963. Thousands of African Americans, ranging from schoolchildren to senior citizens, marched in protest. Although the demonstrators conducted themselves in a nonviolent fashion, police and firefighters attacked the demonstrators with fire hoses, cattle prods, and police dogs, all in clear view of national television cameras. Thousands of demonstrators were dragged off to jail, including King. (It was at this time that King wrote his "Letter from Birmingham Jail," explaining and defending nonviolent direct action.) Pictures of police brutality flashed throughout the nation and the world, touching the consciences of many white Americans.

King was also the driving force behind the most massive application of nonviolent direct action in U.S. history: the great "March on Washington" in August 1963, during which more than 200,000 black and white marchers converged on the nation's capital. The march ended at the Lincoln Memorial, where King delivered his most eloquent appeal, entitled "I Have a Dream."

> I still have a dream. It is a dream deeply rooted in the American dream. I have a dream that one day this nation will rise up and live out the true meaning of its creed: "We hold these truths to be self-evident, that all men are created equal."[b]

It was in the wake of the March on Washington that President John F. Kennedy sent to the Congress a strong civil rights bill that would be passed after his death—the Civil Rights Act of 1964. That same year, King received the Nobel Peace Prize.

White racial violence in the early 1960s, including murders and bombings of black and white civil rights workers, shocked and disgusted many whites in both the North and the South. In 1963 Medgar Evers, the NAACP's state chair for Mississippi, was shot to death by a sniper as he entered his Jackson home. That same year, a bomb killed four young black girls attending Sunday school in Birmingham. On the evening of April 3, 1968, King spoke to a crowd in Memphis, Tennessee, in eerily prophetic terms. "I just want to do God's will. And He's allowed me to go to the mountain. And I've looked over, and I've seen the promised land. I may not get there with you. But I want you to know tonight, that we, as a people will get to the promised land. So I'm happy tonight. I'm not worried about anything. I'm not fearing any man." On the night of April 4, 1968, the world's leading exponent of nonviolence was killed by an assassin's bullet.[c]

[a]Martin Luther King Jr., speech, June 23, 1963, Detroit, Michigan.

[b]Martin Luther King Jr., "I Have a Dream" speech, August 28, 1963, at the Lincoln Memorial, Washington, D.C., printed in David J. Garrow, *Bearing the Cross: Martin Luther King, Jr., and the Southern Christian Leadership Conference* (New York: Vintage Books, 1988), pp. 283–84.

[c]Martin Luther King Jr., speech, April 3, 1968, Memphis, Tennessee, ibid., p. 621.

In the civil rights march of 1963 more than 200,000 people marched peacefully on Washington, D.C., to end segregation. It was here that Martin Luther King Jr. delivered his famous "I Have a Dream" speech.

*Title VI:* Each federal department and agency is to take action to end discrimination in all programs or activities receiving federal financial assistance in any form. This action may include termination of financial assistance to persistently discriminatory agencies.

*Title VII:* It is unlawful for any employer or labor union to discriminate against any individual in any fashion in employment because of the individual's race, color, religion, sex, or national origin. The Equal Employment Opportunity Commission is established to enforce this provision by investigation, conference, conciliation, persuasion, and, if need be, civil action in federal court.

## Affirmative Action: Opportunity versus Results

Although the gains of the civil rights movement were immensely important, these gains were primarily in *opportunity* rather than in *results*. The civil rights movement of the 1960s did not bring about major changes in the conditions under which most African Americans lived in the United States. Racial politics today center around the *actual* inequalities between blacks and whites in incomes, jobs, housing, health, education, and other conditions of life.

**Continuing Inequalities**  The issue of inequality today is often posed as differences in the "life chances" of blacks and whites. Figures can reveal only the bare outline of an African American's "life chances" in this society (see Table 12.4). The average income of a black family is 63 percent of the average white family's income. Over 20 percent of all black families live below the recognized poverty line, whereas less than 10 percent of white families do so. The black unemployment rate is more than twice as high as the white unemployment rate. Blacks are less likely to hold prestigious executive jobs in professional, managerial, clerical, or sales work. They do not hold many skilled craft jobs in industry but are concentrated in operative, service, and laboring positions. The civil rights movement opened up new opportunities for African Americans. But equality of *opportunity* is not the same as equality of *results*.

**U.S. Commission on Civil Rights**
National clearinghouse on information regarding discrimination because of race, color, religion, sex, age, disability, or national origin. Publishes reports, findings and recommendations.
*www.usccr.gov*

**Table 12.4    Minority Life Chances**

| | **Median Income of Families** | | | | |
| | **1970** | **1975** | **1980** | **1985** | **2004** |
|---|---|---|---|---|---|
| White | $10,236 | $14,268 | $21,904 | $29,152 | $49,000 |
| Black | 6,279 | 8,779 | 12,674 | 16,786 | 30,100 |
| Hispanic | (NA) | 9,551 | 14,716 | 19,027 | 34,200 |

| | **Percentage of Persons below Poverty Level** | | | |
| | **1975** | **1980** | **1985** | **2004** |
|---|---|---|---|---|
| White | 9.7% | 10.2% | 11.4% | 8.6% |
| Black | 31.3 | 32.5 | 31.3 | 24.7 |
| Hispanic | 26.9 | 25.7 | 29.0 | 21.3 |

| | **Unemployment Rate** | | |
| | **1980** | **1985** | **2005** |
|---|---|---|---|
| White | 6.3% | 6.2% | 4.0% |
| Black | 14.3 | 15.1 | 10.5 |
| Hispanic | 10.1 | 10.5 | 6.0 |

**Education: Percentage of Persons over Twenty-Five Who Have Completed High School**

| | **1960** | **1970** | **1980** | **1990** | **2004** |
|---|---|---|---|---|---|
| White | 43% | 55% | 69% | 79% | 85% |
| Black | 20 | 31 | 51 | 66 | 80 |
| Hispanic | (NA) | 32 | 44 | 51 | 57 |

**Education: Percentage of Persons over Twenty-Five Who Have Completed College**

| | **1960** | **1970** | **1980** | **1990** | **2004** |
|---|---|---|---|---|---|
| White | 8% | 11% | 17% | 22% | 28% |
| Black | 3 | 4 | 8 | 11 | 17 |
| Hispanic | (NA) | 4 | 8 | 9 | 11 |

*Source: Statistical Abstract of the United States,* various issues; U.S. Census Bureau, *www.census/population;* Bureau of Labor Statistics, *www.bls.gov.*

**affirmative action** Any program, whether enacted by a government or by a private organization, whose goal is to overcome the results of past unequal treatment of minorities and/or women by giving members of these groups preferential treatment in admissions, hiring, promotions, or other aspects of life.

**Policy Choices**    What public policies should be pursued to achieve equality in America? Is it sufficient that government eliminate discrimination, guarantee equality of opportunity, and apply color-blind standards to both blacks and whites? Or should government take **affirmative action** to overcome the results of past unequal treatment of blacks—preferential or compensatory treatment to assist black applications for university admissions and scholarships, job hiring and promotion, and other opportunities for advancement in life? The constitutional question posed by affirmative action programs is whether or not they discriminate against whites in violation of the Equal Protection Clause of the Fourteenth Amendment. A related question is whether or not affirmative action programs discriminate against whites in violation of the Civil Rights Act of 1964, which prohibits discrimination "on account of race," not just discrimination against blacks. Clearly, these are questions for the Supreme Court to resolve.

**Table 12.5   White and Minority Income by Educational Attainment**

| | Annual Mean Income | | | | |
| --- | --- | --- | --- | --- | --- |
| | White | Black | Hispanic | Black/White Ratio | Hispanic/White Ratio |
| Professional Degree | $115,523 | $96,368 | $81,186 | 83% | 75% |
| Bachelor's Degree | 52,479 | 42,285 | 40,949 | 81 | 78 |
| High School Degree | 28,145 | 22,823 | 24,163 | 81 | 86 |
| No High School Degree | 19,264 | 16,516 | 18,981 | 86 | 98 |

*Source:* U.S. Bureau of the Census, 2005. Data for 2002.

**The Bakke Case**   In the absence of a history of racial discrimination, the Supreme Court has been willing to scrutinize affirmative action programs to ensure that they do not directly discriminate against whites. In *University of California Regents v. Bakke* (1978), the Supreme Court struck down a special admissions program for minorities at a state medical school on the grounds that it excluded a white applicant because of his race and violated his rights under the Equal Protection Clause.[71] Allan Bakke applied to the University of California Davis Medical School two consecutive years and was rejected; in both years, black applicants with significantly lower grade point averages and medical aptitude test scores were accepted through a special admissions program that reserved sixteen minority places in a class of one hundred.[72] The University of California did not deny that its admissions decisions were based on race. Instead, it argued that its racial classification was "benign," that is, designed to assist minorities. The special admissions program was designed to (1) "reduce the historical deficit of traditionally disfavored minorities in medical schools and the medical profession"; (2) "counter the effects of societal discrimination"; (3) "increase the number of physicians who will practice in communities currently underserved"; and (4) "obtain the educational benefits that flow from an ethnically diverse student body."

The Supreme Court held that these objectives were legitimate and that race and ethnic origin *may* be considered in reviewing applications to a state school without violating the Fourteenth Amendment's Equal Protection Clause. However, the Court also held that a separate admissions program for minorities with a specific quota of openings that were unavailable to white applicants *did* violate the Equal Protection Clause. The Court ordered the university to admit **Bakke** to its medical school and to eliminate the special admissions program. It recommended that California consider an admissions program developed at Harvard, which considered disadvantaged racial or ethnic background as a "plus" in an overall evaluation of an application but did not set numerical quotas or exclude any person from competing for all positions.

**Affirmative Action as a Remedy for Past Discrimination**   The Supreme Court has continued to approve of affirmative action programs where there is evidence of past discriminatory practices. In *United Steelworkers of America v. Weber* (1979), the Supreme Court approved a plan developed by a private employer and a union to reserve 50 percent of higher paying, skilled jobs for minorities. The Court held that "employers and unions in the private sector [are] free to take such race-conscious steps to eliminate manifest racial imbalances in

**Equal Employment Opportunity Commission (EEOC)** Federal EEOC site with information on what constitutes discrimination by age, disability, race, ethnicity, religion, gender; how to file a charge; and guidance for employers. *www.eeoc.gov*

***Bakke* case** U.S. Supreme Court case challenging affirmative action.

# WHAT DO YOU THINK?

## Do You Favor Affirmative Action?

Americans are divided on the issue of affirmative action. Polls reveal that whites are almost equally divided when the question is posed as general support for "affirmative action." In contrast, blacks and Hispanics are strongly supportive of affirmative action programs for racial minorities.

*Q. "Do you generally favor or oppose affirmative action programs for racial minorities?"*

|  | Favor | Oppose | Unsure |
|---|---|---|---|
| All | 49 | 43 | 8 |
| Whites | 44 | 49 | 7 |
| Blacks | 70 | 21 | 9 |
| Hispanics | 83 | 28 | 9 |

But when the question is phrased in a way that implies minority preference over merit for admission to colleges and universities, then a strong majority of whites favor admission "solely on the basis of merit." Hispanics also favor merit over racial preference, but blacks appeared to be split on the issue.

*Q. "Which comes closer to your view about evaluating students for admission into a college or university? Applicants should be admitted solely on the basis of merit, even if that results in few minority students being admitted. Or, an applicant's race and ethnic background should be considered to help promote diversity on college campuses, even if that means admitting some minority students who otherwise would not be admitted."*

|  | Solely Merit | Race/ Ethnicity | Unsure |
|---|---|---|---|
| All | 69 | 27 | 4 |
| Whites | 75 | 22 | 3 |
| Blacks | 44 | 49 | 7 |
| Hispanics | 59 | 36 | 5 |

Whites believe that black applicants to colleges and universities have the same as or a better chance of admission than white applicants, but blacks believe that white applicants have the advantage.

*Q. "If two equally qualified students, one white and one black, applied to a major U.S. college or university, who do you think would have the better chance of being accepted to the college: the white student, the black student, or would they have the same chance?"*

|  | White Student | Black Student | Same Chance | Unsure |
|---|---|---|---|---|
| All | 31 | 29 | 36 | 4 |
| Whites | 24 | 34 | 38 | 4 |
| Blacks | 67 | 5 | 24 | 4 |
| Hispanics | 44 | 14 | 38 | 4 |

*Source:* As reported in The Polling Report, *www.pollingreport.com*, July 15, 2005.

---

traditionally segregated job categories. We hold that Title VII does not prohibit such . . . affirmative action plans." According to the Court, it would be "ironic indeed" if the Civil Rights Act were used to prohibit voluntary private race-conscious efforts to overcome the past effects of discrimination.[73] In *United States v. Paradise* (1987), the Court upheld a rigid 50 percent black quota system for promotions in the Alabama Department of Safety, which had excluded blacks from the ranks of state troopers prior to 1972 and had not promoted any blacks higher than corporal prior to 1984. In a 5-to-4 decision, the majority stressed the long history of discrimination in the agency as a reason for upholding the quota system. Whatever burdens imposed on innocent parties were outweighed by the need to correct the effects of past discrimination.[74]

**Cases Questioning Affirmative Action**    However, the Supreme Court has continued to express concern about whites who are directly and adversely affected by government action solely because of their race. In *Firefighters Local*

*Union 1784 v. Stotts* (1984), the Court ruled that a city could not lay off white fire-fighters in favor of black firefighters with less seniority.[75] In *City of Richmond v. Crosen Co.* (1989), the Supreme Court held that a minority **set-aside program** in Richmond, Virginia, which mandated that 30 percent of all city construction contracts must go to "blacks, Spanish-speaking, Orientals, Indians, Eskimos, or Aleuts," violated the Equal Protection Clause of the Fourteenth Amendment.[76]

Moreover, the Court has held that racial classifications in law must be subject to "**strict scrutiny.**" This means that race-based actions by government—any disparate treatment of the races by federal, state, or local public agencies—must be found necessary to remedy past proven discrimination, or to further clearly identified, legitimate and "compelling" government interests. Moreover, race-based actions must be "narrowly tailored" and "least restrictive" so as to minimize adverse effects on rights of other individuals. In striking down a federal construction contract set-aside program for small businesses owned by racial minorities, the Court expressed skepticism about governmental racial classifications: "There is simply no way of determining what classifications are 'benign' and 'remedial' and what classifications are in fact motivated by illegitimate notions of racial inferiority or simple racial politics."[77]

### Affirmative Action and "Diversity" in Higher Education

Most colleges and universities in the United States—public as well as private—identify "diversity," a term that refers to racial and ethnic representation in the student body and faculty, as an institutional goal.

University administrators argue that students benefit when they interact with others from different cultural heritages. "Students must be engaged with diverse peers if we expect learning and development to occur," and the existence of a racially and ethnically diverse student body is "a necessary condition" for such engagement. There is some evidence that students admitted under policies designed to increase diversity do well in their postcollege careers. And there are claims that racial and ethnic diversity on the campus improve students' "self-evaluation," "social-historical thinking," and "intellectual engagement."

But despite numerous efforts to develop scientific evidence that racial or ethnic diversity on the campus improves learning, no definitive conclusions have emerged. Educational research on this topic is clouded by political and ideological conflict. There is no evidence that racial diversity does in fact promote the expression of ideas on the campus or change perspectives or viewpoints of students.

### Diversity and Affirmative Action

Even if diversity provides educational benefits, the question arises as to how to achieve it. Diversity is closely linked to affirmative action programs on campuses throughout the nation. When affirmative action programs are designed as special efforts to recruit and encourage qualified minority students to attend college, they enjoy widespread public support. But when affirmative action programs include preferences for minority applicants over equally or better qualified nonminorities, public support falters and constitutional questions arise.

### Diversity as a Constitutional Question

The U.S. Supreme Court has held that the Equal Protection Clause of the Fourteenth Amendment requires that racial classifications be subject to "strict scrutiny." This means that race-based actions by governments—any disparate treatment of the racial or ethnic group by federal, state, or local public agencies, including colleges and universities—must be found necessary to advance a "compelling government interest" and must be "narrowly tailored" to further that interest.[78]

**set-aside program** Program in which a specified number or percentage of contracts must go to designated minorities.

**strict scrutiny** Supreme Court holding that race-based actions by governments can be done only to remedy past discrimination or to further a "compelling" interest and must be "narrowly tailored" to minimize effects on the rights of others.

The U.S. Supreme Court held in 2003 that diversity may be a compelling government interest because it "promotes cross-racial understanding, helps to break down racial stereotypes, and enables [students] to better understand persons of different races." This opinion was written by Justice Sandra Day O'Connor in a case involving the University of Michigan Law School's affirmative action program. In a 5–4 decision, O'Connor, writing for the majority, said the Constitution "does not prohibit the law school's narrowly tailored use of race in admissions decisions to further a compelling interest in obtaining the educational benefits that flow from a diverse student body."[79]

However, in a case involving the University of Michigan's affirmative action program for *undergraduate admissions*, the Supreme Court held that the admissions policy was "not narrowly tailored to achieve respondents' asserted interest in diversity" and therefore violated the Equal Protection Clause of the Fourteenth Amendment. The Court again recognized that diversity may be a compelling interest, but *rejected an affirmative action plan that made race the decisive factor* for even minimally qualified minority applicants. Yet the Supreme Court restated its support for limited affirmative action programs that use race as a "plus" factor, the position the court has held since the *Bakke* case in 1978.[80]

**Race-Neutral Approaches to Diversity**    There is a variety of ways in which diversity can be achieved without using racial preferences in the admission of students. The U.S. Department of Education recommends (1) preferences based on socioeconomic status; (2) recruitment outreach efforts targeted at students from traditionally low-performing schools; and (3) admission plans for students who finish at the top of their high school classes without regard to SAT or ACT scores.[81] California, Texas, and Florida currently give preference to students who stand at or near the top of their class in each of the states' high schools. All three states officially abandoned racial preferences. Yet currently all three states enroll roughly the same numbers of minorities in their colleges and universities that they did before abandoning racial preferences.

**The Absence of a Clear Constitutional Principle**    The Supreme Court's decisions on affirmative action have not yet established a clear and coherent interpretation of the Constitution. No clear rule of law or constitutional principle tells us exactly what is permissible and what is prohibited in the way of racially conscious laws and practices. Nevertheless, over time some general tendencies in Supreme Court policy can be identified. Affirmative action programs are *more likely to be found constitutional* when

- They are adopted in response to a past proven history of discrimination.

- They do not absolutely bar whites or ban them from competing or participating.

- They serve a clearly identified, legitimate, and "compelling governmental interest."

- They are "narrowly tailored" to achieve the government's compelling interest and represent the "least restrictive" means of doing so.

It is important to note that the Supreme Court has never adopted the color-blind doctrine, first espoused by Justice Harlan in his *dissent* from *Plessy v. Ferguson*, that "Our Constitution is color-blind, and neither knows nor tolerates classes among the citizens." If the Equal Protection Clause required the laws of the United States and the states to be truly color-blind, then no racial guidelines, goals, or quotas would be tolerated. Occasionally this view has been expressed in recent minority dissents (see *A Conflicting View:* "The Constitution Should Be Color-Blind").

**FIRE: Foundation for Equal Rights in Education**
Advocacy organization defending individual rights on campus and opposing racial preferences.
*www.thefire.org*

## A CONFLICTING VIEW

### The Constitution Should Be Color-Blind

In 1896 a single voice spoke out against *all* racial classifications—Supreme Court Justice John Harlan opposing segregation: "Our Constitution is color-blind and neither knows nor tolerates classes among the citizens." He was *dissenting* from the Supreme Court's majority opinion in the infamous case of *Plessy v. Ferguson,* which approved the segregationist doctrine of "separate but equal." Unfortunately, the ideal of a color-blind society remains almost as elusive today as it was more than a hundred years ago.

Martin Luther King Jr. had a dream that "our children will one day live in a nation where they will not be judged by the color of their skin but by the content of their character." Can that dream be made a reality?

Over time, the civil rights movement shifted its focus from *individual rights* to *group benefits.* Affirmative action programs classify people by group membership, thereby challenging a belief widely held in the United States—that people be judged on individual attributes such as character and achievement, rather than on race or gender. Racial and gender preferences are currently encountered in hiring and promotion practices in private and public employment and in college and university admissions, scholarships, and faculty recruitment.

Affirmative action programs divide Americans into two classes—those who enjoy legally mandated preferential treatment and those who do not. Majority support for civil rights laws is weakening under growing resentment among those who are denied preferential treatment.

Some early supporters of affirmative action have come to view race-conscious programs as no longer necessary. They argue that disadvantages in society today are based more on class than on race. If preferences are to be granted at all, in their view, they should be based on economic disadvantage, not race.

Misgivings also have been expressed by a few African American scholars about the unfair stigmatizing of the supposed beneficiaries of affirmative action—a resulting negative stereotyping of blacks as unable to advance on merit alone. Race-conscious government policies, they argue, have done more harm than good. African American economist Glenn Loury claims that proponents of affirmative action have an inferiority complex: "When blacks say we have to have affirmative action, please don't take it away from us, it's almost like saying, you're right, we can't compete on merit. But I know that we can compete." Conservative columnist William Bennett says that "toxic" race relations, aggravated by affirmative action, have led to damaging forms of new segregation: "Affirmative action has not brought us what we want—a color-blind society. It has brought us an extremely color-conscious society. In our universities we have separate dorms, separate social centers. What's next—water fountains? That's not good and everybody knows it."

Many argue that affirmative action has caused the civil rights movement to lose widespread public support and instead become contentious and divisive. In fact, civil rights has become such a hot topic that most elected officials now prefer to avoid it. As one anonymous member of Congress put it, "The problem is political correctness—you can't talk openly."

*Source:* Quotations reported in *Newsweek,* February 13, 1996.

## Hispanics in America

Hispanics—a term the U.S. Census Bureau uses to refer to Mexican Americans, Puerto Ricans, Cubans, and others of Spanish-speaking ancestry and culture—are now the nation's largest minority (see Table 12.6). The largest Hispanic subgroup is Mexican Americans. Some are descendants of citizens who lived in the Mexican territory annexed to the United States in 1848, but most have come to the United States in accelerating numbers in recent years. The largest Mexican American populations are found in Texas, Arizona, New Mexico, and California. Puerto Ricans constitute the second largest Hispanic subgroup. Many still retain ties to the commonwealth and move back and forth from Puerto Rico to New York. Cubans make up the third largest subgroup; most have fled from Fidel Castro's Cuba and live mainly in the Miami metropolitan area. Each of these Hispanic groups has encountered a different experience in American life. Indeed,

**Table 12.6    Minorities in America in 2010**

|  | Number (000) | Percent of Population (%) |
|---|---|---|
| Hispanics | 47,756 | 15.5 |
| African Americans | 40,454 | 13.1 |
| Asians | 14,241 | 4.6 |
| All other races[a] | 9,246 | 3.0 |
| Total Population | 308,936 | 100[b] |

[a]Includes American Indian and Alaska Native, Pacific Islanders, and persons identified as being of two or more races.

[b]White alone, not Hispanic = 65.1%.

*Source:* U.S. Bureau of the Census, estimates as of March 18, 2004.

some evidence indicates that these groups identify themselves separately, rather than as Hispanics.[82]

If all Hispanics are grouped together for statistical comparisons, their median family income level is well below that of whites (see Table 12.4). Hispanic poverty and unemployment rates are also higher than those of whites. The percentage of Hispanics completing high school and college education is well below that of both whites and blacks, suggesting language or other cultural obstacles in education. Yet within these overall racial comparisons, there are wide disparities among subgroups as well as among individuals.

**Mexican Americans**    The Mexican American population in the southwestern United States is growing very rapidly; it doubled in size between 1980 and 2000. For many years, agricultural business encouraged immigration of Mexican farm laborers willing to endure harsh conditions for low pay. Many others came to the United States as *indocumentados*—undocumented, or illegal, aliens. In the Immigration Reform Act of 1986 Congress offered amnesty to all undocumented workers who had entered the United States prior to 1982.

Economic conditions in Mexico and elsewhere in Central America continue to fuel immigration, legal and illegal, to the United States. But with lower educational levels, average incomes of Mexican American families in the United States are lower and the poverty rate is higher than the general population. Although Mexican Americans have served as governors of Arizona and New Mexico and have won election to the U.S. Congress, their political power does not yet match their population percentages. Mexican American voter turnout is lower than other ethnic groups, perhaps because many are resident aliens or illegal immigrants not eligible to vote, or perhaps because of cultural factors that discourage political participation.[83]

**Puerto Ricans**    Residents of Puerto Rico are American citizens because Puerto Rico is a commonwealth of the United States. Puerto Rico's commonwealth government resembles that of a state, with a constitution and elected governor and legislature, but the island has no voting members of the U.S. Congress and no electoral votes for president. As citizens, Puerto Ricans can move anywhere in the United States; many have immigrated to New York City.

Median family income in Puerto Rico is higher than anywhere else in the Caribbean, but only half that of the poorest state in the United States. Puerto

**Mexican American Legal Defense League**
Advocacy and litigation on behalf of Latinos, with information on cases dealing with immigration rights.
*www.maldef.org*

## ACROSS THE USA

### Hispanic Populations

The Hispanic population of the United States is concentrated in relatively few states, notably California, Arizona, New Mexico, Texas, and Florida. These are states in which Hispanics exceed 10 percent of the population. In addition Hispanics are 5 to 10 percent of the populations of New York, Massachusetts, Rhode Island, Connecticut, New Jersey, Illinois, Hawaii, Kansas, Colorado, Utah, Wyoming, Nevada, and Washington. Among the states, only Florida, where Cubans predominate in the Hispanic population, regularly votes Republican. In all other states, Hispanics tend to vote Democratic. Texas Hispanics split their vote almost evenly in the 2004 presidential election between Texan George Bush and Massachusetts Senator John Kerry.

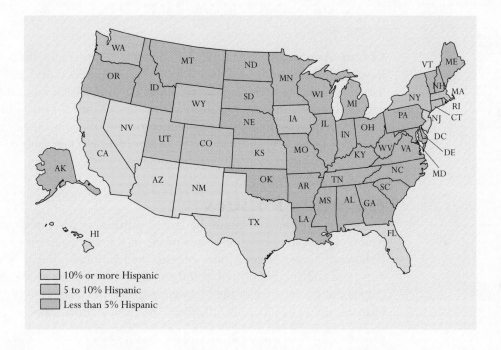

- 10% or more Hispanic
- 5 to 10% Hispanic
- Less than 5% Hispanic

Ricans have not fared as well economically as other Hispanic groups within the United States: Puerto Ricans have lower median family incomes and higher poverty percentages, in part perhaps because of lower workforce participation. One explanation centers on the history of access to federal welfare programs on the island and the resulting social dependency it fostered among some Puerto Rican families.[84]

Puerto Ricans have long debated whether to remain a commonwealth of the United States, apply for statehood, or seek complete independence from the United States. As citizens of a commonwealth, Puerto Ricans pay no U.S. income tax (although their local taxes are substantial) while receiving all the benefits that U.S. citizens are entitled to—Social Security, welfare assistance, food stamps, Medicaid, Medicare, and so forth. If Puerto Rico chose to become a state, its voters could participate in presidential and congressional elections, but its taxpayers would not enjoy the same favorable cost-benefit ratio they enjoy under commonwealth status. Some Puerto Ricans also fear that statehood would dilute the island's cultural identity and force English on them as the national language.

As a state, Puerto Rico would have two U.S. senators and perhaps six U.S. representatives. The island's majority party, the Popular Democratic Party, is closely identified with the Democratic Party, so most of these new members would likely be Democrats. But the island's New Progressive Party, identified with the Republican Party, supports statehood, and many GOP leaders believe their party should appeal to Hispanic voters. If Puerto Ricans were to choose independence, a new constitution for the Republic of Puerto Rico would be drawn up by the islanders themselves.

Only Congress can admit a new state, but Congress is unlikely to act without the full support of Puerto Ricans themselves. Several nonbinding referenda votes have been held in Puerto Rico over the years, the most recent in 1998. Opinion today appears to be closely divided, with commonwealth status edging out statehood by a small margin; independence has never received more than one percent of the vote.

**Cuban Americans**   Many Cuban Americans, especially those in the early waves of refugees from Castro's revolution in 1959, were skilled professionals and businesspeople, and they rapidly set about building Miami into a thriving economy. Although Cuban Americans are the smallest of the Hispanic subgroups, today they are better educated and enjoy higher incomes than the others. They are well organized politically, and they have succeeded in electing Cuban Americans to local office in Florida and to the U.S. Congress.

## Hispanic Politics

Mexican Americans constitute the largest portion, nearly three-quarters, of the nation's Hispanic population. Most reside in the southwestern United States—California, Texas, Arizona, New Mexico, and Colorado. Puerto Ricans in New York, and Cubans and other Central and South Americans in Florida, constitute only about one-quarter of the Hispanic population. Thus, generalizations about Hispanic politics are heavily influenced by Mexican Americans.

**Organizing for Political Activity**   For many decades American agriculture encouraged Mexican American immigration, both legal and illegal, to labor in fields as *braceros*. Most of these migrant farmworkers lived and worked under very difficult conditions; they were paid less than minimum wages for backbreaking labor. Farmworkers were not covered by the federal National Labor Relations Act and therefore not protected in the right to organize labor unions. But civil rights activity among Hispanics, especially among farm workers, grew during the 1960s under the leadership of Cesar Chavez and his United Farm Workers union. Chavez organized a national boycott of grapes from California vineyards that refused to recognize the union or improve conditions. *La Raza*, as the movement was called, finally ended in a union contract with the growers and later a California law protecting the right of farmworkers to organize unions and bargain collectively with their employers. More important, the movement galvanized Mexican Americans throughout the Southwest to engage in political activity.[85]

However, inasmuch as many Mexican American immigrants were noncitizens, and many were *indocumentados* (undocumented residents of the United States), the voting strength of Mexican Americans never matched their numbers in the population. The Immigration Reform and Control Act of 1986 granted amnesty to illegal aliens living in the United States in 1982. But the same act also imposed penalties on employers who hired illegal aliens. The effect of these threatened penalties on many employers was to make them wary of hiring Hispanics, especially as

La Raza National Council of La Raza
Issue positions, programs, news, dedicated to improving life experiences of Hispanic Americans. *www.nclr.org*

permanent employees. At the same time, industries in need of cheap labor—agriculture, health and hospitals, restaurants, clothing manufacturers, and so on—continued to encourage legal and illegal immigration to fill minimum and even subminimum-wage-level jobs with few if any benefits.

**Hispanic Political Power**    Most Hispanics today believe that they confront less prejudice and discrimination than their parents. Nonetheless, in 1994 California voters approved a referendum, Proposition 187, that would have barred welfare and other benefits to persons living in the state illegally. Most Hispanics opposed the measure, believing that it was motivated by prejudice. A federal court later declared major portions of Proposition 187 unconstitutional. And the U.S. Supreme Court has held that a state may not bar the children of illegal immigrants from attending public schools.[86]

Mexican American voter turnout remains weak. Various explanations have been advanced for the lower voter participation of Mexican Americans. Language barriers may still discourage some voters, even though ballots in many states are now available in Spanish. Illegal immigrants, of course, cannot vote. Lower education and income levels are also associated with lower voter turnout. Nonetheless, Hispanic voting is on the increase throughout the nation, and both Democratic and Republican candidates are increasingly aware of the importance of the Hispanic vote.

Overall, most Hispanics identify with the Democratic Party (see Table 12.7). Mexican Americans in the Southwestern states and Puerto Ricans in New York

### Table 12.7    Hispanic Politics

| | Total | Mexican | Puerto Rican | Cuban | Other |
|---|---|---|---|---|---|
| "In politics today do you consider yourself a Republican, a Democrat, an Independent, or something else?" | | | | | |
| Democrat | 37% | 33% | 52% | 29% | 39% |
| Republican | 16 | 15 | 17 | 34 | 12 |
| Independent | 33 | 37 | 17 | 27 | 35 |
| "Do you think abortion should be legal in all cases, illegal in most cases, or illegal in all cases?" | | | | | |
| Legal | 40 | 36 | 60 | 49 | 32 |
| Illegal | 58 | 61 | 39 | 49 | 66 |
| "Do you think the government should provide health insurance for Americans without insurance, or is this something the government should not do?" | | | | | |
| Should | 83 | 83 | 84 | 87 | 86 |
| Should not | 14 | 14 | 15 | 11 | 11 |
| "Should colleges sometimes take a student's racial and ethnic background into consideration when they decide which students to admit, or should they select students without considering their racial or ethnic backgrounds? | | | | | |
| Consider | 22 | 21 | 17 | 17 | 21 |
| Don't consider | 75 | 76 | 78 | 82 | 76 |
| "Do you favor or oppose offering government financial aid or 'vouchers' to pay parents some of the cost of sending their children to private and parochial schools? | | | | | |
| Favor | 40 | 40 | 46 | 49 | 37 |
| Oppose | 18 | 16 | 12 | 22 | 23 |

*Source:* Copyright © *Public Perspective,* a publication of the Roper Center for Public Opinion Research, University of Connecticut, Storrs. Reprinted by permission of Roper Center for Public Opinion Research.

## UP CLOSE

# Republicans and the Latino Vote

Winning the Hispanic vote is increasingly important for the Republican Party. With African American voters regularly giving Democratic candidates 90 percent or more of their vote, the Republican Party cannot afford to lose the vote of what is now the nation's largest minority. It is true that so far Hispanics voters make up only 6 to 8 percent of all voters in presidential elections, even though Hispanics constitute over 12 percent of the nation's population. (African Americans constitute about 12 percent of the population and comprise about 11 percent of the voters on Election Day.) But over time, the growth of the Hispanic population, together with an increase in voter education and participation, will become crucial to Republican victories.

### Bush's Efforts

President George W. Bush has been particularly committed to winning the hearts of Latinos for the GOP. The bilingual president won substantial numbers of Hispanic voters while serving as governor of Texas. In 2000, against democrat Al Gore, Bush won about 36 percent of Hispanic voters nationwide, and in 2004, against Democrat John Kerry, Bush increased that margin to about 42 percent.

### Immigration

President Bush has long supported a new immigration initiative that would allow temporary "guest" workers to cross the border and work in the United States for up to six years. He has also proposed that illegal immigrants be allowed to apply for work visas good for six years, after which they could apply for permanent residency if their taxes are paid and they have no criminal records. The Bush proposal has met with substantial opposition within his own party's Congress members, many of whom oppose giving legal status to people who broke the law to enter the United States. And after 9/11 any effort to relax immigration standards appeared doomed.

### Issues Cited by Latino Voters in 2004

But interestingly, immigration reform appears to be only a modest concern to Hispanic voters. A national survey of Hispanic voters in 2004 reported the following issues of greatest concern to them:

| | |
|---|---|
| Education | 54% |
| Economy/Jobs | 51 |
| Health Care | 51 |
| War on Terror | 45 |
| Crime | 40 |
| Social Security | 39 |
| Moral Values | 31 |
| Taxes | 33 |
| Immigration | 27 |

The issues of concern to Hispanic voters do not appear to be much different from those of non-Hispanic voters.

*Source:* Pew Hispanic Center, Kaiser Family Foundation Survey of Latinos 2004. *www.cis.org/articles*

---

have traditionally supported Democratic candidates, whereas the strong anticommunist heritage among Cuban Americans has fostered a Republican voting tradition in Florida. Hispanics are generally conservative on social issues (opposing abortion, opposing racial preferences, favoring government vouchers to pay parochial school tuitions) but liberal on economic issues (favoring government provision of health insurance for all, favoring a larger federal government with many services). (See *Up Close:* "Republicans and the Latino Vote".)

— Think Again —

Should gender equality receive the same level of legal protection as racial equality?

# Gender Equality and the Fourteenth Amendment

The historical context of the Fourteenth Amendment implies its intent to guarantee equality for newly freed slaves, but the wording of its Equal Protection Clause applies to "any person." Thus the text of the Fourteenth Amendment could be interpreted to bar any gender differences in the law, in the fashion of the once proposed yet never ratified Equal Rights Amendment. But the Supreme Court has not interpreted the Equal Protection Clause to give the same level of protection to gender equality as to racial equality. Indeed, in 1873 the Supreme Court specifically rejected arguments that this clause applied to women. The Court once upheld a state law banning women from practicing law, arguing that "the natural and proper timidity and delicacy which belongs to the female sex evidently unfits it for many of the occupations of civil life. . . . The paramount destiny and mission of women are to fulfill the noble and benign offices of wife and mother. This is the law of the Creator."[87]

**Early Feminist Politics**    The earliest active feminist organizations grew out of the pre–Civil War antislavery movement. There the first generation of feminists—including Lucretia Mott, Elizabeth Cady Stanton, Lucy Stone, and Susan B. Anthony—learned to organize, hold public meetings, and conduct petition campaigns. After the Civil War, women were successful in changing many state laws that abridged the property rights of married women and otherwise treated them as "chattel" (property) of their husbands. By the early 1900s activists were also successful in winning some protections for women in the workplace, including state laws limiting women's hours of work, working conditions, and physical demands. At the time, these laws were regarded as "progressive."

The most successful feminist efforts of the 1800s centered on protection of women in families. The perceived threats to women's well-being were their husbands' drinking, gambling, and consorting with prostitutes. Women led the Anti-Saloon League, succeeded in outlawing gambling and prostitution in every state except Nevada, and provided the major source of moral support for the Eighteenth Amendment (Prohibition).

In the early twentieth century, the feminist movement concentrated on women's suffrage—the drive to guarantee women the right to vote. The early suffragists employed mass demonstrations, parades, picketing, and occasional disruption and civil disobedience—tactics similar to those of the civil rights movement of the 1960s. The culmination of their efforts was the 1920 passage of the Nineteenth Amendment to the Constitution: "The right of citizens of the United States to vote shall not be denied or abridged by the United States or by any State on account of sex." The suffrage movement spawned the League of Women Voters; in addition to women's right to vote, the league has sought protection of women in industry, child welfare laws, and honest election practices.

**Judicial Scrutiny of Gender Classifications**    In the 1970s, the Supreme Court became responsive to arguments that sex discrimination might violate the Equal Protection Clause of the Fourteenth Amendment. In *Reed v. Reed* (1971), it ruled that sexual classifications in the law "must be reasonable and not arbitrary, and must rest on some ground of difference having fair and substantial relation to . . . important governmental objectives."[88] This is a much more relaxed level of scrutiny than the Supreme Court gives to racial classification in the law.

The Supreme Court continues to wrestle with the question of whether some gender differences can be recognized in law. The question is most evident in laws dealing with sexual activity and reproduction. The Court has upheld statutory rape laws that make it a crime for an adult male to have sexual intercourse with a female under the age of eighteen, regardless of her consent. "We need not to be medical doctors to discern that young men and young women are not similarly situated with respect to the problems and the risks of sexual intercourse. Only women may become pregnant, and they suffer disproportionately the profound physical, emotional and psychological consequences of sexual activity."[89]

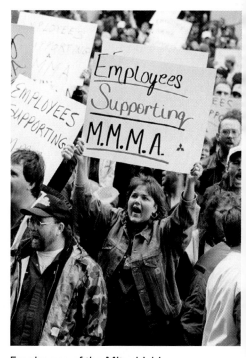

Employees of the Mitsubishi automobile plant in Normal, Illinois, demonstrated outside the offices of the Equal Employment Opportunity Commission in Chicago in April 1996 in support of the company after it became the target of a sexual harassment investigation. The company provided transportation to the demonstration and paid the workers for the day.

**National Organization for Women (NOW)**
Advocacy organization for feminist activists working to protect abortion rights, end discrimination against women, and "eradicate racism, sexism, and homophobia." *www.now.org*

**Title IX** A provision in the Federal Education Act forbidding discrimination against women in college athletic programs.

**Equal Rights Amendment (ERA)**
A proposed constitutional amendment, passed by Congress but never ratified by three-quarters of the states, that would have explicitly guaranteed equal rights for women.

Women's participation in military service, particularly combat, raises even more controversial questions regarding permissible gender classifications. The Supreme Court appears to have bowed out of this particular controversy. In upholding Congress's draft registration law for men only, the Court ruled that "the constitutional power of Congress to raise and support armies and to make all laws necessary and proper to that end is broad and sweeping."[91] Congress and the Defense Department are responsible for determining assignments for women in the military. Women have won assignments to air and naval combat units but remain excluded from combat infantry, armor, artillery, special forces, and submarine duty.

**Title IX and Women's Athletics**  Perhaps no other gender-related law has had more impact on the nation's colleges and universities than **Title IX**, part of the Education Act Amendments of 1972. Title IX prohibits discrimination against women in college and university athletic programs. But what exactly does this mean? It was not until 1978 that the federal government attempted to set forth regulations concerning intercollegiate athletics. Among the stated goals of these regulations were (1) financial support substantially proportionate to the number of male and female athletes; (2) the provision of opportunities to participate in athletics for men and women substantially proportionate to their enrollments; (3) or, where these conditions were not met, a continuing practice of program expansion for female athletes. Football was recognized as unique, because it produces the revenues needed to maintain the entire athletic program of most colleges and universities, so football programs could continue to outspend women's athletics.

The results of Title IX have been impressive. In 2005 there were more than 150,000 female student athletes, a dramatic increase over the 30,000 when the law was passed. Women's teams in the National Collegiate Athletic Association nearly doubled from about 4,800 to 8,400.

But to maintain the proportionality required by the law, the number of men's sports at many universities have failed to expand and indeed many have been cut, especially nonrevenue producing sports such as wrestling. Critics of the law have urged that it be amended to account for perceived differences in interest in athletics between male and female college students.

**The Equal Rights Amendment**  The proposed **Equal Rights Amendment** to the U.S. Constitution, passed by Congress in 1972 but never ratified by the states, was worded very broadly: "Equality of rights under the law shall not be denied or abridged by the United States or any State on account of sex." Had it been ratified by the necessary thirty-eight states, it would have eliminated most, if not all, gender differences in the law. Without the ERA, many important guarantees of equality for women rest on laws of Congress rather than on the Constitution.

## Gender Equality in the Economy

As cultural views of women's roles in society have changed and economic pressures on family budgets have increased, women's participation in the labor force has risen. The gap between women's and men's participation in the nation's workforce is closing over time.[90] With the movement of women into the workforce, feminist political activity has shifted toward economic concerns—gender equality in education, employment, pay, promotion, and credit.

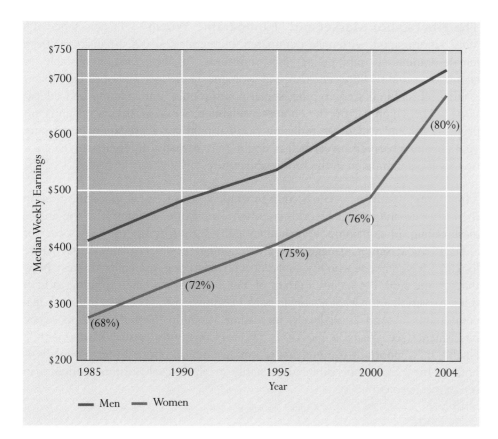

**Figure 12.2** The Earnings Gap: Median Weekly Earnings of Men and Women

The continuing "earnings gap" between men and women reflects a division in the labor market between traditionally male higher paying occupations and traditionally female lower paying positions.

*Note:* Figures in parentheses indicate the ratio of women's to men's median weekly earnings.

*Source:* Bureau of Labor Statistics, *www.bls.gov.*

**Gender Equality in Civil Rights Laws**    Title VII of the Civil Rights Act of 1964 prevents sexual (as well as racial) discrimination in hiring, pay, and promotions. The Equal Employment Opportunity Commission, the federal agency charged with eliminating discrimination in employment, has established guidelines barring stereotyped classifications of "men's jobs" and "women's jobs." The courts have repeatedly struck down state laws and employer practices that differentiate between men and women in hours, pay, retirement age, and so forth.

The Federal Equal Credit Opportunity Act of 1974 prohibits sex discrimination in credit transactions. Federal law prevents banks, credit unions, savings and loan associations, retail stores, and credit card companies from denying credit because of sex or marital status. However, these businesses may still deny credit for a poor or nonexistent credit rating, and some women who have always maintained accounts in their husband's name may still face credit problems if they apply in their own name.

**The Earnings Gap**    Despite protections under federal laws, women continue to earn substantially less than men do. Today women, on average, earn about 76 percent of what men do (see Figure 12.2). This earnings gap has been closing very slowly: In 1985 women earned an average 68 percent of men's earnings. The earnings gap is not primarily a product of **direct discrimination**; women in the same job with the same skills, qualifications, experience, and work record are not generally paid less than men. Such direct discrimination has been illegal since the Civil Rights Act of 1964. Rather, the earnings gap is primarily a product of a division in the labor market between traditionally male and female jobs, with lower salaries paid in traditionally female occupations.

**direct discrimination** Now illegal practice of differential pay for men versus women even when those individuals have equal qualifications and perform the same job.

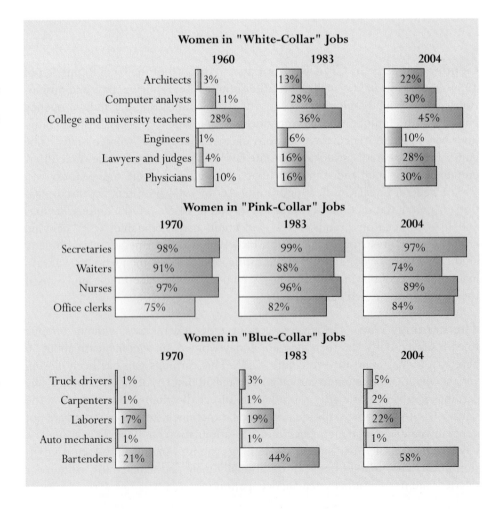

**Feminist.Com**
Web site promoting women's business development, with information and advice.
*www.feminist.com*

**glass ceiling** *"Invisible"* barriers to women rising to the highest positions in corporations and the professions.

### The Dual Labor Market and "Comparable Worth"

The existence of a "dual" labor market, with male-dominated "blue-collar" jobs distinguishable from female-dominated "pink-collar" jobs, continues to be a major obstacle to economic equality between men and women. These occupational differences result from cultural stereotyping, social conditioning, and training and education—all of which narrow the choices available to women. Although significant progress has been made in reducing occupational sex segregation (see Figure 12.3), many observers nevertheless doubt that sexually differentiated occupations will be eliminated in the foreseeable future.

### The "Glass Ceiling"

The barriers to women's advancement to top positions in the corporate and financial worlds are often very subtle, giving rise to the phrase **glass ceiling**. In explaining "why women aren't getting to the top," one observer argues that "at senior management levels competence is assumed. What you're looking for is someone who fits, someone who gets along, someone you trust. Now that's subtle stuff. How does a group of men feel that a woman is going to fit? I think it's very hard." Or, as a woman bank executive says, "The men just don't feel comfortable."[91] And at all levels, increasing attention has been paid to sexual harassment (see *What Do You Think?* "What Constitutes Sexual Harassment?"). Finally, it is important to note that affirmative action efforts by governments—notably the EEOC—are directed primarily at entry-level positions rather than senior management posts.

**Figure 12.3** Gender Differentiation in the Labor Market

Most of the earnings gap between men and women in the U.S. labor force today is the result of the different job positions held by the two sexes. Although women are increasingly entering "white-collar" occupations long dominated by men, they continue to be disproportionately concentrated in "pink-collar" service positions. "Blue-collar" jobs have been the most resistant to change, remaining a male bastion, although women bartenders now outnumber men.

*Sources: Statistical Abstract of the United States, 2001, pp. 380–82; 2004-2005, pp. 388–390.*

**Women in "White-Collar" Jobs**

| | 1960 | 1983 | 2004 |
|---|---|---|---|
| Architects | 3% | 13% | 22% |
| Computer analysts | 11% | 28% | 30% |
| College and university teachers | 28% | 36% | 45% |
| Engineers | 1% | 6% | 10% |
| Lawyers and judges | 4% | 16% | 28% |
| Physicians | 10% | 16% | 30% |

**Women in "Pink-Collar" Jobs**

| | 1970 | 1983 | 2004 |
|---|---|---|---|
| Secretaries | 98% | 99% | 97% |
| Waiters | 91% | 88% | 74% |
| Nurses | 97% | 96% | 89% |
| Office clerks | 75% | 82% | 84% |

**Women in "Blue-Collar" Jobs**

| | 1970 | 1983 | 2004 |
|---|---|---|---|
| Truck drivers | 1% | 3% | 5% |
| Carpenters | 1% | 1% | 2% |
| Laborers | 17% | 19% | 22% |
| Auto mechanics | 1% | 1% | 1% |
| Bartenders | 21% | 44% | 58% |

## WHAT DO YOU THINK?

# What Constitutes Sexual Harassment?

Various surveys report that up to one-third of female workers say they have experienced sexual harassment on the job.[a] But it is not always clear exactly what kind of behavior constitutes "sexual harassment."

The U.S. Supreme Court has provided some guidance in the development of sexual harassment definitions and prohibitions. Title VII of the Civil Rights Act of 1964 makes it "an unlawful employment practice to discriminate against any individual with respect to his [sic] compensation, terms, conditions or privileges of employment because of such individual's race, color, religion, sex, or national origin." In the employment context, the U.S. Supreme Court has approved the following definition of sexual harassment:

> Unwelcome sexual advances, requests for sexual favors, and other verbal or physical conduct of a sexual nature constitute sexual harassment when (1) submission to such conduct is made either explicitly or implicitly a term or condition of an individual's employment; (2) submission to or rejection of such conduct by an individual is used as the basis for employment decisions affecting such individual; or (3) such conduct has the purpose or effect of unreasonably interfering with an individual's work performance or creating an intimidating, hostile, or offensive working environment.[b]

There are no great difficulties in defining sexual harassment when jobs or promotions are conditional on the granting of sexual favors. But several problems arise in defining a "hostile working environment." This phrase may include offensive utterances, sexual innuendoes, dirty jokes, the display of pornographic material, and unwanted proposals for dates. First, it would appear to include speech and hence raise First Amendment questions regarding how far speech may be curtailed by law in the workplace. Second, the definition depends more on the subjective feelings of the individual employee about what is "offensive" and "unwanted" than on an objective standard of behavior easily understood by all. Justice Sandra Day O'Connor wrestled with the definition of a "hostile work environment" in *Harris v. Forklift Systems* in 1993. She held that a plaintiff need not show that the utterances caused psychological injury but that a "reasonable person," not just the plaintiff, must perceive the work environment to be hostile or abusive. Presumably a single incident would not constitute harassment; rather, courts should consider "the frequency of the discriminatory conduct," "its severity," and whether it "unreasonably interferes with an employee's work performance."[c]

What behaviors does a "reasonable person" believe to be sexual harassment? Some polls indicate that women are somewhat more likely to perceive sexual harassment in various behaviors than men (see figure). But neither women nor men are likely to perceive it to include repeated requests for a date, the telling of dirty jokes, or comments on attractiveness—even though these behaviors often inspire formal complaints.

Many university policies go well beyond both Supreme Court rulings and opinion polls in defining what constitutes sexual harassment, including the following: "remarks about a person's clothing" "suggestive or insulting sounds," and "leering at or ogling of a person's body."

[a]*Washington Post National Weekly Edition:* March 7, 1993.

[b]*Mentor Savings Bank v. Vinson,* 477 U.S. 57 (1986).

[c]*Harris v. Forklift Systems,* 126 L. Ed. 2d 295 (1993).

---

**Question**: *Here is a list of some different situations. We're interested in knowing whether you think they are forms of sexual harassment— not just inappropriate or in bad taste, but sexual harassment.*

### Definitely is sexual harassment:

If a male boss makes it clear to a female employee that she must go to bed with him for a promotion
- 91%
- 92%

If a male boss asks very direct questions of a female employee about her personal sexual practices and preferences
- 59%
- 68%

If a female boss asks very direct questions of a male employee about his personal sexual practices and preferences
- 47%
- 57%

If a man once in a while asks a female employee of his to go out on dates, even though she has said no in the past
- 15%
- 21%

If a man once in a while tells dirty jokes in the presence of female employees
- 15%
- 16%

If a male boss tells a female employee that she looks very attractive today
- 3%
- 5%

☐ Men   ☐ Women

*Source:* Roper Organization as reported in *American Enterprise.* September/October 1993, p. 93.

# Summary Notes

- Laws and government are required to protect individual liberty. Yet laws and governments themselves restrict liberty. To resolve this dilemma, constitutions seek to limit governmental power over the individual. In the U.S. Constitution, the Bill of Rights is designed to place certain liberties beyond the reach of government.

- Freedom of religion encompasses two separate restrictions on government: government must not establish religion or prohibit its free exercise. Although the wording of the First Amendment is absolute ("Congress shall make no law . . ."), the Supreme Court has allowed some restrictions on religious practices that threaten health, safety, or welfare.

- The Supreme Court's efforts to maintain "a wall of separation" between church and state have proven difficult and controversial. The Court's banning of prayer and religious ceremony in public schools more than thirty years ago remains politically unpopular today.

- The Supreme Court has never adopted the absolutist position that all speech is protected by the First Amendment. The Court's clear and present danger doctrine and its preferred position doctrine recognize the importance of free expression in a democracy, yet the Court has permitted some restrictions on expression, especially in times of perceived national crisis.

- The Supreme Court has placed obscenity outside the protection of the First Amendment, but it has encountered considerable difficulty in defining "obscenity."

- The Constitution includes a number of important procedural guarantees in the criminal justice system: the writ of habeas corpus; prohibitions against bills of attainder and ex post facto laws; protection against unreasonable searches and seizures; protection against self-incrimination; guarantee of legal counsel; protection against excessive bail; guarantee of a fair public and speedy trial by an impartial jury; the right to confront witnesses and to compel favorable witnesses to testify; and protection against cruel or unusual punishment.

- The Supreme Court has ruled that the death penalty is not a "cruel and unusual punishment," but the Court has insisted on fairness and uniformity of application.

- The original Constitution of 1787 recognized and protected slavery. Not until after the Civil War did the Thirteenth Amendment (1865) abolish slavery. But the Fourteenth Amendment's guarantee of "equal protection of the laws" and the Fifteenth Amendment's guarantee of

voting rights were largely ignored in Southern states after the federal government's Reconstruction efforts ended. Segregation was held constitutional by the U.S. Supreme Court in its "separate but equal" decision in *Plessy v. Ferguson* in 1896.

- The NAACP led the long legal battle in the federal courts to have segregation declared unconstitutional as a violation of the Equal Protection Clause of the Fourteenth Amendment. Under the leadership of Thurgood Marshall, a major victory was achieved in the case of *Brown v. Board of Education of Topeka* in 1954.

- Martin Luther King Jr.'s campaign of nonviolent direct action helped bring remaining racial injustices to the attention of Congress. Key legislation includes the Civil Rights Act of 1964, which bans discrimination in public accommodations, government-funded programs, and private employment.

- Generally the Supreme Court is likely to approve of affirmative action programs when these programs have been adopted in response to a past proven history of discrimination, when they are narrowly tailored so as not to adversely affect the rights of individuals, when they do not absolutely bar whites from participating, and when they serve clearly identified, compelling, and legitimate government objectives.

- Economic conditions in Mexico and other Spanish-speaking nations of the Western Hemisphere continue to fuel large-scale immigration, both legal and illegal, into the United States. But the political power of Mexican Americans, the nation's largest Hispanic group, does not yet match their population percentage. Their voter turnout remains lower than that of other ethnic groups in the United States.

- Gender discrimination in employment has been illegal since the passage of the Civil Rights Act of 1964. Nevertheless, differences in average earnings of men and women persist, although these differences have narrowed somewhat over time. The earnings gap appears to be mainly a product of lower pay in occupations traditionally dominated by women and higher pay in traditionally male occupations. Although neither Congress nor the courts have mandated wages based on comparable worth of traditional men's and women's jobs in private employment, many governmental agencies and some private employers have undertaken to review wage rates to eliminate gender differences.

# Key Terms

| | | | |
|---|---|---|---|
| Free Exercise Clause   422 | symbolic speech   430 | Emancipation Proclamation   446 | *Bakke* case   453 |
| Lemon test   425 | writ of habeas corpus   436 | Jim Crow   446 | set-aside program   455 |
| clear and present danger doctrine   429 | bill of attainder   436 | separate but equal   446 | strict scrutiny   455 |
| preferred position   429 | ex post facto law   436 | de facto segregation   448 | Title IX   464 |
| freedom of expression   430 | search warrant   436 | nonviolent direct action   449 | Equal Rights Amendment (ERA)   464 |
| | exclusionary rule   440 | affirmative action   452 | direct discrimination   465 |
| | plea bargaining   441 | | glass ceiling   466 |

# Suggested Readings

Barker, Lucius J., and Mack H. Jones. *African Americans and the American Political System.* 4th ed. Upper Saddle River, N.J.: Prentice Hall, 1999. Comprehensive analysis of African American politics, examining access to the judicial arena, the interest-group process, political parties, Congress, and the White House.

Bowen, William G., and Derek Curtis Bok. *The Shape of the River.* Princeton, N.J.: Princeton University Press, 1999. An argument by two university presidents that preferential treatment of minorities in admissions to prestigious universities has led to the subsequent success in life by the beneficiaries of the preferences.

Conway, M. Margaret, Gertrude A. Steurnagel, and David W. Ahern. *Women and Political Participation.* 2d ed. Washington, D.C.: CQ Press, 2004. A wide-ranging review of changes in American political culture brought about by women's increasing political clout. Continuing gender differences in representation are explored.

Epstein, Lee, and Thomas G. Walker. *Constitutional Law for a Changing America: Rights, Liberties and Justice.* 5th ed. Washington, D.C.: CQ Press, 2003. An authoritative text on civil liberties and the rights of the criminally accused. It describes the political context of Supreme Court decisions and provides key excerpts from the most important decisions.

Garrow, David. *Liberty and Sexuality: The Right to Privacy and the Making of Roe v. Wade.* New York: Macmillan, 1994.

Historical account of the background and development of the right to sexual privacy.

Hentoff, Nat. *Free Speech for Me—But Not for Thee.* New York: HarperCollins, 1992. Account of how both the right and the left in America try to suppress the opinions of those who disagree with them.

LeMay, Michael, *Perennial Struggle: Race, Ethnicity and Minority Group Relations in the United States,* 2nd ed. Upper Saddle River, N.J.: Prentice Hall, 2005. A description and assessment of minority group strategies—accommodation, separatism, radicalism—in coping with their political and economic status.

Savage, David. *The Supreme Court and Individual Rights.* Washington, D.C.: CQ Press, 2004. An overview of individual rights—freedom of ideas, political participation, due process and criminal rights, equal rights, and personal liberties.

Sullivan, Harold J. *Civil Rights and Liberties: Provocative Questions and Evolving Answers.* 2nd ed. Upper Saddle River, N.J.: Prentice Hall, 2005. Contemporary issues in civil liberties discussed in a question-and-answer format.

Walton, Hanes, and Robert C. Smith. *American Politics and the African-American Quest for Freedom.* 3rd ed. New York: Longman, 2005. Comprehensive text arguing the profound influence that African-Americans have on American politics.

# ★★★ Make It Real

## CIVIL LIBERTIES
The simulation puts the student in the role of NSA policymaker.

## CIVIL RIGHTS
This module contains an excellent interactive timeline on civil rights movements.

# 13 POLITICS, ECONOMICS, AND SOCIAL WELFARE POLICY

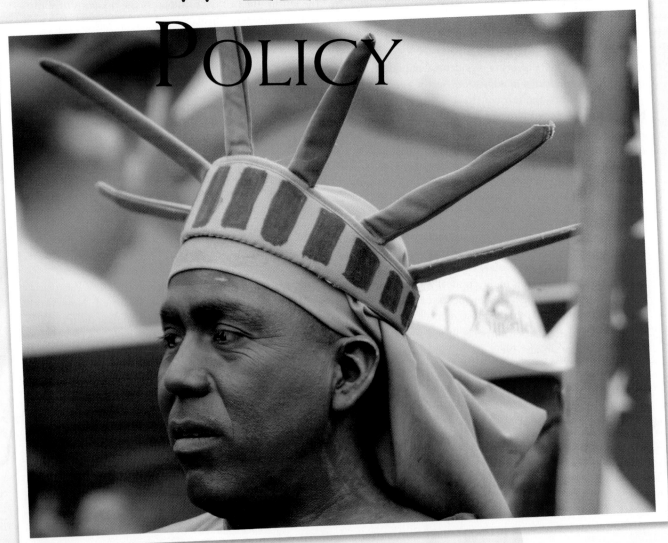

## Chapter Outline

- Politics and Economics
- The Performance of the American Economy
- Economic Globalization
- The Tax Burden
- Tax Politics
- Poverty in the United States
- Social Welfare Policy
- Politics and Welfare Reform
- Health Care in America

## Think About Politics

**1** Do you believe government efforts to manage the economy usually make things better or worse?
Better ☐ Worse ☐

**2** Do you think the trend toward a global economy is a good thing or a bad thing for the United States?
Good thing ☐ Bad thing ☐

**3** Which is more important: holding down the size of government or providing needed services?
Holding down the size of government ☐ Providing needed services ☐

**4** Do you think government welfare programs perpetuate poverty?
Yes ☐ No ☐

**5** Should all retirees receive Social Security benefits regardless of their personal wealth or income?
Yes ☐ No ☐

**6** Should there be a time limit on how long a person can receive welfare payments?
Yes ☐ No ☐

**7** Should government provide health care insurance for all Americans?
Yes ☐ No ☐

*What should government do to encourage economic growth and keep unemployment and inflation low? How is globalization affecting the American economy? Are tax rates too low or too high? Is the government doing enough to assist the aged and the poor? And what should be the government's role in health care?*

# Politics and Economics

Earlier, we observed that one of America's foremost political scientists, Harold Lasswell, defined "politics" as "who gets what, when, and how." One of America's foremost economists, Paul Samuelson, defined "economics" as "deciding what shall be produced, how, and for whom."[1] The similarity between these definitions is based on the fact that both the political system and the economic system provide society with means for deciding about the production and distribution of goods and services. The political system involves *collective* decisions—choices made by communities, states, or nations—and relies on government coercion through laws, regulations, taxes, and so on to implement them. A free-market economic system involves *individual* decisions—choices made by millions of consumers and thousands of firms—and relies on *voluntary exchange* through buying, selling, borrowing, contracting, and trading to implement them. Both politics and markets function to transform popular demands into goods and services, to allocate costs, and to distribute goods and services.

# The Performance of the American Economy

Underlying the power of nations and the well-being of their citizens is the strength of their economy—their total productive capacity. The United States produces about $12 *trillion* worth of goods and services in a single year for its 300 million people—more than $40,000 worth of output for every person.

**Economic Growth**   Gross domestic product (GDP) is a widely used measure of the performance of the economy.[2] GDP is a nation's total production of goods and services for a single year valued in terms of market prices. It is the sum of all the goods and services that people have been willing to pay for, from wheat production to bake sales, from machine tools to maid service, from aircraft manufacturing to bus rides, from automobiles to chewing gum. GDP counts only final purchases of goods and services (i.e., it ignores the purchase of steel by car makers until it is sold as a car) to avoid double counting in the production process. GDP also excludes financial transactions (such as the sale of bonds and stocks) and income transfers

**gross domestic product (GDP)** Measure of economic performance in terms of the nation's total production of goods and services for a single year, valued in terms of market prices.

**economic cycles** Fluctuations in real GDP growth followed by contraction.

**unemployment rate** Percentage of the civilian labor force who are not working but who are looking for work or waiting to return to or to begin a job.

**Bureau of Economic Analysis**
Source of official economic statistics, listed A–Z.
*www.bea.gov*

(such as Social Security, welfare, and pension payments) that do not add to the production of goods and services. Although GDP is expressed in current dollar prices, it is often recalculated in constant dollar terms to reflect real values over time, adjusting for the effect of inflation. GDP estimates are prepared each quarter by the U.S. Department of Commerce; these figures are widely reported and closely watched by the business and financial community.

Growth in real (constant dollar) GDP measures the performance of the overall economy. Economic recessions and recoveries are measured as fluctuations or swings in the growth of GDP. For example, a recession is usually defined as negative GDP growth in two or more consecutive quarters. Historical data reveal that periods of economic growth have traditionally been followed by periods of contraction, giving rise to the notion of **economic cycles**. Prior to 1950, economic cycles in the United States produced extreme ups and downs, with double-digit swings in real GDP. In recent decades, however, economic fluctuations have been more moderate. The United States still experiences economic cycles, but many economists believe that countercyclical government fiscal and monetary policy has succeeded in achieving greater stability (see Figure 13.1).

**Unemployment**  From a political standpoint, the **unemployment rate** may be the most important measure of the economy's performance. The unemployment rate is the percentage of the civilian labor force who are looking for work or waiting to return to or begin a job. Unemployment is different from not working; people who have retired or who attend school and people who do not work because of sickness, disability, or unwillingness are not considered part of the labor force and so are not counted as unemployed. People who are so discouraged about finding a job that they have quit looking for work are also not counted in the official unemployment rate. The unemployed do include people who have been terminated from their last job or temporarily laid off from work, as well as people who voluntarily quit and those who have recently entered or reentered the labor force and are now seeking employment.

**Figure 13.1**
Economic Growth
The tendency for periods of economic growth to alternate with periods of contraction has led to the concept of the business cycle—the idea that at least some fluctuation is normal, even healthy, helping to keep the economy growing in the long run by keeping prices from getting too high. In recent decades, government intervention in the economy appears to have succeeded in reducing, although not in altogether eliminating, the depths of recessions to which the nation was formerly prone.

*Source:* Data from Bureau of Economic Analysis, 2005.

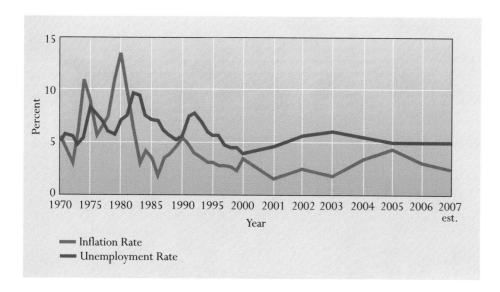

**Figure 13.2**
Unemployment
and Inflation
Economic growth during the
1980s lowered both the
inflation and unemployment
rates, freeing the nation from
the stagflation (combined
inflation and high unemployment) that had characterized
much of the 1970s. Un-
employment rose during the
recession of 1990–91 and
again in 2002–2003. Inflation
has remained relatively low
in recent years.

*Source:* Data from Bureau of Labor
Statistics, 2005.

The unemployment rate is measured each month by the U.S. Department of Labor. It does so by contacting a random sample of more than 50,000 households in many locations throughout the country. Trained interviewers ask a variety of questions to determine how many (if any) members of the household are either working or have a job but did not work at it because of sickness, vacation, strike, or personal reasons (employed); or whether they have no job but are available for work and actively seeking a job (unemployed). The unemployment rate fluctuates with the business cycle, reflecting recessions and recoveries (see Figure 13.2). Generally, unemployment lags behind GDP growth, going down only after the recovery has begun. Following years of economic growth in the 1990s, the nation's unemployment rate fell to near record lows, below 5 percent. The economic slowdown of 2001–02 temporarily pushed unemployment above 5 percent again.

 **Bureau of Labor
Statistics**
The U.S. Department of
Labor's Bureau of Labor
Statistics site contains
monthly information about
the nation's employment rate
plus a wealth of supporting
data. *www.bls.gov*

**Inflation**    Inflation erodes the value of the dollar because higher prices mean that the same dollars can now purchase fewer goods and services. Thus inflation erodes the value of savings, reduces the incentive to save, and hurts people who are living on fixed incomes. When banks and investors anticipate inflation, they raise interest rates on loans in order to cover the anticipated lower value of repayment dollars. Higher interest rates, in turn, make it more difficult for new or expanding businesses to borrow money, for home buyers to acquire mortgages, and for consumers to make purchases on credit. Thus inflation and high interest rates slow economic growth.

In recent years the Fed has been very successful in keeping down the rate of inflation, and as a result, keeping down overall interest rates as well. Low interest rates contributed to the nation's booming economy in the 1990s by encouraging businesses to borrow money for expansion and consumers to buy more on credit. The "soft" economy in 2001–02 inspired the Fed to lower interest rates even further. As the economy strengthened, the Fed gradually raised interest rates.

# Economic Globalization

The American economy is a major force in the global economy. **International trade**—the buying and selling of goods and services between individuals and firms

**international trade** The buying and selling of goods and services between individuals or firms located in different countries.

Just how bad can inflation get? Between the two world wars, inflation in Germany reached such levels that the nation's currency was often weighed, rather than counted, in order to speed transactions.

located in different countries—has expanded rapidly in recent decades. Today almost one-quarter of the world's total output is sold in a country other than the one in which it was produced. The United States exports about 11 percent of the value of its gross domestic product (GDP) and imports about 12 percent. As late as 1970, exports and imports were only about 3 percent of GDP (see Figure 13.3).

**Historic Protectionism** Historically, American business supported high tariffs—taxes on foreign imports. Prior to World War II, U.S. tariffs on imported goods averaged 30 to 50 percent in various decades. This eliminated most foreign competition from U.S. markets. American firms could raise prices to levels just below the price of imported goods with their high tariffs attached. Not only did this improve the profit margins of American manufacturers, it also allowed them to be less efficient than foreign producers and yet survive and prosper under the protection of tariffs. The pressure to cut wages and downsize workforces was less than it would be if U.S. firms had to face foreign competition directly. American

**Figure 13.3**
U.S. World Trade

*Source:* U.S. Bureau of Economic Analysis, December, 2005.

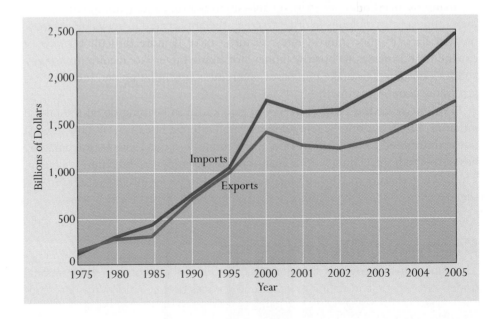

consumers, of course, paid higher prices than they otherwise would if foreign goods could come into the country without tariffs. The policy of high tariffs and quotas—limits on the number of units of specific goods imported into the country—was referred to as **protectionism**.

**Free Trade**   But after World War II, the American economy became the most powerful in the world, and American businesses sought to expand their markets overseas. In order to lower trade barriers in other countries, the United States reduced or eliminated almost all of its own tariffs and import quotas. In effect, the United States became an open market. "Free trade" became a byword of American business, and "protectionism" became a derogatory term.

The argument for **free trade** is that it lowers the price of goods and improves the standard of living in nations that choose to trade with each other. Trade shifts resources (investment capital, jobs, technology, raw materials, etc.) in each nation toward what each does best. If one nation is much better at producing aircraft and another better at producing clothing, then each nation will benefit more from trading than from trying to produce both airplanes and clothing. The efficiencies achieved by trading are said to directly benefit consumers by making available cheaper imported goods. Export industries also benefit when world markets are opened to their products. It is also argued that the pressure from competition from foreign-made goods in the American marketplace forces our own industries to become more efficient—cutting their costs and improving the quality of their goods. Finally, trade expands the menu of goods and services available to trading countries. American consumers gain access to everything from exotic foods and foreign-language movies to Porsches, BMWs, and Toyotas.

**Uneven Benefits of Globalization**   While the U.S. economy has performed very well in recent years, the benefits of that performance have been unevenly distributed. A global economy inspires worldwide competition not only among corporations and businesses but also among workers. America's best educated and most highly skilled workers compete well in the global economy. U.S. export industries have thrived on international trade expansion, adding jobs to the American economy and raising the incomes of their executives, professionals, and skilled high-tech workers. But the global economy offers a huge supply of unskilled and semiskilled workers at very low wages. Increased trade, especially with less developed economies such as Mexico, China, and India, with their huge numbers of low-wage workers, creates competition with America's unskilled and semiskilled workers. It is difficult to maintain the wage levels of American jobs, especially in labor-intensive industries, in the face of competition from low-wage countries. And U.S. corporations can move their manufacturing plants to low-wage countries, for example to northern Mexico, where the transportation costs of moving these products back into the United States are minimal. Harvard economist Richard B. Freeman summarizes the problem:

> An economic disaster has befallen low-skilled Americans, especially young men. Researchers using several data sources—including household survey data from the Current Population Survey, other household surveys, and establishment surveys—have documented that wage inequality and skill differentials in earnings and employment increased sharply in the United States from the mid-1970s through the 1980s and into the 1990s. The drop in the relative position of the less skilled shows up in a number of ways: greater earnings differentials between those with more and less education; greater earnings differentials between older and younger workers; greater differentials between high-skilled and low-skilled occupations; in a wider earnings distribution overall and within demographic and skill groups; and in less time worked by low-skill and low-paid workers.[3]

**protectionism** A policy of high tariffs and quotas on imports to protect domestic industries.

**free trade** A policy of reducing or eliminating tariffs and quotas on imports to stimulate international trade.

**Figure 13.4**
Worsening Inequality
Change in percent
distribution of family
income by quintile,
1980–2000.

*Source: Statistical Abstract of the United States*, 2002 p. 437.

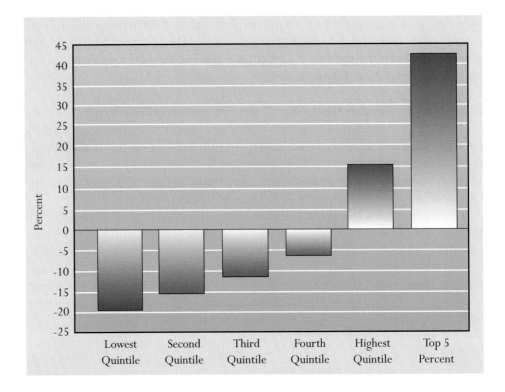

Income inequality has worsened in America along with the growth of international trade (see "Inequality of Wealth and Income" in Chapter 2). Figure 13.4 shows the percentage of losses and gains between 1980 and 2000 for American families in each income class. The nation's lowest income families lost 22 percent of their real income over these years, while the highest income families gained 33 percent in real income. Not all of this increase in inequality can be attributed to the growth of international trade. But, clearly, America's less educated and less skilled workers are at a disadvantage in global competition.

**The Politics of Free Trade**    Over the years both Democratic and Republican presidential administrations have advanced free trade. And Congress has approved the major treaties and organizations designed to institutionalize the global economy (see Table 13.1). The task of the cabinet-level position, International Trade Representative, has been to open up foreign markets to American products. Occasionally the United States has threatened to limit the importation of foreign products in order to force other nations to open up their own markets. And occasionally Congress members from districts adversely affected by foreign competition have opposed specific trade arrangements or, alternatively, called upon the federal government to assist workers displaced by foreign competition. But the thrust of U.S. policy has been to expand free trade.

Democrats in Congress have expressed more reservations about free trade than Republicans. (Democrats often call for "fair trade" in lieu of "free trade.") Democratic Congress members often reflect the views of their party's core constituencies, including labor unions, that fear the adverse effect on wages created by globalization. Environmentalists also complain that foreign corporations are not governed by strong or well-enforced environmental laws in their own countries. An array of other groups frequently demonstrates against globalization at meetings of the World Trade Organization and other international bodies (see *What Do You Think?*: "Does Globalization Help or Hurt America?").

**World Trade Organization (WTO)**
Official WTO site, with trade agreements, including General Agreement on Tariffs and Trade (GATT).
*www.wto.org*

— Think Again —
Which is more important: holding down the size of government or providing needed services?

**Table 13.1    Major International Trade Agreements**

**The World Trade Organization and GATT**

The World Trade Organization (WTO) was created in 1993. Today the WTO includes 149 nations that agree to a governing set of global trade rules. (China joined in 2001.) The WTO is given power to adjudicate trade disputes among countries and monitor and enforce trade agreements, including GATT. GATT, the multinational General Agreement on Tariffs and Trade, was created following World War II for the purpose of encouraging international trade. Over the years GATT has been dominated by banking, business, and commercial interests in Western nations seeking multilateral tariff reductions and the relaxation of quotas. In 1993 the GATT "Uruguay Round" eliminated quotas on textile products; established more uniform standards for proof of dumping; set rules for the protection of intellectual property rights (patents and copyrights on books, movies, videos, and so on); reduced tariffs on wood, paper, and some other raw materials; and scheduled a gradual reduction of government subsidies for agricultural products.

**The International Monetary Fund (IMF) and the World Bank**

The IMF's purpose is to facilitate international trade, allowing nations to borrow to stabilize their balance of trade payments. When economically weak nations, however, incur chronic balance of trade deficits and perhaps face deferral or default on international debts, the IMF may condition its loans on changes in a nation's economic policies. It may require a reduction in a nation's government deficits by reduced public spending and/or higher taxes; or it may require a devaluation of its currency, making its exports cheaper and imports more expensive. It may also require the adoption of noninflationary monetary policies. Currently, the IMF as well as the World Bank are actively involved in assisting Russia and other states of the former Soviet Union to convert to free-market economies.

The World Bank makes long-term loans, mostly to developing nations, to assist in economic development. It works closely with the IMF in investigating the economic conditions of nations applying for loans and generally imposes IMF requirements on these nations as conditions for loans.

**North American Free Trade Agreement (NAFTA)**

In 1993 the United States, Canada, and Mexico signed the North American Free Trade Agreement (NAFTA). Objections by labor unions in the United States were drowned out in a torrent of support by the American corporate community, Democrats and Republicans in Congress, President Bill Clinton, and former President George Bush. NAFTA envisions the removal of tariffs on virtually all products by all three nations over a period of ten to fifteen years. It also allows banking, insurance, and other financial services to cross these borders.

**FTAA AND CAFTA**

Currently the United States and the nations of North, Central, and South America are engaged in negotiations designed to create a free trade area throughout most of the Western Hemisphere. The Free Trade Area of the Americas (FTAA) is to resemble NAFTA. Barriers to trade and investment are to be progressively eliminated. The rules of the World Trade Organization will constitute a base for the FTAA agreements.

Recent U.S. presidents, both Democrats and Republicans, have pressed Congress for "fast-track authority" for trade agreements, essentially requesting that Congress pass presidentially negotiated trade agreements without amendments. In 2002, Congress granted President Bush's request for something quite similar— "trade promotion authority."

While negotiations on FTAA continue, President Bush signed a trade agreement—the Central American Free Trade Agreement (CAFTA)—with five Central American nations (Guatemala, El Salvador, Honduras, Costa Rica, and Nicaragua). CAFTA is based on the NAFTA model and is looked upon in Washington as a stepping stone to the broader FTAA.

# The Tax Burden

The tax burden in the United States is modest compared to burdens in other advanced democracies (see *Compared to What?: "*Tax Burdens in Advanced Democracies*"* on page 592). Federal revenues are derived mainly from (1) individual income taxes, (2) corporate income taxes, (3) Social Security payroll taxes, (4) estate and gift taxes, and (5) excise taxes and custom duties.

**Individual Income Taxes**    The **individual income tax** is the federal government's largest source of revenue (see Figure 13.5). Following tax cuts enacted by Congress in 2001 and 2003, individual income is now taxed at six rates: 10, 15,

**individual income tax** Taxes on individuals' wages and other earned income, the primary source of revenue for the U.S. federal government.

# WHAT DO YOU THINK?

## Does Globalization Help or Hurt America?

While Democratic and Republican presidents and Congresses have supported free trade and given their approval to two major trade agreements, the American public appears to be divided over the benefits of economic globalization.

Q. *Based on what you know or may have heard, do you think the globalization of the world economy is mostly good for the United States, mostly bad for the United States, or doesn't make much difference?*

| | |
|---|---|
| Bad | 22% |
| Good | 38 |
| No difference | 25 |
| Haven't heard/don't know | 14 |

More Americans believe that free trade agreements cost U.S. jobs rather than create U.S. jobs.

Q. *Do you think the trade agreements between the United States and other countries have helped create more jobs in the United States, or have they cost the U.S. jobs, or haven't they made much of a difference?*

| | |
|---|---|
| Cost U.S. jobs | 49% |
| Haven't made much difference | 23 |
| Helped create more U.S. jobs | 21 |
| Don't know | 7 |

It comes as no surprise that higher-income Americans voice greater support for globalization than lower-income Americans. Nor is it much of a surprise that public policy more closely reflects the views of higher-income Americans.

**Question:** *Do you think the trend toward a global economy is a good thing or a bad thing for the country?*

| | Good thing | Bad thing |
|---|---|---|
| $75,000 and up | 69% | 31% |
| $50-75,000 | 65% | 35% |
| $30-49,000 | 61% | 39% |
| $20-29,000 | 60% | 40% |
| Under $20,000 | 56% | 44% |
| Total | 61% | 39% |

☐ Good thing  ☐ Bad thing

*Sources: Washington Post/Newsweek* survey, October 2000 (for first and second questions); Princeton Survey Research, September 1998 (for third question). See *Public Agenda Online* at *www.publicagenda.org.*

---

25, 28, 33, and 35 percent. These are *marginal rates,* a term that economists use to mean additional. That is, income up to the top of the lowest bracket is taxed at 10 percent; additional income in the next bracket is taxed at 15 percent, up to a top marginal rate of 35 percent on income over $311,950 (in 2006). A personal exemption for each taxpayer and dependent, together with a standard deduction for married couples and a refundable earned income tax credit, ensure that low-income earners pay no income tax. (However, they still must pay Social Security

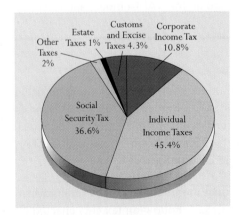

**Figure 13.5** Sources of Federal Income

Individual income taxes make up the largest portion of the federal government's revenues (43 percent). The government also relies heavily on the second largest source of its revenues, Social Security taxes.

*Source:* Budget of the United States Government, 2007.

# COMPARED TO WHAT?

## Tax Burdens in Advanced Democracies

Americans complain a lot about taxes. But from a global perspective, overall tax burdens in the United States are relatively low (see figure). Federal, state, and local taxes in the United States amount to about 30 percent of the gross domestic product (GDP), slightly below the burden carried by the nation's leading competitors, Japan and Germany. U.S. taxes are well below the burdens imposed in Sweden, Denmark, and other nations with highly developed welfare systems.

Top marginal tax rates in many nations were reduced during the 1980s and 1990s. For example, the top rate in Great Britain was lowered from 60 to 40 percent, in Japan from 70 to 30 percent, and in Sweden from 80 to 55 percent. Both in the United States and abroad, the notion that excessively high tax rates discourage work, savings, and investment, as well as slow economic growth, won acceptance (although how high is "excessive" is obviously open to different interpretations). Moreover, in a global economy, with increased mobility of individuals and firms, pressures push nations to keep their top tax rates within reasonable limits. Corporations can shift their assets to low-tax jurisdictions, and high personal income tax rates can even threaten a "brain drain" of talented individuals.

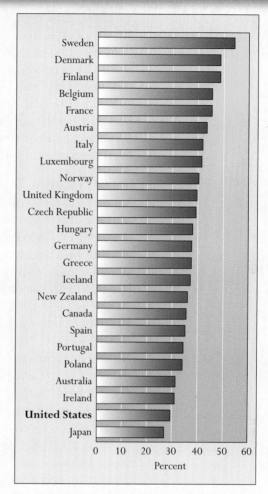

Tax Revenues as a Percentage of GDP

*Source:* OECD, *Figures for 2000. www.oecd.org.*

taxes on wages.) Tax brackets, as well as the personal exemption and standard deduction, are indexed annually to protect against inflation.

Federal government revenues from individual and business income taxes would be substantially higher were it not for special provisions in tax laws that enable taxpayers to avoid paying taxes on often substantial sums of income. Although each of these "loopholes" supposedly has a larger social goal behind it (for example, the deductibility of mortgage interest is supposed to stimulate the purchase and construction of homes, keeping up the value of those assets for current homeowners and keeping the construction industry employed), critics charge that many cost far more than they are worth to society.

**Internal Revenue Service (IRS)**
Official IRS site, with downloadable tax forms, information on tax laws, and tax statistics. *www.irs.gov*

There is a continual struggle between proponents of special tax exemptions to achieve social goals and those who believe the tax laws should be simplified and social goals met by direct government expenditures. Much of the political infighting in Washington involves the efforts of interest groups to obtain exemptions, exclusions, deductions, and special treatments in tax laws.[4]

**Corporate Income Taxes** The corporate income tax provides only about 10 percent of the federal government's total revenue. The Tax Reform Act of 1986 reduced the top corporate income tax from 46 to 34 percent (raised to 35 percent in 1993). However, corporations find many ways of reducing their taxable income often to zero. The result is that many very large and profitable corporations pay little in taxes. Religious, charitable, and educational organizations, as well as labor unions, are exempt from corporate income taxes except for income they may derive from "unrelated business activity."

Who really bears the burden of the corporate income tax? Economists differ over whether the corporate income tax is "shifted" to consumers or whether corporations and their stockholders bear its burden. The evidence on who actually bears the burden of this tax is inconclusive.[5]

**Social Security Taxes** The second largest source of federal revenue is the Social Security tax. It is withheld from paychecks as the "FICA" deduction, an acronym that helps hide the true costs of Social Security and Medicare from wage earners. To keep up with the rising number of beneficiaries and the higher levels of benefits voted for by Congress, including generous automatic cost-of-living increases each year, the Social Security taxes rose to 15.3 percent. (The Social Security tax is 12.4 percent and the Medicare tax is 2.9 percent; all wage income is subject to the Medicare tax, but wage income above a certain level $94,200 in 2006—is not subject to the Social Security tax.)

Taxes collected under FICA are earmarked (by Social Security number) for the account of each taxpayer. Workers thus feel they are receiving benefits as a right rather than as a gift of the government. However, less than 15 percent of the benefits being paid to current recipients of Social Security can be attributed to their prior contributions. Current taxpayers are paying more than 85 percent of the benefits received by current retirees.

Today a majority of taxpayers pay more in Social Security taxes than income taxes. Indeed, combined employer and employee Social Security taxes now amount to over $14,400 for each worker at the top of the wage base. If we assume that the employer's share of the tax actually comes out of wages that would otherwise be paid to the employee, then more than 75 percent of all taxpayers pay more in Social Security taxes than in income taxes.

**Estate and Gift Taxes** Taxation of property left to heirs is one of the oldest forms of taxation in the world. Federal estate taxes begin on estates of $1 million and levy a tax rate that starts at 18 percent and rises to 45 percent for estates worth more than $3 million. Because taxes at death otherwise could be avoided by simply giving estates to heirs while the giver is still alive, a federal gift tax is also levied on anyone who gives gifts in excess of $11,500 annually.

**Excise Taxes and Custom Duties** Federal excise taxes on the consumption of liquor, tobacco, gasoline, telephones, air travel, and other so-called luxury items, together with customs taxes on imports, provide about 3 percent of total federal revenues.

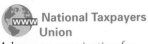 **National Taxpayers Union**
Advocacy organization for taxpayers "to keep what they have earned," with policy papers and data on tax burdens. *www.ntu.org*

# Tax Politics

**progressive taxation**
System of taxation in which higher income groups pay a larger percentage of their incomes in taxes than do lower income groups.

The politics of taxation centers around the question of who actually bears the heaviest burden of a tax—especially which income groups must devote the largest proportion of their income to taxes. **Progressive taxation** requires high-income groups to pay a larger percentage of their incomes in taxes than low-income groups. **Regressive taxation** takes a larger share of the income of low-income groups. **Proportional (flat) taxation** requires all income groups to pay the same percentage of their income in taxes. Note that the *percentage of income* paid in taxes is the determining factor. Most taxes take more money from the rich than the poor, but a progressive or regressive tax is distinguished by the percentages of income taken from various income groups.

**The Argument for Progressivity** Progressive taxation is generally defended on the principle of ability to pay; the assumption is that high-income groups can afford to pay a larger *percentage* of their incomes in taxes at no more of a sacrifice than that required of lower income groups to devote a smaller proportion of their income to taxation. This assumption is based on what economists call *marginal utility theory* as it applies to money; each additional dollar of income is slightly less valuable to an individual than preceding dollars. For example, a $5,000 increase in the income of an individual already earning $100,000 is much less valuable than a $5,000 increase to an individual earning only $10,000 or to an individual with no income at all. Hence, it is argued that added dollars of income can be taxed at higher rates without violating equitable principles.

**The Argument for Proportionality** Opponents of progressive taxation generally assert that equity can only be achieved by taxing everyone at the same percentage of their income, regardless of the size of their income. Progressivity penalizes initiative, enterprise, and the risk taking necessary to create new products and businesses. It also reduces incentives to expand and develop the nation's economy. Highly progressive taxes curtail growth and make everyone poorer.

**Reagan's Reductions in Progressivity** Certainly the most dramatic change in federal tax laws during the Reagan years was the reduction in the progressivity of individual income tax rates (see Figure 13.6). The top marginal tax rate fell from 70 percent when President Reagan took office to 28 percent following enactment of tax reform in 1986. The Tax Reform Act of 1986 reduced fourteen rate brackets to only two rate brackets, 15 and 28 percent.

**regressive taxation** System of taxation in which lower income groups pay a larger percentage of their incomes in taxes than do higher income groups.

**proportional (flat) taxation** System of taxation in which all income groups pay the same percentage of their income in taxes.

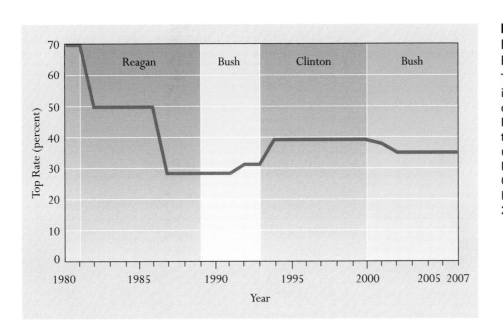

**Figure 13.6** Top Personal Income Tax Rates

The top marginal personal income tax rate fell dramatically during the Reagan Administration, then began to creep upward again under Presidents Bush and Clinton. George W. Bush lowered the top rate in 2001 and again in 2003.

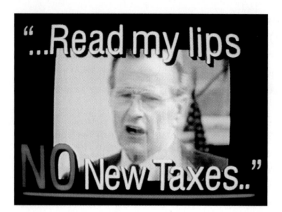

George Bush's pledge "Read my lips, no new taxes" helped him to victory in 1988. But breaking the pledge in 1990 contributed heavily to his defeat in 1992.

**"Read My Lips"**   At the Republican national convention in 1988, presidential nominee George H. W. Bush made a firm pledge to American voters that he would veto any tax increases passed by the Democratic-controlled Congress: "Read my lips! No new taxes." Yet in a 1990 budget summit with Democratic congressional leaders, President Bush agreed to add a top marginal rate of 31 percent to the personal income tax. Breaking his solemn pledge on taxes contributed heavily to Bush's defeat in the 1992 presidential election.

**"Soak the Rich"**   Proposals to "soak the rich" are always politically very popular. President Clinton pushed Congress to raise the top marginal tax rates to 39.6 percent for families earning $250,000. But these new top rates do not raise much revenue, partly because very few people have annual incomes in these categories. Moreover, high rates encourage people to seek tax-sheltered investments—to use their capital less efficiently to create tax breaks for themselves rather than to promote new business and new jobs.

**Bush Tax Cuts**   George W. Bush came into office vowing *not* to make the same mistake as his father, raising tax rates in an effort to compromise with the Democrats. On the contrary, Bush was strongly committed to lowering taxes, arguing that an "economic stimulus" package of additional tax cuts would revive the economy. Bush inspired the Republican-controlled Congress to lower the top marginal rate to 35 percent, and restructure rates through six brackets—10, 15, 25, 28, 33, and 35 percent (see Table 13.2). And the Bush 2003 tax package also contained a variety of new credits and special treatments: Corporate stock dividends are now taxed at a low 15 percent rather than at the same rate as earned income; the marriage penalty was eliminated by making the standard personal deduction for married couples twice that of a single person; the per child tax credit was raised to $1,000 (from $600); and the tax on capital gains—gains made from

**Table 13.2   Marginal Individual Income Tax Rates**

|           | Before 2001 | 2001 | 2007 |
|-----------|-------------|------|------|
| Lowest    | 15%         | 10%  | 10%  |
| to        | 28          | 15   | 15   |
| Highest   | 31          | 27   | 25   |
| Income    | 36          | 30   | 28   |
| Brackets  | 39.6        | 35   | 33   |
|           |             | 38.6 | 35   |

the buying and selling of real estate, stocks and bonds, and so on—was reduced from 20 to 15 percent.

**Who Pays the Federal Income Tax?**    The federal income tax continues to be highly progressive. Progressive rates, together with the personal and standard deductions for families and the earned income tax credit for low-income earners, combined to remove most of the income tax burden on middle- and low-income Americans. Indeed, the lower half of the nation's taxpayers pay less than 4 percent of total income taxes paid to the federal government (see Figure 13.7). Politically, this means that most proposals to reduce income taxes can be branded by opponents as "favoring the rich," inasmuch as the rich pay most of the income tax bill.

Even though marginal tax rates have been reduced substantially since 1980, upper-income Americans pay a much larger share of the federal income tax today than was previously the case. Although top marginal tax rates were reduced from 70 percent to 35 percent, the richest Americans are now paying more of the personal income tax even though their rates are lower than those in effect in 1980. How can one explain the fact that the rich are paying more now even though their tax rates are lower? The answer is that the incentive to earn additional income increases when tax rates decrease. Moreover, the incentive to find loopholes in the tax laws, to avoid receiving taxable income, and even to hide income (that is, to cheat), is reduced when top marginal rates are lowered.

Note that today the top 50 percent of income earners pay virtually all of the nation's personal income tax. Indeed, the top 10 percent of income earners pay about 66 percent of all of the income taxes collected by the federal government, and the top 1 percent pay about a third of all income taxes. This was not the case in 1980 when marginal tax rates were high. At that time the top 10 percent of income earners paid only 49 percent of all income taxes, and the top 1 percent paid only 19 percent of all income taxes.

**www** **Tax Foundation Advocacy**
Organization devoted to making the public "tax conscious," with information, "fiscal facts," and "tax freedom day." *www.taxfoundation.org*

# Poverty in the United States

How much poverty really exists in the United States? It depends on how you define the term "poverty." The official definition used by the federal government focuses on the cash income needed to maintain a "decent standard of living." The official **poverty line** is only a little more than one-third of the median income of

**poverty line** Official standard regarding what level of annual cash income is sufficient to maintain a "decent standard of living"; those with incomes below this level are eligible for most public assistance programs.

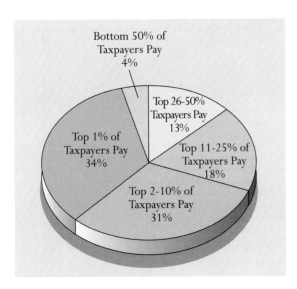

**Figure 13.7**  Who Pays the Federal Personal Income Tax?
Percentage of Total Federal Income Taxes Paid by Income Levels

*Source:* Based on data from The Tax Foundation at *http://www.taxfoundation.org.html.*

all American families. It takes into account the effects of inflation, rising each year with the rate of inflation. (For example, in 1990, the official poverty line for an urban family of four was $13,359 per year; by 2005 the poverty line had risen to about $20,000.)

**Persistent Poverty**    About half of the people on welfare rolls at any one time are *persistently poor,* that is, likely to remain on welfare for five or more years. For these people, welfare is a more permanent part of their lives.

Because they place a disproportionate burden on welfare resources, persistently poor people pose serious questions for social scientists and policymakers. Prolonged poverty and welfare dependency create an **underclass** that suffers from many social ills—teen pregnancy, family instability, drugs, crime, alienation, apathy, and irresponsibility.[6] Government educational, training, and jobs programs, as well as many other social service efforts, fail to benefit many of these people.

**Family Structure**    Poverty and welfare dependency are much more frequent among female-headed households with no husband present than among husband-wife households (see *Up Close:* "Who Are the Poor?"). Traditionally, "illegitimacy" was held in check by powerful religious and social structures. But these structures weakened over time, and the availability of welfare cash benefits, food stamps, medical care, and government housing removed much of the economic hardship once associated with unwed motherhood. Indeed, it was sometimes argued that government welfare programs, however well meaning, ended up perpetuating poverty and social dependency. This argument inspired welfare reform in 1996 (see "Politics and Welfare Reform" later in this chapter).

**Temporary Poverty**    Poor people are often envisioned as a permanent "underclass" living most of their lives in poverty. But most poverty is not long term. Tracing poor families over time presents a different picture of the nature of poverty from the "snapshot" view taken in any one year. For example, over the last decade 11 to 15 percent of the nation's population has been officially classified as poor in any one year. However, only *some* poverty is persistent: about 6 to 8 percent of the population remains in poverty for more than five years. Thus about half of the people who are counted as poor are experiencing poverty for

**underclass** People who have remained poor and dependent on welfare over a prolonged period of time.

**National Center for Children in Poverty**
Columbia University Center with studies and data on children in poverty.
*www.nccp.org*

**Institute for Research on Poverty**
University of Wisconsin Institute leads in research on extent and causes of poverty.
*www.ssc.wsc.edv/irp*

**Figure 13.8**   Number of Poor and Poverty Rate

*Source: http://www.census.gov/hhes/ poverty00/pov00.html*

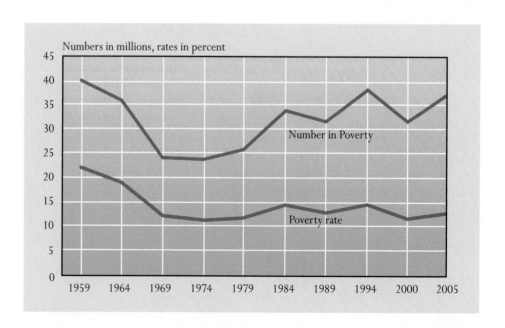

## UP CLOSE

# Who Are the Poor?

Poverty occurs in many kinds of families and in all races and ethnic groups. However, some groups experience poverty (low income) in greater proportions than the national average (see figure).

Poverty is most common among families headed by women. The incidence of poverty among these families is four times greater than that for married couples. These women and their children constitute over two-thirds of all of the persons living in poverty in the United States. About one of every five children in the United States lives in poverty. These figures describe what has been labeled the "feminization of poverty" in the United States. Clearly, poverty is closely related to family structure. The disintegration of the traditional husband-wife family is the single most influential factor contributing to poverty today.

Blacks also experience poverty in much greater proportions than whites. Over the years, the poverty rate among blacks in the United States has been almost three times higher than the poverty rate among whites. Poverty among Hispanics is also significantly greater than among whites.

In contrast, elderly people in America experience less poverty than the nonaged. The aged are not poor, despite the popularity of the phrase "the poor and the aged." The percentage of persons over sixty-five years of age with low incomes is below the national average. Moreover, elderly people are

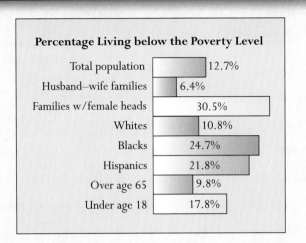

**Percentage Living below the Poverty Level**

| | |
|---|---|
| Total population | 12.7% |
| Husband–wife families | 6.4% |
| Families w/female heads | 30.5% |
| Whites | 10.8% |
| Blacks | 24.7% |
| Hispanics | 21.8% |
| Over age 65 | 9.8% |
| Under age 18 | 17.8% |

much wealthier in terms of assets and have fewer expenses than the nonaged. They are more likely than younger people to own homes with paid-up mortgages. Medicare pays a large portion of their medical expenses. With fewer expenses, elderly people, even with relatively smaller cash incomes, experience poverty differently from the way a young mother with children experiences it. The declining poverty rate among elderly people is a relatively recent occurrence, however. Continuing increases in Social Security benefits over the years are largely responsible for this singular "victory" in the war against poverty.

*Source:* U.S. Bureau of the Census, 2005.

---

only a short period of time. For these temporary poor, welfare is a "safety net" that helps them through hard times.

## Social Welfare Policy

Public welfare has been a recognized responsibility of government in English-speaking countries for many centuries. As far back as the Poor Relief Act of 1601, the English Parliament provided workhouses for the "able-bodied poor" (the unemployed) and poorhouses for widows and orphans, elderly and handicapped people.[7] Today, nearly one-third of the U.S. population receives some form of government benefits: Social Security, Medicare or Medicaid, disability insurance, unemployment compensation, government employee retirement, veterans' benefits, food stamps, school lunches, job training, public housing, or cash public assistance payments. More than half of all families in the United States include at least one person who receives a government check. Thus the "welfare state" now encompasses a very large part of our society.

The major social welfare programs can be classified as either **social insurance** or **public assistance**. This distinction is an important one that has on occasion become a major political issue. If the beneficiaries of a government program are required to have made contributions to it before claiming any of its benefits, and

**social insurance programs**
Social welfare programs to which beneficiaries have made contributions so that they are entitled to benefits regardless of their personal wealth.

**public assistance programs**
Those social welfare programs for which no contributions are required and only those living in poverty (by official standards) are eligible; include food stamps, Medicaid, and Family Assistance.

**Figure 13.9**   Social Welfare Entitlement Programs in the Federal Budget

*Source: Budget of the United States Government, 2007.*

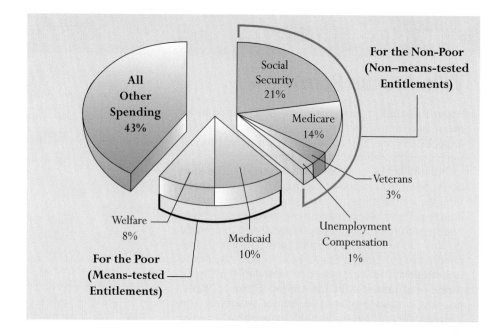

if they are entitled to the benefits regardless of their personal wealth—as in Social Security and Medicare—then the program is said to be financed on the social insurance principle. If the program is financed out of general tax revenues and if recipients are required to show that they are poor before claiming its benefits—as in Temporary Assistance to Needy Families, Supplemental Security Income, and Medicaid—then the program is said to be financed on the public assistance principle. Public assistance programs are generally labeled as "welfare."

**entitlements**  Any social welfare program for which there are eligibility requirements, whether financial or contributory.

**Entitlements**   **Entitlements** are government benefits for which Congress has set eligibility criteria—age, income, retirement, disability, unemployment, and so on. Everyone who meets the criteria is "entitled" to the benefit.

Most of the nation's major entitlement programs were launched either in the New Deal years of the 1930s under President Franklin D. Roosevelt (Social Security, Unemployment Compensation, Aid to Families with Dependent Children, now called Temporary Assistance to Needy Families, and Aid to Aged, Blind, and Disabled, now called Supplemental Security Income) or in the Great Society years of the 1960s under President Lyndon B. Johnson (food stamps, Medicare, Medicaid).

**Social Security**  Social insurance program composed of the Old Age and Survivors Insurance program, which pays benefits to retired workers who have paid into the program and their dependents and survivors, and the Disability Insurance program, which pays benefits to disabled workers and their families.

**Social Security**   Begun during the depression (1935), **Social Security** is now the largest of all entitlements; it comprises two distinct programs. The Old Age and Survivors Insurance program provides monthly cash benefits to retired workers and their dependents and to survivors of insured workers. The Disability Insurance program provides monthly cash benefits for disabled workers and their dependents. An automatic, annual cost-of-living adjustment (COLA) for both programs matches any increase in the annual inflation rate.

With more than 46 million beneficiaries, Social Security is the single largest spending program in the federal budget. About 96 percent of the nation's paid workforce is covered by the program, which is funded by a payroll tax on employers and employees. Retirees can begin receiving benefits at age sixty-two (full benefits at age sixty-five), regardless of their personal wealth or income (see "Senior Power" in this chapter).

**unemployment compensation**  Social insurance program that temporarily replaces part of the wages of workers who have lost their jobs.

**Unemployment Compensation**   **Unemployment compensation** temporarily replaces part of the wages of workers who lose their jobs involuntarily and helps stabilize the economy during recessions. The U.S. Department of Labor oversees the system, but states administer their own programs, with latitude within federal guidelines to define weekly benefits and other program features. Benefits are funded by a combination of federal and state unemployment taxes on employers.

**Supplemental Security Income**   Supplemental Security Income (SSI) is a means-tested, federally administered income assistance program that provides monthly cash payments to needy elderly (sixty-five or older), blind, and disabled people. A loose definition of "disability"—including alcoholism, drug abuse, and attention deficiency among children—has led to a rapid growth in the number of SSI beneficiaries.

**Family Assistance**   Family Assistance, officially Temporary Assistance to Needy Families (formerly AFDC, or Aid to Families with Dependent Children), is a grant program to enable the states to assist needy families. States now operate the program and define "need"; they set their own benefit levels and establish (within federal guidelines) income and resource limits. Prior to welfare reform in 1996, AFDC was a *federal* entitlement program. The federal government now mandates a two-year limit on benefits, a five-year lifetime limit, and other requirements (see "Politics and Welfare Reform" later in this chapter).

**Food Stamps**   The Food Stamp program provides low-income household members with coupons that they can redeem for enough food to provide a minimal nutritious diet. The program is overseen by the federal government but administered by the states.

**Earned Income Tax Credit**   The Earned Income Tax Credit (EITC) is designed to assist the working poor. It not only refunds their payroll taxes but also provides larger refunds than they actually paid during the previous tax year. Thus, the EITC is in effect a "negative" income tax. It was originally passed by a Democratic-controlled Congress and signed by Republican President Gerald Ford in 1975. Over the years EITC payments have increased substantially.

**Supplemental Security Income (SSI)** Public assistance program that provides monthly cash payments to the needy elderly (sixty-five or older), blind, and disabled.

**Family Assistance** Public assistance program that provides monies to the states for their use in helping needy families with children.

**Food Stamp program** Public assistance program that provides low-income households with coupons redeemable for enough food to provide a minimal nutritious diet.

**Earned Income Tax Credit (EITC)** Tax refunds in excess of tax payments for low-income workers.

Most of America's social welfare programs began in either the Great Depression of the 1930s or the War on Poverty in the 1960s. At the outset of the depression, millions of unemployed Americans, like the New Yorkers in a bread line in the photo at left, had only private charities to turn to for survival. The War on Poverty of the 1960s was a reaction to the persistence of extreme poverty, like that of the rural family in the photograph at right, in the midst of the prosperity that followed World War II.

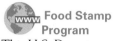

**Food Stamp Program**

This U.S. Department of Agriculture's Food Stamp program site contains information about application procedures, recipient eligibility guidelines, and other relevant subjects. *www.fns.usda.gov/fsp*

**Medicaid** Public assistance program that provides health care to the poor.

— Think Again —

Should there be a time limit on how long a person can receive welfare payments?

However, the program applies only to those poor who actually work and who apply for the credit when filing their income tax.

**Medicaid**  Medicaid is a joint federal-state program providing health services to low-income Americans. Most Medicaid spending goes to elderly and nonelderly disabled people. However, women and children receiving benefits under TANF automatically qualify for Medicaid, as does anyone who gets cash assistance under SSI. States can also offer Medicaid to the "medically needy"—those who face crushing medical costs but whose income or assets are too high to qualify for SSI or Family Assistance, including pregnant women and young children not receiving Family Assistance. Medicaid also pays for long-term nursing home care, but only after beneficiaries have used up virtually all of their savings and income.

## Politics and Welfare Reform

Americans confront a clash of values in welfare policy. Americans are a generous people; they believe government should aid those who are unable to take care of themselves, especially children, disabled people, and elderly people. But Americans are worried that welfare programs encourage dependency, undermine the work ethic, and contribute to illegitimate births and the breakup of families. Although social insurance programs (Social Security, Medicare, and Unemployment Compensation) are politically popular and enjoy the support of large numbers of active beneficiaries, public assistance programs (Family Assistance, SSI, Medicaid) are far less popular. A variety of controversies surround welfare policy in the United States.

**Conflict Over What Causes Poverty**  Americans have different ideas about what causes poverty. Some attribute poverty to characteristics of individuals—drug use, declining moral values, lack of motivation. Others blame the economy—too many part-time and low-wage jobs and a shortage of good jobs. Still others place blame on the welfare system itself. Indeed, prior to welfare reform in 1996, some scholars argued that government itself was a major cause of poverty—that social welfare programs destroyed incentives to work, encouraged teenage pregnancies, and made people dependent on government handouts.[8] They argued that the combination of cash payments, food stamps, Medicaid, and housing assistance unintentionally discouraged people from forming families, taking low-paying jobs, and, perhaps, with hard work and perseverance, gradually pulling themselves and their children into the mainstream of American life.

There is little doubt that poverty and welfare dependency are closely related to family structure. As noted earlier, poverty is much more frequent among female-headed households with no husband present than among husband-wife households. As births to unmarried women rose, poverty and social dependency increased. (In 1970 only 11 percent of births were to unmarried women; by 2000 this figure had risen to 33 percent of all births and 69 percent of minority births.) The troubling question was whether the welfare system ameliorated some of the hardships confronting unmarried mothers and their children, or whether it actually contributed to social dependency by mitigating the consequences of unmarried motherhood. For example, were teenage pregnancies more common because teenagers knew that government benefits were available to young mothers and their children?

**The Politics of Welfare Reform**  A political consensus grew over the years that long-term social dependency had to be addressed in welfare policy. The fact

## UP CLOSE

# Is Welfare Reform Working?

Welfare reform, officially Temporary Assistance to Needy Families, was passed by Congress in 1996; its provisions took effect in 1997. By early 1998 the Clinton Administration, as well as Republican congressional sponsors of welfare reform, was declaring it a success.

The number of cash welfare recipients in the nation has dropped below 5 million—the lowest number in more than twenty-five years. Only about 2 percent of Americans are now on cash welfare—the smallest proportion since 1970. No doubt some of this decline is attributable to strong growth of the economy: declines in welfare rolls began *before* Congress passed its welfare reform law, and some decline may have occurred without reform. Many states had initiated their own reforms under "waivers" from the federal government even before Congress acted.

All states have now developed work programs for welfare recipients. Applicants for welfare benefits are now generally required to enter job-search programs, to undertake job training, and to accept jobs or community service positions.

Yet, although nearly everyone agrees that getting people off welfare rolls and onto payrolls is the main goal of reform, there are major obstacles to the achievement of this goal. First of all, a substantial portion (perhaps 25 to 40 percent) of long-term welfare recipients have handicaps—physical disabilities, chronic illnesses, learning disabilities, alcohol or drug abuse problems—that prevent them from holding a full-time job. Many long-term recipients have no work experience (perhaps 40 per-

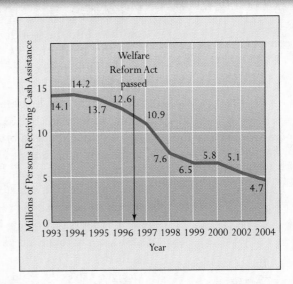

*Source:* Department of Health and Human Services, 2006.

cent), and two-thirds of them did not graduate from high school. Almost half have three or more children, making day-care arrangements a major obstacle. It is unlikely that any counseling, education, job training, or job placement programs could ever succeed in getting these people into productive employment.

Early studies of people who left the welfare rolls following welfare reform suggest that over half and perhaps as many as three-quarters have found work, although most at minimum or near-minimum wages.[a]

[a]*Governing* (April 1999), pp. 21–26.

Programs such as this Riverside, California, "Jobs Club" try to help welfare recipients find jobs in the wake of reforms intended to reduce welfare dependency.

that most nonpoor mothers work convinced many *liberals* that welfare mothers had no special claim to stay at home with their children. And many *conservatives* acknowledged that some transitional assistance—education, job training, continued health care, and day care for children—might be necessary to move welfare mothers into the workforce.

Although President Clinton had once promised "to end welfare as we know it," it was the Republican-controlled Congress elected in 1994 that proceeded to do so. The Republican-sponsored welfare reform bill ended the sixty-year-old federal "entitlement" for low-income families with children—the venerable AFDC program. In its place the Republicans devised a "devolution" of responsibility to the states through federal block grants—**Temporary Assistance to Needy Families**—lump sum allocations to the states for cash welfare payments, with benefits and eligibility requirements decided by the states. Conservatives in Congress imposed tough-minded "strings" to state aid, including a two-year limit on continuing cash benefits and a five-year lifetime limit; a "family cap" that would deny additional cash benefits to women already on welfare who bear more children; the denial of cash welfare to unwed parents under 18 years of age unless they live with an adult and attend school. President Clinton vetoed the first welfare reform bill passed by Congress in early 1996, but as the presidential election neared, he reversed himself and signed the Welfare Reform Act, establishing the Temporary Assistance to Needy Families program. Food stamps, SSI, and Medicaid were continued as federal "entitlements" (see *Up Close:* "Is Welfare Reform Working?").

**Temporary Assistance to Needy Families** Welfare reform program replacing federal cash entitlement with grants to the states for welfare recipients.

# Health Care in America

Historically, most reductions in death rates have resulted from public health and sanitation improvements, including immunizations, clean public water supplies, sanitary sewage disposal, improved diets, and increased standards of living. Many of the leading causes of death today (see Table 13.3), including heart disease, cancer, stroke, and AIDS, are closely linked to heredity, personal habits and lifestyles (smoking, eating, drinking, exercise, stress, sexual practices), and the physical environment—factors over which doctors and hospitals have no direct control. Thus some argue that the greatest contribution to better health is likely to be found in altered personal habits and lifestyles rather than in more medical care. Thanks to improved health care habits as well as breakthroughs in medical technology, Americans are living longer than ever before.

**— Think Again —**

Should government provide health care insurance for all Americans?

**Access to Care**  A major challenge in health care is to extend coverage to all Americans. Today, about 85 percent of the nation's population is covered by either government or private health insurance. Government pays about 43 percent of all health care costs—through Medicare for the aged, Medicaid for the poor, and other government programs, including military and veterans' care. Private insurance pays for about 40 percent of the nation's health costs; the remaining 17 percent is paid directly by patients.

But about 15 percent of the U.S. population—an estimated 45 million Americans—have *no* medical insurance. These include workers and their dependents whose employers do not offer a health insurance plan, as well as unemployed people who are not eligible for Medicare or Medicaid. People who lack health insurance may postpone or go without needed medical care or may be denied medical care by hospitals and physicians in all but emergency situations. Confronted with serious illness, they may be obliged to impoverish themselves in

**Table 13.3    Leading Causes of Death**

| | Deaths per 100,000 Population per Year | | | | |
|---|---|---|---|---|---|
| | **1960** | **1970** | **1980** | **1990** | **2004** |
| All causes | 954.7 | 945.3 | 883.4 | 863.8 | 847.3 |
| Heart disease | 369.0 | 362.0 | 336.0 | 368.3 | 241.9 |
| Stroke (cerebrovascular) | 108.0 | 101.9 | 75.5 | 57.9 | 56.4 |
| Cancer | 149.2 | 162.8 | 183.9 | 203.2 | 197.2 |
| Accidents | 52.3 | 56.4 | 46.7 | 37.0 | 37.0 |
| Pneumonia/Influenza | 37.3 | 30.9 | 24.1 | 32.0 | 22.3 |
| Diabetes | 16.7 | 18.9 | 15.5 | 19.2 | 25.4 |
| Alzheimers | N.A. | N.A. | N.A. | N.A. | 20.4 |
| AIDS | N.A. | N.A. | N.A. | 17.6 | 4.9 |
| Suicide | 10.6 | 11.6 | 11.9 | 12.4 | 11.0 |
| Homicide | 4.7 | 8.3 | 10.7 | 10.0 | 6.1 |

*Source: Centers for Disease Control, www.cdc.gov/nchs/data.*

order to become eligible for Medicaid. Any unpaid medical bills must be absorbed by hospitals or shifted to paying patients and their insurance companies.

**Health Care Costs**    No system of health care can provide as much as people will use. Anyone whose health and life may be at stake will want the most thorough diagnostic testing, the most constant care, the most advanced treatment. Sworn to preserve life, doctors, too, want the most advanced diagnostic and treatment facilities available for their patients. Under conditions of uncertainty in a medical situation—and there is always some uncertainty—physicians are trained to seek more consultations, run more tests, and try new therapeutic approaches. Any tendency for doctors to limit testing and treatment is countered by the threat of malpractice suits; it is always easier to order one more test or procedure than to risk even the tiniest chance that failing to do so will some day be cause for a court suit. So in the absence of restraints, both patients and doctors will push up the costs of health care. Currently, health care costs appear to have stabilized at about 13 percent of the nation's GDP.

**Managed Care Controversies**    Both private and government insurers have made efforts to counter rising costs through **managed care**. Private insurers have negotiated discounts with groups of physicians and with hospitals—**preferred provider organizations (PPOs)**—and have implemented rules to guide physicians about when patients should and should not receive costly diagnostic and therapeutic procedures. Medicare no longer pays hospitals based on costs incurred; instead it pays fixed fees based on primary and secondary diagnoses at the time of admission. Both government and private insurers have encouraged the expansion of **health maintenance organizations (HMOs)**, groups that promise to provide a stipulated list of services to patients for a fixed fee and that are able to provide care at lower total costs than can other providers. Today over 30 percent of Americans are enrolled in HMOs.

But many of the efforts by both private insurers and governments to control costs have created new problems. These include cost-control regulations and

**managed care** Programs designed to keep health care costs down by the establishment of strict guidelines regarding when and what diagnostic and therapeutic procedures should be administered to patients under various circumstances.

**preferred provider organizations (PPOs)** Groups of hospitals and physicians who have joined together to offer their services to private insurers at a discount.

**health maintenance organizations (HMOs)** Health care provider groups that provide a stipulated list of services to patients for a fixed fee that is usually substantially lower than such care would otherwise cost.

restrictions that add to administrative costs and create a mountain of paperwork for physicians and hospitals, and frustration and anger among both health care workers and patients. Doctors and hospitals argue that the *administrative* costs imposed by these cost-control measures far exceed whatever savings are achieved. Patients and doctors complain that preapproval of treatment by insurance companies often removes medical decisions from the physician and patient and places them in the hands of insurance company employees.

**Medicare** Medicare is a two-part program that helps elderly and disabled people pay acute-care (as opposed to long-term-care) health costs. Hospital insurance (Part A) helps pay the cost of hospital inpatient and skilled nursing care. Anyone sixty-five or older who is eligible for Social Security is automatically eligible for Part A benefits. Also eligible are people under sixty-five who receive Social Security disability or railroad retirement disability and people who have end-stage kidney disease. Part A is financed primarily by the 1.45 percent payroll tax collected with Social Security (FICA) withholding. Supplemental Medical Insurance (Part B) is an optional add-on taken by virtually all those covered by Part A. It pays 80 percent of covered doctor and outpatient charges. Small monthly premiums are deducted from Social Security benefit checks to finance it.

**Prescription Drug Coverage under Medicare** The long battle over adding prescription drug coverage to Medicare reached a turning point in 2004 when Congress finally passed by wide margins and President Bush signed such a bill. Americans have long supported the addition of prescription drug benefits to Medicare. And in every election over the previous twenty years both Democrats and Republicans had pledged their support for such a benefit. But it was not until after a prolonged battle over the details of the legislation that Congress finally added the long-awaited prescription drug benefit to Medicare. (The Medicaid program for the poor has paid for prescription drugs since its inception.)

The bill was passed by a Republican-controlled Congress and signed by a Republican president; most Democrats in Congress opposed the bill, claiming that it failed to go far enough in protecting seniors. The AARP provided crucial support for the bill, arguing that later amendments could cure any defects.

To receive prescription drug benefits under Medicare, seniors must enroll in a private plan offered by insurance companies. Participants must pay a modest monthly premium of about $35, as well as an annual deductible of $250. After the deductible is paid, the insurance plan must pay 75 percent of yearly drug costs up to $2,850. The patient must pay all drug costs between $2,850 and $3,600 out-of-pocket—the so-called "coverage gap." After $3,600 in drug costs the plan pays all added costs. All private insurers must at least offer this plan to participate; they may compete by offering additional incentives. In addition to the "coverage gap," critics of the plan note that the federal government does not negotiate with drug companies for lower costs.

**Interest-Group Battles** Interest-group battles over the details of health care policy have been intense. Virtually everyone has a financial stake in any proposal to reorganize the nation's health care system.

- Employers, especially small businesses, are fearful of added costs.

- Physicians strongly oppose price controls and treatment guidelines, as well as programs that take away patient choice of physician or force all physicians into

**Medicare** Social insurance program that provides health care insurance to elderly and disabled people.

www **Medicare**
Official government site explaining eligibility, plan options, appeals, and so forth. *www.medicare.gov*

## A CONSTITUTIONAL NOTE

### Rights versus Entitlements

The Constitution *limits* government. It does not oblige the government to provide any benefits or services to people, such as education, welfare, Social Security, medical care, and so on. Constitutionally speaking, there is no *right* to these benefits. The states, for example, are not obliged by the Constitution to provide public education; the national government is not obliged by the Constitution to provide Social Security or Medicare. These governments do so as a matter of legislation, not as a mandate of the U.S. Constitution. (Of course, if the national or state governments decide to provide such services, they must provide them equally to all persons "similarly situated," that is, they cannot discriminate but must provide "equal protection of laws" under the Fourteenth Amendment.) Political rhetoric often claims a *right* to an education, or to Social Security, or to medical care, or to other important programs. But there are no such rights set forth in the Constitution. Although politically unthinkable, states could abolish public education altogether; Congress could abolish Social Security or Medicare.

However, governments over time have provided benefits and services that people have come to depend upon. The laws granting these benefits set eligibility requirements—age, income, disability, unemployment, and so forth. Everyone who meets these requirements is said to be *entitled* to these benefits by law. Indeed, we have come to refer to these benefits as *entitlements*. But it is important to distinguish between *rights*—limits on government power to protect individuals—and *entitlements*—benefits that governments have enacted for persons who meet specific requirements.

---

health maintenance organizations (HMOs). Support is stronger among those physicians most likely to benefit from low-cost plans—general family practitioners—and weakest among those most likely to lose—medical specialists.

- Psychiatrists, psychologists, mental health and drug abuse counselors, physical therapists, chiropractors, optometrists, and dentists all want their own services covered. Providing such "comprehensive" services greatly increases costs.

- Drug companies want to see prescription drugs paid for, but they vigorously oppose price controls on drugs.

- Hospitals want all patients to be insured but oppose government payment schedules.

- Medical specialists fear that proposals for managed care will result in fewer consultations, and medical manufacturers fear it will limit use of high-priced equipment.

- The powerful senior citizens' lobby wants added benefits—including coverage for drugs, eyeglasses, dental care, and nursing homes—but fears folding Medicare into a larger health care system.

- Veterans' groups want to retain separate VA hospitals and medical services.

- Opponents of abortion rights are prepared to do battle to keep national coverage from including such procedures, whereas many supporters of abortion rights will not back any plan that excludes abortion services.

Although polls show that a majority of Americans are willing to pay higher taxes for comprehensive health care, many are willing to see increases only in "sin taxes"—taxes on alcohol, tobacco, and guns.

# Summary Notes

- The performance of the economy can be measured by GDP growth and the unemployment and inflation rates. Politically the unemployment rate may be the most important of these measures of economic performance.

- Imports and exports grow each year as a percentage of the gross domestic product of the United States. This trend toward globalization has been fostered by U.S. participation in the World Trade Organization, the International Monetary Fund, the World Bank, the North American Free Trade Agreement, and other agreements and treaties in support of free trade. Free trade may benefit the economy as a whole, but it appears to disadvantage poorly educated, low-skilled American workers.

- Tax politics centers on the question of who actually bears the burden of a tax. The individual income tax, the largest source of federal government revenue, is progressive, with higher rates levied at higher income levels. Progressive taxation is defended on the ability-to-pay principle. But half of all personal income, and a great deal of corporate income, is untaxed, owing to a wide variety of exemptions, exclusions, deductions, and special treatments on tax laws. These provisions are defended in Washington by a powerful array of interest groups.

- The Reagan Administration reduced top income tax rates from 70 to 28 percent, believing high rates discouraged work, savings, and investment, and thereby curtailed economic growth. But George Bush agreed to an increase in the top rate to 31 percent. Bill Clinton pushed Congress to raise the top rates to 39.6 percent, arguing that rich people had benefited from Reagan's "trickle down" policies and must now be forced to bear their "fair share." George W. Bush succeeded in getting two tax cut bills through Congress in 2001 and 2003. The bills lowered the top marginal income tax rate to 35 percent, eliminated the marriage penalty, increased child exemptions, and lowered the capital gain rate to 15 percent.

- About 11 to 15 percent of the U.S. population falls below the annual cash income level that the federal government sets as its official definition of poverty.

- Poverty is temporary for many families, but some poverty is persistent—lasting five years to a lifetime. Prolonged poverty and welfare dependency create an "underclass" beset by many social and economic problems. Poverty is most frequent among families headed by single mothers.

- Nearly one-third of the U.S. population receives some form of government payments or benefits. Entitlements are government benefits for which Congress has set eligibility criteria by law. Social Security and Medicare are the largest entitlement programs. The elderly are entitled to these benefits regardless of their income or wealth.

- Social welfare policies seek to alleviate hardship; at the same time they seek to avoid creating disincentives to work. Cash welfare payments may, for example, encourage teenage pregnancies, undermine family foundations, and contribute to long-term social dependency. Welfare reform centers on moving former welfare recipients into the work force. But doing so may require increased spending on education, job training, health care, and child care, and some recipients may never be able to work.

- Welfare reform in 1996 replaced federal entitlements to cash payments with block grants to the states. It also set time limits on welfare enrollment.

- Health care reform centers on two related problems—extending health insurance coverage to all Americans and containing the costs of health care.

- A modest prescription drug insurance plan was added to Medicare for seniors. It is administered through private insurance companies, but fails to cover all drug costs.

- Medicare for the aged and Medicaid for the poor are the largest government health insurance programs. They do not cover the general population. About 15 percent of the population has no health insurance. Only in 2003, after years of interest group conflict, was prescription drug coverage added to Medicare.

# Key Terms

gross domestic product (GDP)  470
economic cycles  470
unemployment rate  470
international trade  471
protectionism  473
free trade  473
individual income tax  475
progressive taxation  478
regressive taxation  479
proportional (flat) taxation  479
poverty line  481
underclass  482
social insurance programs  483
public assistance programs  483
entitlements  484

Social Security   484
unemployment
    compensation   484
Supplemental Security
    Income (SSI)   485

Family Assistance   485
Food Stamp program   485
Earned Income Tax
    Credit (EITC)   485
Medicaid   486

Temporary Assistance to
    Needy Families   488
managed care   489
preferred provider organiza-
    tions (PPOs)   489

health maintenance
    organizations
    (HMOs)   489
Medicare   490

## Suggested Readings

DiNitto, Diana M. *Social Welfare Politics and Policy*. 8th ed. New York: Allyn & Bacon, 2003. A comprehensive overview of social welfare programs—Social Security, Medicare, SSI, cash assistance, Medicaid, food stamps, and so on—and the political controversies surrounding them.

Hays, Sharon. *Flat Broke With Children: Women in the Age of Welfare Reform*. New York: Oxford Press, 2003. Stories of single mothers and welfare workers trying to cope with the harsher rules of welfare reform.

Issak, Robert A. *Globalization Gap*. Upper Saddle River, NJ: Prentice Hall, 2005. Antiglobalization argument that rich nations get richer and poor nations get poorer as a result of international trade.

Jacobs, Laurence R., and Theda S. Kocpol, eds. *Inequality and American Democracy*. New York: Russell Sage Foundation, 2005. A series of essays describing increasing inequality in America and its political and social consequences.

Langren, Robert, and Martin Snitzer. *Government, Business and the American Economy*. Upper Saddle River, N.J.: Prentice Hall, 2001. Comprehensive text on the government's role in the economy.

Rothgeb, John M. Jr. *U.S. Trade Policy*. Washington, D.C.: CQ Press, 2001. Concise text on international trade, including history of GATT, WTO, and NAFTA.

Schiller, Bradley R. *The Economics of Poverty and Discrimination*. 9th ed. Upper Saddle River, NJ: Prentice Hall, 2004. Leading text on poverty and welfare in America.

Sowell, Thomas. *Basic Economics: A Citizen's Guide to the Economy*. New York: Basic Books, 2003. Introduction to economics with an emphasis on public policy. No jargon or equations.

Steger, Manfred B. *Globalism*. Boston: Rowman & Littlefield, 2002. The politics of pro- and antiglobalist groups, with a sharp critique of the ideology of globalism.

Wolff, Edward N. *Top Heavy* (updated edition). New York: Century Foundation, 2002. The study of the increasing inequality of wealth in United States and an argument for taxing financial wealth (bank accounts, stocks, bonds, property, houses, cars, etc.) as well as income.

## Make It Real

### ECONOMIC POLICY
The simulation allows students to try to balance the federal budget.

### SOCIAL POLICY
In this unit, students consider immigration policy options.

# 14 POLITICS AND NATIONAL SECURITY

## | Chapter Outline |

- Power among Nations
- The Legacy of the Cold War
- Nuclear Threats
- When to Use Military Force?
- The War on Terrorism
- Political Support for War in Iraq

# Power among Nations

International politics, like all politics, is a struggle for power. The struggle for power is global; it involves all the nations and peoples of the world, whatever their goals or ideals. As the distinguished political scientist Hans Morgenthau once observed,

> Whatever the ultimate aims of international politics, power is always the immediate aim. Statesmen and peoples may ultimately seek freedom, security, prosperity or power itself. They may define their goals in terms of a religious, philosophic, economic, or social ideal. . . . But whenever they strive to realize their goal by means of international politics, they are striving for power.[1]

The struggle for power among nations has led to many attempts to bring order to the international system.

**Collective Security** Originally, **collective security** meant that *all* nations would join together to guarantee each other's "territorial integrity and existing political independence" against "external aggression" by any nation. This was the idea behind the League of Nations, established in 1919. However, opposition to international involvement was so great in the United States after World War I that, after a lengthy debate, the Senate refused to enroll the United States in the League of Nations. More important, the League of Nations failed to deal with acts of aggression by the Axis Powers—Germany, Japan, and Italy—in the 1930s. During that decade, Japan invaded Manchuria, Italy invaded Ethiopia, and Germany dismembered Czechoslovakia. Finally, when Germany invaded Poland in 1939, World War II began. It cost more than 40 million lives, both civilian and military.

**Formation of the United Nations** Even after World War II, the notion of collective security remained an ideal of the victorious Allied Powers. The Charter of the United Nations, signed in 1945, provided for the following organization:

- The Security Council, with eleven member nations, five of them being permanent members—the United States, the **Soviet Union** (whose membership is now held by Russia), Britain, France, and China—and each having the power to veto any action by the Security Council.

- The General Assembly, composed of all the member nations, each with a single vote.

**collective security**
Attempt to bring order to international relations by all nations joining together to guarantee each other's "territorial integrity" and "independence" against "external aggression."

**Soviet Union**  The Union of Soviet Socialist Republics (USSR) consisting of Russia and its bordering lands and ruled by the communist regime in Moscow, officially dissolved in 1991.

 **State Department**  This U.S. Department of State Web site contains background notes on the countries and regions of the world. *www.state.gov*

**superpowers**  Refers to the United States and the Soviet Union after World War II, when these two nations dominated international politics.

**United Nations**  This United Nations site contains basic information about the world body's mission, member states, issues of concern, institutions, and accomplishments. *www.un.org*

**regional security**  Attempt to bring order to international relations during the Cold War by creating regional alliances between a superpower and nations of a particular region.

**North Atlantic Treaty Organization (NATO)**
Mutual-security agreement and joint military command uniting the nations of Western Europe, initially formed to resist Soviet expansionism.

■ The Secretariat, headed by a Secretary General with a staff at United Nations headquarters in New York.

■ Organizations to handle specialized affairs—for example, the Economic and Social Council, the Trusteeship Council, and the International Court of Justice at The Hague in the Netherlands.

The Security Council has the "primary responsibility" for maintaining "international peace and security." The General Assembly has authority over "any matter affecting the peace of the world," although it is supposed to defer to the Security Council when the council has already taken up a particular security matter. No nation has a veto in the General Assembly; every nation has one vote regardless of its size or power. Most resolutions can be passed by a majority vote.

**The United Nations in the Cold War**  The United Nations (UN) proved largely ineffective during the long Cold War confrontation between the communist nations, led by the Soviet Union, and the Western democracies, led by the United States. The UN grew from its original 51 member nations to more than 150 (191 in 2005), but most of those nations were headed by authoritarian regimes of one kind or another. The Western democracies were outnumbered in the General Assembly, and the Soviet Union frequently used its veto to prevent action by the Security Council. Anti-Western and antidemocratic speeches became common in the General Assembly.

During the Cold War, the UN was overshadowed by the confrontation of the world's two **superpowers**: the United States and the Soviet Union. Indeed, international conflicts throughout the world—in the Middle East, Africa, Latin America, Southeast Asia, and elsewhere—were usually influenced by some aspect of the superpower struggle.

**Regional Security**  The general disappointment with the United Nations as a form of collective security gave rise as early as 1949 to a different approach, **regional security**. In response to aggressive Soviet moves in Europe, the United States and the democracies of Western Europe created the **North Atlantic Treaty Organization (NATO)**. In the NATO treaty, fifteen Western nations agreed to collective regional security: they agreed that "an armed attack against one or more [NATO nations] . . . shall be considered an attack against them all." The United States made a specific commitment to defend Western Europe in the event of a Soviet attack. A joint NATO military command was established (with Dwight D. Eisenhower as its first commander) to coordinate the defense of Western Europe.

After the formation of NATO, the Soviets made no further advances into Western Europe. The Soviets themselves, in response to NATO, drew up the Warsaw Pact, a comparable treaty with their own Eastern European satellite nations. But for many years the real deterrent to Warsaw Pact expansion was not the weak NATO armies, but rather the pledge of the United States to use its strategic nuclear bomber force to inflict "massive retaliation" on the Soviet Union itself in the event of an attack on Western Europe.

The Warsaw Pact disintegrated following the dramatic collapse of the communist governments of Eastern Europe in 1989. Former Warsaw Pact nations—Poland, Hungary, Romania, Bulgaria, and East Germany—threw out their ruling communist regimes and demanded the withdrawal of Soviet troops from their territory. The Berlin Wall was dismantled in 1989, and Germany was formally reunified in 1990, bringing together the 61 million prosperous people of West Germany and the 17 million less affluent people of East Germany. (Unified

Germany continues as a member of NATO.) The Communist Party was ousted from power in Moscow, and the Soviet Union collapsed in 1991.

**NATO Today**    The United States and its Western European allies agree that NATO continues to play an important role in the security of Europe. Indeed, the continued deployment of some level of U.S. troops to NATO is widely considered to be reassurance that the United States remains committed to this security.

In recent years NATO has made the key decision to expand its security protections to the newly democratic nations of Eastern Europe. Three nations—Poland, Hungary, and the Czech Republic—were admitted to NATO in 1998. At that time Russia strongly objected to NATO expansion, viewing it as an incursion of Western powers in the East and a threat to Russia's security. A NATO-Russia Council was created in 2002 to calm Russian fears about NATO's intentions. In 2004 seven additional countries—Bulgaria, Estonia, Latvia, Lithuania, Romania, Slovakia, and Slovenia—were admitted to membership. All of these nations were formerly under the domination of the Soviet Union. NATO now has 26 members.

Yet another question confronting NATO is what role it should play in trying to resolve religious and ethnic conflicts in Eastern Europe. A combination of security and humanitarian concerns drew NATO, with heavy U.S. participation, into the former Yugoslavian province of Bosnia in 1995 to assist in resolving the war among the Serbs, Croats, and Muslims. This was the first deployment of NATO forces *outside* the national boundaries of NATO nations. NATO began acting militarily to halt ethnic conflicts in Kosovo in 1999. NATO forced Serbian President Slobodan Milosovic to withdraw his forces from the largely Muslim province. U.S. air power played the principal role in this engagement.

**The UN Today**    Russia inherited the UN Security Council seat of the former Soviet Union, and its government has generally cooperated in UN efforts to bring stability to various regional conflicts. No longer are these conflicts "proxy" wars between the superpowers. The UN has sent blue-helmeted "peacekeeping" forces to monitor cease-fires in many troubled areas of the world. Yet the United Nations and its Security Council must rely on "the last remaining superpower," the United States, to take the lead in enforcing its resolutions. However, a top-heavy bureaucracy at UN headquarters in New York, together with scandal and inefficiency in UN spending, has eroded support for the UN in the United States.

# The Legacy of the Cold War

For more than forty years following the end of World War II, the United States and the Soviet Union confronted each other in the protracted political, military, and ideological struggle known as the **Cold War**.

**Origins**    During World War II, the United States and the Soviet Union joined forces to eliminate the Nazi threat to the world. The United States dismantled its military forces at the end of the war in 1945, but the Soviet Union, under the brutal dictatorship of Josef Stalin, used the powerful Red Army to install communist governments in the nations of Eastern Europe in violation of wartime agreements to allow free elections. Stalin also ignored pledges to cooperate in a unified allied occupation of Germany; Germany was divided, and in 1948 Stalin unsuccessfully tried to oust the United States, Britain, and France from Berlin in a year-long "Berlin Blockade." Former British Prime Minister Winston Churchill warned the United States as early as 1946 that the Soviets were dividing Europe with an "Iron Curtain." When Soviet-backed communist forces threatened Greece and Turkey

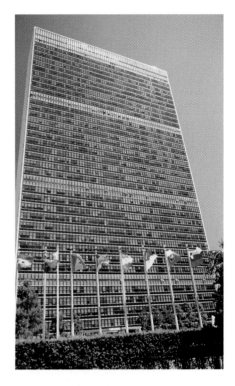

The U.N. Building in New York City symbolizes the hope that nations can resolve problems through collective action. But the United Nations has achieved only limited success in the worldwide war on terror.

**NATO**
The official "North Atlantic Treaty Organization" site contains basic facts about the alliance, current NATO news and issues, and important NATO policies.
*www.nato.int*

**Cold War** Political, military, and ideological struggle between the United States and the Soviet Union following the end of World War II and ending with the collapse of the Soviet Union's communist government in 1991.

— Think Again —
Should the United States and NATO intervene in regional conflicts in Eastern Europe?

**Truman Doctrine** U.S. foreign policy, first articulated by President Harry S Truman, that pledged the United States to "support free peoples who are resisting attempted subjugation by armed minorities or by outside pressures."

**containment** Policy of preventing an enemy from expanding its boundaries and/or influence, specifically the U.S. foreign policy vis-à-vis the Soviet Union during the Cold War.

**Marshall Plan** U.S. program to rebuild the nations of Western Europe in the aftermath of World War II in order to render them less susceptible to communist influence and takeover.

**Korean War Project Organization**
Dedicated to the memory of sacrifices of Americans in Korea, with links to battles, units, and memorials.
*www.koreanwar.org*

**Korean War** Communist North Korea invaded non-Communist South Korea in June 1950, causing President Harry S Truman to intervene militarily, with U.N. support. General Douglas MacArthur defeated the North Koreans, but with China's entry into the war, a stalemate resulted. An armistice was signed in 1953, with Korea divided along nearly original lines.

**Cuban Missile Crisis** The 1962 confrontation between the Soviet Union and the U.S. over Soviet placement of nuclear missiles in Cuba.

in 1947, President Harry S Truman responded with a pledge to "support free people who are resisting attempted subjugation by armed minorities or by outside pressures," a policy that became known as the **Truman Doctrine**.

**Containment**   The United States had fought two world wars to maintain democracy in Western Europe. The new threat of Soviet expansionism and communist world revolution caused America to assume world leadership on behalf of the preservation of democracy. In an influential article in the Council on Foreign Relations' journal *Foreign Affairs*, the State Department's Russia expert George F. Kennan called for a policy of **containment**:

> It is clear that the main element of any United States policy toward the Soviet Union must be that of a long-term, vigilant containment of Russian expansive tendencies. . . .[2]

To implement the containment policy, the United States first initiated the **Marshall Plan**, named for Secretary of State George C. Marshall, to rebuild the economies of the Western European nations. Marshall reasoned that *economically* weak nations were more susceptible to communist subversion and Soviet intimidation. The subsequent formation of NATO provided the necessary *military* support to contain the Soviet Union.

**The Korean War**   The first military test of the containment policy came in June 1950, when communist North Korean armies invaded South Korea. President Truman assumed that the North Koreans were acting on behalf of their sponsor, the Soviet Union. The Soviets had already aided Chinese communists under the leadership of Mao Zedong in capturing control of mainland China in 1949. The United States quickly brought the Korean invasion issue to the Security Council. With the Soviets boycotting this meeting because the council had refused to seat the new communist delegation from China, the council passed a resolution calling on member nations to send troops to repel the invasion.

America's conventional (nonnuclear) military forces had been largely dismantled after World War II. Moreover, President Truman insisted on keeping most of the nation's forces in Europe, fearing that the Korean invasion was a diversion to be followed by a Soviet invasion of Western Europe. But General Douglas MacArthur, in a brilliant amphibious landing at Inchon behind North Korean lines, destroyed a much larger enemy army, captured the North Korean capital, and moved northward toward the Chinese border. Then in December 1950, disaster struck American forces as a million-strong Chinese army entered the conflict. Chinese troops surprised the Americans, inflicting heavy casualties, trapping entire units, and forcing U.S. troops to beat a hasty retreat. General MacArthur urged retaliation against China, but Truman sought to keep the war "limited." When MacArthur publicly protested political limits to military operations, Truman dismissed the popular general. The **Korean War** became a bloody stalemate.

Dwight Eisenhower was elected president in 1952 in large measure because he promised to "go to Korea" to end the increasingly unpopular war. He also threatened to use nuclear weapons in the conflict but eventually agreed to a truce along the original border between North and South Korea. Communist expansion in Korea was "contained," but at a high price: the United States lost more than 38,000 men in the war.

**The Cuban Missile Crisis**   The most serious threat of nuclear holocaust during the entire Cold War was the **Cuban Missile Crisis**. In 1962 Soviet Premier Nikita Khrushchev sought to secretly install medium-range nuclear missiles in Cuba in an effort to give the Soviet Union nuclear capability against U.S. cities. In October 1962 intelligence photos showing Soviet missiles at Cuban bases touched off a thirteen-day crisis. President Kennedy rejected advice to launch an air strike to destroy the missiles before they could be activated. Instead, he publicly announced a naval blockade of Cuba, threatening to halt Soviet missile-carrying vessels at sea by force if necessary. The prospect of war appeared imminent; U.S. nuclear forces went on alert. Secretly, Kennedy proposed to withdraw U.S. nuclear missiles from Turkey in exchange for Soviet withdrawal of nuclear missiles from Cuba. Khrushchev's agreement to the deal appeared to the world as a backing down; Kennedy would be hailed for his statesmanship in the crisis, while Khrushchev would soon lose his job.

**Cuban Crisis**
The October 1962 nuclear missile crisis described day to day, with photos. *www.cubacrisis.net*

**The Vietnam War** When communist forces led by Ho Chi Minh defeated French forces at the battle of Dien Bien Phu, the resulting Geneva Accords divided that country into North Vietnam, with a communist government, and South Vietnam, with a U.S.-backed government. When South Vietnamese communist (Vietcong) guerrilla forces threatened the South Vietnamese government in the early 1960s, President Kennedy sent a force of more than 12,000 advisers and counterinsurgency forces to assist in every aspect of training and support for the Army of the Republic of Vietnam (ARVN) in South Vietnam and authorized a gradual increase in air strikes against North Vietnam. Washington committed more than 500,000 troops to a war of attrition, a war in which U.S. firepower was expected to inflict sufficient casualties on the enemy to force a peace settlement. But over time, the failure to achieve any decisive military victories eroded popular support for the **Vietnam War**.

On January 31, 1968, the Vietnamese holiday of Tet, Vietcong forces blasted their way into the U.S. embassy compound in Saigon and held the courtyard for six hours. The attack was part of a massive, coordinated Tet offensive against all major cities of South Vietnam. U.S. forces responded and inflicted very heavy casualties on the Vietcong. By any military measure, the Tet offensive was a "defeat" for the enemy and a "victory" for U.S. forces. Yet the Tet offensive was Hanoi's greatest *political* victory. Television pictures of bloody fighting in Saigon and Hue seemed to mock President Johnson's promises of an early end to the war.

On March 31, 1968, President Johnson went on national television to make a dramatic announcement: He halted the bombing of North Vietnam and asked Hanoi for peace talks, concluding, "I shall not seek, and I will not accept, the nomination of my party for another term as your president." Formal peace talks opened in Paris on May 13.

The new president, Richard Nixon, and his national security adviser, Henry Kissinger, knew the war must be ended, but they sought to end it "honorably." Even in the absence of a settlement with the communists in Vietnam, Nixon began the withdrawal of U.S. troops under the guise of "Vietnamization" of the war effort. Unable to persuade Hanoi to make even the slightest concession at Paris, President Nixon sought to demonstrate American strength and resolve. In December 1972 the United States unleashed a devastating air attack directly on Hanoi for the first time. Critics at home labeled Nixon's action "the Christmas bombing," but when negotiations resumed in Paris in January, the North Vietnamese quickly agreed to peace on the terms that Kissinger and Le Duc Tho had worked out earlier.

The South Vietnamese government lasted two years after the agreement. In early 1975 Hanoi decided that the Americans would not "jump back in" and therefore "the opportune moment" was at hand for a new invasion. President Gerald Ford's requests to Congress for emergency military aid to the South Vietnamese fell on deaf ears. Saigon (now Ho Chi Minh City) fell to the North Vietnamese in April 1975, and the United States abandoned hundreds of thousands of loyal Vietnamese who had fought alongside the Americans for years.[3] The spectacle of

**Vietnam War** War between non-Communist South Vietnam and Communist North Vietnam from 1956 to 1975, with increasing U.S. involvement, ending with U.S. withdrawal in 1973 and Communist victory in 1975. The war became unpopular in the United States after 1968 and caused President Johnson not to run for a second term. More than 58,000 Americans died in the war.

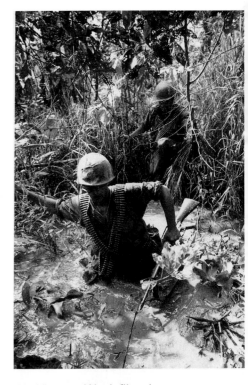

The Vietnam War inflicted more than 47,000 battle deaths on U.S. forces. Units of Army Infantry and Marines slogged through the jungles of Southeast Asia for more than eight years. The Paris Peace Accord, signed in 1973, was ignored by the communist regime in Hanoi; its renewed invasion in 1975 succeeded in capturing all of Vietnam.

U.S. Marines using their rifle butts to keep desperate Vietnamese from boarding helicopters on the roof of the U.S. embassy "provided a tragic epitaph for twenty-five years of American involvement in Vietnam."[4]

**The Vietnam Syndrome**   America's humiliation in Vietnam had lasting national consequences. The United States suffered 47,378 battle deaths and missing-in-action among the 2.8 million U.S. personnel who served in Vietnam. A new isolationism permeated American foreign policy following defeat in Vietnam. The slogan "No more Vietnams" was used to oppose any U.S. military intervention, whether or not U.S. vital interests were at stake. Disillusionment replaced idealism. American leaders had exaggerated the importance of Vietnam; now Americans were unwilling to believe their leaders when they warned of other dangers.

**Rebuilding America's Defenses**   The decision to rebuild Western military forces and reassert international leadership on behalf of democratic values gained widespread support in the Western world in the early 1980s. President Ronald Reagan, British Prime Minister Margaret Thatcher, French President François Mitterrand, and German Chancellor Helmut Kohl all pledged to increase their defense efforts and all held fast against a "nuclear freeze" movement that would have locked in Soviet superiority in European-based nuclear weapons.

The Reagan defense buildup extended through 1985—with increases in defense spending, improvements in strategic nuclear weapons, and, perhaps more important, the rebuilding and reequipping of U.S. conventional forces. The American and NATO defense buildup, together with the promise of a new, expensive, and technologically sophisticated race for ballistic missile defenses, forecast heavy additional strains on the weak economy of the Soviet Union. Thus, in 1985, when new Soviet President Mikhail Gorbachev came to power, the stage was set for an end to the Cold War.

Gorbachev announced reductions in the size of the Soviet military and reached agreements with the United States on the reduction of nuclear forces More important, in 1988 he announced that the Soviet Union would no longer use its military forces to keep communist governments in power in Eastern European nations. This stunning announcement, for which he received the Nobel Peace Prize in 1990, encouraged opposition democratic forces in Poland (the Solidarity movement), Czechoslovakia, Hungary, Bulgaria, Romania, and East Germany. Gorbachev refused to intervene to halt the destruction of the Berlin Wall, despite pleas by the East German hard-line communist leader Erich Honecker.

**The Collapse of Communism**   When hardliners in the Communist Party, the military, and the KGB attempted the forcible removal of Gorbachev in August 1991, democratic forces rallied to his support. Led by Boris Yeltsin, the first elected president of the Russian Republic, thousands of demonstrators took to the streets; Soviet military forces stood aside. Yeltsin emerged as the most influential leader in the nation. The failed coup hastened the demise of the Communist Party. The party lost legitimacy with the peoples of Russia and the other republics.

**The Disintegration of the Soviet Union**   Strong independence movements in the republics of the Soviet Union emerged as the authority of the centralized Communist Party in Moscow waned. Lithuania, Estonia, and Latvia—nations that had been forcibly incorporated into the Soviet Union in 1939—led the way to independence in 1991. Soon all of the fifteen republics of the Soviet Union declared their independence, and the Union of Soviet Socialist Republics officially ceased to exist after December 31, 1991. The red flag with its hammer and sickle atop the Kremlin was replaced with the flag of the Russian Republic.

The Vietnam War Memorial in Washington, D.C., is inscribed with the names of the nearly 50,000 Americans who died in Vietnam. America's defeat fostered a lasting skepticism about the wisdom of foreign military intervention, leading to a new isolationism in foreign policy.

Presidents Vladimir Putin of Russia and George W. Bush of the United States reached agreement in 2002 to reduce their nations' nuclear stockpiles by over 80 percent from Cold War levels.

**Russia after Communism**   The transition from a centralized state-run economy to free markets turned out to be more painful for Russians than expected. Living standards for most people declined, alcoholism and death rates increased, and even average life spans shortened. Ethnic conflict and political separatism, especially in the largely Muslim province of Chechnya, added to Russia's problems. Yeltsin was able to overcome these political challenges and win reelection as president in 1996. But corruption, embezzlement, graft, and organized crime continue to undermine democratic reforms. Poor health eventually forced Yeltsin to turn over power to Vladimir Putin, who himself won election as president of Russia in 2000.

 **Russia EIN News** Business, cultural, political, and scientific news from Russia. *www.einnews.com/russia*

# Nuclear Threats

Nuclear weaponry has made the world infinitely more dangerous. During the Cold War, the nuclear arsenals of the United States and the Soviet Union threatened a human holocaust. Yet, paradoxically, the very destructiveness of nuclear weapons caused leaders on both sides to exercise extreme caution in their relations with each other. Scores of wars, large and small, were fought by different nations during the Cold War years, yet American and Soviet troops never engaged in direct combat against each other.

**Deterrence**   To maintain nuclear peace during the Cold War, the United States relied primarily on the policy of **deterrence**. Deterrence is based on the notion that a nation can dissuade a *rational* enemy from attacking by maintaining the capacity to destroy the enemy's homeland even *after* the nation has suffered a well-executed surprise attack by the enemy. Deterrence assumes that the worst may happen—a surprise first strike against a nation's nuclear forces. It emphasizes **second-strike capability**—the ability of a nation's forces to survive a surprise attack by the enemy and then to inflict an unacceptable level of destruction on the enemy's homeland. Deterrence is really a *psychological* defense against attack; no effective physical defense against a ballistic missile attack exists even today.

**Limiting Nuclear Arms: SALT**   The United States and the Soviet Union engaged in negotiations over nuclear arms control for many years. The development of reconnaissance satellites in the 1960s made it possible for each nation to

─Think Again─

Should the United States destroy all of its nuclear weapons now that the Cold War is over?

**deterrence** U.S. approach to deterring any nuclear attack from the Soviet Union by maintaining a second-strike capability.

**second-strike capability** Ability of a nation's forces to survive a surprise nuclear attack by the enemy and then to retaliate effectively.

Intercontinental Ballistic Missiles (ICBMs) with multiple nuclear warheads, like this MX Peacekeeper being test-fired, threatened a nuclear holocaust during the long Cold War. The START II Treaty in 1993 called for the dismantling of all multiple-warhead missiles, and the Treaty of Moscow in 2002 called for the reduction of total nuclear warheads by 80 percent from Cold War levels.

**SALT I** First arms limitation treaty between the United States and the Soviet Union, signed in 1972, limiting the total number of offensive nuclear missiles; it included the ABM Treaty that reflected the theory that the population centers of both nations should be left undefended.

**ABM Treaty** A formal treaty in 1972 between the United States and the Soviet Union in which each side agreed not to build or deploy antiballistic missiles.

monitor the strategic weapons possessed by the other. Space photography made cheating on agreements more difficult and thus opened the way for both nations to seek stability through arms control.

Following the election of Richard Nixon as president in 1968, the United States, largely guided by former Harvard professor Henry Kissinger (national security adviser to the president and later secretary of state), began negotiations with the Soviet Union over strategic nuclear arms. In 1972 the two nations concluded two and a half years of Strategic Arms Limitation Talks (SALT) about limiting the nuclear arms race. The agreement, **SALT I**, consisted of a treaty limiting antiballistic missiles (ABMs) and an agreement placing a numerical ceiling on offensive missiles. In the **ABM Treaty** both nations pledged *not* to build ballistic missile defenses. This meant that the populations of both nations in effect would be held hostage against a first strike by either nation.

SALT I was the first step forward on the control of nuclear arms; both sides agreed to continue negotiations. After seven years of difficult negotiations, the United States and the Soviet Union produced the lengthy and complicated **SALT II** treaty in 1979. It set an overall limit on "strategic nuclear launch vehicles"—ICBMs, SLBMs, bombers, and long-range cruise missiles—at 2,250 for each side. It also limited the number of missiles that could have multiple warheads (MIRVs). But when the Soviet Union invaded Afghanistan in 1979, President Carter withdrew the SALT II treaty from Senate consideration. However, President Carter, and later President Reagan, announced that the United States would abide by the provisions of the unratified SALT II treaty as long as the Soviet Union did so.

**Reducing Nuclear Arms: START** In negotiations with the Soviets, the Reagan administration established three central principles of arms control—reductions, equality, and verification. The new goal was to be *reductions* in missiles and warheads, not merely limitations on future numbers and types of weapons, as in previous SALT talks. To symbolize this new direction, President Reagan renamed the negotiations the Strategic Arms *Reduction* Talks, or START.

The **START I** Treaty signed in Moscow in 1991 by Presidents George H.W. Bush and Mikhail Gorbachev was the first agreement between the nuclear powers that actually resulted in the reduction of strategic nuclear weapons. The START I Treaty reduced the total number of deployed strategic nuclear delivery systems to no more than 1,600, a 30 percent reduction from the SALT II level.

A far-reaching **START II** agreement, signed in 1993 by U.S. President George H.W. Bush and Russian President Yeltsin, promised to eliminate the threat of a first-strike nuclear attack by either side. Its most important provision was the agreement to eliminate all multiwarhead (MIRVed) land-based missiles. START II also called for the reduction of overall strategic warheads to 3,500.

**The Treaty of Moscow** The capstone of strategic nuclear arms reductions is the Treaty of Moscow, signed by Russian President Vladimir Putin and U.S. President George W. Bush in 2002. This new treaty calls for an overall limit of nuclear warheads at 1,700–2,200 by 2012. Each side may determine for itself the composition and structure of its strategic forces consistent with this limit. The provisions of the START treaties remain unchanged. The effect of the Moscow Treaty, together with earlier reductions in nuclear weapons under the START treaties, will be to reduce the nuclear arsenals of the former adversaries by over 80 percent from Cold War levels (see Figure 14.1).

**Nuclear Terrorism** Even as the threat of a large-scale nuclear attack recedes, the threats arising from "nondeterrable" sources are increasing. Today, the principal

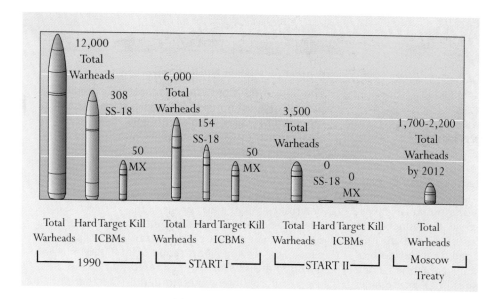

**Figure 14.1**  Strategic Nuclear Arms under START Treaties

Implementation of the START II Treaty will reduce the total number of warheads in both the United States and Russia by over two-thirds and will completely eliminate hard target kill ICBMs.

nondeterrable threats are estimated to be (1) missiles launched by a terrorist nation; (2) unauthorized missile launches by terrorist organizations, and (3) accidental missile launches. Over time global nuclear and ballistic missile proliferation steadily increases the likelihood of these types of threats. Terrorist launches are considered "nondeterrable" because the threat of nuclear retaliation is largely meaningless.

The threat of mass terror weapons—nuclear, chemical, or biological weapons, especially those carried by medium- or long-range missiles—is likely to increase dramatically in the years ahead. North Korea is reported to possess nuclear weapons and to be developing long-range missiles to carry them. Iran has announced its intention to acquire materials for the development of nuclear weapons. Defending against terrorist missile attacks requires the development and deployment of **ballistic missile defense (BMD)** systems, weapons capable of detecting, intercepting, and destroying ballistic missiles while they are in flight. At present there is no defense against a ballistic missile attack on American cities (see *A Conflicting View:* "We Should Defend Ourselves against a Ballistic Missile Attack").

# When to Use Military Force?

All modern presidents have acknowledged that the most agonizing decisions they have made were to send U.S. military forces into combat. These decisions cost lives. The American people are willing to send their sons and daughters into danger—and even to see some of them wounded and killed—but *only* if a president convinces them that the outcome "is worth dying for." A president must be able to explain why they lost their lives and to justify their sacrifice.

**To Protect Vital Interests**    The U.S. military learned many bitter lessons in its long bloody experience in Vietnam. Among those lessons are what became known as the Powell Doctrine, advanced by then Chair of the Joint Chiefs of Staff, General Colin Powell:

- The United States should commit its military forces only in support of vital national interests.

- If military forces are committed, they must have clearly defined military objectives—the destruction of enemy forces and/or the capture of enemy-held territory.

- Any commitment of U.S. forces must be of sufficient strength to ensure overwhelming and decisive victory with the fewest possible casualties.

**SALT II**  Lengthy and complicated treaty between the United States and the Soviet Union, agreed to in 1979 but never ratified by the U.S. Senate, that set limits on all types of strategic nuclear launch vehicles.

**START I**  First treaty between the United States and the Soviet Union that actually reduced the strategic nuclear arms of the superpowers, signed in 1991.

**START II**  A treaty between the United States and Russia eliminating all multiwarhead land missiles and reducing nuclear weapons stockpiles; signed in 2003.

**ballistic missile defense (BMD)**  Weapons systems capable of detecting, intercepting, and destroying missiles in flight.

— Think Again —

Is the president justified in placing U.S. troops in danger where U.S. vital interests are not at stake?

## A CONFLICTING VIEW

# We Should Defend Ourselves against a Ballistic Missile Attack

For over a half-century, since the terrible nuclear blasts at Hiroshima and Nagasaki in Japan in 1945, the world has avoided nuclear war. Peace has been maintained by deterrence—by the threat of devastating nuclear attacks that would be launched in retaliation to an enemy's first strike. But in 1983 President Ronald Reagan urged that instead of deterring war through fear of retaliation, the United States should seek a technological defense against nuclear missiles.

> Our nuclear retaliating forces have deterred war for forty years. The fact is, however, that we have no defense against ballistic missile attack. . . . In the event that deterrence failed, a president's only recourse would be to surrender or to retaliate. Nuclear retaliation, whether massive or limited, would result in the loss of millions of lives. . . .[a]

### "Star Wars"

Reagan's Strategic Defense Initiative (SDI) was a research program designed to explore means of destroying enemy nuclear missiles in space before they could reach their targets. Following President Reagan's initial announcement of SDI in March 1983, the press quickly labeled the effort "Star Wars." In theory, a ballistic missile defense (BMD) system could be based in space, orbiting over enemy missile-launching sites. Should an enemy missile get through the space-based defense, a ground-based BMD system would attempt to intercept warheads as they reentered the atmosphere and approached their targets. SDI included research on laser beams, satellite surveillance, computerized battle-management systems, and "smart" and "brilliant" weapons systems. SDI under President Reagan was a very ambitious program with the goal of creating an "impenetrable shield" that would protect not only the population of the United States but the population of our allies as well.

### Protection against Nuclear Terrorism

The end of the Cold War refocused SDI away from defense against a massive Russian missile attack to more limited yet more likely threats. Today the principal nuclear threats are missiles launched by terrorists or a "rogue state." President Bush redirected SDI toward defending against these more limited yet potentially devastating attacks.

The Gulf War experience demonstrated that deterrence may not protect the United States against a ballistic missile attack by a terrorist regime. The success of the Patriot antiballistic missile in destroying short-range Iraqi Scud missiles during the Gulf War demonstrated that enemy missiles could be intercepted in flight. (The Patriot is a ground-based "tactical" weapon designed to protect specific military targets.) However, developing an effective antiballistic missile that can intercept and destroy another missile in space has proven to be more difficult, although not impossible.

### The Future of BMDs

As a Reagan-era initiative, partisanship has tended to cloud the debate over BMDs. In 1993 President Clinton announced the termination of the separate SDI organization, but he reassured the nation that research would continue on the ground-based ballistic missile defenses. President George W. Bush notified the Russians in 2002 that the United States was withdrawing from provisions of the ABM Treaty of 1972 that prohibited the development, testing, or deployment of new ballistic missile defense systems.

Advanced testing has met with both successes and failures. Intercepting an incoming missile has been compared to "hitting a bullet with a bullet." Even this daunting challenge is further complicated by the likelihood of enemy decoys masking the real warhead; a reliable ballistic missile defense must be able to discriminate between decoys and actual warheads.

President George W. Bush announced a limited deployment of sea-based and ground-based missile interceptors and advanced Patriot missiles in 2004. The president spoke of an incremental growth of U.S. anti-ballistic missile capability directed at potential terrorist attacks.

[a]President Ronald Reagan, *The President's Strategic Defense Initiative*, The White House, January 3, 1985.

- Before committing U.S. military forces, there must be some reasonable assurances that the effort has the support of the American people and their representatives in Congress.

- The commitment of U.S. military forces should be a last resort, after political, economic, and diplomatic efforts have proven ineffective.

President George H.W. Bush argued that his decision to use military force in the Gulf War in 1990–91 met these guidelines: that preventing Iraq's Saddam Hussein from gaining control of the world's oil supply and developing nuclear and chemical weapons were vital national interests; that political and economic sanctions were not effective; and that he had defined clear military objectives—the removal of Iraqi troops from Kuwait and the destruction of Iraq's nuclear and chemical weapon capabilities (see *Up Close:* "The Use of Force: Operation Desert Storm"). And he authorized a large military commitment that led to a speedy and decisive victory.

These guidelines for the use of military force are widely supported within the U.S. military itself.[5] Contrary to Hollywood stereotypes, military leaders are extremely reluctant to go to war when no vital interest of the United States is at stake, where there are no clear-cut military objectives, without the support of Congress or the American people, or without sufficient force to achieve speedy and decisive victory with minimal casualties. They are wary of seeing their troops placed in danger merely to advance diplomatic goals, or to engage in "peacekeeping," or to "stabilize governments," or to "show the flag." They are reluctant to undertake humanitarian missions while being shot at. They do not like to risk their soldiers' lives under "rules of engagement" that limit their ability to defend themselves.

**In Support of Important Political Objectives**   In contrast to military leaders, political leaders and diplomats often reflect the view that "war is a continuation of politics by other means"—a view commonly attributed to nineteenth-century German theorist of war Carl von Clausewitz. Military force may be used to protect interests that are important but not necessarily vital. Otherwise, the United States would be rendered largely impotent in world affairs. A diplomat's ability to achieve a satisfactory result often depends on the expressed or implied threat of military force. The distinguished international political theorist Hans Morgenthau wrote, "Since military strength is the obvious measure of a nation's power, its demonstration serves to impress others with that nation's power."[6]

Currently American military forces must be prepared to carry out a variety of missions in addition to the conduct of conventional war:

- Demonstrating U.S. resolve in crisis situations.

- Demonstrating U.S. support for democratic governments.

- Protecting U.S. citizens living abroad.

- Peacemaking among warring factions or nations.

- Peacekeeping where hostile factions or nations have accepted a peace agreement.

- Providing humanitarian aid often under warlike conditions.

- Assisting in an international war against drug trafficking.

In pursuit of such objectives, recent U.S. presidents have sent troops to Lebanon in 1982 to stabilize the government (Reagan), to Grenada in 1983 to rescue American medical students and restore democratic government (Reagan), to Panama in 1989 to oust drug-trafficking General Manuel Antonio Noriega from power and to protect U.S. citizens (Bush); to Somalia in 1992–93 to provide emergency humanitarian aid (Bush and Clinton); to Haiti in 1994 to restore constitutional government (Clinton) and again to Haiti in 2004 (Bush); and to Bosnia and Kosovo for peacekeeping among warring ethnic factions (see Table 14.1).

**CIA World Factbook**
Nations listed A–Z with geography, people, economy, government, military, and so on, information.
*www.cia.gov/publications/factbook*

## UP CLOSE

# The Use of Force: Operation Desert Storm

Saddam Hussein's invasion of Kuwait on August 2, 1990, was apparently designed to restore his military prestige after an indecisive war against Iran, to secure additional oil revenues to finance the continued buildup of Iraqi military power, and to intimidate (and perhaps invade) Saudi Arabia and the Gulf states, thereby securing control over a major share of the world's oil reserves.

The Iraqi invasion met with a surprisingly swift response by the United Nations, with Security Council resolutions condemning the invasion, demanding an immediate withdrawal, and imposing a trade embargo and economic sanctions. President George H.W. Bush immediately set to work to stitch together a coalition military force that would eventually include thirty nations. Early on, the president described the U.S. military deployment as "defensive," but he soon became convinced that neither diplomacy nor an economic blockade would dislodge Saddam from Kuwait and so ordered the military to prepare an "offensive" option.

The top U.S. military commanders—including the chair of the Joint Chiefs of Staff, General Colin Powell, and the commander in the field, General Norman Schwartzkopf—had been field officers in Vietnam, and they were resolved not to repeat the mistakes of that war. They were reluctant to go into battle without the full support of the American people. If ordered to fight, they wanted to employ overwhelming and decisive military force; they wanted to avoid the gradual escalation, protracted conflict, target limitations, and political interference in the conduct of the war that had characterized the U.S. military's efforts in Vietnam. Accordingly, they presented the president with a plan that called for a very large military buildup involving nearly 500,000 troops. Coalition forces also included British and French heavy armored units, and Egyptian, Syrian, Saudi, and other Arab forces.

From Baghdad, CNN reporters Bernard Shaw and Peter Arnett were startled on the night of January 16 when Operation Desert Storm began with an air attack on key installations in the city. Iraqi forces were also surprised, despite the prompt timing of the attack; Saddam had assured them that the United States lacked the resolve to fight.

The success of the coalition air force was spectacular. American TV audiences saw videotapes of laser-guided bombs entering the doors and air shafts of enemy bunkers. Civilian damage was lower than in any previous air war. After five weeks of air war, intelligence estimated that nearly half the Iraqi tanks and artillery in the field had been destroyed, demoralized troops were hiding in deep

*The Gulf War, labeled "Operation Desert Storm" by the U.S. military, destroyed Iraqi troops in Kuwait and eastern Iraq. President George H. W. Bush ordered a ceasefire after only 100 hours of ground operations. It was hoped that the Iraqi defeat would lead to the ouster of Saddam Hussein, but he survived and strengthened his hold on the Iraqi people.*

shelters, and the battlefield had been isolated and "prepared" for ground operations.

General Schwartzkopf's plan for the ground war emphasized deception and maneuver. While Iraqi forces prepared for attacks from the south and the east coast, he sent heavily armed columns in a "Hail Mary" play—a wide sweep to the west, outflanking and cutting off Iraqi forces in the battle area. On the night of February 24, the ground attack began. Marines breached ditches and minefields and raced directly to the Kuwait airport; army helicopter air assaults lunged deep into Iraq; armored columns raced northward across the desert to outflank Iraqi forces and then attack them from the west, while a surge in air attacks kept Iraqi forces holed up in their bunkers. Iraqi troops surrendered in droves, highways from Kuwait city became a massive junkyard of Iraqi vehicles, and Iraqi forces that tried to fight were quickly destroyed. After 100 hours of ground fighting, President Bush ordered a cease-fire.

The United States had achieved a decisive military victory quickly and with remarkably few casualties. The president resisted calls to expand the original objectives of the war and go on to capture Baghdad, to destroy the Iraqi economy, to encourage Iraq's disintegration as a nation, or to kill Saddam, although it was expected that his defeat would lead to his ouster. Although the war left many political issues unresolved, it was the most decisive military outcome the United States had achieved since the end of World War II.[a] President Bush chose to declare victory and celebrate the return of American troops.

[a]See Harry G. Summers Jr., *On Strategy II: A Critical Analysis of the Gulf War* (New York: Dell, 1992).

**Table 14.1    Major Deployments of U.S. Military Forces Since World War II**

| Year | Area | President |
|------|------|-----------|
| 1950–53 | Korea | Truman |
| 1958 | Lebanon | Eisenhower |
| 1961–64 | Vietnam | Kennedy |
| 1962 | Cuban waters | Kennedy |
| 1965–73 | Vietnam | Johnson, Nixon |
| 1965 | Dominican Republic | Johnson |
| 1970 | Laos | Nixon |
| 1970 | Cambodia | Nixon |
| 1975 | Cambodia | Ford |
| 1980 | Iran | Carter |
| 1982–83 | Lebanon | Reagan |
| 1983 | Grenada | Reagan |
| 1989 | Panama | Bush |
| 1990–91 | Persian Gulf | Bush |
| 1992–93 | Somalia | Bush, Clinton |
| 1994–95 | Haiti | Clinton |
| 1995–2000 | Bosnia | Clinton |
| 1999–2000 | Kosovo | Clinton |
| 2001– | Afghanistan | Bush |
| 2002– | Philippines | Bush |
| 2003– | Iraq | Bush |
| 2004 | Haiti | Bush |

**In Support of the War on Terrorism**    The War on Terrorism creates new conditions for the use of military force.[7] Currently U.S. forces are prepared for:

- Direct attacks against terrorist forces to capture or kill them. These operations are usually carried out by highly trained Special Forces.

- Attacks on nations that harbor terrorists, allow terrorists to maintain bases, or supply and equip terrorist organizations. In 1986, the United States struck at Libya in a limited air attack in response to various Libyan-supported acts of terrorism around the world. In 1993, the United States struck Iraq's intelligence center in Baghdad in response to a foiled plot to assassinate former President George Bush. In 2001, the United States relied principally on Special Forces working in conjunction with tribal forces in Afghanistan to attack Al Qaeda terrorists and to topple the Taliban government that had harbored and supported Al Qaeda.

- **Preemptive attacks** on regimes that threaten to use weapons of mass instruction—chemical, biological, or nuclear weapons—against the United States or its allies, or to supply terrorist organizations with these weapons. Preemptive military action represents a reversal of traditional U.S. policy. Historically the United States acted militarily only in response to a direct attack on its own forces or those of its allies. But it is argued that the Terrorist Attack of 9/11 initiated the current War on Terrorism and that American military actions in the Middle East, including those in Afghanistan and Iraq, are related to the 9/11 attack on America. The argument for preemptive military action was summarized by Secretary of State Condoleezza Rice: "We cannot wait until the smoking gun becomes a mushroom cloud."

— Think Again —

Do you approve of the military attacks led by the United States against targets in Afghanistan?

— Think Again —

Do you favor the United States invading Iraq?

**preemptive attack** The initiation of military action by the United States to prevent terrorists or rogue nations from inflicting heavy damage on the United States.

# The War on Terrorism

**terrorism** Title 22 of the U.S. Code, Section 2656 (d): "The term 'terrorism' means premeditated, politically motivated violence perpetrated against noncombatant targets by subnational groups or clandestine agents, usually intended to influence an audience."

**Terrorism Research Center**

The "Terrorism Research Center" Web site is dedicated to "informing the public of the phenomena of terrorism and information warfare." It contains news, analytical essays on terrorist issues, and many links to other terrorism materials and research sources. *www.terrorism.com*

**Defenselink Terrorism**

Official Defense Department site link to information on terrorism. *www.defenselink.mil/terrorism*

**CIA-Terrorism** Reports, news, facts, regarding terrorism. *www.cia.gov/terrorism*

**Terrorism** is a political act. The deliberate targeting of civilians, the infliction of widespread destruction, and the resulting media portrayals of the pain and suffering of victims are designed to call attention to political grievances and to instill fear in people. (The Latin root of the term, *terrere*, means "to frighten.") The horror of terrorist acts and their unpredictability add to public fear—people can neither anticipate nor prepare for tragedies inflicted upon them. Terrorists hope to undermine the confidence of people in their government to protect them, and so they will conclude that submission to the terrorists' demands is preferable to living in a continuing climate of anxiety and uncertainty.

**Global Terrorism**    Global terrorism has evolved over the years into highly sophisticated networks operating in many countries. The most notable terrorist attacks extend back over thirty years, but the death and destruction wrought by terrorists have dramatically increased (see Table 14.2). Prior to the attacks on New York's World Trade Center and the Pentagon on September 11, 2001, most Americans thought of terrorism as foreign. Terrorist acts on American soil had been rare; the most destructive attack—the Oklahoma City bombing of a federal building in 1995—had been carried out by domestic terrorists. But the 9/11 attacks were on an unprecedented scale and they revealed a sophisticated global plot against America.

A loose-knit network of terrorist cells (Al Qaeda) organized by a wealthy Saudi Arabian, Osama bin Laden, was engaged in global terrorism. Their political grievances included America's support of Israel in Middle East conflicts and an American presence in Islamic holy lands, notably Saudi Arabia. Several nations share these grievances and, more importantly, provided support and haven to Al Qaeda and similar terrorist organizations. The principal base of support and sanctuary for Al Qaeda was the repressive and violent Taliban regime of Afghanistan.

**Declaring War on Terrorism**    On the evening of September 11, President George W. Bush spoke to the American people from the Oval Office in a nationally televised address:

> The pictures of airplanes flying into buildings, fires burning, huge structures collapsing, have filled us with disbelief, terrible sadness, and a quiet, unyielding anger. These mass murders were intended to frighten our nation into chaos and retreat. But they failed; our country is strong. . . . These deliberate and deadly attacks were more than acts of terror. They were acts of war.

The president outlined a broad "response to terrorism" to be fought both at home and abroad through diplomatic, military, financial, investigative, homeland security, and humanitarian means. He warned that the new war on terrorism would require a long-term sustained effort. It would require Americans to accept new restrictions on their lives (see "Terrorism's Threat to Democracy" in Chapter 1). It would require new legislation—an Airport Security Act federalizing security at U.S. airports and instituting new strict security measures, and a Patriot (antiterrorism) Act expanding the authority of the attorney general and federal law-enforcement agencies to fight domestic terrorism (see *A Conflicting View:* "Terrorism Requires Restrictions on Civil Liberties" in Chapter 12). It would require the creation of a new Department of Homeland Security designed to coordinate many federal, state, and local law-enforcement agencies charged with responsibility for dealing with acts of terror (see "The Department of Homeland Security" in Chapter 10).

## PEOPLE IN POLITICS

### Condoleezza Rice

Condoleezza Rice was a trusted Bush insider well before her appointment as secretary of state in 2005. She had served as national security adviser under President Bush in his first term, and along with Vice President Dick Cheney, Secretary of Defense Donald Rumsfeld, and others, she was a staunch supporter of the invasion of Iraq. She lectures in broad terms about "implanting democracy in the Middle East," but, like the president, she defines only a vague strategy to achieve that elusive goal.

Condoleezza Rice was born in Birmingham, Alabama, in 1954, and she observed the violence of early desegregation, including the Birmingham Church bombing that killed four children. Her father was a pastor and her mother a music teacher. Young Condoleezza was a child prodigy who entered college at age fifteen intending to become a concert pianist. But her interests soon turned to international politics, and she graduated Phi Beta Kappa from the University of Denver with a major in political science. She received her master's degree from Notre Dame and then returned to the University of Denver for her Ph.D. in 1981. She accepted a professorship at Stanford University and later became that university's provost. She also joined the staff of the Hoover Institution, a think tank on the Stanford campus occasionally labeled conservative because of its commitment to individualism and free markets around the world. She became a member of the Council on Foreign Relations and joined the boards of Chevron, J.P. Morgan, Transamerica, Hewlett-

Packard, the Hewlett Foundation, the RAND Corporation, and the Carnegie Corporation. (Chevron initially named an oil tanker for her but later changed its name when she went to Washington.)

Rice has been exceptionally well received in world capitals. She speaks several foreign languages, impresses world leaders with her keen intellect, and puts people at ease with her congeniality. She has been instrumental in negotiations, getting the Chinese to side with the United States in pressuring North Korea to give up its nuclear weapons program. But inevitably her legacy as secretary of state will be judged by the outcome in Iraq. Her expressed optimism in democracy is not likely in itself to bring peace to that country. But if significant progress can be achieved in Iraq by 2008, she may be a leading prospect for a place on the Republican presidential ticket.

**Operation "Enduring Freedom"**   The military phase of the war on terrorism began October 7, 2001, when U.S. Air Force and Navy aircraft began attacks on known Al Qaeda bases in Afghanistan and U.S. Special Forces organized and led anti-Taliban fighters, including several tribal groups in a campaign against the Taliban regime. A coalition of nations participated in Operation "Enduring Freedom"; some, including Britain and Canada, contributed troops, while others, including Pakistan, Saudi Arabia, and Uzbekistan, informally allowed U.S. forces to base operations on their territory. Kabul, the capital of Afghanistan, was occupied by anti-Taliban forces on November 13, 2001.

President Bush made it clear that the United States was prepared to act militarily against governments that harbored or gave sanctuary to terrorists. The Taliban regime was ousted from power. By April 2002—six months into Operation Enduring Freedom—Al Qaeda and Taliban forces had been either destroyed or scattered into small groups in the mountainous areas of Afghanistan and neighboring Pakistan. Osama bin Laden himself, however, escaped capture.

A meeting in Bonn, Germany, of various Afghan political and military groups produced general agreement on the installation of a new government in Kabul, headed by Hamid Karzai. But today the Karzai government has less than full

**Table 14.2   Notable Global Terrorist Attacks**

| Date | Number of People Killed | Description | Prime suspect[s] |
|---|---|---|---|
| September 5, 1972 | 17 | Israeli athletes are killed during the Olympics in Munich, Germany | Black September, a Palestinian guerrilla group |
| April 18, 1983 | 63 | The American Embassy in Beirut, Lebanon, is bombed | Hezbollah [Party of God] |
| September 23, 1983 | 112 | A plane crashes in United Arab Emirates after a bomb explodes in the baggage compartment | Unknown |
| October 23, 1983 | 299 | Two truck bombs kill U.S. Marines and French paratroopers in Beirut, Lebanon | U.S. blames groups aligned with Iran and Syria |
| June 23, 1985 | 329 | An Air India jet explodes over the Atlantic Ocean, off the coast of Ireland | The Royal Canadian Mounted Police charge Ajaib Singh Bagri and Ripudaman, two Sikh dissidents, in 2000 |
| November 29, 1987 | 115 | A Korean Air Lines jet explodes over the Burma coast | South Korea suspects North Korean involvement |
| December 21, 1988 | 270 | Pan Am 103 explodes over Lockerbie, Scotland | One Libyan intelligence officer is convicted in a trial in The Hague in 2001, another is acquitted |
| September 19, 1989 | 171 | A French U.T.A. jet explodes over Niger | The Lebanese Islamic Holy War claims responsibility, France holds Libya responsible |
| October 2, 1990 | 128 | A hijacked Xiamen Airlines plane crashes into other parked planes in an airport in China | Unknown |
| March 17, 1992 | 29 | A bomb demolishes the Israeli Embassy in Buenos Aires, Argentina | Unknown |
| February 26, 1993 | 6 | A van filled with explosives explodes in the garage of the World Trade Center, leaving more than 1,000 people wounded | Ramzi Yousef receives a life sentence plus 240 years in 1998; the FBI suspects Osama bin Laden is behind the plot |
| April 19, 1995 | 168 | Oklahoma City truck bomb destroys the Alfred P. Murrah federal building | Timothy McVeigh, executed June 11, 2001 |
| August 7, 1998 | 224 | Car bombs destroy U.S. embassies in Nairobi, Kenya, and Dar Es Salaam, Tanzania | Al Qaeda (Osama bin Laden) |
| October 12, 2000 | 17 | Rubber boat filled with explosives detonates next to USS *Cole* in Yemen | Al Qaeda (Osama bin Laden) |
| September 11, 2001 | 3,000+ | Four U.S. commercial airlines hijacked. Two destroy World Trade Center, one hits the Pentagon, one crashes in Pennsylvania | Al Qaeda (Osama bin Laden) |
| March 11, 2004 | 191 | Bombing of train in Madrid, Spain | Al Qaeda |
| September 3, 2004 | 355 (176 children) | Chechen terrorists attack school in Beslan, Russia | Chechen |
| July 7, 2005 | 58 | Terrorists set off four bombs in London's transit system | Unknown |
| Nov 9, 2005 | 57 | Three hotels bombed in Amman, Jordan | Al Zarqawi, right arm of Osama bin Laden |
| July 11, 2006 | 147+ | Train stations bombed in Mumbai (Bombay), India | Kashmir Muslim separatists |

*Source:* U.S. Department of State, Office of Counterterrorism.

## COMPARED TO WHAT?

### World Opinion about America's War against Terrorism

Europeans were generally sympathetic with the United States following the terrorist attack of 9/11, and generally supported the U.S. military campaign against terrorists in Afghanistan. But opinion in Europe, as well as in the Muslim world, opposed U.S. military action in Iraq. Indeed, over time ratings of the United States have grown markedly less favorable among Europeans, and the United States is now strongly disliked in the Muslim world. An important factor in world opinion about America is the perception that the United States acts internationally without taking into account the interests of other nations.

**Ratings of the United States**

|  | 2002 | | 2004 | |
|---|---|---|---|---|
|  | Favorable | Unfavorable | Favorable | Unfavorable |
| Great Britain | 75% | 16% | 58% | 34% |
| France | 63 | 34 | 37 | 62 |
| Germany | 61 | 35 | 38 | 59 |
| Russia | 61 | 33 | 47 | 44 |
| Turkey | 30 | 42 | 30 | 45 |
| Pakistan | 10 | 58 | 21 | 50 |
| Jordan | 25 | 57 | 5 | 67 |
| Morocco | 27 | 46 | 27 | 46 |

*Source:* Pew Research Center for the People and the Press. *http://www.people-press.org.* Reprinted by permission of Pew Research Center for the People and the Press.

control over Afghanistan; various tribal military chiefs, or "warlords," exercise independent power throughout the country.

**Operation Iraqi Freedom**    At the end of the Gulf War in 1991, the Iraqi regime of Saddam Hussein agreed to destroy all of its chemical and biological weapons and to end its efforts to acquire nuclear weapons. United Nations inspectors were to verify Iraqi compliance with these conditions. But Saddam's regime refused to cooperate; in 1998 he ordered the inspectors out of the country. Over a twelve-year period Iraq violated at least a dozen U.N. resolutions. Following a U.S. military buildup in the region in late 2002, Saddam allowed U.N. inspectors to return but continued to obstruct their work. On March 19, 2003, after giving Saddam a forty-eight hour warning to leave Iraq, the United States and Great Britain launched air strikes designed to eliminate Saddam and his top command.

At different times President Bush stated the purposes of "Operation Iraqi Freedom" as (1) the elimination of Iraq's weapons of mass destruction, (2) a "regime change" for Iraq to end the threat that Saddam posed for his neighbors and to free the Iraqi people from his oppressive rule, and (3) to ensure that Saddam would not harbor or assist terrorist organizations. But President Bush and Secretary of State Colin Powell failed to secure U.N. Security Council approval for military action. Among the permanent members of the Security Council, only the British, with the strong support of Prime Minister Tony Blair, were prepared to offer significant military support for the war against Saddam. Public opinion in America supported military action, but public opinion in Europe opposed it (see *Compared to What:* "World Opinion about America's War against Terrorism"). France and Germany led the diplomatic opposition; Turkey refused to let U.S. troops use its territory to

American and British soldiers and Marines swept into Baghdad in just twenty-one days in 2003 with relatively few casualties. But the subsequent occupation of that country was poorly prepared for, incompetently executed, and terribly costly in soldiers' lives lost.

attack Iraq; and the United States was obliged to rely primarily on Kuwait, Qatar, and the other smaller Gulf states for regional support.

The U.S. military wanted to wage war in the fashion of the successful Gulf War—a period of heavy air bombardment to "prepare the battlefield," followed by a massive ground attack using overwhelming military force. But Secretary of Defense Donald Rumsfeld wanted a "leaner" fighting force in Iraq. He deployed fewer than half of the air, ground, and naval forces that had been used in the Gulf War. And he began the air and ground attacks simultaneously.

American and British soldiers and Marines took just twenty-one days to sweep the 350 miles from the Kuwait border to downtown Baghdad. The British 3rd Armored Division, with Australian support, captured the port city of Basra; the U.S. 3rd Infantry Division moved up the west side of the Euphrates River; and the U.S. 1st Marine Division moved up the east side. Special Operations Forces, together with elements of the 101st Airborne Division, joined Kurdish forces in northern Iraq. Special Operations Forces also acted quickly to secure Iraq's oil fields and prevent their destruction. At first progress was hindered by the requirement that soldiers wear heavy chemical protection gear and carry decontamination equipment. But neither chemical nor biological weapons were used against U.S. forces. The advance on Baghdad was speeded up and the city was captured with precious few casualties.

But the subsequent occupation of Iraq by American troops and attempts to construct a more democratic government in that nation turned out badly. U.S. troops suffered more casualties in the aftermath of the war than during the war itself. Insurgent activity against American and British and other coalition nations' forces, and against Iraqis who appeared to cooperate in the reconstruction of their country, inflicted heavy damage and loss of life. The United States officially turned over sovereignty to an interim Iraqi government before June 30, 2004. The Iraqis voted to ratify a constitution in 2005 and later in the year elected a parliament under that constitution. But no firm plans were announced for the withdrawal of American troops from Iraq.

**American Security Council**
Organization providing summary information on national security threats.
*www.ascusa.org*

**─Think Again─**
Are U.S. military force levels today sufficient to deal with potential regional aggressors such as Iran, Iraq, and North Korea?

# Political Support for War in Iraq

Americans demand quick victory in war. With the exception of World War II, American public support for wars, notably Korea (1950–53) and Vietnam (1965–73), declined steadily as casualties rose and no end appeared in sight. The initial "rally 'round the flag" support for military action begins to wane after the first year of combat. Quick victories with few casualties, as in the Gulf War (1991), inspire support for the president and his decision to go to war. Prolonged stalemates with mounting casualties gradually erode public support for war.

The insurgency in Iraq following the capture of Baghdad in 2003 seemed to surprise Secretary of Defense Donald Rumsfeld. Planning for post-war Iraq appeared nonexistent. Rumsfeld steadfastly refused to send additional U.S. troops to Iraq to handle the insurgency and insisted that a new Iraqi government could eventually recruit and train enough troops to contain the insurgency. President Bush held steady throughout years of rising casualties. By late 2004, polls indicated that Americans, who had strongly supported going to war, had concluded that the war was "not worth it" (see Figure 14.2).

Bush's critics at home and abroad complained bitterly of the president's "unilateralism"—his willingness to go to war without the support of the United Nations. They charged that he misled Congress, the UN and the American

# A CONSTITUTIONAL NOTE

## Congress versus the Commander-in-Chief

The Constitution of 1787 divided war-making powers between the Congress and the president. Article I, Section 8 states that "Congress shall have Power ... to provide for the common Defense ... to declare War. ... to raise and support Armies ... to provide and maintain a Navy ... to make Rules for the Government and Regulation of the land and naval forces." However, Article II, Section 2, states that "the President shall be the Commander-in-Chief of the Army and Navy of the United States." But today wars are not "declared"; instead they begin with military action, and the president is responsible for the actions of the Armed Forces of the United States. Presidents have sent U.S. troops beyond the borders of the United States in military actions on more than 200 occasions. In contrast, Congress has formerly declared war only five times: the War of 1812, the Mexican War in 1846, the Spanish-American War in 1898, World War I in 1917, and World War II in 1941. Congress did *not* declare war in the Korean War (1950–53), the Vietnam War (1965–73), the Persian Gulf War (1991), or the wars in Afghanistan (2002–) or Iraq (2003–). While presidents asked for the support of Congress in these wars, no formal declarations of war were ever made. The Supreme Court has consistently refused to hear cases involving the war powers of the president and Congress.

people about the existence of weapons of mass destruction. Bush's actions alienated our traditional allies—France and Germany—and were opposed by Russia and China and most of the Muslim world. Finally, critics charged that Bush had "no plan" for the reconstruction of Iraq after the fall of Saddam.

Secretary of Defense Rumsfeld continued to refuse to send additional troops to Iraq. He argued that eventually American-trained Iraqi troops would be able to take over the task of providing security for a new, more democratic Iraqi government. He pointed to the successful efforts to write a new Iraqi constitution, the heavy turnout of voters to ratify that constitution, and the even heavier turnout to elect a parliament in 2005. Yet American casualties continued from insurgent attacks, and insurgents attacked newly formed Iraqi troops as well as

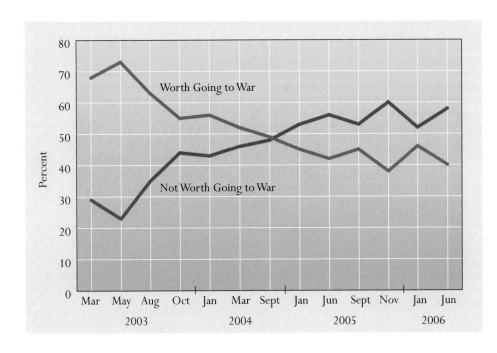

**Figure 14.2** Changing Public Opinion about the War in Iraq

*Q. All in all, do you think it was worth going to war in Iraq, or not?*

Dates of Polls: 2003–March, May, August, October; 2004–January, March, June, September; 2005–January, June, September, November; 2005–June.

*Source: www.pollingreport.com.*

vital infrastructure, including oil supplies, damaging U.S. efforts to create a stable democracy in that country.

Nevertheless, President Bush argued that the war in Iraq was central to the worldwide war against terrorism. The "regime change" in Baghdad (Saddam was captured and placed on trial) removed a base of operations for terrorists. More importantly, President Bush argued forcefully that an abrupt withdrawal ("cut and run") would encourage radical Islamic terrorists around the world.

> Failure is not an option. Iraq would become a safe haven from which terrorists could plan attacks against American interests abroad, and our allies. Middle East reformers would never again fully trust American assurances of support for democracy in human rights in the region. Iraq is the central front in the global war on terror.[8]

Even the Western powers that had initially opposed going to war in Iraq came to see that any defeat of the United States in that country would prove calamitous to the Western world.

# Summary Notes

- The struggle for power is global. Leaders and peoples of the world protect and advance their goals and ideals through the exercise of power.

- There is no world government capable of legislating and enforcing rules of international politics. But various efforts to stabilize relations among nations have been attempted, including the balance-of-power system of alliances in the eighteenth and nineteenth centuries, the collective security arrangements of the League of Nations and the United Nations in the twentieth century, and the regional security approach of the North Atlantic Treaty Organization.

- The United Nations was largely ineffective during the Cold War, the confrontation between the Western democracies led by the United States and communist bloc nations led by the Soviet Union. During these years, the Western nations relied principally on the strength of the North Atlantic Treaty Organization (NATO) to deter war in Europe.

- For nearly fifty years, the Cold War largely directed U.S. foreign and defense policy. The United States sought to contain Soviet military expansionism and world communist revolutionary forces in all parts of the globe. U.S. involvement in the Korean and Vietnam wars grew out of this containment policy.

- During the Cold War years, U.S. and Soviet military forces never engaged in direct combat against each other, although many "proxy" conflicts took place throughout the world. The most serious threat of nuclear war occurred during the Cuban missile crisis in 1962.

- To maintain nuclear peace, the United States relied primarily on the policy of deterrence—dissuading the Soviets from launching a nuclear attack by maintaining survivable second-strike forces capable of inflicting unacceptable levels of destruction in a retaliatory attack.

- In 1970 President Richard Nixon and National Security Adviser Henry Kissinger began negotiations with the Soviet Union with a view to limiting the nuclear arms race. These Strategic Arms Limitation Talks produced the SALT I agreement in 1972, and later, under President Jimmy Carter, the SALT II agreement in 1979. Both agreements set limits on future strategic weapons development but failed to reduce existing weapons stockpiles.

- President Ronald Reagan renamed the negotiations START, emphasizing the goal of reductions in weapons rather than limitations, and stressing equality and verification. The START I (1991) and START II (1993) treaties called for reducing nuclear arsenals by two-thirds from Cold War levels.

- The end of the Cold War followed the ouster of communist governments in Eastern Europe in 1989, the unification of Germany in 1990, the collapse of the Warsaw Pact communist military alliance in 1991, and the dissolution of the Soviet Union in 1991. Russia has inherited most of the nuclear weapons and military forces of the former Soviet Union as well as its seat on the UN Security Council.

- Current threats to peace and security are likely to be posed by regional aggressors. U.S. involvement in the Gulf War in 1990–91 is representative of the type of military action most likely to be undertaken in the future. Current defense policy calls for the United States to be prepared to fight two "Iraqi equivalent wars" "nearly simultaneously."

- The military phase of America's War on Terrorism began October 7, 2001, when U.S. aircraft began attacks on Al Qaeda bases in Afghanistan and U.S. special forces organized and led anti-Taliban Afghan fighters to oust the Taliban regime that had harbored the terrorists. These military actions largely destroyed the terrorist infrastructure in Afghanistan; yet scattered groups of terrorists remain in that country and neighboring Pakistan.

- President George W. Bush warned that the War on Terrorism would be a continuing one, but the variety of ways and means and places of potential terrorist attack make it impossible for the United States to guarantee an end to international terrorism.

- Following the Vietnam War, many military leaders argued that U.S. forces should be used only to protect vital American interests, only in support of clearly defined military objectives, only with sufficient strength to ensure decisive victory with the fewest possible casualties, only with the support of the American people and Congress, and only as a last resort.

- Recent presidents, however, have used military forces to carry out a variety of missions in addition to conventional war, including peacekeeping, antiterrorist, and humanitarian activities. They have argued that the risks were worth taking in light of the importance of the goals.

## Key Terms

collective security   496
Soviet Union   496
superpowers   496
regional security   496
North Atlantic Treaty
   Organization
   (NATO)   496

Cold War   497
Truman Doctrine   498
containment   498
Marshall Plan   498
Korean War   498
Cuban Missile
   Crisis   498

Vietnam War   499
deterrence   501
second-strike
   capability   501
SALT I   502
ABM Treaty   502
SALT II   503

START I   503
START II   503
ballistic missile defense
   (BMD)   503
preemptive attack   507
terrorism   508

## Suggested Readings

Clausewitz, Carl von. *On War*. Edited and translated by Michael Howard and Peter Paret. Princeton, N.J.: Princeton University Press, 1984. The classic theory of war and military operations, emphasizing their political character; first published in 1832.

Combs, Cynthia C. *Terrorism in the 21st Century*. 4th ed. Upper Saddle River, N.J.: Prentice Hall, 2006. History of terrorism, terrorist operations and responses to terrorism, written for those not familiar with the topic.

Hastedt, Glenn P. *American Foreign Policy: Past, Present, Future*. 6th ed. Upper Saddle River, N.J.: Prentice Hall, 2006. A foreign policy text that deals with national security issues within the broader context of foreign policy.

International Institute for Strategic Studies. *The Military Balance*. London: International Institute for Strategic Studies, published annually. Careful description of the military forces of more than 160 countries; this book is considered the most authoritative public information available.

Kegley, Charles W. *The New Global Terrorism*. Upper Saddle River, N.J.: Prentice Hall, 2003. Describing post-9/11 terrorism, its multiple roots, and leading ideas for winning the "war on global terrorism."

Magstadt, Thomas M. *An Empire If You Can Keep It: Power and Principle in American Foreign Policy*. Washington, D.C.: CQ Press, 2004. Comprehensive text on American foreign policy, describing its history, the cold war, the Gulf War, September 11, and the War on Terrorism.

Snow, Donald M. *When America Fights: The Uses of U.S. Military Force*. Washington, D.C.: CQ Press, 2000. Questions U.S. military involvement in "peacekeeping" operations. Discusses the use of force in relation to U.S. national interests.

Summers, Harry G., Jr. *On Strategy II: A Critical Analysis of the Gulf War*. New York: Dell, 1992. Analysis of the Gulf War based on Clausewitz's classic principles of war. The strategic decisions leading to victory in the Gulf contrast markedly with the decisions in Vietnam that led to defeat, a topic covered in Summers's groundbreaking first book, *On Strategy: A Critical Analysis of the Vietnam War* (New York: Dell, 1984).

# Part Six

# CALIFORNIA POLITICS

## Report Card

**ABCNEWS**

Originally Aired: **October 8, 2003**
Program: **Nightline**
Running Time: **17:24**

Public education is one of the great promises of this country. But is America keeping that promise? This ABC News program offers a timely report card on the nation's public education system. Hard-hit by state budget cuts in recent years, the system is also under immense pressure from the No Child Left Behind Act—legislation that demands much of schools but, say critics, provides little funding to help them meet the mandated goals. California has particular challenges because of a growing and diverse student population.

## Critical Thinking Questions

1. What is an unfunded mandate? Give examples of unfunded mandates in the No Child Left Behind Act that are discussed in "Report Card."

2. In "Report Card," author Jonathan Kozol says the "way we finance education in the United States is archaic, chaotic, and utterly undemocratic." What about our education financing leads him to say this?

3. Arnold Schwarzenneger recently vetoed a bill that would have redefined proficiencies in core areas measured by the No Child Left Behind Act. What are arguments against the Federal Government setting standards and defining things such as proficiency?

# 15 CALIFORNIA:
## Historical Perspective

## Chapter Outline

- A Lure and a Challenge: California's Land and Climate
- Native American Settlement
- Spanish Exploration and Settlement
- Mexican Control
- U.S. Annexation
- Early Years of Statehood: The Big Four
- Revolt against the Railroads: The Second California Constitution
- The Progressive Era: Hiram Johnson and Clean Government
- The Twentieth Century: Rapid Economic Growth
- California in the New Millennium

## Think About Politics

**1** Is California in a position to adapt to the global economy?
Yes ☐ No ☐

**2** Should California have stricter energy deregulation guidelines?
Yes ☐ No ☐

**3** Should California give more attention to assisting children in the state who live in poverty?
Yes ☐ No ☐

**4** Should voters in California be able to sign petitions to put specific issues on the ballot?
Yes ☐ No ☐

**5** Should the California legislature increase taxes?
Yes ☐ No ☐

**6** Is California's prison system successful?
Yes ☐ No ☐

**7** Are Californians too impatient with state leadership?
Yes ☐ No ☐

*Historically, California has been considered a trendsetter in American society. Reflecting on the evolution of democracy in California and recent developments in state politics, consider the state's political future.*

## Introduction

Just as democracy has evolved over time in America, so it has evolved in the state of California. In fact, throughout our nation's history, Californians have often led the battle for democracy. Many struggles to preserve and extend freedom and equality have been waged in California, and we will consider many of them throughout these chapters. Some of the most democratic institutions of modern America have originated or reached their greatest development here. But the path of democratic evolution in California has been anything but smooth. Some observers cite California's recent political history as proof that some forms of popular participation can weaken or even paralyze government. Others look to California for hints of what American democracy might become in the twenty-first century. Throughout its history, California has been, for good or ill, a trendsetter in American society. In the words of President Jimmy Carter, "Whatever starts in California unfortunately has an inclination to spread."

The story of California politics is a chronicle of our continuing struggle over the meaning of American democracy. Who are "the people"? How can they be both free and equal? How should the rights of minorities be balanced against the will of majorities? How powerful should our governments be? The answers to questions like these define our democratic ideals and mold our political institutions. Democracy doesn't just happen; it emerges from the continuing clash of real ideals and interests over the course of history. We cannot clearly understand the present or future unless we have a sense of our past.

This chapter describes the events that have shaped California's politics and government over four centuries, from the arrival of the first European explorers to the dawn of the new millennium (see Table 15.1). For 400 years, California has been a state of newcomers, drawn by promises of gold, fertile land, and temperate climate. But as you shall see, the geography of California has been both an attraction and a test for Californians old and new.

| Table 15.1 | Important Events in California History |
|---|---|
| **8,000 years ago** | Chumash Indian tribe settles along the Southern California coast. |
| **1542** | Juan Rodriguez Cabrillo discovers San Diego: he is the first European to land in California, only fifty years after Columbus landed in the Americas. |
| **1577** | Sir Francis Drake explores the California coast and claims the region for Great Britain. |
| **1769** | Father Junipero Serra founds in San Diego the first of twenty-one California missions. |
| **1812** | Russian traders establish Fort Ross near Bodega Bay—according to legend, the Russians acquired the area for three blankets, three pairs of breeches, two axes, three hoes, and some beads. |
| **1821** | Mexico gains its independence from Spain. |
| **1827** | Jedediah Smith crosses the Sierra Nevada range, making him the first American to enter California. |
| **1848** | James Marshall finds gold at Sutter's Mill. |
| **1848** | The Treaty of Guadalupe Hidalgo officially ends the Mexican-American War, resulting in the transfer of Mexican territories, including California, to U.S. control. |
| **1850** | California is admitted to the Union as the thirty-first state. |
| **1851** | The Mariposa Indian War ends with huge numbers of Indians killed in gold country. |
| **1869** | Transcontinental railroad is completed. |
| **1871** | Anti-Chinese riots occur in San Francisco. |
| **1906** | Earthquake and fire destroy much of San Francisco, causing over 3,000 deaths and rendering approximately 300,000 people homeless. |
| **1911** | First motion picture is made in Hollywood. |
| **1937** | Golden Gate Bridge is completed. |
| **1938** | Ten thousand people are arriving each month via U.S. Highway 66, mostly from the Dust Bowl states. |
| **1942** | Japanese Americans and Japanese immigrants are relocated inland. |
| **1955** | Disneyland opens in Anaheim, to be visited by 50 million people in its first ten years. |
| **1962** | California becomes the most populous state. |
| **1965** | Major riots take place in African American sections of Los Angeles. |
| **1968** | Robert Kennedy wins the California presidential primary, but is mortally wounded within minutes of his victory speech. |
| **1971** | American Indian protesters occupy Alcatraz Island in San Francisco Bay. |
| **1977** | Apple II personal computers, developed in "Silicon Valley," are introduced. |
| **1989** | The Loma Prieta earthquake, magnitude 7.1, strikes the San Francisco Bay Area, causing almost $3 billion in damage to San Francisco. |
| **2000** | The Internet industry, primarily located in California, suffers a major decline and over 128,000 workers in the industry lose their jobs. |

---

— Think Again —

What made California attractive to immigrants in the first half of the nineteenth century?

# A Lure and a Challenge: California's Land and Climate

California's climate and geography have played a central role in the state's remarkable development. As Californians move into a post-industrial age increasingly shaped by the forces of technology, we must not overlook the importance of the state's physical environment. California's geography continues to shape the state's social and economic development; it influences government and business policies on energy, water supply, and agriculture. Images of California's balmy weather, bountiful land, and mineral wealth have lured generations of immigrants from around the globe to seek a better life on the shores of the Pacific Ocean.

From the days of the earliest settlers, many of the state's greatest attractions have been found on the coastline. When Gaspar de Portolá's overland expedition first sighted San Francisco Bay in 1769, the explorers discovered one of the world's greatest natural harbors. Besides its scenic beauty, the Northern California coast offered a moderate climate and a wide variety of edible fish and shellfish. Early explorers of the bay and its hinterland reported that huge schools of salmon and other game fish could be easily caught by hand as they passed through the region's inlets and rivers. Venturing inland, settlers found coastal valleys with ample water, fertile soil, and plentiful stands of timber. The redwood, the world's largest tree, would supply new arrivals with some of the toughest and most durable wood on the continent. With adequate water, the soil of these coastal valleys could support almost any type of agricultural production. California's shoreline was blessed with a temperate climate: The seaboard, cooled by the ocean breeze, rarely experienced the scorching summers and harsh winters of the nation's midlands. Most of California enjoys a Mediterranean climate with only two distinct seasons: a cool, wet winter and a mild, dry summer.

An even greater lure than climate for most immigrants to California was the mineral wealth soon discovered in the state's valleys and mountains. The most famous find was, of course, the gold strike at Sutter's Mill on the American River in 1848 that inspired the historic **California Gold Rush**. Many other discoveries followed, and by the twentieth century, California's reserves of oil, chromium, mercury, platinum, and tungsten were proving even more lucrative for their owners than veins of gold.

Mineral wealth created unimaginable personal wealth for a few and thriving communities for many. Developers and promoters fostered dreams of the good life in California; their words would inflame immigrants with visions of flourish-

**California Gold Rush**  The rapid influx of settlers sparked by the discovery of gold at Sutter's Mill on January 24, 1848.

Steep hills overlook the Pacific Ocean at Big Sur on the Northern California coast.

Men and women avidly read news of the California Gold Rush in the painting *California News* by William Sydney Mount.

**Sierra Nevada**  The inland mountain range that makes up half of California's total land area.

ing cities and a great continental union of American states stretching from the Atlantic to the Pacific. For some of these pioneers, the dream would fade among the mountains that guarded the state's western approaches. The jagged granite peaks of the inland **Sierra Nevada** mountain range, which makes up one-half of the state's total land area, are a daunting natural barrier.

The Sierra Nevada range is littered with the grave sites of pioneers consumed by starvation or trapped by winter storms. The legendary ordeals of the Bidwell and Donner parties attest to the early settlers' difficulties in reaching California through the mountains. Jedediah Smith, the famous explorer and fur trapper considered by many to be the first American to enter California, suffered starvation, thirst, and a broiling sun during his many journeys. He said that the Mojave Desert was one of the most desolate places he had seen on earth.

Mountains and deserts make overland access to California hazardous; ocean access is equally difficult. Although the coastline extends over 800 miles, it has only three natural harbors. The Pacific Ocean breeds violent storms, and a strong westward current has always made sailing north along the California coast extremely hazardous. As late as the nineteenth century, sailing ships had less than a 50 percent chance of surviving a voyage of any significant distance northward.[1]

California is a state of diverse subregions. Even those settlers and adventurers fortunate enough to arrive safely in California found it difficult to survive if they settled in one of the state's many inhospitable areas. Without the complex system of irrigation that exists today, large sections of California would still be uninhabited. It is no mystery why most Spanish missions were built along the California coast. Practically all the lowlands of Southern California and the eastern slope of the Sierra Nevada are either desert or semidesert. Prior to the introduction of weather-resistant wheat and modern irrigation, agriculture was very difficult in most of California. Although average yearly rainfall varies from 100 inches on the north coast to 10 inches along the Mexican border, virtually no rain falls in the state during the growing season between May and September.

The earliest Native American inhabitants succeeded in adapting to this severe environment. Estimates vary, but archaeological evidence suggests that these Native Californians have occupied the state for over 6,000 years, fashioning their lifestyles and traditions around the natural landscape and altering few features of their surroundings.[2]

# Native American Settlement

Historians and anthropologists estimate that before the first European settlers arrived, as many as 300,000 Native Americans lived in California, accounting for approximately one-sixth of the population of continental North America. When the Spanish navigator Sebastian Vizcaíno landed at Monterey on December 16, 1602, after a seven-month voyage from Acapulco, he recorded his impressions of the local population in his diary. "The land is thickly populated with numberless Indians, of whom a great many came several times to our camp. They appear to be a gentle and peaceable people. They said by signs that inland there are many settlements. The food which these Indians most commonly eat, besides fish and crustaceans, consists of acorns and another nut larger than a chestnut."[3]

During Vizcaíno's time, native Californians led peaceful, simple lives in almost every region of the state. They spoke some 135 different languages and dialects. Some of the larger tribes were the Shasta, Yurok, Maidu, and Pomo in the north; Miwok, Modoc, Costanoan, Ohlone, and Yokuts in central California; and Shoshone, Chumash, Cahulla, Mojave, and Yuma in the south. Native Californians rarely lived in groups larger than 1,000 persons; more often than not, these groups were based on extended families or clans rather than tribal association. Native communities adapted their cultural and social habits to their surroundings: River and lake communities tended to practice fishing, boat building and agriculture, while woodland communities relied on hunting and acorn gathering. Indians in the desert were especially resourceful, harvesting at least sixty distinct nutritious desert plants and twenty-eight other plants used as narcotics, stimulants, or medicines. Although isolated from the most advanced world civilizations, the California Indians were not as primitive as pioneers often portrayed them. Their cultural progress is clearly illustrated by their use of currency, complex social traits, and artistry in pottery and basket making.

> **Think Again**
> What were the most important features of Native Californian society prior to the arrival of Europeans?

# Spanish Exploration and Settlement

In 1519, Hernán Cortés landed near what is now Vera Cruz, Mexico, and claimed the region for Spain. For the next 300 years, beginning with Juan Rodriguez Cabrillo's discovery of San Diego in 1542, the Spanish gradually expanded the boundaries of "New Spain" northward into the region they would name Alta ("Upper") California. Settlers in this immense new territory were largely ignored by the Spanish colonial government in Mexico. Gaspar de Portola, the Spanish governor of Baja ("Lower") California, and the Franciscan missionary Father Junipero Serra established the first Spanish colony and Franciscan mission at San Diego in 1769. Extending their exploration northward later that year, Portola and his party were unable to find what Vizcaino had identified as "the perfect harbor" at Monterey, but they did discover San Francisco Bay. Not satisfied with the terrain around the bay, Portola founded the settlement of Monterey in 1770, designating it the administrative capital for Spanish settlements in New Spain. Father Serra was so impressed by the nearby countryside that he declared this site the center of his California mission system.[4]

> **Think Again**
> What was the mission system and how did it affect Native Californians?

## WHAT DO YOU THINK?

### Earthquakes: The Ultimate Doom or Reasonable Risk?

As in many tragic occurrences, most inhabitants of the Santa Cruz region and as far north as the San Francisco Bay Area who experienced the Loma Prieta earthquake on October 17, 1989, at approximately 5:00 P.M. will forever remember where they were, if not the details of that day and time. The tremor, registering about 7.1 on the Richter scale, would collapse a section of the San Francisco–Oakland Bay Bridge, bring down or sink buildings, trigger at least twenty-seven fires across San Francisco, slam freeways together, and in the end cause an estimated $6 billion worth of damage within the earthquake zone. Among all the attractive qualities of California, earthquakes provide one conclusive argument for forgoing relocation or even a trip to the great Golden State. The track record for earthquakes in California has been fairly constant. Thousands of earthquakes occur every year in California—10,000 alone in southern California—of which about 100 register a magnitude above 3.0. The largest earthquakes in California's recorded history can be traced back to 1812 at San Juan Capistrano, Fort Tejon (1857), San Francisco (1906), Santa Barbara (1925), Long Beach (1933), San Fernando (1971), and Coalinga (1983). In 1935, Charles Richter, a Caltech scientist, devised the Richter scale, an instrument used to measure earthquake intensity mathematically. Given their propensity for causing immense damage, earthquake tremors attract the most attention; however, the inability of infrastruc-

ture to withstand the aftershocks of an earthquake can be almost as destructive. During the 1906 earthquake, the fires that resulted from falling chimneys and broken stoves caused as much damage as the actual earthquake. There is always the danger that earthquakes will damage vital resources such as dams, reservoirs, power plants, transportation networks, and hospitals. A tsunami in the immediate aftermath of an earthquake poses yet another major threat to safety: The shifting land mass can create massive waves that envelope coastal areas and flood inland waterways and cities and towns at sea level, extending catastrophic damage well beyond the earthquake's epicenter. The Indonesia tsunami of 2004 was a severe reminder of the devastation that can result from this type of natural phenomenon.

The repercussions of Hurricane Katrina have forced many Americans, especially Californians in their earthquake-prone state, to consider how government will respond to natural disasters. Clearly, the performance of the local, state, and federal agencies in response to Katrina was less than adequate. One may wonder, how many Californians are aware of an adequate evacuation plan? Then there is the question of where to evacuate. Many would like to believe that since Loma Prieta, state and local governmental regulations and codes have been more vigorously enforced, and buildings and other structures are now better able to withstand the tremors. The current construction on the San Francisco–Oakland Bay Bridge and the concern over costs has been influenced at least in part by the potential for earthquakes. Within the Office of the Governor, two offices (the Office of Emergency

---

**pueblos** Centers of trade and Spanish civilization during the period of Spanish colonial rule of California.

**presidios** Military outposts during the period of Spanish colonial rule of California.

**The Mission System**    The official colonial policy of Spain dictated the establishment of three distinct organizations at each settlement: missions to provide religious activities for the Indians and convert them to Christianity, **pueblos** as centers of trade and civilization, and **presidios** as military outposts. Although conflicts often arose between the Franciscan friars and the military commanders of the presidios, the three systems of authority generally complemented one another.

Between 1780 and 1821, agriculture and livestock production in the Spanish settlements became increasingly profitable. The export of animal hides to Europe and the newly independent United States was especially lucrative. The mission system founded by Father Serra grew to number twenty-one sites along the coast, from San Diego in the south to Solano in the north. Much of the success of the mission system is attributed to the employment (or as some suggest, exploitation) of Indian labor. Although historians disagree on the severity of the abuse suffered by Indians at the missions, there is no doubt that the mission system contributed little to the ultimate survival of the native Californians. The number of Spanish settlers and administrators was never greater than a few thousand, but they never-

Services and the Office of Homeland Security) have the principal responsibility for managing the response to natural disasters. A bond measure was passed in the 2006 November election ballot sponsored by Governor Schwarzenegger, portions of which are earmarked for the restoration of California levees. The problematic fiscal situation of the state government causes some Californians to wonder whether the fiscal resources are available to respond adequately to a major natural disaster. In addition to responding to the immediate safety and welfare of those affected by the next earthquake, there is also the responsibility of maintaining public order. Many residents in the region affected by the Loma Prieta earthquake reacted with acts of heroism, but sporadic looting did occur in sections of San Francisco. In many of California's highly populated cities, there is the real possibility that any breakdown in the maintenance of law and order during a natural disaster could precipitate the type of anarchy that happened in New Orleans following Hurricane Katrina.

The 100th anniversary of the 1906 San Francisco earthquake and fire, which killed 3,400 people, left tens of thousands homeless, and destroyed the core of the city's business district, has provided many Californians with the opportunity to put the possibility of another earthquake in perspective and consider the reality of such a threat. The truth is that of the ten largest earthquakes recorded in the United States, only one occurred in California: the Fort Tejon earthquake of 1857, registering a 7.9 magnitude. Nevada, Alaska, and Idaho over the last fifty years have had earthquakes that exceeded the 7.1

magnitude of the Loma Prieta earthquake. Californians should be somewhat concerned about the potential occurrence of earthquakes, but rational about that threat as well. The Southern California Earthquake Center (SCEC) recently received a $1.2 million grant to develop an earthquake predictability program. This grant will provide the center with the opportunity to develop a "collaboratory," which is a attempt to establish an earthquake predictability program through collaboration with scientists throughout the world. Tom Jordan, the project's principal investigator and director of the SCEC, concedes that the project as well as earthquake predictability in general is in its infancy, and it will take many years of research to devise a system that can predict when earthquakes will happen. Currently, there are no reliable methods of predicting the locations, times, and magnitudes of destructive faults. According to the SCEC as well as the U.S. Geological Survey, the only way to prevent widespread destruction and death from earthquakes is through advance preparation and adequate response. Only time and the next earthquake will determine whether the residents of California, through their infrastructure and state government, have met this challenge.

*Sources:* "San Francisco Earthquake History 1915–1989," http://www.sfmuseum.net/alm/quakes3.html; "Are Earthquakes Predictable? Southern California Earthquake Center Receives $1.2 Million to Develop Earthquake Predictability Program," Southern California Earthquake Center, http://www.scec.org/research/060118predict.html, *National Earthquake Information Center, U.S. Geological Survey.*

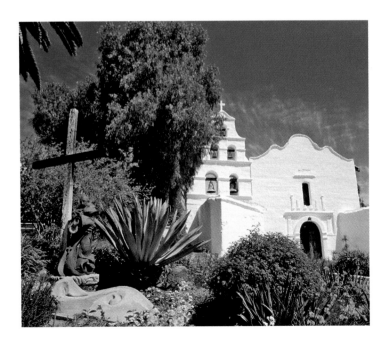

Mission Basilica San Diego de Alcala, built in 1769, was the first of California's Spanish missions.

theless had a profoundly negative effect on the California Indians' freedom of movement, land use, and health. It is clear that the Spanish presence marked the beginning of the end for a vibrant Native American culture and community.[5]

## Mexican Control

Spanish government in California would also come to an end, thanks to various weaknesses in its colonial administration but especially due to Spain's preoccupation with European politics and its overstretched colonial empire. The Spanish monarchy could not withstand the successive military and political challenges of the American and French revolutions and the rise of Napoleonic Europe to its position as a world power. Spanish preoccupation with European challenges and inattention to its colonies abroad provided the impetus for Mexican independence in 1822. However, the new independent Mexican nation was not much more successful in governing California than the Spanish had been. Over the next forty years, the Mexican government was overwhelmed by military coups, political intrigue, and conspiracy. Political instability made it practically impossible for Mexican governors to control a territory extending as far north as present-day Colorado. The few Spanish and Mexican settlers who occupied land in California were largely left to fend for themselves.

**Californios** Mexican settlers of California.

Two factors would strengthen the position of these **Californios**, as the Mexican settlers were known, while making their control over the region much more vulnerable to foreign interests. First was the development of trade with other countries, which increased the number of foreigners traveling to California. Many of the newcomers would remain, bringing an element of self-sufficiency to local settlements and weakening any dependence they once had on the Mexican government. The second factor was the decision by the Mexican government in 1833 to enact a general secularization law, confiscating mission lands and redistributing them to new owners. Major portions of California territory had been administered by Franciscan priests, in cooperation and sometimes competition with local government agencies. The newly independent Mexican government favored a secular society based more on nationalist sentiments than on religious doctrine. Many *Californios* felt that the mission system, which allowed the Catholic church to control vast amounts of land and Indian labor, stifled the growth of an independent economy.[6]

The secularization of church land succeeded in redistributing land to the *Californios* and recent arrivals from Mexico, but secularization created resentment and division among these groups as well. The missions, along with the old colonial administration and the Catholic church, had kept order throughout the state. The disappearance of their authority created a power vacuum. The *Californios* attempted to fill this vacuum with their own local institutions and private organizations, thereby encouraging home rule and greater independence from Mexico. The Mexican government strongly resisted any proposal for more independence by the *Californios*, but the government nevertheless encouraged foreign settlers, particularly American fur trappers and maritime traders who sought a closer economic relationship with the *Californios*. A local movement for American annexation of California soon emerged.[7]

## U.S. Annexation

The poorly trained and ill-supplied troops of the small Mexican army often encountered difficulties with the *Californios* and their American allies. Many Californians considered annexation by the United States inevitable. Confidential discussions regarding annexation had taken place between the *Californios* and Thomas Oliver Larkin, the U.S. consul in California. Influential figures within the United States government were becoming more vocal about the right of America to satisfy its destiny as a world power of continental proportions.

One exponent of this **Manifest Destiny**, Senator Thomas Hart Benton, sought government support for his son-in-law, John C. Frémont, an explorer who by 1845 had led two U.S. Army expeditions to the Pacific Northwest. Today, more than two centuries later, there is still speculation over Frémont's true intentions for California. On the eve of the Mexican-American War of 1846, he took steps to bring large areas of California under American control by mobilizing settlers and pro-American *Californios*, articulating plans to annex California, and providing important topographical information and vital intelligence to the American army. The war that began along the Texas border soon spread to California, where Frémont was already challenging Mexican control through his leadership of the famous yet chaotic **Bear Flag Rebellion**. By January 1847, a force composed of Frémont's Bear Flag rebels and recently arrived U.S. naval and army units accepted the surrender of Mexican and loyal *Californio* military units. A year later, the Treaty of Guadalupe Hidalgo officially ended the Mexican-American War. This agreement (quite similar to an offer rejected earlier by the Mexican government) transferred about 40 percent of Mexico's territory, including California, to the United States in return for a $15 million payment to Mexico. California had become an official territory of the United States, but the region's political and economic future would depend on a number of decisions still to be made.[8]

### The Gold Rush and Statehood for California

One of the pivotal events shaping California's development occurred on January 24, 1848, when James W. Marshall discovered gold while constructing a mill on the American River. Marshall was actually working for John Sutter, who had built a fort in the Sacramento Valley that had become a popular trading post. Although Sutter attempted to keep the discovery secret, news eventually spread. President James Polk mentioned the discovery in his State of the Union address to Congress in December 1848 and encouraged Americans to seek their fortunes in California. By the end of 1849, over 100,000 people had thronged to California in search of easy wealth.

**Manifest Destiny** The belief that the United States had a divinely inspired mission to span the continent of North America.

**Bear Flag Rebellion** A revolt led by John C. Frémont against Mexican control of California in 1846.

*— Think Again —*

What groups benefited the most from the Gold Rush?

A mural by Anton Refregier depicts the Bear Flag of the California Republic being raised in Sonoma, June 1846.

## COMPARED TO WHAT?

# The Spanish Heritage of California and Texas

California and Texas are two very different states politically, culturally, and even economically. Nonetheless, both states share a Spanish heritage that has been the root of important experiences and dilemmas in the contemporary era. Many residents of California and Texas remain somewhat uncomfortable with a legacy that precipitated the rise of Spanish culture in the American Southwest and the Mexican nation-state. Neither state can boast of a history that consistently celebrated its Spanish heritage nor reconciled the differences with Mexican descendants of Spanish colonial rule. Migration, incongruity in language and culture, and economic disparity are only some of the more obvious factors that continue to divide these two American states and the inheritors of the Spanish colonial experience. There continues to be ethnic, political, and civic groups in each state that have sought to address this divide either by acknowledging and embracing the contemporary manifestation of the Spanish legacy or by advocating the perceived presence of two distinct historical and cultural experiences.

### Early Spanish Explorations

Each state has reached its current engagement with Spanish culture from considerably different directions. Texas had a significantly longer history of Spanish colonial rule, beginning in the sixteenth century when the expeditions of Cabeza de Vaca, Coronado, and Alvarado traversed Texas and the Southwest whereas the first large-scale exploration of California would not occur until 1769 with Portola's landing in San Diego. The discovery of rich silver deposits in northern Mexico and the search for remnants of the Great Kingdom of Tejas led to the first Spanish colonial settlement at El Paso del Norte. California was one of the very last frontiers in

North America, an uncharted region until the mid-1800s, isolated by the Pacific Ocean to the west and a series of mountain ranges and desert to the west and south. The relatively flat plains of the Southwest left the region open for a scramble among Spanish, French, and American settlers and profiteers for mineral wealth and commerce at the beginning of the eighteenth century, who converged on the area along the Gulf of Mexico, determined to claim the region north of Mexico, known officially to the Spanish as New Spain, for their respective governments. Having established a presence in Louisiana, anxious French adventurers moved west, but were blocked in Texas by a stronger Spanish colonial system. Until the demise of New Mexico and the advent of American manifest destiny, the Spanish and French would alternate at different periods between a colonial rivalry and amiable trading relations.

### The Spanish Mission System

The Spanish expansion that did take place in California and Texas was largely predicated on the mission system: It was the Franciscan missionaries who laid the foundation for permanent and somewhat productive settlements. The efforts of the Franciscan missionaries are laudable considering their success, however limited, in establishing institutions of the Catholic Church in two very different regions encompassing uniquely difficult conditions. Mission architecture in California and Texas stands not only as a major physical artifact of the Spanish historical presence in the United States, but is also a testament to the dedication and devotion, although often misguided, of the Franciscan missionaries. Some suggest that the Spanish succeeded where other would-be colonial powers failed because of the institutions built by the missionaries. The mission system in Texas was much older and more widespread than in California and by the early nineteenth century would grow to forty-four Franciscan mission sites. Spanish missionaries demonstrated a keen sense of

Although the Gold Rush brought riches to some lucky prospectors and profits to many merchants and outfitters, it also brought serious social problems with unfortunate consequences for the original settlers of California. The Gold Rush years saw increasing murder and abuse of California Indians. Most *Californios* and former Mexican settlers either lost their property outright or were forced into lengthy disputes over land rights. Most American settlers made very little profit from the discovery of gold; even Sutter and Marshall ended their lives in poverty, unable to cope with the onslaught of gold seekers. The insatiable greed of gold miners and merchants stained the pages of California history with racism, price gouging, and lawlessness.

location, having instituted many missions in areas that are now major metropolitan areas in Texas and California. San Antonio and El Paso, two of the largest cities in Texas today, had the largest mission organizations, paralleling the Spanish contributions to the historical development of San Francisco and San Diego in California. Neither state, however, is immune from criticism of the overall accomplishments of the missions, especially in the exploitation of Indian labor. In fairness to the missions, which did provide education, superior farming techniques, and medical care, relations between indigenous peoples and subsequent settlers, including Mexican and American nationals, would prove to be far worse.

### Ethnicity and the Spanish Colonial Experience

In each region, the Europeans would meet indigenous people, but whereas the California Indians were relatively peaceful, the reaction to the Spanish of Indian tribes in Texas varied from inconsistent collaboration to outright warfare. Unlike most Indian groups in California, various tribes in the Southwest engaged in constant warfare prior to arrival of the Spanish. Peace with the Apache and Comanche nations proved elusive for the Spanish, achieved intermittently by the sowing of dissension and transitory military alliances punctuated by periods of conflict. Besides the sheer lack of willing settlers and administrators, the Spanish were largely constrained in California by the geographical conditions. In Texas, the Spanish were constantly forced to retreat from or abandon large areas because of the hostility of Indians. Resistance by Pueblo Indians in modern-day New Mexico and the Apache in East Texas, in particular, prevented the founding of any major Spanish settlements in these regions.

The Spanish legacy in California and Texas poses a number of significant questions about the course of history, particular as that history includes American historical events and how that history has been portrayed. The absence of African slavery in Spanish colonies in California and Texas, when this practice was extremely popular among the English, French, and Portuguese colonies around the same time, is one example of such questions. Indians of the region were forced into slavery and severely mistreated by the Spanish, but rarely replaced when this source of free labor diminished, unlike colonies of other Europeans countries that switched to African slave labor. Was the lack of African slaves in these Spanish colonies merely the result of a supply problem, poor administration, or resistance by the missionaries? California may owe its early antislavery stance, whether voluntary or not, to this decision. The emergence of the so-called **Mestizo** racial group would present yet another series of questions regarding the Spanish legacy. Spanish settlers and colonial administrators would mix with Indians to produce a new race of people that would come to dominate Spanish colonies in South America, outnumbering their Indian ancestors and the Spanish colonialists. Is the relatively brief period of Spanish rule in California a sufficient reason to explain the failure of the Mestizo group to emerge in this state in significant numbers? If the Spanish could cause the birth of a unique group of people within 200 years, could the mixing of various groups in United State today, particularly in a state as diverse as California, bring about a similar metamorphosis in another 200 years? In many respects, the Spanish colonial legacy is still present in both California and Texas in ways that the residents of both states tend to take for granted. The shedding of crocodile tears will not undo past mistakes or miseries; however, lessons may yet be learned from this Spanish heritage.

*Sources:* The Handbook of Texas: Online, www.tsha.utexas.edu/handbook/online/articles/SS/nps1.html; Julian Nava and Bob Barger, *California: Five Centuries of Cultural Contrasts* (Beverly Hills, Calif.: Glencoe Press, 1976); N. Ray Gilmore, and Gladys Gilmore. *Readings in California History* (New York: Thomas Y. Crowell Company, 1966).

Most historians single out 1859 as the year the California Gold Rush came to an end. The discovery of silver at the Comstock Lode in Nevada lured miners with a yen for easy riches out of California, where investment in sophisticated mining technology was needed to extract the remaining gold. Historical data on the California Gold Rush suggest that most of the thousands of "Forty-Niners" never made enough profit to justify their mining operations; only a very few made real fortunes. The miners did, however, cause serious ecological problems that are still evident today, particularly the degradation of rivers and foothills.

**Mestizo** The offspring of a European and an American Indian.

**Legacies of the Gold Rush** The chief legacy of the Gold Rush would be not riches but thousands of new residents, increased commerce, and closer attention from the federal government. It is doubtful that so many people would have risked the perilous journey to California and the hardships they found on arrival were it not for the lure of gold. The mass migration to the gold fields included settlers from around the world, particularly China and South America, thus laying the foundation for California's emerging diversity. The Gold Rush also produced many lucrative and long-lasting commercial opportunities for enterprising migrants. Among the notable examples are Wells Fargo Bank, originally organized by a stage coach express company; the Levi Strauss Company, founded by a tent maker who became a popular clothing manufacturer; and the hundreds of restaurants and retail stores opened by Chinese immigrants who were legally barred from mining. These commercial activities would be financed by Californian investors who acquired their fortunes either directly from the gold mines or from some related business. Most important, however, the Gold Rush hastened the development of governmental institutions in California, creating the state's unique political heritage.

There was considerable indecision over California's political future after American annexation in 1848. Although legally the new territory was governed by the United States Army, self-governing communities soon sprang up, San Francisco being especially noteworthy. Each major political constituency had its own unique design for California government—the former Mexican colonial administrators, southern *Californios* who followed Pablo de la Guerra, northern *Californios* represented by Mariano Vallejo, early settler communities led by John Sutter, former federal officials and agents such as Thomas Larkin and John C. Frémont, the Mormon and merchant community represented by Sam Brannan,

Early Chinese immigrants, who were banned from mining, opened stores and businesses in Chinatown districts.

and various individuals associated with the growing mining interests. Usually years of study and preparation are required before a U.S. territory can be admitted into the Union. A stalemate in Congress over a number of controversial issues regarding slavery, including whether to permit slavery in California, might have caused an even longer delay. Instead, within a year and half of annexation, California's military governor, General Bennett Riley, had issued a call for a constitutional convention that would take the first step for California to be admitted as the thirty-first state.

Hundreds of thousands of people were thronging to the California gold fields, and Congress could not ignore the possibility of losing a large number of its citizens to its newly annexed territory. Unless California became a state, the national government might be unable to take advantage of the Gold Rush. Both the proslavery and antislavery factions in Congress ultimately accepted a compromise proposed by Kentucky Senator Henry Clay, agreeing to admit California as a free state while strengthening the fugitive slave law and leaving the slavery issue open in the other territories.

**Territorial Government**   While Congress debated the compromise, General Riley took the extraordinary step of organizing the new California territorial government without federal approval. He was uneasy with the need to exercise what amounted to a military dictatorship over such disparate groups, and he was anxious to find a prompt replacement for traditional Mexican governmental institutions. So when Congress was finally ready to consider admission of California in 1850, Californians already had a government in waiting: a state constitution, a state legislature, and a state executive.[9]

The institutions of the new government were a mixture of traditions held over from the Spanish and Mexican past, political and commercial expediency, and novel ideas about American society. The first California constitution was strongly influenced by the optimism and inexperience of the forty-eight delegates to the first California constitutional convention, two-thirds of whom were in their twenties and thirties. The convention would rely on the state constitutions of New York and Iowa as models. Six of the delegates represented the *Californios*, who argued for the maintenance of the region's Spanish and Mexican institutions. Although most of their suggestions were voted down, they did succeed in getting Spanish adopted as the official second language of the territory, and they were partly responsible for many of the more progressive features of the new constitution. Even though powerful mining interests created a state government with very limited formal powers, numerous provisions in this first constitution—a free public school system and property rights for women, among others—began the California tradition of innovative solutions for social problems.[10]

# Early Years of Statehood: The Big Four

With the economic power of the Gold Rush and the successful creation of a working government, few doubted that the new state of California would make a major contribution to America's growth and power. But before the state's potential could be realized, the enormous distance between California and the rest of the nation would have to be conquered. In 1860, there were three basic routes to California: a two-month overland trip by horse-drawn wagon from Missouri; a six-month voyage by ship around South America; and a six-week passage from the Gulf of Mexico by way of a 100-mile portage across the malaria-infested isthmus of Panama, followed by another voyage along the Pacific coast. The most

## UP CLOSE

## Levi Strauss: Gold Rush Entrepreneur

The world-famous Levi's jeans were born among the rugged forty-niners in California's gold fields by a 24-year-old German-born New Yorker farsighted enough to realize that what the miners really needed was a durable pair of pants. More than just functional wear, the popular work pants became the cornerstone of a company that epitomized highly successful American entrepreneurship and innovation as well as the constantly evolving and often turbulent nature of American capitalism. Originally a partner in a dry goods business catering to the gold rush onslaught passing through San Francisco, Levi Strauss first used heavy canvas intended for manufacturing tents and wagon covers to create the type of pants that would hold up in the gold fields and other harsh working conditions of the recently arrived Californians. Strauss's pants were soon a hit, but the success of this product was as much due to reliability as it was to the salesmanship of Strauss, who would journey to the mining camps to sell his products, developing a reputation for fairness and reasonable prices.

Once his pants became popular, Strauss refused to become too content with his success, continually altering the style and fabric in response to the needs of the marketplace. Switched from the tough but uncomfortable canvas to "serge de Nimes," a blend of silk and wool made in France, the new pants were soon dubbed "denim." Strauss would transform his denims once again to another European fabric made of cotton, which was called "genes" in Europe, but forever popularized in the United States as "jeans." In 1872, when Jacob Davis, a Nevada tailor who was a regular customer of Levi Strauss, suggested using metal rivets to strengthen the pockets and seams of jeans and asking Strauss to pay for an application to patent the improved pants, other, less open-minded

businesspersons might have disregarded the offer and the still popular feature of jeans might never have been discovered. Strauss not only accepted the deal, he hired Jacob Davis as the manager of his first major manufacturing plant and together they began to introduce a whole line of work clothes, including jackets and shirts, using the rivets.

Highly accomplished in business and now wealthy, Levi Strauss was well-regarded for his sense of humility, insisting on being called simply "Levi." Strauss did join a number of San Francisco merchants in the attempt to finance a local railroad as an alternative to high freight charges of established railroad companies, but that business deal ended in failure. By the beginning of the twentieth century, Levi Strauss turned his successful company over to his four nephews and devoted a large part of his life and fortune to philanthropy and civic improvement. An advocate of education, Strauss generously contributed to a scholarship fund for students at the University of California at Berkeley.

With the passing of Levi Strauss, the clothing company was initially run by David Stern, a nephew of Strauss, who eventually hired his brother-in-law, Walter Haas, Sr. Haas would become the chief executive officer (CEO) of Levi Strauss and Company in 1928 and founder of the well-known San Francisco family, developing a reputation, in the spirit of the founder, for innovation and as a fair employer. When the company opened manufacturing plants in the South, Walter Haas, Sr., for example, insisted that the factories treat African American and white workers equally. In 1958, Walter J. Haas, Jr. inherited the position of CEO of Levi Strauss and Company, having started, according to company legend, as a stock boy. Under the leadership of Haas, Jr., Levi Strauss and Company rode the new wave of jeans' popularity at the end of the 1950s and throughout the 1960s. Jeans became a standard feature of American popular culture and Levi Strauss and Company went international. The Haas family fol-

**transcontinental railroad**
railroad completed in 1869 that linked the east and west coasts of North America.

**Big Four** the founders of the Central Pacific Railroad Company: Collis P. Huntington, Mark Hopkins, Charles Crocker, and Leland Stanford.

practical alternative was a **transcontinental railroad**, which would cut the travel time between New York City and San Francisco down to one week. Theodore Judah, the early California pioneer and railroad-building engineer who first conceived of the transcontinental route, succeeded in convincing four of Sacramento's leading businessmen to invest in his new enterprise.

Three of the four—Collis P. Huntington, Mark Hopkins, and Charles Crocker—were successful merchants during the Gold Rush; the fourth, Leland Stanford, was a lawyer who later became governor of California. Together they formed the Central Pacific Railroad Company and earned their place in California history as the **Big Four**. Obtaining generous loans, grants, and property lowed the altruistic tradition of Levi Strauss, establishing a major charitable foundation and continuing to make generous contributions to educational institutions. Purchasing the Oakland A's baseball team in 1980 when the franchise was threatened with relocation to a more profitable city, Walter J. Haas, Jr., displayed for many his deep ties to the San Francisco Bay Area. Management of Levi Strauss and Company would eventually pass to Robert Haas in 1984, who oversaw Levi Strauss and Company's continued success, which in 1996 had annual sales estimated at $7.1 billion.

Although still very profitable, Levi Strauss and Company has gradually mirrored the fortunes of most major multinational corporations, relying on a foreign workforce while concentrating on marketing, sales, and stock market performance to regain recent losses in market share that caused annual sales to drop to $4 billion in 2005. Personally, Robert Haas, a former Peace Corp volunteer and White House fellow, has been described as "thoughtful," dedicating energy and money to such causes as AIDS research and prevention. "To raise awareness, Haas stood in the lobby of Levi's and distributed information about how HIV is transmitted along with information about prevention."[a] From a business perspective, some accuse Robert Haas of forsaking the company's history of fair labor practices and U.S. manufacturing operations to join the global marketplace. Initially, Levi Strauss and Company refused to join a $20 million settlement of lawsuits "over sweatshop conditions on the U.S. island of Saipan."[b] A group of human rights and labor organizations, including Sweatshop Watch, Global Exchange, and the Asian Law Caucus, brought the lawsuits, claiming that more than 10,000 young women from across Asia were recruited to work in thirty garment factories for up to twelve hours a day, seven days a week, earning $3.05 an hour under harsh conditions that violated U.S. labor laws and human rights standards. Levi Strauss was one of twenty-six other U.S. retailers that subcontracted production to the factories located on Saipan and would eventually settle the lawsuit and adopt Global Sourcing and Operating Guidelines with a pledge to monitor outsourcing practices.

Once again, Levi Strauss and Company is introducing innovation in work wear to meet the perceived demands of the marketplace with the launching of the Levi's RedWire DLX jeans, pants designed to accommodate the iPod. "A control panel sewn directly into the area where most jeans have a coin pocket (at the right hip), means wearers don't have to continually take the iPod out a pocket to adjust the volume or locate a song."[c] The reviews of the high-tech jeans have been mixed, some fashion consultants suggesting the start of a new trend whereas others are predicting failure in a market that is just too narrow. Either way, whether as a clothier of the gold fields, philanthropists, innovators, or simply as a cool bunch of guys, Levi Strauss and his business heirs have forged an important place in the commercial history of California and the United States.

*Sources:* "About Levi Strauss and Company," Levi Strauss and Company Web-site; *www.levistrauss.com/about/*; Pia Sarkar, "Haas to Keep Hand on Levi's/Last of Family to Run Jeans-maker to Stay Active in S.F. Firm," *San Francisco Chronicle*, July 24, 2005; "Levi Strauss and Company," Hoovers: A D&B Company, Information, and Related Industry Information from Hoover's, www.hoovers.com/levi-strauss/ID_40278_/free-co-factsheet.xhtml.

[a]"Levi Strauss" www.referenceforbusiness.com/business/G-L/Strauss-Levi.html
[b]Nikki Bas, Sweatshop Watch, Medea Benjamin, Global Exchange, Joannie C. Chang, and Asian Law Caucus, "Saipan Sweatshop Lawsuit Ends with Important Gains for Workers and Lessons for Activists," Clean Clothes Campaign, January 8, 2005.
[c]Louise Lee, "Sewing Up the iPod Market," BusinessWeek, January 12, 2006.

rights from county, state, and federal governments, the Big Four succeeded in completing the western half of the transcontinental railroad, which joined the track laid by the Union Pacific Railroad Company from the east at Promontory Point in Utah Territory on May 10, 1869.

The Pacific Railway Act of 1862, passed by Congress and signed by President Abraham Lincoln, was especially instrumental in making the transcontinental railroad a reality. The possibility of paying the cost of the Civil War with western gold and silver and the fear that southern sympathizers in California might win the state for the Confederacy convinced the federal government to support the railroad project with enormous sums of money. In addition to federal loans

Picks and shovels, wheelbarrows and one-horse dump carts, black powder and hand drills were the meager tools and materials with which Central Pacific laborers dug and hacked their way over the towering Sierra Nevada mountains of California.

and grants, the act provided land grants that averaged roughly 10 square miles for every mile of track laid. The completion of the transcontinental railroad gave the Big Four virtual control over most of the state's economy.[11]

The completion of the transcontinental railroad ended California's geographic isolation and opened the state up for tremendous commercial expansion. The Big Four would eventually control all major forms of transportation, the industries that used them, and the political institutions that depended on them. They would succeed in acquiring or controlling other local and regional railroad networks, giving them control over almost 85 percent of rail transport in California. In 1870, amid charges of fraud and monopoly, the Central Pacific and Southern Pacific railroad companies would merge to provide rail service to Southern California and the American West.

The Central Pacific had accumulated a huge amount of debt building the transcontinental railroad, and the Big Four were determined to maximize their profits with little regard to business ethics. Even before their rail monopoly was complete, the Big Four began buying up international and domestic steamship lines. With little or no effective state regulation of commerce, the Central Pacific was able to set its own shipping rates for more than thirty years. Corporations that enjoyed close business relations with the Big Four were given preferential treatment. The Standard Oil Company, for example, paid lower shipping rates for its oil and in turn supplied cheap fuel for Central Pacific trains. By exploiting their monopolistic powers to the fullest, the Big Four kept whole industries on the verge of bankruptcy with excessive freight charges. They also profited from the outright sale of the free land grants they received from the federal government, which amounted to nearly 11.4 percent of the land in California. The sale of this land, encompassing much of the state's lumber, mineral, petroleum, and water reserves, was very controversial, resulting in many lawsuits and at least one gun battle, which was immortalized in Frank Norris's muckraking novel *The Octopus*.[12]

Through their Southern Pacific Political Bureau, the railroads determined the course of California's political development. The historian Walton Bean writes,

"Not only did the railroad control the party organizations, but it played them against each other and secretly fostered new factions to keep the old ones in check." The railroad's money "was the power behind almost every political throne and behind almost every insurgent revolt."[13] To avoid being bypassed by the Southern Pacific route through Southern California, the city of Los Angeles agreed to give the company 22 miles of track, land for a depot, and thousands of dollars in subsidies. By subsidizing major newspapers, the Big Four also controlled public opinion in the state for many years. Although the Big Four's domination of California was almost complete by the late 1870s, economic depression throughout the state gave opponents of the railroads the opportunity to break their political power.

## Revolt against the Railroads: The Second California Constitution

California in the late nineteenth century was the home of a vigorous working class, brawny and rugged enough to meet the challenges of an isolated and as yet economically undeveloped society. Even the most prosperous families of California had generally originated with ambitious entrepreneurs who benefited from the exploitation of the state's natural wealth. The state's working class blamed these tycoons for the bank failures, stock fraud, unemployment, and rampant poverty of the nineteenth century. Public condemnation of wealthy merchants and railroad barons like the Big Four triggered a fierce reaction against their domination of state politics. Led by Denis Kearney, an immigrant sailor from Ireland, the **Workingmen's Party** galvanized the spirit of workers throughout the state and won many local elections. Kearney's inflammatory speeches combined denunciation of railroad monopolies with virulent attacks on Chinese workers in California.

The Central Pacific Railroad had recruited unskilled "coolies" from China to build the transcontinental railroad when white railroad workers deserted their

— **Think Again** —

What role did control of transportation networks play in the economic and political history of California in the second half of the nineteenth century? What role did anti-Chinese sentiment play in late-nineteenth-century California politics?

**Workingmen's Party** A political party organized by Denis Kearney to combat the political and economic power of wealthy merchants and railroad barons.

TRIUMPH OF LABOR.

This political cartoon, published in 1878 in San Francisco, backed Denis Kearney and his Chinese labor exclusion policy.

jobs to search for silver in Nevada. These Chinese Californians became a readily available scapegoat for Kearney and the Workingmen's Party, who accused them of undermining the wages of white workers and stealing their jobs. Cultural and physical differences between white and Chinese workers further inflamed the bigotry of the largely uneducated working class. The Workingmen's Party portrayed the Chinese as pawns of the Big Four in a conspiracy to oppress white workers. Kearney and other blue-collar agitators channeled popular outrage into political demands for reform of the state's constitution.

On September 5, 1877, Californians voted to authorize the election of delegates to a convention to be held in Sacramento to reconsider and revise the state constitution of 1849. The 152 delegates who attended the constitutional convention of 1879 included an assortment of Workingmen's Party leaders, representatives of the **Grange** (a nonpartisan farmers' organization), a small contingent from the Republican Party, and various splinter groups. After six months of drafting and debate, they produced a new California constitution more than seven times as long as the Constitution of the United States. The new constitution contained provisions to regulate railroads and corporate influence in the state through regulatory commissions, new corporate tax laws, and restrictions on the power of the state legislature. The greatest accomplishment of the convention may have been the creation of a state railroad commission of three members elected to four-year terms. This commission would have the power to set railroad rates and impose fines for violations of commission regulations. Other new provisions sought to improve the lives of workers by establishing an eight-hour workday for government employees and encouraging the expansion of public education. A majority of the delegates also agreed to constitutional language that restricted Chinese employment and removed the Spanish language from official documents.[14]

**Grange** A farmers' political movement founded in 1867.

This new California constitution made an effort to address economic and political inequality in the state, but the attempted reforms were weakened by divergent interests at the convention, the lack of education of most delegates, and manipulation by powerful interests. Differences among the urban Workingmen's Party, the conservative agrarian interests of the Grange, and the state monopolies represented by a few highly qualified lawyers made it almost impossible to address political and economic injustice in the state. Few delegates from the Workingmen's Party or the Grange had much more than a grade school education; they were hardly able to comprehend California's economic and political problems, much less solve them.

The popularity of the Workingmen's Party and the Grange generated enough votes to ratify the new constitution by a small majority, but doubt and disillusionment with the new government were widespread. In the long run, the California constitution of 1879 would have little meaningful impact on social and economic inequality or the power of the Big Four. The constitutional reforms that the Big Four and other corporate interests could not circumvent through legal loopholes or impede in court were nullified through bribery. The three permanent railroad commissioners charged with regulating and overseeing the railroad were regularly corrupted by the Southern Pacific. It would be easy to blame the Big Four and the corporations for California's problems, but in fact these interests could only corrupt what was already corruptible. The "malefactors of great wealth" had simply perfected techniques of fraud and force practiced against Native Americans, *Californios*, and Chinese ever since the Gold Rush. The constitutional convention of 1878 did, however, demonstrate that democratic principles could provide the impetus for change if citizens were intellectually and ethically prepared to grasp the reins of government.

# The Progressive Era: Hiram Johnson and Clean Government

**Think Again**

How successful was Governor Hiram Johnson's reform effort? What groups opposed his policies and why?

On November 6, 1908, San Francisco's assistant district attorney, Francis J. Heney, was shot and killed in the courtroom while prosecuting city boss Abraham Ruef for corruption. Heney's replacement, assistant DA Hiram Johnson, faced a daunting task: confronting one of the most powerful and most corrupt political organizations in the state. Johnson would rise to the challenge: His conviction of Abe Ruef launched his political career and raised hopes for higher ethical standards in California politics.

To the end of his long political career, Hiram Johnson would embody in California the national Progressive movement, which sought to rid government of corruption and restore democratic principles across America.[15] At the turn of the twentieth century, Johnson was one of many offspring of either Workingmen's Party or Grange members or retainers for the monopolies. Like others of his generation, Johnson had received the benefits of public education, entered a profession, and shared in California's growth. As the new century dawned, while they increasingly assumed the culture and lifestyles of a growing middle class, Johnson and his generation saw their achievement and upward mobility limited by a political and economic system based on graft, greed, and dishonesty. Society was based on whom you knew, not what you knew. Johnson, however, represented the first generation of native Californians, born into an untamed land that fostered rugged individualism and hardness, who used their newly acquired education and status to reject the status quo. Progressivism, the nationwide movement to reform government, provided this new generation of Californians with the ideals and ideology to face the Southern Pacific, other powerful interests, and corruption in government.[16]

"Unquestionably incorruptible and courageous," Hiram Johnson led the California Progressives into government as the newly elected governor of California in 1911. Under his leadership, from 1911 until 1916, when he unsuccessfully ran as Theodore Roosevelt's Bull Moose Party running mate, Governor Johnson pushed through a number of important reform measures that would finally break the near total control of corporate monopolies and corrupt government officials. One of the most significant measures of this period, first as state legislation and later as a constitutional amendment, was the strengthening of the railroad commission to regulate not just the railroads but all public utilities by increasing its size and budget and by requiring that the commissioners be appointed rather than elected. Almost single-handedly, Governor Johnson also got California voters to approve another constitutional amendment that included provisions for the recall, referendum, and initiative, provisions that would provide Californians with avenues for directly participating in government, known as direct democracy.

During his tenure as governor, Johnson guided his fellow Progressives in the state legislature to adopt laws regulating child labor and workmen's compensation, form an employment bureau, set a minimum wage for government employees, and

A banner from the 1912 election campaign for Theodore Roosevelt and Hiram Johnson as the Progressive ("Bull Moose") party candidates for President and Vice President.

reform banking laws. The creation of commissions became a very popular approach for Governor Johnson and the state legislature to keep government honest and democratic. These commissions addressed such issues as conservation, corporations, immigration and housing, irrigation, civil service, and industrial welfare, but the State Board of Control was especially successful in ensuring for the first time that state government was run professionally and prudently, saving California millions of dollars in the first year of its existence.[17]

Although Governor Johnson and the Progressives championed clean and responsive government, their political orientation was anything but radical or even liberal in the contemporary sense. Beneath the Progressive ideological surface lay a deep respect for free-market capitalism and other middle-class values that were often at odds with the interests of the working class in California. During this period, anti-Asian sentiment once again became popular, this time, however, directed at the Japanese, and the Progressives quickly translated this fervor into the **Alien Land bill**. Initially this bill was designed to exclude the Japanese altogether, but because it would cause potential treaty violations with Japan and was constitutionally dubious, the Progressives settled for preventing aliens who were not eligible for citizenship from owning land.

By Governor Johnson's the second term, the Progressives became less inclined to support the interests of labor over business interests, especially when it came to union organizing. Their efforts to regulate morality with legislation—banning, for example, prize fighting, horse race betting, and alcohol consumption—were unpopular. Realizing that their social and economic policies put them at odds with the populist orientation, the Progressives quietly returned to the California Republican Party, with its conservative approach. Governor Johnson hurried this defection when he was elected as U.S. senator and went off to Washington, leaving his California Progressives without a strong leader. Like the constitution of 1879, the California Progressive era has many detractors, considering it not much more than a middle-class revolt. On close analysis, however, it is clear that the Progressives forced state government to be run in a democratic and efficient manner.[18]

**Alien Land bill** A 1913 law that prohibited aliens not eligible for citizenship from owning land.

## The Twentieth Century: Rapid Economic Growth

California's economy made great strides in the early twentieth century. Agricultural production, initially wheat and later fruit and vegetable cultivation, became a multimillion-dollar industry. Agricultural growth was made possible by large-scale water projects such as the Owens Valley Aqueduct, Hoover Dam-Boulder Canyon and Central Valley, and Hetch Hetchy Valley, which also supported large population surges in Southern California. Discoveries of huge oil reserves in Southern California during the 1920s further brightened the state's economic future, coinciding with the rapid growth of the automobile industry. The motion picture industry, headquartered in Hollywood, became a highly lucrative form of popular entertainment, enhancing the state's aura of glamour. California remained, however, geographically isolated from the rest of the nation. Until World War II, passenger air service was restricted to the affluent, which meant that it still took most people days to travel to the West Coast. In 1900, the population of California was barely a million and a half people, ranking well below at least half of the other American states. In fact, during the Great Depression, the state government actually discouraged Americans in the drought-stricken Midwest and eastern portions of the country from coming to California unless they had either money or the promise of a job. This era was vividly depicted in John

A still from the 1940 film *The Grapes of Wrath* shows the Joad family, down-trodden 'Okies' forced to migrate from the Dust Bowl during the Depression.

Steinbeck's tale of the Joad family in his famous novel *The Grapes of Wrath* and many of the songs by the folksinger Woody Guthrie.

**World War II: The Boom Years**    As America entered World War II, California became the major staging area and logistics point for waging war against the Japanese in the Pacific. Almost overnight, the state was transformed with the deployment of over 1.5 million military personnel, the construction of more military installations than in any other state, and the expenditure by the war's end of over $35 billion in federal funds. California also became a major location for defense industries, accounting for 11.9 percent of all U.S. government war contracts and 17 percent of all the matériel produced for the war. Over 1.6 million Americans moved to California during the war, and a large share were employed by companies specializing in aviation, located in Southern California, or shipbuilding, in the north. Forty-four percent of all aircraft and close to 40 percent of all naval and freight ships used during the war were constructed in California. The defense industries, competing with the wartime draft for labor, were obliged to employ a diverse workforce, including minorities and women, who had formerly been denied semiskilled industrial jobs. Such job opportunities dramatically increased the African American population in California and gave the struggle for women's equality a major boost, immortalized by the image of "Rosie the riveter."[19]

*Japanese Internments and the Bracero Program*    The war brought about an impressive array of benefits to California while also sacrificing the livelihood of other Californians for sake of the war effort. Within three months of the bombing of Pearl Harbor, President Franklin Roosevelt issued **Executive Order 9066** resulting in the relocation and internment of 110,000 Japanese legal aliens and American citizens, most of whom came from California. The Japanese in California lost much of their property and other possessions. By implementing the evacuation order, America, particularly in California, lost an element of its moral credibility, which continues as a reminder of the fragility of freedom.[20] To alleviate agricultural labor shortages

**Think Again**

How did World War II contribute to California's rapid growth in the second half of the twentieth century?

**Executive Order 9066**
President Franklin Roosevelt's 1942 order that resulted in the relocation and internment of Japanese legal aliens and American citizens of Japanese descent.

# PEOPLE IN POLITICS

## The Legacy of Upton Sinclair and EPIC

Although not quite as harsh as in other parts of the county, the Great Depression nonetheless had a severe effect on the social and economic conditions in California. By 1934, almost a quarter of the state's population was unemployed and surviving on minimal private relief efforts. A mass migration to California that had begun in the 1920s, grew in the 1930s as the depression worsened in other parts of the country, further straining the economic and social resources of the state. Labor strife was rampant, often resulting in violence and death when striking workers and police and National Guard troops clashed. Leadership in state government was decidedly conservative, exemplified by Governor James "Sonny Jim" Rolph, who was vehemently opposed to the labor movement in California and resisted the New Deal policies of the Roosevelt administration. During this period, the noted author Upton B. Sinclair gradually emerged as a popular figure in California. Having won international notoriety as the author of the still classic work, *The Jungle*, which outlined the dreadful conditions of the Chicago meatpacking industry and led to the enactment of the Pure Food and Drug Act, Sinclair became active in the Socialist Party. Settling in Pasadena, California, in 1915, he was an outspoken critic of government efforts to confront the depression, culminating with his End Poverty in California (EPIC) plan, which he pledged to implement if elected as governor of California.

Sinclair's campaign for governor of California has been considered by many as "The Campaign of the Century," primarily due to his socialist credentials, the extravagant opposition to his candidacy, and the popularity of his EPIC program. Forgoing his socialist roots, Sinclair jumped to the Democratic Party, winning the Democratic nomination for the 1934 gubernatorial election. Through the tract *I, Governor of California, and How I Ended Poverty—A True Story of the Future* and public appearances, the support of influential friends and associates, and the work of a dedicated following disillusioned with the American economic system, Sinclair's campaign and the EPIC program in general became very popular among Californians. Considered utopian, if not unrealistic, by political leaders and activists from both sides of the ideological spectrum, the EPIC program advocated the creation of farming and industrial cooperatives, a progressive and individual income tax, an inheritance tax, property tax relief for small homeowners, a public retirement system, and public works projects. When questioned about the "radical" disposition of the EPIC program, Sinclair insisted that this program really was an attempt to avoid revolution and civil strife with necessary reforms brought about through the democratic process.

Mainstream political and business leaders were appalled by Sinclair's attempt to reform the political and economic institutions in California to which they were inextricably linked, regardless of how popular such reforms were with the average Californian. Business interests, in cooperation with the Republican Party, organized an extremely well-funded campaign against Sinclair that spent as much money supporting the candidacy of the incumbent Republican governor Frank Merriam as it did to discredit Sinclair. During this "Campaign of the Century," a number of innovative campaign techniques were introduced for the first time on a wide scale, including the use of media (radio and motion picture newsreels), direct mail, and the employment of marketing professionals. Dubious tactics coupled with the distortion of Sinclair's own previous writing and record as a member of the Socialist Party served to demonize his image and the EPIC program in the run-up to the election. Few leaders from the Democratic Party actively supported Sinclair, either out of fear of drawing reprisals from the business community, fundamental policy or ideological disagreements, or resentment of his recent entry into party politics. An endorsement by President Roosevelt probably would have helped secured the office of governor for Sinclair—a recent, but still fellow Democrat—but for most of aforementioned reasons, he chose to ignore the campaign. In the end, Frank Merriam triumphed with 1,138,620 votes to 879,537 for Sinclair.

Initially defeated by powerful forces as well as a state ill-prepared for his socio-economic vision, major portions of Sinclair's EPIC program would eventually become cornerstones of the various values and government programs that most Americans now take for granted. Although the notion of farming and industrial cooperatives would never materialize, farm subsidies, tax credits, and even government loans have made government an active partner in commerce. Actively resisted until the 1930s, progressive rates on individual income, corporate and inheritance taxes, and reductions in property taxes for homeowners have become the norm. Social Security remains the popular public retirement system that Sinclair envisioned and some of the major American construction achievements were public works projects. Upton Sinclair lost the "Campaign of the Century," but his programs and ideas may yet win the race to end poverty in California and America.

*Sources:* Leon Harris, *Upton Sinclair: American Rebel* (New York: Thomas Y. Crowell & Co., 1975); Greg Mitchell, *The Campaign of the Century: Upton Sinclair's Race for Governor of California and the Birth of Media Politics* (New York: Random House, 1992); Kevin Starr, *Endangered Dreams: The Great Depression in California* (New York: Oxford University Press, 1996).

A group of Bainbridge Island Japanese citizens marches under Army escort at a Seattle dock headed for Manzanar, California detainment camp as friends and relatives, soon to be evacuated, bid them farewell.

due to the war, the U.S. and Mexican governments instituted the **Bracero Program** in 1942, which granted Mexicans temporary employment status in the United States to cultivate and harvest crops. Although the program did offer employment opportunities to impoverished Mexican farmers, Bracero labor contracts permitted unfair wages, poor working conditions, and oppressive restrictions.

**Bracero Program**  A program granting temporary employment status to Mexicans working in the United States during World War II.

### The Postwar Years: The Boom Continues

In the immediate postwar years, massive federal wartime expenditures, defense industry innovations, sacrifices of workers and armed services, and geographic splendor together propelled California the forefront of the American experience. For the next fifty years, these factors would help California become the epitome of American culture and progress. Such cultural icons as Disneyland, Hollywood, and the surfer scene would set nationwide trends and transform the Golden State into the envy of the world. For World War II defense industries that failed to retool for a peacetime economy, the Cold War created a continued demand for military weapons and technology, applying, for example, the concentration of aviation technology to the development of missile systems. In the spirit of true Progressives, initially under the leadership of Governor Earl Warren, the state government would play a substantial role in guiding California through this era of prosperity, spending massive amounts of funds to facilitate this progress. These massive expenditures resulted in some of the finest public colleges and universities, highways, and health and welfare systems in the world. Yet the state would not be without its problems, most of which remain to this day. The nation's problems were California's problems, just bigger and more noticeable, including the hunt for un-American activities of the 1950s, pockets of urban and rural poverty, degradation of the environment, and escalating crime. Slowly, the problems would seem to be gaining while California's assets were in decline. And when government appeared incapable of addressing this narrowing gap between progress and problem, Californians, utilizing the electoral tools inherited from the Progressives, would act.

### The Late Twentieth Century: Economic Decline

Like most of the world, California has entered a period of resource scarcity, which has posed major dilem-

The surfer of the early 60s is an icon of California culture.

mas and forced hard decisions on the state. One dilemma is the process of globalization, which has caused a great deal of the state's industrial capacity to become obsolete. Beginning in the late 1970s, large quantities of industrial production in California, especially in the steel industry, were supplanted by Asian companies that had started to build a new generation of factories. California, which once produced enough surplus industrial goods to export them, now has ports crowded with incoming Chinese goods. Globalization notwithstanding, the economy of the state was also hurt by the end of the Cold War, which rendered many defense-related industries unnecessary. Stock market failures in the mid-1980s and again at the end of the 1990s and difficulties in the computer industry cost the state in terms of both tax revenue and jobs. California is still a leading exporting state, but it remains competitive thanks primarily to the high-tech sector.

## California in the New Millennium

As California has expanded in population, so has demand for water and energy. With limited rainfall, Californians live with the fear of a major drought, and as a result, most regions of the state have experienced increasing water costs to better manage this precious resource. If there was any one reason why Governor Gray Davis was recalled in 2003, it was due to the state's energy crisis during the preceding two years, which had the dual effect of raising energy prices and limiting supplies. Power outages plagued various regions of the state. Many of the problems associated with the energy crisis, including inadequate energy deregulation guidelines, limited power supplies, and artificially inflated energy prices, continue to haunt Californians.

Water and energy are not the only concerns. According to a statewide poll conducted by the Field Research Corporation in 2005, three out of four Californians identified "the well-being of children" as the issue they were most concerned about.[21] More than 20 percent of the children in the state live in poverty. In 2000–01, almost 2.8 million, or 47 percent, of all public school students participated in the free or reduced-price meal programs offered in California schools. To be eligible for these programs in 2001–02, a family of four had to earn less than $32,653 a year.[22] Education and schools, closely related to the plight of children, was ranked second among issue's of extreme concern.[23] California has the largest school enrollment of any state, fueled by a juvenile population that is growing faster than the adult population. Since the passage of **Proposition 13** in 1978, which severely cut property taxes, the traditional source of education funding, per-pupil spending in public school districts across the state have been well below the national average. Although an attempt was made to restore lost funds through subsequent propositions and legislative acts, large outlays are required to meet the special needs of "English learners," who comprise more than 25 percent of the public school population.[24] Other issues ranked high in this poll, in descending order, were the well-being of seniors, health care, cost of living, war in Iraq, crime and law enforcement, state budget deficit, the economy, the environment, illegal immigration, energy, taxes, and terrorism. Over the past twenty years, crime and law enforcement has stayed high on the list of extreme concerns expressed by Californians, but whereas 71 percent of respondents were extremely concerned in 1986, the number dropped to 56 percent in 2005. The decreasing importance of crime and law enforcement may be related to the gradual decline in crime since 1984 and the explosion of the California prison population, which increased from 43,328 in 1984 to 163,939 in 2004.[25] But incarceration is a severe drain on state revenue, and it

---

*Think Again*

How has globalization changed California in recent decades?

---

**Proposition 13** The 1978 law that severely cut property taxes in California.

raises serious questions regarding the prison system's ability to prevent recidivism (repeat offenders) or to rehabilitate the current inmate population.

Since the Progressive movement more than a century ago, avenues for direct democracy, especially, via the initiative process, have become increasingly popular among Californians. By allowing Californians to place measures on the ballot through petition drives, the initiative process has resulted in the enactment of various popular and controversial laws, including property tax reductions, life imprisonment for habitual criminals, and term limits for state legislators. Such power has caused the executive and legislative branches of government to react rather cautiously to the state's problems while taking steps to insulate themselves from the public's wrath. The state legislature has sought to protect itself by creating safe legislative districts, almost guaranteeing reelection for most members and resisting calls for campaign finance reform, ensuring the accumulation of millions of dollars in campaign contributions from special-interest groups. Although the state has faced annual structural budget deficits of between $4 billion and $10 billion annually since 2001, the public shows little interest in cutting back on programs, and the legislature has been reluctant to increase taxes or cut spending. Any such move would almost certainly face an initiative challenge, which could also result in a further curtailing of legislative power.

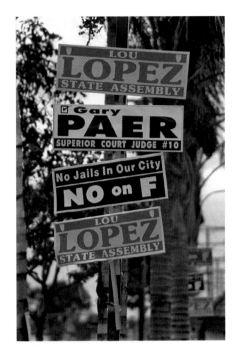

Signs for local propositions and candidates running for office are a familiar sight in California politics.

Governing California from the executive branch, led primarily by the governor, has been even more problematic than the legislature's seeming lack of leadership partly because of the threatened use of direct democracy by an often impatient public and partly because the legislature has become increasingly partisan and hostile to executive branch. It is not uncommon for the radical wings of the governor's own party to rebel against executive policies. No matter how much a governor may oppose an initiative, once it has passed, he is bound to execute the law or policy, which may in turn result in diminished popularity anyway. Despite his opposition, Governor Jerry Brown was forced to implement Proposition 13, causing a massive reduction in state revenue and forcing him to slash thousands of government jobs and services.

Gray Davis, elected governor in 1998, hoped to avoid the pitfalls of California politics. Choosing education, an issue popular with most Californians, as his major policy objective, Davis proclaimed that education would be his first, second, and third priorities and actually authorized $1.8 billion above required funding levels. Because he was adept at steering clear of controversies, however, it was hard to associate Governor Davis with any particular political view or issue. That middle-of-the-road, try-to-please-everyone path would come back to haunt him during the energy crisis of 2001. By not taking a firm stand for or against energy deregulation plans and failing to providing an immediate and concrete solution to the energy crisis that resulted, Governor Davis became vulnerable to attacks from the Republican opposition, which gave the public an identifiable target for its rage over energy price gouging and supply inequities. That rage ultimately fueled a recall campaign that essentially ended the political career of Gray Davis and replaced him with the movie actor Arnold Schwarzenegger.

Historically, California has exemplified bold and innovative approaches to a unique environment that for many years seemed boundless in its potential for growth. Governor Schwarzenegger, irrespective of partisan and personal opinions, embodies that approach, with a persona stemming partly from his action hero film characters, his ability to convey confidence, and his rags-to-riches notoriety.

Schwarzenegger's success in the recall campaign and popularity in office clearly met the desire of Californians for a strong but extraordinary leader who did not fit the profile a the stereotypical professional politician. And during his first year in office, Governor Schwarzenegger was bold and innovative in using the initiative—the very weapon used to circumvent politicians—and his charisma to promote propositions granting him greater authority on budget matters and a $19 billion bond arrangement. A year later, however, the power of his personality and another attempt to use the initiative to gain even more budgetary power, force competitive legislative elections, and take on public service unions would be stopped cold by the power of special-interest groups coupled with an unpopular special election that was crowded with too many controversial and complicated initiatives. The governor has retreated momentarily, but he has demonstrated daring and audaciousness that is certain to be refined and repackaged for his next political battle. Whether or not he can exploit these qualities to regain the advantage will determine the future of his political career.

# Summary Notes

- California contains some of the nation's most spectacular natural attributes, including excellent natural harbors and redwood forests. Early explorers found a livable climate, abundant sea life, fertile soil, large sources of timber, and ample quantities of wild game in different parts of the state. But the landscape also presented natural challenges, including nearly impenetrable mountain ranges, deserts, a treacherous coastline, and a lack of substantial water resources.

- The Spanish explorers who arrived in California found the Indians already living there—an estimated population of 300,000—to be peaceful and simple. Determined to establish a colonial presence in California, the mission system, under the initial leadership of Father Junipero Serra, became the foundation of the Spanish settlement of California.

- Upon gaining independence from Spain in 1822, the Mexican government's control over the California region was plagued by political and social disorders, which made administration of the territory practically impossible. In 1833, the Mexican government would secularize church land, which had the short-term effect of redistributing land to the *Californios* and recent Mexican arrivals.

- Led by John C. Frémont, who by 1845 had led two U.S. Army expeditions to the Pacific Northwest, Americans gradually settled the California territory, establishing a presence that would become official when the U.S. government annexed California after the Mexican-American War of 1846.

- At first, there was some indecision regarding California's political future upon American annexation in 1848, but the discovery of gold at the start of that year hastened the call for a constitutional convention, and Congress quickly admitted California as the thirty-first state. The dominate mining interests in the region imposed a very limited model of state government but also included in the state's first constitution numerous farsighted provisions, such a free public school system and property rights for women.

- Lacking a reliable and rapid means of transportation to the rest of the United States, California benefited greatly from the ultimate success of the group of businessmen, known as the Big Four, who built the western portion of the transcontinental railroad. Led by Denis Kearney, the Workingmen's Party succeeded in calling for a state constitutional convention that drastically altered the California constitution, incorporating provisions that regulated railroads and corporate influence and other important reformist ideas but also certain notions that were not so reform-minded, such as restricting Chinese employment. The provisions of the altered constitution were, however, generally circumvented by the Big Four and other corporate interests through legal loopholes or outright bribery.

- Led by Hiram Johnson, California Progressives successfully advocated for a number of important reform measures that would finally break the near total control of corporate monopolies and corrupt government officials. One of the most important and lasting reforms of the Progressive era were provisions for the recall, referendum, and initiative, laws that would provide Californians with avenues for directly participating in government.

- California had since the beginning of the twentieth century made great strides as a state, particularly in economic growth. California remained, however, geographically isolated from the rest of the nation. As America entered World War II, California became the major staging area and logistics point for the waging of war against the Japanese in the Pacific. Almost overnight, the state was transformed with the deployment of over 1.5 million military personnel, the construction of more military installations than any other state, and major expenditures by the federal government.

■ In years following World War II, under the leadership of Governor Earl Warren, the state government would play a substantial role in guiding California through an era of prosperity, spending massive amounts on public education, infrastructure, and health and welfare systems. This prosperity would begin to decline the late 1970s when large segments of industrial production in California were forced to compete with foreign manufacturers. The scarcity of resources would start to become a problem for Californians, culminating with the recall of Governor Gray Davis, who was removed from office in 2002 in a recall campaign that resulted in the election of Arnold Schwarzenegger.

## Key Terms

California Gold Rush  523
Sierra Nevada  524
pueblos  526
presidios  526
Californios  528

Manifest Destiny  529
Bear Flag Rebellion  529
Mestizo  531
transcontinental
  railroad  534

Big Four  534
Workingmen's
  Party  537
Grange  538
Alien Land bill  540

Executive Order
  9066  541
Bracero Program  543
Proposition 13  544

## Suggested Reading

Didion, Joan. *Slouching Toward Bethlehem*. New York: Farrar, Straus and Giroux, 1967; Delta Edition, 1968.

Fradkin, Philip L. *The Seven States of California: A Human and Natural History*. New York: Henry Holt and Company, 1994.

Gentry, Curt. *The Last Days of the Late, Great State of California*. Sausalito, Calif.: Comstock Edition, 1968.

Gilmore, N. Ray, and Gladys Gilmore, eds. *Readings in California History*. New York: Thomas Y. Crowell, 1966.

Hale, Dennis, and Jonathan Eisen. *The California Dream*. New York: Collier Books, 1968.

Kotkin, Joel, and Paul Grabowicz. *California, Inc*. New York: Rawson, Wade, 1982.

McWilliams, Carey. *California: The Great Exception*. New York: Current Books, 1949.

Royce, Josiah. *California from the Conquest in 1846 to the Second Vigilance Committee in San Francisco*. New York: Knopf, 1948.

# 16 DEMOCRACY, CALIFORNIA STYLE:
## Political Participation

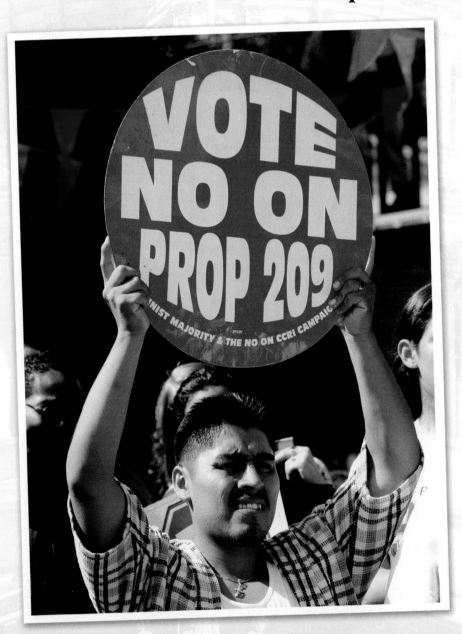

## Chapter Outline

- Voting: Who Can Vote?
- Elections
- Direct Democracy: California's Electoral Dilemma
- Campaigning for Votes
- Empowering California Voters

Political participation should be an important duty in our society, where we take pride in the freedoms that have evolved from the development of democratic government. Yet the level of political participation by Californians is not drastically different from that seen among people living under despotic rule. There is an inexhaustible list of reasons why so many Californians opt out of political participation, many of which are founded on misconceptions about the American political process. For example, one of the most common justifications for not voting is that "my vote doesn't count." There are many variations on this complaint, but the most persuasive—not completely unfounded—is that the electoral college, not average Americans, elects the president of the United States, so why bother? Californians also cite the registration and voting process, which seems inconvenient and unnecessarily complicated, requiring registration weeks in advance of an election.

In California, similar perceptions about voting have resulted in low voter turnout rates over the past decade. Even the figure for the 2004 presidential election—a 75.9 percent statewide turnout rate—is deceiving because it actually represents 75.9 percent of Californians who bothered to register, not the eligible voters who failed to register. Of the approximately 36 million residents of California, about 22 million are eligible to vote. When the polls closed on November 2, 2004, over 12 million ballots had been cast, but 4 million registered Californians did not vote and about 5.5 million eligible voters had not registered and therefore could not vote. And remember, this was a high-turnout election. Seven months earlier, for a primary that included major propositions on school funding and a proposal for the state to borrow $15 billion, the voter turnout rate was 43.6 percent. Turnout in the 2002 elections was lower still.[1]

Sadly, the wealthiest and most populous state in the Union has been among the twenty states with the lowest turnout rates since 1998. Young adults are especially unlikely to vote. According to the Pew Charitable Trusts, "Two of every three 18- to 25-year-olds do not vote, and at least 40 percent are not even registered to vote."[2] Considering the enormous amount of money California spends on higher education, the result of an annual budget process that is inherently political, students and recent graduates have an inherent interest in choosing their elected representatives.

As you will see in this chapter, Californians have the opportunity to vote on many different types of candidates and issues, some of which involve millions of votes and other less than 10,000. The results of the 2000 presidential election, which George W. Bush won on the basis of a

527-vote margin in a single state, remind us of the importance of each individual vote.

On the other hand, many Californians do value their ability to participate in government. Elections in California offer all U.S. citizens who meet the basic requirements the opportunity to have their say on national issues as well as concerns close to home.

## Voting: Who Can Vote?

⊣Think Again⊢

In what ways has it become easier to vote in California in recent years?

Any person who is 18 years old, a citizen of the United States, a resident of California, and a county resident for at least fifteen days prior to the election may register to vote. Registered voters who have recently moved to another county may still be able to vote by absentee ballot or by voting at their former polling place. Recent residents may vote for president of the United States if they apply for a presidential ballot at least seven days prior to the election. Individuals who have been declared mentally incompetent by a court of law or convicted felons who are either incarcerated or on parole are disqualified from voting. Reregistration is required if the prospective voter has moved, completed an official name change, or changed political party affiliation. Registering to vote in California and most other states was made significantly more convenient when Congress passed the **National Voter Registration Act**, the so-called Motor Voter Law. This law requires the states to allow citizens to register by mail and to accept a universal mail-in voter registration form. It also specifies that voter registration forms be made available at public agencies and requires that the department of motor vehicles incorporate voter registration into the process of applying for or renewing a driver's license or obtaining nondriver identification. Made much less complicated in recent years, an increasing number of Californians are choosing to vote using an absentee ballot. Voters can apply for permanent absentee voter status or request an absentee ballot for a particular election.

**National Voter Registration Act** Law designed to make it easier for voters to register to vote and to maintain their registration.

A woman fills in a form while registering to vote at a registration table in Bexar County, California.

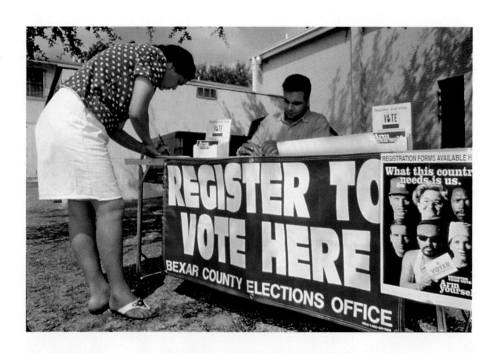

# UP CLOSE

## Voter Rights

Would it matter to many Californians who consistently refuse to vote that this feature of democratic government was judiciously guarded by the founders of California's state government, a large number of whom came from states where there had been a property-owning requirement for voting? Would certain segments of California's nonvoters take the electoral process a little more seriously if they realized that 100 years ago, these judicious guardians of California democracy would have prevented them from voting? There are of course Californians who for one reason or the other will never vote. On the other hand, maybe there are some nonvoters who simply cannot appreciate this aspect of their civic duty and the struggle to gain this civil right. When the California constitution was first written in 1849, restricting voting to white male citizens of the United States and Mexico, the forefathers of the Golden State appreciated the power of this right by excluding the people whom they thought were not worthy of voting. They did realize that if there was any chance of joining the union of states to which most of the delegates gave cultural and political allegiance, their work at the convention would have to meet minimal standards of democracy. It would be difficult to know their exact motivations, but chances are they either doubted the intellectual abilities of every other category of Californian or were fearful of these groups' electoral choices. Had they predicted the widespread apathy toward the electoral process that we see today, California might have been spared years of ill will. A number of historians have speculated that the few *Californios* at the convention, while harboring attitudes of superiority toward California's Indians, nonetheless argued for granting them the right to vote based on Spanish and Catholic notions of the divine universality of man. This argument was persuasive enough to secure for Indians constitutional provisions that at least gave the state legislature the discretion, by a two-thirds vote, to grant Indian voting rights in the future. Not necessarily a major advance for the California Indian, who would suffer a generation of indignities before this provision was exercised, it could very well have been that one early expression of tolerance that planted the seed for California's subsequent forward-looking approach to suffrage. At the convention, this position may well have caused suspicions about *Californios* and subsequent limits on the expansion of their suffrage. The terms of the Treaty of Guadalupe Hidalgo dictated that men who had lived in California prior to annexation by the U.S. government would be eligible for citizenship and the right to vote. The California constitution required that those men be white, causing large groups of transient Mexicans and *Californios* with mixed Indian heritage to be excluded. The subsequent lack of voting power would result in laws such as the foreign miners' tax, which had the effect of driving most of the *Californios* out of the gold fields.

Although numbering around 1,000 and subjected to institutional and cultural racism, the small African American community in California at the beginning of statehood realized the importance of voting. The first California constitution essentially permitted African Americans to be disqualified from testifying in court trials, which in a number of instances caused African Americans to lose their property or to be unfairly convicted. With the right to vote, such disqualifications became more difficult to legally justify, and as early as 1856, the African American community conducted conventions to pressure the state legislature to grant suffrage, which it did in 1865. Chinese immigrants, probably due to their large numbers—at least 15,000 had worked on the transcontinental railroad alone— would have to wait much longer for voting rights. Often the focus of physical attacks, the Chinese suffered long-term repression through the use of the democratic process in California, which generated a series of laws beginning in 1854 that made them subject to discriminatory taxes, deportation, and jail. The Japanese immigrants that would arrive later in large numbers would be subjected to similar laws that remained valid until the 1950s. In fact, the fear of Asians' and Indians' gaining voting rights prompted the California state legislature to refuse to ratify the Fifteenth Amendment to the United States Constitution granting all male citizens the right to vote regardless of race or background, knowing that they ultimately would be forced to comply with this national law anyway.

California was one of the first states in the Union to extend suffrage to women, which it did in 1911, a full eight years before the passage of the Nineteenth Amendment in 1920, which outlawed denying the right to vote based on gender. One of the initial reforms of the Progressives, after numerous attempts to expand suffrage to women, this amendment to the California constitution narrowly won approval by 3,500 votes. Joan Jensen and Gloria Ricci Lothrop wrote in California Women: A History that "the enfranchisement of women, one antagonist claimed, would add middle-class votes to the ranks of those opposing labor, cause friction between husbands and wives because of divided political loyalties, and ultimately fail because women could be too easily swayed or would vote for 'foolish moral measures.'[a] Again on display are the sentiments of Californians who in a perverse perspective wanted

[a]Joan M. Jensen and Gloria Ricci Lothrop, *California Women: A History* (San Francisco: Boyd & Fraser, 1987), pp. 65–66.

to limit franchisement precisely because of the value they attached to this right. Imagine the plight of Julia Morgan, an architect who established a flourishing practice in California after receiving an engineering degree from the University of California at Berkeley in 1894, collaborated on building designs for UC Berkeley and Mills College in Oakland, and designed the enormous Hearst Castle in San Simeon—but could not vote. It was in fact the growing role of women in the workforce that spurred the formation of a variety of women's clubs such as the State Nurses' Association, the Mothers' Congress, and Native Daughters of the Golden West that waged and won the battle for women's suffrage.

The passage of the Fifteenth Amendment and other laws that expanded suffrage would not prevent certain forces within California from restricting voting rights. In 1894, for example, the state legislature adopted an English literacy requirement to vote, denying the right to vote to any male person who was unable to read in English or write his name. Often applied more stringently to the Latino population of California than to European immigrant communities, many of which also had limited English skills, the state court in *Castro* v. *State of California* would in 1970 toss out this literacy requirement. The series of voters' rights provisions adopted by the federal government over the past

sixty-five years would expand suffrage, but various advocacy groups charge that subtle forms of disenfranchisement continue to exist in California. Redistricting continues to be one of these subtleties, affecting millions but conducted by a relatively small group that draws electoral districts throughout California often in blatant attempts to consolidate or divide whole groups of voters. In *Garza* v. *County of Los Angeles* and *Gomez* v. *City of Watsonville*, the Ninth Circuit Court of Appeals found that the Latino populations had been prevented, due to the drawing of racially polarized districts, from participating effectively in the political process.

The struggle to expand suffrage equally to all Californians does continue, offering most the choice of joining this enduring endeavor at its most basic level through the act of voting. Nonvoting is another choice, satisfying the differing groups of individuals who for various reasons value voting enough to continue in the task of excluding whole groups of eligible Californians.

*Sources:* Julian Nava and Bob Barger, *California: Five Centuries of Cultural Contrasts.* (Beverly Hills, CA: Glencoe Press, 1976); Mexican American Legal Defense and Educational Fund and William C. Velasquez, "California Congressional Redistricting Plan: Supplement to MALDEF-WCVI Congressional Redistricting Plan," July 2001.

**Think Again**

How have primary elections in California changed since their introduction in 1866?

**direct primary elections** Elections in which voters choose the candidates who will compete in a subsequent general election.

**cross-filing** A system that allowed a candidate to represent multiple parties.

**closed primary system** An election system that permits registered members of a political party to vote only for their party's candidates.

**blanket primary** A primary election in which all voters can vote for any candidate, regardless of party affiliation.

# Elections

In California, there are three basic types of elections: state primary elections, state general elections, and special elections.

**State Primary Elections**    Until the turn of the twentieth century, candidates for elected office throughout the United States were nominated or simply chosen at autocratic party conventions, and the average voter had no say in the selection of candidates for general elections. The California Progressives promoted **direct primary elections**. In 1908, California passed a constitutional amendment that made primaries mandatory, less partisan, and more democratic. Although the primary underwent another change when **cross-filing**, a system that allowed a candidate to represent multiple parties, was abolished in 1959, many Californians remain dissatisfied with the **closed primary system**, which requires registered members of a political party to vote only for their party's candidates.[3]

In 1996, adoption of Proposition 198 transformed the California primary to a **blanket primary**, in which all registered voters could vote for any candidate, regardless of political affiliation. After its use in the 1998 statewide primary election, the blanket primary was contested in the courts by both the Democratic and Republican national parties, which feared both that party supporters would vote as independents and that each party would encourage its supporters to act as "spoilers" by voting for the opposing party's least popular candidates. The spoilers' actions would attempt to guarantee that their party's general election candidate faced the weakest opposition candidate.

In 2000, the United States Supreme Court declared California's blanket primary in violation of the political party's First Amendment right of association, forcing the state to adopt a modified closed primary system. Under this system, voters may decline to state their party affiliation in any primary election if this is authorized by the rules of a political party. Otherwise, voters may only receive a ballot for the party for which they are registered.

State primaries are usually held on the first Tuesday after the first Monday in June of even-numbered years; presidential primaries are conducted on the first Tuesday after the first Monday in March. Traditionally, the California presidential primary took place in June as well, but as other states moved their primaries earlier, the California primary became increasingly irrelevant. As a result, the presidential primary was moved to March as of the 2000 election year. Since then, a number of questions and doubts have been raised about the new date, partly because the statewide primary is still held in June. In response to these concerns, Governor Arnold Schwarzenegger recently signed into law provisions for returning all California primaries to June.

Much of the state primary is taken up by nonpartisan elections at the municipal and county levels. The state constitution specifies that candidates for a nonpartisan office, such as a city council member or district attorney, must receive 50 percent or more of the vote. If no candidate receives a majority, the two candidates with the most votes must face each other in a runoff during the general election. Because statewide primaries in nonpresidential years attract low voter turnout, many Californians miss the opportunity to vote for local elected officials.

**State General Elections**    The state **general election** takes place on the first Tuesday after the first Monday in November of even-numbered years. At general elections, voters choose among the nominees chosen during the primaries. Regular or "midterm" general state elections generally have lower voter turnout than presidential elections. The state's fifty-five electors for the electoral college are chosen according to the rules of the two Democratic and Republican state party organizations. The Democratic state party organization permits each member of the California Democratic congressional delegation to choose one elector, and the Republican party state party organization allows major figures and officials in the state party organization to act as electors. On rare occasions, a **special election** will be held in California to fill vacancies in Congress or the state legislature or conduct a recall. The governor can call a special election in the attempt to win the approval of one or more initiatives by the voters, but such efforts—including a tax limitation initiative sponsored by Governor Ronald Reagan in 1973, a school voucher initiative in 1993 by Governor Pete Wilson, and the most recent attempt by Governor Arnold Schwarzenegger to get approval for initiatives on budget restrictions and on teacher evaluation policy—failed at the polls.[4]

An electoral legacy of the Progressives is the provision for partisan as well as nonpartisan elections. **Partisan elections** account for slightly more than 10 percent of the elections that are conducted in California and include all statewide executive offices, with the exception of the superintendent of education, insurance commissioner, congressional representatives, and state legislators. The election of judges and all local and county elections are **nonpartisan elections**. In these elections, no party designation can be used on the ballot, although local and county elected officials still receive partisan support and express partisan opinions.

Along with nonpartisan elections, Progressive reforms were apparent in attempts to design ballots that would minimize the number of offices and items (short ballots)

**general election** An election in which candidates compete directly for election to a given office.

**special election** An election called to address a specific issue prior to the next regularly scheduled election.

**partisan election** An election in which candidates are identified by party affiliation.

**nonpartisan election** An election in which candidates are not identified by party affiliation.

## UP CLOSE

# Circumventing Campaign Finance Law: California's Independent Expenditure Committees

In 2000, voters passed Proposition 34, the Campaign Contributions and Spending Limits and Disclosure initiative, one of the few limits on campaign funding to survive a legal challenge. The restrictions imposed by Proposition 34 can be circumvented, however, through a huge loophole that allows for almost unlimited amounts of money to be spent by independent expenditure committees on a campaign. Under Proposition 34 guidelines, individual direct contributions are capped at $3,300 for each legislative candidate and $22,300 for each statewide campaign during an election. Independent expenditure committees in California can, on the other hand, spend unlimited sums on a campaign as long as these committees do not coordinate their support or contributions with a candidate or members of a campaign organization. It has been said that politics makes for strange bedfellows and the collection of "fellows" in independent expenditure committees may be even more peculiar. There are literally hundreds of committees that are registered with the Office of the California Secretary of State that will very often assume names that conceal intent or ideological orientation.

The one common denominator for the most effective independent expenditure committees is their ability to accumulate considerable amounts of money. Political consultants are the key players in determining how contributions from the independent expenditure committees are channeled, serving as intermediaries who, while not directly involved with a campaign or candidate, make recommendations regarding financial support on the basis of knowledge of the candidate or issue and personal and professional relationships with members of a campaign organization. The monetary clout of the independent expenditure committees largely comes from special interest groups, usually from either the business community or labor unions, that make large donations to a committee in support of a favorite candidate or issue. In addition to the loose restrictions on campaign spending, special interest groups also appreciate the anonymity that the committees provide. Corporate sponsors of the Alliance for California's Tomorrow committee included Sempra Energy ($100,000), Pacific Gas and Electric Co. ($75,000), and Hollywood Park and Bay Meadows racetracks ($50,000 each). Unlike campaign organizations that must make regular contribution disclosures, the independent expenditure committees are only required to disclose the source of their funds at the end of an election period, further shrouding the true political motivations of the support. These committees are also a means for individual businesses and other organizations to pool

---

**Table 16.1** Partisan Differences in Political Participation Rates, by Party Registration

|  | By Party Registration (%) | | | | |
|---|---|---|---|---|---|
|  | Democrat | Republican | Independent | Not Registered | IPI |
| Vote regularly | 62 | 67 | 47 | 13 | 0.13 |
| Sign petitions | 44 | 43 | 43 | 21 | 0.07 |
| Attend local meetings | 42 | 39 | 40 | 32 | 0.03 |
| Write to elected officials | 32 | 35 | 30 | 12 | 0.08 |
| Contribute money | 23 | 34 | 16 | 7 | 0.14 |
| Attend rallies | 18 | 16 | 17 | 8 | 0.07 |
| Participate in political party work | 10 | 8 | 4 | 3 | 0.15 |

*Note:* The reference populations are adult citizens for political participation.

*Sources:* PPIC Statewide Surveys (August, October, and November 2002). *The Ties That Bind: Changing Demographics and Civic Engagement in California,* S. Karthick Ramakrishnan and Mark Baldassare 2004.

their funds and make a major impact on either the success or defeat of a particular campaign.

Rather than contribute money directly, the independent expenditure committees typically fund campaign activities separate from a campaign organizations', such as mailers, radio time, billboards, phone banks, polling, and election-related research, but for committees with deep pockets, television advertisement for or against a particular candidate or measure can really make the difference in a campaign. Television ads are extremely expensive and most major campaign donors would be unable to make an equivalent contribution directly to a campaign under legal limits. The California Correctional Peace Officers Association has one of the more active independent expenditure committees, which spent $200,000 on assemblyman and former parole agent Rudy Bermudez of Norwalk and $165,000 on Assemblyman Tom Harman, a Republican from Huntington Beach. The work of the independent expenditure committees comes in many forms, including spending on local candidates such as Oakland mayoral candidate Ignacio De La Fuente, who got help from Californians United, a committee tied to state senate president pro tem Don Perata, D-Oakland. The African American Political Empowerment Committee surfaced during the June 2006 primary election and was typical of the aberrant quality of independent expenditure committees, accusing Board of Equalization candidate Judy Chu of accepting big tobacco, HMOs, and drug company campaign support in a mailer while actually receiving contributions from two major tobacco companies. The $9 million that was donated by the family of millionaire Sacramento developer Angelo Tsakopoulos for independent expenditures in support of the "Phil Angelides for Governor" primary campaign generated the most controversy regarding independent expenditures

during this 2006 election. The expenditure was unexpected and caused misjudgments by Steve Westly and his campaign organization, the other front-runner for the Democratic nomination who was ultimately defeated.

The impact of the independent expenditure committees on elections and politics in California varies, but it would be unrealistic to think that the large expenditure of money on a campaign does not coincide with the "pay to play" principle of American politics and limits the effectiveness of the average California voters who don't pay. As long as the California courts associate the spending of money on a campaign with First Amendment rights, using however much money it takes to say something for or about a candidate or issue, the chances of restricting independent expenditure committees are remote. Although involving a bit more work for the average voter, California disclosure laws do provide some defense against massive independent expenditures. The Office of the Secretary of State, through the *Cal-Access* database, furnishes information on contributions that have been received and made by a wide range of individuals and groups, including independent expenditure committees. The data are made available after an election, but *Cal-Access* can be useful in tracking the history of contributions to a particular candidate or campaign, suggesting that "where there is smoke, there is usually fire."

*Sources:* Phillip Matier and Andrew Ross, "Free-Spending Special Interests Exert Big Influence," *San Francisco Chronicle,* June 7, 2006; John Howard, "The Rise of the IE," *Capitol Weekly,* May 18, 2006, http://www.capitolweekly.net/news/article.html?article_id=717; Andy Furillo, "Big Money Still Finds its Way to Hot Races," Sacramento Bee, http://www.sacbee.com/content/politics/ca/elections.

and that listed candidates by office rather than by party (office block ballots). The intent of the Progressives was to create a simple, nonpartisan—or perhaps antiparty—ballot. The short ballot eventually became impractical as the number of offices and ballot measures grew, but the listing of candidates by office remains on the current long ballot. The long ballot has complicated the voting process by forcing the voter to make important decisions on a long list of candidates and issues without the luxury of voting for a slate of candidates grouped by political party.[5]

# Direct Democracy: California's Electoral Dilemma

Three avenues for direct democracy—the recall, the referendum, and the initiative—have been unique features of the political landscape in California, especially in their broad application and controversial outcomes. In many ways, direct democracy continues to accomplish the goals of the Progressives when

This portion of a long ballot covers a wide range of state and county issues on which citizens register their votes.

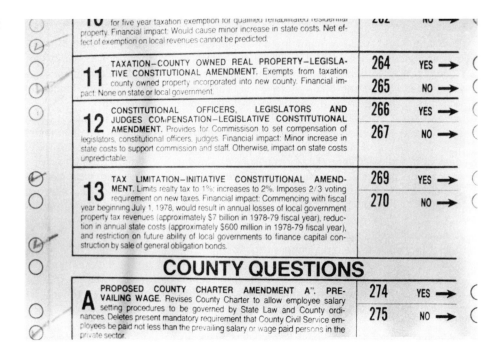

they led the state in enacting these provisions in 1911. The Progressives wanted Californians to have the political power to circumvent an unresponsive state legislature or executive branch. Hiram Johnson proclaimed in 1911 that the avenues for direct democracy "were attempts to bring the government closer to the people," with the hope that "we may yet live in a free republic."[6] However, the Progressives might be surprised and saddened by the influence that wealth, interest groups, and partisanship have over these democratic practices today.

**The Recall** The **recall** is a constitutional procedure that allows for the removal from public office of any person who has proved to be poorly qualified, corrupt, or incompetent. Originally, the Progressives used the recall to target judges who favored corporate interests and corrupt politicians.[7] The recall was one of the most popular constitutional reform proposals in 1911, approved by over 76 percent of the voters.[8]

The two major phases of the recall process are the signature-gathering stage and the election stage. The process begins with a petition that outlines the reasons why an official should be removed from office. A recall petition cannot be circulated against an officeholder during the first six months of his or her term of office. To recall a statewide official, the number of signatures on a recall petition must equal or exceed 12 percent of the total votes cast in the last general election. When attempting to recall a state legislator, judge, member of the Board of Equalization, or countywide officeholder, signatures equal to 20 percent or more of the last vote for the office are required. Sponsors of a recall campaign have 160 days to file signed petitions with the secretary of state. The appropriate office must verify and certify the signatures and petition and forward them to the governor, who is required to call for a recall election between sixty and eighty days after certification.

During the election stage of the recall process, voters vote on two separate issues: First, they will decide whether to recall the officeholder, and then they may select a replacement. Candidates for the office must submit a petition signed by registered voters that equal 1 percent or more of the vote cast for that office during the last election and pay a registration fee. During the election stage, the

**recall** A procedure by which voters can remove an elected official from office before to the end of the official's term.

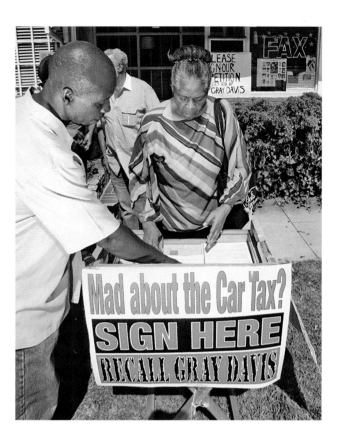

Citizens sign a petition for the recall of California Governor Gray Davis.

officeholder is in the difficult position of having to respond to charges in the recall statement as well as campaigning against any replacement candidates.

A simple majority of voters can recall an officeholder, and the replacement candidate who receives the most votes will fill the vacant position. Every vote cast for recall is counted, regardless of whether the voter selects a replacement candidate, but a vote for a replacement candidate will be counted only if the voter responded to the recall question.

Until recently, the recall process was never used successfully against a statewide officeholder and had been used only a few times against state legislators. A number of local officials have been recalled, including an El Dorado County supervisor, Cabrillo Unified School District trustees, Placer County fire protection district board members, Del Norte County school board members, and city council members in Amador, Brisbane, and Grass Valley. Many recall petitions against statewide officials have been circulated over the years, including ones seeking to remove Governors Pat Brown and Ronald Reagan, but all were primarily symbolic until 2003 and the recall of Governor Gray Davis.

*The Recall of Gray Davis*    As unfortunate as the recall election on October 7, 2003, may have been for Governor Gray Davis and his supporters or how gratifying it was for Rescue California and the many other committees that formed to oust the governor, the importance of this successful recall can be found in the convergence of various political and economic issues and trends affecting California and the attempt to resolve them. When taking into account the historical ineffectiveness of the recall process against statewide officials, the reelection of Governor Davis only eleven months earlier, and the dominance of the Democratic Party in California, more than a few political pundits were stunned by the recall results. On close analysis, however, the fact that 55 percent of California voters would take the unprecedented step of removing Governor Davis was a logical reaction to crit-

|Think Again|

**What led to the recall of Governor Gray Davis in October 2003?**

Democrat Gray Davis reacts to the crowd's applause during a victory celebration in November, 1998. Davis defeated Republican rival Dan Lungren to become the state's first Democratic governor in 16 years.

**deregulation** The removal of government restrictions on businesses or industries.

ical dilemmas facing California in 2002. The statewide energy crisis, probably more than any other factor, caused Californians to become extremely dissatisfied with their state government and to seek some remedy to an increasingly intolerable situation. The **deregulation** of energy production and consumption in 1998 resulted in a complicated statewide power generating system that suffered from out-of-state ownership, dwindling energy resources, lack of oversight, and unscrupulous business tactics. This energy conundrum led to a dramatic rise in energy costs and a dramatic drop in supply, punctuated by the infamous "rolling blackouts." Soon thereafter, Internet-based and microcomputer companies headquartered in California, which had made substantial tax contributions to the state general fund, began to experience commercial and economic difficulties, resulting in significant financial losses for that industry as well as the California economy. An unexpected 20 percent decrease in state tax revenues in 2000 was followed by a large state budget deficit equal to over one-quarter of the total budget, which most Californians were unwilling to cover through higher taxes. Davis's inability to convince Californians that he, as the chief executive officer of the state, could solve these and other mounting problems made him a likely target for the average resident's wrath. Under the leadership of Darrell Issa, a wealthy businessman and member of the U.S. House of Representatives, a wide collection of Republican Party elected officials, activists, and supporters formed recall committees and raised millions of dollars to wage sustained attacks on Governor Davis' leadership qualities and channel voter disenchantment toward the recall process.

California gubernatorial candidate Arnold Schwarzenegger addresses supporters during a campaign stop, September 2003, in Santa Maria, California.

In the midst of the sudden economic decline, the energy crisis, and the unusual statewide recall campaign, Californians were astonished yet again by the decision of Arnold Schwarzenegger, bodybuilder, film star, and successful businessman without any professional political experience, to run in the recall election to replace Gray Davis as governor. In a field of 135 replacement candidates, including five major and independent party contenders, Schwarzenegger captured 48.6 percent of the vote, acutely demonstrating the displeasure of Californians with conventional professional politicians and their desire for a confident, self-made, seemingly independent, and charismatic leader.[9] The recall election was also another reminder of the effectiveness of expensive modern campaign techniques such as television political advertisements and professional signature-gathering services. Rather than the popular or grassroots efforts that the Progressives envisioned would grow out of the avenues for direct democracy, all three mechanisms have in recent years favored interest groups and individuals capable of raising millions of dollars. The Schwarzenegger replacement campaign accounted for nearly half of all campaign contributions among all the replacement candidates, more than $22 million.[10]

**The Initiative**    In his insightful book *Paradise Lost: California's Experience, America's Future*, the award-winning journalist Peter Schrag writes:

> The passage of Proposition 13 serves as a convenient way of dividing the post–World War II era in California between that postwar period of optimism, with its huge investment in public infrastructure and its strong commitment to the development of quality education systems and other public services, and a generation of declining confidence and shrinking public services.[11]

With the passage of Proposition 13 in 1978, politics underwent a drastic change as the **initiative** process became a popular avenue for Californians and the interest groups representing them to repudiate the lawmaking authority of representative government and invoke change.

Before the enactment of Proposition 13, the initiative process was used sparingly, although there was a flurry of initiative activity soon after the passage of the three avenues for direct democracy in 1911. In the attempt to politically empower Californians and make California politics more democratic, the Progressives led the state to adopt the **direct initiative**, which allows Californians to *directly* propose and enact a law or constitutional amendment. The Progressives could have chosen a process that requires the legislature to passage citizen-proposed laws, a practice still used in nine states, but by instead implementing the direct initiative, the Progressives placed lawmaking power firmly in the hands of any resident who had the wherewithal to place a proposed law on the ballot through a petition circulation process.

Today, that process requires valid signatures of registered voters equal to 5 percent or more of the votes cast in the last gubernatorial election to propose a law

**⊢Think Again⊣**

What accounts for the increase in the use of the initiative in recent years?

**initiative**  A process by which voters can directly propose and enact a law or constitutional amendment.

**direct initiative**  An initiative that allows voters to propose and enact a law or constitutional amendment without the intervention of the state legislature.

Supporters wearing stickers that read "Save the American Dream, vote Yes on 13" celebrate the overwhelming lead taken by Proposition 13 in early returns in the California primary.

and 8 percent or more to propose a constitutional amendment. According to the state constitution, an initiative must be limited to one subject, and it may not name a person to office and grant a duty or power to a private corporation. After the state attorney general's office prepares a title and summary of the proposed law or amendment and forwards a copy to the secretary of state, supporters of the initiative have 150 days to gather signatures. Once the petition process is completed, arguments for and against the initiative are printed in a ballot pamphlet that is mailed to all registered voters, and the initiative is placed on the ballot for next scheduled election. In campaigning for passage of an initiative, a group or individual must file campaign expenditure statements, but there are no restrictions on the amount of money that can be received and spent. Approval of an initiative requires a simple majority of those voting on the initiative. Once an initiative is passed, it can be changed or invalidated only by another initiative or a successful legal challenge. It has become a common practice for opponents of an approved initiative to file a lawsuit within days of the election in the hope that a legal technicality or judicial doctrine will prevent the law from going into effect.

Through the power of judicial review, state and federal courts can invalidate a new law enacted by the initiative process if one of those courts determines that the initiative violates the federal or state constitution or federal law. Judicial review by state courts is, however, not an option if the initiative resulted in a change to the state constitution. On very rare instances, state courts have intervened before an initiative election, almost always to enforce the single-subject rule, the constitutional provision that restricts an initiative to one subject. Since 1986, nearly two-thirds of the popular initiatives approved by the voters were challenged in the courts, and half of those were either partially or totally invalidated.[12]

For example, the crowds that gather at Indian reservations across California to gamble would probably be surprised to learn the that California Supreme Court originally struck down Proposition 5, the 1998 initiative allowing Nevada-style casinos on Indian reservations. Passed by 63 percent of the voters, Proposition 5 permitted gambling on Indian reservations and established regulatory and revenue-sharing guidelines, pitting a group of California Indian casino owners against Governor Pete Wilson and Nevada casino and California racetracks owners. Nearly six months after the election, the California Supreme Court ruled 6–1 that the initiative violated the 1984 California State Lottery Act, an initiative constitutional amendment that banned casino-style gambling in the state. The supreme court ruling later became irrelevant when incoming Governor Gray Davis concluded an agreement regarding the scope of Indian casino gambling with all the California Indian casino owners.[13]

Legal challenges to California initiatives are more likely to come from federal courts than from state courts. The state constitutional requirement that forces California state court judges and justices to face election after being appointed is one commonly held justification for the reluctance of state courts to invalidate initiatives passed by the very voters they will eventually confront. Federal judges and justices, on the other hand, serve for life and experience no such pressure. Another view finds that federal courts have less appreciation for the "popular" democracy practiced in California, focusing instead on their responsibility to uphold the U.S. Constitution, especially as it pertains to civil liberties and the power of the federal government. California courts, on the other hand, are torn by their responsibility to uphold both constitutions. The invalidation by the U.S. Supreme Court of initiatives granting Californians a blanket primary and establishing limits on campaign contributions are two instances in which the Court found that initiatives approved by California voters were contrary to First Amendment rights.

The passage of Proposition 215, which permitted the use of marijuana for medical purposes in California, provides a good example of the delicate legal balance the federal courts must adopt when attempting to enforce federal statutes and constitutional provisions while respecting states' rights. After almost nine years of legal uncertainty regarding the freedom of Californians to ignore federal drugs laws and the authority of federal law enforcement agencies to prevent the medical use of marijuana, the U.S. Supreme Court finally addressed this dilemma in *Gonzales v. Raich*, when it ruled in a 6–3 decision that the federal government has the authority under the commerce clause of the U.S. Constitution to prevent the use, sale, and cultivation of marijuana, thereby effectively invalidating Proposition 215. The Court did not, however, take the next legal step of finding Proposition 215 to be unconstitutional.[14] Needless to say, a large number of Californians have been displeased with this and various other court rulings that have nullified state initiatives. Some attempt to place checks on the power

---

**Table 16.2   Propositions Invalidated**

### Propositions Entirely Invalidated, 1986–2000

| Proposition | | Reason Invalidated | Court |
|---|---|---|---|
| 49 | Nonpartisan Offices | U.S. Const. First Amendment | Federal |
| 68 | Legislative Campaign Spending Limits | Conflicting Proposition received more votes | State |
| 105 | Disclosures to Consumers, Voters, and Investors | Addressed more than a single subject | State |
| 164 | Term Limits | [never enforced] | [Federal] |
| 198 | Open Primaries | U.S. Const. First Amendment | Federal |
| 208 | Campaign Contributions and Spending Limits | U.S. Const. First Amendment | Federal |
| 225 | Congressional Term Limits | U.S. Const. Article V | State |

### Propositions Substantially Invalidated, 1986–2000

| | | | |
|---|---|---|---|
| 73 | Campaign Financing | U.S. Const. First Amendment | Federal |
| 187 | Illegal Aliens, Ineligibility for Public Services | Federal preemption | Federal |
| 8 | Tribal Gaming | Cal. Const. Act | State |

### Propositions Invalidated in Part, 1986–2000

| Proposition | | Reason invalidated | Court |
|---|---|---|---|
| 65 | Safe Drinking Water | Some applications preempted by federal law others not | Federal and State |
| 103 | Insurance Rates, Regulation | Insurance rate rollback and required contributions to nonprofits invalid remainder of initiative valid | State |
| 115 | Criminal Laws | Constitutional amendment conforming California construction to the federal constitution was an unlawful constitutional revision remainder of initiative valid | State |
| 132 | Marine Resources | Application in some contexts preempted by federal law | Federal |

*Source:* University of California Hastings College of the Law, *Ballot Measures and Judicial Review, 1986–2000*, by David J. Jung and Janis M. Crum, **PLRI REPORTS**, Fall 2000. This report was prepared by the Public Law Research Institute at Hastings College of the Law. It does not represent the views or policies of Hastings College of the Law, its Board of Directors or its faculty.

of judicial review, an almost impossible task against federal courts, could well be the next target of the volatile political tendencies of the California electorate.

Californians have used the initiative to change or influence municipal or county government more often than at the state level. The process follows slightly different rules. The signature-gathering period is slightly longer (180 days), and the number of signatures required to place an initiative on the ballot at the county level is based on the number of votes cast in that county during the last gubernatorial election. At the municipal level, the signature-gathering requirement is based on the total number of registered voters in that municipality.

Although the number of initiatives qualified by petition and adopted grew moderately in the 1980s, the successful passage of Proposition 13 in 1978 popularized the initiative as a means of attempting to address major issues. Proposition 13 also showed that the ability to pass an initiative depends on access to generous financial support and professional campaign management.

<table>
<tr><td>

|Think Again|

**In what ways has Proposition 13 served as a model for subsequent initiative efforts?**

</td></tr>
</table>

*Proposition 13*   Proposition 13 grew out of the rapid rise in residential property taxes throughout the 1970s and the highly visible antitax advocacy of Howard Jarvis and Paul Gann, two representatives of the California real estate industry.[15] In 1978, Jarvis and Gann spearheaded the successful passage of Proposition 13, an initiative for a constitutional amendment that limited the total property tax to 1 percent of the assessed value of each parcel or residential home and further limited the annual increase in assessment to 2 percent. The initiative also required that any general tax increases be approved by a majority of voters and that increases in "special taxes," to fund such things as local transportation, would need to be approved by two-thirds of the voters. Similarly, the state legislature was prohibited from passing any tax increases without a two-thirds vote in each chamber. Proposition 13 benefited Californians who had lived or planned to live in their homes for a long period of time and those who were able to find moderately priced real estate. As a result of Proposition 13, California residents continue to pay property taxes that are considerably lower than elsewhere in the nation, but the result has been a severe reduction in the amount of funds available to state and local governments. California schools were especially affected by the reduction in property taxes, formerly a traditional source of funding for local education.

<table>
<tr><td>

|Think Again|

**How has the referendum shaped the course of constitutional change in California?**

</td></tr>
</table>

*Formula for a Successful Initiative*   The passage of Proposition 13 not only popularized the initiative but also provided the campaign formula that gives the proponents of initiatives a better than even chance in winning the approval of the voters. The first feature of the post–Proposition 13 initiative formula is to keep the campaign message simple. In the case of Proposition 13, even though the actual language of the initiative involved complicated tax policy and real estate jargon, the basic campaign message was "If you want lower taxes, vote for Proposition 13." Numerous sources of electoral data and studies, as well as the outcomes of initiative elections, suggest that when in doubt or unclear about the intention of an initiative, voters will cast a no vote every time.

Unfortunately, Proposition 13 and many other successful initiative campaigns achieved that simplicity of message through the distortion or omission of central details of the initiative.[16] For example, the campaign managers of Proposition 205, another initiative in 1998 to permit casino-style gambling on Native American land in California, omitted most references to "gambling" or "casinos" in their media advertisements.

The second feature of the formula involves the creation of an organizational framework or committee that can stimulate interest, especially among registered

| **Table 16.3** | **California Ballot Propositions Since 2000** |
|---|---|

**March 7, 2000**

- *1A* – Passed – Gambling on Tribal Lands. Legislative Constitutional Amendment.
- *12* – Passed – Safe Neighborhood Parks, Clean Water, Clean Air, and Coastal Protection Bond Act of 2000.
- *13* – Passed – Safe Drinking Water, Clean Water, Watershed Protection, and Flood Protection Bond Act.
- *14* – Passed – California Reading and Literacy Improvement and Public Library Construction and Renovation Bond Act of 2000.
- *15* – Failed – The Hertzberg-Polanco Crime Laboratories Construction Bond Act of 1999.
- *16* – Passed – Veterans Homes Bond Act of 2000.
- *17* – Passed – Lotteries. Charitable Raffles. Legislative Constitutional Amendment.
- *18* – Passed – Murder: Special Circumstances. Legislative Initiative Amendment.
- *19* – Passed – Murder BART and CSU Peace Officers. Legislative Initiative Amendment
- *20* – Passed – California State Lottery. Allocation for Instructional Materials. Legislative Initiative Amendment.
- *21* – Passed – Juvenile Crime. Initiative Statute.
- *22* – Passed – Limit on Marriages. Initiative Statute.
- *23* – Failed – 'None of the Above' Ballot Option. Initiative Statute.
- *24* – Removed from ballot by order of the California Supreme Court.
- *25* – Failed – Election Campaigns. Contributions and Spending Limits. Public Financing. Disclosures. Initiative Statute.
- *26* – Failed – School Facilities. Local Majority Vote. Bonds, Taxes. Initiative Constitutional Amendment and Statute.
- *27* – Failed – Elections. Term Limit Declarations for Congressional Candidates. Initiative Statute.
- *28* – Failed – Repeal of Proposition 10 Tobacco Surtax. Initiative Statute.
- *29* – Passed – 1998 Indian Gaming Compacts. Referendum Statute.
- *30* – Failed – Insurance Claims Practices. Civil Remedies Referendum.
- *31* – Failed – Insurance Claims Practices. Civil Remedy Amendments. Referendum.

**November 7, 2000**

- *32* – Passed – Veterans' Bond Act of 2000. A.B. 2305.
- *33* – Failed – Legislature. Participation in Public Employees' Retirement System. A.C.A. 12.
- *34* – Passed – Campaign Contributions and Spending Limits. Disclosure. S.B. 1223.
- *35* – Passed – Public Works Projects. Use of Private Contractors for Engineering and Architectural Services. Initiative.
- *36* – Passed – Drugs. Probation and Treatment Program. Initiative.
- *37* – Failed – Fees, Vote Requirements. Taxes. Initiative.
- *38* – Failed – School Vouchers. State-Funded Private and Religious Education. Public Schoolfunding. Initiative.
- *39* – Passed – School Facilities. 55% Local Vote. Bonds, Taxes. Accountability Requirements. Initiative.

**March 5, 2002**

- *40* – Passed – The California Clean Water, Clean Air, Safe Neighborhood Parks, and Coastal Protection Act of 2002. AB 1602.
- *41* – Passed – Voting Modernization Bond Act of 2002. (Shelley-Hertzberg Act). AB 56.
- *42* – Passed – Transportation Congestion Improvement Act. Allocation of Existing Motor Vehicle Fuel Sales and Use Tax Revenues for Transportation Purposes Only. Legislative Constitutional Amendment. ACA 4.
- *43* – Passed – Right to Have Vote Counted. ACA 9.
- *44* – Passed – Chiropractors. Unprofessional Conduct. SB 1988.
- *45* – Failed – Legislative Term Limits. Local Voter Petitions. Initiative.

**November 5, 2002**

- *46* – Passed – Housing and Emergency Shelter Trust Fund Act of 2002. S.B. 1227.
- *47* – Passed – Kindergarten-University Public Education Facilities Bond Act of 2002. A.B. 47.
- *48* – Passed – Court Consolidation. A.C.A. 15.
- *49* – Passed – Before and After School Programs. State Grants. Initiative.
- *50* – Passed – Water Quality, Supply and Safe Drinking Water Projects. Coastal Wetlands Purchase and Protection. Bonds. Initiative.
- *51* – Failed – Transportation. Distribution of Existing Motor Vehicle Sales and Use Tax. Initiative.
- *52* – Failed – Election Day Voter Registration. Voter Fraud Penalties. Initiative.

*(continued)*

**Table 16.3** California Ballot Propositions Since 2000

**October 7, 2003**

- *53* – Failed – Funds Dedicated for State and Local Infrastructure. Legislative Constitutional Amendment. A.C.A. 11.
- *54* – Failed – Classification by Race, Ethnicity, Color, or National Origin. Initiative Constitutional Amendment.

**March 2, 2004**

- *55* – Passed – Kindergarten-University Public Education Facilities Bond Act of 2004.
- *56* – Failed – State Budget, Related Taxes, and Reserve. Voting Requirements. Penalties. Initiative Constitutional Amendment and Statute.
- *57* – Passed – The Economic Recovery Bond Act.
- *58* – Passed – The California Balanced Budget Act.

**November 2, 2004**

- *1A* – Passed – Protection of Local Government Revenues.
- *59* – Passed – Public Records, Open Meetings. Legislative Constitutional Amendment.
- *60* – Passed – Election Rights of Political Parties. Legislative Constitutional Amendment.
- *60A* – Passed – Surplus Property. Legislative Constitutional Amendment.
- *61* – Passed – Children's Hospital Projects. Grant Program. Bond Act. Initiative Statute.
- *62* – Failed – Elections. Primaries Initiative Constitutional Amendment and Statute.
- *63* – Passed – Mental Health Services Expansion, Funding. Tax on Personal Incomes Above $1 Million. Initiative Statute.
- *64* – Passed – Limits on Private Enforcement of Unfair Business Competition Laws. Initiative Statute.
- *65* – Failed – Local Government Funds, Revenues. State Mandates. Initiative Constitutional Amendment.
- *66* – Failed – Limitations on "Three Strikes" Law. Sex Crimes. Punishment. Initiative Statute.
- *67* – Failed – Emergency Medical Services. Funding. Telephone Surcharge. Initiative Constitutional Amendment and Statute.
- *68* – Failed – Non-Tribal Commercial Gambling Expansion. Tribal Gaming Compact Amendments. Revenues, Tax Exemptions. Initiative Constitutional Amendments and Statute.
- *69* – Passed – DNA Samples. Collection Database. Funding. Initiative Statute.
- *70* – Failed – Tribal Gaming Compacts. Exclusive Gaming Rights. Contributions to State. Initiative Constitutional Amendment and Statute.
- *71* – Passed – Stem Cell Research. Funding. Bonds. Initiative Constitutional Amendment and Statute.
- *72* – Failed – Health Care Coverage Requirements. Referendum.

**November 8, 2005**

- *73* – Failed – Termination of Minor's Pregnancy. Waiting Period and Parental Notification. Initiative Constitutional Amendment.
- *74* – Failed – Public School Teachers. Waiting Period for Permanent Status. Dismissal. Initiative Statute.
- *75* – Failed – Public Employee Union Dues. Required Employee Consent for Political Contributions. Initiative Statute.
- *76* – Failed – School Funding. State Spending. Initiative Constitutional Amendment.
- *77* – Failed – Reapportionment. Initiative Constitutional Amendment.
- *78* – Failed – Prescription Drugs. Discounts. Initiative Statute.
- *79* – Failed – Prescription Drug Discounts. State-Negotiated Rebates. Initiative Statute.
- *80* – Failed – Electric Service Providers. Regulation. Initiative Statute.

**June 6, 2006**

- *81* – California Reading and Literacy Improvement and Public Library Construction and Renovation Bond Act of 2006.
- *82* – Public Preschool Education. Tax Increase on Incomes Over $400,000 for Individuals; $800,000 for Couples.

**Table 16.3    California Ballot Propositions Since 2000** *(continued)*

**November 7, 2006**

- *1A* – Passed – Protection of Transportation Funding.
- *1B* – Passed – Highway Safety, Traffic Reduction, Air Quality, and Port Security.
- *1C* – Passed – Housing and Emergency Shelter Trust Fund Act of 2006.
- *1D* – Passed – Kindergarten-University Public Education Facilities Bond Act of 2006.
- *1E* – Passed – Disaster Preparedness and Flood Prevention Act of 2006.
- *83* – Passed – Comprehensive Registered Sex Offender Laws (popularly known as "Jessica's Law").
- *84* – Passed – Bonds for clean water, flood control, state and local park improvements, etc.
- *85* – Failed – Parental Notification before Termination of Teen's Pregnancy (second attempt at Proposition 73).
- *86* – Failed – Increase on Cigarette Tax.
- *87* – Failed – Funding for alternative forms of energy.
- *88* – Failed – Property Parcel Tax to fund for Education.
- *89* – Failed – Campaign Finance Restrictions, including a corporate tax increase.
- *90* – Passed – Eminent Domain Restrictions.

**References**

- *California Secretary of State - Elections & Voter Information - Initiative Update*

voters, and generate endorsements from celebrities and politicians. The more "grassroots" such an entity becomes, the better. Howard Jarvis started his antitax crusade with a group called the United Organizations of Taxpayers, which quickly spun off similar groups to spread the tax rollback message. Jarvis became personally identified with the tax revolt, publicizing the initiative in frequent speaking engagements and media appearances with a personal style that apparently resonated with prospective voters.

The third feature of the formula entails the application of the most advanced campaign techniques available, backed by generous financial support. Both sides of Proposition 13 raised and spent large sums on the campaign, but it was the proponents who most effectively used the most current campaign techniques and secured victory at the polls. Jarvis retained Bill Butcher and Arnold Forde to manage a direct mail operation that raised thousands of dollars and convinced thousands of targeted registered voters to support Proposition 13 at the polls. Butcher and Forde professionalized the initiative campaign process by employing such techniques as direct mail petitions and computer-generated letters to property owners.[17] The effectiveness of the Butcher-Forde partnership on the Proposition 13 campaign led to the adoption even more advanced techniques in subsequent initiative campaigns and the growth of what is now known as the "initiative industrial complex." In the aftermath of Proposition 13, many campaign consultants and public relations firms that formerly concentrated on electing candidates switched to managing initiative campaigns. Political scientists and journalists have suggested that the growth of these firms is a major reason the initiative has become a fixture of California electoral politics. The large sum of money such firms can earn by managing initiative campaigns creates an incentive for them to encourage an interest group or wealthy individual to sponsor an initiative. For the representatives of interest groups, elected officials, and major corporate interests, attempting to pass an initiative, especially when the conditions of post–Proposition 13 formula converge, can be easier than achieving a public policy objective through the state legislature. The legislative process inevitably involves almost endless lobbying, large campaign contributions to individual legislators, trade-offs, and side deals. With the initiative, by contrast, few concessions need to be made.

Howard Jarvis, California tax fighter, announces the formation of the American Tax Reduction Movement in front of Internal Revenue Service Headquarters in 1978.

## ACROSS THE USA

# Reforming Campaign Finance: California and Connecticut

In 2000, the California Supreme Court invalidated Proposition 208, a campaign financing reform law that imposed a series of significant restrictions on the way candidates raised money. The California legislature, fearing that an even tougher initiative would be placed on the ballot, rushed to fill the void with Proposition 34, another campaign financing law that was approved by the voters and met judicial concerns. Since its passage, campaign finance law under the provisions of Proposition 34 have been soundly criticized as an ineffective means of limiting the amount of money contributed to candidates in the state. Although Proposition 208 set contribution limits from an individual at $250 for assembly and senate candidates and $500 for gubernatorial candidates, Proposition 34 raised those limits to $3,000 for assembly and senate candidates and $22,300 for governor. Other contributions could come from small contributor committees, political parties, political action committees (PACs), and soft money donations. These critics are particularly worried about the formation of and spending by independent expenditure committees that can raise unlimited funds to promote a certain candidate as long as they do not coordinate or work directly with a candidate's campaign committee. Proposition 34 guidelines have received high grades for its disclosure rules and the availability of online access to current contribution records. Enforcement of the Proposition 34 campaign guidelines have in general been disappointing, resulting in far fewer investigations and prosecutions of reported and confirmed campaign violations than expected. California's Fair Political Practices Commission (FPPC), responsible for implementing and enforcement of Proposition 34 restrictions, has complained that the agency's funding has not kept pace with its increased workload, allowing numerous campaign spending violations to avoid scrutiny. Even with limits on campaign contributions, California continues to be one of a handful of states that have no limits on the total amount of money that a candidate can raise and spend, and exceeds every other state in the amount of money contributed to most candidates for the legislature and statewide offices. The size and wealth of California can explain some aspects of the state's campaign financing largess, but Californians have long been concerned about the actual purpose of campaign contributions in California. In 2004, California Assembly and California State Senate candidates raised an average of $403,456 and $555,196, respectively, amounts that may insulate legislators from most constituents and favor special interests. In fact, one huge loophole to emerge from Proposition 34 has been the practice of "bundling," a means of contributing through third parties when an individual contribution limit to a particular candidate has been reached. Bundling has been used by like-minded individuals who want to pool contributions, but it is also used by big-money donors to go beyond contribution limits by using the names of friends and family members over eighteen years of age to make additional individual contributions.

One solution to California's inability to adequately address campaign financing may be found in the recent campaign finance law passed in Connecticut, touted as one of the nation's toughest. Not only does this law place strict limits on campaign contributions, but it creates a publicly funded election system that includes all statewide elections. The Connecticut legislature did not reach this juncture easily, forced somewhat down the road to publicly finance campaigns in the wake of a corruption scandal in 2005 that resulted in a prison sentence for former governor John G. Rowland and convictions of state legislators for accepting gifts from contractors. In an effort to limit the influence of special interests, the law bans political contributions from lobbyists and state contractors. Approximately $17 million in public funds (generated from unclaimed property and checks that end up in the state's general fund) will be allocated each year for political campaigns. Candidates are required to raise a minimum amount of funds to qualify for public campaign funds. Any ambivalence that the Connecticut legislature may have had about publicly financed elections was overcome by the extensive and persistent grassroots lobbying effort led by the Connecticut Citizen Action Group, Connecticut Common Cause, the Connecticut League of Women Voters, and various civil rights, labor, and environmental organizations. Ultimately, supporters of Connecticut's new campaign financing law would like to believe that publicly financed campaigns give ordinary people, unable or unwilling to make large contributions, a greater voice in the electoral process.

One year after the passage of Connecticut's new campaign finance law, the California legislature is in the process of crafting a similar law for state elections. Assembly Bill 583, introduced by assemblywoman Loni Hancock, D-Berkeley, won approval in the assembly and would provide an estimated $106 million in the first years to all candidates for state office who met "qualifying contributions" limits, and was passed by the senate but voted down on November 7, 2006. Participation in the California version of publicly financed elections would be voluntary, yet proponents of the bill feel that there would be pressure on most candidates to accept public funding to avoid the perception of being a special-interest candidate. The bill already has many detractors, principally among the Republican opposition in the legislature, who believe that publicly financed elections run counter to free speech and consider such government funding of campaigns a waste of state revenue.

Back in Connecticut, the very grassroots organizations that strongly advocated for passage of publicly financed campaigns are now concerned that the original bill has a number of features that could weaken its effectiveness and even implementation. Groups that favor and oppose the law are both concerned about the power given to the court in repealing the law; allowances for in-kind contributions in the form of advertising, mailing, and consultants; and potential equal protection violations regarding

the treatment of independent and minor party candidates. Whether the Connecticut legislature, which has the responsibility of addressing these concerns, will act accordingly remains to be seen. Or will the flow of campaign contributions, like water, simply find other indirect routes to the candidate?

*Sources:* Alex Knott, "California Awash in Campaign Cash, Potentials for Conflict of Interest," The Center For Public Integrity, January 25, 2001; State Elections Overview 2004, The Institute on Money In State Politics; Bill Ainsworth, "Cash Flow," *California Journal*, February, 2002, pp. 54–57; Edwin Garcia, "Campaigns Could Be Publicly Funded," *Contra Costa Times*, January 31, 2006; Connecticut Common Cause, "Connecticut's campaign finance law needs urgent changes," www.commoncause.org; Susan Haigh, "Connecticut OKs Campaign Finance Bill," *The Capital Times*, December 1, 2005.

*Problems with Initiatives*    Surveys of Californians conducted by the Public Policy Institute of California suggest that the initiative is very popular, but a significant majority "think that the ballot wording for citizens' initiatives is often too complicated and confusing for voters to clearly understand what would happen" if the measure passed.[18] The surveys also reveal that slightly more than half of Californians have more confidence in the initiative process than in the public policy decisions made by the governor and state legislature. Conversely, respondents feel that there are too many propositions on the state ballot.[19]

During his first two years in office, Governor Schwarzenegger introduced initiatives in two different elections, winning in the first attempt with the approval in 2004 of his California Balanced Budget Act, a constitutional amendment designed to make state government more fiscally responsible and provide the governor with greater authority on budget matters. The governor's second try at the polls resulted in the defeat of all four initiatives he sponsored in the 2005 special election, which included attempts to restrict teacher employment rights, limit the use of union dues for political purposes, constrain state spending and increase the budget authority of the governor, and strip the state legislature of its redistricting power. The campaigns of the four failed Schwarzenegger initiative campaigns largely disregarded the key features of the initiative formula, choosing instead to rely on the perceived popularity of the governor. Whether or not this repudiation at the polls will have any long-term effects on the political future of Governor Schwarzenegger and the initiative as an instrument for change remains to be seen, but he was reelected by a margin of 56% to 39% in the November 2006 election.

*Reforming the Initiative Process*    As more and more initiatives find their way on to the ballot, an increasing number of reports and commissions, such as the *Citizen's Commission on Ballot Initiatives* and the *California Constitution Revisions Commission*, have found problems in the initiative process and recommend implementation of a wide variety of reforms. Critics charge that too often the initiative process fails as an adequate avenue for direct democracy because of the dominance of special-interest groups, excessive campaign spending, poorly and deceptively written proposals, and a lack of accountability. Various recommended reforms from

|Think Again|

How has the preponderance of nonpartisan elections shaped California politics?

groups inside as well as outside government have largely centered on preelection review of initiative proposals, greater disclosure of financial sources and proponents, an increased legislative role, and more stringent qualifying requirements. Considering the lack of any meaningful change in the initiative process after over a decade of discussion, review, and debate, Californians remain as wary of such changes as with difficulties associated with the process.

**referendum**  A process by which voters can demand the review and approval of a particular legislative action by the voters.

**The Referendum**   The **referendum** has been commonly referred to as the least popular avenue of direct democracy. That observation is generally true, but on closer analysis, there is evidence to suggest that the two types of referendum in California, *petition* and *compulsory*, have in recent times played a growing and critical role in state politics.

**petition referendum**  A procedure that allows voters to request that all or part of a law be submitted to the voters for approval.

*The Petition Referendum*   Of the two types of referendum, the protest **petition or referendum** is closer to the spirit of the Progressive movement, as it allows voters to request that all or part of a law be submitted to the voters for approval, often preventing a piece of legislation from taking effect. All laws that have been recently passed by the state legislature and signed by the governor, with the exception of urgency statutes, statutes calling elections, or statutes providing for tax levies or appropriations for current expenses of the state, can be subjected to a petition.

Before a petition can be placed on a ballot, supporters must obtain the signatures of a number of registered voters equal to 5 percent or more of the votes for all candidates in the last gubernatorial election. The petition is considered one of the most difficult opportunities for direct democracy because of the relatively short time proponents have to gather the hundreds of thousands of signatures required (ninety days after enactment of the law). Once the required number of signatures is presented and certified by the secretary of state, the petition will be voted on during the next general election or special statewide election. A simple majority of voters will determine whether the law will be retained or invalidated.

Although the use of the petition has been infrequent, especially in comparison to the initiative, there has been a slight increase over the past twenty years. From 1942 until 1970, only one petition successfully qualified for the ballot, but between 1982 and 2005, the number grew to seven.[20] For the 2000 primary election, insurance claim practices became the target of the seldom-used petition, providing a good example of how direct democracy can produce unintended outcomes. The two insurance claim practices referendums, Propositions 30 and 31, were placed on the 2000 primary election ballot in response to two laws passed by the legislature and signed by the governor that would permit third-party lawsuits. These laws gave accident victims the right to sue insurance companies that denied, delayed, or attempted to "lowball" insurance claims resulting from an automobile accident. Under previous California law, a person who felt that an accident settlement was unsatisfactory or unfair could only file a complaint with the Department of Insurance or reject the settlement and sue the individual responsible for causing the accident, but the person could not sue an insurance company for unfair claims practices.[21]

The insurance industry objected to the new laws and had the financial muscle to overcome the difficulties of qualifying two petitions for the ballot. During the campaign phase leading up to the 2000 primary election, the insurance industry spent large sums of money convincing voters that the insurance claims practice laws would cause auto insurance premiums to skyrocket and that the laws would benefit personal injury attorneys, not consumers. Consumer groups argued that the insurance companies regularly deny claims, delay insurance payments, or pay only minimal costs of accident victims. They repeatedly cited the enormous profits that insurance companies made in the course of such business practices. In the end, the voters agreed with the insurance companies and rejected Propositions 30 and 31 by 68 and 71 percent, respectively.

*The Compulsory Referendum*    The legislative or **compulsory referendum** has generated much more attention and use than the petition referendum, principally because it is an approval device for the state legislature. The compulsory nature of this type of referendum is the consequence of the state constitution, which requires that all debts and liabilities and all constitutional amendments that originate in the state legislature must be passed by a two-thirds vote of each house of the legislature and approved by a majority of the voters during the next scheduled primary or general election. Almost every regularly scheduled election since 2000 has included a compulsory referendum that authorizes a bond act.

The issuance of bonds—in most cases **general obligation bonds**, state debt that is backed by the "full faith and credit of the state"—has become a popular means for the state government to raise revenue without raising taxes. General obligation bonds are generally used to finance major projects or long-term services rather than regular government operating costs. Such bonds place an obligation on future taxpayers and will ultimately cost them far more than the funds received, as a result of the interest that must be paid on the bond. Governor Schwarzenegger's response to California's budget woes in 2004 was to encourage the state legislature to enact the Economic Recovery Bond Act soon after taking office. This $15 billion bond scheme gave the state a much-needed infusion of funds and was the last electoral victory by Governor Schwarzenegger before various propositions that he supported were defeated at the polls.

Constitutional amendments are also often cast as compulsory referendums. Amendments have covered a wide variety of issues and services, including court consolidation, gambling, transportation, election rights, and surplus property. The compulsory referendum method in California is relatively straightforward and can easily be a regular part of the state electoral process. A noted University of California political science professor, Bruce E. Cain, has found that the more deliberative methods of constitutional change in the state, involving either a constitutional convention or constitutional revision commissions, have been eclipsed by more direct methods, including legislative constitutional amendments. The result, according to Cain, is that constitutional change in California lacks the "integrated perspective" of constitutional conventions or revision commissions and that the shift from "revision to amendment may be misshaping California state structure in important and predictable ways."[22] Evidently, the ability of the state legislature to enact constitutional amendments through the compulsory referendum process has been a major contributor to California's high ranking among states that change their constitutions often.

As with the initiative, California residents may also attempt to subject county or municipal laws or ordinances to a referendum, but there are a number of noticeable differences compared to statewide referendums. The time period allowed for gathering signatures cities and counties is longer (180 days) than the ninety days allowed to qualify a statewide referendum, and all proposals or petitions are submitted to the city or county clerk. Although most local referendums are also approved by a majority vote, local bond measures, with the exception of education bonds, must be passed by a two-thirds majority. Rather than follow the general law for cities and counties, whose election provisions are established

**compulsory referendum** A constitutional requirement that all debts and liabilities over $3 million and constitutional amendments that originate in the state legislature must be passed by a two-thirds vote of all the members elected to each house of the state legislature and approved by a majority of the voters during the next scheduled primary or general election.

**general obligation bonds** State debt that is backed by the "full faith and credit of the state."

Governor Ronald Reagan being interviewed regarding the death penalty, February 1972 in San Francisco.

by the state legislature, many local governments have adopted charters with prescribed procedures, including the referendum, that are unique to the region and type of government.

## Campaigning for Votes

Any election, whether for president of the United States, an initiative, or a seat on the city council, is the culmination of a political campaign, and California campaigns reflect the distinctive nature of the politics practiced in this state. If there was any one indication of the importance of voting, campaigns should be it, involving hundreds of millions of dollars, sophisticated technology and techniques, and the commitment of time and energy by people who are often working as unpaid volunteers. For many Californians, campaigns may not generate a large amount of excitement, particularly since the rise in television political advertising, but even with the subtleties of contemporary campaigning techniques, registered voters are still the targets of serious efforts to determine how they will vote and how to influence their voting decisions. There are, of course, many types of campaigns in California, distinguished by the office being filled, the number of candidates, and the level of resources and money. In California, some of the major influences on the strategies and operations of a campaign are nonpartisan qualification, voter records, interest groups, state geography, and mass communication. (See Table 16.4.)

**Nonpartisan Qualification**   Due to Progressive era reforms that made most elective offices nonpartisan, the role of political parties in California is not as significant as it is in other states. Voters are essentially left without a party label as a signal of the candidate's political orientation. The absence of party labels has encouraged a greater sense of independence among California voters compared to voters in other states. According to the Public Policy Institute of California, "The largest change in the electorate since 1994 is the addition of 1.4 million 'decline to state' or independent voters (1.5 million to 2.9 million), which led to a 7 percentage point increase (11% to 18%) in their share of the electorate."[23] The governorships

**Table 16.4** "Which of these information sources do you think has the biggest effect on voters' decisions to vote yes or no on citizens' initiatives?"

| | | Party Registration | | | |
| | All Adults | Democrat | Republican | Other Voters | Likely Voters |
| --- | --- | --- | --- | --- | --- |
| Voter information guide | 23% | 24% | 27% | 18% | 27% |
| News stories in the media | 38 | 35 | 36 | 43 | 35 |
| Government and independent websites | 7 | 6 | 6 | 7 | 5 |
| Paid political commercials | 26 | 29 | 25 | 27 | 28 |
| Other | 2 | 2 | 2 | 2 | 2 |
| Don't know | 4 | 4 | 4 | 3 | 3 |

*Source:* From *Occasional Paper*, "The California Initiative Process Background and Perspective," by J. Fred Silva. Resource Material for *The Speaker's Commission on The California Initiative Process*, November 2000, Public Policy Institute of California.

of Hiram Johnson, Earl Warren, and now Arnold Schwarzenegger are good examples of candidates who succeeded during their campaigns in convincing California voters of their political independence, drawing many voters from the opposite party. Even Ronald Reagan, who began his campaign for governor with very partisan credentials, astutely developed the image of a "citizen-politician." Political scientists and California journalists have suggested that nonpartisan elections tend to favor the Republican Party, which is able to compensate for the absence of a party label with well-funded, well-organized campaign organizations. Another advantage for the Republicans in nonpartisan elections comes from their traditionally higher voter turnout in elections where overall voter turnout is low.

In California, partisan elections are few in number, consisting of races for congressional representatives, state legislators, and most statewide elective offices, but their importance cannot be overstated. In the current era, with the exception of governor, the majority of Democratic voters in California tends to produce a majority of Democratic officeholders in partisan contests.

**Voter Records**   Voter registration information is extremely important in identifying the ideological background and basic personal information about voters that campaigns use to determine their strategies and tactics. State party organizations attempt to register as many potential voters as possible with the hope that they will vote for their party or a particular candidate. Few of the individuals—or deputy registrars, as they are known officially—who actually register prospective voters are volunteers engaged in fulfilling some civic duty. Most are somehow connected to a political party or interest group either directly or hired specifically to register prospective voters in a given area. In California, the Democratic Party has normally been the most active party in conducting voter registration drives, a key factor in its ability to remain the dominant political party. The registration of new Democratic Party voters is, however, often inconsequential, canceled out by low Democratic Party turnout between general elections and the high number of Democratic voters who are purged from election records either because they failed to vote in the last election or had a change of address.

Political parties often concentrate voter registration drives in areas where their party support is high or where the population is increasing. Both of these factors are significant in California, which tends to have high concentrations of party loyalists and an expanding and mobile population. All the voter information that is gathered during the registration process can be purchased from all county election offices in California. These reports contain data used to build mailing, telephone, precinct canvassing, and poll watcher lists. Voter registration data also serve to measure trends among registered voters. Using voting records from previous elections, a campaign organization can analyze the voting outcome of one voter precinct or a cluster of precincts for a particular election and attempt to find patterns or make forecasts.

The wide differences in voter registration rates throughout the state frequently present strategic dilemmas for state political party organizations that must decide the focus of campaign efforts. Does the Democratic Party, for example, concentrate its financial and human resources in Marin County, where voter registration is regularly above 80 percent, 40 percent vote by absentee ballot, and the Democratic Party is in the majority, or in Imperial County, where registration is slightly above 50 percent, 13 percent vote by absentee ballot, and the majority is also Democratic? The relative affluence of Marin County, with a median household income of $71,306, is an important source of political contributions in addition to high Democratic Party voter turnout. Yet the ideological principles of the Democratic Party are closer to the working-class population of Imperial County, which has a median household income of $31,870, a higher percentage of registered Democrats, and a greater opportunity to expand the number of registered Democratic voters.[24]

A working-class neighborhood that is predominantly Democratic but voted overwhelmingly to pass a "law and order" proposition could potentially be convinced to vote for another proposition sponsored by conservatives or for a Republican candidate who is able to downplay his or her party label. The tendency of California voters to lean toward nonpartisanship or to switch parties in gubernatorial elections makes the analysis of voter information a necessity.

**Interest Groups**   Interest groups are formal organizations of people who share a common outlook or social circumstance and who band together in the hope of influencing government policy. In California, there are many interest groups and government policies that these groups seek to influence.

The governorship of Arnold Schwarzenegger epitomizes the significance as well as the perils of the relationship between elected officials or candidates and interest groups. In the twelve months following his election in 2003, Governor Schwarzenegger broke every fundraising record, accumulating approximately $26.6 million, nearly twice the amount raised by Governor Gray Davis during his first year in office.[25] Most of the money was contributed to committees set up by Governor Schwarzenegger to support his ballot measures, thereby avoiding the $21,000 limit on individual contributions to candidates, and much of it can be traced to interest groups with a stake either in these propositions or in other laws and decisions before the state government. The size and origin of these political contributions have resulted in repeated accusations of influence peddling. In response, the governor and representatives of these interest groups have said that the contributions were merely supporting Schwarzenegger's ideological and leadership direction.[26] Many of the contributors represented industries, such as finance, insurance, automobile, health care, and pharmaceuticals, that evidently did receive some consideration or assistance through the policies and decisions of the Schwarzenegger administration, while other supporters in entertainment, real estate, and technology have received intangible returns. Moreover, the return on this money to the governor has been mixed—it helped him

**Table 16.5    Top Ten Contributors to Legislators 2001 Legislative Session**

| | |
|---|---|
| 1. California Correctional Peace Officers Association | $2,307,565 |
| 2. California Teachers Association | $1,950,538 |
| 3. Philip Morris Companies | $1,305,194 |
| 4. Service Employees International Union | $1,235,899 |
| 5. California Medical Association | $1,191,291 |
| 6. Edison International and Subsidiaries | $1,066,790 |
| 7. Pacific Gas & Electric Company | $1,062,861 |
| 8. California Dental Association | $1,058,585 |
| 9. Agua Caliente Band of Cahuilla Indians | $1,050,805 |
| 10. California School Employees Association | $1,050,135 |

*Source:* California Common Cause. *Top Ten Contributors to California Legislators and Legislative Campaigns: The 1999–2000 Election Cycle and the 2001 Legislative Session.* www.commoncause.org/states/california

get two important propositions passed in 2004 but was irrelevant in 2005 when the voters rejected four propositions he supported.

The same dilemmas crop up at each level of electoral politics and are probably most pronounced at the local level, where political contributions and other resources become scarce. The early 2000s boom in the California real estate market has made local government especially vulnerable to interest groups associated with real estate development. An in-depth report on campaign contributions in the Sacramento metropolitan area in 2002 revealed that the biggest political contributors were developers, land speculators, contractors, and building tradespeople. The report found "regionally, that one campaign dollar out of four came from development and real estate. In slow-growth Yolo County, however, that statistic is one dollar out of six. And in burgeoning Placer County, it's nearly one campaign dollar out of two."[27] Still, the representatives of these real estate industry interest groups deny any wrongdoing, asserting that they are only supporting the best-qualified candidates, that they often make contributions in communities where they have no business interests, and that political donations are only one of many types of charitable giving. This same report also revealed that land development often makes strange bedfellows, bringing the real estate industry and trade unions together to back candidates who are prodevelopment.[28]

**Geography**    The geography of California, which encompasses numerous geographic regions within one political entity, is yet another major influence on the outcome of elections. James Q. Wilson, the noted political scientist, observed that the conservative tendencies of Southern California have a lot to do with the tradition of property and automobile ownership, emphasizing individual accomplishment and initiative rather than dense urban settings where there is a proliferation of organizations and the individual is more likely to join a group. Wilson goes on to say that the large number of newcomers to Southern California and highly mobile residents "are more likely to vote the way established institutions— newspapers, churches, labor unions, business firms—tell them to vote."[29] The low-density and single-family neighborhoods that have spread across Southern California have made the more personal door-to-door campaigning more difficult. As housing developments multiply in every part of California, aspects of

⊢**Think Again**⊣

How does the geography of California influence the outcome of elections?

Wilson's thesis on Southern California politics are becoming apparent in other regions as well. The suburban trend in California is causing residents of the state to disconnect from established political traditions and vote more as individuals or independents.

Various generalities regarding the geopolitics of California are vital to understanding who gets elected where, but some caution should be exercised due to the many exceptions that mirror California's diverse landscape. Political commentators often suggest that the Republican Party tends to be concentrated in Southern California and that Northern California is the stronghold of the Democrats. The Los Angeles metropolitan area, though in the south, is nevertheless solidly Democratic. The San Francisco Bay Area is one of the most liberal regions in the country, but 40 miles to the east, you are in Republican country. The major cities along the coast of California tend to be Democratic, again with various exceptions, while the sparsely populated eastern side of the state is much more conservative. In 2004, out of the top ten Democratic Party counties with the highest percentage of party registration, seven were adjacent to the coast, while in the top ten Republican Party counties with the highest percentage of party registration, nine were inland and five were located in Northern California.[30]

The party orientation of these areas will determine not only what type of candidates will be elected but also their campaign strategy. A school board candidate, despite the nonpartisan designation, will be less likely to campaign on the promise of a school bond in a fiscally conservative Republican-dominated district. These geopolitical considerations have in fact become more institutionalized as the state legislature has been inclined to draw district boundaries that create safe state legislative districts for both political parties. This trend has disturbed both liberal and conservative elected officials and private citizens, from the political advocacy group Common Cause to Governor Schwarzenegger himself. In fact, Schwarzenegger unsuccessfully attempted to get the approval of an initiative that would have stripped the state legislature of its power to redistrict. The major point of the geopolitics of California is that where residents of the state live has a lot to do with whether their votes will really make a difference.

| Think Again |

Why is television advertising so important in California political campaigns?

**Mass Communication**    The use of mass communication has been vital to the efforts of political parties and candidates in reaching voters. Of all the major influences on an election, mass communication is probably the most significant, and at the cornerstone of mass communication is television. In the past, campaigning was a personal activity. Candidates were expected to give many speeches, engage in debates, and walk precincts. Except for a small number of local elections, these tactics are fast becoming obsolete. Potential voters rarely meet with a candidate face-to-face.

In her book *Phantom Politics: Campaigning in California*, Mary Ellen Leary explores how the mass media have changed the way politics is practiced in California, using the election of Jerry Brown as governor in 1974 as the campaign case study. Quoting a professional campaign manager and media consultant with "15 years of Los Angeles political experience," Leary writes:

> There are three key factors in a political campaign these days," he said in his staccato manner. "No. 1 is television, No. 2 is television, No. 3 is television. In all our survey work, we ask people why they voted the way they did, and it always comes up television.[31]

And television advertising for any purpose, much less politics, is expensive. During the campaign season leading up to the November 2005 special election, the cost of a 30-second advertising spot in the Los Angeles market started at roughly $3,000.

**Table 16.6**  California Markets: Political Advertising
August 1–October 16, 2005

**Local Market Detail: California**
In the 11 markets that make up the state of California, 44,122 political commercials aired between August 1–October 16, 2005. "Vote No on Proposition 79" had the most activity, with over 18,000 commercials airing. In fact, referendum-related advertising accounted for 43,996 or 99.7% of the spots during this period.

| Market | Spot TV. Units | Spot TV. GRP: P18 |
| --- | --- | --- |
| Los Angeles | 7,796 | 9,237 |
| San Francisco-Oakland-San Jose | 5,660 | 6,574 |
| San Diego | 5,182 | 8,535 |
| Sacramento-Stockton-Modesto | 5,076 | 10,024 |
| Fresno-Visalia | 4,667 | 8,919 |
| Santa Barbara-Sanmar-San Luis Obispo | 3,119 | 5,583 |
| Bakersfield | 2,967 | 5,073 |
| Chico-Redding | 2,919 | 5,141 |
| Palm Springs | 2,713 | 4,242 |
| Monterey-Salinas | 2,145 | 3,771 |
| Eureka | 1,878 | 2,821 |
| Grand Total | 44,122 | 69,920 |

*Source:* Nielsen Monitor-Plus. Nielsen Media Research, www.nielsenmedia.com

As the election drew closer, that figure shot to $10,000. Nationally, six of the top ten television political advertising markets are in California, and the Los Angeles advertising market was second only to the New York metropolitan area in the number of political commercials aired between August 1 and October 16, 2005.[32]

The proliferation of cable and satellite stations makes these outlets affordable alternatives to expensive network television advertising for local campaigns that want to go beyond traditional forms of campaigning. Candidates may also arrange for appearances at debates and forums televised on the local government channels and local-access programs and may even sponsor their own local-access programming. News reports on television, on radio, and in newspapers provide free political publicity, especially for campaigns that can afford to hire media consultants or "spin doctors" who maximize the quality and quantity of a candidate's news media exposure. Of course, getting exposure on local and regional media outlets presents certain challenges, since there is no guarantee that media coverage will be positive. For their part, media organizations attempt to portray candidates in a "fair and balanced manner" within their regular news programming formats. Media outlets have the additional pressure of having to cover the election process at a time when their parent companies are more inclined to favor entertainment programming over news. An investigation of local nightly news broadcasts in eleven markets including Los Angeles found that a typical half-hour of local news consisted of these segments:[33]

Advertising: 8 minutes 51 seconds

Sports and weather: 6 minutes 21 seconds

Elections: 3 minutes 11 seconds

    Presidential coverage: 2 minutes

    Noncandidate coverage (initiatives, referendums): 45 seconds

    All other races (local, state, and federal): 30 seconds

Crime: 2 minutes 34 seconds

Local interest: 1 minute 56 seconds

Teasers, intros, music: 1 minute 43 seconds

Health: 1 minute 22 seconds

Other: 1 minute 12 seconds

Unintentional injury: 55 seconds

Business and economy: 47 seconds

Government (nonelection coverage): 28 seconds

Iraq: 25 seconds

Foreign policy: 13 seconds

In the Los Angeles area, on the four stations included in the investigation, between 1 and 3 percent of all news stories were about local campaigns. As a media outlet for political campaigns, radio is clearly less attractive than television, but it suffers from similar constraints. The one bright spot for radio is the proliferation of talk radio programming and round-the-clock news, which has become increasingly popular among California's many commuters. Newspapers, unlike talk radio, must strive to treat each candidate fairly and provide accurate reporting, even though that may require focusing more on a particular candidate. As circulation rates continue to fall, newspapers have also slowly introduced more entertainment content in the attempt to lure readers, especially amid a California lifestyle at least partially driven by Hollywood. Other mass communication techniques, such as direct mail and telephone solicitation, though not as effective as the mass media in reaching large segments of the population, can still facilitate contact with prospective voters with greater efficiency than traditional face-to-face campaigning.

To a large extent, mass communication techniques were pioneered in California during the 1934 gubernatorial race, the so-called campaign of the century between the "socialist" Democratic candidate, Upton Sinclair, and the Republican governor, Frank Merriam. For the first time in California campaign history, an ad agency, Lord & Thomas (later merged into Foote, Cone & Belding) managed Merriam's political campaign. Employing marketing techniques, including direct mail and the targeting of specific groups, led that campaign to victory.[34] The success of Lord & Thomas precipitated an explosion of political consultants that specialized in political marketing, and each successive generation of consultants has raised the bar of mass market campaigning ever since. Later, the firm of Spencer & Roberts would be instrumental in the 1970 election of Ronald Reagan by introducing computer technology to political marketing. The work of the legendary Butcher-Forde political consulting firm on the Proposition 13 campaign, again adopting novel techniques such as designing a solicitation letter to resemble a tax bill, was another milestone in political marketing. Today, for campaigns that lack the funds to acquire media advertisement, direct mail has become the mainstay. Behind each direct mail piece are often sophisticated technologies and techniques designed to target various categories of voters using words, colors, and layout styles that have been tested through focus groups and computer simulations.

An ad from a group calling itself San Franciscans for Preservation Planning promotes strong citywide preservation policies in San Francisco and the election of candidate Tom Ammiano for mayor.

The campaign is indeed an intricate process with a number of major influences, but all of these influences lead to a single choice on the part of the voter: The voter can simply take the passive role, generally ignoring these influences or, worse, going along with them and voting with little conviction. The voter can also take an active role in the electoral process by downplaying the influences and making electoral decisions based on a reasonable weighing of accumulated information. The latter requires a considerable amount of work, but at worst, the voter will cast a ballot for a losing candidate or proposition.

## Empowering California Voters

Nonvoters usually harbor misguided notions about why elections are unimportant or why their vote would make no difference, but a wealth of evidence bears out the value of the electoral process in a democratic society. The founders of the American Republic viewed elections as vital to establishing a functional democracy, as did the Progressives in California, who provided residents of the state with extraordinary powers to influence government directly.

Many Californians understand the importance of voting but feel intimidated by the process. Many regular voters complain of complicated ballot information, made even more confusing by the large amount of campaign literature, signs, and advertisements. Such intimidation is not surprising considering the lack of education or training that residents receive about the California electoral process. Gallant efforts are being made at the secondary school level through mock elections, model government, and student council elections, but such efforts are ultimately simulations of the process in a very controlled environment. Any contact with the California electoral process will be a fleeting experience for most residents, and in the absence of strong political party organizations in most communities, voters really are on their own. This sense of electoral isolation can be overcome by taking the necessary steps to understand the process and navigate through voting procedures.

The first step to becoming an empowered voter is to realize that voters do have power. Almost every aspect of life in California—roads, taxes, schools, water, even

> **┤Think Again├**
>
> What steps have been taken to help empower California voters?

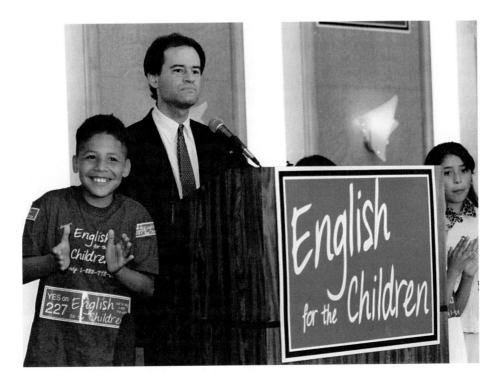

Reformer Ron Unz stands with applauding kids at a rally for the English for the Children campaign against bilingual education in California in 1998.

the air we breathe—especially at the local level, is affected by the electoral process. Once that fact is realized, the next step is to clearly understand voting procedures. The California Voter Foundation found that many infrequent California voters were not familiar with absentee voting and that "half of the infrequent voters surveyed said they had never voted absentee." [35] Absentee voting in California has been simplified over the years, particularly through temporary mail-in ballot provisions. In a large number of counties, after simply downloading forms requesting a mail-in ballot, the voter can complete the registration and voting process by mail within two weeks of an election.

Another example of an electoral procedure often overlooked by prospective voters is the right under California law to take up to two hours off from work without loss of pay to vote on election day. Various organizations and government agencies that exist to inform prospective voters of electoral procedures and voters rights. The League of Women Voters provides assistance to voters, publishes election information, conducts an assortment of voter education programs, and serves as a clearinghouse for similar organizations.

The next major step to becoming an empowered voter is to know what is being voted on. It has often been said that an uninformed voter is worse than a non-voter because the uninformed voter stands a good chance of voting for candidates or issues that they really oppose, canceling out the true intent of their vote. In 1996, Proposition 209 appeared on the ballot as the "California Civil Rights Initiative." The name succeeded in deceiving many uninformed voters, who thought they were voting in favor of civil rights. The initiative that voters actually passed effectively ended affirmative action by prohibiting all race- and gender-based considerations in California public education, contracting, and employment. Voters can avoid or minimize this type of electoral deception by becoming informed.

Newspapers are the first line of defense in combating voter manipulation, providing most of the basic information that is needed to understand the issues of a campaign. Although newspapers do have biases at the journalist, editor, or ownership level that affect content, the newspaper is still an important source of information if used comprehensively, which means reading and comparing the features, news stories, editorials, and letters to the editor, which may offer different perspectives on a given issue. The voter ballot guide published by the California secretary of state offers important descriptions of the ballot, but the voter should expect a minimal amount of objectivity in these guides and a lot of partisan arguments. Campaign literature is frequently full of inaccuracies, distortions, and embellishments, but for the observant voter or a voter willing to invest a little time in the information-gathering process, such literature does contain subtle clues that can help determine the worthiness of the candidates. California election law requires that all campaign mailings list the name of the sponsoring organization or individual and reveal the name of the financial backer—though sometimes this is done in tiny, difficult-to-read print. The election slate postcards sent by political party organizations or unions that list all the candidates and propositions endorsed by that group are sometimes more informative in terms of who and what they do *not* list or endorse, especially when similar groups are endorsing those missing candidates or propositions.

|Think Again|

What are the challenges of making the transition to electronic voting machines?

# Vote-Counting Difficulties in California

Since 2004, problems with electronic voting machines in California have occurred. The roots of these difficulties lie in mandates from the federal government encouraging states to modernize the election process. [36] Electronic voting machines are

A touch-screen voting machine is demonstrated during a news conference in Sacramento.

supposed to offer a faster way of voting and tabulation. Yet in 2004, Diebold Election Systems agreed to pay a $2.6 million settlement to the state of California after Bill Lockyer, the attorney general, found that Diebold representatives misled the secretary of state about the level of security and certification of its electronic voting machines.[37] Prior to the problems with Diebold electronic voting machines in California, Walden O'Dell, the chief executive officer of Diebold and an active Republican supporter of President George W. Bush, was already viewed with suspicion by many state officials when he promised in a fundraising letter to deliver Ohio's electoral votes for President Bush in 2004.

In 2005, problems again plagued electronic voting machines in California, manufactured this time by Election Systems and Software. Malfunctions occurred with the computerized touch screen and software, resulting in incorrect vote counts. Company spokespersons asserted that the problems were attributable either to operator error or to incorrect coding on ballots.[38] California voters may have to wait a little longer for all the technical bugs to be worked out before fully realizing the application of innovative technology to the election process.

## Beyond Electoral Politics

Representative democratic government in the United States almost seems to begin and end with the electoral process, but in reality, there are a number of other avenues open to Californians who want to participate in politics. Some of the more common activities include attending local meetings, writing to elected officials, contributing money, attending rallies, and participating in political party work. The rate of nonvoting political participation in California, compared to the rest of the nation, varies considerably for different types of activities, according to the Public Policy Institute of California. Analyzing data collected from a 2002 statewide survey and national elections studies, PPIC found that while on the average, the rest of the nation contributes twice as much money to political causes

> **Think Again**
>
> Aside from elections, what other avenues of political participation are open to Californians?

and attends rallies and works for political parties at slightly higher rates, a higher percentage of Californians attend meetings on community affairs, and they write to elected officials about as much as people in the rest of the country. After voting, attending meetings on community affairs is the most popular form of political participation in California, performed by approximately 35 percent of the state population. This level of political participation should not be particularly surprising, considering the size of the state and the dominant role of the state government. For every major quality-of-life issues—parks and recreation, water, transportation, irrigation, education—some governmental or quasi-governmental body holds public meetings.

The second most popular form of political participation in California is writing to an elected official, an activity performed by about 20 percent of adult citizens. Letters carry enormous weight in the decisions of government officials. Consequently, the 20 percent of Californians who write letters to government officials exercise a disproportionate amount of influence on government. Monetary contributions to political parties, candidates, and campaigns, as the third most common form of political participation, are made by less than 7 percent of the population. The fact that only one of every fourteen residents makes political contributions is somewhat unexpected, considering that California contributes the largest total amount of money to electoral campaigns and other political causes of all the states in the nation. Assuming that contributions result in even greater influence over government officials than letter writing, once again it appears that a small proportion of the population has an inordinate amount of influence. Less than 10 percent of the state population attended rallies or worked for a political party. The physical activity and time required would naturally make these activities the least attractive, especially when compared to the relatively low rates for the other forms of participation.[39]

## California's Tradition of Unconventional Political Participation

Unconventional political participation has long been a fixture in California, ebbing and flowing with the changing attitudes and demographics of the state's residents. The popular soapbox rallies and demonstrations of the Kearneyites and labor unions of the late nineteenth century laid the foundation for a succession of unconventional political movements and actions throughout the decades such as the End Poverty in California campaign of the 1930s, the 1943 "zoot suit" riots in Los Angeles, the Berkeley free-speech movement and Vietnam protests in the 1960s, and the environmental protests that erupted dramatically in the 1970s. In fact, a number of nationally recognized unconventional political movements, including the Black Panther Party and the La Raza Unida Party, had their start in California.

There are many different ways of engaging in unconventional political action, but the peaceful demonstration has in the current era become the most popular form. The demonstration is used for a variety of political purposes, depending on the issue and the number of people involved. It is regularly used to get the attention of governmental leaders, and each year, many groups descend on the state capitol, particularly during periods of government budget cutbacks, to visibly demonstrate their concern over a political issue. In 2002, for example, faced with

---

**|Think Again|**

What forms of nonconventional political activity are most common, and when do they tend to be used?

major budget cuts to the California Community College system, close to 10,000 students and community college employees from across the state marched through Sacramento and rallied at the steps of the capitol. That mass demonstration, like all such efforts, was designed to physically and loudly exhibit the displeasure of a large group of people and their willingness to express that displeasure during the next election. Some demonstrations are intended to gain media attention in the hope of increasing public support for a concern or cause, usually involving smaller numbers of people.

Demonstrations, like other types of unconventional political activities, generally occur when all conventional avenues for political expression are closed. Unconventional activities in California reflect the diversity of the state and can sometimes descend into violence, as in the horrific riots unleashed in Los Angeles in the wake of the verdict in the Rodney King trial. Although the level of unconventional political activity has been waning in California since the 1970s, the potential for the rapid resurgence of this type of political participation lingers on the periphery of conventional state politics. The point of unconventional political action runs counter to long-term organization and commitment, usually relying on a dramatic political act or a series of acts to force conventional recognition of the issue or cause. For better or worse, California's diversity encompasses an assortment of differences, many of which are so divergent as to produce groups irremediably frustrated with conventional politics. The frustrations of groups in California seeking political solutions to such issues as animal rights, environmental degradation, border security, abortion, and drug laws, to name

Students protest cuts in state funding for community colleges in Los Angeles.

only a few, present long-term challenges to the political stability of the state. Whether those frustrations will be addressed peaceably through recognition by the conventional political process or become detrimental will largely depend on how well California convinces its people to express their will through the democratic process.

# Summary Notes

- In California, voting as a form of political participation has occurred at low turnout rates since the mid-1990s. For example, during the statewide voter turnout rate was 43.6 percent, and turnout in the 2002 elections was lower still.

- Any person who is eighteen years of age, a citizen of the United States, a resident of California, and a county resident for at least fifteen days prior to an election may register to vote. Registering to vote in California and most other states has been made significantly more convenient when Congress passed the National Voter Registration Act.

- In California, there are three basic types of elections: state primary elections, state general elections, and special elections.

- Another electoral legacy of the Progressives is provision for both partisan and nonpartisan elections. Partisan elections consume slightly more than 10 percent of the elections that are conducted.

- As one of the first states to provide Americans with avenues for direct democracy, the recall, referendum, and initiative have been unique features of the political landscape in California.

- In California, some of the major influences on the strategies and operations of a campaign are nonpartisan qualification, voter records, interest groups, state geography, and mass communication. The absence of party labels for most

candidates has been a major factor in encouraging a greater sense of independence among California voters.

- The geography of California is sometimes described in terms of the numerous geographic subregions that are generally dominated by one of the two major political parties. The Republican party tends to be concentrated in Southern California, while Northern California is the stronghold of the Democrats. As a Democratic stronghold, the Los Angeles metropolitan area is the exception to the rule of partisan politics in Southern California.

- The use of mass communications has been vital to political parties and candidates to elective office determined to reach millions of California voters. Nationally, six of the top ten television political advertising markets are in California. Mass communication techniques were pioneered in California during the 1934 gubernatorial "Campaign of the Century" between the "socialist" Democratic candidate, Upton Sinclair, and the Republican Governor Frank Merriam.

- Absentee voting in California has been simplified over the years, particularly with temporary mail-in ballot provisions.

- California has a long history of nonconventional political participation that often increases as the demographics of the state residents change. The "Kearneyites" and labor unions of the late nineteenth century often resorted to violent forms of nonconventional action.

# Key Terms

National Voter
   Registration Act   550
direct primary
   elections   552
cross-filing   552
closed primary system   552

blanket primary   552
general election   553
special election   553
partisan election   553
nonpartisan
   election   553

recall   556
deregulation   558
initiative   559
direct initiative   559
referendum   568
petition referendum   568

compulsory
   referendum   569
general obligation
   bonds   569

# Suggested Readings

Cronin, Thomas E. *Direct Democracy: The Politics of the Initiative, Referendum and Recall.* Cambridge, Mass.: Harvard University Press, 1989.

League of Women Voters of California Education Fund. *Guide to California Government.* 14th ed. Sacramento: League of Women Voters of California, 1992.

Leary, Mary Ellen. *"Elusive Candidates." Phantom Politics Campaigning in California.* Washington, D.C.: Public Affairs, 1977.

Lee, Eugene C., and Willis D. Hawley, Eds. *The Challenge of California with a Concise Introduction to California Government.* Boston: Little, Brown & Company, 1970.

Lubenow, Gerald C., and Bruce E. Cain, Eds. *Governing California: Politics, Government, and Public Policy in the Golden State.* Institute of Governmental Studies Press, University of California, 1997.

Magleby, David. *Direct Legislation: Voting on Ballot Propositions in the United States.* Baltimore: The John Hopkins University Press, 1984.

Mitchell, Greg. *The Campaign of the Century: Upton Sinclair's Race for Governor of California and the Birth of Media Politics.* New York: Random House, 1992.

Olin, Spencer C., Jr. *California's Prodigal Son: Hiram Johnson and the Progressives, 1911–17.* Berkeley: University of California Press, 1968.

Owens, John R., Edmond Costantini, and Louis F. Weschler. *California Politics and Parties.* London: Macmillan, 1970.

Schrag, Peter. *California: America's High-Stakes Experiment.* Berkeley: University of California Press, 2006.

Schrag, Peter. *Paradise Lost: California's Experience, America's Future.* Berkeley: University of California Press, 2004.

Shultz, Jim. *The Initiative Cookbook: Recipes and Stories from California's Ballot Wars.* San Francisco: The Democracy Center, 1996.

Starr, Kevin. *California: A History.* New York: Modern Library-Random House, 2005.

# 17 THE CALIFORNIA STATE LEGISLATURE

## Chapter Outline

- The Role of the California Legislature
- The Making of a California State Legislator
- The Legislative Universe
- Leadership in the State Legislature
- The Legislative Committee System
- The Legislative Process
- The Hidden View of Lawmaking

## Think About Politics

1 Do lobbyists and other representatives have a positive impact on California's political system?
Yes ☐ No ☐

2 Should the terms of California state legislators be limited?
Yes ☐ No ☐

3 Should California reform the reapportionment and redistricting process?
Yes ☐ No ☐

4 Should legislators introduce bills that have little chance of being approved but are used to advance their political career?
Yes ☐ No ☐

5 Should California continue to require balanced budget approval by a two-thirds majority in both chambers?
Yes ☐ No ☐

6 Are California legislators overpaid?
Yes ☐ No ☐

7 Would California benefit from a part-time legislature?
Yes ☐ No ☐

*Many California State legislators are influenced by lobbyists and other representatives, oftentimes having a direct impact on the passage of state laws.*

★   ★   ★

## Introduction

Academics and journalists alike typically describe the passage of **Proposition 140** in 1990, a constitutional initiative limiting the terms of office for California state legislators, as a reaction to the unsavory opinion that many California residents have about the state legislature. A quick scan of California history will reveal that such feelings are not new and that there have been numerous attempts to reform the structure and procedures of the state legislature and to hold that body accountable to the principles of representative democracy. Staying true to such principles has been and continues to be difficult, considering the diversity of interests that have been so much a part of California's development. Too often the legislature has chosen to favor the special interests over the demands of the average resident. Rather than dedicate state resources for the greatest good of the greatest many, the California legislature regularly divides large portions of these resources among diverse groups for reasons both altruistic and self-serving. In the process, a "**Third House**" has emerged, consisting of lobbyists and other representatives, often armed with millions of dollars and detailed information, to assist lawmakers in selecting the most worthy cause or interest. Periodically inspired by a history of charismatic leaders or popular ideas about government, Californians have forced reform and the reconstitution of the state legislature to reflect prevailing attitudes. At times contrary to democratic principles, efforts to make the legislature more responsive have only resulted in a different set of problems for the state.

## The Role of the California Legislature

Known unflatteringly as "the legislature of a thousand drinks" during its early sessions, the California state legislature suffered from a bad reputation as well as constitutional impediments. Embracing the prevailing minimalist notions of government, the original mining and merchant interests that dominated early California created a state government at the first state constitutional convention that was prone to party machine politics and corruption. As the fortunes of the Southern Pacific Railroad grew, these weaknesses allowed the railroad interests to dominate the state legislature as it had every other major aspect of California society. In fact, the attempt and eventual failure to limit the power of the Southern Pacific through the

**Figure 17.1**
This historic document lists the president and senators of California and identifies their district, geographic origin, emigration date, profession, age, and marital status.

THE NAMES OF THE PRESIDENT AND SENATORS
OF THE
FIRST SENATE OF THE STATE OF CALIFORNIA
Convened at the Capitol at San Jose, December the 15th, One Thousand Eight Hundred and Forty Nine.

| Names. | District Representing. | Place of Nativity. | State from whence Emigrated. | When Emigrated | Profession or Occupation. | Age. | |
|---|---|---|---|---|---|---|---|
| John McDougal, | Lt Gov'r and Pres't of Senate, | Ohio, | Indiana, | Dec'r 1848 | Merchant, | 32 | Married. |
| Nathaniel Bennett, | San Francisco, | New York, | New York, | Dec'r 1848 | Lawyer, | | Single. |
| David C. Broderick, | San Francisco, | Washington, D. C. | New York, | April, 1849 | Merchant, | 31 | Single. |
| John Bidwell, | Sacramento, | New York, | Missouri, | May, 1841 | Farmer, | 30 | Single. |
| William R. Bassham, | San Jose, | Tennessee, | Tennessee, | April, 1843 | Merchant, | 28 | Single. |
| E. Kirby Chamberlin, | San Diego and Los Angeles, | Connecticut, | Ohio, | June, 1849 | Physician & Surgeon, | 44 | Widower. |
| Elisha O. Crosby, | Sacramento, | New York, | New York, | Feb'y, 1849 | Counsellor at Law, | 34 | Married. |
| David F. Douglass, | San Joaquin, | Tennessee, | Texas, | Dec'r, 1848 | Wagoner, | 29 | Single. |
| Pablo de la Guerra, | Santa Barbara & St. Luis Obispo, | Santa Barbara, | | | Ranchero, | 30 | Married. |
| William D. Fair, | San Joaquin, | Virginia, | Mississippi, | Feb'y, 1849 | Lawyer, | 28 | Single. |
| Thomas J. Green, | Sacramento, | North Carolina, | Massachusetts, | April, 1849 | Farmer. | 44 | Married. |
| Alexander W. Hope, | Los Angeles and San Diego, | Virginia, | Illinois, | April, 1848 | Mountaineer, | 26 | Single. |
| Elcan Heydenfeldt, | San Francisco, | South Carolina, | Louisiana, | July, 1849 | Lawyer, | 28 | Married. |
| Benjamin S. Lippincott, | San Joaquin, | New York, | New Jersey, | March, 1846 | Merchant, | 31 | Single. |
| G. B. Post, | San Francisco, | New Jersey, | New York, | 1849 | Merchant, | | Single. |
| Henry E. Robinson, | Sacramento, | Connecticut, | Louisiana, | March, 1849 | Merchant, | 36 | Single. |
| Nelson Taylor, | San Joaquin, | Connecticut, | New York, | July, 1847 | Merchant, | 29 | Married. |
| Mariano G. Vallejo, | Sonoma, | Monterey, Cala., | | | Ranchero, | 42 | Married. |
| Thomas L. Vermeule, | San Joaquin, | New Jersey, | New York, | 1847 | Counsellor at Law, | 31 | Married. |
| Selim E. Woodworth, | Monterey, | New York, | New York, | April, 1846 | Merchant, | 34 | Single. |

**Proposition 140**
A constitutional initiative limiting the terms of office for California state legislators.

**"Third House"** Collective term for lobbyists and special-interest representatives.

|Think Again|

How have corruption and partisanship marred the California legislature in recent decades?

constitutional convention of 1878–79 was partly the consequence of the control the Southern Pacific had over state legislators. Rather than reform the state legislature to address corruption and the excessive monopolistic influence on government, the Progressives sought to limit the political power of the legislative body, particularly as an instrument for special interests and political parties. Important aspects of the state legislature's power were reduced by Progressive reforms that enlarged the state bureaucracy, empowered the governor, and institutionalized nonpartisanship. Highly qualified potential candidates were discouraged from running for a legislative body that was essentially a part-time responsibility that met every other year, had limited support staff and no office space, and was poorly paid. By the early 1920s, as the Progressive era in California was coming to an end, partisanship and special interests slowly crept back into the state legislature, taking full advantage of its weakened condition. Few individuals in California politics have received more notoriety for their ability to take advantage of these weaknesses than the infamous Art Samish. From the 1920s until 1953, when he was convicted of federal income tax evasion, Samish was the consummate lobbyist, employing his now well known political tactic of "select and elect." "I didn't care whether a man was a Republican or a Democrat or a Prohibitionist. I didn't care whether he voted against free love or for the boll weevil. All I cared about was how he voted on legislation affecting my clients."[1] In his popular book, *The Secret Boss of California*, Samish explains that his success in lobbying the state legislature was based on selecting the individuals that he thought would support his clients' interest and providing the funds to get them elected. He confessed that the $1,200 annual salary for California legislators was a weakness that he readily exploited:

> Some of the legislators augmented their income by outright bribes from some of my lobbying colleagues, and occasionally they got caught at it. That was stupid, both on the part of the legislators and the lobbyists. There were other, strictly legal ways of adding to the income of the lawmakers and simultaneously making them friendly to your organization.

Supposing the senator or assemblyman was a lawyer, as many of them were. Well, then you could see that the worthy barrister was hired on a retainer or received important cases on behalf of your clients. Or if Mr. Legislator engaged in the insurance business, you could assure him of some lucrative policies provided by your clients. It was all very simple.[2]

By the early 1960s, it became clear to the political forces in California that the state had outgrown the curbs on legislative power and other aspects of state government and, in 1963, the state legislature authorized the **Constitutional Revision Commission**. In 1966, the commission issued its final report, recommending the revision of various articles of the California constitution that addressed the three branches of state government and the state bureaucracy: these changes were passed into law by the legislature later that year. The new laws had the overall affect of professionalizing the state legislature by requiring a full-time commitment, establishing compensation that was equivalent to a full-time salary set by the legislature, instituting conflict-of-interest restrictions, and providing a living expense allowance. This process had already been underway when full-time professionals, such as the legislative analyst in 1941 and the legislative auditor in 1955, were added to the legislative staff, and the legislature has since made funding available to provide support staff for individual members and committees.[3] By 1971, California was judged to have one of the best legislatures in the Union and certainly remains one of the best paid. Until the passage of Proposition 13 in 1978, the state legislature presided over one of the most grandiose policy agendas in the history of California under the leadership of the Democratic Party. Throughout this period, the legislature succeeded in enacting a wide range of laws that addressed water development, civil rights, postsecondary education funding, social welfare, and highway construction and still managed to maintain a budget surplus. Then, almost out of nowhere, a legislature riding high on a string of achievements ran into a brick wall built on the conservative backlash of California voters.

Public aversion to the state legislature was predicated on a number of factors that began with the election of Ronald Reagan, who defeated the incumbent Democratic governor, Edmund G. "Pat" Brown Sr., and adopted a leadership style that promoted conservative attitudes favoring limited government, elements of which remain popular today. The state legislature has been fighting an uphill battle ever since, due as much to its own dysfunction as to partisan politics and distortions of reality. Major corruption scandals in the 1980s and 1990s that ensnarled state legislators in FBI undercover operations caused a tremendous amount of embarrassment for the state legislature. The undercover operations resulted in the conviction of a number of legislators and legislative aides, the humiliation of many other lawmakers, and greater public awareness of the corruptibility of the state legislature by the increasingly sophisticated and well-financed "third house" of lobbyists and special-interest groups that shower the state legislature with millions of dollars and special privileges. Amid the accusations of impropriety, the state legislature grew increasingly partisan, due in part to the emergence of divided government upon the successive election of two Republican governors, George Deukmejian and Pete Wilson, who faced a Democratic-controlled legislature. The major economic recession of the early 1990s, coupled with shrinking state government resources, tended to inflame partisan differences, especially during the annual budget process. Gridlock became commonplace, most noticeably in the budget process. Since the late 1970s, Californians have come to expect that the legislature and the governor will fail to meet statutory deadlines set for passage of the state budget.

Enduring the weight of the public criticism, the state legislature is nonetheless charged, by the outcome of the electoral process, with developing, funding, and

**Constitutional Revision Commission** Commission created in 1963 to revise and reform the California constitution.

overseeing policies that affect the quality of life in California. The challenges California state legislators face are nothing short of daunting:

> Think of the learning curve facing each new legislator, who must master the intricacies associated with every aspect of legislating, from how a bill is introduced and ushered through the legislative process to the solving of constituent problems, from the nuances of budget-making to the complexities inherent in nearly every policy sphere. To cast intelligent votes on a range of issues, a rookie's brain must ricochet among teacher tenure, insurance regulation, renewable energy, welfare reform, public employee pensions, coastal protection, pesticide regulation, auto emission standards, affordable housing, trial-court funding, smog-check programs, highway construction, mass transit, earthquake retro-fitting, local tax base, water marketing, agriculture, urban sprawl, state parks, prison overcrowding, death penalty, abortion funding, Medi-Cal eligibility, assault weapons, Internet pornography, class-size reduction, vehicle license fees, workers' compensation, reapportionment, immigration law, border policy, nursing home inspections, child-care centers, electricity deregulation, oil depletion allowances, Indian gaming, tax breaks for filmmakers, election law, fund-raising restrictions, legislative ethics, Proposition 13 over-haul, ATM fees—the list surges across the legislative landscape like a river gone mad.[4]

## The Making of a California State Legislator

|Think Again|

**What is the background of a typical California state legislator?**

Although regularly subjected to harsh criticism, California legislators are confronted by an extremely challenging responsibility that necessitates long working hours, attention to detail, sociability, public scrutiny, management skills, and an in-depth understanding of how government works. The legal qualifications for the state legislature are quite minimal, requiring only that the candidate be a U.S. citizen, 18 years of age or older, who has been a resident of California for three years and a resident of a legislative district for one year immediately before the election for that office. The actual pathways to a seat in the California legislature are, however, by and large restricted to individuals with experience as locally elected officials or as professional staff members in local, county, or state political party organizations or representative governments. For the state senate, the most obvious stepping-stone is election to the state assembly. Faced with term limits, most state assembly members will attempt to continue their legislative careers by filling the state senate seats being vacated by members of that body who have also been "termed out." A large number of members in the state assembly usually begin their political careers as either city council members or school board trustees, and although most advance gradually—serving, for example, as a county supervisor along the way—it is not unusual for a council-member to make the leap directly to the assembly. Local elected office is especially important for gaining name recognition among at least a portion of the voters in a legislative district and building a network of supporters. Another large group of assembly members get their start in politics working on the staff of a state legislator or in a position within a local or state political party organization. Candidates running for a seat in the state legislature who have served with distinction as party functionaries or legislative aides normally forgo prior experience in elected office. If they demonstrate the qualities necessary to serve in the state legislature and a seat becomes available, the local or state party organization or party leader can be instrumental in generating financial support that will often overcome the lack of name recognition. The two major political parties continue to play a major role in determining which individuals will run and stand the best chance of winning. Most members of the legislature maintain a political action committee (PAC) or an individual campaign contribution fund and will generally contribute this money to fellow party members who are campaigning for legislative seats in the state.

Because most incumbent members of the state legislature have not faced competitive elections in recent years, the transfer of PAC money to challengers has become increasingly common. In 1985, the California Commission on Campaign Financing asserted in its report *The New Gold Rush: Financing California's Legislative Campaigns:*

> Transfers have mixed effects on campaigns. In some cases they enhance competition, help new candidates with poor fundraising power, immunize some transfer recipients from special interest influence, allow candidates to spend less time fundraising and more time debating issues and offset the advantages of wealthy candidates. In a 1982 Santa Barbara Assembly race, for example, a lesser-funded Democratic candidate defeated a wealthier Republican by a narrow 50.6% margin only after receiving $122,000 in transfers from Assembly Speaker Brown.[5]

Other vocations that seem to give candidates an edge in running for an assembly seat are law, journalism, education, and law enforcement, but even individuals with these backgrounds still need substantial financial or political party support.

Possessing the mandatory personal qualities and the support of political organizations, interest groups, and elected officials are really the only prerequisites for advancing to the election stage in becoming a state legislator. As difficult as accumulating these prerequisites may be for prospective candidates, the state legislative campaign and election are fraught with political intrigue, high-stakes strategies, and power plays that will test and very often quash the mettle of even California's most experienced and adroit politicians.

**Electing the California Legislator**   Considering that the reelection rate for California state legislators has been well over 90 percent and that the vast majority of assembly members will successfully make the jump to the state senate, it is safe to assume that the relatively brief tenure of a state legislator is generally a secure job. Candidates for the state legislature must first win the election, a course of action that is often beset by any number of obstacles, not to mention the demands of the campaign process. Even incumbents, who are rarely successfully challenged, are not totally immune to the ambitious politicians in their districts and political party who might gain an edge through funding or popularity. The timing of a decision to run for a seat in the state senate amid considerations of term limits have posed serious threats to the survival of senate incumbents. Assembly members may be tempted to sacrifice portions of their three-term limit in the assembly to challenge an incumbent in the state senate from an adjacent legislative district. Completing the three-term limit in the assembly and waiting an additional two years while a popular state senator completes his or her two-term limit may avoid a competitive election—or not. The potential and frequently unexpected maneuverings of legislative electoral politics, such as a rising personality on the local political scene, a personal scandal, or controversial issues or policies, can radically alter the fortunes of both challengers and incumbents. In *The Third House: Lobbyists, Money, and Power in Sacramento,* Dan Walters writes:

> Allen Hoffenblum, a veteran political consultant, has listed five essential factors in a winning legislative campaign: a competitive district, one in which the candidate has at least a theoretical chance to win; a candidate that meets at least minimum personal qualifications; a well-organized and experienced campaign team; a realistic campaign strategy; and as the bottom line, enough money to carry out the strategy. And how much is enough? That can vary widely, depending on the district and the circumstances. In a district with a lopsided

---

|Think Again|

What role do political action committees play in California politics?

---

|Think Again|

How have term limits shaped the nature of political leadership in California?

party registration, where the primary winner is certain to be elected in November and there's little conflict in the primary, as little as $100,000 might do it. But in a highly competitive "swing" district and/or one in which competing factions are battling in the primary—two Latino organizations have been struggling for dominance in Los Angeles, for example—it would not be unusual for an Assembly seat campaign to consume a million dollars, and Senate seats can easily cost several million.[6]

The legislative incumbent, on the other hand, must try to prevent this type of candidate and campaign from emerging. The electoral defeat of former Republican State Senator Richard Rainey, who represented the seventh senate district on the eastern fringe of the San Francisco Bay Area, is an example of the very rare occasion when an incumbent can lose. Vulnerable even before the 2000 election year as a result of a district equally divided along party lines and a low-key demeanor, Rainey was challenged by Assemblyman Tom Torlakson, a moderate Democrat who had good name recognition in his district, got heavy financial support from his party, and by Rainey's own admission, ran an aggressive campaign. Such defeats have become rare, however, as incumbents in the state legislature have increasingly taken the steps necessary to protect their seats. Both parties have closed ranks, sharing and directing campaign funds and creating safe districts, but the accumulation of large campaign funds by individual members of the legislature between elections, which could easily be as much as half a million dollars, is one of the more convincing methods of scaring off would-be challengers.

The real electoral contests for legislative seats usually take place during the state primary campaigns and elections. One consequence of term limits are the open seats that become available every two years when up to one-third of the state legislators are forced out of office. In the absence of an incumbent, the opportunity for members of political parties in California to win the nomination as the candidate representing his or her party for a seat in the legislature in the general election has dramatically improved. The partisan nature of legislative elections allows political parties to become deeply involved in the primary campaign and election. Although most primary candidates for the legislature run campaigns independent of political parties, party involvement can range from outright recruitment of primary candidates to discouraging the candidacy of party members who threaten to take votes away from a favored candidate. The extent of political party involvement in a legislative electoral race will largely depend on the strength and depth of local or regional party organizations, which tend to be high in urban areas and low in rural communities. The role of political parties in the primary election process can be complicated, full of intricacies related to personality, demographics, personal relationships, and campaign contributions, but two factors—legislative **reapportionment** and **redistricting**—more than any others, generally determine the outcome of a primary or general election. In recent years, reapportionment and redistricting have become controversial issues, seen more as a means of "fixing" legislative districts to guarantee the election of party favorites than as a neutral constitutional responsibility of the state legislature. The design of legislative district has been constant in California politics, however, and is likely to remain controversial as long as reapportionment and redistricting play an influential role in the election of a partisan state legislature.

**reapportionment**
Redistribution of representation in a legislative body.

**redistricting** Drawing new boundaries for election districts.

**Reapportionment and Redistricting**   Throughout California history, there has been a recurring quandary regarding how Californians should be represented. The constitutions of the United States and California give the state legislature the power to create federal and state legislative districts based on the national census

## UP CLOSE

## Latino Legislators: The Long and Difficult Road to the California Legislature

When the California legislature convened for the first time in 1850, eight *Californios* legislators, native-born Californians of Mexican descent, would join that body, many of whom were participants in the first constitutional convention of 1848–49. Notable among them were Andres Pico, Mariano Vallejo, and Pablo de la Guerra, former military and political leaders prior to the American annexation of California. Within a few years, however, almost all of these representatives would be gone as a result of a widespread concerted effort to suppress Californians who did not adequately reflect the cultural, political, and economic vision of the emerging American settler population. Not only were most of the constitutional provisions advocated by the native-born legislators discarded (e.g., bilingual government documents), but a series of laws were enacted over the next fifty years that discriminated against the *Californios* and other ethnic minorities. The *Californios* saw their landholdings illegally whittled away by American squatters and filibusters, making the possibility of election to the state legislature even more difficult. By the late 1850s, there would be less than a handful of Latino legislators in California despite the large number of Latinos in the state, especially in the south. When Miguel Estudillo's term ended in the state senate in 1911, he would be the last Mexican American to serve in the state legislature until the 1960s. The redistricting and apportionment process that regularly fragmented Latino communities made electing representatives from these districts very difficult. The large Latino East Los Angeles community, for example, was parceled out to nine assembly districts, seven state senate districts, and six congressional districts; eventually, the Latino population in these districts rarely amounted to more than 20 percent.

A major turning point occurred following the defeat of the Latino candidate for the Los Angeles City Council, Edward Roybal, who with supporters of his failed campaign, founded the Community Political Organization (CPO) in September 1947, the first broad-based Mexican American organization dedicated to political organizing. Although in 1949, the CPO, later renamed the Community Service Organization (CSO), succeeded in helping Roybal become the first Latino elected to the Los Angeles City Council since 1881, few other Latinos were elected during the 1950s. In 1959, the political organizing capacity

of Latino communities in California was strengthened when the Mexican American Political Association (MAPA) was formed, joining the CSO in a large-scale effort to recruit candidates and register Latinos to vote. In 1962, these efforts paid off when Philip L. Soto and John Moreno became the first Latino legislators to be elected since the turn of the century.

A Democrat from Santa Fe Springs, John Moreno represented the 51st District in the assembly from 1962 until 1964. Phil Soto, also a Democrat and from La Puente, represented the 50th assembly district from 1962 to 1966. Assemblyman Soto, a founding member of the United Farm Workers (UFW) organization, used his position in the assembly to promote the plight of California agricultural workers and worked closely with Cesar Chavez during the Delano farmworkers' strike. Assembly members Moreno and Soto would establish a precedent for other Latino candidates to the California legislature, but their tenures would be shortened. Moreno's reelection bid in 1964 was essentially cancelled out by another Latino candidate in the Democratic primary who split the Latino vote in the 51st District, allowing the Anglo-American candidate to garner enough votes to grab the nomination. Soto was reelected in 1964, but in 1965 the California legislature was forced to reapportion district boundaries by the California Supreme Court, and assembly speaker Jesse Unruh chose Soto's district to carve up, diluting his Latino constituency and costing him reelection in 1966. Unruh justified this decision on the need to maintain high numbers of registered Democrats in the districts within and surrounding Los Angeles County, which in Phil Soto's district were Latino voters.

By 1968, Latino communities in California were once again without representation in the state legislature, but the past experiences of Soto and Moreno, the emergence of significant Latino organizations, the election of Edward Roybal to the U.S. House of Representatives in 1963, and the growing Latino population would forge a movement destined to transform Latino politics in California. The first two modern-day state legislators demonstrated how Latinos could be elected, but the founding of the Mexican American Legal Defense and Educational Fund (MALDEF) in 1968 in San Antonio, Texas, would be instrumental in keeping the political playing field level through legal challenges to electoral practices that restricted Latino participation. Other Latino political organizations were formed, including Californios for Fair Representation, which organized chapters throughout California that provided political education programs and voter registration drives. At the federal level, Congressman Roybal pressed the government to investigate violations of voter rights acts and would become one of the founding members of the Congressional Hispanic Caucus, serving in Congress until 1993. As the Latino population grew in the 1970s and 1980s, often becoming the majority in certain state legislative districts, it became increasingly more difficult to split up Latino voters. This numerical advantage gradually brought about the election of Latino legislators, who then solidified their power base in the state legislature by forming the Chicano Legislative Caucus, a legislative body that for the first time in the legislature's history could establish legislative priorities and an agenda dedicated to the interests of Latinos throughout California. Today, Latinos hold 25 percent of the seats in the state assembly and three of the last five assembly speakers were Latino members. One enduring legacy of the struggle for Latino representation has to be the legislative achievements of Nell Soto, political activist and wife of the pioneering legislator Phil Soto, who was told by her husband as he lay dying in 1997 "that it was her turn to move up."[a] At 80 years old, state senator Nell Soto will be termed out of the senate after being first elected to the assembly in 1998. An eyewitness to the historic struggle for Latino political empowerment and herself an architect of political and social reforms, Nell Soto may well be best remembered for her warning to Jesse Unruh after the assembly speaker altered the boundaries of her husband's district: "I'm going to work against you every chance I get."[b]

[a] Rojas, Aurelio, "Legacy of Respect: Trailblazing Latina Activist and Lawmaker Nell Soto Going Strong at 80," *Sacramento Bee* Capitol Bureau, Sunday, June 18, 2006, *sacbee.com*.
[b] Ibid.

*Sources:* Pitt, Leonard, *The Decline of the Californios* (Berkeley and Los Angeles: University of California Press, 1970).
Latino Legislative Caucus History and Purpose—California Latino Legislative Caucus, http://democrats.assembly.ca.gov/LatinoCaucus/history_purpose.htm; "Chicano Representation in California: Taking Control of their Destiny." HispanicVista Columnists, Hispanicvista.com. http://www.hispanicvista.com/HVC/Columnist/jschmal/070405jpschmal.htm

---

**⊢Think Again⊣**

Why have California voters repeatedly rejected efforts to reform the reapportionment and redistricting process?

conducted every ten years. California's bicameral (two-chamber) legislature is one of the smallest in the nation in proportion to the size of its population, which is the largest in the nation. Only fourteen states have smaller legislatures, and most have far fewer people.[7] The relatively small size of the California legislature has resulted in some of the largest legislative districts in the country. The average assembly district contains about 425,000 residents, and a state senate district has twice as many. The state legislature determines what portions of the population of California are contained in senate and assembly legislative districts.

From the granting of statehood to the modern era, California has suffered from a dilemma similar to the one the American founders faced when considering representation in Congress, which was ultimately solved through what is known as the Great Compromise (see Chapter 2). In California, the opposing sides were political leaders from urban and rural regions, each accusing the other of using the drawing of district boundaries to gain political advantage. The "not so great" compromise implemented in 1930 was the Federal Plan, which established a state senate composed of forty geographic districts that give no county more than one district and permit no more than three counties to share a single district. The state senate would thus provide equal representation to each county or groups of smaller counties. Representation in the eighty-seat assembly would remain apportioned on the basis of population.

During the 1940s and 1950s, the population of California expanded dramatically, primarily in the urban areas, with Southern California, particularly Los Angeles County, experiencing the greatest gains:

Los Angeles County's population increased from 2.2 million in 1930 to almost 7 million in the mid-1960s. Under the Federal Plan, these 7 million residents were represented by one state Senator, while only 17,000 inhabitants of three rural counties in the North also had one Senator. In other words, in theory at least, a resident of one of these three rural counties had 425 times the "voting power" in the state Senate than a resident of Los Angeles.[8]

The Federal Plan's end came in 1964 when the U.S. Supreme Court ruled in *Reynolds* v. *Sims* that the equal protection clause of the U.S. Constitution requires that the seats in both houses of a bicameral state legislature must be apportioned on the basis of population, and in reaction to this ruling, the state legislature passed the California Reapportionment Act of 1965, mandating that legislative districts for both houses contain relatively equal numbers of people.[9]

The controversy over legislative reapportionment and the redrawing of district boundaries over the past three decades has had less to do with the composition of legislative districts and more about who is doing the reapportioning and redistricting. Since the 1970s, when the Democrats solidified their control over the state legislature, Republican governors, including Ronald Reagan in 1971 and 1973 and Pete Wilson in 1991, vetoed redistricting plans that they labeled as attempts to gerrymander districts to favor Democrats running for Congress and the state legislature. Those plans were eventually revised in a less partisan manner by court-appointed retired appellate judges. Legislative veterans such as Phil Burton, a legendary member of both the state legislature and the U.S. Congress and brother of the former state senate president pro tempore, John Burton, became adept at affecting the electoral outcome of certain races by including all the registered Republican voters into one district (a practice known as "packing") while splitting the Republican Party base of voters of another district into different districts ("cracking"). In the 1980s, various initiatives and referendums were introduced in an attempt to remove redistricting power from the state legislature, but they either failed to qualify for the ballot, were rejected by the voters, or were avoided by legislative compromises. The redistricting and reapportionment process in 2001 was largely a bipartisan exercise that resulted in the creation of safe legislative districts for both major parties. These districts, according to political analyst Daniel Weintraub, "were designed to protect the jobs of those then in office, provide opportunities for legislators seeking to move up and freeze the partisan divide as it stood between Democrats and Republicans."[10] Critics of this last redistricting process—which have included a wide range of significant political actors, from Governor Arnold Schwarzenegger to Chellie Pingree, the president of Common Cause, a public advocacy group—charge that the legislature has engaged in a gerrymandering of legislative districts that makes a mockery of the legislative electoral process. Yet when the voters were once again given the opportunity to strip the state legislature of the power to redraw districts through an initiative sponsored by Governor Schwarzenegger in 2005, they chose to reject the initiative. Various justifications can be offered for this rejection, many based on political considerations and others on ignorance of the process, but one prevailing view suggests that voters are not convinced that the partisanship or manipulation associated with redistricting and reapportionment will disappear by simply changing the parties responsible for the process.

## The Legislative Universe

Every two years, after each general election, the state legislature begins its legislative session starting in December, and legislators once again (or for the first time) enter a very exclusive environment composed of a highly select membership with the unprecedented responsibility of making laws for one of the most important states in the Union. The organization and functions of the state legislature are based on Article 4 of the state constitution, which governs **standing rules** and **joint rules**. These laws and rules provide the legislature with self-governing powers, allowing almost total independence from any other public or

---

**┤Think Again├**

What are the Standing and Joint rules of the legislature, and why are they important?

**standing rules** Rules that ensure that the legislature operates in an efficient and civil manner.

**joint rules** Guidelines for cooperation between the two chambers of the legislature.

private authority and control over almost every aspect of the offices. Most of the standing rules for the state legislature are carried over from one session to the next but can be altered, amended, or repealed during each session. The standing rules also ensure that the legislature operates in an efficient and civil manner, covering such as areas as meeting times, order of business, number and membership of committees, duties of officers, rules of debate, and votes required on legislative action. The standing rules for the senate and assembly are similar, but there are differences that reflect the structural distinctions between the two chambers. Relations between the two chambers are defined by the joint rules, which establish guidelines for cooperation. The effectiveness of the rules are determined by the way they are applied and can be used as much to slow, corrupt, or even prevent the completion legislative functions as they are used to facilitate legislative responsibilities.

**Legislative Functions**   Although the state constitution prescribes lawmaking as the main responsibility of the California legislature, it has taken on many other duties that have become vital to legislating. Although not necessarily prescribed directly by the California constitution, these other vital functions compel the legislator to adopt qualities of an educator, accountant, personnel director, public relations executive, and law enforcement officer. Understanding these functions will help the constituent better appreciate the workload of California legislators, differentiate between actual and fabricated negative perceptions, and participate in the legislative function.

*Lawmaking*   The lawmaking responsibility of the assembly and the state senate focuses largely on drafting, reviewing, and ultimately voting on bills (proposed laws). Thousands of laws are passed every year that address a broad range of issues, many of which are designed to protect the public and others to benefit a powerful interest group. Bills that are introduced in the state senate or assembly carry the designation SB or AB, a number, and usually the name of the author. The ability to vote on and propose bills is the most important service expected of legislators. California state law or statues are divided into twenty-nine different codes—for example, Business and Professions, Fish and Game, and Military and Veterans—that regulate almost all major aspects of life in California. A modification or repeal of a law or merely one section regulating, say, the alcohol content of wine coolers sold in California, how much concert tickets can be marked up, or whether nurses can work twelve-hour shifts, can mean the loss or gain of millions of dollars for a particular industry. Although only members of the state legislature may introduce bills for consideration, lobbyists, state and federal government officials, and private citizens often ask to participate in the drafting of a particular bill or serve as important sources of information during the drafting process. Once the basic idea of a bill is conceived, it is the job of the Legislative Counsel, the law office of the legislature, to reformat the bill to meet legal technicalities. All laws must be passed by a majority in both chambers and go into effect on first day of the following calendar year (January 1). Bills approved by the legislature that take effect immediately involve the state budget, calling elections, introducing tax levies, immediate fiscal allocations, and urgency bills. Urgency bills are intended to address matters of urgency, and require a two-thirds majority vote in both chambers.

One of the most important as well as controversial types of proposed laws are known as "juice" bills—bills written to benefit a particular group, usually engaged in business. The consideration and passage of a "juice" bill usually results in large campaign contributions and other benefits to the author or sponsor of the bill and

---

┤Think Again├

What is the scope of the lawmaking power of the California legislature?

---

**"juice" bills**  Bills written to benefit a particular group, usually engaged in business.

other legislators who have played influential roles in getting the bill passed. The "juice" that flows from a bill to benefit a particular legislator is often inadvertent, the result of the representation provided to interests in the legislator's district. For example, such a bill might benefit a particular industry that will in turn employ thousands of people in that legislator's district. There have also been many instances of California legislators seeking or actually writing "juice" bills for their own personal enrichment. One flagrant example occurred in 1988, when the FBI set up a sting operation using a phony company, Gulf Shrimp Fisheries of Mobile, Alabama, that succeeded in getting a number of Democratic and Republican California assembly members to sponsor two bills that would have allowed Gulf Shrimp Fisheries to sell tax-exempt industrial development bonds to finance construction of a food-processing facility in California. The FBI caught on videotape many of the assembly members accepting thousands of dollars for their work on the bills, which easily passed in both chambers but was vetoed by Governor Deukmejian, who had been tipped off by the FBI about the anticorruption sting operation.[11]

There are very important bills that are introduced purely for the good of the public without any direct financial benefit to anyone. Many of these bills are in response to the requests of administrative agencies of the state government regarding the broadening or narrowing of regulatory powers. Bills from that arise from the concerns of a partisan official of the executive branch of government may be politically hard for a fellow party member in the legislature to ignore. Bills are often generated from the personal interest of a legislator in solving social problems, and at other times they are a response to media attention on a particular issues. Although for decades, the state legislature has passed various laws that have benefited the California Community College system and has been very reluctant to cut that budget, this educational community does not have a powerful lobbying group or union to bestow large contributions, nor does it have a constituency that is known to turn out in great numbers at the polls. Most legislators, who probably have a community college in their district, realize the value of the educational services that these colleges provide to their constituents, and legislators may even have attended a community college at some point in their lives. The efforts of Candy Lightner, who founded Mothers Against Drunk Driving (MADD), after her teenage daughter was killed by a drunk driver, demonstrated the power of media attention to generate important bills in the state legislature. After years of lawmakers resisting attempts to lower blood alcohol levels for motorists, in large part due to powerful liquor industry lobbyists, Lightner ignited public interest and extensive media coverage through her compelling personal story and organization. Under intense public scrutiny, the legislature eventually passed a series of bills that lowered blood alcohol levels and increased the penalties for drunk driving.[12]

A MADD bulletin board details Mothers Against Drunk Diving events.

Many bills that have little or no chance of being approved are introduced solely to advance a legislator's political career. Some of these bills will satisfy a small segment of a legislator's constituency back home that their concerns are being heard. At times such frivolous bills are intended to get media attention. Senator John Vasconcellors received plenty of media attention for introducing a bill that proposed to lower the voting age to 14. A bill to require the California Buildings Standards Commission to include *feng shui* in design principles was another such wasted legislative effort. The problem presented by these exercises in futility is that they consume the valuable time of legislators and staff, who are required to subject such legislation to the normal process, and the fiscal resources that accompany these efforts.

## UP CLOSE

# An Ethical Legislature?

Over the past two decades, the California legislature has established a formidable array of ethics laws that are thought to be some of the toughest in the nation. These laws can be found in provisions of the California Constitution, the Political Reform Act, and other sections of the Government Code and are intended to prevent inappropriate behavior and conflicts of interests among the members and staff of the state legislature. Restrictions and limits imposed by these laws affect such areas as gifts from lobbyists, speaker fees, and donations. Legislative resources theoretically may only be used only for legislative purposes and not for personal benefit or to advance a campaign. The members and staff of the legislature are required to attend an ethics orientation course once every two years, and both houses of the California legislature have ethics committees that are responsible for overseeing enforcement of ethics laws. The legislature went as far as creating the Fair Political Practices Commission in 1974 to investigate complaints of unethical behavior, especially as such behavior relates to the electoral process. And yet, there continues to be accusations of corruption and influence peddling in the state legislature. The California Nurses Association, as one rationale for its Clean Money Initiative, noted that "as many as 13% of all corporations operating in California paid no state income tax in 2004 while spending millions of dollars on political contributions 'that have unduly influenced public policy and fueled public disenchantment with our political system.'"[a] Funding shortfalls and the lack of resources forced the Fair Political Practices Commission (FPPC) in 2005 to terminate the investigation of 225 cases of campaign law and ethics violations out of a record high 1,751 complaints, many inevitably involving the state legislature. In October 2005, assembly member Sarah Reyes, her campaign committee, and its campaign treasurer were fined $23,000 by the California FPPC for failing to disclose $80,000 in donations her campaign made to other Democratic candidates and $105,000 in late contributions received by her campaign in 2000.

Should Californians be surprised at the seemingly unavoidable occurrence of unethical behavior by the state legislature? Angry, yes; surprised, not really. As unfortunate and detrimental as it may be to the democratic process of representative government, unethical activities by state legislators goes back to the early days of the California legislature. George E. Mowry, in his important work *The California Progressives*, describes the depths of unethical behavior on display during the 1906 legislative session, during which the assembly

> had on its pay roll thirty-six sergeants of arms, ten doorkeepers for four doors, eighteen watchmen, the same number of porters, seven postmistresses, twenty-seven engrossing and enrolling clerks, thirty-one 'straight clerks,' and forty other people. Later investigations showed that a newspaperman drawing full pay from his paper was also in the pay of both houses, that a high school student drew a full salary, and those persons who never left Los Angeles for the term of the session received regular checks from the state.[b]

The efforts of the Progressives to clean house in the state legislature are now legendary, and for a while, their sense of righteousness prevailed in state government as they employed the initiative at critical junctures to prevent corrupt or unethical actions or policies. Once the Progressive fervor dissipated, leaving a vacuum in political party influence to be filled with a crowd of special groups that flocked to the state legislature, it was business as usual. By 1949, the ethics in the state legislature had declined to an all-time low, so writes the noted California observer Carey McWilliams in his classic book *California: The Great Exception*.

> Decisive power rests not with the people but with the Canners' League, the Wine Institute, and the other organized trade, crop and industry organizations. The California legislature, indeed, closely resembles the "chamber of corporations" under Italian fascism. Curiously, the legislators have failed to catch the meaning of the new dispensation; that is, they have failed to form their own trade association and retain a lobbyist. Their salary is still $1,200 a year. However, as the Philbrick Report revealed, most of them manage to do very well.[c]

---

[a]"California Nurses to Sponsor Clean Money Initiative—To Stem Corruption of Elections, Ballot Campaigns," California Nurses Association, *www.calnurses.org*.

[b]Mowry, George E., *The California Progressives* (Chicago: Quadrangle Books, 1951), pp. 62–63.
[c]McWilliams, Carey. *California: The Great Exception* (New York: Current Books, 1949), p. 213.

*Jesse "Big Daddy" Unruh left the legislature to run for Governor against Ronald Reagan in 1970. He was also a candidate for Mayor of Los Angeles in 1973. After losing both elections, he was elected State Treasurer in 1974. He served as treasurer from 1975 until his death in 1987.*

One justification for the reform of the California legislature in the 1960s was to finally put an end to the influence of special interest groups through professionalizing the structure and members of the institution. Increased salary and benefits, professional staff, and full-time schedules, it was reckoned, would put legislators beyond the expertise and favors of lobbyists. The now immortal words of former speaker of the assembly Jesse "Big Daddy" Unruh and chief architect of this professionalized legislature—"If you can't eat their food, drink their booze, screw their women and then vote against them, then you don't belong here"—became the supposed credo of the new and improved California legislature. But in reality, "Big Daddy" and just about everyone in the legislature did commit all of these acts and still voted for "them." Very early in his career, Unruh accepted contributions from oil companies and other big businesses. Most observers of capitol politics during the Unruh years concede that the flow of influence and any unethical acts were contained by the heightened sense of partisanship under Unruh's position as speaker of the assembly. Partisanship, the drive for professionalism in the 1960s, and the moderate costs of a legislative campaign caused a reversal of roles, whereby the state legislative leaders began to dictate to the special interest groups and lobbyists, unlike the days of the "secret boss of California" Artie Samish's tactics of "selecting and electing" legislators to serve his corporate clients. Jesse Unruh accepted thousands of dollars in campaign contributions and organized fundraisers at which lobbyists were expected to con-

tribute up to $1,000, but that money was generally used to elect other Democrats.

By the late 1970s, as the cost of campaigns and the amount of money available to individual members of the California legislature began to rise, the level of ethical behavior on the part of legislators started to fall. An FBI sting operation in the 1980s successfully netted a number of assembly and state senate members, both Democrats and Republicans, and members of their staff who had blatantly taken money to influence legislation. In 1990, state senator Joseph Montoya became the symbol of this scandal-ridden period and the first California legislator in thirty-six years to be convicted of corruption on seven counts of extortion, racketeering, and money laundering. Ironically, Montoya began his career on a platform of high ethics and political reform; by the time he was convicted, he had become popularly known among lobbyists as "El Bandito." Montoya climbed the political ranks gradually, from the city council of La Puente to mayor, then on to the assembly and finally the state senate, where he was awarded chairpersonship of the powerful Business and Professional Committee. Practically every business in California could be affected by the laws that flowed from this committee and, as chairperson, Montoya would control it favorably for those lobbyists and business interests that contributed to his cause. Although earning $37,500 per year as a state senator, Montoya managed to become a millionaire while in office, acquiring real estate worth more than $2 million. On June 29, 1988, Montoya's undoing came when he agreed to help get a special bill passed in return for a $3,000 check from an undercover FBI Agent.

Before Californians condemn unethical practices in the state legislature too harshly, they might want to assess the level of ethics that are exhibited in everyday life. Government, in the immortal words of Benjamin Franklin, is really only as good as the people, and the ethical standards of the California legislature will only be as high as the residents of this state raise it.

*Sources:* Ethical Standards, California State Legislature, www.legislature.ca.gov; Furillo, Andy, "FPPC Gets Briefing on Staff Woes: Board Takes No Action but Hands Out a Series of Fines," *Sacramento Bee,* October 13, 2005; "Fresno Lawmaker Fined $23,000 for Campaign Disclosure Violations," Associated Press, August 5, 2004; Curtius, Mary, "States Offer Grim Look at Curbing Corruption," *Los Angeles Times,* February 28, 2006; Cannon, Lou, *Ronnie and Jesse: A Political Odyssey* (Garden City, N.Y.: Doubleday, 1969); Bernstein, Dan, "Some in Limbo 4 Years after FBI's Capitol Raid," *Sacramento Bee,* August 16, 1992; Gunnison, Robert B., "Capitol Probe: FBI Reportedly Told Deukmejian About Its Sting," *San Francisco Chronicle,* August 30, 1988; Roberts, Jerry, " 'Poor Kid' Montoya Got Rich in Office," *San Francisco Chronicle,* February 3, 1990.

**resolutions** Formal statements explaining a decision or expressing an opinion.

In addition to changes or additions to California statutes, the state legislature may also propose and pass constitutional amendments and **resolutions**. The depth of the California constitution, nearly ten times as long as the U.S. Constitution, necessitates regular amending that the legislature is empowered to perform. Any constitutional amendment proposed by the state legislature, known as an ACA for the assembly or SCA for the senate, must be passed by a two-thirds vote in both chambers and then ratified by a majority of the voters. There are a number of different types of resolutions that are considered and regularly approved by the legislature, consisting of concurrent (ACR or SCR), joint (AJR or SJR), and house resolutions (AR or SR), most commonly defined as the sentiments or opinions of the legislative body.

Resolutions are regularly used by the legislature to recognize the achievements of a particular individual. Concurrent resolutions can originate in either chamber but must be passed in both chambers to go into effect and usually authorize the forming of joint temporary committees, requesting information from the state agencies, adopting joint rules, and establishing the time the legislature may recess during a session. Joint resolutions, which can also originate in either chamber and require approval by a majority of legislators in both chambers, express the collective position of the California legislature on matters of public interest. Each chamber may pass a house resolution that pertains directly to its concerns or the conduct of its business; such resolutions normally involve the adoption of rules, the selection of committees, the allocation of funds, the appointment of officers, and the hiring of employees.

⊣Think Again⊢

What are the main features of the annual budget process in California?

*Lawmaking and the Annual Budget Process*    The most important aspect of the lawmaking function is the passage of the annual state budget, which is essentially treated as a bill. The annual budget for the state of California reflects the size of the state and requires detailed consideration and substantial interaction between the legislature and the executive branch. The budget process begins with the governor, who prepares the annual budget and must submit it to both chambers of the legislature by January 10. After the receipt and introduction in both chambers, the annual budget is referred to the Senate Budget and Fiscal Review Committee and the Assembly Budget Committee, which will in turn refer sections of the budget to subcommittees by major subject areas such as education or health and human services. Both the governor and the state legislature are obligated by the state constitution to complete a balanced annual budget that meets other constitutional budgetary mandates such as the allocation of 40 percent of the general fund to education. After conducting hearings, the subcommittees will issue reports with recommendations regarding funding levels and other actions in specific areas of the budget, which will be sent back to the Senate Budget and Fiscal Review Committee and the Assembly Budget Committee. These committees will review the subcommittee reports, revise the total budget package, and send a completed annual budget to the full body of their respective legislative chambers for debate and vote. Following passage by both chambers, any differences between the assembly and senate versions of the budget are worked out in a conference committee that is comprised of members from both chambers. The compromise budget that will emerge from the conference committee will be submitted to the full membership of each chamber for a final vote.

The legislature is constitutionally bound to pass a balanced budget by an extraordinary or two-thirds majority in both chambers. The two-thirds majority rule, which is extremely rare in other states, has proved to be a major hurdle in passing the budget in recent years due to the narrow majorities that the Democrats have had in both houses. In the budget process, the minority Republican Party has been the dominant player, refusing to provide the votes needed for passage of the budget unless the Democrats relent on aspects of the spending plan. This dilemma has contributed to the state government's inability to meet specific guidelines and deadlines that the legislature is mandated to follow once it receives the budget proposal, particularly in meeting the June 15 deadline for passage and delivery of the budget back to the governor.

*Representation*    The notion of representative or indirect democracy is founded on the principle that voters designate a relatively small number of people to represent their interests; those representatives then meet in a legislative body to make decisions on behalf of the entire citizenry. In the California legislature, representing the interests of Californians through lawmaking and other legislative responsibilities is made especially difficult by the diversity, size, and wide disparity in wealth of the state. Besides fulfilling the democratic ideal, representation can be an important factor in the reelection of state legislators. California legislators have adopted various methods of representation in response to the wide-ranging conditions in California, but the one universal and most basic approach to representation is known as **casework**.

Each year, the state legislature allocates a substantial amount of funds for legislators to maintain offices and staff in the state capitol as well as the home districts that are dedicated to assisting constituents with problems and questions that arise. "Casework is across the board" in the 71st District of Assemblyman Todd Spitzer in Orange, California, according one of his district staffers. "It can be everything from DMV problems to questions about real estate licensing."[13] Staff members encourage constituents to record their complaints or requests for assistance in letter form. The opening of a file on each constituent contact is the first step in handling casework in Assemblyman Spitzer's district office. The office staff often ends up referring constituents to the appropriate organization or service. "We act as middlemen a lot," commented the staff member. Staff members will attempt to resolve the problems or issues associated with a state government agency or department through telephone inquiries to the office in question and follow up with letters. The district office staff will generally expect state agencies to contact the constituent in writing and notify the district office of the final disposition of the constituent's concern. Some of the more basic methods legislators employ to keep in touch with their districts include conducting town hall meetings, surveys of constituent interests, newsletters and recognition of constituent achievements.

The 42nd Assembly District staff of Assemblyman Paul Koretz, who represents the Hollywood–West Los Angeles area, provides a good example of the organization and focus of a legislator's district office in conducting casework and related constituency services. The organizational structure begins with the district director, who is in direct contact with Assemblyman Koretz and largely responsible for supervising the group of field representatives that responds to casework requests. Each of the field representatives is responsible for specific issue areas: For example, one takes care of health care, public education, and transportation, and another's responsibilities include the environment and animal and public safety. Assemblyman Koretz complements the work of the field representatives with a "labor liaison" position that directly interacts with unions in the district. The district office has also organized a health care advisory committee that conducts community outreach activities.[14]

Representation comes in many different varieties, whether based on the geographic conditions, social or cultural background of constituents, specific policy issues, or personal interests. Legislators will attempt to identify which of these con-

**casework** The direct assistance legislators offer in response to requests from their constituents.

ditions most affect the majority of their constituents, especially the ones that vote, and tailor their legislative agenda, district office organization, committee assignments, and often votes on issues in the legislature to their constituencies. Representation is undoubtedly very difficult for California legislators who must spend a significant proportion of their time learning about the legislature as rapidly as possible before being forced into retirement as a result of term limits. The unusually large number of constituents in California districts and the diverse array of special interests inside as well as outside a California legislator's district make the representation function even more difficult. Most legislators seem to have resolved this dilemma by focusing on the groups or individuals that will best demonstrate their appreciation for the efforts of the legislator. There is plenty of evidence that supports the notion that money in the form of campaign contributions is a key factor in acquiring representation from legislators on a given issue. The substantial sums of campaign contributions from groups such the California Correctional Peace Officers Association and California Indian casino owners to both Democratic and Republican legislators, considering the generous benefits correction officers have received over the years and the easing of former prohibitions on gambling in California, has made a difference in gaining the attention of legislators.

─┤**Think Again**├─

Why has the California legislature had a poor record on oversight in recent decades?

**oversight function** The responsibility for supervising the implementation of all laws and the government officials charged with implementing them.

*Oversight*   Although legislators have the primary responsibility of making laws, they are also responsible for overseeing the implementation of all laws as they were originally intended and the government officials who are charged with implementing them. Certain constitutional powers granted to the state legislature, most notably for shaping the annual state budget, conducting public hearings, and the impeachment and removal of elected officials, can be powerful restraints on a wayward or incompetent organization of the executive branch. Former Senator Jim Costa, a Democrat who represented the 16th Senate District, deems the **oversight function** "highly important to making the legislature a coequal branch of government." Senator Costa notes, however, that the California legislature does not typically do oversight well because "this work is labor intensive and time intensive, and it takes a dedicated legislator to do it properly. We tend to emphasize oversight only when there is a major crisis or a legislator has a deep interest in a particular area." Although not fashionable," Senator Costa concedes, "oversight work can be rewarding when you do it well."[15]

Legislative investigations of the California Department of Corrections have been some of the most disheartening but nonetheless important instances of legislative oversight. In 2000, State Senator Richard Polanco, chair of the Joint Legislative Committee on Prison Construction and Operation, along with two other state senators, took the extraordinary step of conducting hearings at Valley State Prison for Women and the Central California Women's Facility at Chowchilla, California, to hear testimony from prisoners, prison advocacy groups, and Department of Corrections staff on "alleged medical abuse and neglect endured by women inside." The testimony heard from more than a dozen prisoners detailed inadequate medical care that resulted in serious illnesses being left untreated for months and misdiagnoses that caused the deaths of at least two inmates who were mistakenly given tuberculosis medicine.[16] Five years later, conditions at both women's prisons remain problematic, prompting State Senator Jackie Speier to take the even greater extraordinary action of leading a delegation of state senators from the women's caucus, to spend the night at Valley State Prison for Women to determine the nature of the conditions at first hand. Senator Speier, who chaired the Senate Select Committee on Government Oversight, "found conditions that I believe are unacceptable for pregnant inmates, in terms of the quality of attention they receive and the lack of programming in their facilities. Many women had not had a Pap smear or a mammogram in a number of years."[17] Speier was particularly troubled by the fact that the cost of health care in state prisons for women is 60 percent more expensive than in institutions for men, yet reports to the Senate Select Committee on Government Oversight and her own observations at the Valley State Prison for Women indicate that the quality of health care was substandard. Speier would introduce seven bills related to prison reform, addressing a wide range of issues, but such reforms continue to face an uphill battle, primarily against the California Correctional Peace Officers Association, which is resistant to budget-cutting measures and legislative scrutiny.

Patterned after the advice and consent power of the U.S. Senate, an important part of the oversight function is the state senate's power to confirm or reject many of the appointments of the governor. These appointments, literally in the hundreds, include the heads of state departments and agencies and various positions on state boards and commissions. Unlike the U.S. Senate, judicial appointments are not reviewed or confirmed by the state senate. The state senate confirmation process begins with hearings and background investigations conducted by the Senate Rules Committee, including testimony from individuals that either supports or questions a nominee's qualifications. The committee then issues a recommendation of approval or disapproval of the nominee to the entire membership of the state senate. A majority of votes in the full state senate is required to confirm the nomination. Legislators will have to ultimately approve someone for vacant government positions, but the confirmation process can still be a very partisan affair, especially with a state government that over the years has often been divided between a Republican governor and Democratic-controlled legislature. In the instances of divided state government, it is almost inevitable that a number of major appointments will be rejected, although the true intentions of a nomination may have more to do with political payback than the real desire by the governor to nominate the most qualified candidate. Other rejected appointments are clearly the result of ideological differences between the two parties. One such rejection occurred when Cindy Tuck, a consultant for the California Council for Environmental and Economic Balance, a coalition of business, labor, and public officials, was nominated by Governor Schwarzenegger to head the California Air Resources Board. Stating in senate hearings that she did not intend to represent business interests and was not clearly affiliated with any political party, Tuck even got the Democratic senate president pro tem, Don Perata, to concede that she was a "very impressive individual." Public criticism from groups such as the Los Angeles Physicians for Social Responsibility, accusing Tuck of being a longtime professional lobbyist for polluting industries that were consistently opposed to California clean air regulations, convinced the state senate to rejected her nomination, which it did on a 21–14 vote.[18]

**The Partisan Caucus**    Much of the action taken in the California legislature is based on the decisions of the legislative **party caucuses**, which are groups of legislators from the same party that form a formal association to pursue the interests of the party as those interests relate to the work of the legislature. The Democratic and Republican Parties have the two main legislative party caucuses in each of the chambers. The most important tasks of the caucuses are to elect legislative leaders, set policy goals, and support the election of fellow legislators. Party members from each chamber are not legally bound to participate in the activities of their party caucus, but most legislators appreciate the benefits of this interaction or fear the repercussions of not being actively involved and supporting the policies that result

**party caucus** Legislators from the same party who meet to establish group goals, policies, and strategies.

from caucus meetings. Assembly Speaker Jesse Unruh began the tradition of having the speaker elected in the Democratic assembly caucus in 1963, despite the constitutional provision that calls for the speaker to be elected by the full membership of the assembly. The gesture was designed to achieve a greater sense of party unity and has been in place ever since.[19] Life for legislators who do not follow the dictates of their respective party caucuses can be rather difficult. When, for example, in 2004, Assemblyman Joe Canciamilla formed a moderate Democratic caucus known as the Mod Squad, which opposed many of the policies that came out of the Democratic assembly caucus and cooperated with a number of moderate Republicans, the assembly leadership was quick to strip him of his committee chair.[20] In 2003, during tense budget negotiations, Senate Republican minority leader Jim Brulte warned that he would personally campaign against any member of the Republican caucus who joined the Democrats in voting for a tax increase.

In addition to the party caucuses in both chambers, there are seven other caucuses, representing ethnic, gender, Internet, and "smart-growth" issues and concerns. Most of these caucuses were formed as a result of a perceived lack of attention given to the concerns of these groups by the party caucuses. Recently, there has been some controversy among the Latino and Asian Pacific Islander caucuses, in which all the members are from the Democratic Party, regarding whether to admit Latino and Asian Republican members. Although the Latino caucus continues to resist the membership of Republican Latinos on the grounds of policy interests, the Asian caucus continues to debate the issue. Ultimately, the Asian caucus will have to resolve whether the caucus on the one hand should be inclusive of all Asian Pacific Islander members of the legislature or whether the financial contributions that the Democratic assembly leadership makes to this caucus and the potential ideological divisions that may result are good reasons to keep the Republicans out.

**Legislative Compensation**   In 2005, California legislators remained the highest-paid legislators in the nation, with an annual base salary of $110,880, which is established by an independent citizens' commission. For comparison's sake, the salary of legislators in New York State was $79,500 per year, and members of the Nevada state legislature received $130 per day for a maximum of sixty days in the legislative session. In addition to their salaries, California legislators receive a per diem of $138 each day their chamber is in session.[21] Additional benefits include an automobile, a cell phone, health insurance, and funds to hire staff and rent office space in their districts. There are of course at least two ways to judge this salary and the benefits. Is this level of compensation simply in line with what a corporate executive would expect, especially considering that California is the nation's largest and wealthiest state? Or does this compensation package make it more difficult for the legislator to truly appreciate the financial constraints that most of his or her constituents must face—and if they wanted a corporate-level compensation package, shouldn't they have chosen a different career? (See Table 17.1.)

## Leadership in the State Legislature

For better or worse, term limits have reduced a substantial amount of the power and stature of leadership positions. The people who held these positions were once prodigious forces in the statewide political arena, competing with governors for dominance over the state government and for media attention. Top legislative leadership positions also were frequent launch pads for election to the state executive office and beyond. Speaker Jesse M. Unruh was largely respon-

## Table 17.1   Annual Compensation for California Legislators

California has the highest paid legislators in the nation. The seven-member California Citizens Compensation Commission was created in June 1990, as a result of the passage of Proposition 112, to determine the salaries and benefits for members of the legislature and other statewide offices. The Governor appoints all seven commissioners, who then serve for overlapping six-year terms.

California legislators elected after 1990 are not eligible for a pension.

**Assembly and State Senate Salary:**          $110,880
Assembly speaker, State Senate president pro tempore and Minority leader are paid $127,572;
Majority leader and second-ranking Minority Leader are paid $119,196.

**Per Diem Living Expenses:**          $27,500 ($152 per day)
Approximate tax-free annual funds provided to each member for each day the legislature is in session. This is not set by the California Citizens Compensation Commission, but by the California Victim Compensation and Government Claims Board.

**Car Allowance:**          $6,000 ($500 per month)
For purchase of a vehicle on two-year loan and $350 monthly for a four-year loan.

**Dental:**          $1,596.84 ($133 per month)

**Vision:**          $364.68 ($30 per month)

**Family Health Insurance:**          $3,852 ($21 per month)
Monthly cost toward family health insurance, ranging from $321 to $807, depending on number of covered dependents.

*Source: California Citizens Compensation Commission: Fact Sheet.* www.dpa.ca.gov; Martin, Mark, Gledhill Lyndia, "Nation's highest paid legislators get raise: first boost in 7 years ups pay to $110 as state battle deficit." *San Francisco Chronicle,* May 24, 2005.

sible for establishing the model for powerful legislative leadership for that lasted more than three decades. An advocate of a professional legislature in the 1960s, Unruh is also known for introducing an organized partisan approach to the legislature that continues today. Unruh and subsequent state senate leaders derived their influence from a professionalism that tended to concentrate power, erect a partisan bulwark against stagnation, and encourage the financial largess of special-interest groups. The era of powerful legislative leaders would end with Willie Brown, the longest-standing assembly speaker, who was the epitome of the Unruh era politician. Known for his fundraising prowess and flamboyance, Speaker Brown frequently demonstrated an astute understanding of legislative politics and was the ultimate consensus builder. Today, the formal powers remains intact, but the ability of legislative leaders to promote a productive legislature during the one term that most serve in this capacity curtails their ability to organize a political agenda, build trust and confidence, and establish relationships in both houses and the executive branch.

**Assembly Speaker**   The selection of **assembly speaker** has in recent history been a turbulent process, full of political intrigue and backstabbing, often severely testing the relationships and loyalties among assembly members. With the Democrats firmly in power for some time, the selection of the assembly speaker has been

**assembly speaker** The presiding officer of the California state assembly.

⊣Think Again⊢

What are the powers of the
Assembly Speaker?

an intraparty contest, compelling ambitious assembly members seeking the speak-ership to cultivate factions that will provide the necessary votes when the election for assembly speaker takes place in the Democratic Party caucus. The tradition of electing the speaker in the Democrat-controlled assembly is usually a rough-and-tumble game of who can stab who in the back first. Jesse Unruh was a minor exception to that rule largely because of his tactless manner, chairmanship of the then powerful Ways and Means Committee, and popularity with lobbyists, all of which allowed him to simply bully his way into the assembly speaker position. Others, such as Bob Moretti, Leo McCarthy, and Willie Brown, were considerably more subtle but no less cunning. McCarthy and Brown actually competed to oust Moretti in the middle of his two-year term as speaker, with the prize going to McCarthy, who won by a 26–22 vote in the Democratic caucus. Brown would soon after launch a failed attack on McCarthy, establishing a pattern of enlisting the support of Republicans to grab power that would reappear periodically throughout his career.[22] Even with term limits, the struggle for the assembly speakership within the Democratic caucus has been no less malicious, exemplified by the rise of Fabian Nuñez, who ended up beating out four other candidates, including the front-runner, Jenny Oropeza. Amid accusations that he secretly agreed to back Oropeza, Nuñez publicly denied that any deal was made, convincing various factions of the Democratic Party caucus to support his candidacy. Nuñez, who assumed the position of assembly speaker at age 36, had never held office before and had served only one year as an assembly member. His ascendancy may yet become another model for legislative leadership that now focuses on youthful aspirants who could hold on to this important leadership position for two terms.[23]

Similar in many respects to the speaker of U.S. House of Representatives, the assembly speaker position was made especially powerful by the California constitution and the standing rules of the assembly, elements of which remain potent even with term limits. In theory, the position of assembly speaker is a feature of the parliamentary system of deliberative assemblies, with the main responsibility of maintaining order in a neutral or non-partisan manner. The partisan nature of legislative politics in California compels the assembly speaker to use the position for very partisan objectives. Considering the range of the assembly speaker's parliamentary authority, it would not be an exaggeration to suggest that this position is probably the second most powerful political official in the state, after the governor. Specific qualities of the assembly speaker's parliamentary powers are derived from the following responsibilities and duties:

- Determines the number and titles of standing committees, special committees, and subcommittees

- Arranges the schedule for committee meetings

- Appoints members of the assembly standing committees, special committees, and subcommittees

- Appoints chairs and vice-chairs of all assembly committees

- Appoints the majority floor leader

- Appoints three members of the assembly to serve on conference committees

- Directs the Rules Committee in the referral of bill to specific committees

- Serves as the ex officio nonvoting member of all assembly committees

- Presides over the assembly and can appoint assembly members as a temporary replacements as necessary

- Assigns office space in the capitol to assembly members

The authority of the assembly speaker is very similar to the role of a judge in a court setting, which includes recognizing the right of members to speak during debates and clarifying parliamentary procedure and rules of the assembly. The one organizational limitation of the assembly speaker's power is the inability to appoint members to the Rules Committee. Because of the partisan nature of the state legislature, the assembly speaker is somewhat indebted as well as accountable to the majority party but, as the presiding officer, may be forced to enlist the support of the opposition through compromise, tactics used by Speakers Unruh and Brown, especially in their ability to gain and retain their positions. Consequently, the assembly speaker must often walk a very fine line between using the enormous authority of the position to facilitate the policymaking or legislative imperative of the assembly and protecting his or her political party. The supremacy of the assembly speaker does attract the generosity of special-interest groups, which see this position as the most direct and important access point for influencing the lawmaking function. Consequently, the assembly speaker is a main beneficiary as well as a fountainhead for campaign contributions The legislative skills and longevity of Willie Brown during his tenure as assembly speaker attracted campaign contributions, like a magnet: During the 1991–92 election cycle, he received approximately $5.3 million in contributions; his Republican counterpart at the time, Assembly Minority Leader Bill Jones, could muster only $1.2 million.[24] Despite the social consciousness and working-class orientation of the Democratic Party's registered voters and party platform, Speaker Brown was regularly the top recipient of campaign contributions from the oil and tobacco industry.[25] However difficult it may be for an assembly speaker to accept large sums of money from special-interest groups, that money is vital to the assembly speaker's responsibility of maintaining his or her party's majority in the assembly. Dispensing large sums of campaign contributions or directing generous donors to fellow assembly members and to the party, in accordance with relatively lax California campaign finance laws during election time, is the key to maintaining this majority.

**Partisan Assembly Leaders**    Although the California constitution specifies only the assembly speaker as the presiding officer of the assembly, a number of other leadership positions are derived from the partisan divisions among assembly members.

*Majority Floor Leader, Assistant Majority Leader, Whip, and Assistant Whip*    Although elected by the majority party caucus, the assembly speaker is largely responsible for the selection of these positions, which serve as the Assembly Speaker's personal liaison with the majority party. The majority floor leader supervises this team of assembly members who represent the speaker on the floor, clarifying assembly proceedings and parliamentary procedures such as motions and points of order and promoting unity among the party membership. These positions are especially important in coordinating the majority party's efforts to pass legislation and in facilitating two-way communication between the speaker and the assembly membership. In an environment where assembly members may be reluctant to express personal feelings and positions, the majority floor leader conveys personal opinions to the assembly speaker and gauges the sentiments of the entire assembly membership. The individuals who are selected for these positions generally serve at the discretion of the assembly speaker and hence are expected to perform whatever duties will support the position of the assembly speaker and their party, which may include fundraising, policy development, campaign management, and interacting with lobbyists. Thanks to the constant influx of new members with minimal experience in the legislature, the floor leadership has become increasingly important to the performance of the assembly. Legislative leadership

| Think Again |
What role do partisan Assembly and Senate leaders play in the legislative process?

positions adhere to a pecking order, and assembly members who are chosen to fill these position expect to rise as higher positions become vacant. Fabian Nuñez was chosen by the Speaker Herb Wesson to serve as majority whip soon after entering the assembly, an experience that clearly played a role in his subsequent election to the assembly speaker position.

*Speaker Pro Tempore and Assistant Speaker Pro Tempore*   Appointed by the assembly speaker, the speaker pro tempore presides over floor sessions in the absence of the speaker, and the assistant speaker pro tempore presides over floor sessions in the absence of the speaker and the speaker pro tempore.

*Minority Floor Leader*   Elected by the minority party caucus, the minority floor leader is generally considered the leader of the minority party in the assembly and is responsible for representing the minority party caucus or minority party on the floor of the assembly. To some extent, the minority floor leader is an assembly speaker in wating as the leader of the party in opposition. There is an considerable amount of pressure on the minority floor leader to assist in the reelection of assembly members from the minority party, which in recent years has been the Republican Party. And when the minority party does lose seats, the party caucus has been quick to replace the minority floor leader, a decision that was made at least four times between 1998 and 2001. In March 2001, for example, Assemblyman Bill Campbell had served only four months as assembly minority leader when assembly Republicans voted unanimously to remove him in favor of Assemblyman Dave Cox. Although Cox considered the ouster of Campbell "a family matter," other assembly members quietly complained that he had not been aggressive enough in establishing the Republican caucus's agenda on California's energy crisis.[26]

*Assistant Minority Floor Leader*   The assistant minority floor leader fulfills roles very similar to the assembly majority leadership positions, but with a much smaller membership, as the minority party has limited legislative power. Because of the rapid change in minority floor leaders, however, opportunities for the assistant minority floor leader to assume the top spot are greatly enhanced.

California State Assembly Speaker of the House Herb Wesson and Assembly Minority Leader Dave Cox share a laugh after agreeing on a budget at the State Capitol Building during a marathon State Assembly session.

## PEOPLE IN POLITICS

# The Rapid Rise of Fabian Nuñez

Since the advent of term limits for California legislators, the power and prestige of the assembly speaker has been significantly reduced, now that he or she typically rotates out every two years when that particular legislative officer's term has expired. Once predicated on a majority vote of the membership, the speaker's tenure presently suffers from a tenuous disposition that makes commitments, relationships, and alliances difficult to solidify. Rising rapidly to this transitory leadership position, Fabian Nuñez promises to be a notable exception to the recent line of successive assembly speakers who have mostly disappeared from the main stage of state politics. Assuming the speaker's post at age thirty-six in 2005, the second youngest to hold the job and appearing even younger, Nuñez has already established himself as a paradoxical leader, defying second-guesses about his legislative goals. In fact, his rapid rise to the speaker spot was clouded in controversy over accusation of double-dealing, backstabbing, and outright lies when he vied among three other Democratic assembly members for the top position, causing considerable acrimony within the assembly's Democratic caucus. When the final vote for assembly speaker was taken, Nuñez's age, political savvy, and backroom deals made all the difference. His chances of landing any major legislative leadership position got a huge boost when his predecessor, Herb Wesson, appointed him as the assembly majority whip in his freshman year. Although his lack of experience as a legislative leader and as a legislator in general, not having held any elective office before coming to the assembly, has been the cause of missteps and a credibility gap. Nuñez will not be termed out until 2008, giving him the chance of serving as speaker for an unprecedented five years since term limits were enacted.

Despite his hasty climb to the top, Nuñez grew up in circumstances that were less than ideal. One of twelve siblings, he was born in the United States and later raised in the Logan Heights section of San Diego, although he lived in Tijuana, Mexico, until age eight. Life in San Diego included selling subscriptions for the *San Diego Union-Tribune* newspaper and working as a gardener for the family business as well as honing his skills as a reputed amateur boxing champion. His formal education prepared him to enter Pitzer College in Claremont where he earned a B.A. in political science and education while engaging in political activism and Latino protest politics. Establishing himself in the Los Angeles political landscape through a string of influential positions, such as the political director for the Los Angeles County Federal of Labor from 1996–2000 and later as government affairs director for the Los Angeles Unified School District, Nuñez was first elected to the assembly in

2002, representing the 46th District. Nuñez has been closely associated with labor organizations and issues, exemplified by the long list of financial contributions from labor unions. As a strong supporter of liberalizing laws affecting immigrants, Nuñez backed legislation that would permit illegal immigrants to obtain driver's licenses. The proposed law hurt the standing of the Democrats in the assembly, which was unpopular among many Californians and was ultimately opposed by Governor Schwarzenegger. Notwithstanding a substantial record of "progressive" positions, Nuñez is not unsympathetic to the interests of big business and affluent groups in California. In March 2006, Nuñez made public his intention to introduce a bill that would grant telecommunications companies state-issued franchises, which would bypass current law that requires telecommunications companies to negotiate separate cable franchise agreements with each municipality in California. The telecommunications companies, dominated by AT&T and Verizon, are anxious to roll out $4.4 billion in upgrades of phone lines to high-speed fiber optic lines with the capacity to transmit Internet and video signals faster than DSL, and want to avoid having to conclude individual municipal franchise agreements, which they consider time-consuming, cumbersome, and outdated. Consumer advocates from groups such as the Utility Reform Network are critical of the plan because they fear state-issued franchises will permit the cable companies to concentrate on serving upper-income customers while disregarding middle-to low-income cable customers and will leave local communities with little control over programming and public utility right-of-way issues. Whether Nuñez will become the champion of fiber optics or suffer through accusations of corporate cronyism remains to be seen.

With potentially more time to lead the assembly than recent speakers—if the Democrats can maintain their majority and he can contain any interparty challenges—Fabian Nuñez could use these years to launch a gubernatorial or even congressional campaign. Nuñez will only have reached his early forties when termed out in 2008, much younger than most of the former assembly speakers who quietly slipped out of the state capital scene and into political oblivion. Already quite a different type of Speaker who is clearly on the fast track, it seems that Californians will be hearing about Nuñez for some time.

*Sources:* Official Web site of Fabian Nuñez, California State Assembly; Goldmacher, Shane, "Nuñez to Sponsor Major Cable Deregulation Bill," *Capitol Weekly,* March 23, 2006; Rojas, Aurelio, "Legacy of Respect: Trailblazing Latina activist and lawmaker Nell Soto Going Strong at 80," *Sacramento Bee* Capitol Bureau. Sunday, June 18, 2006, sacbee.com; Kearns, Jeff, "Dems Divided," *Sacramento News and Review,* December 25, 2003, http://www.newsreview.com/sacramento.

*President of the Senate*   The constitution of California designates the lieutenant governor of California as the president of the senate, similar to the position of the vice president of the United States in the U.S. Senate. And like the vice president, the lieutenant governor's role in the state senate is largely ceremonial, with the exception of having the authority to cast a tie-breaking vote. The lieutenant governor may also be invited periodically to preside on ceremonial occasions, such as the opening of the session. The lieutenant governor is elected independent of the governor in statewide elections, slightly enhancing or detracting acknowledgment by the state senate, depending on the majority party. The position of lieutenant governor is often seen as a springboard for election as governor, Gray Davis being the most recent example, and any chance to increase name recognition, including appearances in the state senate, is actively sought.

## Partisan State Senate Leaders

*President Pro Tempore*   The president pro tempore is the actual leader of the state senate, elected by the members at the beginning of each session. As the presiding officer of the senate, the president pro tem, as the position is commonly known, has much less power than the assembly speaker, the natural counterpart of the president pro tem in the assembly. Like the U.S. Senate, the state senate was designed to be more "deliberative" as a result of its smaller number of members, decentralized leadership structure, and longer terms of office. The committee chairpersons in the state senate maintain a large degree of legislative power and are responsible for making critical decisions about bills that pass through their committees.

Whatever leadership power may exist outside the responsibilities of the committee chairs is exercised by the senate's five-member Rules Committee, which has legislative powers that are equivalent to those of the assembly speaker. The power of the president pro tem is based on his or her designation as chair of the Rules Committee. The committee is composed of two senators from each party, who are nominated by their party caucuses and also must receive 21 votes from the full senate. This composition and the powers invested in the Rules Committee causes the senate to be slightly less partisan, and the president pro tem must be much more cautious of backdoor dealing, especially by his or her two fellow party members on the committee. In recent years, the state senate has become increasingly partisan, thanks to the strong leadership styles of former President pro tem David Roberti (who served in this position for almost as long as Willie Brown served as assembly speaker), Bill Lockyer, and John Burton. As a result of the senate power to confirm gubernatorial appointments, the president pro tem has the opportunity to interact much more with the executive branch of state government than any assembly leader and as a result has greater political leverage either within his or her party or with the opposition, depending on the partisan orientation of the governor. There is considerable pressure on the president pro tem, as on the assembly speaker and the assembly leadership, to keep current members in office through assistance with fundraising and campaign management.

*Senate Majority Leader and Majority Whip*   The senate majority leader and whip are chosen by the majority caucus and serve as the main floor managers for the president pro tempore and the majority party, fulfilling responsibilities that are not very different from those of their counterparts in the assembly.

*Senate Minority Leader*   The senate minority leader (also known as the "Republican leader") holds the second most powerful position in the senate. Elected by members of the minority caucus, the senate minority leader speaks for the minority party, maintains party discipline, and interacts with the president pro tempore to

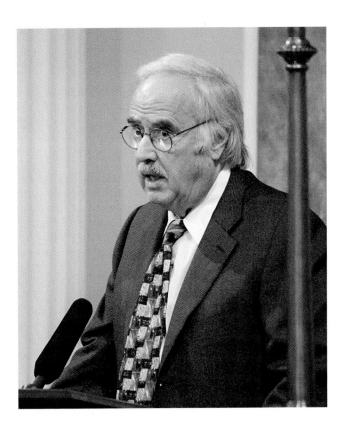

President Pro Tem of the Senate John Burton (D-San Francisco) speaks before California Governor Arnold Schwarzenegger gives his first State address, in the State Assembly Chamber at the State Capitol.

set the senate's order of business. As a member of the Rules Committee, the senate minority leader is in good position to cut deals and take advantage of the decentralized and deliberative nature of the senate. The Republicans have been fortunate to have had a number of strong minority leaders in the past, the most notable being Ross Johnson, who developed a reputation for great intellect, a trait that can be significant in the deliberative senate. Jim Brulte, termed-out as minority leader in 2006, established a tough track record in the assembly and continued in like fashion in the senate.

*Minority Whip*    The minority whip is essentially an assistant to the senate minority leader, who is elected by the minority caucus and helps count potential votes on matters that present particular party concerns.

### Nonmember Officers

*Chief Sergeant-at-Arms*    The chief sergeant-at-arms, elected by the total membership of the senate, is responsible for order on the senate floor and in committees and meetings. The chief sergeant-at-arms works closely with the California Highway Patrol and the assembly security personnel to maintain the security of the capitol and senate offices statewide.

*Chief Clerk and Legislative Secretary*    These positions are nonpartisan and nonmember officers elected by the majority of the membership at the start of each session. The chief clerk serves as a legislative officer and parliamentarian and the secretary as the primary recordkeeper.

## The Legislative Committee System

With between 5,000 and 6,000 bills introduced each legislative session, the committee system is a logical approach to delegating proposed laws of a specific type

# WHAT DO YOU THINK?

## Is California Ready for a Part-Time Legislature?

The idea of a part-time legislature in Sacramento may not mean very much to the average Californian, especially those residents aware of the myriad issues facing the state. "How could the law-making function of the most populous and third-largest state, known for its complexity, possibly operate under a part-time schedule?" some may ask. As weird as this legislative status may sound, however, there are a number of considerations that could compel greater attention to and discussion of this idea, including how well—or not—part-time legislatures work in other states. A full-time legislature is a relatively new feature of government in California history. From 1850 until 1966, the legislature was actually a part-time body. Back in the early sixties, the consensus among legislators, other government officials, and the general public—partly based of the work of a constitutional revisions commission—was that the state had outgrown the legislature's part-time schedule. The full-time legislature would professionalize the work and staff of the legislature, limit special interest influence, produce greater independence among members, and provide more time to consider important issues. Since the switch to a full-time legislature, there has been a growing group of political leaders who question the results of this conversion. Over ten years ago, Tom McClintock, then a former assembly member and director of the Claremont Institute's Golden State Policy Center and currently a state senator, suggested that California should return to part-time legislators: "The shift to a full-time legislature was a well-intentioned experiment that has failed to achieve any of its stated objectives after thirty years. Indeed, in every instance, it has moved the state further away from those objectives."[a] There is naturally some debate over whether the California state legislature has become a more professional body at a time when its popularity has not grown very substantially since the imposition of term limits on state legislators in 1990 with the passage of Proposition 140. Term limits were seen as the cure for a legislature that many thought exhibited numerous symptoms of a dysfunctional law-making institution: gridlock, corruption, careerism, and fiscal irresponsibility. Term limits notwithstanding, similar charges continue to follow the California legislature.

Advocates of a part-time California legislature have been floating the idea for many years now and look to the rest of the nation to support their argument for limiting the amount of time legislators spend in the state's capital. Of the fifty states, only eleven can truly qualify as full-time legislatures. The

national Conference of State Legislatures' standard classification starts with "red states," in which legislators operate on a full-time basis, served by a large staff and paid a competitive salary. In the middle are "white states," hybrids of the full- and part-time legislatures, usually involving somewhat more time than a part-time legislator's schedule, moderate staff size, and pay that is commensurate with the hours on the job. Then there are the "blue states," definitely part-time in all aspects of the legislative office, particularly in the low salary afforded each member. Understandably, the larger states tend to have "red" legislatures and the "blue" states are most often small. The "white" legislatures are a mixed bag, including Hawaii and Texas.

The state of Georgia presents an interesting model for Californians contemplating part-time legislative status. There are numerous contrasts between the two states, considering that Georgia is the twenty-fourth largest in the nation, ranks tenth in total population at 8,186,453, and has an annual state governmental budget of about $18 billion. The positive outcomes of Georgia's part-time legislature do offer some grounds for comparison when examining the results of the full-time California legislature, which most political commentators suggest are less than stellar, the idea being that if they can do that, why can't we? The General Assembly, as the Georgia legislature is known, is composed of a house of representatives consisting of 180 members and a state senate with 56 members, one of the largest state legislatures in nation. This part-time legislature meets for forty days each year for the two-year terms of office for both houses, although the governor can call the general assembly into special session. In 2005, each legislator was paid $16,524 annually and allotted $128 per diem. The Georgia legislature comes very close to the traditional or citizen-legislator model, prescribing regular interaction with constituents to best fulfill the representative function. The Government Performance Project awarded Georgia an overall "B" rating as opposed to the "C–" that California received. Regarded as a competent financial manager, the Georgia state government, largely because of the work of the legislature, has produced balanced budgets and timely financial reports. The legislature passes its budget on time, usually at least one month before the start of its fiscal year. This fiscal attentiveness has resulted in a fully funded pension system and a very high credit ranking for the state. The citizen-legislator model of the Georgia legislature was in full display when it passed laws addressing sex offenders, class-size reduction, denying state services to illegal immigrants, and restrictions on eminent domain during its 2006 session.

In California, Governor Arnold Schwarzenegger has been one of the more vocal advocates of reducing the time California legislators spend in Sacramento. Specifically, the governor is displeased with the

[a]McClintock, Tom, "California Should Return To Part-Time Legislators," *Contra Costa Times*, (Opinion), August 5, 1995.

## Table 1   Red, White, and Blue Legislatures

| Red | Red Light | White | | Blue Light | Blue |
|---|---|---|---|---|---|
| California | Alaska | Alabama | Missouri | Georgia | Montana |
| Michigan | Illinois | Arizona | Nebraska | Idaho | New Hampshire |
| New York | Florida | Arkansas | North Carolina | Indiana | North Dakota |
| Pennsylvania | Ohio | Colorado | Oklahoma | Kansas | South Dakota |
| | Massachusetts | Connecticut | Oregon | Maine | Utah |
| | New Jersey | Delaware | South Carolina | Mississippi | Wyoming |
| | Wisconsin | Hawaii | Tennessee | Nevada | |
| | | Iowa | Texas | New Mexico | |
| | | Kentucky | Virginia | Rhode Island | |
| | | Louisiana | Washington | Vermont | |
| | | Maryland | | West Virginia | |
| | | Minnesota | | | |

## Table 2   Average Job Time, Compensation, and Staff Size by Category of Legislature

| Category of Legislature | Time on the Job (1) | Compensation (2) | Staff per Member (3) |
|---|---|---|---|
| Red | 80% | $68,599 | 8.9 |
| White | 70% | $35,326 | 3.1 |
| Blue | 54% | $15,984 | 1.2 |

*Notes*:

1. Estimated proportion of a full-time job spent on legislative work including time in session, constituent service, interim committee work, and election campaigns.

2. Estimated annual compensation of an average legislator including salary, per diem, and any other unvouchered expense payments.

3. Ratio of total legislative staff to number of legislators.

*Source: NCSL, 2004*

large number of bills, most of which have very little chance of being passed, that are produced by the full-time legislature. Gary Kovall, a legal scholar and fellow at the Rose Institute for State and Local Government, commented in the *California Journal* of August 2004 that "Really, the Legislature is part-time now. They [lawmakers] waste most of the year and cram deadlines and then dump huge, controversial provisions into bills at the eleventh hour."[b] Still, it is hard to argue for a part-time legislature given the sheer size and complexity of law-making issues facing California. Representing some of the biggest state legislative districts in the nation, California legislators must be at least symbolically responsive to large and diverse interests. Kovall proposes limiting the legislative session, "while maintaining a bipartisan interim commission that would make recommendations for legislation, thus giving lawmakers a leg up on worthy bills." There may be very serious and well-thought-out ideas about reducing the time California legislators spend in Sacramento, but any switch to a less than full-time schedule faces numerous barriers, the least of which is generating public attention. The state legislature could lead the effort to change its schedule by putting a revision of the California Constitution on the ballot or approving a constitutional convention charged with tackling this issue. The two-thirds vote that is required for both methods (as well as conventional wisdom) suggests that the legislature will not be tampering with their schedule anytime soon. The part-time legislature could happen as an initiative in the reformist spirit of Proposition 140. Whether it will happen and "part-time" would really be as good for California as it is for the Georgia legislature is an as yet unanswered question.

*Sources:* "Full- and Part-Time Legislatures," NCSL Backgrounder—National Conference of State Legislatures, June, 2004 (updated October, 2005); www.georgiaencyclopedia.org—*Georgia General Assembly*; "Legislator Compensation 2005," NCSL Backgrounder–National Conference of State Legislatures, updated November 1, 2005; 2005 State Report Cards: Georgia State Government, Government Performance Project, http://results.gpponline.org; Bluestein, Greg, "Lawmakers Gavel a Frenzied Election-year Session to its End," Associated Press, April 2, 2006.

[b]Howard, John, "The Part-Time Legislature," *California Journal*, August 2004.

to a small group of legislators who either have the expertise or the interest to determine their merits. As in the U.S. Congress, state legislative committees are where most of the work of the legislature takes place, and they are the proving ground for legislators who aspire to higher leadership or are interested in developing a particular expertise. To a large extent, the committees reflect the vital concerns and wealth of the state, and considering the size and complexity of California, committee work can be extremely important.

**standing committees** The permanent committees of the legislature; also known as *policy committees.*

**Standing Committees**   Standing committees, also known as policy committees, are the permanent committees of the legislature that act as the clearinghouses for bills that are introduced in the legislature and will from time to time handle important action required of the state legislature, executive oversight and confirmations being two of the most obvious. When a legislator is elected, a serious effort is made to appoint that member to several committees that will mirror his or her qualifications and interests. Other factors, such as the legislator's standing in the party and personal idiosyncrasies of the legislative leaders, also influence committee assignments. The size of standing committees varies, depending on the standing rules adopted for each legislative session; they can have as few as seven members or as many as twenty-five. The names of committees may also change from session to session and between chambers, but both chambers generally have committees that address similar areas. Probably the most important type of standing committees are the *fiscal committees,* which review the annual state budget and all other bills that create financial obligations for the state. Although each chamber adjusts the number of standing committees at the start of the legislative session, there are usually approximately twenty-three standing committees in the state senate and twenty-nine committees in the assembly. Each committee is managed by a chairperson who is empowered by the rules of each chamber to maintain order and keep the committee focused. The committee chairs also have a special partisan responsibility to guarantee that the interests of the party in power reported by each bill; bills that do not pass muster are "killed" in committee. One of the most important powers of most committee chairs is the ability to set the agenda for committee meetings, thereby focusing attention on

---

**Table 17.2   State Senate Standing Committees**

| | |
|---|---|
| Agriculture | Health |
| Appropriations | Human Services |
| Banking, Finance and Insurance | Judiciary |
| Budget and Fiscal Review | Labor and Industrial Relations |
| Business, Professions and Economic Development | Local Government |
| Education | Natural Resources and Water |
| Elections, Reapportionment and Constitutional Amendments | Public Employment and Retirement |
| | Public Safety |
| Energy, Utilities and Communications | Revenue and Texation |
| Environmental Quality | Rules |
| Governmental Organization | Transportation and Housing |
| Government Modernization, Efficiency and Accountability | Veterans Affairs |

*Source:* California State Senate.

certain issues and downplaying or ignoring others. The scope of many standing committees is so wide-ranging as to necessitate the creation of subcommittees to address one portion of a broader issue, service, or problem. Members from the parent standing committee serve on the subcommittees. The work of the standing committees largely consists of gathering information about a particular bill to determine if it is worthy of a vote by the assembly or state senate, correcting perceived problems through an amendment process, or simply preventing the bill from advancing to the full body. The information-gathering process is conducted partly by a committee support staff and partly through the hearing process. During the hearing process, a variety of supporters, detractors, and neutral experts will provide testimony on the merits of a bill. Committee hearings permit interested parties to give their views concerning a particular bill. The hearings also place the legislators in the public eye, allowing them the opportunity to appear competent and knowledgeable as well as to increase their standing with the constituents in their home districts. To handle "juice" bills that are introduced, legislators have applied a special recognition to certain committees that attract the attention of generous special-interest groups that seek to influence proposed laws. These "juice" committees are sought after by legislators, who see them as a means of generating the ever-important campaign contributions.

### Select Committees

**Select committees** are temporary committees formed to conduct investigations of issues or problems that either not specifically related to a standing committee or that is of special interest to a legislator. These committees do not handle or create legislation and at best will generate a report that could be the basis for a bill. In recent years, a deluge of select committees have been set up in both chambers, some by legislators who are sincerely concerned about a specific problem and others by legislators who use the select committee to grab media attention through high-profile hearings and enhance their legislative résumé. At last count, there were thirty-four select committees in each chamber, addressing such matters as the health insurance crisis and the West Nile virus.

**select committees**
Temporary committees formed to conduct investigations of issues or problems that are either not specifically related to a standing committee or of special interest to a legislator.

### Conference Committees

**Conference committees** are based on the constitutional provision that requires a bill to be passed in both legislative bodies before it can become law. The conference committee is charged with the task of reconciling any differences that may arise between the two different versions of a bill. Composed of three members of each chamber, the conference committee becomes significant when the two chambers are controlled by different political parties. Otherwise, chances are that any differences between the two versions of a bill are worked out by the partisan leadership of both chambers long before it reaches the conference committee stage.

**conference committees**
Committees charged with the task of reconciling any differences that may arise between two different versions of a bill.

### Joint Committees

There are six **joint committees** in the state legislature that are intended to facilitate the work of the legislature by bringing together equal numbers of legislators from both chambers to address specific issues and policy areas. Although joint committees do not usually review proposed laws, they do provide an important forum for the entire legislature to attempt to reach a consensus and present a unified voice to the public on important matters. Two of the more noteworthy joint committees are the Joint Legislative Budget Committee and the Joint Rules Committee.

**joint committees**
Committees that bring together equal numbers of legislators from both chambers to address specific issues and policy areas.

### Rules Committees

Each chamber has a **rules committee**. The five-member Rules Committee of the state senate is considered to be the executive committee of the Senate, with the authority to assign senators to committees, appoint committee chairs, refer bills, assign office space and support staff, and set the overall

**rules committees**
Committees charged with the administration of the legislature and defining the rules of its operation.

## Table 17.3   Assembly Standing Committees

Committee on Aging and Long-Term Care
Committee on Agriculture
Committee on Appropriations
Committee on Arts, Entertainment, Sports, Tourism, and Internet Media
Committee on Banking and Finance
Committee on Budget
Committee on Business and Professions
Committee on Education
Committee on Elections and Redistricting
Committee on Environmental Safety and Toxic Materials
Committee on Governmental Organization
Committee on Health
Committee on Higher Education
Committee on Housing and Community Development
Committee on Human Services
Committee on Insurance
Committee on Jobs, Economic Development, and the Economy
Committee on Judiciary
Committee on Labor and Employment
Committee on Local Government
Committee on Natural Resources
Committee on Public Employees, Retirement and Social Security
Committee on Public Safety
Committee on Revenue and Taxation
Committee on Rules
Committee on Transportation
Committee on Utilities and Commerce
Committee on Veterans Affairs
Committee on Water, Parks and Wildlife

*Source:* California State Assembly.

policy direction of the senate. The authority of the state senate president pro tempore is derived from his or her position as the chair of this committee.

The assembly Rules Committee is chaired by the assembly speaker or the speaker's appointee and is responsible for selecting and supervising assembly support staff. Its administrative responsibilities include overseeing the finances of the assembly and proposing changes in house rules.

## The Legislative Process

After a bill has been introduced into either chamber by its author, it is numbered and referred to a committee. To allow members of the public and the press to become informed about a specific proposal, no committee action may take place until a bill has been in print for thirty days. The members of the committee may recommend approval of a bill and send it to the chamber floor without alteration, may suggest modifications to a bill and recommend that it be passed on the floor as amended, or may allow a bill to die in committee. The great majority of bills that fail to be enacted into law are killed in committee. The reality of passing a bill is complicated and generally hidden from public view (see Table 17.4).

> ┤Think Again├
>
> How does the reality of the passage of bills in California differ from the formal process?

**Table 17.4    Key Terms In California Legislative Procedure**

**Across the Desk**

The official act of introducing a bill, resolution, or proposed amendment. The measure receives a number and becomes a public document.

**Adjournment Sine Die**

Final adjournment of the legislature; regular sessions of the legislature, and any special session not previously adjourned, are adjourned sine die at midnight on November 30 of each even-numbered year.

**Call of the House**

On motion from the floor to place a call of the house, the presiding officer directs the Sergeant-at-Arms to lock the chambers and bring in the absent members (by arrest, if necessary) to vote on a measure under consideration. Action is not taken on an item under call until the call is lifted, at which time it must be immediately voted on.

**Chapter**

When a bill has been passed by the Legislature and enacted into law, the Secretary of State assigns the bill a "chapter number" such as "Chapter 123, Statutes of 1992," which is subsequently used to refer to the measure in place of the bill number.

**Committee of the Whole**

The Assembly or Senate meeting as a committee for the purpose of receiving information.

**Daily Journal**

Produced by the Assembly and Senate respectively the day after a floor session. Contains roll call votes on bills heard in policy committees and bills considered on the floor, and other official action taken by the body. Any official messages from the Governor are also included. A member may seek approval to publish a letter in the Journal on a specific legislative matter. At the end of a legislative session, the Journals are bound.

**First Reading**

Each bill introduced must be read three times before final passage. The first reading of a bill occurs when it is introduced.

**Motion**

A formal proposal for action made by a legislator during a committee hearing or floor session.

**Quorum**

A simple majority of the membership of a committee or the Assembly or Senate; the minimum number of legislators needed to begin conducting official business. The absence of a quorum is grounds for immediate adjournment of a committee hearing or floor session.

*Source:* Adapted from Senate Select Committee on Citizen Participation in Government. *The Legislative Process: A Citizens Guide to Participation,* pp. 18–31.

# The Hidden View of Lawmaking

The state capitol building is no more secure than the typical government building, and most hearings and legislative offices are open to the public. There are various written records of legislative work and proceedings, not to mention daily newspapers, that most Californians assume will preserve the free and open ideal of representative democracy. Yet in the state capitol, all too often the dysfunction and disappointments that many people associate with the legislative process are not necessarily hidden by backroom deals or shadowy figures but are shrouded by a process that is manipulated beyond the point of comprehension or even recognition. And therein lies the problem: How can Californians fix or reform a process that is convoluted and obscure? Not many years ago, a bill was proposed in the state legislature that provides a good example of the manipulation of the legislative process and a starting point in understanding what needs to be fixed. The proposed bill would allow insurance companies to give discounts to drivers who had no gaps in their automobile coverage. The argument of the bill's backers inside as well as outside the state legislature was that if you stayed with your insurance company for a period of time, you should be entitled to a discount. Consumer advocates for the insurance industry, who had supported Proposition 103, the 1988 insurance reform initiative, pointed out that the law prohibited companies from discriminating against uninsured motorists who wanted to get coverage. The consumer advocate also found that people in the military and new drivers, through no fault of their own, would have gaps in their auto insurance coverage and would pay what the advocates thought would be an unfair higher rate.[27] The advocate's view prevailed in the standing committee where the bill was originally sent, which stalled consideration of the bill in the hope that it would die there. Meanwhile, the insurance lobbyists for a large insurance company that had contributed at least $1 million to the politicians in Sacramento, $25,000 of which had gone to the bill's author, were putting pressure on the legislative leaders to intervene. First, using his "fast track" powers, the presiding officer of the legislative body referred the insurance bill ahead of all others bills to a particular committee unrelated to the insurance industry. That unrelated committee, led by the committee chairperson at the direction of the presiding officer, engaged in the "gut and amend" tactic. This legislative tactic involves taking out the contents of an unrelated bill, which in this case would have expanded prostate cancer research, and inserting the language of the insurance bill. Any attempt to hold hearings on the bill were subjected to repeated postponements until the last seventy-two hours of the session. At 8:30 A.M. on a Saturday, the unrelated committee held an obligatory fifteen-minute hearing before unanimously voting to pass the bill on to the full chamber. Once on the floor of both chambers, the bill was passed into law.[28]

# Summary Notes

- Academics and journalists alike typically describe the passage of Proposition 140 in 1990, a constitutional initiative limiting the terms of office for California state legislators, as a reaction to the unsavory opinion that many California residents have regarding the state legislature. Despite that effort to eliminate career politicians beholden to special interest groups, a "third house" has emerged in California legislative politics, consisting of lobbyists and other representatives seeking to influence legislators.

- Embracing the prevailing minimalist notions of government, the original mining and merchant interests that dominated early California created a state government at the first state constitutional convention that was prone to party machine politics and corruption. The Progressives sought to limit the political power of the legislative body, particularly as an instrument for special interests and political parties.

- In 1966, the state legislature was professionalized, instituting a full-time schedule, increased compensation, and conflict-of-interest restrictions. By 1971, California was judged to have one of the best legislatures in the United States.

- Major corruption scandals in the 1980s and 1990s that ensnared state legislators in FBI undercover sting operations caused tremendous embarrassment. Amid the accusation of impropriety, the state legislature grew increasingly partisan, partly due to the emergence of divided government with successive Republican governors and a Democrat-controlled legislature.

- Candidates for the state legislature must be U.S. citizens, 18 years of age or older who have lived in California for three years and in a legislative district for one year immediately before the election for that office. Candidates for the state legislature typically have had experience working as local elected officers, staff members for a state legislator or state political party organization, or in various positions in law, journalism, education, or law enforcement.

■ The reelection rate for California state legislators has been well over 90 percent, and a large number of assembly members will later win election to the state senate. The real electoral contests for legislative seats usually take place during the state primary campaigns and elections.

■ The state legislature is largely self-governing, almost totally independent from any other public or private authority. Standing rules in both chambers ensure that the legislature operates in an efficient and civil manner.

■ All laws must be passed by a majority in both chambers, and most take effect on January 1 of the following year. Any constitutional amendment proposed by the state legislature must be approved by a two-thirds vote in both chambers and then ratified by a majority of the voters.

■ The most important aspect of the lawmaking function is the passage of the annual state budget, which is essentially treated as a bill. The budget process begins with the governor, who prepares the annual budget and must submit it to both chambers of the legislature by January 10. After receipt and introduction in both chambers, the annual budget is referred to the Senate Budget and Fiscal Review Committee and the Assembly Budget Committee. Following passage by both chambers, any differences between the assembly and senate versions of the budget are worked out in a conference committee.

■ California legislators have adopted various methods of representation in response to the wide-ranging conditions in California, but the one universal and most basic approach to representation is known as casework. Representation may be based on geographic conditions, social or cultural background of constituents, specific policy issues, or personal interests.

■ State legislators are also responsible for overseeing the implementation of all laws as they were originally intended and the government officials who are charged with implementing them. Certain constitutional powers granted to the state legislature to oversee the shaping of the annual state budget, the conduct public hearings, and the impeachment and removal of elected officials.

■ The Democratic and Republican Parties have the two main legislative party caucuses in each of the chambers. The most important tasks of the caucuses are to elect legislative leaders, set policy goals, and support the election of fellow legislators.

■ The assembly speaker is very powerful and is responsible for maintaining order during the formal sessions of the assembly. One of the main functions of all legislative leaders outside of the legislative process is to help assembly members from their own party win reelection.

■ The California constitution designates the lieutenant governor as the president of the senate. The president pro tempore is the actual leader of the senate, elected by the members at the beginning of each session. The president pro tem's true power is realized as the chair of the five-member senate Rules Committee, which has powers. The senate majority leader is the second-most powerful person in the senate.

■ Most of the work of the legislature takes place in legislative committees. Standing committees are the permanent committees of the legislature. There are six joint committees in the state legislature that are intended to address specific issues and policy areas. Both chambers have rules committees, which issue rules on how bills will be treated, and conduct the executive functions of each chamber.

# Key Terms

| | | | |
|---|---|---|---|
| Proposition 140  586 | redistricting  590 | casework  599 | select committees  613 |
| "Third House"  586 | standing rules  593 | oversight function  600 | conference committee  613 |
| Constitutional Revision | joint rules  593 | party caucus  602 | joint committees  613 |
| Commission  587 | "juice bills"  594 | assembly speaker  603 | rules committees  613 |
| reapportionment  590 | resolutions  598 | standing committees  612 | |

# Suggested Readings

Beek, Joseph Allan. *The California Legislature.* Sacramento: California Office of State Printing, 1980.

Block, A.G., and Claudia Buck, eds. *1999–2000 California Political Almanac.* 6th ed. California, 1999.

Jacobs, John. *A Rage for Justice: The Passion and Politics of Phil Burton.* Berkeley: University of California Press, 1995.

Michael, Jay, Dan Walters, and Dan Weintraub. *The Third House: Lobbyist, Money, and Power in Sacramento.* Berkeley:

Public Policy Press, Institute of Governmental Studies, University of California, 2002.

Mills, James R. *A Disorderly House: The Brown–Unruh Years in Sacramento.* Berkeley: Heyday Books, 1987.

Richardson, James. *Willie Brown.* Berkeley: University of California Press, 1996.

Samish, Arthur H., and Bob Thomas. *The Secret Boss of California: The Life and High Times of Art Samish.* New York: Crown, 1971.

# 18 THE CALIFORNIA EXECUTIVE AND BUREAUCRACY

### Chapter Outline

- Governor: Supreme Executive Authority
- Becoming Governor
- The California Plural Executive

## Introduction

The legislature can make laws that shape and influence life in California, and the state judiciary will enforce compliance with those laws, but it is the state's executive branch that is responsible for governing the Golden State, and a number of performance reviews indicate that the California state government has not done so well. The Government Performance Project, a 2005 research project that evaluated and graded all fifty states in four areas—how well they managed the money, people, infrastructure, and information of the state government—concluded that California merited an overall grade of C–[1]. The only other C– in the study was given to the state of Alabama. Of the four areas of evaluation, considered essential to successfully implementing executive functions, the management of money was deemed the most problematic for California. Management of state revenues suffered from low credit ratings, an underfunded state pension system, chaotic state purchasing systems, inadequate financial controls and reporting systems, and insufficient revenue sources. The people or personnel aspects that contribute to the state's low grade suffer from the absence of centralized workforce planning and training programs. The report discovered that hiring for state jobs had been frozen, recruitment activities were "fragmented, sporadic and reactive," and one-fifth of all state workers were employed under expired labor contracts. One good sign was the below-average number of employee grievances among California state workers. The project report commended the California Department of Transportation (referred to in the report as the DOT and also known in California as Caltrans) for innovative highway management systems but criticized the overall management of the state infrastructure (for example, state buildings) in California. The report found inconclusive measurements of infrastructural needs and the siphoning of maintenance funds to support operating requirements. Commending most individual state agencies for the compiling information on performance, the project report was critical of the state government's reluctance to use this information for state budgeting purposes. Residents of California can easily access information regarding state services and programs on the Internet, including vehicle registrations, voter registration, downloading income tax forms, and applying for unemployment benefits, but most transactions with state government involving, for example, renewing driver's licenses, filing business sales tax, or applying for food stamps or Medicaid have to be completed offline. A great deal of the project's findings were confirmed by the California Performance Review, a four-volume report produced by key California government officials and industry representatives that made roughly 1,200 individual recommendations covering 280 issue areas.

**619**

Many Californians will attest to a comfortable life regardless of inadequate government performance. Others might suggest that superior accomplishments in various sectors of the state economy and social system are realized either in spite of or as the result of ineffective state government. Californians have grown accustomed to the reputation of the state as a mecca of sorts for innovation, wealth, and natural beauty, but there are indications that this reputation is gradually being eroded by the increasing inability of the executive branch to effectively carry out the laws and regulations of the state government. This erosion is too often evident in the simplest of services, perhaps a government office under-staffed at lunch hour, or in the long-term consequences of overcrowded prisons. Even more than providing the framework to better understanding the powers and duties of the executive, ideally, this chapter will encourage an ongoing and informed assessment of the state government in California as well as the development of effective methods to more competently and resourcefully serve the residents of this state.

## Governor: Supreme Executive Authority

Any understanding of the **executive branch** of California's government is based first and foremost on the role of the **governor**, who according to the California constitution is vested with "supreme executive power" to ensure that the laws of the state are faithfully executed. As a result of this power, the governor usually attracts the most blame when problems arise and not much praise when things are going well. Field poll trends of job performance ratings for California governors since 1959 report approval ratings for five of the last seven governors below 40 percent at some point while in office. Only Ronald Reagan and George Deukmejian consistently had the approval of a majority of Californians.[2]

The concentration of power within the office of governor in California is not the case in other states. For example, in Texas, the governor's power is severely curtailed, and the office is something of a part-time job. In California, the governor has the authority to affect the operations of the state government. The constitution of California identifies the governor as the sole official representative in communication between the state and federal governments and other states of the United States. Over the years, successive California governors have used this authority to further strengthen this position with formal and informal powers that affect all branches of government. Hiram Johnson, the Progressive governor of California at the turn of the twentieth century, was the chief architect and promoter of sweeping changes made to the duties of governor as well as the structure of state government.

The state legislature receives the governor's spending plan for the state, which it treats as a proposed law. Whatever changes are made after passage can be subjected to further changes by the governor's use of **line-veto powers**, allowing for the elimination or reduction of all or part of the state budget. The governor also has the power to call the state legislature into special session for a specific purpose. When called into an **extraordinary session**, the state legislature cannot take up any legislative matter other than the one specified by the governor. Early in his term, Gray Davis called an extraordinary session of the legislature to address education, but such sessions usually fall short of producing any meaningful legislation. At the beginning of each year and legislative session, the governor is expected to present a "State of the State" address, informing the legislature of the conditions of the state and recommending a course of legislative action. All proposed laws that are passed by the legislature are subject to approval or veto by the governor. That veto can be overridden by the state legislature by a two-

---

— Think Again —

What are the consequences of the concentration of power in the hands of the governor in California?

**executive branch** Branch of government responsible for carrying out laws.

**governor** Supreme executive of a state vested with the power to ensure that the state's laws are carried out.

George Deukmejian was sworn into office as California's 35th governor on January 3, 1983.

## Table 18.1  Functions of Government

All levels of government in California carry out a variety of tasks, but the vast majority of those responsibilities can be narrowed down to one or more of the following functions.

*Direct services:* Local government provides most of the direct services to residents of California. Although the state does deliver certain large-scale services, it is most concerned with monitoring funding allocations and actual implementation.

*Financing:* The distribution of funds is the one of the most typical functions of government, often to private agencies, subcontractors or community-based levels of government.

*Regulations:* As modern society evolves, there is a constant need to regulate human behavior and development. Establishing rules and standards can be extremely effective, especially when government officials are knowledgeable of the regulated area or very unpopular if applied haphazard or randomly.

*Purchasing:* Government procurement of goods and services is a function that has traditionally involved abuse and corrupt acts by private industry and government officials alike. Government purchases are vital to the delivery of public services and make major contributions to the state and local economies.

*Resource transfers:* There are a myriad of ways that government can transfer resources and just about as many reasons for such actions. Subsidies are one of the more common ways that government can transfer resources. Government official must, however, proceed with caution as resource transfers can result in financial loss for the taxpayers.

*Source:* Little Hoover Commission, "Historic Opportunities: Transforming California State Government."

thirds vote in both legislative chambers. Informally, the governor can threaten or actually use the initiative process, as Governor Schwarzenegger successfully did in 2004, to circumvent the legislative function of the state legislature. A popular governor can be an effective tool in promoting an initiative campaign.

The power of the California chief executive over the state judiciary begins with the authority to appoint judges and state supreme court justices to fill vacancies before they are confirmed by subsequent elections and to fill newly created judgeships. The outcome of any trial in California, with the exception of impeachments, can be altered through the governor's **clemency powers**—the right to grant pardons, commutation of sentences, and reprieves. Any use of clemency powers has to be reported to the state legislature. In circumstances pertaining to fugitives from justice under the laws of another state, it is the responsibility of the governor to order extradition. Other law enforcement powers allow the governor to offer rewards, not exceeding $50,000, for information leading to the arrest and conviction of suspects for certain crimes. There is a very good possibility that a governor who serves two terms will appoint a fair number of judges and probably a few justices to the appellate or supreme court, giving the governor the power to influence the political or judicial philosophy of certain courts. The conservative majorities on the California supreme court during the 1980s and 1990s tended to favor the conservative or Republican perspective on laws and initiatives.

As the chief executive officer of the state government, the governor is directly responsible for a vast state bureaucracy and can appoint thousands of people as department and agency heads or to other influential government posts. The nucleus or control center of the governor's authority is his office, staffed by a wide range of professionals who either facilitate communications and relations with other parts of government or act as advisers on critical matters and policy. Probably one of the most important members in the Office of the Governor is

**line-veto power** The power to veto individual items in a larger law.

**extraordinary session** A special session of the state legislature called by the governor for a specific purpose.

**clemency powers** The right to pardon or commute the sentences of convicted persons.

Governor Ronald Reagan greets a large crowd of enthusiastic supporters gathered at Leisure World, a retirement community.

the chief of staff, who is expected to manage the day-to-day operations of that office as well as serve as the governor's closest adviser. Other major areas of the Office of the Governor are constituent affairs, communications, appointments, legal affairs, legislative affairs, policy development, the first lady's office, scheduling, and protocol. In addition to the governor's immediate staff, there are a number of offices, such as the state Office of Emergency, Office of Planning and Research, and Military Department, that carry out specific functions and are usually independent of other parts of the California state government and are administered by or report directly to the governor or his office. (See Table 18.2.)

The governor has direct authority over eleven major departments and agencies (Department of Food and Agriculture; Labor and Workforce Development Agency; Business, Transportation and Housing Agency; Department of Education; Environmental Protection Agency; Health and Human Services Agency; Department of Finance; Resources Agency; Department of Veterans Affairs; State and Consumer Services; and Department of Corrections and Rehabilitation), which implement the policies of the governor through the statutory mandates of the department or agency. Most of these departments and agencies have between four and thirteen subareas that are responsible for one aspect of the overall mission of the department or agency. For example, the California Highway Patrol is one of twelve subdepartments, offices, agencies, and programs within the California Business, Transportation and Housing Agency. The one exception is the secretary of education, a position that has no real authority over the Department of Education and serves in an advisory role to the governor. Each of these eleven departments and agencies is headed by a secretary, who collectively form the governor's cabinet.

The governor may also choose to reorganize departments and agencies of the state executive branch by expanding, consolidating, or eliminating aspects of the state bureaucracy with the consent of the state legislature. Although the plural executive offices (described later in this chapter) are chosen by election, the governor can fill unexpired terms of such offices upon confirmation by the legislature. Constitutional provisions designate the governor as commander in chief of the

**Table 18.2   Managerial Ranks**

*Political appointees.*  The State employs 3,370 political appointees who are exempt from the civil service system. Not all political appointees are managers.

*Career Executive Assignments (CEA).* The CEA position is a senior management position that confers exempt status—like political appointees—on persons from within the civil service system. In 2004 there were 1,224 CEAs in state service.

*Management classifications.* Select state jobs are classified—or defined—as managers. Management positions are part of the civil service system, but not covered under the collective bargaining process. In 2004 there were 2,813 state employees designated as managers.

*Supervisory classifications.*  Like managers, state supervisors have civil service protections, but are not part of the bargaining process. In 2004 there were 23,610 state supervisors.

*Resource transfers:* There are a myriad of ways that government can transfer resources and just about as many reasons for such actions.  Subsidies are one of the more common ways that government can transfer resources. Government officials must, however, proceed with caution as resource transfers can result in financial loss for the taxpayers.

*Source:* Liale Hoover Commission.

---

California National Guard with the authority to activate the National Guard during periods of state emergency. In the attempt to exert the authority of the office over the state government, the governor also has the prerogative to issue executive orders. In 2001, for example, Governor Gray Davis issued executive order D-23-01, which required that the Independent System Operator (ISO), the state energy regulatory agency, take certain steps to address the California energy crisis.

# Citizen-Governor Persona

Despite the perhaps less-than-stellar reputations that both Reagan and Schwarzenegger had prior to running for governor, each campaigned on the notion that they were not career politicians but represented the interests of common citizens who were fed up with entrenched government and run-of-the-mill politicians. Although Reagan had been identified with right-wing political views, during his campaign he moved to the center and focused on making commonsense sound bites that emphasized a "business approach to government" and the value of "work ethics." This approach resonated with voters who had grown wary of the radicalism and cultural revolution of the late 1960s that had caused so many difficulties for the incumbent governor, Edmund "Pat" Brown. In 2003, faced with an energy crisis and a series of other problems, voters had again lost faith with the typical model of Californian politician, and Schwarzenegger typified change not so much in what he said as in his desire as a Californian to make things better, and his credentials as a successful bodybuilder, businessman, and actor made people feel he could indeed lead the state in a new direction. Unlike the career politician, these credentials were characteristics that the average Californian actually admired.

# Humble Background

As candidates, both Reagan and Schwarzenegger would generate wide personal appeal for having emerged from humble beginnings. Each could claim to be a self-made man, without the benefits enjoyed by many traditional politicians who either came from wealthy families or owed their success to some benefactor or political party association. It was well known that Reagan's father was an alcoholic and that young Ronald worked his way up through the Hollywood ranks, starting as a sports announcer. Schwarzenegger, the son of an Austrian police officer, fit the classic model of immigrants in the American melting pot, working hard and eventually integrating themselves into mainstream American society.

## Partner Wife

A large number of Californians, like other Americans, continue to adhere to the notion that behind (or next to) every strong leader is a strong women, and indeed, a strong and visible partner can often take the heat off a politician who may run into difficult situations. In her role as the prospective first lady to candidate Reagan, Nancy Reagan had the ability to convey the lifelong partner ideal, a sense of class, and the importance of the traditional family structure. As a former actor herself, she got just enough attention to project these qualities to a wide public audience. For Ronald Reagan, Nancy served to humanize his gubernatorial campaign, which at times suffered from his often aloof and scripted appearance. In recent years, political aides and associates have revealed that Nancy Reagan's role was far greater than most people realized and that in addition to shielding the governor from difficult situations and individuals, she often provided her husband with important political advice. Arnold Schwarzenegger's wife, Maria Shriver, although significantly different from Nancy Reagan, has nonetheless been an asset to the current governor. Her liberal credentials as a Kennedy clan member undoubtedly brought over a number of Democratic fence-sitters in the recall campaign. As the image of a supportive and loving wife, Shriver was extremely important in dispelling various charges regarding inappropriate sexual conduct against her husband. Schwarzenegger's macho and at times chauvinistic persona, cultivated during his acting career, is significantly moderated by Shriver, whose feminine poise was honed in her career in broadcast journalism.

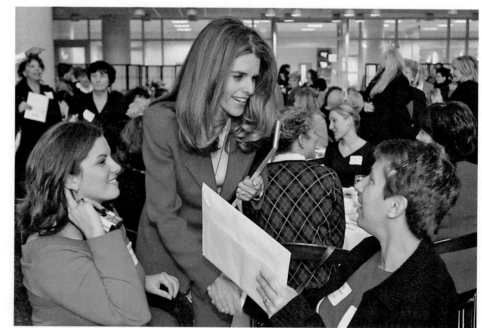

Maria Shriver, wife of Governor Arnold Schwarzenegger, introduces herself to Mary Davenport, a member of the Best Buddies program, during a luncheon held in Shriver's honor. Shriver spoke about her family, her job, and her commitment to volunteerism. Best Buddies is a program founded by a member of Shriver's family to help the developmentally disabled.

# A Nonpublic Side

Both Reagan and Schwarzenegger are know to have "other sides" that in Reagan's case never fully emerged to hurt what would prove to be a relatively successful career in politics. Reagan's personal views reflected a far-right-wing conservatism. An early supporter of Barry Goldwater, the archconservative who was regarded as fanatical by many Americans during his presidential campaign against Lyndon Johnson in 1964, Reagan clearly was not eager to display those tendencies when running for governor of California. Some political insiders and others who had the opportunity to interact with Reagan also suggest that he was not a knowledgeable executive leader, another feature of his personality that was never a liability due to a tendency toward aloofness and a talent for public speaking. Schwarzenegger, for his part, has many miles to travel in his political career, and he too has "baggage." Having overcome rumors of inappropriate sexual conduct as a younger man, there have also been implications that his business dealings could present conflict-of-interest issues for him as governor. One such conflict arose from a relationship that Schwarzenegger had with *Muscle & Fitness* magazine, which advertises nutritional supplements, and his veto of a bill that would have placed certain prohibitions on these supplements. It may serve Arnold well in the future to take a few pages from the Reagan playbook and rely a bit more on his advisers and Maria.

**Party Leadership and State Spokesperson**   The governor is generally assumed by the public to be leader of his or her political party as a result of the partisan nature of the office as well as its visibility and influence. Aware of the immense power of the governor over state government, fellow political party members readily defer to the leadership of this office on partisan matters and policies. There is no formal way the governor can control the party organization, and there are always subtle disagreements that occur between fellow party members in the state legislature. A majority of California Democrats, both inside and outside state government, were not content with Governor Davis's pro–capital punishment stance, and fiscally conservative Republicans in the state legislature have publicly taken issue with the moderate budget proposals of Governor Schwarzenegger. Having the Office of the Governor and the state legislature controlled by the same party does tend to make it easier to carry out the duties of state government. Difficulties that occur in passing a state budget under divided government, for example, rarely arise when the executive and legislative branches are of the same party. Elected as the one statewide official representing the entire state government, the governor retains the ceremonial role as head of state. In this role, the governor performs perfunctory duties that might include ribbon-cutting gatherings or appearing at public celebrations, which can be extremely important in shaping public opinion or promoting policy goals. As the one state government figure that most Californians can identify, the position as spokesperson for the state can be extremely important. Many political insiders attribute Ronald Reagan's popularity and high approval rating as governor less to his policy achievements than to his effectiveness as a public speaker. This role does have it difficulties, however, if the governor has not had a successful policy agenda and is not well received by the public. Facing such a predicament, Gray Davis saw his approval rating drop from a high of 62 percent during his first year in office to 22 percent, the lowest rating on record, when he was finally recalled.[3]

# Becoming Governor

The importance and power of the office of governor of California attracts highly qualified candidates to a usually very competitive election. In addition to acquiring the enormous resources required of most high-stakes elections in California, successful gubernatorial candidates either have expertise in the management of state governmental affairs or a charismatic personality that appeals to a broad range of Californians. Before running for governor, however, the candidate must meet very basic qualifications. All candidates must be citizens of the United States, registered voters, 18 years of age or older, and residents of California for at least five years immediately preceding the election. The term of office for the governor of California is four years beginning on the Monday after January 1 following the election and is limited to two terms.

The election for governor begins with the primary election in June. In recent years, candidates for office have usually had experience in government, either as mayor of a large metropolitan city, or as attorney general or lieutenant governor, but it has been very rare for members of the state legislature to win the nomination. The ability to raise large amounts of campaign contributions has been an even more important factor in the race for governor. Since the election of Ronald Reagan in 1966, television has become the main campaign vehicle for this statewide office, offering candidates statewide access to potential voters, and television advertising is very expensive. During the 1998 Democratic gubernatorial primary, corporate executive Al Checchi and Congresswomen Jane Harman together spent more than $50 million, and Gray Davis added roughly $9 million in campaign spending.[4] Six months into his first term in office, Governor Davis had raised over $6.1 million for his reelection campaign, breaking campaign contribution records until the recall election, after which Governor Schwarzenegger accumulated of approximately $26.6 million by the end of his first year in office.[5] Since the election of Hiram Johnson in 1911, more than twice as many Republicans as Democrats have served as governor. In the past half-century, the general election for governor has been quite competitive, with only two exceptions: the election of

Arianna Huffington ran for governor as an Independent candidate. She fought to get special interest money out of politics and filed papers with the California Attorney General for an initiative for public financing of elections.

# PEOPLE IN POLITICS

## Susan Kennedy: Democrat Joins Schwarzenegger Republicans

Sacramento insiders are not sure how long the relationship will last, but when Governor Arnold Schwarzenegger hired Susan Kennedy as his chief of staff, he continued his habit of bewildering—as well as angering—a lot of politicians and state government bureaucrats from both parties. At forty-five, Kennedy assumed the role of chief of staff after spending most of her political career aligned with the Democratic Party, either in high-level government positions or as a top party official. Chosen to be deputy chief of staff and cabinet secretary by former Governor Gray Davis, she demonstrated an acute administrative ability as the governor's principal liaison with over 100 state agencies, departments, boards, and commissions and in the coordination of major policies, including the development of the $100 billion state budget. Proving her mettle during the California energy crisis, Kennedy organized the activities of more than a dozen state agencies that succeeded in generating more than 1,300 megawatts of additional power while directing "Flex Your Power," considered one of the most successful energy conservation campaigns ever conducted. Kennedy's political experience extends to the Washington, D.C., beltway, where she served as the Communications Director for U.S. Senator Dianne Feinstein, handling a wide range of duties that included the development of legislation and policy initiatives, media relations, and community outreach. In 1992, Kennedy was chosen as the executive director of the California Democratic Party, winning high marks for her management of dynamic Get Out the Vote campaigns, which were extremely important in the election of Feinstein and Barbara Boxer to the U.S. Senate. In her last position before joining the Schwarzenegger administration, Kennedy was one of four commissioners on the California Public Utilities Commission (CPUC). Appointed by former governor Davis, she developed a pro-industry reputation that has been severely criticized by many consumer groups. In fact, her positions on a number of key decisions by the CPUC was likely a key factor in her recruitment by Schwarzenegger.

Early in 2004, the CPUC had approved a Telecommunications Consumer Bill of Rights. One year later, over the objections of the California attorney general, every state district attorney, and a slew of consumer advocates, the bill of rights was suspended at the insistence of Kennedy, who contended that they would impose an unreasonable burden and restrictions on the wireless industry, despite a stream of complaints alleging false advertising and fraudulent business practices. In supporting the merger of telecommunications giants AT&T and SBC, Kennedy would again be denounced by industry watchdogs who felt the merger circumvented CPUC regulations. Controversy is nothing new to Kennedy, who endured unflattering scrutiny during an episode in the Davis administration that involved the approval of a contract between the state government and the Oracle Corporation, which was followed by a $25,000 donation from the software company to Governor Davis. The multi million-dollar contract, which was eventually canceled, and the subsequent donation caused suspicions of wrongdoing that were traced back to Kennedy, who had signed the memo approving the Oracle deal.

Controversy aside, the selection of Kennedy offered Governor Schwarzenegger yet another opportunity to display his skill in neutralizing his opposition with unpredictable acts or policies, for example, the hype surrounding whether he would really run in the recall campaign or labeling Democrats "girlie men." Having already established her pro-industry credentials, a stance that has been central to the political career and previous policy mandates of Schwarzenegger, Kennedy brings invaluable state government experience as well as insight into the Democratic party to the Schwarzenegger administration. In fact, as the executive director of the California Democratic Party, Kennedy worked under Phil Angelides, who was the party chairman and the Democratic Party gubernatorial candidate for the 2006 general election. Having failed to enact a series of relatively conservative policies through the initiative process, could Kennedy's appointment signal more nonpartisan direction for Schwarzenegger, in the spirit of former Governor Earl Warren? Regardless, Schwarzenegger disheartened many of the party faithful with the Kennedy appointment. One Republican activist, Steve Frank, summed up the reaction among the party's rank and file, suggesting that "Politics is built on loyalty, trust and experience. How are you going to ask a volunteer to trust an administration that's headed by a former California Democratic Party leader?"[a] Many Democrats can't be too happy either, considering that Kennedy is now working for the governor who replaced Gray Davis, her former boss.

The personal background and aspects of Kennedy's politics could cause long-term dissension among Republicans in Sacramento and across the state and force a large number of hardcore Republicans to turn their backs on Schwarzenegger. Not

[a]Ainsworth, Bill, "Governor appoints Democrat to Run Staff," *San Diego Union-Tribune*, December 1, 2005, http://signonsandiego.com.

only will many conservative Republican activists never accept Kennedy's pro-choice stance, they were undoubtedly appalled by her former position as executive director of the California Abortion Rights League as well as her openly gay lifestyle. In reality, however, California is a relatively liberal state where politics has for some time been dominated by the Democratic Party. Failing to push through a conservative agenda during the 2005 special election and sinking in opinion polls, the governor has few other choices but to reach some degree of peaceful accommodation with the Democrats if he is to survive politically. Susan Kennedy does have the skills and background to help him achieve that rapprochement and refocus his political agenda—if the partisan players from both parties can overlook past deeds and accept the fact that she is the governor's chief of staff.

*Sources:* Hoard, John, and York, Anthony, "Schwarzenegger hires former Gray Davis Aide Susan Kennedy as Chief of Staff," *Capital Weekly News,* November 29, 2005, http://www.capitolweekly.net "Susan P. Kennedy—Commissioner California Public Utilities Commission," http://www.tmcnet.com/voip/conference/ca05/susan-kennedy.aspx; "California Suspends Wireless Bill of Rights," http://www.consumeraffairs.com/news04/205/cpuc_wireless.html.

Ronald Reagan in 1966, who overwhelmingly beat the incumbent, Pat Brown, and Gray Davis's landslide victory in 1998 over Dan Lungren.

**Gubernatorial Style** The past governors of California have come from varied personal backgrounds; in fact, only three of the last nine were natives of the state. Since the governorship of Earl Warren, governors had law degrees and long careers in government service—with the exception of Ronald Reagan and Arnold Schwarzenegger. Historically, California voters have used the office of governor as an engine for change, electing inexperienced governors in the case of Reagan and Schwarzenegger and turning out incumbents such as Brown and Davis when the state faced critical issues that the most visible executive of government appeared incapable of solving. Interestingly, the Democratic majority in the state legislature generally survived these critical times, which included urban riots and college campus unrest in the 1960s and the energy crisis in 2001.

The last nine governors, can actually be sorted into either of two categories: master stewards of government policy and "citizen-politician." Although Earl Warren and Goodwin Knight were the last of the Progressive era Republican governors who embraced a spirit of bipartisanship, they were nonetheless experienced politicians who served in various government posts and will be remembered more for their policies and politics than as public personalities. Governors George Deukmejian and Pete Wilson were hardly charismatic leaders, but with the solid backing of the Republican Party, they faced the governance of California with an unflinching resolve. When asked why he ran for the office of governor, Deukmejian is said to have replied, "Attorneys general don't appoint judges; governors do." Wilson will long be remembered for the budget impasse between the governor and state legislature that forced the state to operate without a budget for a record sixty-one days. Disregarding the potential damage in public opinion and the wrath of unpaid state employees and creditors during his first term, Wilson exhibited a toughness during this episode that contributed to his reputation for firm leadership. These governors also demonstrated moderate tendencies, exemplified by Deukmejian's ability to compromise with a Democrat-controlled legislature lead by the flamboyant assembly speaker, Willie Brown, and by Wilson's moderate Republican ideological values. That Gray Davis was one of the professional politician types may in part explain his downfall, becoming only the second governor in U.S. history to be recalled from office. A consummate policy wonk and political strategist, overshadowed throughout most of his political career by more popular politicians, Davis had the ambition, superior knowledge of California politics, and aptitude for fundraising to over-

---

**Think Again**

What kinds of individuals have been elected governor in recent years? What might this tell us about the California electorate?

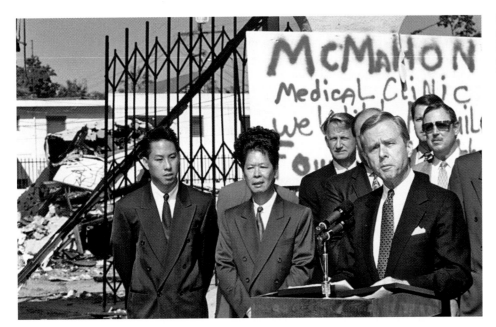

Governor Pete Wilson speaks to community leaders outside a destroyed shopping center after the 1992 Los Angeles riots.

come his incapacity to generate enthusiasm about his campaigns or actions as governor.[6]

Californians have at times heralded true leaders of state government based on force of personality and words rather than on track record or managerial competence. Governor Pat Brown, often described as "backslapping" or the "amiable owl," was the last of the pretelevision politicians. Without the benefits of sophisticated media technology and manipulation, Governor Brown was able to emanate statesmanship through a seemingly endless series of public appearances and by carefully cultivating affable relationships with key political figures. Many Californians disagreed with his ideological orientation, but few questioned his honesty or his courage, and these traits won him many votes. Brown had, for example, opposed capital punishment, even though most Californians were in favor of it. Unfortunately, he is less well known for the major policy achievements of his administration, most notably in education and racial equality, than he is for his loss to a challenger after having served two terms in office (this before there were term limits). In 1966, Brown became a victim of his own failure to master an emerging media technology that transformed his gracious statesmanlike demeanor into the image of a "stumblebum."[7] In defeating Brown in 1966, Ronald Reagan's media savvy, perfected after years as a Hollywood actor and pitchman for major corporations, was essential in conveying uncomplicated conservative solutions to complex problems and issues at a time when many voting mainstream Americans were uncomfortable with the rapid pace of social change. Although most California governors probably harbor hopes of being propelled by state politics to the White House, Reagan is the only one who has reached that goal. Reagan's record as governor is open to debate, and analysts see little of his rhetorical affirmations reflected in effective state policies, but his words, projected astutely via television to millions of Californians, resonated and reassured, pushing California to the right of the ideological spectrum and forever granting him the title of Great Communicator. Jerry Brown was a governor with the force of personality and words who built on a popular name in California politics, that of his "governor dad," a leadership style that subscribed to leadership by example. He was assumed to be honest because he had gone to divinity school, and his degrees in Latin and Greek established that he was smart. Governor

Jerry Brown served as Governor for two terms, elected in 1974 and reelected in 1978. Brown is now the Mayor of Oakland, California.

Brown did not just say he wanted to cut taxes and government waste; he lived it by refusing to live in the grandiose new governor's mansion or use the state-owned limousine, choosing instead to rent a modest apartment in Sacramento and drive a state-issued Plymouth—superficial acts, to be sure, but nonetheless actions that provided interesting media material about a governor who could otherwise be nondescript. Jerry Brown will be remembered for his social consciousness as governor, making appointments that reflected the diversity of California and signing the first state farm labor law. As the novelty of his personality waned in his second term, however, and the passage of Proposition 13, the property tax–cutting measure, reignited a conservative impulse nurtured under the reign of Ronald Reagan, Brown's vision was often at odds with conventional California politics. In many ways, Arnold Schwarzenegger is a composite of his various citizen-politician predecessors. He initially embraced the backslapping, amiable approach, particularly with members of the state legislature, and sought staged media attention to the point of eschewing public debates during his campaign in favor of focused media appearances. Unafraid to capitalize on his action movie stardom or employ offbeat insinuations, such as referring to state legislators as "girlie men," Schwarzenegger has used these incidents to garner maximum media exposure as a means of instituting a solidly Republican plan to shape California's government. In a new spin on the gubernatorial leadership style, once in the spotlight, the "Governator" continues to astonish his audience and confound the opposition with a tendency to do the unexpected. Filling key appointments with Democrats and going directly to the voters with initiatives to reform state government and raise revenue caused some bewilderment all across political landscape of California. Although Governor Schwarzenegger has had a number of his initiatives defeated at the polls, his reelection by an overwhelming margin in the November 2006 election was the culmination of a shrewd but successful political strategy. Whether this sleight-of-hand strategy will result in major policy accomplishments and a lengthy political career or simply confuse voters to the point of voting no remains to be seen.

## The California Plural Executive

**plural executive** The group of independently elected officials responsible for carrying out the laws of a state.

The **plural executive** has experienced some changes over the years, but in the main, it is very similar to the structure defined by the first California constitution of 1850. In contrast to the federal government but like the executive governments in most states, the plural executive in California is a collection of elected officers who share power with the governor. Members of the plural executive are elected at the same time as the governor, serve the same four-year term of office, and are limited to two terms. The development of the plural executive at the state level was an attempt to institute an elaborate system of separation of powers and checks and balances for the executive branch of government. In California, although the plural executive tends to foster independence among the major components of the state bureaucracy and permit the voters to select the heads of this bureaucracy, constitutional authority over the plural executive favors the governor, owing especially to the governor's power to develop and control the budgetary process. Ideally, the structure and democratic orientation of the plural executive does encourage leaders of the state bureaucracy to speak openly and honestly about the condition of government.

**lieutenant governor** The official who serves as acting governor when the governor is unable to carry out his or her duties.

**Lieutenant Governor**    The **lieutenant governor** is essentially the understudy for the governor, assuming that office in the event of a vacancy and serving as acting governor should the governor be impeached, absent, or temporarily disabled. In the absence of the lieutenant governor, succession to the office of governor goes to the

Lieutenant Governor Cruz Bustamante shakes hands with supporters at a "Get Out the Vote" and "Vote 'No' on the Recall" rally held by the UFW.

officers of the state legislature and in their absence to officers of the plural executive. Because all members of the plural executive, especially the lieutenant governor, must run for election independent of the governor, there is a good chance that the lieutenant governor will be a member of a different political party than the governor. This can cause some consternation for the governor, who must entrust the reigns of state government to the lieutenant governor when traveling out of state. Mike Curb, the Republican lieutenant governor during the term of Democratic Governor Jerry Brown, had many opportunities to act as interim governor for Brown, who for much of 1979 and early 1980 was out of state campaigning for the Democratic presidential nomination. Taking advantage of Brown's absence, Curb vetoed legislation that Brown would probably have signed and issued executive orders not at all in keeping with the governor's policies. Although many of Curb's actions as interim governor were contested in court, most were upheld and provided a precedent for the latitude afforded to lieutenant governors when serving as acting governor.

The California constitution also recognizes the lieutenant governor as the president of the state senate, a position with the sole legislative responsibility of casting a vote in the event of a tie in the senate when all forty members are voting. Otherwise, the lieutenant governor's legislative responsibilities are generally ceremonial, for example, presiding over the state senate during the State of the State address by the governor. Over the years, the lieutenant governor has been given additional duties related to executive departments and agencies, which include, ex officio or by virtue of being lieutenant governor, membership on the Board of Regents of the University of California, chairperson of the Commission for Economic Development, member of the State Lands Commission and the California Emergency Council, trustee of the California State University system, and many other positions either as vice-chair or member.

## Attorney General

As the top legal officer in the state and head of the California Department of Justice, the **Attorney General**, much like the attorney general for the federal

> ### Think Again
> What constitutional provisions create a likelihood of friction between the governor and lieutenant governor?

> ### Think Again
> What are the responsibilities of the attorney general? What kinds of agendas have governors assigned to the attorney general?

**Attorney General** The state's top legal officer.

## UP CLOSE

# California's Problematic Health Care Safety Net

Imagine you just started a job and the health care benefit hasn't kicked in yet, or you are between jobs and have no health care insurance at all. Worse, you have a young child who comes down with a fever but no insurance to pay to take her to a doctor. At best, you may be able to prove indigence and qualify for Medi-Cal, the state medical insurance program. Any earned income above the established poverty level will, however, make you ineligible for that program. There is the Healthy Families program that provides medical coverage for children of parents who are low-income, but make too much money to qualify for Medi-Cal. That program will cover your children, not you. And then hopefully you don't live in a county where there is a waiting list to receive Healthy Families care. The last resort, if you are without any money at all or are unable to use a credit card, would be to go to your nearest emergency ward, which by law must treat everyone regardless of income. If you are lucky, there won't be too long of a wait and an overworked medical staff.

This is the predicament in which over six million residents of California without health insurance consistently find themselves. In a near perfect world, the state government would be there with some sort of health care safety net to catch those who simply do not have the financial resources or employment benefits to gain access to health care. The truth is that eight out of ten uninsured are from working families. In fact, California has one of the highest rates of uninsured in the nation at 21 percent of the population, compared to the national average of 17 percent. There are another six million residents who receive

Medi-Cal, a combination of federal and state funds, which is administered at the state level by the Medical Care Services Division of the California Department of Health Services. Most Medi-Cal claimants are covered by some type of managed care program in their county, the largest being the Medi-Cal Managed Care (MCMC) program that serves twenty-two counties and covers about half of all Medi-Cal patients statewide. The MCMC, financed through Medi-Cal funding, is much like the typical HMO, in which one health care facility or organization manages all of a patient's health care needs. County governments largely have the responsibility of administering the Medi-Cal program at the local level and find it increasingly difficult to implement the program because of increasing health care costs and caseloads and stagnant state budget allocations. Medi-Cal program participants also face certain anxieties: compliance with reporting requirements, the erosion of benefits due to state budget cuts, and the reluctance of many doctors to participate in the Medi-Cal program.

In California, the average cost of health care coverage for families increased by 70 percent since 2000, going from about $5,904 annually in 2000 to $10,013 in 2004.[a] Spending by state government for the health care safety net has on the other hand remained fairly flat between 1994 and 2005, accounting for an annual average increase of 4.2 percent for each Medi-Cal participant.[b] Under the weight of the budget constraints that the California state government has endured over the years, there is simply not enough money to go around. Even with increased revenue for the 2006–07 $131 billion state budget, approximately $35 billion going to Medi-Cal, there will still be about a

[a]Budget brief, August 2005, California Budget Project, p. 1.
[b]Budget brief, August 2005, California Budget Project, p. 2.

government, has many distinct responsibilities at various levels of government that are sometimes at odds At times, the attorney general is responsible for the enforcement of California law, and in other circumstances, this government official must defend other California government officials against accusations regarding violations of laws and regulations. Because of these varied duties, the attorney general is often regarded as second only to the governor in authority and statewide influence. Serving as the legal council to all branches of California government, the most time-consuming of all California Department of Justice duties, the attorney general is expected to render legal opinions for executive officers and represent these officials in court proceedings as well as prepare all titles and summarizations for statewide ballot measures.

As the top law enforcement officer of the state, the attorney general is expected to maintain a central registry of law enforcement records and files, supervise state law enforcement training programs, assist local civil and criminal investigations, and investigate and prosecute major civil and criminal misconduct.

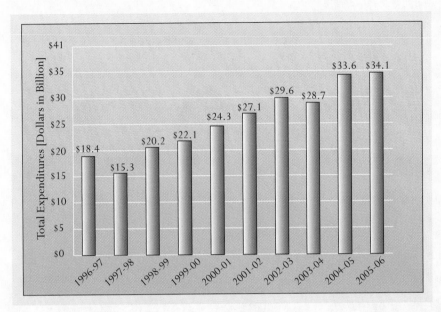

**Figure 18.1**   Medi-Cal Spending, 1996–07 to 2005–06

budget line for the Healthy Families program was increased in the 2006–07 budget and Democrats in the state legislature and Governor Schwarzenegger were in agreement over a plan to add $23 million to extend the Healthy Families program to cover all children in California, but the Republican legislators blocked that allocation on the grounds that the program would cover the children of undocumented immigrants and encourage illegal immigration.

Clearly, one of the major challenges facing the nation as well as California is to come to terms with the problem of available health care and its escalating costs. Although the state government under the leadership of Governor Schwarzenegger has demonstrated a willingness to bring the public allocation of funds for health care under control, many wonder whether the long-term effect will be to increase the number of people without any health care options. The goal of covering all children in California may be one policy progression that will encourage the further expansion of health care coverage in the future. The major challenge of any policy will be to devise a fiscal matrix that compensates health care professionals fairly for adequate if not good, reasonably priced, health care for the average resident of California.

$3.3 billion deficit. In response to the state's fiscal uncertainties, the state government has implemented a number of methods to cap Medi-Cal costs, including the reduction of payments to certain providers by 5 percent, increased reporting requirements, and the elimination of the second year of transitional Medi-Cal benefits for former welfare recipients. Governor Schwarzenegger is also proposing an overall restructuring of the Medi-Cal program that will be phased in over the next three or four years, saving the state government roughly $150 million by 2008–09. This restructuring would establish monthly premiums for certain families that could range between $4 to $27 per month, limit dental services, force almost all Medi-Cal participants into managed care programs, and process Medi-Cal applications through a centralized vendor instead of county welfare offices. The

*Source:* Budget Backgrounder—California Budget Project, March 2005, p. 2. "Budget Still Stuck on Immigration," *Sacramento Bee*, June 20, 2006, p. A3; Medi-Cal Program — Budget Backgrounder, California Budget Project, March, 2005; Robitaille, Stephen, "A Tattered Safety Net," *California Journal*, March, 2004, p. 9.

After being elected, most attorneys general will concentrate one or more major law enforcement areas either as a result of campaign promises or at the request of the governor. As attorney general of California, Pat Brown was asked by Governor Earl Warren to focus on organized crime and on his own initiative launched a major investigation into accusation of brutality at state mental hospitals.[8] Stanley Mosk, before going on to be the longest-serving associate justice of the California supreme court, created new divisions in the California Department of Justice to prosecute antitrust, consumer fraud, and investment fraud cases. He is also credited with laying the groundwork for the Peace Officers' Standards and Training (POST) academies. The next attorney general, Thomas C. Lynch, established a consumer bureau and directed the California Justice Department toward enforcement of environmental laws. Evelle Younger was elected to the office of attorney general in 1970 and adopted a tough stance on crime and college campus protests of the era. His successor, George Deukmejian, was also a "law and order" attorney general who established the California Crime Watch prevention program and

Attorney General Bill Lockyer joined former governor Gray Davis, film director-activist Rob Reiner and Chris Albrecht, CEO of HBO Television to announce California's acquisition of the 2,960-acre Ahmanson Ranch in the Santa Monica Mountains for its preservation as a parkland.

PRESERVING OPEN SPACE

successfully argued to uphold the "use a gun, go to prison" and death penalty laws before the California supreme court. He was also instrumental in the development of the Campaign to Eradicate Marijuana Planting (CAMP) in California. John van de Kamp followed Deukmejian in 1979, taking steps to modernize the Department of Justice's scientific and technological resources and pioneering the use of DNA forensic investigations. Although van de Kamp was on record for his personal opposition to the death penalty, he actively enforced the applications of the California death penalty law and limited appeals by condemned prisoners. Elected to the office on a "tough on crime" position, Dan E. Lungren was the force behind the "three strikes and you're out" mandatory twenty-five years to life sentencing law as well as "Megan's law," the statute that established a database of convicted child molesters. Capital punishment was restarted under his direction of the California Department of Justice after a twenty-five-year interval. Attorney General Bill Lockyer has focused on efforts to enforce environmental law, beginning his tenure in 1999 by supporting lawsuits to ban two-stroke-engine watercraft from Lake Tahoe. Pledging the efforts and resources of the California Department of Justice to fight illegal discrimination and racism in California, Lockyer nonetheless continues to actively pursue most of the "tough on crime" positions of his predecessors. Despite record seizures of marijuana plants during his terms, Lockyer is an advocate of California's medical marijuana law and has been critical of attempts by the federal government to enforce federal drug laws regarding the cultivation and sale of marijuana.[9]

The attorney general is directly responsible for supervising all district attorneys and sheriff's departments throughout the state. At the direction of the attorney general, the California Department of Justice may intervene in any county that is not considered to be uniformly and adequately enforcing state laws and regulations. Additionally, county grand juries may be convened by the attorney general to investigate allegations or evidence of wrongdoing.

**Controller**    Acting as the state's chief financial officer, the **controller** is responsible for all financial transactions involving the state government and local jurisdictions. The controller endorses the disbursement of state funds and oversees the maintenance of all state financial records through uniform accounting methods. The signature of the controller is readily apparent on the approximately 112,000 warrants (state equivalent of checks) that are written daily. The controller may issue periodic reports at the request of the state legislature regarding the fiscal ramifications of state operations and may also release special reports regarding the management of public revenue that in the past have included an audit of the California Department of Parks and Recreation and an investigation of fraud in the Medi-Cal program. The controller is the chief tax collector, monitoring the correct payment of taxes and authorizing court action for the recovery of delinquent tax debt. The controller orders regular financial audits of state and local governments to determine that all public funds are spent according to California law. The controller is also a member of many different boards and commissions, including the Board of Equalization, Franchise Tax Board, State Lands Commission, and State Board of Control.[10]

The role of the controller has not been without controversy. Some observers have argued that there are simply too many agencies responsible for state revenue and expenditure matters, citing the Board of Equalization, Franchise Tax Board, and Department of Finance as only the most important of the fiscally related agencies, and that the controller's job really should be folded into the purview of the governor. Others defend the controller's independence as a means of safeguarding against potential fiscal impropriety, which is more likely to occur by an official controlled by the governor or a political appointee. The audits or reports released by the Office of the Controller, especially those that find financial waste or impropriety, may not be as well received from the guilty government agencies as they would from the public. In fact, many are downright embarrassing, such as the audits conducted under the supervision of Kathleen Connell, the California controller in 1998, that "found ways to save the state more than a billion dollars, including $457 million in the Medi-Cal program, $121 million in the state prison system and $100 million in the state lottery."[11] One report regarding millions being wasted in the state Department of Education's adult education programs led to an investigation by the FBI.

One major drawback of the controller post is that it often attracts candidates who do not have a background in accounting or fiscal management and are using the position as a springboard to higher elected political office. A controller motivated by politics may be prone to inattentiveness and actual incompetence or lack the qualifications necessary for the professional demands of the office. Although Kathleen Connell and Steve Westy did have backgrounds in fiscal management, the biographies of other former controllers, such as Alan Cranston, who later became U.S. senator, and Gray Davis, a future governor, were less clear about similar experiences.

**State Treasurer**    If the controller is the chief account of the state, the **state treasurer** is the chief banker or financial consultant. The most basic responsibility of the state treasurer is to account for state bank deposits, supervising the receipt of funds to the state as well as the payment of state funds authorized by the controller, but it is important to note that this officer exercises little or no discretion in this duty and most other responsibilities associated with this position. A daily report, known as the daily clearance, must be filed with the controller, under the direction of the state treasurer, disclosing the amount of money that

**Think Again**

What kinds of controversies have sometimes emerged over the Office of the Controller?

**controller** The state's chief financial officer.

**state treasurer** The state's chief banker and financial consultant.

was disbursed during the preceding day and the source of these funds. As chair of the Pooled Money Investment Board and many other boards and commissions, the state treasurer is responsible for directing the investment of surplus state funds. Moreover, the state treasurer is charged with selling all state bonds. At the request of either chamber of the state legislature and the governor during specified times in the year, the state treasurer is required to present written reports on the fiscal standing of the state.

Many of the duties of the director of finance, which is a position in the governor's cabinet, coincide with the state treasurer's, implying that the office of state treasurer may be somewhat redundant. There is the possibility that the state treasurer could use information about the financial status of the state as a means of criticizing political opponents who happen to be the governor or state legislators. Again, the independence of this office seems to outweigh, at least among the public, any concerns about redundancy or partisanship.

**Secretary of State**   The main functions of the California **secretary of state** are the administration of elections and supervision of state records and government documents. Serving as the state's chief elections officer, the secretary of state oversees the voter registration process throughout the state, certifies certain nominations and statewide ballot measures, supervises the publishing and printing of ballot pamphlets, compiles reports of statewide voter turnout and election results, and enforces election laws. Not one of the higher-profile offices in the California plural executive, the secretary of state has in recent years taken on increasing importance as the job of administering elections has become clouded by the vote-counting controversies that arose in several states in the 2000 and 2004 presidential elections and accompanying the introduction of electronic voting machines. This responsibility has been complicated by a number of new federal laws, especially the **Help America Vote Act**, which require states to certify new voting equipment, create a statewide fraud-resistant voter registration list, and institute voting procedures and facilities that are accessible to disabled and non-English-speaking voters. These mandates have made the job of secretary of state during the administrations of Kevin Shelley and Bruce McPherson especially daunting, having had to administer such changes in the electoral process throughout a decentralized election system of fifty-eight California county voter registrar offices that independently handle registrations and election procedures. In 2006, Secretary of State McPherson faced the dilemma of being unable to certify by the June deadline federally mandated electronic voting machines due to technical malfunctions and security flaws.[12] As a member of the plural executive, elected on a partisan ballot, McPherson had to be concerned about potential allegations of partisan manipulation of votes through the certification of faulty voting machines.

Allegations of partisanship on the part of the secretary of state are not restricted to the voting and election process, which during the term of Secretary of State McPherson surfaced over the registration of political parties. Three days after removing the Peace and Freedom Party from the June 2006 ballot, McPherson reversed himself and qualified the party for a place on the ballot. He originally disqualified the party under the California election code, which requires that a party either have registered voters equal to at least 1 percent of the number of votes cast in the previous gubernatorial election or had a candidate receive 2 percent of the votes cast in that election.[13] Facing accusations of incompetence or political motivations and a threatened lawsuit, McPherson put the Peace and Freedom Party back on the ballot, based on "historical precedent."[14]

---

**— Think Again —**

Why has the Office of the Secretary of State taken on greater importance in recent years?

**secretary of state**
California's administrator of elections and supervisor of state records and archives.

**Help America Vote Act**
Federal law mandating certain measures to modernize voting procedures.

As the chief custodian of the state archives and records, the job of secretary of state is considerably quieter. The California state archives contain more than 100 million permanent government records, 20,000 maps and architectural drawings, 250,000 photographs, 7,500 video and recordings, and hundreds of historical artifacts. The secretary of state is also responsible for countless records of official acts, including laws and resolutions, articles of incorporation, and financial transactions. The passage of the Political Reform Act of 1974 made the Office of the Secretary of State the repository for the various registration forms, financial statements, and expenditure reports filed by candidates, elected officials, campaign organizations, political parties, and lobbyists. The secretary of state is expected to maintain this repository in a fair and open manner that will bring greater transparency to the financing of campaigns. As custodian of the Great Seal of California, the secretary of state is accountable for how and where that seal is affixed.[15]

The resignation of Secretary of State Kevin Shelley in 2005 reveals how the once modest and largely supraclerical office of the secretary of state has emerged as a position that can generate significant political influence as well as unwanted public scrutiny and partisan temptations. Shelley's problems apparently began with a report in the *San Francisco Chronicle* that he had received what appeared to be illegal contributions toward his election campaign. The story eventually led to audits by the controller's office and a grand jury investigation. These investigations resulted in the charge that as secretary of state, Shelley had diverted $1.5 million in federal Help America Vote Act grants to hire Democratic Party workers. Further questions surfaced regarding whether other funds were illegally channeled to political supporters of the secretary of state. Before long, the media had also found that staff members in Shelley's office had filed charges of verbal abuse and sexual harassment. The combination of unlawful and embarrassing charges drove Shelley to resign.[16] Ultimately, the Shelley affair demonstrates how overly partisan acts and bad choices can cause members of the plural executive to stray from constitutional or statutory guidelines and lead to their downfall and disgrace.

**Superintendent of Public Instruction**    Possessing limited formal political power, the **superintendent of public instruction** is generally forced to compete with the policymaking power of the California Board of Education, budget control of the state legislature, self-governing school districts, and the executive authority of the Governor. Designated as a nonpartisan office, the influence of the superintendent of public instruction is mainly derived from being the sole publicly elected person responsible for matters of public education. This sense of public accountability gives this office a commanding voice on educational matters and the development of educational policy. As secretary and executive officer of the eleven-member Board of Education, the superintendent of public instruction can influence or encourage the policies of the board, but the Board of Education as a whole establishes educational policy. Exercising the policy decisions of the board as executive officer makes the superintendent of public instruction directly responsible for monitoring public school attendance, distributing funds to school districts, overseeing state educational curriculum, and managing federal educational programs.

**superintendent of public instruction**  The elected official responsible for matters of public education in California.

Although nonpartisan for electoral purposes, the superintendent of public instruction can nonetheless become very political. Three-term Superintendent Bill Honig was forced to resign his office in 1992 after being convicted of conflict-of-interest charges. Honig had been a very vocal advocate of education in California and used his office to force various educational reforms that often drew mixed reactions from government leaders, the education community, and

**Proposition 98** California law requiring that 40 percent of the state general fund be reserved for education.

the public. Honig was a major force behind the passage of **Proposition 98**, which required that 40 percent of the state general fund be reserved for education. The measure was an attempt to restore educational funding lost to Proposition 13, but it severely limited the fiscal discretion of the legislature and the governor. The charges against Honig and his subsequent conviction stemmed from an investigation that learned that the Department of Education, under Honig's direction, had made payments to his wife's education-related firm.[17] At about the same time, in a move to strip Honig and any subsequent superintendent of public instruction of power, the Republican-dominated State Board of Education, mostly appointed by Republican Governor Pete Wilson, launched a legal battle that later ended with an California appellate court ruling that confirmed the transfer of the superintendent's policymaking power to the Board of Education and local school districts. The Democratic-controlled state legislature introduced legislation that attempted to restore the power of the superintendent, but the bill was subsequently vetoed by Governor Wilson.[18]

**─Think Again─**

What challenges are faced by the State Insurance Commissioner?

**Proposition 103** California law imposing the regulation of insurance rates and creating the elected position of state insurance commissioner.

**state insurance commissioner** Official responsible for oversight of the insurance industry and enforcement of insurance regulations in California.

**State Insurance Commissioner** Established in 1959, the State Insurance Department was headed by a gubernatorial appointee until 1988, when the passage of **Proposition 103**, an insurance initiative sponsored by California consumer groups and endorsed by Ralph Nader, was passed. This measure imposed the regulation of insurance rates and created the elected position of **state insurance commissioner**. Funded by a portion of insurance fees, the State Insurance Department, at the direction of the nonpartisan state insurance commissioner, monitors the financial condition of insurance companies operating in California, licenses companies and insurance professionals, approves workers' compensation rates, publishes annual financial statements of insurance companies in California, and provides information about insurance rates. Although designated as a nonpartisan member of the California plural executive, the recent line of state insurance commissioners have aligned themselves with either pro-industry or consumer interests that tend to have very partisan orientations. The dilemma is whether to initiate or enforce policies that will result in fair and beneficial insurance services for consumers or to promote a healthy business environment for insurance companies that employ thousands of workers and sustain related industries. Elected as the first state insurance commissioner in 1990, John Garamendi is credited with bringing a proconsumer perspective to the State Insurance Department, which prior to Proposition 103 had developed a pro–insurance industry reputation. Although consumers did experience some insurance premium rebates, many of the insurance reforms mandated by Proposition 103 were tied up in court, and insurance consumers lost their chief advocate when Garamendi left office to run for governor.

In 1994, even before Charles "Chuck" Quackenbush was elected as the second state insurance commissioner, he was regarded as the pro–insurance industry candidate, due largely to the $2.4 million in industry contributions that financed 70 percent of his election campaign. Two years into his first term, Quackenbush was criticized by the state's auditor general for failing to respond aggressively to complaints about the insurance industry in California.[19] Nevertheless, Quackenbush was elected in 1998 to a second term. Not long thereafter, the insurance commissioner was the target of investigations that alleged he concluded a settlement highly favorable to insurance companies that had deceived victims of the Northridge earthquake. The investigation by the state attorney general's office revealed that Quackenbush had agreed not to fine the companies or to finalize a report on Northridge earthquake claims-handling violations.[20] In compensation for his looking the other way, the investigation charged, Quackenbush compelled various insurance companies to contribute over $4 million to nonprofit foundations the insurance commissioner had created. As the investigation widened, exposing at one point $3 million the foundations had spent on political advertising featuring Quackenbush, the commissioner felt obliged to resign.[21]

Workers' compensation benefits emerged as a major issue during the early 2000s, illustrating the contradictions or inequities that often arise in the business community over practices that benefit one industry at the disadvantage of other industries and the tenuous role that government must adopt in resolving such conflicts. By 2003, California businesses were paying the highest rates in the nation to cover employees with workers' compensation insurance provided by private insurance companies as required by California law and insurance industry regulations. Threatening to relocate to other states to avoid these high rates, many companies charged that California's workers' compensation law created an unfavorable businesses environment in California. The private insurance companies that provided workers' compensation coverage contended that they were forced to charge high rates due to the coverage required by insurance regulations. In 2004, pledging to fix the workers' compensation system, Governor Schwarzenegger got the state legislature to enact a law that lowered workers' compensation insurance costs for California businesses through limits on coverage for hospital costs, outpatient surgery, and permanent disability claims.[22] Workers' compensation insurance rates decreased by 37.8 percent. Reelected as insurance commissioner in 2002, John Garamendi faced the precarious position of supporting the new workers' compensation regulations, widely applauded by the California business community; denouncing private insurance companies that failed to pass on all of the windfall profits from the new regulations to businesses in the form of even lower premiums; and investigating the charges of injured workers, unions, and health care professionals citing various inequities in the new regulations.[23]

The travails of the Department of Insurance and the state insurance commissioner over the years demonstrates the difficulty that all plural executive officers face in enforcing California regulations and laws while considering the divergent interests of California residents. Even with certain safeguards, such as the nonpartisan designation of the insurance commissioner, inequities and official abuse persist. Yet the dilemmas of the plural executive also illustrate the ability of government to fashion tentative solutions, solutions that will inevitably unravel without constant scrutiny and some measure of impartiaity.

**Board of Equalization**   The **Board of Equalization**, created by constitutional amendment in 1879, consist of four voting members, who represent Board of Equalization districts of roughly 8 million people each throughout the state, and the state controller, who serves as an ex officio member. Each board member must reside in his or her respective district one year preceding election to this partisan office. Although the Board of Equalization has a variety of duties and responsibilities, its most basic task is to adopt rules, based on state laws, governing the collection and payment of property, sales, excise, and special taxes. Its property tax responsibilities are focused on setting and evaluating guidelines for the assessment policies of the fifty-eight county assessors, who establish property values and corresponding tax liabilities in their respective counties. The Board of Equalization has the authority to directly assess taxes on utilities, insurance companies, items for sale, and the use of certain goods. The board also acts as a quasi-judicial body, hearing and adjudicating appeals on the decisions of the Franchise Tax Board, which administers the state income tax, bank and corporate taxes, and a variety of other taxes and fees.[24]

**Board of Equalization**
California body that makes rules, based on state laws, governing the collection and payment of property, sales, excise and other taxes.

Like most segments of the plural executive, the Board of Equalization walks a tightrope of governance, balancing what is necessary for the health of the state against what residents of the state desire. Had the Board of Equalization in the 1970s foreseen the perceived inequity between the tax surplus accumulated by state government and public dissatisfaction over rising property tax bills and sounded the alarm, some analysts suggest, the resulting backlash of Proposition 13, which brought dramatic property tax reductions and the loss of a large portion of government revenue, might have been avoided. Since the advent of Proposition 13, the "tax burden" has been a major public policy issue, generating a plethora of special-interest and advocacy groups that regularly petition, criticize, and even sue the Board of Equalization. When the board, for example, began considering a new proposal to tax certain prescription drugs, including cosmetic botox, the Citizens Against Unfair Health Care Taxes was formed, and a campaign was launched branding the proposed tax a "dangerous precedent" and calling on residents of California to write or call their local Board of Equalization member.[25] Another effort by the board, this time allowing a tax credit or refund to companies that manufacture equipment, was severely criticized by California tax advocacy and reform groups and even one former Board of Equalization member. At issue was a decade-old manufacturers' investment credit enacted during the economic recession of the 1990s in California to help a declining manufacturing sector. Although the effect of this tax credit law was minimal and it was allowed to expire in 2003, many companies were nonetheless given the credit for equipment purchases made prior to the expiration of the tax law, amounting to $80 million in refunds. Most of the criticism of the Board of Equalization approval of the refund surfaced when tax reform advocacy groups learned that the eighteen companies that received the tax credit, most of them technology firms, had not paid any corporate taxes in recent years because of the accumulation of other tax credits. Senate Appropriations Committee Chair Carole Migden (D–San Francisco), a former chair of the Board of Equalization, pointed out, "These are refunds for taxes not even paid. It is scandalous." In letters to the board, members of the California Tax Reform Association and the Foundation for Taxpayer and Consumer Rights accuse the board of "coddling California corporate welfare queens."[26]

— Think Again —

What plans did Governor Schwarzenegger have to reform California's many boards and commissions? What opposition did he encounter?

**California Boards and Commissions**   According to the California Performance Review project initiated by Governor Schwarzenegger, there are an estimated 339 boards and commissions scattered across the executive branch of California government.[27] Historically, these boards and commissions originated during the late nineteenth century when the Progressives sought to circumvent the partisan influence of corrupt political "bosses" and "machines" that loaded government departments and agencies with their cronies. The Progressive idea was that the governor, sometimes with the consent of the state legislature, would appoint presumably nonpartisan professionals to boards and commissions who would bring expert knowledge and experience to the management of state government affairs. Today, the vast majority of these boards and commissions function as appendages of the major departments and agencies, focusing on a specific aspect of the mission of these organizations. In most instances, the members of boards and commissions are appointed to fixed terms by the governor and the state legislature and cannot be removed. The Board of Parole Hearing is a subsection of the Department of Corrections and Rehabilitation and is one example of a board with an important mandate under the authority of the governor through the department secretary. The duties and tasks of the state boards and commissions vary considerably, from simply offering guidance on a subject to acting in a quasi-judicial capacity or establishing policy and standards. Many departments and agencies have the authority to create boards and commissions independent of the governor and the state legislature. There are a number of boards and commissions that derive their authority from government statutes and, although members are appointed by the governor and the state legislature, are designed to be independent of all branches of government. Examples of these types of boards and commissions include the Fair Political Practices Commission, charged with regulating campaign contributions and spending; the Little Hoover Commission, a state oversight agency that promotes efficient government; and the Public Utilities Commission, which is responsible for ensuring reasonable and safe utility and transportation services. In recent years, various advocacy groups and political leaders have complained of what they feel is an excessive number of boards and commissions that very often duplicate efforts, unnecessarily complicate and decentralize decisionmaking, and waste valuable resources and funds.

In response to the criticism of boards and commissions, Governor Schwarzenegger had planned to abolish as many as eighty-eight of them. In his 2005 annual address to the state legislature, he portrayed the boards as expensive and "unnecessary" and gave the impression that they were filled with partisan appointees who were not very productive. The governor planned to fold most of the tasks of the abolished boards and commissions into other existing departments, the Consumer Services Agency receiving the majority of these duties. Administrative law judges and advisory panels set up by departments would, under Schwarzenegger's plan, also assume the work of abolished boards and commissions. The governor also wanted to limit the power of the state legislature to appoint a number of members to boards and commissions and warned that he could take his plan to reorganize the state boards and commissions directly to the voters as an initiative.[28] But a month later, Governor Schwarzenegger was forced to drop the proposal, encountering opposition from a wide variety of special-interest groups as well as from Democratic and Republican members of the state legislature. One of the most common criticisms of the plan was that decisions and actions that are normally made or at least discussed during the public meetings of boards and commissions would be hidden from public view if the work of boards and commissions were shifted to state bureaucrats. Another concern was the elimination of public input that has been an important function of boards and commissions, which ordinarily include a combination of appointees from both the private and public sectors of the state. Probably the most damning criticism was the charge that much of the proposal to abolish eighty-eight boards and commissions was motivated by politics or special relationships with the governor. Critics support this charge by citing the governor's decision to keep the New Motor Vehicle Board, which is a favorite of the California car dealers who have been big Schwarzenegger supporters, and the California Film Commission, composed in part of fellow actor friends of the governor. Schwarzenegger hopes nevertheless to find ways of streamlining the state government.[29]

**The Plural Executive and the Third House**     If Californians look closely at the campaign contributions to plural executive officers, they will see the increasing broad influence of the "third house", the army of lobbyists that represent special-interest groups that seek to shape the decisions of government officials. Like members of the state legislature, the officers of the plural executive must face the question of whether the campaign contributions that they accept from special-

## WHAT DO YOU THINK?

# The California Performance Review—Quality Control or Just Hype?

One key goal in Governor Schwarzenegger's first State of the State address was to make state government more efficient through a major reorganization. Stressing his earnestness in this task, the governor said "Every governor proposes moving boxes around to reorganize government. I don't want to move boxes around; I want to blow them up."[a] Schwarzenegger initiated his goal of "blowing up the boxes" with the creation of the California Performance Review Commission to conduct a "top-to-bottom review of California state government." In the end, the review and recommendations of the commission were repackaged in a watered-down version for public release, and eventually were withdrawn altogether by Schwarzenegger, who faced mounting criticisms over his reorganization plan amid other political difficulties.

Although not implemented, the Report of the California Performance Review (CPR)—"Government for the People for a Change"—remains as a resource for understanding the problems of California state government and ways to improve its performance. Serving as volunteers, members of the CPR commission were drawn from a wide variety of legislators, state government employees, corporate personnel, and representatives of the non-profit community. Over six months of work by the commission went into producing a report that was 2,500 pages in length and included over 1,000 recommendations that purportedly would have saved the state roughly $32 billion within five years. Listed below are highlights of the recommendations contained in the CPR report, which are subdivided into seven basic categories.

### General Government

Frankly, there is not much that is new in this section of the report. Although the commission calls for reducing and consolidating certain agencies and departments, it also calls for adding workers in specific areas such as tax collection and audit staff. Another redundant theme in this section calls for greater use of online governmental services. Many agencies are employing online services, which cost governments time and money in constructing and maintaining Web sites. There was the recommendation to institute a multistate lottery, saving California administrative overhead and enlarging the jackpot to attract more participants. Other points included two-year vehicle registration periods and stronger agreements with Native American casino owners to address the local effects of casinos.

### Health and Human Services

Once again, consolidation was the main theme in this section. The commission proposed combining various state health and human service agencies and eliminating others, but it was not clear whether the commission was calling for fewer—but larger—agencies at the state level. Centralizing the procurement process for durable medical equipment and using a competitive bidding method was encouraging; however, it still involves a massive state agency susceptible to fraud and waste.

### Education, Training, and Volunteerism

This section contained a number of commonsense as well as controversial ideas, many of which sounded promising, but would require intense coordination and implementation. One commonsense idea was synchronizing the educational process in public schools with workforce preparation through forums and increased dialogue. Granting school districts greater flexibility to enter into alternative arrangements for a wide range of services normally mandated by the state could be a good idea if the state can somehow guarantee this flexibility will not be abused. Another interesting recommendation was to allow California community colleges to award bachelor's degrees in rural communities and in high-demand disciplines. There is some doubt as to whether the four-year colleges would also find this recommendation interesting. One downright radical proposal was to require students attending Califor-

interest groups and business representatives have any significant influence on their decisions and actions. From a broad legal point of view, as long as the executive officers do not engage in cash-for-deal transactions and comply with the individual donor limits, they are generally free to accept as many contributions they wish. The reality of accepting this money, however, raises questions regarding the donors' true interests and whether tacit cash-for-deal arrangements have been made. The campaign experience of Governor Gray Davis during the Democratic gubernatorial primary, in which he faced Al Checci and Jane Harman, two independently wealthy opponents, suggests why many candidates are preoccupied with raising campaign funds. Had he not taken an aggressive but successful personal

CHAPTER 18 • THE CALIFORNIA EXECUTIVE AND BUREAUCRACY **643**

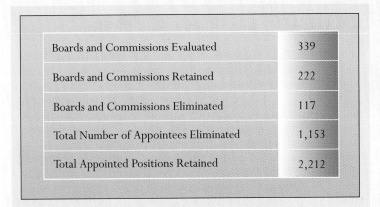

| | |
|---|---|
| Boards and Commissions Evaluated | 339 |
| Boards and Commissions Retained | 222 |
| Boards and Commissions Eliminated | 117 |
| Total Number of Appointees Eliminated | 1,153 |
| Total Appointed Positions Retained | 2,212 |

**Figure 1** California Boards and Commissions: CPR Review and Recommendations

nia public colleges and universities to perform sixteen hours of community service.

### Infrastructure

Once again, the commission proposes a considerable amount of consolidation of agencies engaged in building or maintaining the state's infrastructure. It is very probable that state agencies would respond to these recommendations by stating that they are either already doing so or do not have sufficient staff. There is the suggestion that the state government provide a builders' risk insurance program for private contractors working on state projects. This program would cut insurance costs for contractors and the state government and potentially stabilize insurance rates. The commission wants transportation funds and taxes to be used only for transportation infrastructure and would exempt infill and mixed-use development projects from environmental review procedures.

### Resource Conservation and Environmental Protection

The commission is especially concerned about informing the public about environmental issues and suggests creating a single office dedicated to responding to public inquiries about environmental protection, using automated or online systems (e-government) to facilitate this effort. Otherwise, the emphasis is on combining or streamlining a wide range of environmental and conservation programs that include toxic cleanup, waste reduction, pollution prevention, water management, and real estate management.

### Public Safety

The major recommendation in this section combines the more than eighty current separate state entities into one department of public safety and homeland security. Although most of these entities are related to public safety and security issues, the commission also folds into this proposed department investigative units that handle state medical and disability insurance fraud cases and victim assistance programs.

### Statewide Operations

In this section there is a strong emphasis on technology upgrades and instituting performance standards and measures. The commission found that there is no coordination of the state's information technology and calls for a new technology division to fulfill this function. It would also add a statewide enterprise architect to bring state government IT up to industry standards. Other IT-related recommendations include instituting a single state government portal or Web site, advertising on state Web sites to generate revenue, electronic fee collection, and introducing voice-over Internet protocol (VOIP). The introduction of touch-screen terminals and digital photo technology were also suggested as ways to make state government, especially at the field office level, more efficient. A long list of proposals were offered by the commission regarding performance standards, particularly as they are related to agency funding, training, salary, job duties, and incentives. The emphasis was on making the delivery of state government services more customer-oriented, rewarding those workers who embrace this concept and penalizing those who do not. Last, the commission felt the state constitution needed to be amended to allow for a biennial budget process. A two-year budget, according to this recommendation, would support a more comprehensive approach to planning and the projection of revenue.

*Source:* Delsohn, Gary, "Governor to Ditch Cuts," *Sacramento Bee,* February 17, 2005, p. A1; California Performance Report, http://cpr .ca.gov/report/cprrpt.

fundraising approach or lacked contacts that would net him large contributions in his campaigns for executive office, Davis would not have been able to compete against the personal fortunes of his opponents. (Checci's spending earned him the nickname "checkbook Checci" during the primary campaign.) In an examination of Governor Davis's fundraising prowess, in Cynthia H. Craft wrote:

> The spadework is perhaps made all the easier by the power and prestige of the office Davis now holds. But show up he must. "Successful fund-raising is not something you can do without the active involvement of the candidate. People expect to see the candidate," South testified in trial. "They expect to have some access to the candidate and the process.[30]

# COMPARED TO WHAT?

## California and Nevada Governments Grapple with Gambling

The state of Nevada has become the gambling capital of the United States and maybe even the world, and its success in this form of adult entertainment is establishing the example for daring entrepreneurs and state governments across America in search of similar fortunes. The Nevada gaming industry, centered in Las Vegas, is now legendary, transforming Las Vegas first from a sleepy truck stop intersecting Highways 15 and 95 on the way to Los Angeles to the hub of the hip life, now spread throughout the state, combining qualities of resort recreation with gambling. In Las Vegas at least, the gaming goldmine continues to bring prosperity to the state, boosting employment well above the national norm, producing business growth, generating construction, and providing the state government with a steady flow of tax revenue. Tourism, largely the result of the gaming industry, is the state's most important economic activity, furnishing well over $10 billion each year in revenue for Nevada's economy. Gaming has consistently paid over 47 percent of the cost of state government, enabling Nevada to spend a significant sum on education and social services while keeping taxes lower for other traditional state revenue sources. In fact, Nevada has no corporate or income tax, reflecting the state government's conservative approach to governing. It is very difficult for the Nevada state government to avoid catering to an industry that employs half of the state's workers either directly in the gambling trade or indirectly through other types of service industries.

Across the border, Indian casinos in California have become a new and fierce competitor in the effort to lure gamblers and other patrons. In 1999, after a long legal battle and twelve state and local ballot measures, fifty-nine California Indian tribes signed a tribal gaming agreement concluded by then governor Gray Davis on behalf of state government, essentially legalizing substantially expanded categories of gambling that would be restricted to Indian reservations. On March 7, voters approved this agreement in the form of Proposition 1A by nearly a 2-to-1 margin. Since that time, of the 107 federally recognized native tribes in California, over forty are currently operating casinos and many are accumulating fortunes, earning since 2001 over $5 billion in gaming dollars annually. In addition to cutting significantly into the profits of the Nevada gaming industry, the Indian casinos have in various ways altered the manner in which the California government operates. One of the most noticeable effects has been the hundreds of millions of dollars directors of Indian casinos have contributed to members of the California state government. Not unlike the scenario surrounding the convicted Washington lobbyist Jack Abramoff, the California Indian casino organizations have contributed to almost all influential members of government, including major amounts to both Gray Davis and Arnold Schwarzenegger and current candidates in November 2006 elections. All three of Californias last governors, including Schwarzenegger, have been responsible for negotiating what cut the state will take in Indian casino revenue. These negotiations got off to a bumpy start with former governor Pete Wilson, who objected to the use of slot machines and the level of state control over gambling on Indian reservations. Intense bargaining and lobbying has resulted in millions of dollars in gambling revenue being distributed to local governments and to the state government. The distribution of these funds actively involves the state controller, whose office holds such funds in special accounts, arranges methods of dispersal, and advises local governments on the use of these funds. The Attorney General's Office is responsible for regulating gambling in California and the expansion of gaming in California has caused concern

This access was implied during the attempt to pass SB773 in the state legislature, a 2001 consumer privacy bill that would strengthen a 1999 federal law safeguarding financial information that consumers list on loan and credit applications. The bill was set for passage after making its way through the various different legislative committees and watered down a bit by way of the amendment process, but it fell into limbo awaiting Governor Davis's decision either to sign or veto the bill. That decision must have been especially difficult for the governor, who during the six-month period leading up to the completion of legislative work on the bill had received at least $500,000 from banking and insurance com-among numerous law enforcement officials over the tendency of organized crime groups to gravitate toward gambling activity. Former attorney general Dan Lungren, in the Department of Justice 1996 Organized Crime in California Report, mentioned that a number of attempts have been made by organized crime groups to infiltrate Indian gambling operations and warned that the California tribal governments were unprepared to identify "unscrupulous subjects." Casinos and hotels on Indian reservations are springing up in various locations of California, often in rural or remote areas, from Palm Springs to Sonoma County and environmental and safety issues have caused the state government environmental agencies to express apprehension regarding some of these construction projects. Nevada state government has until recently resisted any suggestion of a state-run lottery and is one of only ten states without one. The natural competition between casino-style gambling and a lottery may yet draw the California Department of Education into the orbit of Indian casinos with a demand for a share of casino profits if portions of the already negligible amount of lottery money that goes to education shifts to the Indian casinos.

If the results of a 2003 study conducted by the University of Nevada at Las Vegas Center for Business and Economic Research are accepted, the California state government may be in store for a host of social problems that the center has linked to the gambling industry in Nevada. The study found that the social problems resulting from gambling costs the state between $300 million to $450 million annually in services—costs that basically cancel out the state tax revenue received from the gaming industry. Nevada has, according to the study, an estimated 20,000 to 40,000 pathological gamblers. In addition to the cost of treatment programs provided by the state, the financial drain of compulsive gamblers can be found in missed work, productivity losses, unemployment compensation, and a number of other factors that adversely affect state revenue. The report did exclude the costs related to suicide and attempted suicide, a serious issue for compulsive gamblers, who have the highest rates of any addicted group. Las Vegas—representing the peak of success for the gaming industry, although stuck in the middle of a desert—also illustrates some of the worst qualities of urban life, qualities that have not evolved over generations of urban decay, but have emerged from one generation and are linked inextricably to the gambling industry. The reluctance of the state and local governments to contribute sufficient funds for social services and the low-income communities filled with the low-wage workers so vital to the operations of the casinos, that have sprouted up away from the Strip are making Las Vegas an increasingly problem-ridden city.

For most of California's history, Indians within the state have suffered the worst indignities of any group of Californians and, until the advent of casinos, were largely forgotten on reservations, many of which were the sites of deplorable conditions. Most Indian tribes are now using the wealth generated from gambling to fund health care and education for their people and to develop a sustainable economic base for the future. In the short term, this wealth is based on gambling and, regardless of how Indians may be using it or how entertaining or popular it becomes, it is ultimately predicated on losing. In the competition with Nevada casinos, many wonder whether there will always be enough gamblers to go around. Will the California state government become wary, not unlike the government in Nevada, of the golden egg that has been laid by Indian casinos thus far, or will that state government have the foresight and fortitude to cash out before the losing hand is played?

*Sources:* John Stearns, "Gaming referendum ushers in new beginning for Indian Tribes," *Reno Gazette-Journal,* http://www.rgi.com/news2/specialreport/part1.htm; Glenn F. Bunting, "Tribes Watch Their Own Casinos," *Los Angeles Times,* October 19, 2004, http://www.latimes.com; P. A19; Roger Dunstan, "Gambling in California," *California Research Bureau,* January, 1997, http://www.library.ca.gov/CRB/97/03/crb97003.html; Rod Smith, "Problem Gambling's Social Cost High, Report Says," *Las Vegas Review-Journal,* February 13, 2003, http://reviewjournal.printthis.clickability.com; Rod Smith, Hubble Smith and John G. Edwards, "Nevada Defies Jobless trend," *Las Vegas Review Journal,* August 7, 2004, http://www.reviewjournal.com.

panies.[31] In the end, Davis did sign the bill, but only after aides from the governor's office and banking and insurance company lobbyists worked together to rewrite it. Another bill in 2000, AB1963, which would have required credit card companies to disclose information on their billing statements to help consumers better understand the cost of making the minimum payment on their debt, wasn't as fortunate under Governor Davis's pen. Shelley Curran, a policy analyst with the West Coast Regional Office of the Consumers Union, commented, "It is particularly frustrating that the Governor vetoed this measure since it enjoys strong popular support and passed by such a wide margin when it was considered by lawmakers in Sacramento."[32]

The relationship between campaign contributions from lobbyists and the officers of the plural executive is often unclear. How should Californians perceive the California Attorney General's Invitational golf tournament sponsored by the Barona Band of Mission Indians, owners of a San Diego County casino? Should Californians believe that the $25,000 a "celebrity sponsor" paid to attend the tournament had no bearing on the former Attorney General Bill Lockyer's constitutional and statutory responsibility to regulate California's thriving Indian gambling industry?[33] Should Californians think anything odd about the $355,000 that former State Treasurer and gubernatorial candidate Phil Angelides received over a three-year period from the law firm of Milberg Weiss, one of six law firms chosen to represent the state pension system that are selected by the state pension board, of which Treasurer Angelides is a member?[34] During the 2002 campaign for statewide executive offices, every winning candidate, with the exception of former Insurance Commissioner John Garamendi, who spent the least, outspent their opponents by at least twice as much money, all easily surpassing $1 million.

If Californians believe the findings of Government Performance Project, the 2005 research project mentioned at the beginning of this chapter, and other problems we have pointed out, the California executive is in need of reform. Just what direction this reform should take and how it will be initiated raises a profound series of questions. Acknowledging some of the issues highlighted in this chapter may be a good way to start answering these questions and lead Californians down the road to reform.

# Summary Notes

- The constitution of California identifies the governor as the sole official representative with executive powers that include budget authority, the state government and line-veto powers, As the chief executive officer of the state government, the governor is directly responsible for appointing departments and agency heads, judges, commissioners, and state board members.

- All candidates for governor must be citizens of the United States, registered voters, 18 years of age or older, and California residents for at least five years immediately preceding the election.

- The plural executive in California is a collection of elected officers who share power with the governor and serve a four-year term of office that is limited to two terms. The development of the plural executive at the state level was an attempt to institute an elaborate system of separation of powers and checks and balances for the executive branch of government.

- The lieutenant governor is the "understudy" for the governor, assuming that office in the event of a vacancy and serving as acting governor should the governor be impeached, absent, or temporarily disabled. The lieutenant governor also serves as the president of the state senate, a position with the sole responsibility of casting a vote in the event of a tie when all forty members are voting.

- The top legal officer in the state, the attorney general, is the head of the California Department of Justice. The attorney general is responsible for the enforcement of California law, for defending other government officials against accusations regarding violations of laws and regulations, and for preparing the titles and summaries of all statewide ballot measures.

- The state's chief financial officer, the controller is responsible for all financial transactions involving the state government and local jurisdictions. The controller endorses the disbursement of state funds, oversees the maintenance of all state financial records through uniform accounting methods, and may issue periodic reports at the request of the state legislature regarding the fiscal ramifications of state operations.

- The state treasurer is the state's chief banker or financial consultant, responsible for state bank deposits, state investments. supervising the receipt of funds and the payment of state funds authorized by the controller.

- The main functions of the California secretary of state are the administration of elections and supervision of state records and government documents. The state's chief elections officer, the secretary of state oversees the voter registration process throughout the state, certifies certain nominations and elections, supervises the publishing and printing of ballot pamphlets, compiles reports of statewide voter turnout and election results, and enforces election laws.

■ Possessing limited formal political power, the nonpartisan superintendent of public instruction participates in the policymaking process of the State Board of Education, works with the state legislature on education laws and policy, advises local school districts, and serves as the chief spokesperson on matters of public education.

■ Originally established in 1959, the State Insurance Department was headed by a gubernatorial appointee until 1988, when the passage of Proposition 103 created the elected position of state insurance commissioner. The commissioner directs, the California Department of Insurance, which monitors insurance companies operating in California.

■ The Board of Equalization, created by constitutional amendment in 1879, consists of four voting members who adopt rules governing the collection and payment of property, sales, excise, and special taxes and set and evaluate guidelines for the property tax assessment policies of the county assessors throughout the state.

■ A large number of boards and commissions either work closely with the major departments and agencies, focusing on a specific aspect of the mission of these organizations, or act independently, developing policy or providing expertise in a specific policy area. Most members of boards and commissions are appointed to fixed terms by the governor and the state legislature and cannot be removed.

## Key Terms

executive branch    620
governor    620
line-veto power    621
extraordinary session    621
clemency powers    621

plural executive    630
lieutenant governor    630
Attorney General    631
controller    635
state treasurer    635

secretary of state    636
Help America
    Vote Act    636
superintendent of public
    instruction    637

Proposition 98    638
Proposition 103    638
state insurance
    commissioner    638
Board of Equalization    639

## Suggested Readings

Baldassare, Mark. *California in the New Millennium.* Berkeley: University of California Press, 2000.

Burns, John F., and Richards J. Orsi, Eds. *Taming the Elephant: Politics, Government, and Law in Pioneer California.* Berkeley: University of California Press 2003.

Cannon, Lou. *Ronnie to Jesse: A Political Odyssey of Two Political Champions.* Garden City, N.Y.: Doubleday, 1969.

Rapoport, Roger. *California: The Political Odyssey of Pat and Jerry Brown.* Berkeley, Calif.: The Nolo Press, 1982.

Rarick, Ethan. *California Rising: The Life and Times of Pat Brown.* Berkeley: University of California Press, 2004.

Walters, Dan. *The New California: Facing the 21st Century.* Sacramento: California Journal Press, 1992.

# 19 THE CALIFORNIA JUDICIARY

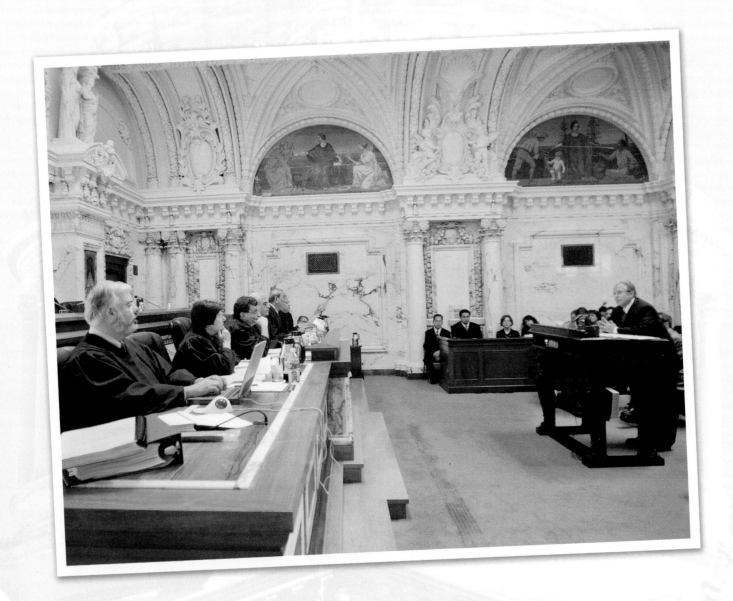

## Chapter Outline

- The California Court System
- The Variations in California Law
- The California Jury System
- Police Powers and the Prosecution
- Trends in the California Judicial System
- Punishment in California
- Reforming the California Judicial System

## Think About Politics

1 Should plea bargains be encouraged to decrease state caseloads?
Yes ☐ No ☐

2 Should the use of alternative dispute resolution be encouraged?
Yes ☐ No ☐

3 Has California's Three-Strikes law been effective?
Yes ☐ No ☐

4 Should California reevaluate its stance on the death penalty?
Yes ☐ No ☐

5 Does California's jury system need to be reformed?
Yes ☐ No ☐

6 Should state District Attorneys be more highly scrutinized?
Yes ☐ No ☐

7 Should state prisons work to rehabilitate prisoners?

*The role of juries in the California judicial system is extremely important. Consider the impact that verdicts handed down by juries in high profile cases such as the O.J. Simpson trial have had on the overall perception of the state's judicial system.*

★   ★   ★

## Introduction

The legal framework for the California state government begins with the California constitution, which is more than four times as long as the U.S. Constitution and the foundation for the twenty-nine codes that contain statutes covering almost every aspect of life in California. The details and procedures that further define the areas covered by these twenty-nine codes are contained in the California Administrative Codes, regulations created by hundreds of agencies in California. Regardless of how much California college students may enjoy their American government course, Title 5, Section 40404 of the California Administrative Code requires that all California State University (CSU) students pass a CSU-accredited American government course to qualify for graduation. Common sense dictates that food service workers should wash their hands, but according to Section 114020(f) of the California Health and Safety Code, "Gloves shall be worn when contacting food and food contact surfaces if the employee has any cuts, sores, rashes, artificial nails, nail polish, rings (other than a plain ring, such as a wedding band), uncleanable orthopedic support devices, or fingernails that are not clean, trimmed, and smooth." Violation of this section is "punished by a fine of not less than twenty-five dollars ($25) or more than one thousand dollars ($1,000) or by imprisonment in the county jail for a term not exceeding six months, or by both fine and imprisonment." The California Penal Code is probably the most widely known of the codes, covering a long list of antisocial behavior and penalties, from disturbing the peace to the death penalty. California Code 415 provides a broad description of disturbing-the-peace violations. Most cities have municipal codes that are more specific, such as Title 10 of San Jose's municipal code, titled "Public Peace, Morals and Welfare," which prohibits any person from disturbing the "peace, quiet and comfort of any neighborhood by creating therein any disturbing or unreasonable loud noise." Punishment of this code violation is outlined as well, stipulating that a second violation within twelve hours of the first warning by a police officer, will result in a the levying of "response fee." These laws are microscopic examples of the multitude of laws that the vast majority of Californians willingly obey, often without much thought or concern. Social contract theorists, discussed in Chapter 2, reasoned that individuals existed in a "state of nature," meaning that people were essentially born free. The formation of societies ruled by organized governments, so said these theorists in the Western tradition, should be based on a contract of sorts that, while restricting certain freedoms, like the freedom not to study American government, wear gloves in the food service industry—nails or no nails—or play loud music, provide protection to the overall society. In many societies today, the "contract" is arbitrary and unconditional. The American version of the social contract is constantly challenged, sustained, and occasionally revised through the judicial system. However unfair, extreme, or incorrectly laws may be applied, the California judicial system, in the American tradition of jurisprudence, provides the opportunity for reviewing what may be an excessive restriction of personal freedom or conditions not relevant to the "contract."

## The California Court System

The California court system is the largest in the nation, with more than 2,000 judicial officers and 18,000 court employees who handle approximately 9 million cases each year. The court system is very similar to the pyramidlike structure of the federal court system, with superior or trial courts spread throughout California's fifty-eight counties at the base, six appellate court districts in the middle, and one state supreme court at the top. All California judges and justices are required by the Code of Judicial Ethics to "be faithful to the law regardless of partisan interests, public clamor or fear of criticism." Courts can be very deceptive places. A great deal of expense and care go into erecting courthouses—commonly constructed with stone, granite, and solid wood—designed to reinforce an atmosphere of professional, official, and eternal enforcement of the state's laws. A certain formal decorum is compulsory, starting with the black robe of the judges and justices, formal attire of the court's participants, and sober ambience, all of which are enforced by administrative rules and laws. Yet despite this correctness and ambience, the very worst aspects of California society are on display every day in these courtrooms. It is important to remember throughout this chapter that the judicial system really is the fine line between chaos or absolute government and a civil society (see Figure 19.1).

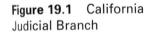

**Figure 19.1** California Judicial Branch

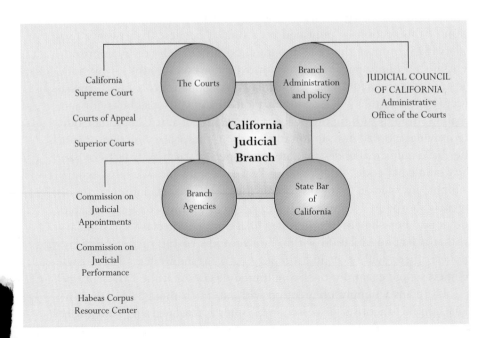

**Superior Courts**    The entry point for the enforcement of California law and the settlement of conflicts or disagreements is the California **superior courts**, adjudicated or administered by 1,499 authorized judges and 437 commissioners and referees.[1] In 1998, California voters approved **Proposition 220**, a constitutional amendment that consolidated superior and municipal courts into a single superior court with original jurisdiction over all cases that enter the court system, generally consisting of felonies, misdemeanors, and traffic and civil cases. In consolidating these courts, the judicial system, in cooperation with the state legislature, was attempting to provide greater flexibility in how court cases were assigned and make more efficient use of state funding allocations. Of the roughly 9 million cases that are filed annually, 8.5 million are dealt with by superior courts at over 400 locations. Superior courts also have appellate jurisdiction for small claims cases. Over the past forty years, the superior courts have experienced major increases in caseload, the greatest growth occurring in criminal cases. Efforts to lessen this caseload has caused an increase in the use of **plea bargains**, formal agreements between the district attorney's office and the defendant to forgo a trial. Family matters have become the largest part of the superior courts' civil case workload. Matters involving family law and other specific legal areas are heard in special superior court departments. Specialty superior courts have been developed to address specific kinds of cases and more effectively comply with recent initiatives and statutes, principally in nonviolent drug and domestic violence cases, and to coordinate efforts with other agencies within the justice system.[2] California is one of the first states in the nation to initiate the **drug court** as an alternative to the traditional criminal justice process for drug law offenders, offering options other than incarceration, supervising drug treatment programs, and having specially trained California judges and other court professionals deal with prevention and relapse issues. Small claims court is another type of special court where civil disputes involving less than $7,500 are resolved quickly and inexpensively. The parties to a small claims case are not allowed representation by an attorney in court. The filing fees are relatively inexpensive, and the rules of this court are simple and structured to allow a person without much legal knowledge to present his or her case. In many small claims courts, commissioners take the place of judges and usually inform both parties of the court's ruling by mail.[3]

**Court of Appeals**    California has six appellate districts, headquartered in San Francisco (First District), Los Angeles (Second District), Sacramento (Third District), San Diego (Fourth District), Fresno (Fifth District), and San Jose (Sixth District), with a total of 105 justices. Each district of the California **court of appeals** has a presiding justice and a number of associate justices serving on panels of three justices that review approximately 25,000 requests for an appeal each year.[4] Upon completion of a superior court trial, the losing party has the right to appeal the ruling to the California court of appeals, with the exception of death penalty cases, which must go straight to the state supreme court. Appeals are usually reviewed in the appellate district where the superior court that originally heard the case was located. The appellate process in the California court of appeals begins with the filing of the notice of appeal and written arguments, known as briefs, from both sides of the case. Appellate courts do not review new evidence or assess the credibility of witnesses. Required by the California constitution to issue a decision within ninety days of accepting a case, the appellate courts first review the written record of the case to determine if the trial court properly interpreted the law and applied legal procedures correctly. The appellate court justices also read the briefs and hear oral arguments by the parties to the case before issuing a

—**Think Again**—

What kinds of cases do California's superior courts handle? Which areas of adjudication have grown most rapidly in recent years?

**superior courts**  Entry point for the enforcement of California law and the settlement of conflicts or disagreements.

**Proposition 220**  A California constitutional amendment that consolidated superior and municipal courts into a single superior court with original jurisdiction over all cases that enter the court system.

**plea bargain**  A formal agreement between the district attorney's office and a defendant to forgo a trial in exchange for a guilty plea.

**drug court**  An alternative criminal justice venue for drug law offenders.

—**Think Again**—

What steps must appellate courts take when handling appeals? What can't they do when considering the validity of a lower court's decision?

**court of appeals**  Court that has the power to consider or hear an appeal.

California Supreme Court Chief Justice Ronald George administers the oath of office to Arnold Schwarzenegger, California's 38th Governor.

written statement, known as the opinion, of the panel's decision. At least two justices on the panel must concur on the final ruling of the court.[5]

The California court of appeals does have original jurisdiction in cases challenging confinement (habeas corpus), ordering government to act (writs of mandamus), requesting review of judicial action (writs of certiorari), and requesting restraint on certain actions. This court will also review appeals of the decisions made by certain quasi-judicial bodies such as the Workers' Compensation Appeals Board, Agricultural Labor Relations Board, Public Employment Relations Board, Department of Alcoholic Beverage Control Board, and Public Utilities Commission (see Figure 19.2).[6]

**Think Again**

What role has the state Supreme Court played in shaping the evolution of the California judicial system?

**supreme court** The highest court in a state, the decisions of which are binding on all lower courts.

**Supreme Court**   The California **supreme court** is the highest court in the state, and its decisions are binding on all other California courts. It is in reality the "court of last resort." There are seven supreme court justices, including the chief justice.

The California constitution gives the state supreme court appellate jurisdiction (the power to review decisions) over the California court of appeals. With the exception of death penalty cases, which it must review under the provisions of the California constitution, the supreme court has discretion over what cases it will review and as a result will review only a small number of the thousands of cases that it receives annually. As the highest court in California, the supreme court is expected to decide important legal questions and issues and maintain the uniformity or consistency of California law. The supreme court also has original jurisdiction in cases involving writs of mandamus, writs of certiorari, prohibitions, and habeas corpus. Special matters that can come before the supreme court are reviews of the recommendations by the Commission on Judicial Performance and the State Bar of California regarding disciplinary action against judges and attorneys for misconduct. The supreme court also reviews the appeals of the decisions by the Public Utilities Commission. In deciding a case, at least four of

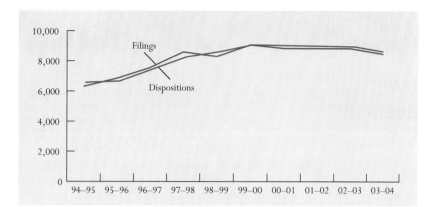

**Figure 19.2** Total Supreme Court Filings and Dispositions 1994–1995 to 2003–2004

*Source: 2005 Annual Report, Cornerstones of Democracy: California Courts Enter a New Era of Judicial Branch Independence,* Judicial Council of California, Administrative Office of the Court.

the seven supreme court justices must agree on the final decision. The procedure for reviewing cases, other than its discretion, is very similar to the process in the California court of appeals. In recent years, most criminal cases and about two-thirds of the civil cases that were appealed to either appellate court were affirmed or found to be without legal errors or to have properly followed legal procedures. When a case was reversed or found to have involved errors by the appellate courts, it was almost always sent back to the trial court for retrial to apply the correct law or procedures.[7]

**Alternative Dispute Resolution**    In many California counties, especially densely populated ones, it can take up to two years before a civil lawsuit can reach the trial stage. Not only has the criminal and civil caseload grown dramatically, straining the resources of the California court system, but the legal procedures required by civil law cases in particular, such as discovery and the taking of depositions, can cause major delays in court action and involve costly fees for both the court and attorneys. In response to these legal impediments, the Judicial Council of California, local courts, and various legal associations are increasingly encouraging the use of **alternative dispute resolution (ADR)** as a way of expediting the legal process. There are many variations of ADR, some of which facilitate narrow aspects of the legal process, but the two major forms are mediation and arbitration. Until recently, ADR was largely restricted to specific situations such as contract negotiation and business disputes and use by experienced legal professionals. California superior courts have become much more proactive in encouraging the use of ADR resources, regularly making referrals to private legal firms and forming cooperative relations with nonprofit organizations that provide free or low-cost ADR services. When parties to a conflict of some sort opt for mediation, they are basically getting an impartial person to help the parties reach a mutually acceptable resolution of the dispute. A mediator will not make a final decision but will try to get the parties to communicate and ultimately agree on a settlement. Arbitration, by contrast, does involve an impartial binding or nonbinding decision by an outside party after all the arguments and evidence have been presented. Arbitration is less formal, expensive, and time-consuming than a trial. Parties that choose binding arbitration waive their right to a trial and agree to accept the arbitrator's decision as final.

As ADR becomes more popular and the number of private firms that specialize in this alternative to formal court trials continue grow, there have been concerns that the costs may be as prohibitive as the formal legal process for the average Californian. In some cases, mediators can charge hundred of dollars per hour for ADR services. The state legislature has taken up this issue but must walk

---Think Again---

Why has alternative dispute resolution (ADR) grown more popular in recent years?

**alternative dispute resolution (ADR)** Non-court-centered options for resolving disagreements, such as mediation and arbitration.

## PEOPLE IN POLITICS

### Janice Rogers Brown: California's Controversial Justice Reaches U.S. Appellate Court

There is a reasonably good chance that within the next ten years another Californian, appellate court justice Janice Rogers Brown, could be nominated and confirmed as a justice of the U.S. Supreme Court. The Republicans in the U.S. Senate, aided by President George W. Bush and other influential Republicans, fought a hard-won battle to secure her confirmation to the U.S. Court of Appeals. The high regard in which Justice Brown is held in the Republican Party was illustrated by the persistence of her Senate sponsors, who reintroduced her nomination after Democrats launched a filibuster that stalled her confirmation for two years. If the Republicans can regain control of the nomination and confirmation process of U.S. Supreme Court justices and vacancies materialize, Justice Brown's experience and background will make her a very appealing candidate to that bench. For Californians, the judicial elevation of Janice Rogers Brown offers the opportunity to better understand the state judicial system that essentially produced this nationally recognized jurist. More than any other factor, Justice Brown's ascension implies that California may not be as liberal, at least within its legal circles, as previously thought.

Born in Greenville, Alabama, Brown came to California with her mother as a teenager and began her college education at California State University, Sacramento. Widowed with one child as a college student, she succeeded in obtaining her law degree from the University of California at Los Angeles School of Law. Taking a position first as legal counsel to the state legislature, she went on to the attorney general's office where she was instrumental in successfully defending the state against a class-action suit that accused the state of underpaying a group of female state workers. Justice Brown's work on this case earned her the admiration of then-governor Pete Wilson, who initially appointed her as deputy secretary and general legal counsel to the State of California Business, Transportation, and Housing Agency and later as legal advisor to the governor and eventually legal affairs secretary in the Wilson cabinet. Although from a liberal Democratic family, somewhere along her career path Brown adopted conservative political views coupled with evangelical Christian beliefs. These beliefs were clearly inconsequential to the moderately conservative politics of former governor Wilson, who first nominated Brown as an associate justice to the California Court of Appeals for the Third District in 1994 and then as an associate justice to the California Supreme Court. The judicial career of Janice Brown almost ended at the appellate level when the California Commission on Judicial Nominees Evaluation found her unqualified for the California Supreme Court, citing inexperience, the lack of minimum qualifications, and her tendency to insert conservative views into opinions. Despite this evaluation, for the first time in its seventeen-year history,

a fine line between limiting the financial incentives to legal professionals or dumbing down legal procedures and attempting to structure adequate dispute resolution for the average resident.

**Judicial Qualifications and Selection**   All California court judges and justices must first have been an attorney with the ability to practice law or have served as a judge in California for at least ten years immediately preceding election or appointment. The governor fills superior court vacancies through appointment. Otherwise, these judges are elected to six-year terms by voters on a nonpartisan ballot in the county where the superior court is located. Appellate or supreme court justices are appointed by the governor but must first be evaluated by the California State Bar's Commission on Judicial Nominees and confirmed by the Commission on Judicial Appointments. This commission, composed of the chief justice of California, the state attorney general, and a senior presiding justice of the California court of appeals, will review the nomi-

Governor Wilson ignored the commission's findings and went ahead with the appointment.

As the first African American woman appointed to the California Supreme Court, Brown took decidedly conservative positions that were often laced with abrasive observations, reserved in a number of instances for her fellow justices. Throughout her nine years on the California Supreme Court, the legal opinions of Justice Brown generally mirrored the moderately conservative trend of the court apart from a number of a dissenting opinions in which she felt the interpretation of the court was either too liberal or contrary to the founding principles of the United States Constitution. In the body of her opinions, she is most noted for favoring private property rights, opposing affirmative action, and supporting a state law requiring girls under the age of eighteen to notify their parents before getting an abortion. One of Justice Brown's most cited opinions is *Hi-Voltage Wire Works v. City of San Jose* in 2000. At issue was the city's public-works program that required applicants for contracts to engage in special outreach efforts to recruit disadvantaged subcontractors, explicitly implying that those subcontractors should be racial minorities. Writing for the majority, Justice Brown's opinion upheld the California voter-approved initiative, Proposition 209, that bans race and gender preferences by government and found that the proposition not only forbids specific quotas, but also bans any subtle and long-term goals for race and gender inclusion.

Despite her conservative legal approach, 76 percent of the California voters approved her retention as an associate justice of the California Supreme Court during the 1998 California general election. If California's liberal community or civil libertarians had any difficulty accepting her often inflammatory judicial and political views, such opposition was extremely hard to notice, unlike the intense outcry over the legal positions of former chief justice Rose Bird and the successful campaign to oust her from the California Supreme Court by conservatives and Republican party activists. Justice Brown's opinions while on the California Supreme Court did attract the attention of conservative legal groups, such the Federalist Society, and members of the Republican Party from across the country and she became a sought-after speaker. Unlike other conservative members of the California Supreme Court as well as other state court justices throughout the country, this attention and her compelling personal story made her a likely nominee for the U.S. Court of Appeals for the District of Columbia. The D.C. Circuit of the U.S. Court of Appeals is considered one of the most important courts in the United States after the Supreme Court. This court oversees the actions of federal agencies and its rulings have serious consequences for national policies and law. Although it may be premature to suggest that Justice Brown's position on the U.S. Court of Appeals will be a stepping-stone to the nation's highest judicial body, her experience at the California bar clearly has been beneficial to what has so far been a successful judicial career.

*Sources:* David D. Kirkpatrick, "New Judge Sees Slavery in Liberalism," *New York Times,* June 9, 2005, http://www.nytimes.com; "NWPC Opposes the Confirmation of Janice Rogers Brown," National Women's Political Caucus, April 26, 2005, http://www.nwpc.org; George Raine, "Not Qualified Judge Review Shifts Spotlight to Commission," SFGate.com, April 29, 1996, http://www.sfgate.com; Resume of Janice R. Brown, Office of Legal Policy, U.S. Department of Justice, http://www.usdoj.gov/olp/brownresume.htm; Harold Johnson, and Timothy Sandefur, "Judging Janice Rogers Brown," FrontPageMagazine.com, November 5, 2003, http://www.frontpagemag.com/Articles.

nee's qualifications, conduct public hearings, and confirm the appointment if it finds the nominee qualified to serve. After the nominee is confirmed and admitted as an appellate or supreme court justice, the appointment must be approved by a majority of voters at the next general election; the term of service is twelve years.

**The Judicial Council**  The **Judicial Council** is the governing body of the California courts and has the responsibility of establishing guidelines for these courts, submitting recommendations to the governor and state legislature regarding the judicial system, and adopting and revising the California Rules of Court. The twenty-seven-member Judicial Council is chaired by the chief justice of the state supreme court, and also includes fourteen judges appointed by the chief justice, four attorneys appointed by the board of governors of the State Bar Board of California, one member chosen from each house of the legislature, and six advisory members. As the workload of the California judicial system grows and

**Judicial Council** The body that governs California's courts.

becomes increasingly complex, especially with the advent of new technology, the Judicial Council is expected to continuously review and evaluate methods of meeting these current challenges. If a new policy or method is initiated in the California court system, chances are that the Council was behind it.

## The Variations in California Law

The work of California courts is largely predicated on interpreting California law, codes, regulations, and ordinances broadly classified as either civil or criminal law. California laws, like most laws in the tradition of American jurisprudence, are "living" articles of California society, evolving gradually in large part but sometimes subject to rapid change. Rapid change to the California legal system is often the result of voters, who can affect the body of California law through the initiative and referendum. The initiative process in particular regularly generates laws that are more reactions to social attitudes than to farsightedness or detailed study. More than a decade after passage of **Proposition 184**, the "three-strikes" law, Californians may be tempted to ask whether they are any safer now than before the passage of this initiative. Some would suggest that the slight decrease in crime is a positive sign, while others will point to a prison population that has grown, partly due to individuals convicted under Proposition 184, to be not only the largest in the nation but also a breeding ground for generations of crime and criminals. The champions of the initiative process have been more attracted to the sensationalism of crime, devoting few resources to producing and passing successful measures that addressed civil law issues. The passage of initiatives addressing the insurance industry and tort reform are the rare examples of initiative topics that have sought to alter civil law, and such change has been limited in scope.

**Proposition 184** The "three strikes" law imposing a 25-years-to-life imprisonment for a third felony offense.

**civil law** The area of law dealing with relations between private citizens.

**Civil Law**   **Civil law** is intended to help people settle conflicts or disputes that they ordinarily cannot solve themselves. California civil law encompasses a wide variety of topics, consisting of general civil, family, juvenile, landlord-tenant, probate, and small claims law. General civil law, which focus on contracts, damage to property, and injury, is an extremely broad category. California Civil Code 3342, commonly known as the "dog bite" statute, imposes strict liability on the owner of a dog that bites someone. According to the statute, the dog only has to bite once, even if no puncture to the skin results, for the dog owner to be liable for the actions of that dog. Although this statute may appear pretty straightforward, harm caused by a dog's barking is not covered by the "dog bite" statute, illustrating the many gradations, exceptions, and difficulties inherent in solving disputes among people in court.

**tort law** The area of law dealing with any wrongdoing that results in legal action for damages.

Litigation explosion in California has been another source of concern regarding general civil law over the past thirty years. Detractors of litigation, particularly when it involves California **tort law**, which is any wrongdoing that results in legal action for damages, propound that Californians are encouraged by lawyers to take just about all real or imagined disputes to court. Another view considers litigation a just means of resolving disputes that may involve discrimination, product safety, worker rights, and environmental degradation and finds the problem of abuse in the rules and procedures and not in the act of litigation itself. The expense of litigation alone, such advocates suggest, is beyond the resources of most people anyway. For many years now, California has been the setting for various legal battles between a number of different industries and trial

Attorneys present their case before the judge at a civil hearing.

lawyers over the ability to sue and the monetary limits on damages awarded by California courts. Two main advocacy organizations, the California Medical Association and the Consumer Attorneys of California, have clashed repeatedly over limits on malpractice cases and awards. By lobbying the state legislature, spending millions in the process, the California Medical Association has been able to get the passage of laws that imposed limits on contingency fees, eliminated multiple payment of court awards, qualified the rules for the payment of malpractice awards in installments, and placed limits on pain-and-suffering damages. The insurance industry has been less successful in containing what has been also seen by some as frivolous insurance lawsuits in California. However, the insurance industry and trial lawyers continue to skirmish over workers' compensation, and many more battles are expected in the future.

Family law tends to take of up most of the time and effort of the California courts that handle civil law cases. These civil law matters usually involve divorce, child support, and child custody. Since the 1980s, the Judicial Council has tried to address the rise in family law cases by introducing a number of special programs and offices such as the Statewide Office of Family Court Services, child support commissioners, family law facilitators, and the Center for Families, Children and the Courts. **Probate law** largely pertains to the personal affairs of an individual and how those personal affairs will be handled in the event that a person becomes incapacitated. Typical probate cases involve wills or trusts, guardianship, name changes, and adoptions, but the field has become increasingly controversial in California due to instances or accusations of elder abuse as it relates to the estate or financial assets of the elderly. The state legislature recently added the Elder Abuse and Dependent Adult Civil Protection Act to the Welfare and Institutions Code in reaction to a wave of financially abusive situations affecting California's large aging population. In 2003, most alleged perpetrators of financial elder abuse were adult children or other family members involving misappropriation of income or assets, charging excessive fees, or obtaining money or property by undue influence.[9]

**probate law**  The area of law governing cases that pertain to the personal affairs of an individual.

## Criminal Law
California has established a considerable reputation nationally for crime due in large part to the long list of highly publicized or infamous crimes

that have been tried in California courts. In fact, these cases have been so well publicized and have so frequently involved heinous acts that they have tended to set or influence state and national standards in criminal justice. Throughout the 1950s, Caryl Chessman, sentenced to death for a rape conviction under dubious evidence, caused the nation to reflect on capital punishment. In the 1960s, the various trials of Black Panther members and political activist Angela Davis had the affect of politicizing the court process. The murder trial of Charles Manson and his "family" in the 1970s energized a statewide and nationwide get tough-on-crime approach. In the 1980s, the McMartin preschool child molestation case captured national media attention, stirring questions about being judged guilty before having the chance to prove one's innocence and the quality of investigations by law enforcement agencies. In the early 1990s, the acquittal of four police officers charged with the beating of Rodney King and the subsequent Los Angeles riots raised important issues regarding equality before the law and the resulting lawlessness. And not long after that, the murder of Polly Klaas and the acquittal of O. J. Simpson generated yet another get tough-on-crime backlash. The consequences of California's high-profile criminal cases as well as the prevailing popularity of pro-law-and-order attitudes among most people in this large state have put intense pressure on all levels of the criminal justice system to avoid the perception of coddling criminals while maintaining the appearance of fairness and professionalism in enforcing **criminal law**.

**criminal law** The area of law dealing with crime and the legal punishment of criminal offenses.

**California Penal Code** The listing of all crimes defined by statutes.

**felony** A crime for which a person may be sentenced to imprisonment in the state prison or to death.

**misdemeanor** A crime for which a person may be imprisoned in a county jail for usually a year or less and/or fined.

**infraction** Any public offense punishable by a fine.

*corpus delicti* The elements of a crime.

**determinate sentence** The choices for punishment for a crime that can be imposed by a judge.

Law enforcement begins with the **California Penal Code**, which contains all crimes defined by statutes. In the California Penal Code, offenses are divided into two major categories: felonies and misdemeanors. **Felonies** are crimes for which a person may be sentenced to imprisonment in the state prison, or to death. **Misdemeanors** are lesser crimes for which a person may be imprisoned in a county jail for usually a year or less and/or fined. **Infractions** are classified in California as public offenses and normally pertain to municipal ordinances or codes and are punishable by fines only. A parking ticket is probably the best example of an infraction. An individual charged with an infraction is not entitled to a trial by jury or public defense.[10]

Every criminal law in California must reflect the notion of **corpus delicti** or elements of a crime. Establishing *corpus delicti* begins with proving that the actions specified in the law really did happen and that there was intent or the accused knowingly planned to commit the crime outlined in the law. Once the accused is found guilty in a California court, according to the penal code, a **determinate sentence** will generally be imposed, which means that the judge will have the choice of three punishments, in most cases defined by the number of years in prison, for example, a six-year, twelve-year, or sixteen-year sentence. If any sentence other than the middle sentence is selected, the judge must explain in writing what aggravating facts justify the lower or higher sentence. California does have elements of "indeterminate sentencing." The best example is the "three strikes and you're out" law that was enacted by the state legislature and by the electorate in Proposition 184. This law imposes an indeterminate twenty-five years–to–life imprisonment and other "enhancements" (lengthening of sentences for the commission of felony offenses) for anyone who had been previously convicted of two or more serious and/or violent felonies. Violation of California criminal law is also punishable by consecutive sentencing, a period of confinement in prison for each separate crime, or concurrent sentencing, one sentence for multiple crimes.[11] In 1984, Peter Chan helped plan the robbery of a jewelry store in Los Angeles, scouting out the location of the robbery, obtaining weapons, and arranging the getaway car, but was never actually present during the crime. Two Los Angeles

# UP CLOSE

## The Wendland Case and the Right to Die

In 2001, the California Supreme Court addressed the issue of the right to die in the *Conservatorship of Wendland*, a case very similar to that of Terri Schiavo, which made national headlines in 2005. Although not quite as sensational, the Wendland case was also very controversial, highlighting the major issues involved the right to die, including when life support may be withdrawn, which family member decides, and the role of the court in determining the proper course of action. Unable to communicate, eat, drink, or use the bathroom because of injuries that resulted from a 1993 auto accident, Robert Wendland languished for two years, in the opinion of immediate family members and medical professionals who were closely monitoring his condition. In 1995, his wife, Rose, and three children favored removing his feeding and hydration tube, believing that statements made by Mr. Wendland before the accident supported this course of action. Doctors familiar with his case as well as the hospital ethics panel supported the immediate family's wishes. Mr. Wendland's mother and sister, however, did not approve of the plan to withdraw artificial life support. They could point to his ability to convey "yes" or "no" answers to simple questions, among other factors, and challenged the decision to end his life in court.

Robert Wendland died of pneumonia prior to a decision in the case, but his wife asked the state supreme court to rule anyway in an attempt to clarify the law for similar cases in the future. In establishing new restrictions on the right to end life support for the terminally ill who are unable to speak for themselves, the court said in a unanimous decision that a relative or friend who requests such action must present "clear and convincing evidence" that the patient really wanted to die and that death would be in his or her best interests. The court did state that the decision to terminate the life of minimally conscious patients was a fundamental right under California's privacy laws and that any restrictions by the government must be justified by a compelling state interest. That fundamental right, however, had to be substantiated by either a designated agent for such health care decisions, specific written instructions completed prior to incapacitation by the patient, or a persistent vegetative state of the patient. The court based its decision on a conscious patient's constitutional right to life and the notion that a decision to terminate life is irreversible. The court added that any decision must be supported by strong evidence of the patient's desire to terminate life-supports. And so, had Mr. Wendland lived, his wife and children would not have been able to have his life terminated.

The Wendland case presents a very difficult question, whether legal or moral or both, that will probably never be answered in a clear-cut manner. The most unfortunate aspect of such circumstances, as Rose Wendland conceded, is that in the absence of specific instructions, the decision of life or death for minimally conscious patients is ultimately in the hands of people in "three-piece suits and black robes." The simplest way of dealing with these occurrences is to complete a valid durable power of attorney for health care decisions or through an advance health care directive. Using the durable power of attorney or health care directive, a person may provide instructions that determine the conditions under which he or she would not want to continue receiving life-sustaining treatment. Establishing specific instructions is extremely important because, as was seen in the Wendland case, the distinction between minimally conscious and fully alive can vary, including such physical conditions as brain death, irreversible coma, persistent vegetative state, or semi-consciousness. Without a durable power of attorney or health care directive, the court is responsible for appointing a conservator if the minimally conscious patient is incapable of making decisions about his or her own welfare.

Less than 20 percent of Americans execute durable power of attorney or health care directives, despite national surveys that suggest most people would rather have their lives terminated than be sustained through artificial means. Although it is possible that a young person could suffer from severe incapacitation, for example, it is very unlikely that they would consider completing instructions to address such remote medical conditions. In the absence of specific directives or agents, most people simply have to continue to hope they will pass quickly, the legal system will act in their best interests, or the miracles of modern medicine will alleviate such dilemmas.

*Sources:* Margaret C. Crosby, "The Right to Die California Supreme Court Ruling in Wendland Case Should Spur Us to Protect Our Rights," Staff Attorney, *ACLU—The Newspaper of ACLU of Northern California,* Autumn, 2001, http://www.aclunc.org/aclunews; Claire Cooper, "New Curbs Placed on Right to Die," *Sacramento Bee,* August 10, 2001; "Top California Court Rules in 'Right to Die' Case," The World Federation of Right to Die Societies," August 9, 2001, http://www.worldrtd.net/news/world/?id=485; Amy L. McEvoy, "California Health Care Decisions Law and the Right to Die," Drobny Law Offices, Inc., http://www.drobnylaw.com/articles/die.html.

California courts have been the scene of many high-profile criminal cases, including the trials of O.J. Simpson and Scott Peterson, both accused of murder. Simpson was acquitted of murdering his ex-wife, Nicole Brown Simpson and her friend, Ron Goldman. Peterson was found guilty of murdering his wife, Laci.

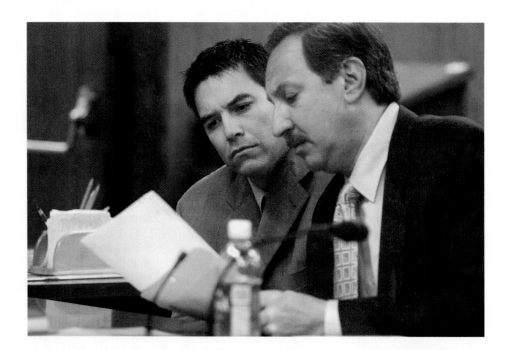

police officers were shot, however, in the commission of the crime, one fatally. Based on the intent and action of the crime, according to the criminal statute, Chan qualified for a charge of first-degree murder. California criminal law stipulates that all principals to a crime are equally guilty, including those who aid and abet other parties to commit a crime, regardless of whether a participant was present during the crime. The jury nonetheless found Chan guilty of murder in the second-degree. Second-degree murder normally carries a fifteen years–to–life sentence with the possibility of parole. The judge chose instead to essentially impose a life sentence by sentencing Chan to thirty-eight years to life by making other criminal violations associated with Chan's case consecutive.[12]

# The California Jury System

In California, as in most states, the jury is a fundamental part of the California legal system, ideally guaranteeing fairness in the decision of guilt or innocence of the accused in a court trial. Many political observers and social critics suggest a growing tendency among Americans to avoid the obligations of civic duty. The reluctance of Californians to actively participation in the jury process is not that different. Among the few civic obligations requested of Californians, participation in a jury requires prospective jurors to absent themselves from normal routine, enter an unfamiliar environment, interact with strangers, bear long hours of inactivity, and judge those accused of criminal as well as distasteful and embarrassing acts. Despite these inconveniences and discomforts, many Californians realize the importance of this duty of citizenship and comply with the obligation to serve. In California, to serve as a juror, you must be a U.S. citizen 18 years of age or older, with a conversational understanding of the English language, who lives in the county of service, has not served on a jury in the past twelve months and is not currently on a grand jury or on another jury, and is free of parole commitments. For most jurors, the jury experience will begin and end with the waiting period prior to the selection process. A large jury pool waiting to be selected for a case can often be a major inducement, especially in civil matters, for the settlement of a case. Once the court case does start, the jury selection process, known as **voir dire**, allows the defense and prosecution interview potential jurors and to ask the judge to excuse certain jurors due to a perceived bias or unsuitability to serve. Throughout the trial, it is the responsibility of the jury to hear the evidence and decide questions of fact, while the judge's concern is to address questions of law. After the facts of a case have been presented, the jury must act on the instructions of the judge, which normally involves the relevant law and the degree of proof required to reach a verdict. In California courts, parties to a civil trial must prove guilt or innocence by a "preponderance of evidence"; in a criminal trial, the jurors must be convinced "beyond a reasonable doubt."

The state of California pays jurors $15 per day starting on the second day of service, and transportation costs; an exception is government employees, who are entitled to receive full pay and benefits from their employers while on jury duty. The length of jury service in California is based on a "one-day or one-trial jury service" obligation during a twelve-month period. Failure to fulfill jury duty, unless this duty has been excused or postponed, could result in a fine up to $1,500 or time in the county jail.

The role of juries in the California judicial system has been the source of a great deal of criticism in recent decades, stemming in large part from the acquittal of the accused in a number of high-profile court cases. The verdicts in the O. J. Simpson and Rodney King cases fanned suspicions that jurors are influenced by factors other than a sense of justice and often rely more on cultural mores and personal experience than on the evidence presented at the trial. In the aftermath of these trials, there were various calls from inside and outside the judicial system for drastic changes to the jury system. The California District Attorneys Association has called on the state legislature to abolish the unanimous verdict and to permit juries in California to convict or acquit whenever ten of twelve jurors agree on a verdict. Anyone who has witnessed a highly publicized trial on televi-

---

**Think Again**

Who can serve on a jury in California and how are jurors selected for participation in a trial?

Why do so many people avoid jury service in California?

What role does the county grand jury play in the California judicial system?

---

**voir dire** The process of selecting a jury (from an Old French expression meaning "speak the truth").

## WHAT DO YOU THINK?

# The Evolving Dimensions of Capital Punishment

Throughout California history, capital punishment is the one criminal justice issue that inevitably resurfaces at some point, usually brought on by an imminent execution of a prisoner convicted under questionable circumstances or issues of cruel and unusual punishment. Not unlike the Caryl Chessman clemency campaign of the 1950s, the death sentence of Crips gang founder and anti-gang children's author Stanley "Tookie" Williams produced an international crusade that sparked widespread discussions of criminal justice, morality, and redemption. In the end, Governor Schwarzenegger, seemingly forced by the broad public support for capital punishment, Williams's unrepentant stance, and the ideology of his political party, denied a mass appeal for clemency. Attitudes about the death penalty have been fairly constant since this punishment was reinstated in California during the 1970s, but there have been distinct changes over the decades, suggesting that Californians may be due for another major reappraisal.

Prior to statehood, the most common form of execution in California was the firing squad. After California was admitted into the Union, hanging became the preferred method of execution, but attitudes about this practice, reflecting many of the concerns about capital punishment expressed today, underwent significant change over a ninety-year period. At first, hangings were carried out in public. William B. Shepard was executed in San Francisco on July 28, 1854, after being convicted of murder four months earlier. Shepard was escorted by carriage up Broadway and Pacific Streets to the Presidio, where a scaffold had been erected in a location capable of accommodating the mob of 10,000 people that would eventually gather. Addressing the crowd before his death, Shepard turned and proclaimed: "I have been tried and convicted of the murder of my friend, Henry C. Day. All I have to ask of you now is your prayers. I am innocent. As I expect forgiveness from God, which I truly expect and know I have. I am innocent." The newspapers of the day frequently denounced such public executions, and the spectacles they became, gradually moving opinions away from such local exhibitions. By 1872, the county sheriff was given the responsibility of carrying out executions, which were moved behind the walls of county jail or to a "convenient private place in the county." By 1891, executions were moved once again by constitutional amendment, this time inside the walls of state prisons.

Increasingly seen as inhumane and uncivilized for a society surrounded by modernity, hanging gave way to the use of the gas chamber in California in 1937. The state prison at San Quentin became the site of the state's only lethal gas chamber and was used to execute 194 prisoners between 1938 and 1967. Beginning in 1967, courts across the country faced legal challenges to the constitutionality of the death penalty on Eighth Amendment grounds; for most death penalty sentences, there was an appellate process that would take years. The U.S. Supreme Court eventually approved execution as a legitimate form of punishment in 1972, but required most

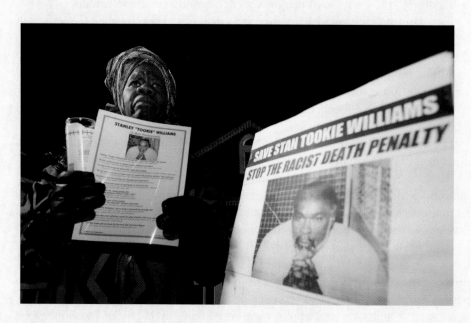

Queen Mother Dr. Delois Blakely, Community Mayor of Harlem, outside the gates of San Quentin State Prison, holds a vigil to protest the execution of Stanley "Tookie" Williams. Governor Arnold Schwarzenegger refused to commute his sentence of death by lethal injection, which was carried out on December 13, 2005.

states to enact laws that could be administered without violating the Eighth Amendment. Between 1972 and 1993, the California legislature would rewrite death penalty legislation a number of times, finally creating a law that would withstand legal challenges and pave the way for the execution of Robert Alton Harris in 1992. Two years later, David Mason would be one of the last condemned prisoners to be executed by lethal gas, not long before the U.S. Ninth Circuit Court of Appeals ruled in 1996 that the gas chamber constituted cruel and unusual punishment. The court found that the suffering of prisoners executed by gas at San Quentin was "impermissibly cruel," and accounts of the process describe the condemned in a state of pain and extreme anxiety not unlike a heart attack victim, often dying minutes after being exposed to hydrocyanic gas. According to a witness to a San Quentin gas chamber execution, when the gas is administered, the condemned prisoner will often give the appearance of extreme terror, pain, and strangling as the skin turns purple, eyes bulge, and drooling occurs.

In 1996, serial killer William Bonin became the first condemned prisoner to die of lethal injection, a process that was thought to be more humane, involving the injection of two needles into the veins of the prisoner's arms. Over the years, the costs associated with carrying out the death penalty would increase dramatically. Although the actual cost of the lethal injection chemicals is about $200, the expense of housing a prisoner on death row is considerably higher than the $34,150 in annual costs for the average prisoner. The Death Penalty Information Center estimates that the average cost of eleven executions over twenty-seven years was $250 million. The number of inmates on death row has grown as well: in 1990, 272 condemned prisoners on San Quentin's death row was thought high but has now shot up to 650. Most of the condemned will stay on death row for an average of 17.5 years and will be forty-nine at the time of their executions.

Many pro-death penalty advocates assumed that with rewritten laws and the acquiescence of the state and supreme courts on capital punishment, the road would be clear for regular executions. In February 2006, however, that road was once again blocked, this time indefinitely when a California judge ruled for a defendant who charged that prison officials were not qualified to administer the lethal injection without the supervision of qualified medical personnel. Medical professionals in California have generally resisted participating in executions on the grounds that the American Medical Association in particular, other medical groups, and professional ethics prohibit such activities. The respected British medical journal *The Lancet* reported in 2005 that in a study of lethal injections, half of the inmates were conscious enough throughout the process to experience suffering and that the failure to employ medically trained personnel in the process led to flaws in the administering of the lethal drugs. The final report of the study recommended that the practice be terminated.

*Sources:* William Carlsen, "Appeal Rejected—California Killer Moves Closer to Execution," *San Francisco Chronicle,* January 17, 1990, p. A1; "Hangings," San Francisco History, http://www.sfgenealogy.com/sf/history/hghan.htm; Claire Cooper, "Judge Bars State's Gas chamber—Calls It Cruel, Antiquated; Injection still Available," *Sacramento Bee,* October 5, 1994, p. A1. Gina Holland, "Executions By Lethal Injection Are Under Scrutiny Across the Country," Associated Press, February 26, 2006. Venise Wagner, "Tookie Williams: The Co-founder of the Crips Street Gang Shows his True Colors. *Mother Jones,* March/April, 2001; "History of Capital Punishment in California," California Department of Corrections and Rehabilitation, www.cya.ca.gov; "Death Penalty in California is Very Costly," Death Penalty Information Center, www.deathpenaltyinfo.org; "Medical Journal, The Lancet: Inmates Probably Conscious During Lethal Injections," Death Penalty Information Center, www.deathpenaltyinfo.org.

sion cannot help but wonder what effect the excessive media exposure is having on the outcome of the trial and the ability of the jurors to reach a fair verdict. Jurors worry about a decision that will be scrutinized in the media, and there is the possibility of financial rewards from media organizations for jurors willing to report on behind-the-scenes court proceedings. In reality, such high-profile cases are exceedingly rare.

A far more common problem facing thousands of courtrooms throughout California every day is the lack of participation, which has plagued the jury process in California to the point that the Blue Ribbon Commission on Jury Service Improvement convened by the Judicial Council of California concluded in 1996 that "the jury system is on the brink of collapse."

The American Tort Reform Association cited the avoidance of jury service by Californians as a serious problem in which "barely a quarter of those summoned for jury duty actually serve." The result of this reluctance to serve, the association

The jury in the case of the Menendez brothers, who were found guilty of murdering their parents, holds a press conference at the conclusion of the trial.

pointed out, is that "the system imposes a disproportionate share of the jury service burden on those willing to serve, which means these good citizens must serve more often."[13] The Judicial Council of California's Blue Ribbon Commission on Jury Service Improvement did make twenty-nine recommendations to remedy problems associated with the jury process, the most significant being these:

- Use of the National Change of Address System to update jury source lists to reduce the problem of undeliverable summonses

- Placing a hold on driver's license renewals of persons who fail to respond to jury summonses

- Creation of childcare programs for jurors who have children in their care

- Adoption of the one-day, one-trial system

- Implementation of a telephone standby system

- Increasing juror fees to $40 for each day after the first day and $50 after the thirteenth day.

- Requiring employers to pay employees for at least three days of jury service and providing tax credits to employers who voluntarily pay employees absent for more than three days due to jury service

Since the Blue Ribbon Commission report, only a few of the commission's recommendations have been implemented, most requiring enactment by the state legislature. Of the recommendations listed, only the National Change of Address System, "one-day, one-trial system," and telephone standby system are now widely used in California courts. Jury fees were increased, but only to the current $15-per-day rate. The problems associated with the jury process raises broader questions about the commitment to justice among Californians. Most

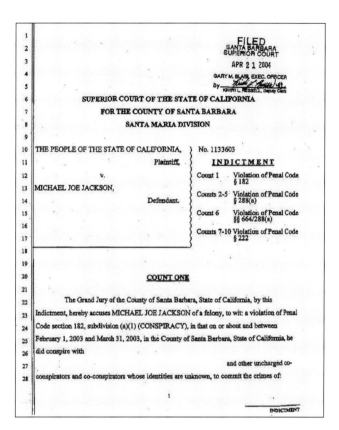

The front page of the Santa Barbara county grand jury indictment handed down April 21, 2004 against entertainer Michael Jackson outlines the charges made against the singer.

Californians abhor the instances of abuse by law enforcement officials, but criticisms by people who intentionally avoid their responsibility to the judicial system place the fairness in the California court system in jeopardy and undermine one of the most basic American democratic principles.

Aside from the regular juries of the California superior courts, the California constitution requires each county to impanel a grand jury every year. Selected by superior court judges, the **county grand jury** serves for a term of one year with the possibility of extensions of service and has the responsibility of "inquiring into public offenses committed or triable within the county, and may present them to the court by indictment" upon a finding of sufficient evidence. Because of the time and effort required by this process, the grand jury is rarely used to bring indictment, most California courts choosing instead to employ preliminary hearings to determine if sufficient evident exist for a trial. The California grand jury is required, based on provisions of the penal code, to make an annual examination of the operations, accounts, and records of the county government and special districts within the county and inquire into the conditions and management of state prisons within the county. The powers of the grand jury are derived from the ability to access all public records of county, municipal, and special-district government agencies within the county; investigate and report on the operations of local government; hire, with the permission of the superior court, experts such as auditors and accountants; and inquire into the sale, transfer, or ownership of any property that may or should be under the control of the state. The grand jury also has the responsibility of responding to complaints from residents of the county regarding the performance of local government officials or employees. Government agencies that are the target of a grand jury investigation and report are required by law to respond to specific recommendations by the

**county grand jury** In California, a jury that investigates public offenses committed or triable within the county.

**Figure 19.2** California
Penal Code Section 893-9

**California Penal Code Section 893-9**

P893. (a) A person is competent to act as a grand juror only if he possesses each of the following qualifications: (1) He is a citizen of the United States of the age of 18 years or older who shall have been a resident of the state and of the county or city and county for one year immediately before being selected and returned. (2) He is in possession of his natural faculties, of ordinary intelligence, of sound judgment, and of fair character. (3) He is possessed of sufficient knowledge of the English language.

(b) A person is not competent to act as a grand juror if any of the following apply: (1) The person is serving as a trial juror in any court of this state. (2) The person has been discharged as a grand juror in any court of this state within one year. (3) The person has been convicted of malfeasance in office or any felony or other high crime. (4) The person is serving as an elected public officer. 894. Sections 204, 218, and 219 of the Code of Civil Procedure specify the exemptions and the excuses which relieve a person from liability to serve as a grand juror.

grand jury, but the grand jury has no enforcement power, and government agencies are under no legal obligation to implement these recommendations.

The grand jury is considered one of the few local bodies that provide a public watchdog function over the operations of local government.[14] Over the years, the grand jury has been criticized for being unrepresentative of the community at large, shrouded in secrecy due to the rules governing investigations, and overly influenced by the county district attorney's office.

If, however, the public chooses to read the hundreds of reports issued by grand juries in California's fifty-eight counties, it is rare not to find information that is critical to the process of improving the performance of local government. In El Dorado County, for example, the grand jury found that the county mental health department failed to spend funds earmarked for a program to help children with severe emotional problems remain with their families. The grand jury for the county cited a lack of oversight of the special mental health program and uncovered discrepancies between services planned for children in the program and what was actually delivered.[15] An investigation by the San Joaquin County civil grand jury was prompted by complaints against the Tracy city manager's office, alleging that the assistant city manager used her influence to hire a former colleague, violated policy and procedures, and discriminated against racial minorities in making the appointment, among a number of other related complaints. The grand jury discovered that the assistant city manager did "display what appears to be a marked pattern of favoritism and cronyism, a) by changing the Oral Board Examination questions and tailoring them to favor the candidate with whom she had a previous work relationship." The grand jury did not, however, find "improper or unfair employment practices exercised against minorities."[16]

## Police Powers and the Prosecution

**Police Powers** When most Californians hear the term *police*, they tend to visualize the typical police officer, armed and in paramilitary dress. Although the typical municipal police officer has the broadest public authority, there are literally hundreds of individuals inside and sometimes outside government who have police powers. These police powers are intended for the enforcement of existing

California State University police officer and police dog search a dumpster outside Cox Arena in San Diego during a basketball tournament.

laws as outlined by the Tenth Amendment of the U.S. Constitution and Articles 11 and 12 of the California constitution. The enforcement of these laws, necessitating the granting of police powers to do so, extends to health inspectors, university and community college public safety officers, and even humane society workers, who can be empowered in California to make arrests, carry firearms, use force, and serve warrants. One section of a recent bill in the California state assembly was interpreted by the National Alliance of Homeowners as granting police powers to homeowners' associations. Instead of requiring the use of a "peace officer" to enforce a court order preventing an occupant from gaining physical access to a housing unit, this section of the bill would permit representatives of the homeowners' association to enforce such court orders.[17]

It is unfortunate that so many members of California society see a distinction between the duties of an official with police powers and existing law. The controversial aspect of this distinction stems from how far police officers can stray from the law in effectively executing their duties. One perspective suggests that law enforcement includes many gray areas, unlike laws, which are written to be as specific as possible, and that to see police work in black and white hues will only invite lawlessness. Racial profiling is one examples of the techniques used in law enforcement that while not codified—and, some people would suggest, unconstitutional—can be useful in bringing some criminals to justice. Certain California laws, civil libertarians argue, actually encourage the police to violate the law, pointing specifically to the Police Safety Officers Procedural Bill of Rights Act, which imposes limits on investigations, internal hearings, and punishment of police officers. California law specifies that most police disciplinary records and citizen complaints against officers be kept secret, unlike at least thirty states that permit partial or complete public access to police personnel records. Despite the merits or failings of either position, the accused or the individual subjected to unlawful action of those with police powers must have their day in court, where the legality of such actions will ideally be either affirmed or denied.[18]

── Think Again ──

What criticisms have been made of the actions of California district attorneys in recent years?

**district attorney** The principal public prosecutor in a county.

# The Prosecution

Each California county has a **district attorney** who is the principal public prosecuting officer. The office of district attorney is of great importance in the administration of criminal law, responsible for investigation of alleged crimes, gathering evidence, submitting formal criminal charges, and representing the state or "the people" in court trials. District attorneys are under a great deal of social pressure to remove criminals or lawbreakers from society and as a result cannot help but have a certain sensitivity to accusations of being "soft on crime." Regardless of how much investigative work is conducted by police officers and how secure they feel in having captured a perpetrator, it is ultimately the DA's decision to attempt to seek punishment. The position of the DA is naturally made more difficult by the growing number of laws that people in California can violate. Fairly recent additions to the long list of criminal laws consist of increased penalties for driving under the influence of intoxicating drugs, high-technology crime, gang violence, environment pollution, family violence, and sexual assault.[19]

Unfortunately, in the pursuit of crime and violators of California law, California DAs have faced allegations of impropriety. In 2006 the *San Jose Mercury News* reported on a three-year investigation it had conducted of the Santa Clara County criminal justice system and found that "in nearly 100 cases, the prosecution has engaged in questionable conduct that bolstered its efforts to win convictions. Some Santa Clara County prosecutors withheld evidence that could have helped defendants, some defied judges' orders and some misled juries during closing arguments."[20] Members of the Santa Clara County District Attorney's Office, in interviews with *San Jose Mercury News* reporters, conceded some concern about the findings of the investigation while defending other actions as being either proper conduct that was wrongly criticized or "problems that amounted to nothing more than honest mistakes." In response, the report found that "while many errors were isolated incidents, others fell into patterns that suggested broader problems. And certain prosecutors engaged in questionable behavior in multiple cases, suggesting either sloppiness or a deliberate disregard for ethical rules."[21] It would be unfair to lump every DA's office into the category of problems presented by this article, and considering the number of hardened criminals that exist in California society, there is plenty of room for mistakes to be made and still find justified ways of convicting such criminals. This article does clearly illustrate that mistakes, whether inadvertent or intentional, are made and that perhaps closer scrutiny of the work of county DAs' offices could help prevent such mistakes and cause Californians to become more sensitive about enforcement of the law.

── Think Again ──

What role has the state Supreme Court played in shaping the evolution of the California judicial system?

# Trends in the California Judicial System

One of the best ways to appreciate trends in the California judicial system is to focus on the composition and decisions of the California supreme court. More than any one type of court in California, the state's supreme court is in a position to influence not only decisions in lower courts through the establishment of precedents, but also the actions of the legislative and executive levels of government through the power to interpret California law. Often that interpretation goes beyond the rights and obligations listed in the U.S. Constitution and federal statutes. First of all, since statehood, the composition and views of the California supreme court justices have been determined by the ideological orientation of

Supporters march to protest the California Supreme Court's overturning the city of San Francisco's decision to permit same sex marriages.

the governor, who may have the opportunity to make enough appointments to influence the direction of the court. Once on the bench, it has been rare for the justices of the California supreme court not to adhere to the ideological perspective of the governor who appointed them. Second, these justices must either assume a judicially active stance, establishing precedent or overturning past rulings and taking an active role in judicial affairs, or maintain judicial restraint, relying on precedent and established law and refraining from using the courts to influence society. Three decades ago, the California supreme court took a major swing to the left with the appointments by Governor Jerry Brown of three liberal justices, including Chief Justice Rose Bird, who became the first woman on the court. Known for its diversity (it also had the first African American), that court quickly developed a reputation for liberal tendencies and an activist perspective of the law. Major California supreme court cases during this period affirmed positions on labor rights (in favor), capital punishment (against), and the rights of criminal defendants and tenants. This Bird court ended, after ten years of liberal and activist rulings, when three of the court's most liberal justices lost their confirmation elections in 1987. Conservative politicians and activists specifically targeted Chief Justice Rose Bird during this election, branding her as soft on crime and spending millions to emphasize this point to the voters.[22]

The subsequent elections of George Deukmejian and Pete Wilson as Republican governors guaranteed a conservative majority on the California supreme court that exists to this day. There are currently six registered Republicans and one Democrat on the court, led by Chief Justice Ronald M. George. Although almost all owe their positions to appointments by Republicans, the court has exercised a moderate judicial philosophy, taking a pro-law-and-order stance while moving to the center on many social issues. The California supreme court does tend to support widely publicized legal positions that mirror the political agenda of the California Republican Party. Governor Arnold Schwarzenegger apparently wanted to maintain this moderate direction when he replaced the rather conservative justice Janice Rogers Brown, who became a federal appellate judge, with Carol A. Corrigan, a moderate Republican.

The current California supreme court has taken decidedly conservative positions, routinely upholding death penalty convictions, even when, for example, the cases involved coerced confessions. The court moved quickly to overturn the decision by the city of San Francisco to permit same-sex marriages, raising the issue of the inconsistency of the city's decision with California law. In cases pitting the California business community against employees or consumers, the judicial scorecard suggests that the George court will in most instances go with the former. The court did in 1996 allow judges the discretion to waive the third strike when confronted with a third-time offender under the "three-strikes" law and faced the wrath of California antiabortion advocates after a 4–3 ruling that overturned a state law requiring parental consent for abortions performed on minors. The latter ruling was seen, to the displeasure of many prominent Republicans, as too broad an interpretation of civil liberty protections provided by the state constitution.[23] The civil libertarian tendencies of the court where on display again in a 2004 case in which the court unanimously overturned the conviction of a 15-year-old student who was charged with violating the state's criminal threat statue after writing a poem about "dark themes."[24] The court has established a pattern of leaning toward the conservative position in interpreting the California constitution, state law, and lower court cases while refraining from absolute doctrines and leaving some room for more moderate interpretations of similar cases that may surface in the future. This pattern can be found in a case where the California supreme court in 2002 permitted a city to test all job applicants for drugs while blocking drug tests for employees who sought promotions for nonsecurity positions.[25] Almost three years before the Terry Schiavo drama, in Florida, the California supreme court essentially prevented a terminally ill patient from being removed from life support despite his expressed wish to family members that he be removed from such equipment in the event that he could not have an active life. Although the court did agree that the termination of life support is a fundamental right under California's "privacy guarantee" and that any restrictions on the right to die must be weighed against a compelling state interest, it also found that, a patient's right to die must be supported either by a person designated to make such decisions or the patient's own written instructions exercised for a patient who is not mentally conscious.[26] Since the 1970s, many Californians have become sensitive about the court's ability to nullify or significantly alter initiatives. The court's strongest weapon against initiatives heading to the ballot is the **single-subject rule**, which is required of initiatives by the California constitution and monitored by the California supreme court. Essentially, initiatives may address only one major subject or policy. In the 1990s, the court removed parts of Proposition 115, the Victims' Bill of Rights initiative, and revised Proposition 103, the proconsumer insurance industry initiative, to the advantage of insurance companies. The George court has had a number of opportunities to reshape initiatives through legal challenges, including the slew of initiatives in the 2005 special election, a number of which were seen as legally dubious, but so far the court has shown restraint.[27] Californians should not expect any major deviation from moderate Republican ideological views while Chief Justice George is leading the court, especially on law-and-order issues. For many, it should be comforting to know that the court has not taken far-right positions and its past rulings have demonstrated a commitment to respect the civil liberties of state residents.

**single-subject rule** Ballot initiatives may contain only one subject of policy.

# Punishment in California

The average Californian would like to believe that the conviction of a criminal who has broken the law puts an end to a societal menace and perhaps brings closure to survivors of a horrible nightmare. What really happens is that convicted criminal is shuttled from one venue to another to serve the imposed sentence. The convicted are, however, still very much on earth. The "three-strikes" law has increased the possibility that criminals convicted of a series of crimes will spend a lifetime in prison, but not without continuing to have repercussions on California society. The "three-strikes" law is but one factor among many that have caused the California prison population to explode over the past fifteen years. California has the third-largest penal system in the world, surpassed only by those of China and the United States. Its $5.7 billion annual budget is one of the largest single state fiscal liabilities, and this financial outlay has bought a system that suffers from overcrowding, extreme violence, corruption, and substandard services. The philosophy of rehabilitation in state prison was officially discarded more than twenty-five years ago under Governor Jerry Brown, but has resurfaced by Governor Schwarzenegger. The rash of recent state prison problems, however, including rapid turnover of corrections heads, prison riots, poor medical services, and federal investigations, has pushed rehabilitation far down his list of priorities. Many private citizens and employees of the California Department of Corrections would welcome a takeover of the department by the federal government. Nine out of every ten inmates will be released eventually, but with the **recidivism rate** approaching 80 percent, the chances of the recently released going back to jail are high. There was some hope among lawmakers and prison reform advocacy groups, as well as the voters who approved **Proposition 36**, that convicts who would normally do time for the violation of certain drug offenses would instead get treatment at a rehabilitation facility. Considering that eight out of ten felons have substance abuse problems, this program seemed to be a step in a more constructive direction. After a number of years in use, however, the program has had mixed results. Over 25 percent of program participants never actually receive drug abuse treatment, and a large number are arrested within a year for a new drug offense.[28]

**recidivism rate** The percentage of inmates who are convicted of another crime after their release from prison.

**Proposition 36** Initiative that created diversion program for individuals convicted of offenses.

The California Youth Authority, dedicated to educating and rehabilitating offenders sentenced by juvenile court, has been plagued by antiquated facilities, undertrained employees, and violence. This prison features dormitory-style rooms.

If there is any good news, it is that violent crime statistics in 2006 were slightly down and arrests for various categories of crime were up. More important, various government and nonprofit agencies have conducted serious studies of the California Department of Corrections Department that contain well-thought-out recommendations for prison reform. Reports from the Hoover Commission, a nonpartisan group of state legislators and influential private citizens, and the state legislative analyst's office recommend expanding community-based services and residential housing, implementing parole reforms, improving evaluation measures, and upgrading inadequate information technology systems, among many other innovations. Most of the recent studies of the department, including the work of these two agencies, generally endorsed Governor Schwarzenegger's reorganization plan for Corrections in 2004. Whether or not the plan will survive the numerous legislative and bureaucratic barriers and promote significant change remains unknown, especially when taking into account the powerful California Correctional Peace Officers Association, a public service union that from a labor-management perspective may find certain aspects of the plan objectionable. The greatest challenge facing the corrections system, implied in the aforementioned studies and well-known assertions by key players, is the capacity to reduce the California prison population enough to save funds that can be used for rehabilitation and other programs that will better prepare inmates and parolees to become productive citizens.[29]

## Reforming the California Judicial System

Unlike the California prison system, reform in the California judicial system has been under way for awhile now, and there have been a number of tangible, if not entirely obvious, improvements. The court unification process (begun in 1998), which eliminated the municipal courts, has not generated many complaints and has apparently streamlined the California court system. Given the difficult task of implementing Proposition 36, the mandated drug diversion program, the court system does at least have a program up and running to benefit numerous offenders. The "one-day, one-trial" reform of the jury process has been a major step toward longer-term reforms of the jury process, and the Judicial Council continues to provide funds to support pilot programs and special services. The council's promotion of alternative dispute resolution resources remains popular among segments of the public, and thanks to plans for expansion and statutory adjustments to address professional and community-related concerns, ADR could reduce demand on the congested court system. Public opinion polls have indicated that many Californians question the fairness and sense of justice afforded by the court system. Among the problems associated with the system, most of which are due simply to the large number of people dependent on it, the ethical and moral standards of public and private legal professionals have generated widespread criticism. It is reasonable to suggest that most Californians hope that the courts are one of the few institutions in society committed to fairness and ethics. Whether or not those responsible for this system can reconcile the need for law and order with "justice" will determine the how fair and ethically the people living in California will be treated. Real change can come from normal routines or interactions that promote safer communities, good citizenship, civic responsibility, crime prevention, and ethical behavior—the types of interactions that will prevent people from having to enter the judicial system as either victims or as suspects.

# UP CLOSE

# Exonerations in California and Louisiana

In 2006, Kenneth Marsh was awarded $756,900, the largest compensation for wrongful imprisonment in California history. Under state law, Marsh, who was wrongfully imprisoned for twenty-one years, was entitled to $100 for every day he was wrongfully incarcerated. For years, Marsh's girlfriend and the mother of the toddler he was convicted of murdering, wrote letters to anyone who would listen, seeking assistance in getting the case reopened, having few doubts that Marsh was innocent. Several years ago, San Diego County district attorney Bonnie Dumanis agreed to review the case and determined, based on a medical examination of the evidence, that reasonable doubt did exist in the Marsh case and so supported his release. Sadly, twenty-one years before, police investigators had informed the then San Diego district attorney that there was insufficient evidence of a crime, but he decided to file charges anyway.

California has a rather dismal record in the number and circumstances surrounding exonerations. Out of the top ten states for the number of exonerations between 1989 and 2003, California is ranked fourth. California has a very large prison population, an important factor that numerous legal scholars suggest contributes to the large number of unjustly convicted. Because of its size, there is a tendency to employ plea-bargaining procedures and rush from case to case. Exonerations could imply that the state government is finally correcting its judicial mistakes and that the release of wrongfully convicted prisoners is generally a good policy. Although partially

### Table 1   Exonerations by State

| Rank | State | Number of Exonerations |
|------|-------|------------------------|
| 1 | Illinois | 54 |
| 2 | New York | 35 |
| 3 | Texas | 28 |
| 4 | California | 27 |
| 5 | Louisiana | 17 |
| 6 | Massachusetts | 16 |
| 7 | Florida | 15 |
| 8 | Pennsylvania | 13 |
| 9 | Oklahoma | 11 |
| 10 | Missouri | 10 |

*Source: The Journal of Criminal Law & Criminology* Vol. 95, No. 2, Page 541. Copyright © 2005 by Northwestern University, School of Law.

true, exonerations also suggest that mistakes were made, raising the issue of quality control in California's legal system, or, just how many mistakes have been made? In a 2004 report on the wrongly convicted, *San Francisco* magazine found that 63 percent of wrongful convictions involved serious police error or misconduct and 47 percent occurred when the prosecutor committed errors or acted improperly. Imagine for a moment that it is in fact the police who committed or were an accessory to the crime for which you have been falsely accused. One of the most brazen incidences of police misconduct that caused mass exonerations occurred in 1999, when it was discovered that the CRASH (Community Resources Against Street Hoodlums) unit of the Rampart division of the Los Angeles Police Department had routinely lied on arrest reports, shot and killed or wounded unarmed suspects and innocent bystanders, and committed many other crimes. The subsequent investigation led to the release of over 150 individuals who had been framed by CRASH officers and then forced to plead guilty to false felony gun or drug charges.

It would be unfair to single out the California judicial system without acknowledging that wrongful convictions are a national problem. Out of the top ten states for the number of exonerations between 1989 and 2003, Louisiana is fifth, just behind California. In Louisiana, the problem is particularly acute because of the inadequate number of public defenders' offices. The *Shreveport Times* reported that the National Legal Aid and Defender Association studied one rural parish in Louisiana, discovering that the court-appointed attorneys had doubled the 150-case maximum normally assigned to each public defender. One lawyer identified in the study said that it was not uncommon for a public defender to have eighteen minutes to prepare for a second-degree murder trial. And this study took place before Hurricane Katrina. Louisiana's worst exonerated-prisoner case may lack in the sheer quantity of the Ramparts case, but surpassed in stark terror any California exoneration in recent memory. In 1984, John Thompson was convicted of murdering a hotel operator in New Orleans. Just two days before his scheduled execution in 2002, the fourth Circuit Court of Appeals ruled that Thompson's case merited a new trial after an investigator working on behalf of his defense council discovered blood sample evidence that the prosecution had intentionally hidden. A jury later acquitted Thompson of the charges. This incident is particularly frightening when one considers that Louisiana is tenth on the list of executions carried out by state (California is sixteenth).

Various news and media reports raise the suspicion that the wrongful convictions in California may be a common occurrence. When threatened with charges under the three-strikes law, a large number of innocent people in the California justice system, according to the *San Francisco* magazine report, accept deals and plead guilty to crimes they didn't commit rather than gamble on the outcome of a trial that could result in the automatic life sentence of a third strike. The truly disheartening aspects of exonerations occurs when the innocent fight and hopefully win their freedom, while the guilty go unpunished. Attempting to find the real perpetrator is made especially difficult after years of delay: evidence gets lost, witnesses relocate, and recollections grow faint. Perhaps with the acknowledgment that wrongful convictions are a wider problem than previously thought, slightly less pressure will be placed on the judicial system to put someone—anyone—away, rather than be sure before proceeding; the general public will pay closer attention to the practices of that system; and the quality of police work and adjudication will improve to the point that wrongful convictions become rare. At the moment, at least in California, they are not.

*Sources*: Jim Sanders, "Exonerated Convict Gets Compensation for Time," *Sacramento Bee*, January 21, 2006; "Gideon plus 43: Indigent Defense Still Awaits Solution," *Shreveport Times*, March 20, 2006; Susan Finch, "Wrongfully Convicted Get Ally on Bench." *Times Picayune*, August 21, 2005; "Exonerations in the United States: 1989 Through 2003; Northwestern University School of Law, *Journal of Criminal Law and Criminology*, 95, 2 (2005); 533–34, 541.

# Summary Notes

- The California legal system derives its authority and police powers from the California constitution, twenty-nine codes that contain statutory law, and the California Administrative Codes. The California court system, responsible for administering and adjudicating these laws, is the largest in the nation; The court system is composed of superior or trial courts, six appellate court districts, and the state supreme court at the top.

- The entry point for the enforcement of California law and the settlement of conflicts or disagreements is the California superior courts, consisting of 1,499 authorized judges and 437 commissioners and referees. In 1998, California courts were giving superior courts the authority to hear cases that would normally be heard in municipal courts.

- There are six appellate districts with a total of 105 justices. Each district has a presiding justice and a number of associate justices serving on panels of three justices that review approximately 25,000 requests for an appeal each year. The California court of appeals does have original jurisdiction in cases involving habeas corpus, writs of mandamus, writs of certiorari, and restraints on certain actions.

- The California supreme court is the highest court in the state, and its decisions are binding on all other California courts. There are seven supreme court justices, one of whom serves as chief justice. With the exceptions of death penalty cases, which it must review under the California constitution, the supreme court has discretion over the cases it will accept for review.

- All California court judges and justices must have practiced law or served as a judge in California for at least ten years preceding election or appointment. The governor fills vacancies in California courts through appointment, but judges and justices must eventually be confirmed by the voters in an election.

- The jury is a fundamental part of the state legal system, determining guilt or innocence of the accused in a court trial. A juror must be a U.S. citizen, 18 years of age or older who understands English, lives in the county of service, has not served for at least a year, is not currently on any jury, and is not on parole. After the facts of a case have been presented, the jury must act as instructed by the judge regarding relevant law and degree of proof required to reach a verdict.

- The California constitution requires each county to impanel a grand jury every year. Selected by superior court judges, the grand jury serves for one year and can be extended. It can investigate public offenses, issue indictments, conduct an annual examination of the operations of countys government and special districts, and inquire into the conditions and management of state prisons located the county.

- Each California county has a district attorney who is the principal prosecuting officer. The district attorney is responsible for investigating alleged crimes, gathering evidence, submitting formal criminal charges, and representing the state or its people in court trials.

- The "three-strikes" law has increased the possibility that the worst criminals will spend a lifetime in prison. Nine out of every ten inmates in California will eventually be released, but 80 percent of them will be arrested for new crimes.

# Key Terms

superior courts 651
Proposition 220 651
plea bargain 651
plea bargain 651
court of
  appeals 651
supreme court 652

alternative dispute
  resolution (ADR) 653
judicial council 655
Proposition 184 656
civil law 656
tort law 656
probate law 657

criminal law 658
California Penal
  Code 658
felony 658
misdemeanor 658
infraction 658
*corpus delicti* 658

determinate sentence 658
county grand jury 665
district attorney 668
voir dire 661
single-subject rule 670
recidivism rate 671
Proposition 36 671

# Suggested Readings

Abramson, Leslie. *The Defense Is Ready: Life in the Trenches of Criminal Law.* New York: Simon & Schuster, 1997.

Friedman, Lawrence, and Robert Percival. *Roots of Justice: Crime and Punishment in Alameda Country California, 1870–1910.* Chapel Hill: University of North Carolina Press, 1981.

Grodin, Joseph R. *In Pursuit of Justice: Reflections of a State Supreme Court Justice.* Berkeley: University of California Press, 1989.

Judicial Council of California Administrative Office of Court. *A Visitor's Guide to the California Supreme Court.* San Francisco, September 2004.

Payton, George T. *Concepts of California Criminal Law.* San Jose, Calif.: Criminal Justice Services, 1995.

Stolz, Preble. *Judging Judges: The Investigation of Rose Bird and the California Supreme Court.* New York: Free Press, 1981.

# 20 LOCAL GOVERNMENT IN CALIFORNIA

## Chapter Outline

- California County Government
- Funding County Government
- The Legal Framework and Formation of Cities
- The City Council
- The Municipal Bureaucracy

- Special Districts
- School Districts in California
- Councils of Government
- The Future of Local Government

## Think About Politics

**1** Should the state government support contract cities?
Yes ☐ No ☐

**2** Should California encourage the use of public utilities?
Yes ☐ No ☐

**3** Would stricter laws enforcing growth management benefit California?
Yes ☐ No ☐

**4** Is California's current tax structure adequate to fund county governments?
Yes ☐ No ☐

**5** Are redevelopment zones helping to improve California?
Yes ☐ No ☐

**6** Are government officials abusing California's eminent domain powers?
Yes ☐ No ☐

**7** Should California provide vouchers or monetary support to private schools?
Yes ☐ No ☐

*California residents depend on local governments for services vital to everyday life. Imagine life without local government. How might your life be affected?*

★   ★   ★

## Introduction

Local governments exist in a precarious position, overshadowed by the larger issues of state and national governments, especially as the process of globalization reduces the barriers between nations and causes governments increasingly to confront international concerns. Yet just about all Californians depend on local government to provide and protect the basic necessities of daily life. The devastation caused by Hurricane Katrina in 2005 brought into sharp focus both the importance and the failings of local governments in responding to a disaster and aiding victims. Criticism of the federal government's inability to anticipate and react promptly was matched by the near total breakdown of local governments in the Gulf region, allowing already catastrophic conditions to become even more desperate. An immediate response in the wake of Hurricane Katrina could have been mounted only by local governments and in too many instances, but particularly in the case of the city of New Orleans, this response suffered from failed warning systems, inadequate emergency resources, poor coordination, and technological disintegration. To their credit, municipal governments surrounding the Gulf region provided the most immediate and critical assistance to the victims of this emergency and continue to shoulder the burden of integrating Hurricane Katrina victims even in the conspicuous absence of the federal government. The devastating effects of this natural disaster should be a reminder of the vital and imperative responsibility local governments have to local residents, especially in earthquake-prone California, and the need to constantly reappraise and upgrade the resources of these governments.

The ability of local governments to provide vital services to communities throughout California is legally determined by the state government. This relationship is advanced by **Dillon's Rule**, a nineteenth century legal interpretation named after an Iowa judge that allows local governments to have only those power specially delegated to them by state law.[1] California is one of eight states that give local governments the option to exercise a considerable amount of authority beyond the dictates of Dillon's Rule. The four basic units of local government in California are cities,

**Dillon's Rule** Legal interpretation that local governments have only the powers specially delegated to them by state law.

counties, special districts, and regional bodies. How far these units of government can stray from the dictates of Dillon's Rule is specified in the California Government Code.

# California County Government

### Historical Roots of California's Counties

**Think Again**

What are the historical roots of the California county system?

Historically, counties were the principal administrative unit used by the absolute monarchs of Europe to govern wide areas, most noticeably where large cities or towns were lacking. Throughout much of the American colonial period, the superiority of the county governing unit prevailed, with most county officials being appointed by the colonial or state governor and the most important administrative duties for a region taking place at the center of county government. As the nation grew, two models of county government emerged that to some extent remain today and on occasion are a source of conflict between counties and state governments or between cities and counties. The weaker model of county authority developed in the American Northeast, where cities and towns were more established and closer together, limiting the need for a strong county government. The larger cities and towns of this region increasingly began to assume duties and services formerly conducted by the county government. In the South and on the western frontier, the strong county model continued to be important in taming expansive wilderness regions where established settlements were sparse. The democratization of the American experience served to empower the strong county model as residents of the county gradually chose to elect county officials, but that also led counties on the eventual collision course with the authority of state government.[2]

The formation of counties was absolutely vital to the growth and administration of early California, which was an unusually large state that during its first fifty to seventy-five years had a small population and dispersed settlements. In fact, the county government's importance was demonstrated by the conflicts that arose among county residents over where the county "seat" or county government offices would be located. Without the benefit of modern transportation or roads, the distances between settlements and centers of commerce and these county seats made the conduct of official business very difficult. In the effort to spread government authority and favor other less scrupulous interests, the early California legislature simplified the process of establishing new counties. Formation of counties was entirely up to the state legislature, which often complied with the requests of wealthy individuals or a large group of settlers without much investigation or scrutiny. Counties have always been viewed in varying degrees throughout California history by the state government as "legal subdivisions of the state."

Prior to a number of reforms efforts, county government in California was susceptible to corrupting influences, and it was not uncommon for counties to experience periods of virtual lawlessness. Between 1860 and 1890, California historical records are full of major disputes and incidents of crime either involving issues of county governance or necessitating the intervention of county officials. There are reports of gun battles among residents of Lassen and Plumas Counties over disputed territory, of a San Diego sheriff and his appointed deputies who, acting as tax collectors, retained portions of all taxes, and of an all-powerful Los Angeles County judge of sessions who had almost feudal authority over the county government. The situation in Klamath County got so out of hand that in 1875, the county was abolished and its territory divided among four different counties.[3]

Gradually, the state government brought some order to the administration of California counties. Beginning in 1879 with the first major revision of the California constitution and a series of state legislative acts, a framework was created to bring uniformity to all California counties. County governments were given police powers and required to designate a grand jury, a superior court, justices of the peace, a superintendent of schools, a board of education, a board of equalization, a treasurer, a recorder, a tax collector, a license collector, an assessor, an auditor, a public administrator, and constables.[4]

The California Progressives built on this reformist trend by advocating for the passage of a state constitutional amendment that gave California counties the option of **home rule** charter authority, making California the first state in the nation to grant county residents the authority to tailor their local charters to the needs and interests of their respective counties. A general law on counties was also established for those counties that did not choose to embrace home rule and write county charters. This **general law** prescribes the duties, obligations, offices, and basic template for county government, although scholars and government officials have noted that there are few practical differences in government organization between general-law and charter counties. After a rash of charter adoptions by California counties, (Los Angeles County was the first in the nation to adopt a home rule charter), the drafting of these charters in California slowed dramatically and eventually stopped at thirteen of the state's fifty-eight counties, including seven of the largest. Home rule charters are particularly useful to highly populated counties that require flexibility and political power in responding to problems or issues that smaller counties do not usually encounter. Initially, many of the home rule charter counties used this flexibility to incorporate the governmental reforms of the Progressive era into county government, particularly by establishing a civil service system for county officers and other types of employees. The city and county government of San Francisco would emerge as a unique form of home rule charter that combined the two into a single consolidated government with an eleven-member board of supervisors.[5]

**home rule** A county's right to tailor its local charter to its own needs and interests.

**general law** A standard list of the duties, obligations, offices, and structure of county government.

**Board of Supervisors**    The governmental structure of California counties is largely determined, with the exception of the thirteen home rule charter counties, by the California constitution and the California Government Code. These laws are implemented by a **county board of supervisors**, which is also prescribed by government code. Anyone interested in becoming a member of the board of supervisors must be a registered voter residing in the county district and must run as a nonpartisan candidate for election. The board of supervisors, whose members serve four-year terms of office, exercises both legislative and executive power and in a number of instances has quasi-judicial authority. Legislative power is based on the ability to pass, by a simple majority of the board, resolutions, board orders, and county ordinance. County ordinances are the equivalent of statutes or laws passed by the state legislature and can be used by the board of supervisors to regulate a wide range of actions and behaviors as long the ordinances do not conflict with state law. There are different types of ordinances: Urgency ordinances are intended for the immediate protection of the public in matters of health, safety, and civility, and statutory ordinances address procedural or common affairs. This lawmaking power is especially important as the means of proposing revenue-raising sources such as taxes, assessments, and fees. The board of supervisors can propose these levies, but voters within the county must approve them.

———Think Again———

What are the responsibilities of the county board of supervisors?

**county board of supervisors** Board responsible for implementing the provisions of a county's charter.

**Figure 20.1** Total 2003–04 County Expenditures by Function and Other Financing Uses.

*Source:* 2003–04 Counties Annual Report, California State Controller's Office.

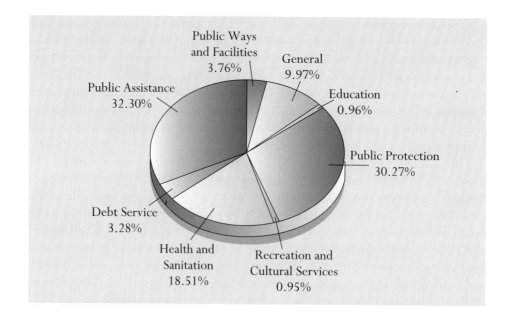

The board of supervisors' most basic executive responsibility is to oversee most county departments and programs. The word *oversee* in this context is almost literal, as the board of supervisors is prohibited from directing or controlling the day-to-day operations of a specific county department. Powers typically used in this oversight function involve requests for regular reports from department heads, approval of county ordinances and orders, development of county priorities, control of all county property, endorsement of the annual budget, and allocation of funds for specific expenditures. Supervision of a number of elected county officers is limited by the dual accountability that these officers have to both the board of supervisors and members of the statewide executive branch. For example, the county district attorney and sheriff are accountable to the attorney general on law enforcement matters and to the board of supervisors in areas related to the legal obligations of the county. The board does have the authority to establish a joint-powers agreement or joint-powers agency with another public agency or local government. Joint-powers agreements are usually created to provide a service or fulfill a need that encompasses two or more local governments or is beyond the resources or boundaries of the county government. Joint-powers agreements often give the board of supervisors some leverage with municipal and other local governments that benefit from the county's economies of scale—for example, in the use of the sheriff's office's central countywide dispatcher station by local municipal police departments. Common quasi-judicial powers of the board of supervisors are used to settle claims made against the county, examine and audit through subpoena power the financial records of other county officers and departments, and serve as an appellate body in department-level decisions involving land use and tax issues. Member of the board of supervisors will often facilitate intergovernmental relations as members of various government commissions and boards. Air quality management boards for the various regions throughout California usually mandate that counties within these districts be represented by at least one member of the board of supervisors.[6]

**Unincorporated Communities and Contract Cities**   There are communities within counties that are not incorporated as cities for various reasons — lack of political will or interest, a limited resource or tax base, geographic remoteness, or underdevelopment. Incorporation normally gives cities a certain degree of independence based on the general law for cities as prescribed by the California constitution. Lacking that independence, unincorporated areas become the responsibility of county governments based on state law. As the basic unit of government for unincorporated areas, counties are charged with providing the same services to an unincorporated area that a municipal government would provide for the municipality. In California, one in every five state residents lives in an unincorporated area, which amounts to approximately 6.4 million people. San Francisco is the only one of California's fifty-eight counties that does not have an unincorporated area. Unincorporated areas can be found in isolated mountain and desert regions, farming areas, suburban housing tracts, and inner-city areas and vary widely in socioeconomic conditions.[7] State regulations mandate that county governments encourage the formation of **municipal advisory councils (MACs)**, elected by residents of unincorporated areas to furnish representation in matters affecting their communities. MACs have very limited governmental authority and are largely dependent on the county supervisors representing the district where the unincorporated areas are located to serve as an advocate for their interests on the board of supervisors. Administering these areas can be very difficult for county governments, which are already responsible for a variety of services to all residents and local governments within the county.

There are many incorporated or independent cities across California identified as **contract cities**, which contract with county government for major municipal services, principally in the areas that are normally assumed by municipal governments, such as police and fire protection, animal control, and public works. Since their inception in the 1960s, contract cities have grown dramatically in number, and the services porvided by county governments are often instrumental in helping cities incorporate that initially lack a strong tax base and facilities. In many instances, county governments welcome the opportunity to maximize their productivity and to receive revenue for contract services that might otherwise go to fully independent municipal governments. The arrangements between county governments and contract cities have generated disputes over the costs that counties may charge for contracted services, and many fully incorporated cities have criticized contract city agreements as an unfair use of county general tax revenues to subsidize incorporated cites. The state legislature has tried to resolve such issues through guidelines, with mixed results, but the scramble by a long list of local and state governmental units for increasingly scarce tax revenues guarantees that the concept of contract cities will remain controversial. In the future, depending on political interests and the fortunes of local government, contract cities could develop into a popular idea that eliminates redundancy in the delivery of local services, or they could fall by the wayside due to the fiscal difficulties of county governments.[8]

**County Bureaucracy**    County governments are responsible for providing a variety of services to all county residents. Many of these services, including the sheriff's, district attorney's and assessor departments, are required by the California constitution, and other services have been instituted in the absence of other local governmental authority. According to a report by the County Supervisors Association in 1958, counties performed 22 basic functions in 1850. That number grew to 167 in larger counties in 1909, and in 1958, counties were performing 900 separate functions.[9] The explosion of housing developments in California and the accompanying rise in population have placed an enormous strain on the capacity of county governments. The size and composition of the county bureaucracy does vary from county to county, depending on geographic conditions,

**municipal advisory council (MAC)** A council formed by the citizens of unincorporated areas to provide representation in matters affecting their communities.

**contract cities** Incorporated or independent cities that contract with counties for the provision of major municipal services.

# WHAT DO YOU THINK?

## Public Power in California

Since the California energy crisis in 2001, the private energy companies that operate in the state, and their regulation, have been the focus of public attention. During this crisis, however, there was very little consideration of public power or the possibility of the state government simply assuming direct responsibility for providing power to the residents of the state. For many, such considerations would be heresy in a country and state that takes pride in free market capitalism and that has had marginal faith in government bureaucracies. Though sacrilegious to some, there are cities and regions in California that have been getting their power from public utilities for quite a while. In fact, the shift toward deregulating the California energy market, which is widely seen as the cause of the energy crisis, was a major step away from government involvement. That step began in September 1996, when the state legislature passed AB 1890, allowing energy customers to choose their electricity supplier, separating the companies that transmit power from the companies that distribute power, and permitting electricity to be auctioned off as a commodity. Making deregulation work proved quite difficult, leading to energy shortages that caused "rolling blackouts," increased consumer prices, and the financial decline of major California and out-of-state energy producers. Still, the public and the media remain very reluctant to examine how California public power utilities have fared either before or during the energy crisis. It seems that Californians readily accept public water districts, rarely ever seriously considering the privatization of the water supply, but public power is simply not open to debate. Despite the dominance of private power providers and the lack of any widespread discussion on the matter, power has been supplied by publicly-owned utilities in California since the turn of the twentieth century.

Most publicly owned power utilities began as electricity was gradually being used to power electric lights in the late 1800s. Cities generally had the choice of signing on with the Pacific Gas and Electric Company, assuming control of the many failing power companies, or exercising provisions in state law for the formation of special districts to establish their own power agencies. For cities such as Los Angeles, creating a public power utility was a natural extension of the water district that was formed, which, through its aqueducts, provided an

*The Hetch Hetchy reservoir in the Sierra Mountains separates California and Nevada.*

inexpensive source of hydroelectric power to the city. The first power plant of the Los Angeles Department of Water and Power (LADWP) was built in 1905 at Division Creek in the Owens Valley to supply power for the construction of the infamous Owens Valley aqueduct. In 1909, the Bureau of Los Angeles Aqueduct Power was formed under the direction of Ezra F. Scattergood as chief electrical engineer. The city charter of Los Angeles, enacted in 1925, included language that made the distribution of water and power the official responsibility of the municipal government. A similar situation evolved, although not on the scale of the LADWP, in San Francisco in the aftermath of the 1906 earthquake and fire, which left the city without a reliable water supply. In response to this need, the state legislature granted the City and County of San Francisco the authority to build the Hetch Hetchy aqueduct, stretching 160 miles from Yosemite National Park and Stanislaus National Forest. In addition to water, the Hetch Hetchy aqueduct also generated hydroelectric power that would be divided between the city's municipal needs and the Modesto and Turlock Irrigation Districts. One example of the various municipalities that were self-starters in the production of energy was the city of Anaheim, where the residents decided in 1894 that the city could operate its own electric utility for less than the bids proposed by private companies and, as a result of a 103 to 5 vote, approved the start-up of the Anaheim Public Utility Electric Department. Other cities, such as Alameda and Lodi in 1906 and 1910, respectively, acquired the facilities of private power companies within their city limits and municipalized the production of energy.

Most cities across California either could not or did not want to compete with the financial and technological juggernaut that grew to be the Pacific Gas and Electric Company (PG&E), which formed in 1905 from a merger of the California Electric Light Company and the San Francisco Gas and Electric Company. Until deregulation of the energy industry in California in 1995, PG&E monopolized power production in northern California through great financial leverage and the ability to discover and exploit natural gas as an energy source within as well as outside California. Two other investor owned companies, Southern California Edison and San Diego Gas and Electric, would eventually monopolize energy production and transmission in Southern California. The true entrepreneurial and technological success of these companies resulted from their capability and capacity to not only generate electricity, but to also transmit power along high voltage transmission lines and provide gas through a complex system of pipelines, distribute energy and gas directly to millions of customers, and establish metering and billing systems. Of the massive power grid covering California, PG&E would eventually own 46 percent of its transmission lines.

Despite the expansion and monopoly of the three major investor-owned power companies, public power utilities remain an important source of power in the state. Nationally, California is sixteenth in the number of public power utilities. The forty-seven public power utilities that now spread throughout the state vary dramatically in size and structure, with many that are not much more than municipal bureaus that receive fees from private power producers within city limits according to state law, and others that function as power-producing special districts. LADWP is the nation's largest publicly owned utility and the third largest electric utility in California, with generating resources that reach into the power plants in Arizona, Nevada, and Utah. Another large publicly owned utility is the Sacramento Municipal Utility District; founded in the 1920s, it is the fifth largest electric utility in California and relies on hydroelectric power sources from a variety of state and federal facilities. Although many of the publicly owned power districts and departments generally claim that their cost to customers is between 10 % to 15 % cheaper than private companies, other energy analysts dispute these claims. In a report entitled "The California Electricity Crisis:

Causes and Policy Options," by the Public Policy Institute of California, Christopher Weare found that, though public power producers did provide energy at a lower cost to consumers, the differences in costs were the result of advantages that public utilities received from federal low-cost hydroelectric generating facilities, the exemption of state and federal taxes, and publicly financed debt arrangements. The report also cites potential inefficiencies that arise within public bureaucracies that limit the effectiveness of public utilities. Public energy providers are, according to the report, in a better position to invest in technology to expand and improve energy production because they are not subject to changes in financial markets and the constraints of the profit motive. The evolution of public power utilities does continue, seen most vividly in the expansion of the City of Alameda Bureau of Electricity into telecommunications. The residents of Alameda approved a measure in 1998 allowing the utility, now known as Alameda Power and Telecom, to offer telecommunication services and products. Since that time, Alameda Power and Telecom has completed a fiber optic link of the twenty-two Alameda Unified School District sites and has begun offering cable television and high-speed Internet services to residential customers. It is unlikely that most Californians will discard their private power suppliers anytime soon, but considering the recent performance of the energy industry in California, the public power utilities in the select communities across the state are not going away either, and at some point may become the answer to an uncertain energy future.

*Sources:* George Avalos and Matt Sebastian, "Powerhouse from the Past Now Struggles for Survival," *Contra Costa Times,* January 28, 2001, p. 1. "LADWP: A Century of Service: History of Water and Power in LA," Los Angeles Department of Water and Power, http://www.ladwp.com; "Electric," City of Anaheim: Anaheim Public Utilities, http://www.anaheim.net; "Plugged In: The History of Power in Los Angeles," http://www.usc.edu/isd/archives/la/historic/power/; "Power," http://sfwater.org/main.cfm/MSC_ID/15; "History," About Us: Lodi Electric Utility, http://www.lodielectric.com/about/history.php; "History," Alameda Power and Telecom, http://www.alamedapt.com/aboutus/history.html; "Public Power Costs Less," 2006–07 Annual Directory & Statistical Report, American Public Power Association, http://www.APPAnet.orgChristopherWeare, "The California Electricity Crisis: Causes and Policy Options," Public Policy Institute of California, 2003.

## COMPARED TO WHAT?

# Smart Growth in Oregon and California

There are few areas south of Lake Tahoe and east of the Sierras that have not experienced residential housing development. Although single-family home ownership has become the ideal in California, fulfilling this American dream has caused an endless list of social malaise, the least of which include assessment fees, financially strapped school districts, gridlock, environmental degradation, and social detachment. The propensity for California cities to build out has increased housing development, local tax revenue, demand in the service industry, and pockets of urban revitalization. Can California have, many residents ask, the benefits of growth without the various problems that tend to follow in its path? The answer in California over the last decade has been the concept of "smart growth," an approach that employs, depending on the region and political and philosophical beliefs of local residents, any number of techniques that include urban growth boundaries, development charges or fees, building caps, and zoning ordinances. Unfortunately, the prognosis on smart growth in California among various scholars, planning professionals, and even most residents willing to take a hard look at their own locales or region, is not encouraging. Capping the number of housing units that can be built in a city, for example, usually comes either during or immediately after a housing construction boom. Thus, the cap tends to create an enlarged housing market rather than maintaining current or past qualities of the local community. The use of urban growth boundaries in California often simply shifts development to adjacent areas just outside city boundaries. The relatively high cost of housing in California has made development charges or fees less effective, as they can often be transferred to the homebuyer or renter without much notice. Zoning is one of the most often used techniques for managing growth in California, but tends to be a very blunt instrument that frequently produces unintended results. For example, it is very difficult to use zoning to create a mixed-use neighborhood, especially without strict adherence to a detailed plan for growth. Consequently, even as many cities zone out most types of commercial development within residential areas to make way for further development, local commuting residents constantly complain about an inadequate local employment market. Frequently, smart growth in California is the cause of increases in the price of single-family homes and decreases in the availability of affordable housing. Most experts on growth in the state agree that local control of plans is the biggest problem facing growth management. Although they concede that home rule is a noble idea, there are too many pressures on local governments, including local lobbying by developers, intercity rivalries, tax revenue, and demographic preferences, to leave growth planning solely in the realm of city councils. Local decisions on growth are regularly based on political compromises of a city council that may have more to do with political expediency than on sound policy.

Oregon is considered by many planning professionals to have the most advanced growth management system in the country. The principal feature of growth management in Oregon is the major role the state government plays in laying the groundwork for

stages of development and socioeconomic characteristics. But there are a number of county officers and departments that are common to all or nearly all counties because of the vital nature of the services they deliver.

**County Administrator**   As far as the board of supervisors is concerned, the **county administrator** is probably the most important position in the county bureaucracy. Known by various titles in county government (chief executive, county manager, and administrative director are some), the county administrator has a dual set of responsibilities, half of which involves supplying the board of supervisors with reports and information to make critical decisions and determine policy. The annual county governmental budget is one of the most important items that is prepared by the county administrator and submitted to the board of supervisors for review and approval. This responsibility necessitates close interaction with other county officials who account for aspects of the county's finan-

**county administrator**
Official responsible for providing the board of supervisors with reports and information and managing the day-to-day operations of county government.

the cities to follow in developing a growth plan. Before local government can adopt new development plans or modify existing plans, the state Land Conservation and Development Commission must review and approve them. The state government has various "sticks and carrots" to force local governments to comply with statewide goals for growth, including tax revenue distribution and the ultimate authority to issue building permits. Oregon's Smart Development initiative mandates basic requirements for each city or region that encourages cities to embrace mixed-use plans, transportation alternatives, and person-friendly urban and suburban designs. Each city is required to have a comprehensive plan that is consistent with the statewide and county planning goals. Cities in Oregon are also required to have urban growth boundaries. Cities must adhere to a number of factors when drawing these boundary lines, which address such issues as need factors, growth expectations, economic development, environmental concerns, and retention of agricultural land. Protecting open space is another important part of the Oregon approach: 300 miles of greenway along the Willamette River, for example, must be protected by the cities adjacent to the river. Probably one of the most radical elements of Oregon's growth management system is the requirement that fast-growing cities or cities with populations over 25,000 have a twenty-year supply of land within their urban growth boundaries. This mandate is designed to meet future challenges in housing—that twenty-year supply must include provisions for affordable housing.

Clearly, California and Oregon have probably as many dissimilarities as similarities and population influx is undoubtedly one of the biggest differences.

Each state does have its challenges and it appears that Oregon is making a greater effort to address the problems associated with growth. Interestingly, both states have a well-endowed unitary state system of government, whereby the state legislature and executive governments have the authority to dictate policy to county and municipal governments. Oregon chooses to utilize that power and California has not, at least when it comes to growth. Oregon's imperative in growth management has been to preserve agricultural lands, a large part of its economy that has experienced major reductions in recent years. Oregon does lack the population density of California, affording it the luxury of tight controls on the planning process that occurs in its cities. The relatively large population in California creates a sizable group of special interests that advocate for short-sighted policies and commercialism over livability concerns. No doubt, Oregonians can look south and see how they don't want to grow—maybe, Californians will gaze north to find some new ideas about growing smarter.

*Sources:* "New Growth Management Guidelines," Sierra Club Mother Lode Chapter, http://motherlode.sierraclub.org/conservation.html; "Ballot Box Planning and Growth Management," produced by Local Government Commission and based on a research report by Solimar Research Group; "The Link Between Growth Management And Housing Affordability: The Academic Evidence," A discussion paper prepared for The Brookings Institution Center on Urban and Metropolitan Policy, February, 2002; "Growth Management Programs: A Comparison of Selected States." Florida Department of Community Affairs, July 31, 2000. http://www.dca.state.fl.us/growth/pdf/states.pdf; "Myths & Facts About Oregon's Urban Growth Boundaries," 1000 Friends of Oregon, http://www.friends.org/resources/myths.html.

cial health, including the auditor-controller, the treasurer, the tax collector, and the assessor. The other half of the county administrator's duties is to manage the day-to-day operations of county government, normally involving coordination of county department functions and providing administrative guidance. Any major initiative or action by a county department must ordinarily be approved by the county administrator, who must determine countywide ramifications and relevance to county policy and fiscal resources.

**District Attorney**   As a constitutionally elected county official and the public prosecutor of criminal violations, the district attorney owes allegiance to the state attorney general. The DA is the top law enforcement officer for the county and has wide latitude in deciding which laws will be enforced in the county. For example, after passage of the medical marijuana initiative, various DAs turned a blind eye to flagrant marijuana use, even though it was technically still illegal.

The influence of the DA can be felt in all superior courts adjudicating misdemeanor as well as felony violations, beginning with the investigation, decision to indict, and prosecution. Interaction with the board of supervisors is limited, but the district attorney can influence the operations of county government as the legal adviser to the county grand jury, which regularly conducts investigations and issues reports regarding the performance of county government. Violations of certain civil ordinances, such as environmental regulations, are prosecuted by the DA, and this tends to strengthen the authority of the board of supervisors, which passes those ordinances and relies on the force of law to maintain healthy conditions within the county. The board of supervisors can in turn affect the work of the DA through its control over the county governmental budget and administrative functions. The sensationalism of crime and punishment often brings a certain element of notoriety to the DA that in various counties around the state overshadows the board of supervisors.

**sheriff** County officer whose chief duty is to enforce California state law and county ordinances, usually outside of incorporated cities.

**Sheriff** The **sheriff** was one of the first elected county offices created by the first version of the California constitution and has undergone numerous alterations in duties and responsibilities. Between 1851 and 1868, for instance, the sheriff was responsible for tax collection in many counties.[10] In most counties today, the sheriff's chief duty is to enforce California state law and county ordinances, usually in areas outside of incorporated cities. In this law enforcement role, the sheriff, like the district attorney, is directly accountable to the state attorney general. The sheriff also works very closely with the county superior court system and supports many of the functions of the county government. In superior courts, the sheriff is considered an officer of the court, and deputy sheriffs provide security and courtroom assistance to judges as bailiffs, a duty that most sheriffs' departments have taken over from the county marshall's office. In support of local law enforcement agencies and the court system, the sheriffs of most counties operate the county jail, where almost all prisoners within the county are held either during trial or to serve short-term sentences. Interaction between the sheriff's department and the board of supervisors is based first and foremost on county budget allocations, including various monetary benefits to the sheriff. Many of the operations of the sheriff's department are financed by the county budget, and this allocation gives the board a certain amount of leverage. Various departments that are administered by the board of supervisors, such as the Probation Department, are closely involved with the operations of the sheriff's department, providing the board with additional leverage over the sheriff, but of course, such relationships can flow both ways. In most counties, the coroner's office is combined with the sheriff's department, supporting criminal investigations as well as attending to deaths of unidentified persons.

**assessor** County officer whose principal duty is to determine the value of property within the county.

**Assessor** The **assessor** is another constitutionally elected county officer whose principal duty is to determine the value of property within the county. Important aspects of the assessor's obligations are making accurate annual property assessments and maintaining a wide range of records and information related to property within the county. These are extremely important in setting property tax rates. The assessor's office staff maintains forms, compiles state-required reports, arranges for the mapping of county land, and responds to public requests for information and documents. Although the board of supervisors oversees the duties of the assessor, the state Board of Equalization has the statutory authority to establish standards for county property assessment and reviews the assessment procedures and records of the county assessor's office.

**County Clerk**   Except in a few counties where the post is appointed, the **county clerk** is an elected official responsible for the public records of the county, including birth and death certificates and marriage licenses. The county clerk is also empowered to perform civil marriage ceremonies. When not supervising the maintenance of public records, the county clerk acts as the main clerk to the board of supervisors, conducting official clerical duties during board meetings and maintaining all board records. In most counties, the county clerk is responsible for registering voters and maintaining voter records and other election information and records.

**county clerk** Officer responsible for the public records of the county.

**Other County Fiscal Officers**   Chief accountant for the county government, the auditor-controller is elected in all but four of California's fifty-eight counties.[11] This officer monitors the county budget and disbursements and organizes the county government accounting system. The auditor-controller supervises processing of the county payroll and oversees the long-term debt obligations of the county. Most audits of county departments are either conducted or arranged by the auditor-controller. The positions of treasurer and tax collector are typically combined, and the people who hold these posts are usually elected by the voters and have many duties that are determined by state laws and regulations. The tax collector is obligated to generate tax bills and conduct tax collection proceedings. The financial assets of the county and county investments are under the supervision of the treasurer. The treasurer oversees all county bond obligations and is closely involved in county pension boards or systems.

**Other Major County Departments**   The county counsel is the chief civil legal officer of the county. This appointed officer is responsible for providing legal services to the board of supervisors and county departments and also prosecutes most civil actions in which the county or its officers are a party. The County Health Services Department, led by a director, attends to the health-related issues of the county. This department usually consumes a large part of the county budget, particularly in health care services to low-income residents of the county, but also administers a wide range of offices and programs, including alcohol and drug dependency programs, detention facilities, and environmental health and public health services. The County Probation Department is mandated by the California Government Code to advise the courts on punishment for certain crimes, usually requiring less than a year in the county jail, and supervising probation restrictions imposed by the court. The County Probation Department also manages a wide range of juvenile offender and nonoffender programs. This department is led by a chief probation officer, who is appointed by the board of supervisors.

Another department of major importance is the County Public Works Department, which manages the county's public infrastructure. The maintenance of county roadways is normally the central concern of the County Public Works Department, but other areas of responsibility, especially in unincorporated areas, can include waste disposal systems, flood control systems, and street lighting. In the past, the County Social Services or Welfare Department operated a wide variety of programs for the indigent and low-income residents of a county, based on a combination of funding allocations from the state and federal governments. With the passage of federal welfare reform laws, these departments have shifted much of their organizational focus to the coordination of training programs and employment development. They do continue to provide vital social services for children and the aging.

Think Again

How did Proposition 13 change the nature of county funding? What challenges did it present to county government?

# Funding County Government

Since the passage of Proposition 13, the statewide initiative that resulted in a major reduction in property tax revenue, county governments have faced a precarious fiscal situation. Counties were especially reliant on property tax revenue to fund numerous countywide services. In the aftermath of Proposition 13, control over the distribution of property tax revenue was transferred from local governments to the state, reducing revenue that remained in the county by approximately 39 percent. Unlike cities, counties have limited taxing power, and that power does not extend beyond unincorporated areas. In response to the property tax shortfall experienced by counties, the California state government directly funds many county health and welfare programs as well as specific categories of county responsibility, particularly law enforcement, the courts, and transportation. County funding currently comes from five distinct sources: 31 percent from the state government, 21 percent from property tax allocations, 17 percent from the federal government, 13 percent businesses and corporate taxes, and the balance from a variety of fees and interest on deposits and investments.[12]

The unstable fiscal situation that most California counties must endure has for the most part been addressed through a combination of creative funding schemes and reduction of services. Such schemes can go very wrong, and county governments throughout the state constantly wonder how responsibilities will be met in that event, particularly in terms of traditional financial obligations that include pension funds, health care, and road maintenance. The fiscal crisis of Orange County in 1994 is a glaring example of what can go awry when county governments attempt to get too creative in generating revenue. For many years, the Orange County treasurer was able to overcome the budget shortfall created by Proposition 13 by generating substantial income through interest earned on securities that yielded high returns. In 1994, this amounted to roughly 12 percent of revenue to Orange County, compared to an average of 3 percent in interest received by most other counties. Attempting to increase this revenue source,

**Figure 20.2** 2003–04 Total County Revenues by Source and Other Financing Source Excluding Transfers In

*Source:* 2003–04 Counties Annual Report, California State Controller's Office

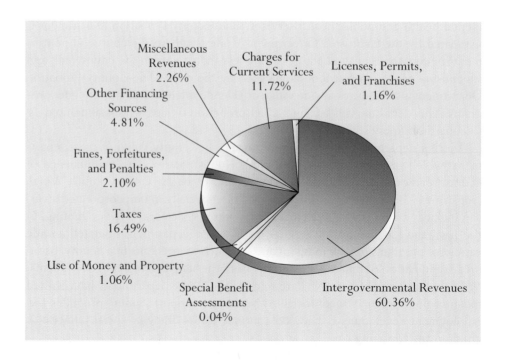

the county Treasurer began to borrow investment money at the rate of $2 for every $1 of county funds on deposit and reinvesting these borrowed funds in additional securities. Eventually, the Federal Reserve Board began raising interest rates, making it nearly impossible for Orange County to repay its loans, losing about $1.64 billion in the process. The county government ultimately was forced to declare bankruptcy on December 6, 1994. Although county residents voted down a proposal for a half-cent sales tax increase to pay off the accumulated debt, relief came with a financial recovery plan that diverted tax funds from other county agencies, sold county bonds, and included financial assistance from the state legislature. About eighteen months after declaring bankruptcy, Orange County returned to fiscal solvency, but its experience remains a vivid example to all local governments of the perils in financing local government.[13]

# The Legal Framework and Formation of Cities

For better or for worse, municipal governments are the major influences on the direction that California cities will take. These units of government are tied to state government in many respects, but unlike county governments, they exercise a considerable amount of independence. For most municipal governments, the dictates from state government are founded on aspects of the California constitution and the general law on municipal government, which prescribes the basic obligations that every California city must satisfy. By 1890, cities had gained the right to create home rule charters. Since then, the constitutional and other statutory provisions regarding city charters have evolved, giving chartered cities the opportunity to "make and enforce all laws and regulations in respect to municipal affairs, subject only to the restrictions and limitations provided in their several charters."[14] In 1896, the state legislature amended the state constitution to subject all cities without home rule charters to a general law that is detailed in the California Government Code. The general law and government code mandate a wide variety of duties that city governments must carry out, necessitating, for example, the formation of planning commissions and the drafting of a general plan. How these duties will be implemented in a specific city is reflected in the municipal ordinances or codes, the laws governing a municipality. In addition to municipal codes, many cities maintain other subcategories of regulations, special zoning or building codes being an obvious example. Each city is authorized to enforce these ordinances or codes, the violation of which normally constitutes a misdemeanor or an infraction. Most cities have separate "rules of procedure" for the actual proceedings and actions of a city council and rules governing the municipal civil service.

The process of forming a city begins with a resolution by the county board of supervisors or by a petition signed by at least 25 percent of the voters living in the area requesting consideration of incorporation. The petition and the accompanying proposal for incorporation are presented to the **local agency formation commission** (LAFCO), a countywide commission that conducts studies and public hearings to determine the feasibility of establishing a city. If LAFCO approves the proposal to incorporate, the board of supervisors will again hold public hearings and in the absence of any disputes over the proposal will call an election in which approval by a majority of voters living within the proposed city is needed for incorporation.[15] To date, 478 California cites have incorporated, 83 of them choosing to write charters and the rest remaining under the general law.[16] If a

> **Think Again**
>
> What are the main features of the incorporation process?

**local agency formation commission (LAFCO)** A countywide commission that conducts studies and public hearings to determine the feasibility of establishing a new city.

Aerial view of modern-day
San Francisco.

View of San Francisco,
c.1875.

city decides to disincorporate, which has not been done since 1972, that decision will ultimately be determined by a majority of voters in a special election.
California cities do have the right to expand or consolidate with other cities or
areas under certain circumstances. State laws and regulations covering annexation allow cities to expand into unincorporated areas as long as the area is con-
tiguous to the city and in the same county. Annexation must be reviewed and
approved by LAFCO and follows procedures that are similar to incorporation.
The consolidation of two cities is a very complicated process that requires majority approval of voters in both cities.[17]

## The City Council

City councils are the elected bodies that govern California cities. The city council is for a number of reasons the cornerstone of American democracy and is
responsible for making decisions that have immediate as well as long-term conse-

quences on the daily lives of residents of this nation. If there was ever an example of why each vote counts, it is the city council. In many municipal elections, 200 or 300 votes can make the difference in whether a city elects council members who are dedicated to the health of the entire city and have the professional qualifications to make informed decisions or ones who are influenced by special interests and have little understanding of the complex issues California cities face. Candidates for a nonpartisan city council seat must be registered voters 18 years of age or older who live in the city. Voters do have the option to circumvent the decisions of the council using the initiative or referendum or to recall a council member via the electoral process.

Once elected, the city council, except in the larger California cities, is considered a part-time office with a four-year term. The general law gives cities the option of five-, seven-, or nine-member city councils; the vast majority have five-member councils. The main responsibilities of a city council are to enact local ordinances (laws), determine municipal policies, approve programs and budgets, and levy local taxes. The city council is the one body that is accountable for providing the direction that a city will take and is regarded by most city residents as a body of problem solvers. This role can be especially tough on city council members, who are expected to approach all problems as neither too big nor too small.

The system of governance adopted by city governments is a major factor in the way a city council handles the issues and problems of its city. Governance in California cities are organized around one of three basic of models, although city councils frequently modify these models to reflect the unique qualities of their particular city. Most California cities use the **council-manager model**, a system that emphasizes the political leadership and policymaking qualities of the council as a whole while vesting administrative authority in a full-time professional manager. Another legacy of the Progressives, the council-manager model was

**council-manager model**
Model of city government that emphasizes the political leadership and policymaking qualities of the council as a whole, while vesting administrative authority in a full-time professional manager.

City Councilman Eric Garcetti speaks at the dedication of CA Distinguished School, Santa Monica Blvd. Community Charter School.

Governor Arnold Schwarzenegger (center) was joined by former Oakland Mayor Jerry Brown (right) and former Los Angles Mayor James Hahn (left) at a press conference with California's law enforcement, fire personnel, and local government after meeting with them to invoke emergency powers to order payments to cities and counties without legislative approval at the State Capitol. He exercised his executive branch power so the scheduled payments are ensured.

**weak mayor–council model**
Model of city government that emphasizes the mayor's role as facilitative leader.

**strong mayor–council model** Model of city government that gives the mayor direct authority over the city government, including the city manager.

designed to facilitate the part-time restrictions of the office of council member and place the day-to-day management of a city under the control of a professional administrator theoretically beyond political pressures. It was hoped that this arrangement would prevent council members from becoming too powerful or entrenched. There are provisions for a mayor in the council-manager model, but the post is usually filled either by someone chosen by the city council or by the council member who receives the most votes in the city council election. Mayors under this model most often serve only two years and are largely responsible for presiding over city council meetings, and conducting ceremonial functions. The second model is the **weak mayor–council** model, with a mayor who uses popular appeal to lead the city government. Although the mayor in the weak mayor–council model does not have much more administrative power than the mayor in the council-manager model, this mayor, having been directly elected to the position, can in theory count on broader support, has a wider understanding of the community, and usually serves a four-year term. Of the 478 incorporated cities in California, 147 have directly elected mayors, many of whom serve in city governments that follow a third model, the **strong mayor–council** model. Again, subject to modifications, this model gives the mayor direct authority over the city government, including the city manager. The mayor's powers are similar to the authority of executive offices such as the governor, and the city council acts as a legislative body, approving or disapproving policies submitted by the mayor and providing checks and balances on the city government. This model is generally employed in California's larger cites, where the mayor is a full-time office and has broad powers over the municipal government.[18]

There has been much debate in California over which model is the most efficient as well as democratic, and all have received a fair share of criticism. Despite its progressive legacy, the council-manager model has been criticized for empowering and politicizing the municipal bureaucracy, and because of the part-time restrictions on council members, the affairs of local government are often hidden from the public. The city of San Diego is the one of the most recent cities to switch from the council-manager model to a semblance of the strong mayor–council model after suffering a wave of corruption scandals involving the city bureaucracy and the council.[19] An example of the weak mayor–council model can be found in the city of Sacramento, which various political commentators suggest has worked with a minimum of problems due to the election of mayors who have generally been popular among city residents.[20] The strong mayor–council model is a mainstay of California's larger cities, such as San Francisco, Oakland, and Los Angeles, and is best suited for cities that face an assortment of difficult issues on a daily basis. This model has attracted such strong personalities and political leaders as former Assembly Speaker Willie Brown, former governor Jerry Brown, and Antonio Villaraigosa, another former assembly speaker. This model does tend to encourage the concentration of political and city resources within the mayor's office and is thus open to charges of misuse of power. The demands of the office of the mayor, in the strong mayor–council model, especially during elections, can blur the lines between political interests and the needs of the city.

San Francisco Mayor Willie Brown (1996–2004) gives a thumbs up when asked about the state providing more money to local governments during his appearance before the Sacramento Press Club Wednesday, May 15, 2002.

**Democracy in Action: The City Council Meeting**    Conducting city council meetings is one of the most important duties of the city council. These meeting provide the public with a rare opportunity to interface with elected leaders on a regular basis and to address a broad range of concerns and problems facing the community. It is true that other elected governments hold regular public meetings, including counties and special districts, but these governments tend to have either a very broad or a very narrow focus that usually precludes the interest of the general public except under special circumstances. City council meetings, by contrast, can be popular affairs for city residents, who often consider them a forum of sorts, and they provide opportunities for the city council to disseminate and gather information and fulfill statutory requirements. However long and tedious or devoid of significant topics council meetings may become, they are nevertheless a public setting where council members are expected to appear professional and in command. The ability to present these qualities well usually leads to reelection, a supportive community, a responsive city bureaucracy, and often a boost toward higher office, whereas habitually poor performance at city council meetings can lead to defeat in the next election.

For the public, besides the inevitable dreariness, city council meetings can be very confusing due largely to the terminology and the parliamentary procedures that are followed. Some understanding of these aspects of city council meetings will make them more interesting and perhaps even revealing. The agenda is the basic framework of the council meeting—the schedule of items to be covered. The Brown Act, a law named after Ralph M. Brown, the former California assembly man who wrote it, requires that local governments hold their meetings in pub-

United States Senator Dianne Feinstein (left), Los Angeles Mayor Antonio Villaraigosa (center) and Governor Arnold Schwarzenegger (right) call for passage of federal legislation that would ban human reproductive cloning but would allow therapeutic stem cell research to go forward. Since the state's passage of Proposition 71, California has led the nation in efforts by states to fund embryonic stem cell research.

lic, except under special circumstances. One important part of this law compels local governments to post the agenda of regular public meetings seventy-two hours before the meeting takes place, giving the public enough time to research the major items to be addressed if so desired. Items are placed on the agenda at the request of the council or city staff members. The agenda generally follows a specific format and structures the council meeting in the following order:

1. *Study sessions* often take place before the meeting, allowing time for the council to publicly review a special issue without taking any formal action.

2. *Closed sessions* are closed to the general public and usually entail a personnel matter or pending litigation that requires confidentiality.

3. *Call to order or roll call* signals the start of the official meeting and identifies the council members in attendance. The roll call will determine if there is a *quorum*, the minimum number of council members that are required to be present to make the meeting official and to validly approve any action that necessitates a vote.

4. *Council member reports and remarks* is the time when council members may make brief announcements or informal comments.

5. *Public remarks and comments* is the time when the audience can address the council on issues that are not on the agenda. Most cities impose a three- to five-minute time limit on each speaker, and no council action or discussion is conducted during this period.

6. *The consent calendar* includes multiple matters that are considered to be routine or procedural items that require the approved of the council, which will vote to adopt the entire list of items without separate discussions of the items. Items can be removed from the consent calendar at the request of a member of the council or the public prior to the vote to adopt.

7. *Approval of minutes* is another procedural matter that requires a vote of approval by the council. The minutes are the record of the previous meeting and are made official by this vote.

A citizen speaks out during a public water board hearing in Orange County.

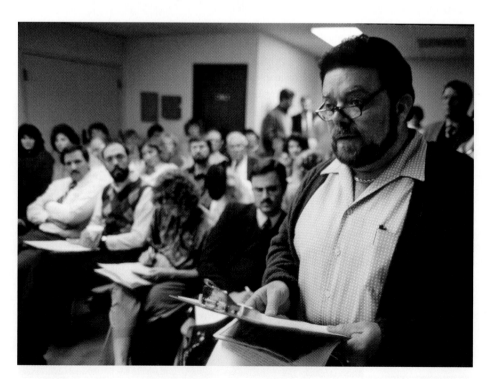

"blighted" and are on the fringe of a downtown area or on waterfront property, there is the constant fear that local government officials, who often experience pressure from local real estate interests, see their neighborhoods as the perfect location for redevelopment. These opportunities introduce upscale housing and commercial projects that not only increase local tax revenue, but are also a subtle method of changing the demographics of a particular area or the city in general. Small businesses and landowners that tend to be located in downtown areas or in areas where a greater portion of excess land exists are especially susceptible to eminent domain actions by local government. The often limited number of and lack of organized representation among small commercial interests makes fighting the redevelopment plans of local government that much harder.

The New London decision has incited various constituencies throughout California that either had long-term concerns about redevelopment or now view their communities as potential redevelopment areas, and the state legislature has responded with a number of bills designed to tighten up the rules for eminent domain and the redevelopment process. One bill, AB 590, would prohibit the acquisition of private property for private business development. There are two proposed constitutional amendments originating in the state senate: one prohibits the taking of "owner-occupied" residential property for private use and the other requires property taken under eminent domain to be owned and occupied by the condemner and can only be used for public purposes. A senate bill (SB 1099) prohibits the use of eminent domain for "agricultural property." A ballot initiative has also been qualified for the ballot—the Protecting Our Homes Act—requiring a government agency to occupy seized property or rent it to the public, increasing the amounts governments must pay for seized property, and many other provisions mentioned in the legislative proposals. Government officials and some civic leaders quite naturally submit that such proposed laws will increase the price of property, limiting the ability of governments to obtain property for a wide variety of uses and making it much more difficult for local governments to redevelop areas that truly are blighted. The issue of eminent domain and redevelopment certainly presents multi-sided dilemmas both for property owners and those who value the attractiveness and economic vitality of their municipality. A scan of our respective communities for instances of redevelopment plans that either went terribly wrong or truly benefited the residents as a whole might be a good start to resolving this complicated subject.

*Sources:* Erik Kancler, "This Land is Our Land: Why Eminent Domain Is Nothing to Fear—So Long as Its Abuses Can Be Curbed," *Mother Jones,* March 18, 2005, http://www.motherjones.com; James Keene, "What Will Kelo Mean in California?" California State Association of Counties, Housing and Land Use: Eminent Domain, http://www.csac.counties.org; Carol Lloyd, "Are California Bay Area Cities Abusing Eminent Domain as a Redevelopment Tool?" *San Francisco Chronicle,* March 7, 2005, http://www.sfgate.com; Patrick Hoge, "Property Seizure Revolt Heads for California Ballot Initiative Would Limit Use of Eminent Domain," *San Francisco Chronicle,* June 26, 2006, p. A1, http://www.sfgate.com

increasing pressure due to the public's heightened perception of crime and the fact that police departments consume a large portion of the municipal budget. City government maintains a very precarious relationship with the police department, being dependent on the vital services that the department provides but at the same time concerned about the perceived independence of the police department. The nature of police work tends to generate a large numbers of civil litigation and workers' compensation claims that can be a serious financial drain on city revenue.

**Boards and Commissions**  City boards and commissions are important government units outside the municipal bureaucracy that not only support implementation of municipal laws, ordinances, and plans but also offer local residents the opportunity to participate in the governing of the city. State laws and regulations mandate that cities appoint local residents to a **planning commission**, which is responsible for advising the city council on the adoption and administration of zoning laws and building regulations. Planning commissions are regarded as an important body in shaping the appearance of a city, and even though public interest is not always as high as it should be, the participation of

**planning commission**
Commission responsible for advising the city council on the adoption and administration of zoning laws and building regulations.

local residents on these commissions are a credit to the tradition of American democracy. In recent years, there has been some controversy over the role of police commissions. Important as they are in responding to instances of police misconduct and facilitating relations between the community and police departments, there is nevertheless some concern that these commissions either weaken the crime-fighting ability of the police or have little real authority, especially in cities where there has long been tension between law enforcement agencies and city residents. Other types of commissions commonly formed by city government that reflect this participatory strain are design review boards, human relations boards, parks and recreation boards, and youth commissions.

## Special Districts

— Think Again —

**What kinds of needs do special districts help address? What kinds of criticisms have been leveled against special districts?**

**special district** Legal district formed to meet a specific need in an area or community.

In the late 1800s, farmers in the San Joaquin Valley were faced with an unpredictable water supply, a local government unable to address the problem, and what many charged was a "water monopoly" that charged fluctuating rates and resisted expanding irrigation. By 1887, C. C. Wright, a Central Valley schoolteacher and lawyer who had been elected to the state legislature on the campaign platform of enacting irrigation district law, drafted and ultimately won passage of the Wright Act, giving small regions the right to form local water districts that would act as subdivisions of the state government and to finance these districts with bond sales.[21] Since the passage of the Wright Act, there has been a wave of state laws encouraging the formation of other types of **special districts** to meet a specific need in an area or community. These districts now furnish Californians with a wide variety of services, in such areas as aviation, cemeteries, drainage, fire protection, health care, irrigation, and transit. Some of them are confined to small communities, and others serve millions of people. Over 85 percent of California's approximately 5,000 special districts provide a single service.

There are independent districts and dependent districts. Independent districts are truly separate from state, county, and local governments, operating with independent elected boards of directors and revenue sources.[22] There are about twice as many independent special districts as dependent districts, exemplified by the massive East Bay Municipal Utility District, which supplies water to parts of the San Francisco Bay Area. Dependent districts, as the name implies, are subject to local governments. A large number of the recreational areas in the Sacramento region are dependent special districts that have board members appointed by the Sacramento County Board of Supervisors. Special districts also exist in the form of enterprise districts, offering services for fees, or non-enterprise districts, which make services available to benefit an entire community. Water districts are the most common enterprise districts (which are in fact the most numerous type of special district), and fire protection districts are an example of non-enterprise districts.

The process of forming a special district begins when registered voters put together a proposal that is submitted to the local agency formation commission for review and possible approval. It the proposal is approved by LAFCO and passes the pubic hearing requirements, voters within the proposed district will have the opportunity to approve or disapprove the proposal. A two-thirds vote in favor of the proposal is required if the new special district plans to levy any new taxes.[23]

The funding of special districts generally comes from service fees, property tax revenues, and bond sales. Probably the best example of a fee paid for the services of a special district are the charges listed on a typical water bill. For districts in which it would be difficult or impractical to charge a fee, such as fire protection, a property tax is assessed. Annual assessments on homeowners in a Northern California special district normally include $5 for mosquito and vector control services, $10 for emergency medical services, $77 for street lighting, $191 for sanitation district services, and $3 to the water district.

Special districts will sometimes gamble and put a bond measure on the ballot, but such electoral exercises have been less popular with the voters in recent years. Bond measures can be initiated by both enterprise and non-enterprise special districts, but general obligation bonds (see Chapter 25) require two-thirds majority approval at the polls. The costs to the homeowner for bonds vary widely, from about $9 on the annual tax bill for a bond for a regional park district to $40 for a school district bond. Special districts that rely on property tax assessments recently suffered a major loss in revenue when the state legislature exempted special districts from a deal in 2004 that would limit future property tax shifts from local governments to the state. The exemption, which will cost many special districts millions and will likely result in increased rates, demonstrates the uncertainly in revenue sources that all segments of California's government currently face.[24]

**Fiscal and Political Accountability**    One of the major criticisms of special districts revolves around the issue of fiscal accountability. Concern, especially from taxpayer advocacy groups, has focused on the large reserves in funds that some special districts maintain while continuing to tax and assess fees at a constant level, particularly in independent special districts. In 2000, the California Taxpayers Association singled out the Water Replenishment District of Southern California (WRD) as an obvious culprit, describing how that district "has overcharged water users for nearly a decade, amassed unconscionable reserves, and grew top heavy with highly paid administrators and consultants."[25] Various reports on special districts by the State Auditor's Office, Controller's Office, and Little Hoover Commission suggest that the financial reserves of many districts are hidden, purposely or not, from public view and that certain districts do not include fixed and other assets when reporting these reserves. This implies that machinery or land that could be disposed of for millions of dollars is often omitted from financial statements in some special districts. Another criticism centers on the many enterprise special districts, especially water districts, that have the ability to charge fees for services but also receive property tax assessments. Of course, numerous special districts continue to struggle financially, particularly in the case of non-enterprise districts like parks and recreational areas. The broader issue, however, is the level of overall accountability.[26]

Advocacy groups for special districts and even the districts themselves believe that accountability is built into the structure of these types of governments, primarily through the voters, who elect the boards of directors that manage districts. They also refer to oversight by the state government, which requires special districts to submit annual financial reports to the state controller, and the state laws mandating public hearings, debt levels, and record keeping. There is also the watchful eye of LAFCO, regularly conducting special studies that review ways to reorganize and refine the sphere of influence of special districts. Many government leaders and private Californians think otherwise, suggesting that most residents of special districts usually know very little about operations in their district; know even less about the board members who run for election; rarely, if ever, attend regular district meetings, let alone hearings; and have difficulty understanding the districts' financial statements. A study conducted by the

## UP CLOSE

# LAFCO Rules

There are few cities and counties within California that are not experiencing some form of growth, whether stretching beyond their original boundaries or struggling to extend vital services to areas with new residential housing. The demand for housing in particular is drastically changing the landscape of the state in ways that would never have been imagined ten years ago. In fact, over the last decade, some cities have doubled in population. Overseeing growth among California counties are the Local Agency Formation Commissions (LAFCOs) charged with discouraging urban sprawl and encouraging the orderly formation and development of local government agencies. In the aftermath of the World War II, California experienced a period of rapid expansion not unlike the building boom occurring today. By the late 1950s, it became clear to government leaders and many residents of the state that this unchecked expansion was creating a host of problems, not the least of which were many new local governmental agencies and boundaries that were poorly created, leaving whole communities without vital services and in precarious economic and social conditions. In 1959, a study by the Commission on Metropolitan Area Problems recommended the creation of Local Agency Formation Commissions, which was formally adopted by the state legislature in 1963. Since its inception, the statute mandating LAFCOs has undergone two major revisions by the state legislature in order to keep abreast of the evolving land-use issues and demands on local government in California.

### Goals

A major goal of any LAFCO is to determine whether the proposals for the formation of new local government agencies are feasible. In this task, a LAFCO reviews and approves the formation of cities and special districts that will meet the needs of residents in terms of vital services, affordable housing, economic opportunity, and the conservation of natural resources. LAFCOs are expected to make every effort to preserve agricultural land resources, considering the effect proposed local government formations have on these types of land areas. Another major goal of the LAFCOs is to prevent as much as possible the incidences of urban sprawl. During the early post-World War II period throughout the United States, massive residential housing tracts were developed without much thought for long-term consequences. Some obvious effects of urban sprawl, which are still somewhat evident today, were the lack of adequate transportation systems, educational institutions, water management, emergency services, and open space. LAFCOs were intended to promote the formation of local governmental agencies that would avoid these problems of urban sprawl.

### Organization

Each county in California has a LAFCO, usually composed of a seven-member commission that includes two city council members, two county supervisors, two members of special districts, and one public member who is chosen by the members of the commission. Each agency that has a member on the LAFCO is expected to contribute to a portion of the

Little Hoover Commission in 2000 found that many districts fail to even consider many basic steps that could be taken to involve the public and community leaders. The commission also discovered that in its current state, LAFCO suffered from understaffing, underfunding, and a lack of ability to challenge the status quo. Suggestions for improving accountability begin with the special districts themselves. One suggestion is greater transparency in financial accounting, using, for example, financial statement summaries, and increasing the clarity of billing statements. Greater public disclosures are seen as necessary, involving full explanations of fiscal reserves, plans, and needs. Various reports found that some districts have outlived their usefulness and should be either consolidated or abolished. The Little Hoover Commission report pointed out that twenty-four of California's seventy-four health care districts no longer operated hospitals, yet nearly all continued to exist, having fallen under the radar of both government and public scrutiny.[27]

LAFCO budget. LAFCOs conduct regular meetings that are open to the public and are required to hold public hearings when a proposal or review is under consideration, offering the public the opportunity to comment.

### Responsibilities

The major responsibilities of the LAFCOs consist of coordinating reasonable and timely changes to local governmental boundaries; conducting special studies and reviews that recommend the most efficient governmental structure and services; and assisting in the resolution of differences or problems between local governmental agencies.

### Authority

Any boundary changes that are requested by a local governmental agency must first be approved by the LAFCOs. Although the LAFCOs do not have the power to initiate boundary expansion, they can propose the dissolution or consolidation of special districts. Cities will typically request the approval of the annexation of unincorporated land located adjacent to the city. LAFCOs also determine the spheres of influence of all local governmental agencies. A sphere of influence is an area outside of the normal boundaries or service area of a governmental agency, but is likely to be included within normal boundaries of an agency some time in the future. A sphere of influence is a buffer of sorts that prevents the overlapping of boundaries and service areas and is reviewed by LAFCO every five years. LAFCOs are required to conduct municipal service reviews (MSR) periodically, which are comprehensive studies of the services that are provided by local governments and special districts to the residents of a specific area. These reviews ascertain whether services are being delivered properly, identify opportunities for greater coordination and cooperation, and are the basis for determining the size and composition of sphere-of-influence areas.

In reality, the power of LAFCOs is very limited when it comes to land use and special district services within cities. Unless restricted by state law or regional agreements, cities are really free to develop as they see fit. The power of LAFCOs is most often applied to unincorporated areas and the service areas of special districts, such as water or fire districts. The revisions of state law regarding LAFCOs have been generally effective in causing these bodies to be especially sensitive to the annexation of land and the formation of new cities. The City of Bakersfield, for example, just recently got permission from the Kern County LAFCO to add roughly 100 square miles after years of restricting the city's growth because of what it perceived as a poor record for protecting farmland. The approval did come with the condition that the City of Bakersfield would not immediately develop on agricultural land and refrain from requesting another expansion of their sphere of influence for five years. Although not the most widely known local governmental agency, the work of the LAFCOs can offer a good idea of how a region will look, and the special district services it will receive, in the future.

*Sources:* Welcome to LAFCO, http://lafco.marin.org/; "What is LAFCO?— History," California Association of Local Agency Formation Commissions, http://www.calafco.org/about.htm; James Burger, "City's Sphere of Influence Grows after LAFCO Vote, *Bakersfield Californian*, January 25, 2006.

# School Districts in California

California school districts tend to fall into a special category of local government, in part owing to their lack of autonomy, but with elected officials, a constituency, and a set of rules, they qualify as government institutions. As a result of pressure from families across California not long after statehood, public school districts started out as local entities receiving minimal support from the state government. However, both local and state educational agencies have consistently failed to keep pace with California's public school needs. As Howard De Witt notes in *The California Dream*, "By 1860 many judged public school education a dismal failure in California as less than 25% of the eligible students attended school."[28] One the state's first superintendents of public instruction expressed his disgust with early school allocations, which he claimed amounted to $1 for every $3 spent on prisons. Public schools gradually improved with the reform measures of Superintendent John Swett in the mid-1860s and later with the Progressives,

> ── Think Again ──
> How are school districts in California funded? What are the consequences of this arrangement?

who sought to impose uniform educational standards in public education.[29] Slow migration into California kept the state's school-age population low, allowing adequate educational funding levels to be reached by the turn of the twentieth century, although communities of racial minorities were persistently plagued by inferior educational programs and poor school districts. School districts were such local developments that each type of school had its own district, prompting efforts spanning over a hundred years by the state government to consolidate elementary, middle, and high schools into unified school districts. In 1932, there were 3,579 school districts, compared to the 1,056 districts that remain today. By the end of World War II, California school districts had again fallen behind as the school-age population exploded, thanks to the arrival of defense industry workers and returning soldiers.[30] By 1948, some 27,000 children were forced into part-time attendance in Los Angeles schools because of the shortage of facilities.[31] To the credit of the Warren and Brown gubernatorial administrations, a share of the postwar period of prosperity was spent on the public school system. As the state government became increasingly involved in education, local school districts and the school boards that oversaw them gradually relinquished greater portions of control to the state.

Most parents with children in public schools would like to believe that locally elected school boards are accountable for overseeing public education in their communities. Successive governors, state legislatures, and state boards of education have, however, assumed a growing share of this oversight through a series of laws and budget allocations, beginning with the State Educational Code, which has grown to five volumes of laws and regulations that influence almost every aspect of school functions. The California Board of Education, backed by its funding recommendations, now sets state educational policies for approving curriculum, textbooks, assessment methods, and student standards of performance. Since the passage of Proposition 13 in 1978, which dramatically cut property taxes, the traditional funding source for local school districts, almost all property taxes have shifted to the state government, which now directly allocates approximately 85 percent of school districting funding, as opposed to a 50–44 percent

An ESL teacher speaks Spanish to her students during a lesson in this California classroom.

ratio between state and local funding sources for school districts in most states nationwide.[32] Despite what parents may believe, the funding system in California has caused school districts to lose a great deal of local control over educational plans while becoming frequent targets of angry parents, teachers, and students who blame the school boards for policies mandated by the state that regularly involving funding or programming cuts. The approval by the voters of Proposition 98 in 1988 was an attempt to respond to funding reductions in education as a result of Proposition 13 by requiring that the state government allocate 40 percent of the general fund to education, but this initiative did not restore local revenue sources to the school districts. School districts lose even more control to the categorical programs that the state government creates to direct or earmark funds to special or specific purposes. Although most categorical programs are usually designed with the best of intentions, they defy the notion of locally controlled school districts.

School districts are continually subjected to the policies that result from the initiative process and the will of California voters. The control of state government over individual school districts has served to place education high on the political agenda of political leaders and various interest groups in California, causing these leaders and groups to use the initiative process to shape educational policy. Consequently, there have been numerous initiatives over the years, some with a genuine concern for influencing the quality of education and others that use education to further other political interests. During the 2005 California election, two of the eight items on the ballot dealt with education-related issues. One of the most controversial initiatives approved by voters was Proposition 227, which limited the use of bilingual educational programs in California public schools. The wealth of research validating the importance and success of bilingual education programs was not enough to convince the voters, many of whom used this initiative to express anti-immigrant sentiments.

At the school district level, the locally elected school boards, usually with four or five members, are left with the responsibility of deciding how to spend whatever funds are left according to prescribed laws. The local allocation process puts the school board face-to-face with employees and members of the local community, who usually demand costly services but nearly always have to settle for less. Contract negotiations between representatives of the school boards and employee unions and the decision to cut arts or athletic programs can be very combative. Local or county school bond measures can be one means of generating local revenue outside of state government controls. School district bond measures have become a popular method of raising local revenue, generating growing resistance among local residents, who resent the frequency with which they are proposed and their increasing failure at the polls. The board of trustees for a school district must also be activity engaged in the implementation of the state curriculum, managing facilities maintenance and construction plans, hiring a management team, quasi-judicial functions, and ceremonial duties. These obligations are clearly evident on the agenda of a typical Fresno Unified School Board District meeting:

- Voting on the appointments of an administrator of human resources and assistant superintendent for K–6 school leadership

- Voting on the appointment of two program managers

- Announcement of the positive evaluation given to the superintendent

- Recognition of a retiring employee after thirty-five years of service.

- Voting on two board resolutions that recognized Week of the School Administrator and the National School Breakfast Program.

- Voting on the recommendation of the school board administration to allow seniors who have met academic credit requirements to participate in graduation exercises regardless of whether they took the California High School Exit Examination.[33]

Each school district has a superintendent of schools (or superintendent of education) who assists the trustees of a school district in their official duties, most noticeably as the administrator of the day-to-day operations of the school district, much like the city manager of municipal government. The superintendent is responsible for the supervision of financial controls, recruitment and hiring, coordination of curriculum development, student services, report drafting, evaluation procedures, and many other tasks. The superintendent and the board of trustees form a mutually dependent relationship that is based on clear and effective policy development and decision making by the board and sound management by the superintendent.

**Reforming California Schools**   Despite California's relative prosperity, the state's public school students perform poorly. The high numbers of low-income students and students with limited proficiency in English in present major challenges for school districts. Political leaders and educational advocacy groups have responded to these challenges with a series of proposals for educational reform. The federal government plays a significant role in the process of education in California, as it does in most states, through the funding of federal education programs, many of which support the reform process in California. There are literally hundreds of educational programs in California that are supported by various federal agencies and departments—the U.S. Department of Education in particular—but one of the most recent is the somewhat controversial **No Child Left Behind** (NCLB). This federal law represents a very broad effort by the federal government to impose educational reform across the county by requiring that all schools make every attempt to adopt student proficiency standards. According to this law, federal funding would be reduced for states that fail to adopt the provisions and for schools that do not meet certain proficiency standards. After years of contentious discussions with the government and the California educational community, the state had developed public school accountability and proficiency assessment tests, but a number of conflicts between NCLB programs and California assessment measurements remain unresolved.

Educational reform at the state level has centered on class size reduction, charter schools, vouchers, and "high-stakes" testing and accountability standards. In 1996, the state legislature enacted a law to provide funding for school districts that reduced class size as well as funds to build additional schools. Various studies have indicated that although class sizes were reduced fairly rapidly, such efforts tended to benefit more affluent schools, and teacher quality, measured by experience and credentials, dropped. Charter schools have become relatively popular in California; the state was the second in the nation to authorize their use, in 1992. California is now fifth among all states in the number of charter schools, which are designed to grant more local control of funding, educational programs, and facilities and have school site governing bodies. Although charter schools remain popular, whether they actually increase academic performance is unclear. The

**No Child Left Behind Act (NCLB)** Federal law imposing educational reform throughout the country by requiring that all schools adopt student proficiency standards.

policy to provide vouchers or monetary support to private schools has not taken root in California, and two ballot initiatives to institute vouchers in the state have failed. Attaching "high stakes" to the outcomes of standardized tests has been very popular among states, and in 1999 the California legislature passed the Public School Accountability Act, largely involving monetary and nonmonetary awards to schools that met performance standards on statewide academic assessment tests. Under this act, schools that failed to meet certain academic standards would initially receive assistance but could ultimately face closure if they are unable to demonstrate improvement. Considering that public school students in California have consistently scored lower than the national average on standardized tests, it may prove very difficult for the state government to compel school districts to comply with the Public School Accountability Act.[34]

# Councils of Government

The federal and state governments have attempted to respond to the needs of local governments by encouraging the formation of regional organizations that bring municipal and county governments together to address common issues and problems. Although generally unable to deliver direct services, these regional organizations, established through federal and state statues, have been designated **councils of government** (COGs) and granted the power to allocate funds and monitor compliance with various types of regulations. Through joint-powers agreements, COGs have facilitated the pooling of city and county resources and serve as collective planning bodies of governments within one region to exchange ideas and develop regionwide policy. Designated as metropolitan planning organizations by the federal government, COGs are required to devise regional plans for transportation, growth management, environmental quality controls, and economic development. In turn, the federal government ties the allocation of federal funds, especially for transportation, to the completion and substance of these plans. Metropolitan transportation COGs can be found across the state and are one of the few types of COGs that generate long-term tangible outcomes using a regional approach. Many of California's mass transit systems and policies on highway construction are the direct result of COG collaborated efforts. Most major regions have "associations of government" COGs that provide information and planning services, but the functions of these COGs rarely go beyond the consultative stage. Issues related to growth are among the toughest for the COGs to achieve regional agreements and coordination. Cities, in particular, are still very reluctant to relinquish any authority on development and often reject COG plans to limit growth in favor of expanding development plans.

# The Future of Local Government

Local governments are the primary governmental units where the average citizen can make a real and immediate contribution. The number of Californians who recognize this fact and actually get involved will determine the future success or failure of local governments. Funding California's local governments will require the serious attention of all citizens. It is clear that the state never really recovered from the Proposition 13 tax cuts, and at some point, a reckoning will be required. Too many Californians continue to blame the current fiscal dilemma on "welfare" when in fact spending on social services could stop altogether and there would still be fiscal difficulties. It seems that a large number of Californians take the services that they receive, especially from local governments, for granted, and a

---

**Think Again**

What kinds of issues prompt the creation of a Council of Government (COG)? What role do they generally play in the policy process?

**councils of government (COGs)** Regional organizations that bring municipal and county governments together to address common issues and problems.

reality check of some type may be in order. Education in California, representing one of the most important functions of local government, will also merit the close attention of all residents. Regardless of the number of school-age children any Californian may have, they will make large tax contributions to an educational system that in general is not working very well. More money might help, but there is no guarantee, particularly when considering how few of these students regularly complete their homework and the large numbers who waste millions of dollars due to behavior problems that cause major disruptions to the education process. Quality education must be extended to all residents, for the future requires an educated workforce and a thinking public. Size is yet another major topic in the future of local government. California cities are growing, but are they becoming better places to live? Have cities outlived their usefulness as the suburban model continues to spread, and are counties in fact better equipped to address the move toward metropolis? But what do Californians lose as they become more suburban? These concerns and questions, as they relate to local government, are within the reach of most Californians. Will they grasp them?

## Summary Notes

- The relationship between the California state government and local governments is based on Dillion's Rule, the notion that local governments have only the power specially delegated to them by state law and is one of eight states that give local governments the option to exercise authority beyond Dillion's Rule. The four basic units of local governments in California are cities, counties, special districts, and regional bodies.

- The formation of counties in California was absolutely vital to the growth and administration of the state. The California constitution was revised to establish uniformity among all California counties. County governments were given police powers and required to designate a grand jury, a superior court, and various departments.

- The California Progressives further revised the Constitution and state law, granting California counties the option of home rule charter authority. A general law was also established for the remaining counties, prescribing the duties, obligations, offices, and form for county government. Of the fifty-eight counties in California, thirteen have home rule charters, including seven of the state's largest counties.

- Counties are governed by a county board of supervisors, which is also prescribed by government code. The board of supervisors, whose members serve four-year terms of office, exercises both legislative and executive power and in a number of instances has quasi-judicial authority, and has the authority to propose methods of raising revenue, with the approval of the voters. The board of supervisors is prohibited from directing or controlling the day-to-day operations of a specific county department but may use governing powers to oversee the operations of the county government.

- County ordinances are the equivalent of statutes or laws passed by the state legislature and can be used by the board of supervisors to regulate a wide range of actions and behaviors as long such ordinances do not conflict with state law.

- County governments are also responsible for communities in unincorporated areas, providing the same basic services that a municipal government would provide. In California, one in five state residents lives in an unincorporated area, which amounts to approximately 6.4 million people.

- Contract cities contract with county governments for the provision of municipal services in areas normally assumed by municipal governments, such as police and fire protection, animal control, and public works. The number of contract cities has grown dramatically since their inception in the 1960s.

- The county administrator supplies the board of supervisors with reports and information on which to base decisions and policies and manages the day-to-day operations of the county government.

- As the public prosecutor of criminal violations, the district attorney's first allegiance is to the state attorney general. The DA is the top law enforcement officer for a county and has wide latitude in deciding which laws will be enforced.

- The county sheriff was one of the first elected county offices created by the first version of the California constitution. The sheriff's department in most counties works closely with the county superior court system and supports many of the functions of the county government, including administrator of the county jails.

- The assessor is a constitutionally elected county officer whose principal duty is to determine the value of property within the county. The assessor and staff must produce accurate records of annual property assessments and maintain records and information related to property within the county.

- The county clerk, an elected position in most counties, is responsible for the public records of the county, including birth and death certificates and marriage licenses. The county clerk also performs marriage ceremonies, maintains public election records, supervises the registration of voters, and acts as the main clerk for the board of supervisors.

- Although municipal governments exercise a considerable amount of independence, the state government authority over municipal governments is founded on aspects of the California constitution and the general law on municipal government. Since 1890, when cities gained the right to create home rule charters, other statutory provisions regarding city charters have evolved, giving chartered cities the opportunity to make and enforce all laws and regulations with respect to municipal affairs.

- The process of forming an incorporated city begins with a resolution by the county board of supervisors or by a petition signed by at least 25 percent of the voters living in the area seeking incorporation and later involves public hearings conducted by the Local Agency Formation Commission (LAFCO). To date, California has 478 incorporated cites, 83 of them with charters.

- City councils with five (the usual number), seven, or nine members are the elected bodies that govern California cities. They are generally organized around one of three basic of models: the council-manager model, the weak mayor–council model, or the strong mayor–council model. Municipal boards and commissions also perform valuable services.

- State laws provide for the formation of special districts to meet specific needs in an area or community, such as water, waste management, and transportation. The funding of special districts generally comes from service fees, property tax revenues and bond sales. As the state government has become the principal funding source for education, local school districts and the school boards that oversee them have relinquished more and more control to the state.

- Another type of local government that is often regional in scope is the council of government (COG). Granted the power to allocate funds and monitor compliance with various types of regulations, COGs serve as collective planning bodies that exchange ideas and develop policy.

# Key Terms

Dillon's rule   677
home rule   679
general law   679
county board of
   supervisors   679
municipal advisory
   council (MAC)   681
contract cities   681
county administrator   684

sheriff   686
assessor   686
county clerk   687
local agency formation commission (LAFCO)   689
council-manager
   model   691
weak mayor–council
   model   692

strong mayor–council
   model   692
city manager   696
city attorney   696
city clerk   696
city treasurer   696
planning
   commission   699
special district   700

No Child Left
   Behind Act
   (NCLB)   706
councils of
   government
   (COGs)   707

# Suggested Readings

*Budget: Perspectives and Issues.* Sacramento: Legislative Analyst's Office.

League of California Cities. *A Primer on California City Finance.* March 2005.

Krolak, Richard. *California's Budget Dance: Issues and Process.* Sacramento: California Journal Press, 1990.

Senate Advisory Commission on Cost Control in State Government. *California's Budget Process: Improving Quality, Cost-Efficiency, Effectiveness and Accountability in State Government.* Sacramento: The Commission, 1999.

Senate Select Committee on Citizen Participation in Government. *The Budget Process: A Citizen's Guide to Participation.* Sacramento: California Senate Publications.

Silva, J. Fred, and Elisa Barbour. *The State–Local Fiscal Relationship in California: A Changing Balance of Power.* Public Policy Institute of California, 1999.

# 21 CALIFORNIA FISCAL POLICY

## Chapter Outline

- The California Structural Budget Gap
- The California Budget: Politics and Key Players
- Major Sources of State Revenue
- Major State Expenditures
- Financing Local Government
- The California Budget Process
- The Effect of the Direct Democracy on the Budget Process
- The State Economy: The Foundation of Fiscal Policy
- The Future of the California Political Economy
- Review

## Think About Politics

**1** Should California give tax credits to corporations that move into enterprise zones?
Yes ☐ No ☐

**2** Is California fiscally disciplined?
Yes ☐ No ☐

**3** Is borrowing money a good revenue source for the state of California?
Yes ☐ No ☐

**4** Should counties be allowed to increase the state sales tax?
Yes ☐ No ☐

**5** Should a minimum of 40% of the state's general fund be spent on K-12 public education?
Yes ☐ No ☐

**6** Should the state government be forced to commit funding resources to support the goals of ballot measures?
Yes ☐ No ☐

**7** Is migration to California helping the state's economy?
Yes ☐ No ☐

*Currently, California is faced with a significant structural budget gap. Consider the factors that contributed to this gap, and how the state might overcome its fiscal problems.*

## Introduction

Studying the fiscal systems and conditions of state and local governments is often contradictory and convoluted, but it has direct consequences for most people living in California. Californians will pay thousands of their hard-earned dollars to state and local governments to finance a wide variety of services that may or may not have an effect on their lives. The paying and spending of tax revenues do not necessarily correspond to how average Californians manage their financial affairs and often foster certain illusions, misconceptions, and anxieties among state residents. Most people in the state have grown accustomed to the buying and selling mentality of our free-market society, where one generally pays for what one gets. When it comes to government finances, however, it is not that simple, and in this era of increased scarcity, the funding of government has become even more complex. A large number of products and services that were once taken for granted have become more prohibitive in cost. Using six categories of family expense—housing and utilities, child care, transportation, food, health care, and miscellaneous expenses and taxes—the California Budget Project calculates the cost of raising a family in California. Comparing the reports for the Los Angeles region in 1999 and 2005, it is possible to obtain a better idea of why Californians may be reluctant to fork over their income for taxes and other forms of state revenue. Although salaries did increased by about one-third from 1999 to 2005, total estimated monthly expenses for a single-parent family living in Los Angeles went from $3,056 in 1999 to $4,502 in 2005. Health care costs in particular, for such a family, rose from $193 in 1999 to $545 in 2005.[1] These costs varied throughout the state, but in almost every region, they did escalate, prompting Californians to become even less inclined to hand their money over to the government for services that very often offer intangible returns.

There are obvious services that most residents enjoy and are willing to finance, usually involving education, public safety, recreation, water, and other services that are either vital to our health and safety or make our lives more comfortable. These services, as with basic family expenses, also increase over time as the cost for materials used by government grow and government employees demand higher wages. Should the government deny raises to public servants because residents of the state don't want to pay higher taxes? There are other services that are less obvious, for example, the California Environmental Protection Agency, the Office of Emergency Services, and the Division of Occupational Safety, which definitely help keep us safe and healthy but may often be out of sight and mind when it comes to paying taxes. Then there are the expenses of government that provide no direct benefit but force Californians to accept certain philosophical notions about social responsibility—notions, for example, that oblige the state government to provide income and health care to disabled residents. The moral obligations of state government are normally the hardest for taxpayers to willingly accept, and programs such as "welfare" are commonly cited as potential areas to cut government spending. Subjected to cer-

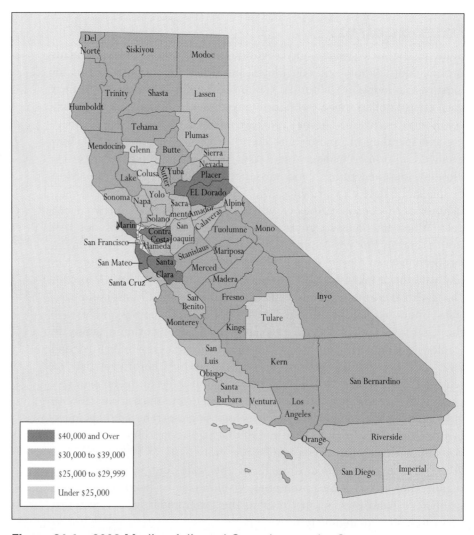

**Figure 21.1**    2003 Median Adjusted Gross Income by County

*Source: Annual Report 2004, Franchise Tax Board.*

tain reforms mandated by the federal government beginning in 1996, "welfare" is now limited to five years in most cases and annually costs the state about 5 percent of the state budget to essentially furnish assistance for about half a million recipients, most of them children, out of the approximately 34 million state residents. Is the cost of this aid to families in need a moral imperative that taxpayers can no longer afford? The average Californian would probably think not, but it is tempting to ponder when there are no other easily recognizable areas in the state budget to cut.

In some circles, the consternation about paying taxes is not so much the purpose but the methods, which different tax reform groups believe regularly encourage waste and mismanagement. One common solution, such groups propose, is to run government more like a business. Individuals in these circles want desperately to believe that the principles of an efficiently managed business, encompassing precise accounting methods, dedicated personnel, and a marketable product or service, will cure governmental inefficiency and possibly save them tax dollars. Often left out of this comparison is the profit motive, the central feature of any business but inappropriate for any government organization and impossible to achieve for most. A more appropriate standard might be an enhanced sense of professionalism among government organizations, but that of course does not usually come cheap. The illusions about government financing run both ways, and government bureaucrats themselves are frequently guilty of taking a cavalier approach to the use of government funds or of treating the public as customers who really do have the choice to take their business elsewhere. All too often, public servants and individuals who benefit from government services forget who is ultimately paying the bills. For many years now, the state government in California has faced serious budget problems—what many economists and budget experts are calling a structural budget gap—which in some respects are made worst by delusions about how much money the state receives and how its is spent. Although the residents of California entrust the legislature and executive branches of state government with the responsibility to pull the state out of this mess, they are limited by the fact that confronting fiscal realities is too often synonymous with political suicide.

## The California Structural Budget Gap

Most governments, and businesses for that matter, endure difficult financial periods. California governors going back as far as Ronald Reagan encountered difficulties in balancing the state budget. California is, however, endowed with a resource-rich economy, and all governors, in cooperation with the state legislature up to Governor Gray Davis, found differing methods of achieving governmental solvency. When Governor Davis took office in 1999, California was prospering economically and the state government produced a balanced budget. In fact, at the end his predecessor's term, the state government had about $4 billion in reserve, but that money went either to finance tax cuts or to restore cuts in programs that had suffered during lean budgetary years. Still, for the next couple of years into the Davis administration, the state government's financial situation remained stable, thanks to the thriving economy, especially in high-tech industries. Any attempt to conserve excess revenue to the state during this period was dispelled by major increases in spending for a number of governmental services, but especially for education, a major campaign promise by Davis that was supported by the state legislature. During these boom years, state government took the opportunity to reduce fees, enact special tax breaks, and extend health

— Think Again —

What factors contributed to the creation of California's current budget problems? How has Governor Schwarzenegger responded to these problems?

**Figure 21.2** 2004
General Fund Sources

*Source: Annual Report 2004,* Franchise
Tax Board.

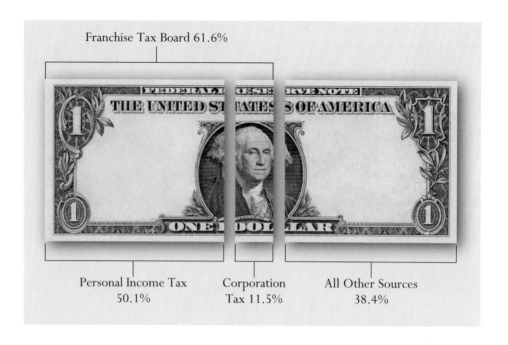

Franchise Tax Board 61.6%

Personal Income Tax
50.1%

Corporation
Tax 11.5%

All Other Sources
38.4%

**structural budget gap** A
long-term excess of state
expenditures over state
revenues.

coverage to uninsured children. Spending by the state government shot up to
between 25 and 35 percent. Then, in early 2001, the high-tech industry suffered
a major decline, and with it went about 15 percent of the state tax revenue. Soon
after that, the state was hit with the energy crisis, forcing the state government
to spend $6 billion of its cash reserves to shore up the energy industry. Making
the financial situation even worse was a slide in the stock market that delivered
yet another major revenue loss to the California state government. By the time
Arnold Schwarzenegger took office in 2003, the state was confronted with the
realities of a **structural budget gap**.[2]

The difference between a structural budget gap and a budget problem or
deficit is that the gap tends to be either permanent or at least long-term. In most
developing nations, a gap between the money that they accumulate and the cost
of government services has existed for decades. Many carry a national debt, used
to bridge the gap, which even in prosperity could never be paid off. The California state government is now inching toward a similar situation. California's government revenue problems started with the passage of Proposition 13 in 1978,
resulting in a massive property tax cut, and the state government has been trying
desperately to make up that loss in revenue ever since. For a while, the successive
line of governors have been able to fill the gap with short-term measures, such as
shifting funds from one department to another, deferring payments on state debt
and other long-term costs, internal borrowing from special funds, and external
borrowing. These financial tactics work well as long as there is the promise of
future funds to eventually balance the books, but since 2002, no future revenue
sources have materialized.

Upon taking office, Governor Schwarzenegger campaigned for and got the
approval of a $15 billion bond measure, essentially borrowing the California
state government out of the structural budget gap. Borrowing, in combination
with slight increases in revenue in fiscal 2005–06, got California over the gap.
The governor's proposed budget for 2006–07 assumes that the state will take in
just over $92 billion and spend close to $98 billion, leaving a deficit—a budget
gap—of about $6 billion.[3] Deficit or not, Governor Schwarzenegger must walk a
very fine line in proposing this budget, addressing the needs and interests of the

various political players who will benefit directly or indirectly from the state government's revenue and expenditure plan.

# The California Budget: Politics and Key Players

There is little doubt in the minds of the elected officers of the executive and state legislators that the budget is where reality and ideas part. The annual budget reflects the priorities of the state government, and most Californians would like to believe that these priorities correspond to California's best interests. These leaders and legislators owe their positions to political considerations, not prudent economics, and can be counted on to listen very carefully to concerns about the budget from the individuals and groups that are responsible for their political success. Governor Jerry Brown was adamantly opposed to Proposition 13 and vigorously campaigned against it, but when it was approved by the voters, he advocated many of its tax-cutting features.[4] As governor of California, Ronald Reagan was forced to backpedal on his "small is good" approach to state government and sign into law a budget that was based on a tax increase. The governor is the ringmaster of the California budget circus, but the star performer of that show is clearly the state legislature. This drama becomes especially intense for the governor when the state legislature is controlled by the opposing party, which has been the case for four of the last six governors. That legislative body will first and foremost want to craft a budget that will cater to members' voting constituents and the special-interest groups that helped them get elected. For the Democrats in the legislature, who tend to represent a wide range of interests, providing for their supporters in the annual budget can be difficult and costly for California taxpayers. The annual state budget is full of tax breaks as well as generous funding of certain departments that benefit businesses, unions, and seniors. For years, the Democrat-controlled legislature has given a hefty tax credit to corporations that moved into "enterprise zones" and hired local residents, despite complaints that many businesses were taking advantage of the program and not

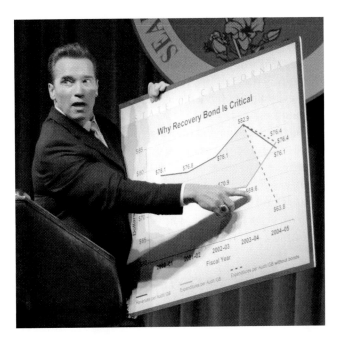

Governor Arnold Schwarzenegger announced a $99 billion state budget for 2004–2005 that included $4.1 billion for full state reimbursement to local governments of lost Vehicle License Fee revenues and honored his commitment to education with increased spending.

producing the intended results.[5] Interest groups have a large stake in the budget plan and will not hesitate to use information, campaign contributions, and the initiative process to influence what the budget supports and how it is financed. It is no secret that the oil companies located in California have contributed heavily to the elections of statewide officers and state legislators and will receive a number of annual tax breaks, such as an oil depletion allowance worth about $28 million, a manufacturer's investment credit that can be as high as $40 million, and a drilling allowance that deducts roughly $10 million from their taxes.[6] Legislators have balanced the weaknesses they may have on budgetary matters, the consequences of term limits, and the necessity of having to learn budget details quickly, with a large staff of personal aides, committee consultants, party caucus staff, and research staff. The elected statewide officers of government are another source of political pressure and influence on budgetary matters, especially from the treasurer and controller, who have direct responsibilities for financial aspects of the government. During 2005, Phil Angelides, the state treasurer, was a very vocal critic of the fiscal policies of the Schwarzenegger administration, a position that observers of state capitol politics feel stemmed from his Democratic partisan politics, his perspective on budget developments, and his decision to run for governor. The **Legislative Analyst's Office** (LAO) is supposed to be the one governmental entity in the state budget drama not closely associated with any one character or plot. Created in 1941 as the first nonpartisan legislative fiscal office in the country, the LAO is headed by a legislative analyst who is responsible for examining the state budget and making recommendations to the state legislature regarding the fiscal efficiency of state government.[7] Its Web site is full of detailed analyses of the state budget and reports on the performance of specific departments and agencies. Theoretically serving all 120 members of the state legislature, the LAO, particularly Elizabeth Hill, who has served as the legislative analyst for sixteen years, has received high marks from members of both parties in the legislature for a nonpartisan approach to budgetary matters. Provisions in **Proposition 140**, mandating term limits, also cut 60 percent of the LAO's budget, making certain detailed budget analyses and the former practice of scrutinizing specific fiscal bills nearly impossible.[8] There are a number of external but nonetheless important budget politics players from so-called citizen advocacy groups that specialize in state government fiscal policy. The California Taxpayers Association and the California Tax Reform Association are two of the major statewide organizations that purportedly represent the private citizens' view, but it often is very difficult for these groups to submerge their ideological leanings. These groups have been important in providing an alternative perspective on budget policy and are often found testifying at state legislative committee hearings.

All of these players and many others too obscure to mention here will converge when the time comes to determine the most complete accounting of state government revenue and whether there will be enough to spend on state government expenditures. These decisions are complicated by the various sources of revenue and what appears to be the growing list of government expenses. A reasonably clear understanding of revenue and expenditures is extremely important in forming rational opinions about the state government's financial predicament.

**Legislative Analyst's Office (LAO)** The office responsible for analyzing the California state budget and making recommendations to the state legislature regarding the fiscal efficiency of state government.

**Proposition 140** Law that established term limits and cut 60 percent of the LAO budget.

— Think Again —
What are the most important sources of state revenue?

# Major Sources of State Revenue

One of the most controversial and most misunderstood aspects of government, revenue is the fuel that powers the engine of government. Ultimately, most of

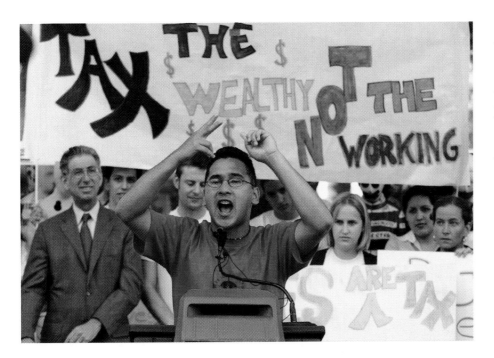

Former State Treasurer Phil Angelides (left) joined the University of California and California State student associations, and the "Stop the Cuts" Coalition of students from 20 universities to protest Governor Schwarzenegger's higher education cuts and student fee hikes.

the revenue of the state will find it way into the state's **general fund**, the major pool of money used to finance government. Most of California's revenue is derived from taxes, although in recent years, borrowing has become much more popular. The question these days among leaders in the executive and legislative branches of California government is not whether to borrow but how much. There are still taxes that generate very large sums of money for the state, and despite the grumbling of "no new taxes," this extremely important way of raising revenue will probably be around for a while. "Fairness" is one of the fundamental

**general fund** The pool of money used to finance the California state government.

## Table 21.1   General Fund Revenues

|  | 2003 | | 2004 | | |
|---|---|---|---|---|---|
|  | **Amount (Millions)** | **Percent of Total** | **Amount (Millions)** | **Percent of Total** | **Percent Change** |
| **Franchise Tax Board Sources:** | | | | | |
| Personal Income Tax | $33,991.2 | 46.6 | $38,539.7 | 50.1 | 13.4 |
| Corporation Tax | 6,959.6 | 9.4 | 8,811.6 | 11.5 | 28.3 |
| Subtotal | $40,860.8 | 56.0 | $47,351.3 | 61.6 | 15.9 |
| **Other Revenue Sources** | | | | | |
| Retail Sales and Use Tax | $22,781.3 | 31.2 | $24,435.7 | 31.8 | 7.3 |
| Insurance Company Tax | 1,993.1 | 2.7 | 2,222.6 | 2.9 | 11.5 |
| Estate, Gift, and Inheritance Tax | 782.0 | 1.1 | 539.8 | 0.7 | –31.0 |
| Alcoholic Beverage Excise Tax | 303.2 | 0.4 | 311.1 | 0.4 | 2.6 |
| Cigarette Tax | 114.8 | 0.2 | 121.2 | 0.2 | 5.5 |
| Other Revenues & Investment Interest | 6,131.6 | 8.4 | 1,901.8 | 2.5 | –69.0 |
| **Subtotal** | $32,106.0 | 44.0 | $29,532.1 | 38.4 | –8.0 |
| **Total General Fund Revenues** | $72,966.8 | 100.0 | $76,883.5 | 100.0 | 5.4 |

*Source:* Annual Report 2004, Franchise Tax Board.

## COMPARED TO WHAT?

# California and Minnesota: Approaches to Fiscal Policy

The Government Performance Project of 2005 offers a good opportunity to compare the performance of the fifty state governments, and the budget policies of California and Minnesota in particular, which are at opposite ends of the performance scale in this category. The Government Performance Project (GPP) is one of the only comprehensive and independent analyses available on the quality of state government throughout the country and has been conducting the performance reports on state governments since 1997. The independence of the GPP is at least somewhat assured by its support from the Pew Charitable Trusts, which has a solid reputation for supporting as well as conducting nonpartisan research projects. In the 2005 GPP rating of state governments, Minnesota earned an overall B+ grade and an A– for the management of money. The GPP basically uses five standard criteria for grading money management: long-term outlook, budget process, structural balance, contracting/purchasing, and financial control/reporting.

### Long-Term Outlook

According to the 2005 GPP report, Minnesota has a strong forecasting capability and adheres to long-term budgeting. The state has a fairly well-funded public pension system, low debt levels, and a good credit rating at Aa1. Minnesota uses a variety of methods and groups to forecast revenue, including private consultants and economic analysis models. Revenue forecasts in California are largely con-

ducted for purposes of budgetary planning by the Department of Finance, which is an executive department. Both of the state's public employee pension systems are underfunded, a financial liability that in the future will have to be solved either through increased payroll deductions or tax increases, or decreased pension benefits. California continues to amass a large debt and its bond rating is the worst in the nation.

### Budget Process

Minnesota regularly passes the state budget by the specified deadlines. The budget process is considered to be very transparent, offering state residents the opportunity to publicly discuss fiscal policy through advisory groups, public hearings, and town hall meetings and to submit budgetary input on a state government Web site that in 2004 received over 1,800 comments and suggestions. The budget process in California regularly runs past the required budget deadlines and, according to the GPP, is often driven by the state electoral initiatives. The observations by the GPP on the initiative process may be a bit distorted as there are a number of ways the state legislature and governor of California can circumvent the effects of initiatives, either by increasing taxes or reducing the budget.

### Structural Balance

In the balance of revenue and expenditures, Minnesota's tax revenue sources are very similar to the percentages of personal income tax, sales tax, and other sources in California, although Minnesota does have a corporate tax rate that is roughly 1 percent higher than the rate in California. Minnesota

principles of tax policy, and governmental leaders spend long hours trying to devise methods of avoiding being unfairly criticized for heaping the tax burden on one particular group. A "fair" tax policy is very difficult to achieve simply because of the dilemma in deciding whether to tax everyone equally, regardless of how much fairness is involved, or vice versa. A progressive tax is one that takes a greater percentage from individuals with higher incomes than from those with lower incomes. A *regressive tax* imposes a heavier burden on people who are less able to pay the specified tax. Applied to income, it is a tax that takes a greater percentage of income from people with low incomes than from those with high incomes.

**Personal Income Tax**    Adopted in 1935, the state income tax is the largest source of state revenue, accounting for about 40 percent of the state's general fund. California's income tax is a progressive tax. There are six state income tax rates, that beginning at 1.0 percent of total annual income and ending at 9.3 perearmarks motor vehicle sales and license and gas taxes to support its transportation system. The tax rates in each state are considered to be relatively high in comparison to the rest of the nation and the residents of both states pay significantly more in federal taxes than is received in services from the federal government. The Tax Foundation ranks these two states very close to the bottom of the fifty states in having a favorable business tax climate. Both states have instituted hiring freezes, but the Minnesota state government appears more inclined to impose layoffs and across-the-board and targeted spending cuts than the California state government. California does rely much more on bonds to finance its government and balance the state budget and has consistently used transportation-related taxes and fees for non-transportation expenditures.

### Contracting/Purchasing

The Minnesota state government is the main procurement agent for most levels of government in the state and has passed laws requiring the oversight of outside contractors that includes performance measures to monitor and evaluate contract performance. The California state government does not have a single or central system for contracting and purchasing goods and services for government operations. Each state agency or department is largely responsible for its own procurement system, which tends to vary dramatically in efficiency and level of sophistication.

### Financial Controls/Reporting

The Minnesota state government is known to generate financial reports within a reasonable period of time and is fairly proficient in linking cost analysis with performance information and the impact of proposed legislation. Twice a year, state agencies and departments are required to submit reports on expenditures and operational performance that are available to the public at a "Department Results" Web site. The California state government also produces financial reports in a timely manner, but with the exception of the fiscal reports that are prepared by the Legislative Analyst's Office, there is little evidence of an effort to connect cost analysis with government performance or spending.

Conventional wisdom would suggest that California has a significantly higher number of factors that complicates its fiscal management: its border with Mexico, large urban populations, relatively high cost of living, and avenues for direct democracy. Interestingly, both states received very similar percentages of tax revenue, but it seems that the high grade Minnesota received from the Government Performance Project was closely associated with fiscal discipline, a practice that has eluded the California state government. Following Minnesota's example in strong forecasting methods, a transparent budget process, centralized procurement procedures, and public and elaborate cost analysis with performance requirements will not necessarily drastically increase the amount of revenue or lower expenditures in California. Such practices might provide state legislators and executive officers with a bit more fiscal backbone, potentially reduce some waste that inevitably occurs in huge government bureaucracies, and dispel fiscal misconceptions among voters who are endowed with ballot-box budgeting powers.

*Sources:* State Report Cards: California and Minnesota State Government Performance 2005, Government Performance Project, http://results.gpponline.org; The Tax Foundation, Tax Research Areas. http://www.taxfoundation.org.

cent, the top rate. The precise numbers can drastically change from year to year, but it is safe to assume that under the current income tax system in California, between 1 and 5 percent of the wealthiest Californians pay at least half of the total income taxes collected.[9] The state legislature has been trying to add a 10 percent bracket for single residents making between $143,000 and $286,000 or married couples earning between $286,843 and $573,686 and an 11 percent bracket for single residents earning over $286,843 and married couples who made over $573,686, but so far, these new rates have been resisted.[10]

**Sales Tax**    The second largest amount of tax dollars comes from the state sales tax, consisting of about 28 percent of the general fund. Sales taxes are generally considered regressive because they impose a heavier burden on those less able to bear it. Though this condition may not strictly apply to the purchase of a luxury item, it is relevant to the buying of necessities. Although the statewide sales tax rate is set at 7.25 percent of the retail price of purchased goods, most counties

**Figure 21.3** California Personal Income Annual Growth

*Source: California Economic Indicators, January–February, 2005, California Department of Finance.*

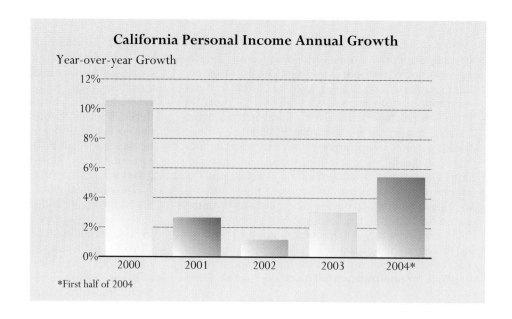

**California Personal Income Annual Growth**

Year-over-year Growth

*First half of 2004

have taken the opportunity to increase the sales tax, with voter approval, to fund various local expenditures such as transportation. Many cities and counties set the basic sales tax rate at 8.25 percent, but it can go higher—it is currently 8.50 percent in San Francisco. There have been numerous complaints among Californians over the years about the unevenness with which the sales tax is applied. The charge that certain industries are exempt from the sales tax is usually countered with the argument that the government is merely attempting to restrain its tax policy. For example, according to the Revenue and Taxation Code, a state resident will pay no tax on seeds that produce food for humans but will pay a tax on seeds that produce nonfood plants. Moreover, if the seeds are purchased by mail and the company does not have a physical presence in the county of the final destination, that sale will be subject only to the statewide rate of 7.25 percent.

**Corporate Taxes**   Various types of taxes are placed on businesses and corporations that operate in California, most of which are subject to the basic rate of 8.84 percent of profits that are earned in the state, commonly known as a *franchise tax*. For any business transaction that somehow involves selling products or services outside the state or a company outside the state conducting business in California, a corporate tax on profits is levied. The tax rate on banks and financial institutions is determined by the **Franchise Tax Board** and will vary from year to year between 10 percent and 12 percent; the corporate tax rate for the insurance industry in California has been significantly lower. All corporations that are taxed by the state government generated roughly 10 percent of state revenue.[11]

**Franchise Tax Board**   The board that sets tax rates for banks and financial institutions in California.

**excise tax**   A sales tax imposed only on specific goods.

**Excise Taxes**   Often labeled a "sin tax," an **excise tax** is a selective sales tax, imposed only on the sale of specific goods. In California, those specific goods include tobacco, alcoholic beverages, and gasoline. Tobacco is hit hardest by excise taxes, comprising two separate types of taxes, the first being a surtax on each pack of cigarettes, clearly identified by a stamp, paid for by the distributor. There is also a tobacco tax levied on all tobacco products, and at least one initiative has been passed over the past decade that puts a special tax on cigarettes to fund smoking prevention, health-related programs, and youth activities. The construction and maintenance of highways in California have traditionally been financed through a tax on gas and diesel fuel. Taxes on fuel are split between an 18-cent-per-gallon excise tax and a sales tax, but in recent years, the funds generated from these taxes have been shifted to other areas of state expenditures. Excise taxes account for approximately 4 percent of the general fund and are considered regressive. With the introduction of fuel-efficient automobiles, some state legislators and transportation and taxation experts suggest that taxing miles driven rather than the gas would be a more equitable way of paying for California's highways and would provide some relief from escalating fuel prices.[12]

**Bond Debt**   Most politicians these days are especially sensitive to any consideration of raising taxes and instead are increasingly using bonds to pay for government expenditures that current levels of revenue cannot meet, although the use of bonds can be problematic because voter approval is required in most instances. Although bonds are traditionally used for major state-funded construction projects, Governor Schwarzenegger drafted a $15 billion bond plan, approved by the voters, to address a budgetary shortfall. The use of bonds is basically an opportunity for the state government to borrow, and bonds come in three basic varieties. *General obligation bonds* are backed by the "full faith and credit" of the state government and are a form of long-term financing that is slowly paid back by state revenue, which in most circumstances comes from taxpayers. These so-called GO bonds can be used on just about any type of government expenditure at the state level. *Revenue bonds* are used to finance a government facility that will generate funds, which will be used to pay back the bond debt.[13] In a rare display of bipartisanship, the state legislature and Governor Schwarzenegger jointly supported a series of bond measures approved by the voters in the November 2006 elections that will generate close to $40 billion for transportation, housing, schools, and levees. Many members of the state government as well as private citizens worry about the long-term repercussions of relying on borrowing. Although bonds avoid resorting to highly unpopular increases in taxes, they can take between nine and fourteen years to pay off and end up costing much more in interest than the amount originally borrowed. California's bond rating has dropped considerably over the years, and there is some doubt about the effect that the continued use of bonds will have on that rating in the future. Another type of bond debt, *lease-revenue bonds*, became popular with the California state government in the 1980s. Use of these bonds requires only a majority vote of the state legislature, and they are usually sold to finance the construction and renovation of state facilities. Borrowing funds through lease-revenue bonds is typically small, but the interest rates on these bonds tend to be higher than on GO bonds.[14]

**Federal Contributions**   Budgetary trends over the course of the Bush administration have been to reduce spending on a long list of federal programs that directly benefit Californians. Education is heavily supported in California by the federal government, particularly in vocational, basic adult, preschool, and disadvantaged student programs. Low-income Californians are the direct beneficiaries of federal spending on child care, food assistance, and housing. Other major federal allocations to California are earmarked for statewide water treatment and a series of block grants to local government, most notably the Community Development Block Grant (CDBG), an important funding stream for a wide variety of community development projects that are administered by local governments.[15] Californians have received less federal funding per dollar of federal taxes paid than the average state. For example, in 1992, California received 93 cents in federal expenditures on each taxable dollar but only 79 cents in 2004, and even lower returns can be anticipated if the federal government continues to pursue in funding reductions.[16]

> **Think Again**
>
> Why is bond debt often seen as a more attractive way of raising revenue than tax increases?

**Other Revenue Sources**   In addition to taxes and bonds, the state government receives small amounts of revenue from a number of different sources, supporting the notion that every little bit helps. In 1972, property taxes accounted for about 30 percent of the revenue that went to state and local governments, a large portion earmarked for education.[17] As a result of Proposition 13, that amount is down to 13 percent, most of which goes to state government, with small portions going back to local government. Motor vehicle fees and other sources in the revenue mix contribute on the average about 13 percent of the all revenue the state receives.[18] Interest earned on state deposits and the lottery, which funds education costs, are very small forms of revenue to the state government, and both tend to be unpredictable.

## Major State Expenditures

This topic really presents a challenge to all Californians who care how their hard-earned tax dollars are being spent and a particular challenge to those who believe that those dollars are being wasted. It would be silly to suggest that no waste occurs in the state government, but the arguments about the squandering of state government revenue are also often misplaced when considering that the state budget for 2006–07 will be close to $100 billion; clearly, curtailing the fraudulent activities of parents receiving public assistance would hardly amount to a drop in the bucket. The time really has come for Californians to take a good look at the state's expenditures and find the fat to cut out if tax increases are to be avoided.

**Education**   Passed in 1988, Proposition 98 requires the state government to spend a minimum of 40 percent of the general fund on K–12 public school education. Propostion 98 is credited with significantly raising spending per pupil in California after falling to forty-seventh in the nation in the aftermath of Proposition 13. Nonetheless, even though an awful lot of money goes to education in California, the number of students continues to climb, and overall educational results have been less than stellar. With the exception of California community colleges, funding for higher education in California has slipped as students at the

*Think Again*

What kinds of programs are part of California's health and human services budget?

Teachers and administrators attempt to create a budget in light of cuts to school programs by the state.

## UP CLOSE

# The Protection and Education of Children

A large share of the expenditures prescribed by the state budget goes to fund programs intended for the protection and education of children residing in California. These tasks are performed at the expense of state residents who have become increasingly sensitive about their tax burden and periodically pressure the state government into budget-cutting policies or attempts to scale back the budget themselves through the initiative process, often sacrificing expenditures for California's youth. Proposition 13 placed the financing of education in serious jeopardy, and public assistance to families is still usually the first to be reduced when the state government needs to trim costs. This lack of enthusiasm about funding programs that support the welfare of children is not unlike the values, philosophy of governance, and laws embraced by the founders of the California state government over a century ago, whose solution to this expense was not to finance such expenditures at all. At the time, fortunes both within and outside the gold fields were being realized, and a very large number of children were treated, with the tacit approval of government, very much like adults. The chronicles of Eliza Woodson Burhans-Farnham offers a poignant observation of one of the "saddest features" she witnessed in the California gold country of the 1850s:

> The children participate in all the vices of their elders. I saw boys, from six upward, swaggering through the streets, begirt with scarlet sash, in exuberant collar and bosom, segar in mouth, uttering huge oaths, and occasionally treating men and boys at the bars.

Burhans-Farnham continues with a description that would be unimaginable today, prevented in large part by social programs and the enforcement of laws and regulations at considerable cost to the taxpaying public:

> A mother with whom I was talking saw from my window her son, a young hopeful boy of ten, walk into a rum-shop opposite, and call up two or three men and large boys to drink. I called her attention to the fact, not knowing that she had a son. "Yes," she said, sadly, "that is my boy."

Continuing in her line of questioning, Burhans-Farnham asks, "And is it possible that you cannot prevent him?" "No, he washes his own gold, and gets from three to five dollars a week; and he will spend that for what he pleases." Not satisfied with the justification, Burhans-Farnham persists in her questions to the mother, who replies:

*The Cypress College Day Care, which has operated since 1975, became a victim of cutbacks during California's budget crisis when it had to close its doors to the 51 children enrolled in the center.*

> There are so many boys in town that do what you see him do, that it is impossible to stop one; and the fact is, that up here our boys grow old very fast anyhow. There is no school to send them to, and no church, and it's useless trying to make good boys of them, when they see men behave so badly and hear so much swearing and bad language.

During the early days of California state government, the line between child and adulthood was so blurred that boys, often as young as 12, where sentenced to San Quentin and Folsom prisons. One of the bright spots in the welfare of children during this initial period was the leadership of John Swett, who as superintendent of education succeeded in expanding education throughout California. During the 1860s, he is credited with abolishing tuition for public schools, encouraging school districts to build better schools, and lengthening the school year.

Illustrating the harsh conditions that a very large number of the children in San Francisco continued to endure in the 1890s, James Flamant writes:

> Those interested in the praiseworthy efforts of preventing crime among the juvenile element of the state will regretfully acknowledge that a fearful state of demoralization exists among the lower classes, where examples of depravity, degradation and excessive intemperance are held above the impressionable youth until their stings have penetrated his weakened mind, and poisoned a life which might otherwise have been faultless.

By this time, the plight of children in San Francisco was beginning to be addressed, and Flamant describes the effort in the following comments:

To meet this midway or mixed class of otherwise innocent transgressors and castaways, we can proudly boast of possessing, free from the state, two institutions meeting all the requirements necessary on saving and caring for such cases—the Boys' and Girls' Aid Society of California and the Youths' Directory, the former being nonsectarian and the latter under Catholic control, although, in many cases, caring for Protestant children.

Not only was the Boys' and Girls' Aid Society of California "free from the state," according to Flamant, but it was also "self-supporting," "laying aside each month a surplus." No doubt the society's "self-supporting" knack must have been derived from the "good work" that is depicted by the author. "Lodging and board at a nominal charge are furnished to working children without suitable homes or care in the city."

As the influence of Progressives grew in the early years of the twentieth century, the state government attempted to take a more active role in establishing a sense of professionalism and supervision in the care of children, though still not providing much money. In 1903, the state government established the Board of Charities to evaluate and report on various types of institutions, including those that cared for children. By 1908, the board recommended the removal of children from many unfit orphan asylums and began what is known today as the foster care program. The Progressives would institute other policies in attempting to alleviate youth-related problems that were suspect in intent, if not down right repressive. The policy of relying on private charitable organizations to care for children would continue through the Progressive period and into the 1920s, but foster care was favored by state and county governments because of the deplorable conditions in many of the "asylums." The response to child labor by the Progressives at the turn of the century was to enact labor laws that limited the working hours of children to eight hours per day. Eugenic sterilization was another social policy from the California Progressive era that would continue well into the into the 1930s as a means of preventing the problems of youth by simply thwarting any attempt to reproduce among those deemed genetically unfit for child rearing. Minors themselves were sometimes the targets of the sterilization policy if they demonstrated "deviant" behavior and the susceptibility to premature parenthood.

As California moved into the industrial boom years of the 1920s, the combination of high employment rates, private charitable activities, and state government policies tended to mask the plight of children across the state. The harsh economic conditions brought on by the depression of the 1930s, however, dissipated whatever social supports existed for children living in poverty in California. Parents were rendered destitute, donations to private relief agencies dried up or fell dramatically short, and even the traditional labors of children were now being performed by adults. The consolidation of various charitable agencies in Los Angeles County to form the Family Welfare Association at the beginning of the Great Depression became a model approach to alleviating rampant poverty, especially among children. Through the coordination of resources and the administrative capacity of agencies that included the American Red Cross, the American Legion, and the Children's Protective Association, the Family Welfare Association expanded its relief efforts in Los Angeles from 1,187 families in 1931 to 18,071 in 1932, but even this level of service proved inadequate. Most racial minorities in California were excluded from most charitable activities from the founding of the state to well into the twentieth century. Indian children, at least until the Progressive era, were not only the victims of wholesale neglect but were often forced into varying forms of bondage with the approval of state laws and local ordinances. Ethnic and racial minorities in California were usually somewhat successful in forming mutual aid societies and educational institutions, many of which remain today. Jewish family service organizations could be found in most major California cities dating back to the 1850s, developing a fine reputation for their nonsectarian and nondiscriminatory relief activities.

Initially, Californians were reluctant to back proposals to increase government spending, despite the obvious need of so many residents during the 1930s for government intervention, resolutely rejecting Proposition 9 in 1932, an income tax plan to fund schools and other social programs. Another income tax proposal was passed by the state legislature in 1933 only to be vetoed by Governor James "Sunny Jim" Rolph. The passage of the Social Security Act of 1935 by Congress, as a part of the New Deal programs of the federal government, provided state governments with funds for the care of children through the Aid to Dependent Children program. This program formed the foundation for statewide relief efforts in California that were administered by a state bureaucracy expanded under the leadership of Governor Frank Merriam, who did sign into law an income tax bill in 1935, and by Colbert Olsen, elected in 1939 on a New Deal platform and the first Democratic governor in California since 1895. The federal Aid to Dependent Children program, later to become Aid to Families with Dependent Children, for the first time guaranteed to all children in California the necessities of life through income security to their families. This program was supplemented with state resources that were increasingly taking the shape of a child welfare system in the post–World War II period of prosperity. In 1948, Governor Earl Warren held the first Statewide Youth Conference in Sacramento, attended by an estimated 2,200 social service administrators, child welfare professionals, and youth advocates. By the 1960s, California's relative economic success, progressive attitudes, and interventionist approach of government fueled the expansion of social services that were considered some of the most generous in the nation. Today, California implements a wide range of federal and state-funded child welfare programs through a county-based social service system that is overseen by the California Department of Human Services and the California Child Welfare Services agency as well as the California Department of Education and the numerous unified school districts. Close to half of the current budget of the state is consumed by these programs, which many Californians have been less willing to pay for in recent years, but alternatives to these costs will likely be reminiscent of

the past: neglect, child labor, increased crime, lost childhood, and dysfunctional adults.

*Sources:* Eliza Woodson Burhans-Farnham *California, In-Doors and Out; or, How We Farm, Mine and Live Generally in the Golden State,* New York: Dix, Edwards, 1856, pp. 358–359; James Flamant, "Child-Saving Charities in This Big Town," San Francisco History, http://www .sfgenealogy.com/sf/history/hgcsc.htm, May 28, 1893; Janna Braun, "A Lifeline: Social Services to Protect and Serve," Making It in L.A., http://www-scf.use.edu/~jour556/issues/services.shtml; David R. Doerr, "Conformity: The Impossible Dream," *Cal-Tax Digest,* March 1997, http://www.caltax.org/MEMBER/digest/mar97/mar97-3.htm; "Our History," California Department of Corrections and Rehabilitation, http://www.cya.ca.gov/DivisionsBoards/DJJ/about/history .html; Diane F. Reed and Kate Karpilow, *Understanding the Child Welfare System in California* (Oakland: California Center for Research on Women and Families, 2002).

California state universities and the University of California have experienced steep fee increases. Spending on higher education in the 2006–07 budget proposal was slightly down from the 12.8 percent that was allocated during 1999–2000. Funding for California's community colleges has remained fairly constant, but this share of the budget has been regularly criticized as inadequate.

**Health and Welfare**    The bulk of the approximately 28 percent of the general fund allocated for the health and welfare of state residents is consumed by a wide range of health care services that are administered by the counties. These services extend health care coverage to low-income families, low-income elderly, and the disabled through the Medi-Cal program. Surprisingly, the state budget allocation for health care has remained fairly constant in comparison to the skyrocketing costs of private health care providers. Roughly 25 percent of the health and welfare budget line goes to Temporary Assistance for Needy Families (TANF) and CalWORKs, the companion program that supports employment development, education and training, and child care services for TANF participants. Other sizable social service programs financed through the general fund are the Supplemental Security Income (SSI) and Supplementary Security Payment (SSP) programs, helping low-income seniors and people with disabilities cover basic living expenses.

**Corrections**    Alarming growth in the California Department of Corrections is pushing up the price tag for incarcerating a prison population that has grown sevenfold since the 1980s to 170,000 inmates. The current cost of about $8.1 billion, or 6.4 percent of the state budget, is barely supporting the costs of maintaining thirty-three prisons that are at twice their intended capacity and considered some of the worst in the nation. There is no shortage of reasons why California prisons are overcrowded, some of which have to do with high recidivism rates, and tough sentencing policies, but unless new approaches are adopted or drastic measures are taken, the prison population is projected to increase (to 193,000 inmates by 2011), and so will the annual costs.[19]

**Other Expenditures**    Almost three-fourths of the state budget is devoted to public education, health and human services for low-income residents, and corrections in California. The remaining fourth is split among seven major fund-

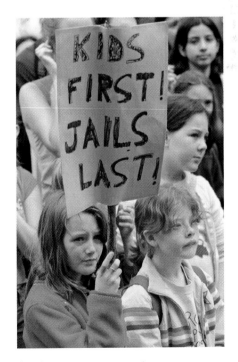

Students, parents, teachers and supporters protested cuts to education spending at the California State Capitol building.

Visitors to Yosemite National Park were forced to vacate as a result of the national budget crisis. One visitor, lined up to leave the campground, flies an American flag upside down in protest of the cuts that forced the park to close.

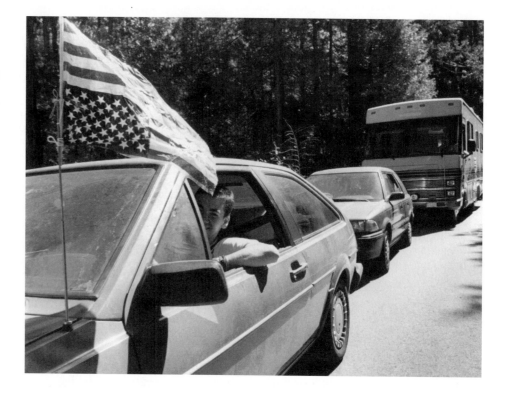

ing categories that include a wide variety of departments and agencies that have suffered major cutbacks and whose directors can be regularly heard complaining about the lack of funds to complete their mission satisfactorily. Because funds are basically locked into the top three spending areas for statutory, public safety, or public health reasons, there is probably little chance of seeing any increases in the budgets of environmental protection, state government resources, business and housing, consumer services, judicial administration, or workforce development agencies. Transportation would normally be included among these spending areas, but there has recently been serious political pressure to commit highway user taxes and motor vehicle fees and bond measures to transportation improvement.

## Financing Local Government

---Think Again---
How is local government financed in California?

Since the passage of Proposition 13, the amount of revenue generated by county and municipal governments has decreased substantially. The loss of local property tax funds to local government has made county governments largely dependent on budgetary allocations from the state government. California county governments have always had a difficult time financing their operations, and the loss of property tax funds has made that task even harder. Almost 31 percent of county revenue comes from the state to finance state-mandated programs and services that are administered by the county government, the biggest and most expensive being health and welfare services.[20] Administering these services can be problematic for county government because they are rarely funded at the total or true costs of the services provided. In addition to federal funds for special initiatives usually associated with state-mandated functions, the other revenue sources that go to county government for so-called general-purpose functions including property taxes redistributed from the state, special fees, charges for current services, and a variety of smaller forms of revenue. California county governments are experiencing a tight financial situation as residents of local cities remain dependent on them for various services, ranging from voter registration to county jail services, while the county governments receive a diminishing share of state and local revenues. Counties may receive additional revenue by providing services to municipal governments through contract city arrangements, but such contracts have become somewhat controversial, as outlined in Chapter 24.

City governments do have considerably more flexibility in revenue sources but are to a large extent on their own when it comes to raising this revenue. Typical sources of revenue to cities are derived from service charges for utilities, licenses and permits, a portion of state sales taxes, redistribution of property taxes from the state government, and an assortment of smaller forms of revenue. Cities may impose an additional percentage point on sales taxes that they are allowed by the state to retain, and this has become a major form of revenue to California cities and a significant influence on municipal policy to promote retail sales establishments, especially the "big box" stores or "megastores" that generate a lot of sales revenue for municipal governments. Depending on the city, other revenue sources, such as a developer fees and business license and hotel taxes, can provide revenue. Many cities are also increasingly attempting to institute the **Mello-Ross Community Facilities District**, which is a financing tool that local governments can use to levy special taxes or assessments for designated community improvements, such as freeway interchanges, library services, or recreation programs. To institute a Mello-Ross fee, the voters living in the designated community must consent by a two-thirds voting margin.

**Mello-Ross Community Facilities District** A financing tool that local governments can use to levy special taxes or assessments for designated community improvements, such as freeway interchanges, library services, or recreation programs.

The fiscal future of counties and cities was improved when voters passed Proposition 1A in 2004, a ballot measure that comes very close to basically prohibiting the state government from shifting any additional local tax revenues back to the general fund. Proposition 13 and the transfer of most property tax revenues to the state government began a process by the state government of periodically raiding the revenue sources of local governments, most recently the local portion of sales and highway user taxes, to avoid state government budget deficits.[21] In return for the prohibition instituted by Proposition 1A, the California county governments did have to agree to transfers of $2.6 billion between 2004 and 2006 to the state government. The fiscal relationship between local and state governments is getting increasingly complicated as both levels of government search for equitable and creative methods of funding services. Take, for example, the recent introduction of the "Triple Flip," instituted in 2004 as a part of Proposition 57, the California Economic Recovery Bond Act. Under the Triple Flip, essentially a revenue-swapping procedure, the local government's portions of the sales tax are shifted to the state. In return, a portion of local property taxes that are normally used for local education will be held by the county governments and used to reimburse the county and city governments for the lost sales tax revenue during January and May of each year. The state government will make up the loss in local educational funding through the minimum-funding guarantee of Proposition 98.[22]

# The California Budget Process

Anyone who is employed by the state government, is heavily taxed or maybe not taxed enough, or has some other vested interest in the budget of the California state government will be focused on the budget process that gradually unfolds over the course of the first six, and possibly many more months of the year. It is tempting to call this process a cycle, as it consists of a recurring sequence of specific steps that must follow state laws and legislative procedures. For the last few years, however, it is difficult to predict what the final budget will look like and whether or not there will be some last-minute "discovery." During the term of

**Think Again**

How does the governor develop his or her Executive Budget Proposal? What are the key steps in the budget approval process?

# WHAT DO YOU THINK?

## Understanding Municipal Budgets

For the average Californian, city government is the most clearly identifiable source of direct services from any government entity or agency. City dwellers depend on municipal governments for a wide range of services that are vital to maintaining adequate living conditions, including police protection, utilities, and roadways. Unfortunately, city residents often fail to fully comprehend the cost of these functions, especially when it comes to paying taxes. Understanding the municipal budget can help residents appreciate the juggling act most city governments must perform to finance the delivery of vital services and in convincing their residents to participate in local governance, because, after all, it is ultimately our money that fund these services. After reading this brief feature and possibly conducting further studies on this subject, perhaps you could determine some innovative ways of saving money or increasing funding for your city.

The municipal budgets of most California cities are in reality very complex listings of revenue and expenditures that involve many subcategories and state regulations and laws and ordinances. The following information is merely an introduction that will ideally encourage further investigation. Despite the complexity of municipal budgets the two major components, revenue and expenditures, contain a number of basic features that are the foundation for the spending plan of most municipal governments.

### Municipal Revenue Sources

The revenue that flows to city governments is placed in a variety of funds or accounts that determine how that money will be used based on state law and the conditions associated with the allocation of certain funds. Special revenue funds contain money that must be used for a special purpose. For example, portions of the gas tax that the state government collects are allocated to municipal governments and can only be used on transportation-related expenditures. Enterprise funds are used to support the delivery of specific services, such as utilities, and contain the fees that are collected for these services. The general fund is an all-purpose account that is used at the discretion of the city government.

### Sales Taxes

The statewide sales and use tax rate is 7.25 percent with 5 percent going to the state, 1 percent that is shared by cities and counties, 0.5 percent allocated to cities and counties for the Public Safety Fund, 0.5 percent for the state's Local Revenue Fund, and 0.25 that goes to cities and counties for transportation purposes. Municipal governments are permitted to retain a portion of the sales tax, usually around 1 percent above the basic rate of 7.25 that is received on goods sold in a particular city if residents of the county vote to institute this additional amount on a county-wide basis. Municipal governments have come to rely heavily on sales taxes, which is one reason cities tend to encourage the influx of the ample sales-tax-generating big box retail establishments.

### Property Tax

Since the passage of Proposition 13, the state government largely determines how property taxes will be spent, dividing these funds between state expenditures, counties, school districts, special districts, and cities. Property taxes account for between 15 and 20 percent of the total city budget, depending on the services that are provided by a city. When fire protection is delegated to a fire district, a portion of the property tax is allocated to the fire district rather than to the city. Conversely, an additional share of property taxes will be captured if the city has a redevelopment agency and has designated sections of the city as redevelopment zones.

### Vehicle License Fee (VLF)

The VLF is actually a tax on the ownership of registered vehicles that is collected by the state Department of Motor Vehicles and allocated to cities and counties based on population. Since 1998, the state government has substantially reduced this tax, subsidizing portions that go to local government with funds directly from the state general fund. The amount of money that the VLF contributes to the total city revenue varies, ranging between 16 and 24 percent.

### Utility User Tax

Approximately 150 California cities charge a utility user tax of some types at rates that can be as low as 1 percent to as much as 11 percent to the users of various types of utilities that could include telephone, electricity, gas, water, and cable television. This tax will contribute, for the cities that charge utility user taxes, about 15 to 20 percent to the municipal general fund. These taxes are generally not very popular with businesses as well as the residents of a city and can be difficult to impose.

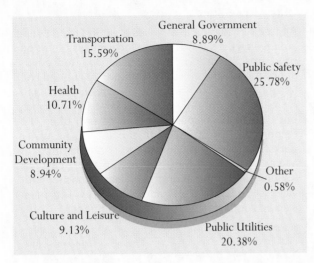

*Source:* California State Controller Cities Annual Report, 2003–04.

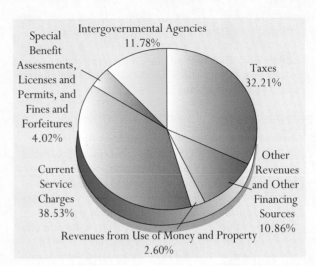

*Source:* California State Controller Cities Annual Report, 2003–04.

## Miscellaneous Municipal Taxes

The business license tax and the transient occupancy tax are examples of taxes typically imposed by most municipal governments. Business license tax rates vary throughout California and usually provide about 3–6 percent to the general fund of a city. Cities also have the option to adopt a transient occupancy tax, that is, a hotel/motel tax imposed on individuals who stay for no longer than thirty days in some type of lodging facility. Rates for this tax are usually between 4 and 15 percent and most often go directly into the general fund, but some city councils earmark a portion of this tax to support tourism or commercial development-related activities in their cities. Cities sometimes impose an assessment fee that, although not technically a tax, gives all the appearances of such and is levied on a specific district or area to pay for specific improvements or services. Infrastructure for a new housing development is often financed through assessments.

## Enterprise Service Charges and Fees

There is a long list of services that are provided by municipal governments; and rather than support these operations with taxes, cities charge residents a specific fee. These fees and charges compose a large part of municipal revenue and differ greatly in how they are collected. In some instances the city provides the service directly to residents; in other circumstances it contracts the service out to a private company and either pays that company directly or takes a percentage of the fees that are received. Common enterprise services are garbage, water, sewage, harbor/marina, and airport services.

## Intergovernmental Revenue

Municipal governments receive funds or grants from the state and federal government for special programs or projects or are reimbursed for the cost of a service or operation required by state law. Local police and housing departments are typical beneficiaries of intergovernmental revenue, but such funds usually are not permanent and often have to be matched with funds from local revenue sources.

## Municipal Expenditures

Expenditures obviously differ from city to city depending on a variety of factors, but the needs of a city typically determines the spending plan. Cities with a high crime rate will have to spend more money on public safety whereas cities with a large commercial sector will allocate funds for community development in order to attract patrons of local businesses.

## Public Safety

Public safety is the largest expenditure for cities and the most important one to its residents. The amount spent in this category depends in part on whether the city has its own fire department or can rely on a fire district. The twenty-four-hour nature of this service and the fact that it is prone to lawsuits and expensive disability claims are only a couple of the reasons for its high costs.

## Public Utilities

Private companies provide a large number of the utilities that residents require, but there are some utilities, such as sewage and water that have traditionally been operated by the public works departments and other divisions within municipal government. Considering the scale of a city-wide utility and the cost of its equipment, labor, and materials, public utilities can be quite expensive to municipal governments.

### Transportation

It is rare that transportation services pay for themselves; they usually end up costing a city more than it receives in any transportation-related revenue. Most California cities spend the bulk of their transportation funds on road maintenance as public transportation is typically provided by a special transportation district or agency. Rarely does a city ever totally meet its road construction or maintenance needs, a daunting task considering that automobile use shows few signs of decreasing.

### Other Expenditures

Although most health services are conducted at the county level, cities often fund local clinics, nutrition programs, hazardous waste, disposal, and emergency medical services. The funding of cultural and leisure services, commonly known as parks and recreation, is not only used to maintain city parks, but also to host special programs and often are responsible for special attractions such as water parks. The community development department of a city oversees a long list of functions such as building and engineering services, inspection services and planning operations—all of which must also be supported by the municipal budget.

*Source:* Michael Coleman, "Special Report: A Primer on California City Finance," Western City—League of California Cities, November 2002, http://www.cacities.org; California State Controller Cities Annual Report 2003–04.

Governor Schwarzenegger the California Department of Finance has in two different fiscal years announced that the state had accumulated more tax revenue than anticipated. It is doubtful anyone could have predicted that the 1992 budget process would end up being sixty-five days overdue.

**Executive Budget Plan**    The governor is required by California law to submit a spending plan, the **executive budget plan**, to the state legislature by January 10, nearly eighteen months before the fiscal year officially ends on June 30. In reality, the development of the state budget begins six months before the January deadline, when the heads of state departments and agencies first submit their budget requests to the California Department of Finance for review and to gradually make budget recommendations to the governor. Because the California state government, like most governments, operates on a pay-as-you-go system and really does not know how much revenue, especially in taxes, it will take in until the end of the fiscal year, the projections made by Department of Finance regarding future revenue are very important to the governor in devising a new budget plan. Once these projections have been made and the budgets of individual state governmental organizations are analyzed, the governor is free to authorize the final budget. In the past, many observers would suggest that incrementalism, the basing of the current year budget on what the department or agency got the previous year, dominated the budget process. But in the current age of limited revenue resources, no part of the California state government is sacred, and there is always the possibility that any state government organization could suffer a budget cut. State law mandates that every budget be balanced, with equal amounts of revenue and expenditures. The governor can create the illusion of a balance budget by deferring payments, shifting balances, or even reorganizing government. In addition to submitting it to the state legislature, the budget is first made public in printed form, usually with some fanfare. Do not be fooled, however; that budget has many miles to travel and could be a drastically different creature by the time the governor finally signs the budget into law.

**executive budget plan**  The spending plan for the state of California that the governor must submit to the state legislature by January 10 each year.

**The Legislative Budget Approval Process**    The system of checks and balances in California's state government is evident in the adoption of the state budget, which, after being devised by the governor, must be approved by the state legislature in the form of a bill or proposed legislation in time for the start of the state fiscal year on July 1 and ending on the last day of June. And so, on or before January 10, the state budget will be introduced in the legislature and automatically assigned to the Assembly Budget and Senate Budget and Fiscal Review Committees, reviewed for a number of weeks, and then parceled out by subject to the appropriate subcommittees. At about the same time, the Legislative Analyst's Office will draft an extensive analysis of the budget, citing, in what is supposed to be a nonpartisan approach, the weak and strong points of this financial document. It is not uncommon for the LAO analysis to be critical of the governor's spending and revenue-generating plan, usually attracting significant media attention. For example, public criticism by Elizabeth Hill, the legislative analyst, of a welfare reform spending plan prepared by the office of Governor Pete Wilson and later of revenue estimates submitted by the Department of Finance under Governor Gray Davis drew significant media coverage.[23]

From about late February until the final vote on the budget bill, which should happen by June 15 according to the California constitution, a number of important steps will take place that can influence the numbers in the state budget. Whatever critique of the budget made by the LAO will pass quickly, and the focus will shift to the hearings that are conducted by the subcommittees of the state legislature. In most instances, the members of the legislative subcommittees know in advance the gist of the testimony to be given by department heads and representatives of particular interest groups, and these hearings remain under the tight control of the committee chairs. Although the Assembly Budget and Senate Budget and Fiscal Review Committees will seriously consider figures from the Department of Finance, LAO analysis, extensive work by the committee staff, and the subcommittee reports based on testimony and committee research, any real revision of the governor's original spending plan in the state legislature will be heavily dependent on political pressures that the state legislature will experience and that can emerge at any moment. Governor Schwarzenegger and the state legislature had originally planned to cut $7.3 million in state tourism funding for the 2005–06 budget in response to severe revenue limitations. Before the governor could sign the final budget package, however, the California Lodging Industry Association and other California travel and hospitality industry associations

## Table 21.2   Key Budget Terms

**APPROPRIATION**   money set apart in the budget or by a piece of legislation, for a specific use.

**AUGMENTATION**   an increase in an appropriation.

**BLUE PENCIL**   the California Constitution grants the governor "line item veto" authority to reduce or eliminate any item of appropriation from any bill including the budget bill.

**BUDGET CHANGE PROPOSAL (BCP)**   document prepared by a state agency to propose and document budget changes to maintain or to change the existing level of service; and is used in preparing the governor's budget.

**CAPITAL OUTLAY**   expenditures which result in acquisition of or addition to major fixed assets, such as buildings.

**CONTINUING APPROPRIATION**   amount available each year under a permanent constitutional or statutory expenditure authorization which is automatically renewed each year.

**FUNGIBLE**   special funds which may be transferred to the General Fund.

**SPECIAL FUNDS**   funds where monies have been collected for user fees or where revenues are set aside for a particular use.

An Assembly Sargent-At-
Arms intern delivers copies
of the state budget bill to
Assembly members' desks
at the Capitol in
Sacramento.

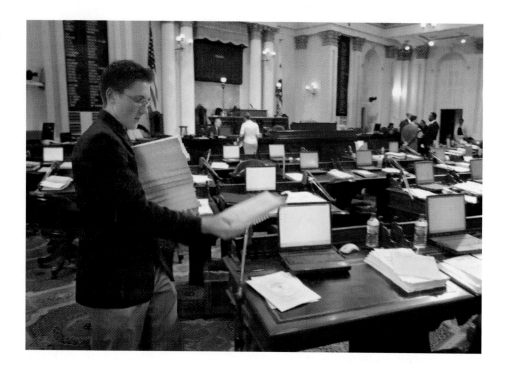

rapidly mobilized lobbyist and industry supporters who lobbied, wrote letters, and called legislators. The result was restoration of the full $7.3 million for the California Travel and Tourism Commission to spend promoting tourism in the state, California's third-largest industry.[24]

**May revise**  A revised
projection of California's
financial picture conducted
by the head of the State
Department of Finance and
economists from private
industry.

**May Revise**   Another major step in the budget process is the **May revise**, a revised projection of the state's financial picture that is conducted by the head of the Department of Finance and economists from private industry. The governor will have worked on the budget long before it was publicly released and sent to the state legislature, and during that time, revenue and expenditures will probably have changed for the better or for the worse. Conducting this review of the financial situation of the state in May has a lot to do with the April 14 tax-filing deadline, offering the state the most accurate view of the amount of revenue that the state will receive before the final budget should be voted on in June. The Department of Finance, under the direction of the governor, will revise the original budget plan numbers either upward or downward to reflect the current financial picture of the state and the governor's spending priorities and submit this revision to the budget subcommittees of the state legislature, which are bound by law and procedure to accept it. The May revise of the state budget will be an important influence on the budget, but that revised budget can be adjusted in the committees of the legislature, which will make a series of recommendations starting in the subcommittees and additional changes in the full committees before moving on to the full membership of the assembly and state senate for a final vote.

**Two-Thirds Requirement and the Conference Committee**   California is one of the few states in the Union that requires two-thirds of the members in each house of the state legislature to approve the budget. For most of California's legislative history, this constitutional rule was a mere formality, but starting in the 1990s, for various reasons, including term limits and increasing partisanship in the state legislature, this requirement has caused passage of the budget to be delayed almost every year. One of the biggest problems of the two-thirds rule is that it effectively gives the minority party an equal voice in crafting the budget in

Governor Arnold Schwarzenegger takes questions from reporters at a press conference, after sending his revised state budget plan to the Legislature. The $102.8 billion spending plan relied on across-the-board spending cuts and avoided tax increases to plug a shortfall of over $9 billion.

the legislature if the majority party lacks a two-thirds majority in both chambers. Unless members of the minority party vote with the majority, the budget bill has no chance of passing, and that gives the minority the leverage to advance its budgetary interests or philosophy. Although there have been many calls from various individuals and groups inside and outside the legislature to abolish this requirement and to adopt simple-majority passage, there is no denying that the two-thirds requirement builds consensus. Once the budget is finally approved, neither party can realistically disavow the outcome of the spending plan.

Regardless of whatever motivations that legislators may have in not approving the budget, the governor must have revenue to carry out the executive duties of the state government, and in 1990, Governor George Deukmejian called together the four party leaders in both chambers to resolve budgetary issues that were preventing passage of the state budget. Ever since, the so-called Big Five have been a sort of court of last resort, hammering out unresolved budgetary issues. The dynamics of this group change from year-to-year, depending on the party affiliation of the governor and spending priorities, but the governor usually has the most leverage thanks to the power to use the line-veto power and the ability to encourage fellow party members in the legislative leadership to cooperate. It does appear that the legislature is growing more dependent on the Big Five, evidenced by the growing tendency to leave *all* unresolved matters to this highly select group. The strength of partisanship in the state legislature in recent years is clear from the strict adherence to the final decision of the Big Five by the members of the state legislature, who could reject such compromises through their votes on the budget bill but do not. The negotiations that take place among the Big Five are really supposed to happen in the conference committee of the state legislature, where the legislative leaders and committee chairs work out differences in the versions of the budget bill that were passed in either chamber. The Democratic party has controlled both chambers for some time, and so the barrier presented by the two-thirds requirement has, except on rare occasions, made the conference committee meeting unnecessary. In reality, the Big Five negotiations have taken the normal back-door dealings, so much a part of the legislative process, to new heights.[25]

**Final Budget Approval by the Governor**    The budget process comes to a close with the signature of the governor on the budget bill. If the typical steps of the budget process are followed, the signing of the budget by the governor is only a formality. Whatever problems there may have been in adopting the final budget were worked out among the Big Five. The governor of California, unlike the president of the United States, does have line-item veto power, the ability to reduce or reject any particular item in the state budget. When a governor decides to "blue-pencil" a specific amount, it is usually for symbolic reasons that all inside players have anticipated. The final budget usually runs to over 1,000 pages, which the governor has little time to scrutinize for items to veto, and the governor may not eliminate any budget item that is mandated by law.

## The Effect of the Direct Democracy on the Budget Process

——— Think Again ———

How has the passage of initiatives by the public shaped the California budget process?

Commonly known as "ballot-box budgeting," the initiative process in California has had a profound effect on the budget process in a variety of ways. Of all the initiatives passed throughout the history of California, approximately half have had a direct impact on state government fiscal matters, and some 40 to 50 percent of the state budget is locked into certain expenditures as a result of initiative statutes or constitutional amendments based on initiatives. There are variations in the fiscal effects of initiatives, the most blatant being propositions such as Proposition 13, which specifically mandated changes in tax or fiscal policies of the state government; Proposition 98, requiring that 40 percent of the general fund be spent on education; and Proposition 10, which increased the tax on tobacco products by 50 cents to fund early childhood educational development programs. There are also initiatives that do not involve changes in taxes but do authorize bonds for specific purposes. There have been a considerable number of such initiatives, authorizing bond issues for natural resource preservation (Proposition 70), rail transportation (Proposition 116), and water project (Proposition 50), and voters can expect a slew of similar initiatives in the future. Bonds that are passed as ballot measures, very often originating in the state legislature, give voters the impression that this is a painless way of raising revenue instead of increasing taxes, despite the fact that residents of California end up paying a lot more than the original bond amount. Some initiatives are not necessarily intended to alter fiscal policy but have that effect when implemented. Proposition 184, the "three-strikes" initiative, has greatly increased the California prison population, causing a dramatic rise in the cost of the correctional system.[26]

There are two major opinions on the fiscal effect of initiatives and referendums on the budget process, the first suggesting that initiatives constrain the capacity of elected officials to make decisions regarding fiscal policy. By forcing the state government to commit funding resources to support the goals of ballot measures or replacing revenue that has been decreased by initiatives, elected officials have found it difficult to craft a balanced budget and adjusting spending policies to new or emerging problems or societal needs. The paralyzing effect of direct democracy on fiscal policy is further demonstrated, so say the critics of ballot-box budgeting, by the difficulty of altering or removing ballot measures, which in California can be repealed or amended only through the mechanisms of direct democracy.[27]

Other observers of California government have found that rather than the initiative alone, other aspects of the budget process also influence the fiscal policies of the state. Educational costs, some suggest, would probably not be much lower than the amount locked in by Proposition 98, which requires the state government to spend 40 percent of the budget on education, considering that the cost per pupil as a result of this initiative has not risen above the national median cost per pupil. There have been periods of relatively stable financial conditions for the California state government, for example, during at least half of Governor Gray Davis's tenure, when the state actually had a budget surplus, despite the existence of Proposition 13, which critics believed condemned California to eternal indebtedness. There is no law or regulation preventing the state legislature from passing tax increases if an initiative has an adverse effect on the fiscal health of the state. The problems is not the initiative, say advocates of the initiative; the budget quandary is the result of poor leadership.[28]

# The State Economy: The Foundation of Fiscal Policy

When analyzing the expenditures and revenue of state government, it is often easy to lose sight of the foundation for sound fiscal policies: a healthy economy. If the economy is going well, chances are that the government will have more than enough revenue to meet its responsibilities. Over the past decade, California has been riding an economic roller coaster that in the late 1990s was on the way up but fell quickly with the drop in the productivity and investment outcomes of the computer industry, major losses in the stock market, and changes in the global economy. Slowly, the California economic situation appears to be climbing again as unemployment has declined slightly for many regions, real estate transactions remain stable, population continues to grow, the overall business climate continues to provide opportunities for growth, and government revenue is experiencing slight increases.[29]

The unemployment rate is always a good indicator, albeit incomplete, of the state of any economy, local or national. In Caiifornia, the unemployment rate has stayed fairly stable at about 5.4 percent over the three years 2002–2005. A good measure of this rate is to remember the near 10 percent unemployment rate of the early 1990s, when California suffered a severe recession. An unemployment rate above 5 percent is not intolerable, but it is not great either. It appears from some obvious and also less obvious statistics and signs that employment trends for retail trade, information services, professional and business services, education, and health services will be very favorable. Other major business areas that generate substantial employment are showing declining trends, particularly manufacturing, government services, and financial services.[30] California, like much of the rest of the nation, has been moving to a service economy, losing manufacturing capacity to the global marketplace. Not necessarily a negative trend, this shift does decrease the labor opportunities for large segments of the state's workforce. As the industrial capacity of China grows, the industrial sector of California will probably decline even further, based in part on the state's location along the Pacific Rim and the cost of labor in the state.

The real estate market has been especially significant in California, which for many years now has expanded the housing stock, construction projects and jobs, and a wide variety of services. Costs have also increased to the point that home ownership for the many Californians is out of reach, but relief may be in sight for first-time home buyers, as home prices are slowly starting to drop. A major plunge in home sales and prices will, however, cause substantial declines in job growth and financial markets.

Migration to California has become intensely debated recently, especially regarding people who come from abroad. The question as to whether migration is good or bad in the long run depends partly on who is immigrating and what aspects of their presence are being observed. There is much evidence to support the notion that California would have a labor shortage, especially in select industries, without migrations to the state. The consumption of goods and services by recent arrivals is yet another plus. Migrants can also cause social services and infrastructure to become overburdened, requiring increased government revenue, as well as social problems that result from recent arrivals who for various reasons cannot become integrated into the society. The current unemployment rate suggests that migration to California has not created a major labor shortage, but as the population of immigrants becomes more integrated and more educated, competition in all sectors of the state economy could increase dramatically.

Although many California based businesses complain of a poor business climate, citing housing, energy, and insurance costs as well as government regulations and taxes, the actual number of businesses that have left the state is relatively small. Even with the negative aspects of the California commercial sector, few other markets in the United States can campete with the population size and consumer spending power of the state features that may be more important to a company than the accommodation of its business operations.

## The Future of the California Political Economy

Think Again

What are the major trends in the contemporary California economy?

The role of the state government in the California economy is largely based on the condition of the state budget and how the government crafts that budget. At a minimum, the state government attempts to refrain from policies that will hurt the state's economy. Limiting revenue, which should be kept within the economy while maintaining adequate services for the public, is the ideal, and on this objective, the California state government receives mixed reviews. Although state government leaders have avoided large tax increases, the government has not performed particularly well, using education, public safety, and commercial activity as measures. The shift to using bonds to finance government could be the answer to regaining acceptable performance levels, but too many bonds create debt that is difficult to repay. Yet many Californians take government services for granted without giving much thought to what those services cost. Then there is the question as to whether the business sector is paying its fair share of taxes. Most California-based businesses probably are, but there are industries that earn large profits that hardly pay the same percentage in taxes as middle-income families. Then there are the government leaders, who will always have a difficult time formulating and implementing policies that are equitable and are forward-looking when well-funded special-interest groups can influence their actions by almost guaranteeing their reelection. Addressing the numerous critical issues facing the future of California will require considerable effort. The population is expected to grow dramatically by the end of the decade to over 40 million residents, and there may not be enough affordable housing, health care, and education resources to go around. California already has the seventh highest percentage of residents without health insurance in the nation.[31] The notion of performance standards has become popular in government and industry, but could it be that the fiscal health of the state is inextricably tied to every Californian's maintaining a basic level of individual and organizational performance that is first and foremost equitable and forward-looking?

# Summary Notes

■ The annual state budget reflects the priorities of the state government. Interest groups have a very large stake in the budget plan and regularly use information, campaign contributions, and the initiative process to influence what the budget supports and how it is financed.

■ Most of California's revenue is derived from taxes, although borrowing has become a popular alternative. The state income tax is the largest source of state revenue, accounting for about 40 percent of the state's general fund. The second largest amount of tax dollars comes from the state sales tax, consisting of about 28 percent of the general fund. Various taxes are placed on businesses and corporations that operate in California, most of which are subject to a basic rate of 8.84 percent of profits that are earned in the state, commonly known as the franchise tax. An excise tax is a selective sales tax imposed only on the sale of specific goods.

■ The California state government is increasingly using bonds to finance government expenditures. The use of bonds by state government is dominated by general obligation bonds which are backed by the state government, and revenue bonds, used to finance a government facility that will generate funds utilized to service the bond debt. Another form of major revenue to the state comes from the federal government, which funds a wide range of programs.

■ A large part of state budget expenditures is earmarked for education based on Proposition 98, which requires the state government to spend a minimum of 40 percent of the general fund on public school education. Approximately 28 percent of the general fund is allocated for the health and welfare of state residents. The remaining expenditures are currently divided among the California prison system, various state programs and services, and transportation costs, which are normally financed through highway user taxes and motor vehicle fees.

■ Since the passage of Proposition 13, the amount of revenue generated by county and municipal governments has decreased substantially. Almost 31 percent of county revenue comes from the state to finance state-mandated programs. Typical sources of revenue to cities are derived from service charges for utilities, licenses, and permits, a portion of state sales taxes, redistribution of property taxes from the state government, and an assortment of smaller forms of revenue.

■ The governor is required by California law to submit the executive budget plan to the state legislature by January 10. The state budget will be introduced in the legislature, but will also be reviewed by the Legislative Analyst's Office and the Department of Finance. (California is one of the few states that requires two-thirds of the members in each house of the state legislature to approve the budget.)

■ The initiative process has had a profound effect on the budget process in California. About half of the initiatives passed in California have had a direct impact on state government fiscal matters.

# Key Terms

structural budget gap   714
Legislative Analyst's Office
   (LAO)   716

Proposition 140   716
general fund   717
Franchise Tax Board   720

excise tax   720
Mello-Ross Community
   Facilities District   727

executive budget plan   730
May revise   732

# Suggested Reading

*Budget: Perspectives and Issues.* Sacramento: Legislative Analyst's Office.

Krolak, Richard. *California's Budget Dance: Issues and Process.* Sacramento: California Journal Press, 1990.

League of California Cities. *A Primer on California City Finance.* March 2005.

Senate Advisory Commission on Cost Control in State Government. *California's Budget Process: Improving Quality, Cost-*

*Efficiency, Effectiveness and Accountability in State Government.* Sacramento: The Commission, 1999.

Senate Select Committee on Citizen Participation in Government. *The Budget Process: A Citizen's Guide to Participation.* Sacramento: California Senate Publications.

Silva, J. Fred, and Elisa Barbour. *The State–Local Fiscal Relationship in California: A Changing Balance of Power.* Public Policy Institute of California, 1999.

# California Constitution of 1879

ARTICLE 1 DECLARATION OF RIGHTS

## SEC. 1.

All people are by nature free and independent and have inalienable rights. Among these are enjoying and defending life and liberty, acquiring, possessing, and protecting property, and pursuing and obtaining safety, happiness, and privacy.

## SEC. 2.

(a) Every person may freely speak, write and publish his or her sentiments on all subjects, being responsible for the abuse of this right. A law may not restrain or abridge liberty of speech or press.

(b) A publisher, editor, reporter, or other person connected with or employed upon a newspaper, magazine, or other periodical publication, or by a press association or wire service, or any person who has been so connected or employed, shall not be adjudged in contempt by a judicial, legislative, or administrative body, or any other body having the power to issue subpoenas, for refusing to disclose the source of any information procured while so connected or employed for publication in a newspaper, magazine or other periodical publication, or for refusing to disclose any unpublished information obtained or prepared in gathering, receiving or processing of information for communication to the public.

Nor shall a radio or television news reporter or other person connected with or employed by a radio or television station, or any person who has been so connected or employed, be so adjudged in contempt for refusing to disclose the source of any information procured while so connected or employed for news or news commentary purposes on radio or television, or for refusing to disclose any unpublished information obtained or prepared in gathering, receiving or processing of information for communication to the public.

As used in this subdivision, "unpublished information" includes information not disseminated to the public by the person from whom disclosure is sought, whether or not related information has been disseminated and includes, but is not limited to, all notes, outtakes, photographs, tapes or other data of whatever sort not itself disseminated to the public through a medium of communication, whether or not published information based upon or related to such material has been disseminated.

## SEC. 3.

(a) The people have the right to instruct their representatives, petition government for redress of grievances, and assemble freely to consult for the common good.

(b) (1) The people have the right of access to information concerning the conduct of the people's business, and, therefore, the meetings of public bodies and the writings of public officials and agencies shall be open to public scrutiny.

(2) A statute, court rule, or other authority, including those in effect on the effective date of this subdivision, shall be broadly construed if it furthers the people's right of access, and narrowly construed if it limits the right of access. A statute, court rule, or other authority adopted after the effective date of this subdivision that limits the right of access shall be adopted with findings demonstrating the interest protected by the limitation and the need for protecting that interest.

(3) Nothing in this subdivision supersedes or modifies the right of privacy guaranteed by Section 1 or affects the construction of any statute, court rule, or other authority to the extent that it protects that right to privacy, including any statutory procedures governing discovery or disclosure of information concerning the official performance or professional qualifications of a peace officer.

(4) Nothing in this subdivision supersedes or modifies any provision of this Constitution, including the guarantees that a person may not be deprived of life, liberty, or property without due process of law, or denied equal protection of the laws, as provided in Section 7.

(5) This subdivision does not repeal or nullify, expressly or by implication, any constitutional or statutory exception to the right of access to public records or meetings of public bodies that is in effect on the effective date of this subdivision, including, but not limited to, any statute protecting the confidentiality of law enforcement and prosecution records.

(6) Nothing in this subdivision repeals, nullifies, supersedes, or modifies protections for the confidentiality of proceedings and records of the Legislature, the Members of the Legislature, and its employees, committees, and caucuses provided by Section 7 of Article IV, state law, or legislative rules adopted in furtherance of those provisions; nor does it affect the scope of permitted discovery in judicial or administrative proceedings regarding deliberations of the Legislature, the Members of the Legislature, and its employees, committees, and caucuses.

## SEC. 4.

Free exercise and enjoyment of religion without discrimination or preference are guaranteed. This liberty of conscience does not excuse acts that are licentious or inconsistent with the peace or safety of the State. The Legislature shall make no law respecting an establishment of religion.

A person is not incompetent to be a witness or juror because of his or her opinions on religious beliefs.

### SEC. 5.

The military is subordinate to civil power. A standing army may not be maintained in peacetime. Soldiers may not be quartered in any house in wartime except as prescribed by law, or in peacetime without the owner's consent.

### SEC. 6.

Slavery is prohibited. Involuntary servitude is prohibited except to punish crime.

### SEC. 7.

(a) A person may not be deprived of life, liberty, or property without due process of law or denied equal protection of the laws; provided, that nothing contained herein or elsewhere in this Constitution imposes upon the State of California or any public entity, board, or official any obligations or responsibilities which exceed those imposed by the Equal Protection Clause of the 14th Amendment to the United States Constitution with respect to the use of pupil school assignment or pupil transportation. In enforcing this subdivision or any other provision of this Constitution, no court of this State may impose upon the State of California or any public entity, board, or official any obligation or responsibility with respect to the use of pupil school assignment or pupil transportation, (1) except to remedy a specific violation by such party that would also constitute a violation of the Equal Protection Clause of the 14th Amendment to the United States Constitution, and (2) unless a federal court would be permitted under federal decisional law to impose that obligation or responsibility upon such party to remedy the specific violation of the Equal Protection Clause of the 14th Amendment of the United States Constitution.

Except as may be precluded by the Constitution of the United States, every existing judgment, decree, writ, or other order of a court of this State, whenever rendered, which includes provisions regarding pupil school assignment or pupil transportation, or which requires a plan including any such provisions shall, upon application to a court having jurisdiction by any interested person, be modified to conform to the provisions of this subdivision as amended, as applied to the facts which exist at the time of such modification.

In all actions or proceedings arising under or seeking application of the amendments to this subdivision proposed by the Legislature at its 1979-80 Regular Session, all courts, wherein such actions or proceedings are or may hereafter be pending, shall give such actions or proceedings first precedence over all other civil actions therein.

Nothing herein shall prohibit the governing board of a school district from voluntarily continuing or commencing a school integration plan after the effective date of this subdivision as amended.

In amending this subdivision, the Legislature and people of the State of California find and declare that this amendment is necessary to serve compelling public interests, including those of making the most effective use of the limited financial resources now and prospectively available to support public education, maximizing the educational opportunities and protecting the health and safety of all public school pupils, enhancing the ability of parents to participate in the educational process, preserving harmony and tranquility in this State and its public schools, preventing

the waste of scarce fuel resources, and protecting the environment.

(b) A citizen or class of citizens may not be granted privileges or immunities not granted on the same terms to all citizens. Privileges or immunities granted by the Legislature may be altered or revoked.

### SEC. 8.

A person may not be disqualified from entering or pursuing a business, profession, vocation, or employment because of sex, race, creed, color, or national or ethnic origin.

### SEC. 9.

A bill of attainder, ex post facto law, or law impairing the obligation of contracts may not be passed.

### SEC. 10.

Witnesses may not be unreasonably detained. A person may not be imprisoned in a civil action for debt or tort, or in peacetime for a militia fine.

### SEC. 11.

Habeas corpus may not be suspended unless required by public safety in cases of rebellion or invasion.

### SEC. 12.

A person shall be released on bail by sufficient sureties, except for:

(a) Capital crimes when the facts are evident or the presumption great;

(b) Felony offenses involving acts of violence on another person, or felony sexual assault offenses on another person, when the facts are evident or the presumption great and the court finds based upon clear and convincing evidence that there is a substantial likelihood the person's release would result in great bodily harm to others; or

(c) Felony offenses when the facts are evident or the presumption great and the court finds based on clear and convincing evidence that the person has threatened another with great bodily harm and that there is a substantial likelihood that the person would carry out the threat if released.

Excessive bail may not be required. In fixing the amount of bail, the court shall take into consideration the seriousness of the offense charged, the previous criminal record of the defendant, and the probability of his or her appearing at the trial or hearing of the case.

A person may be released on his or her own recognizance in the court's discretion.

### SEC. 13.

The right of the people to be secure in their persons, houses, papers, and effects against unreasonable seizures and searches may not be violated; and a warrant may not issue except on probable cause, supported by oath or affirmation, particularly describing the place to be searched and the persons and things to be seized.

### SEC. 14.

Felonies shall be prosecuted as provided by law, either by indictment or, after examination and commitment by a magistrate, by information.

A person charged with a felony by complaint subscribed under penalty of perjury and on file in a court in the county where the felony is triable shall be taken without unnecessary delay before a magistrate of that court. The magistrate shall immediately give the defendant a copy of the complaint, inform the defendant of the defendant's right to counsel, allow the defendant a reasonable time to send for counsel, and on the defendant's request read the complaint to the defendant. On the defendant's request the magistrate shall require a peace officer to transmit within the county where the court is located a message to counsel named by defendant.

A person unable to understand English who is charged with a crime has a right to an interpreter throughout the proceedings.

### SEC. 14.1.

If a felony is prosecuted by indictment, there shall be no post-indictment preliminary hearing.

### SEC. 15.

The defendant in a criminal cause has the right to a speedy public trial, to compel attendance of witnesses in the defendant's behalf, to have the assistance of counsel for the defendant's defense, to be personally present with counsel, and to be confronted with the witnesses against the defendant. The Legislature may provide for the deposition of a witness in the presence of the defendant and the defendant's counsel.

Persons may not twice be put in jeopardy for the same offense, be compelled in a criminal cause to be a witness against themselves, or be deprived of life, liberty, or property without due process of law.

### SEC. 16.

Trial by jury is an inviolate right and shall be secured to all, but in a civil cause three-fourths of the jury may render a verdict. A jury may be waived in a criminal cause by the consent of both parties expressed in open court by the defendant and the defendant's counsel. In a civil cause a jury may be waived by the consent of the parties expressed as prescribed by statute.

In civil causes the jury shall consist of 12 persons or a lesser number agreed on by the parties in open court. In civil causes other than causes within the appellate jurisdiction of the court of appeal the Legislature may provide that the jury shall consist of eight persons or a lesser number agreed on by the parties in open court.

In criminal actions in which a felony is charged, the jury shall consist of 12 persons. In criminal actions in which a misdemeanor is charged, the jury shall consist of 12 persons or a lesser number agreed on by the parties in open court.

### SEC. 17.

Cruel or unusual punishment may not be inflicted or excessive fines imposed.

### SEC. 18.

Treason against the State consists only in levying war against it, adhering to its enemies, or giving them aid and comfort. A person may not be convicted of treason except on the evidence of two witnesses to the same overt act or by confession in open court.

### SEC. 19.

Private property may be taken or damaged for public use only when just compensation, ascertained by a jury unless waived, has first been paid to, or into court for, the owner. The Legislature may provide for possession by the condemnor following commencement of eminent domain proceedings upon deposit in court and prompt release to the owner of money determined by the court to be the probable amount of just compensation.

### SEC. 20.

Noncitizens have the same property rights as citizens.

### SEC. 21.

Property owned before marriage or acquired during marriage by gift, will, or inheritance is separate property.

### SEC. 22.

The right to vote or hold office may not be conditioned by a property qualification.

### SEC. 23.

One or more grand juries shall be drawn and summoned at least once a year in each county.

### SEC. 24.

Rights guaranteed by this Constitution are not dependent on those guaranteed by the United States Constitution.

In criminal cases the rights of a defendant to equal protection of the laws, to due process of law, to the assistance of counsel, to be personally present with counsel, to a speedy and public trial, to compel the attendance of witnesses, to confront the witnesses against him or her, to be free from unreasonable searches and seizures, to privacy, to not be compelled to be a witness against himself or herself, to not be placed twice in jeopardy for the same offense, and to not suffer the imposition of cruel or unusual punishment, shall be construed by the courts of this State in a manner consistent with the Constitution of the United States. This Constitution shall not be construed by the courts to afford greater rights to criminal defendants than those afforded by the Constitution of the United States, nor shall it be construed to afford greater rights to minors in juvenile proceedings on criminal causes than those afforded by the Constitution of the United States.

This declaration of rights may not be construed to impair or deny others retained by the people.

### SEC. 25.

The people shall have the right to fish upon and from the public lands of the State and in the waters thereof, excepting upon lands set aside for fish hatcheries, and no land owned by the State shall ever be sold or transferred without reserving in the people the absolute right to fish thereupon; and no law shall ever be passed making it a crime for the people to enter upon the public lands within this State for the purpose of fishing in any water containing fish that have been planted therein by the State; provided, that the legislature may by statute, provide for the season when and the conditions under which the different species of fish may be taken.

### SEC. 26.

The provisions of this Constitution are mandatory and prohibitory, unless by express words they are declared to be otherwise.

### SEC. 27.

All statutes of this State in effect on February 17, 1972, requiring, authorizing, imposing, or relating to the death penalty are in full force and effect, subject to legislative amendment or repeal by statute, initiative, or referendum.

The death penalty provided for under those statutes shall not be deemed to be, or to constitute, the infliction of cruel or unusual punishments within the meaning of Article 1, Section 6 nor shall such punishment for such offenses be deemed to contravene any other provision of this constitution.

### SEC. 28.

(a)  The People of the State of California find and declare that the enactment of comprehensive provisions and laws ensuring a bill of rights for victims of crime, including safeguards in the criminal justice system to fully protect those rights, is a matter of grave statewide concern.

The rights of victims pervade the criminal justice system, encompassing not only the right to restitution from the wrongdoers for financial losses suffered as a result of criminal acts, but also the more basic expectation that persons who commit felonious acts causing injury to innocent victims will be appropriately detained in custody, tried by the courts, and sufficiently punished so that the public safety is protected and encouraged as a goal of highest importance.

Such public safety extends to public primary, elementary, junior high, and senior high school campuses, where students and staff have the right to be safe and secure in their persons.

To accomplish these goals, broad reforms in the procedural treatment of accused persons and the disposition and sentencing of convicted persons are necessary and proper as deterrents to criminal behavior and to serious disruption of people's lives.

(b) Restitution. It is the unequivocal intention of the People of the State of California that all persons who suffer losses as a result of criminal activity shall have the right to restitution from the persons convicted of the crimes for losses they suffer.

Restitution shall be ordered from the convicted persons in every case, regardless of the sentence or disposition imposed, in which a crime victim suffers a loss, unless compelling and extraordinary reasons exist to the contrary. The Legislature shall adopt provisions to implement this section during the calendar year following adoption of this section.

(c) Right to Safe Schools. All students and staff of public primary, elementary, junior high and senior high schools have the inalienable right to attend campuses which are safe, secure and peaceful.

(d) Right to Truth-in-Evidence. Except as provided by statute hereafter enacted by a two-thirds vote of the membership in each house of the Legislature, relevant evidence shall not be excluded in any criminal proceeding, including pretrial and post conviction motions and hearings, or in any trial or hearing of a juvenile for a criminal offense, whether heard in juvenile or adult court. Nothing in this section shall affect any existing statutory rule of evidence relating to privilege or hearsay, or Evidence Code, Sections 352, 782 or 1103. Nothing in this section shall affect any existing statutory or constitutional right of the press.

(e) Public Safety Bail. A person may be released on bail by sufficient sureties, except for capital crimes when the facts are evident or the presumption great. Excessive bail may not be required. In setting, reducing or denying bail, the judge or magistrate shall take into consideration the protection of the public, the seriousness of the offense charged, the previous criminal record of the defendant, and the probability of his or her appearing at the trial or hearing of the case. Public safety shall be the primary consideration.

A person may be released on his or her own recognizance in the court's discretion, subject to the same factors considered in setting bail. However, no person charged with the commission of any serious felony shall be released on his or her own recognizance.

Before any person arrested for a serious felony may be released on bail, a hearing may be held before the magistrate or judge, and the prosecuting attorney shall be given notice and reasonable opportunity to be heard on the matter.

When a judge or magistrate grants or denies bail or release on a person's own recognizance, the reasons for that decision shall be stated in the record and included in the court's minutes.

(f) Use of Prior Convictions. Any prior felony conviction of any person in any criminal proceeding, whether adult or juvenile, shall subsequently be used without limitation for purposes of impeachment or enhancement of sentence in any criminal proceeding. When a prior felony conviction is an element of any felony offense, it shall be proven to the trier of fact in open court.

(g) As used in this article, the term "serious felony" is any crime defined in Penal Code, Section 1192.7(c).

### SEC. 29.

In a criminal case, the people of the State of California have the right to due process of law and to a speedy and public trial.

### SEC. 30.

(a) This Constitution shall not be construed by the courts to prohibit the joining of criminal cases as prescribed by the Legislature or by the people through the initiative process.

(b) In order to protect victims and witnesses in criminal cases, hearsay evidence shall be admissible at preliminary hearings, as prescribed by the Legislature or by the people through the initiative process.

(c) In order to provide for fair and speedy trials, discovery in criminal cases shall be reciprocal in nature, as prescribed by the Legislature or by the people through the initiative process.

### SEC. 31.

(a) The State shall not discriminate against, or grant preferential treatment to, any individual or group on the basis of race, sex, color, ethnicity, or national origin in the operation of public employment, public education, or public contracting.

(b) This Section shall apply only to action taken after the Section's effective date.

(c) Nothing in this Section shall be interpreted as prohibiting bona fide qualifications based on sex which are reasonably necessary to the normal operation of public employment, public education, or public contracting.

(d) Nothing in this Section shall be interpreted as invalidating any court order or consent decree which is in force as of the effective date of this Section.

(e) Nothing in this Section shall be interpreted as prohibiting action which must be taken to establish or maintain eligibility for any federal program, where ineligibility would result in a loss of federal funds to the State.

(f) For the purposes of this Section, "State" shall include, but not necessarily be limited to, the State itself, any city, county, city and county, public university system, including the University of California, community college district, school district, special district, or any other political subdivision or governmental instrumentality of or within the State.

(g) The remedies available for violations of this Section shall be the same, regardless of the injured party's race, sex, color, ethnicity, or national origin, as are otherwise available for violations of then-existing California antidiscrimination law.

(h) This Section shall be self-executing. If any part or parts of this Section are found to be in conflict with federal law or the United States Constitution, the Section shall be implemented to the maximum extent that federal law and the United States Constitution permit. Any provision held invalid shall be severable from the remaining portions of this Section.

# APPENDIX

## The Declaration of Independence

Drafted mainly by Thomas Jefferson, this document, adopted by the Second Continental Congress and signed by John Hancock and fifty-five others, outlined the rights of man and the rights to rebellion and self-government. It declared the independence of the colonies from Great Britain, justified rebellion, and listed the grievances against George III and his government. What is memorable about this famous document is not only that it declared the birth of a new nation, but that it set forth with eloquence our basic philosophy of liberty and representative democracy.

IN CONGRESS, JULY 4, 1776 (The unanimous Declaration of the Thirteen United States of America)

## Preamble

When, in the course of human events, it becomes necessary for one people to dissolve the political bands which have connected them with another, and to assume, among the powers of the earth, the separate and equal station to which the laws of nature and of nature's God entitle them, a decent respect to the opinions of mankind requires that they should declare the causes which impel them to the separation.

### New Principles of Government

We hold these truths to be self-evident; that all men are created equal, that they are endowed by their Creator with certain unalienable rights, that among these are life, liberty, and the pursuit of happiness.

That, to secure these rights, governments are instituted among men, deriving their just powers from the consent of the governed.

That whenever any form of government becomes destructive of these ends, it is the right of the people to alter or to abolish it, and to institute new government, laying its foundation on such principles, and organizing its powers in such form, as to them shall seem most likely to effect their safety and happiness. Prudence, indeed will dictate that governments long established should not be changed for light and transient causes; and accordingly all experience hath shown that mankind are more disposed to suffer while evils are sufferable, than to right themselves by abolishing the forms to which they are accustomed. But when a long train of abuses and usurpations, pursuing invariably the same object, evinces a design to reduce them under absolute despotism, it is their right, it is their duty, to throw off such government, and to provide new guards for their future security.

### Reasons for Separation

Such has been the patient sufferance of these colonies; and such is now the necessity which constrains them to alter their former systems of government. The history of the present king of Great Britain is a history of repeated injuries and usurpations, all having in direct object the establishment of an absolute tyranny over these states. To prove this, let facts be submitted to a candid world.

He has refused his assent to laws, the most wholesome and necessary for the public good.

He has forbidden his governors to pass laws of immediate and pressing importance unless suspended in their operation till his assent should be obtained; and when so suspended, he has utterly neglected to attend to them.

He has refused to pass other laws for the accommodation of large districts of people, unless those people would relinquish the right of representation in the legislature, a right inestimable to them, and formidable to tyrants only.

He has called together legislative bodies at places unusual, uncomfortable, and distant for the depository of their public records, for the sole purpose of fatiguing them into compliance with his measures.

He has dissolved representative houses repeatedly, for opposing, with manly firmness, his invasions on the rights of people.

He has refused, for a long time after such dissolutions, to cause others to be elected; whereby the legislative powers incapable of annihilation, have returned to the people at large for their exercise; the state remaining, in the mean-time, exposed to all the dangers of invasion from without and convulsions within.

He has endeavored to prevent the population of these states; for that purpose obstructing the laws of naturalization of foreigners, refusing to pass others to encourage their migration hither, and raising the conditions of new appropriations of lands.

He has obstructed the administration of justice, by refusing his assent to laws for establishing judiciary powers.

He has made judges dependent on his will alone for the tenure of their offices, and the amount and payment of their salaries.

He has erected a multitude of new offices, and sent hither swarms of officers to harass our people and eat out their substance.

He has kept among us, in times of peace, standing armies, without the consent of our legislature.

He has affected to render the military independent of, and superior to, the civil power.

He has combined with others to subject us to jurisdiction foreign to our constitution and unacknowledged by our laws, giving his assent to their acts of pretended legislation:

For quartering large bodies of armed troops among us;

For protecting them, by a mock trial, from punishment for any murders which they should commit on the inhabitants of these states;

For cutting off our trade with all parts of the world;

For imposing taxes on us without our consent;

For depriving us, in many cases, of the benefits of trial by jury;

For transporting us beyond seas, to be tried for pretended offenses;

For abolishing the free system of English laws in a neighboring province, establishing therein an arbitrary government, and enlarging its boundaries, so as to render it at once an example and fit instrument for introducing the same absolute rule into these colonies;

For taking away our charters, abolishing our most valuable laws, and altering, fundamentally, the forms of our governments;

For suspending our own legislatures, and declaring themselves invented with power to legislate for us in all cases whatsoever.

He has abdicated government here, by declaring us out of his protection and waging war against us.

He has plundered our seas, ravaged our coasts, burned our towns, and destroyed the lives of our people.

He is at this time transporting large armies of foreign mercenaries to complete the works of death, desolation, and tyranny already begun with circumstances of cruelty and perfidy scarcely paralleled in the most barbarous ages and totally unworthy of the head of a civilized nation.

He has constrained our fellow-citizens, taken captive on the high seas, to bear arms against their country, to become the executioners of their friends and brethren, or to fall themselves by their hands.

He has excited domestic insurrections among us, and has endeavored to bring on the inhabitants of our frontiers the merciless Indian savages, whose known rule of warfare is an undistinguished destruction of all ages, sexes, and conditions.

In every stage of these oppressions we have petitioned for redress in the most humble terms; our repeated petitions have been answered only by repeated injury. A prince whose character is thus marked by every act which may define a tyrant is unfit to be the ruler of a free people.

Nor have we been wanting in attention to our British brethren. We have warned them, from time to time, of attempts by their legislature to extend an unwarrantable jurisdiction over us. We have reminded them of the circumstances of our emigration and settlement here. We have appealed to their native justice and magnanimity; and we have conjured them, by the ties of our common kindred, to disavow these usurpations, which would inevitably interrupt our connections and correspondence. They, too, have been deaf to the voice of justice and of consanguinity. We must, therefore, acquiesce in the necessity which denounces our separation, and hold them, as we hold the rest of mankind, enemies in war, in peace, friends.

We, therefore, the representatives of the United States of America, in General Congress assembled, appealing to the Supreme Judge of the world for the rectitude of our intentions, do, in the name and by authority of the good people of these colonies, solemnly publish and declare, that these united colonies are, and of right ought to be, free and independent states; that they are absolved from all allegiance to the British crown, and that all political connection between them and the state of Great Britain is, and ought to be, totally dissolved; and that, as free and independent states, they have full power to levy war, conclude peace, contract alliances, establish commerce, and do all other acts and things which independent states may of a right do. And, for the support of this declaration, with a firm reliance on the protection of Divine Providence, we mutually pledge to each other our lives, our fortunes, and our sacred honor.

# The Federalist, No. 10, James Madison

*To the People of the State of New York:* Among the numerous advantages promised by a well-constructed union, none deserves to be more accurately developed than its tendency to break and control the violence of faction. The friend of popular governments, never finds himself so much alarmed for their character and fate, as when he contemplates their propensity to this dangerous vice. He will not fail, therefore, to set a due value on any plan which, without violating the principles to which he is attached, provides a proper cure for it. The instability, injustice, and confusion introduced into the public councils, have, in truth, been the mortal diseases under which popular governments have everywhere perished; as they continue to be the favourite and fruitful topics from which the adversaries to liberty derive their most specious declamations. The valuable improvements made by the American constitutions on the popular models, both ancient and modern, cannot certainly be too much admired; but it would be an unwarrantable partiality, to contend that they have as effectually obviated the danger on this side, as was wished and expected. Complaints are everywhere heard from our most considerate and virtuous citizens, equally the friends of public and private faith, and of public and personal liberty, that our governments are too unstable; that the public good is disregarded in the conflicts of rival parties; and that measures are too often decided, not according to the rules of justice, and the rights of the minor party, but by the superior force of an interested and over-bearing majority. However anxiously we may wish that these complaints had no foundation, the evidence of known facts will not permit us to deny that they are in some degree true. It will be found, indeed, on a candid review of our situation, that some of the distresses under which we labour have been erroneously charged on the operation of our governments; but it will be found, at the same time, that other causes will not alone account for many of our heaviest misfortunes; and, particularly, for that prevailing and increasing distrust of public engagements, and alarm for private rights, which are echoed from one end of the continent to the other. These must be chiefly, if not wholly, effects of the unsteadiness and injustice, with which a factious spirit has tainted our public administrations.

By a faction, I understand a number of citizens, whether amounting to a majority or minority of the whole, who are united and actuated by some common impulse of passion, or of interest, adverse to the rights of other citizens, or to the permanent and aggregate interests of the community.

There are two methods of curing the mischiefs of faction: the one, by removing its causes; the other, by controlling its effects.

There are again two methods of removing the causes of faction: the one, by destroying the liberty which is essential to its existence; the other, by giving to every citizen the same opinions, the same passions, and the same interests.

It could never be more truly said, than of the first remedy, that it was worse than the disease. Liberty is to faction what air is to fire, an aliment without which it instantly expires. But it could not be a less folly to abolish liberty, which is essential to political life, because it nourishes faction, than it would be to wish the annihilation of air, which is essential to animal life, because it imparts to fire its destructive agency.

The second expedient is as impracticable, as the first would be unwise. As long as the reason of man continues fallible, and he is at liberty to exercise it, different opinions will be formed. As long as the connection subsists between his reason and his self-love, his opinions and his passions will have a reciprocal influence on each other; and the former will be objects to which the latter will attach themselves. The diversity in the faculties of men, from which

the rights of property originate, is not less an insuperable obstacle to an uniformity of interests. The protection of these faculties is the first object of government. From the protection of different and unequal faculties of acquiring property, the possession of different degrees and kinds of property immediately results; and from the influence of these on the sentiments and views of the respective proprietors, ensues a division of the society into different interests and parties.

The latent causes of faction are thus sown in the nature of man; and we see them everywhere brought into different degrees of activity, according to the different circumstances of civil society. A zeal for different opinions concerning religion, concerning government, and many other points, as well of speculation as of practice; an attachment to different leaders ambitiously contending for preeminence and power; or to persons of other descriptions whose fortunes have been interesting to the human passions, have, in turn, divided mankind into parties, inflamed them with mutual animosity, and rendered them much more disposed to vex and oppress each other, than to cooperate for their common good. So strong is this propensity of mankind, to fall into mutual animosities, that where no substantial occasion presents itself, the most frivolous and fanciful distinctions have been sufficient to kindle their unfriendly passions and excite their most violent conflicts. But the most common and durable source of factions, has been the various and unequal distribution of property. Those who hold, and those who are without property, have ever formed distinct interests in society. Those who are creditors, and those who are debtors, fall under a like discrimination. A landed interest, a manufacturing interest, a mercantile interest, a moneyed interest, with many lesser interests, grow up of necessity in civilized nations, and divide them into different classes, actuated by different sentiments and views. The regulation of these various and interfering interests forms the principal task of modern legislation, and involves the spirit of the party and faction in the

necessary and ordinary operations of the government.

No man is allowed to be a judge in his own cause; because his interest will certainly bias his judgment, and, not improbably, corrupt his integrity. With equal, nay, with greater reason, a body of men are unfit to be both judges and parties at the same time; yet what are many of the most important acts of legislation, but so many judicial determinations, not indeed concerning the right of single persons, but concerning the rights of large bodies of citizens? And what are the different classes of legislators, but advocates and parties to the causes which they determine? Is a law proposed concerning private debts? It is a question to which the creditors are parties on one side, and the debtors on the other. Justice ought to hold the balance between them. Yet the parties are, and must be, themselves the judges; and the most numerous party, or, in other words, the most powerful faction, must be expected to prevail. Shall domestic manufacturers be encouraged, and in what degree, by restrictions on foreign manufacturers are questions which would be differently decided by the landed and the manufacturing classes; and probably by neither with a sole regard to justice and the public good. The apportionment of taxes, on the various descriptions of property, is an act which seems to require the most exact impartiality; yet there is, perhaps, no legislative act, in which greater opportunity and temptation are given to a predominant party to trample on the rules of justice. Every shilling, with which they overburden the inferior number, is a shilling saved to their own pockets.

It is in vain to say, that enlightened statesmen will be able to adjust these clashing interests, and render them all subservient to the public good. Enlightened statesmen will not always be at the helm; nor, in many cases, can such an adjustment be made at all, without taking into view indirect and remote considerations, which will rarely prevail over the immediate interest which one party may find in disregarding the rights of another, or the good of the whole.

The inference to which we are brought is, that the *causes* of faction cannot be removed; and that relief is only to be sought in the means of controlling its *effects*.

If a faction consists of less than a majority, relief is supplied by the republican principle, which enables the majority to defeat its sinister views, by regular vote. It may clog the administration, it may convulse the society; but it will be unable to execute and mask its violence under the forms of the Constitution. When a majority is included in a faction, the form of popular government, on the other hand, enables it to sacrifice to its ruling passion or interest, both the public good and the rights of other citizens. To secure the public good, and private rights, against the danger of such a faction, and at the same time to preserve the spirit and the form of popular government, is then the great object to which our inquiries are directed. Let me add, that it is the great desideratum, by which alone this form of government can be rescued from the opprobrium under which it has so long laboured, and be recommended to the esteem and adoption of mankind.

By what means is this object attainable? Evidently by one of two only. Either the existence of the same passion or interest in a majority, at the same time, must be prevented; or the majority, having such coexistent passion or interest, must be rendered, by their number and local situation, unable to concert and carry into effect schemes of oppression. If the impulse and the opportunity be suffered to coincide, we well know that neither moral nor religious motives can be relied on as an adequate control. They are not found to be such on the injustice and violence of individuals, and lose their efficacy in proportion to the number combined together; that is, in proportion as their efficacy becomes needful.

From this view of the subject, it may be concluded, that a pure democracy, by which I mean a society consisting of a small number of citizens, who assemble and administer the government in person, can admit of no cure for the mischiefs of faction. A common passion or interest will, in almost every case, be felt by a majority of the whole; a communication and concert, results from the form of government itself; and there is nothing to check the inducements to sacrifice the weaker party, or an obnoxious individual. Hence, it is, that such democracies have ever been spectacles of turbulence and contention; have ever been found incompatible with personal security, or the rights of property; and have in general been as short in their lives, as they have been violent in their deaths. Theoretic politicians, who have patronized this species of government, have erroneously supposed, that by reducing mankind to a perfect equality in their political rights, they would, at the same time, be perfectly equalized and assimilated in their possessions, their opinions, and their passions.

A republic, by which I mean a government in which the scheme of representation takes place, opens a different prospect, and promises the cure for which we are seeking. Let us examine the points in which it varies from pure democracy, and we shall comprehend both the nature of the cure and the efficacy which it must derive from the union.

The two great points of difference, between a democracy and a republic, are, first, the delegation of the government, in the latter, to a small number of citizens, elected by the rest; secondly, the greater number of citizens, and greater sphere of country, over which the latter may be extended.

The effect of the first difference is, on the one hand, to refine and enlarge the public views, by passing them through the medium of a chosen body of citizens, whose wisdom may best discern the true interest of their country, and whose patriotism and love of justice, will be least likely to sacrifice it to temporary or partial considerations. Under such a regulation, it may well happen, that the public voice, pronounced by the representatives of the people, will be more consonant to the public good, than if pronounced by the people themselves, convened for the purpose. On the other hand the effect may be inverted. Men of factious tempers, of local prejudices, or of sinister designs, may by intrigue, by corruption, or by other means, first obtain the suffrages, and then betray the interest of the people. The question resulting is, whether small or extensive republics are most favourable to the election of proper guardians of the public weal; and it is clearly decided in favour of the latter by two obvious considerations.

In the first place, it is to be remarked that, however small the republic may be, the representatives must be raised to a certain number, in order to guard against the cabals of a few; and that however large it may be, they must be limited to a certain number, in order to guard against the confusion of a multitude. Hence, the number of representatives in the two cases not being in proportion to that of the constituents, and being proportionally greatest in the small republic, it follows, that if the proportion of fit characters be not less in the large than in the small republic, the former will present a greater option, and consequently a greater probability of a fit choice.

In the next place, as each representative will be chosen by a greater number of citizens in the large than in the small republic, it will be more difficult for unworthy candidates to practice with success the vicious arts, by which elections are too often carried; and the suffrages of the people being more free, will be more likely to centre in men who possess the most attractive merit, and the most diffusive and established characters.

It must be confessed, that in this, as in most other cases, there is a mean, on both sides of which inconveniences will be found to lie. By enlarging too much the number of electors, you render the representatives too little acquainted with all their local circumstances and lesser interests; as by reducing it too much, you render him unduly attached to these, and too little fit to comprehend and pursue great and national objects. The federal constitution forms a happy combination in this respect; the great and aggregate interests being referred to the national, the local and particular to the state legislatures.

The other point of difference is, the greater number of citizens, and extent of territory, which may be brought within the compass of republican, than of democratic government; and it is this circumstance principally which renders factious combinations less to be dreaded in the former, than in the latter. The smaller the society, the fewer probably will be the distinct parties and interests composing it; the fewer the distinct parties and interests, the more frequently will a majority be found of the same party; and the smaller the number of individuals composing a majority, and the smaller the compass within which they are placed, the more easily will they concert and execute their plans of oppression. Extend the sphere, and you take in a greater variety of parties and interests; you make it less probable that a majority of the whole will have a common motive to invade the rights of other citizens; or if such a common motive exists, it will be more difficult for all who feel it to discover their own strength, and to act in unison with each other. Besides other impediments, it may be remarked, that where there is a consciousness of unjust or dishonourable purposes, communication is always checked by distrust, in proportion to the number whose concurrence is necessary.

Hence, it clearly appears, that the same advantage, which a republic has over a democracy, in controlling the effects of faction, is enjoyed by a large over a small republic—is enjoyed by the union over the states composing it. Does this advantage consist in the substitution of representatives, whose enlightened views and virtuous sentiments render them superior to local prejudices, and to schemes of injustice? It will not be denied that the representation of the union will be most likely to possess these requisite endowments. Does it consist in the greater security afforded by a greater variety of parties, against the event of any one party being able to outnumber and oppress the rest? In an equal degree does the increased variety of parties, comprised within the union, increase the security? Does it, in fine, consist in the greater obstacles opposed to the concert and accomplishment of the secret wishes of an unjust and interested majority? Here, again, the extent of the union gives it the most palpable advantage.

The influence of factious leaders may kindle a flame within their particular states, but will be unable to spread a general conflagration through the other states; a religious sect may degenerate into a political faction in a part of the confederacy; but the variety of sects dispersed over the entire face of it, must secure the national councils against any danger from that source; a rage for paper money, for an abolition of debts, for an equal division of property, or for any other improper or wicked project, will be less apt to pervade the whole body of the union than a particular member of it; in the same proportion as such a malady is more likely to taint a particular county or district, than an entire state.

In the extent and proper structure of the union, therefore, we behold a republican remedy for the diseases most incident to republican government. And according to the degree of pleasure and pride we feel in being republicans, ought to be our zeal in cherishing the spirit, and supporting the character of federalists.

## The Federalist, No. 51, James Madison

To what expedient, then, shall we finally resort, for maintaining in practice the necessary partition of power among the several departments as laid down in the Constitution? The only answer that can be given is that as all these exterior provisions are found to be inadequate the defect must be supplied, by so contriving the interior structure of the government as that its several constituent parts may, by their mutual relations, be the means of keeping each other in their proper places. Without presuming to undertake a full development of this important idea I will hazard a few general observations which may perhaps place it in a clearer light, and enable us to form a more correct judgment of the principles and structure of the government planned by the convention.

In order to lay a due foundation for that separate and distinct exercise of the different powers of government, which to a certain extent is admitted on all hands to be essential to the preservation of liberty, it is evident that each department should have a will of its own; and consequently should be so constituted that the members of each should have as little agency as possible in the appointment of the members of the others. Were this principle rigorously adhered to, it would require that all the appointments for the supreme executive, legislative, and judiciary magistracies should be drawn from the same fountain of authority, the people, through channels having no communication whatever with one another. Perhaps such a plan of constructing the several departments would be less difficult in practice than it may in contemplation appear. Some difficulties, however, and some additional expense would attend the execution of it. Some deviations, therefore, from the principle must be admitted. In the constitution of the judiciary department in particular, it might be inexpedient to insist rigorously on the principle: first, because peculiar qualifications being essential in the members, the primary consideration ought to be to select that mode of choice which best secures these qualifications; second, because the permanent tenure by which the appointments are held in that department must soon destroy all sense of dependence on the authority conferring them.

It is equally evident that the members of each department should be as little dependent as possible on those of the others for the emoluments annexed to their offices. Were the executive magistrate, or the judges, not independent of the legislature in this particular, their independence in every other would be merely nominal.

But the great security against a gradual concentration of the several powers in the same department consists in giving to those who administer each department the necessary constitutional means and personal motives to resist encroachments of the others. The provision for defense must in this, as in all other cases, be made commensurate to the danger of attack. Ambition must be made to counteract ambition. The interest of the man must be connected with the constitutional rights of the place. It may be a reflection on human nature that such devices should be necessary to control the abuses of government. But what is government itself but the greatest of all reflections on human nature? If men were angels, no government would be necessary. If angels were to govern men, neither external nor internal controls on government would be necessary. In framing a government which is to be administered by men over men, the great difficulty lies in this: you must first enable the government to control the governed; and in the next place oblige it to control itself. A dependence on the people is, no doubt, the primary control on the government; but experience has taught mankind the necessity of auxiliary precautions.

This policy of supplying, by opposite and rival interests, the defect of better motives, might be traced through the whole system of human affairs, private as well as public. We see it particularly displayed in all the subordinate distributions of power, where the constant aim is to divide and arrange the several offices in such a manner as that each may be a check on the other— that the private interest of every individual may be a sentinel over the public rights. These inventions of prudence cannot be less requisite in the distribution of the supreme powers of the State.

But it is not possible to give to each department an equal power of self-defense. In republican government, the legislative authority necessarily predominates. The remedy for this inconveniency is to divide the legislature into different branches; and to render them, by modes of election and different principles of action, as little connected with each other as the nature of their common functions and their common dependence on the society will admit. It may even be necessary to guard against dangerous encroachments by still further precautions. As the weight of the legislative authority requires that it should be thus divided, the weakness of the executive may require, on the

other hand, that it should be fortified. An absolute negative on the legislature appears, at first view, to be the natural defense with which the executive magistrate should be armed. But perhaps it would be neither altogether safe nor alone sufficient. On ordinary occasions it might not be exerted with the requisite firmness, and on extraordinary occasions it might be perfidiously abused. May not this defect of an absolute negative be supplied by some qualified connection between this weaker department and the weaker branch of the stronger department, by which the latter may be led to support the constitutional rights of the former, without being too much detached from the rights of its own department?

If the principles on which these observations are founded be just, as I persuade myself they are, and they be applied as a criterion to the several State constitutions, and to the federal Constitution, it will be found that if the latter does not perfectly correspond with them, the former are infinitely less able to bear such a test.

There are, moreover, two considerations particularly applicable to the federal system of America, which place that system in a very interesting point of view.

*First.* In a single republic, all the power surrendered by the people is submitted to the administration of a single government; and the usurpations are guarded against by a division of the government into distinct and separate departments. In the compound republic of America, the power surrendered by the people is first divided between two distinct governments, and then the portion allotted to each subdivided among distinct and separate departments. Hence a double security arises to the rights of the people. The different governments will control each other, at the same time that each will be controlled by itself.

*Second.* It is of great importance in a republic not only to guard the society against the oppression of its rulers, but to guard one part of the society against the injustice of the other part. Different interests necessarily exist in different classes of citizens. If a major-

ity be united by a common interest, the rights of the minority will be insecure. There are but two methods of providing against this evil: the one by creating a will in the community independent of the majority—that is, of the society itself; the other, by comprehending in the society so many separate descriptions of citizens as will render an unjust combination of a majority of the whole very improbable, if not impracticable. The first method prevails in all governments possessing an hereditary or self-appointed authority. This, at best, is but a precarious security; because a power independent of the society may as well espouse the unjust views of the major as the rightful interests of the minor party, and may possibly be turned against both parties. The second method will be exemplified in the federal republic of the United States. Whilst all authority in it will be derived from and dependent on the society, the society itself will be broken into so many parts, interests and classes of citizens, that the rights of individuals, or of the minority, will be in little danger from interested combinations of the majority. In a free government the security for civil rights must be the same as that for religious rights. It consists in the one case in the multiplicity of interests, and in the other in the multiplicity of sects. The degree of security in both cases will depend on the number of interests and sects; and this may be presumed to depend on the extent of country and number of people comprehended under the same government. This view of the subject must particularly recommend a proper federal system to all the sincere and considerate friends of republican government, since it shows that in exact proportion as the territory of the Union may be formed into more circumscribed Confederacies, or States, oppressive combinations of a majority will be facilitated; the best security, under the republican forms, for the rights of every class of citizen, will be diminished; and consequently the stability and independence of some member of the government, the only other security, must be proportionally increased. Justice is the end of government. It is the end of civil society. It ever has been and ever will be pursued until it be obtained, or until liberty be lost in the pursuit. In a society under the forms of which the stronger faction can readily unite and oppress the weaker, anarchy may as truly be said to reign as in a state of nature, where the weaker individual is not secured against the violence of the stronger; and as, in the latter state, even the stronger individuals are prompted, by the uncertainty of their condition, to submit to a government which may protect the weak as well as themselves; so, in the former state, will the more powerful factions or parties be gradually induced, by a like motive, to wish for a government which will protect all parties, the weaker as well as the more powerful. It can be little doubted that if the State of Rhode Island was separated from the Confederacy and left to itself, the insecurity of rights under the popular form of government within such narrow limits would be displayed by such reiterated oppressions of factious majorities that some power altogether independent of the people would soon be called for by the voice of the very factions whose misrule had proved the necessity of it. In the extended republic of the United States, and among the great variety of interests, parties, and sects which it embraces, a coalition of a majority of the whole society could seldom take place on any other principles than those of justice and the general good; whilst there being thus less danger to a minor from the will of a major party, there must be less pretext, also, to provide for the security of the former, by introducing into the government a will not dependent on the latter, or, in other words, a will independent of the society itself. It is no less certain that it is important, notwithstanding the contrary opinions which have been entertained that the larger the society, provided it lie within a practicable sphere, the more duly capable it will be of self-government. And happily for the *republican cause*, the practicable sphere may be carried to avery great extent by a judicious modification and mixture of the *federal principle*.

# PRESIDENTS AND VICE PRESIDENTS

1. George Washington (1789)
   John Adams (1789)

2. John Adams (1797)
   Thomas Jefferson (1797)

3. Thomas Jefferson (1801)
   Aaron Burr (1801)
   George Clinton (1805)

4. James Madison (1809)
   George Clinton (1809)
   Elbridge Gerry (1813)

5. James Monroe (1817)
   Daniel D. Tompkins (1817)

6. John Quincy Adams (1825)
   John C. Calhoun (1825)

7. Andrew Jackson (1829)
   John C. Calhoun (1829)
   Martin Van Buren (1833)

8. Martin Van Buren (1837)
   Richard M. Johnson (1837)

9. William H. Harrison (1841)
   John Tyler (1841)

10. John Tyler (1841)

11. James K. Polk (1845)
    George M. Dallas (1845)

12. Zachary Taylor (1849)
    Millard Fillmore (1849)

13. Millard Fillmore (1850)

14. Franklin Pierce (1853)
    William R. King (1853)

15. James Buchanan (1857)
    John C. Breckinridge (1857)

16. Abraham Lincoln (1861)
    Hannibal Hamlin (1861)
    Andrew Johnson (1865)

17. Andrew Johnson (1865)

18. Ulysses S. Grant (1869)
    Schuyler Colfax (1869)
    Henry Wilson (1873)

19. Rutherford B. Hayes (1877)
    William A. Wheeler (1877)

20. James A. Garfield (1881)
    Chester A. Arthur (1881)

21. Chester A. Arthur (1881)

22. Grover Cleveland (1885)
    T.A. Hendricks (1885)

23. Benjamin Harrison (1889)
    Levi P. Morton (1889)

24. Grover Cleveland (1893)
    Adlai E. Stevenson (1893)

25. William McKinley (1897)
    Garret A. Hobart (1897)
    Theodore Roosevelt (1901)

26. Theodore Roosevelt (1901)
    Charles Fairbanks (1905)

27. William H. Taft (1909)
    James S. Sherman (1909)

28. Woodrow Wilson (1913)
    Thomas R. Marshall (1913)

29. Warren G. Harding (1921)
    Calvin Coolidge (1921)

30. Calvin Coolidge (1923)
    Charles G. Dawes (1925)

31. Herbert C. Hoover (1929)
    Charles Curtis (1929)

32. Franklin D. Roosevelt (1933)
    John Nance Garner (1933)
    Henry A. Wallace (1941)
    Harry S Truman (1945)

33. Harry S Truman (1945)
    Alben W. Barkley (1949)

34. Dwight D. Eisenhower (1953)
    Richard M. Nixon (1953)

35. John F. Kennedy (1961)
    Lyndon B. Johnson (1961)

36. Lyndon B. Johnson (1963)
    Hubert H. Humphrey (1965)

37. Richard M. Nixon (1969)
    Spiro T. Agnew (1969)
    Gerald R. Ford (1973)

38. Gerald R. Ford (1974)
    Nelson A. Rockefeller (1974)

39. James E. Carter Jr. (1977)
    Walter F. Mondale (1977)

40. Ronald W. Reagan (1981)
    George H.W. Bush (1981)

41. George H.W. Bush (1989)
    James D. Quayle III (1989)

42. William J.B. Clinton (1993)
    Albert Gore (1993)

43. George W. Bush (2001)
    Richard Cheney (2001)

# SUPREME COURT JUSTICES

*Current Supreme Court Justices*

1. John G. Roberts (Chief Justice)
2. Antonin Scalia (Associate Justice)
3. John Paul Stevens (Associate Justice)
4. Samuel A. Alito Jr. (Associate Justice)
5. Anthony M. Kennedy (Associate Justice)
6. Ruth Bader Ginsburg (Associate Justice)
7. David H. Souter (Associate Justice)
8. Clarence Thomas (Associate Justice)
9. Stephen G. Breyer (Associate Justice)

*Former Supreme Court Chief Justices*

1. John Jay (1779–1795)
2. John Rutledge (1795)
3. Oliver Ellsworth (1996–1800)
4. John Marshall (1801–1835)
5. Roger Brooke Tancy (1836–1864)
6. Salmon Portland Chase (1864–1873)
7. Morrison R. Waite (1874–1888)
8. Melville Weston Fuller (1888–1910)
9. Edward Douglas White (1910–1921)
10. William Howard Taft (1921–1930)
11. Charles Evans Hughes (1930–1941)
12. Harlan Fiske Stone (1941–1946)
13. Fred M. Vison (1946–1953)
14. Earl Warren (1953–1969)
15. Warren E. Burger (1969–1986)
16. William H. Rehnquist (1986–2005)

*Former Supreme Court Associate Judges*

1. James Wilson (1789–1798)
2. William Cushing (1790–1810)
3. John Blair Jr. (1790–1796)
4. James Iredell (1790–1799)
5. Thomas Johnson (1792–1793)
6. William Paterson (1793–1806)
7. Samuel Chase (1796–1811)
8. Bushrod Washington (1799–1829)
9. Alfred Moore (1800–1804)
10. William Johnson (1804–1834)
11. H. Brockholst Livingston (1807–1328)
12. Thomas Todd (1807–1826)
13. Gabriel Duvall (1811–1835)
14. Joseph Story (1812–1845)
15. Smith Thompson (1823–1843)
16. Robert Trimble (1826–1828)
17. John McLean (1830–1861)

18. Henry Baldwin (1830–1844)
19. James M. Wayne (1835–1867)
20. Philip P. Barbour (1836–1841)
21. John Catron (1837–1865)
22. John McKinley (1838–1852)
23. Peter V. Daniel (1842–1860)
24. Samuel Nelson (1845–1872)
25. Levi Woodbury (1845–1851)
26. Robert C. Grier (1846–1870)
27. Benjamin R. Curtis (1851–1857)
28. John A. Campbell (1853–1861)
29. Nathan Clifford (1858–1881)
30. Noah H. Swayne (1862–1881)
31. Samuel F. Miller (1862–1890)
32. David Davis (1862–1877)
33. Stephen J. Field (1863–1897)
34. William Strong (1870–1880)
35. Joseph P. Bradley (1870–1892)
36. Ward Hunt (1873–1882)
37. John Marshall Harlan (1877–1911)
38. William B. Woods (1881–1887)
39. Stanley Matthews (1881–1889)
40. Horace Gray (1882–1902)
41. Samuel Blatchford (1882–1893)
42. Lucius Q. C. Lamar (1888–1893)
43. David J. Brewer (1890–1910)
44. Henry B. Brown (1891–1906)
45. George Shiras Jr. (1892–1903)
46. Howell E. Jackson (1893–1895)
47. Rufus W. Peckham (1896–1909)
48. Joseph McKenna (1898–1925)
49. Oliver Wendell Holmes Jr. (1902–1932)
50. William R. Day (1903–1922)
51. William H. Moody (1906–1910)
52. Horace H. Lurton (1910–1914)
53. Willis Van Devanter (1911–1937)
54. Joseph Rucker Lamar (1911–1916)
55. Mahlon Pitney (1912–1922)
56. James Clark McReynolds (1914–1941)
57. Louis D. Brandeis (1916–1939)
58. John H. Clark (1916–1922)
59. George Sutherland (1922–1938)
60. Pierce Butler (1923–1939)
61. Edward T. Sanford (1923–1930)
62. Owen J. Roberts (1930–1945)
63. Benjamin Nathan Cardozo (1932–1938)
64. Hugo Black (1937–1971)
65. Stanley F. Reed (1938–1957)

66. Felix Frankfurter (1939–1962)
67. William O. Douglas (1939–1975)
68. Frank W. Murphy (1940–1949)
69. James F. Byrnes (1941–1942)
70. Robert H. Jackson (1941–1954)
71. Wiley B. Rutledge (1943–1949)
72. Harold H. Burton (1945–1958)
73. Tom C. Clark (1949–1967)
74. Sherman Minton (1949–1956)
75. William J. Brennan Jr. (1956–1990)

76. John Marshall Harlan II (1955–1971)
77. Charles E. Whittaker (1957–1962)
78. Potter Stewart (1958–1981)
79. Byron R. White (1962–1993)
80. Arthur J. Goldberg (1962–1965)
81. Abe Fortas (1965–1969)
82. Thurgood Marshall (1967–1991)
83. Harry A. Blackmun (1970–1994)
84. Lewis F. Powell Jr. (1972–1987)
85. Sandra Day O'Connor (1981–2005)

# PRESIDENTIAL ELECTIONS AND VOTING

| Year | Number of States | Candidates | Party | Popular Vote* | Electoral Vote[†] | Percentage of Popular Vote |
|------|------------------|------------|-------|---------------|-------------------|----------------------------|
| 1789 | 11 | George Washington | No party designations | | 69 | |
|      |    | John Adams | | | 34 | |
|      |    | Other Candidates | | | 35 | |
| 1792 | 15 | George Washington | No party designations | | 132 | |
|      |    | John Adams | | | 77 | |
|      |    | George Clinton | | | 50 | |
|      |    | Other Candidates | | | 5 | |
| 1796 | 16 | John Adams | Federalist | | 71 | |
|      |    | Thomas Jefferson | Democratic Republican | | 68 | |
|      |    | Thomas Pinckney | Federalist | | 59 | |
|      |    | Aaron Burr | Democratic Republican | | 30 | |
|      |    | Other Candidates | | | 48 | |
| 1800 | 16 | Thomas Jefferson | Democratic Republican | | 73 | |
|      |    | Aaron Burr | Democratic Republican | | 73 | |
|      |    | John Adams | Federalist | | 65 | |
|      |    | Charles C. Pinckney | Federalist | | 64 | |
|      |    | John Jay | Federalist | | 1 | |
| 1804 | 17 | Thomas Jefferson | Democratic Republican | | 162 | |
|      |    | Charles C. Pinckney | Federalist | | 14 | |
| 1808 | 17 | James Madison | Democratic Republican | | 122 | |
|      |    | Charles C. Pinckney | Federalist | | 47 | |
|      |    | George Clinton | Democratic Republican | | 6 | |
| 1812 | 18 | James Madison | Democratic Republican | | 128 | |
|      |    | DeWitt Clinton | Federalist | | 89 | |
| 1816 | 19 | James Monroe | Democratic Republican | | 183 | |
|      |    | Rufus King | Federalist | | 34 | |
| 1820 | 24 | James Monroe | Democratic Republican | | 231 | |
|      |    | John Quincy Adams | Independent Republican | | 1 | |
| 1824 | 24 | John Quincy Adams | | 108,740 | 84 | 30.5 |
|      |    | Andrew Jackson | | 153,544 | 99 | 43.1 |
|      |    | William H. Crawford | | 46,618 | 41 | 13.1 |
|      |    | Henry Clay | | 47,136 | 37 | 13.2 |
| 1828 | 24 | Andrew Jackson | Democrat | 647,286 | 178 | 56.0 |
|      |    | John Quincy Adams | National Republican | 508,064 | 83 | 44.0 |
| 1832 | 24 | Andrew Jackson | Democrat | 687,502 | 219 | 55.0 |
|      |    | Henry Clay | National Republican | 530,189 | 49 | 42.4 |
|      |    | William Wirt | Anti-Masonic | | 7 | |
|      |    | John Floyd | National Republican | 33,108 | 11 | 2.6 |
| 1836 | 26 | Martin Van Buren | Democrat | 765,483 | 170 | 50.9 |
|      |    | William H. Harrison | Whig | | 73 | |
|      |    | Hugh L. White | Whig | | 26 | |
|      |    | Daniel Webster | Whig | 739,795 | 14 | 49.1 |
|      |    | W. P. Mangum | Whig | | 11 | |
| 1840 | 26 | William H. Harrison | Whig | 1,274,624 | 234 | 53.1 |
|      |    | Martin Van Buren | Democrat | 1,127,781 | 60 | 46.9 |

(continued on page A-14)

# PRESIDENTIAL ELECTIONS AND VOTING

| Year | Number of States | Candidates | Party | Popular Vote* | Electoral Vote† | Percentage of Popular Vote |
|------|------|------|------|------|------|------|
| 1844 | 26 | **James K. Polk** | Democrat | 1,338,464 | 170 | 49.6 |
|  |  | Henry Clay | Whig | 1,300,097 | 105 | 48.1 |
|  |  | James G. Birney | Liberty | 62,300 |  | 2.3 |
| 1848 | 30 | **Zachary Taylor** | Whig | 1,360,967 | 163 | 47.4 |
|  |  | Lewis Cass | Democrat | 1,222,342 | 127 | 42.5 |
|  |  | Martin Van Buren | Free Soil | 291,263 |  | 10.1 |
| 1852 | 31 | **Franklin Pierce** | Democrat | 1,601,117 | 254 | 50.9 |
|  |  | Winfield Scott | Whig | 1,385,453 | 42 | 44.1 |
|  |  | John P. Hale | Free Soil | 155,825 |  | 5.0 |
| 1856 | 31 | **James Buchanan** | Democrat | 1,832,955 | 174 | 45.3 |
|  |  | John C. Frémont | Republican | 1,339,932 | 114 | 33.1 |
|  |  | Millard Fillmore | American ("Know Nothing") | 871,731 | 8 | 21.6 |
| 1860 | 33 | **Abraham Lincoln** | Republican | 1,865,593 | 180 | 39.8 |
|  |  | Stephen A. Douglas | Democrat | 1,382,713 | 12 | 29.5 |
|  |  | John C. Breckinridge | Democrat | 848,356 | 72 | 18.1 |
|  |  | John Bell | Constitutional Union | 592,906 | 39 | 12.6 |
| 1864 | 36 | **Abraham Lincoln** | Republican | 2,206,938 | 212 | 55.0 |
|  |  | George B. McClellan | Democrat | 1,803,787 | 21 | 45.0 |
| 1868 | 37 | **Ulysses S. Grant** | Republican | 3,013,421 | 214 | 52.7 |
|  |  | Horatio Seymour | Democrat | 2,706,829 | 80 | 47.3 |
| 1872 | 37 | **Ulysses S. Grant** | Republican | 3,596,745 | 286 | 55.6 |
|  |  | Horace Greeley | Democrat | 2,843,446 | * | 43.9 |
| 1876 | 38 | **Rutherford B. Hayes** | Republican | 4,036,572 | 185 | 48.0 |
|  |  | Samuel J. Tilden | Democrat | 4,284,020 | 184 | 51.0 |
| 1880 | 38 | **James A. Garfield** | Republican | 4,453,295 | 214 | 48.5 |
|  |  | Winfield S. Hancock | Democrat | 4,414,082 | 155 | 48.1 |
|  |  | James B. Weaver | Greenback-Labor | 308,578 |  | 3.4 |
| 1884 | 38 | **Grover Cleveland** | Democrat | 4,879,507 | 219 | 48.5 |
|  |  | James G. Blaine | Republican | 4,850,293 | 182 | 48.2 |
|  |  | Benjamin F. Butler | Greenback-Labor | 175,370 |  | 1.8 |
|  |  | John P. St. John | Prohibition | 150,369 |  | 1.5 |
| 1888 | 38 | **Benjamin Harrison** | Republican | 5,447,129 | 233 | 47.9 |
|  |  | Grover Cleveland | Democrat | 5,537,857 | 168 | 48.6 |
|  |  | Clinton B. Fisk | Prohibition | 249,506 |  | 2.2 |
|  |  | Alson J. Streeter | Union Labor | 146,935 |  | 1.3 |
| 1892 | 44 | **Grover Cleveland** | Democrat | 5,555,426 | 277 | 46.1 |
|  |  | Benjamin Harrison | Republican | 5,182,690 | 145 | 43.0 |
|  |  | James B. Weaver | People's | 1,029,846 | 22 | 8.5 |
|  |  | John Bidwell | Prohibition | 264,133 |  | 2.2 |
| 1896 | 45 | **William McKinley** | Republican | 7,102,246 | 271 | 51.1 |
|  |  | William J. Bryan | Democrat | 6,492,559 | 176 | 47.7 |
| 1900 | 45 | **William McKinley** | Republican | 7,218,491 | 292 | 51.7 |
|  |  | William J. Bryan | Democrat; Populist | 6,356,734 | 155 | 45.5 |
|  |  | John C. Woolley | Prohibition | 208,914 |  | 1.5 |

# PRESIDENTIAL ELECTIONS AND VOTING

| Year | Number of States | Candidates | Party | Popular Vote* | Electoral Vote[†] | Percentage of Popular Vote |
|---|---|---|---|---|---|---|
| 1904 | 45 | **Theodore Roosevelt** | Republican | 7,628,461 | 336 | 57.4 |
| | | Alton B. Parker | Democrat | 5,084,223 | 140 | 37.6 |
| | | Eugene V. Debs | Socialist | 402,283 | | 3.0 |
| | | Silas C. Swallow | Prohibition | 258,536 | | 1.9 |
| 1908 | 46 | **William H. Taft** | Republican | 7,675,320 | 321 | 51.6 |
| | | William J. Bryan | Democrat | 6,412,294 | 162 | 43.1 |
| | | Eugene V. Debs | Socialist | 420,793 | | 2.8 |
| | | Eugene W. Chafin | Prohibition | 253,840 | | 1.7 |
| 1912 | 48 | **Woodrow Wilson** | Democrat | 6,296,547 | 435 | 41.9 |
| | | Theodore Roosevelt | Progressive | 4,118,571 | 88 | 27.4 |
| | | William H. Taft | Republican | 3,486,720 | 8 | 23.2 |
| | | Eugene V. Debs | Socialist | 900,672 | | 6.0 |
| | | Eugene W. Chafin | Prohibition | 206,275 | | 1.4 |
| 1916 | 48 | **Woodrow Wilson** | Democrat | 9,127,695 | 277 | 49.4 |
| | | Charles E. Hughes | Republican | 8,533,507 | 254 | 46.2 |
| | | A. L. Benson | Socialist | 585,113 | | 3.2 |
| | | J. Frank Hanly | Prohibition | 220,506 | | 1.2 |
| 1920 | 48 | **Warren G. Harding** | Republican | 16,143,407 | 404 | 60.4 |
| | | James M. Cox | Democrat | 9,130,328 | 127 | 34.2 |
| | | Eugene V. Debs | Socialist | 919,799 | | 3.4 |
| | | P. P. Christensen | Farmer-Labor | 265,411 | | 1.0 |
| 1924 | 48 | **Calvin Coolidge** | Republican | 15,718,211 | 382 | 54.0 |
| | | John W. Davis | Democrat | 8,385,283 | 136 | 28.8 |
| | | Robert M. La Follette | Progressive | 4,831,289 | 13 | 16.6 |
| 1928 | 48 | **Herbert C. Hoover** | Republican | 21,391,993 | 444 | 58.2 |
| | | Alfred E. Smith | Democrat | 15,016,169 | 87 | 40.9 |
| 1932 | 48 | **Franklin D. Roosevelt** | Democrat | 22,809,638 | 472 | 57.4 |
| | | Herbert C. Hoover | Republican | 15,758,901 | 59 | 39.7 |
| | | Norman Thomas | Socialist | 881,951 | | 2.2 |
| 1936 | 48 | **Franklin D. Roosevelt** | Democrat | 27,752,869 | 523 | 60.8 |
| | | Alfred M. Landon | Republican | 16,674,665 | 8 | 36.5 |
| | | William Lemke | Union | 882,479 | | 1.9 |
| 1940 | 48 | **Franklin D. Roosevelt** | Democrat | 27,307,819 | 449 | 54.8 |
| | | Wendell L. Willkie | Republican | 22,321,018 | 82 | 44.8 |
| 1944 | 48 | **Franklin D. Roosevelt** | Democrat | 25,606,585 | 432 | 53.5 |
| | | Thomas E. Dewey | Republican | 22,014,745 | 99 | 46.0 |
| 1948 | 48 | **Harry S Truman** | Democrat | 24,105,812 | 303 | 49.5 |
| | | Thomas E. Dewey | Republican | 21,970,065 | 189 | 45.1 |
| | | J. Strom Thurmond | States' Rights | 1,169,063 | 39 | 2.4 |
| | | Henry A. Wallace | Progressive | 1,157,172 | | 2.4 |
| 1952 | 48 | **Dwight D. Eisenhower** | Republican | 33,936,234 | 442 | 55.1 |
| | | Adlai E. Stevenson | Democrat | 27,314,992 | 89 | 44.4 |
| 1956 | 48 | **Dwight D. Eisenhower** | Republican | 35,590,472 | 457* | 57.6 |
| | | Adlai E. Stevenson | Democrat | 26,022,752 | 73 | 42.1 |

*(continued on page A-16)*

# PRESIDENTIAL ELECTIONS AND VOTING

| Year | Number of States | Candidates | Party | Popular Vote* | Electoral Vote† | Percentage of Popular Vote |
|------|------------------|------------|-------|---------------|-----------------|----------------------------|
| 1960 | 50 | John F. Kennedy | Democrat | 34,227,096 | 303† | 49.9 |
|      |    | Richard M. Nixon | Republican | 34,108,546 | 219 | 49.6 |
| 1964 | 50 | Lyndon B. Johnson | Democrat | 42,676,220 | 486 | 61.3 |
|      |    | Barry M. Goldwater | Republican | 26,860,314 | 52 | 38.5 |
| 1968 | 50 | Richard M. Nixon | Republican | 31,785,480 | 301 | 43.4 |
|      |    | Hubert H. Humphrey | Democrat | 31,275,165 | 191 | 42.7 |
|      |    | George C. Wallace | American Independent | 9,906,473 | 46 | 13.5 |
| 1972 | 50 | Richard M. Nixon‡ | Republican | 47,165,234 | 520 | 60.6 |
|      |    | George S. McGovern | Democrat | 29,168,110 | 17 | 37.5 |
| 1976 | 50 | Jimmy Carter | Democrat | 40,828,929 | 297 | 50.1 |
|      |    | Gerald R. Ford | Republican | 39,148,940 | 240 | 47.9 |
|      |    | Eugene McCarthy | Independent | 739,256 | | 0.9 |
| 1980 | 50 | Ronald Reagan | Republican | 43,201,220 | 489 | 50.9 |
|      |    | Jimmy Carter | Democrat | 34,913,332 | 49 | 41.2 |
|      |    | John B. Anderson | Independent | 5,581,379 | | 6.6 |
| 1984 | 50 | Ronald Reagan | Republican | 53,428,357 | 525 | 59.0 |
|      |    | Walter F. Mondale | Democrat | 36,930,923 | 13 | 41.0 |
| 1988 | 50 | George H. W. Bush | Republican | 48,901,046 | 426 | 53.4 |
|      |    | Michael Dukakis | Democrat | 41,809,030 | 111 | 45.6 |
| 1992 | 50 | Bill Clinton | Democrat | 43,728,275 | 370 | 43.2 |
|      |    | George Bush | Republican | 38,167,416 | 168 | 37.7 |
|      |    | H. Ross Perot | United We Stand, America | 19,237,247 | | 19.0 |
| 1996 | 50 | Bill Clinton | Democrat | 45,590,703 | 379 | 49.0 |
|      |    | Bob Dole | Republican | 37,816,307 | 159 | 41.0 |
|      |    | H. Ross Perot | Reform | 7,866,284 | | 8.0 |
| 2000 | 50 | George W. Bush | Republican | 50,456,169 | 271 | 48.0 |
|      |    | Al Gore | Democrat | 50,996,116 | 266 | 48.0 |
|      |    | Ralph Nader | Green | 2,767,176 | 0 | 3.0 |
| 2004 | 50 | George W. Bush | Republican | 62,040,606 | 286 | 50.7 |
|      |    | John Kerry | Democrat | 59,028,109 | 251 | 48.3 |
|      |    | Ralph Nader | Independent | 411,304 | 0 | 1.0 |

*Percentage of popular vote given for any election year may not total 100 percent because candidates receiving less than 1 percent of the popular vote have been omitted.

†Prior to the passage of the Twelfth Amendment in 1904, the electoral college voted for two presidential candidates; the runner-up became Vice President. Data from Historical Statistics of the United States, Colonial Times to 1957 (1961), pp. 682–683, and The World Almanac.

*Because of the death of Greeley, Democratic electors scattered their votes.

*Walter B. Jones received 1 electoral vote.

†Harry F. Byrd received 15 electoral votes.

‡Resigned August 9, 1974: Vice President Gerald R. Ford became President.

# PARTY CONTROL OF CONGRESS

| Congress | Years | Party and President | Senate DEM. | REP. | OTHER | House DEM. | REP. | OTHER |
|---|---|---|---|---|---|---|---|---|
| 57th | 1901–03 | R  T. Roosevelt | 29 | 56 | 3 | 153 | 198 | 5 |
| 58th | 1903–05 | R  T. Roosevelt | 32 | 58 | — | 178 | 207 | — |
| 59th | 1905–07 | R  T. Roosevelt | 32 | 58 | — | 136 | 250 | — |
| 60th | 1907–09 | R  T. Roosevelt | 29 | 61 | — | 164 | 222 | — |
| 61st | 1909–11 | R  Taft | 32 | 59 | — | 172 | 219 | — |
| 62d | 1911–13 | R  Taft | 42 | 49 | — | 228 | 162 | 1 |
| 63d | 1913–15 | D  Wilson | 51 | 44 | 1 | 290 | 127 | 18 |
| 64th | 1915–17 | D  Wilson | 56 | 39 | 1 | 230 | 193 | 8 |
| 65th | 1917–19 | D  Wilson | 53 | 42 | 1 | 200 | 216 | 9 |
| 66th | 1919–21 | D  Wilson | 48 | 48 | 1 | 191 | 237 | 7 |
| 67th | 1921–23 | R  Harding | 37 | 59 | — | 132 | 300 | 1 |
| 68th | 1923–25 | R  Coolidge | 43 | 51 | 2 | 207 | 225 | 3 |
| 69th | 1925–27 | R  Coolidge | 40 | 54 | 1 | 183 | 247 | 5 |
| 70th | 1927–29 | R  Coolidge | 47 | 48 | 1 | 195 | 237 | 3 |
| 71st | 1929–31 | R  Hoover | 39 | 56 | 1 | 163 | 267 | 1 |
| 72d | 1931–33 | R  Hoover | 47 | 48 | 1 | 216 | 218 | 1 |
| 73d | 1933–35 | D  F. Roosevelt | 59 | 36 | 1 | 313 | 117 | 5 |
| 74th | 1935–37 | D  F. Roosevelt | 69 | 25 | 2 | 322 | 103 | 10 |
| 75th | 1937–39 | D  F. Roosevelt | 75 | 17 | 4 | 333 | 89 | 13 |
| 76th | 1939–41 | D  F. Roosevelt | 69 | 23 | 4 | 262 | 169 | 4 |
| 77th | 1941–43 | D  F. Roosevelt | 66 | 28 | 2 | 267 | 162 | 6 |
| 78th | 1943–45 | D  F. Roosevelt | 57 | 38 | 1 | 222 | 209 | 4 |
| 79th | 1945–47 | D  Truman | 57 | 38 | 1 | 243 | 190 | 2 |
| 80th | 1947–49 | D  Truman | 45 | 51 | — | 188 | 246 | 1 |
| 81st | 1949–51 | D  Truman | 54 | 42 | — | 263 | 171 | 1 |
| 82d | 1951–53 | D  Truman | 48 | 47 | 1 | 234 | 199 | 2 |
| 83d | 1953–55 | R  Eisenhower | 47 | 48 | 1 | 213 | 221 | 1 |
| 84th | 1955–57 | R  Eisenhower | 48 | 47 | 1 | 232 | 203 | — |
| 85th | 1957–59 | R  Eisenhower | 49 | 47 | — | 234 | 201 | — |
| 86th | 1959–61 | R  Eisenhower | 64 | 34 | — | 283 | 154 | — |
| 87th | 1961–63 | D  Kennedy | 64 | 36 | — | 263 | 174 | — |
| 88th | 1963–65 | D { Kennedy / Johnson | 67 | 33 | — | 258 | 176 | — |
| 89th | 1965–67 | D  Johnson | 68 | 32 | — | 295 | 140 | — |
| 90th | 1967–69 | D  Johnson | 64 | 36 | — | 248 | 187 | — |
| 91st | 1969–71 | R  Nixon | 58 | 42 | — | 243 | 192 | — |
| 92d | 1971–73 | R  Nixon | 55 | 45 | — | 255 | 180 | — |
| 93d | 1973–75 | R { Nixon / Ford | 57 | 43 | — | 243 | 192 | — |
| 94th | 1975–77 | R  Ford | 61 | 38 | — | 291 | 144 | — |
| 95th | 1977–79 | D  Carter | 62 | 38 | — | 292 | 143 | — |
| 96th | 1979–81 | D  Carter | 59 | 41 | — | 277 | 158 | — |
| 97th | 1981–83 | R  Reagan | 47 | 53 | — | 243 | 192 | — |
| 98th | 1983–85 | R  Reagan | 46 | 54 | — | 269 | 166 | — |
| 99th | 1985–87 | R  Reagan | 47 | 53 | — | 253 | 182 | — |
| 100th | 1987–89 | R  Reagan | 55 | 45 | — | 258 | 177 | — |
| 101st | 1989–91 | R  Bush | 55 | 45 | — | 260 | 175 | — |
| 102d | 1991–93 | R  Bush | 57 | 43 | — | 267 | 167 | 1 |
| 103d | 1993–95 | D  Clinton | 59 | 43 | — | 258 | 176 | 1 |
| 104th | 1995–97 | D  Clinton | 46 | 54 | — | 204 | 230 | 1 |
| 105th | 1997–99 | D  Clinton | 45 | 55 | — | 207 | 227 | 1 |
| 106th | 1999–01 | D  Clinton | 45 | 55 | — | 211 | 223 | 1 |
| 107th | 2001–03 | R  Bush | 50 | 50 | — | 212 | 221 | 2 |
| 108th | 2003–05 | R  Bush | 49[a] | 51 | — | 206 | 228 | 1 |
| 109th | 2005–07 | R  Bush | 45[a] | 55 | — | 202 | 230 | 1 |
| 110th | 2007–09 | R  Bush | 51[b] | 49 | — | 230 | 205 | — |

[a]Including Vermont independent Jim Jeffords.
[b]Including Vermont independent Bernie Sanders and Connecticut independent Joe Lieberman.

# GLOSSARY

**ABM Treaty** Treaty in 1972 between the U.S. and the Soviet Union in which each side agreed not to build or deploy antiballistic missiles.

**abolition movement** Social movement before

**adjudication** Decision making by the federal bureaucracy as to whether or not an individual or organization has complied with or violated government laws and/or regulation.

**adversarial system** Method of decision making in which an impartial judge or jury or decision maker hears arguments and reviews evidence presented by opposite sides.

**advice and consent** The constitutional power of the U.S. Senate to reject or ratify (by a two-thirds vote) treaties made by the president.

**affirmative action** Any program, whether enacted by a government or by a private organization, whose goal is to overcome the results of past unequal treatment of minorities and/or women by giving members of these groups preferential treatment in admissions, hiring, promotions, or other aspects of life.

**affirmative racial gerrymandering** Drawing district boundary lines to maximize minority representation.

**agenda setting** Deciding what will be decided, defining the problems and issues to be addressed by decision makers.

**Alien Land bill** A 1913 law that prohibited aliens not eligible for citizenship from owning land.

**alternative dispute resolution (ADR)** Non-court-centered options for resolving disagreements, such as mediation and arbitration.

**amendment** Formal change in a bill, law, or constitution.

**amicus curiae** Literally, "friend of the court"; a person, private group or institution, or government agency that is not a party to a case but participates in the case (usually through submission of a brief) at the invitation of the court or on its own initiative.

**Anti-Federalists** Those who opposed the ratification of the U.S. Constitution and the creation of a strong national government.

**appeal** In general, requests that a higher court review cases decided at a lower level. In the Supreme Court, certain cases are designated as appeals under federal law; formally, these must be heard by the Court.

**appellate jurisdiction** Particular court's power to review a decision or action of a lower court.

**apportionment** The allocation of legislative seats to jurisdictions based on population. Seats in the U.S. House of Representatives are apportioned to the states on the basis of their population after every ten-year census.

**appropriations act** Congressional bill that provides money for programs authorized by Congress.

**assembly speaker** The presiding officer of the California state assembly.

**assessor** County officer whose principal duty is to determine the value of property within the county.

**Attorney General** The state's top legal officer.

**authoritarianism** Monopoly of political power by an individual or small group that otherwise allows people to go about their private lives as they wish.

**authorization** Act of Congress that establishes a government program and defines the amount of money it may spend.

**Bakke case** U.S. Supreme Court case challenging affirmative action.

**balanced budget** Government budget in which expenditures and revenues are equal, so that no deficit or surplus exists.

**ballistic missile defense (BMD)** Weapons systems capable of detecting, intercepting, and destroying missiles in flight.

**Bear Flag Rebellion** A revolt led by John C. Frémont against Mexican control of California in 1846.

**beliefs** Shared ideas about what is true.

**bicameral** Any legislative body that consists of two separate chambers or houses; in the United States, the Senate represents 50 state-wide voter constituencies, and the House of Representatives represents voters in 435 separate districts.

**Big Four** the founders of the Central Pacific Railroad Company: Collis P. Huntington, Mark Hopkins, Charles Crocker, and Leland Stanford.

**bill of attainder** Legislative act inflicting punishment without judicial trial; forbidden under Article I of the Constitution.

**Bill of Rights** Written guarantees of basic individual liberties; the first ten amendments to the U.S. Constitution.

**bipartisanship** Agreement by members of both the Democratic and the Republican parties.

**blanket primary** A primary election in which all voters can vote for any candidate, regardless of party affiliation.

**Board of Equalization** California body that makes rules, based on state laws, governing the collection and payment of property, sales, excise and other taxes.

**Bracero Program** A program granting temporary employment status to Mexicans working in the United States during World War II.

**briefs** Documents submitted by an attorney to a court, setting out the facts of the case and the legal arguments in support of the party represented by the attorney.

**budget maximization** Bureaucrats' tendencies to expand their agencies' budgets, staff, and authority.

**budget resolution** Congressional bill setting forth target budget figures for appropriations to various government departments and agencies.

**bureaucracy** Departments, agencies, bureaus, and offices that perform the functions of government.

**cabinet** The heads (secretaries) of the executive departments together with other top officials accorded cabinet rank by the president; only occasionally does it meet as a body to advise and support the president.

**California Gold Rush** The rapid influx of settlers sparked by the discovery of gold at Sutter's Mill on January 24, 1848.

**California Penal Code** The listing of all crimes defined by statutes.

**Californios** Mexican settlers of California.

**campaign strategy** Plan for a political campaign, usually including a theme, an attempt to define the opponent or the issues, and an effort to coordinate images and messages in news broadcasts and paid advertising.

**capitalism** Economic system asserting the individual's right to own private property and to buy, sell, rent, and trade that property in a free market.

**capture theory of regulation** Theory describing how some regulated industries come to benefit from government regulation and how some regulatory commissions come to represent the industries they are supposed to regulate rather than representing "the people."

**casework** Services performed by legislators or their staff on behalf of individual constituents.

**censure** Public reprimand for wrongdoing, given to a member standing in the chamber before Congress.

**centralized federalism** Model of federalism in which the national government assumes primary responsibility for determining national goals in all major policy areas and directs state and local government activity through conditions attached to money grants.

**chain of command** Hierarchical structure of authority in which command flows downward; typical of a bureaucracy.

**challengers** In politics, a reference to people running against incumbent officeholders.

**checks and balances** Constitutional provisions giving each branch of the national government certain checks over the actions of other branches.

**circuit courts** The twelve appellate courts that make up the middle level of the federal court system.

**city attorney** The legal adviser to the city council.

**city clerk** Official responsible for the preparation and maintenance of minutes, ordinances, resolutions, agreements, and other legal documents.

**city treasurer** Official whose chief responsibility is to audit and examine all investments made by authorized city personnel.

**civil cases** Noncriminal court proceedings in which a plaintiff sues a defendant for damages in payment for harm inflicted.

**class action suits** Cases initiated by parties acting on behalf of themselves and all others similarly situated.

**class conflict** Conflict between upper and lower social classes over wealth and power.

**class consciousness** Awareness of one's class position and a feeling of political solidarity with others within the same class in opposition to other classes.

**classical liberalism** Political philosophy asserting the worth and dignity of the individual and emphasizing the rational ability of human beings to determine their own destinies.

**clear and present danger doctrine** Standard used by the courts to determine whether speech may be restricted; only speech that creates a serious and immediate danger to society may be restricted.

**clemency powers** The right to pardon or commute the sentences of convicted persons.

**closed rule** Rule that forbids adding any amendments to a bill under consideration by the House.

**cloture** Vote to end debate—that is, to end a filibuster—which requires a three-fifths vote of the entire membership of the Senate.

**Cold War** Political, military, and ideological struggle between the United States and the Soviet Union following the end of World War II and ending with the collapse of the Soviet Union's communist government in 1991.

**collective security** Attempt to bring order to international relations by all nations joining together to guarantee each other's "territorial integrity" and "independence" against "external aggression."

**common market** Unified trade area in which all goods and services can be sold or exchanged free from customs or tariffs.

**communism** System of government in which a single totalitarian party controls all means of production and distribution of goods and services.

**compulsory referendum** A constitutional requirement that all debts and liabilities over $3 million and constitutional amendments that originate in the state legislature must be passed by a two-thirds vote of all the members elected to each house of the state legislature and approved by a majority of the voters during the next scheduled primary or general election.

**concurrent powers** Powers exercised by both the national government and state governments in the American federal system.

**concurring opinion** Opinion by a member of a court that agrees with the result reached by the court in the case but disagrees with or departs from the court's rationale for the decision.

**confederation** Constitutional arrangement whereby the national government is created by and relies on subnational governments for its authority.

**conference committee** Meeting between representatives of the House and Senate to reconcile differences over provisions of a bill passed by both houses.

**confirmation** The constitutionally required consent of the Senate to appointments of high-level executive officials by the president and appointments of federal judges.

**congressional hearings** Congressional committee sessions in which members listen to witnesses who provide information and opinions on matters of interest to the committee, including pending legislation.

**congressional investigation** Congressional committee hearings on alleged misdeeds or scandals.

**congressional session** Each Congress elected in November of even-numbered years meets the following January 3 and remains in session for two years. Since the first Congress to meet under the Constitution in 1789, Congresses have been numbered by session (for example, 107th Congress 2001–2003, 108th Congress 2003–2005, 109th Congress 2005–2007).

**conservatism** Belief in the value of free markets, limited government, and individual self-reliance in economic affairs, combined with a belief in the value of tradition, law, and morality in social affairs.

**constituency** The votes in a legislator's home district.

**constitution** The legal structure of a political system, establishing governmental bodies, granting their powers, determining how their members are selected, and prescribing the rules by which they make their decisions. Considered basic or fundamental, a constitution cannot be changed by ordinary acts of governmental bodies.

**constitutionalism** A government of laws, not people, operating on the principle that governmental power must be limited and government officials should be restrained in their exercise of power over individuals.

**Constitutional Revision Commission** Commission created in 1963 to revise and reform the California constitution.

**containment** Policy of preventing an enemy from expanding its boundaries and/or influence, specifically the U.S. foreign policy vis-à-vis the Soviet Union during the Cold War.

**contingency fees** Fees paid to attorneys to represent the plaintiff in a civil suit and receive in compensation an agreed-upon percentage of damages awarded (if any).

**continuing resolution** Congressional bill that authorizes government agencies to keep spending money for a specified period at the same level as in the previous fiscal year; passed when Congress is unable to enact final appropriations measures by October 1.

**contract cities** Incorporated or independent cities that contract with counties for the provision of major municipal services.

**controller** The state's chief financial officer.

**cooperative federalism** Model of federalism in which national, state, and local governments work together exercising common policy responsibilities.

*corpus delicti* The elements of a crime.

**council-manager model** Model of city government that emphasizes the political leadership and policymaking qualities of the council as a whole, while vesting administrative authority in a full-time professional manager.

**council of government (COG)** Council comprised of representatives of other governments in a defined region of the state.

**county administrator** Official responsible for providing the board of supervisors with reports and information and managing the day-to-day operations of county government.

**county board of supervisors** Board responsible for implementing the provisions of a county's charter.

**county clerk** Officer responsible for the public records of the county.

**county grand jury** In California, a jury that investigates public offenses committed or triable within the county.

**court of appeals** Court that has the power to consider or hear an appeal.

**covert action** Secret intelligence activity outside U.S. borders undertaken with specific authorization by the president, acknowledgment of U.S. sponsorship would defeat or compromise its purpose.

**criminal law** The area of law dealing with crime and the legal punishment of criminal offenses.

**cross-filing** A system that allowed a candidate to represent multiple parties.

**Cuban Missile Crisis** The 1962 confrontation between the Soviet Union and the U.S. over Soviet placement of nuclear missiles in Cuba.

**de facto segregation** Racial imbalances not directly caused by official actions but rather by residential patterns.

**defendants** Parties against whom a criminal or civil suit is brought.

**deferrals** Items on which a president wishes to postpone spending.

**deficit** Imbalance in the annual federal budget in which spending exceeds revenues.

**delegated, or enumerated, powers** Powers specifically mentioned in the Constitution as belonging to the national government.

**delegates** Accredited voting members of a party's national presidential nominating convention.

**democracy** Governing system in which the people govern themselves, from the Greek term meaning "rule by the many."

**democratic ideals** Individual dignity, equality before the law, widespread participation in public decisions, and public decisions by majority rule, with one person having one vote.

**deregulation** Lifting of government rules and bureaucratic supervision from business and professional activity.

**determinate sentence** The choices for punishment for a crime that can be imposed by a judge.

**deterrence** U.S. approach to deterring any nuclear attack from the Soviet Union by maintaining a second-strike capability.

**devolution** Passing down of responsibilities from the national government to the states.

**Dillon's Rule** Legal interpretation that local governments have only the powers specially delegated to them by state law.

**diplomatic recognition** Power of the president to grant "legitimacy" to or withhold it from a government of another nation (to declare or refuse to declare it "rightful").

**direct democracy** Governing system in which every person participates actively in every public decision, rather than delegating decision making to representatives.

**direct discrimination** Now illegal practice of differential pay for men versus women even when those individuals have equal qualifications and perform the same job.

**direct initiative** An initiative that allows voters to propose and enact a law or constitutional amendment without the intervention of the state legislature.

**direct primary elections** Elections in which voters choose the candidates who will compete in a subsequent general election.

**discharge petition** Petition signed by at least 218 House members to force a vote on a bill within a committee that opposes it.

**discretionary funds** Budgeted funds not earmarked for specific purposes but available to be spent in accordance with the best judgment of a bureaucrat.

**dissenting opinion** Opinion by a member of a court that disagrees with the result reached by the court in the case.

**district attorney** The principal public prosecutor in a county.

**district court** Primary trial court in Texas. It has jurisdiction over criminal felony cases and civil disputes.

**diversity** Term in higher education that refers to racial and ethnic representation among students and faculty.

**divided party government** One party controls the presidency while the other party controls one or both houses of Congress.

**division of labor** Division of work among many specialized workers in a bureaucracy.

**drafting a bill** Actual writing of a bill in legal language.

**drug court** An alternative criminal justice venue for drug law offenders.

**dual federalism** Early concept of federalism in which national and state powers were clearly distinguished and functionally separate.

**Earned Income Tax Credit (EITC)** Tax refunds in excess of tax payments for low-income workers.

**economic cycles** Fluctuations in real GDP growth followed by contraction.

**Electoral College** The 538 presidential electors apportioned among the states according to their congressional representation (plus 3 for the District of Columbia) whose votes officially elect the president and vice president of the United States.

**elitism** Political system in which power is concentrated in the hands of a relatively small group of individuals or institutions.

**Emancipation Proclamation** Lincoln's 1862 Civil War declaration that all slaves residing in rebel states were free. It did not abolish all slavery; that would be done by the Thirteenth Amendment.

**end of history** The collapse of communism and the worldwide movement toward free markets and political democracy.

**entitlements** Any social welfare program for which there are eligibility requirements, whether financial or contributory.

**enumerated powers** Powers specifically mentioned in the Constitution as belonging to the national government.

**Equal Rights Amendment (ERA)** Proposed amendment to the Constitution guaranteeing that equal rights under the law shall not be denied or abridged on account of sex. Passed by Congress in 1972, the amendment failed to win ratification by three of the necessary three-fourths of the states.

**equality of opportunity** Elimination of artificial barriers to success in life and the opportunity for everyone to strive for success.

**equality of results** Equal sharing of income and material goods regardless of one's efforts in life.

**equal-time rule** Federal Communications Commission (FCC) requirement that broadcasters who sell time to any political candidate must make equal time available to opposing candidates at the same price.

**excise tax** A sales tax imposed only on specific goods.

**executive branch** Branch of government responsible for carrying out laws.

**executive budget plan** The spending plan for the state of California that the governor must submit to the state legislature by January 10 each year.

**Executive Order 9066** President Franklin Roosevelt's 1942 order that resulted in the relocation and internment of Japanese legal aliens and American citizens of Japanese descent.

**ex post facto law** Retroactive criminal law that works against the accused; forbidden under Article I of the Constitution.

**exclusionary rule** Rule of law that evidence found in an illegal search or resulting from an illegally obtained confession may not be admitted at trial.

**executive agreement** Agreement with another nation signed by the president of the United States but less formal (and hence potentially less binding) than a treaty because it does not require Senate confirmation.

**executive order** Formal regulation governing executive branch operations issued by the president.

**executive privilege** Right of a president to withhold from other branches of government confidential communications within the executive branch; although posited by presidents, it has been upheld by the Supreme Court only in limited situations.

**externalities** Costs imposed on people who are not direct participants in an activity.

**extraordinary session** A special session of the state legislature called by the governor for a specific purpose.

**extremism** Rejection of democratic politics and the assertion of the supremacy of the "people" over laws, institutions, and individual rights.

**Family Assistance** Public assistance program that provides monies to the states for their use in helping needy families with children.

**fascism** Political ideology in which the state and/or race is assumed to be supreme over individuals.

**Federal Election Commission (FEC)** Agency charged with enforcing federal election laws and disbursing public presidential campaign funds.

**federalism** A constitutional arrangement whereby power is divided between national and subnational governments, each of which enforces its own laws directly on its citizens and neither of which can alter the arrangement without the consent of the other.

**"feeding frenzy"** Intense media coverage of a scandal or event that blocks out most other news.

**felony** A crime for which a person may be sentenced to imprisonment in the state prison or to death.

**filibuster** Delaying tactic by a senator or group of senators, using the Senate's unlimited debate rule to prevent a vote on a bill.

**first reading** Introduction of a bill in the house or the senate and its referral to a committee by the presiding officer.

**fiscal year** Yearly government accounting period, not necessarily the same as the calendar year. The federal government's fiscal year begins October 1 and ends September 30.

**focus group** In a political context, a small number of people brought together in a comfortable setting to discuss and respond to themes and issues, allowing campaign managers to develop and analyze strategies.

**Food Stamp Program** Public assistance program that provides low-income households with coupons redeemable for enough food to provide a minimal nutritious diet.

**Franchise Tax Board** The board that sets tax rates for banks and financial institutions in California.

**franking privilege** Free use of the U.S. mails granted to members of Congress to promote communication with constituents.

**Free Exercise Clause** Clause in the First Amendment to the Constitution that prohibits government from restricting religious beliefs and practices.

**free market** Free competition for voluntary exchange among individuals, firms, and corporations.

**free-riders** People who do not belong to an organization or pay dues, yet nevertheless benefit from its activities.

**free trade** A policy of reducing or eliminating tariffs and quotas on imports to stimulate international trade.

**freedom of expression** Collectively, the First Amendment rights to free speech, press, and assembly.

**front-end strategy** Presidential political campaign strategy in which a candidate focuses on winning early primaries to build momentum.

**front loading** The scheduling of presidential primary elections early in the year.

**general election** An election in which candidates compete directly for election to a given office.

**general fund** The pool of money used to finance the California state government.

**general law** A standard list of the duties, obligations, offices, and structure of county government.

**general obligation bonds** State debt that is backed by the "full faith and credit of the state."

**gerrymandering** Drawing district boundary lines for political advantage.

**glass ceiling** "Invisible" barriers to women rising to the highest positions in corporations and the professions.

**government** Organization extending to the whole society that can legitimately use force to carry out its decisions.

**governor** Supreme executive of a state vested with the power to ensure that the state's laws are carried out.

**grand jury** Jury charged only with determining whether sufficient evidence exists to support indictment of an individual on a felony charge; the grand jury's decision to indict does not represent a conviction.

**Grange** A farmers' political movement founded in 1867.

**grants-in-aid** Payments of funds from the national government to state or local governments or from a state government to local governments for specific purposes.

**gridlock** Political stalemate between the executive and legislative branches arising when one branch is controlled by one major political party and the other branch by the other party.

**gross domestic product (GDP)** Measure of economic performance in terms of the nation's total production of goods and services for a single year, valued in terms of market prices.

**health maintenance organizations (HMOs)** Health care provider groups that provide a stipulated list of services to patients for a fixed fee that is usually substantially lower than such care would otherwise cost.

**Help America Vote Act** Federal law mandating certain measures to modernize voting procedures.

**home rule** Power of a country or a local government to pass laws affecting local affairs, so long as those laws do not conflict with state or federal laws.

**home style** Activities of Congress members specifically directed at their home constituencies.

**honeymoon period** Early months of a president's term in which his popularity with the public and influence with the Congress are generally high.

**horse-race coverage** Media coverage of electoral campaigns that concentrates on who is ahead and who is behind, and neglects the issues at stake.

**ideology** Consistent and integrated system of ideas, values, and beliefs.

**impeachment** Equivalent of a criminal charge against an elected official; removal of the impeached official from office depends on the outcome of a trial.

**impersonality** Treatment of all persons within a bureaucracy on the basis of "merit" and of all "clients" served by the bureaucracy equally according to rules.

**implementation** Development by the federal bureaucracy of procedures and activities to carry out policies legislated by Congress; it includes regulation as well as adjudication.

**implied powers** Powers not mentioned specifically in the Constitution as belonging to Congress but inferred as necessary and proper for carrying out the enumerated powers.

**impoundment** Refusal by a president to spend monies appropriated by Congress; outlawed except with congressional consent by the Budget and Impoundment Control Act of 1974.

**incidence** Actual bearer of a tax burden.

**income transfers** Government transfers of income from taxpayers to persons regarded as deserving.

**incorporation** In constitutional law, the application of almost all of the Bill of Rights to the states and all of their subdivision through the Fourteenth Amendment.

**incremental budgeting** Method of budgeting that focuses on requested increases in funding for existing programs, accepting as legitimate their previous year's expenditures.

**incumbent** Candidate currently in office seeking reelection.

**incumbent gerrymandering** Drawing legislative district boundaries to advantage incumbent legislators.

**independent counsel ("special prosecutor")** A prosecutor appointed by a federal court to pursue charges against a president or other high official. This position was allowed to lapse by Congress in 1999 after many controversial investigations by these prosecutors.

**individual income tax** Taxes on individuals' wages and other earned income, the primary source of revenue for the U.S. federal government.

**information** Document formally charging a person with a misdemeanor.

**information overload** Situation in which individuals are subjected to so many communications that they cannot make sense of them.

**infraction** Any public offense punishable by a fine.

**intergovernmental relations** Network of political, financial, and administrative relationships between units of the federal government and those of state and local governments.

**international trade** The buying and selling of goods and services between individuals or firms located in different countries.

**issue ads** Ads that advocate policy positions rather than explicitly supporting or opposing particular candidates.

**Jim Crow** Second-class-citizen status conferred on blacks by Southern segregation laws; derived from a nineteenth-century song-and-dance act (usually performed by a white man in blackface) that stereotyped blacks.

**joint committees** Committees that bring together equal numbers of legislators from both chambers to address specific issues and policy areas.

**joint rules** Guidelines for cooperation between the two chambers of the legislature.

**judicial activism** Making of new law through judicial interpretations of the Constitution.

**Judicial Council** The body that governs California's courts.

**judicial review** Power of the courts, especially the Supreme Court, to declare laws of Congress, laws of the states, and actions of the president unconstitutional and invalid.

**judicial self-restraint** Self-imposed limitation on judicial power by judges deferring to the policy judgments of elected branches of government.

**"juice" bills** Bills written to benefit a particular group, usually engaged in business.

**jurisdiction** Power of a court to hear a case in question.

**Korean War** Communist North Korea invaded non-Communist South Korea in June, 1950, causing President Harry S Truman to intervene militarily, with U.N. support. General Douglas MacArthur defeated the North Koreans, but with China's entry into the war, a stalemate resulted. An armistice was signed in 1953, with Korea divided along nearly original lines.

**laboratories of democracy** A reference to the ability of states to experiment and innovate in public policy.

**left** A reference to the liberal, progressive, and/or socialist side of the political spectrum.

**Legislative Analyst's Office (LAO)** The office responsible for analyzing the California state budget and making recommendations to the state legislature regarding the fiscal efficiency of state government.

**legitimacy** Widespread acceptance of something as necessary, rightful, and legally binding.

**Lemon test** To be constitutional, a law must have a secular purpose; its primary effect must neither advance nor inhibit religion; and it must not foster excessive government entanglement with religion.

**Leninism** The theories of Vladimir Lenin, among them that advanced capitalist countries turned toward war and colonialism to make their own workers relatively prosperous.

**libel** Writings that are false and malicious and are intended to damage an individual.

**liberalism** Belief in the value of strong government to provide economic security and protection for civil rights, combined with a belief in personal freedom from government intervention in social conduct.

**libertarian** Opposing government intervention in both economic and social affairs, and favoring minimal government in all sectors of society.

**lieutenant governor** The official who serves as acting governor when the governor is unable to carry out his or her duties.

**limited government** Principle that government power over the individual is limited, that there are some personal liberties that even a majority cannot regulate, and that government itself is restrained by law.

**line-item veto** Power of the chief executive to reject some portions of a bill without rejecting all of it.

**line-veto power** The power to veto individual items in a larger law.

**litmus test** In political terms, a person's stand on a key issue that determines whether he or she will be appointed to public office or supported in electoral campaigns.

**lobbyist** Person working to influence government policies and actions.

**local agency formation commission (LAFCO)** A countywide commission that conducts studies and public hearings to determine the feasibility of establishing a new city.

**logrolling** Bargaining for agreement among legislators to support each other's favorite bills, especially projects that primarily benefit individual members and their constituents.

**majority leader** In the House, the majority-party leader and second in command to the Speaker; in the Senate, the leader of the majority party.

**majority opinion** Opinion in a case that is subscribed to by a majority of the judges who participated in the decision.

**malapportionment** Unequal numbers of people in legislative districts resulting in inequality of voter representation.

**managed care** Programs designed to keep health care costs down by the establishment of strict guidelines regarding when and what diagnostic and therapeutic procedures should be administered to patients under various circumstances.

**Manifest Destiny** The belief that the United States had a divinely inspired mission to span the continent of North America.

**mandate** Perception of popular support for a program or policy based on the margin of electoral victory won by a candidate who proposed it during a campaign; direct federal orders to state and local governments requiring them to perform a service or to obey federal laws in the performance of their functions.

**mandatory spending** Spending for program committments made by past congresses.

**markup** Line-by-line revision of a bill in committee by editing each phrase and word.

**Marshall Plan** U.S. program to rebuild the nations of Western Europe in the aftermath of World War II in order to render them less susceptible to communist influence and takeover.

**Marxism** The theories of Karl Marx, among them that capitalists oppress workers and that worldwide revolution and the emergence of a classless society are inevitable.

**mass media** All means of communication with the general public, including television, newspapers, magazines, radio, books, recordings, motion pictures, and the Internet.

**May revise** A revised projection of California's financial picture conducted by the head of the State Department of Finance and economists from private industry.

**means-tested spending** Spending for benefits that is distributed on the basis of the recipient's income.

**Medicaid** Public assistance program that provides health care to the poor.

**Medicare** Social insurance program that provides health care insurance to elderly and disabled people.

**Mello-Ross Community Facilities District** A financing tool that local governments can use to levy special taxes or assessments for designated community improvements, such as freeway interchanges, library services, or recreation programs.

**merit system** Selection of employees for government agencies on the basis of competence, with no consideration of an individual's political stance and/or power.

**Mestizo** The offspring of a European and an American Indian.

**metro government** Local government in which city and county governments consolidate to avoid duplication of public services.

**minority leader** In both the House and Senate, the leader of the opposition party.

**Miranda warning** Requirement that persons arrested be informed of their rights immediately after arrest.

**misdemeanor** A crime for which a person may be imprisoned in a county jail for usually a year or less and/or fined.

**mobilize** In politics, to activate supporters to work for candidates and turn out on Election Day.

**monetary policy** Economic policies involving the money supply, interest rates, and banking activity.

**"Motor Voter Act"** Federal mandate that states offer voter registration at driver's licensing and welfare offices.

**muckraking** Journalistic exposés of corruption, wrongdoing, or mismanagement in government, business, and other institutions of society.

**municipal advisory council (MAC)** A council formed by the citizens of unincorporated areas to provide representation in matters affecting their communities.

**name recognition** Public awareness of a candidate—whether they even know his or her name.

**National Security Council (NSC)** "Inner cabinet" that advises the president and coordinates foreign, defense, and intelligence activities.

**National Supremacy Clause** Clause in Article VI of the U.S. Constitution declaring the constitution and laws of the national government "the supreme law of the land" superior to the constitutions and laws of the states.

**National Voter Registration Act** Law designed to make it easier for voters to register to vote and to maintain their registration.

**nationalism** Belief that shared cultural, historical, linguistic, and social characteristics of a people justify the creation of a government encompassing all of them, the resulting nation-state should be independent and legally equal to all other nation-states.

**Necessary and Proper Clause** Clause in Article I, Section 8, of the U.S. Constitution granting Congress the power to enact all laws that are "necessary and proper" for carrying out those responsibilities specifically delegated to it. Also referred to as the Implied Powers Clause.

**negative campaigning** Speeches, commercials, or advertising attacking a political opponent during a campaign.

**New Deal** Policies of President Franklin D. Roosevelt during the depression of the 1930s that helped form a Democratic Party coalition of urban working-class, ethnic, Catholic, Jewish, poor, and Southern voters.

**new federalism** Attempts to return power and responsibility to the states and reduce the role of the national government in domestic affairs.

**newsmaking** Deciding what events, topics, presentations, and issues will be given coverage in the news.

**No Child Left Behind Act (NCLB)** Federal law imposing educational reform throughout the country by requiring that all schools adopt student proficiency standards.

**nonpartisan election** An election in which candidates are not identified by party affiliation.

**nonviolent direct action** Strategy used by civil rights leaders such as Martin Luther King Jr., in which protesters break "unjust" laws openly but in a "loving" fashion in order to bring the injustices of such laws to public attention.

**North Atlantic Treaty Organization (NATO)** Mutual-security agreement and joint military command uniting the nations of Western Europe, initially formed to resist Soviet expansionism.

**obligational authority** Feature of some appropriations acts by which an agency is empowered to enter into contracts that will require the government to make payments beyond the fiscal year in question.

**open rule** Rule that permits unlimited amendments to a bill under consideration by the House.

**open seat** Seat in a legislature for which no incumbent is running for reelection.

**original intent** Judicial philosophy under which judges attempt to apply the values of the Founders to current issues.

**original jurisdiction** Refers to a particular court's power to serve as the place where a given case is initially argued and decided.

**outlays** Actual dollar amounts to be spent by the federal government in a fiscal year.

**override** Voting in Congress to enact legislation vetoed by the president; requires a two-thirds vote in both the House and Senate.

**oversight** Congressional monitoring of the activities of executive branch agencies to determine if the laws are being faithfully executed.

**oversight function** The responsibility for supervising the implementation of all laws and the government officials charged with implementing them.

**packing** Redistricting in which partisan voters are concentrated in a single district, "wasting" their majority vote and allowing the opposition to win by modest majorities in other districts.

**paradox of democracy** Potential for conflict between individual freedom and majority rule.

**parole** Early release of an inmate from prison, subject to certain conditions.

**partial preemption** Federal government's assumption of some regulatory powers in a particular field, with the stipulation that a state law on the same subject as a federal law is valid if it does not conflict with the federal law in the same area.

**partisan election** An election in which candidates are identified by party affiliation.

**party caucus** Legislators from the same party who meet to establish group goals, policies, and strategies.

**party unity** Percentage of Democrats and Republicans who stick with their party on party votes.

**party vote** Majority of Democrats voting in opposition to a majority of Republicans.

**passport** Evidence of U.S. citizenship, allowing people to travel abroad and reenter the United States.

**petit (regular) jury** Panel of citizens that hears evidence in a civil lawsuit or a criminal prosecution and decides the outcome by issuing a verdict.

**petition referendum** A procedure that allows voters to request that all or part of a law be submitted to the voters for approval.

**photo ops** Staged opportunities for the media to photograph the candidate in a favorable setting.

**plaintiffs** Parties initiating suits and claiming damages. In criminal cases, the state acts as plaintiff on behalf of an injured society and requests fines and/or imprisonment as damages. In civil suits, the plaintiff is the injured party and seeks monetary damages.

**planning commission** Commission responsible for advising the city council on the adoption and administration of zoning laws and building regulations.

**plea bargaining** Practice of allowing defendants to plead guilty to lesser crimes than those with which they were originally charged in return for reduced sentences.

**plea bargain** A formal agreement between the district attorney's office and a defendant to forgo a trial in exchange for a guilty plea.

**plural executive** The group of independently elected officials responsible for carrying out the laws of a state.

**pluralism** Theory that democracy can be achieved through competition among multiple organized groups and that individuals can participate in politics through group memberships and elections.

**pocket veto** Effective veto of a bill when Congress adjourns within ten days of passing it and the president fails to sign it.

**political action committees (PACs)** Organizations that solicit and receive campaign contributions from corporations, unions, trade associations, and ideological and issue-oriented groups, and their members, then distribute these funds to political candidates.

**political culture** Widely shared views about who should govern, for what ends, and by what means.

**political equality** Belief that the law should apply equally to all and that every person's vote counts equally.

**political parties** Organizations that seek to achieve power by winning public office.

**political science** The study of politics: who governs, for what ends, and by what means.

**politically correct (PC)** Repression of attitudes, speech, and writings that are deemed racist, sexist, homophobic (anti-homosexual), or otherwise "insensitive."

**politics** Deciding who gets what, when, and how.

**poll taxes** Taxes imposed as a prerequisite to voting; prohibited by the Twenty-fourth Amendment.

**pork barreling** Legislation designed to make government benefits, including jobs and projects used as political patronage, flow to a particular district or state.

**poverty line** Official standard regarding what level of annual cash income is sufficient to maintain a "decent standard of living"; those with incomes below this level are eligible for most public assistance programs.

**power of the purse** Congress's exclusive, constitutional power to authorize expenditures by all agencies of the federal government.

**precedent** Legal principle that previous decisions should determine the outcome of current cases; the basis for stability in law.

**preemption** Total or partial federal assumption of power in a particular field, restricting the authority of the states.

**preferred position** Refers to the tendency of the courts to give preference to the First Amendment rights to speech, press, and assembly when faced with conflicts.

**preferred provider organizations (PPOs)** Groups of hospitals and physicians who have joined together to offer their services to private insurers at a discount.

**presidios** Military outposts during the period of Spanish colonial rule of California.

**prior restraint** Government actions to restrict publication of a magazine, newspaper, or books on grounds of libel, obscenity, or other legal violations prior to actual publication of the work.

**probate law** The area of law governing cases that pertain to the personal affairs of an individual.

**program budgeting** Identifying items in a budget according to the functions and programs they are to be spent on.

**progressive taxation** System of taxation in which higher income groups pay a larger percentage of their incomes in taxes than do lower income groups.

**proportional (flat) taxation** System of taxation in which all income groups pay the same percentage of their income in taxes.

**Proposition 13** The 1978 law that severely cut property taxes in California.

**Proposition 36** Initiative that created diversion program for individuals convicted of offenses.

**Proposition 98** California law requiring that 40 percent of the state general fund be reserved for education.

**Proposition 103** California law imposing the regulation of insurance rates and creating the elected position of state insurance commissioner.

**Proposition 140** Law that established term limits and cut 60 percent of the LAO budget.

**Proposition 140** A constitutional initiative limiting the terms of office for California state legislators.

**Proposition 184** The "three strikes" law imposing a 25-years-to-life imprisonment for a third felony offense.

**Proposition 220** A California constitutional amendment that consolidated superior and municipal courts into a single superior court with original jurisdiction over all cases that enter the court system.

**protectionism** A policy of high tariffs and quotas on imports to protect domestic industries.

**public goods** Goods and services that cannot readily be provided by markets, either because they are too expensive for a single individual to buy or because if one person bought them, everyone else would use them without paying.

**pueblos** Centers of trade and Spanish civilization during the period of Spanish colonial rule of California.

**radicalism** Advocacy of immediate and drastic changes in society, including the complete restructuring of institutions, values, and beliefs. Radicals may exist on either the extreme left or extreme right.

**ratification** Power of a legislature to approve or reject decisions made by other bodies. State legislators or state conventions must ratify constitutional amendments submitted by Congress. The U.S. Senate must ratify treaties made by the president.

**reapportionment** Redistribution of representation in a legislative body.

**recall** A procedure by which voters can remove an elected official from office before to the end of the official's term.

**recession** Decline in the general level of economic activity.

**recidivism rate** The percentage of inmates who are convicted of another crime after their release from prison.

**Reconstruction** The Post–Civil war period when the Southern states were occupied by federal troops and newly freed African Americans occupied many political offices and exercised civil rights.

**redistricting** Drawing new boundaries for election districts following each ten-year census.

**referenda** Proposed laws or constitutional amendments submitted to the voters for their direct approval or rejection, found in state constitutions but not in the U.S. Constitution.

**referendum** A process by which voters can demand the review and approval of a particular legislative action by the voters.

**regional security** Attempt to bring order to international relations during the Cold War by creating regional alliances between a superpower and nations of a particular region.

**regressive taxation** System of taxation in which lower income groups pay a larger percentage of their incomes in taxes than do higher income groups.

**regulation** Development by the federal bureaucracy of formal rules for implementing legislation.

**remedies and reliefs** Orders of a court to correct a wrong, including a violation of the Constitution.

**representational federalism** Assertion that no constitutional division of powers exists between the nation and the states but the states retain their constitutional role merely by selecting the president and members of Congress.

**representative democracy** Governing system in which public decision making is delegated to representatives of the people chosen by popular vote in free, open, and periodic elections.

**Republican Party** One of the two main parties in American politics, it traces its origins to the antislavery and nationalist forces that united in the 1850s and nominated Abraham Lincoln for president in 1860.

**reserved powers** Powers not granted to the national government or specifically denied to the states in the Constitution that are recognized by the Tenth Amendment as belonging to the state governments. This guarantee, known as the Reserved Powers Clause, embodies the principle of American federalism.

**resolutions** Formal statements explaining a decision or expressing an opinion.

**restricted rule** Rule that allows specified amendments to be added to a bill under consideration by the House.

**retail politics** Direct candidate contact with individual voters.

**retrospective voting** Voting for or against a candidate or party on the basis of past performance in office.

**rider** Amendment to a bill that is not germane to the bill's purposes.

**right** A reference to the conservative, traditional, anticommunist side of the political spectrum.

**roll-call vote** Vote of the full House or Senate on which all members' individual votes are recorded and made public.

**rule** Stipulation attached to a bill in the House of Representatives that governs its consideration on the floor, including when and for how long it can be debated and how many (if any) amendments may be appended to it.

**rule of four** At least four justices must agree to hear an appeal (writ of certiorari) from a lower court in order to get a case before the Supreme Court.

**rules committees** Committees charged with the administration of the legislature and defining the rules of its operation.

**safe seat** Legislative district in which the incumbent regularly wins by a large margin of the vote.

**salient issues** Issues about which most people have an opinion.

**SALT I** First arms limitation treaty between the United States and the Soviet Union, signed in 1972, limiting the total number of offensive nuclear missiles; it included the ABM Treaty that reflected the theory that the population centers of both nations should be left undefended.

**SALT II** Lengthy and complicated treaty between the United States and the Soviet Union, agreed to in 1979 but never ratified by the U.S. Senate, that set limits on all types of strategic nuclear launch vehicles.

**search warrant** Court order permitting law-enforcement officials to search a location in order to seize evidence of a crime; issued only for a specified location, in connection with a specific investigation, and on submission of proof that "probable cause" exists to warrant such a search.

**second-strike capability** Ability of a nation's forces to survive a surprise nuclear attack by the enemy and then to retaliate effectively.

**secretary of state** California's administrator of elections and supervisor of state records and archives.

**secular** In politics, a reference to opposition to religious practices and symbols in public life.

**select committees** Temporary committees formed to conduct investigations of issues or problems that are either not specifically related to a standing committee or of special interest to a legislator.

**selective perception** Mentally screening out information or opinions with which one disagrees.

**senatorial courtesy** Custom of the U.S. Senate with regard to presidential nominations to the judiciary to defer to the judgment of senators from the president's party from the same state as the nominee.

**seniority system** Custom whereby the member of Congress who has served the longest on the majority side of a committee becomes its chair and the member who has served the longest on the minority side becomes its ranking member.

**separate but equal** Ruling of the Supreme Court in the case of *Plessy v. Ferguson* (1896) to the effect that segregated facilities were legal as long as the facilities were equal.

**separation of powers** Constitutional division of powers among the three branches of the national government—legislative, executive, and judicial.

**set-aside program** Program in which a specified number or percentage of contracts must go to designated minorities.

**sheriff** County officer whose chief duty is to enforce California state law and county ordinances, usually outside of incorporated cities.

**Sierra Nevada** The inland mountain range that makes up half of California's total land area.

**single-subject rule** Ballot initiatives may contain only one subject of policy.

**slander** Oral statements that are false and malicious and are intended to damage an individual.

**social contract** Idea that government originates as an implied contract among individuals who agree to obey laws in exchange for protection of their rights.

**social insurance programs** Social welfare programs to which beneficiaries have made contributions so that they are entitled to benefits regardless of their personal wealth.

**social mobility** Extent to which people move upward or downward in income and status over a lifetime or generations.

**Social Security** Social insurance program composed of the Old Age and Survivors Insurance program, which pays benefits to retired workers who have paid into the program and their dependents and survivors, and the Disability Insurance program, which pays benefits to disabled workers and their families.

**socialism** System of government involving collective or government ownership of economic enterprise, with the goal being equality of results, not merely equality of opportunity.

**socialization** The learning of a culture and its values.

**solicitor general** Attorney in the Department of Justice who represents the U.S. government before the Supreme Court and any other courts.

**sound bites** Concise and catchy phrases that attract media coverage.

**sovereign immunity** Legal doctrine that individuals can sue the government only with the government's consent.

**Soviet Union** The Union of Soviet Socialist Republics (USSR) consisting of Russia and its bordering lands and ruled by the communist regime in Moscow, officially dissolved in 1991.

**Speaker of the House** Presiding officer of the House of Representatives.

**special district** Legal district formed to meet a specific need in an area or community.

**special election** An election called to address a specific issue prior to the next regularly scheduled election.

**spin doctor** Practitioner of the art of spin control, or manipulation of media reporting to favor one's own candidate.

**splinter party** Third party formed by a dissatisfied faction of a major party.

**splintering** Redistricting in which a strong minority is divided up and diluted to prevent it from electing a representative.

**spoils system** Selection of employees for government agencies on the basis of party loyalty, electoral support, and political influence.

**standard partial preemption** Form of partial preemption in which the states are permitted to regulate activities already regulated by the federal government if the state regulatory standards are at least as stringent as the federal government's.

**standing** Requirement that the party who files a lawsuit have a legal stake in the outcome.

**standing committee** Permanent committee of the House or Senate that deals with matters within a specified subject area.

**standing committees** The permanent committees of the legislature; also known as *policy committees*.

**standing rules** Rules that ensure that the legislature operates in an efficient and civil manner.

**stare decisis** Judicial precept that the issue has already been decided in earlier cases and the earlier decision need only be applied in the specific case before the bench; the rule in most cases, it comes from the Latin for "the decision stands."

**START I** First treaty between the United States and the Soviet Union that actually reduced the strategic nuclear arms of the superpowers, signed in 1991.

**START II** A treaty between the United States and Russia eliminating all multiwarhead land missiles and reducing nuclear weapons stockpiles; signed in 2003.

**state insurance commissioner** Official responsible for oversight of the insurance industry and enforcement of insurance regulations in California.

**state treasurer** The state's chief banker and financial consultant.

**statutory laws** Laws made by act of Congress or the state legislatures, as opposed to constitutional law.

**strict scrutiny** Supreme Court holding that race-based actions by government can be done only to remedy past discrimination or to further a "compelling" interest and must be "narrowly tailored" to minimize effects on the rights of others.

**strong mayor–council model** Model of city government that gives the mayor direct authority over the city government, including the city manager.

**structural budget gap** A long-term excess of state expenditures over state revenues.

**subcommittees** Specialized committees within standing committees; subcommittee recommendations must be approved by the full standing committee before submission to the floor.

**subcultures** Variations on the prevailing values and beliefs in a society.

**subpoenas** Court orders requiring people to testify in court or before grand juries or to produce certain documents.

**suffrage** Legal right to vote.

**Sullivan rule** Court guideline that false and malicious statements regarding public officials are protected by the First Amendment unless it can be proven they were known to be false at the time they were made or were made with "reckless disregard" for their truth or falsehood.

**superdelegates** Delegates to the Democratic Party national convention selected because of their position in the government or the party and not pledged to any candidate.

**superintendent of public instruction** The elected official responsible for matters of public education in California.

**superior courts** Entry point for the enforcement of California law and the settlement of conflicts or disagreements.

**superpowers** Refers to the United States and the Soviet Union after World War II, when these two nations dominated international politics.

**Supplemental Security Income (SSI)** Public assistance program that provides monthly cash payments to the needy elderly (sixty-five or older), blind, and disabled.

**supreme court** The highest court in a state, the decisions of which are binding on all lower courts.

**survey research** Gathering of information about public opinion by questioning a representative sample of the population.

**swing states** States that are not considered to be firmly in the Democratic or Republican column.

**symbolic speech** Actions other than speech itself but protected by the First Amendment because they constitute political expression.

**tag** Rule that allows an individual senator to postpone a committee hearing on any bill for at least forty-eight hours, a delay that can be fatal to a bill during the closing days of a legislative session.

**takings clause** The Fifth Amendment's prohibition against government taking of private property without just compensation.

**tariff** Tax imposed on imported products (also called a customs duty).

**tax avoidance** Taking advantage of exemptions, exclusions, deductions, and special treatments in tax laws (legal).

**tax evasion** Hiding income and/or falsely claiming exemptions, deductions, and special treatments (illegal).

**tax expenditures** Revenues lost to the federal government because of exemptions, exclusions, deductions, and special-treatment provisions in tax laws.

**taxes** Compulsory payments to the government.

**television malaise** Generalized feelings of distrust, cynicism, and powerlessness stemming from television's emphasis on the negative aspects of American life.

**Temporary Assistance to Needy Families** Welfare reform program replacing federal cash entitlement with grants to the states for welfare recipients.

**terrorism** Title 22 of the U.S. Code, Section 2656 (d): "The term 'terrorism' means premeditated, politically motivated violence perpetrated against noncombatant targets by subnational groups or clandestine agents, usually intended to influence an audience."

**Texas court of criminal appeals** Nine-member court with final appellate jurisdiction over criminal cases.

**Texas supreme court** Nine-member court with final appellate jurisdiction over civil lawsuits.

**"Third House"** Collective term for lobbyists and special-interest representatives.

**third party** Political party that challenges the two major parties in an election.

**third reading** Final presentation of a bill before the full house or senate.

**ticket splitter** Person who votes for candidates of different parties for different offices in a general election.

**Title IX** A provision in the Federal Education Act forbidding discrimination against women in college athletic programs.

**tort law** The area of law dealing with any wrongdoing that results in legal action for damages.

**total preemption** Federal government's assumption of all regulatory powers in a particular field.

**totalitarianism** Rule by an elite that exercises unlimited power over individuals in all aspects of life.

**transcontinental railroad** railroad completed in 1869 that linked the east and west coasts of North America.

**Truman Doctrine** U.S. foreign policy, first articulated by President Harry S Truman, that pledged the United States to "support free peoples who are resisting attempted subjugation by armed minorities or by outside pressures."

**trustees** Legislators who feel obligated to use their own best judgment in decision making.

**turnover** Replacement of members of Congress by retirement or resignation, by reapportionment, or (more rarely) by electoral defeat, usually expressed as a percentage of members newly elected.

**unanimous consent agreement** Negotiated by the majority and minority leaders of the Senate, it specifies when a bill will be taken up on the floor, what amendments will be considered, and when a vote will be taken.

**underclass** People who have remained poor and dependent on welfare over a prolonged period of time.

**unemployment compensation** Social insurance program that temporarily replaces part of the wages of workers who have lost their jobs.

**unemployment rate** Percentage of the civilian labor force who are not working but who are looking for work or waiting to return to or to begin a job.

**unfunded mandates** Mandates that impose costs on state and local governments (and private industry) without reimbursement from the federal government.

**unitary system** Constitutional arrangement whereby authority rests with the national government; subnational governments have only those powers given to them by the national government.

**U.S. Solicitor General** The U.S. government's chief legal council, presenting the government's arguments in cases in which it is a party or in which it has an interest.

**values** Shared ideas about what is good and desirable.

**veto** Rejection of a legislative act by the executive branch; in the U.S. federal government, overriding of a veto requires a two-thirds majority in both houses of Congress.

**Vietnam War** War between non-Communist South Vietnam and Communist North Vietnam from 1956 to 1975, with increasing U.S. involvement, ending with U.S. withdrawal in 1973 and Communist victory in 1975. The war became unpopular in the U.S. after 1968 and caused President Johnson not to run for a second term. More than 58,000 Americans died in the war.

**visa** A document or stamp on a passport allowing a person to visit a foreign country.

**voir dire** The process of selecting a jury (from an Old French expression meaning "speak the truth").

**War Powers Resolution** Bill passed in 1973 to limit presidential war-making powers; it restricts when, why, and for how long a president can commit U.S. forces and requires notification of and, in many cases, approval by Congress.

**Watergate** The scandal that led to the forced resignation of President Richard M. Nixon. Adding "gate" as a suffix to any alleged corruption in government suggests an analogy to the Watergate scandal.

**weak mayor–council model** Model of city government that emphasizes the mayor's role as facilitative leader.

**whips** In both the House and Senate, the principal assistants to the party leaders and next in command to those leaders.

**whistle-blower** Employee of the federal government or of a firm supplying the government who reports waste, mismanagement, and/or fraud by a government agency or contractor.

**White House press corps** Reporters from both print and broadcast media assigned to regularly cover the president.

**Workingmen's Party** A political party organized by Denis Kearney to combat the political and economic power of wealthy merchants and railroad barons.

**writ of certiorari** Writ issued by the Supreme Court, at its discretion, to order a lower court to prepare the record of a case and send it to the Supreme Court for review. Most cases come to the Court as petitions for writs of certiorari.

**writ of habeas corpus** Court order directing public officials who are holding a person in custody to bring the prisoner into court and explain the reasons for confinement; the right to habeas corpus is protected by Article I of the Constitution.

**zero-based budgeting** Method of budgeting that demands justification for the entire budget request of an agency, not just its requested increase in funding.

# NOTES

## Chapter 1

1. Harold Lasswell, *Politics: Who Gets What, When, How* (New York: McGraw-Hill, 1936).
2. For a discussion of various aspects of legitimacy and its measurement in public opinion polls, see M. Stephen Weatherford, "Measuring Political Legitimacy," *American Political Science Review* 86 (March 1992): 140–55.
3. Thomas Hobbes, *Leviathan* (1651).
4. John Locke, *Treatise on Government* (1688).
5. See Barbara S. Gamble, "Putting Civil Rights to a Popular Vote," *American Journal of Political Science* 41 (January 1997): 245–69.
6. James Madison, Alexander Hamilton, and John Jay, *The Federalist Papers* (New York: Mentor Books, 1961), No. 10, p. 81. Madison's *Federalist Papers*, No. 10 and No. 51, are reprinted in the Appendix.
7. E. E. Schattschneider, *Two Hundred Million Americans in Search of a Government* (New York: Holt, Rinehart & Winston, 1969), p. 63.
8. Harold Lasswell and Daniel Lerner, *The Comparative Study of Elites* (Stanford, Calif.: Stanford University Press, 1952), p. 7.
9. C. Wright Mills's classic study, *The Power Elite* (New York: Oxford University Press, 1956), is widely cited by Marxist critics of American democracy, but it can be read profitably by anyone concerned with the effects of large bureaucracies—corporate, governmental, or military—on democratic government.
10. In *Who Rules America?* (New York: Prentice Hall, 1967) and its sequel, *Who Rules America Now?* (New York: Prentice Hall, 1983), sociologist G. William Domhoff argues that America is ruled by an "upper class" who attend the same prestigious private schools, intermarry among themselves, and join the same exclusive clubs. In *Who's Running America?* (New York: Prentice Hall, 1976) and *Who's Running America? The Clinton Years* (New York: Prentice Hall, 1995), political scientist Thomas R. Dye documents the concentration of power and the control of assets in the hands of officers and directors of the nation's largest corporations, banks, law firms, networks, foundations, and so forth. Dye argues, however, that most of these "institutional elites" were not born into the upper class but instead climbed the ladder to success.
11. Yale political scientist Robert A. Dahl is an important contributor to the development of pluralist theory, beginning with his *Preface to Democratic Theory* (Chicago: University of Chicago Press, 1956). He often refers to a pluralist system as a *polyarchy*—literally, a system with many centers of power. See his *Polyarchy* (New Haven, Conn.: Yale University Press, 1971), and for a revised defense of pluralism, see his *Democracy and Its Critics* (New Haven, Conn.: Yale University Press, 1989).

## Chapter 2

1. Gunnar Myrdal, *An American Dilemma* (New York: Harper, 1944).
2. See Martin Luther King, Jr., "Letter from Birmingham City Jail," April 16, 1963.
3. For a discussion of the sources and consequences of intolerance in the general public, see James L. Gibson, "The Political Consequences of Intolerance: Cultural Conformity and Political Freedom," *American Political Science Review* 86 (June 1992): 338–52.
4. Alexis deTocqueville, *Democracy in America*, orig. 1835 (New York: Penguin Classic Books, 2003). See also Aurelian Craiutu and Jeremy Jennings, "The Third Democracy: Tocqueville's Views of America After 1840," *American Journal of Political Science* 98 (August 2004): 391–404.
5. Quoted in *The Ideas of Equality*, ed. George Abernathy (Richmond, Va.: John Knox Press, 1959), p. 185; also in Herbert McClosky and John Zaller, *The American Ethos: Public Attitudes toward Capitalism and Democracy* (Cambridge, Mass.: Harvard University Press, 1984), p. 72.
6. Quoted in Richard Hofstadter, *The American Political Tradition* (New York: Knopf, 1948), p. 45. Historian Hofstadter describes the thinking of American political leaders from Jefferson and the Founders to Franklin D. Roosevelt.
7. For a discussion of how people balance the values of individualism and opposition to big government with humanitarianism and the desire to help others, see Stanley Feldman and John Zaller, "The Political Culture of Ambivalence: Ideological Responses to the Welfare State," *American Journal of Political Science* 36 (February 1992): 268–307.
8. Lawrence R. Jacobs and Theda Skocpol, eds., *Inequality and American Democracy* (New York: Russell Sage Foundation, 2005).
9. Greg J. Duncan, *Years of Poverty, Years of Plenty* (Ann Arbor: University of Michigan Press, 1984); Isabel Sawhill, *Income Mobility in the United States* (Washington, D.C.: Urban Institute, 1996).
10. American Security Council, *The Illegal Immigration Crisis* (Washington, D.C.: ASC, 1994).
11. *Sale v. Haitian Centers Council*, 125 L. Ed. 2d 128 (1993).
12. Poll figures in this section are derived from the Pew Research Center for the People and the Press, "Religion and American Life," August 24, 2004. *www.people-press.org*
13. *Congressional Quarterly*, March 7, 2005.
14. See Stephen Earl Bennett, "Americans' Knowledge of Ideology, 1980–92," *American Politics Quarterly* 23 (July 1995): 259–78.
15. For evidence that ideological consistency increases with educational level, see William G. Jacoby, "Ideological Identification and Issue Attitude," *American Journal of Political Science* 35 (February 1991): 178–205.
16. Richard Hofstadter, *The Paranoid Style in American Politics* (New York: Knopf, 1965).
17. Francis Fukuyama, *The End of History and the Last Man* (New York: Free Press, 1992).
18. See Robert Kimball, *Tenured Radicals* (New York: Harper & Row, 1990).
19. Herbert Marcuse, *One-Dimensional Man* (Boston: Beacon Press, 1964).
20. Allan Bloom, *The Closing of the American Mind* (New York: Simon & Schuster, 1987), p. 15.

# Chapter 3

1. In *Federalist Papers*, No. 53, James Madison distinguishes a "constitution" from a law: a constitution is "established by the people and unalterable by the government, and a law established by the government and alterable by the government."

2. Another important decision on opening day of the Constitutional Convention was to keep the proceedings secret. James Madison made his own notes on the convention proceedings, and they were published many years later. See Max Ferrand, ed., *The Records of the Federal Convention of 1787* (New Haven, Conn.: Yale University Press, 1911).

3. See Edward Millican, *One United People: The Federalist Papers and the National Idea* (Lexington: University Press of Kentucky, 1990).

4. See David Brian Robertson, "Madison's Opponents and Constitutional Design," *American Political Science Review* 99 (May 2005): 225–43.

5. Charles A. Beard, *An Economic Interpretation of the Constitution* (New York: Macmillan, 1913).

6. Robert E. Brown, *Charles Beard and the Constitution* (Princeton, N.J.: Princeton University Press, 1956).

7. James Madison, *Federalist Papers*, No. 10, reprinted in the Appendix.

8. Alexander Hamilton, *Federalist Papers*, No. 78.

# Chapter 4

1. The states are listed in the order in which their legislatures voted to secede. While occupied by Confederate troops, secessionist legislators in Missouri and Kentucky also voted to secede, but Unionist representatives from these states remained in Congress.

2. *Texas v. White*, 7 Wallace 700 (1869).

3. James Madison, *Federalist Papers*, No. 51, reprinted in the Appendix.

4. Ibid.

5. The arguments for "competitive federalism" are developed at length in Thomas R. Dye, *American Federalism: Competition among Governments* (Lexington, Mass.: Lexington Books, 1990).

6. David Osborne, *Laboratories of Democracy* (Cambridge, Mass.: Harvard Business School, 1988).

7. Morton Grodzins, *The American System* (Chicago: Rand McNally, 1966), pp. 8–9.

8. Ibid., p. 265.

9. Charles Press, *State and Community Governments in the Federal System* (New York: Wiley, 1979), p. 78.

10. *Garcia v. San Antonio Metropolitan Transit Authority*, 469 U.S. 528 (1985).

11. See Michael S. Greve, *Real Federalism: Why It Matters, How It Could Happen* (Washington, D.C.: AEI Press, 1999).

12. *U.S. v. Lopez*, 514 U.S. 549 (1995).

13. *Seminole Tribe of Florida v. Florida*, 517 U.S. 44 (1996).

14. *Alden v. Maine*, 67 U.S.L.W. 1401 (1999).

15. *Printz v. U.S.* 521 U.S. 890 (1997).

16. *Brzonkala v. Morrison* (2000).

17. *Federal-State-Local Relations: Federal Grants in Aid*, House Committee on Government Operations, 85th Cong., 2d sess., p. 7.

18. Craig Volden, "Intergovernmental Political Competition in American Federalism," *American Journal of Political Science* 49 (April 2005): 327–42.

# Chapter 5

1. John E. Filer, Lawrence W. Kenny, and Rebecca B. Morton, "Redistribution, Income, and Voting," *American Journal of Political Science* 37 (February 1993): 63–87.

2. Sidney Verba, Kay Scholzman, Henry Brady, and Norman Nie, "Citizen Activity: Who Participates? What Do They Say?" *American Political Science Review* 87 (June 1993): 303–18.

3. See Katherine Tate, "Black Political Participation in the 1984 and 1988 Presidential Elections," *American Political Science Review* 85 (December 1991): 1159–76.

4. Gerald Pomper, *Elections in America* (New York: Dodd, Mead, 1968).

5. Morris P. Fiorina, *Retrospective Voting in American National Elections* (New Haven, Conn.: Yale University Press, 1988).

6. See Jamie L. Carson, "Strategy, Selection and Candidate Competition in U.S. House and Senate Elections", *Journal of Politics* 67 (February 2005): 1–26.

7. Alan I. Abramowitz, "Incumbency, Campaign Spending, and the Decline of Competition in U.S. House Elections," *Journal of Politics* 53 (February 1991): 55–70.

8. Herbert Alexander, as quoted in Richard R. Lau et al., "The Effects of Negative Political Advertisements," *American Political Science Review* 93 (December 1999): 851–75.

9. Lee Sigelman and Emmett H. Buell Jr., "You Take the High Road and I'll Take the Low Road? The Interplay of Attack Strategies and Tactics in Presidential Campaigns," *The Journal of Politics* 46 (May 2003): 518–31; Richard R. Lau and Gerald M. Pomper, "Effectiveness of Negative Campaigning in U.S. Senate Elections," *American Journal of Political Science* 46 (January 2002): 47–66.

10. Ted Brader, "Striking a Responsive Chord: How Political Ads Motivate and Persuade Voters by Appealing to Emotions," *American Journal of Political Science* 49 (April 2005): 388–405.

11. Paul Friedman, Michael Franz, and Kenneth Goldstein, "Campaign Advertising and Democratic Citizenship," *American Journal of Political Science* 48 (October 2004): 723–41.

12. Thomas M. Holbrook and Scott D. McClung, "The Mobilization of Core Supporters," *American Journal of Political Science*, 49 (October 2005): 689–703.

13. Center for Responsive Politics, *The Big Picture: The Money Behind the 2000 Elections* (Washington, D.C., 2001).

14. In the important U.S. Supreme Court decision in *Buckley v. Valeo* in 1976, James L. Buckley, former U.S. senator from New York, and his brother, William F. Buckley, the well-known conservative commentator, argued successfully that the laws limiting an individual's right to participate in political campaigns—financially or otherwise—violated First Amendment freedoms. Specifically, the U.S. Supreme Court held that no government could limit individuals' rights to spend money or publish or broadcast their own views on issues or elections. Candidates can spend as much of their own money as they wish on their own campaigns. Private individuals can spend as much as they wish to circulate their own views on an election, although their contributions to candidates and parties can still be limited. The Court, however, permitted governmental limitations on parties and campaign organizations and allowed the use of federal funds for financing campaigns. *Buckley v. Valeo*, 424 U.S. 1 (1976).

15. *McConnell v. Federal Elections Commission* 540 U.S. 93 (2003).

16. *Randall v. Sorrell*, June 26, 2006.

17. See Paul-Henri Guvian and Audrey A. Haynes, "Presidential Nominating Campaigns," *P.S. Political Science and Politics* 36 (April 2003): 175–80.

18. Lynn Vavreck, Constantine J. Spiliotes and Linda L. Fowler, "The Effects of Retail Politics in the New Hampshire Primary," *American Journal of Political Science* 46 (July 2002): 595–610.

19. William G. Mayer, "Forecasting Presidential Nominations," *P.S. Political Science and Politics* 36 (April 2003): 153–58.

20. Matthew A. Baum, "Talking the Vote: Why Presidential Candidates Hit the Talk Show Circuit," *American Journal of Political Science* 49 (April 2005): 213–34.

21. University-based political scientists rely heavily on a series of National Election Studies, originated at the Survey Research Center at the University of Michigan, which have surveyed the voting-age population in every presidential election and most congressional elections since 1952.

22. See Martin P. Wattenberg, *The Rise of Candidate-Centered Politics* (Cambridge, Mass.: Harvard University Press, 1991).

23. Responsibility for the economy, however, is also affected by the voters' partisanship, ideology and views about whether the president or Congress is chiefly responsible. See Joseph J. Rudolph, "Who's Responsible for the Economy?," *American Journal of Political Science* 47 (October, 2003): 698–713.

24. For an argument that voters look ahead to the economic future and reward or punish the president based on rational expectations, see Michael B. MacKuen, Robert S. Erickson, and James A. Stimson, "Peasants or Bankers? The American Electorate and the U.S. Economy," *American Political Science Review* 86 (September 1992): 680–95.

25. See Herbert F. Weisberg, "The Structure and Effects of Moral Predispositions in Contemporary American Politics", *Journal of Politics* 67 (August 2005): 646–68.

# Chapter 6

1. For an overview of the mass media in American politics, see Doris A. Graber, *Mass Media and American Politics*, 6th ed. (Washington, D.C.: CQ Press, 2002).

2. Pew Research Center for People and the Press. http://people-press.org June, 2000.

3. See Lance Bennett, *News: The Politics of Illusion*, 4th ed. (White Plains, N.Y.: Longman, 2001).

4. E. E. Schattschneider, *The Semisovereign People* (New York: Holt, Rinehart & Winston, 1961), p. 68.

5. William A. Henry, "News as Entertainment," in *What's News*, ed. Elie Abel (San Francisco: Institute for Contemporary Studies, 1981), p. 133.

6. Shanto Iyengar, *Is Anyone Responsible? How Television Frames Political Issues* (Chicago: University of Chicago Press, 1991).

7. Graber, *Mass Media*, p. 35.

8. Matthew A. Baum, "Sex, Lies, and War: How Soft News Brings Foreign Policy to the Inattentive Public," *American Political Science Review* 96 (March, 2002): 91–109.

9. Larry Sabato, Mark Stencel, and S. Robert Lichter, *Peep Show? Media Politics in an Age of Scandal* (Lanham, Md.: Rowman & Little-field, 2001).

10. Ben J. Wattenberg, *The Good News Is the Bad News Is Wrong* (New York: Simon & Schuster, 1984).

11. Ted Smith, "The Watchdog's Bite," *American Enterprise* 2 (January/February 1990): 66.

12. Larry Sabato, *Feeding Frenzy: How Attack Journalism Has Transformed American Politics* (New York: Free Press, 1991).

13. Graber, *Mass Media*, p. 946.

14. S. Robert Lichter, Stanley Rothman, and Linda S. Lichter, *The Media Elite* (Bethesda, Md.: Adler and Adler, 1986).

15. David Prindle, "Hollywood Liberalism" *Social Science Quarterly* 71 (March 1993): 121.

16. David C. Barker, "Rushed Decisions: Political Talk Radio and Vote Choice," *Journal of Politics* 61 (May 1999): 527–39.

17. Diana C. Mutz and Byron Reeves, "The New Videomalaise: Effects of Televised Incivility on Political Trust," *American Political Science Review* 99 (February 2005): 1–15.

18. Marcus Prior, "News Versus Entertainment; How Increasing Media Choice Widens Gaps in Political Knowledge and Turnout," *American Journal of Political Science* 49 (July 2005): 577–592.

19. Julianne F. Flowers, Audrey A. Haynes, and Michael H. Crespin, "The Media, the Campaign, and the Message," *American Journal of Political Science* 47 (April 2003): 259–73.

20. See David S. Castle, "Media Coverage of Presidential Primaries," *American Politics Quarterly* 19 (January 1991): 13–42; Christine F. Ridout, "The Role of Media Coverage of Iowa and New Hampshire," *American Politics Quarterly* 19 (January 1991): 43–58.

21. *Media Monitor* Vol. 14 (November/December, 2000).

22. *New York Times v. U.S.*, 376 U.S. 713 (1971).

23. *New York Times v. Sullivan*, 376 U.S. 254 (1964).

24. See Arthur Lupia and Tasha S. Philpot "Views from Inside the Net," *Journal of Politics* 67 (November, 2005): 1122–42.

25. *Reno v. American Civil Liberties Union* 117 S.Ct. 2329 (1997).

26. Bernard Cohen, *The Press and Foreign Policy* (Princeton, N.J.: Princeton University Press, 1963), p. 16.

27. Austin Ranney, *Channels of Power* (New York: Basic Books, 1983), p. 81.

28. Benjamin J. Page, Robert Y. Shapiro, and Glen R. Dempsey, "What Moves Public Opinion," *American Political Science Review* 81 (March 1987): 23–43.

29. National Institute of Mental Health, *Television and Behavior* (Washington, D.C.: Government Printing Office, 1982).

30. Brandon Centerwall, "Exposure to Television as a Risk Factor for Violence," *American Journal of Epidemiology* 129 (April 1989): 643–52.

# Chapter 7

1. Gaetano Mosca, *The Ruling Class* (New York: McGraw-Hill, 1939), p. 51.

2. E. E. Schattschneider, *Party Government* (New York: Holt, Rinehart & Winston, 1942), p. 1.

3. Geofrey C. Layman and Thomas M. Carsey, "Party Polarization and Conflict Extension in the American Electorate," *American Journal of Political Science* 46 (October 2002): 786–802.

4. Since 1954, only Presidents Kennedy, Johnson, and Carter (all Democrats) worked with their party's majorities in both houses of Congress; President Clinton enjoyed Democratic Party control of the Congress only in his first two years in office. George W. Bush is the only Republican president in a half century to serve with a Republican majority in both the House and Senate. See Harold W. Stanley and Richard C. Niemi, *Vital Statistics on American Politics* (Washington, D.C.: CQ Press, 2003).

5. See Thomas R. Dye and Susan Mac-Manus, *Politics in States and Communities*, 11th ed. (Upper Saddle River, N.J.: Prentice Hall, 2003).

6. *National Election Study*, 2000.

7. Conventions continue to play a modest role in nominations in some states:
   • Colorado: Parties may hold a preprimary convention to designate a candidate to be listed first on the primary ballot. All candidates receiving at least 30 percent of the delegate vote will be listed on the primary ballot.
   • Connecticut: Party conventions are held to endorse candidates. If no one

challenges the endorsed candidate, no primary election is held. If a challenger receives 20 percent of the delegate vote, a primary election will be held to determine the party's nominee in the general election.

- New York: Party conventions choose the party's "designated" candidate in primary elections. Anyone receiving 25 percent of the delegates also appears on the ballot.
- Utah: Party conventions select party's nominees.
- Illinois, Indiana, Michigan, and South Carolina: Party conventions nominate candidates for some minor state offices.

8. For an argument that primary elections force parties to be more responsive to voters, see John G. Geer and Mark E. Shere, "Party Competition and the Prisoner's Dilemma: An Argument for the Direct Primary," *Journal of Politics* 54 (August 1992): 365–74.

9. For an up-to-date listing of state primaries and relevant information about them, see *The Book of the States*, published biannually by the Council of State Governments, Lexington, Kentucky.

10. Congressional Quarterly, *National Party Conventions 1811–1996* (Washington, D.C.: CQ Press, 1997).

11. For evidence that the national party conventions raise the poll standings of their presidential nominees, see James E. Campbell, Lynna L. Cherry, and Kenneth A. Wink, "The Convention Bump," *American Politics Quarterly* 20 (July 1992): 287–307.

12. See John A. Clark, John M. Bruce, John H. Kessel, and William G. Jacoby, "I'd Rather Switch Than Fight: Lifelong Democrats and Converts to Republicanism among Campaign Activists," *American Journal of Political Science* 35 (August 1991): 577–97.

13. For a scholarly debate over realignment, see Byron E. Schafer, ed., *The End of Realignment: Interpreting American Election Eras* (Madison: University of Wisconsin Press, 1991).

14. Gary Miller and Norman Schofield, "Activists and Partisan Realignment in the United States," *American Political Science Review* 97 (May 2003): 245–60.

15. James Madison, *Federalist Papers*, No. 10, reprinted in the Appendix.

16. Political scientist David Truman's classic definition of an interest group: "any group that is based on one or more shared attitudes and makes certain demands upon other groups or organizations in society." See *The Governmental Process* (New York: Knopf, 1971), p. 33.

17. Gale Research Company, *Encyclopedia of Associations* (Detroit: Gale Research, 2004).

18. Frank R. Baumgartner and Beth L. Leech, "Interest Niches and Policy Bandwagons: Patterns of Interest Group Involvement in National Politics," *The Journal of Politics* 63 (November 2001): 1191–1213.

19. Jeffrey M. Berry, *The New Liberalism: The Rising Power of Citizen Groups* (Washington, D.C.: Brookings Institution Press, 1999).

20. For both theory and survey data on the sources of interest-group mobilization, see Jack L. Walker, *Mobilizing Interest Groups in America: Patrons, Professions, and Social Movements* (Ann Arbor: University of Michigan Press, 1991).

21. Kay Lehmann Scholzman, "What Accent the Heavenly Chorus? Political Equality and the American Pressure System," *Journal of Politics* 46 (November 1984): 1006–32; see also Jeffrey M. Berry, Kent E. Portney, and Ken Thomson, *The Case for Participatory Democracy* (Washington, D.C.: Brookings Institution Press, 1994).

22. Center for Responsive Politics, *Influence, Inc. 2000* (Washington, D.C., 2001).

23. Jeffrey M. Berry, *The New Liberalism* (Washington D.C.: Brookings Institution Press, 1999).

24. For evidence that vote buying on congressional roll calls is rare, see Janet M. Grenzke, "Shopping in the Congressional Supermarket: The Currency Is Complex," *American Journal of Political Science* 33 (February 1989): 1–24. But for evidence that committee participation by members of Congress is influenced by political action committee money, see Richard L. Hall and Frank W. Wayman, "Buying Time: Moneyed Interests and the Mobilization of Bias in Congressional Committees," *American Political Science Review* 84 (September 1990): 797–819.

25. Robert H. Salisbury, "Who You Know versus What You Know: The Use of Government Experience by Washington Lobbyists," *American Journal of Political Science* 33 (February 1989): 175–95.

26. *Brown v. Board of Education of Topeka*, 349 U.S. 294 (1955).

# Chapter 8

1. James Madison, *Federalist Papers*, No. 10, reprinted in the Appendix.

2. Quoted in Jay M. Schafritz, *The Harper Collins Dictionary of American Government and Politics* (New York: HarperCollins, 1992), p. 56.

3. See David Auerswald and Forrest Maltzman, "Policymaking through Advice and Consent: Treaty Consideration by the United States Senate," *Journal of Politics* 65 (November 2003): 1097–1110.

4. *McGrain v. Doughterty*, 273 U.S. 13J (1927).

5. *Baker v. Carr*, 369 U.S. 186 (1962), *Wesberry v. Sanders*, 370 U.S. 1 (1964).

6. *Gray v. Sanders*, 322 U.S. 368 (1963).

7. *Department of Commerce v. U.S. House of Representatives*, 525 U.S. 316 (1999).

8. *Gaffney v. Cummings*, 412 U.S. 763 (1973).

9. *Davis v. Bandemer* 478 U.S. 109 (1986).

10. *Vieth v. Jubelirer* 241 F. Supp. 2d 478 (2004).

11. *League of United Latin American Citizens v. Perry*, June 28, 2006.

12. Scott W. Desposato and John R. Petrocik, "The Variable Incumbency Advantage: New Voters, Redistricting, and Personal Vote," *American Journal of Political Science* 47 (January 2003): 18–32

13. *Thornburg v. Gingles*, 478 U.S. 30 (1986).

14. *Shaw v. Reno*, 125 I. Ed. 2d 511 (1993).

15. *Miller v. Johnson*, 115 S. Ct. 2475 (1995).

16. See Roger H. Davidson and Walter J. Oleszek, *Congress and Its Members*, 9th ed. (Washington, D.C.: CQ Press, 2004).

17. David Lublin, *The Paradox of Representation: Racial Gerrymandering and Minority Interests in Congress* (Princeton, NJ.: Princeton University Press, 1997). See also David Lublin and D. Stephen Voss, "The Missing Middle," *Journal of Politics* 65 (February 2003). 227–37.

18. *Georgia v. Ashcroft*, 539 U.S. 461 (2003).

19. For an in-depth analysis of who decides to run for Congress and who does not, see Linda L. Fowler and Robert D. McClure, *Political Ambition: Who Decides to Run for Congress* (New Haven, Conn.: Yale University Press, 1990).

20. See Michael K. Moore and John R. Hibbing, "Situational Dissatisfaction in Congress: Explaining Voluntary Departures," *Journal of Politics* 60 (November 1998): 1088–1107.

21. *U.S. Term Limits v. Thornton*, 115 S.C. 1842, (1995).

22. See Gary Jacobson, *The Politics of Congressional Elections*, 5th ed. (New York: HarperCollins, 2000).

23. See David Epstein and Peter Zemsky, "Money Talks: Deterring Quality Challengers in Congressional Elections," *American Political Science Review* 89 (June 1995): 295– 322.

24. See Thomas E. Mann and Raymond Wolfinger, "Candidates and Parties in Congressional Elections," *American Political Science Review* 84 (September 1990): 545–64.

25. See Mary T. Hanna, "Political Science Caught Flat-Footed by Midterm Elections," *Chronicle of Higher Education*, November 30, 1994, pp. B1–2.

26. See Richard Fenno, *Going Home: Black Representatives and Their Constituents* (Chicago: University of Chicago Press, 2003).

27. Paul S. Herrnson, J. Celeste Lay, and Atiya Kai Stokes, "Women Running 'As Women'," *Journal of Politics* 65 (February 2003): 244–55.

28. See Glen S. Krutz, "Issues and Institutions: 'Winnowing' in the U.S. Congress," *American Journal of Political Science* 49 (April 2005) 313–26.

29. U.S. House of Representatives, Commission on Administrative Review, *Administrative Reorganization and Legislative Management*, 95th Cong., 1st sess, H. Doc. 95–232, pp. 17–19.

30. Richard F. Fenno, *Home Style* (Boston: Little, Brown, 1978).

31. Roger H. Davidson and Walter J. Oleszek, *Congress and Its Members* 814 (Washington, D.C.: CQ Press, 2000).

32. Glenn R. Parker, *Characteristics of Congress* (Upper Saddle River, N.J.: Prentice Hall, 1989), p. 30.

33. Richard F. Fenno, *The Making of a Senator: Dan Quayle* (Washington, D.C.: CQ Press, 1989), p. 119. Also cited in Davidson and Oleszek, *Congress and Its Members*, 9th ed., p. 120.

34. Davidson and Oleszek, *Congress and Its Members*, 9th ed., p. 129.

35. Barbara Sinclair, "The Emergence of Strong Leadership in the House of Representatives," *Journal of Politics* 54 (August 1992): 657–84.

36. Gary W. Cox and Eric Magar, "How Much Is Majority Status in the U.S. Congress Worth?" *American Political Science Review* 93 (June 1999): 299–310.

37. Davidson and Oleszek, *Congress and Its Members*, 9th ed. p. 161.

38. John R. Hibbing, *Congressional Careers* (Chapel Hill: University of North Carolina Press, 1991).

39. See Charles Stewart and Tim Groseclose, "The Value of Committee Seats in the United States Senate," *American Journal of Political Science* 43 (July 1999): 963–73.

40. Larry Markinson, *The Cash Constituents of Congress* (Washington, D.C.: CQ Press, 1992).

41. Donald Matthews, *U.S. Senators and Their World* (New York: Vintage Books, 1960).

42. David Rohde, Norman J. Ornstein, and Robert L. Peabody, "Political Change and Legislative Norms," in *Studies of Congress*, ed. Glenn R. Parker (Washington, D.C.: CQ Press, 1985), p. 175.

43. See John R. Hibbing, "Contours of the Modern Congressional Career," *American Political Science Review* 85 (June 1991): 405–28.

44. Richard Fenno, *Power of the Purse* (Boston: Little, Brown, 1965), p. 620.

45. See David R. Mayhew, *Divided We Govern* (New Haven, Conn.: Yale University Press, 1991); Sarah A. Binder, "The Dynamics of Legislative Gridlock," *American Political Science Review* 93 (September 1999): 519–33.

46. *Congressional Quarterly Weekly Report*, November 23, 1991, p. 3437.

# Chapter 9

1. For an argument that presidents encourage people to think of them as "the single head of government and moral leader of the nation who speaks for all of the people," see Barbara Hinckley, *The Symbolic Presidency: How Presidents Portray Themselves* (New York: Routledge, 1991).

2. See Theodore Lowi, *The Personal President* (Ithaca, N.Y.: Cornell University Press, 1987).

3. Presidential address to Congress, September 20, 2001.

4. See Michael Less Benedict, *The Impeachment and Trial of Andrew Johnson* (New York: Norton, 1973).

5. William Howard Taft, *Our Chief Magistrate and His Powers* (New York: Columbia University Press, 1938), p. 138, reprinted in *The Presidency*, ed. John P. Roche (New York: Harcourt Brace Jovanovich, 1964), p. 23.

6. Quoted in Arthur B. Tourtellot, *Presidents on the Presidency* (New York: Doubleday, 1964), pp. 55–56.

7. *Youngstown Sheet & Tube Co. v. Sawyer*, 343 U.S. 579 (1952).

8. *United States v. Nixon*, 418 U.S. 683 (1974).

9. *Nixon v. Fitzgerald*, 457 U.S. 731 (1982).

10. *Clinton v. Jones*, 520 U.S. 681 (1997).

11. Quoted in Richard Neustadt, *Presidential Power* (New York: Wiley, 1960), p. 9.

12. See Paul Brace and Barbara Hinckley, "The Structure of Presidential Approval," *Journal of Politics* 53 (November 1991): 993–1017.

13. See Suzanne L. Pancer, "Toward an Understanding of 'Rally' Effect," *Public Opinion Quarterly* 59 (September, 1995): 526–46; Wave J. Aetherington and Michael Nelson: "Anatomy of a Rally Effect," *P.S. Political Science and Politics* 36 (January, 2003): 37–42.

14. John Mueller, *War, Presidents, and Public Opinion* (New York: Wiley, 1973).

15. See George C. Edwards and B. Dan Wood, "Who Influences Whom," *American Political Science Review* 93 (June 1999): 327–44.

16. Garry Young and William B. Perkins, "Presidential Rhetoric, the Public Agenda, and the End of Presidential Television's 'Golden Age,'" *Journal of Politics* 67 (November 2005): 1190–1205.

17. Michael Bailey, Lee Sigelman, and Clyde Wilcox, "Presidential Persuasion on Social issues," *Political Research Quarterly* 56 (March 2003): 49–58.

18. George C. Edwards and Stephen J. Wayne, *Presidential Leadership*. 6th ed. (Belmont, Calif.: Wadsworth, 2003), p. 118.

19. Lawrence R. Jacobs and Robert Y. Schapiro, *Politicians Don't Pander* (Chicago: University of Chicago Press, 2000).

20. Brandice Canes-Wrone and Kenneth W. Shotts, "The Conditional Nature of Presidential Responsiveness to Public Opinion," *American Journal of Political Science* 48 (October 2004): 690–706.

21. *Youngstown Sheet & Tube Co. v. Sawyer*, 343 U.S. 579 (1952).

22. Kenneth R. Mayer, "Executive Orders and Presidential Power," *Journal of Politics* 61 (May 1999): 445–66; Christopher J. Deering and Forrest Maltzman, "The Politics of Executive Orders," *Political Research Quarterly* 52 (December 1999): 767–83.

23. See also Jeffrey E. Cohen, *The Politics of the U.S. Cabinet* (Pittsburgh: University of Pittsburgh Press, 1988).

24. John Kingdon, *Agenda, Alternatives, and Public Policies* (Boston: Little, Brown, 1984), p. 25.

25. See Daniel E. Ingberman and Dennis A. Yao, "Presidential Commitment and the Veto," *American Journal of Political Science* 35 (May 1991): 357–89; and Samuel B. Hoff, "Saying No," *American Politics Quarterly* 19 (July 1991): 310–23.

26. For a discussion of the factors affecting the use of the presidential veto, see John T. Woolley, "Institutions, the Election Cycle, and the Presidential Veto," *American Journal of Political Science* 35 (May 1991): 279–304.

27. *Clinton v. City of New York*, 524 U.S. 417 (1998).

28. G.J.A. O'Toole, *Honorable Treachery: A History of U.S. Intelligence from the American Revolution to the CIA* (New York: Atlantic Monthly Press, 1991).

29. National Commission on Terrorist Attacks upon the United States, *The 9/11 Commission Report*, New York: W.W. Norton, 2004.

30. *Mora v. McNamara*, 389 U.S. 934 (1964); *Massachusetts v. Laird*, 400 U.S. 886 (1970). The Court specifically refused to intervene in the conduct of the Vietnam War by presidents Johnson and Nixon.

31. Jules Witcover, *Crap Shoot: Rolling the Dice on the Vice Presidency* (New York: Crow Publishing, 1992).

# Chapter 10

1. "Red tape" derives its meaning from the use of reddish tape by seventeenth-century English courts to bind legal documents. Unwrapping court orders entangled one in "red tape." See Herbert Kaufman, *Red Tape: Its Uses and Abuses* (Washington, D.C.: Brookings Institution, 1977).
2. H. H. Gerth and C. Wright Mills, *From Max Weber* (New York: Oxford Press, 1958).
3. Max Neiman, *Defending Government: Why Big Government Works* (Upper Saddle River, N.J.: Prentice Hall, 2000).
4. James Q. Wilson, *Bureaucracy: What Government Agencies Do and Why They Do It* (New York: Basic Books, 1989).
5. William Niskanen, *Bureaucracy and Representative Government* (Chicago: Aldine, 1971).
6. The constitutional question of whether Congress can establish an executive branch commission and protect its members from dismissal by the president was settled in *Humphrey's Executor v. United States* (1935). Franklin Roosevelt fired Humphrey from the Federal Trade Commission despite a fixed term set by Congress. Humphrey died shortly afterward, and when the executors of his estate sued for his back pay, the Supreme Court ruled that his firing was illegal.
7. See Nicholas Henry, *Public Administration and Public Affairs*, 7th ed. (Upper Saddle River, N.J.: Prentice Hall, 1999), Chapter 11.
8. Quoted in U.S. Civil Service Commission, *Biography of an Ideal: A History of the Civil Service System* (Washington, D.C.: Government Printing Office, 1973), p. 16.
9. See John D. Huber and Nalan McCarty, "Bureaucratic Capacity, Delegation, and Political Reform," *American Political Science Review* 98 (August 2004) 481–494.
10. Paul C. Light, *Thickening Government: Federal Hierarchy and the Diffusion of Accountability* (Washington, D.C.: Brookings Institution, 1995).
11. David Osborne and Ted Gaebler, *Reinventing Government* (New York: Addison-Wesley, 1992).
12. Al Gore, *Creating a Government That Works Better and Costs Less* (Washington, D.C.: Government Printing Office, 1993).
13. William G. Howell and David E. Lewis, "Agencies by Presidential Design," *Journal of Politics* 64 (November 2002): 1098–1114.
14. Daniel P. Carpenter, "Protection Without Capture," *American Political Science Review* 98 (November 2004): 613–31.
15. Robert Crandell and Jerry Ellig, *Economic Deregulation and Consumer Choice* (Fairfax, Va.: Center for Market Processes, 1997).
16. General Accounting Office, *Regulatory Enforcement Fairness Act Report*, 1999.
17. Thomas D. Hopkins, *Regulatory Costs in Profile* (Washington, D.C.: Center for the Study of American Business, 1996).
18. Richard K. Vedder, "Federal Regulation's Impact on the Productivity Slowdown: A Trillion Dollar Drag," *Policy Study*, Center for the Study of American Business, July 1996.
19. For research suggesting that the appointive power is a more important instrument of political control of the bureaucracy than budgets or legislation, see B. Dan Wood and Richard W. Waterman, "The Dynamics of Political Control of the Bureaucracy," *American Political Science Review* 83 (September 1991): 801–28.
20. See Joel D. Aberbach, *Keeping a Watchful Eye: The Politics of Congressional Oversight* (Washington, D.C.: Brookings Institution, 1990).
21. Evidence of the effectiveness of interventions by members of Congress in local offices of federal agencies is provided by John T. Scholz, Jim Twombly, and Barbara Headrick, "Street-Level Political Controls over Federal Bureaucracy," *American Political Science Review* 85 (September 1991): 829–50.
22. Bradley Cannon and Michael Giles, "Recurring Litigants: Federal Agencies before the Supreme Court," *Western Political Quarterly* 15 (September 1972): 183–91; Reginald S. Sheehan, "Federal Agencies and the Supreme Court," *American Politics Quarterly* 20 (October 1992): 478–500.

# Chapter 11

1. Alexis de Tocqueville, *Democracy in America* (1835; New York: Mentor Books, 1956), p. 75.
2. Felix Frankfurter, "The Supreme Court and the Public," *Forum* 83 (June 1930): 332.
3. Alexander Hamilton, *Federalist Papers*, No. 78 (New York: Modern Library, 1937), p. 505.
4. *Marbury v. Madison*, 1 Cranch 137 (1803).
5. *Brown v. Board of Education of Topeka*, 347 U.S. 483 (1954).
6. *Roe v. Wade*, 410 U.S. 113 (1973).
7. *Lawrence v. Texas* (June 26, 2003).
8. *Buckley v. Valeo*, 424 U.S. 1 (1976).
9. *U.S. v. Morrison* (May 15, 2000).
10. *Ex parte Milligan*, 4 Wallace 2 (1866).
11. *Youngstown Sheet & Tube Co. v. Sawyer*, 343 U.S. 579 (1952).
12. *United States v. Nixon*, 418 U.S. 683 (1974).
13. *Clinton v. Jones*, 520 U.S. 681 (1997).
14. *West Virginia Board of Education v. Barnette*, 319 U.S. 624 (1943).
15. Quoted in Henry J. Abraham, *Justices and Presidents*, 3rd ed. (New York: Oxford University Press, 1992), p. 7.
16. Quoted in Charles P. Curtis, *Lions under the Throne* (Boston: Houghton Mifflin, 1947), p. 281.
17. Lee Epstein and Thomas G. Walker, *Constitutional Law for a Changing America*, 3rd ed. (Washington, D.C.: CQ Press, 1998), pp. 33–34.
18. William O. Douglas, "Stare Decisis," *Record*, April 1947, cited in Henry J. Abraham, *The Judicial Process* (New York: Oxford University Press, 1968), p. 58.
19. *Flast v. Cohen*, 392 U.S. 83 (1968).
20. *Gideon v. Wainwright*, 372 U.S. 335 (1963).
21. *Missouri v. Jenkins*, 110 S.C. 1651 (1990).
22. *Morrison v. Olson*, 487 U.S. 654 (1988).
23. Robert Scigliano, *The Supreme Court and the Presidency* (New York: Free Press, 1971), pp. 147–48.
24. See Bryon J. Moraski and Charles R. Shipan, "The Politics of Supreme Court Nominations," *American Journal of Political Science* 43 (October 1999): 1069–95.
25. See Charles R. Shipan and Megan L. Shannon, "Delaying Justices, *American Journal of Political Science* 47 (October, 2003): 654–68; Sarah A. Binder and Forrest Maltzman, "Senatorial Delay in Confirming Federal Judges," *American Journal of Political Science* 46 (January 2002): 190–99.
26. At one time the U.S. Supreme Court was legally required to accept certain "writs of appeal," but today very few cases come to the Court in this fashion.
27. *University of California Regents v. Bakke*, 438 U.S. 265 (1978).
28. See Lee Epstein et al., *The Supreme Court Compendium*, 3rd ed. (Washington, D.C.: CQ Press, 2002).
29. Thomas Marshall, *Public Opinion and the Supreme Court* (New York: Unwin Hyman, 1989), p. 97.
30. Lee Epstein and C. K. Rowland, "Debunking the Myth of Interest Group Invincibility," *American Political Science Review* 85 (1991): 205–17.
31. James L. Gibson et al., "Measuring Attitudes toward the United States Supreme Court," *American Journal of Political Science* 47 (April 2003): 354–67; Stephen P. Nicholson and Robert H. Howard, "Framing Support for the Supreme Court

in the Aftermath of *Bush v. Gore*," *Journal of Politics* 65 (August 2003): 676–95.

32. President Andrew Jackson's comments came in response to the Court's ruling in the case of *Cherokee Nation v. Georgia* (1831) and *Worcester v. Georgia* (1832), which forbade the federal or state governments from seizing Native American lands and forcing the people to move. Refusal by Jackson, an old "Indian fighter," to enforce the Court's decisions resulted in the infamous "Trail of Tears," the forced march of the Georgia Cherokees that left one-quarter of them dead along the path west.

33. *Grove City College v. Bell*, 465 U.S. 555 (1984).

34. *Pollock v. Farmer's Loan*, 158 U.S. 601 (1895).

# Chapter 12

1. James Madison, *Federalist Papers*, No. 10, reprinted in the Appendix.

2. *West Virginia Board of Education v. Barnette*, 319 U.S. 624 (1943).

3. *Reynolds v. United States*, 98 U.S. 145 (1879).

4. *Pierce v. Society of Sisters*, 268 U.S. 510 (1925).

5. Opening public meetings with prayer was ruled constitutional as "a tolerable acknowledgment of beliefs widely held among the people of this country." *Marsh v. Chambers*, 463 U.S. 783 (1983).

6. *Lemon v. Kurtzman*, 403 U.S. 602 (1971).

7. *Muebler v. Adams*, 463 U.S. 388 (1983).

8. *Tilton v. Richardson*, 403 U.S. 672 (1971).

9. *Lambs Chapel v. Center Moriches Union Free School District*, 508 U.S. 384 (1993).

10. *Rosenberger v. University of Virginia*, 515 U.S. 819 (1995).

11. *Walz v. Tax Commission*, 397 U.S. 664 (1970).

12. *Board of Education v. Mergens*, 497 U.S. 111 (1990).

13. *McGowan v. Maryland*, 366 U.S. 429 (1961), and *Braunfeld v. Brown*, 366 U.S. 599 (1961).

14. *County of Allegheny v. ACLU*, 492 U.S. 573 (1989).

15. *Edwards v. Aguillard*, 482 U.S. 578 (1987).

16. *Engel v. Vitale*, 370 U.S. 421 (1962).

17. *Abington School District v. Schempp*, 374 U.S. 203 (1963).

18. *Wallace v. Jaffree*, 472 U.S. 38 (1985).

19. *Lee v. Weisman*, 505 U.S. 577 (1992).

20. *Santa Fe Independent School District v. Doe*, 120 S.Ct. 2266 (2000).

21. *Schenck v. United States*, 249 U.S. 47 (1919).

22. *Gitlow v. New York*, 268 U.S. 652 (1925).

23. *Schenck v. United States*, 249 U.S. 47, 52 (1919).

24. *Whitney v. California*, 274 U.S. 357, 377 (1927), concurring opinion.

25. *Thomas v. Collins*, 323 U.S. 516 (1945).

26. *Tinker v. Des Moines Independent Community School District*, 393 U.S. 503 (1969).

27. *Texas v. Johnson*, 491 U.S. 397 (1989).

28. *Virginia v. Black*, 538 U.S. 343 (2003).

29. *New York Times v. Sullivan*, 376 U.S. 254 (1964).

30. *Griswold v. Connecticut*, 381 U.S. 479 (1965).

31. *Roe v. Wade*, 410 U.S. 113 (1973).

32. *Harris v. McRae*, 448 U.S. 297 (1980).

33. *Planned Parenthood v. Casey*, 510 U.S. 110 (1992).

34. *Stenberg v. Carbart*, June 28, 2000.

35. *Bowers v. Hardwick*, 478 U.S. 186 (1986).

36. *Lawrence v. Texas* (June 26, 2003).

37. *Gertz v. Robert Welch, Inc.*, 418 U.S. 323 (1974).

38. *Reno v. American Civil Liberties Union*, 117 S.Ct. 2329 (1997).

39. James Madison, *Federalist Papers*, No. 46.

40. *Ex parte Milligan*, 4 Wallace 2 (1866).

41. *United States v. Watson*, 423 U.S. 411 (1976).

42. *Payton v. New York*, 445 U.S. 573 (1980).

43. *Escobedo v. Illinois*, 378 U.S. 478 (1964).

44. *Miranda v. Arizona*, 384 U.S. 436 (1966).

45. *Spano v. New York*, 360 U.S. 315 (1959).

46. *Gideon v. Wainwright*, 372 U.S. 335 (1963).

47. *Escobedo v. Illinois*, 378 U.S. 478 (1964).

48. *Miranda v. Arizona*, 384 U.S. 436 (1966).

49. *Mapp v. Ohio*, 367 U.S. 643 (1961).

50. *United States v. Leon*, 468 U.S. 897 (1984).

51. *Illinois v. Perkins*, 497 U.S. 177 (1990).

52. *U.S. v. Marion*, 404 U.S. 307 (1971).

53. *Barker v. Wingo*, 407 U.S. 514 (1972).

54. U.S. Department of Justice, *The Prevalence of Guilty Pleas* (Washington, D.C.: Government Printing Office, 1984).

55. *U.S. v. Perez*, 9 Wheat 579 (1824).

56. *Heath v. Alabama*, 474 U.S. 82 (1985).

57. *Furman v. Georgia*, 408 U.S. 238 (1972).

58. *Gregg v. Georgia*, 428 U.S. 153 (1976); *Proffitt v. Florida*, 428 U.S. 242 (1976); *Jurek v. Texas*, 428 U.S. 262 (1976).

59. *Ring v. Arizona*, June 24, 2002.

60. *Atkins v. Virginia*, June 20, 2002.

61. *Roper v. Simmons*, March 1, 2005.

62. *Dred Scott v. Sandford*, 60 U.S. 393 (1857).

63. *Sweatt v. Painter*, 339 U.S. 629 (1950).

64. *Brown v. Board of Education of Topeka*, 347 U.S. 483 (1954).

65. The Supreme Court ruled that Congress was bound to respect the Equal Protection Clause of the Fourteenth Amendment even though the amendment is directed at states, because equal protection is a liberty guaranteed by the Fifth Amendment. *Bolling v. Sharpe*, 347 U.S. 497 (1954).

66. *Brown v. Board of Education of Topeka* (II), 349 U.S. 294 (1955).

67. *Alexander v. Holmes Board of Education*, 396 U.S. 19 (1969).

68. *Swann v. Charlotte-Mecklenburg County Board of Education*, 402 U.S. (1971).

69. *Milliken v. Bradley*, 418 U.S. 717 (1974).

70. Martin Luther King Jr., "Letter from Birmingham City Jail," April 16, 1963.

71. *University of California Regents v. Bakke*, 438 U.S. 265 (1978).

72. Bakke's overall grade point average was 3.46, and the average for special admissions students was 2.62. Bakke's MCAT scores were verbal, 96; quantitative, 94; science, 97; general information, 72. The average MCAT scores for special admissions students were verbal, 34; quantitative, 30; science, 37; general information, 18.

73. *United Steelworkers of America v. Weber*, 443 U.S. 193 (1979).

74. *United States v. Paradise*, 480 U.S. 149 (1987).

75. *Firefighters Local Union 1784 v. Stotts*, 467 U.S. 561 (1984).

76. *City of Richmond v. Crosen Co.*, 488 U.S. 469 (1989).

77. *Adarand Construction v. Pena*, 132 L. Ed., 2d 158 (1995).

78. *Hopwood v. Texas*, 116 S.Ct. 2581 (1996).

79. *Grutter v. Bollinger* (June 23, 2003).

80. *Gratz v. Bollinger* (June 23, 2003).

81. U.S. Department of Education, Office of Civil Rights, "Race-neutral Alternatives in Postsecondary Education," March 2003.

82. Rudolpho O. de la Garza et al., *Latino Voices: Mexican, Puerto Rican, and Cuban Perspectives on American Politics* (Boulder, Colo.: Westview Press, 1992).

83. See F. Luis Garcia, *Latinos in the Political System* (Notre Dame, Ind.: Notre Dame University Press, 1988).

84. Linda Chavez, "Tequila Sunrise: The Slow but Steady Progress of Hispanic Immigrants," *Policy Review* (Spring 1989): 64–67.

85. Peter Mathiessen, *Sal Si Puedes: Cesar Chavez and the New American Revolution* (New York: Random House, 1969).

86. *Plyer v. Doe*, 457 U.S. 202 (1982).

87. *Bradwell v. Illinois*, 16 Wall 130 (1873).

88. *Reed v. Reed*, 404 U.S. 71 (1971).

89. *Michael M. v. Superior Court of Sonoma County*, 450 U.S. 464 (1981).

90. *Rostker v. Goldberg*, 453 U.S. 57 (1981).

91. *Statistical Abstract of the United States*, 2002, p. 440.

92. Susan Fraker, "Why Women Aren't Getting to the Top," *Fortune*, April 16, 1984, pp. 40–45.

# Chapter 13

1. Paul Samuelson, *Economics*, 12th ed. (New York: McGraw-Hill, 1985), p. 5.
2. For an argument that the money supply expands in election years in most democracies, see Edward R. Tufte, *Political Control of the Economy* (Princeton, N.J.: Princeton University Press, 1978).
3. GDP differs very little from gross national product, GNP, which is often used to compare the performance of national economies.

4. For a revealing case study of interest-group efforts to maintain tax breaks during the struggle over the Tax Reform Act of 1986, see Jeffrey H. Birnbaum and Alan S. Murray, *Showdown at Gucci Gulch* (New York: Random House, 1986).
5. Joseph A. Pechman, *Federal Tax Policy*, 5th ed. (Washington, D.C.: Brookings Institution, 1987).

6. Christopher Jenks and Paul E. Peterson, eds., *The Urban Underclass* (Washington, D.C.: Brookings Institution, 1991). See also William A. Kelso, *Poverty and the Underclass* (New York: New York University Press, 1994).
7. See Michael B. Katz, *In the Shadow of the Poorhouse* (New York: Basic Books, 1996).
8. See Charles Murray, *Losing Ground* (New York: Basic Books, 1984).

# Chapter 14

1. Hans Morgenthau, *Politics among Nations*, 5th ed. (New York: Knopf, 1973), p. 27.
2. George F. Kennan, writing under the pseudonym "X," "Sources of Soviet Conduct," *Foreign Affairs* 25 (July 1947): 25.
3. Frank Snepp, *Decent Interval* (New York: Random House, 1977).

4. George C. Herring, *America's Longest War* (New York: Random House, 1979), p. 262.
5. See Caspar W. Weinberger, "The Uses of Military Force," *Defense* (Arlington, Va.: American Forces Information Services Survey, 1985), pp. 2–11.
6. Morgenthau, *Politics among Nations*, p. 80.

7. President George W. Bush, *National Security Strategy 2006*, March 16, 2006, www.whitehouse.gov.
8. President George W. Bush, *National Strategy for Victory in Iraq*, November 1, 2005, www.whitehouse.gov.

# Chapter 15

1. Nava, Julian and Bob Barger. *California: Five Centuries of Cultural Contrasts.* Beverly Hills: Glencoe Press, 1976. p. 10–11.
2. Ibid. p. 28.
3. Gilmore, N. Ray, and Gladys Gilmore. *Readings in California History.* New York: Thomas Y. Crowell Company, 1966. p. 9–12.
4. Op. cit. Nava and Barger, p. 69–86.
5. Robinson, W. W. *Land in California.* Berkeley: University of California Press, 1948. p. 23–32.
6. Dewitt, Howard. The California Dream. Dubuque: Hendall/Hunt Publishing Company, 1997. p. 53–68.
7. Ibid. p. 15–20.

8. Ibid. p. 76–83.
9. Op. cit. Nava, p. 170.
10. Dewitt, op cit. p. 100–103.
11. Cleland, Robert G., *From Wilderness to Empire: History of California.* New York: Alfred A. Knopf Inc. 1959. p. 168–174.
12. Mowry, George E., *The California Progressives.* Chicago" Quadrangle Books, 1963. p. 8–12.
13. Bean, Walton. *Boss Ruef's San Francisco.* Berkeley: University of California Press, 1952. p. 5.
14. Op. cit., Nava and Barger p. 259–260.
15. Op. cit. Mowry p. 18–21.
16. Ibid. p. 36.
17. Ibid. p. 116–134.

18. Ibid. p. 135–157.
19. Starr, Kevin, *California: A History.* New York: The Modern Library, 2005. p. 235–244.
20. Ibid. p. 226–227.
21. "Major Issues Facing Californians." San Francisco: Volume 2 Field Research Corporation, March, 2005.
22. "Who Are California's Students?" EdSource 2002.
23. Op. cit. Field Research Corporation.
24. Ibid.
25. "Historical Trends 1984–2004." California Department of Corporations and Rehabilitation Offender Information Services Branch Data Analysis Unit.

# Chapter 16

1. Report of Registration, January 2, 2004. California Secretary of State California, <http://www.ss.ca.gov/elections/ror_01022004.htm>.
2. "Youth Voting 2004." The Pew Charitable Trusts-Supporting Civic Life. <http://pewtrusts.com/ideas/ index.cfm?issue=7.
3. Owens, John R., Edmond Costantini, and Louis F. Weschler. *California Politics and Parties.* London: Macmillan, 1970. p. 90–92.
4. "Special Elections in California" Hot Topic: Library. Institute of Government Studies, University of California, Berkeley. <http://www.igs.berkeley.edu/library/HTSpecialElectioninCalifornia.html>.

5. Op. cit. Owens p. 103–106.
6. Mowry, George E. *The California Progressives.* Chicago: Quadrangle Books, 1963. p. 149.
7. Ibid. p. 140.
8. Ibid. p. 149.
9. "2003 California recall." <http://wikipedia.org/wiki/2003_California_recall>.
10. Ibid.
11. Schrag, Peter. *Paradise Lost: California's Experience, America's Future.* Berkeley: University of California Press, 2004. p. 10.
12. Price, Charles M. "Shadow Government." California Government and Politics, Annual: 2001–2002. Edited by A.G. Block and Charles M. Price. Sacramento: California Journal/Statenet 2001. p. 72–74.

13. "Tribes Vow to Fight Casino Ruling" *Gambling Magazine.* <http://www.gamblingmagazine.com/articles/41/41-216.htm>.
14. "U.S. Supreme Court Rules on Medical Marijuana." *Marijuana Policy Project.* 30 Dec. 2005 <http://www.mpp.org/raich/>.
15. Soble, Ronald L. "Homeowners Get Tax News, Vow to Back Prop. 13," *Los Angeles Times* May 19, 1978: p. 1, 20.
16. Matthews, Jay. "California Transformed by 'Prop 13'" *Los Angeles Times* May 23, 1988: A4. Also in Fairbanks, Robert. "Prop. 13's Super Salesman" *Los Angeles Times* May 17, 1978: p. 24.; Boyarsky, Bill. "Grass Roots on Airwaves to Push 13" *Los Angeles Times* May 28, 1978: p. 18; Reich,

Kenneth. "Jarvis Riding Wave of Public Anger" *Los Angeles Times* June 8, 1978: p. 18.

17. Op. cit. Schrag p. 146–147.

18. "The California Initiative Process—How Democratic Is It?" Public Policy Institute of California. Feb. 2002 http://www.ppic.org/content/pubs/OP_202XXOP.pdf p. 4–5.

19. Ibid. p. 1–4.

20. Allswang, J. *California Initiatives and Referendums: 1912–1990,* (Los Angeles: Edmund G. Brown Institute of Public Affairs, 1991).

21. "Insurers to Seek Referendum to Repeal New 'Bad Faith' Law." *California Policy Bulletins* 2.18 (Oct. 18, 1999). Jan. 2, 2006 <http://ca.rand.org/statebulls/bulletins/xstatebull218.html>.

22. Cain, Bruce E. "Constitutional Revision in California: The Triumph of Amendment Over Revision." Working paper. University of California, Berkeley. p. 2 .

23. "California Voter and Party Profiles" *Just the Facts.* Public Policy Institute of California. August, 2005. <http://ww.ppic.org/content/pubs/JTF_VoterProfilesJTF.pdf>.

24. Marin and Imperial County info.

25. Berthelsen, Christian. "Governor Sets Money-raising Record." *San Francisco Chronicle* Nov. 17, 2004: A1.

26. Talev, Margaret. "Corporate Donations Defended." *Sacramento Bee* Aug. 27, 2003.

27. Korber, Dorothy. "Growth Lobby a Growing Business, Records Show." *Sacramento Bee* Dec. 8, 2002: A1.

28. Ibid.

29. Hale, Dennis and Jonathan Eisen. *The California Dream.* New York: Collier Books, 1968. "The Political Culture of Southern California" by James Q. Wilson p. 217.

30. Op. cit. Report of registration.

31. Leary, Mary Ellen. "Elusive Candidates." *Phantom Politics Campaigning in California.* Washington D.C.: Public Affairs, 1977. p. 20.

32. Rains, George, "Election 2005: Analysis—Costly TV ads doing little to sway voters." San Francisco Chronicle, Saturday, October 29, 2005. p. B-2.

33. Kaplan, Martin, Ken Goldstein, and Matthew Hale. "Local News Coverage of the 2004 Campaigns: An Analysis of Nightly Broadcasts in 11 Markets." Working paper, Feb. 15, 2005. Lear Center Local News Archive, Los Angeles. p. 12.

34. Ibid.

35. Mitchell, Greg, *The Campaign of the Century.* New York: Random House, 1992 p. 201–202.

36. Gentry, Curt, *The Last Days of the Late, Great State of California.* Sausalito: Comstock Edition 1968. p. 77–79.

37. "Strategies for Improving California Voter Participation." *The California Voter Foundation.* Jan. 14, 2006. <http://www.calvoter.org/issues/votereng/votpart/strategies.html>.

38. Yamamura, Kevin, "Voting act puts counties in bind," San Francisco Chronicle, January 2, 2006. p. A1.

39. Hardy, Michael, "Diebold pays $2.6-million to settle California lawsuit," Federal Computer Week.

40. Williams, Juliet, "State election official threatens to block use of voting machines," Associate Press, December 24, 2005. p. A11.

41. Ramakrishnan, S. Karthick (Subramanian Karthick), Mark Baldassare. "The ties that bind: changing demographics and civic engagement." San Francisco Public Policy Institute of California. p. 9–18.

# Chapter 17

1. Samish, Arthur H., and Bob Thomas. *The Secret Boss of California; the Life and High Times of Art Samish.* New York: Crown, 1971. p. 35.

2. Ibid. p. 35–36.

3. Ross, Ruth A., and Barbara S. Stone. *California's Political Process.* New York: Random House, 1973. p. 91–92.

4. Block, A G., and Claudia Buck, eds. *California Political Almanac.* 6th ed. California Journal, 1999. p. 19, 123–124.

5. *The New Gold Rush: Financing California's Legislative Campaigns.* California Commission on Campaign Financing. Los Angeles: Center for Responsive Government, 1985. p. 8.

6. Michael, Jay, Dan Walters, and Dan Weintraub. *The Third House: Lobbyist, Money, and Power in Sacramento.* Berkeley: Berkeley Public Policy Press, 2002. p. 75 .

7. "Current Number of Legislators, Terms of Office and Next Election Year." Chart. National Conference of State Legislatures. <http:www.ncsl.org>.

8. Owens, John R., Edmond Costantini, and Louis F. Weschler. *California Politics and Parties.* London: The Macmillan Company, 1970. p. 285–286.

9. Ibid. p. 286.

10. Weintraub, Daniel. "Governor Should Be Bold, Call for New Lines." *The Sacramento Bee* Dec. 5, 2004, sec. Forum: E1.

11. Gunnison, Robert B. "Capital Probe; FBI Reportedly Told Deukmejian About Its Sting." *The San Francisco Chronicle* Aug. 30, 1988, sec. News: p. A1.

12. Op. cit. Michael p. 95–96.

13. Staffer of Assemblyman Todd Spitzer. Telephone interview. Feb. 3, 2006.

14. Ibid.

15. Paul Koretz, California Assembly Member, Forty-second Assembly District <http://democracts.assembly.ca.gov/members/a42/Constituent Services.

16. *Legislative Effectiveness Committee Meeting Summaries.* Assembly on State Issues Meeting, National Conference of State Legislatures. Washington DC, December 2000. <http://www.ncsl.org>.

17. Ibid.

18. Ibid.

19. Szymanski, Katie. "Women Prisoners Tell All At State Hearing." *Bay Area Reporter* Oct. 19, 2000. Feb. 2, 2006 <www.aegis.com>.

20. Ibid.

21. Katayama, Lisa. "Reforming California's Prisons: an Interview with Jackie Speier." *Mother Jones* July 7, 2005. Feb. 4, 2006. <www.motherjones.com>.

22. Ibid.

23. Delsohn, Gary. "Rejected Air Board Boss Gets New Post." *The Sacramento Bee* Sept. 29, 2005, sec. Main News: p. A3.

24. Op. cit. Owens p. 302.

25. Sanders, Jim. "Some Moderates Claim Pressure by Nunez." *The Sacramento Bee* Jan. 9, 2005, Metro Final ed., sec. Main News: p. A3.

26. *Legislator Compensation 2005.* National Conference of State Legislatures. Washington DC. <http://www.ncsl.org>.

27. Richardson, James, *Wllie Brown: A Biography.* Berkeley: University of California Press, 1996. p. 220–231.

28. Kearns, Jeff. "Dems Divided." *Sacramento News and Review* Dec. 25, 2003. <http://www.newsreview.com/sacramento>.

29. Richardson, James D. "Willie Brown: the Member's Speaker." 1994. <http://www.aliciapatterson.org>. p. 2.

30. Fred M. Monardi Ph.D., Edith D. Balbach Ph.D., Stella Aguinaga MScN, MPH, and Stanton A. Glantz Ph.D., "Shifting Allegiances: Tobacco Industry Political Expenditures in California January 1995—March 1996" (April 1, 1996). *Center for Tobacco Control Research and Education. Tobacco Control Policy Making: United States.* Paper CA1996. http://repositories.cdlib.org/ctcre/tcpmus/CA1996.

31. The Associated Press. "Assembly GOP Votes for New Minority Leader." *Berkeley Daily Planet* Mar. 27, 2001. <www.berkeleydailyplanet.com>.

32. "FTCR Praises Veto of Mercury Insurance Surcharge." *The Foundation for Taxpayer and Consumer Rights.* Sept. 30, 2002. <http://www.consumerwatchdog.org>.

33. "Above the Rules: How California Legislators Subvert the Public Interest-and Even the Expressed Will of the Voters." *San Francisco Chronicle* Sept. 22, 2002. <http://www.sfgate.com>.

# Chapter 18

1. *The Government Performance Project: Grading the States '05.* Washington D.C., 2005. <http://results.gpponline.org/>.
2. "Field Poll Trend of Job Performance Ratings of California Governors." *The Field Poll.* <http://field.com>.
3. "Executive Order D-23-01," Executive Orders - February 2001 http://www.governor.ca.gov/state/govsite/gov_pressroom_index.jsp?BV_SessionID=@@.
4. Op. cit. Field Poll.
5. Block, A. G., and Claudia Buck, eds. *California Political Almanac.* 6th ed. California Journal, 1999. p. 36–37.
6. Craft, Cynthia H. "Gray Davis: Show me the money," Edited by A.G. Block and Charles Price. *California Government and Politics Annual 2001–2002.* Sacramento: California Journal/Statenet, 2001. p. 10.
7. "Governors of California," http:/www.governor.ca.gov/govsite/govgallery/h/biography/governor.
8. Rarick, Ethan, *California Rising: The Life and Times of Pat Brown.* Berkeley: The University of California Press, 2006.
9. "Mike Curb." *Wikipedia.* <http:/en.wikipedia.org>.
10. Op. cit. Rarick p. 68.
11. "Stanley Mosk, 24th Attorney General." *Office of the Attorney General.* California Department of Justice. <http://ag.ca.gov>.
12. "Thomas C. Lynch, 25th Attorney General." *Office of the Attorney General.* California Department of Justice. <http://ag.ca.gov>. and "Ex-State Attorney General Thomas Lynch Dies At 82." *The San Francisco Chronicle* May 30, 1986.
13. "George Deukmejian, 27th Attorney General." *Office of the Attorney General.* California Department of Justice. <http://ag.ca.gov>.
14. "John Van De Kamp, 28th Attorney General." *Office of the Attorney General.* <http://ag.ca.gov>.
15. "Daniel E. Lungren. 29th Attorney General." *Office of the Attorney General.* California Department of Justice. <http://ag.ca.gov>.
16. "Bill Lockyer.30th Attorney General."
*Office of the Attorney General* California Department of Justice. <http://ag.ca.gov>.
17. "Responsibilities of the Controller's Office." *California State Controllers Office: Steve Westly.* California State Controllers Office. <http://www.sco.ca.gov>.
18. Op. cit. Block, A. G., and Claudia Buck. p. 57.
19. Williams, Juliet. "State Election Official Threatens to Block Use of Voting Machines." *Contro Costa Times* Dec. 24, 2005. p. A11.
20. Smith, Dan. "Peace Party Back on June 6 Ballot." *The Sacramento Bee* Feb. 4, 2006. p. A3.
21. "Statement Regarding Peace and Freedom Party's Qualification for the June 6, 2006 Primary Election Ballot." *California Secretary of State Bruce McPherson.* State of California. <http://www.ss.ca.gov>.
22. "The Secretary of State." *California Secretary of State Bruce McPherson.* State of California. <http://www.ss.ca.gov>.
23. Williams, Lance, and Christian Berthelsen. "Shelley's Shock Soul Searching." *The San Francisco Chronicle* Feb. 6, 2005, A1.
24. Mangold, Kirsten. "The Race for Superintendent of Public Instruction: DiMarco, Easton Tangle for the Job of Schools' Chief." *California Journal* 1994 <www.calvoter.org/archive>.
25. Chavez, Ken. "Wilson Vetoes Bill to Boost Instruction Offices Powers, Would Have Reversed Increase in Education Panel Clout." *The Sacramento Bee* Sept. 9, 1983, p. A6.
26. Schrag, Peter. "Paradise Lost: California's Experience, America's Future." Berkeley: University of California Press, 2004. p. 197.
27. Ellis, Virginia, and Carl Ingram. "Whistle-Blower Emerges in Quackenbush Probe." *The Los Angeles Times* June 23, 2000.
28. Bazar, Emily. "Quake Insurers Taken to Court." *The Sacramento Bee* 21 Nov. 2000, sec. Main News: p. A1.
29. Walters, Dan. "Schwarzenegger's Only Big Gain-Workers' Comp-is At Risk." *The Sacramento Bee* Nov. 20, 2005.
30. Chan, Gilbert. "Workers' Comp Cost Dropped." *The Sacramento Bee* Jan. 2, 2006, sec. Business: D1.
31. Op. cit. Block, A. G., and Claudia Buck. p. 70–72.
32. "Citizens Against Unfair Health Taxes: California Chapter." *Citizens Against Unfair Health Care Taxes.* <http://www.stophealthcaretaxes.com>.
33. Halper, Evan. "California Ok's $80 Million in Tax Refunds to Companies." *Los Angeles Times* Jan. 26, 2005.
34. "Evaluating California's Board and Commissions," California Performance Review Project. <http://cpr.ca.gov/report/cprrpt/frmfunc/bdscmm.htm.
35. "Consumer Advocates Assail Gov. Schwarzenegger's Plan to Abolish Independent Regulatory Boards Called Blow to Public Interest. Cabinet Member Says Citizens Will Have Input." *The Los Angeles Times* Jan. 8, 2005, sec. California: B12.
36. Martin, Mark, and Lynda Gledhill. "Governor Finds Trouble At Home . . . Overhaul Plan: He Drops Proposal to Abolish 88 Board." *The San Francisco Chronicle* Feb. 18, 2005. <http://sfgate.com>. p. 31–32.
37. Op. cit. Craft p. 12.
38. Salladay, Robert. "Consumer Privacy Bill Could Be Weakened/Davis Aids Conferring with Industry Lobbyist." *The San Francisco Chronicle* Aug. 3, 2001. <http://sfgate.com>.
39. "Press Release: California Governor Vetoes Credit Card Disclosure Bill." *Consumers Union.* Sept. 29, 2000. <http://www.consumersunion.org>.
40. "Campaign Finance Reformers See Gaming Conflict," Gambling Magazine—Issues & Ideas, 1999. http://www.gamblingmagazine.com/article/26/26–302.htm.
41. McCoy, Kevin. "Campaign Contributions or Conflicts of Interest?" *USA Today* Oct. 9, 2001. <http://www.sirotalaw.com>.

# Chapter 19

1. "California Office of Administrative Law." California Code Regulations. Thomson/West. 2006. <http://weblinks.westlaw.com/Find/Default.wl?DB=CA%2DADC%2DTOC%3BADCCAT . . . >.
2. "Find Law for Legal Professionals." *Health and Service Code Section 113950–113970.* <http://caselaw.lp.findlaw.com/cacodes/hsc/113950–113970.html>.
3. Ibid.
4. California Penal Code 415.
5. "San Jose Municipal Code." Title 10: Public Peace, Morals and Welfare. <http://www.amlegal.com/nxt/gateway.dll/California/sanjose/title10publicpeacemoralsandw . . . >.
6. Ibid.
7. California Courts, "What Appellate Justices Do". <http://www.courtinfo.ca.gov/courts/courtsofappeal/1stDistrict/do.htm>.
8. "Judicial Council of California," *Fact*
*Sheet: California Judicial System. Administrative Office of the Courts.* San Francisco: January 2003.
9. Ibid.
10. Ibid.
11. "A Visitor's Guide to the California Supreme Court." *Judicial Council of California Administrative Office of Court.* San Francisco: September 2004.
12. "California Courts: Self-Help Center:

Small Claims: Small Claims Basics." http://courtinfo.ca.gov/selfhelp/smallclaims/scbasics.htm.

13. Op. cit. "Judicial Council of California".

14. Op. cit. California Courts, "What Appellate Justices Do".

15. Op. cit. "Judicial Council of California".

16. Ibid.

17. Op. cit. "A Visitor's Guide to the California Supreme Court".

18. "How Appellate and Supreme Court Justices are selected," California Courts of Appeals: 1st District: San Francisco <http://www.courtinfo.ca.gov/courts/courtsofappeal/1stDistrict/selected.htm>.

19. "Overview of the California State Court System," Self Service Center—Superior Court of Santa Clara, 2006. <http://www.scselfservice.org/home/overview.htm>.

20. "Civil Liability under the California Dog Bite Statute." The Dog Bite Statute. Civil Code section 3342 <http:www.dogbitelaw.comPAGES/civil.htm>.

21. "National Center on Elder Abuse." Abuse of Adults 60 + 2004 Survey of Adult Protective Services. Washington, DC. February 2006.

22. Payton, George T., *Concepts of California Criminal Law.* San Jose: Criminal Justice Services, 1995. p. 125–131.

23. Amar, Vikram. "An Important Sentencing Ruling from the California Supreme Court: Despite the U.S. Supreme Court's Recent Sentencing Upheaval, California's System is Held to be Valid." June 24, 2005. <http://writ.news.findlaw.com/scripts/printer_friendly.pl?page=/amar/20050624.html>.

24. Abrams, Leslie, *The Defense Is Ready: Life in the Trenches of Criminal Law.* New York: Simon and Schuster, 1997. p. 183–204.

25. "Jurors: The Basics" and "Step 1–3," California Courts: Guide to California Jury Service. <http://www.courtinfo.ca.gov/jury/step1.htm>.

26. Klerman, Daniel. "American Tort Reform Association: Bringing Greater Fairness, Predictability and Efficiency to the Civil Justice System." A Look at California Juries Participation, Shortcomings and Recommendations. <http://www.atra.org/reports/CA_juries/>.

27. "The California Grand Jurors' Association." *History of the California Grand Jurors' Association.* http://www.nvo.com/cgja/grandjuryback groundinformation/ and Jameson, Marianne. "The Grand Jury." *A Brief Historical Overview. California Grand Jurors Association.*

28. LockeBee, Cathy, "Grand jury cites unspent funds," Sacramento Bee, January 12, 2006. p. G1.

29. "Final Report: Case #0404—City of Tracy," 2004–2005 San Joaquin County Civil Grand Jury.

30. "Assemblywoman Kehoe Pushing for Police Powers for Homeowner Associations." American Homeowners Resource Center, June 21, 2002. <http://www.ahrc.com/new/index.php/src/news/sub/press-rel/action/ShowMedia/id/190>.

31. "State Law protects Officers from Disclosure of Complaints." *SFGate.com.* February 9, 2006. <http://www.sfgate.com/cgibin/article.cgi?file=/c/a/2006/02/09/MNUFMAIN.DTL&type=p . . . >.

32. CDAA Specialized Newsletters. California District Attorney's Association, 2006. <http://www.cdda.org/grantpubs/index.htm>.

33. Tulsky, Fredric. "Review of More Than 700 Appeals Finds Problems Throughout the Justice System: First five parts." *Mercury News.* January 22, 2006. <http://www.mercurynews.com/mld/mercurynews/news/special_packages/stolenjustice/13674876.htm>.

34. Ibid.

35. Ibid.

36. Walters, Dan. "The Question on Rose Bird." *Sacramento Bee.* January 20, 1985. p. A3.

37. Egelko, Bob. "Ronald George," Edited by A.G. Block and Charles Price. *California Government and Politics Annual 2001–2002.* Sacramento: California Journal/Statenet, 2001. p. 22–24.

38. "California Supreme Court Upholds Student's First Amendment Rights Conviction of 'George T' for Writing Dark Poems Overturned." The American Civil Liberties Union of Northern California Press Release July 22, 2004. <http://www.aclunc.org.pressrel/040722-georget.html>.

39. Op. cit. Egelko.

40. Crosby, Margaret. "The Right to Die California Supreme Court Ruling in Wendland Case Should Spur Us to Protect Our Rights." ACLU News—The Newspaper of the ACLU of Northern California. Autumn 2001.

41. Price, Charles M., "Shadow Government." Edited by A.G. Block and Charles Price. *California Government and Politics Annual 2001–2002.* Sacramento: California Journal/Statenet, 2001. p. 72–74.

42. Howard, John. "Waiting for Judgment Day." California Journal, May 2004.

43. Macallair, Daniel. "The Death of Prison Reform." Sign on SanDiego.com: *The San Diego Union Tribune.* January 18, 2006. http://www.signonsandiego.com/union-trib/20060118/news_lz1e18macalla.html.

# Chapter 20

1. Richardson Jr., Jesse J., Meghan Zimmerman, and Robert Puentes. *Is Home Rule the Answer? Clarifying the Influence of Dillon's Rule on Growth Management.* The Brookings Institution Center on Urban and Metropolitan Policy. 2003. <http://www.brookings.edu>.

2. "The History of County Government." *National Association of Counties.* <http://www.naco.org>.

3. Purdy, Tim I., "Lassen's Past," Lassen County History and Culture: Narrative History. <http://www.psln.com/pete/history.htm>.

4. *The Historical Records of County Government in California.* 2nd edition California State Archives, 2004. p. 70.

5. Sonenshein, Raphael J. The Prospect for County Charter Reform in California. Department of Political Science, California State University, Fullerton, 2001. p. 14–16.

6. "County Structure." *California State Association of Counties.* <http://www.csac.counties.org>.

7. Sokolow, Alvin D. "Caring for Unincorporated Communities." San Lorenzo Express March–April, 2000. <http://www.sanlorenzoexrpess.com>.

8. History of Contract Cities, California Contract Cities Association. <http://www.contracities.org>.

9. Op. cit. *The Historical Records of County Government in California.* p. 71.

10. Ibid. p. 63.

11. "County Offices: Auditor-Controller." *California State Association of Counties.* <http://www.csac.counties.org>.

12. "Lean on Me: California's Local Governments Rely on State Money More Than Those in Rest of Nation." Public Policy Institute of California. Jan. 27, 2003. <http://www.ppic.org>.

13. "When Government Fails: The Orange County Bankruptcy—A Policy Summary," Public Policy Institute of California. March 18, 1998.

14. Meeker, Amanda. An Overview of the History of Constitutional Provisions Dealing with Local Government. California Constitutional Revision Commission. <http://www.library.ca.gov>. p. 4.

15. "Guide to Government, California State Government." Smart Voter. <http://www.smartvoter.org>.

16. "Types of Cities." *League of California Cities.* <http://www.cacities.org>.

17. Op. cit. "Guide to Government".

18. Speer, Robert. "Measure A, Nasty Politics and the Leadership Gap." Chico News and Review, March 13, 2006. <http://www.newsreview.com/chico/Home>.

19. McCarthy, Kevin F., Fae W. Archibald, and Brian Weatherford. "Facing the Challenge of Implementing Proposition F in San Diego." Rand Corporation, 2005.
20. Op. cit. Speer.
21. "Dreams Become Reality," Modesto Irrigation District, 1987 <http://www.mid.org>.
22. "About Special Districts." California Special Districts Association. <http://www.csda.net>.
23. "Frequently Asked Questions." California Special Districts Association. <http://www.csda.net>.
24. Fine, Howard. "Special Districts Get Stuck with Bigger Tax Losses Than Planned." Los Angeles Business Journal, 2004. <http://www.findarticles.com>.

25. Titel, Marc, and Roger Wagner. "Tightening Controls Over California's Special Districts: Lessons Learned From the WRD." Cal-Tax Digest, July 2000. <http://www.caltax.org>.
26. Terzian, Richard R. "Special Districts: Relics of the Past or Resources for the Future?" Cal-Tax Digest, July 2000. <http://www.caltax.org>.
27. Ibid.
28. Dewitt, Howard. *The California Dream.* Dubuque: Hendall/ Hunt Publishing Company, 1997. p. 182.
29. Ibid. p. 182–183.
30. "District Organization." California Department of Education. State of California. <http://www.cde.gov>.

31. McWilliams, Carey, *California: The Great Exception.* New York: Current Books, 1949. p. 18.
32. "How Do California's School Boards Compare?" Stanford News Service. Stanford University. <http://www.stanford.edu/dept/news>.
33. "Board Briefs—News from the School Board Meeting," Fresno Unified School District, February 22, 2006.
34. Carrol, Stephen J., Cathy Krop, Jeremy Arkes, Peter A. Morrison, and Ann Flanagan. "California's K-12 Public Schools: How Are They Doing?" Santa Monica: Rand Corporation, 2005.

# Chapter 21

1. "Making Ends Meet: How Much Does It Cost to raise a Family In California?" California Budget Project. 1999 and 2005 Reports.
2. Rabin, Jeffrey. "State Spent Its Way Into Budget Crisis." Los Angeles Times, October 29, 2002.
3. "Governor's Budget- Summary Charts." 2006–07 Total Revenues and Transfers. <http://www.ebudget.ca.gov/BudgetSummary/SUM/1249561.html>.
4. Schrag, Peter. *Paradise Lost: California's Experience, America's Future.* Berkeley: University of California Press, 2004. p. 153–154.
5. Guynn, Jessica. "Corporate Tax Break in Jeopardy." The Contra Costa Times, 15 March 2006. p. C1.
6. "Oil and Gas Tax Breaks." 2002 Update, California Tax Reform Association.
7. "LAO Facts." Legislative Analyst's Office. <http://www.lao.ca.gov/LAOMenus/LAOFacts.aspx>. p. 8.
8. Vanzi, Max. "Liz Hill: Here Today, Here Tomorrow." The California Journal. July 1999.
9. "Annual Report 2004," California Franchise Tax Board, p. 1–29. http://www.ftb.ca.gov.
10. "Summary Analysis of Amended Bill,"(AB 6) California Franchise Tax Board. Amended May 27, 2005 and June 15, 2005.
11. Reference: Sections 6358 and 6373, Revenue and Taxation Code.
12. Op. cit. "Annual Report 2004," p. 31–51 and S.M., Newcomb. "California: Bank and Financial Corporation v. General Corporation Taxation." The CPA Journal. May 1990.

13. McClintock, Tom. "Highway Robbery." 17 November 2004. <http://www.tommcclintock.net/blog//2004_11_01_archive.html>.
14. Thompson, Don. "Governor, Others Working to Salvage Bond Measure." The Contra Costa Times, March 13, 2006. p. A12 and "Governor Releases Proposed 2006–07 Budget.," California Budget Project. 19 January 2006. Sacramento.
15. "Budget Background: A Mini-Primer On Bonds." *California Budget Project.* February 2006. Sacramento.
16. "Budget Brief: What Would The President's Proposed Budget Mean For California." California Budget Project. February 2006. Sacramento, California.
17. "Research Areas: California—The Facts On California's Tax Climate," The Tax Foundation, 2006. <http://www.taxfoundation.org/research/topic/15.html>.
18. Op. cit. Schrag. p. 154.
19. Silva, J. Fred and Elisa Barbour. "The State-Local Fiscal Relationship in California: A Changing Balance of Power." Public Policy Institute of California. 1999.
20. Warren, Jenifer. "Jail Population Expected to Rise by Thousands." The Contra Costa Times. April 23, 2006. p. A4 <http://republican.sen.ca.gov/web/mcclintock/article_print.asp?PID=286>.
21. Op. cit. Silva and Barbour.
22. "A Primer on California City Finance." League of California Cities. Reprinted from Western City Magazine, March 2005. p. 6.
23. "Special Notice: How Local Governments Will Be Reimbursed for the Upcoming Reduction in the Local Sales

and Use Tax Rate." State Board of Equalization. June 2004.
24. Op. cit. Vanzi.
25. "Tourism Funding Restored." California Lodging Industry Association. August 6, 2005. <http://www.clia.org/print.cfm?newsid=181>.
26. McClintock, Tom. "Big Five, Big Mistake." State Senator Tom McClintock 19th District. February 3, 2005. http://republican.sen.ca.gov/web/mcclintock/article_print.asp?PID=287.
27. Matsusaka, John. "Direct Democracy and Fiscal Gridlock: Have Voter Initiatives Paralyzed the California Budget.?" *Marshall School of Business.* Los Angeles.
28. Ibid.
29. Ibid.
30. Lieser, Tom. "California's Economic Outlook: Looking Beyond the State Budget," UCLA Anderson Forecast. University of California - Los Angeles.
31. Said, Carolyn. "A 'Fragile Economy' Ahead." San Francisco Chronicle, March 29, 2005. p. C1.
32. "The Hardest Part of Politics: The California Budget." The California Agenda/Public Policy Lecture by Bill Hauck, California Business Roundtable and Jean Ross, California Budget Project. Edmund G. "Pat" Brown Institute of Public affairs, California State University, Los Angeles. June 7, 2005.

# PHOTO CREDITS

**Part Six**   San Francisco Chronicle/ Corbis—NY

**Chapter 15**   page 520, Michael Newman/PhotoEdit Inc.; page 523, Everton, Macduff/Getty Images Inc.—Image Bank; page 524, The Long Island Museum of American Art, History and Carriages; page 527, Darrell Gulin/Getty Images; page 529, The Granger Collection; page 532, Corbis/Bettmann; page 536, UPI/Corbis/Bettmann; page 537, The Granger Collection; page 539, The Granger Collection; page 541, Photofest; page 543 top of page, UPI/Corbis/Bettmann; page 543 bottom right, The Granger Collection; page 545, Spencer Grant/PhotoEdit Inc.

**Chapter 16**   page 548, Kim Kulish/ SABA/Corbis/SABA Press Photos, Inc.; page 550, Bob Daemmrich/Stock Boston; page 556, AP Wide World Photos; page 557, David McNew, Getty Images; page 558 top of page, Eric Draper/AP Wide World Photos; page 558 bottom left, Michael A. Mariant/AP Wide World Photos; page 559, M.C. Lendon/AP Wide World Photos; page 565, UPI/Corbis/ Bettmann; page 570, Corbis/Bettmann; page 576, Rachel Epstein/PhotoEdit Inc.; page 577, AP Wide World Photos; page

579, Rich Pedroncelli/AP Wide World Photos; page 581, AP Wide World Photos.

**Chapter 17**   page 584, Corbis/Bettmann; page 586, Library of Congress; page 595, Sherpard Sherbell/Corbis/SABA Press Photos, Inc.; page 597, Corbis/Bettmann; page 596, Mark Costantini/San Francisco Chronicle/Corbis—NY; page 609, Ken James/Corbis—NY.

**Chapter 18**   page 618, Lucy Nicholson/ Corbis—NY; page 620, California Governor's Office; page 622, Corbis/ Bettmann; page 624, Rich Pedroncelli/AP Wide World Photos; page 626, Kenneth James/Corbis—NY; page 629, Nick Ut/AP Wide World Photos; page 630, Roger Rossmeyer/ Corbis—NY; page 631, Darryl Bush/San Francisco Chronicle/ Corbis—NY; page 634, Jim Ruymen/ Corbis/Reuters America LLC.

**Chapter 19**   page 648, Paul Sakuma/ Pool/Corbis/Bettmann; page 652, Brendan McDermid/epa/Corbis—NY; page 657, A. Ramey/PhotoEdit Inc.; page 660 top, AP Wide World Photos, page 660 middle, AP Wide World Photos; page 662, John G. Mabanglo/epa/Corbis—NY; page 664, Myung Chun/L.A. Daily News/Corbis/

Sygma; page 665, Handout/Corbis/Reuters America LLC; page 667, Jeff Topping/ Corbis/Reuters America LLC; page 669, David Paul Morris/Getty Images; page 671, Monica Almeida/New York Times Agency.

**Chapter 20**   page 676, Chad Ehlers/The Stock Connection; page 682, Andrei Sarna-Wojcicki/U.S. Geological Survey, Denver; page 690 top, American Photographer (19th century)/The Bridgeman Art Library International; page 690 middle, Cameron Davidson/The Stock Connection; page 691, Michael Newman/PhotoEdit Inc.; page 692, Ken James/Corbis—NY; page 693 top, P.F. Bentley/Getty Images/ TimeLife Pictures; page 693 bottom, Gene Blevins/Corbis—NY; page 694, Spencer Grant/PhotoEdit Inc.; page 704, Spencer Grant/PhotoEdit Inc.

**Chapter 21**   page 710, Kimberly White/ Corbis/Reuters America LLC; page 715, Ken James/Corbis—NY; page 717, Ken James/ Corbis—NY; page 722, Michael Newman/ PhotoEdit, Inc.; page 723, Robert Harbison/ Robert Harbison; page 724, Kim Kulish/ Corbis—NY; page 726, Olga Shalygin/AP Wide World Photos; page 732, Rich Pedroncelli/AP Wide World Photos; page 733, Ken James/Corbis—NY.

# INDEX

## A

A. C. Nielsen, 181
*AARP The Magazine*, 182, 234
ABC, 44, 175, 188, 190, 317
*Abington Township v. Schempp*, 427
ABM Treaty, defined, 504
Abortion rights, 45, 431–432
    partial birth abortion, 432
Abramoff, Jack, 234, 644
"Absence of malice," 196
Academic radicalism, 51–52
Access, defined, 232
*Access Hollywood*, 182
Accuracy in Media, 186
Adams, John, 61, 63, 83, 334, 337, 339
Adjudication, defined, 347
Administrative Procedures Act, 377
Adros, Edmund, 58
Adversarial system, defined, 397
Advice and consent, 248–249
    defined, 248
Affirmative action, 451–457
    courts and, 453–455, 456
    defined, 452
    higher education, 455
Affirmative racial gerrymandering, 256
    defined, 255
AFL-CIO, 225, 226
African Americans, 34
    Congress, 267–268
Age Discrimination Act, 128
Agenda setting, 179–180
    defined, 179
Agnew, Spiro, 307
Agricultural growth, 540
Agriculture, U.S. Department of, 238, 351
Agua Caliente Band of Cahuilla Indians, 573
Aid to Families with Dependent Children, 126
Air Force Association, 225
Alameda Power and Telecom, 683
Albrecht, Chris, 634
*Alden v. Maine*, 122
Alien and Sedition Acts of 1798, 112
Alien Land bill, defined, 540
Alito, Samuel A., Jr., 398, 402, 404, 406, 410
Allen, George, 214
Alliance for California's Tomorrow, 554
Al Qaeda, 510, 511, 512
Alternative dispute resolution (ADR), defined, 653
Alvarado, Pedro de, 530
Amendment. *See also* Individual amendments
    defined, 78
American Association of Retired Persons (AARP), 225, 232, 233, 234, 492
American Bankers Association, 225, 235
American Bar Association (ABA), 225
    Commission on Women and the Profession, 269

American Civil Liberties Union (ACLU), 18, 41, 44, 225, 239, 406
American Conservative Union (ACU), 42, 225, 229
American Council of Life Insurance, 230
American Farm Bureau Federation, 225
American Federation of State, County, and Municipal Employees (AFSCME), 225, 226, 227, 288
American Federation of Teachers (AFT), 225, 226, 235
American Gas Association, 225
American Hospital Association, 230, 235
American Indian Movement, 225
American Iron and Steel Institute, 225
American Israel Public Affairs Committee, 225
American Journalism Review, 198
American Legion, 19, 225, 724
American Medical Association (AMA), 225, 230, 235, 663
*American National Law Journal*, 269
American Petroleum Institute, 225
American Political Science Association, 5
American Red Cross, 724
American Security Council, 225
Americans for Constitutional Action, 225
Americans for Democratic Action (ADA), 44, 225, 229
*American Spectator*, 176
Americans United for Separation of Church and State, 41, 425
Americans with Disabilities Act (ADA) of 1990, 128
American Tax Reduction Movement, 565
American Tort Reform Association, 663
American Truckers Association, 225
Amicus curiae, 239, 407
Amtrak, 356
Anaheim Public Utility Electric Department, 682
Anderson, John, 222
Angelides, Phil, 627, 646, 716, 717
Annapolis Convention, 61
Annenberg Public Policy Center, 197
Anthony, Susan B., 227, 463
Anti-Defamation League of B'nai B'rith, 45, 225, 227, 426
Anti-Federalists, 77, 79, 82
Anti-Saloon League, 227, 463
Appeal, defined, 392
Appellate jurisdiction, defined, 392
Apportionment, defined, 251
Appropriation, 731
Appropriations act, defined, 368
Army Association, 225
Arnett, Peter, 508
Arrests, 438

Article I, of the U.S. Constitution, 87–91, 248, 314, 424, 436, 444
Article II, of the U.S. Constitution, 91–93
Article III, of the U.S. Constitution, 93–94
Article IV, of the U.S. Constitution, 94–95, 115, 444
Articles of Confederation, 59–61, 64, 66, 75, 105
Article V, of the U.S. Constitution, 95, 111
Article VI, of the U.S. Constitution (The National Supremacy Clause), 70, 71, 95, 111
Article VII, of the U.S. Constitution, 95
Asbestos Hazard Emergency Act, 128
Ashcroft, John, 439
Asian Law Caucus, 535
Assembly Bill , 566
Assembly Budget Committee, 598, 731
Assembly leaders, partisan, 605–608
Assembly speaker, 603–605
    defined, 603
Association of American Railroads, 230
Association of Trial Lawyers of America, 225, 226, 235
AT&T, 230, 607, 627
Attorney General, 631–646
Augmentation, 731
Authoritarianism, defined, 14
Authorization, defined, 368
Automobile Dealers Association, 225

## B

*Baker v. Carr*, 82, 251, 391
*Bakke* case, 456
    defined, 453
Bakker, Tammy Faye, 228
Ballistic missile defense (BMD)
    defending, 506
    defined, 505
Bargaining, and the legislative process, 294
Bay Meadows, 554
Bean, Walton, 536
Beard, C. A., 66, 67
Bear Flag Rebellion, defined, 529
Beliefs, 25–26
    defined, 26
*Bell Curve, The* (Herrnstein and Murray), 33
Bennett, Robert, 389
Bennett, William, 389
Bentsen, Lloyd, 337
Bermudez, Rudy, 555
Bernanke, Ben, 356
Bernstein, Carl, 313
*Better Homes and Gardens*, 182
Bicameral, defined, 246
Biden, Joseph R., Jr., 214, 403
Bidwell party, 524
Big Four, defined, 534

Big-money contributors, 151–152
Bill of attainder, 424
    defined, 436
Bill of Rights, 12, 79, 82, 423, 431, 442
    defined, 78
Bills, becoming a law, 287
Bin Laden, Osama, 162, 510, 512
Bipartisan Campaign Finance Reform Act, 155
Bipartisanship, defined, 288
Bird, Rose, 669
Black, Hugo, 86, 410
Black Entertainment Television, 182
Blackmun, Harry, 402, 409, 410
Black Panther Party, 580
Black Panthers, 658
Blair, Tony, 309, 330, 513
Blakely, Delois, 662
Blanket primary
    defined, 552
    and the U.S. Supreme Court, 553
Block grant, 125
Blue Cross/Blue Shield, 230
Blue pencil, 731
Board of Education, of California, 637–638
Board of equalization, 639–640
    defined, 639
Board of Parole Hearing, 640
Boeing Company, 230
Bolten, Joshua B., 377
Bond debt, 721
Bonin, William, 663
Bork, Robert H., 401, 402, 405
Boston University, 44
Boxer, Barbara, 44, 45, 268
Braddock, E., 63
Brady, James S., 435
Brady Handgun Violence Protection Act, 122
*Brady Law*, 435
Brandeis, Louis D., 109, 429
Brannan, Sam, 532
Braun, Carol Moseley, 268
Brennan, William J., 402, 410, 442
Breyer, Stephen G., 402, 406, 410, 413
Bribery, defined, 233
Briefs, 393–394
    defined, 394
Brooklyn College, 45
Brown, Edmund G. "Pat," 587, 623, 628, 629, 704
Brown, Janice Rogers, 654–655, 669
Brown, Jerry, 545, 574, 629, 630, 631, 669, 671, 692, 693, 715
Brown, Linda, 239, 398
Brown, Pat, 557
Brown, Ralph M., 693
Brown, Willie, 604, 605, 608, 628, 693
Brown Act, 693
*Brown v. Board of Education of Topeka*, 82, 112, 117, 239, 336, 388, 391, 398, 406, 411, 447
Brulte, Jim, 602
*Buckley v. Valeo*, 157, 388

Budget
    Congress and, 381
    house and senate committees, 368
    president's, 367–368
    process, 366
Budget and Accounting Act, 322, 381
Budget and Impoundment Control
    Act of 1974, 314
Budget change proposal (BCP), 731
Budgeting, politics of, 369–372
Budget maximization, defined, 348
*Budget of the United States Government*,
    362, 367, 381
Budget resolution, defined, 368
Budgets
    effect of direct democracy on,
        734–735
    executive plans, 730–732
    key terms, 731
    municipal, 728–730
    politics, 715–716
    process, 727–734
Bull Moose Party, 539
Bureaucracy
    budgetary process, 362–369
    bureaucratic power, 343–349
    congressional constraints,
        376–380
    defined, 344
    democracy and, 357–360
    dismissing a federal employee,
        359
    federal, 345, 349–357
    interest groups and, 380
    judicial constraints on, 380–381
    nature of, 343
    politics of, 360–362
    politics of budgeting, 369–372
    regulating America, 375–376
    regulatory battles, 372–375
Bureau of Alcohol, Tobacco,
    Firearms, and Explosives
    (ATF), 434, 435
    Supreme Court and, 395–397
Bureau of Justice Statistics, 443
Bureau of Los Angeles Aqueduct
    Power, 682
Bureau of the Census, 252
Burger, Warren, 402, 409, 410
Burhans-Farnham, Eliza Woodson,
    723
Burton, John, 593, 608
Burton, Phil, 593
Bush, George H. W., 6, 45, 163, 167,
        170, 219, 290, 308, 334,
        335, 337, 338, 339, 353,
        356, 399
    approval ratings and, 316, 317
    court nominations of, 406
    debate with Clinton and Perot,
        165
    debate with Dukakis, 164
    Gulf War, 507–508
    influence on court policy, 414
    party leadership and, 319
    personality, 317
    START, 504
    success with Congress, 328
    taxes, 482
Bush, George W., 6, 19, 125, 129,
        145, 155, 163, 167, 168,
        169, 170, 172, 219, 234,
        284, 285, 305, 308, 330,
        334, 335, 338, 352, 353,

356, 363, 377, 404, 439,
        462, 506, 550, 579
    court nominees of, 401–402, 404
    debate with Gore, 165
    debate with Kerry, 165
    influence on court policy, 414
    media and, 317, 318
    party control of the House and
        Senate and, 263
    presidential style, 321
    Republican victories in '02 and
        '04, 264–267
    success with Congress, 326–327
    taxes, 482–483
    Treaty of Moscow, 504
    vs. John F. Kerry, 162
    War on Terrorism, 509–516
Bush, Prescott, 308
*Bush v. Gore*, 413
Business Roundtable, 225, 230
Bustamante, Cruz, 631
Butcher, Bill, 565, 576
Byrd, Robert, 283

**C**

Cabeza de Vaca, Ivar Nuñez, 530
Cabinet, 322–323
    defined, 322
    department functions, 351
Cabrillo, Juan Rodriguez, 525
Cain, Bruce E., 569
*Cal-Access*, 555
Calhoun, John C., 112, 116
California
    ballot propositions since 2000,
        563–564
    beyond electoral politics,
        579–580
    budget politics, 715–716
    budget process, 727–734
    early years of statehood, 533–537
    elections, 552–555
    electoral dilemma, 555–570
    empowering the voters, 577–578
    events in history, 522
    executive branch, 545
    and gambling, 644
    land and climate, 522–525
    legislative budget approval,
        730–732
    Mexican control, 528
    Native American settlement, 525
    in the new millennium, 544–546
    political advertising in, 575
    the Progressive era, 539–540
    Proposition 57, 727
    Proposition 5, 560
    Proposition 9, 724
    Proposition 98, 722, 727
    Proposition 1A, 727
    Proposition 184, 656, 658
    Proposition 115, 670
    Proposition 140, 585, 586, 610,
        716
    Proposition 116, 734
    Proposition 103, 638
    Proposition 13, 544, 545, 559,
        562, 565, 704, 705, 707,
        715, 722, 723, 726
    Proposition 34, 554, 566
    Proposition 36, 671
    Proposition 215, 561
    Proposition 220, 651
    Proposition 227, 705

Proposition 209, 578, 655
    second constitution, 537–538
    Spanish exploration and
        settlement, 525–528
    Spanish heritage of, 530–531
    structural budget gap, 713–715
    the twentieth century, 540–544
    unconventional political
        participation, 580–582
    U.S. annexation, 528–533
    vote-counting difficulties,
        578–579
*California: The Great Exception*
    (McWilliams), 596
California, University of, 717
    Board of Regents, 631
California, University of Berkeley,
    552, 569
California, University of Los
    Angeles, 654
California Abortion Rights League,
    628
California Administrative Codes,
    649
California Air Resources Board, 601
California Balanced Budget Act, 567
California Board of Education, 704
California Budget Project, 711
California Buildings Standards
    Commission, 595
California Business, Transportation,
    and Housing Agency, 622
California Civil Rights Initiative, 578
California Commission on
    Campaign Financing, 589
California Community College
    system, 581, 595
*California Constitution Revisions
    Commission*, 567
California Correctional Peace
    Officers Association, 555,
    573, 600, 601, 672
California Council for
    Environmental and
    Economic Balance, 601
California county government
    assessor, 686
    county administration, 684–685
    county bureaucracy, 681–684
    county clerk, 687
    district attorney, 685–686
    funding, 688–689
    historical roots of, 678–679
    sheriff, 686
    unincorporated communities and
        contract cities, 679–680
California Crime Watch, 633
California Dental Association, 573
California Department of
    Corrections, 671, 672, 725
California Department of Education,
    635, 645
California Department of Justice,
    633
California Department of Parks and
    Recreation, 635
California Department of
    Transportation, 619
California District Attorneys
    Association, 661
*The California Dream* (De Witt), 703
California Economic Recovery Bond
    Act, 727
California Electric Light Company,
    683

California Emergency Council, 631
California Environmental Protection
    Agency, 712
California Environmental Quality
    Act (CEQA), 697
California Film Commission, 641
California Gold Rush, 530, 531
    defined, 523
    legacies of, 532–533
California Government Code, 679,
    687
California Indian casino owners, 600,
    644
*California Journal*, 611
California judicial system
    reforming, 672–674
    trends in, 668–670
California law, variations in,
    656–661
California legislature
    committee system, 609–614
    compensation, 602, 603
    electing, 589–590
    hidden view of lawmaking,
        615–616
    leadership in, 602–609
    legislative process, 614–615
    legislative universe, 593–602
    making of, 588–593
    part-time, 610–611
California Lodging Industry
    Association, 731
California Medical Association, 573,
    657
California National Guard, 623
California Nurses Association, 596
California Penal Code, 649
California Performance Review,
    640–643
*California Progressives, The* (Mowry),
    596
California Public Utilities
    Commission (CPUC), 627
California Reapportionment Act of
    1965, 593
California School Employees
    Association, 573
California's Fair Political Practices
    Commission (FPPC), 566
California State Lottery Act, 560
California State University (CSU),
    631, 649, 654, 717
California Taxpayers Association,
    701, 716
California Tax Reform Association,
    716
California Teachers Association, 573
California Travel and Tourism
    Commission, 732
California Voter Foundation, 578
*California Women: A History* (Lothrop),
    551
California Youth Authority, 671
Californios, 530, 532, 538, 591
    defined, 528
    and voter rights, 551
Californios for Fair Representation,
    591
Caltech, 526
Calvert, C. *See* Lord Baltimore
CalWORKs, 725
Campaign finance, regulating,
    154–157
Campaign finance law,
    circumventing, 554–555

Campaign finance reform, 566–567
Campaigning, 570–577. *See also*
    Presidential campaign
  effects of, 147
  election costs, 147–149
  and geography, 573–574
  and interest groups, 572–573
  and mass communications,
    574–577 .
  nonpartisan qualification,
    570–571
  raising cash, 149–151
  strategies, 143–147
  voter records, 571–572
Campaign strategy, defined, 143
Campaign to Eradicate Marijuana
    Planting (CAMP), 634
Campbell, Bill, 606
Canciamilla, Joe, 602
*Capital Gang*, 187
Capital improvement project, 697
Capitalism, defined, 26
Capital outlay, 731
Capital punishment, in California,
    662–663
Capture theory of regulation,
    372–374
  defined, 372
Career Executive Assignments
    (CEA), 623
Carnegie Corporation, 511
Carpenters & Joiners Union, 235
Carswell, G. Harrold, 402
Carter, Jimmy, 80, 199, 214, 219,
    282, 290, 305, 327, 352,
    359, 521
  court nominations, 406
  debate with Ford, 164
  debate with Reagan, 164
  deregulation of the airline
    industry, 374
  party leadership and, 319
  personality, 317
  presidential style, 321
  Sandanista regime in Nicaragua
    and, 330
  success with Congress, 327–328
Case Act of 1972, 331
Casework, defined, 272, 380, 599
Castro, Fidel, 330
*Castro v. State of California*, 552
Categorical grant, 124–125
Caucus, defined, 211
CBS, 175, 188, 190, 193, 317
CBS News, 145
Censure, defined, 298
Census Act of 1976, 252
Center for Families, Children and
    the Courts, 657
Center for Media and Public Affairs,
    181
Center for Responsive Politics,
    238
Center for Voting and Democracy,
    163
Central American Free Trade
    Agreement (CAFTA), 477
Central Intelligence Agency (CIA),
    332–333, 352, 363, 364
Centralized federalism, defined, 119
Central Pacific Railroad Company,
    534, 536, 537
Chain of command, 343
  defined, 41
*Challenger*, 303–305

Challengers, 146
  defined, 142
Chamber of Commerce of the U.S.,
    230
Chan, Peter, 658–661
Chase, Salmon P., 103
Chavez, Cesar, 460, 591
Checci, Al, 626, 642, 643
Checks and balances, defined, 72
Cheney, Dick, 264, 285, 308, 337,
    511
  presidential confidant, 338
Chertoff, Michael, 352
Chessman, Caryl, 658, 662
Chevron, 511
*Chicago Tribune*, 182
Children, protecting and education
    of, 723–725
Children's Defense Fund, 225, 269
Children's Protective Association,
    724
Child Welfare Services, California,
    725
Chinese immigrants, 532, 537
  scapegoat for Workingmen's Party,
    538
  and voter rights, 551
Christian Broadcasting Network
    (CBN), 228
Christian Coalition, 225, 227, 228,
    288
Chu, Judy, 555
Churchill, Winston, 333, 499
Circuit courts, defined, 393
Cities
  city council, 690–695
  legal framework and formation of,
    689–690
Citizens Against Unfair Health Care
    Taxes, 640
*Citizen's Commission on Ballot Initiatives*,
    567
Citizenship, 37–40
  natural born vs. naturalized, 51
City attorney, defined, 696
City clerk, defined, 696
City manager, defined, 696
City treasurer, defined, 696
Civil cases, defined, 397
Civil disobedience, 8
Civil law, 656–657
  defined, 656
Civil Rights, Office of, 405
Civil Rights Act of 1957, 445
Civil Rights Act of 1968, 445
Civil Rights Act of 1964, 112, 227,
    267, 293, 445, 449–451, 452
  Title VII, 465, 467
Civil rights acts, 448–451
Civil Rights Acts of 1866, 1871, and
    1875, 445
Civil Service Reform Act of 1978,
    359
Claremont Institute, Golden State
    Policy Center, 610
Clark, Wesley, 214
Class action suits, 400
  defined, 398
Class conflict, defined, 33
Class consciousness, defined, 33
Classical liberalism, defined, 26
Clausewitz, Karl von, 507
Clay, Henry, 533
Clean Air Act, 128
Clean Money Initiative, 596

Clear and present danger doctrine,
    defined, 429
Clemency powers, defined, 621
Clinton, Bill, 6, 45, 123, 125, 126,
    167, 168, 170, 172, 199,
    214, 219, 250, 251, 260,
    263, 269, 290, 311, 334,
    337, 356, 362, 399, 400, 406
  approval ratings, 316
  debate with Bush and Perot, 165
  debate with Dole, 165
  influence on court policy, 414
  judicial review and, 389
  Paula Jones suit of, 314, 389
  personality, 317
  presidential style, 321
  success with Congress, 327
Clinton, Hillary Rodham, 44, 147,
    214, 250, 268, 269, 311, 399
Closed primaries, 212–213
  defined, 212
Closed primary system, defined, 552
Closed rule, defined, 284
Cloture, defined, 284
CNBC, 175, 188
CNN, 175, 176, 178, 188, 190, 199,
    317
Coalition, defined, 233
Code of Federal Regulations, 376
Code of Judicial Ethics, 650
Cohen, Bernard, 198
Cold War, 499–503
  defined, 499
Collective security, 497–498
  defined, 498
Collins, Susan, 268
Colonial Charters, 58
Columbia University
  Law School, 406
  National Center for Children in
    Poverty, 484
Comedy Central's *Daily Show*, 182
Commander-in-Chief, 68–69, 247,
    248
  vs. Congress, 515
Commerce, U.S. Department of,
    350, 351
Commission for Economic
    Development, 631
Commission on Judicial
    Performance, 652
Committee to Reelect the President
    (CREEP), 313
Commodity Futures Trading
    Commission, 354
Common Cause, 225, 227, 574, 593
Common market, defined, 68
Communications Decency Act of
    1996, 197, 202, 433
Communism, 50
  collapse of, 502
  defined, 49
*Communist Manifesto, The* (Marx and
    Engels), 48
Community Development Block
    Grants (CDBGs), 697, 721
Community Political Organization
    (CPO), 591
Community Resources Against Street
    Hoodlums (CRASH), 673
Compulsory referendum, 569–570
  defined, 569
Comstock Lode, 531
*Conan O'Brien*, 183, 190, 201
Concurrent powers, 111–114

defined, 114
Concurring opinion, defined, 409
Confederation, 104
  defined, 105
Conference committee, defined,
    286, 613
Confirmation, defined, 249
Congress. *See also* House of
    Representatives; Legislative
    branch; Senate
  apportionment and redistricting,
    251–256
  background of members in, 258
  budget and, 381
  checks on judiciary, 414–415
  committee, 278–283
  competition for seats, 257–259
  customs and norms, 292–296
  decision making in, 286–292
  Democratic dominance of, 262
  election and reelection, 256–
    262
  ethics in, 296–299
  floor, 283–284
  floor voting, 284–286
  home style, 272–273
  life in, 267–272
  lobbying, 291
  party and leadership, 273–278
  party fortunes in, 262–267
  pay and perks, 271–272
  personal values in, 292
  powers of, 245–251
  staff, 270
  support agencies, 270–271
  term limits, 259–260
  vs. Commander-in-Chief, 515
  workload, 271
Congressional Budget Office (CBO),
    271
Congressional elections, 260–262
  campaign financing, 261–262
  independence of, 260
  reelection, 261
Congressional hearings, 249–250
  defined, 249
Congressional Hispanic Caucus, 592
Congressional investigation, defined,
    250
*Congressional Quarterly*, 327
Congressional Research Service
    (CRS), 270
Congressional session, defined, 246
Connecticut Compromise, 64–65
Connell, Kathleen, 635
Conservatism, 41–46
  defined, 42
Conservatives, and federalism, 127
*Conservatorship of Wedland*, 659
Constituency
  defined, 289
  influence of, 289–291
Constitution, 57–59. *See also* U.S.
    Constitution
  Anti-Federalists and, 82
  change in, 78–84
  conflict in Philadelphia, 62–66
  consensus in Philadelphia, 62
  decision-making bodies, 72
  defined, 58
  economic issues and, 66–68
  government structure and, 70–72
  national security and, 68–70
Constitution, California, 596, 598
  Article 11, 667

Constitution, California (*continued*)
Article 12, 667
and county government, 679
Constitutional Convention, 61
Constitutional government, 14
Constitutionalism, 57–59
defined, 58
Constitutional Revision
Commission, defined, 587
Constitution of the United States,
538
Constitution Society, 60
Consumer Attorneys of California,
657
Consumer Federation of America,
225, 227
Consumer Product Safety
Commission (CPSC), 354
Consumer Services Agency, 641
Consumers Union, 646
Containment, defined, 500
Continental Congress, 58
Contingency fees, defined, 399
Continuing appropriation, 731
Continuing resolution, defined, 369
Contract cities, defined, 681
Controller, defined, 635
Convention, 214–217
defined, 214
Coolidge, Calvin, 339
Cooperative federalism, 116–119
defined, 116–119
Cornell Law School, Legal
Information Institute, 394
Cornwallis, Lord C., 59, 63
Coronado, Francisco V-zquez, 530
*Corpus delicti*, defined, 658
Corrections and Rehabilitation,
Department of, 640
Corrigan, Carol A., 669
Cortes, Hernandez, 525
Corzine, Jon, 148, 150
Costa, Jim, 600
Council for Excellence in
Government, 9, 10
Council-manager model, defined,
691
Council of Economic Advisors, 356
Council on Foreign Relations, 511
Councils of government (COGs),
707
County board of supervisors,
679–680
defined, 679
County clerk, defined, 687
County grand jury, 665–666
defined, 665
County probation department, 687
County Public Works Department,
687
County Social Services, 687
County Supervisors Association, 681
Court of appeals
California, 651–652, 654
defined, 651
Courts. *See* Judicial system
Court system, California,
650–656
judicial branch, 650
Covert actions, 332–333
defined, 332
Cox, Dave, 606
Cracking, 593
Craft, Cynthia H., 643
Cranston, Alan, 45, 635

Crédit Mobilier, 250
Credit Union National Association,
235
Criminal defendants, rights of,
436–441
Criminal law, 657–661
defined, 658
Crocker, Charles, 534
Cross-filing, defined, 552
*Crossfire*, 187
C-SPAN, 278
Cuban Americans, 460
Cuban Missile Crisis, 500–501
defined, 500
Curb, Mike, 631
Curran, Shelley, 645
*Current Affair, A*, 182
Custis, Martha, 63

**D**

*Daily News*, 182
D'Alesandro, Thomas, 277
*Dallas Morning News*, 182
Danforth, John, 405
Daschle, Tom, 265
*Das Kapital* (Marx), 48
*Dateline NBC*, 182
*David Letterman*, 183, 188, 190, 201
Davis, Angela, 658
Davis, Gray, 544, 545, 560, 620,
623, 625, 626, 627, 634,
635, 642, 643, 645, 713,
731, 735
and California gambling, 644
fundraising of, 572
recall of, 557–559
victory over Dan Lungren, 628
Davis, Jacob, 534
Day, Henry C., 662
Dealignment, defined, 219
Dean, Howard, 160, 162
Dean, John, 313
Death penalty, 441–444
Declaration of Independence, 10, 25,
58–59, 251
De facto segregation, defined,
448
Defendants, defined, 397
Defense, U.S. Department of, 7,
351, 353, 363, 364, 379
Defense Intelligence Agency (DIA),
363
Defense of Marriage Act, 115
Deferrals, defined, 314
De La Fuente, Ignacio, 555
Delegated powers, 110–111
defined, 110
Delegates, 292
defined, 215
Democracy
American, 21
around the world, 11
bureaucracy and, 357–360
defined, 9–10
direct, 14–16, 21, 73
paradox of, 12–14
terrorism and, 18–19
*Democracy in America* (Tocqueville), 27
Democracy Net, 18
Democratic ideals, defined, 10
Democratic National Committee,
313
Democratic Party, 206, 208–210,
217. *See also* Political parties

Congressional organization,
273–275
dominance in Congress, 262
racial gerrymandering and, 256
revival, 263–264
Democratic Party of California, 542,
553, 571–572, 574, 604
Denver, University of, 511
Deregulation, defined, 374, 558
Desegregation, 447–448
Determinate sentence, defined, 658
Deterrence, defined, 503
Deukmejian, George, 587, 620, 628,
633, 634, 669
Devolution, 125–126
defined, 126
political obstacles to, 127
De Witt, Howard, 703
Diebold Election Systems, 579
Dillon's Rule, 677–678
defined, 677
Diplomatic recognition, defined, 330
Direct democracy, 14–16, 21, 73
defined, 14
Direct discrimination, defined, 465
Direct initiative, defined, 559
Direct primary elections, defined,
552
Discharge petition, defined, 283
Discretionary funds, defined,
348
Dissenting opinion, defined, 409
District attorney, 685–686
defined, 668
District courts, 392–393
defined, 392
Divided party government, defined,
211, 288
Division of labor, 343
defined, 344
Dole, Bob, 163, 167, 168, 219, 263
debate with Clinton, 165
Dole, Elizabeth, 268
Donner party, 524
Douglas, William O., 391, 410, 431
Double jeopardy, 441
Drafting a bill, defined, 281
*Dred Scott* decision, 415, 444
Drudge, Matt, 198
Drug court, defined, 651
Drug Enforcement Agency (DEA),
Supreme Court and, 395
Dual federalism, 116
defined, 116
Dukakis, Michael, 219, 337
debate with Bush, 164
Dumanis, Bonnie, 673

**E**

Earned Income Tax Credit (EITC),
487
Earnings gap, 465
Earthquakes, 526–527
East Bay Municipal Utility District,
700
Economic cycles, defined, 472
Economic globalization, 473–477
uneven benefits of, 475–476
Economic growth, 472
*An Economic Interpretation of the
Constitution of the United States*
(Beard), 67
Economic Recovery Bond Act, 569
Economics

performance of the American
economy, 471–473
and politics, 471
Edelman, Marian Wright, 269
Edison Electric Institute, 230
Edison International and
Subsidiaries, 573
Education, U.S. Department of, 343,
351, 352, 353, 456, 706
Education Act Amendments of 1972,
Title IX, 464
Edwards, John, 160, 214, 337
Ehrlichman, John, 313
Eighteenth Amendment, to the U.S.
Constitution (Prohibition),
81, 99, 227, 463
Eighth Amendment, to the U.S.
Constitution, 96, 391, 424,
437, 441, 444
Eisenhower, Dwight D., 6, 117, 199,
293, 306, 335, 336, 337,
362, 428
presidential style, 321
Elder Abuse and Dependent Adult
Civil Protection Act, 657
Elections, democratic, 136–139
Election Systems and Software, 579
Electoral College, 163
defined, 161
Electoral system vs. interest-group
systems, 223–224
Eleventh Amendment, to the U.S.
Constitution, 81, 97
Elitism, 16–17
defined, 16
Emancipation Proclamation, defined,
446
Emergency Services, California
Office of, 527
EMILY's List, 153, 235, 236
Eminent domain, 698
End of history, defined, 50
End Poverty in California Plan
(EPIC), 542, 580
Energy, U.S. Department of, 351,
363, 364
E! Network, 182
Engels, Friedrich, 48
*Engel v. Vitale*, 427
*Entertainment Tonight*, 182, 183
Entitlement programs, 486
Entitlements, defined, 486
Enumerated powers, 110–111, 123,
124
defined, 78, 110
Enumeration, 252
Environmental Defense Fund, 225,
355
Environmental Protection Agency
(EPA), 128, 347, 354, 355,
375
Equal Employment Opportunity
Commission (EEOC), 354,
374, 405
Equality, 27–30, 444
opportunity, 28–29
political, 28
results, 29
Equality of opportunity, 28–29
defined, 28
Equality of results, defined, 29
Equal Rights Amendment (ERA),
463, 464
defined, 80
Equal-time rule, defined, 194

*Escobedo v Illinois*, 440
Espionage Act of 1917, 429
Ethics in Government Act of 1978, 399
Ethnicity, 34–40
European Union (EU), 104, 106–107
Excise tax, defined, 720–721
Exclusionary rule, defined, 440
Executive agreement, 331–332
defined, 331
Executive branch, checks and balances and, 74
Executive branch, defined, 620
Executive budget plan, defined, 730
Executive order, defined, 320
Executive order D-23-01, 623
Executive Order 9981, 320
Executive Order 9066, 320, 541
Executive Order 11246, 320
Executive power, 83, 310–312, 339
Executive privilege, 312–314
defined, 312
*Ex parte Milligan*, 389, 436
Ex post facto laws, 424
defined, 436
Externalities, defined, 9
*Extra*, 182
Extraordianary session, 620
defined, 621
Extremism, defined, 46

**F**

Fairness, 29–30
Fair Political Practices Commission (FPPC), 596, 641
Fair tax policy, 718
Falwell, Jerry, 228
Family Assistance, 126, 485, 488. *See also* Temporary Assistance to Needy Families
defined, 487
*Family Circle*, 182
Family Leave Act of 1993, 282
Family Medical Leave Act, 45
Family Religious Council, 41
Family Welfare Association, 724
Fascism, defined, 48
Faubus, O., 117
Federal Bureau of Investigation (FBI), 352, 358, 635
Supreme Court and, 395
Federal Communications Act of 1934, 202
Federal Communications Commission (FCC), 146, 193–194, 202, 321, 347, 354, 373, 376
Federal contributions, 721
Federal courts
caseload, 396
geographic boundaries, 395
jurisdiction of, 394
structure of, 393
Federal Election Campaign Act of 1974, 155
Federal Elections Commission (FEC), 354
defined, 154
Federal Emergency Management Agency (FEMA), 111, 346, 352
Federal Energy Regulatory Commission, 354

Federal grants, state-local dependency on, 125
Federal Highway Act of 1916, 118, 293
Federal Home Loan Bank, 354
Federal income tax, 483
Federalism, 70
centralized, 119
coercive, 127–129
conservatives, 127
cooperative, 116–119
defined, 105
dual, 116
enemy of uniformity, 108
evolution of American, 114–121
Hurricane Katrina and, 110
liberals, 127
new, 119
original design, 110–114
political obstacles to, 127
reasons for, 105–110
representational, 120–121
revived, 121–123
same-sex marriage and, 115
state-centered, 116
*Federalist Papers, The*, 12, 76, 77, 311, 434
Federal laws, interpreting, 389–390
Federal Maritime Commission, 354
*Federal Register*, 347, 376
Federal Reserve Board (FRB), 321, 354, 373, 689
Federal Reserve System "Fed," 355, 356, 473
Federal Trade Commission (FTC), 354
Feeding frenzy, defined, 185
Feinstein, Dianne, 45, 268, 693
Felony, defined, 658
Feng shui, 595
Ferraro, Geraldine, 337
FICA, 480, 492
Field Research Corporation, 544
Fifteenth Amendment, to the U.S. Constitution, 81, 117, 171, 251, 445, 446
and California state legislature, 551, 552
Fifth Amendment, to the U.S. Constitution, 37, 96, 391, 407, 423, 431, 437, 438–439, 440
Filibusters, 285
court nominees and, 401–402
defined, 284
FIRE: Foundation for Equal Rights in Education, 456
First Amendment, to the U.S. Constitution, 14, 95, 193, 196, 391, 423, 431, 433, 555, 560
freedom of speech, 429–431
Internet and, 197
No Establishment Clause, 425, 426, 427, 428
Supreme Court, 407
First Amendment Center, 422
Fiscal committees, 612
Fiscal year, defined, 367–368
Flamant, James, 723
Floor voting, 284–286
Focus group, defined, 144
Food and Drug Administration (FDA), 353, 354, 373

Food stamp program, 488
defined, 487
Foote, Cone & Belding, 576
Forbes, John, 63
Ford, Gerald R., 80, 199, 305, 307, 309, 310, 313, 337, 435, 501
court appointees of, 409
debate with Carter, 164
success with Congress, 328
Forde, Arnold, 565, 576
Ford Motor Company, 230
Foreign Intelligence Surveillance Act of 1978 (FISA), 364
Foreign policy, 330–331
Fortas, Abe, 402, 410
*48 Hours*, 182
Fourteenth Amendment, to the U.S. Constitution, 37, 51, 81, 98, 117, 251, 391, 398, 425, 431, 432, 445–446, 456, 493
Equal Protection Clause, 251, 255, 407, 432, 446, 452, 453, 456
gender equality and, 462–464
Fourth Amendment, to the U.S. Constitution, 96, 423, 431, 437
FOX, 317
Fox News, 44, 175, 187, 188, 190
Franchise Tax Board, defined, 720
Frank, Barney, 298
Frankfurter, Felix, 390
Franking privilege, defined, 143, 273
Franklin, Benjamin, 246, 597
Freedom House, 11, 12
Freedom of Access to Clinics Act, 45
Freedom of expression, defined, 430
Freedom of Information Act, 377, 378
Free Exercise Clause, defined, 422
Freeman, Richard B., 475
Free market, defined, 8
Free trade
defined, 475
politics of, 476
Free Trade Areas of the Americas (FTAA), 477
Frèmont, John C., 529, 532
Fresno Unified School Board District, 705
Friedman, Milton, 471
Friends of the Earth, 355
Frist, Bill, 214, 277, 285, 402
Front-end strategy, 160–161
defined, 160
Front-loading, defined, 161
Frost, D., 44
Fund raising, 153
Fungible, 731
*Furman v. Georgia*, 442

**G**

Gambling, California and Nevada, 644–645
Garamendi, John, 638, 639, 646
Garfield, James A., 306, 357
Garner, John Nance, 337
Garza, Juan, 443
*Garza v. County of Los Angeles*, 552
Gay marriage, and the Supreme Court, 432–433
Gender gap, voting and, 167
General Agreements on Tariffs and Trade (GATT), 476, 477
General election, defined, 553

General elections, 213–214
defined, 213
General Electric (GE), 230
General fund, defined, 717
General law, defined, 679
General Motors Corporation, 230, 343
General obligation bonds, 721
defined, 569
Generation gap, news, 177
Geneva Accords, 501
George, Ronald M., 652, 669, 670
Gephardt, Dick, 160
Gerry, Elbridge, 253
Gerrymandering, 253–254, 593
defined, 253
incumbent, 255
racial, 255, 256
Gettysburg Address, 14, 251
G.I. Bill of Rights, 293
*Gideon v. Wainwright*, 440
Gingrich, Newt, 262, 263, 275
Ginsburg, Douglas, 402
Ginsburg, Ruth Bader, 402, 406, 410, 413
*Gitlow v. New York*, 429
Giuliani, Rudolph, 214, 269, 337
Glass ceiling, defined, 466
Global Exchange, 535
Goldberg, Arthur, 402
Goldman, Ron, 660
Goldwater, Barry, 145, 199, 337, 406, 625
*Gomez v. City of Watsonville*, 552
*Gonzales v. Raich*, 561
*Good Housekeeping*, 182
GOP (Grand Old Party), 264. *See also* Republican Party
Gorbachev, Mikhail, 333, 504
Gore, Al, 163, 167, 168, 169, 172, 214, 219, 337, 338, 362
debate with Bush, 165
personality, 317
Government
constitutional, 14
defined, 4
limited, 13
purposes of, 7–9
trust in, 6
Government, functions of, 621
Government Accountability Office (GAO), 371, 379
defined, 270
Governmental politics, 3–7
Government corporations, 356
Government Performance Project (GPP), 619, 646, 718
Governor
becoming, 626–630
California plural executive, 630–631
citizen-governor persona, 623
defined, 620
gubernatorial style, 628–630
humble backgrounds, 623–624
nonpublic, 625
partner wife, 624
supreme executive authority, 620–623
Graber, D., 182
Grace Commission, 362, 371
Grand jury, 393
Grange, defined, 538
Grant, Ulysses S., 250

Grants-in-aid, defined, 123
*Grapes of Wrath, The* (Steinbeck), 541
Grassroots lobbying, defined, 233
Great Compromise. *See* Connecticut Compromise
Great Depression, 303, 540, 542
Greenpeace, 225
Greenspan, Alan, 356
*Gregs v. Georgia*, 443
Gridlock, 295–296
    defined, 295, 328
Griswold, Estelle, 431
Gross domestic product (GDP), 8, 471–472, 474
    defined, 9, 472
Guerra, Pablo de la, 532, 591
Gulf War, 506–508
Gun control, 435
Gun-Free School Zones Act of 1990, 121
Guthrie, Woody, 541

**H**
Haas, Robert, 535
Haas, Walter J., Jr., 534, 535
Haas, Walter J., Sr., 534
Habeus corpus, 424, 437
Hahn, James, 692
Haldeman, H. R., 313
Hamilton, Alexander, 60, 66, 75, 76, 77, 83, 117, 311
Hancock, J., 59
Hancock, Loni, 566
*Hannity and Colmes*, 163
*Hardball*, 163, 187
Harlan, John Marshall, 402, 410, 456, 459
Harman, Jane, 626, 642
Harman, Tom, 555
*Harper's Weekly*, 145
Harris, Robert Alton, 663
*Harris v. Forklift Systems*, 467
*Harvard Law Review*, 404
Harvard University, 282
    John F. Kennedy School of Government, 44
    Law School, 404
Hastert, Dennis, 275, 277
Hastings, Alcee, 415
Hatch Act, 358
Hayes, Rutherford B., 446
Haynsworth, Clement, 402
Health and Human Services, U.S. Department of, 351, 352, 353
Health care, American, 490–493
Health Maintenance Organizations (HMOs), 493
    defined, 491
Hearst Castle, 552
Help America Vote Act, 637
    defined, 636
Heney, Francis J., 539
Henry, Patrick, 77
Heritage Foundation, 27
Herrnstein, Richard J., 33
Herschensohn, Bruce, 45
Hetch Hetchy reservoir, 682–683
Hewlett Foundation, 511
Hewlett-Packard, 511
Hill, Anita, 405
Hill, Elizabeth, 716, 731
Hispanics
    American, 33–34, 457–460

Congress, 268
    politics, 460–462
Hitler, Adolf, 48
*Hi-Voltage Wire Works v. City of San Jose*, 655
Hobbes, Thomas, 26
Ho Chi Minh, 501
Hoffenblum, Allen, 589
Hofstadter, Richard, 47
Hollywood Park, 554
Holmes, Oliver Wendell, 429
Holy Cross, College of the, 405
Home Builders Association, 225
Homeland Security, California office of, 527
Homeland Security, U.S. Department of, 19, 129, 351, 352, 353, 363, 364
Home rule, defined, 105, 679
Homestead Act, 293
Home style, 272–273
    defined, 272
Honeymoon period, 326–327
    defined, 326
Honig, Bill, 637–638
Hoover, Herbert, 305
Hoover Commission, 362
Hoover Dam-Boulder Canyon, 540
Hoover Institution, 511
Hopkins, Mark, 534
Horse-race coverage, defined, 191
House of Representatives, 246. *See also* Congress; Senate
    impeachment and, 250
    impeachment of Bill Clinton, 269
    Judiciary Committee, 269
    vs. Senate, 247
House Rules Committee, 283–284
House Ways and Means Committee, 297, 298
Housing and Urban Development, U.S. Department of, 351, 352
*Houston Chronicle*, 182
Howard University Law School, 406
Human Services, California Department of, 725
Humphrey, Hubert, 199
Hunt, E. Howard, Jr., 313
Huntington, Collis P., 534
Hurricane Katrina, 110, 673, 677
Hussein, Saddam, 309, 507, 513, 515
Hutchison, Kay, 268

**I**
IBM, 343
Ideological organizations, defined, 229
Ideology, 41–46
    age and, 47
    antidemocratic, 47–49
    defined, 41
Immigration, 34–40
    illegal, 37
Immigration and Naturalization Service (INS), 37, 352
Immigration Reform and Control Act of 1986, 37, 460
Impeachment, 250
    defined, 308
    presidential, 308–310
Impersonality, 343
    defined, 344
Implementation, 344–347
    defined, 344

Implied powers, defined, 111
Impoundment, defined, 314
Income inequality, 30–32
Income transfers, defined, 9
Incorporation, defined, 422
Incremental budgeting, 370–371
    defined, 370
Incumbency, advantages of, 139–143, 259
Incumbent gerrymandering, defined, 255
Incumbents, 146
    defined, 139
    redistricting and, 259
Independent counsel, defined, 399
Independent system operator (ISO), 623
Individual income tax, defined, 477
Individual liberty, 421–422
Inequality, of income, 30–32
Inflation, 473
Information overload, defined, 198
Infraction, defined, 658
Initiative, 559–562
    defined, 559
    problems with, 567
    reforming the process, 567–568
*Inside Edition*, 44, 182
Intelligence
    community, 365
    reorganizing after 9/11, 363–364
Interest-group battles, health care and, 492–493
Interest-group influence, 291
Interest groups, 18, 205
    bureaucracy and, 380
    defined, 224
    power of, 223–224
    Washington, 224–229, 285–292
    Washington lobbyists, 229–230
Interest groups, in California, 572–573
Intergovernmental relations, defined, 105
Intergovernmental revenue, 729
Interior, U.S. Department of, 351
Internal Revenue Service (IRS), 157, 347–348, 354, 376, 479, 565
    Supreme Court and, 395
International Brotherhood of Electrical Workers, 226, 227, 235
International Brotherhood of Teamsters, 225, 226, 227, 235
International Ladies' Garment Workers Union, 225
International Monetary Fund (IMF), 477
International trade, 473
Internet, in politics, 197–198
Interstate commerce, 118
Interstate Commerce Clause, 123
Interstate Commerce Commission (ICC), 374
Iran-Contra investigation, 250
Iron triangles, 237–238, 239
    defined, 238
Issue ads, defined, 151
Issue voting, 171–172
*It Takes a Village* (Clinton), 269

**J**
Jackson, Andrew, 312, 357, 358, 412
Jackson, Janet, 193, 202

Jackson, Jesse, 44
Jackson, Michael, 665
James II, 58
Japanese internment, 544
Jarvis, Howard, 565
Jay, John, 76, 77
Jefferson, Thomas, 29, 61, 145, 310, 311, 314, 339, 444
    classical liberalism, 26, 42
    Declaration of Independence, 10, 58
    doctrine of nullification, 112
    Louisiana Purchase and, 293
Jeffords, Jim, 264
Jensen, Joan, 551
Jim Crow, defined, 446
Johnson, Andrew, 250, 310, 311
Johnson, Hiram, 539–540, 556, 571, 626
Johnson, Lyndon B., 6, 121, 145, 199, 293, 320, 334, 339, 352
    appointment of Thurgood Marshall, 406
    approval ratings and, 315
    Great Society program, 326, 486
    presidential style, 321
    success with Congress, 327
    Vietnam War, 501
Joint committees, defined, 613
Joint-powers agreements, 680
Joint rules, defined, 593
Jones, Bill, 605
Jones, Paula Corbin, 389
Jordan, Tom, 527
J.P. Morgan, 511
Judicial activism, defined, 391
Judicial branch, checks and balances and, 74
Judicial Council, defined, 655–656
Judicial Council of California, Blue Ribbon Commission on Jury Service Improvement, 663, 664
Judicial power, 385–390
Judicial review, 74–75, 80–82, 388–389
    defined, 74, 81, 386
    power of, 415
Judicial self-restraint, defined, 390
Judicial system, U.S. *See also* Supreme Court, U.S.
    activism vs. self-restraint, 390–392
    checking court power, 411–415
    federal court structure and jurisdiction, 392–397
    judicial power, 385–390
    politics and the Supreme Court, 409–411
    politics of selecting judges, 399–403
    rules of judicial decision making, 397–399
    selection, 403–406
    Supreme Court decision making, 406–409
Judiciary Act of 1789, 387
Judiciary Committee, of the House of Representatives, 269
"Juice" bills, defined, 594
*Jungle, The* (Sinclair), 542
Jurisdiction, defined, 392
Jury system, of California, 661–666
Justice, U.S. Department of, 250, 253, 350, 351, 352
    solicitor general, 407

# K

Kearney, Denis, 537, 538
*Kelo v. The City of New London*, 698–699
Kemp, Jack, 337
Kennedy, Anthony, 122, 402, 410, 413
Kennedy, Edward M. "Ted," 155, 281, 282, 283, 290, 561
  party leadership and, 319
Kennedy, John F., 6, 170, 199, 200, 282, 311, 339
  Cuban Missile Crisis, 501
  debate with Nixon, 164
  success with Congress, 327
Kennedy, Joseph P., 282
Kennedy, Joseph P., Jr., 282
Kennedy, Robert F., 282, 435
Kennedy, Susan, 627–628
Kennedy-Kassebaum Act of 1996, 282
Kerry, John F., 160, 167, 168, 169, 170, 171, 172, 214, 219, 337
  debate with Bush, 165
  personality, 317
  Swift Boat Veterans for Truth, 145
  vs. George W. Bush, 162, 309
Khrushchev, Nikita, 500
Killer amendments, 284
King, Larry, 163, 194
King, Martin Luther Jr., 8, 227, 435, 448–451, 457
King, Rodney, 581, 658, 661
King Center, The, 7, 448
Kissinger, Henry, 501, 504
Klass, Polly, 658
Knight, Goodwin, 628
Korean War, 515
  defined, 500
Koretz, Paul, 599
Kovall, Gary, 611
Kucinich, Dennis, 160

# L

Labor, U.S. Department of, 351, 352, 353, 473, 487
Laboratories of democracy, defined, 109
Laborers Union, 235
*Ladies Home Journal*, 182
La Follette, R. M., 220, 222
*Lancet, The*, 663
*La Raza*, 460
La Raza Unida Party, 580
Larkin, Thomas, 532
*Larry King Live*, 44, 188, 190, 194
Lasswell, Harold, 471
Latino legislators, 591
Lawmaking, 594–598
*Lawrence v. Texas*, 432
Lazio, Rick, 147, 269
Leader-follower relations, 295
League of Nations, 331, 497
League of Women Voters, 18, 225, 227, 233, 463, 578
Lear, Norman, 153
Leary, Mary Ellen, 574
Lease-revenue bonds, 721
Le Duc Tho, 501
Lee, Richard Henry, 59
Lee, Robert E., 117
Left, defined, 46
Legal fees, 398–399
Legislative Analyst's Office (LAO), defined, 716

Legislative branch. *See also* Congress
  checks and balances and, 74
Legitimacy, 8
  defined, 5
Lemon test, defined, 425
Lenin, V., 48
Leninism, defined, 48
Leno, Jay, 182, 183, 188, 190, 201
Letterman, David, 163, 182, 183
Levi Strauss and Company, 532, 534–535
Lewinsky, Monica, 311
Libel, 431
  defined, 194
Liberalism, 41–46
  defined, 43
Liberals, and federalism, 127
Libertarian, defined, 46
Library of Congress, 270
Liddy, G. Gordon, 313
Lieberman, Joe, 160, 337
Lieutenant governor, 630–631
  defined, 630
Lightner, Candy, 595
Limited government, defined, 13
Lincoln, Abraham, 14, 19, 27, 145, 264, 436
  Emancipation Proclamation, 312
  judicial review and, 389
Line-item veto, 328–329
  defined, 328
Line-veto power, 620
  defined, 621
Litigation, defined, 238
Litmus test, defined, 400
Little Hoover Commission, 641, 701, 702
Lobbying
  art of, 231–238
  bureaucracy, 236–238
  courts, 238–239
  defined, 231
  ethics, 233–235
Lobbyists, 229–230
  defined, 229
Local agency formation commission (LAFCO), 689–690, 700, 701
  defined, 689
  rules, 702–703
Local government
  financing, 726–727
  future of, 707–708
Locke, J., 10, 26, 42, 58, 59
Lockheed Martin, 230
Lockyer, Bill, 608, 634, 646
Logrolling, defined, 295
Lord Baltimore, 58
Lord & Thomas, 576
Los Angeles Department of Water and Power (LADWP), 682, 683
Los Angeles Physicians for Social Responsibility, 601
*Los Angeles Times*, 182
Lothrop, Gloria Ricci, 551
Louisiana Purchase, 293
Lungren, Dan E., 558, 634
Lynch, Thomas C., 633

# M

Machine, defined, 210
Machinists/Aerospace Workers Union, 227, 235
Madison, James, 387, 434
  Bill of Rights, 78

direct democracy, 12, 21
  federalism, 112, 121
  ratification, 76, 77
  separation of powers, 72
  Shays's Rebellion, 60
Magna Carta, 57
Majoritarianism, defined, 224
Majority leader, defined, 276
Majority opinion, 408–409
  defined, 408
Malapportionment, defined, 251
Managed care, defined, 491
Management classifications, 623
Mandates, 129, 138
  defined, 128
Manifest Destiny, defined, 529
Manson, Charles, 658
Mao Zedong, 500
*Mapp v. Ohio*, 440
Marbury, William, 387
*Marbury v. Madison*, 75, 81, 386, 415
Marcy, William, 357
Marist College, 44
Markup, 281–283
  defined, 282
Marsh, Kenneth, 673
Marshall, George C., 500
Marshall, James W., 529
Marshall, John, 117
  judicial review, 75, 81, 415
  Supreme Court politics and, 387
Marshall, Thurgood, 239, 406, 410, 442, 447
Marshall Plan, defined, 500
Martinez, Mel, 265
Marx, K., 48
Marxism, 51
  defined, 48
Mason, David, 663
Mason, G., 82
Massachusetts Institute of Technology (MIT), 356
Mass communications, and campaigning, 574–577
Mass media, defined, 176
Mayflower Compact, 58
May Revise, defined, 732
McCain, John, 155, 214, 308
McCarthy, Leo, 604
McClintock, Tom, 610
McCord, James W., Jr., 313
McCorvey, Norma, 431
*McCulloch v. Maryland*, 117
McGovern, George, 199
McGwire, Mark, 278
McPherson, Bruce, 636
McVeigh, Timothy, 443
McWilliams, Carey, 596
Media
  bias, 186
  business of, 181–183
  effects, 198–202
  freedom vs. fairness, 193–194
  libel and slander, 194–196
  mediated elections, 188–192
  polarization of, 188
  power of, 175–178
  power sources, 178–181
Medicaid, 293, 432, 459, 485, 486, 492
  defined, 488
Medi-Cal Managed Care (MCMC), 632–633, 635, 725
Medicare, 121, 234, 237, 293, 459, 485, 493
  defined, 492

Meehan, Martin T., 257
*Meet the Press*, 163, 187
"Megan's law," 634
Mello-Ross Community Facilities District, defined, 727
Merit system, 357–358
  defined, 357
Merit Systems Protection Board, 359, 360
Merriam, Frank, 542, 576, 724
Mestizo, defined, 531
Mexican-American Legal Defense and Educational Fund (MALDEF), 225, 591
Mexican American Political Association (MAPA), 591
Mexican Americans, 458
Mexican-American War, 529
Mexican War, 515
Michigan, University of, 456
Miers, Harriet, 402, 404
Migden, Carole, 640
Milberg Weiss, 646
Military force, 505–509
  protecting vital interests, 505–507
  support of important political objectives, 507–509
  War on Terrorism, 509
Miller, William, 337
Mills College, 552
Minority leader, defined, 276
*Miranda v. Arizona*, 440
Misdemeanor, defined, 658
Mission Basilica San Diego de Alcala, 527
Mission system, 526–528
Mitchell, John, 313
Mobilization against AIDS, 45
Mobilize, defined, 147
Mondale, Walter, 219, 336
  debate with Reagan, 164
Montoya, Joseph, 597
Moreno, John, 591
Moretti, Bob, 604
Morgan, Julia, 552
Morgenthau, Hans, 507
Morrill Land Grant Act of 1862, 118
Mosca, Gaetano, 205
Moscow, Treaty of, 504
Moseley Braun, Carol, 160
Mosk, Stanley, 633
Mothers Against Drunk Driving (MADD), 124, 224, 225, 229, 595
Mothers' Congress, 552
Motion Picture Association of America, 225
Motor Voter Law, 550
Mott, Lucretia, 227, 463
Mount, William Sydney, 524
MoveOn, 225
Mowry, George E., 596
MSNBC, 175, 188, 190
MTV News, 182
Muckraking, defined, 185
Municipal advisory council (MAC), defined, 681
Municipal bureaucracy, 695–700
Municipal expenditures, 729
Municipal revenue sources, 728
Municipal taxes, 729
Murkowski, Lisa, 268
Murray, C., 33
*Muscle & Fitness*, 625
Mussolini, B., 48
Myers, Michael "Ozzie," 298

# N

Nader, Ralph, 222, 227
Name recognition, defined, 142, 189
NARAL Pro-Choice America, 225, 229, 233, 239, 405, 431
*Nation*, 176
National Association for the Advancement of Colored People (NAACP), 18, 225, 239
   Legal Defense Fund, 406, 447
National Association of Broadcasters, 181, 225
National Association of Counties, 225, 229
National Association of Home Builders of the U.S., 235
National Association of Letter Carriers, 225, 227
National Association of Manufacturers, 225
National Association of Real Estate Boards, 225
National Association of Realtors, 230, 235
National Association of Scholars, 51
National Association of State Legislators, 225
National Audubon Society, 355
National Auto Dealers Association, 235
National Beer Wholesalers Association, 235
National Cattlemen's Association, 225
National Change of Address System, 664
National Coalition to Abolish the Death Penalty, 442
National Conference of State Legislators, 225, 229
National Constitution Center, 58
National Council of Churches, 225, 227
National Counterterrorism Center, 363
National Education Association (NEA), 225, 226, 227, 288
National Endowment for Democracy, 12
National Farmers Union, 225
National Federation of Independent Business, 225
*National Geographic*, 182
National Governors Association, 225, 229
National Grange, 225
National Imagery and Mapping Agency (NIMA), 363
National Intelligence Director (NID), 332, 363
National Intelligence Estimates (NIEs), 363
Nationalism, defined, 62
National Labor Relations Act, 293
National Labor Relations Board (NLRB), 347, 354, 373
National League of Cities, 225, 229
National Legal Aid and Defender Association, 673
National Milk Producers Federation, 225
National Organization for Women (NOW), 227, 233, 239, 405, 464

National Public Radio (NPR), 188
National Reconnaissance Office (NRO), 363
National Resources Defense Council, 225
*National Review*, 176
National Rifle Association (NRA), 19, 225, 229, 288
National Right to Life Committee, 225, 229, 288
National security, and the Constitution, 68–70
National Security Act of 1947, 364
National Security Agency (NSA), 363
National Security Council (NSC), defined, 323
National Small Business Association, 225
National Supremacy Clause, 64, 70, 71, 111
   defined, 112
National Taxpayers Union, 225, 480
National Urban League, 18–19, 225
National Voter Registration Act, defined, 550
National Voter Registration Act of 1993, 128
National Wildlife Federation, 225, 355
Native Americans, 538
Native American settlement, 525
Native Daughters of the Golden West, 552
Naturalized citizenship, 51
Natural Resources Defense Council, 355
Nature Conservancy, 225
Navy Association, 225
NBC, 175, 188, 190, 317
NBC-Universal, 184
Necessary and proper clause, 117
   defined, 111
Negative campaigning, 144, 145
   defined, 144
Nevada, and gambling, 644
Nevada at Las Vegas, University of, Center for Business and Economic Research, 645
New federalism, defined, 119
*New Gold Rush: Financing California's Legislative Campaigns, The*, 589
New Hampshire primary, 159–160
New Jersey, College of. *See* Princeton University
New Jersey Plan, 64
New Motor Vehicle Board, 641
*New Republic*, 176
New Rules Project, 14
News, vs. entertainment, 187–188
NewsCorp, 184
Newsmaking, 178–179
   defined, 178
*Newsweek*, 176, 317
*New York Post*, 182
*New York Times*, 176, 182, 193, 317
*New York Times v. Sullivan*, 195
New York University, 356
Nguyen Van Thieu, 332
9/11, 309, 352
   reorganizing intelligence after, 363–364
   War on Terrorism, 510
9/11 Commission, 363

Nineteenth Amendment, to the U.S. Constitution, 81, 99, 171, 251, 463
   and California state legislature, 551
Ninth Amendment, to the U.S. Constitution, 97, 424, 431
Ninth Circuit Court of Appeals, of California, 552
Nixon, Richard M., 6, 170, 307, 337, 339
   approval ratings, 316
   court appointees of, 409
   debate with Kennedy, 164, 200
   ERA and, 80
   executive agreement with South Vietnam, 332
   executive power, 83
   judicial review, 389
   media and, 199
   People's Republic of China and, 330
   personality, 317
   presidential pardon of, 310
   resignation of, 250, 312
   success with Congress, 328
   Vietnam War, 334, 501
   War Powers Resolution of 1973, 248
   Watergate scandal, 248, 313, 314, 412–414
No Child Left Behind Act (NCLB), 128, 706
Nomination, defined, 210
Nominee, defined, 210
Nonpartisan election, defined, 211, 553
Nonviolent direct action, defined, 449–451
Noriega, Manuel Antonio, 507
Norris, Frank, 536
North American Free Trade Agreement (NAFTA), 477
North Atlantic Treaty Organization (NATO), 330, 331, 498–499
   defined, 498
Northwest Ordinance of 1787, 118
Not in my back yard (NIMBY), 109
Notre Dame, University of, 511
Nuclear Regulatory Commission (NRC), 354
Nuclear threats, 503–505
   terrorism, 505
Nuñez, Fabian, 604, 606, 607

# O

Obama, Barack, 265, 268
Obligational authority, defined, 368
O'Brien, Conan, 163, 182, 183
Obscenity, and the law, 433
Occupational Health and Safety Administration (OSHA), 353, 354, 356
Occupational Safety, Division of (California), 712
O'Connor, Sandra Day, 255, 406, 410, 413, 432, 456, 467
*Octopus, The*, 536
O'Dell, Walden, 579
Office of Emergency Services (California), 712
Office of Management and Budget (OMB), 271, 322, 347, 364–367, 373, 377

Office of Personnel Management (OPM), 359
Oklahoma, University of, 405
Oklahoma City bombings, 510
Olsen, Colbert, 724
O'Neill, Thomas P. "Tip," 267
Open primaries, defined, 213
Open rule, defined, 284
Open seat, defined, 257
Operation Desert Storm, 508
Operation Enduring Freedom, 510–512
Operation Iraqi Freedom, 513–514
*Oprah Winfrey*, 183
Oracle Corporation, 627
O'Reilly, B., 42, 44
*O'Reilly Factor, The*, 44, 163, 187, 188
Organizational sclerosis, defined, 224
Organized labor, 225, 226–227
Original intent, 390–391
   defined, 390
Original jurisdiction, defined, 392
Oropeza, Jenny, 604
Outlays, defined, 368
Override, defined, 328
Oversight, defined, 248
Oversight function, defined, 600–601
Owens Valley Aqueduct, 540, 682

# P

Pacific Gas and Electric Company (PG&E), 554, 573, 682, 683
Pacific Railway Act of 1862, 535
Packing, defined, 254
Packwood, Robert, 45, 298
Palmeiro, Rafael, 278
*Paradise Lost: California's Experience, America's Future* (Schrag), 559
Paradox of democracy, 12–14
   defined, 12
Partial preemption, defined, 128
Partisan election, defined, 553
Partisanship, sources of congressional, 286–288
Party caucus, 601–602
   defined, 601
Party identification, 218
   defined, 217
Party leadership, president and, 318–319
Party polarization, defined, 209
Party unity, defined, 286
Party vote, 217–220
   defined, 286
Passports, 39–40
   defined, 39
Paterson, William, 64
PATRIOT Act, 439
Patriotism, U.S., 18–20
Patriot missiles, 506
Patronage, defined, 210
Peace and Freedom Party, 636
Peace Officers' Standards and Training (POST), 633
Pearl Harbor, 303
Pelosi, Nancy, 257, 277
Pelosi, Paul, 277
Penal code, defined, 658
Penn, William, 58
People for the American Way, 40, 153, 185, 225, 239, 405
Perata, Don, 555

Perot, Ross, 222
  debate with Bush and Clinton, 165
Persian Gulf War, 515
Personal income tax, 718
Peterson, Laci, 660
Peterson, Scott, 660
Petition referendum, defined, 568–569
Petit (regular) juries, defined, 393
Pew Charitable Trusts, 549
Pew Research Center, 178, 188
*Phantom Politics: Campaigning in California* (Leary), 574
Pharmaceutical Research and Manufacturers of America, 230
Philbin, Regis, 163
Philip Morris Companies, 230, 573
Photo ops, defined, 146
Pico, Andres, 591
Pingree, Chellie, 593
Pitzer College, 607
Plaintiff, defined, 397
Planned Parenthood, 45, 225
*Planned Parenthood of Pennsylvania v. Casey*, 411, 432
Planning commission, 699–700
  defined, 699
Platform, 215–216
  defined, 215
Plea bargaining, defined, 441
Plea bargains, defined, 651
Pledge of Allegiance, 428
*Plessy v. Ferguson*, 446, 447, 456, 457
Pluralism, 17–21
  defined, 17
Pocket veto, defined, 328
Polanco, Richard, 600
Police powers, 666–667
Police Safety Officers Procedural Bill of Rights Act, 667
Policy leadership, 319
Political action committees (PACs), 273, 589
  defined, 153
  money distribution, 235
Political appointees, 623
Political culture, 25–26
  defined, 26
Political equality, defined, 28
Politically correct (PC), defined, 51
*Politically Incorrect*, 182, 183
Political organizations, 205
Political parties, 205. *See also* Democratic Party; Republican Party
  defined, 206
  democratic government and, 205–211
  election organizers, 211–214
  two-party system, 220–223
Political Reform Act of 1974, 596, 637
Political science, defined, 3
Politics
  defined, 3
  governmental vs. nongovernmental, 3–7
  individual participation in, 135
  news, 183–188
  religion in, 40–41
  support for War in Iraq, 514–516
Polk, James, 529
Polling Report, The, 216

*Pollock v. Farmer's Loan*, 415
Pooled Money Investment Board, 636
Poor Relief Act of 1601, 485
Pork barreling, defined, 272
Portol·, Gaspar de, 523, 525
Poverty, in the U.S., 483–485
Poverty line, defined, 483–484
Powell, Colin, 308, 337, 505, 513
Powell, Lewis, 121, 402, 409, 410
Powell Doctrine, 505
Power, among nations, 497–499
Power of the purse, defined, 248
Precedent, defined, 391
Precinct, defined, 211
Preemption, defined, 128
Preemptive attack, defined, 509
Preferred position, 429–430
  defined, 429
Preferred provider organizations (PPOs), defined, 491
President
  chief executive, 319–325
  chief legislator and lobbyist, 325–329
  Commander-in-Chief, 333–336
  constitutional powers of, 306–314
  executive power, 310–312
  global leader, 306, 329–333
  managing the government, 306
  media and, 317
  military force in domestic affairs, 335
  party leadership, 318–319
  personality vs. policy, 317–319
  policy leadership of, 305
  political resources of, 314–317
  presidential power, 303–306
  styles of, 321
Presidential, appointments, 320–321
Presidential campaign. *See also* Campaigning
  general election, 161–163
  primary race, 158–161
  voter decision, 163–172
Presidential debates, 162–163, 164–165
Presidential Election Campaign Fund, 149
Presidential impoundment, 314
Presidential pardons, 310
Presidential perks, 325
Presidential primaries, defined, 214
Presidential succession, 306–308
President pro tempore, 276, 608
Presidios, defined, 526
Presler, Larry, 298
Primary elections
  defined, 210
  types of, 212–213
*Primetime Live*, 182
Princeton University, 404
Prior restraint, defined, 193
Privacy, 431
Privacy Act, 377
Probate law, defined, 657
Pro-Choice America, 431
Proclamation of Neutrality, 310
Professional associations, 225–226
Program budgeting, defined, 372
Progressive movement, 539–540, 555, 558, 577
Progressives, 703, 724
Progressive taxation, defined, 480

Prohibition, 79
Property tax, 728
Proportional (flat) taxation, defined, 481
Proportional representation, defined, 223
Proposition 57, 727
Proposition 5, 560
Proposition 9, 724
Proposition 98, 722, 727
  defined, 638
Proposition 1A, 727
Proposition 184, 656, 658
Proposition 115, 670
Proposition 140, 585, 610
  defined, 586, 716
Proposition 116, 734
Proposition 103, defined, 638
Proposition 13, 545, 559, 562, 565, 704, 705, 707, 715, 722, 723, 726
  defined, 544
Proposition 36, defined, 671
Proposition 215, 561
Proposition 220, 651
Proposition 227, 705
Proposition 209, 578, 655
Prosecution, 668
Protectionism, 474–475
  defined, 475
Public assistance programs, defined, 485
Public Citizen, Inc., 45, 225, 227
Public goods, defined, 7
*Public Interest*, 176
Public Interest Research Groups (PIRGs), 225
Public money, 149
Public Policy Institute of California, 570, 579
Public relations, 231–232
  defined, 231
Public safety, 729
Public Safety Fund, 728
Public School Accountability Act, 707
Public utilities, 729–730
Public Utilities Commission, 652
Pueblos, defined, 526
Puerto Ricans, 458–460
Punishment, in California, 671–672
Putin, Vladimir, 11, 504

**Q**

Quackenbush, Charles, 638, 639
Quayle, Dan, 337, 338
Quid pro quo, 297

**R**

Race, 34–40
  voting and, 167
Racial gerrymandering, 255, 256
Radicalism, defined, 46
Raiding, defined, 213
Rainbow Coalition, 225
Rainey, Richard, 590
RAND Corporation, 196, 511
Randolph, Edmund, 64
Ranking majority-party member, 281
Ranking minority member, defined, 278
Ranney, Austin, 198

Rather, Dan, 145
Ratification, defined, 75
*Reader's Digest*, 182
Reagan, Nancy, 624
Reagan, Ronald, 6, 170, 219, 250, 290, 305, 308, 353, 356, 399, 404, 410, 435, 553, 557, 570, 593, 625, 630, 715
  approval ratings and, 316
  attempted assassination of, 306
  debate with Carter, 164
  debate with Mondale, 164
  defeat of Pat Brown, 587
  deregulation and, 374
  federal grant cutbacks, 125
  and federal tax laws, 481
  governor campaign strategy, 623
  Grace Commission, 362
  humble background of, 623–624
  influence on court policy, 414
  media and, 317
  party leadership, 319
  personality, 317
  presidential style, 321
  START and, 504
  Star Wars, 506
  success with Congress, 326–327, 328
  Supreme Court nominees of, 401
Realignment, defined, 220
Reapportionment, 252, 590–593
  defined, 590
Recall, 556–559
  defined, 556
  of Gray Davis, 557–559
Recidivism rate, defined, 671
Reciprocity, and the legislative process, 294–295
Redistricting, 252–253, 590–593
  defined, 252, 590
  incumbents and, 259
Referenda, defined, 72
Referendum, defined, 568
Regional security, defined, 498
*Regis and Kelly*, 182
Regressive tax, 718
Regressive taxation, defined, 481
Regulation, defined, 347
Rehnquist, William, 121, 402, 404, 406, 409, 410, 413, 427
Reid, Harry, 280
Reiner, Rob, 634
Religion, in politics, 40–41
Remedies and relief, defined, 399
*Reno v. American Civil Liberties Union*, 197
Representational federalism, 120–121
  defined, 120
Representative democracy, 14–16, 21
  defined, 15
Republicanism, 70–71
  defined, 62
Republican Party, 206, 208–210, 217. *See also* GOP (Grand Old Party); Political parties
  Congressional organization and, 273–275
  racial gerrymandering and, 256
  revolution, 262–263
  victories in '02 and '04, 264–267
Republican Party, of California, 538, 540, 553, 571–572, 574
Requests for proposals (RFPs), 357

Re-redistricting, 254
Reregulation, 374
Rescissions, 314
Reserved powers, 112–114, 123, 124
   defined, 114
Resolutions, defined, 598
Resource transfers, 623
Responsible party model, defined, 206
Restricted rule, defined, 284
Retail politics, defined, 160
Retrospective voting, defined, 138
Revenue and Taxation Code, 720
Revenue bonds, 721
Revenue sources, other, 722
Revolving doors, defined, 238
Reynolds, Mel, 298
Reynolds v. Sims, 593
Rice, Condoleezza, 214, 309, 509, 511
Richards, Ann, 308
Richter, Charles, 526
Rider, defined, 284
Right, defined, 46
Right to bear arms, 434–435
Riley, Bennett, 533
Roberti, David, 608
Roberts, John G., Jr., 398, 402, 403, 404, 406, 410
Robertston, Pat, 228
Roe v. Wade, 82, 388, 391, 400, 401, 403, 404, 431–432
Roll-call vote, defined, 286
Rolph, James, 542, 724
Romney, Mitt, 214
Roosevelt, Franklin D., 303, 312, 320, 331, 333, 336, 337, 356, 541, 542
   communist Russia and, 330
   interstate commerce and, 118
   lengthy tenure of, 306
   media and, 199, 414
   New Deal, 119, 126, 486
   Social Security Act and, 293
   Supreme Court and, 414
Roosevelt, Theodore, 220, 222, 339, 539
Rose Law Firm, 269
Rostenkowski, Dan, 297, 298
Rousseau, J. J., 26
Roybal, Edward, 591
Ruef, Abe, 539
Rule, defined, 283
Rule of four, defined, 407
Rules Committee, 608
Rules committees, 613–614
   defined, 613
Rumsfeld, Donald, 309, 511, 514, 515
Runoff primary, defined, 213
Rural districts, 265
Rush Limbaugh Show, 188

S
Sacramento County Board of Supervisors, 700
Safe Drinking Water Act, 128
Safe seat, defined, 259
Sales tax, 719–720, 728
SALT I, 503–504
   defined, 504
SALT II, 504–505
   defined, 505
Samish, Art, 586, 597
Samuelson, Paul, 471

San Diego Gas and Electric, 683
San Diego Union-Tribune, 607
San Francisco, 673, 674
San Francisco Gas & Electric Company, 683
San Jose Mercury News, 668
SBC Communications, 235, 627
Scalia, Antonin, 123, 402, 406, 410, 413
Schattschneider, E. E., 179
Schering-Plough Corporation, 230
Schilling, Curt, 278
School districts, California, 703–707
   reforming California schools, 706–707
School prayer, 426–427
Schrag, Peter, 559
Schwartzkopf, Norman, 508
Schwarzenegger, Arnold, 545–546, 553, 567, 571, 593, 607, 625, 626, 630, 639, 669, 671, 672, 692, 693, 721, 733
   and California gambling, 644
   California Performance Review, 640–642
   campaign strategy, 623
   and chief of staff, 627–628
   and Economic Recovery Bond Act, 569
   fundraising of, 572
   and health care, 633
   humble background of, 623–624
   and a part-time legislature, 610–611
   and the recall election, 558
   redistricting initiative, 574
   and state tourism, 731
   and the structural budget gap, 714–715
Search warrant, 436–438
   defined, 436
Second Amendment, to the U.S. Constitution, 95–96, 423, 434–435
Second-strike capability, defined, 503
Secretary of state, defined, 636–637
Secret Boss of California, The (Samish), 586
Secret Service, 352
Secular, 40–41
   defined, 40
Securities and Exchange Commission (SEC), 321, 347, 354, 373
Sedition Act of 1918, 429
Segregation, 112
Select Committee on Campaign Practices. See Watergate Committee
Select committees, defined, 613
Selective perception, defined, 200
Seminole Tribe v. Florida, 122
Sempra Energy, 554
Senate, 246. See also Congress; House of Representatives
   floor traditions, 284
   vs. House of Representatives, 247
   women in, 296
Senate Budget and Fiscal Review Committee, 598
Senate Ethics Committee, 298
Senate Foreign Relations Committee, 249
Senate Judiciary Committee, 405

Senatorial courtesy, defined, 401
Seniority system, defined, 281
Seniors Coalition, 230
Separate but equal, defined, 446
Separation of powers, 106
   defined, 72
Serra, Father Junipero, 525, 526
Service Employees International Union, 226, 235, 573
Set-aside program, defined, 455
Seventeenth Amendment, to the U.S. Constitution, 81, 82, 98–99, 251
Seventh Amendment, to the U.S. Constitution, 96, 424
Sexual conduct, and the Supreme Court, 432
Sexual harassment, 467
Sharpton, Al, 160
Shaw, Bernard, 508
Shaw v. Reno, 255, 256
Shays, D., 60
Shays's Rebellion, 60
Shelley, Kevin, 636–637
Shreveport Times, 673
Shriver, Maria, 624
Sierra Club, 18, 45, 225, 288, 364
Sierra Nevada, defined, 524
Simpson, Nicole Brown, 660
Simpson, O. J., 199, 658, 660, 661
Simpson-Mazzoli Act, 37
Sinclair, Upton, 542, 576
Single-issue groups, defined, 229
Single-subject rule, defined, 670
"Sin" tax, 720
Sirica, John J., 313
Sixteenth Amendment, to the U.S. Constitution, 81, 98, 118, 415
Sixth Amendment, to the U.S. Constitution, 96, 398, 424, 437, 440–441
60 Minutes, 175, 182
Slander, 431
   defined, 194
Slavery, and the Constitution, 65, 444–445
Smith, Adam, 26
Smith, Jedediah, 524
Smith-Hughes Act of 1917, 118
Snowe, Olympia, 268
Social contract, defined, 7
Social insurance programs, defined, 485
Socialism, defined, 49
Socialist Party USA, 49
Socialization, defined, 181
Social mobility, 32–34
   defined, 32
Social Security, 121, 234, 485, 488, 492, 493
   defined, 486
   taxes, 478–479, 480
Social Security Act, 293, 724
Social Welfare policy, 485–488
Solicitor General, defined, 407, 411
Sony, 184
Sosa, Sammy, 278
Soto, Nell, 592
Soto, Phillip L., 591, 592
Sound bites, defined, 146, 192
Souter, David H., 402, 406, 410, 413
Southeastern Legal Foundation, 412
Southern California Earthquake Center (SCEC), 527
Southern California Edison, 683

Southern Christian Leadership Conference (SCLC), 225, 227, 449
Southern Methodist University, 404
Southern Pacific Political Bureau, 536
Southern Pacific Railroad, 585
Southern Poverty Law Center, 412
Sovereign immunity, defined, 397
Soviet Union, 497–498
   defined, 498
   disintegration of, 502–503
Spanish-American War, 515
Spanish settlement, 525–528
Speaker of the House, 275–276
   defined, 275
Special district, 700–703
   defined, 700
Special election, defined, 553
Special funds, 731
Special prosecutor, defined, 399
Speier, Jackie, 600–601
Spencer & Roberts, 576
Spin doctor, defined, 160
Spitzer, Todd, 599
Splintering, defined, 253
Spoils system, defined, 357
St. Clair, Arthur, 250
Stalin, Josef, 333
Standard Oil Company, 536
Standard partial preemption, defined, 128
Standing, defined, 397
Standing committee, defined, 278, 612–613
Standing rules, 593–594
   defined, 593
Stanford, Leland, 534
Stanford University, 406, 511
Stanton, Elizabeth Cady, 227, 463
Stare decisis, defined, 391
Starr, Kenneth, 311, 399
Starr Report, 311
START, 504
START I, 504–505
   defined, 505
START II, 504–505
   defined, 505
Star Wars, 506
State, U.S. Department of, 351, 353, 363, 364
State Bar of California, 652
   Commission on Judicial Appointments, 652
   Commission on Judicial Nominees, 652
State-centered federalism, 116
State Education Code, California, 704
State expenditures, major, 722–726
State insurance commissioner, 638
   defined, 638
State Lands Commission, 631
State militias, 434
State Nurses' Association (California), 552
State of the Union Address, 317
State revenue, sources of, 716–722
State senate leaders, partisan, 608–609
State treasurer, 635–636
   defined, 635
Statewide Office of Family Court Services, 657

Statewide Youth Conference, 724
Statutory laws, defined, 389
Stern, David, 534
Stern, Howard, 193, 202
Stevens, John Paul, 406, 409, 410, 413
Stewart, Potter, 402, 410
Stone, Lucy, 227, 463
Strauss, Levi, 534
Strict scrutiny, 455
Strong mayor-council model, defined, 692
Structural budget gap, defined, 714–715
Studds, Gerry, 298
Subcommittees, defined, 279
Subcultures, 25–26
    defined, 26
Suburban districts, 265
Sullivan rule, 195–196
    defined, 196
Superintendent of public instruction, 637–638
    defined, 637
Superior Courts of California, defined, 651
Superpowers, defined, 498
Supervisory classifications, 623
Supplemental Security Income (SSI), 486, 488, 725
    defined, 487
Supplementary Security Payment (SSP), 725
Supreme Court, U.S., 19, 197, 202, 256, 428, 435, 438, 440, 441, 442, 446, 453, 456, 662. See also Judicial system, U.S.
    appeals to, 395
    apportionment and, 251–252, 255
    Bush v. Gore, 413
    California blanket primary, 553
    decision making, 406
    Dred Scott decision, 415, 444
    Gonzales v. Raich, 561
    Pollock v. Farmer's Loan, 415
    Reynolds v. Sims, 593
Supreme Court of California, 652–653, 654
    defined, 652
    Proposition 5, 560
Sutter, John, 529
Sweatshop Watch, 535
Swett, John, 703, 723
Swing states, 161–162
    defined, 161
Symbolic president, 303
Symbolic speech, defined, 430

T
Taft-Hartley Act of 1947, 312
Taliban, 511
Taney, Roger, 444
Tariff, defined, 66
Tax burden, 477–480
Taxes
    Constitution and, 66–68
    defined, 66
Tax politics, 480–483
Tax Reform Act of 1986, 480, 481
Telecommunications Consumer Bill of Rights, 627
Television, power of, 175–176
Television malaise, defined, 200

Temporary Assistance for Needy Families (TANF), 486, 489, 725. See also Family Assistance
    defined, 490
Temporary poverty, 484–485
Tennessee Valley Authority, 356, 424
Tenth Amendment, to the U.S. Constitution, 97, 424, 667
Terrorism
    civil liberties and, 439
    defined, 510
    democracy and, 18–19
    notable global attacks, 512
    war on, 308
Terrorism Research Center, 19, 510
Texas, re-redistricting, 254
Texas, Spanish heritage of, 530–531
Texas v. Johnson, 430
Third Amendment, to the U.S. Constitution, 96, 423, 431
Third House, 585
    defined, 586
Third House: Lobbyists, Money, and Power in Sacramento, The (Walters), 589
Thirteenth Amendment, to the U.S. Constitution, 81, 97–98, 117, 415, 425, 444, 445
Thomas, Clarence, 401, 402, 405, 406, 410, 413
Thompson, John, 673
Thornberry, Homer, 402
Thornburg v. Gingles, 255
Time, 176, 182, 317
Time Warner, Inc., 184
Title IX
    defined, 464
    women's athletics and, 464
Tobacco Institute, 225
Tocqueville, A. de, 27, 28, 385
Torlakson, Tom, 590
Torricelli, Robert, 298
Tort law, defined, 656
Totalitarianism, 13–14
    defined, 13
Total preemption, defined, 128
Tower, John, 353
Trade associations, 225
    defined, 225
Traficant, James A., 298
Transamerica, 511
Transcontinental railroad, defined, 534
Transportation, U.S. Department of, 351
Transportation Security Administration (TSA), 352
Treasury, U.S. Department of, 67, 351, 353, 354, 363, 364, 381
Treaties, 331
Treaty of Guadalupe Hidalgo, 529, 551
Trinity College, 277
Triple flip, 727
Truman, Harry, 336, 339, 362
    executive orders and, 320
    judicial review and, 389
    Korean War and, 334
    presidential power and, 312, 314
    treaties, 331
Truman Doctrine, 293
    defined, 500
Trustees, defined, 292
Tuck, Cindy, 601
Turner, Ted, 199

Turnover, defined, 259
TV Guide, 182
Twelfth Amendment, to the U.S. Constitution, 81, 97
Twentieth Amendment, to the U.S. Constitution, 81, 99
Twenty-fifth Amendment, to the U.S. Constitution, 81, 100–101, 306, 307
Twenty-first Amendment, to the U.S. Constitution, 81, 99
Twenty-fourth Amendment, to the U.S. Constitution, 81, 100, 171
Twenty-second Amendment, to the U.S. Constitution, 81, 99–100, 306
Twenty-seventh Amendment, to the U.S. Constitution, 81, 101
Twenty-sixth Amendment, to the U.S. Constitution, 81, 101, 171
Twenty-third Amendment, to the U.S. Constitution, 81, 100
20/20, 175, 182

U
Unanimous consent agreement, defined, 284
Underclass, defined, 484
Unemployment, 472–473
    and inflation, 473
Unemployment compensation, 486–487
    defined, 486
Unemployment rate, 472–473
    defined, 472
Unfunded mandates, defined, 129
Union Pacific Railroad Company, 535
Unitary system, 104
    defined, 105
United Auto Workers, 225, 226, 227, 235
United Farm Workers (UFW), 460, 591
United Mine Workers, 226
United Nations
    formation of, 497–498
    today, 499
United Nations Charter, 331
United Organization of Taxpayers, 565
United Parcel Service (UPS), 235
United Postal Workers, 225
United States, troubles confronting as new nation, 59–62
United States v. Miller, 435
United States v. Morrison, 388
United States v. Richard M. Nixon, 313, 314
United Steelworkers of America, 225, 226, 227
University of California Regents v. Bakke, 407, 453
Unruh, Jesse M., 591, 597, 602, 604
Unz, Ron, 577
Urban districts, 265
Urban Institute, 127
Urban League. See National Urban League
U.S. Border Patrol, 352
U.S. Catholic Conference, 225
U.S. Chamber of Commerce, 225

U.S. Coast Guard, 352
U.S. Conference of Mayors, 225, 229
U.S. Constitution, 12, 19, 21, 87–101, 252, 593, 598. See also Constitution
    Article I, 72, 87–91, 248, 424, 436, 444
    Article II, 72, 91–93, 399
    Article III, 72, 93–94, 414
    Article IV, 94–95, 115, 444
    Article V, 95
    Article VI, National Supremacy Clause, 70, 71, 95, 111, 388, 415
    Article VII, 95
    First Amendment, 14, 95, 193, 196, 391, 407, 423, 425, 426, 427, 428, 429–431, 433, 555, 561
    Second Amendment, 95–96, 423, 434–435
    Third Amendment, 96, 423, 431
    Fourth Amendment, 96, 423, 431, 437
    Fifth Amendment, 37, 96, 391, 407, 423, 431, 437, 438–439
    Sixth Amendment, 96, 398, 424, 437, 440–441
    Seventh Amendment, 96, 424
    Eighth Amendment, 96, 424, 437, 441, 444
    Ninth Amendment, 97, 424, 431
    Tenth Amendment, 97, 424, 667
    Eleventh Amendment, 81, 97
    Twelfth Amendment, 81, 97
    Thirteenth Amendment, 81, 97–98, 117, 415, 425, 444, 445
    Fourteenth Amendment, 37, 51, 81, 98, 117, 251, 255, 391, 398, 407, 425, 431, 432, 445–446, 452, 453, 456, 462–464, 493
    Fifteenth Amendment, 81, 98, 117, 171, 251, 445, 446, 551, 552
    Sixteenth Amendment, 67, 81, 98, 118, 415
    Seventeenth Amendment, 81, 82, 98–99, 251
    Eighteenth Amendment (Prohibition), 81, 99, 227, 391, 463
    Nineteenth Amendment, 81, 99, 171, 251, 463, 551
    Twentieth Amendment, 81, 99
    Twenty-first Amendment, 81, 99
    Twenty-second Amendment, 81, 99–100, 306
    Twenty-third Amendment, 81, 100
    Twenty-fourth Amendment, 81, 100, 171
    Twenty-fifth Amendment, 81, 100–101, 306, 307
    Twenty-sixth Amendment, 81, 101, 171
    Twenty-seventh Amendment, 81, 101
    Bill of Rights, 78, 79, 82, 423, 431, 442
    executive branch and, 319–320
    judicial interpretations of, 80–82

U.S. Constitution (*continued*)
  nullified California state
    initiatives, 561
  prisoners captured in battlefields,
    438
  ratification conflict, 75–77
U.S. Court of Appeals, 393–394,
  401, 428, 435
U.S. Customs Service, 352
U.S. Geological Survey, 527
U.S. Information Agency, 9
U.S. Marine Corps, 343
*U.S. News & World Report*, 176, 317
U.S. Solicitor General, defined, 411
*U.S. vs. Lopez*, 121
USA PATRIOT Act, 19, 364
*USA Today*, 182
Utility Reform Network, 607
Utility user tax, 728

**V**

Vallejo, Mariano, 532, 591
Values, 25–26
  defined, 26
Van Buren, Martin, 339
van de Kamp, John, 634
Vasconcellos, John, 595
Vehicle license fee (VLF), 728
Verizon Communications, 230, 607
Versailles Treaty, 331
Veterans Affairs, U.S. Department
  of, 351
Veterans of Foreign Wars of the
  United States, 19, 225
Veto, defined, 328
Viacom, 184
Vice President, 336–339
Victims' Bill of Rights, 670
Vietnam Veterans of America, 225
Vietnam War, 501–502, 515
  defined, 501

Villaraigosa, Antonio, 693
Violence against Women Act of
  1994, 123
Virginia, University of, 35
Virginia Plan, 64, 65
Virginia Polytechnic Institute (VPI),
  123
Visa, defined, 40
Vizcaíno, Sebastian, 525
Voir dire, defined, 661–666
Voltaire, 26
Voluntary prayer, 428
Voter qualifications, and the
  Constitution, 65–66
Voter Rights, 551
Voting, 135–136
  difficulties in California, 578–579
  requirements, 550–552
Voting Rights Act of 1965, 255, 267,
  268, 293, 445

**W**

Wadsworth, J., 58
Wallace, George C., 112, 220, 222
*Wall Street Journal*, 176, 182, 317
Wal-Mart Stores, 235
Walt Disney, 184
Walters, Dan, 589
Ward, defined, 211
War of 1812, 515
War on Terrorism, 509–514
  world opinion on, 513
War Powers Resolution of 1973,
  334–335
  defined, 334
Warren, Earl, 402, 409, 410, 440,
  544, 571, 627, 628, 633,
  704, 724
Warsaw Pact, 498
Washington, George, 58, 63, 64, 82,
  306, 310, 332

Articles of Confederation and, 61
  constitutional power of the
    president, 306
  national security and, 68
  presidential power and, 83
  Shays's Rebellion and, 60
Washington, Martha. *See* Custis,
  Martha
*Washington Monthly*, 176
*Washington Post*, 176, 182, 193, 313,
  317
Watergate Committee, 250
Watergate scandal, 248, 312–313,
  314, 317, 333, 399
  defined, 312
Water Replenishment District of
  Southern California (WRD),
  701
Weak mayor-council model, defined,
  692
Weber, Max, 343
*Weekly Standard*, 176
Welfare and Institutions Code, 657
Welfare reform, politics and,
  488–490
Wellesley College, 269
Wells Fargo Bank, 532
Wendland, Robert, 659
Wendland, Rose, 659
Wesson, Herb, 606, 607
Westy, Steve, 635
Whips, defined, 276
Whistle-blowers, defined, 361
White, Byron, 402, 410
White House press corps, defined,
  317
White House staff, 323–325, 326
Whitewater Committee, 250
Whittaker, Charles, 402
Wilderness Society, 225, 355
*William Jefferson Clinton v. Paula Corbin
  Jones*, 314, 389

Williams, Stanley "Tookie," 662
Wilson, James Q., 573–574
Wilson, Pete, 553, 560, 587, 593,
  638, 655, 669, 731
Wilson, Woodrow, 306, 352
Winfrey, Oprah, 163, 182, 183
Wisconsin, University of, Institute
  for Research on Poverty, 484
*Woman's Day*, 182
Women, in Congress, 268–270
Woodward, Bob, 313
Workingmen's Party, 538
  defined, 537
World Bank, 477
World Trade Organization (WTO),
  476, 477
World War I, 515
World War II, 515
Wright, C. C., 700
Wright, Susan, 389
Wright Act, 700
Writ of certiorari, 652
  defined, 407
Writ of habeas corpus, 19, 652
  defined, 436
Writ of mandamus, 652
Writ of prohibitions, 652

**Y**

Yale University, 269, 404
  School of Law, 405
Yeltsin, Boris, 504
Young Americans for Freedom (YAF),
  43
Younger, Evelle, 633
*Youngstown Sheet & Tube Co. v. Sawyer*,
  389

**Z**

Zero-based budgeting, defined, 371